STATISTICAL HANDBOOK ON THE SOCIAL SAFETY NET

STATISTICAL HANDBOOK ON THE SOCIAL SAFETY NET

Fernando F. Padró

ORYX STATISTICAL HANDBOOKS

GREENWOOD PRESS
Westport, Connecticut • London

Library of Congress Cataloging-in-Publication Data

Padró, Fernando F.
    Statistical handbook on the social safety net / Fernando F. Padró.
      p.   cm.—(Oryx statistical handbooks)
    International in scope, but with a focus on the United States.
    Includes bibliographical references and index.
    ISBN 1–57356–516–4 (alk. paper)
    1. Public welfare—Statistical services—Electronic information resources.   2. Human
services—Statistical services—Electronic information resources.   3. Economic assistance,
Domestic—Statistical services—Electronic information resources.   I. Title: Social safety
net. II. Title. III. Series.
    HV51.P33   2004
    025.06'361—dc22   2004043641

British Library Cataloguing in Publication Data is available.

Library of Congress Catalog Card Number: 2004043641
ISBN: 1–57356–516–4

First published in 2004

Greenwood Press, 88 Post Road West, Westport, CT 06881
An imprint of Greenwood Publishing Group, Inc.
www.greenwood.com

Printed in the United States of America

The paper used in this book complies with the
Permanent Paper Standard issued by the National
Information Standards Organization (Z39.48–1984).

10 9 8 7 6 5 4 3 2 1

This book is dedicated to my father, Dr. Fernando Padró—who spent his entire career working in the public health arena and showed me the importance of the role of government in helping its people—and to my mother, Helen K. Padró who made me think of the importance between balancing the interests of individuals and governments.

Contents

Tables and Figures

Acknowledgments

This book has been a great learning experience for me and one that has come to life because of the support and many kindnesses on the part of a number of individuals. If there are kudos to be had for this book, they are due to their efforts. All of the shortcomings are strictly my responsibility.

First of all, I want to thank Dr. Eleanora von Diehsen who first asked me to write this book and got me on my way and Dr. Judith Bazler who encouraged me to take on this project.

The writing of this volume profited from the encouragement and enthusiasm given me by Paul Longo. He unselfishly read portions of the manuscripts and talked me through some issues, always providing excellent suggestions and additional food for thought. The assistance of Mr. Michael DeCotis and Ms. Megan Jones was instrumental in bringing together the unruly amount of data collected in anticipation of this book. Both helped me in the selection and organization of the data.

I also want to thank Ms. Sarah Colwell and Mr. Andrew Hudak, whose assistance with the editing and printing processes have been invaluable. Their communication, understanding, patience, and support were and are the reasons for completing this project; they made this book better by their questions and suggestions after I thought I was through with it all.

Finally, to my wonderful wife Trudy, thanks for putting up with me for the duration. I cannot tell you how grateful I am that you understood what this project meant and your willingness to be there when I needed it.

Introduction

When I took the first survey of my undertaking, I found our speech copious without order, and energetick without rules: wherever I turned my view, there was perplexity to be disentangled, and confusion to be regulated; choice was to be made out of boundless variety, without any established principle of selection; adulterations were to be detected, without a settled test of purity; and modes of expression to be rejected or received, without the suffrages of any writers of classical reputation or acknowledged authority.

Samuel Johnson

This book is written with two principal purposes in mind. The first purpose is to provide background statistical information to the reader who is interested in or is looking to do basic research on the subject of a national social safety net. The second purpose is to provide those individuals interested in writing grants in areas such as community development, social equity, or workforce development a single text source for socioeconomic data on key indicators that will help them in their task of generating justifications for their proposals.

This book does not attempt to be comprehensive in the sense that it discusses the social safety net from a basic perspective and offers basic statistics from government and nongovernment sources. A comprehensive book discussing the nuances of safety nets in detail, providing all available data, and giving equal attention to private as well as public activities in different countries, is a task simply too great for one volume. Like Samuel Johnson found out in writing his famous English dictionary, choices have to be made out of the endless variety of programs and information about those programs.

Moreover, this book does not address the pros and cons of providing a safety net to a nation's citizenry. To put it mildly, almost all aspects of the social safety net are controversial. There are many supporters and detractors of the systems nations put in place. Those in support of having a public safety net have as the basis of their argument moral obligation, rights, and quality of life. Rebecca Blank (1997) identifies eight of the most common arguments for government assistance to the poor: (1) investment in the future of a society, (2) risk sharing—government insurance against future economic risk, (3) human dignity, (4) capacity to respond enhances the moral responsibility to assist the poor, (5) the administrative capacity of the government is better than that of the private sector, (6) equity, (7) the protection of those that would be hurt if there is a market failure, and (8) the economic rights of citizens to be full participants in the society. Those seen as detractors have an argument that, at its most basic distillation, follows the sentiments expressed by Ogden Nash's poem *Common Sense*:

> Why did the Lord give us agility
> If not to evade responsibility?

Those not in favor of extensive safety net programs are interested in (1) accountability, (2) avoiding system abuse, (3) cost containment, (4) self-sufficiency, (5) over-reaching intrusion of the government into personal lives and the erosion of personal freedoms, and (6) in the United States, limiting the role and scope of the federal government in order to allow states greater latitude of freedom in defining what it is their citizens need. The issues on both sides are given attention in chapter 1 so that the reader can make up his or her mind while becoming familiar with the seesawing of the evolutionary political and social trends shaping programs and resource allocations.

The information itself is not always easy to access. It exists in many government databases at various levels; it is identified and published by a number of private and public organizations interested in public policy, social, and economic issues. Basic research into the field of social safety nets crosses into a number of fields. First one must go and find demographic information and economic analysis—economics. Second, one must go into the fields of history, political science, policy, and social work in order to determine the issues that shape and influence the numbers generated. Third, one—on occasion—needs to also go to the fields within philosophy in order to understand the implications behind the influences of trends. Fourth and finally, depending on need, one needs to delve into the psychology of the system itself, the programs, and the individuals providing and receiving the benefits of the safety net. These different academic disciplines look at the same institutions and come up with different data and approaches to evaluate the success and merit of these entities and their programs. There is no better example of this than when doing a basic blind search on the Internet. Writing the term *safety net* by itself will not lead to too many sites with useful leads. Adding the prefix terms *social* or *economic* will provide more leads and some even to the same sites and information. However, for the most part, any investigator using the Internet for these data will end up in two very different avenues and still with not much information unless the investigator has a greater in-depth knowledge of what needs to be found.

Two caveats should be mentioned before proceeding any further. The first warning is that the paradigm of the social safety net throughout much of the Western world is changing. This means that the data themselves are limited in certain respects, and longitudinal comparisons will yield unfortunate results. It also means that the policies and the institutions, as well as data collection itself, have changed, mostly from about 1996 onwards. The second caution is probably the most important: There is no standard definition of the term social safety net. The term is so often used in official and unofficial documents and academic studies that there is a built-in assumption about what it means. However, a careful look at these documents and research clearly shows that the assumptions are shaped by the needs of those doing the writing, and depends on the field in which the research is done or the discussion advanced.

From a data analysis perspective, how any society determines its view of "social justice" and individual "right" (in terms of being able to make a claim to the government and not just as a form of freedom to act) colors how the statistical data that is compiled must be treated. A nation that believes in the entitlement of individuals as a form of wealth redistribution may be proportionately higher when compared to nations whose outlook of social justice is one of fairness of opportunity and not a form of shifting wealth from one element of society to another. The data may be the same; however, the data reflect a different purpose and mission as defined by formal and informal policy. Not taking the differences into account means that the reader, when using this data in a report, will find himself or herself creating a weaker argument because of technical inconsistencies. The researcher is looking at the surface issues at the expense of the underlying ones that are more significant. For those individuals who are looking at performing a statistical analysis, this could mean a Type I error.

For the reader who is doing a cross-cultural perspective, the focus on the forces that shapes data is even more important. There are different forms of government in different localities; different norms and references apply. When working in non-Western cultures, or those that are considered to have less complex or sophisticated social structures, this need to focus on the precursors that define action assists in at least reducing the potential for cultural bias.

This book mainly focuses on information about the United States and the various components of its social safety net. Yet, for perspective purposes, a few initial comparative comments are in order. According to Goodin, Headey, Muffels, and Dirven (1999), the United States' approach to social safety nets is typical of countries belonging to the Organization for Economic Co-operation and Development (OECD). They see the United States as an example of what they term a "liberal welfare regime" as exemplified by the nineteenth-century philosopher John Stuart Mill's notions of freedom and autonomy, emphasizing the separating out those "unwilling to work from those genuinely unable to do so" (44). By extension, the argument has to go one more step. The United States' safety net ensures that maintaining a high degree of personal responsibility for consequences does not minimize risk-taking by individuals. The social background remains one in which individuals have to maintain a bargaining relationship in terms of employment, consumption, asset development and maintenance, and risk management. In this system, "a just society would be one in which inequalities in wealth were acceptable provided that the people at the top of the heap got there as a result of effort and skill" (Wilson, 1993, 73).

These points of view contrast dramatically with the corporatist and socialist (social democratic) systems such as those enacted by Germany and the Netherlands, two countries that are, to some extent, examples of the processes that are being considered for the European Union as a model for a meta-level social safety net in Europe.

Corporatist philosophy presupposes that "everything in capitalist society is in principle open to negotiation" (Cawson, 1986, 14) and that the basis of a social relationship is based on a compact between those groups within society who have more power than those who have less. The idea is that those traditionally seen to be the "weaker" classes still often control the methods of production and, therefore, it is in everyone's interest to ensure that their interests are met as well. Bargaining takes on the form of negotiations, and the individual becomes an element within the aggregate of an interest group. The individual notion of risk is muted (if not blunted) through the notions of rationality of thought emanating from similar interests because, as John Rawls believes, "The intuitive idea is that since everyone's well-being depends upon a scheme of cooperation without which no one could have a satisfactory life, the division of advantages should be such as to draw forth the willing cooperation of everyone taking part in it, including those less well situated" (1971, 15).

The social democratic belief structure is somewhat different than the corporatist due to its concern with promoting welfare through the economic sphere (Goodin et al., 1999). not unlike the liberal regime. However, as Goodin and coauthors also write, the ultimate goal of social democracies is to achieve social equality as a means of eliminating poverty. Tax transfers are done in two ways, through the manipulation (control) of market forces as well as through traditional taxing structures. Risk-taking is reduced or mitigated because of government intercession, structured on the premise that material and social limitations upon the individual's ability to act and move are "broken down, and replaced with rules laid down by legislation and collective agreements" (Myrdal, 1963, 86) that, in turn, allow more freedom because these rules can be accepted or overturned by vote, and are thus less arbitrary, less individuous. Like with the corporatist state, individual interest is channeled through spheres of interests within government and entities such as the labor unions.

The comparison between these three countries—and political systems—makes apparent the many number of programs and levels of benefits provided to their citizens (a key distinction which is discussed in greater detail in Chapter 1). For readers in the United States, what becomes apparent is not only the additional layers of bureaucracy but the redistributive component that is built in to these systems (for example, Germany's and the Netherlands' guarantee of a minimum standard of living). Interestingly enough, one approach does come across in common: the participative or insurance component to the welfare programs. They may vary in contributions and participation requirements, but they are similar in that contributions still make up a significant portion of the retirement and health schemes.

HOW THE BOOK IS ORGANIZED

The book's overall organization breaks down to three sections. The first three chapters discuss the definition of a social safety net (chapter 1); the economic health of nations, principally that of the United States (chapter 2); and how nations, again, mainly the United States, define poverty and use that definition to provide services (chapter 3). Each of these chapters are augmented with tables that assist the reader to develop a better picture of what the narrative is presenting and/or illustrating about the impact the issues have on the safety net.

The second section presents a narrative and data about the traditional safety net programs available in the United States and other countries based on the notions of insurance—people contributing in order to "buy" benefits for later or when needed. Chapter 4 is on old age, survivors, and disability insurance (OASI and DI, or OASDI), better known in the United States as Social Security, with data to provide comparisons with how selected countries provide these benefits. Chapter 5 discusses unemployment insurance and worker compensation in the United States (the second tier of the Social Security Act of 1935) with some international comparative data. Chapter 6 presents information on the public health programs known in the United States as Medicare and Medicaid, two programs not developed until the 1960s. Comparative data are provided as a means to illustrate the extent of coverage and resources allocated to public health. Chapter 7 reviews the new paradigm impacting the welfare system in the United States as defined by the Temporary Assistance for Needy Families Act (TANF) that replaced the paradigm of public welfare first enacted as part of the Social Security Act of 1935, the Aid to Families and Dependent Children (AFDC)

program. Comparative data from other selected countries is provided. Chapter 8 centers on supplemental income programs based on the concept of the negative income tax and other benefit programs such as housing.

The last section focuses on women's (chapter 9) and children's public safety net issues (chapter 10). These are provided separate attention because of the dual impact that the safety net has on these two groups. Women are impacted because of longevity, the increase in the divorce rate and, more critically, the traditional notions of family that encouraged women to stay at home (see Navarro, 2000). Staying at home means lower or no income and typically, lower paying jobs. The traditional policies mean that women do not have as lengthy a track record at work, of contributions to the health and retirement schemes, and the expectations that their benefits are tied to the head of household (defined as main wage earner). The result is that women receive less and are more prone to poverty as they age (see Lindbeck, 1999). The concern over children is best summed up by the statement that "children growing up in poor single-parent families face a double-negative effect in their lives: living in poverty and living with only one parent" (Blank, 1997, 41). The change in social expectations and *mores* have meant that the situation of children seems to be worsening rather than improving, leading both sides of the political spectrum to make demands on existing programs that may or may not improve their well-being. One camp is basically thinking of turning the clock back to when the opprobrium of bastardry had an impact on the status of the child, through collection of unpaid support regardless of a man's ability to pay, or through the forced marriage of unmarried parents. In both cases, the penalty is the loss of other benefits. The other camp prefers expanded government oversight to ensure the health and welfare of children. The view is that the government has a compelling reason to break families apart in order to ensure the children's welfare.

Even though education and its institution fit the definition of the term social safety net as given in chapter 1, education does not have its own chapter in this volume. Like other texts in this area, this book only provides a passing reference to education when talking about public welfare issues. The reason is one of size and scope. The emphasis of this book is to look at those institutions focusing on meeting what Herzberg, Mausner, and Snyderman (1959) refer to as "hygienic needs." The reason for this is because education requires its own separate treatment. It is this author's view (no different than many who have had to make this consideration in the past) that the structural, political, philosophical, historic, economic, and technical differences between basic education and higher education requires that each aspect of the educational system be given its own distinct analysis and then brought together into a coherent whole.

SOURCES OF DATA

The chapters in this book rely on data from numerous sources. There was no one source of data, no one great study that was the basis for the numbers; instead, the book provides information from many sources. Even so, there are certain key sources that readers can refer to for doing further, more detailed and refined research in this area.

One of the goals is to use as many freely accessible Internet sources as possible, so that readers can go and begin to search for more detailed information on their own. As stated at the beginning of this discussion, searching the Internet can be a tricky proposition.

For data on the United States, three excellent places to further search are the U.S. Bureau of Labor Statistics at http://www.bls.gov, and the U.S. Census Bureau with its site http://www.census.gov, in particular the Statistical Abstract found at http://www.census.gov/statab/www/. Other federal government Web sites that provide significant staging areas for readers to continue their research are in the following list. These may land you back to the Census Bureau site; however, these sites contain other information that may be useful to the reader in the performance of research and/or writing grants. Whether to begin at the Statistical Abstract and Census sites or go to these other sites first really depends on how well defined the research or grant topics are and if there is only a need for very specific data. If there is a need to investigate policy matters, regulations, legislation, and court cases, then it may be more profitable to begin sorting these issues out before collecting data.

- The Social Security Administration at http://www.ssa.gov
- The U.S. Health and Human Services at http://www.hhs.gov
- The U.S. Health and Human Services Office of the Assistant Secretary for Planning and Evaluation at http://www.aspe.hhs.gov
- The U.S. Administration for Children and Families at http://www.acf.hhs.gov
- Centers for Medicare and Medicaid Services at http://www.cms.gov
- The Catalog of Federal Domestic Assistance at http://www.cfda.gov
- The U.S. Department of Labor at http://www.dol.gov
- The U.S. Department of Labor Employment and Training Administration at http://www.doleta.gov
- The U.S. Department of Labor Women's Bureau at http://www.dol.gov/wb
- The U.S. Department of Commerce at http://www.doc.com
- The Office of Management and Budget (OMB) at http://www.whitehouse.gov
- The U.S. Government Accounting Office (GAO) at http://www.gao.gov
- The U.S. Office of Housing and Urban Development (HUD) at http://www.hud.gov

Each state has equivalent government agencies with useful Web sites—too many sites to mention here. Readers looking for specific data for states should locate the state equivalents.

Many states have a Department of Economic Security or its equivalent, a Department of Health, a Department of Children Services or equivalent, and a Bureau of Statistics or equivalent. Because many programs are run by states but regulated and significantly funded by the federal government, those interested in policies and procedures, eligibility guidelines, benefits and services, and timelines should consider these Web sites early on in their research activities. These sites often have statistical data as well, although do not be surprised to end up at a federal database such as that available through the Census Bureau or Bureau of Labor Statistics. Sites often referred to in the preparation of this book come from the states of Minnesota and California. Other state department or program Web sites used in writing this text are from Maryland, Illinois, Pennsylvania, and Texas.

Nongovernment Web sites that provide good starting points for follow-up work include the following list. There are many others available, but when preparing and researching materials and data for this book, the author found himself going to these sites with greater frequency.

- Carnegie Corporation at http://www.carnegie.org[1]
- Center on Budgeting and Policy Priorities at http://www.cbpp.org
- Center for Women Policies Studies at http://www.centerwomenpolicy.org
- Econdata.Net at http://www.econdata.net/content_quicklinks.html
- The Ford Foundation at http://www.fordfound.org
- Heritage Foundation at http://www.heritage.org
- The Robert Wood Johnson Foundation at http://www.rwjf.org
- The Joint Center on Poverty Research at http://www.jcpr.org
- The Henry J. Kaiser Family Foundation at http://www.kff.org
- The W.K. Kellogg Foundation at http://www.wkkf.org
- 'Lectric Law Library at http://www.lectlaw.com
- Legal Information Institute at the Cornell University Law School at http://www.law.cornell.edu
- The Library of Economics and Liberty (Liberty Fund, Inc.) at http://www.econlib.org
- The Charles Stewart Mott Foundation at http://www.mott.org
- The Rockerfeller Foundation at http://www.rockfound.org
- The Urban League at http://www.urban.org

For international material and international comparative data, there are a number of free sources available through the Internet. Some are not the most user-friendly, and language can be an issue at times, although in most instances English materials are available. A few sites provide only statistics, others statistics and policies, and others only provide technical and advanced information rather than at a superficial or introductory level. Some of these sites will not allow the reader to download information from one's computer; either the request has to be done through e-mail and the data sent by hand, or access can be achieved through a registration fee or equivalent. Nevertheless, the sites below provide a solid framework for those interested in performing comparative analyses.

- Columbia University's International Clearinghouse on International Developments in Child, Youth and Family Policies Web site. Retrieved from: http://www.childpolicyintl.org/contexttablessocexp/table243.pdf
- European Parliament (EuroParl) at http://www.europarl.eu.int/plenary/default_en.htm
- EuReporting at http://www.plg.at/euroreporting
- European System of Social Indicators (EUSI) at http://www.gesis.org/en/social_monitoring/social_indicators/EU_Reporting/
- Eurostat at http://www.europa.eu.int
- The International Labor Organization at http://www.ilo.org
- The International Monetary Fund (IMF) at http://www.imf.org
- The Organization for Economic Co-operation and Development (OECD) at http://www.oecd.org
- The Social Science Information Gateway (SOSIG) at http://www.sosig.ac.uk/statistics/
- The United Nations Development Program at http://www.undp.org
- The United Nations Educational, Scientific and Cultural Organization (UNESCO), for research documents, at http://www.unesco.org
- The United Nations Educational, Scientific and Cultural Organization (UNESCO) Institute for Statistics at http://portal.unesco.org/uis/ev.php?URL_DO=DO_TOPIC&URL_SECTION=201
- The United Nations Children's Fund (UNICEF) at http://www.unicef.org
- The United Nations Department of Economic and Social Affairs, Statistics Division at http://unstats.un.org/unsd/methods/inter-natlinks/nd_natstat.htm
- The United States Central Intelligence Agency (CIA) with its "World Factbook" at http://www.cia.gov/cia/publications/factbook
- The U.S. Social Security Administration through its "Social Security Programs Throughout the World" at http://www.ssa.gov/
- The World Bank at http://www.worldbank.org

When looking for data for individual countries, there is a question of whether to look at a country from the outside or from within. The sites in the preceding list provide that external view for countries that an investigator wants to review. However, the following Web sites found available in various nations provided the author—and will provide the reader—with much useful information.

- In Australia, the Australia Bureau of Statistics at http://www.abs.au
- In Canada, Statistics Canada at http://www.statcan.ca/start.html
- In Germany, the Federal Statistics Office at http://www.destatis.de/e_home.htm
- In Japan, the Statistics Bureau of the Ministry of Public Management, Home Affairs, Posts and Telecommunications at http://www.stat.go.jp/english/index.htm
- In South Korea, the Korea National Statistics Office at http://www.nso.go.kr/eng/index.shtml
- In the United Kingdom, National Statistics Online at http://www.ons.go.uk

The United Nations Statistics Office provides links to statistical information Web sites of numerous member nations at http://unstats.un.org/unsd/methods/inter-natlinks/sd_natstat.htm. For those who may want to look for library sources nearby or write to national agencies, the Statistical Abstract of the United States also provides the names of agencies and the addresses of the statistical abstracts generated in the OECD countries, Slovakia, and Russia.[2]

HOW TO ACCESS THE DATA IN THE BOOK

The tables provided in each chapter of the book are not discrete in that they only refer to concepts in that chapter; the contrary is the case. In many instances, the information in the tables can be used when thinking about topics described in other chapters. Therefore, readers are going to have to refer to data throughout the text. The use of the index in this regard will be indispensable. The tables are meant to be illustrative of the topics discussed (except for chapter 1), but because the social safety net is intertwined in such a way that programs, regulations, allocations, and data crosscut through the various chapter categories. It is hoped that the need to have to relate data tables in one chapter to another or to a set of chapters mitigates the potential inconvenience of needing to do so, and that the benefits in having information accessible in one volume from such diverse sources compensates for the difficulties.

The tables in chapter 1 do not focus on the discussion preceding them unless otherwise specified. Most of the information made available here is of a demographic nature, allowing readers access to basic data that begins to create the picture that will be further enhanced by reading the remaining appropriate portions of the book. These tables act as a frame of reference so that, based on need, readers can establish ties to data to meet specific requirements.

The sources of data for this book are numerous, as exemplified by the number of Web sites available as access points to research the topic. There are some references that are used more frequently than others; however, statistical references, studies, articles, reports, and Web site–based tables are used to describe key aspects of that part of the social safety net.

To research and put the ideas surrounding social safety nets in perspective, a comment made by the playwright George Bernard Shaw comes to mind: "Remember, to be a critic, you must be not only a bit of an expert in your subject, but you must also have literary skill, and trained critical skill too—the power of analysis, comparison &c." (1955, pp. 3–4). In this attempt at making sense of the safety net structure, particularly in the United States, each chapter includes the primary bibliographic references for the tables found in each chapter in the book for the reader needing or wanting to investigate these sources in greater detail. Readers are encouraged to look at these sources themselves, to replicate this investigation if it suits their research or writing agenda. These are only reference points in a map that is very large, broad, and full of interdisciplinary connections. To understand the social safety net, policy has to be looked at from a demographics and economics point-of-view. To impress how effective these programs are, then the need is to look at who is eligible, who received benefits, and what the consequences of the policies supporting these benefits are. The question of "are people being served?" is an important one in terms of how many and how much—how much is allocated for the program, how much each beneficiary receives. Is this enough? Does this meet social expectation and demands? Alas, much social activity, in order to be understood as a function, has to look at the economic numbers indicating allocation and deployment in order to determine results.

NOTES

1. Full reports will have to be ordered; however, there are abridged reports that are accessible to those searching the Web site.

2. The OECD countries are Australia, Austria, Belgium, Canada, the Czech Republic, Denmark, Finland, France, Germany, Greece, Hungary, Iceland, Ireland, Italy, Japan, Luxembourg, Mexico, the Netherlands, New Zealand, Norway, Poland, Portugal, South Korea, Spain, Sweden, Switzerland, Turkey, and the United Kingdom.

BIBLIOGRAPHY

Blank, R.M. (1997). *It takes a nation: A new agenda for fighting poverty.* New York: Russell Sage Foundation.

Goodin, R.E., Headey, B., Muffels, R., and Dirven, H.J. (1999). *The real worlds of welfare capitalism.* Cambridge: Cambridge University Press.

Herzberg, F., Mausner, B., and Snyderman, B. (1959). *The motivation to work.* New York: John Wiley and Sons.

Lindbeck, A. (1999). Welfare state dynamics. In Buti, M., Franco, D., and Pench, L.R., eds. *The welfare state in Europe: Challenges and reforms.* Cheltenham, UK: Edward Elgar, 71–89.

Myrdal, G. (1960). *Beyond the welfare state.* New Haven, CT: Yale University Press.

Navarro, V. (2000). The political economy of the welfare state in developed capitalist countries. In Navarro, V., ed. *The political economy of social inequalities: Consequences for health and quality of life.* Amityville, NY: Baywood, 121–169.

Rawls, J. (1971). *A theory of justice.* Cambridge, MA: Harvard University Press.

Shaw, G.B. (1955). Personal letter to R. Golding Bright, April 30, 1894. In Shaw, G.B. (introduction and notes by E.J. West). *Advice to a young critic and other letters.* New York: Crown Publishers.

Wilson, J.Q. (1993). *The moral sense.* New York: Free Press.

1. What Does the Term *Social Safety Net* Mean?

THE DEFINITION OF A SOCIAL SAFETY NET

In all too many instances the concept of a **social safety net** is automatically equated with "welfare." True enough, welfare (or a derived equivalent) makes up a significant component of any social safety net; however, not all social programs are only providing subsistence handouts for the poor. A social safety net is there to meet the needs of those who need assistance in one form or another. Workplace standards, labor well-being, workforce development programs, individual retirement income protections, health care, and quality of life concerns are also important parts of a social safety net. So is education, particularly in its ability to foment social mobility in terms of moving to where the opportunities are, as well as the ability to climb the "social ladder" by the dint of one's abilities and efforts. For the purposes of this text, the social safety net is defined by the following criteria:

(a) government or programs (at national, state or province, and/or local levels) that are designed to assist those needing assistance to maintain a basic standard of living as defined by the community;

(b) defined by the powers that be as appropriate to provide available resources to those deemed eligible;

(c) possibly also supported by private philanthropic or community-based non-government organizations (NGOs) whose purpose is to assist those in need of assistance in accordance to their own interests; and

(d) whose performance can be measured in economic and social terms relating to the ability of the participants to at the least maintain, if not enhance, their quality of life.

This definition attempts to avoid emphasizing one competing philosophy of social interaction over another. To begin with, the definition does not take sides in establishing a preference toward a social welfare state where the focus is the redistribution of wealth through entitlement programs. On the other hand, the definition cannot just gravitate around the fact that all government programs by their own volition focus on the common weal, or the well-being of the nation's citizens (at least of those who have a recognized franchise), regardless of governmental level or actual purpose. Therefore, departments or agencies whose duties and responsibilities are in national defense or foreign policy do not qualify. Department, agencies, and programs that do qualify to meet the definition created herein are those social programs whose direct purpose is to provide a service and/or benefit that is deemed equitable and appropriate by that nation's (or internal political subunit, if applicable) social norms and laws.

THE APPROACHES TAKEN BY THIS DEFINITION OF A SOCIAL SAFETY NET

This definition reflects a four-prong approach toward defining a safety net. The first element considered is based on a government's legal authority to provide social programs. In the United States, for example, the legal right to generate social programs emanates from its legal concept of a state's police power. According to *Black's Law Dictionary* (1957), the reference to police power in this instance means that the state's legislature is given the power to "make, ordain, and establish all manner of wholesome and reasonable laws . . . for the good and welfare . . . insuring to each [citizen] an uninterrupted enjoyment of all of the privileges conferred upon him by the laws of his country" (1317). It can be argued that most governments base their actions toward providing services to their citizens as an expansion of their power to protect their interests. An excellent description of this argument is to be found in the 1925 California Supreme Court decision of *Miller v. Board of Public Works*, 195 Cal.477, 485, 234 Pac. 381:

> In its inception the police power was closely concerned with the preservation of the public peace, safety, morals and health without specific regard for "the general welfare." The increasing complexity of our civilization and institutions later gave rise to cases wherein the promotion of the public welfare was

held by the courts to be a legitimate object for the exercise of the police power. As our civic life has developed so has the definition of the "public welfare" until it has been held to embrace regulations "to promote the economic welfare, public convenience and general prosperity of the community."

The second consideration in generating the definition of a social safety net is to look at a nation's or state's (province's) institution to determine access to them. A social safety net is made up of institutions that not only provide a benefit, but do so for those who are in need of assistance to make ends meet, in other words, ensuring the well-being of those citizens who need help in order to make it from day to day. Often, these are the programs that are referred to as those providing welfare services for the poor.

It is not unusual for these "welfare" benefits to go to specific groups. Chapter 1 of the *World Bank Participation Sourcebook* (World Bank, 1996) defines the situation as well as can be found anywhere:

Who Are the Poor?

The poor include people in remote and impoverished areas. Women and children make up a large proportion of the very poor, which also includes people marginalized by virtue of their race and ethnicity as well as those disadvantaged by circumstances beyond their control, such as disabilities and natural or man-made disasters. Some of the poorest people live in countries characterized by weak governments and civil strife.

As an aside, a comment needs to be made at this time: Because the poor are generally less educated and less organized than other more powerful stakeholders, because they are more difficult to reach, and because the institutions that serve them are often weak, interventions targeting the poor must often be small, context-specific, and resource-intensive.

The third consideration toward a definition is to provide an outlook regarding how combine policy and program offerings and access to these programs. A model on how to pursue this amalgamation is the World Bank's Comprehensive Development Framework (CDF). As the World Bank report points out:

The basic elements of the CDF are not new. What is new is their joint articulation as a guide to development assistance. First, development constraints are structural and social and cannot be overcome through economic stabilization and policy adjustment alone—they require a *holistic, broad-based approach.* Second, policy reform and institutional development cannot be imported or imposed: without domestic *ownership,* reforms and investments are not sustainable. Third, successful development requires *partnerships* among government, local communities, the private sector, civil society, and development agencies. Fourth, development activities must be guided and judged by *results.* (World Bank, 1999, 1, italics in original)

The criteria identified in this report provide the following items to consider:

Short term versus long term: Social transformation and institutional development require long-term and sustained efforts.

Comprehensiveness versus selectivity. Speed versus broad-based ownership: For both of these considerations, sustainable reform requires broad-based ownership. Yet partners may disagree about the distinctive roles of the state, the private sector, and civil society.

Ownership versus conditionality: Thought of in terms of access to programs as well as eligibility, conditions, and time limitations.

Country capacity and ownership: "Countries . . . often lack the capacity to coordinate aid." Governments, civil society, the private sector, and external donors may have different agendas, requiring a gradual approach to consensus building. The larger and more diverse the partners, the higher the transaction costs and the greater the difficulty of combining ownership and partnership. Where country commitment is lacking, coherent views may be perceived as "ganging up."

Country-led partnership versus donor accountability: Mainly applicable for comparative data of developing countries. All development assistance agencies are accountable to their authorities, so placing an unresponsive government in control involves risks. The challenge is to find common ground and achieve results over the long term through patient nurturing of reform and capacity building.

Results-orientation versus local capacity: Country-based programs versus global public goods. Again, a better focus for developing countries. Development assistance efforts and approaches are focused at the project and country levels. With globalization, development problems require multilateral solutions and stronger links between national strategies and international policies.

Put these all together and that is why the World Bank (1995) says

safety nets address humanitarian concerns and temper the immediate political costs to governments implementing radical reforms. Over the long term, safety nets can strengthen human capital development, especially among the most deprived parts of society.

But not all social safety nets are replicable or sustainable. They run the risk of entrenching themselves in a government's social development strategy and burdening public finances and institutions. Thus the strategy should be to seek an appropriate balance, consistent with the needs of broadly based growth and long-term investment in the social sectors. More systematic piloting is needed to develop appropriate policy prescriptions for the design of cost-effective safety nets.

The fourth consideration into the making of a working definition of a social safety net is the acknowledgment that all assistance programs are not necessarily the result of government activity. In the United States for example, there is still a very strong history and presence of private agencies and organizations coming to the aid of those who need assistance. There are a number of international private organizations whose mission it is to provide assistance on a short-term basis in times of crises, or for a longer duration in order to combat hunger, disease, or social maladies. It must be noted that often times, these private entities collaborate closely with the national, regional and/or local governments, but on occasions, for whatever reason, these do not cooperate and have either a distant or antagonistic relationship with Government Agencies.

WHY IS THERE A CONTROVERSY OVER THE NOTION OF A SOCIAL SAFETY NET?

The notion of a social safety net is controversial because it is representative of a society's philosophical views on itself, the division of labor and wealth, the role of government in the private affairs of its citizens, the status of the poor, and the role that the government and private sectors should play in assisting the poor. Simply put, the controversy exists because it brings attention to a society's definition of "social justice." This happens because as C. Wright Mills in his 1963 essay, *The Sociology of Stratification*, points out:

> In almost any community in every nation there is a high and a low, and in many societies, a big in-between.
>
> If we go behind what we can thus casually observe while standing on street corners, and begin seriously to observe in detail the 24-hour cycle of behavior and experience, the 12-month cycle, the life-long biography of people in various cities and classification of people in terms of the social distribution of valued things and experiences; to find out just which people regularly expect to and do receive many of the available valued things and experiences, and, on every level, why. (305)

These discussions become personalized because there is a tendency to equate social responsibility with individual integrity (see Dworkin, 1986, 213). At the basis of any debate (and the inherent controversy) on social issues of any kind is the notion of justice as equated by fairness. Fairness is seen in terms of those who feel they receive it and those who do not. According to John Rawls,

> the primary subject of justice is the basic structure of society, or more exactly, the way in which the major social institutions distribute fundamental rights and duties and determine the division of advantages from social cooperation. . . . Taken together as one scheme, the major institutions define [the individual's] rights and duties and influence in their life-prospects, what they can expect to be and how well they can hope to do. (1971, 7)

More to the point, does fairness translate to "entitlement"? Is entitlement a right? There are many types of rights, such as those generated from a mutually agreed to contract, those identified by law, those emanating from our sense of what is acceptable and unacceptable, and those framed from the interaction between political agents. In all these instances the one common thread is the creation of an obligation followed by the integrity to go through with that obligation. An entitlement takes the obligation from one that is voluntary or discretionary to one that becomes permanent or nondiscretionary through the means of law and regulatory compliance (see Kelsen, 1952, 8).

From another point of view, social inequity is based on the simple fact that not everyone is able to make the same amount of money, have the same degree of prestige and the same capacity to access, generate, and maintain power. Individual differences, levels of opportunity, and the ability to take advantage of opportunity means that some individuals progress further than their peers and amass greater rewards than the others. The discussion of a national safety net simply centers about how that society views this built-in inequity and what it does to address the issue. There is a corollary issue here as well, that of how willing the members of that community are to help to reduce the impact that this inequity has on all members' ability to self-actualize to the best of their ability.

Ideally, government agencies are charged with the responsibility of administering those processes that lead to the well-being of its citizens, and to meeting the needs of the people that these agencies serve. The bureaucratic processes of these agencies are ostensibly there to ensure that there is a way to define how things are done, as well as to provide accountability for how well these agencies are meeting their duties and responsibilities. Policy, as made through legislative, judicial, and administrative (executive) decision-making avenues, is there to provide the guidance and direction—the duties and responsibilities—that shape the form of these agencies. Following the procedural aspects of government agencies is not difficult. In fact, most of the numbers that readers of this text want are those accountability numbers that show what they are doing and how they are doing it in terms of (1) types of programs generated and administered, (2) access to the programs, (3) people served, (4) resources allocated, and (5) measures of effectiveness and efficiency.

What is difficult to gauge and what varies the meaning of the five types of data are the adjudicatory, regulatory, and statutory guidelines that create, administer, maintain, and influence the programmatic component of the government agencies. One has to be careful to apply the Greek historian Thucidides' distinction regarding cause and effect. It is somewhat easy to determine the surface causes, but it takes care and effort to ensure that what, on the surface, seems to be the link is not, in effect, a Band-Aid for deeper and less apparent yet truer causes of what is in fact happening.

The controversy is given additional fuel when the notions of rights, obligations, and entitlement are woven together under the form of human rights. For example, the United Nations Development Programme (UNDP) takes a broad vision of how it defines human rights, in particular, as it desires to draw out "the complex relationship between human development and human rights" (2000, iii). The basis is in the belief in equity. Rawls (1971) indicates that there is an expectation of equity "when an exception is to be made when the established rule works an unexpected hardship" (237–238). Therefore, the term "equitable" for the purposes of this text means that individuals expect to be treated fairly by the governments' bureaucracies, that those who can and should use the system will receive the full benefits of what is duly owed them.

LEGAL ISSUES LEADING TO THE DEVELOPMENT OF THE SOCIAL SAFETY NET

The rise of the notions of the social safety net has its roots primarily in the late nineteenth century, with some of the earliest utilitarian notions on the role of government first conceived by Jeremy Bentham and Wilhelm von Humboldt during the latter stages of the eighteenth century. However, the social safety net is pretty much a twentieth-century evolutionary phenomenon, with the current use of the term coming to life in only the early 1980s.

The evolution of social safety nets reflects a change in a nation's legal philosophy based on the state having a legitimate role in assisting those who require assistance. John Locke (1764) initially makes the argument that a government of laws is in place to take into account the discretion of the public good. Yet, the key question asked early on is one, as posited by Sir Frederick Pollock, of "how far the State ought to exercise general control over the private actions of its citizens" (1911, 130). To quote Bentham:

> Ethics then, in as far as it is the art of directing a man's actions in [respect to affecting his happiness], may be termed the art of discharging one's duties to one's self. . . . In as far as his happiness, and that of any other person or persons whose interests are considered, . . . may be said to depend upon his *duties to others*, . . . his *duty to his neighbour*. . . . A man's duty to his neighbour is accordingly partly negative and partly positive: to discharge the negative branch of it, is *probity*: to discharge the positive branch, *beneficence*.
>
> Now private ethics has happiness at its end: and legislation can have no other. Private ethics concerns every member, that is the happiness and the actions of every member, of any community that can be proposed; and legislation can concern no more. Thus far, then, private ethics and the art of legislation go hand in hand. The end they have, or ought to have, in view, is of the same nature. . . . The very acts they ought to be conversant about, are even in a *great measure* the same. Where then lies the difference? . . . There is no case in which a private man ought to not to direct his own conduct to the production of his own happiness . . . but there are cases in which the legislator ought not . . . to attempt to direct the conduct of the several other members of the community. (1789/1988, 312–314, italics in original)

Social changes at the beginning of the twentieth century and the resulting Great Depression of the late 1920s and 1930s formed the background that provided the need for a different approach to the questions Bentham and later Pollock present us. The fullness of the impact resulting from such a widespread collapse of the economy demonstrated the weakness of the institutions in place to assist those who needed help. In short, the network of private assistance agencies was overwhelmed and incapable of meeting the demand placed on them. As Felix

Frankfurter observed in an address he gave in 1912 prior to becoming Associate Justice of the U.S. Supreme Court,

> The tremendous economic and social changes of the last fifty years have inevitably reacted upon the functions of the state. More and more government is conceived as the biggest organized social effort for dealing with social problems. Our whole evolutionary thinking leads to the conclusion that economic independence lies at the foundation of social and moral well-being. (1962, 4)

In the United States, the watershed year for legal its social safety net was 1937. At this point, the United States Supreme Court changed its view, retreating as it were from its laissez faire constitutionalism and limited federalism to extended federal government participation through Congress' power to regulate interstate commerce. In *Chas. C. Steward Machine Co. v. Davis*, 301 U.S. 548, 57 S. Ct. 883, 81 L. Ed. 1279 (1937) the Court upholds the constitutionality of the tax imposed by the Social Security Act of 1935. On the same day, in *Helvering v. Davis*, 301 U.S. 619, 57 S. Ct. 904, 81 L. Ed. 1307 (1937), Justice Cardozo, speaking for the Court, states that:

> The conception of the spending power advocated by Hamilton and strongly reinforced by Story has prevailed, yet difficulties are left when the power is conceded. The line must still be drawn between one welfare and another, between particular and general. . . . The discretion, however, is not confined to the courts. The discretion belongs to Congress, unless the choice is clearly wrong, a display of arbitrary power, not an exercise of judgment. . . . Nor is the concept of general welfare static. Needs that were narrow or parochial a century ago may be interwoven in our day with the well-being of the Nation.

In a number of societies, legal procedures gravitate around the identified rights of citizens. It is the result of nullifying the belief that government speaks for the people under the concept of *Rex est lex loquens*—royal prerogative based on the view that the king is the law speaking. The definition of the social safety net is thus prescribed by those notions of personal liberty that define the nation's standards of how much intrusion the government is allowed into the lives of everyday citizens. A nation generates prohibitions to national governments by furnishing guarantees to individual citizens. The ethical and moral notions of duty, equity, and fairness are codified through this point of reference as it is reevaluated over time, based on the dynamic processes influencing the definitions of what is right and what is not. Furthermore, as Franklin Roosevelt indicated in his Constitution Day Speech of 1937, rights were put in place "not only to protect minorities against intolerance of majorities, but to protect majorities against the enthronement of minorities."

In the United States, individual rights are based on the Bill of Rights that make up the first ten amendments to the U.S. Constitution. After World War II, Japan ratified a new constitution (with its own Bill of Rights) in 1947 based on many of the notions espoused in the U.S. Constitution and the later U.N. Declaration of Human Rights of 1948; In Europe, as part of the changes after World War II that eventually led to the formation of the European Union, the series of treaties between the member countries that upheld and updated the notions of human rights as originally defined in the European Convention for the Protection of Human Rights and Fundamental Freedoms of 1950. Table 1.1 at the end of the chapter provides a side-by-side comparative view of what these basic freedoms are under their respective jurisdictions.

An analysis of these three lists of rights indicates that there is a contractual relationship based on a reciprocal relationship between the state and the individual. Often, it is a response to prior experiences where the government was seen as the oppressor, as exemplified in practice by the English Bill of Rights of 1689, the U.S. Bill of Rights, and later clearly articulated in the preamble of the Universal Declaration of Human Rights of 1948. These rights are written broadly enough to support the normative definitions of duties and obligations on the part of citizens and the government without losing their meaning with the passage of time, or reinterpretation renders them moot. Through their existence, there has to be a reconciliation process as measured through public debate and legislation. Individual rights as written out are not absolute in favor of the citizen, but emphasize the notions of egalitarianism. Rights are balanced in order to allow for the continued existence of the government as long as it follows defined legitimate legal practice, and allows individuals to exercise their freedom of action in pursuit of their individual welfare. Edward Coke, Attorney General to Queen Elizabeth I, makes the comment that these rights provide the basis of the common law:

> *Rectum*, right is taken here for law, in the same sense that *jus*, often is so called. 1. Because it is the right line, whereby justice distributative is guided, and directed, . . . that is, to do justice and right according to the rule of law and custom . . . which is called common right . . . is called common law. . . . 2. The law is called *rectum*, because it discovers, that which is tort, crooked, or wrong, for as right signifies law, for tort, crooked, or wrong, signify injury, and . . . against right. . . . 3. It is called right, because it is the best birthright the subject has, for thereby his goods, lands, wife, children, his body, life, honor, and estimation are protected from injury, and wrong. (1649, Ch. 29)

In the United States, this means that an individual right or freedom can be limited by the government when the action generated by the exercise of personal rights is "directed to inciting or producing imminent lawless action and is likely to incite such action" (*Brandenburg v. Ohio*, 395 U.S. 444, 89 S. Ct. 1827, 23 L. Ed. 2d 430 [1969]) As Associate Justice Louis Brandeis in his concurring opinion in *Whitney v. California* (274 U.S. 357, 47 S. Ct. 641, 71 L. Ed. 1095 [1927]) writes:

> [The] exercise [of the rights of free speech and assembly] is subject to restriction, if the particular restriction proposed is required in order to protect the state from destruction or from serious injury, political, economic, or moral. . . .
>
> Those who won our independence believed that the final end of the state was to make men free to develop their faculties; and that in its government the deliberative forces should prevail over the arbitrary. . . . Believing in the power of reason as applied to public discussion, they eschewed silence coerced by law. . . . Recognizing the tyrannies of governing majorities, they amended the Constitution so that free speech and assembly should be guaranteed.

KEY ECONOMIC AND HISTORICAL ISSUES INFLUENCING THE DEVELOPMENT OF THE SOCIAL SAFETY NET

The acceptance of a social safety net reflects the accompanying change in economic philosophy from one that is laissez faire or marketplace-centered to one where the government is seen as a mechanism to assist those who have been left behind because of economic challenges. The basis of capitalistic economic theory as espoused by classical economists such as Adam Smith in his *Wealth of Nations* and David Ricardo's *Principles of Political Economy* reflects the view that "the barriers must be removed, but once they are removed, modern capitalism—or free enterprise—becomes established of itself" (Parsons, 1968, 157). Smith suggests that the market is the cure for all ills, that government should not intrude. Yet, for the purposes of this text, Ricardo's notions that supply and demand determines the limits of distribution of wealth is particularly worth noting because, as Paul Samuelson writes, "To Ricardo the most important thing in economics was the laws of distribution of the national product among the great classes of society: wages for workers, profits for capitalists, and rents for landowners. With a total social pie limited in its growth, what went to one social class had to be taken away from another" (1976, 842).

These beliefs, for the most part, remain the bases of the market theory economy in the United States until about the time of the Great Depression. However, there is another school of thought that came about that also impacted and continues to impact the economic course of other nations. The socialist school, based on Karl Marx's *Capital* published in 1867, that focuses on the role of labor rather than business cycles. Ironically enough, what Marx does is to take on Ricardo's notions of the distribution of wealth as seen above and tie it together with John Locke's view toward value in human labor and the potential for conflicts in interests. Marx also brings into the equation Thomas Malthus' views of diminishing results vis-à-vis the need for efficiency based on the pressures brought on from overpopulation—in other words, reduction of wages.

One of the important aspects of Marx's work is his emphasis on the bargaining power of labor based on the fact workers make more than it costs employers to pay them wages and provide the necessary environment and tools to produce. This is better known as the relative wage.

> What Marx did was to show "how a moral and historical element" enters into wages, so that the value of the worker's labor power varies over time and place. In addition, Marx explained how wages can in fact rise during a period of intense

accumulation, although its "increase at best means but a quantitative decrease in of the unpaid labor, which the worker must perform. This decrease can never proceed to the point at which it would endanger the system itself." (Linder, 1977, 85)

It is worth noting that as an economic theory as such, Marx's views, at least in the mind of most Western experts, are seen as academic because many of the theories he used or was arguing against were being overturned or changed by contemporaries. What remains is the impact of his insights on how historical, political, and social elements have in the formation of social class and its structure.

Moving forward into the twentieth century, general consensus was that classical economic theories were incapable of explaining or handling the Great Depression. The "neoclassical" economists had not really moved beyond these basic tenets of laissez faire theories. Their focus was on microeconomics as applied to the rise of monopolies imperfect competition (Samuelson, 1976). The thought of a self-correcting business cycle did not seem to fit the era of "big business" and the influences these brought to their communities. The Depression may have begun in the United States, but it spread all over the world. President Herbert Hoover, who had a reputation as a progressive and was seen as having made tremendous accomplishments, utilized the tried and true methods of the existing system to no avail. Hoover believed that voluntary cooperation between the private sector and government was the way to maintain a stable society; yet, he believed in a restricted role of government, especially as it related to price regulations, which were stifling to competition.

The election of Franklin Roosevelt in 1932 paved the way for a new economic order based on the ideas postulated by John Maynard Keynes. Roosevelt's approach was to try to find something that would get things straightened out again.

> The depression that started in mid-1929 was a catastrophe of unprecedented dimensions for United States. The dollar income of the nation was cut in half before the economy hit bottom in 1933. Total output fell by a third, and unemployment reached the unprecedented level of 25 percent of the work force. The depression was no less a catastrophe for the rest of the world. As it spread to other countries, it brought lower output, higher unemployment, hunger, and misery everywhere. (Friedman and Friedman, 1981, 62)

In his groundbreaking work, *General Theory of Employment, Interest and Money* (1936), John Maynard Keynes shifted economic thought to one of full employment. As far as he was concerned, the role of government was to place people in work even if it meant running deficit spending through borrowing. This last was a very radical departure from previous thinking because the role of government had to be limited and government spending had to be balanced; indeed, Keynes ideas were a full repudiation of Say's law of supply always creating its own demand. Many of the New Deal era programs and legislation were indebted to the notion that government spending was the way to revive purchasing power (Leuchtenburg, 1963). As Linder (Linder and Sensat, 1977) pointed out, "Keynesianism

turned out to be the theoretical-ideological program that best synthesized the practical requirements of capitalism" (248).

> What Marx had diagnosed as a distributional struggle to be settled by Power, Keynes saw as a problem of insufficient demand to be remedied by expertise. If the leaders of capitalism insisted on treating problems of demand as though they were problems of supply, and on screwing down the wages of workers in order to restore profits, then a class war could easily arise which would vindicate Marx's prophesy. (Skidelsky, 1992, 439)

Keynes departed from Ricardo and the neoclassicists in thinking that the economy would be voluntarily consuming 100 percent of all of its full-employment income, with demand maintaining full employment. Instead, he saw the lower rates of return on investment from a steady system as possibly leading to stagnation with chronic unemployment. He thought the incentive for investment becomes so low in a steady system because it reduces risk-taking and, in turn, this generates indifference to invest and a preference to hoard money (resulting in stagnation). The laissez faire system to him did not possess an effective self-corrective system. What he visualized was the

> economy as an aggregate quantity of output, resulting from two streams of demand: consumption demand and investment demand. . . . [T]he level of employment depends on the level of aggregate demand for goods and services; if the demand falls short of supply, supply—the society's level of income—has to adjust downwards to bring it back to equality with demand; this equality being the condition of a "stable equilibrium at . . . a level of full employment." The revolutionary thought was that people could be unemployed due to a "lack of effective demand," and not because "they had priced themselves out of jobs." (Skidelsky, 544, 545)

In sum, for Keynes, government's role is to offset the problems that ensue from an excess of savings on the part of those who no longer see investment as an incentive to make money. The government does this by propping up the economy to increase or maintain a high level of demand which, in turn, maintains the need for continued full employment. According to John Kenneth Galbraith (1972), Keynes approach is given qualified but quite explicit support in the United States by the passage of the Employment Act in 1946, in its recognition "that unemployment and insufficient output would respond to positive policies" (52).

Keynes is also worth noting in this discussion because, in spite of his many supporters, there are many detractors from both sides of the political spectrum. The political left sees Keynsianism as too conservative. Markets, a market-type economy, and the systems supporting that type of economy remain intact, as does private property. Keynes sees solutions based on the practical and actual, focusing on political needs and realities rather than the social obligations and responsibilities to a community. Worst of all, to use Galbraith's comment, "Keynes even made legitimate what the governments of all of the industrial countries, including the United States, were already doing" (1981, 67). This is why Linder (Linder and Sensat, 1977) writes the following:

> Keynes made the attempt to conceptualize the practical policy measures undertaken to keep alive a bankrupt socioeconomic formation. . . . Keynsianism seeks to protect capitalism from the revolutionary political forces capitalism has given rise to. Thus in the political aspect of political economy . . . the Keynsians have clearly not "overcome" that aspect of neoclassical economics which tends to deny the existence and/or importance of social classes. . . .
>
> What Keynes succeeded in doing was to lend support to the notion of the survival of a capitalism rid of its blemishes at a time when it could no longer be a progressive society even without the inevitable periodic crises. . . .
>
> Keynes insists on seeing this solution within the framework of a society that continues to give birth to such crises. . . .
>
> The Keynsian misconception of the real processes of characterizing capitalist production is due to the failure to recognize that "the economy can be stabilized" in accordance with the needs of a "healthy" capitalism only if money is spent as capital—that is, the purchase of means of production and labor power—and only if subsequently the labor power is expended in a . . . manner [that] produces surplus value which can be accumulated.
>
> Thus it is not the paid labor of the workers employed by the state investments that leads to increased total income, but only the increase of the productively employed workers. On the other hand, the total income cannot exceed the increase of paid labor if only government expenditures take place, for these by their very nature are not surplus-value producing.
>
> Keynsian fiscal policy is able to come to grips with certain "difficulties" only by shifting the expression of underlying contradictions either to another sphere or to the future. This is a built-in contradiction . . . for to the extent that is is successful in . . . recreating conditions of profitability it must at the same time lay the groundwork for the next cycle deriving from the contradictions inherent in the self-expansion of value. (244, 282, 289, 343)

The political right decries that Keynsianism is the basis of the rise of socialism and the welfare state. For example, Henry Hazlitt (1979) is of the opinion that:

> One of the worst results of the retention of the Keynsian myths is that it not only promotes greater and greater inflation, but that it systematically diverts attention away from the real causes of our unemployment, such as excessive union wage-rates, minimum wage laws, excessive and prolonged unemployment insurance, and overgenerous relief payments.
>
> But the inflation, though in part often deliberate, is today mainly the consequence of other government economic interventions. It is the consequence, in brief, of the Redistributive State—of all the policies of expropriating money from Peter in order to lavish it on Paul. . . .
>
> But instead of passing any such single measure, and bringing our ruin in one single swoop our government has preferred to enact a hundred laws that effect such a redistribution on a partial and selective basis. These measures may miss some needy groups entirely; but on the other hand they may shower upon other groups a dozen different variety of benefits, subsidies, and other handouts. These include, to give a random list: Social Security, Medicare, Medicaid, unemployment insurance, food stamps, veterans' benefits, farm subsidies, subsidized housing, rent subsidies, school lunches, public employment on make-work jobs, Aid to Families with Dependent Children, and direct relief of all kinds, including aid to the aged, the blind, and the disabled. (204–205)

Basically, deficits, inflation, and higher taxation in the name of economic redistribution is what Keynes is all about. The business cycle indicates that government spending goes down in the good times, but begins anew when the cycle is down. This last elements means the need for additional taxes to make up the cost of borrowing funds that the government may not have but are needed in order to keep full employment going. Fueling the cost of borrowing is "that there is no longer an incentive for thrift" (Zoffler, 1980, 237) and savings.

For conservative economists, Keynsianism becomes the chief justification used in the formation and maintenance of "big government." Big government is seen in Orwellian terms, with Big Brother now believing itself to have the right to intrude into people's lives. The experiences of the Great Depression, the resulting New Deal programs to combat the depression, and World War II cements the economics of a mixed economy in the United States after the war, where the federal government has a key role in leveling the playing field of the markets in order to ensure fairness and equity to U.S. citizens. Conservative economists see this new paradigm on government as referee as emanating from a negative perspective. This conservative point of view is reflected in Milton and Rose Friedman's (1981) conclusion about what came to pass:

> World War II interrupted the New Deal, while at the same time strengthened greatly its foundations. The war brought unprecedented control by government over details of economic life: fixing of prices and wages by edict, rationing of consumer goods, prohibition of the production of some civilian goods, allocation of raw materials and finished products, control of imports and exports. . . .
>
> The war's effect on public attitudes was the mirror image of the depression's. The depression convinced the public that capitalism was defective; the war, that centralized government was efficient. Both conclusions were false. The depression was produced by a failure of government, not of private enterprise. As to the war, it is one thing for government to exercise great control temporarily for a single overriding purpose shared by almost all citizens and for which almost all citizens are willing to make heavy sacrifices; it is a very different thing for government to control the economy permanently to promote a vaguely defined "public interest" shaped by the enormously varied and diverse objectives of its citizens. (85–86)

From about 1945 until 1973, national economies throughout the world were categorized under three basic "-isms": capitalism, socialism, and Marxism. In practice, all three had one thing in common, the existence of a welfare state. The difference between these three economies was the degree and level of resources given to support the infrastructure of providing social equity to the citizens of the country in question. The

Arab oil crisis of 1973 brought home the new reality of a reestablished global economy that was fueled through the existence of interdependence, and with the new reality came a reevaluation of the basic tenets that came out from the 1930s.

The United States represented the capitalistic view; however, it was more accurately a mixed economy because it was a mix of government regulation and private enterprise. The New Deal became the Fair Deal under Truman and eventually the Great Society under Johnson. The impact of regulation was to provide a level playing field for workers, owners, and consumers. Government was the means by which to ensure social justice. Under this form of capitalism, in the United States it also suggests a continued increase in the role, power, and influence of the federal government—to many, at the expense of the states' rights to self-regulation. Think in terms of the following assumptions as applying:

- Adequate technology exists to produce enough for everybody.
- All members of society should participate in some way in this production process [understanding that participation is a voluntary process].
- Those who have contributed in the past or have the potential to contribute in the future to the production process should be under a social safety net.
- Those who do not participate in the production process should be seen as "deviants." (Chatterjee, 1999, 3)

The former Soviet Union's communist state represented a planned economy, with industry owned and controlled by the state. Under the rhetoric utilized by the supporters of this system, the key was that the state and all its all activity was worker controlled. Personal incentive had to be subjected to the will and the need of the state and its citizens. Ironically, communism's exercise of economic planning under the Soviet regime (especially under Stalin) was foreign to Marx's point of view. Also ironic was that decision-making became centralized to the point that only the top leaders and those recognized for their support and ability to serve the Party and the State were allowed to participate. Assumptions applying in this system as identified by Chatterjee (1999) were:

- Regardless of technology, all persons have a responsibility to participate in the production process.
- Whatever is produced will be distributed, not by the principle of who contributed most to the production process, but by the principle of who has the most need.
- Those who do not subscribe to the interpretation of this doctrine (usually a dominant political party) are deviants.

The third economy, what is colloquially known as socialism, came to life in most of Europe and Japan. Socialism after World War II was a synthesis between the remaining elements of the prewar market economy and pluralistic interests, where identified and accepted interest groups provided input into government decisions. The Bretton Woods Conference[1] findings and agreements on monetary reform made in 1944 and adopted in the late 1940s meant that the U.S. dollar became the standard for monetary transactions in order to provide for monetary stability; however, the perspective was to use the legacy of the war to revive the economy and ensure the social rights of citizens.

In many European countries and others that accepted this mode of economic and political life, the following rationales for government actions were typical (Samuelson, 1976, 871–872):

1. Government ownership of productive resources
2. Planning
3. Redistribution of income
4. Peaceful and democratic evolution

According to Samuelson, sometimes production for use rather than profit was advocated. Moreoever, workers and professionals were encouraged to learn craftmanship and hone their sense of social service "so that they will be guided by motives other than those of our 'acquisitive society'" (872). The payoff was to be a cradle-to-grave system to increase their individual well-being and an acceptable minimum standard of life.

> The urge for economic equalization is everywhere present and it is commonly proclaimed as a principle. Its sphere of operation is not limited to taxation and redistributional expenditure schemes like those for various forms of social insurance. It enters into, and determines, the scope of all other state intervention.
>
> The important thing is that it then becomes one of the main driving forces behind the general trend towards increasing the volume of state intervention. . . . Generally, the less privileged groups in democratic society, as they become aware of their interests and their political power, will be found to press for even more state intervention in practically all fields. Their interest clearly lies in having individual contracts subordinated as much as possible to general norms laid down in laws, regulations, administrative dispositions, and semi-voluntary agreements between apparently private, but in reality, quasi-public organizations. (Myrdal, 1963, 38)

The economic systems that these countries put in place were directly tied to social policies, with the resulting welfare regimes characterized by:

- a distinctive set of fundamental *values*;
- a distinctive analysis of what produces social *welfare*, and connected to that, a distinctive analysis of why some people *fail to benefit* from that process; and
- deriving from that analysis, a distinctive *policy response* to such people's failures to benefit from the productive process, together with a distinctive way of constructing the *social goal* which that response is aimed at achieving and a distinctive set of *threats* to be avoided in the process. (Goodin et al., 2000, 38, italics in original)

Governments had to interfere in order to bring about the recovery from the ravages of war. The economic structures of most of these countries were not the only ones destroyed.

Many of the political and social institutions were badly damaged as well. There was no steady economic surplus to provide welfare support. There was little beyond survival at the individual level; therefore, the market had to be individual and collective in thought and action at the same time. Wealth creation and distribution (and redistribution for those who could not recover at the same rate as others) had to go hand in hand. This demanded a political structure that could accommodate both elements in a meaningful way.

In Europe, government intervention meant that various governments had to pool their resources in order to leverage their resources in a manner that increased their efficiency. For example, in order to administer the aid package coming from the United States under the Marshall Plan, the European nations created the Organization for European Economic Cooperation (OEEC). In 1950, France advocated that it, Germany, and other European nations combine their coal and steel. The result was the formation of the European Coal and Steel Community (ECSC) in 1952. Then came the formation of the European Atomic Energy Community (Euratom) in 1957 along with the development under the Treaty of Rome that same year of the European Economic Community, the forerunner to what is now the European Union (EU).

After 1973, most of the noncommunist economies were forced to review their economic policies in order to cope with the notions that a global economy not only influences national economies but drive them as a result of adding foreign considerations to a national economy. The increase in uncertainty and volatility meant that many of the old assumptions either collapsed entirely or needed rethinking. The Arab oil embargo of 1973 resulted in a recession—if not actual depression—in many countries as a result of the inflationary spiral resulting from a quadruple increase in price. The United States for the first time realized that its resources were indeed finite, that it simply could not just keep creating revenues to meet its programmatic needs. Europe also felt the pressure, more so because of the destabilization of their monetary system they had in the late 1960s and early 1970s combined with the decision by the United States to "float" the dollar. Basically, the dual negative regime of high unemployment and high inflation meant that most countries running deficits to maintain domestic programs at their accustomed levels had to borrow more to pay for their dependency on foreign oil. The inflationary period that followed created many strains in government programs at all levels. Priorities had to be made in relation to budget allocations as these defined national interests. The arguments boiled down to the question of equity versus efficiency because the basic presumption that there is sufficient profit or wealth derived from production to take care of welfare needs was no longer easily seen to be anymore. The arguments reflected the view that domestic welfare issues were a drain on national resources and, thus, a drag on economic growth (see Goodin et al., 2000).

By the 1980s, the so-called Reagan Revolution meant a reevaluation of the role of the federal government in the United States. The economic slowdown, along with the high inflation and unemployment, that started as an effect of the 1973 embargo were making their presence felt by the time Ronald Reagan became president in 1981. At the beginning of the decade, the U.S. was the largest creditor nation in the world, but by 1987 it became the largest debtor nation. The looming imbalance was seen as an actual threat to the continued well-being of the nation itself. Consequently, the advocates of "supply-side" economics, also referred to as neoliberals, began their advocacy of retreating from the concepts of demand economics supported by the followers of Keynes. The name of the game was to spur the economy by stimulating business. Tax cuts and business credits were the means of economic expansion vis-à-vis the generating of jobs and increased personal income. The result was not as expected, as Lester Thurow (1985) pointed out: government spending rose because of national defense, "a form of public consumption . . . but that does not make it any less government spending" (309). Thurow also observed that the tax cuts reduced the personal savings rate instead of increasing it as expected. In sum, consumption increased, so did the demand for products and services.

The new conservatism focused on monetarism (the increase of money supply) supply-side economics rather than on demand-side economics. Parenthetically, it also meant a desire to return to a greater role of state government in defining needs and revenue allocations. Tax cuts were seen as important because the money was better utilized by individuals rather than by the government. Particularly vulnerable were social programs. Their administrative bureaucracy was very expensive, making these programs inefficient. The notion of equity itself was challenged as well because of concerns that many recipients were at worst abusing the system or, at the least, encouraged by these programs to become dependent on the subsidies these programs provided rather than going out and working for a living. Therefore, there also arose a question of effectiveness.

The economic basis of this reevaluation is based on what is termed the Laffer curve, named after the economist Arthur Laffer. This curve points out that there are two tax rates disastrous to government revenues. At a one hundred percent (100 percent) tax rate, all production stops because all revenues go to the government. At zero percent (0 percent), the opposite is true; production is maximized, but the government receives no revenue. The trick is to find an optimal point where interests balance out—in other words, how much tax the government can claim and collect without stifling the interest to work. Therein lays its controversy: At what point of taxation is work stifled and tax revenues reduced? The focus is on productivity, at the market level and, by implication, at the individual level within the workplace. But as Zoffer (1980) suggests, the Laffer curve "does not come to grips with the real problem, which is the role of government in the economy and not the amount of taxes collected to pay for government activities" (110).

Germany and Japan came into their own in economic terms by the 1970s. Other economies also rebuilt themselves after the War and could be termed successful, albeit at a more modest level because of their smaller size and available resources. However, as alluded to earlier in this chapter, Europe in the 1970s (and some other countries following their economic examples) saw the fulfillment of welfare states in the postwar years leading "to expectations of benefits and services which outstripped the capacity of states to finance them" (Cawson, 1986, 90). The economic imbalance was accompanied by a perception problem on the part of the public, which became critical of the decision-making process in social services. These were seen as private and undemocratic, unresponsive to consumer convenience and to public complaints, with an over-reliance on their own experts from their civil servants ranks (George and Wilding, 1985).

The two major political models of socialism that developed throughout Europe are referred to as *social democracies*, as seen in Scandinavia and the *corporatist state*, such as Germany. In both types of socialism, the center of action is based on citizens controlling the means of national production. Class politics, socialist economics, and redistributive social welfare characterize the Scandinavian model (Goodin et al., 2000). The basis for both types is the maintenance of social equality and security via the strong connection between the government and its citizens. Its reasoned doctrine is the use of government regulation as the means of controlling resources for the purposes of reducing/eliminating poverty, providing for national welfare by subsidizing quality of life programs, controlling unemployment, and market intervention.

Corporatism "represents a fusion of the processes of interest representation and policy implementation into a reciprocal relationship between the state and organised interests" (Cawson, 1986, 18). These interests are based on (1) group politics, (2) communitarian economics, and (3) mutualist policies where the fundamental value is social cohesion and integration (Goodin et al., 2000). Bargaining can be said to exist within an economic framework absent of many forms or pressures of competition. Competition is reduced because it recognized the interests of the various elements within the state. Interest mediation occurs because

> The state may not be either an arena for which interests contend or another interest group with which they must compete, but a constitutive element engaged in defining, distorting, encouraging, regulating, licensing and/or repressing the activities of associations—and backed in its efforts, at least potentially, by coercive actions and claims to legitimacy. (Schmitter, 1982, 260–261)

Overcentralization was the complaint faced by many of these countries. Between 1945 and the early 1970s many of these governments ignored employment policy, something that could not be ignored by the 1980s when the worldwide economic slowdown made work a scarce commodity (George and Wilding, 1985). The reason that unemployment was ignored was because high productivity was linked with high employment. With increased unemployment came the additional pressures on states that were already challenged with the need to pay for their dependency on foreign sources of energy. The oil crisis brought with it higher national debts and inflation levels along with higher unemployment. In societies whose main purpose was the redistribution of wealth, the question of who has input thus became one of more than idle interest. The result was a renewed interest in the discussion of a private economy, with a particular emphasis on the reexamination on the role of government ownership of key industries. The best example of this was Great Britain where in 1979 Margaret Thatcher was elected prime minister, heading a conservative government whose interest it was to dismantle many of the cherished elements of the social welfare state in that country.

The 1980s and 1990s saw other economic changes that further influenced the political aspects of policy-making throughout the world. One change was the dismantling of the Berlin Wall in 1989, an event that signaled the end of the communist system as a viable social and economic alternative to capitalism and socialism. It was accompanied by the reunification of Germany and the tremendous costs associated in bringing the former East Germany up to par with the conditions and expectations of the former West Germany. Many of these costs were associated with social safety net concerns, and these costs had a serious impact on the German economy and its ability to meet the demands of resource reallocation.

Germany's reunification meant adding 17 million citizens to a country that already had about 63 million in its census rolls. Many of the costs had to do with bringing the East German infrastructure up to date and standards found in West Germany. The costs were estimated to cost about $100 billion USD, subsidized by temporary taxes on West German citizens. The continuation of the taxes reflected a redirection of resources to modernize an obsolete infrastructure as well as its collateral subject-matter of pollution, trying to integrate a system that represented a lower standard living, and a continued preference by East Germans for their social programs. It ended up with the collapse of East German industry and high unemployment, with overall German economic growth averaging about 1 percent and unemployment hovering at the 10 percent level (Clark, 2002). It also was seen as a major reason for the early weakness of the newly minted euro currency (Hanley, 2002, 3). While making Germany the largest and ostensibly the most powerful nation in Europe, the impact was that Germany had to retrench, rethink, and reduce some of its contributions to the European Union. Nevertheless, reunification also provided a renewed interest in sharing resources and working as a key player in a greater European community.

A second event was the continuing evolutionary process in Europe toward a federation of nations, exemplified by the creation of the European Monetary Union through the adoption of the Maastricht Treaty. "The Treaty provide[d] for economic and monetary union to be introduced by the end of the century in three successive stages according to a precise timetable," actually begun in 1990 (European Union Economic and Monetary Affairs, 2002). According to Levine (1999), "To join the union, applicants were required to 'converge' by this year on four criteria: low inflation, a narrow range of interest rates, stable exchange rates, and budget deficits no greater than three percent of GDP."

At first, agreements centered on following prohibitions set forth in the treaty on certain behaviors by national central banks. The next level of agreements gravitated around rules of public financing, and the third stage focused on binding budgetary and monetary rules. The most visible impact of these changes was the adoption of a single currency—the euro—that came into existence on January 1, 2002. This evolutionary process reflected a regional attempt at streamlining the socioeconomic and supporting political processes in a progressively more regional than individual state manner, all in the name of improved efficiency and accountability as a means to meet the needs of the citizens of the member states. Paradoxically, this evolutionary process toward increased centralism at the potential expense of national sovereignty provided an example of the socialist philosophy in action while providing a marked contrast to the decentralization and government downsizing that was seen in the United States at the time.

A third event was the ability of the United States to regain its status as the top economic powerhourse as the result of (1) increased productivity (reversing the trend of the 1970s and 1980s), (2) improved quality control, (3) technological innovations in the areas of information technology and biotechnology, which led to improving human capital, (4) rapid expansion in various economic sectors and the various investment markets, and most unexpectedly, (5) a very low rate of inflation. Small and large businesses contributed to this resurgence, highlighting the impact that quality and adaptability in the planning process had on corporate success. Joseph Juran (2000) identified the aspects of quality that led the resurgence: customer focus, quality as a top priority, strategic quality planning, benchmarking, continuous improvement, training in managing for quality, quality from suppliers as well as manufacturers, partnering, employee empowerment, motivation, meaningful measures to follow these concepts, and not delegating managerial responsibility for quality. Some industries such as the semiconductor and steel industries made a comeback from the brink of competitive collapse; other industries like computer disk drive makers and pharmaceuticals weathered strong foreign competition in the 1970s and 1980s (Mowery, 1999). Mowery also points out that:

> U.S. competitive resurgence . . . relied on the close proximity of U.S. producers and demanding, innovative users in large domestic market. In addition, the rapid growth of desktop computing in the United States during the 1980s was aided by the availability of imported desktop systems and components, which kept product prices low and propelled adoption of this technology at a faster pace than most Western European economies or in Japan, where trade restrictions and other policies kept desktop prices higher. The rapid domestic adoption of desktop computing contributed to the growth of a large packaged software industry . . . This virtuous circle was further aided by the restructuring of the U.S. telecommunications industry that began in the 1980s. (1999, 4–5)

Economic resurgence brought forth a series of discussions, some old, some newer, some transposed. On the social front, the need to accommodate this new technology to the everyday work and personal life meant a renewed emphasis on training. The lowering of unemployment meant that those that remained out of work were either incapable of working or lacked the skills. Employers from the 1970s onward complained about the poor level of education provided in the Pre K–12 public school systems in the country. Many provided evidence that a number of high school graduates lacked the necessary reading, writing, and computation skills necessary to become effective workers. Some companies such as Motorola moved to meet this challenge with the formation of Motorola U. However, other employers did not feel it their responsibility (even for cost effectiveness reasons) to do so because of the direct and indirect cost to the employers in resources and time away from production. This combined with a social and government reexamination of the effectiveness of the school system. Terrence Bell, the then U.S. Secretary of Education, published *A Nation at Risk* in 1983. The title said it all: the public education system had serious flaws in meeting the needs of an educated citizenry and a competent workforce. The technological revolution that was seen in the 1980s and 1990s now added a new complication, the need to update and upgrade skills. More and more of the machinery required to do work meant a need to learn how to use new equipment as well as pursuing a different way of thinking. The center of interest became these questions: Who should do the training? Who picks up the tab? How much training is needed? Who will benefit from the training? Who should be trained in order to meet the employment shortfalls?

Economic resurgence from a socioeconomic-political perspective meant that although it became the greatest debtor nation through a negative balance of trade fueled by its citizen's desires for cheap products (labor costs being cheaper in other parts of the world) and an even higher standard of living, by 1996 the United States was able to establish a balanced budget. From a historical perspective, this was a return to one of the country's panaceas up to the Great Depression and the formation of the New Deal. The other historical panacea that came to the forefront was the reduction of the national debt. Moves were made to reduce the debt under the Clinton administration; however, a debate centered over the use of the budget surpluses. Should there be a continued emphasis in reducing the national debt? Should there be significant tax cuts because individuals have a right to their own money and have a better idea on what to do with it? Should some of the funds be used to provide "appropriate" assistance to those in need that are not benefiting from the improved economic circumstances and opportunities? Much of the credit for balancing the budget was given to the downsizing of government and a retrenchment in government intrusion into individual affairs along with improved economic performance in the private sector. The argument crystallized into the neoliberal supply-side economic espousing personal responsibility and a degree of government laissez faire versus social capitalism that posits government as the referee and protector from the abuses emanating out of the built-in inequities of those who receive the benefits from private enterprise.

A fourth event was the rising tide of illegal immigration to the so-called industrialized countries by people seeking to improve their personal lot, resulting from the formation of a global economy. A major problem in the United States because of the number of people coming across the border with Mexico from Mexico and other parts of Latin America or via boats from the Caribbean area and from the Far East, illegal immigration also became a major problem in other Western countries, especially in Europe. This brought forth many issues that went beyond the economic costs of providing services to these individuals. Illegal immigration brought out issues such as displacement of labor combined with the desire for cheap labor, human rights issues (for example, smuggling, safety of transportation, slavery, and racism), organized crime, confusion in national immigration processes because of the need to distinguish between asylum seekers and those simply looking for a better life, straining of bilateral and multilateral relationships based on the demand to repatriate illegal immigrants to their land of origin, the "brain drain" created in the country of origin, and the lack of opportunity in the land of origin that made these individuals to immigrate illegally in the first place. The crux of these matters was the need for a concerted effort based "on the principle of different treatment for refugees compared with economic migrants" (Castles and Loughana, 2002, 2) in order to remain compliant to the 1951 United Nations Refugee Convention and the 1967 Protocols on Refugees.

Legal immigration has been seen as a national benefit; illegal immigration was seen as a drain on the economy. Governments continued to research the various types of immigration because, as Australia's Minister of Immigration and Multicultural and Indigenous Affairs Philip Ruddock (2001) pointed out,

> governments have to make sure immigration has an unequivocally positive impact depending on its composition. This is critical to obtaining public confidence in immigration. . . . Immigration is also the only thing that will eventually keep our labour force from going into decline. This is a point that the populations of Japan and many nations in Europe have already reached. It is not surprising to see these countries now grappling with the need to develop a formal migration program to supplement their declining labour force . . . . [G]iven the very substantial budgetary and economic costs, it is important that a fair balance is struck between the extent to which these costs are borne by taxpayers and society in general.

Illegal immigration also left its impact on those countries that acted and continue to be the roadways to the United States and Europe. A number of these countries not only saw a number of illegal immigrants pass through their borders, they saw a number of their own citizens make the decision themselves. Mexico provided the greatest number of illegal immigrants to the United States, as well as being the gateway for many immigrants from other parts of Central and South America. Turkey was a gateway to Europe because of its location and for meeting the demand for foreign workers. Both countries were denounced for not making their boundaries more impermeable while incapable of sustaining strong enough national economies to provide work for their citizens. Repatriation was

not a viable option because the jobs did not exist in the first place. This was why it was written of Turkey that

> Recent international developments, cross-border or civil conflicts, economic hardships as well as hunger, famine and epidemics, the desire for a better lifestyle and widespread human rights violations have led millions of people to migrate to developed countries through legal or illegal means. . . . [T]he financial burden on our country, which is generally a transit rather than a target country, is very high. Not a single positive contribution has been made through our projects prepared under the "Sharing the Burden" projects presented to the EU. European countries directly benefit from this, but instead of cooperating with our country to share this burden, they have failed to exert any efforts to solve this problem. They ignore all our efforts and voice unfair criticisms, both of which have the effect of straining our cooperative goodwill. (Sayin, 2002)

Another issue spawned from illegal immigration was the reliance on remittances, the amount of funds that these immigrants returned to their country of origin to help their families or facilitate the migration of some of the other family members. Remittances became an example of one element of the global economy, the transference of funds based on the need to find cheap labor. Common for legal as well as illegal immigrants, and as seen in Table 1.2, they added up to the point that the nations of origin end up relying on this transfer of funds to provide needed infusion of cash. In a current analysis, Arno Tanner (2002) suggested that the three countries he researched (Canada, New Zealand, and Switzerland) made considerations pertaining national immigration policy "mainly by themselves, and leading to often economically satisfactory but socially questionable outcomes" (27). Further analysis of the EU discussions at a summit in Seville in June 2002 within their Parliament prior to that meeting also demonstrated that the extension of this observation applies more than not when considering immigration issues.[2] The EU "has adopted a holistic approach on migration and asylum issues . . . however this discourse has not been translated into concrete action" (Hurwitz, 2002, 11).

A fifth event was the role that stock markets played as barometers of national economic strength. Traditionally perceived as a predictor of performance, the stock market has become, in the eyes of many, an actual indicator of current performance. The changes measured by the Standard and Poor's 500 have been considered as one of the ten criteria for the leading economic indicator index. Yet, for many policymakers it seemed the stock market was now perceived to be an actual macroeconomic indicator of its own, because stock market prices reflected real economic activity rather than market expectations. As Burgstaller (2002) suggested,

> Rising asset prices, for instance, will improve balance sheets of firms and banks, and the market value of assets owned by households will increase. Credit costs decrease and the borrowing capacity of firms and households to finance current consumption and investment should enhance (IMF, 2000).

As asset markets are responsible for more and more capital movement in comparison with the trade of goods we might expect an additional channel from stock prices to the real economy via the exchange rate. A decrease in stock prices causes a reduction in wealth of domestic investors which in turn leads to lower demand for money and lower interest rates. These lower interest rates encourage capital outflows, ceteris paribus, which in turn are the cause of currency depreciation (Granger et al., 1998). Stock prices lead exchange rates with positive correlation according to this reasoning. (1)

The period from about 1991 through 2001 saw an unprecedented economic upturn in the United States led through technological innovations, also known as the "dot.com" era. The emphasis became capital formation through stock offerings, and the goal of corporate profits truly became one of meeting shareholder expectations. However, the economic upturn was not as strong in Europe or Japan, having been sporadic in terms that only certain aspects of the national economies seemed to have moved forward. The focus on the market as an economic indicator meant that capital formation and investment became primary over other economic and social concerns. Europe and Japan—really for the first time in their postwar experience—had to deal with unemployment and underemployment, along with working out issues of what to do with nationalized industries and overcentralized economic policies. And as the slowdown became more pervasive in Japan, these issues also crossed their borders into other Asian economies, most notably South Korea's. A study of Singapore's stock market indicated that there were some relationships between stock market and economic performance (Leigh, 1997); yet, contrary to expectations, Burgstaller's (2002) analysis indicated that the stock markets in Austria, Japan, and the United States did not "have predictive content for real variables like industrial production" (9).

Probably more significant, however, was a sixth event, the formation of a new basis of economic activity: the information age. The technological advances represented through the creation of supercomputers and later personal computers and the accompanying telecommunications revolution allowed for new capital formation and the creation of new types of jobs, although these were mainly in the service rather than industrial sector. This change from the industrial-age economy to a high-technology-focused information-age and service-sector economy demanded greater freedoms and degrees of participation on the part of individuals and a number of businesses. Its backdrop was the crystallization of a world economy, but one that was different to what existed in the late nineteenth and early twentieth centuries.

Twenty years ago no one talked of the "world economy." The term then was "international trade." The change in term . . . bespeaks a profound change in economic reality. Twenty or thirty years ago the economy outside the borders of a nation—and especially outside the borders middle-sized or large nation—could still be seen as different, as separate, as something that could be safely ignored in dealing with the domestic economy and in domestic economic policy. That, as the evidence makes unambiguously clear, is sheer delusion today. (Drucker, 1995, 144)

The information age also brought forth an individualized sense of entrepreneurship along with a new way of doing business at the national and international levels. As Peter Drucker indicated back in 1985 while all of this was developing, the new technology accompanying the electronics revolution of the information age is entrepreneurial management. Many of the advances were generated by individuals acting on their own, or in work environments that fostered innovation and individualized thinking. Intelligence became a form of capital with a potential specific value in its own right. The question of who owned an individual's intellectual capital came to the fore once again: Does a society have the right to impose its will on an individual's ability? Also, this renewed emphasis on individual action from an economic perspective reopened the question of an individual's obligation to his or her community and nation. The issues were personal control and moral obligations or, if one prefers, the choice of whether or not to share.

The new demands and ways of doing business in an information age emphasized the seventh event worth consideration, the reestablishment of the global economy. As Robert Reich pointed out, "In the global enterprise, the bonds between company and country—between them and us—are rapidly eroding." Multinational corporations that came to life in the 1950s, some having already been major players in their nation economies prior to World War II, made national borders a moot point in certain regards by the 1970s. The 1990s saw a another twist in the global market. Again, as Reich noted, "cross-border ownership is booming: Americans are buying into global companies based in Europe and East Asia; Europeans and Asians are buying into companies based in the United States" (1991, 77).

By the 1990s these corporations became the backbone of the now emerged global economy. As Ferdows pointed out, three realities became apparent in the emerging world economy: (1) the liberalization of international trade accompanied with capital mobility, (2) increased technology, and (3) deregulation. Tariffs were reduced worldwide from an average of 40 percent in 1940 to 7 percent in 1990 through a series of multinational agreements (1997). The existence of multinational corporations directly challenged the notions of nationalized industries. Illustrative of the challenge was the Turin European Council's identification of the emerging global economy as a major challenge facing the European Union. The reduction of tariffs made national boundaries more permeable to goods from the outside. Increased sophistication of manufacturing and product development meant the need to have easy access to world-class suppliers. Finally, the pressure of getting a product from the drawing board into production meant a stronger incentive for these global firms to focus on the efficiencies received from paying attention to the first two realities. In sum, global businesses became better at leveraging their resources to get out a quality product.

The global economy made these multinational firms as players in national economies and their social structures. The question became one of their role in maintaining quality-of-life issues such as environmental concerns and social well-being.

Did companies—and do they now—have a moral or legal obligation to ensure that they practiced public responsibility as part of their operations? The discussion also presented itself in terms of whether the laissez-faire global market influences should be curbed through the reestablishment of a social market economy structure by governments. Stuart Hart wrote that it is easy to state the case in terms that these corporations are the cause of many of the problems. Taking from his terminology, corporations were seen as guilty of social upheavals in many developing nations that led to impoverished customers, degraded environment, failing political systems, and unraveling societies. Yet, as Hart also pointed out,

> The root of the problem—explosive population growth and rapid economic development in the emerging economies—are political and social issues that exceed the mandate and the capabilities of any corporation. At the same time, corporations, are the only organizations that have the technology, global reach, and, ultimately, the motivation to achieve sustainability. (1997, 67)

The seventh and recent event that had an impact on world and national affairs was the attack on New York City by terrorists on September 11, 2001. Combined with the economic slowdown in the United States that begun in 2000 and some of the impacts on revenue generation and distribution resulting from the passing of a tax cut earlier in 2001, this meant the elimination of the country's budget surplus and a return to deficit spending. The United States, along with Germany and Japan, returned to a recession economy during 2001. However, the United States also returned to a "wartime" economic outlook where defense spending was reviewed in anticipation of a war on terrorism that may require troops and material to be sent throughout the world. Deficit spending quit being a negative term because the cause was deemed appropriate; the budget is indicative of the role of government, revealing its purposes to others even though at times they can be contradicting commitments (Wildavsky, 1992).

The main impact of September 11th was the creation of instability and the perception that the United States was finally vulnerable to terrorism. As analysts were saying at the time,

> confidence in the strength and resilience of the US economy and the invincibility of the US dollar had been severely damaged prior to September 11, that the successful attacks that day on the nerve center of world capitalism had damaged confidence further, and that under such circumstances US consumers who have prevented a lapse into recession to date will hardly be encouraged to go on a spending spree. (*Asia Times*, September 18, 2001, Editorial)

The attack cast doubt over the U.S. economy and its ability to rebound and once again be the main economic engine in the global economy. The attack has made the many interested groups, organizations, associations, businesses, industries, and so on, reanalyze the economy and its impact on society. A potential reprioritization of programs and who should subsidize them—if at all—began, with new considerations fueling old political paradigms and philosophies.

For the United States, the question now became one of how to build an internal defense infrastructure (the first one since the Civil War), to maintain economic prosperity while ensuring the well-being of those living in the United States, and keep a balance between revenues and expenditures. The economic slowdown reinvigorated the ideological discussion of tax revenues and the need of social programs on the lines of the role of the federal government: either it is too big and needs to be curtailed, or it is not big enough and the need justifies additional resources and/or programming. It brought forth once again the issue of fair share. As Wildavsky observed in 1974:

> At this point it is necessary to distinguish "fair share" from another concept, "the base." The base is the general expectation among the participants that programs will be carried on at close to the going level of expenditures but it does not necessarily include all activities. . . . "Fair share" means not only the base an agency has established but also the expectation that it will receive some proportion of funds. . . . "Fair share" then, reflects a convergence of expectations on roughly how much the agency is to receive in comparison to others. (17)

CULTURAL CONSIDERATIONS INFLUENCING THE PERCEPTIONS TOWARD SOCIAL SAFETY NETS

Cultural outlooks influence laws and economic structures because they represent theories of human nature. The social movements representing the status quo or conversely attempting to change the community provide the framework of legitimate activity as represented by a community's laws, its economic systems, its government definition and structure, and other organized social interaction. Individuals, government agencies, nongovernment agencies, businesses, and industries all reflect the culture that generates them. They do so by using procedures that are accepted by society, defining their existence by meeting the needs of the community, and presenting themselves as meeting those needs. To ignore their role is to try to wish away that most basic level of influences on what happens in that community, state, region, or nation.

In Western societies, particularly in the United States more so than in England and mainland Europe, there were two social philosophies that led to movements impacting the outlook toward social safety nets and how governments provided services under their police powers of protecting the interests of their citizens. The first and most famous of these philosophies was referred to as "social Darwinism" as espoused in the late nineteenth century. The second social philosophy was first identified by the famous German social historian Max Weber, referring to how the "Protestant Ethic" is the foundation for capitalism and individual success within a capitalistic society. These philosophies waned—more slowly than one would expect—after World War II, evolving to a one that emphasizes human rights, individual participation, and a more ecological perspective on individual responsibility. However, the latent influences of these ways of thinking did not or have not completely disappeared because of their deep roots in Western thought, particularly in the spheres of influence dominated by Anglo-Saxon thinking.

The Views of Social Darwinism

Cynthia Eagle Russett (1976) provides the best description of how the United States came to adopt this view:

> Americans accepted Darwinism [by the end of the nineteenth century].... They measured it with their minds, not their pocket books. The American business community did, it is true, obey the precepts of pragmatism, and continued to do its affairs ... with small regards for finespun theories. But intellectuals took Darwinism with great seriousness from the first. They realized the challenge thrown up by Darwinian social theory to the fluid society of industrial America.... They proposed not to abandon Social Darwinism but to tame it, to make it at last truly social. In this they achieved a dual success—the beginning of a sophisticated social science and the establishment of a collective theory of society. The United States had moved into the twentieth century; it now had a twentieth-century social philosophy. (119–120)

And in Europe, the publication of *The Origin of Species By Means of Natural Selection* in 1859 provided the catalyst for the rethinking of the role of man and society based on biological models, giving the nineteenth and early twentieth centuries what Oscar Spengler (1956) disparagingly calls the "spiritual unity" of the age:

> Darwinism—that is to say, that totality of very varied and discrepant ideas, in which the common factor is merely the application of the causality principle to living things ... —was known in all details to the 18th century.... From Schopenhauer to Shaw, everyone has been, without being aware of it, bringing the same principle into form. Everyone (including even those ... [who] knew nothing of Darwin) is a derivative of the evolution idea ... whether he issues it with a biological or economic imprint. (369–370)

Social Darwinism, for better or worse, is equated with the notion of the survival of the fittest. Darwin puts forth the view, based on his studies of ecosystems, that competition between variants of a species determines which one survives and which one becomes extinct. In his words,

> [Natural selection] leads to the improvement of each creature in relation to its organic and inorganic conditions of life, and consequently, in most cases, to what must be regarded as an advance in organisation.
>
> Natural selection also leads to divergence of character; for the most organic beings diverge is structure, habit, and constitution, by so much the more can a large number be supported on the area.... Therefore, during the modification of the descendants of any one species, and during the incessant struggle of all species to increase in numbers, the more diversified the descendants become, the better will be their chance of success in the battle of life. (1859/1952, 63)

Others have juxtaposed these words into a human social context in the nineteenth and twentieth centuries. At the most basic level, Darwin has been meant to support the laissez faire approach by government toward meeting social ills. To this way of thinking as exemplified by Konrad Lorenz for example, natural selection, as part of the evolutionary process is the bedrock of all human phenomena which "might be approached and explained by economic, religious, ethical, or political considerations" (Fromm, 1973, 31). Or as Herbert Spencer preached, take *laissez-faire* quite literally; do not interfere because "evolution will bring about the progressive adjustment of internal relations to external relations unless we muck it up" (Young, 1990).

The basic premise, seemingly, was that to help the weaker is a disservice to them and to the society as a whole. It also tied into the traditionally accepted notions in the West of self-reliance, in which adversity is seen as a means of improving oneself. Self-preservation was equated with ability on one hand, and in a more trenchant form, evolution itself. Thorstein Veblen wrote,

> The evolution of social structures has been a process of natural selection of institutions.... Institutions are not only in themselves the result of a selective and adaptive process which shapes the prevailing or dominant types of spiritual attitude and aptitudes; they are at the same time special methods of life and of human relations, and are therefore in their turn efficient factors of selection. So that in the changing institutions in their turn make for a further selection of individuals endowed with the fittest temperament. (1953, 131)

This observation supported Thomas Huxley's view that the role of science and education is to make the working class' work more effective (Irvine, 1955).

One notion that made social Darwinism attractive was "its complete abandonment of the subjective for an objective point of view" (Parsons, 1968, 115). As a concept, it reduced human behavior to concrete variables rather than philosophical conjecturing. As a theory, it provided a unifying approach to the psychology of individuals and socioeconomic behavior. More important, social Darwinism could and did provide a means of reconciling the sciences with the notions of morality and morals espoused by many of the mainstream religious practices of the day, at least as it related to human behavior and practices. (This is not to be confused with the natural selection view of evolution that was attacked in the famous Scopes "Monkey Trial" of 1925.) Evolution was a process, meaning that although it had its false starts and "dead ends," human existence was not anarchical per sé, but had an intrinsic sense of order. This was well summed up by Matthew Arnold when he wrote by 1875, "Thus, in our eyes, the very framework and exterior order of the State, whoever may administer the State, is sacred, and culture is the most resolute enemy of anarchy, because of the great hopes and designs for the State which culture teaches us to nourish" (1966, 204).

Thoughts Typical of the "Protestant Ethic"

The second social consideration prevalent in Anglo-Saxon thinking that still has not gone completely away and impacts some of the social thinking in the United States and elsewhere in the Western world is what the German social historian Max Weber termed the "Protestant ethic." His comments demonstrate another component of a social doctrine that was prevalent in the nineteenth and twentieth centuries and is still around today, although in a more latent form.

Writing about the situation in Germany in his work, *The Protestant Ethic and the Spirit of Capitalism*, originally written in 1904–1905, Weber put forth the proposition that it seems that those individuals who are mostly successful in the acquisition of wealth believe or tend to adopt the views typically attributed to Protestants of hard work and progress. Whereas Darwin's notions of evolution were seen as antireligious, here is an argument that cloaks many of the sentiments espoused by the social Darwinists with the cloak of religious propriety.

Weber states right off that "man is dominated by the making of money, by acquisition as the ultimate purpose of his life" (1958, 53). He prefaces this view by commenting, "the impulse to acquisition, pursuit of gain, of money, of the greatest amount of money, has in itself nothing to do with capitalism. . . . One may say that it has been common to all sorts and conditions of men at all times and in all countries of the earth, wherever the objective possibility of it is or has been given" (17). His thesis takes on two forms. First, that those in the West were the ones that were able to establish and utilize their legal and social systems to their benefit through the elements of trade. From this perspective, Weber then provides his view on the principal characteristics of modern capitalism. Second, that the inherent notions particularly evident in the Protestant ethic provide the moral as well as ethical underpinnings for individuals to act in such a manner that is, by itself, the catalyst for acquisition and personal improvement. What he refers to the spirit of capitalism is based on his belief that "the magical and religious forces, and the ethical idea of duty based upon them, have in the past always been among the most important formative influences on conduct" (27).

For the purposes of this narrative, the discussion shall center on the second point, but only at a somewhat superficial level. In particular, the point worth emphasizing is on the importance of wanting to work. According to Weber, the Protestant ethic values work as a virtue. It is a virtue because work, as an indicator of purpose for working for the greater good, is a calling ordained by God. More to the point, the Puritanical concept of work, as part of the division of labor in the community, is important because personal character "is to be known by its fruits" (161).

Provide there are, then, two duties: one to work and a second one to stewardship over one's possessions. The first duty means that indolence cannot be tolerated, even from the rich. Wealth is bad "ethically in so far as it is a temptation to idleness and sinful enjoyment of life" (163). However, wanting to be poor is worse. As Weber writes later in the same paragraph,

To wish to be poor was, it was often argued, the same thing as wishing to be unhealthy; it is objectionable as a glorification

of works and derogatory to the glory of God. Especially begging, on the part of one able to work, is not only the sin of slothfulness, but a violation of the duty of brotherly love according to the Apostle's own words. (163)

The second duty refers to the belief that all things come from God. "Man is only a trustee of the goods which have come to him through God's grace. He must, like the servant in the parable, give an account of every penny entrusted to him" (170).

As Weber sees it, this means that the use of acquired goods needs to be used in balance, to glorify God by saving, being provident, and not using money for frivolous purposes or luxuries. The ideal under these premises is the middle-class home because it avoids ostentation and the sins of excess. The middle-class home is also the indicator of sound judgment and the "rational" use of wealth. The middle class thus becomes the moral yardstick by which social behavior is measured.

Weber's assertions work closely with the then held notions espoused by the social Darwinists. It provides a moral argument, indicating that those who do not measure up are somehow deficient and lacking. People have to help themselves, to fend for themselves. Those asking for a handout that can work should work, and not rely on the goodness of others. This point of view serves to support a belief that those needing assistance are trying to avoid work and that the best help anyone can give an individual in need is to get that person working and fending for him or herself.

THE FIRST ELEMENTS OF THE SOCIAL SAFETY NET IN THE UNITED STATES: UNEMPLOYMENT AND OLD-AGE INSURANCE

On the side of relief we have extended material aid to millions of our fellow citizens.

On the side of recovery we have helped to lift agriculture and industry from a condition of utter Prostration.

But, in addition to these immediate tasks of relief and of recovery we have properly, necessarily and with overwhelming approval determined to safeguard these tasks by rebuilding many of the structures of our economic life and reorganizing it in order to prevent a recurrence of collapse.

It is childish to speak of recovery first and reconstruction afterward. In the very nature of the processes of recovery we must avoid the destructive influences of the past. We have shown the world that democracy has within it the elements necessary to its own salvation. (Franklin D. Roosevelt, Message to Congress, June 8, 1934)

The United States' federal government began to establish its social safety nets in response to the plight of citizens during the Great Depression. Private charitable organizations could not provide assistance to the degree it was required, neither could state-based programs. As President Roosevelt stated above, the collapse was economic as well as personal.

Up to this point, traditionally, welfare was the province of state and local governments whenever government had to become involved; usually, assistance was provided through private charity by community or church organizations. Initially under the Hoover Administration, and then under Roosevelt's New Deal, in spite of many reservations based on traditional societal expectations, the federal government decided to step in because of the scale of reform that was needed. The new watchwords for these reforms became recovery, reform, and security (Freedman, 1967, 223). Legislation had to be passed to make needed changes to the banking and finance sectors. Assistance legislation had to be generated to stabilize farm prices and help farmers keep their farms. Business regulations had to be worked out in order to provide a "fair" working environment for citizens. Along the way, there was a realization that individual assistance was also needed because so many had lost their assets, real and paper. Frances Perkins, Roosevelt's Secretary of Labor, in a speech titled "The Roots of Social Security" in 1962 summed up the situation best:

> I suppose the roots—the idea that we ought to have a systematic method of taking care of the material needs of the aged—really springs from that deep well of charitableness which resides in the American people, and the efforts and the struggles of charity workers and social workers to handle the problems of people who were growing old and had no adequate means of support. . . .
>
> People were so alarmed that all through the rest of 1929, 1930, and 1931, the specter of unemployment—of starvation, of hunger, of the wandering boys, of the broken homes, of the families separated while somebody went out to look for work—stalked everywhere. The unpaid rent, the eviction notices, the furniture and bedding on the sidewalk, the old lady weeping over it, the children crying, the father out looking for a truck to move their belongings himself to his sister's flat or some relative's already overcrowded tenement, or just sitting there bewilderedly waiting for some charity officer to come and move him somewhere. I saw goods stay on the sidewalk in front of the same house with the same children weeping on top of the blankets for 3 days before anybody came to relieve the situation!
>
> I've always said, and I still think we have to admit, that no matter how much fine reasoning there was about the old-age insurance system and the unemployment insurance prospects—no matter how many people were studying it, or how many committees had ideas on the subject, or how many college professors had written theses on the subject—and there were an awful lot of them—the real roots of the Social Security Act were in the great depression of 1929. Nothing else would have bumped the American people into a social security system except something so shocking, so terrifying, as that depression.

The creation of the American social welfare state in the 1930s "rested on the assumption that a just society could be secured by imposing a welfare state on a capitalist foundation" (Leuchtenburg, 1963, 165). President Herbert Hoover's attempt to generate solutions through voluntary cooperation of the business community proved insufficient and forced him to "abandon old assumptions about the sufficiency of voluntary measures and support a progressive program that implied more extensive federal intervention" (Link, 1955, 371). Yet, the changes made were done in an environment that had to balance experimentalism, pragmatism, and acceptance. This meant an emphasis of building and maintaining self-pride and self-reliance; programs could not be seen as a handout to people. The idea was to give insurance instead of welfare, to blunt the negative impacts of economic downturns rather than having a de facto right to a minimum quality of life. The government had to provide individual assistance alongside systems-wide reform and collective assistance. This meant looking at problems from a "clinical" needs assessment perspective, identifying potential solutions, and having the flexibility to make changes when the identified solution did not work. Above all else, it meant taking a look at what worked, to identify benchmarks of best practice and offer these in a manner that was politically tolerable to the inherent conservative beliefs in Congress and shared by many others throughout the country.

The social safety net, consequently, looked somewhat like the tax-based programs that had been formed in Germany under Bismark in the 1880s and in England from the time of the Asquith government prior to World War I: social security. Both countries had set forth programs providing unemployment insurance and a government sponsored pensioner's scheme. England's 1911 National Insurance Act was a combination of social assistance through an adaptation or extension of traditional poor-laws and worker insurance that also included unemployment insurance (Bourguignon, 2002). Bismark's social program was "run by the State rather than private companies, . . . compulsory for some groups of workers and of course that it was subsidized so as to provide the appropriate incentive for workers to indeed collectively accumulate savings to cover their old age, their invalidity, their sickness leaves or their funeral" (Bourguignon, 2002, 8).

Creating the social safety net was a difficult undertaking balancing the pragmatism of incremental politics because it left the administration of the social security programs "completely in the hands of the Federal Government as opposed to the States" (Freedman, 1967, 224). Besides, because "unemployment relief often was treated in public debates as the sole source of strain, the ideological content of the relief question obscured the complex nature of the latter" (Howard, 1968, 45). The Social Security Act, signed into law on August 14, 1935, established the two social insurance programs for the unemployed and for senior citizens. The act also provided the states with federal grant-in-aid for the means-tested assistance to seniors and the blind that gave help to those that were either ineligible for social security or whose benefits were insufficient to provide "a basic living" (United States House of Representatives, Committee on Ways and Means, 2000, section 1, 2). It was not until 1939 that Congress made Social Security into a family program by adding benefits to dependents of retired workers and surviving dependents of deceased workers. Even so, the program still excluded broad categories of workers such as domestic workers and agricultural laborers.

The Social Security Act of 1935 did provide two new wrinkles: Aid to Families with Dependent Children (AFDC), and maternal and child welfare grants. Both of these programs were designed to give public assistance for those individuals deemed to be in need. AFDC's purpose was to provide cash assistance to children who had been deprived of support from one of their parents. It was not such a stretch in thinking because it focused on what happened to children whose wage-earning parent (usually the father) died or could not be accounted for. Payments were provided to the children and not the surviving parent. The provisions for mother and child welfare were on promoting the health and welfare of mothers and children in rural and economically hard hit areas. Both were based on federal and state partnerships, with the federal government providing the funds and the state performing the actual administration and documentation, with the federal government having a priori approval of each state's program. This is why, for example, the amount of funds received by AFDC clients varied in accordance to where they lived.

The Social Security Act programs were insurance programs because recipients had to contribute into them. All employees had to pay a tax based on a percentage of accrued income, with these taxes collected through payroll deductions at the time of payment. This new tax could not be deducted against income tax because it was a contribution the employee was making toward his or her retirement or collecting unemployment benefits when out of work. Employers that had eight or more employees also had to pay a tax based on having employees working for them. Employers were expected to also provide a contribution toward their employees' retirement or assist them by helping fund the unemployment insurance fund.

THE EVOLUTION OF THE SOCIAL SAFETY NET IN THE UNITED STATES

Increased interest in social programs led to the creation of new programs and adaptation of New Deal programs started during the Great Depression to augment program offerings as well as increasing the pool of eligible participants. Many of these changes occurred in the areas of education and labor, with two major examples that had a significant impact being the G.I. Bill of 1944 and the Fair Labor Standards Act of 1949. In 1953, as a result of a study led by Herbert Hoover, there was a restructuring of the cabinet-level positions and the executive branch that led to the establishment of the Department of Health, Education and Welfare, now known as the Department of Health and Human Services. The Eisenhower campaign showed how much the notion of the social safety net had become accepted in society. It became clear "that many of the great innovations of these programs had become accepted elements in Republican as well as Democratic thinking" (Butts and Cremin, 1953, 474).

After the 1930s, the next significant period of new program enactment in the social safety net in the United States occurred in the 1960s under the Johnson administration, in what is referred to as the Great Society. One of the main reasons for the expansion was the Civil Rights movement taking on a new meaning as a result of the Warren Court and its decisions during the 1950s and 1960s, the most notable of which

was the end of desegregation in *Brown v. Topeka Board of Education* in 1954. One of the effects the movement had was to redefine services to some of the heretofore disenfranchised elements of the society in the United States. The creation of the Medicare and Medicaid programs was seen as only two of the major steps that had to be taken in a much larger assault on poverty (Brinkley, 1993).

The federal government took on the position that it had a responsibility to equalize the opportunities and social services available to U.S. citizens (Patterson, 1990). The welfare programs that came into being at this time and subsequently until the 1990s, not only in education but in healthcare and public housing, seem to echo Theodore Schultz's view that

> While land per se is not the critical factor in being poor, the human agent is: investment in improving population quality can significantly enhance the economic prospects and welfare of poor people. Child care, home and work experience, the acquisition of information and skills through schooling, and other investments in health and schooling can improve population quality. (1981, 7)

Therefore, over the years, the social safety net programs in the United States became a combination of social insurance programs, opportunity programs (equality of opportunity through training and/or education) and public assistance programs (programs for the needy funded through general revenues). Social Security, unemployment insurance and Medicare (1964) became the three principal components of the social insurance approach to individual assistance. The public assistance programs that came to life were the AFDC, supplemental social security in 1974 (a combination of the original efforts at helping the elderly and the blind and later included the disabled), food stamps (1961), Medicaid (1965), earned income tax credit (1975), and subsidized housing (1988).

Opportunity assistance programs were developed later. The Comprehensive Employment and Training Act of 1973 (CETA) formally recognized the importance that training has on employment opportunities. CETA provided state and local government with grants for employment and job training for poor, disadvantaged, and undertrained individuals. It brought together and expanded on previous existing efforts enumerated under the Manpower Development and Training Act of 1962 and other legislation from that period. CETA, however, was terminated in 1983 due to budgetary constraints and replaced by a lesser-funded training program under the Job Training and Partnership Act of 1982 (JTPA). In turn, the JTPA was terminated in 1998 with the passage of the Workforce Investment Act of 1998 (WIA). WIA was set up to establish a comprehensive system of job training and placement services for adults and eligible youth. WIA was bolstered by the creation of the Welfare-to-Work Program (WtW) set up as part of the Welfare-to-Work and Child Support Amendments of 1999. WtW allowed for public assistance recipients who qualified to receive training opportunities to enhance their ability to become enrolled and leave welfare roles based on their abilities to get a job.

THE CONSERVATIVE AGENDA TOWARD THE SOCIAL SAFETY NET IN THE UNITED STATES: THE PARADIGM SHIFT OF WELFARE TO WORKFARE (THE UNITED STATES AS THE LEAD CASE)

> The transition of the nation's human services programs from income maintenance to self-sufficiency requires a systems-wide paradigm shift that affects people, culture, processes, procedures, information, and information systems. (United States Department of Health and Human Services, 2000)

The expansion of the social safety net came about because public demand coincided with a time of economic expansion, so the money was available to support these programs. However, the times of plenty came to an end by the early 1970s, and by the end of that decade all levels of government were hard pressed to generate sufficient revenues to meet their obligations. One of the effects of economic and government retrenchment was the need to reassess the whole fabric of the social safety net. Although the concepts of welfare had already become an accepted expectation of most constituents on both sides of the political spectrum, the system was seen as inefficient and rife with abuse. For some, the administrative costs had to be scaled back. For others, this meant the development of "entitlement mentality" in those who the system was supposed to help rather than a focus on the traditionally held notions of self-reliance. Between 1960 and 1975, the percent of the gross domestic product (GDP) expended in the area of the social safety net grew from about 10 percent to 19 percent. By the period of 1992 to 1995, the United States was down to spending about 10.5 percent of its GDP on social safety net issues (United Nations Development Programme, 1997).

Ronald Reagan came into office stating that he represented the "typical" belief that the welfare system and most of the social safety net had to be scaled back. Although this set the table for the paradigm shift that was to come in 1996, the one thing that neoliberal economic politicians learned was that the social security aspect of the safety net was sacrosanct. Ironically enough, it was the Reagan administration that coined the term *social safety net* as a means of demonstrating that social security was "off limits" along with the other insurance type programs. To quote DiNitto and Dye (1987),

> Originally, the Reagan administration asserted that it would protect the "truly needy" by not making significant cuts in many of the income security programs. These programs included: Social Security, Medicare, Unemployment Compensation, veterans' benefits, Supplemental Security Income, Head Start, summer jobs for disadvantaged youths and free school lunches and breakfasts. The Reagan administration referred to these as the "social safety net programs." Note, however, that many of these programs belong to what is known as the "upper tier" of social welfare benefits. This upper tier consists largely of social insurance programs which are funded through payroll taxes. . . . Many of the programs which constitute the "lower tier" of social welfare. . . . were not included in the safety net and were targeted for substantial budget savings. Thse included: Aid to Families with Dependent Children,

Food Stamps, Medicaid, housing assistance, CETA, social services, compensatory education, and legal services. (38)

Subsequent discussions during the 1980s and 1990s seemed to center around the notion of income maintenance and the significant normative issues raised by income maintenance for those people in poverty and the role of work in their lives. The following comparison places these issues into question forms identified by Andrew Dobelstein (1996, 131–132) to describe the debate about the social safety net that crystallized during this time. The current answers to these questions became the basis of workfare, the paradigm shift that came to life through legislation in 1996.[3]

QUESTIONS ABOUT THE DEFINITION AND DISTRIBUTION OF BENEFITS UNDER THE WORK-TO-WORKFARE PARADIGM SHIFT

Benefit Definition and Distribution

1. Should poverty be defined in relation to individual conditions or by a model?
2. Should in-kind benefits and non-wage income (e.g., social security) be included in the measurement, or should only earned income be included?
3. Should both cash and in-kind benefits be distributed, and, if so, in what proportion to each other?
4. Should income maintenance be made available to the family, or to the individual? How should a family be defined?
5. Should it come from general revenue taxes, or from other contributions (such as Social Security) and, if so, in what proportion?

Work or Welfare

1. *Work and welfare*: Should welfare be given to people who work but do not earn enough by working?
2. *Work in place of welfare*: Should welfare be used to enforce work and discourage dependency?
3. *Work incentives*: Should incentives, such as child care, be given to support some kind of workers? All workers? Should these work incentives be counted as welfare?
4. *Ability to work*: Who is capable of working, and who determines this? For example, should teenagers be expected to work?
5. *Availability of work*: Should people be required to work at low-paying, dead-end jobs that have little social usefulness?
6. *Work and other values*: Should rewards be given to those who do work, such as retirement benefits, paid vacations, free medical care?

The greatest concern was over the costs of Social Security and health care. By the end of the 1980s, the federal government was spending around $300 million for Social Security and Medicare while it was spending close to $75 million on its major public assistance programs (Patterson, 1990). Social

Security taxes paid by wage earners increased from a range of $38 to $50 in 1950, to $767 to $1,014 in 1980, and then to a range between $2,318 and $3,682 in 1999 (United States House of Representatives, Committee on Ways and Means, 2000). In 1939, 43.6 million civilian employees paid taxes while 24 million were covered under the old-age and survivor and disability insurance (OASI) and disability insurance (DI). By 1980, 98.9 million paid into the system while 89.3 million were receiving benefits. By 1990, 117.8 million wage earners contributed into the "insurance" systems, with 111.3 million individuals receiving benefits. Also according to the *Green Book of 2000* data, Medicare costs rose from $2.597 billion for Part A and $798,000,000 for Part B coverage in 1967, to $24.288 billion for Part A and $10.746 billion for Part B in 1980, to $66.7 billion for Part A and $43.022 billion for Part B in 1990, to $114.883 billion for Part A and $65.213 for Part B in 1995.[4] Medicaid (indigent health care) total costs for the federal and state governments rose from $1.658 billion in 1966, to $25.781 billion in 1980, to $72.492 billion in 1990, to $156.395 billion in 1995.

SSI program costs for the federal government and states rose from a combined total of $5.246 billion in 1974, to $7.940 billion in 1980. By 1990 the costs rose to $16.599 billion, and by 1994 at $25.870 billion. Total federal and state costs for AFDC were at $22.018 billion, and increased to $30.091 billion by 1995.

The first calls for reexamination began under the Nixon administration, but the full-blown demand for this need to look over these programs did not come about until the Reagan administration. The first Clinton administration was not able to get through its healthcare reform that would have increased the amount of funds provided in the areas of healthcare then and now currently provided for under Medicare and Medicaid; instead a major shift in the social services paradigm occurred as the result of the takeover of Congress by the Republicans in 1996. Nixon's attempt at reassessment was based on a way to bring the states back as the determiners of what was needed under their jurisdictions. The Reagan administration's "new federalism" was a broader attack on the federal government's role and size. The attack was based on the notion that the "tax and spend" liberals that ran the federal government had policies that had the impact of fiscally and morally bankrupting the country. A weak economy combined with a massive budget deficit—a significant portion of which was the result of the payoffs to maintain social programs—that needed to be controlled forced many to look at the decisions responsible for such a situation. Social services were also reassessed as part of an overall attempt at budget cutbacks throughout all the federal departments and programs. Ironically, the Reagan administration added to the deficit as a result of its spending in other areas such as defense, tax reduction, deregulation of businesses, and privatization of services.

A big issue of Reagan's new federalism was the view that many of the social safety net programs went against the grain of what it was to be American. Worse still, a number of these programs and services condoned and, in their view, advocated morally wrong programs such as abortion, keeping families

apart (single head of household definitions for receiving benefits), and keeping people dependent instead of allowing them the ability to return to work. It did not help matters that some of the changes seemed to conflict with existing welfare programs, creating a ripple effect that made it more difficult, for example, to get some of the people off welfare and back to work. The question became one of what were acceptable alternatives in terms of economics and social mores.

From the 1980s onwards, cost reductions and increased state decision-making resulted from a repackaging of program funding approaches. According to Gilbert, Specht, and Terrell (1993),

> To deal with these concerns, the New Federalism decategorized federal aid. When Ronald Reagan took office in 1981, a major plank in his domestic platform was to consolidate multiple, detailed, categorical grants into a limited number of block grants.... [Seventy-seven] categorical grants-in-aid were collapsed into 9 block grants under the Omnibus Budget Reconciliation Act of 1981. For example, 10 separate grants that provided state aid for addressing different aspects of alcohol, drug abuse, and mental health were combined to 1 new block grant, streamlining administration, reducing paperwork, and giving the states increased discretion to define programs as they chose. Thirty-seven categoricals in education were similarly consolidated, as were 27 in health. (204)

The ostensible streamlining kept administrative costs down, achieving its quest for a "mean and lean" social welfare system (Goodin et al., 1999). Between 1983 and 1992, Goodin and coauthors evaluate the social safety net in the United States as being one that

> certainly does not provide any more than they need to escape from poverty: instead it errs in the opposite direction, standardly giving poor people less than they need. Nor does [it] . . . generally give benefits to many who do not need them: again, it errs instead in the opposite direction, not paying benefits to substantial proportions of those who are in need. (244)

Prior to the 1996 midterm congressional election, the Republican Party's new agenda was demarcated in its *Contract with America* (Republican Members of the House of Representatives, 1996). It provided a platform of change that gave a voice and form to many of the concerns and interests of those who criticized the social safety net structure as it existed. Its core values were three in number: accountability, responsibility, and opportunity. According to the Republicans, accountability was needed because government was too big, that too many unelected bureaucrats in Washington, D.C. were too entrenched and therefore unresponsive to the public's needs. Responsibility was needed because bigger government has and tends to usurp personal responsibility from families and individuals. And opportunity was needed because too many regulations and harsh tax laws put the American dream out of reach for so many. The signers vowed that if the Republicans won control of at least the House and Senate that they would focus on pursuing the following legislative course of action:

1. THE FISCAL RESPONSIBILITY ACT: A balanced budget/tax limitation amendment and a legislative line-item veto to restore fiscal responsibility to an out-of-control Congress, requiring them to live under the same budget constraints as families and businesses.

2. THE TAKING BACK OUR STREETS ACT: An anti-crime package including stronger truth-in-sentencing, "good faith" exclusionary rule exemptions, effective death penalty provisions, and cuts in social spending from this summer's "crime" bill to fund prison construction and additional law enforcement to keep people secure in their neighborhoods and kids safe in their schools.

3. THE PERSONAL RESPONSIBILITY ACT: Discourage illegitimacy and teen pregnancy by prohibiting welfare to minor mothers and denying increased AFDC for additional children while on welfare, cut spending for welfare programs, and enact a tough two-years-and-out provision with work requirements to promote individual responsibility.

4. THE FAMILY REINFORCEMENT ACT: Child support enforcement, tax incentives for adoption, strengthening rights of parents in their children's education, stronger child pornography laws, and an elderly dependent care tax credit to reinforce the central role of families in American society.

5. THE AMERICAN DREAM RESTORATION ACT: A $500 per child tax credit, begin repeal of the marriage tax penalty, and creation of American Dream Savings Accounts to provide middle class tax relief.

6. THE NATIONAL SECURITY RESTORATION ACT: No U.S. troops under U.N. command and restoration of the essential parts of our national security funding to strengthen our national defense and maintain our credibility around the world.

7. THE SENIOR CITIZENS FAIRNESS ACT: Raise the Social Security earnings limit which currently forces seniors out of the work force, repeal the 1993 tax hikes on Social Security benefits and provide tax incentives for private long-term care insurance to let Older Americans keep more of what they have earned over the years.

8. THE JOB CREATION AND WAGE ENHANCEMENT ACT: Small business incentives, capital gains cut and indexation, neutral cost recovery, risk assessment/cost-benefit analysis, strengthening the Regulatory Flexibility Act and unfunded mandate reform to create jobs and raise worker wages.

9. THE COMMON SENSE LEGAL REFORM ACT: "Loser pays" laws, reasonable limits on punitive damages and reform of product liability laws to stem the endless tide of litigation.

10. THE CITIZEN LEGISLATURE ACT: A first-ever vote on term limits to replace career politicians with citizen legislators.

The republican agenda impacted the social safety net in that it clearly indicated that there was to be a reduction in social program spending in favor of stronger criminal laws and enforcement (items 2 and 3); a reduction in welfare (item 3); a formal focus in reducing illegitimate births by creating stricter eligibility rules (item 3); a "tough" entry and exit provisions for benefits-eligibility in social safety net programs (item 3); the expansion of parental rights in the education process of their children and a reinforcement of the central role of families in American society in the care of family members such as the elderly (item 4); an increase in the amount of tax relief and other incentives to the middle class (item 5); assistance for senior citizens through tax relief to keep more of their assets, to help in long-term health care, and allow them remain in the workforce if they so desire (item 7); and new job creation through unfunded mandate reforms (item 8). With a Republican Congressional win in 1996, this agenda became the controlling policy perspective in Washington.

Not all of these legislative acts passed; in fact, most did not, especially as originally proposed. However, from these items, what came through via the passage in 1996 of the Personal Responsibility and Work Opportunity Reconciliation Act was a new paradigm that changed the nature of the social safety net. The focus now became block grants, to states, state-based decisions of limited lifetime welfare benefits, streamlined program services and administration, greater emphasis on keeping families together as a requirement for receiving and maintaining benefits, and most important of all, that beneficiaries need to return to work as soon as possible and get off the welfare rolls. In sum, fewer can qualify and these benefits have a lifetime amount that add up to a total of five years. The idea now was that if one needs helps, is eligible for it, and is granted benefits, help is available, but only until the claimant can return to the workforce. Nevertheless, the new paradigm did not significantly impact Social Security or any of the other so-called insurance programs like unemployment and disability.

THE SOCIAL SAFETY NET FROM 1996 TO PRESENT

Felix Frankfurter observed back in 1936 that "the tremendous implication of the existence of an enlarged governmental responsibility for the welfare of the people" (Frankfurter, 1962, 241) is that government institutions will remain because of continued need and an organizational desire to continue in existence. As he put it, "Alphabetical agencies will continue, or analphabetical agencies will take their place" (241). This was the case as the programs under the banner of AFDC were transformed under a new program called Temporary Assistance for Needy Families (TANF).

Under the auspices of the Personal Responsibility and Work Opportunity Reconciliation Act of 1996 (PRWORA), what was a categorical grant program gave way to a block grant program, albeit funded at the largest annual amount funded under AFDC. As indicated in the *Green Book 2000*:

> The law entitles States to fixed block grants ($16.5 billion annually) for 6 years to operate programs of their own design, but imposes time limits on receiving welfare without working, lifetime benefit time limits, and minimum work participation rates. Within these limits, it allows States to reduce their own spending on behalf of children. The 1996 law also sharply expands funding for child care. (United States House of Representatives, Committee on Ways and Means, 2000, section 7, 1/72–2/72).

TANF's main purpose was to

1. provide assistance to needy families so that children may be cared for in their own homes or those of relatives;

2. end the dependency of needy parents on government benefits by promoting job preparation, work, and marriage;

3. prevent and reduce incidences of out-of-wedlock pregnancies; and

4. encourage the formation and maintenance of two-parent families. (Section 7, 3/72)

What the paradigm shift in the social safety net reduces itself to is that it is a transition from an income maintenance perspective where the government is ensuring that a minimum income is maintained to one of self-sufficiency where individuals make their own decisions and, as a result, are able to fend for themselves by making sufficient income through their ability to work. The difference in this shift is reflected in Chart 1.1.

Chart 1.1
Characteristics of the Old Paradigm (Income-Maintenance) and the New Paradigm (Self-Sufficiency)

Characteristics of an Income Maintenance Program

Primary goal—Timely and accurate benefits.

Rule-based decisions—Eligibility decisions are based in rules. There is a "right answer" in any given decision. Individuals are held accountable for getting the answer right.

Process focus—How things must be done is very clear in the program.

Managers know the answers—Management structure needs to minimize mistakes in the program and ensure consistency.

Error avoidance—Individuals are extensively trained to avoid costly errors, resulting in a focus on what can't be done. Individuals try to operate as much as possible in "black and white" clarity in decision-making in order to reduce problems in the program.

Limited expectations—Focus is on certifying client needs and lack of resources as part of the eligibility process. Program is geared to help people by providing for their basic needs since they have demonstrated in the eligibility process that they are not doing so for themselves.

Services provided for or to clients—Staff have ultimate authority and expertise to get clients benefits.

Entitlement system—All who are eligible must receive all benefits for which they are eligible and to which they are entitled.

Characteristics of a Self-Sufficiency Program

Primary goal—Decreasing dependence on public assistance through work and other resources.

Principle-based decisions—Self-sufficiency service decisions are based on principles, outcomes, and an assessment of the individual situation. There is not one "right answer." Individuals are held accountable for making decisions that reflect principles/outcomes.

Outcome focus—What must be achieved is very clear in the program. Principles guide the how.

Managers know how to get people to ask good questions—Management structure needs to facilitate experimentation, keep focus on outcomes and principles, and move good decision-making to the front-line level.

Experiment—Individuals are extensively trained to experiment with the best ways to reach outcomes, resulting in a focus on what can be done. Individuals operate primarily in areas of many shades of gray. New leadership and team structures result from this focus on service outcomes and experimentation.

High expectations—Focus is on discovering client strengths and resources. There are high expectations of the client. There is a social contract in which the basic support services are provided in exchange for participation in actitivies leading to self-sufficiency.

Services provided with clients—Staff can't "make" clients self-sufficient. Staff can only work with clients on process, taking part in process, not controlling it.

Temporary assistance—Wide range of choices made at State, local, and worker level that influences the type of benefits provided.

Source: United States Department of Health and Human Services. (2000). *Welfare reform information technology*, table 1.

OTHER NATIONS CONSIDERING THE PARADIGM SHIFT

Spurred on by the passage of the landmark welfare reform legislation—the Personal Responsibility and Work Opportunity Reconciliation Act of 1996—States have made tremendous progress toward the critical goal of moving families from welfare to work. More families are entering employment, earnings are up, and caseloads are down. (U.S. Department of Health and Human Services Administration for Children and Families, Office of Family Assistance, 2001)

The worth of government institutions is based on their ability to meet the needs of legislation and their supporting mandate as well as those individuals or groups they are meant to serve. The overriding question is the one asked by Lisa Newton (1977, 154): "Can human institutions ever be pronounced good, as tending to fulfill human nature, or bad as tending to warp or injure it?" Lowi and Ginsberg (1990) best sum up the basis of the social safety net in the United States as established in 1932 to its present day when they point out that

Americans have traditionally conceived of those living in poverty as two distinct classes, the "deserving poor" and the "undeserving poor." The deserving poor were the widows and orphans and others rendered dependent by such misfortune as national disaster or injury in the course of honest labor. The undeserving poor were able-bodied persons unwilling to work, transients from their communities, or others of whom, for various reasons the community did not approve. (699)

Advocates and critics of the new paradigm shift in the United States' social safety net focus their arguments from the perspective of the deserving and undeserving. For some who advocate for these changes, the dramatic decrease in the number of welfare recipients is an indication that the system is working, that costs and efficiency along with appropriate incentives mean that people can fend for themselves. For others who criticize the impact of these programs, the numbers are deceiving because they do not clearly track those that no longer qualify for the various programs and therefore are unaccounted. The increase in request for aid from private sources is a clear indication that the poor are being hurt. Ironically, both sides indicate that there is an income gap that does not seem to help those in the bottom but actually exacerbate the problems of those individuals in the lower socioeconomic strata. Where they differ is in the role that individualism plays in personal decisions in contrast to a collectivistic evaluation of personal decisions in determining self-actualization and personal well-being.

The United States is not alone in reassessing its commitment toward social services. Europe, Australia, and parts of Asia are looking at what the United States is doing in changing services from an entitlement viewpoint to one of individual responsibility. For example, most of Europe, because of the pressures emanating from high unemployment faced in the 1990s, finds itself with the problem of how to avoid social exclusion while not overtaxing their economies' abilities toward producing wealth. This is one reason why in 1996, the European Union Parliament adopted a report that identified the following recommendations:

- a reasonable, growth-oriented approach to budgetary discipline;
- an investment policy which stimulates public and private investment;
- a taxation policy and social welfare structures which act as an incentive to employment creation; and
- an active education, training and re-training policy at Community and national level, particularly in high technology sectors. (Employment in Europe, 1996 Annual Report)

Japan finds itself having to work through the throes of a slow economy that has led to the need of layoffs and significant unemployment for the first time, creating a tension within the social structure because of the need to readjust the thinking about lifetime employment and the assurance for a minimum standard of living for all citizens. South Korea, also in the midst of an economic slowdown, downsizing in the workforce and declining wages, is looking at the role that government has in providing assistance to those that now need help. It is looking for a vision to follow as it considers implementing needed reforms (Park, 1999). Unemployment compensation measures are passed to strengthen the social safety net; however, these are having a hard time keeping up with the need, mainly because of the macroeconomic and social policy changes that are required in order to rectify intrinsic challenges within their corporate and financial structures (Cho, 1999). Wages need to keep pace with productivity (Shin, 1999). Australia is looking for a means of simplifying and reducing the impact that wage increases have on the labor market and the economy in general. The Australian government's perspective is that a tax transfer system is the most effective way of helping low-income earners and addressing poverty (Commonwealth of Australia, 2002). Their interest is in reducing administrative and program benefit costs while still maintaining the social guarantees mandated under their laws. High employment, improved living standards, low inflation, international competitiveness, and higher productivity are key (Workplace Relations Act of 1996 as quoted in Australian Industry Group and Engineering Employers' Association, South Australia, 2001), but these must be achieved in a manner that allows them to be met.

Chatterjee (1999, 152–155) posits that at the international level, there are a number of lessons learned from the social safety net movements in the twentieth century. These are:

1. Industrialization is a sufficient condition for the evolution of the welfare state.

2. The welfare state relies on one or more styles of redistribution. In practice, it seeks equity.

3. Capitalist industrialism is a better developer of efficiency than is socialist industrialism. Any form of industrialism is a better developer of efficiency than is a preindustrial economy.

4. Capitalist industrial societies almost invariably create a society with a class hierarchy. Class-related politics and the way in which a national culture prioritizes its vulnerable roles are factors that influence redistribution.

5. A popular trend in the welfare states of the First World has been to promise benefits on the basis of citizenship.

6. Regardless of whether redistributionist policies are based on citizenship (and role) or reciprocity (and role), they are distributions resulting from past activities.

7. A two-tiered system of redistribution is clearly visible in most welfare states. What can be appropriately redistributed through these two tiers and who should be the targets of it has not been settled.

8. Welfare states' redistributionist policies have not dealt well with indigenous populations.

9. All people should be encouraged to participate in an asset-building program.

10. A great mistake may have been made in removing stigma and other social controls from illegitimacy. In many settings, the inability to control illegitimacy has led to social conditions in which that behavior is routine.

What the United States is doing is providing an experiment per sé that is taking into account or at least illustrating most—if not all—of these ten lessons. A complex economy requires some form of government intrusion into the lives of individuals. Equity, as defined by Justinian as the instrument to "render every man his due" is an important consideration because the question of who is deserving and who is not is central to whether the government has a right to intrude into personal affairs. In the United States this takes on additional meaning because of constitutional guarantees of due process, personal rights such as the right to privacy and the notion of self-determination. Yet, government action has to be efficient in terms of administration and program costs. It is the dilemma of the effectiveness-efficiency paradox at the economic, social, political, and programmatic levels that makes the United States an experiment that others want to observe and use as an example of what to do or not do. Goodin, Headey, Muffels, and Dirven (1999) come to the conclusions that (1) the social democratic welfare regime is at least as good—and usually better—than other systems in respect of all of the social objectives typically set for the various types of social safety nets as well as achieving economic objectives, and (2) that over time, "government interventions can cure most things" (263). If this is the case, the example of the United States is not a strong one; yet, others are still looking to see what is successful and potentially replicated. In this period of increasing globalization and the challenges it brings to nations, their infrastructures, and their social safety net, it seems that there is still much to be settled.

NOTES

1. In 1947, this agreement also forged the creation of three international organizations that are still operating and are influential today: (1) the General Agreement on Tariffs and Trade (GATT), today also known as the World Trade Organization; (2) the International Bank for Reconstruction and Development (IBRD), known today as the World Bank; and (3) and the International Monetary Fund (IMF).

2. Paper presented at the United Nations–World Institute for Development Economics Research (UNUWIDER) Conference on Poverty, International Migration, and Asylum in Helsinki, Finland, 27–28 September, 2002.

3. Table 1.4 represents most of the key legislative acts and creation of federal agencies that shaped the United States' response to social safety net issues between the years 1933 and 1996. Table 1.4 represents the laws passed after the 1996 paradigm shift as brought about by the Personal Responsibility and Work Opportunity Reconciliation Act. While not all-inclusive, key legislative acts and executive orders impacting the development of the social safety net are identified in order to provide a basic overview of the breadth of the programs that came about. Some of these seem to have little bearing on the development of social programs at a prima facie level; however, these illustrate the interrelationship that social programs have with a nation's economic and political agenda. Also note that while Republican administrations are traditionally viewed as antagonistic toward the issue of social welfare, Republican administrations have also had to deal with and enacted legislation and other administrative regulations to continue tweaking the program. They may have preferred contractions in these programs, but the results were still to continue the programs and, in some instances, increase their size.

4. Part A coverage is defined as inpatient hospital care for the first 60 days of inpatient hospital services in a benefit period; skilled nursing facility up to 100 days following hospitalization for those who need nursing or rehabilitation services; home healthcare visits for persons needing skilled nursing care on an intermittent basis, or physical therapy, or speech therapy; or hospice care for terminally ill patients with a life expectancy of 6 months or less. Part B coverage generally pays 80 percent of approved amount, most often under a fee schedule of the following services:

- doctor's services such as surgery, consultation, and home/ office/institutional visits;
- other medical health benefits such as laboratory and other diagnostic tests, X-rays and other radiation therapy, outpatient hospital services, rural health clinical services, DME, home dialysis supplies and equipment, artificial devices (other than dental), physical and speech therapy, and ambulance services;
- specified preventive services that include an annual screening mammography for all women over 40, a screening Pap smear and pelvic exam once every 3 years (except for women with a high risk of cervical cancer), specified colorectal screening procedures, diabetes self-management training services, bone-mass measurements for high-risks persons, and prostate cancer screenings;
- drugs and vaccines, but only for imunosuppresive drugs for a minimum of 36 months following a covered organ transplant, certain oral cancer drugs, erythropoietin (EPO) for treating anemia in persons with chronic kidney failure, and flu shots, pneumococcal pneumonia vaccines, and hepatitis B vaccines for those at risk;
- home health services that include an unlimited number of medically-necessary home health benefits for persons not covered under Part A.

PRINCIPAL SOURCES FOR ILLUSTRATIONS

Acma, B. (2002). *Economic consequences of international migration: Case study of Turkey.* Paper retrieved from: http://Widerunu.edu/conference/conference2002-3/conference-2002-3-programme.htm.

Casey, B., and Yamada, A. (2002). Getting older, getting poorer? A study of earnings, pensions, assets, and living arrangements of older people in nine countries. OECD's *Labour Market and Occasional Papers No. 60.*

Organization of Economic Co-operation and Development. (2003). *Tables and Figures of Ageing.* Retrieved from: http://www.occd.org/dataoccd/27/44/2345400.pdf.

United States Census Bureau. (2002). *Statistical abstract of the United States 2002.* Washington, D.C.: Government Printing Office. Retrieved from: http://www.census.gov/statab/www/.

World Bank. (2003). The international economy and prospects for developing countries. *Global Economic Prospects and the Developing Countries 2003,* pp. 1–43. Retrieved from: http://www.worldbank.org/ prospects/gep2003/ full.htm.

BIBLIOGRAPHY

Acma, B. (2002). *Economic consequences of international migration: Case study of Turkey.* Paper presented at the United Nations–World Institute for Development Economic Research (UNUWIDER) Conference on Poverty, International Migration, and Asylum in Helsinki, Finland, 27–28 September 2002. Retrieved from: http://Widerunu.edu/conference/conference2002-3/conference-2002-3-programme.htm.

Arnold, M. (1966). *Culture and anarchy.* London: Cambridge University Press.

Asia Times. (September 18, 2001). US economy: Not dead by a longshot. In *Asia Times Online,* Editorial Section. Retrieved from: http://www.atimes.com/editor/CI18Ba01.html.

Australian Industry Group and Engineering Employers' Association, South Australia. (2001). *2001 safety net review case.* Retrieved from: http://www.airgroup.asn.au/pdf/safetynet01ver3.pdf.

Bentham, J. (1789/1988). *The principles of morals and legislation.* Amherst, NY: Prometheus Books.

Black's law dictionary, 4th ed. (1957). St. Paul, MN: West Publishing Co.

Bourguignon, F. (2002). *Social protection in industrial countries: Which lessons for LAC countries?* World Bank. Retrieved from: http://lnweb18.worldbank.org/External/lac/lac.nsf/92fc607f00 e4de4a852568cf00633afd/9491670c24b2801185256aaa0045 3118/$FILE/lacjune.pdf.

Brinkley, A. (1993). *The Unfinished Nation: A concise history of the American people, volume II: From 1865.* New York: McGraw-Hill.

Brown, A. (1997). ReWORKing Welfare Technical Assistance for States and Localities: A How-to Guide Work First, How to Implement an Employment-Focused Approach to Welfare Reform. In *Welfare to work overview references, appendix A.* Washington, D.C.: U.S. Dept. of Health and Human Services.

Burgstaller, J. (2002). *Are stock returns a leading indicator for real macroeconomic developments?* Linz: Johannes Keppler University Department of Economics Working Paper No. 0207. Retrieved from: http://www.economics.uni-linz.ac.at/paper/wp0207.pdf.

Butts, R.F., and Cremin, L.A. (1953). *A history of education in American culture.* New York: Henry Holt and Company.

Castles, S., and Loughana, S. (2002). *Trends in asylum migration to industrialised countries:1990–2001.* Paper presented at the United Nations–World Institute for Development Economic Research (UNUWIDER) Conference on Poverty, International Migration, and Asylum in Helsinki, Finland, 27–28 September 2002. Retrieved from: http://Widerunu.edu/conference/conference2002-3/conference-2002-3-programme.htm.

Cawson, A. (1986). *Corporatism and political theory.* Oxford: Basil Blackwell.

Chambers, D.E. (1986). *Social policy and social programs: A method for the practical public policy analyst.* New York: McMillan Press.

Chatterjee, P. (1999). *Repackaging the welfare state.* Washington, D.C.: National Association of Social Workers.

Cho, D. (1999). Korea's response to the crisis: Korea's structural adjustments. In *Korean Economic Institute of America Monograph.* Washington, D.C. Retrieved from: http://www.keia.com/economy99.pdf.

Clark, A. (September 28, 2002). Germany regains its self-confidence. *Australian Financial Review,* 25.

Coke, E. (1649). Chapter 29: Magna Carta. In *Second institutes of the laws of England.* Retrieved from: http://kancrn .kckps.k12.ks .us/Harmon/breighm/ccmgdex.html.

Commonwealth of Australia. (1 March 2002). *Commonwealth submission: Safety net review—Wages 2001–2002.* Retrieved from: http://airc.gov.au/safetynet_review/dewr/commonwealth_ submission.pdf.

Darwin, C. (1859/1952). *The origin of species by means of natural selection.* Chicago: Encyclopedia Britannica.

DiNitto, D.M., and Dye, T.R. (1987). *Social welfare: Politics and public policy.* 2nd ed. Englewood Cliffs, NJ: Prentice Hall.

Dobelstein, A.W. (1996). *Social welfare: Policy and analysis.* Chicago: Nelson-Hall Publishers.

Drucker, P.F. (1985). *Innovation and entrepreneurship: Practices and principles.* New York: Harper and Row.

Drucker, P.F. (1995). *Managing in a time of great change.* New York: Truman Talley Books/Plume.

Dworkin, R. (1986). *Law's empire.* Cambridge, MA: Belknap Press.

European Parliament. (2000). *European Parliament factsheet 2.1.1. Respect for fundamental rights in the EU—general development.* Retrieved from: http://www.europarl.eu.int/factsheets/ 2_1_1_en.htm.

European Parliament. (2002). *Report on Employment in Europe–1996.* European Parliament Website. Retrieved from: http:// europa.eu.int/scadplus/leg/csv/cha/c10204g.htm.

European Union Economic and Monetary Affairs. (2002). *From Rome to Maastricht: A brief history of EMU.* Retrieved from: http://www.europa.eu.int/scadplus/printversion/en/lvb/l25007 .htm.

Ferdows, K. (March–April 1997). Making the most of foreign factories. *Harvard Business Review,* 73–88.

Frankfurter, F. (1962). *Law and politics.* New York: Capricorn Books.

Freedman, M. (1967). *Roosevelt and Frankfurter: Their correspondence, 1928–1945.* Boston: Little, Brown, and Company.

Friedman, M., and Friedman, R. (1981). *Free to choose.* New York: Avon.

Fromm, E. (1973). *The anatomy of human destructiveness.* New York: Holt, Rinehart and Winston.

Galbraith, J.K. (1972). *Economics, peace and laughter*. New York: Times Mirror.

Galbraith, J.K. (1981). *A life in our times: Memoirs*. Boston: Houghton Mifflin.

Gallagher, L.J. (1998*). A shrinking portion of the safety net: General assistance from 1989 to 1998*. Retrieved from: http://newfederalism.urban.org/html/anf_a36.html.

George, V., and Wilding, P. (1985). *Ideology and social welfare*. London: Routledge.

Gilbert, N., Specht, H., and Terrell, P. (1993). *Dimensions of social welfare policy*. 3rd ed. Englewood Cliffs, NJ: Prentice-Hall.

Goodin, R.E., Headey, B., Muffels, R., and Dirven, H.J. (1999). *The real worlds of welfare capitalism*. Cambridge: Cambridge University Press.

Hanley, T.R. (2002). *German economic issues: An informed questions paper*. Washington, D.C. National Defense university. Retrieved from: http://www.ndu.edu/nwc/writing/AY02/5604/SeminarO5604BestPaper.rtf.

Hart, S.L. (January–February 1997). Strategies for a sustainable world. *Harvard Business Review*, 67–76.

Hazlitt, H. (1979). *Economics in one lesson*. New York: Arlington House.

Herzberg, F., Mausner, B., and Snyderman, B. (1959). *The motivation to work*. New York: John Wiley and Sons.

Howard, J.W., Jr. (1968). *Mr. Justice Murphy: A political biography*. Princeton, NJ: Princeton University Press.

Hurwitz, A. (2002). *The externalization of EU policies on migration and asylum: Agreements and comprehensive approaches*. Paper presented at the United Nations–World Institute for Development Economic Research (UNUWIDER) Conference on Poverty, International Migration, and Asylum in Helsinki, Finland, 27–28 September 2002. Retrieved from: http://Widerunu.edu/conference/conference2002-3/conference-2002-3-programme.htm.

Irvine, W. (1955). *Apes, angels, and Victorians; the story of Darwin, Huxley, and evolution*. New York: Time Incorporated.

Juran, J.M. (2000). How to think about quality. In Juran, J.M., Godfrey, A.B., Hoogstoel, R.E., and Schilling, E.G., Eds. *Juran's quality handbook*. 5th ed. New York: McGraw-Hill, 2.1–2.18.

Kelsen, H. (1952). *Principles of International Law*. [I.] New York: Bingham & Company, Inc.

Leigh, L. (1997). *Stock market equilibrium and macroeconomic fundamentals*. Paper by the International Monetary Fund, Policy Development and Review Department. Retrieved from: http://www.imf.org/external/pubs/ft/wp/wp9715.pdf.

Leuchtenburg, W.E. (1963). *Franklin D. Roosevelt and the New Deal, 1932–1940*. New York: Harper Torchbooks.

Levine, R.A. (November 1999). The European Monetary Union once seemed unimaginable. The questions now are What will it lead to? and Will Britain join? *Atlantic Monthly*. Retrieved from: http://www.theatlantic.com/issues/99nov/9911euroland.htm.

Linder, M., and Sensat, J., Jr. (1977). *Anti-Samuelson macroeconomics volume I: Basic ideological concepts, crises, and Keynsianism*. New York: Urizen Books.

Link, A.S. (1955). *American epoch: A history of the United States since the 1890's*. New York: Alfred A. Knopf.

Locke, J. (1764). *Two treatises of government*. Retrieved from: http://history.hanover.edu/early/locke/j-l2-001.htm.

Lowi, T.J., and Ginsberg, B. (1990). *American government: Freedom and power*. New York: W.W. Norton and Company.

Mead, L.M. (2001). *Governmental quality and welfare reform*. Madison, WI: Institute for Research on Poverty, Discussion Paper no. 1230-01. Retrieved from: http://www.ssc.wisc.edu/irp/pubs/dp123001.pdf.

Mills, C.W. (1963). The sociology of stratification. In Horowitz, C.I., ed. *Power, politics and people: The collected essays of C. Wright Mills*. New York: Ballantine Books, 305–323.

Mowery, D.C. (1999). America's economic resurgence (?): An overview. In Mowery, D.C., ed. *U.S. Industry in 2000: Studies in Competitive Performance*. Washington, D.C.: National Academies Press, 1–16. Retrieved from: http://books.nap.edu/books/0309061792/html/1.html#pagetop.

Myrdal, G. (1960). *Beyond the welfare state*. New Haven, CT: Yale University Press.

Newton, L.H. (1977). The political animal. In Pennock, J.R., and Chapman, J.W., eds. *Human nature in politics, nomos XVII*. New York: New York University Press, 142–156.

Park, J. (1999). Government reform in Korea. In *Korean Economic Institute of America monograph*. Washington, D.C. Retrieved from: http://www.keia.com/ economy99.pdf.

Park, S.I. (1999). The labor market policy and social safety net in Korea: After the 1997 crisis. CNAPS Working Paper. New York: Brookings Institute. Retrieved from: http://www.brook.edu/fp/cnaps/papers/1999_park.htm.

Parsons, T. (1968). *The structure of social action*. Two volumes. New York: Free Press.

Patterson, T.E. (1990). *The American democracy*. New York: McGraw-Hill.

Perkins, F. (1962). *The roots of Social Security*. Address delivered at Social Security Administration Headquarters, Baltimore, MD on October 23, 1962. Retrieved from: http://www.ssa.gov/history/perkins5.html.

Pollock, F. (1911). *An Introduction to the History of the Science of Politics*. London: Macmilland and Co., Limited.

Rawls, J. (1971). *A theory of justice*. Cambridge, MA: Harvard University Press.

Reich, R.B. (March–April 1991). Who is them? *Harvard Business Review*, 77–88.

Republican Members of the House of Representatives. (1996). *Republican contract with America*. Retrieved from: http://www.house.gov/house/Contract/ CONTRACT.html.

Roosevelt, F.D. (1934). *Message to Congress reviewing the broad objectives and accomplishments of the Administration, June 8, 1934*. Retrieved from: http://www.ssa.gov/history/fdrstmts.html#message2.

Roosevelt, F.D. (1937). *Constitution Day speech, Washington, D.C.* Retrieved from: http://newdeal.feri.org/court/fdr03.htm.

Ruddock, P. (2001). *Economic impact of immigration*. Speech given at the Economic Impact of Immigration Seminar in Canberra, 1 March 2001.

Russett, C.E. (1976). *Darwin in America: The intellectual response, 1865–1912*. San Francisco: W.H. Freeman and Company.

Samuelson, P. (1976). Optimal contracts for redistribution. In Grieson, R.E., ed. *Public and urban economics*. Lexington, MA: Lexington Books, 179–190.

Samuelson, P.A. (1976). *Economics*. 10th ed. New York: McGraw-Hill.

Sayin, M. (July–August 2002). Illegal Immigration. *Newspot*, number 34. Retrieved from: http://www.byegm.gov.tr/YAYINLARIMIZ/newspot/2002/july-aug/news34.htm.

Schmitter, P.C. (1982). Reflections on where the theory of neo-corporatism has gone and where the proxis of neo-corporatism may be going. In Lembruch, G. and Schmitter, P.C., eds. *Patterns of corporatist policy-making*. Beverly Hills: Sage Publications.

Schultz, T.W. (1981). *Investing in people: The economics of population quality*. Berkeley, CA: University of California Press.

Shin, D. (1999). Labor market reform. In *Korean Economic Institute of America monograph*. Washington, D.C. Retrieved from: http://www.keia.com/economy99.pdf.

Skidelsky, R. (1992). *John Maynard Keynes, volume II: The economist as saviour*. London: Penguin Books.

Spengler, O. (1961). *The decline of the West, volume one: Form and actuality*. New York: Alfred A. Knopf.

Tanner, A. (2002). Country of Origin and Domestic Responsibility Argumentation in National Labour Immigration Policy–Brain Drain and Domestic Racism Focused. Presented at the United Nations–World Institute for Development Economics Research (UNUWIDER) Conference on Poverty, International Migration, and Asylum in Helsinki, Finland 27–28 September 2002. Retrieved from: http:// wider.unu.edu/conference/conference-2002-3/conference/020papers/tanner.pdf.

Thurow, L.C. (1985). *Zero-sum solution: Building a world-class American economy*. New York: Simon and Schuster.

Uccello, C.E., and Gallagher, L.J. (1998). *The state-based part of the safety net*. Washington, D.C.: Urban Institute, Series A-4. Retrieved from: http://newfederalism.urban.org/html/anf_a4.htm#authors.

United Nations. (1948). *Universal declaration of human rights*. Retrieved from: http://www.yale.edu/lawweb/avalon/un/unrights.htm#art30.

United Nations Development Programme. (1997). *Human development report 1997*. New York: Oxford University Press.

United Nations Development Programme. (2000). *Human development report 2000*. New York: Oxford University Press.

United States Department of Health and Human Services Administration for Children and Families, Office of Family Assistance. (2000a). *Third annual report to Congress*. Retrieved from: http://www.acf.dhhs.gov/programs/opre/director.htm.

United States Department of Health and Human Services Administration for Children and Families, Office of Family Assistance. (2001). *Helping families achieve self-sufficiency*. Retrieved from: http://www.acf.dhhs.gov/programs/ofa/funds2htm#executive.

United States Department of Health and Human Services. (2000b). *Welfare reform information technology: A study of issues in implementing information systems for the Temporary Assistance for Needy Families (TANF) Program*. Retrieved from: http://www.acf.dhhs.gov/programs/oss/WRITReport/WRITbody.htm#background.

United States House of Representatives, Committee on Ways and Means. (2000). *The 2000 Green Book: Background material and data on programs within the jurisdiction of the Committee on Ways and Means*. Retrieved from: http://aspe.hhs.gov/2000gh.

Veblen, T. (1953). *The theory of the leisure class*. New York: New American Library.

Weber, M. (1958). *The Protestant ethic and the spirit of capitalism*. New York: Charles Scribner's Sons.

Wildavksy, A. (1992). *The new politics of the budgetary process*. 2nd ed. New York: HarperCollins.

Wildavsky, A. (1974). *The politics of the budgetary process*. 2nd ed. Boston: Little, Brown and Company.

Wilson, J.Q. (1993). *The moral sense*. New York: Free Press.

World Bank. (November 1999). *1999 annual review of development effectiveness: Toward a comprehensive development strategy*. Annual Review NUMBER: 19905. Retrieved from: http://wbln0018.worldbank.org/oed/oeddoclib.nsf/11d38e62c269811285256808006a0022/0bd1230e97bb5505852568420056a30f?OpenDocument.

World Bank. (1995). *Structural adjustment and the poor*. Precis NUMBER: 96. Retrieved from: http://wbln0018.worldbank.org/oed/oeddoclib.nsf/992b8c4bfe826f7185256885007c60b5/94fcbe62f3a22b39852567f5005d89f0?OpenDocument.

World Bank. (1996). *The World Bank Participation Sourcebook*. Retrieved from: http://www.worldbank.org/wbi/sourcebook/sb0002.htm.

Young, R.M. (1990). Herbert Spencer and "inevitable" progress. In Marsden, G., ed. *Victorian values: Personalities and perspectives in nineteenth-century society*. New York: Longman, 1990, 147–157. Retrieved from: http://human-nature.com/rmyoung/papers/paper84h.html.

Zoffer, G.R. (1980). *Economic sanity or collapse*. New York: McGraw-Hill.

Table 1.1
Comparison Between Three Documents Defining Individual Rights: The U.S. Constitution, the European Convention for the Protection of Human Rights and Fundamental Freedoms, and the Japanese Constitution

U.S. Constitution, Bill of Rights	European Convention for the Protection of Human Rights and Fundamental Freedoms (1950)	Japanese Constitution (1947)
		Article 11: Guarantee of fundamental human rights
		Article 12: Guarantee that the freedoms and rights of the people shall be responsible for the pursuit of public welfare
Amendment 1 • Freedom of religion • Freedom of speech • Freedom of the press • Freedom for peaceable assembly • Petition government for redress of grievances.	• Freedom of religion and confession (Prais [1976] ECR 1589, 1599) • Freedom of association (Gewerkschaftsbund, Massa et al. [1974] 917, 925) • Freedom of expression and publication (VBVB, VBBB [1984] 9 et seq., 62). • Respect for family life (Commission v. Germany [1989] 1263)	*Article 13:* Right to life, liberty, and the pursuit of happiness to the extent that it does not interfere with the public welfare as consideration in legislation and in other governmental affairs
		Article 16: Right of peaceful petition for the redress of wrongs
		Article 17: Every person may sue for redress as provided by law from the State or a public entity
		Article 19: Freedom of thought and conscience
		Article 20: • Freedom of religion • Separation of church and state
		Article 21: • Freedom of assembly • Freedom of association • Freedom of speech • Freedom of the press • Freedom of all other forms of expression • No censorship shall be maintained, nor shall the secrecy of any means of communication be violated.
Amendment 2 Right to keep and bear arms		
Amendment 3 No solider shall in time of peace be quartered in any house without the owner's consent, nor in time of war but in a manner prescribed by law.		

Table 1.1 (*continued*)

U.S. Constitution, Bill of Rights	European Convention for the Protection of Human Rights and Fundamental Freedoms (1950)	Japanese Constitution (1947)
Amendment 4 • Right against unreasonable searches and seizure of persons, houses, papers, and effects • Government must demonstrate probable cause and the warrant shall describe place to be searched, and person or thing to be seized.	• Privacy (National Panasonic [1980] ECR 2033, 2056 et seq.) • Property (Her [1979] ECR 3727, 3745 et seq.)	*Article 33:* • No person shall be apprehended except upon warrant issued by a competent judicial officer • Warrant must specify the offense with which the person is charged *Article 35:* • Right to be secure in homes • Right against search and seizures of papers and effects except upon warrant issued for adequate cause • Warrant has to describe the place to be searched and things to be seized, or except as provided by Article 33 • Each search or seizure shall be made upon separate warrant issued by a competent judicial officer
Amendment 5 • Cannot be held to answer for a capital crime or otherwise similar act without an indictment • Cannot be exposed to double jeopardy • Right not to self-incriminate • Right not to be deprived of life, liberty, or property without due process of law • Private property will not be taken for public use without just compensation.	• Inviolability of residence (Hoechst AG v. Commission [1989] 2919) • Equal treatment (Klöckner-Werke AG [1962] ECR 653) • Non-discrimination (Defrenne v. Sabena [1976] ECR 455)	*Article 14:* • Equality under the law • No discrimination in political, economic, or social relations because of race, creed, sex, social status, or family origin • Peers and peerage shall not be recognized or inherited *Article 18:* • No person shall be held in bondage of any kind *Article 29:* • Right to right to own or to hold property • Private property may be taken for public use upon just compensation *Article 31:* • Right of legal due process *Article 38:* • Right not to self-incriminate • Confession made under compulsion, torture or threat, or after prolonged arrest or detention shall not be admitted in evidence • Conviction or punishment must be made with evidence beyond the confession of the accused *Article 39:* Cannot be exposed to double jeopardy

Table 1.1 (*continued*)

U.S. Constitution, Bill of Rights	European Convention for the Protection of Human Rights and Fundamental Freedoms (1950)	Japanese Constitution (1947)
Article 6 • Right to a speedy and public trial by an impartial jury wherein the crime was committed • Right to be informed as to the nature and cause of the accusation • Right to be confronted with the witnesses against the individual • Right to force witnesses to appear in individual's favor • Right to have assistance of counsel for individual's defense	• Entitlement to effective legal defense and a fair trial (Johnston v. Chief Constable of the Royal Ulster Constabulary [1986] 1651 et seq.; Pecastaing v. Belgium [1980] 691 et seq., 716)	*Article 34:* • No person shall be arrested or detained without being informed of the charges against that person • Right to the immediate privilege of counsel • Right not to be detained without adequate cause • Upon demand of any person, cause must be immediately shown in open court in the presence of accused and counsel *Article 37:* • Right to a speedy and public trial by an impartial tribunal • Right to be confronted with the witnesses against the individual • Right to force witnesses to appear in individual's favor • Right to have assistance of Counsel for individual's defense
Article 7 • Right of trial by jury • Right of appeal through appropriate legal procedures		*Article 32:* Right of access to courts *Article 40:* In the case of acquittal, any individual can sue the State for redress as provided for by law
Article 8 • Right not to be forced to pay excessive bail or fines • Right against the infliction of cruel and unusual punishments	• Human dignity (Casagrande [1974] ECR 773)	*Article 24:* • Marriage based on mutual consent of both sexes • Equal rights of husband and wife • Laws to be based on individual dignity and the essential equality of the sexes are the bases of choice of spouse, property rights, inheritance, choice of domicile, divorce, and other matters pertaining to marriage and the family *Article 36:* • Prohibition of infliction of torture by any public officer • Prohibition against cruel punishments

Table 1.1 (continued)

U.S. Constitution, Bill of Rights	European Convention for the Protection of Human Rights and Fundamental Freedoms (1950)	Japanese Constitution (1947)
Article 9 Enumeration of these rights do not mean or deny or disparage other rights retained by the people	• Freedom of Profession (Her [1979] 3727) • Freedom of Industry (Usinor [1984] 4177 et seq.)	*Article 22:* • Freedom to choose and change residence • Freedom to choose occupation to the extent that it does not interfere with the public welfare *Article 27:* • Right and the obligation to work • Standards for wages, hours, rest, and other working conditions fixed by law • Prohibition of child labor
Article 10 Powers not delegated to the federal government by the U.S. Constitution, nor prohibited by it to the states, are reserved to the states, or to the people	• Freedom of trade (International Trade Association [1970] 1125, 1135 et seq.) • Freedom of competition (France [1985] 531) • Medical secrecy (Commission v Federal Republic of Germany [1992] ECR 2575)	*Article 28:* • Right of workers to organize and bargain collectively *Article 23:* • Academic freedom *Article 25:* • Right to a quality of life (minimum standards of wholesome and cultured living) • State shall promote the extension of social welfare and security, and of public health *Article 26:* • Compulsory education of boys and girls • Right to receive an equal education correspondent to their ability, as provided for by law. *Article 30:* • Right of citizens to be taxed

Source: EU data adapted from European Parliament, 2000.

Table 1.2
Top Fifteen Developing Country Receivers of
Remittances: 1999

Rank	Country	$ Million	% of GDP
1	India	11,097	2.61
2	Philippines	7,016	8.9
3	Mexico	6,649	1.7
4	Turkey	4,529	2.3
5	Egypt	3,196	4.0
6	Morocco	1,918	5.5
7	Bangladesh	1,803	4.1
8	Pakistan	1,707	2.7
9	Dominican Republic	1,613	11
10	Thailand	1,460	1.1
11	Jordan	1,460	21.2
12	El Salvador	1,379	12.3
13	Nigeria	1,292	3.5
14	Yemen	1,202	24.5
15	Brazil	1,192	0.2

Source: Acma, B. (2002). *Economic Consequences of International Migration: Case Study of Turkey.* Retrieved from http://Widerunu.edu/conference/conference2002-3/conference-2002-3-programme.html.

Table 1.3
**Key Legislative Acts and Developments in the Social Safety Net
in the United States: 1932 to 1996**

Year	Administration	Legislation/Agency Created	Action/Importance
1932	Hoover	Reconstruction Finance Corporation	Shifted some relief efforts to the federal government.
1932	Hoover	Emergency Relief Act of 1932	Provides states with a $300 million loan package to support local relief efforts.
1933	Roosevelt	Glass-Steangal Act	Established the Federal Deposit Insurance Corporation (FDIC), giving the government the ability to curb irresponsible speculation by banks.
1933	Roosevelt	Federal Emergency Relief Program (FERA)	Program ended in 1936. Programs shifted to the WPA.
1933	Roosevelt	National Industrial Recovery Act (NIRA)	Created the Public Works Administration (PWA). It administered construction of public works such as bridges, dams, housing developments, and public buildings. Also made loans to states and local governments for similar projects.
1933	Roosevelt	National Industrial Recovery Act (NIRA)	Created the National Recovery Administration (NRA). Drew up over 500 regulatory codes of fair practice for various industries. Also set up a "blanket code" of a maximum workweek of 35 to 40 hours, the abolition of child labor, and a minimum wage of 30 to 40 cents per hour. Declared unconstitutional by the U.S. Supreme Court in 1935.
1933	Roosevelt	Civilian Conservation Corps (CCC)	A federal relief program tied to public works program that generates government-sponsored projects in order to generate employment.
1933	Roosevelt	Civil Works Administration (CWA)	Shut down in 1934. Hired laborers for temporary federal government sponsored construction projects.
1933	Roosevelt	Agricultural Adjustment Act (AAA)	Reduced crop production to eliminate surpluses and control the lowering prices of farm products. The U.S. Supreme Court declared many aspects of this act illegal in 1936.
1933	Roosevelt	Tennessee Valley Authority (TVA)	Created an independent public projects agency to provide for energy needs in rural areas as well as to generate jobs.
1933	Roosevelt	Frazier-Lemke Bank Bankruptcy Act	Enabled some farmers to regain their land even after it had been foreclosed.
1934	Roosevelt	National Housing Act of 1934	Created the Federal Housing Administration to insure loans made by private lending institutions to middle-class owners to repair or modernize their homes, or buy new ones.
1934	Roosevelt	Federal Securities Act	Created the Securities and Exchange Commission (SEC) to oversee and regulate exchange practices in the stock market.
1935	Roosevelt	Works Progress Administration (WPA)	Replaced CWA, FERA, and PWA. Purpose was to provide jobs for unemployed that could work.
1935	Roosevelt	National Youth Administration (NYA)	Provided assistance to those aged 16 to 25 who wanted to continue their education by providing them with part-time jobs.
1935	Roosevelt	Social Security Act (SSA)	Unemployment insurance (SSA Title III), retirement supplement, and relief package. This bill provided many of the provisions that later became known as "welfare" through the creation of the Aid to Families with Dependent Children (AFDC) program (SSA Title IV), which was replaced by the Temporary Aid for Needy Families (TANF) as of 1996.
1935	Roosevelt	Resettlement Administration	Provided loans for farmers to relocate from poor producing lands to better land.

(continued)

Table 1.3 (*continued*)

Year	Administration	Legislation/Agency Created	Action/Importance
1935	Roosevelt	Rural Electrification Administration	Provided electrical power to farmers through the creation of cooperatives.
1935	Roosevelt	Wagner Act	Provided for government protection of the exclusive right of labor unions to collective bargaining.
1935	Roosevelt	National Labor Relations Act	Created National Labor Relations Board (NLRB) to ensure against unfair labor practices.
1937	Roosevelt	National Housing Act of 1937	Provided assistance to low-income families.
1937	Roosevelt	Bankhead-Jones Tenancy Act	Created the Farm Security Administration to replace the Resettlement Administration. Continued to provide loans to resettling farmers and aided migrant workers by establishing a chain of sanitary migratory camps.
1938	Roosevelt	Fair Labor Standards Act	Formally put in place a minimum wage (40 cents per hour), created the 40 hour work week, and made employment of children under the age of 16 illegal.
1939	Roosevelt	Relief Act	Put an 18-month cap on an individual's eligibility to participate in the WPA job program.
1939	Roosevelt	Social Security Amendments of 1939	Transformed Social Security from a retirement program for workers into a family-based economic security program by adding two new categories of benefits: (1) payments to the spouse and minor children of a retired worker (so-called dependents benefits) and (2) survivors benefits paid to the family in the event of the premature death of a covered worker.
1944	Roosevelt	Servicemen's Readjustment Act (G.I. Bill of Rights)	Provided opportunity for returning servicemen to receive federal funds to pursue education or training.
1946	Truman	National School Lunch Act	Authorized assistance to states to assist in providing adequate foods and facilities for the establishment and operation of nonprofit school lunch programs.
1946	Truman	Employment Act	Established the Council of Economic Advisers.
1947	Truman	Labor-Management Relations Act (Taft-Hartley Act)	Made it illegal to require a person be in a union to get a job. Allowed states to pass "right-to-work" laws limiting the establishment of unions in workplaces, and also provided the president with the power to issue an injunction to call a 10-week "cooling off" period prior to striking.
1949	Truman	Fair Labor Standards Act Amendments	Raised minimum wage from 40 to 75 cents an hour.
1949	Truman	National Housing Act of 1949	Provided for the construction of low-income housing (810,000 units) and subsidies for long-term rent.
1950	Truman	Social Security Amendments of 1950	Extended coverage and expanded benefits of the Federal old-age and survivors insurance program (approx. 10 million). Broadened and increased grants to states for public assistance to permanently and totally disabled, needy individuals, also to maternal and child health and child welfare services.
1953	Eisenhower	Department of Health, Education and Welfare	New cabinet-level department providing aid and limited oversight of education programs, protecting the health of all Americans, and providing essential human services, especially for those who are least able to help themselves. In 1980, this department split into two cabinet-level departments, the Department of Education and Health and the Department of Human Services.
1954	Eisenhower	School Milk Program Act	Provided funds for purchase of milk for school lunch programs.

Table 1.3 (*continued*)

Year	Administration	Legislation/Agency Created	Action/Importance
1954	Eisenhower	Social Security Amendments of 1954	Established first disability program under the Social Security Act.
1954	Eisenhower	Educational Research Act	Authorized cooperative arrangements with universities, colleges, and state educational agencies for educational research.
1956	Eisenhower	Social Security Amendments of 1956	Provided monthly insurance benefits to eligible disabled workers from ages 50 to 65.
1958	Eisenhower	National Defense Education Act (NDEA)	Federal effort to improve elementary and secondary education, particularly in the fields of science, mathematics, and foreign languages.
1959	Eisenhower	Landrum-Griffin Labor Management Act	Protected union funds through requirements for labor organizations to file annual financial reports as well as reports regarding certain labor relations practices from union officials, employers, and labor consultants. Also established standards for the election of union officers.
1960	Eisenhower	Social Security Amendments of 1960	Removed minimum age requirement of 50 for eligible disabled workers to receive benefits.
1961	Kennedy	Area Redevelopment Act	Provided for training or retraining of persons in redevelopment areas.
1962	Kennedy	Manpower Development and Training Act	Provided training for the unemployed and underemployed (new training or skills upgrading).
1962	Kennedy	Migrant Health Act	Provided support for clinics serving agricultural workers.
1963	Kennedy	Vocational Education Act	Increased federal support of vocational education schools and vocational education programs.
1963	Kennedy	Higher Education Facilities Act	Provided grants and loans for classrooms, libraries, and laboratories in public community colleges and technical institutes, as well as undergraduate and graduate facilities at other colleges and universities.
1963	Kennedy	Equal Pay Act	Law banned wage discrimination based on gender in jobs requiring equal skills, effort, and responsibility.
1964	Johnson	Civil Rights Act of 1964	Title I: presumption that literacy equated with a sixth-grade education in English.
			Title VII: outlaws discrimination in various forms of employment on the basis of race, religion, and sex. The Equal Employment Opportunity Commission (EEOC) is formed to enforce Title VII.
1964	Johnson	Economic Opportunity Act	Established the Job Corps program and the creation of education and training activities and of community action programs through Head Start, Follow Through, and Upward Bound, and the Volunteers in Service to America (VISTA). Also authorized grants for college work-study programs for students from low-income families. Authorized support for work-training programs to provide education and vocational training and work experience opportunities in welfare programs.
1964	Johnson	Food Stamp Act	Nationalized a pilot project initiated in 1961: a voucher scheme where public assistance recipients and other eligible low-income individuals are able to receive coupons of certain worth that are redeemable for food.
1965	Johnson	Medicare and Medicaid (Social Security Act, Titles XVIII and XIX respectively)	First significant attempt at providing comprehensive healthcare to millions of Americans.

Table 1.3 (*continued*)

Year	Administration	Legislation/Agency Created	Action/Importance
1965	Johnson	Older Americans Act	Nutritional and social programs for the aged.
1965	Johnson	Department of Housing and Urban Development Act	Established Housing and Urban Development (HUD) as a cabinet-level department.
1965	Johnson	Elementary and Secondary Education Act (ESEA)	Provided federal aid to school children with substantial numbers of children from unemployed families or those making less than $2,000 per year.
1965	Johnson	Higher Education Act	Provided grants for university community service programs and college libraries. Also provided grants to strengthen developing institutions and teacher training programs, providing assistance with undergraduate instructional equipment. Authorized insured student loans, established a National Teacher Corps, and provided for graduate teacher training fellowships.
1966	Johnson	Adult Education Act	Provided grants to states for the encouragement and expansion of educational programs for adults. Also provided assistance for the training of teachers of adults, a program previously under the Economic Opportunity Act of 1964.
1967	Johnson	Age Discrimination in Employment Act	Prohibited employment discrimination against persons 40 years of age or older.
1967	Johnson	Social Security Amendments of 1967	Provided for the payment of benefits to disabled widows and widowers age 50 or older.
1967	Johnson	Education Professions Development Act	Amended the Higher Education Act of 1965, giving impetus to improving the quality of teaching and to help meet critical shortages of adequately trained educational personnel.
1968	Johnson	Vocational Education Amendments of 1968	Provided for a National Advisory Council on Vocational Education.
1968	Johnson	Handicapped Children's Early Education Assistance Act	Authorized preschool and early education programs for handicapped children.
1968	Johnson	Civil Rights Act of 1968	Made refusing to sell or rent a dwelling based on race or religion illegal.
1970	Nixon	Occupational Safety and Health Act (OSH)	Created the Occupational Safety and Health Administration (OSHA). Mandated to set standards and conduct inspections to ensure that employers are providing safe and healthful workplaces. Also allowed to require that employers adopt certain practices, means, methods or processes reasonably necessary and appropriate to protect workers on the job.
1970	Nixon	National Commission on Libraries and Information Services Act	Established the National Commission on Libraries and Information Science with mission to effectively utilize the nation's educational resources.
1972	Nixon	Equal Employment Opportunity Act	Expanded Civil Rights Act of 1964 to public sector employees.
1972	Nixon	Education Amendments of 1972	Established the National Institute of Education (NIE). Set up federal matching grants for state Student Incentive Grants. Prohibited sex bias in admission to vocational, professional, and graduate schools, and public institutions of undergraduate higher education. Title IX: equality of women programming in sports.
1972	Nixon	Social Security Amendments of 1972	Created the Supplementary Security Income (SSI) (SSA Title XVI) program. It provided cash assistance for the aged, blind, and disabled. Begun in 1974. The Amendments also provided Medicare and

Table 1.3 (*continued*)

Year	Administration	Legislation/Agency Created	Action/Importance
			Medicaid protection for Social Security disability recipients. Set up indexing by tying cost of living allowance (COLA) increases tied to the Consumer Price Index (CPI).
1973	Nixon	Older Americans Comprehensive Services Amendment of 1973	Expanded comprehensive programs of health, education, and social services to older citizens.
1973	Nixon	Comprehensive Employment Training Program (CETA)	Provided states and local governments with grants combining training with direct employment opportunities. Extended and expanded provisions in the Manpower Development and Training Act of 1962, Title I of the Economic Opportunity Act of 1962, Title I of the Economic Opportunity Act of 1964, and the Emergency Employment Act of 1971 as in effect prior to June 30, 1973.
1973	Nixon	Rehabilitation Act	Section 503: required employers with federal contracts or subcontracts that exceed $10,000 to take affirmative steps to hire, retain, and promote qualified individuals with disabilities.
1974	Nixon	Employee Retirement Income Security Act (ERISA)	Provided regulation to employers who offer pension or welfare benefit plans for their employees. Imposed a wide range of fiduciary, disclosure and reporting requirements on fiduciaries of pension and welfare benefit plans and those having dealings with these plans.
1974	Nixon	Housing and Community Development Act	Consolidated programs into Community Development Block Grant (CDBG) program. Formation of Section 8 tenant-based certificates increased low-income tenants' choice of housing.
1975	Ford	Child Support Enforcement program	Provided for a grant-in-aid program with incentives to states to improve state efforts in the area of child support. States were allowed to keep 75% of collected payments from absent parent whose children received AFDC.
1975	Ford	Amendments to Civil Rights Act of 1965	Broadened anti-discrimination efforts to protect other language minorities such as Hispanics and Native Americans.
1975	Ford	Age Discrimination Act	Prohibited discrimination on the basis of age in programs or activities receiving federal financial assistance.
1975	Ford	Education for All Handicapped Children Act (Public Law 94-142)	Required that that all handicapped children have available a free appropriate education designed to meet their unique needs.
1975	Ford	Earned Income Tax Credit	Part of the individual income tax process, designed to have the effect of providing additional revenue to poor families. Provided tax reductions and wage supplements for low- and moderate-income working families. Expanded in 1986, 1990 and 1993, and 2001. Used extensively from 1994 as an antipoverty measure.
1977	Carter	Health Care Financing Administration	Separate management of Medicare and Medicaid from the Social Security Administration.
1977	Carter	Youth Employment and Demonstration Projects Act	Established a youth employment training program that promoted education-to-work transition, literacy training, bilingual training, and attainment of certificates of high school equivalency (GED).
1977	Carter	Career Education Incentive Act	Established a career education program for elementary and secondary schools.
1978	Carter	Amendments to Civil Rights Act of 1964	Added prohibition of employment due to pregnancy or related disabilities. Mandated that pregnancy or related medical conditions be treated in the same light as a disability and eligible for medical and liability insurance.

Table 1.3 (*continued*)

Year	Administration	Legislation/Agency Created	Action/Importance
1978	Carter	Middle Income Student Assistance Act	Modified provisions for student financial assistance programs to allow middle-income as well as low-income students attending college or other postsecondary institutions to qualify for federal education assistance.
1980	Carter	Social Security Disability Amendments of 1980	Strengthened work incentives in both the disability insurance and SSI programs by providing a disabled individual who completes a 9-month trial work period with an additional 15-month period within which to test his or ability to work while retaining disability status. Also provided that in determining whether a disabled individual's earnings demonstrate substantial gainful activity, the amount of such earnings will be reduced by the amount of impairment-related work expenses incurred by the individual. Abolished the system of individual state agreements to ensure uniform administration of mandates.
1982	Reagan	Job Training Partnership Act (JTPA)	Provided for a training and employment program. It replaced CETA. JTPA was replaced by the passage of the Workforce Investment Act of 1998.
1983	Reagan	Social Security Amendments of 1983	One-half of social security benefits as taxable income for taxpayers whose adjusted gross income, combined with half their benefits and any tax-exempt interest they may have, exceeds $25,000 for a single taxpayer and $32,000 for married taxpayers filing jointly. Benefits received by married taxpayers filing separately are taxable without regard to other income.
1984	Reagan	Migrant and Seasonal Agricultural Worker Protection Act	Provided safeguards for most migrant and seasonal agricultural workers in their interactions with farm labor contractors, agricultural employers, agricultural associations, and providers of migrant housing.
1984	Reagan	Carl D. Perkins Vocational Education Act	Replaced the Vocational Education Act of 1963. Provided aid to the states to make vocational education programs accessible to all persons, including handicapped and disadvantaged, single parents and homemakers, and the incarcerated.
1986	Reagan	Federal Employee's Retirement System Act	Required federal employees hired after 1983 to be covered under Social Security. Heretofore, federal employees belonged to the CSRS program.
1988	Reagan	Job Opportunities and Basic Skills (JOBS)	Purpose was to assist the poor in moving from welfare to work; federal support for childcare initiated.
1988	Reagan	McKinney Act	Provided healthcare to the homeless.
1988	Reagan	Family Support Act	Stressed the mutual obligation of government and welfare recipient to promote self-sufficiency of AFDC families.
1990	G. Bush	Americans with Disabilities Act	Prohibited private firms, state and local government employers with 15 or more employees, and employment agencies from discriminating on the basis of disability.
1990	G. Bush	Cranston-Gonzalez National Affordable Housing Act	Created HOME housing block grant that emphasizes home ownership and tenant-based assistance.
1990	G. Bush	Omnibus Budget Reconciliation Act	Established two new state child care grant programs: The Child Care and Development Block Grant and the At-risk Child Care Program.
1990	G. Bush	Budget Enforcement Act	Removed Social Security taxes and benefits from calculations of the budget.

Table 1.3 (*continued*)

Year	Administration	Legislation/Agency Created	Action/Importance
1993	Clinton	Family and Medical Leave Act (FMLA)	Required employers of 50 or more employees to give up to 12 weeks of unpaid, job-protected leave to eligible employees for the birth or adoption of a child or for the serious illness of the employee or a spouse, child, or parent.
1993	Clinton	Student Loan Reform Act	Phased in a financial aid for college and other postsecondary institution students a system of direct lending designed to provide savings for taxpayers and students.
1994	Clinton	Goals 2000: Educate America Act	Formed a new federal partnership through a system of grants to states and local communities to reform the nation's education system.
1994	Clinton	School-To-Work Opportunities Act	Established a national framework within which states and communities can develop School-To-Work Opportunities systems to prepare young people for first jobs and continuing education. The framework was to develop a system of programs that include work-based learning, school-based learning, and connecting activities components leading to a high school diploma (or its equivalent), a nationally recognized skill certificate, or an associate degree (if appropriate) that would help in getting that first job.
1996	Clinton	Health Insurance Portability and Accountability Act	Protected health insurance coverage for workers and their families when they change or lose their jobs.
1996	Clinton	The Personal Responsibility and Work Opportunity Reconciliation Act	Placed lifetime limits on receiving AFDC payments by replacing AFDC with the Temporary Assistance for Needy Families (TANF). Provided for block grants to states for temporary assistance to eligible individuals. Required that persons applying for old-age, survivor, and disability insurance (OASDI) must provide proof of citizenship, nationals, or aliens who are lawfully present in the USA.
1996	Clinton	Senior Citizens' Right to Work Act	Relaxed earning limits for seniors who reached federal retirement age (currently at 65).
1996	Clinton	Contract with America Advancement Act	Prohibited disability insurance and SSI eligibility to individuals whose drug addiction and/or alcoholism is a contributing factor material to the finding of disability.
1996	Clinton	Public Law 104-193 (General Welfare Reform Bill)	Title III: imposed state obligations to provide child support for each child receiving assistance under TANF, foster care adoption, and Medicaid. Other sections identified key administrative requirements for welfare programs.

Table 1.4
Legislation Impacting the Social Safety Net Under the New Paradigm:
1997 to 2000

Year	Administration	Legislation/Agency Created	Action/Importance
1997	Clinton	Balanced Budget Act of 1997	Provided that despite restrictions imposed in 1996, non-citizens lawfully residing in the USA who were receiving SSI remain eligible. Established the Welfare to Work (WtW) grant program. Made amendments that allowed states to exempt significant numbers of able-bodied adults without dependents from new work requirements, and more than doubled federal funding for employment and training programs for food stamp recipients. Also established State's Children Health Insurance Program.
1998	Clinton	Workforce Investment Act	Replaced JTPA. It provided financial assistance for a comprehensive system of job training and placement services for adults and eligible youth.
1998	Clinton	Deadbeat Parents Punishment Act	Imposed two new categories of felony offenses for parents avoiding the payment of child support.
1999	Clinton	Welfare-to-Work and Child Support Amendments of 1999	Removed the requirement that long-term TANF recipients must meet additional barriers to employment in order to be eligible for WtW. TANF recipients became eligible for WtW if they received assistance for at least 30 months (whether consecutive or not), if they are within 12 months of reaching their TANF time limit, or if they have exhausted their receipt of TANF due to time limits.
1999	Clinton	Foster Care Independent Act	Enforced restriction for prisoners and created new sanctions to deter abuse by people improperly receiving benefits.
1999	Clinton	Ticket to Work and Work Incentives Improvement Act	Amended the Social Security Act, expanding the availability of healthcare coverage for working individuals with disabilities and establishes a Ticket to Work and Self-Sufficiency Program within the Social Security Administration to provide such individuals with meaningful opportunities to work.
2000	Clinton	Social Security Amendments of 2000	Eliminated earnings limit for seniors who have reached federal retirement age, effective as of 2000.

Table 1.5
Overall Population of the United States: 1960 to 2001

[In thousands, except percent (180,671 represents 180,671,000). **Estimates as of July 1.** Total population includes Armed Forces abroad; civilian population excludes Armed Forces.]

Year	Total Population	Total Percent change [1]	Resident population	Civilian population	Year	Total Population	Total Percent change [1]	Resident population	Civilian population
1960	180,671	1.60	179,979	178,140	1981	229,966	0.98	229,466	227,818
1961	183,691	1.67	182,992	181,143	1982	232,188	0.97	231,664	229,995
1962	186,538	1.55	185,771	183,677	1983	234,307	0.91	233,792	232,097
1963	189,242	1.45	188,483	186,493	1984	236,348	0.87	235,825	234,110
1964	191,889	1.40	191,141	189,141	1985	238,466	0.90	237,924	236,219
1965	194,303	1.26	193,526	191,605	1986	240,651	0.92	240,133	238,412
1966	196,560	1.16	195,576	193,420	1987	242,804	0.89	242,289	240,550
1967	198,712	1.09	197,457	195,264	1988	245,021	0.91	244,499	242,817
1968	200,706	1.00	199,399	197,113	1989	247,342	0.95	246,819	245,131
1969	202,677	0.98	201,385	199,145	1990	250,132	1.13	249,623	247,983
1970	205,052	1.17	203,984	201,895	1991	253,493	1.34	252,981	251,370
1971	207,661	1.27	206,827	204,866	1992	256,894	1.34	256,514	254,929
1972	209,896	1.08	209,284	207,511	1993	260,255	1.31	259,919	258,446
1973	211,909	0.96	211,357	209,600	1994	263,436	1.22	263,126	261,714
1974	213,854	0.92	213,342	211,636	1995	266,557	1.18	266,278	264,927
1975	215,973	0.99	215,465	213,789	1996	269,667	1.17	269,394	268,108
1976	218,035	0.95	217,563	215,894	1997	272,912	1.20	272,647	271,394
1977	220,239	1.01	219,760	218,106	1998	276,115	1.17	275,854	274,633
1978	222,585	1.06	222,095	220,467	1999	279,295	1.15	279,040	277,841
1979	225,055	1.11	224,567	222,969	2000	282,339	1.09	282,125	280,939
1980	227,726	1.19	227,225	225,621	2001	285,024	0.95	284,797	283,624

1. Percent change from immediate preceding year.

Source: United States Census Bureau. (2002). *Statistical Abstract of the United States 2002*. Washington, D.C.: Government Printing Office. Retrieved from http://www.census.gov/prod/2003pubs/02statab/pop.pdf.

Table 1.6
Components of Population Change, Projections: 2005 to 2050

[286,549 represents 286,549,000. Resident population. Based on middle series of assumptions.]

Year	Population as of Jan. 1 (1,000)	Calendar year — Net increase Total (1,000)	Calendar year — Net increase Percent [1]	Births (1,000)	Deaths (1,000)	Net migration [2] (1,000)	Rate per 1,000 midyear population — Net growth rate	Birth rate	Death rate	Net migration rate [2]
2005	286,549	2,443	0.9	4,045	2,480	878	8.5	14.1	8.6	3.1
2010	298,710	2,425	0.8	4,283	2,578	720	8.1	14.3	8.6	2.4
2015	311,069	2,521	0.8	4,476	2,695	740	8.1	14.3	8.6	2.4
2020	323,724	2,530	0.8	4,613	2,840	757	7.8	14.2	8.7	2.3
2025	336,566	2,621	0.8	4,736	3,033	918	7.8	14.0	9.0	2.7
2030	349,789	2,688	0.8	4,878	3,257	1,067	7.7	13.9	9.3	3.0
2040	376,123	2,601	0.7	5,286	3,702	1,018	6.9	14.0	9.8	2.7
2050	402,420	2,699	0.7	5,661	3,952	990	6.7	14.0	9.8	2.5

1. Percent of population at beginning of period.
2. Covers net international migration and movement of Armed Forces, federally affiliated civilian citizens, and their dependents.

Source: United States Census Bureau. (2002). *Statistical Abstract of the United States 2002*. Washington, D.C.: Government Printing Office. Retrieved from http://www.census.gov/prod/2003pubs/02statab/pop.pdf.

Table 1.7
Households, Families, Subfamilies, and Married Couples:
1980 to 2000

[**In thousands, except as indicated (80,776 represents 80,776,000). As of March.** Based on Current Population Survey; includes members of Armed Forces living off post or with their families on post, but excludes all other members of Armed Forces; Minus sign (-) indicates decrease]

Type of unit	1980	1985	1990	1995	1997	1998	1999	2000	Percent change 1980-90	Percent change 1990-2000
Households	**80,776**	**86,789**	**93,347**	**98,990**	**101,018**	**102,528**	**103,874**	**104,705**	16	12
Average size	2.76	2.69	2.63	2.65	2.64	2.62	2.61	2.62	(X)	(X)
Family households	59,550	62,706	66,090	69,305	70,241	70,880	71,535	72,025	11	9
Married couple	49,112	50,350	52,317	53,858	53,604	54,317	54,770	55,311	7	6
Male householder [1]	1,733	2,228	2,884	3,226	3,847	3,911	3,976	4,028	66	40
Female householder [1]	8,705	10,129	10,890	12,220	12,790	12,652	12,789	12,687	25	17
Nonfamily households	21,226	24,082	27,257	29,686	30,777	31,648	32,339	32,680	28	20
Male householder	8,807	10,114	11,606	13,190	13,707	14,133	14,368	14,641	32	26
Female householder	12,419	13,968	15,651	16,496	17,070	17,516	17,971	18,039	26	15
One person	18,296	20,602	22,999	24,732	25,402	26,327	26,606	26,724	26	16
Families	**59,550**	**62,706**	**66,090**	**69,305**	**70,241**	**70,880**	**71,535**	**72,025**	11	9
Average size	3.29	3.23	3.17	3.19	3.19	3.18	3.18	3.17	(X)	(X)
With own children [2]	31,022	31,112	32,289	34,296	34,665	34,760	34,613	34,605	4	7
Without own children [2]	28,528	31,594	33,801	35,009	35,575	36,120	36,922	37,420	18	11
Married couple	49,112	50,350	52,317	53,858	53,604	54,317	54,770	55,311	7	6
With own children [2]	24,961	24,210	24,537	25,241	25,083	25,269	25,066	25,248	-2	3
Without own children [2]	24,151	26,140	27,780	28,617	28,521	29,048	29,703	30,062	15	8
Male householder [1]	1,733	2,228	2,884	3,226	3,847	3,911	3,976	4,028	66	40
With own children [2]	616	896	1,153	1,440	1,709	1,798	1,706	1,786	87	55
Without own children [2]	1,117	1,332	1,731	1,786	2,138	2,113	2,270	2,242	55	30
Female householder [1]	8,705	10,129	10,890	12,220	12,790	12,652	12,789	12,687	25	17
With own children [2]	5,445	6,006	6,599	7,615	7,874	7,693	7,841	7,571	21	15
Without own children [2]	3,261	4,123	4,290	4,606	4,916	4,960	4,948	5,116	32	19
Unrelated subfamilies	360	526	534	674	615	575	522	571	48	7
Married couple	20	46	68	64	50	41	50	37	(B)	(B)
Male reference persons [1]	36	85	45	59	77	72	64	57	(B)	(B)
Female reference persons [1]	304	395	421	550	487	463	408	477	39	13
Related subfamilies	1,150	2,228	2,403	2,878	2,907	2,870	2,901	2,984	109	24
Married couple	582	719	871	1,015	1,012	947	1,029	1,149	50	32
Father-child [1]	54	116	153	195	244	250	281	201	(B)	31
Mother-child [1]	512	1,392	1,378	1,668	1,651	1,673	1,591	1,634	169	19
Married couples	**49,714**	**51,114**	**53,256**	**54,937**	**54,666**	**55,305**	**55,849**	**56,497**	7	6
With own household	49,112	50,350	52,317	53,858	53,604	54,317	54,770	55,311	7	6
Without own household	602	764	939	1,079	1,062	988	1,079	1,186	56	26
Percent without	1.2	1.5	1.8	2.0	1.9	1.8	1.9	2.1	(X)	(X)

B. Not shown; base less than 75,000.

X. Not applicable.

1. No spouse present.

2. Under 18 years old.

Source: United States Census Bureau. (2002). *Statistical Abstract of the United States 2002*. Washington, D.C.: Government Printing Office. Retrieved from http://www.census.gov/prod/2003pubs/02statab/pop.pdf.

Table 1.8
Households by Age of Householder and Size of Household: 1980 to 2000

[In millions (80.8 represents 80,800,000). As of March. Based on Current Population Survey.]

Age of householder and size of household	1980	1985	1990	1995	1999	2000 Total [1]	2000 White	2000 Black	2000 His-panic [2]
Total	80.8	86.8	93.3	99.0	103.9	104.7	87.7	12.8	9.3
Age of householder:									
15 to 24 years old	6.6	5.4	5.1	5.4	5.9	5.9	4.5	1.0	0.9
25 to 29 years old	9.3	9.6	9.4	8.4	8.5	8.5	6.7	1.3	1.1
30 to 34 years old	9.3	10.4	11.0	11.1	10.3	10.1	8.1	1.4	1.3
35 to 44 years old	14.0	17.5	20.6	22.9	24.0	24.0	19.8	3.1	2.5
45 to 54 years old	12.7	12.6	14.5	17.6	20.2	20.9	17.5	2.6	1.5
55 to 64 years old	12.5	13.1	12.5	12.2	13.6	13.6	11.6	1.5	0.9
65 to 74 years old	10.1	10.9	11.7	11.8	11.4	11.3	9.9	1.1	0.6
75 years old and over	6.4	7.3	8.4	9.6	10.2	10.4	9.5	0.8	0.4
One person	18.3	20.6	23.0	24.7	26.6	26.7	22.3	3.6	1.3
Male	7.0	7.9	9.0	10.1	11.0	11.2	9.2	1.6	0.7
Female	11.3	12.7	14.0	14.6	15.6	15.5	13.1	2.0	0.6
Two persons	25.3	27.4	30.1	31.8	34.3	34.7	30.1	3.4	1.9
Three persons	14.1	15.5	16.1	16.8	17.4	17.2	13.8	2.5	1.8
Four persons	12.7	13.6	14.5	15.3	15.0	15.3	12.8	1.7	1.9
Five persons	6.1	6.1	6.2	6.6	7.0	7.0	5.7	0.9	1.3
Six persons	2.5	2.3	2.1	2.3	2.4	2.4	1.8	0.4	0.6
Seven persons or more	1.8	1.3	1.3	1.4	1.3	1.4	1.1	0.2	0.5

1. Includes other races, not shown separately.
2. Hispanic persons may be of any race.

Source: United States Census Bureau. (2002). *Statistical Abstract of the United States 2002.* Washington, D.C.: Government Printing Office. Retrieved from http://www.census.gov/prod/2003pubs/02statab/pop.pdf.

Table 1.9
Persons Living Alone by Sex and Age: 1980 to 2000

[As of March (18,296 represents 18,296,000). Based on Current Population Survey.]

Sex and age	Number of persons (1,000) 1980	1985	1990	1995	2000	Percent distribution 1980	1985	1990	1995	2000
Both sexes	18,296	20,602	22,999	24,732	26,724	100	100	100	100	100
15 to 24 years old	1,726	1,324	1,210	1,196	1,144	9	6	5	5	4
25 to 34 years old	[1]4,729	3,905	3,972	3,653	3,848	[1]26	19	17	15	14
35 to 44 years old	([1])	2,322	3,138	3,663	4,109	([1])	11	14	15	15
45 to 64 years old	4,514	4,939	5,502	6,377	7,842	25	24	24	26	29
65 to 74 years old	3,851	4,130	4,350	4,374	4,091	21	20	19	18	15
75 years old and over	3,477	3,982	4,825	5,470	5,692	19	19	21	22	21
Male	6,966	7,922	9,049	10,140	11,181	38	39	39	41	42
15 to 24 years old	947	750	674	623	556	5	4	3	3	2
25 to 34 years old	[1]2,920	2,307	2,395	2,213	2,279	[1]16	11	10	9	9
35 to 44 years old	([1])	1,406	1,836	2,263	2,569	([1])	7	8	9	10
45 to 64 years old	1,613	1,845	2,203	2,787	3,422	9	9	10	11	13
65 to 74 years old	775	868	1,042	1,134	1,108	4	4	5	5	4
75 years old and over	711	746	901	1,120	1,247	4	4	4	5	5
Female	11,330	12,680	13,950	14,592	15,543	62	62	61	59	58
15 to 24 years old	779	573	536	572	588	4	3	2	2	2
25 to 34 years old	[1]1,809	1,598	1,578	1,440	1,568	[1]10	8	7	6	6
35 to 44 years old	([1])	916	1,303	1,399	1,540	([1])	4	6	6	6
45 to 64 years old	2,901	3,095	3,300	3,589	4,420	16	15	14	15	17
65 to 74 years old	3,076	3,262	3,309	3,240	2,983	17	16	14	13	11
75 years old and over	2,766	3,236	3,924	4,351	4,444	15	16	17	18	17

1. Data for persons 35 to 44 years old included with persons 25 to 34 years old.

Source: United States Census Bureau. (2002). *Statistical Abstract of the United States 2002.* Washington, D.C.: Government Printing Office. Retrieved from http://www.census.gov/prod/2003pubs/02statab/pop.pdf.

Table 1.10
Family Groups with Children Under 18 Years Old by Race
and Hispanic Origin: 1980 to 2000

[In thousands. As of March (32,150 represents 32,150,000). Family groups comprise family households, related subfamilies, and unrelated subfamilies. Excludes members of Armed Forces except those living off post or with their families on post. Based on Current Population Survey.]

Race and Hispanic origin of householder or reference person	1980	1990	1995	2000 Total	2000 Family households	2000 Subfamilies Total	2000 Subfamilies Related	2000 Subfamilies Unrelated
All races, total [1]	**32,150**	**34,670**	**37,168**	**37,496**	**34,605**	**2,890**	**2,346**	**544**
Two-parent family groups	25,231	24,921	25,640	25,771	25,248	523	512	11
One-parent family groups	6,920	9,749	11,528	11,725	9,357	2,368	1,834	534
Maintained by mother	6,230	8,398	9,834	9,681	7,571	2,110	1,633	477
Maintained by father	690	1,351	1,694	2,044	1,786	258	201	57
White, total	**27,294**	**28,294**	**29,846**	**30,079**	**28,107**	**1,973**	**1,558**	**415**
Two-parent family groups	22,628	21,905	22,320	22,241	21,809	433	422	11
One-parent family groups	4,664	6,389	7,525	7,838	6,298	1,540	1,136	404
Maintained by mother	4,122	5,310	6,239	6,216	4,869	1,347	995	352
Maintained by father	542	1,079	1,286	1,622	1,429	193	140	53
Black, total	**4,074**	**5,087**	**5,491**	**5,530**	**4,782**	**748**	**642**	**106**
Two-parent family groups	1,961	2,006	1,962	2,135	2,093	41	41	-
One-parent family groups	2,114	3,081	3,529	3,396	2,689	706	600	106
Maintained by mother	1,984	2,860	3,197	3,060	2,409	651	550	101
Maintained by father	129	221	332	335	280	55	50	5
Hispanic, total [2]	**2,194**	**3,429**	**4,527**	**5,503**	**4,814**	**688**	**596**	**92**
Two-parent family groups	1,626	2,289	2,879	3,625	3,423	203	194	9
One-parent family groups	568	1,140	1,647	1,877	1,391	486	402	84
Maintained by mother	526	1,003	1,404	1,565	1,145	420	347	73
Maintained by father	42	138	243	313	246	66	55	11

-. Represents or rounds to zero.

1. Includes other races, not shown separately.

2. Hispanic persons may be of any race.

Source: United States Census Bureau. (2002). *Statistical Abstract of the United States 2002.* Washington, D.C.: Government Printing Office. Retrieved from http://www.census.gov/prod/2003pubs/02statab/pop.pdf.

Table 1.11
Families by Number of Own Children under 18 Years Old: 1980 to 2000

[As of March (59,550 represents 59,550,000) and based on Current Population Survey.]

Race, Hispanic origin, and year	Number of families (1,000)					Percent distribution				
	Total	No children	One child	Two children	Three or more children	Total	No children	One child	Two children	Three or more children
ALL FAMILIES [1]										
1980	59,550	28,528	12,443	11,470	7,109	100	48	21	19	12
1990	66,090	33,801	13,530	12,263	6,496	100	51	20	19	10
1995	69,305	35,009	14,088	13,213	6,995	100	51	20	19	10
2000	72,025	37,420	14,311	13,215	7,080	100	52	20	18	10
Married couple	55,311	30,062	9,402	10,274	5,572	100	54	17	19	10
Male householder [2]	4,028	2,242	1,131	483	171	100	56	28	12	4
Female householder [2]	12,687	5,116	3,777	2,458	1,336	100	40	30	19	11
WHITE FAMILIES										
1980	52,243	25,769	10,727	9,977	5,769	100	49	21	19	11
1990	56,590	29,872	11,186	10,342	5,191	100	53	20	18	9
1995	58,437	30,486	11,491	10,983	5,478	100	52	20	19	9
2000	60,251	32,144	11,496	10,918	5,693	100	53	19	18	9
Married couple	48,790	26,981	8,023	8,970	4,816	100	55	16	18	10
Male householder [2]	3,081	1,652	885	400	144	100	54	29	13	5
Female householder [2]	8,380	3,511	2,588	1,548	732	100	42	31	18	9
BLACK FAMILIES										
1980	6,184	2,364	1,449	1,235	1,136	100	38	23	20	18
1990	7,470	3,093	1,894	1,433	1,049	100	41	25	19	14
1995	8,093	3,411	1,971	1,593	1,117	100	42	24	20	14
2000	8,664	3,882	2,101	1,624	1,058	100	45	24	19	12
Married couple	4,144	2,050	838	754	501	100	49	20	18	12
Male householder [2]	706	427	196	62	21	100	60	28	9	3
Female householder [2]	3,814	1,405	1,066	807	536	100	37	28	21	14
HISPANIC FAMILIES [3]										
1980	3,029	946	680	698	706	100	31	22	23	23
1990	4,840	1,790	1,095	1,036	919	100	37	23	21	19
1995	6,200	2,216	1,408	1,406	1,171	100	36	23	23	19
2000	7,561	2,747	1,791	1,693	1,330	100	36	24	22	18
Married couple	5,133	1,710	1,139	1,276	1,008	100	33	22	25	20
Male householder [2]	658	412	141	68	38	100	63	21	10	6
Female householder [2]	1,769	625	511	350	284	100	35	29	20	16

1. Includes other races, not shown separately.
2. No spouse present.
3. Hispanic persons may be of any race.

Source: United States Census Bureau. (2002). *Statistical Abstract of the United States 2002*. Washington, D.C.: Government Printing Office. Retrieved from http://www.census.gov/prod/2003pubs/02statab/pop.pdf.

Table 1.12
Families by Size and Presence of Children: 1980 to 2000

[**In thousands, except as indicated (59,550 represents 59,550,000). As of March.** Excludes members of Armed Forces except those living off post or with their families on post. Based on Current Population Survey.]

Characteristic	Number					Percent distribution				
	1980	1985	1990	1995	2000	1980	1985	1990	1995	2000
Total.	59,550	62,706	66,090	69,305	72,025	100	100	100	100	100
Size of family:										
Two persons	23,461	25,349	27,606	29,176	31,455	39	40	42	42	44
Three persons	13,603	14,804	15,353	15,903	16,073	23	24	23	23	22
Four persons.	12,372	13,259	14,026	14,624	14,496	21	21	21	21	20
Five persons	5,930	5,894	5,938	6,283	6,526	10	9	9	9	9
Six persons.	2,461	2,175	1,997	2,106	2,226	4	4	3	3	3
Seven or more persons . .	1,723	1,225	1,170	1,213	1,249	3	2	2	2	2
Average per family	3.29	3.23	3.17	3.19	3.17	(X)	(X)	(X)	(X)	(X)
Own children under age 18:										
None	28,528	31,594	33,801	35,009	37,420	48	50	51	51	52
One.	12,443	13,108	13,530	14,088	14,311	21	21	20	20	20
Two	11,470	11,645	12,263	13,213	13,215	19	19	19	19	18
Three	4,674	4,486	4,650	5,044	5,063	8	7	7	7	7
Four or more	2,435	1,873	1,846	1,951	2,017	4	3	3	3	3
Own children under age 6:										
None	46,063	48,505	50,905	53,695	57,039	77	77	77	77	79
One.	9,441	9,677	10,304	10,733	10,454	16	15	16	15	15
Two or more	4,047	4,525	4,882	4,876	4,533	7	7	7	7	6

X. Not applicable.

Source: United States Census Bureau. (2002). *Statistical Abstract of the United States 2002.* Washington, D.C.: Government Printing Office. Retrieved from http://www.census.gov/prod/2003pubs/02statab/pop.pdf.

Table 1.13
Population by Country: 1990 to 2010

[5,283,755 represents 5,283,755,000. Population data generally are de facto figures for the present territory. Population estimates were derived from information available as of spring 2000. East Timor became independent of Indonesia, but population data will not be available until the next update of the International Data Base. Minus sign (-) indicates decrease.]

Country or area	Midyear population (1,000)				Population rank, 2001	Annual rate of growth, [1] 2000-2010 (percent)	Population per sq. mile, 2001	Area (sq. mile)
	1990	2000	2001	2010, proj.				
World	5,283,755	6,080,142	6,157,401	6,823,635	(X)	1.2	122	50,580,319
Afghanistan	14,750	25,889	26,813	33,864	39	2.7	107	250,000
Albania	3,258	3,490	3,510	3,827	128	0.9	332	10,579
Algeria	25,341	31,194	31,736	36,589	34	1.6	35	919,591
Andorra	53	67	68	74	204	1.0	388	174
Angola	8,056	10,145	10,366	12,646	71	2.2	22	481,351
Antigua and Barbuda.	63	66	67	71	206	0.6	394	170
Argentina	32,634	36,955	37,385	41,082	31	1.1	35	1,056,637
Armenia	3,366	3,344	3,336	3,365	130	0.1	290	11,506
Australia	17,022	19,165	19,358	20,925	53	0.9	7	2,941,285
Austria	7,718	8,131	8,151	8,278	86	0.2	255	31,942
Azerbaijan.	7,200	7,748	7,771	8,221	87	0.6	232	33,436
Bahamas, The	257	295	298	315	176	0.7	77	3,888
Bahrain.	500	634	645	737	162	1.5	2,700	239
Bangladesh	109,897	129,194	131,270	150,392	8	1.5	2,539	51,703
Barbados	263	274	275	287	178	0.4	1,658	166
Belarus.	10,215	10,367	10,350	10,294	73	-0.1	129	80,154
Belgium	9,969	10,242	10,259	10,340	76	0.1	879	11,672
Belize	191	249	256	320	179	2.5	29	8,803
Benin	4,656	6,396	6,591	8,411	95	2.7	154	42,710
Bhutan	1,598	2,005	2,049	2,476	142	2.1	113	18,147
Bolivia	6,574	8,153	8,300	9,499	85	1.5	20	418,683
Bosnia and Herzegovina . . .	4,424	3,836	3,922	4,103	121	0.7	199	19,741
Botswana	1,304	1,576	1,586	1,502	147	-0.5	7	226,012
Brazil	151,053	172,860	174,469	186,823	5	0.8	53	3,265,061
Brunei.	258	336	344	408	174	1.9	169	2,035
Bulgaria	8,894	7,797	7,707	7,006	88	-1.1	181	42,683
Burkina Faso	9,037	11,946	12,272	15,424	65	2.6	116	105,714
Burma	38,519	41,735	41,995	43,674	27	0.5	165	253,954
Burundi.	5,285	6,055	6,224	7,669	99	2.4	628	9,903
Cambodia	8,965	12,212	12,492	15,233	64	2.2	183	68,154
Cameroon	11,761	15,422	15,803	19,202	60	2.2	87	181,251
Canada.	27,791	31,278	31,593	34,253	35	0.9	9	3,560,219
Cape Verde	349	401	405	431	172	0.7	260	1,556
Central African Republic. . . .	2,803	3,513	3,577	4,135	127	1.6	15	240,533
Chad	6,018	8,425	8,707	11,616	83	3.2	18	486,178
Chile	13,128	15,154	15,328	16,727	61	1.0	53	289,112
China [2]	1,138,895	1,261,832	1,273,111	1,359,141	1	0.7	354	3,600,930
Colombia.	32,859	39,686	40,349	46,109	28	1.5	101	401,042
Comoros.	429	578	596	773	163	2.9	712	838
Congo (Brazzaville) [3].	2,218	2,831	2,894	3,491	132	2.1	22	131,853
Congo (Kinshasa) [3].	37,991	51,965	53,625	69,846	23	3.0	61	875,521
Costa Rica	3,027	3,711	3,773	4,306	124	1.5	193	19,560
Cote dÍvoire	11,919	15,981	16,393	20,003	57	2.2	134	122,780
Croatia	4,508	4,282	4,334	4,505	117	0.5	199	21,829
Cuba	10,545	11,142	11,184	11,526	67	0.3	261	42,803
Cyprus	681	758	763	801	158	0.5	214	3,568
Czech Republic	10,310	10,272	10,264	10,157	75	-0.1	338	30,365
Denmark.	5,141	5,336	5,353	5,474	105	0.3	327	16,359
Djibouti	370	451	461	579	166	2.5	54	8,486
Dominica.	73	72	71	70	202	-0.2	244	290
Dominican Republic	7,098	8,443	8,581	9,884	84	1.6	459	18,680
Ecuador	10,317	12,920	13,184	15,518	62	1.8	123	106,888
Egypt	56,106	68,360	69,537	79,811	15	1.5	181	384,344
El Salvador	5,100	6,123	6,238	7,293	98	1.7	780	8,000
Equatorial Guinea.	368	474	486	604	164	2.4	45	10,830
Eritrea	2,945	4,136	4,298	5,709	119	3.2	92	46,842
Estonia	1,573	1,431	1,423	1,372	148	-0.4	82	17,413
Ethiopia	48,335	64,117	65,892	82,312	18	2.5	152	432,310
Fiji	738	832	844	958	156	1.4	120	7,054
Finland	4,986	5,167	5,176	5,228	107	0.1	44	117,942
France	56,735	59,330	59,551	61,069	21	0.3	283	210,668
Gabon	1,069	1,208	1,221	1,309	151	0.8	12	99,486
Gambia, The	962	1,367	1,411	1,833	149	2.9	366	3,861
Georgia	5,457	5,020	4,989	4,815	111	-0.4	185	26,911
Germany.	79,380	82,797	83,030	84,616	12	0.2	614	135,236
Ghana	15,360	19,534	19,894	22,650	50	1.5	224	88,811
Greece	10,158	10,602	10,624	10,758	69	0.1	210	50,502
Grenada	92	89	89	91	197	0.2	682	131
Guatemala	9,630	12,640	12,974	16,194	63	2.5	310	41,865
Guinea	5,936	7,466	7,614	9,281	89	2.2	80	94,927
Guinea-Bissau	996	1,286	1,316	1,614	150	2.3	122	10,811
Guyana.	742	697	697	729	160	0.4	9	76,004
Haiti	6,028	6,868	6,965	7,950	94	1.5	655	10,641
Honduras	4,772	6,250	6,406	7,683	97	2.1	148	43,201
Hungary	10,372	10,139	10,106	9,831	77	-0.3	283	35,653
Iceland	255	276	278	289	177	0.4	7	38,707
India.	850,558	1,014,004	1,029,991	1,168,205	2	1.4	897	1,147,950
Indonesia	188,651	224,784	228,438	259,743	4	1.4	324	705,189
Iran	55,717	65,620	66,129	73,772	17	1.2	105	631,660

Table 1.13 (*continued*)

Country or area	Midyear population (1,000)				Population rank, 2001	Annual rate of growth,[1] 2000-2010 (percent)	Population per sq. mile, 2001	Area (sq. mile)
	1990	2000	2001	2010, proj.				
Iraq	18,135	22,676	23,332	29,672	44	2.7	139	167,556
Ireland	3,508	3,797	3,841	4,161	123	0.9	144	26,598
Israel	4,512	5,842	5,938	6,645	100	1.3	757	7,849
Italy	56,758	57,634	57,680	57,409	22	-	508	113,521
Jamaica	2,463	2,653	2,666	2,851	135	0.7	638	4,181
Japan	123,537	126,550	126,772	127,252	9	0.1	832	152,411
Jordan	3,262	4,999	5,153	6,486	108	2.6	146	35,344
Kazakhstan	16,708	16,733	16,731	17,276	55	0.3	16	1,049,150
Kenya	23,767	30,340	30,766	33,068	36	0.9	140	219,788
Kiribati	71	92	94	115	195	2.3	340	277
Korea, North	20,019	21,688	21,968	23,753	49	0.9	473	46,490
Korea, South	42,869	47,471	47,904	51,097	25	0.7	1,264	37,911
Kuwait	2,142	1,974	2,042	2,788	144	3.5	297	6,880
Kyrgyzstan	4,390	4,685	4,753	5,444	113	1.5	62	76,641
Laos	4,210	5,497	5,636	6,993	102	2.4	63	89,112
Latvia	2,672	2,405	2,385	2,252	139	-0.7	96	24,903
Lebanon	3,147	3,578	3,628	4,056	125	1.3	918	3,950
Lesotho	1,732	2,143	2,177	2,339	140	0.9	186	11,718
Liberia	2,190	3,164	3,226	4,073	131	2.5	87	37,189
Libya	4,140	5,115	5,241	6,447	106	2.3	8	679,359
Liechtenstein	29	32	33	35	213	0.8	523	62
Lithuania	3,702	3,621	3,611	3,560	126	-0.2	143	25,174
Luxembourg	382	437	443	493	168	1.2	444	998
Macedonia, The Former Yugoslav Republic of	1,893	2,041	2,046	2,115	143	0.4	206	9,928
Madagascar	11,522	15,506	15,983	20,993	58	3.0	71	224,533
Malawi	9,219	10,386	10,548	11,621	70	1.1	290	36,324
Malaysia	17,504	21,793	22,229	26,144	48	1.8	175	126,853
Maldives	216	301	311	400	175	2.8	2,683	116
Mali	8,228	10,686	11,009	14,349	68	2.9	23	471,042
Malta	359	392	395	420	173	0.7	3,184	124
Marshall Islands	46	68	71	100	201	3.9	1,013	70
Mauritania	1,984	2,668	2,747	3,561	134	2.9	7	397,838
Mauritius	1,074	1,179	1,190	1,280	152	0.8	1,667	714
Mexico	84,446	100,350	101,879	114,995	11	1.4	137	742,486
Micronesia, Federated States of	109	133	135	141	191	0.6	497	271
Moldova	4,398	4,431	4,432	4,535	116	0.2	341	13,012
Monaco	30	32	32	33	214	0.4	41,235	1
Mongolia	2,218	2,616	2,655	3,040	136	1.5	4	604,247
Morocco	24,686	30,122	30,645	35,301	37	1.6	178	172,317
Mozambique	14,276	19,105	19,371	20,504	52	0.7	64	302,737
Namibia	1,409	1,771	1,798	1,908	146	0.7	6	317,873
Nauru	9	12	12	14	223	1.9	1,491	8
Nepal	19,325	24,702	25,284	30,758	40	2.2	479	52,819
Netherlands	14,952	15,892	15,981	16,617	59	0.4	1,220	13,104
New Zealand	3,360	3,820	3,864	4,228	122	1.0	37	103,734
Nicaragua	3,643	4,813	4,918	5,839	112	1.9	106	46,430
Niger	7,627	10,076	10,355	13,140	72	2.7	21	489,073
Nigeria	92,483	123,338	126,636	155,588	10	2.3	360	351,649
Norway	4,242	4,481	4,503	4,677	115	0.4	38	118,865
Oman	1,773	2,533	2,622	3,523	137	3.3	32	82,031
Pakistan	113,975	141,554	144,617	171,373	7	1.9	481	300,664
Palau	15	19	19	22	219	1.4	108	177
Panama	2,388	2,808	2,846	3,150	133	1.1	97	29,340
Papua New Guinea	3,825	4,927	5,049	6,171	110	2.3	29	174,405
Paraguay	4,236	5,586	5,734	7,162	101	2.5	37	153,398
Peru	21,989	27,013	27,484	31,471	38	1.5	56	494,208
Philippines	65,037	81,160	82,842	97,898	13	1.9	720	115,124
Poland	38,119	38,646	38,634	38,691	30	-	329	117,571
Portugal	9,923	10,048	10,066	10,183	78	0.1	285	35,382
Qatar	481	744	769	970	157	2.6	181	4,247
Romania	22,866	22,411	22,364	21,930	47	-0.2	251	88,934
Russia	148,082	146,001	145,470	142,328	6	-0.3	22	6,592,817
Rwanda	6,962	7,229	7,313	7,876	91	0.9	759	9,633
Saint Kitts and Nevis	41	39	39	40	211	0.4	279	139
Saint Lucia	140	156	158	177	189	1.3	671	236
Saint Vincent and the Grenadines	107	115	116	119	193	0.3	886	131
Samoa	170	179	179	176	185	-0.2	163	1,100
San Marino	23	27	27	31	216	1.3	1,180	23
Sao Tome and Principe	119	160	165	219	187	3.1	445	371
Saudi Arabia	15,847	22,024	22,757	30,546	45	3.3	27	829,996
Senegal	7,360	9,987	10,285	13,221	74	2.8	139	74,131
Seychelles	73	79	80	83	198	0.4	453	176
Sierra Leone	4,227	5,233	5,427	6,930	103	2.8	196	27,653
Singapore	3,016	4,152	4,300	5,776	118	3.3	17,849	241
Slovakia	5,263	5,408	5,415	5,475	104	0.1	287	18,842
Slovenia	1,896	1,928	1,930	1,947	145	0.1	247	7,819
Solomon Islands	335	466	480	610	165	2.7	45	10,633
Somalia	6,675	7,253	7,489	9,922	90	3.1	31	242,216
South Africa	38,176	43,421	43,586	41,108	26	-0.5	92	471,444
Spain	39,351	39,997	40,038	40,157	29	-	208	192,819
Sri Lanka	17,193	19,239	19,409	20,832	51	0.8	776	24,996

Table 1.13 (*continued*)

Country or area	Midyear population (1,000)				Population rank, 2001	Annual rate of growth,[1] 2000-2010 (percent)	Population per sq. mile, 2001	Area (sq. mile)
	1990	2000	2001	2010, proj.				
Sudan	26,627	35,080	36,080	45,485	33	2.6	39	917,375
Suriname	395	431	434	450	169	0.4	7	62,344
Swaziland	852	1,083	1,104	1,216	155	1.2	166	6,641
Sweden	8,559	8,873	8,875	8,882	82	-	56	158,927
Switzerland	6,838	7,262	7,283	7,385	92	0.2	474	15,355
Syria	12,436	16,306	16,729	20,606	56	2.3	235	71,062
Tajikistan	5,332	6,441	6,579	8,007	96	2.2	119	55,251
Tanzania	26,224	35,306	36,232	44,957	32	2.4	106	342,100
Thailand	55,052	61,231	61,798	66,291	19	0.8	313	197,595
Togo	3,691	5,019	5,153	6,245	109	2.2	245	21,000
Tonga	92	102	104	123	194	1.8	376	277
Trinidad and Tobago	1,198	1,176	1,170	1,115	154	-0.5	590	1,981
Tunisia	8,207	9,593	9,705	10,661	81	1.1	162	59,985
Turkey	56,085	65,667	66,494	73,322	16	1.1	223	297,591
Turkmenistan	3,668	4,518	4,603	5,431	114	1.8	24	188,456
Tuvalu	9	11	11	13	224	1.5	1,095	10
Uganda	17,186	23,318	23,986	31,395	42	3.0	311	77,108
Ukraine	51,658	49,153	48,760	46,193	24	-0.6	209	233,089
United Arab Emirates	1,951	2,369	2,407	2,763	138	1.5	75	32,278
United Kingdom	57,621	59,508	59,648	60,602	20	0.2	639	93,278
United States	249,948	275,563	278,059	300,118	3	0.9	79	3,539,227
Uruguay	3,106	3,334	3,360	3,600	129	0.8	50	67,035
Uzbekistan	20,624	24,756	25,155	29,280	41	1.7	146	172,741
Vanuatu	154	190	193	221	184	1.5	34	5,699
Venezuela	19,325	23,543	23,917	27,134	43	1.4	70	340,560
Vietnam	66,338	78,774	79,939	90,192	14	1.4	636	125,622
Yemen	12,023	17,479	18,078	24,637	54	3.4	89	203,849
Zambia	7,851	9,582	9,770	11,482	80	1.8	34	285,992
Zimbabwe	10,103	11,343	11,365	11,057	66	-0.3	76	149,293
OTHER								
Montenegro	565	680	674	713	161	0.5	126	5,333
Serbia.[2]	9,201	9,982	10,003	9,954	79	-	293	34,116
Taiwan [2]	20,279	22,191	22,370	23,873	46	0.7	1,796	12,456
AREAS OF SPECIAL SOVEREIGNTY AND DEPENDENCIES								
American Samoa	47	65	67	81	205	2.1	873	77
Anguilla	8	12	12	14	222	1.8	345	35
Aruba	67	70	70	73	203	0.5	939	75
Bermuda	58	63	64	67	208	0.6	3,357	19
Cayman Islands	26	35	36	42	212	1.8	354	100
Cook Islands	18	20	21	22	218	0.9	222	93
Faroe Islands	47	45	46	48	210	0.6	84	541
French Guiana	116	173	178	214	186	2.1	5	34,421
French Polynesia	202	249	254	291	180	1.5	179	1,413
Gaza Strip [4]	643	1,132	1,178	1,651	153	3.8	8,009	147
Gibraltar	29	28	28	28	215	0.2	11,935	2
Greenland	56	56	56	56	209	-	(Z)	131,931
Guadeloupe	378	426	431	468	170	0.9	634	680
Guam	134	155	158	184	190	1.7	754	209
Guernsey	63	64	64	66	207	0.3	859	75
Hong Kong	5,688	7,116	7,211	7,981	93	1.1	18,883	382
Jersey	84	89	89	92	196	0.3	1,978	45
Macau	352	446	454	527	167	1.7	73,448	6
Man, Isle of	69	73	73	77	200	0.5	324	227
Martinique	374	415	418	448	171	0.8	1,023	409
Mayotte	90	156	163	231	188	3.9	1,125	145
Montserrat	11	6	8	10	225	4.3	196	39
Netherlands Antilles	189	210	212	228	182	0.8	572	371
New Caledonia	168	202	205	230	183	1.3	28	7,243
Northern Mariana Islands	44	72	75	99	199	3.1	405	184
Puerto Rico	3,537	3,916	3,937	4,088	120	0.4	1,138	3,459
Reunion	597	721	733	829	159	1.4	759	965
Saint Helena	7	7	7	8	226	0.6	46	158
Saint Pierre and Miquelon	6	7	7	7	227	0.2	74	93
Turks and Caicos Islands	12	18	18	24	220	3.0	109	166
Virgin Islands	104	121	122	133	192	1.0	904	135
Virgin Islands, British	16	20	21	25	217	2.0	359	58
Wallis and Futuna	14	15	15	17	221	0.9	146	106
West Bank [4]	1,255	2,020	2,091	2,765	141	3.1	960	2,178
Western Sahara	191	245	251	301	181	2.1	2	102,703

-. Represents or rounds to zero.

X. Not applicable.

Z. Less than one person per square mile.

1. Computed by the exponential method.

2. With the establishment of diplomatic relations with China on January 1, 1979, the U.S. government recognized the People's Republic of China as the sole legal government of China and acknowledged the Chinese position that there is only one China and that Taiwan is part of China.

3. "Congo" is the official short-form name for both the Republic of Congo and the Democratic Republic of the Congo. To distinguish one from the other the U.S. Dept. of State adds the capital in parentheses. This practice is unofficial and pro-visional.

4. The Gaza Strip and West Bank are Israeli occupied with interim status subject to Israeli/Palestinian negotiations. The final status is to be determined.

Source: United States Census Bureau. (2002). *Statistical Abstract of the United States 2002*. Washington, D.C.: Government Printing Office. Retrieved from http://www.census.gov/prod/2003pubs/02statab/intlstat.pdf.

Table 1.14
Age Distribution by Country: 2001 and 2010

[In percent]

Country or area	2001 Under 15 years old	2001 65 years old and over	2010, proj. Under 15 years old	2010, proj. 65 years old and over
World	29.6	7.0	30.0	8.6
Afghanistan	42.2	2.8	53.0	3.9
Albania	29.5	7.0	26.7	9.3
Algeria	34.2	4.1	33.5	5.2
American Samoa	38.4	5.0	38.1	8.5
Andorra	15.3	12.6	15.3	17.1
Angola	43.3	2.7	53.4	3.4
Argentina	26.5	10.4	27.3	12.3
Armenia	23.2	9.7	18.2	10.3
Aruba	21.3	10.2	18.6	14.6
Australia	20.6	12.5	20.4	15.2
Austria	16.6	15.4	14.8	18.1
Azerbaijan	28.9	7.1	26.0	7.3
Bahamas, The	29.4	6.1	27.0	8.7
Bahrain	29.6	3.0	29.6	4.8
Bangladesh	35.0	3.4	34.5	4.5
Barbados	21.7	8.9	19.8	9.7
Belarus	17.9	13.9	15.5	13.5
Belgium	17.5	16.9	16.1	18.1
Benin	47.3	2.3	59.4	3.1
Bermuda	19.4	11.2	18.2	14.6
Bolivia	38.5	4.5	37.4	5.7
Bosnia and Herzegovina	20.1	9.1	19.1	12.6
Brazil	28.6	5.5	26.4	7.5
Bulgaria	15.1	16.7	11.0	16.3
Burkina Faso	47.5	2.9	59.1	3.5
Burma	29.1	4.8	26.5	5.5
Burundi	46.8	2.8	56.1	3.1
Cambodia	41.3	3.5	47.3	4.5
Cameroon	42.4	3.4	49.5	4.7
Canada	18.9	12.8	18.2	15.5
Cape Verde	42.8	6.5	36.7	6.8
Central African Republic	43.2	3.8	47.8	4.7
Chad	47.7	2.8	65.0	3.7
Chile	27.3	7.4	25.1	10.2
China	25.0	7.1	22.5	8.9
Colombia	31.9	4.8	33.1	6.6
Congo (Brazzaville)	42.4	3.3	50.7	3.9
Congo (Kinshasa)	48.2	2.5	63.2	3.2
Costa Rica	31.4	5.3	30.5	7.3
Cote d'Ivoire	46.2	2.2	54.9	3.1
Croatia	18.2	15.2	19.6	16.7
Cuba	21.0	9.9	18.1	12.5
Czech Republic	16.1	13.9	13.2	15.8
Denmark	18.6	14.9	17.9	17.2
Dominican Republic	34.1	4.9	36.0	6.9
Ecuador	35.8	4.4	37.9	6.0
Egypt	34.6	3.8	34.9	5.2
El Salvador	37.7	5.1	41.7	6.4
Estonia	17.1	14.8	13.7	15.6
Ethiopia	47.2	2.8	60.3	3.6
Finland	18.0	15.0	16.3	17.3
France	18.7	16.1	18.0	17.3
French Guiana	30.5	5.5	34.4	8.9
Gabon	33.3	5.9	35.8	8.5
Gambia, The	45.2	2.7	58.1	3.8
Germany	15.6	16.6	14.3	20.1
Ghana	41.2	3.5	39.4	4.4
Greece	15.0	17.7	14.7	19.8
Greenland	26.7	5.4	22.8	7.9
Grenada	37.0	3.9	32.2	2.8
Guam	35.1	6.2	37.2	8.7
Guatemala	42.1	3.6	50.4	4.9
Guinea	43.1	2.7	50.5	3.5
Guinea-Bissau	42.1	2.9	50.8	3.9
Guyana	28.2	4.9	25.7	6.1
Haiti	40.3	4.2	41.6	5.1
Honduras	42.2	3.6	46.0	5.1
Hungary	16.6	14.7	13.9	15.6
Iceland	23.2	11.8	21.1	13.5
India	33.1	4.7	33.6	6.1
Indonesia	30.3	4.6	31.9	6.7
Iran	33.0	4.6	28.5	5.3
Iraq	41.6	3.1	50.3	3.9
Ireland	21.6	11.4	22.7	13.4
Israel	27.4	9.9	28.9	11.3
Italy	14.2	18.3	13.1	20.5
Jamaica	29.7	6.8	26.3	7.6

Country or area	2001 Under 15 years old	2001 65 years old and over	2010, proj. Under 15 years old	2010, proj. 65 years old and over
Japan	14.6	17.5	14.5	21.9
Jordan	37.2	3.3	39.6	5.6
Kazakhstan	26.7	7.2	24.9	7.8
Kenya	41.9	2.8	38.0	3.7
Korea, North	25.5	6.8	24.6	10.7
Korea, South	21.6	7.3	21.6	10.6
Kuwait	28.8	2.4	37.0	4.2
Kyrgyzstan	35.0	6.1	36.9	6.1
Laos	42.7	3.3	51.5	3.9
Latvia	16.6	15.3	12.4	16.2
Lebanon	27.6	6.7	29.0	8.1
Libya	35.4	3.9	41.5	5.5
Lithuania	18.7	13.6	15.8	14.5
Luxembourg	18.9	14.1	20.3	16.3
Macau	22.7	7.2	21.0	9.1
Madagascar	45.0	3.2	60.2	3.9
Malawi	44.4	2.8	45.0	3.4
Malaysia	34.5	4.2	37.2	6.1
Mali	47.2	3.1	62.1	3.8
Mauritania	46.1	2.3	59.9	2.9
Mexico	33.3	4.4	33.2	6.3
Monaco	15.3	22.5	15.1	24.1
Mongolia	33.0	3.9	31.9	4.8
Montenegro	21.7	12.1	21.7	13.8
Morocco	34.4	4.7	34.7	6.1
Mozambique	42.7	2.8	43.1	3.5
Nepal	40.3	3.5	46.5	4.8
Netherlands	18.4	13.7	17.6	16.0
New Zealand	22.4	11.5	22.2	13.6
Nicaragua	39.0	2.9	40.2	4.2
Niger	48.0	2.3	60.0	3.0
Nigeria	43.7	2.8	53.5	3.8
Norway	20.0	15.1	19.2	16.2
Oman	41.5	2.4	59.2	4.0
Pakistan	40.5	4.1	41.9	5.3
Panama	30.1	6.0	27.7	8.3
Paraguay	38.9	4.7	46.8	6.6
Peru	34.4	4.8	34.3	6.7
Philippines	36.9	3.7	40.1	5.2
Poland	18.4	12.4	15.7	13.1
Portugal	17.0	15.6	16.8	17.1
Romania	17.9	13.5	15.5	14.1
Russia	17.4	12.8	14.9	12.7
Rwanda	42.4	2.9	41.2	3.0
Samoa	31.9	5.7	23.2	6.9
Saudi Arabia	42.5	2.7	58.0	5.1
Senegal	44.1	3.1	53.6	4.0
Serbia	19.7	15.1	18.2	15.5
Sierra Leone	44.7	3.1	57.6	4.4
Singapore	17.9	7.0	22.1	10.5
Slovakia	18.9	11.5	15.4	12.9
Slovenia	16.1	14.3	14.1	16.0
Somalia	44.5	2.8	61.5	3.4
South Africa	32.0	4.9	26.8	5.8
Spain	14.6	17.2	13.9	18.5
Sri Lanka	26.0	6.6	24.4	8.9
Sudan	44.6	2.1	52.8	3.5
Swaziland	45.5	2.6	49.8	3.5
Sweden	18.2	17.3	14.9	19.2
Switzerland	17.0	15.3	15.0	18.2
Syria	39.9	3.2	44.8	4.3
Taiwan	21.2	8.8	21.4	11.1
Tajikistan	41.2	4.6	45.9	5.2
Tanzania	44.8	2.9	54.6	3.9
Thailand	23.4	6.6	23.7	9.2
Trinidad and Tobago	24.1	6.7	17.9	7.9
Tunisia	28.7	6.1	25.4	7.9
Turkey	28.4	6.1	26.2	8.1
Uganda	51.1	2.1	66.0	2.6
Ukraine	17.3	14.1	14.4	13.9
United Arab Emirates	28.9	2.4	28.7	6.7
United Kingdom	18.9	15.7	17.1	17.0
United States	**21.1**	**12.6**	**21.6**	**14.4**
Uruguay	24.4	13.0	25.7	14.3
Uzbekistan	36.3	4.6	37.5	5.0
Venezuela	32.1	4.7	30.7	6.6
Vietnam	32.1	5.4	30.9	6.2
Yemen	47.2	3.0	65.0	3.5
Zambia	47.4	2.5	54.2	3.0
Zimbabwe	38.7	3.6	32.6	4.4

1. With the establishment of diplomatic relations with China on January 1, 1979, the U.S. government recognized the People's Republic of China as the sole legal government of China and acknowledged the Chinese position that there is only one China and that Taiwan is part of China.

2. "Congo" is the official short-form name for both the Republic of Congo and the Democratic Republic of the Congo.

Source: United States Census Bureau. (2002). *Statistical Abstract of the United States 2002.* Washington, D.C.: Government Printing Office. Retrieved from http://www.census.gov/prod/2003pubs/02statab/intlstat.pdf.

Table 1.15
Foreign or Foreign-Born Population and Labor Force in Selected OECD Countries:
1988 and 1999

[In Australia, Canada, and the United States the data refer to people present in the country who are foreign born. In the European countries and Japan they generally refer to foreigners and represent the nationalities of residents]

Country	Foreign population [1]				Foreign labor force [2]			
	Number (1,000)		Percent of total population		Number (1,000)		Percent of total labor force	
	1988	1999	1988	1999	1988	1999	1988	1999
United States [3]	[4]19,767	28,180	7.9	10.3	[4]11,565	16,114	9.4	11.7
Australia [3]	[5]3,965	4,419	22.9	23.3	[5]2,182	2,310	25.7	(NA)
Austria	344	748	4.5	9.2	161	334	5.4	10.0
Belgium	869	897	8.8	8.8	[6]291	(NA)	7.2	(NA)
Canada [3]	[5]4,343	(NA)	16.1	(NA)	[5]2,681	(NA)	18.5	(NA)
Denmark.	142	259.4	2.8	4.9	65	(NA)	2.2	(NA)
France	[7]3,714	3,263	6.8	(NA)	1,557	1,594	6.4	5.8
Germany	4,489	7,344	7.3	8.9	1,911	3,545	7.0	8.8
Italy	645	1,252	1.1	2.2	[5]285	748	1.3	3.6
Japan	941	1,556	0.8	1.2	[8]86	126	0.1	0.2
Luxembourg	106	159.4	27.4	36.0	[9]69	146	39.9	57.3
Netherlands	624	651.5	4.2	4.1	176	(NA)	3.0	(NA)
Spain.	360	801	0.9	2.0	58	173	0.4	1.0
Sweden	421	487	5.0	5.5	220	222	4.9	5.1
Switzerland	1,007	1,369	15.2	19.2	[10]608	701	16.7	18.1
United Kingdom	1,821	2,208	3.2	3.8	871	1,005	3.4	3.7

NA. Not available.

1. Data are from population registers except for France (census), the United Kingdom (labor force survey), Japan and Switzerland (register of foreigners) and Italy, and Spain (residence permits).

2. Includes unemployed except for Italy, Luxembourg, Netherlands, and United Kingdom. Data for Austria, Germany, and Luxembourg are from social security registers, for Denmark from the register of population. Data for Italy, Spain, and Switzerland are from residence or work permits. Figures for Japan and Netherlands are estimates. Data for other countries are from labor force surveys.

3. Census data except 1999 data for the United States from Current Population Survey.

4. 1990 data.

5. 1991 data.

6. 1989 data.

7. 1982 data.

8. 1992 data.

9. Includes cross-border workers.

10. Foreigners with an annual residence permit or a settlement permit who engage in gainful activity. Seasonal and cross-border workers are excluded.

Source: United States Census Bureau. (2002). *Statistical Abstract of the United States 2002.* Washington, D.C.: Government Printing Office. Retrieved from http://www.census.gov/prod/2003pubs/02statab/intlstat.pdf.

Table 1.16
Total Population Growth Estimates and Projections in OECD Countries[1]

	1960	1970	1980	1990	2000	2010	2020	2030	2040	2050
United States	1.7	1.2	0.9	1.0	0.9	0.7	0.6	0.5	0.3	0.2
Japan	1.2	1.0	1.1	0.6	0.3	0.0	-0.3	-0.5	-0.6	-0.6
Germany	0.6	0.7	0.1	0.1	0.4	0.0	-0.1	-0.2	-0.3	-0.4
France	0.9	1.1	0.6	0.5	0.4	0.3	0.1	0.0	-0.1	-0.2
Italy	0.6	0.7	0.5	0.1	0.0	-0.3	-0.5	-0.7	-0.8	-1.0
United Kingdom	0.3	0.6	0.1	0.2	0.2	0.1	0.1	0.0	-0.2	-0.3
Canada	2.7	1.8	1.4	1.2	1.1	0.9	0.8	0.6	0.4	0.4
Australia	2.3	2.0	1.5	1.5	1.1	0.9	0.8	0.6	0.4	0.4
Austria	0.2	0.6	0.1	0.2	0.6	0.2	-0.1	-0.3	-0.5	-0.7
Belgium	0.6	0.5	0.2	0.1	0.2	0.0	-0.1	-0.2	-0.4	-0.5
Czech Republic	0.7	0.3	0.5	0.0	-0.1	-0.2	-0.3	-0.5	-0.7	-0.9
Denmark	0.7	0.7	0.4	0.0	0.3	0.1	-0.1	-0.2	-0.4	-0.4
Finland	1.0	0.4	0.4	0.4	0.4	0.1	0.1	-0.1	-0.3	-0.3
Greece	1.0	0.5	0.9	0.6	0.4	-0.1	-0.4	-0.6	-0.7	-0.8
Hungary	0.7	0.3	0.4	-0.3	-0.3	-0.4	-0.5	-0.6	-0.7	-0.7
Iceland	2.1	1.5	1.1	1.1	1.0	0.8	0.6	0.4	0.2	0.0
Ireland	-0.5	0.4	1.4	0.3	0.6	0.7	0.7	0.4	0.3	0.2
Korea	2.1	2.5	1.8	1.2	0.9	0.6	0.4	0.2	0.0	-0.3
Luxembourg	0.6	0.8	0.7	0.5	1.2	0.6	0.2	-0.1	-0.3	-0.4
Mexico	2.9	3.2	2.9	2.1	1.7	1.3	1.0	0.8	0.5	0.3
Netherlands	1.3	1.3	0.8	0.6	0.5	0.1	-0.1	-0.2	-0.4	-0.6
New Zealand	2.2	1.7	1.0	0.8	1.4	0.9	0.8	0.6	0.5	0.4
Norway	0.9	0.8	0.5	0.4	0.5	0.4	0.3	0.1	0.0	-0.1
Poland	1.8	1.0	0.9	0.7	0.2	0.1	0.0	-0.2	-0.3	-0.4
Portugal	0.5	0.2	0.8	0.1	0.0	-0.1	-0.3	-0.4	-0.5	-0.7
Spain	0.8	1.0	1.1	0.5	0.1	-0.1	-0.4	-0.5	-0.7	-0.9
Sweden	0.6	0.7	0.3	0.3	0.4	0.1	0.1	-0.1	-0.2	-0.2
Switzerland	1.3	1.4	0.2	0.8	0.8	0.3	0.0	-0.2	-0.4	-0.6
Turkey	2.8	2.5	2.3	2.4	1.7	1.3	1.0	0.8	0.6	0.4
OECD Total	1.3	1.2	1.0	0.8	0.7	0.5	0.3	0.2	0.0	-0.1
Memorandum item: Total population, in millions										
OECD Total	774.3	872.5	962.2	1043.2	1117.7	1170.1	1207.7	1228.9	1231.9	1220.9

1. Average annual percent change over ten years to date shown.

Source: Organization of Economic Co-operation and Development. (2003). *Tables and Figures on Ageing.* OECD Web site. Retrieved from http://www .oecd.org/dataoecd/27/44/2345400.pdf. OECD Copyright. Reproduced by permission of the OECD.

Table 1.17
Elderly Population Growth Estimates and Projections in OECD Countries[1]

	Population aged 65 and over									
	1960	1970	1980	1990	2000	2010	2020	2030	2040	2050
United States	2.7	1.9	2.2	2.0	1.0	1.2	3.0	2.7	0.7	0.3
Japan	2.7	3.2	3.7	3.4	3.9	2.4	1.7	-0.1	0.5	-0.1
Germany	2.3	2.4	1.4	-0.3	1.3	1.9	0.7	1.7	0.6	-0.6
France	1.1	2.1	1.4	0.5	1.7	0.7	2.1	1.4	0.8	-0.1
Italy	1.9	2.3	2.4	1.6	1.8	1.1	0.9	1.2	0.9	-0.9
United Kingdom	1.2	1.6	1.7	0.6	0.4	0.7	1.6	1.5	0.6	-0.3
Canada	2.5	2.2	3.3	3.0	2.5	2.0	3.2	2.8	0.9	0.4
Australia	2.7	1.9	2.9	3.0	1.9	1.9	3.1	2.4	1.4	0.6
Austria	1.7	2.2	1.0	-0.1	0.4	1.3	1.4	2.3	1.1	-0.3
Belgium	1.4	1.7	0.9	0.6	1.2	0.5	1.7	1.7	0.4	-0.5
Czech Republic	1.3	3.6	1.4	-0.6	0.8	1.2	2.7	0.8	0.8	0.7
Denmark	2.2	2.2	2.0	0.8	0.0	1.2	1.8	1.0	0.5	-0.8
Finland	1.8	2.8	3.1	1.5	1.4	1.4	2.9	1.2	-0.2	-0.3
Greece	2.9	3.6	2.6	1.0	3.2	1.1	0.8	0.9	1.0	0.2
Hungary	2.8	2.8	1.9	-0.4	0.6	0.4	1.5	0.1	0.8	0.8
Iceland	2.4	2.6	2.2	1.9	1.8	1.4	3.0	2.8	1.3	0.6
Ireland	0.0	0.4	1.0	0.8	0.6	1.5	2.8	2.2	1.4	1.7
Korea	3.0	2.4	3.3	4.0	3.9	3.9	3.2	4.2	2.3	0.5
Luxembourg	1.6	2.3	1.5	0.4	1.9	1.5	1.9	1.9	0.9	-0.1
Mexico	3.3	2.4	1.7	2.5	3.6	3.7	4.0	4.0	3.9	2.4
Netherlands	2.8	2.5	2.1	1.7	1.3	1.5	2.7	2.0	0.8	-0.8
New Zealand	1.8	1.6	2.6	1.9	1.9	1.7	2.9	2.6	1.3	0.6
Norway	2.3	2.3	1.9	1.4	0.0	0.8	2.4	1.6	1.0	-0.4
Poland	2.8	4.6	3.0	0.6	1.9	0.6	3.0	1.7	0.4	1.4
Portugal	1.8	1.7	2.1	2.8	1.5	0.7	1.0	1.3	1.5	0.4
Spain	2.0	2.8	2.0	3.1	2.2	0.7	1.0	1.7	1.6	0.1
Sweden	2.2	2.1	2.1	1.2	0.2	1.3	1.8	0.9	0.4	-0.4
Switzerland	1.8	2.7	2.2	1.1	1.0	1.6	2.0	2.3	0.9	-0.6
Turkey	3.6	4.8	3.1	1.4	4.9	2.6	3.5	4.0	3.4	2.6
OECD Total	2.2	2.4	2.2	1.6	1.8	1.6	2.2	2.0	1.1	0.4
Memorandum item: Total population aged 65 and over, in millions										
OECD Total	66.2	83.6	103.6	121.5	145.8	170.2	211.2	256.5	286.9	298.1

1. Average annual percent change over ten years to date shown.

Source: Organization of Economic Co-operation and Development. (2003). *Tables and Figures on Ageing.* OECD Web site. Retrieved from http://www .oecd.org/dataoecd/27/44/2345400.pdf. OECD Copyright. Reproduced by permission of the OECD.

Table 1.18
Elderly Population Estimates and Projections in OECD Countries

	Population aged 65 and over, in thousands									
	1960	1970	1980	1990	2000	2010	2020	2030	2040	2050
United States	17,101	20,667	25,793	31,478	34,834	39,321	52,705	68,673	73,692	75,899
Japan	5,397	7,371	10,560	14,809	21,614	27,389	32,491	32,239	33,809	33,323
Germany	8,370	10,641	12,213	11,872	13,444	16,247	17,468	20,721	22,027	20,794
France	5,317	6,535	7,525	7,932	9,413	10,087	12,389	14,275	15,402	15,285
Italy	4,674	5,863	7,420	8,738	10,412	11,609	12,733	14,415	15,745	14,377
United Kingdom	6,119	7,198	8,491	9,050	9,433	10,162	11,859	13,757	14,545	14,107
Canada	1,343	1,677	2,309	3,117	3,972	4,856	6,678	8,806	9,669	10,057
Australia	870	1,046	1,397	1,883	2,284	2,766	3,758	4,756	5,456	5,811
Austria	849	1,051	1,163	1,153	1,206	1,377	1,581	1,991	2,226	2,151
Belgium	1,095	1,292	1,413	1,499	1,695	1,775	2,093	2,476	2,582	2,464
Czech Republic	836	1,190	1,374	1,289	1,397	1,569	2,057	2,233	2,420	2,600
Denmark	485	605	738	802	804	908	1,083	1,198	1,260	1,157
Finland	319	422	572	667	771	888	1,176	1,319	1,289	1,253
Greece	687	980	1,267	1,399	1,908	2,124	2,299	2,504	2,765	2,820
Hungary	903	1,194	1,438	1,383	1,474	1,538	1,778	1,804	1,946	2,108
Iceland	14	18	23	27	32	37	50	66	75	79
Ireland	317	331	365	398	423	492	648	803	926	1,096
Korea	832	1,052	1,453	2,144	3,152	4,639	6,366	9,565	12,024	12,665
Luxembourg	34	43	49	51	62	72	87	105	114	114
Mexico	1,698	2,155	2,563	3,294	4,671	6,686	9,867	14,665	21,579	27,336
Netherlands	1,034	1,324	1,628	1,920	2,177	2,522	3,278	3,994	4,328	3,978
New Zealand	205	239	310	374	450	530	707	910	1,034	1,093
Norway	398	500	603	692	690	744	939	1,106	1,219	1,176
Poland	1,706	2,680	3,600	3,833	4,647	4,935	6,657	7,915	8,250	9,468
Portugal	705	832	1,021	1,343	1,553	1,670	1,853	2,100	2,430	2,536
Spain	2,499	3,305	4,010	5,430	6,745	7,210	7,945	9,414	11,029	11,154
Sweden	895	1,099	1,354	1,522	1,552	1,761	2,106	2,305	2,404	2,314
Switzerland	539	702	875	981	1,087	1,278	1,561	1,967	2,145	2,024
Turkey	972	1,550	2,099	2,403	3,876	5,000	7,021	10,386	14,494	18,825
OECD Total	66,213	83,563	103,626	121,482	145,778	170,193	211,233	256,468	286,885	298,062

Source: Organization of Economic Co-operation and Development. (2003). *Tables and Figures on Ageing.* OECD Web site. Retrieved from http://www .oecd.org/dataoecd/27/44/2345400.pdf. OECD Copyright. Reproduced by permission of the OECD.

Table 1.19
Median Age Estimates and Projections in OECD Countries

	1960	1970	1980	1990	2000	2010	2020	2030	2040	2050
United States	29.6	28.2	30.1	32.8	35.8	37.8	39.0	40.6	41.8	42.1
Japan	25.5	29.0	32.6	37.4	41.2	43.8	46.9	49.3	49.5	49.0
Germany	34.7	34.3	36.4	37.7	40.0	44.1	46.9	47.6	48.7	48.4
France	33.0	32.3	32.5	34.7	37.6	40.3	42.3	43.6	44.1	43.9
Italy	31.3	32.9	34.0	37.4	40.6	44.9	49.0	52.2	53.0	53.2
United Kingdom	35.4	33.7	34.6	36.1	38.2	41.2	42.7	43.6	44.8	44.5
Canada	26.4	26.0	29.2	32.8	36.8	40.0	41.6	42.8	43.4	42.6
Australia	29.6	27.6	29.4	32.2	35.3	38.0	39.8	41.2	42.1	42.2
Austria	35.4	33.9	34.7	35.6	37.8	41.8	45.1	47.4	49.4	50.2
Belgium	35.2	34.5	34.1	36.5	39.3	42.6	44.9	46.3	47.2	46.8
Czech Republic	32.8	33.5	33.0	35.2	37.5	40.4	44.7	49.1	51.8	53.3
Denmark	33.0	32.5	34.3	37.1	39.0	41.8	44.0	43.7	44.2	44.4
Finland	28.2	29.6	32.8	36.4	39.4	42.3	43.5	44.6	45.2	44.5
Greece	29.1	33.4	34.2	36.1	39.4	43.0	46.6	50.1	52.3	52.5
Hungary	32.1	34.1	34.4	36.4	38.1	39.8	43.3	46.3	48.2	49.2
Iceland	25.4	24.6	26.9	30.0	32.9	35.5	37.9	40.0	42.0	43.3
Ireland	29.8	27.6	26.4	29.1	32.3	34.7	38.0	40.4	40.7	41.2
Korea	19.2	19.0	21.8	26.9	31.5	36.0	39.8	42.3	43.6	44.4
Luxembourg	35.2	35.4	34.8	36.5	37.8	40.3	42.6	44.4	45.6	46.1
Mexico	17.5	16.7	17.2	19.7	23.3	27.0	30.7	34.3	37.3	39.5
Netherlands	28.8	28.6	31.3	34.5	37.8	42.1	45.7	46.7	47.6	47.8
New Zealand	27.4	25.6	28.3	31.1	34.0	36.3	37.8	39.3	40.3	40.6
Norway	34.4	33.0	33.3	35.4	37.4	40.3	42.2	42.7	43.6	43.8
Poland	26.5	28.2	29.6	32.3	35.1	37.3	40.6	44.3	46.3	46.0
Portugal	28.0	28.6	29.1	34.5	37.3	40.5	44.5	48.0	49.4	50.0
Spain	29.6	30.2	30.3	33.9	37.9	42.3	46.9	51.4	54.1	54.3
Sweden	36.2	35.4	36.3	38.3	40.0	42.7	44.9	45.3	46.8	46.3
Switzerland	32.5	32.0	34.8	36.4	38.4	42.3	45.6	47.3	48.7	49.4
Turkey	20.3	19.1	19.8	22.2	25.6	29.6	33.0	35.4	37.7	39.1
OECD average (unweighted)	29.7	29.6	30.9	33.6	36.5	39.6	42.4	44.5	45.8	46.2

Source: Organization of Economic Co-operation and Development. (2003). *Tables and Figures on Ageing.* OECD Web site. Retrieved from http://www .oecd.org/dataoecd/27/44/2345400.pdf. OECD Copyright. Reproduced by permission of the OECD.

Table 1.20
Births and Birth Rates by Race, Sex, and Age in the United States: 1980 to 2000

[**Births in thousands. (3,612 represents 3,612,000). Births by race of mother.** Excludes births to nonresidents of the United States.]

Item	1980	1985	1990	1993	1994	1995	1996	1997	1998	1999	2000
Live births [1]	**3,612**	**3,761**	**4,158**	**4,000**	**3,953**	**3,900**	**3,891**	**3,881**	**3,942**	**3,959**	**4,059**
White	2,936	3,038	3,290	3,150	3,121	3,099	3,093	3,073	3,119	3,134	3,194
Black	568	582	684	659	636	603	595	600	610	607	623
American Indian	29	34	39	39	38	37	38	39	40	41	42
Asian or Pacific Islander	74	105	142	153	158	160	166	170	173	182	201
Male	1,853	1,928	2,129	2,049	2,023	1,996	1,990	1,986	2,016	2,028	2,077
Female	1,760	1,833	2,029	1,951	1,930	1,903	1,901	1,895	1,925	1,934	1,982
Males per 100 females	105	105	105	105	105	105	105	105	105	106	105
Age of mother:											
Under 20 years old	562	478	533	514	518	512	503	493	494	485	478
20 to 24 years old	1,226	1,141	1,094	1,038	1,001	966	945	942	965	982	1,018
25 to 29 years old	1,108	1,201	1,277	1,129	1,089	1,064	1,071	1,069	1,083	1,078	1,088
30 to 34 years old	550	696	886	901	906	905	898	887	889	892	929
35 to 39 years old	141	214	318	357	372	384	400	410	425	434	452
40 to 44 years old	(NA)	(NA)	(NA)	(NA)	(NA)	(NA)	72	76	81	83	90
45 to 49 years old	(NA)	(NA)	(NA)	(NA)	(NA)	(NA)	3	3	4	4	4
Birth rate per 1,000 population	**15.9**	**15.8**	**16.7**	**15.5**	**15.2**	**14.8**	**14.7**	**14.5**	**14.6**	**14.5**	**14.7**
White	15.1	15.0	15.8	14.7	14.4	14.2	14.1	13.9	14.0	14.9	14.1
Black	21.3	20.4	22.4	20.5	19.5	18.2	17.8	17.7	17.7	18.4	17.6
American Indian	20.7	19.8	18.9	17.8	17.1	16.6	16.6	16.6	17.1	17.8	17.1
Asian or Pacific Islander	19.9	18.7	19.0	17.7	17.5	17.3	17.0	16.9	16.4	17.7	17.8
Plural birth ratio [2]	19.3	21.0	23.3	25.2	25.7	26.1	27.4	28.6	30.0	30.7	31.1
White	18.5	20.4	22.9	24.9	25.5	26.0	27.5	28.7	30.2	30.9	31.2
Black	24.1	25.3	27.0	28.7	29.4	28.8	29.8	30.9	32.0	32.9	34.0
Fertility rate per 1,000 women [3]	**68.4**	**66.2**	**70.9**	**67.6**	**66.7**	**65.6**	**65.3**	**65.0**	**65.6**	**65.9**	**67.5**
White [3]	65.6	64.1	68.3	65.4	64.9	64.4	64.3	63.9	64.6	65.1	66.5
Black [3]	84.9	78.8	86.8	80.5	76.9	72.3	70.7	70.7	71.0	70.1	71.7
American Indian [3]	82.7	78.6	76.2	73.4	70.9	69.1	68.7	69.1	70.7	70.7	71.4
Asian or Pacific Islander [3]	73.2	68.4	69.6	66.7	66.8	66.4	65.9	66.3	64.0	66.6	70.7
Age of mother:											
10 to 14 years old	1.1	1.2	1.4	1.4	1.4	1.3	1.2	1.1	1.0	1.9	0.9
15 to 19 years old	53.0	51.0	59.9	59.6	58.9	56.8	54.4	52.3	51.1	50.6	48.5
20 to 24 years old	115.1	108.3	116.5	112.6	111.1	109.8	110.4	110.4	111.2	112.0	112.3
25 to 29 years old	112.9	111.0	120.2	115.5	113.9	111.2	113.1	113.8	115.9	118.8	121.4
30 to 34 years old	61.9	69.1	80.8	80.8	81.5	82.5	83.9	85.3	87.4	90.6	94.1
35 to 39 years old	19.8	24.0	31.7	32.9	33.7	34.3	35.3	36.1	37.4	39.3	40.4
40 to 44 years old	3.9	4.0	5.5	6.1	6.4	6.6	6.8	7.1	7.3	8.4	7.9
45 to 49 years old	0.2	0.2	0.2	0.3	0.3	0.3	0.3	0.4	0.4	1.4	0.5

NA. Not available.

1. Includes other races not shown separately.

2. Number of multiple births per 1,000 live births.

3. Per 1,000 women, 15 to 44 years old in specified group. The rate for age of mother 45 to 49 years old computed by relating births to mothers 45 years old and over to women 45 to 49 years old.

Source: United States Census Bureau. (2002). *Statistical Abstract of the United States 2002.* Washington, D.C.: Government Printing Office. Retrieved from http://www.census.gov/prod/2003pubs/02statab/vitstat.pdf.

Table 1.21
Teenager Births and Birth Rates by Race, Sex, and Age in the United States: 1990 to 2000

[Birth rates per 1,000 women in specified group.]

Item	1990	1992	1993	1994	1995	1996	1997	1998	1999	2000
NUMBER OF BIRTHS										
All races, total [1] . . .	521,826	505,415	501,093	505,488	499,873	494,272	489,211	484,975	476,050	468,990
15-17 years.	183,327	187,549	190,535	195,169	192,508	186,762	183,324	173,252	163,588	157,209
18-19 years.	338,499	317,866	310,558	310,319	307,365	307,509	305,886	311,724	312,462	311,781
White.	354,482	342,739	341,817	348,081	349,635	346,509	342,029	340,894	337,888	333,013
15-17 years	114,934	118,786	121,309	126,388	127,165	124,031	121,864	116,699	111,624	106,786
18-19 years	239,548	223,953	220,508	221,693	222,470	222,477	220,164	224,195	226,264	226,227
Black.	151,613	146,800	143,153	140,968	133,694	131,059	130,401	126,865	121,166	118,954
15-17 years	62,881	63,002	63,156	62,563	59,112	56,218	54,883	50,062	45,919	44,618
18-19 years	88,732	83,798	79,997	78,405	74,582	74,841	75,518	76,803	75,247	74,336
BIRTH RATE										
All races, total [1] . . .	59.9	60.7	59.6	58.9	56.8	54.4	52.3	51.1	49.6	48.5
15-17 years.	37.5	37.8	37.8	37.6	36.0	33.8	32.1	30.4	28.7	27.4
18-19 years.	88.6	94.5	92.1	91.5	89.1	86.0	83.6	82.0	80.3	79.2
White.	50.8	51.8	51.1	51.1	50.1	48.1	46.3	45.4	44.6	43.6
15-17 years	29.5	30.1	30.3	30.7	30.0	28.4	27.1	25.9	24.8	23.6
18-19 years	78.0	83.8	82.1	82.1	81.2	78.4	75.9	74.6	73.5	72.7
Black.	112.8	112.4	108.6	104.5	96.1	91.4	88.2	85.4	81.0	79.4
15-17 years	82.3	81.3	79.8	76.3	69.7	64.7	60.8	56.8	52.0	50.4
18-19 years	152.9	157.9	151.9	148.3	137.1	132.5	130.1	126.9	122.8	121.3

1. Includes races other than White and Black.

Source: United States Census Bureau. (2002). *Statistical Abstract of the United States 2002.* Washington, D.C.: Government Printing Office. Retrieved from http://www.census.gov/prod/2003pubs/02statab/vitstat.pdf.

Table 1.22
Proportion of Young Adults Living with Their Parents

	Men		Women	
	Age category			
	25-29	30-34	25-29	30-34
Canada	25	11	13	6
Finland	0	0	4	2
Germany	33	15	13	3
Italy	76	33	50	20
Japan	59	36	48	28
Netherlands	26	5	5	1
United Kingdom	22	7	9	4
United States	19	9	12	6

Note: The coding of the relationship to household head is based on the original definition of each country. Because the numbers are obtained by income survey data, the numbers could be different from those given in national censuses.

The Swedish definition of household in the survey is based on "tax units." Therefore, the data is not shown in this chart.

Source: Casey, B. & Yamada, A. (2002). Getting older, getting poorer? A study of earnings, pensions, assets, and living arrangements of older people in nine countries. OECD's *Labour Market and Occasional Papers No. 60.* Retrieved from http://www.olis.oecd.org/OLIS/2002DOC.NSF/LINKTO/DEELSA-ELSA-WD(2002)4. OECD Copyright. Reproduced by permission of the OECD.

Table 1.23
**Money Income of Households in United States—Median Income by Race
and Hispanic Origin, in Current and Constant (2000) Dollars: 1980 to 2000**

[In dollars.]

Year	Median income in current dollars					Median income in constant (2000) dollars				
	All house-holds [1]	White	Black	Asian, Pacific Islander	His-panic [2]	All house-holds [1]	White	Black	Asian, Pacific Islander	His-panic [2]
1980	17,710	18,684	10,764	(NA)	13,651	35,238	37,176	21,418	(NA)	27,162
1985	23,618	24,908	14,819	(NA)	17,465	36,246	38,226	22,742	(NA)	26,803
1986	24,897	26,175	15,080	(NA)	18,352	37,546	39,474	22,742	(NA)	27,676
1987 [3]	26,061	27,458	15,672	32,226	19,336	38,007	40,044	22,856	46,998	28,199
1988	27,225	28,781	16,407	32,267	20,359	38,309	40,499	23,087	45,404	28,648
1989	28,906	30,406	18,083	36,102	21,921	38,979	41,002	24,385	48,683	29,560
1990	29,943	31,231	18,676	38,450	22,330	38,446	40,100	23,979	49,369	28,671
1991	30,126	31,569	18,807	36,449	22,691	37,314	39,101	23,294	45,145	28,105
1992 [4]	30,636	32,209	18,755	37,801	22,597	36,965	38,863	22,630	45,611	27,266
1993	31,241	32,960	19,533	38,347	22,886	36,746	38,768	22,975	45,105	26,919
1994	32,264	34,028	21,027	40,482	23,421	37,136	39,166	24,202	46,595	26,958
1995	34,076	35,766	22,393	40,614	22,860	38,262	40,159	25,144	45,603	25,668
1996	35,492	37,161	23,482	43,276	24,906	38,798	40,623	25,669	47,307	27,226
1997	37,005	38,972	25,050	45,249	26,628	39,594	41,699	26,803	48,415	28,491
1998	38,885	40,912	25,351	46,637	28,330	41,032	43,171	26,751	49,212	29,894
1999	40,816	42,504	27,910	51,205	30,735	42,187	43,932	28,848	52,925	31,767
2000	42,151	44,232	30,436	55,525	33,455	42,151	44,232	30,436	55,525	33,455

NA. Not available.

1. Includes other races not shown separately.

2. Persons of Hispanic origin may be of any race.

3. Beginning 1987, data based on revised processing procedures and not directly comparable with prior years.

4. Based on 1990 census population controls.

Source: United States Census Bureau. (2002). *Statistical Abstract of the United States 2002.* Washington, D.C.: Government Printing Office. Retrieved from http://www.census.gov/prod/2003pubs/02statab/income.pdf.

Table 1.24
Money Income of Families in United States—Median Income by Race and Hispanic Origin, in Current and Constant (2000) Dollars: 1980 to 2000

Year	Median income in current dollars					Median income in constant (2000) dollars				
	All families [1]	White	Black	Asian, Pacific Islander	His-panic [2]	All families [1]	White	Black	Asian, Pacific Islander	His-panic [2]
1980 [3]	21,023	21,904	12,674	(NA)	14,716	41,830	43,583	25,218	(NA)	29,281
1985 [3]	27,735	29,152	16,786	(NA)	19,027	42,564	44,739	25,761	(NA)	29,200
1986 [4]	29,458	30,809	17,604	(NA)	19,995	44,425	46,462	26,548	(NA)	30,154
1987 [4]	30,970	32,385	18,406	(NA)	20,300	45,166	47,230	26,843	(NA)	29,605
1988	32,191	33,915	19,329	36,560	21,769	45,297	47,723	27,199	51,445	30,632
1989	34,213	35,975	20,209	40,351	23,446	46,135	48,511	27,251	54,412	31,616
1990	35,353	36,915	21,423	42,246	23,431	45,392	47,398	27,506	54,243	30,085
1991	35,939	37,783	21,548	40,974	23,895	44,514	46,798	26,689	50,750	29,596
1992 [5]	36,573	38,670	21,103	42,255	23,555	44,129	46,659	25,463	50,985	28,421
1993 [6]	36,959	39,300	21,542	44,456	23,654	43,472	46,226	25,338	52,290	27,822
1994 [6]	38,782	40,884	24,698	46,122	24,318	44,638	47,058	28,427	53,087	27,990
1995 [7]	40,611	42,646	25,970	46,356	24,570	45,599	47,884	29,160	52,050	27,588
1996	42,300	44,756	26,522	49,105	26,179	46,240	48,925	28,993	53,679	28,618
1997	44,568	46,754	28,602	51,850	28,142	47,687	50,026	30,603	55,478	30,111
1998	46,737	49,023	29,404	52,826	29,608	49,317	51,729	31,027	55,742	31,243
1999	48,950	51,224	31,778	56,316	31,663	50,594	52,945	32,846	58,208	32,727
2000	50,890	53,256	34,192	61,511	35,054	50,890	53,256	34,192	61,511	35,054

NA. Not available.

1. Includes other races not shown separately.

2. Persons of Hispanic origin may be of any race.

3. Recording of amounts for earnings from longest job increased to $299,999.

4. Implementation of a new March CPS processing system.

5. Implementation of 1990 census population controls.

6. Introduction of 1990 census sample design.

7. Full implementation of the 1990 census-based sample design and metropolitan definitions, 7,000 household sample reduction, and revised race edits.

Source: United States Census Bureau. (2002). *Statistical Abstract of the United States 2002.* Washington, D.C.: Government Printing Office. Retrieved from http://www.census.gov/prod/2003pubs/02statab/income.pdf.

Table 1.25
Money Income of Families in United States—Distribution by Family Characteristics and Income Level: 2000

[(72,388 represents 72,388,000).]

Characteristic	Number of families (1,000)	Income level (1,000)							Median income (dollars)
		Under $15,000	$15,000 to $24,999	$25,000 to $34,999	$35,000 to $49,999	$50,000 to $74,999	$75,000 to $99,999	$100,000 and over	
All families	**72,388**	**6,910**	**8,308**	**8,704**	**11,521**	**15,543**	**9,118**	**12,282**	**50,890**
Age of householder:									
15 to 24 years old.	3,489	911	722	564	545	484	136	128	26,536
25 to 34 years old.	12,824	1,540	1,484	1,709	2,250	3,052	1,397	1,392	45,890
35 to 44 years old.	18,581	1,384	1,599	1,879	2,906	4,506	2,820	3,487	58,084
45 to 54 years old.	16,225	850	1,056	1,271	2,153	3,776	2,815	4,304	68,082
55 to 64 years old.	9,662	824	927	1,023	1,537	2,040	1,285	2,027	55,718
65 years old and over	11,606	1,402	2,520	2,258	2,131	1,685	666	945	32,852
White.	60,222	4,787	6,456	7,119	9,604	13,371	8,073	10,810	53,256
Black	8,814	1,757	1,478	1,247	1,482	1,474	676	700	34,192
Hispanic origin [1]	7,728	1,259	1,411	1,187	1,398	1,385	617	471	35,054
Northeast	13,422	1,212	1,247	1,492	1,967	2,907	1,847	2,748	56,128
Midwest	16,646	1,319	1,750	1,828	2,611	3,981	2,417	2,740	54,576
South	26,602	3,004	3,399	3,473	4,456	5,438	2,915	3,916	46,009
West	15,719	1,375	1,912	1,910	2,487	3,217	1,939	2,878	51,034
Type of family:									
Married-couple families	55,611	2,968	4,928	5,947	8,753	13,231	8,246	11,537	59,184
Male householder, wife absent .	4,252	595	657	679	793	847	348	331	37,529
Female householder, husband absent	12,525	3,347	2,723	2,078	1,975	1,465	524	413	25,794
Unrelated subfamilies	528	212	158	88	29	33	2	5	17,339
Education attainment of householder: [2]									
Total	**68,899**	**6,000**	**7,587**	**8,140**	**10,977**	**15,059**	**8,982**	**12,155**	**52,166**
Less than 9th grade	4,178	1,003	1,088	748	610	464	166	98	24,946
9th to 11th grade (no diploma) . . .	6,026	1,291	1,275	1,043	998	942	286	191	28,878
High school graduate (includes equivalency)	21,502	2,055	2,834	3,151	4,133	5,099	2,439	1,791	44,248
Some college, no degree.	12,593	886	1,284	1,574	2,315	3,102	1,690	1,742	51,642
Associate degree	5,869	261	497	643	1,003	1,499	1,010	955	57,814
Bachelor's degree or more.	18,732	504	609	982	1,918	3,953	3,390	7,378	84,172
Bachelor's degree.	12,016	330	446	743	1,429	2,782	2,166	4,119	77,245
Master's degree	4,518	122	109	178	360	873	894	1,983	91,126
Professional degree	1,161	27	19	43	59	129	164	720	100,000
Doctorate degree	1,036	26	34	18	69	169	166	555	100,000

1. Persons of Hispanic origin may be of any race.
2. Persons 25 years old and over.

Source: United States Census Bureau. (2002). *Statistical Abstract of the United States 2002.* Washington, D.C.: Government Printing Office. Retrieved from http://www.census.gov/prod/2003pubs/02statab/income.pdf.

Table 1.26
Share of Aggregate Income Received by Each Fifth and Top 5 Percent of Families:
United States, 1980 to 2000

[**Families as of March of the following year (60,309 represents 60,309,000).** Income in constant 2000 CPI-U-RS adjusted dollars.]

Year	Num-ber of fami-lies (1,000)	Income at selected positions (dollars)					Percent distribution of aggregate income					
		Upper limit of each fifth					Low-est 5th	Sec-ond 5th	Third 5th	Fourth 5th	Highest 5th	Top 5 percent
		Lowest	Sec-ond	Third	Fourth	Top 5 percent						
1980	60,309	20,693	34,840	49,346	69,243	109,436	5.3	11.6	17.6	24.4	41.1	14.6
1985	63,558	20,388	35,122	50,877	74,016	121,185	4.8	11.0	16.9	24.3	43.1	16.1
1986	64,491	21,113	36,344	52,963	76,263	125,773	4.7	10.9	16.9	24.1	43.4	16.5
1987 [1]	65,204	21,289	36,725	53,670	77,775	126,805	4.6	10.7	16.8	24.0	43.8	17.2
1988	65,837	21,251	36,842	54,175	78,668	129,458	4.6	10.7	16.7	24.0	44.0	17.2
1989	66,090	21,580	37,757	55,018	80,302	133,449	4.6	10.6	16.5	23.7	44.6	17.9
1990	66,322	21,630	37,292	53,978	78,951	131,425	4.6	10.8	16.6	23.8	44.3	17.4
1991	67,173	21,056	36,056	53,259	78,020	127,356	4.5	10.7	16.6	24.1	44.2	17.1
1992 [2]	68,216	20,166	35,805	53,090	77,283	127,914	4.3	10.5	16.5	24.0	44.7	17.6
1993 [3]	68,506	19,961	35,287	52,965	78,565	133,127	4.1	9.9	15.7	23.3	47.0	20.3
1994 [3]	69,313	20,649	36,026	54,097	80,568	138,170	4.2	10.0	15.7	23.3	46.9	20.1
1995 [4]	69,597	21,412	37,037	55,002	81,136	138,845	4.4	10.1	15.8	23.2	46.5	20.0
1996	70,241	21,513	37,512	55,845	82,332	139,924	4.2	10.0	15.8	23.1	46.8	20.3
1997	70,884	22,026	38,519	57,368	85,598	146,672	4.2	9.9	15.7	23.0	47.2	20.7
1998	71,551	22,792	39,773	59,113	88,313	153,215	4.2	9.9	15.7	23.0	47.3	20.7
1999	72,031	23,593	40,930	61,395	91,041	160,248	4.3	9.9	15.6	23.0	47.2	20.3
2000	72,388	24,000	41,000	61,378	91,700	160,250	4.3	9.8	15.5	22.8	47.4	20.8

1. Implementation of a new March CPS processing system.
2. Based on 1990 census population controls.
3. Introduction of new 1990 census sample design.
4. Full implementation of the 1990 census based sample design and metropolitan definitions. 7,000 household sample reduction and revised race edits.

Source: United States Census Bureau. (2002). *Statistical Abstract of the United States 2002.* Washington, D.C.: Government Printing Office. Retrieved from http://www.census.gov/prod/2003pubs/02statab/income.pdf.

Table 1.27
Global Conditions Affecting Growth in Developing Countries and World GDP Growth

(percentage change from previous years, except interest rates and oil price)

	Current estimate		Current forecasts			Global Development Finance 2002 forecasts	
	2000	2001	2002	2003	2004	2002	2003
Global conditions							
World trade (volume)	13.1	0.5	2.9	7.0	8.0	1.8	8.3
Inflation (consumer prices)							
G-7 OECD countries[a,b]	1.9	1.7	0.9	1.2	1.5	0.9	1.6
United States	3.4	2.8	1.5	2.1	2.3	1.5	2.4
Commodity prices (nominal $)							
Commodity prices, except oil ($)	1.3	9.1	5.0	5.8	4.4	1.3	7.3
Oil price ($, weighted average), $/bbl	28.2	24.4	25.0	23.0	20.0	20.0	21.0
Oil price (% change)	56.2	13.7	2.7	8.0	13.0	17.9	5.0
Manufactures export unit value ($)[c]	2.1	1.4	0.5	3.0	2.2	0.5	3.6
Interest rates							
LIBOR, 6 months (US$, percent)	6.6	3.6	1.8	1.5	3.1	2.3	4.0
EURIBOR, 6 months (euro, percent)	4.5	4.2	3.4	3.2	3.8	3.0	4.0
GDP (growth)[d]							
World	3.8	1.1	1.7	2.5	3.1	1.3	3.6
Memo item: World GDP (ppp)[e]	4.5	2.1	2.8	3.4	4.0	2.4	4.3
High-income countries	3.5	0.7	1.5	2.1	2.7	0.9	3.3
OECD countries[f]	3.4	0.8	1.4	2.1	2.6	0.8	3.1
United States	3.8	0.3	2.3	2.6	3.1	1.3	3.7
Japan	2.1	0.3	0.0	0.8	1.3	1.5	1.7
Euro Area	3.7	1.5	0.8	1.8	2.6	1.2	3.3
Non-OECD countries	6.8	0.7	2.3	3.7	5.3	2.7	5.3
Developing countries	5.2	2.9	2.8	3.9	4.7	3.1	4.9
East Asia and Pacific[f]	7.0	5.5	6.3	6.1	6.4	5.6	7.1
Europe and Central Asia	6.6	2.3	3.6	3.4	3.6	3.2	4.3
Transition countries	6.4	4.6	3.5	3.3	3.5	3.4	4.0
Latin America and the Caribbean	3.7	0.4	1.1	1.8	3.7	0.5	3.8
Excluding Argentina	4.5	1.2	0.7	1.9	3.6	2.1	4.3
Middle East and North Africa	4.2	3.2	2.5	3.5	3.7	2.7	3.3
Oil exporters	3.6	2.4	2.4	3.7	3.6	2.2	2.8
Diversified economies	3.7	4.3	2.2	2.7	3.6	3.1	4.4
South Asia	4.8	4.4	4.6	5.4	5.8	4.9	5.3
Sub-Saharan Africa	3.2	2.9	2.5	3.2	3.8	2.6	3.6
Memorandum items							
Developing countries							
Excluding the transition countries	5.0	2.6	2.7	4.0	4.9	3.1	5.1
Excluding China and India	4.6	1.7	1.5	2.8	3.8	2.0	4.1

Note: OECD = Organization for Economic Co-operation and Development, bbl = barrel, EURIBOR = European interbank offered rate, LIBOR = London interbank offered rate, ppp = purchasing power parity.

a. Canada, France, Germany, Italy, Japan, the United Kingdom, and the United States.
b. In local currency, aggregated using 1995 GDP weights.
c. Unit value index of manufactures exports from the G-5 countries to developing countries, expressed in U.S. dollars.
d. GDP in 1995 constant dollars: 1995 prices and market exchange rates.
e. GDP measured at 1995 purchasing power parity (international dollar) weights.
f. Republic of Korea income classification changed from middle to high income (July 2002). Both forecasts were adjusted for this revision.

Source: World Bank. (2003). The international economy and prospects for developing countries. *Global Economic Prospects and the Developing Countries 2003*, pp. 1–43. Retrieved from http://www.worldbank.org/prospects/gep2003/chap1.pdf.

Figure 1.1
Growth of Working-Age Population Decelerates

(annual growth of population for ages 15 to 65)

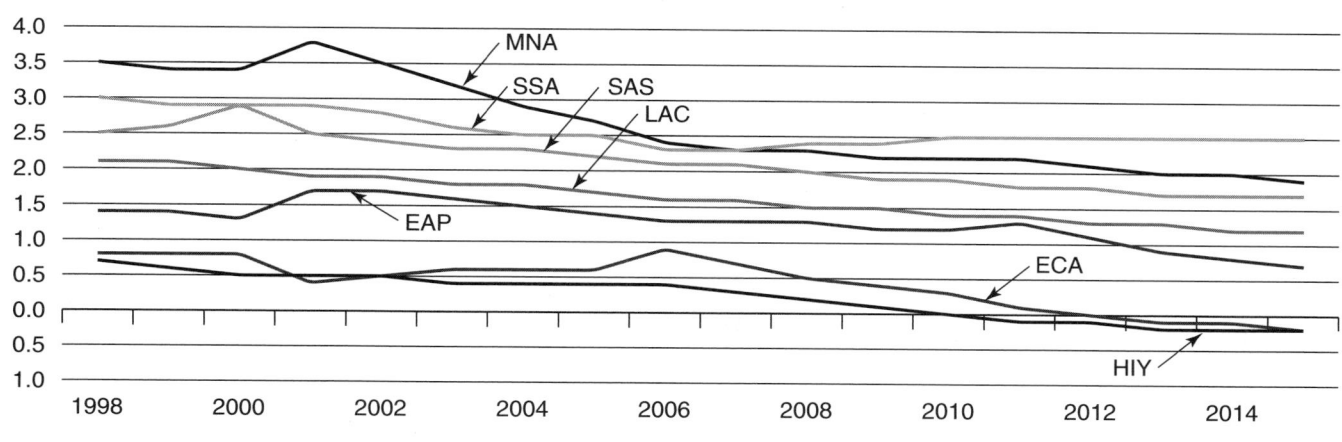

Note: HIY refers to high-income countries; SSA refers to Sub-Saharan Africa; EAP refers to East Asia and Pacific; SAS refers to South Asia; ECA refers to Eastern Europe and Central Asia; MNA refers to Middle East and North Africa; LAC refers to Latin America and the Caribbean.

Source: World Bank. (2003). The international economy and prospects for developing countries. *Global Economic Prospects and the Developing Countries 2003*, pp. 1–43. Retrieved from http://www.worldbank.org/prospects/gep2003/chap1.pdf.

Table 1.28
Savings as Percent of GDP in Various Regions of the World

	1997–2001			2015		
	Savings (S)	Investment (I)	Capital inflows (KA)	Savings (S)	Investment (I)	Capital inflows (KA)
Total	22.4	22.5	0.1	20.5	20.5	0.0
High income	22.0	21.9	0.1	18.6	19.0	0.4
Low and middle income	24.2	24.7	0.5	26.0	24.9	1.1
European Union	20.8	20.4	0.4	17.5	17.4	0.1
Japan	29.8	27.5	2.2	26.0	25.4	0.6
United States	17.5	19.5	2.0	14.5	16.3	1.9
Rest of high income	30.8	26.1	4.7	24.9	23.2	1.7
East Asia and Pacific	36.9	33.9	3.0	35.0	29.3	5.8
South Asia	21.3	22.2	0.9	23.7	23.5	0.2
Middle East and North Africa	26.2	21.4	4.8	23.1	22.2	0.9
Sub-Saharan Africa	13.9	17.6	3.7	19.0	20.1	1.1
Europe and Central Asia	21.9	22.6	0.7	22.0	27.1	5.1
Latin America and the Caribbean	17.9	21.7	3.7	20.5	20.6	0.0

Note: The columns (S), (I), and (KA) represent, respectively, the national saving rate, the national investment rate, and the capital account, all as a share of GDP. The values for 2015 are simulated values from the global general equilibrium model (maintained by the Development Economics Prospects Group). The values for the 1997–2001 period represent the average observed values from the World Bank's statistical databases. For the high-income countries, these values are the 1997–1999 or 1997–2000 averages, depending on data availability. For the totals, the averages cover only the years 1997–1999.

Source: World Bank. (2003). The international economy and prospects for developing countries. *Global Economic Prospects and the Developing Countries 2003*, pp. 1–43. Retrieved from http://www.worldbank.org/prospects/gep2003/chap1.pdf.

Table 1.29
Social Expenditures as a Percentage of GDP in OECD Countries

	1980	1981	1982	1983	1984	1985	1986	1987	1988	1989	1990	1991	1992	1993	1994	1995	1996	1997
United States	12.8	12.9	13.4	13.6	12.6	12.5	12.7	12.6	12.5	12.6	13.0	14.1	14.7	14.9	14.9	15.0	14.9	14.5
Japan	10.6	11.0	11.4	11.7	11.5	11.5	11.9	12.1	11.8	11.7	11.5	11.5	12.0	12.6	13.2	14.1	14.1	14.3
Germany	22.7	23.5	23.7	23.2	22.9	23.6	23.5	23.8	23.8	22.9	22.2	24.3	25.8	26.3	26.2	26.6	26.7	26.2
France	22.9	24.6	25.5	26.0	26.3	26.6	26.4	26.2	26.0	25.2	26.5	27.0	27.8	29.2	29.2	29.3	29.3	29.4
Italy	18.3	19.8	20.3	21.4	20.9	21.3	21.3	21.5	21.6	21.8	23.8	25.7	26.8	27.1	26.8	25.8	26.0	26.4
United Kingdom	19.0	20.5	20.9	21.5	21.8	21.7	22.0	21.3	19.9	19.3	19.6	21.1	23.3	24.0	23.3	23.0	22.6	21.4
Canada	13.6	13.9	16.4	16.6	16.3	16.6	16.7	16.5	16.2	16.4	17.6	19.5	20.2	20.2	19.1	18.1	17.3	16.6
Australia[1]	12.0	12.1	12.7	13.9	13.9	14.0	14.1	14.0	13.2	13.3	14.5	15.7	16.8	16.9	16.6	18.3	18.3	17.9
Austria	22.2	..	..	..	..	23.8	..	..	..	..	23.6	23.8	24.4	25.9	26.5	26.3	26.2	25.3
Belgium	24.3	25.9	26.6	26.9	26.2	27.1	26.9	26.6	26.2	25.2	25.5	26.3	26.3	27.5	26.9	27.0	27.5	23.5
Czech Republic	..	..	..	..	..	..	..	..	..	..	..	16.8	17.3	18.7	19.0	18.6	18.5	19.4
Denmark	29.4	29.8	30.0	30.4	28.9	28.1	27.2	27.9	29.1	29.4	28.5	29.5	30.0	31.6	32.4	31.8	31.7	30.8
Finland	18.5	19.0	20.3	20.9	21.8	22.8	23.4	23.8	23.3	23.1	24.8	29.9	33.9	34.0	33.1	31.2	31.0	28.7
Greece	11.4	13.3	15.6	16.2	16.7	17.5	17.3	17.6	17.3	18.1	21.7	21.0	20.7	21.1	21.1	21.3	21.9	22.0
Iceland	..	..	..	..	..	..	..	..	..	..	..	..	..	..	18.2	18.6	18.2	17.8
Ireland	17.0	17.1	17.8	17.9	17.3	22.1	22.3	21.5	20.1	18.4	18.7	19.5	19.9	19.9	20.0	19.3	18.5	17.6
Korea	..	..	..	..	..	..	..	..	..	..	3.6	3.5	3.7	3.8	3.8	4.0	4.3	4.8
Luxembourg	23.3	25.0	24.2	24.4	23.0	22.8	22.3	23.1	22.2	21.5	21.7	22.3	22.6	23.2	22.6	23.4	23.6	22.4
Mexico[2]	..	..	..	..	..	1.8	1.8	2.0	2.2	2.8	3.3	3.7	4.0	4.2	4.7	7.3	7.4	7.9
Netherlands	27.4	28.4	30.0	30.2	29.0	27.5	27.2	27.3	26.9	26.5	28.0	28.1	28.6	28.8	26.9	26.0	25.3	24.2
New Zealand	20.0	18.8	19.4	19.7	18.6	19.5	20.4	20.6	21.1	22.2	22.4	22.7	22.7	21.5	20.2	19.5	19.7	20.9
Norway	18.5	..	..	..	..	19.7	..	..	24.9	25.9	26.0	27.2	28.4	28.1	28.0	27.6	26.2	25.1
Poland	..	..	..	..	..	..	..	..	..	..	..	16.2	23.1	27.4	26.7	25.6	25.1	25.2	24.5
Portugal	11.1	12.0	11.2	11.3	11.2	11.4	12.2	12.5	12.9	12.4	14.1	15.1	15.8	17.3	17.3	17.8	18.3	18.7
Spain	15.7	16.9	16.8	17.5	17.2	18.0	17.8	17.6	18.2	18.4	19.1	19.9	20.7	21.7	21.3	20.6	20.6	19.9
Sweden	28.8	29.7	29.9	30.2	29.0	30.0	30.1	30.3	30.9	30.3	31.1	33.1	36.2	36.7	35.3	33.0	32.5	31.9
Switzerland	14.8	14.5	15.5	15.9	16.1	15.9	16.1	16.3	16.4	16.1	16.3	17.4	18.9	20.4	20.6	20.9	21.7	22.4
Turkey	5.3	4.7	4.8	5.1	4.7	4.4	4.6	4.9	5.4	6.4	7.6	8.1	8.6	8.6	8.0	7.7	6.7	6.5

1. Prior to 1995, data on "superannuation pensions" and "superannuation lump sum" is not available.
2. Prior to 1995, social expenditure were underestimated, particularly with regard to old age cash benefits.

Source: Organization of Economic Co-operation and Development. (2003). *Tables and Figures on Ageing.* OECD Web site. Retrieved from http://www .oecd.org/dataoecd/27/44/2345400.pdf. OECD Copyright. Reproduced by permission of the OECD.

2. The Budgetary and Economic Contexts of Social Safety Nets

The previous chapter makes the point that all analyses of social safety nets combine law, policy, and economic considerations and data. A person interested in finding out about and generating an analysis on social safety nets cannot simply look at data focusing on programs, benefits given and received, demographics, and immediate consequences to eligible and noneligible individuals. The researcher needs to consider economic indicators to flesh out demographic concerns; policy in the form of laws, regulations, reports, government and nongovernment reports, political argumentation, and third-party commentaries; and, also, how policy considerations are tied together through the **budget** and the budgetary process that sets out to define revenue sources and identify what will be funded and what will not, by how much or how little (e.g., through an unfunded legislative mandate).

The purpose of this chapter and the next is to provide an introduction and some insights to the budgetary and economic aspects of the social safety net. This chapter describes the budgetary process and its implications to the social safety net. It then proceeds to discuss economic indicators as a means of helping the reader establish a basis for analyzing social safety nets. These indicators are normally referred to as **macroeconomic** indicators because these data provide a reference point to determine the national wherewithal to provide services and the nation's ability to allocate funds to budgeted programs that represent national interest and political/social philosophy. The next chapter deals with the specific merger between economic and policy underpinnings in determining what, in most instances, is the key to access benefits in the public welfare component of the social safety net: the definition of poverty.

BUDGETS AND THE SAFETY NET

The complexity of the budgetary process—the large numbers of wide-ranging yet uncertain consequences—reveals that the purposes of budgets are as varied as the purposes of the people who make them. (Wildavsky, 1992, 7)

A student of social programs needs to look at and understand what a budget indicates and the story it does not tell. The importance of the budget rests in the relationship it demonstrates between government interests, policies, and the actual expenditures met. "Budgeting is translating financial resources into human purposes" (Wildavsky, 2001, 179). Laws create and direct. Regulations provide guidelines for the systematic administration of what the law says must be. Budgets, as statements of planned revenues and spending for a given year, therefore, are the end-product of the legislative process, because they identify which programs are funded (and at times, which are not), the amount of resources available to that program for administration (it may all be in money, but it translates into personnel, equipment, and support structures), funds to be provided to eligible beneficiaries, and (at times) length of program and benefit offerings (again, by limiting the existence of a program by only providing for funds or continuation of funding to a specified limit). Requests for proposals (RFPs) leading to grant funding are an excellent example of this last point.

Because budgeting translates ideas into actions, budgeting, as Lowi and Ginsberg (1990) write, is "the quintessential constituent policy" (646). There is an inherent conflict of interest resulting from different interested parties (from within and outside the programs, direct or indirect bystanders) demanding **allocations**, particularly when there is a shrinking resource base due to economic downturns and/or increased pressure to reduce taxes. Therefore, it is a stakeholder driven process which many would see either as a bottoms-up process because of its decentralized nature, or a **special interest**–access process resulting from the perception that lobbying groups and campaign contribution practices limit the voices to those who "feed the trough." The budgetary process is also a status seeking game. As Peter Drucker (1974) wrote a while back, "it is the budget, after all, that measures performance and importance" (p. 143).

Government budgets in the area of social safety net programs do not include private activity on the part of nongovernment organizations (NGOs) or philanthropic organizations, many who provide significant funds and services to assist people in need. These are completely separate entities. NGOs may come together in the form of service providers who receive funds from the government as a result of a grant award; otherwise, the source of funding, policies, and approaches to services remains independent. The discussion in this section only represents government-based budgeting activity.

In the best of times, establishing a budget may take between twelve to fifteen months from about summer of the previous year.[1] But as has happened in the United States for some time, it may take longer as a result of the political tensions between parties, especially when the executive branch is of one party while the legislative branch is either split between the two main political parties or outright controlled by the opposing party. Add to this that the federal budget is not a cash management account but "a summary of what policymakers want the financial flows to be during any given time period" (United States House of Representatives, Committee on Ways and Means, 2000, 7), and what one gets is a determination—or at least an impression—of who controls the provisions and bases of allocations as well as the systems of services delivery (Gilbert, Specht, and Terrell, 1993).

In the United States, as with many other countries, the term *budget* as we have referred to it so far is misleading because so many programs have been taken out of the annualized budgetary process and, in this regard, put "off-budget."[2] At present, the two principal entities that are kept off the budget are social security (and its Trust Fund Administration program) and the Postal Service.

To some, this may diminish the importance of the budgetary process because key programs representing significant **outlays** (funds disbursed or the net between refunds and reimbursements) and expenditures are no longer part of the equation (Lowi and Ginsberg, 1990). Aaron Wildavsky (2001) goes so far as to flatly state that the government budget is no longer the yardstick to use as the monetary measure of the public use of public financial resources, because the budget no longer is sufficiently comprehensive. Other critics take on the opinion that the practice of placing programs off-budget violates the spirit of the Balanced Budget Act of 1997 (see Utt, 1998). An even more extreme position is that the practice of having off-budget programs allows decreased public accountability and scrutiny because the decisions are not part of the day-to-day framework.[3] At present, approximately two-thirds of all federal spending avoids the traditional appropriations process (Heniff, 2001).

However, the purpose of analyzing government programs within the social safety net is to be able to identify the key programs and levels of funding. The difficulty arises when only looking at the budget and not tying it to the political activity shaping policy. For that, it is imperative to determine what is off-budget as well as on-budget and try to figure out why.

The rationale behind putting programs off-budget is so that the outlays are (1) not counted against that year's total allocation either as a surplus or deficit, (2) not restricted to the political and financial vicissitudes based on year-to-year accounting and financing, (3) maintain the integrity between the purpose of the program to its intended beneficiaries, and (4) like with social security, hope to maintain and extend program solvency. To illustrate this point,

> Legislation enacted in 1980 (the Budget Enforcement Act, included in Public Law 101-508) removed Social Security taxes and benefits from calculations to the budget. In large part, this was done to prevent Social Security from masking the size of Federal budget deficits and to protect it from benefit cuts motivated by budgetary concerns. (United States House of Representatives Committee on Ways and Means, 2000, section 1, p. 7/75)

By definition, off-budget programs are not counted against annual budgets and their imposed limitations due to provisions in current laws. The built-in irony is that the impetus is not to establish a "shell game;" instead the idea is to provide for continuity and stability, the two perceptions implicit in having an annual cycle in the budget (Wildavsky, 2001).

At the national level, the United States outlays for budgeted items either from appropriation acts (permitting funding for agencies and their activities), **entitlements** (such as social security or unemployment insurance), or **appropriated entitlements** (where Congress must still make a grant through an appropriation bill; see Wildavsky, 1992; Heniff, 1999). Appropriation acts are the traditional method of generating outlays. Also known as discretionary spending, the annual appropriation process follows a two-step process: (1) the **authorization** measure that creates or allows the continuation of an agency or program, as well as authorize the subsequent enactment of appropriations; and (2) the enactment of appropriations to provide funds for the authorized agency or program (Heniff, 2001).[4] This process results in allowing agencies and programs to incur obligations and generate payments from the U.S. Treasury.

Entitlements are guaranteed benefits for those who qualify and are eligible to receive the benefits until predefined limits are met. These obligations are open-ended, meaning recipients are able to get benefits regardless of the budgeted total. Amounts and limits are adjusted through indexing, the most common reference being the **consumer price index (CPI)**. More important is that the decision-making process to providing authorization and allocations takes different routes than those that are part of the appropriations process. Because of the amounts involved, this has the effect, in Wildavsky's (1992) opinion, of putting the budget on "automatic pilot" because the increased amount of obligations is based on prior authorizations rather than on current obligations set forth in the typical appropriations process.

Generally, benefits are distributed directly by the federal government to the beneficiaries in the form of cash or **in-kind** payments, or disbursed through grants to state and local authorities; however, payments to states often do not include the costs of program administration. **Entitlement programs** differ from other forms of commitments in the budgetary process in four ways:

1. Entitlements do no specify spending totals; compensation is based on the sum legislatively mandated to beneficiaries.

2. Totals are "guesstimates" that are based on the number of qualified beneficiaries and the amounts to which they are entitled.

3. The authority to spend these funds does not have a time limit but continues as long as the program exists.

4. Unlike other programs, these do not involve the House and Senate Appropriation Committees in any meaningful way. (United States House of Representatives Committee on Ways and Means, 2000)

Appropriated entitlements are obligations that combine elements of the appropriations process and entitlement outlays. Medicaid and parts of the veterans programs are example of programs funded in this manner. The way this budgeting approach works is that the authorizing statute provides the authority to spend, but Congress must pass an annual grant of funds in order to pay the obligations (see Wildavsky, 1992).

The process so far discussed is what occurs at the federal level. What often happens in the United States, as somewhat identified above, is that many aspects of the social safety net are funded by the federal government giving states the funds to run these programs. States administer these programs in accordance to federal guidelines set forth in the authorizing legislation and other regulatory compliance mechanisms to ensure that states administer these programs in a consistent manner.

Once the budget is set, there are various ways in which to distribute the funds to those programs that create a partnership between federal, state, and local government agencies. Originally developed under the Johnson and Nixon administrations, the most popular of these in the social safety net arena is the grant-in-aid. There are three categories of grants-in-aid: categorical grants, block grants, and general revenue sharing. Gilbert, Specht, and Terrell (1993) identify four types of conditions that states have to follow in order to receive federal funds based on the stipulations set forth in the authorizing legislation, supporting appropriation acts, and regulations set forth in other regulatory compliance mechanisms.

1. program conditions—these identify the purpose of the grant;

2. financial conditions—these governing the arrangement for matching funds;

3. beneficiary conditions—these establish eligibility requirements; and

4. procedural conditions—these specifying planning, administrative, and reporting procedures.

The federal government (more typically when under Democratic control) was partial to categorical grants because these imposed all of the aforementioned conditions on the states on how to use the programs. Block grants (preferred by a majority of Republican officials) differed in that they gave state and local governments much greater freedom of action

in how to use these funds. The states were free to use the funds as they deemed appropriate within mandated federal limits and regulations. Revenue-sharing was an attempt to give the states even more control of funds, with the federal government allowing states unrestricted use of these funds and local governments limited discretion on which programs to use the funds. Revenue-sharing was—and is—the least-favored of grant-in-aid revenues because Congress loathes giving up some of the control over policy and resource allocation to support its policy interests.

ECONOMIC INDICATORS AND THEIR USE IN THE ANALYSIS OF SOCIAL SAFETY NETS

It is the first task of modern political economy to *describe*, to *analyze*, to *explain*, and to *correlate* the behavior of production, unemployment, prices, and similar phenomena. To be significant, descriptions must be more than a series of disconnected narratives. They must be fitted into a systematic pattern—i.e., constitute true analysis. (Samuelson, 1976, 7)

[The] specification for data needs for economic policy must originate from economic and social research agendas, because research provides the information that is ultimately decisive for policy making. . . . Thus, perceiving, developing and unmet need for economic data requires knowledge of economic research and policy analyses, and the ability to communicate with analytic users of data. (Triplett, 1991, 158, italics in original)

The setting of the budget requires forecasting on the part of the executive and legislative branches in order to determine resource, availability of resources, and the ability to distribute these resources in order to meet the nation's policy interests. There is a need to look forward, and economic data help planners and policymakers forecast (Mark, 1998). Forecasting relies on the use of economic data in order to find out a pattern between the health of the economy based on its ability to generate resources (goods, services, and money) and the costs to maintain the ability to consume the resources. Economic statistics, in effect, provide information to interested individuals and are used by the policymakers as a means of understanding the economy and prospective issues (Triplett, 1991).

Economics involves the production, distribution, and consumption of goods and services mainly through institutions that "affect how people earn their living and fulfill their needs" (Gilbert, Specht, and Terrell, 1993, 5). One thing that is needed, among other items, that can be a limiting factor when looking merely at economic data is a better understanding of the behavior of individuals (Griliches, 1985). Therefore, economic data has to be placed within the context of social and political policy analysis in order to make the linkage with individual behavior as it relates to choices and quality of life. For the sake of simplicity—hopefully not to the point of reductionistic fallacy—income drives consumer spending, although other factors play a role: changes in employment, wealth, prices, and interest rates (Mark, 1998).

Nobel Prize winner Herbert Simon's (1974) theory of "bounded rationality" postulates that reality imposes limits on what many would hope to be rationally derived. In other words, decisions are arrived at as a result of looking at properly defined and collected information about the appropriateness of goals and the success in meeting these goals. He identifies three limitations with which decisionmakers must deal: (1) psychological limitations, (2) limitations of "values and those conceptions of purpose" which influence decisions (40), and (3) limitations imposed by the extent of knowledge attained about relevant things regarding the work to be done. These are what the budgeting process represents. It is the economic data that influences the decision-making machinae of what becomes funded and what does not by governments and by organizations, businesses, and industries; these change the views on the strengths and weaknesses of the economy and impact the forecasts that are the basis of program development or maintenance, expenditures, and investments (see Mark, 1998).

Economic analysis, at least as suggested here, gravitates around data integration, using Triplett's (1991) definition: "any activity that compares, combines, or unites data from different surveys or sources according to a conceptual, organizing framework" (169). A point that always arises is one of accuracy. For example, another Nobel Prize winner, Theodore Schultz states that "economists find it difficult to comprehend the preferences and scarcity constraints that determine the choices poor people make" (1981, 3). There is a gap between data and its utilization that can lead to inadequate or outright bad policy decisions (see Richman and Labate, 1993; Triplett, 1991). One reason for the collection of data and its dissemination is to reduce uncertainty about what is happening and what is needed. Lacking credible information can easily translate to "poorer growth prospects as well as the prospects of more pronounced cyclical behavior" (Ehrlich, 1997, 14). A criticism that can be made—which Oskar Morgenstern made as far back as 1950—is whether economic data was accurate enough for what it were being used for. Griliches (1985) says there are at least three interrelated and overlapping causes for the difficulties in comprehending individual behavior: (1) the model used to look at the data is incomplete or incorrect; (2) the units measured are wrong, not allowing for heterogeneity (individuality) of responses; or (3) data inaccuracy relative to what it purports to measure. As he sees it, "At the macro level . . . it is common to assume away the underlying heterogeneity of the individual actors and analyze the data within the framework of the 'representative' firm or 'average' individual, ignoring the aggregation difficulties associated with such concepts" (198).

Furthermore, there is a need to understand that data gathering is typically done by government agencies and the information is used by others who, for the most part, are outside the system. With this being the case, what Tripplet (1991) has to say is worth noting: "Agency staffs do not understand analysis or communicate well with analytical users; whatever their potential for understanding . . . they do not in fact talk with analytical users very frequently because of lack of understanding or organizational lines of communications between statistic users and statistics producers" (160).

Data is what the analysts make of them, how they use them, and the interpretation made from the data. The casual reader cannot assume that the information is infallible, while the avid researcher cannot fully rely on economic indicators without the use of supporting information. In the United States, the reporting system of economic indicators is in place for the purpose of detecting cyclical swings and analyzing the impact that the cycles have on the nation, its business interests, and its citizens. However, the changing type and rate of activities challenges the ability to keep accurate and up-to-date data. Changes brought forth through participation in the global economy have required a reassessment of information needed; what was once a minor concern is now critical. Globalization is a "major transformation in the territorial organization of economic activity and of political-economic power" (Sassen, 1999, 17). So, as changes in the economy and social life of the nation increases, there is pressure on the reporting systems to keep up and, particularly when the rate of change is very fast, there is a lag between the data and the use of the data in analysis (and why the need to use lagging economic indicators). One of the complaints—the warning as it were that also applies to the reading of this text—is that the information used by casual readers and experts is already outdated and may not meet immediate exigencies. Also, there is always the concern and fear of politicizing data, to make it look and say what a government agency or program wants to reflect. The manipulation may not be overt or purposeful on the part of who presents the data, but a subtle influence may be present because of a preference for a particular attitude or approach, or because of aspects of the *REALPOLITIK* that ensures that agency's or program's survival or, more to the point, that of the individuals employed therein.

Social safety nets address humanitarian concerns and temper the immediate political costs to governments implementing reforms (World Bank, 1995). Most economic and political discussions on the social safety net are ultimately about the quality of life measured as the ability to be able to enjoy life and generate a personal sense of well-being and satisfaction. There are issues that generate a perception of satisfaction, of avoiding deprivation, and/or having good or improved health. But as Nussbaum and Sen (1993) point out, economic measures such as the **gross national product (GNP)** are insufficient to measure quality of life. They advance the suggestion that there is a need to ask about how the redistribution of resources impacts individual lives. Another way of saying what Nussbaum and Sen are suggesting: social safety nets have the capability to strengthen **human capital** development in most nations over the long term, particularly among the most deprived parts of society (World Bank, 1995)—assuming there is the social and political will to do so, along with the economic resources to allow for human capital development.

This is where the policy considerations enter the analysis picture. Traditional leading economic indicators such as employment, income distribution, housing measures, health indicators, and educational attainment need to be tied to the social norms of expectations vis-à-vis rights (who is entitled to what), obligations (actual commitments), and merit (who is deserving). Of particular interest when looking at the social safety net is how social rights, obligations, and merit stack up when compared to other forms of expectations such as national defense, environmental concerns, access, and ability to consume goods.[5]

One of the most heated discussions in the politics of nearly all nations is about who is poor and who is not. Almost as heated is the follow-up discussion as to what type of help the poor need, how much of it, and for how long. The controversy at both levels of the argument rests in what government officials, other interested observers, and those needing the assistance use to define **poverty** and the nation's resources. Further complicating everything are the divergent moral and political views and expectations atempting to influence domestic and foreign policies. Because of the moral and political views, one of the considerations becomes who are the "deserving" poor and who are the "undeserving" poor.

The United States generates two official definitions of poverty, one for statistical purposes and the other to establish eligibility criteria. There are slight variations between the two, but for the most part, the formulae used to determine them are based on looking at pretax earnings and comparing these earnings against the cost of living. The accuracy of the formulae is a subject of controversy, with attempts underway to find a better formula to determine who is poor and who deserves to receive assistance. How controversial the definition is can be seen in the poll undertaken by the Kaiser Foundation and Harvard University's Kennedy School of Government in 2001 that points out that there is a significant perceptual difference between the U.S. government's official poverty line and that understood by individuals (National Public Radio, 2001). Another example is the study by Haveman and Wolf (2001) suggesting that in spite of significant asset development by many families, the decade of the '90s "brought an unexpected increase in asset poverty for groups that are generally viewed as particularly not vulnerable (such as whites and college-educated families), and a sizeable reduction in asset for vulnerable population groups such as racial minorities and single-parent families" (Abstract). The subject of the definition of poverty is one that is discussed in greater detail in chapter 3.

"To concern ourselves with the welfare state is to concern ourselves with entitlements" (Garnham, 1999, 113). The social safety net is a discussion of government responses to the traditional inequities that exist in a society as a means of ensuring the well-being or welfare of its members. Even in agricultural societies that are typically considered less complex, most of the people are born poor (Schultz, 1981). The ever-present pressure is on making the correct decisions between available resources and providing the greatest good resulting from the allocation and use of these resources.

One of the major segments of the social safety net is what many consider the traditional system of welfare. Goodin,

Headey, Muffels, and Dirven (1999) are of the opinion that the traditional notions of welfare have to have six moral values to help individuals and through which they should be evaluated:

promoting economic efficiency;

reducing poverty;

promoting social equality;

promoting social integration and avoiding social exclusion;

promoting social stability; and

promoting autonomy. (22)

These moral points make sense if Rawls' (1971) opinion that most individuals are rational and are willing to make decisions on a collective best interest is applicable most of the time. James Wilson (1993) has a different point of view: that there is a degree of fairness in the unequal distribution of wealth based on risk-taking, vis-à-vis effort and skill). More bluntly, as Frank Oppenheim (1977) observes, "those who enjoy political, social and especially economic advantages are seldom benevolent to such a degree as to make it rational for them willingly to forgo these benefits for the sake of bringing the underprivileged up to an equal common level" (284).

The gathering of economic data is a decentralized process within the U.S. Federal government. The system has been around since the 1940s

collecting various quantity and price series on a continuous basis, with the primary purpose of producing aggregate level indicators such as price indexes and national income account series, supplemented by periodic surveys of population numbers and production and expenditure patterns to be used primarily in updating the various aggregate series. (Griliches, 1985, 196)

The decentralization makes collection and access more difficult. The agencies are not directly linked to coordinate their activities (see Triplett, 1991). Thus, to a person just beginning to look at finding information about the safety net or for non-economists looking for economic and demographic data for research and/or funding purposes, the important question becomes: What key demographic and economic indicators should be considered? Chart 2.1 provides some generic areas to consider, along with specific available demographic and economic indicators or survey or study results, and the source on the Internet where the information can be accessed. The list of indicators and sources is not all-inclusive, but it does provide a significant amount of information that can serve as means of initiating research on the subject. Some of the information will repeat source material in other chapters while the remainder come from different sources; remember, this list is to assist in looking at the major socioeconomic framework while the information from other chapters is geared specifically to those topics and often includes information not found on the Internet. Yet, for those looking for sources, the list of Web sites provided in the introduction and here provide the best starting points. In keeping with the tenor of the other parts of this book, the focus is on

Chart 2.1
Economic Indicators by Research Purpose and Internet Sources Where Indicators May Be Found

Purpose	Economic indicator	Source
Demographics	• 2000 census • United States foreign-born population • Population (national, regional, state, metro and non-metro portions)	• U.S. Census Bureau (http:// www .census.gov/main/www/cen2000.html) • U.S. Census Bureau (http://www .census.gov/population/www/ socdemo/foreign.html) • U.S. Department of Commerce Bureau of Economic Analysis (http:// www.bea.doc.gov/bea/ regional/reis/)
Employment	• Labor force statistics • National employment, hours, and earnings • State and area employment, hours, and earnings • Covered employment and wages • Local area unemployment statistics • Geographic profile • Mass layoff statistics • National longitudinal surveys	• U.S. Bureau of Labor Statistics (http://data.bls.gov/cgi-bin/ surveymost?gp)
Occupation	• Job openings and labor turnover survey • Occupational employment statistics • Occupational employment and wages • Industry-specific occupational employment and wage estimates • Job patterns for minorities and women in private industry	• U.S. Bureau of Labor Statistics (http://data.bls.gov/cgi-bin/ surveymost?gp) • U.S. Bureau of Labor Statistics (http://www.bls.gov/oes/home.htm) • U.S. Equal Employment Opportunity Commission (http://www.eeoc.gov/ stats/jobpat.html)
Income, compensation and working conditions	• National income and product accounts (NIPA) tables • State and local personal income • Wage and salary summary estimates • Work stoppage data • Employee benefit survey • Employer cost index • Employer cost for employee compensation • Safety and health statistics (OSH) • Total wages, covered employee • Taxable wages • Ratio of taxable to total wages • Current population survey • Statistics on income	• U.S. Department of Commerce Bureau of Economic Analysis (http://www.bea.doc.gov/) • U.S. Bureau of Labor Statistics (http://data.bls.gov/cgi-bin/ surveymost?gp) • U.S. Department of Labor, Workforce Development Center (http:// workforcesecurity.doleta.gov/ unemploy/ finance.asp) • U.S. Census Bureau (http://www .census.gov/hhes/www/income.html) • Internal Revenue Service (IRS) (http://www.irs.ustreas.gov/taxstats/ index.html)

(continued)

Chart 2.1 (*continued*)

Purpose	Economic indicator	Source
Productivity and technology/output and trade	• Major sector productivity and cost index • Major sector multifactor productivity index • Foreign labor statistics	• U.S. Bureau of Labor Statistics (http://data.bls.gov/cgi-bin/ surveymost?gp)
	• Statistics of U.S. businesses • U.S. trade balance	• U.S. Census Bureau (http://www .census.gov/csd/susb/susb.htm) • U.S. Census Bureau (http://www .census.gov/foreign-trade/ balance/ index.html)
	• Food consumption data • Agricultural indicators	• U.S. Department of Agriculture, Economic Research Service (ERS) (http://www.ers.usda.gov/Data/)
Prices	• Consumer price index (CPI)—its different versions [with preferred being CPI-U] • Producer price index (PPI)—industry and commodity data • Import/export price indexes	• U.S. Bureau of Labor Statistics (http://data.bls.gov/cgi-bin/ surveymost?gp)
Economic activity/assets	• Gross domestic product (GDP) • Gross state product (GSP) • GDP by Industry • "Economic Census" reports	• U.S. Department of Commerce Bureau of Economic Analysis (http:// www.bea.doc.gov/) • U.S. Census Bureau (http://www .census.gov/epcd/www/econ97.html)
	• Gross national product (GNP)	• Central Intelligence Agency (http:// www.cia.gov/cia/publications/ factbook/geos/gm.html.
	• FDIC statistics on banking	• Federal Deposit Insurance Corporation (FDIC) (http://www.fdic.gov/ bank/index.html)
Quality of life/health	• Poverty tables • Dynamics of economic well-being: Poverty • Birth rates • Death rates • Mortality rates • Marriages and divorces • Fetal death data • National survey of family growth • National death index	• U.S. Census Bureau (http://www .census.gov/hhes/www/poverty.html) • Central Intelligence Agency (http:// www.cia.gov/cia/publications/ factbook/geos/gm.html. • U.S. Department of Health and Human Services, Center for Disease Control, National Center for Health Statistics (for each state) (http://www .cdc.gov/nchs/fastats/default.htm) • U.S. Department of Health and Human Services, Center for Disease Control, National Center for Health Statistics (http://www.cdc.gov/nchs/)
	• American community survey	• U.S. Census Bureau (http://www .census.gov/acs/www/)

Chart 2.1 (*continued*)

Purpose	Economic indicator	Source
	• Bankruptcy filings	• American Bankruptcy Institute (ABI) World (http://www.abiworld.org/stats/newstatsfront.html)
	• State income inequality	• Economic Policy Institute/Center on Budget and Policy Priorities (http://www.cbpp.org/1-18-00sfp.htm)
	• Food and nutrition data	• U.S. Department of Agriculture (http://www.fns.usda.gov/fns/research/research.htm)
	• Consumer expenditure survey (CEX)	• U.S. Bureau of Labor Statistics (http://www.bls.gov/cex/home.htm)
	• Educational attainment	• U.S. Census Bureau (http://www.census.gov/population/www/socdemo/educ-attn.html)
	• Elementary and secondary school data (CCD) • Postsecondary education data (PEDS) • American housing survey	• U.S. Department of Education, National Center for Educational Statistics (http://nces.gov/) • U.S. Census Bureau (http://www.census.gov/hhes/www/housing/ahs/nationaldata.html)
	• HUD data sets	• U.S. Department of Housing and Urban Development (http://www.huduser.org/datasets/pdrdatas.html)
	• Childstats.gov: International comparisons	• http://www.childstats.gov/intnlindex.asp (ties into U.S. Census Bureau data)
Transfer payments	• Federal expenditures by state • Federal aid to states	• U.S. Census Bureau (http://www.census.gov/prod/www/abs/fed-exp.html) • U.S. Census Bureau (http://www.census.gov/prod/www/abs/fas.htm)

using U.S.-based materials rather than an international comparative approach as a launching pad for research activities.

To begin to get an idea of the "big picture," the GNP and the **gross domestic product (GDP)** provide in overall dollar amounts and percent changes a quick view of the total output of the economy at the national level.[6] Overall, these two indicators give the impression of the potential for the nation's income, setting the table for the analysis of the resources a nation has available to it when meeting social needs. The **gross state product (GSP)** provides a similar overview for each state in the United States.

GNP and GDP should not be used to determine specific definitions of policy items such as the definition of poverty because they become more tenuous as the information is less reliable. This is more evident when the data is broken down to a **per capita** basis. The World Bank, in recognition of this

flaw, has made technical changes in the measurement of the GNP and now use a method referred to as the **gross national income (GNI)**. Nevertheless, these indicators are only as valid and reliable as the data that provides the information. The real caveat is still in the nature of trying to read policy into what is, in effect, only a first step in determining national income and what it breaks down to in terms of the counted members of the population base.

For those interested in comparative analysis between different types of social welfare systems and their overarching social safety net structure, or simply engaged in doing a country-to-country comparison, the GDP and the GDP per capita are two of the better starting points because they show how national wealth translates to individual participation in that wealth. For example, in the United States, the 2001 per capita GDP is estimated at $36,300, making it the world's strongest economy. This contrasts, for example, with Japan's per capita GDP of about $27,200; Germany's amount of $26,200; France's capacity of $25,400; Sweden's and Singapore's estimated figure of $24,700; Australia's $24,000; the United Kingdom's $21,100; South Korea's $18,000; the Czech Republic's $14,400; South Africa's $9,400; Poland's $8,800; Russia's $8,300; India's $2,500; and Nigeria's $840 (Central Intelligence Agency, 2002).

Another reason why the GDP is a good baseline indicator is that many of the risks that affect families and individuals are essentially those of consumption (Bourguignon, 2002). Consumption needs may exceed current market income, as Bourguignon points out. The GDP provides those measures of production that allow consumption (spending) to occur. Three items become apparent under this analysis that are highly related to each other: (1) the amount of disposable income a family or individual can accumulate, (2) savings rate, and (3) debt load. When consumption needs exceed income capacity, then saving becomes a moot point because of the need to expend money in order to meet one's consumption needs.

Along with getting and keeping assets, one of the first places one looks when thinking of a social safety net is in the area of hourly wages or salary. The reason for this is a simple one: salary and wage levels are a basic indicator and indirect predictor of poverty. The **inflation** rate and the CPI indicate the costs associated with living in a community. The definition of poverty is in part based on how much it costs to live. Income rates, earned and unearned, and the unemployment rate provide a description of how much money a person makes for the purpose of having a meaningful life. How much money one is able to garner also equates with a quality of life—in other words whether or not a person or a family are living at a subsistence level or if they have discretionary income to pursue interests and goods or services to meet their wants, not just their needs. The social safety net structure is designed to actually meet the gap between what an individual or family makes and the amount it takes to meet the obligations incurred from securing housing, food, transportation, and other incidental costs that make up the day-to-day lives of people. For example, one component of the social safety net, the federal **minimum wage**, is currently at $5.15 per hour. This translates into full-time annual earnings of $10,300. A proposal under consideration in 2001 called for an immediate increase of $.60 per hour, followed by increases of $.50 on January 1, 2002, and $.40 on January 1, 2003, which would have increased the minimum wage to $6.65 per hour, increases that did not occur due to the economic slowdown discernible as of the fall of 2001, especially after the September 11 attack. Some states have minimum wage laws (often referred to as living wage laws) that mandate a higher minimum than the level set under federal law. For a current guide to state laws, go to the U.S. Department of Labor's web site at http://www.dolgov/esa/minwage/america.htm.

Indicators like the GDP and some of its specific subcomponents also demonstrate the impact the role that the global economy is having on nations, their citizens—in particular their poor—and the safety net structure that is present to assist the poor. Opening markets throughout the world and the ensuing flow of products, technologies, jobs, and other forms of intellectual capital seems to be bringing greater volatility in domestic financial systems, especially in countries where financial systems were weak in the first place. The reduction in capital and a lessened demand for unskilled labor lead to lower wages, at least in the short-term and these translate into higher poverty rates (Agénor, 2002). Higher poverty rates in systems where the resources are weak, or where the infrastructure is not fully developed or comprehensive, signifies a heightened interest in the negotiation and communication processes as an avenue to meet the demand in fighting poverty. Importation of goods and services as a percent of the GDP is one form of assessing how globalization affects employment and the creation of wealth (see Henten, 1999).

When there is a desire or need for international data for comparative purposes or specific analysis based on a conceptual framework, the Internet sources listed in the introduction also provide a good launching point. However, as indicated in the introduction, there are other Internet and non-Internet sources available that are very useful (and are often available to download for a reasonable price). The United Nations' *Human Development Reports* and the *United Nations Programme Reports*; the Organization for Economic Co-operation and Development (OECD) reports and economic and social safety net indicators for member nations; the World Bank, and the International Monetary Fund (IMF) reports and statistical compilations are excellent sources the reader should explore. Many nations have their own sources of information, quite a bit of it through the Internet. Australia and South Korea are examples. Japan also has plenty of information available through the Internet, but it is easier to access this information through indirect sources (in other words, from other countries or international agencies).

For those utilizing international data and analyses, it is critical to remember what has been said in various ways up to this point in this chapter, the previous chapter, and even the introduction: How any society determines its view of social justice and individual rights (in terms of being able to make a claim to the government and not just as a form of freedom to act) colors how statistical data must be treated. A nation that is committed to wealth redistribution through individual entitlement may be ranked proportionately higher when compared to nations whose outlook of social justice is based on fairness of opportunity and not redistribution of wealth from one element of society to another. The data may be identical; however, the same data may reflect a different purpose and mission as defined by formal and informal policy norms. Not taking such differences into account means that the reader, when using this data in a report, could find himself or herself creating a skewed or misleading argument because of technical inconsistencies in data definition and measurement. As the cliché goes, make sure to "compare apples with apples and oranges with oranges."

The information in the following tables are representative of some of the macroeconomic indicators alluded to in this chapter. The sources of these tables may be different, the reason for this being that the attempt is to present longitudinal information whenever possible. These are, in effect snapshots of what has transpired and what data is available at the time of writing this chapter. For all intensive purposes, the data presented here is already historical and not immediate. Some will remain current because more current versions of the data are not yet available. The real purpose of these data is to provide the reader with useful information for research or grant-writing purposes, but rather than serve as a final reference these tables (and this book as a whole) should be considered as a compass for where to go, for more detailed and elaborate research and analysis.

NOTES

1. In general, the budgeting calendar and overall process works like this:

January–March: The president and the Office of Management and Budget (OMB) consider revenue and expenditure forecasts and set general guidelines for federal agencies. Agencies then set their budget requests.

April–July: Agencies prepare and submit requests to the OMB.

August–October: OMB reviews requests from agencies, holding hearings with senior agency officials.

November–December: OMB sends the revised budget to the president (pending final appeals to the president, Congressional message is prepared).

January: President presents next year's budget to Congress.

February–May: Standing committees review proposal as does the Congressional Budget Office (CBO).

May–June: House and Senate budget committees present first concurrent resolution, setting major outlay totals in major categories.

July–September: House and Senate appropriation committees and subcommittees prepare detailed appropriation bills. Reconciliation of differences worked out between subcommittees and committees. House and Senate vote on second concurrent resolution.

September–October: House and Senate pass the different appropriation bills by major functional category. President signs, or presidential veto may be overridden by two-thirds vote in House and Senate.

October 1: Beginning of new federal fiscal year.

2. List of functional and subfunctional categories in the U.S. federal budget (Heniff, 2001a). Usually, the first seventeen functional items are for policy areas and the last three for nonprogrammatic concerns. *Note*: Functions in bold denote author's identification of programs involved within the safety net structure.

Functional categories

National defense (050)
International affairs (150)
General science, space, and technology (250)
Energy (270)
Natural resources and environment (300)
Agriculture (350)
Commerce and **housing credit** (370)
Transportation (400)

Community and regional development (450)
Education, training, employment, and social services (500)
Health (550)
Medicare (570)
Income security (600)
Social security (650)
Veterans benefits and services (700)
Administration of justice (750)
General government (800)
Net interest (900)
Allowances (920)
Undistributed offsetting receipts (950)

Subfunctional categories

Department of Defense—Military (051); atomic energy defense activities (053); defense-related activities (054)

International development and humanitarian assistance (151); international security assistance (152); conduct of foreign affairs (153); foreign information and exchange activities (154); international financial programs (155)

General science and basic research (251); space flight, research, and supporting activities (252)

Energy supply (271); energy conservation (272); emergency energy preparedness (274); energy information policy, information, and regulation (276)

Water resources (301); conservation and land management (302); recreational resources (303); pollution control and abatement (304); other natural resources (306)

Farm income stabilization (351); agricultural research and services (352)

Mortgage credit (371); postal Service (372); **deposit insurance** (373); other advancement of commerce (376)

Ground transportation (401); air transportation (402); water transportation (403); other transportation (407)

Community development (451); area and regional development (452); disaster relief and insurance (453)

Elementary, secondary, and vocational education (501); higher education (502); research and **general education aids (503); training and employment (504); other labor services (505); social services (506)**

Healthcare services (551); health research and training (552); consumer and occupational health and safety (554)

Medicare (571)

General retirement and disability insurance (excluding social security) (601); federal employment retirement and disability (602); unemployment compensation (603); housing assistance (604); food and nutrition assistance (605); other income security (609)

Social security (651)

Income security for veterans (701); veterans education, training, and rehabilitation (702); hospital and medical care for veterans (703); veterans housing (704); other veterans benefits and services (705)

Federal law enforcement activities (751); federal litigative and judicial activities (752); federal correctional activities (753); criminal justice assistance (754)

Legislative functions (801); executive direction and management (802); central fiscal operations (803); general property and records management (804); central personnel management (805); general purpose fiscal assistance (806); other general government (808); deductions for offsetting receipts (809)

Interest on the public debt (901); **interest received by on-budget trust funds (902); interests received by off-budget trust funds (903)**; other interests (908)

Varies by year

Employer share, employee retirement (on-budget) (951); employer share, employee retirement (off-budget) (952); rents and royalties on the Outer Continental Shelf (953); sale of major assets (954); other undistributed offsetting receipts (959)

3. At the state and local level (as well as the federal), there is a concern because of the rise of off-budget enterprises (also known as OBEs, shadow governments, or special districts) that operate through the use of public funds to further their interests, some having the ability to generate tax-exempt revenue bonds to finance ventures (see Morgan and England, 1999).

4. Also referred to as the authorization-appropriation process.

5. An aspect of the traditional definition of quality of life is the access that individuals have to leisure and recreational activities. The thought here is that quality of life equates with the potential for spending time away from work as a means of improving psychological well-being through the enjoyment of what they are able to choose, in terms of avocational activities or the consumption of goods. The European Union believes that the quality of life is determined by long-term availability in sufficient quantity and of adequate quality of resources such as water, air, land, space, and raw materials (European Union, 2003).

6. The GDP, however, is the primary indicator used by economists and policy makers. There are two basic approaches used by the United Nations to measuring the GDP: (1) the expenditure approach and (2) the income approach.

(1) Adding up expenditures on all final goods and services produced

$$GDP = Consumption + Investment + Government\ spending + Net\ exports$$

$$Net\ exports = exports - imports$$

(2) Adding all expenditures on all income earned by the suppliers of resources used to produce the total output during the year

$$GDP = Aggregate\ income = Wages + Rent + Interest + Profit$$

To illustrate the type of information that goes into making the GDP, in the United States, sources of information that enter into the GDP formula include the following (see Mark, 1998)

- Personal consumption expenditures
- Retail sales
- Unit auto and truck sales
- Value of new total private construction
- Exports/imports of machinery
- Residential investment
- Housing starts
- Change in business inventories
- Manufacturing and trade inventories
- Net exports of goods and services
- Merchandise exports and imports
- Government consumption expenditures and gross investment
- Federal outlays
- CPI
- PPI
- Non-petroleum merchandise export and import price indexes
- Values and quantities of petroleum imports

PRINCIPAL SOURCES FOR ILLUSTRATIONS

Columbia University. (2003). *Social protection expenditures in europe as a percent of the GDP and per capita (in euros) 1991–2000*. The International Clearinghouse on International Developments in Child, Youth and Family Policies Web site. Retrieved from: http://www.childpolicyintl.org/contexttablessocexp/table243.pdf.

Columbia University. (2003). *Taxation scheme in OECD countries 1999*. The International Clearinghouse on International Developments in Child, Youth and Family Policies Web site. Retrieved from: http://www.childpolicyintl.org/contexttablespublicsector/table 222.pdf.

Moody, J.S. (April 2003). America celebrates Tax Freedom Day. *Special Report*, vol. 122. Washington, D.C.: Tax Foundation. Retrieved from: http://www.taxfoundation.org/SR122.pdf.

Organization of Economic Co-operation and Development. (1998). News release on *Revenue statistics of OECD countries 1965–1997*. Retrieved from: http://www1.oecd.org/media/publish/PB98-33A.pdf.

Organization of Economic Co-operation and Development. (2003). OECD Statistics at OECD Web site. Retrieved from: http://www.oecdwash.org/DATA/STATS/incometaxrates.pdf.

Social Security Administration. (2001). *Annual statistical supplement, 2001 to the Social Security Bulletin*. Baltimore: Social Security Administration, Office of Policy. Retrieved from: http://www.ssa.gov/statistics/Supplement/2001/supp01.pdf.

United Nations Development Programme. (2003). *Human Development Report 2003*. New York: Oxford University Press. Retrieved from: http://www.undp.org/hdr2003/pdf/hdr03_complete.pdf.

United States Census Bureau. (2002). *Statistical abstract of the United States 2002*. Washington, D.C.: Government Printing Office. Retrieved from: http://www .census.gov/statab/www/.

United States Department of Labor. (2001). *Report on the American workforce*. Washington, D.C.: Government Printing Office. Retrieved from: http://www.bls.gov/opub/rtaw/rtawhome.htm.

United States Department of Labor (2003). *Characteristics of minimum wage workers: 2002*. Washington, D.C.: Bureau of Labor Statistics. Retrieved from: http://www.bls.gov/cps/minwage2002pdf.pdf.

BIBLIOGRAPHY

Agénor, P.R. (2002). *Does globalization hurt the poor?* Draft version of September 9, 2002. Washington, D.C.: World Bank. Retrieved from: http://econ.worldbank.org/files/20957_wps2922.pdf.

Bourguignon, F. (2002). *Social protection in industrial countries: which lessons for LAC countries?* World Bank. Retrieved from: http://lnweb18.worldbank.org/External/lac/lac.nsf/92fc607f00e4de4a852568cf00633afd/9491670c24b2801185256aaa00453118/$FILE/lacjune.pdf.

Bureau of Economic Analysis. (2002). *Regional accounts data*. Retrieved from: http://www.bea.gov/bea/regional/data.htm.

Central Intelligence Agency. (2002). *The world fact book 2002*. Retrieved from: http://www.cia.gov/cia/publications/factbook/geos/gm.html.

Chatterjee, P. (1999). *Repackaging the welfare state*. Washington, D.C.: National Association of Social Workers.

Deardorff, A.V. (2001). *Deardorff's glossary of international economics*. Retrieved from: http://www-personal.umich.edu/~alandear/glossary/.

DiNitto, D.M., and Dye, T.R. (1987). *Social welfare: Politics and public policy*. 2nd ed. Englewood Cliffs, NJ: Prentice Hall.

Dobelstein, A.W. (1996). *Social welfare: Policy and analysis*. 2nd ed. Chicago: Nelson-Hall Publishers.

Drucker, P. (1974). *Management: Tasks, responsibilities, practices*. New York: Harper and Row.

Dworkin, R. (1986). *Law's empire*. Cambridge, MA: Belknap Press.

Ehrlich, E. (March/April 1997). The downside of bad data. *Challenge*, vol. 40 (2), pp. 13–37.

European Union. (2003). *The Eurostat concepts and definion database*. Retrieved from: http://forum.europa.eu.int/irc/dsis/coded/info/data/coded/en/all.htm.

Garnham, N. (1999). Amartya Sen's "Capabilities" approach to the evaluation of welfare: Its applications to communications. In Calabrese, A., and Burgelman, J.C., eds. *Communication, citizenship, and social policy: Rethinking the limits of the welfare state*. Lanham, MD: Rowman and Littlefield Publishers, pp. 113–124.

Gilbert, N., Specht, H., and Terrell, P. (1993). *Dimensions of social welfare policy*. 3rd ed. Englewood Cliffs, NJ: Prentice Hall.

Goodin, R.E., Headey, B., Muffels, R., and Dirven, H.J. (1999). *The real worlds of welfare capitalism*. Cambridge: Cambridge University Press.

Griliches, Z. (May 1985). The use and abuse of econometrics: Data and econometricians—the uneasy alliance. *American Economics Review*, vol. 75 (2), pp. 196–200.

Haveman, R., and Wolff, E.N. (2001). *Who are the poor?: Levels, trends, and composition, 1983–1998*. Madison, WI: Institute for Research on Poverty, Discussion Paper no. 1227-01. Retrieved from: http://www.ssc.wisc.edu/irp/pubs/dp122701.pdf.

Hazlitt, H. (1972). *The foundations of morality*. 2nd ed. Los Angeles: Nash Publishing.

Heniff, B, Jr. (1999). Entitlements and appropriated entitlements in the federal budget process. Senate Budget Committee Democratic Caucus Budget Background, *Fact sheet on the Senate budget process, RS20129*. Retrieved from: http://budget.senate.gov/democratic/crsbackground/entitlements.html.

Heniff, B., Jr. (March 5, 2001). Overview of the authorization-appropriation process. *CRS Reporting for Congress*. Washington, DC: CRS Web. Retrieved from: http://www.senate.gov/reference/resources/pdf/RS20371.pdf.

Heniff, B., Jr. (March 5, 2001a). Functional categories of the federal budget. *CRS Reporting for Congress*. Washington, DC: CRS Web. Retrieved from: http://www.house.gov/rules/98-280.pdf.

Henten, A. (1999). Will information societies be welfare societies? In Calabrese, A., and Burgelman, J.C., eds. *Communication, citizenship, and social policy: Rethinking the limits of the welfare state*. Lanham, MD: Rowman and Littlefield Publishers, pp. 77–90.

Homans, G.C. (1950). *The human group*. New York: Harcourt, Brace and Company.

Jansson, B.B. (1994). *Social policy: From theory to policy practice*. 2nd ed. Pacific Grove, CA: Brooks/Cole Publishing Company.

Lowi, T.J., and Ginsberg, B. (1990). *American government: Freedom and power*. New York: W.W. Norton and Company.

Mark, R.R. (1998). A primer on short-term linkages between key economic data series. *Economic Bank Review* (Federal Reserve Bank of Atlanta), vol. 83 (2), pp. 50–54.

Morgan, D.R., and England, R.E. (1999). *Managing urban America*. 5th ed. New York: Chatham House Publishers.

Morgenstern, O. (1950). *On the accuracy of economic observations*. Princeton, NJ: Princeton University Press.

National Public Radio. (2001). *NPR/Kaiser/Kennedy School Poll on Poverty in America*. Menlo Park, CA: Henry J. Kaiser Foundation. Retrieved from: http://www.kff.org/content/2001/3118/Summary.pdf.

Nussbaum, M., and Sen, A. (1993). Introduction. In Nussbaum, M., and Sen, A., eds. *The Quality of Life*. Oxford: Claredon Press.

Oppenheim, F.B. (1977). Rationality and egalitarianism. In Pennock, J.R., and Chapman, J.W., eds. *Human nature in politics*. New York: New York University Press, pp. 280–285.

Rawls, J. (1971). *A theory of justice*. Cambridge, MA: Harvard University Press.

Richman, L.S., and Labate, J. (March 8, 1993). Why the economic data mislead us. *Fortune*, vol. 125 (5), pp. 108–112.

Samuelson, P.A. (1976). *Economics*. 10th ed. New York: McGraw-Hill Book Company.

Sassen, S. (1999). The state and the new geography of power. In Calabrese, A., and Burgelman, J.C., eds. *Communication, citizenship, and social policy: Rethinking the limits of the welfare state*. Lanham, MD: Rowman and Littlefield Publishers, pp. 17–31.

Schultz, T.W. (1981). *Investing in people: The economics of population quality*. Berkeley, CA: University of California Press.

Simon, H.A. (1974). *Administrative behavior: A study in decision-making processes in administrative organizations*. New York: Free Press.

Triplett, J.E. (1991). The federal statistical system's response to emerging data needs. *Journal of Economic and Social Measurement*, vol. 17, pp. 155–177.

United States House of Representatives, Committee on Ways and Means. (2000). *The 2000 Green book: Background Material and Data on Languages within the Jurisdiction of the Committee on Ways and Means*. Retrieved from: http://aspe.hhs.gov.

Utt, R.D. (March 31, 1998). *Why moving transportation trust funds "off budget" threatens taxpayers*. Washington, DC: Heritage Foundation (Executive memorandum no. 519). Retrieved from: http://www.heritage.org/Research/Budget/em519.cfm.

Wildavsky, A. (1992). *The new politics of the budgetary process*. 2nd ed. New York: HarperCollins.

Wildavsky, A. (2001). *Budgeting and governing*. New Brunswick, NJ: Transaction Publishers.

Wilson, J.Q. (1993). *The moral sense*. New York: Free Press.

World Bank. (1995). *Structural adjustment and the poor*. Precis NUMBER: 96. Retrieved from: http://wbln0018.worldbank.org/oed/oeddoclib.nsf/992b8c4bfe826f7185256885007c60b5/94fcbe62f3a22b39852567f5005d89f0?OpenDocument.

Table 2.1
Gross Domestic Product (GDP) in Current and Real (1996) Dollars

[In billions of dollars (527.4 represents $527,400,000,000).]

Item	1960	1970	1980	1985	1988	1989	1990	1991	1992	1993	1994	1995	1996	1997	1998	1999	2000	2001
CURRENT DOLLARS																		
Gross domestic product	527.4	1,039.7	2,795.6	4,213.0	5,108.3	5,489.1	5,803.2	5,986.2	6,318.9	6,642.3	7,054.3	7,400.5	7,813.2	8,318.4	8,781.5	9,268.6	9,872.9	10,208.1
Personal consumption expenditures	332.3	648.9	1,762.9	2,712.6	3,356.6	3,596.7	3,831.5	3,971.2	4,209.7	4,454.7	4,716.4	4,969.0	5,237.5	5,529.3	5,856.0	6,250.2	6,728.4	7,064.5
Durable goods	43.3	85.0	214.2	363.3	450.2	467.8	467.6	443.0	470.8	513.4	560.8	589.7	616.5	642.5	693.2	760.9	819.6	858.3
Nondurable goods	152.9	272.0	696.1	928.8	1,082.9	1,165.4	1,246.1	1,278.8	1,322.9	1,375.2	1,438.0	1,497.3	1,574.1	1,641.6	1,708.5	1,831.3	1,989.6	2,055.1
Services	136.1	292.0	852.7	1,420.6	1,823.5	1,963.5	2,117.8	2,249.4	2,415.9	2,566.1	2,717.6	2,882.0	3,047.0	3,245.2	3,454.3	3,658.0	3,919.2	4,151.1
Gross private domestic investment	78.9	152.4	477.9	736.3	821.1	872.9	861.7	800.2	866.6	955.1	1,097.1	1,143.8	1,242.7	1,390.5	1,538.7	1,636.7	1,767.5	1,633.9
Fixed investment	75.7	150.4	484.2	714.5	802.7	845.2	847.2	800.4	851.6	934.0	1,034.6	1,110.7	1,212.7	1,327.7	1,465.6	1,578.2	1,718.1	1,692.4
Change in business inventories	3.2	2.0	-6.3	21.8	18.5	27.7	14.5	-0.2	15.0	21.1	62.6	33.0	30.0	62.9	73.1	58.6	49.4	-58.4
Net exports of goods and services	2.4	1.2	-14.9	-114.2	-106.3	-80.7	-71.4	-20.7	-27.9	-60.5	-87.1	-84.3	-89.0	-89.3	-151.7	-250.9	-364.0	-329.8
Exports	25.3	57.0	278.9	303.0	446.9	509.0	557.2	601.6	636.8	658.0	725.1	818.6	874.2	966.4	964.9	989.8	1,102.9	1,050.4
Imports	22.8	55.8	293.8	417.2	553.2	589.7	628.6	622.3	664.6	718.5	812.1	902.8	963.1	1,055.8	1,116.7	1,240.6	1,466.9	1,380.1
Government consumption expenditures and gross investment	113.8	237.1	569.7	878.3	1,036.9	1,100.2	1,181.4	1,235.5	1,270.5	1,293.0	1,327.9	1,372.0	1,421.9	1,487.9	1,538.5	1,632.5	1,741.0	1,839.5
Federal	65.9	116.4	245.3	413.4	462.6	482.6	508.4	527.4	534.5	527.3	521.1	521.5	531.6	538.2	539.2	564.0	590.2	615.7
National defense	55.2	90.9	169.6	312.4	355.9	363.2	374.9	384.5	378.5	364.9	355.1	350.6	357.0	352.6	349.1	364.5	375.4	399.0
State and local	47.9	120.7	324.4	464.9	574.3	617.7	673.0	708.1	736.0	765.7	806.8	850.5	890.4	949.7	999.3	1,068.5	1,150.8	1,223.8
CHAINED (1996) DOLLARS																		
Gross domestic product	2,376.7	3,578.0	4,900.9	5,717.1	6,368.4	6,591.8	6,707.9	6,676.4	6,880.0	7,062.6	7,347.7	7,543.8	7,813.2	8,159.5	8,508.9	8,856.5	9,224.0	9,333.8
Personal consumption expenditures	1,510.8	2,317.5	3,193.0	3,820.9	4,279.5	4,393.7	4,474.5	4,466.6	4,594.5	4,748.9	4,928.1	5,075.6	5,237.5	5,423.9	5,683.7	5,968.4	6,257.8	6,450.3
Durable goods	(NA)	(NA)	(NA)	(NA)	481.5	491.7	487.1	454.9	479.0	518.3	557.7	583.5	616.5	657.3	726.7	817.8	895.5	955.6
Nondurable goods	(NA)	(NA)	(NA)	(NA)	1,315.1	1,351.0	1,369.6	1,364.0	1,389.7	1,430.3	1,485.1	1,529.0	1,574.1	1,619.9	1,686.4	1,766.4	1,849.9	1,883.3
Services	(NA)	(NA)	(NA)	(NA)	2,477.2	2,546.0	2,616.2	2,651.8	2,729.7	2,802.5	2,886.2	2,963.4	3,047.0	3,147.0	3,273.4	3,393.2	3,527.7	3,633.4
Gross private domestic investment	272.8	436.2	655.3	863.4	902.8	936.5	907.3	829.5	899.8	977.9	1,107.0	1,140.6	1,242.7	1,393.3	1,558.0	1,660.1	1,772.9	1,630.8
Fixed investment	(NA)	(NA)	(NA)	(NA)	887.1	911.2	894.6	832.5	886.5	958.4	1,045.9	1,109.2	1,212.7	1,328.6	1,480.0	1,595.4	1,716.2	1,682.6
Change in business inventories	(NA)	(NA)	(NA)	(NA)	18.4	29.6	16.5	-1.0	17.1	20.0	66.8	30.4	30.0	63.8	76.7	62.1	50.6	-61.7
Net exports of goods and services	(NA)	(NA)	(NA)	(NA)	-112.1	-79.4	-56.5	-15.8	-19.8	-59.1	-86.5	-78.4	-89.0	-113.3	-221.1	-316.9	-399.1	-408.7
Exports	87.5	159.3	334.8	341.6	473.5	529.4	575.7	613.2	651.0	672.7	732.8	808.2	874.2	981.5	1,002.4	1,034.9	1,133.2	1,081.7
Imports	108.0	223.1	324.8	490.7	585.6	608.8	632.2	629.0	670.8	731.8	819.4	886.6	963.1	1,094.8	1,223.5	1,351.7	1,532.3	1,490.4
Government consumption expenditures and gross investment	661.3	931.1	1,020.9	1,190.5	1,307.5	1,343.5	1,387.3	1,403.4	1,410.0	1,398.8	1,400.1	1,406.4	1,421.9	1,455.4	1,483.3	1,531.8	1,572.6	1,628.6
Federal	(NA)	(NA)	(NA)	(NA)	586.9	594.7	606.8	604.9	595.1	572.0	551.3	536.5	531.6	529.6	525.4	536.7	545.9	560.3
National defense	(NA)	(NA)	(NA)	(NA)	446.8	443.3	443.2	438.4	417.1	394.7	375.9	361.9	357.0	347.7	341.6	348.6	349.0	365.3
State and local	(NA)	(NA)	(NA)	(NA)	721.4	749.5	781.1	798.9	815.3	827.0	848.9	869.9	890.4	925.8	957.7	994.7	1,026.3	1,067.5

NA. Not available.

Source: United States Census Bureau. (2002). *Statistical Abstract of the United States 2002.* Washington, D.C.: Government Printing Office. Retrieved from http://www.census.gov/prod/2003pubs/02statab/income.pdf.

Table 2.2
Gross State Product (GSP) in Current and Real (1996) Dollars

[In billions of dollars (5,706.7 represents $5,706,700,000,000).]

State	Current dollars					Chained (1996) dollars[1]				
	1990	1995	1997	1998	1999	1990	1995	1997	1998	1999
United States	5,706.7	7,309.5	8,225.0	8,752.4	9,309.0	6,630.7	7,434.0	8,093.4	8,508.0	8,934.1
Alabama..............	71.6	95.5	104.2	109.0	115.1	83.2	96.6	102.6	105.7	110.1
Alaska...............	24.8	24.8	26.6	25.0	26.4	27.8	26.4	26.1	25.3	25.9
Arizona..............	68.9	104.6	122.3	133.5	143.7	79.0	105.4	120.8	131.3	140.1
Arkansas	38.4	53.8	59.1	61.6	64.8	44.1	54.7	58.6	60.3	62.8
California	798.9	925.9	1,045.3	1,125.6	1,229.1	927.6	941.9	1,029.2	1,096.6	1,185.6
Colorado.............	74.7	109.0	129.6	141.1	153.7	87.0	111.2	127.3	136.9	147.0
Connecticut...........	98.9	118.6	135.0	143.2	151.8	117.3	120.8	132.6	138.7	145.3
Delaware	20.3	27.6	31.3	33.9	34.7	25.0	28.2	30.1	31.7	31.9
District of Columbia	40.4	48.4	50.5	52.2	55.8	50.9	49.7	49.3	49.7	51.8
Florida..............	258.3	344.8	389.5	416.4	442.9	303.7	350.6	382.3	401.9	420.3
Georgia	141.4	203.5	235.7	255.5	275.7	164.8	206.4	231.8	246.6	260.8
Hawaii..............	32.3	37.2	38.5	39.6	40.9	38.1	37.9	37.7	37.9	38.3
Idaho...............	17.7	27.2	29.4	31.2	34.0	20.0	27.4	29.3	31.2	34.1
Illinois	275.8	359.5	400.3	424.8	445.7	317.9	364.1	394.5	413.0	429.5
Indiana..............	110.8	148.4	163.0	176.1	182.2	127.0	150.0	161.1	171.6	176.0
Iowa	55.8	71.7	81.7	83.1	85.2	63.4	73.1	81.5	82.4	84.0
Kansas..............	51.5	64.1	73.0	76.8	80.8	59.8	65.6	72.1	75.0	78.0
Kentucky	67.9	91.5	101.5	107.6	113.5	77.5	92.8	100.2	104.2	107.5
Louisiana	94.9	112.2	123.5	125.3	129.0	108.0	116.5	120.7	123.6	124.4
Maine...............	23.5	28.0	30.4	32.1	34.1	27.8	28.3	30.0	31.1	32.3
Maryland	115.0	139.5	154.6	164.3	174.7	137.1	142.1	151.5	157.9	164.8
Massachusetts...........	160.0	197.5	223.6	240.9	262.6	187.2	200.5	219.7	233.6	251.9
Michigan.............	190.8	254.2	279.5	291.6	308.3	225.1	258.3	276.0	283.8	295.6
Minnesota............	100.4	131.8	152.3	162.5	173.0	116.6	133.8	150.4	158.4	167.1
Mississippi	39.2	54.6	58.7	61.4	64.3	44.9	55.4	57.8	59.6	61.9
Missouri	104.8	139.5	155.8	163.9	170.5	122.8	141.9	153.4	158.8	162.9
Montana.............	13.4	17.5	18.9	19.9	20.6	15.5	17.9	18.6	19.3	20.0
Nebraska............	33.5	44.1	49.3	51.7	53.7	38.6	45.2	48.9	50.7	52.2
Nevada	31.6	49.4	59.2	64.3	69.9	37.1	50.1	57.5	61.0	64.6
New Hampshire..........	23.9	32.4	37.5	41.2	44.2	27.3	32.6	37.1	40.7	43.5
New Jersey............	217.0	271.4	300.0	316.5	331.5	253.6	275.0	294.1	304.8	315.4
New Mexico	27.2	42.2	47.8	49.2	51.0	29.4	42.7	47.6	50.3	51.9
New York	502.2	597.6	663.4	710.9	754.6	593.4	609.1	651.1	688.1	728.9
North Carolina..........	141.1	194.6	221.6	236.5	258.6	162.6	197.5	218.1	227.5	240.8
North Dakota...........	11.5	14.5	15.9	17.0	17.0	13.2	15.0	15.8	16.9	16.7
Ohio	230.0	295.7	326.5	346.8	362.0	265.9	299.2	322.1	337.7	348.9
Oklahoma..	57.8	70.0	79.4	83.0	86.4	66.1	71.8	78.1	81.7	84.0
Oregon..	57.8	81.1	97.5	103.5	109.7	66.5	81.3	97.1	103.7	110.1
Pennsylvania...........	249.9	318.8	347.3	364.9	383.0	291.5	322.9	340.9	352.1	364.9
Rhode Island...........	21.6	25.7	29.4	30.5	32.5	25.5	26.2	28.8	29.2	30.6
South Carolina..........	66.1	86.9	95.4	101.2	106.9	76.0	87.8	94.3	98.2	102.3
South Dakota	13.0	18.3	19.8	20.9	21.6	15.1	18.7	19.7	20.6	21.3
Tennessee	95.0	136.8	151.7	161.8	170.1	110.5	138.6	149.2	156.4	161.7
Texas...............	388.1	513.9	608.6	645.2	687.3	439.5	527.7	597.9	636.2	668.5
Utah	31.4	46.3	55.1	59.0	62.6	36.3	47.0	54.0	56.9	59.7
Vermont	11.8	14.0	15.5	16.2	17.2	13.4	14.1	15.3	15.9	16.6
Virginia..............	148.2	189.0	212.1	228.0	242.2	174.5	192.5	207.9	218.4	225.1
Washington............	115.5	151.3	175.2	191.8	209.3	136.6	154.0	172.2	185.3	198.9
West Virginia...........	28.3	36.3	38.3	39.4	40.7	31.8	36.6	37.7	38.2	39.1
Wisconsin............	100.4	133.7	148.2	158.3	166.5	115.3	135.2	146.9	155.0	161.5
Wyoming	13.4	14.9	16.2	16.5	17.4	14.3	15.6	16.0	16.5	17.2

1. For chained (1996) dollar estimates, states will not add to U.S. total.

Source: United States Census Bureau. (2002). *Statistical Abstract of the United States 2002.* Washington, D.C.: Government Printing Office. Retrieved from http://www.census.gov/prod/2003pubs/02statab/income.pdf.

Table 2.3

Consumer Price Index, All Urban Consumers (CPI-U) by Major Groups: 1980 to 2001

[1982-84=100 except as noted. Represents annual averages of monthly figures. Reflects buying patterns of all urban consumers. Minus sign (-) indicates decrease.]

Year	All items	Com- modities	Serv- ices	Food	Energy	All items less food and energy	Food and bever- ages	Shelter	Trans- porta- tion	Medical care	Apparel	Educa- tion and commu- nication[1]
1980	82.4	86.0	77.9	86.8	86.0	80.8	86.7	81.0	83.1	74.9	90.9	(NA)
1987	113.6	107.7	120.2	113.5	88.6	118.2	113.5	121.3	105.4	130.1	110.6	(NA)
1988	118.3	111.5	125.7	118.2	89.3	123.4	118.2	127.1	108.7	138.6	115.4	(NA)
1989	124.0	116.7	131.9	125.1	94.3	129.0	124.9	132.8	114.1	149.3	118.6	(NA)
1990	130.7	122.8	139.2	132.4	102.1	135.5	132.1	140.0	120.5	162.8	124.1	(NA)
1991	136.2	126.6	146.3	136.3	102.5	142.1	136.8	146.3	123.8	177.0	128.7	(NA)
1992	140.3	129.1	152.0	137.9	103.0	147.3	138.7	151.2	126.5	190.1	131.9	(NA)
1993	144.5	131.5	157.9	140.9	104.2	152.2	141.6	155.7	130.4	201.4	133.7	85.5
1994	148.2	133.8	163.1	144.3	104.6	156.5	144.9	160.5	134.3	211.0	133.4	88.8
1995	152.4	136.4	168.7	148.4	105.2	161.2	148.9	165.7	139.1	220.5	132.0	92.2
1996	156.9	139.9	174.1	153.3	110.1	165.6	153.7	171.0	143.0	228.2	131.7	95.3
1997	160.5	141.8	179.4	157.3	111.5	169.5	157.7	176.3	144.3	234.6	132.9	98.4
1998	163.0	141.9	184.2	160.7	102.9	173.4	161.1	182.1	141.6	242.1	133.0	100.3
1999	166.6	144.4	188.8	164.1	106.6	177.0	164.6	187.3	144.4	250.6	131.3	101.2
2000	172.2	149.2	195.3	167.8	124.6	181.3	168.4	193.4	153.3	260.8	129.6	102.5
2001	177.1	150.7	203.4	173.1	129.3	186.1	173.6	200.6	154.3	272.8	127.3	105.2
PERCENT CHANGE[2]												
1980	13.5	12.3	15.4	8.6	30.9	12.4	8.5	17.6	17.9	11.0	7.1	(NA)
1987	3.6	3.2	4.2	4.1	0.5	4.1	4.0	4.7	3.0	6.6	4.4	(NA)
1988	4.1	3.5	4.6	4.1	0.8	4.4	4.1	4.8	3.1	6.5	4.3	(NA)
1989	4.8	4.7	4.9	5.8	5.6	4.5	5.7	4.5	5.0	7.7	2.8	(NA)
1990	5.4	5.2	5.5	5.8	8.3	5.0	5.8	5.4	5.6	9.0	4.6	(NA)
1991	4.2	3.1	5.1	2.9	0.4	4.9	3.6	4.5	2.7	8.7	3.7	(NA)
1992	3.0	2.0	3.9	1.2	0.5	3.7	1.4	3.3	2.2	7.4	2.5	(NA)
1993	3.0	1.9	3.9	2.2	1.2	3.3	2.1	3.0	3.1	5.9	1.4	(NA)
1994	2.6	1.7	3.3	2.4	0.4	2.8	2.3	3.1	3.0	4.8	-0.2	3.9
1995	2.8	1.9	3.4	2.8	0.6	3.0	2.8	3.2	3.6	4.5	-1.0	3.8
1996	3.0	2.6	3.2	3.3	4.7	2.7	3.2	3.2	2.8	3.5	-0.2	3.4
1997	2.3	1.4	3.0	2.6	1.3	2.4	2.6	3.1	0.9	2.8	0.9	3.3
1998	1.6	0.1	2.7	2.2	-7.7	2.3	2.2	3.3	-1.9	3.2	0.1	1.9
1999	2.2	1.8	2.5	2.1	3.6	2.1	2.2	2.9	2.0	3.5	-1.3	0.9
2000	3.4	3.3	3.4	2.3	16.9	2.4	2.3	3.3	6.2	4.1	-1.3	1.3
2001	2.8	1.0	4.1	3.2	3.8	2.6	3.1	3.7	0.7	4.6	-1.8	2.6

NA. Not available.

1. Dec. 1997 = 100.

2. Change from immediate prior year.

Source: United States Census Bureau. (2002). *Statistical Abstract of the United States 2002.* Washington, D.C.: Government Printing Office. Retrieved from http://www.census.gov/prod/2003pubs/02statab/prices.pdf.

Table 2.4
CPI-U for Selected Items and Groups: 1980 to 2001

[1982-84 = 100 except as noted. Annual averages of monthly figures.]

Item	1980	1990	1995	1996	1997	1998	1999	2000	2001
All items	82.4	130.7	152.4	156.9	160.5	163.0	166.6	172.2	177.1
Food and beverages	86.7	132.1	148.9	153.7	157.7	161.1	164.6	168.4	173.6
Food	86.8	132.4	148.4	153.3	157.3	160.7	164.1	167.8	173.1
Food at home	88.4	132.3	148.8	154.3	158.1	161.1	164.2	167.9	173.4
Cereals and bakery products	83.9	140.0	167.5	174.0	177.6	181.1	185.0	188.3	193.8
Cereals and cereal products	84.2	141.1	167.1	168.9	169.5	171.5	175.0	175.9	178.7
Cereal	76.3	158.6	192.5	190.0	187.5	189.9	195.2	198.0	199.7
Rice, pasta, and cornmeal	90.9	122.0	140.2	144.2	148.8	150.5	151.9	150.7	154.6
Bakery products	83.8	139.2	167.4	176.1	181.1	185.4	189.4	194.1	201.3
White bread	85.9	136.4	165.5	177.5	183.8	187.3	192.5	199.1	208.3
Cookies, cakes, and cupcakes	81.5	142.7	169.1	174.1	179.2	181.2	185.0	187.9	192.0
Meats, poultry, fish and eggs	92.0	130.0	138.8	144.8	148.5	147.3	147.9	154.5	161.3
Meats	92.7	128.5	135.5	140.2	144.4	141.6	142.3	150.7	159.3
Beef and veal	98.4	128.8	134.9	134.5	136.8	136.5	139.2	148.1	160.5
Uncooked ground beef and related products	104.6	118.1	116.1	114.3	116.4	116.1	118.4	125.2	135.5
Pork	81.9	129.8	134.8	148.2	155.9	148.5	145.9	156.5	162.4
Bacon	73.5	113.4	120.0	148.9	164.0	152.0	151.5	177.5	184.6
Chops	82.9	140.2	144.2	153.0	155.2	146.8	143.5	152.2	159.0
Ham	85.5	132.4	139.6	149.2	156.3	150.0	147.0	152.7	157.3
Poultry	93.7	132.5	143.5	152.4	156.6	157.1	157.9	159.8	164.9
Fish and seafood	87.5	146.7	171.6	173.1	177.1	181.7	185.3	190.4	191.1
Canned fish and seafood	93.7	119.5	125.5	125.9	128.4	132.6	131.5	127.4	127.3
Eggs	88.6	124.1	120.5	142.1	140.0	135.4	128.1	131.9	136.4
Dairy and related products	90.9	126.5	132.8	142.1	145.5	150.8	159.6	160.7	167.1
Fruits and vegetables	82.1	149.0	177.7	183.9	187.5	198.2	203.1	204.6	212.2
Fresh fruits and vegetables	81.8	(NA)	206.0	211.8	215.4	231.2	237.2	238.8	247.9
Fresh fruits	84.8	170.9	219.0	234.4	236.3	246.5	266.3	258.3	265.1
Apples	92.1	147.5	183.5	202.3	199.6	202.3	200.1	212.6	213.9
Bananas	91.5	138.2	153.8	159.0	159.6	160.9	159.4	162.5	166.6
Oranges, tangerines	72.6	160.6	224.5	239.3	226.1	251.5	337.0	257.0	271.7
Fresh vegetables	79.0	151.1	193.1	189.2	194.6	215.8	209.3	219.4	230.6
Potatoes	81.0	162.6	174.7	180.6	174.2	185.2	193.1	196.3	202.3
Lettuce	77.8	150.3	221.2	185.7	200.1	229.1	208.3	228.1	233.8
Tomatoes	81.9	160.8	188.3	198.2	213.6	239.2	224.1	234.7	250.0
Processed fruits and vegetables [1]	(NA)	(NA)	(NA)	(NA)	(NA)	(NA)	(NA)	105.6	109.0
Nonalcoholic beverages and beverage materials	91.4	113.5	131.7	128.6	133.4	133.0	134.3	137.8	139.2
Carbonated drinks	86.6	112.1	119.5	119.9	118.3	117.5	118.8	123.4	125.4
Coffee	111.6	117.5	163.1	149.2	168.0	163.4	154.8	154.0	146.7
Food away from home	83.4	(NA)	149.0	152.7	157.0	161.1	165.1	169.0	173.9
Alcoholic beverages	86.4	129.3	153.9	158.5	162.8	165.7	169.7	174.7	179.3
Alcoholic beverages at home	87.3	123.0	143.1	146.8	149.5	150.6	153.7	158.1	161.1
Beer ale, and other malt beverages	84.8	123.6	143.9	147.4	148.2	148.5	151.9	156.8	160.7
Distilled spirits	89.8	125.7	145.7	147.5	150.8	152.7	156.2	162.3	168.0
Wine	89.5	114.4	133.6	139.3	145.5	147.3	149.4	151.6	151.5
Alcoholic beverages away from home	82.9	144.4	176.5	182.7	189.4	195.0	201.0	207.1	215.2
Housing	81.1	128.5	148.5	152.8	156.8	160.4	163.9	169.6	176.4
Shelter	81.0	140.0	165.7	171.0	176.3	182.1	187.3	193.4	200.6
Owners' equivalent rent of primary residence [2]	(NA)	144.8	171.3	176.8	181.9	187.8	192.9	198.7	206.3
Fuels and utilities	75.4	111.6	123.7	127.5	130.8	128.5	128.8	137.9	150.2
Fuels	74.8	104.5	111.5	115.2	117.9	113.7	113.5	122.8	135.4
Fuel oil and other	86.1	99.3	88.1	99.2	99.8	90.0	91.4	129.7	129.3
Gas (piped) and electricity	71.4	109.3	119.2	122.1	125.1	121.2	120.9	128.0	142.4
Electricity	75.8	117.4	129.6	131.8	132.5	127.4	126.5	128.5	137.8
Utility natural gas service	65.7	97.3	102.9	107.2	114.6	112.4	113.0	132.0	158.3
Water and sewerage maintenance	74.0	150.2	196.5	204.5	210.0	217.3	222.0	227.5	234.6
Garbage and trash collection [3]	(NA)	171.2	241.2	246.0	250.5	256.7	263.8	269.8	275.5

Table 2.4 (*continued*)

Item	1980	1990	1995	1996	1997	1998	1999	2000	2001
Household furnishings and operations	86.3	113.3	123.0	124.7	125.4	126.6	126.7	128.2	129.1
Furniture and bedding	88.0	115.7	130.9	134.1	134.5	135.0	134.9	134.4	132.2
Bedroom furniture	83.5	118.5	136.4	139.3	141.5	141.3	141.0	138.4	136.6
Housekeeping supplies	83.2	125.2	137.1	141.1	143.1	145.7	148.1	153.4	158.4
Apparel	90.9	124.1	132.0	131.7	132.9	133.0	131.3	129.6	127.3
Men's and boy's apparel	89.4	120.4	126.2	127.7	130.1	131.8	131.1	129.7	125.7
Women's and girl's apparel	96.0	122.6	126.9	124.7	126.1	126.0	123.3	121.5	119.3
Infants' and toddlers'	85.5	125.8	127.2	129.7	129.0	126.1	129.0	130.6	129.2
Footwear	91.8	117.4	125.4	126.6	127.6	128.0	125.7	123.8	123.0
Transportation	83.1	120.5	139.1	143.0	144.3	141.6	144.4	153.3	154.3
Private transportation	84.2	118.8	136.3	140.0	141.0	137.9	140.5	149.1	150.0
New vehicles	88.5	121.4	141.0	143.7	144.3	143.4	142.9	142.8	142.1
New cars	88.4	121.0	139.0	141.4	141.7	140.7	139.6	139.6	138.9
New trucks [3]	(NA)	121.6	145.9	149.5	151.4	151.1	152.0	151.7	150.7
Used cars and trucks	62.3	117.6	156.5	157.0	151.1	150.6	152.0	155.8	158.7
Motor fuel	97.4	101.2	100.0	106.3	106.2	92.2	100.7	129.3	124.7
Motor vehicle maintenance and repair	81.5	130.1	154.0	158.4	162.7	167.1	171.9	177.3	183.5
Motor vehicle insurance	82.0	177.9	234.3	243.9	251.6	254.3	253.8	256.7	268.1
Motor vehicle fees [1]	(NA)	(NA)	(NA)	(NA)	(NA)	102.5	103.8	107.3	109.3
Public transportation	69.0	142.6	175.9	181.9	186.7	190.3	197.7	209.6	210.6
Airline fares	68.0	148.4	189.7	192.5	199.2	205.3	218.8	239.4	239.4
Medical care	74.9	162.8	220.5	228.2	234.6	242.1	250.6	260.8	272.8
Medical care commodities	75.4	163.4	204.5	210.4	215.3	221.8	230.7	238.1	247.6
Prescription drugs and medical supplies	72.5	181.7	235.0	242.9	249.3	258.6	273.4	285.4	300.9
Nonprescription drugs and medical supplies[4]	(NA)	120.6	140.5	143.1	145.4	147.7	176.7	149.5	150.6
Medical care services	74.8	162.7	224.2	232.4	239.1	246.8	255.1	266.0	278.8
Professional services	77.9	156.1	201.0	208.3	215.4	222.2	229.2	237.7	246.5
Hospital and related services	69.2	178.0	257.8	269.5	278.4	287.5	299.5	317.3	338.3
Recreation [1]	(NA)	(NA)	(NA)	(NA)	(NA)	(NA)	102.0	103.3	104.9
Video and audio	100.7	80.8	73.9	71.3	99.4	100.1	100.7	101.0	101.5
Cable television [3]	(NA)	158.4	200.7	212.6	228.7	245.2	254.6	266.8	278.4
Photography [1]	(NA)	(NA)	(NA)	(NA)	(NA)	(NA)	99.4	99.2	99.0
Sporting goods	88.5	114.9	123.5	123.4	122.6	121.9	120.3	119.0	118.5
Other recreational goods [1]	(NA)	(NA)	(NA)	(NA)	(NA)	97.1	92.3	87.8	84.6
Pets, pet products and services [1]	(NA)	(NA)	(NA)	(NA)	(NA)	101.5	103.4	106.1	109.7
Recreation services [2]	(NA)	(NA)	(NA)	(NA)	(NA)	102.4	106.9	111.7	116.1
Recreational reading materials	(NA)	(NA)	(NA)	(NA)	179.0	184.1	186.1	188.3	191.4
Tobacco and smoking products	72.0	181.5	225.7	232.8	243.7	274.8	355.8	394.9	425.2
Personal care	81.9	130.4	147.1	150.1	152.7	156.7	161.1	165.6	170.5
Personal care services	83.7	132.8	151.5	156.6	162.4	166.0	171.4	178.1	184.3
Education and communication [1]	(NA)	(NA)	(NA)	(NA)	(NA)	(NA)	101.2	102.5	105.2
Education [1]	(NA)	(NA)	(NA)	(NA)	(NA)	97.3	102.1	107.0	112.5	118.5
Educational books and supplies	71.4	171.3	214.4	226.9	238.4	250.8	261.7	279.9	295.9
Tuition, other school fees and child care	71.2	175.7	253.8	267.1	280.4	294.2	308.4	324.0	341.1
College tuition and fees	70.8	175.0	264.8	279.8	294.1	306.5	318.7	331.9	348.8
Communication [1]	(NA)	(NA)	99.0	100.3	100.0	97.1	95.9	93.0	93.4
Postage [1]	76.2	125.1	160.3	160.3	160.3	160.3	165.1	165.1	171.5
Delivery services [1]	(NA)	(NA)	(NA)	(NA)	100.0	104.2	110.0	114.5	123.0
Information and information processing [1]	(NA)	(NA)	98.9	100.3	100.0	96.9	95.4	92.8	92.3
Telephone services [1]	(NA)	(NA)	(NA)	(NA)	(NA)	(NA)	100.1	98.5	99.3
Telephone services, local charges [1]	72.8	149.3	160.4	160.8	163.1	165.7	168.7	175.6	184.8
Telephone services, long distance charges [1]	(NA)	(NA)	(NA)	(NA)	100.0	99.9	98.6	97.8	88.8
Cellular telephone services [1]	(NA)	(NA)	(NA)	(NA)	100.0	91.7	81.1	76.0	68.1
Information and information processing other than telephone services [5]	(NA)	(NA)	61.0	53.9	47.4	34.8	28.2	25.9	21.3
Personal computers and peripheral equipment [1]	(NA)	(NA)	(NA)	(NA)	100.0	64.2	47.2	41.1	29.5
Computer software and accessories [1]	(NA)	(NA)	(NA)	(NA)	100.0	90.0	88.2	85.4	79.1
Computer information processing services [1]	(NA)	(NA)	(NA)	(NA)	100.0	103.3	96.0	96.4	98.1
All commodities	86.0	122.8	136.4	139.9	141.8	141.9	144.4	149.2	150.7
All commodities less food	85.7	117.4	129.8	132.6	133.4	132.0	134.0	139.2	138.9
Energy	86.0	102.1	105.2	110.1	111.5	102.9	106.6	124.6	129.3

NA. Not available.

1. December 1997 = 100.
2. December 1982 = 100.
3. December 1983 = 100.
4. December 1986 = 100.
5. December 1988 = 100.

Source: United States Census Bureau. (2002). *Statistical Abstract of the United States 2002.* Washington, D.C.: Government Printing Office. Retrieved from http://www.census.gov/prod/2003pubs/02statab/prices.pdf.

Table 2.5
International Economic Performance through the Measure of GDP

HDI rank	GDP US$ billions 2001	GDP PPP US$ billions 2001	GDP per capita US$ 2001	GDP per capita PPP US$ 2001	GDP per capita annual growth rate (%) 1975-2001	GDP per capita annual growth rate (%) 1990-2001	GDP per capita Highest value during 1975-2001 (PPP US$)	Year of highest value	Average annual change in consumer price index (%) 1990-2001	Average annual change in consumer price index (%) 2000-01
High human development										
1 Norway	166.1	133.7	36,815	29,620	2.6	2.9	29,620	2001	2.2	3.0
2 Iceland	7.7	8.5	27,312	29,990	1.7	2.1	29,990	2001	2.9	6.4
3 Sweden	209.8	215.1	23,591	24,180	1.4	1.7	24,180	2001	1.8	2.4
4 Australia	368.7	491.8	19,019	25,370	1.9	2.7	25,370	2001	2.2	4.4
5 Netherlands	380.1	436.2	23,701	27,190	1.9	2.3	27,190	2001	2.4	4.5
6 Belgium	229.6	262.5	22,323	25,520	2.0	1.9	25,520	2001	1.9	2.5
7 United States	10,065.3	9,792.5 a	35,277	34,320 a	2.0	2.1	34,592	2000	2.7	2.8
8 Canada	694.5	843.2	22,343	27,130	1.5	2.1	27,130	2001	1.7	2.5
9 Japan	4,141.4	3,193.0	32,601	25,130	2.6	1.0	25,309	2000	0.6	-0.7
10 Switzerland	247.1	203.2	34,171	28,100	1.0	0.3	28,100	2001	1.5	1.0
11 Denmark	161.5	155.4	30,144	29,000	1.6	2.0	29,000	2001	2.1	2.4
12 Ireland	103.3	124.4	26,908	32,410	4.2	6.8	32,410	2001	2.4	4.9
13 United Kingdom	1,424.1	1,420.3	24,219	24,160	2.1	2.5	24,160	2001	2.8	1.8
14 Finland	120.9	126.8	23,295	24,430	2.0	2.6	24,430	2001	1.6	2.6
15 Luxembourg	18.5	23.7	42,041	53,780	4.0	4.2	53,780	2001	2.0	2.7
16 Austria	188.5	217.4	23,186	26,730	2.1	1.8	26,730	2001	2.2	2.7
17 France	1,309.8	1,420.0	22,129	23,990	1.7	1.5	23,990	2001	1.6	1.6
18 Germany	1,846.1	2,086.8	22,422	25,350	1.8	1.2	25,350	2001	2.2	2.5
19 Spain	581.8	828.4	14,150	20,150	2.2	2.2	20,150	2001	3.7	3.6
20 New Zealand	50.4	73.7	13,101	19,160	0.9	2.0	19,160	2001	1.8	2.6
21 Italy	1,088.8	1,429.7	18,788	24,670	2.0	1.4	24,670	2001	3.5	2.8
22 Israel	108.3	125.9	17,024	19,790	2.0	2.0	20,376	2000	8.9	1.1
23 Portugal	109.8	181.9	10,954	18,150	3.0	2.6	18,150	2001	4.3	4.4
24 Greece	117.2	184.7	11,063	17,440	1.0	2.0	17,440	2001	8.3	3.4
25 Cyprus	9.1	16.1 b	12,004	21,190 b	4.8	3.2	21,190	2001	3.5	2.0
26 Hong Kong, China (SAR)	161.9	167.1	24,074	24,850	4.5	2.1	25,037	2000	4.9	-1.6
27 Barbados	2.8	4.2	10,281	15,560	1.3	2.1	15,560	2001	2.5	2.6
28 Singapore	85.6	93.7	20,733	22,680	5.1	4.4	23,804	2000	1.6	1.0
29 Slovenia	18.8	34.1	9,443	17,130	..	3.0	17,130	2001	22.0 c	9.4
30 Korea, Rep. of	422.2	714.2	8,917	15,090	6.2	4.7	15,090	2001	4.9	4.1
31 Brunei Darussalam	..	..	..	..	-2.2 c	-0.7 c	..	..	..	..
32 Czech Republic	56.8	150.5	5,554	14,720	..	1.3	14,720	2001	7.3 c	4.7
33 Malta	3.6	5.2 b	9,172	13,160 b	4.5	3.8	13,427	2000	3.0	2.9
34 Argentina	268.6	424.4	7,166	11,320	0.4	2.3	12,827	1998	7.4	-1.1
35 Poland	176.3	365.3	4,561	9,450	..	4.4	9,450	2001	23.1	5.5
36 Seychelles	0.6	..	6,912	..	2.5	0.1	..	..	2.1	6.0
37 Bahrain	7.9	10.5	12,189	16,060	1.1 c	1.9	16,126	2000	0.8	..
38 Hungary	51.9	125.7	5,097	12,340	0.9	2.1	12,340	2001	19.2	9.1
39 Slovakia	20.5	64.6	3,786	11,960	(.) c	1.9	11,960	2001	8.5 c	7.3
40 Uruguay	18.7	28.2	5,554	8,400	1.4	2.1	9,256	1998	30.2	4.4
41 Estonia	5.5	13.9	4,051	10,170	-0.5 c	1.6	10,501	1989	18.9 c	5.7
42 Costa Rica	16.1	36.7	4,159	9,460	1.2	2.8	9,529	2000	15.1	11.2
43 Chile	66.5	141.6	4,314	9,190	4.1	4.7	9,190	2001	8.3	3.6
44 Qatar	16.5 d	..	28,132 d	..	..	..	..	..	2.7	1.4
45 Lithuania	12.0	29.5	3,444	8,470	..	-1.6	11,031	1990	27.0 c	1.2
46 Kuwait	32.8	38.2 b	16,048	18,700 b	-0.7 c	-1.0 c	29,396	1979	2.0	1.7
47 Croatia	20.3	40.2	4,625	9,170	..	2.1	9,313	1990	72.1	4.8
48 United Arab Emirates	..	..	..	..	-3.7 c	-1.6 c	..	..	..	..
49 Bahamas	4.8 d	5.0	15,797 d	16,270	1.5 c	0.1 c	..	..	2.0	2.0
50 Latvia	7.5	18.2	3,200	7,730	-0.7	-1.0	10,243	1989	25.0 c	2.5

Table 2.5 (*continued*)

HDI rank	GDP US$ billions 2001	GDP PPP US$ billions 2001	GDP per capita US$ 2001	GDP per capita PPP US$ 2001	GDP per capita annual growth rate (%) 1975-2001	GDP per capita annual growth rate (%) 1990-2001	GDP per capita Highest value during 1975-2001 (PPP US$)	Year of highest value	Average annual change in consumer price index (%) 1990-2001	Average annual change in consumer price index (%) 2000-01
51 Saint Kitts and Nevis	0.3	0.5	7,609	11,300	5.4 c	3.9	11,377	2000	3.4 c	..
52 Cuba	..	..	..	..	..	3.7 c	..	..	..	..
53 Belarus	12.2	76.0	1,226	7,620	..	-0.6	8,078	1990	294.7 c	61.1
54 Trinidad and Tobago	8.8	11.9	6,752	9,100	0.7	2.9	9,100	2001	5.7	..
55 Mexico	617.8	838.2 b	6,214	8,430 b	0.9	1.5	8,581	2000	18.6	6.4
Medium human development										
56 Antigua and Barbuda	0.7	0.7	9,961	10,170	4.4 c	2.7	10,223	2000	..	..
57 Bulgaria	13.6	55.3	1,690	6,890	(.) c	-0.6	8,012	1988	105.3	7.4
58 Malaysia	88.0	208.3 b	3,699	8,750 b	4.1	3.9	8,996	1997	3.4	1.4
59 Panama	10.2	16.7	3,511	5,750	0.8	2.1	5,821	2000	1.1	0.3
60 Macedonia, TFYR	3.4	12.5	1,676	6,110	..	-0.9	6,990	1991	8.0 c	-0.7
61 Libyan Arab Jamahiriya	34.1 d	..	6,453 d	..	..	..	..	..	..	..
62 Mauritius	4.5	11.8	3,750	9,860	4.7 c	3.9	9,860	2001	6.7	5.4
63 Russian Federation	310.0	1,027.9	2,141	7,100	-1.2	-3.5	10,326	1989	85.9 c	21.5
64 Colombia	82.4	302.8	1,915	7,040	1.5	0.8	7,539	1997	19.5	8.7
65 Brazil	502.5	1,268.6	2,915	7,360	0.8	1.4	7,360	2001	161.6	6.9
66 Bosnia and Herzegovina	4.8	24.3	1,175	5,970	..	20.5 c	..	..	..	..
67 Belize	0.8	1.4	3,258	5,690	2.8	1.6	5,690	2001	1.8	1.2
68 Dominica	0.3	0.4	3,661	5,520	3.5 c	1.7	5,756	2000	1.8	1.9
69 Venezuela	124.9	139.5	5,073	5,670	-0.9	-0.6	7,619	1977	45.9	12.5
70 Samoa (Western)	0.3	1.1	1,465	6,180	0.4 c	2.0	6,180	2001	3.6	3.8
71 Saint Lucia	0.7	0.8	4,222	5,260	4.1 c	0.7	5,529	1999	2.7	0.1
72 Romania	38.7	130.7	1,728	5,830	-1.3 c	-0.1	7,325	1987	92.8	34.5
73 Saudi Arabia	186.5	285.3	8,711	13,330	-2.1	-1.1	23,294	1980	0.8	-0.5
74 Thailand	114.7	391.7	1,874	6,400	5.4	3.0	6,763	1996	4.6	1.7
75 Ukraine	37.6	213.3	766	4,350	-7.5 c	-7.4	9,303	1989	200.4 c	..
76 Kazakhstan	22.4	96.8	1,503	6,500	..	-1.9	7,948	1989	54.8 c	8.4
77 Suriname	0.8	..	1,803	..	(.)	2.6	..	..	88.0 c	..
78 Jamaica	7.8	9.6	3,005	3,720	0.2	-0.5	4,174	1975	21.4	7.0
79 Oman	19.8 d	29.0	8,226 d	12,040	2.3 c	0.6 c	..	..	(.)	-1.1
80 St. Vincent & the Grenadines	0.4	0.6	3,047	5,330	3.9	2.5	5,402	2000	2.2	0.8
81 Fiji	1.7	4.0	2,061	4,850	1.0	1.7	4,961	1999	3.3	4.3
82 Peru	54.0	120.4	2,051	4,570	-0.7	2.4	5,310	1981	23.8	2.0
83 Lebanon	16.7	18.3	3,811	4,170	4.0 c	3.6	4,244	1998	..	..
84 Paraguay	7.2	29.4	1,279	5,210	0.6	-0.6	6,052	1981	12.5	7.3
85 Philippines	71.4	301.1	912	3,840	0.1	1.0	3,946	1982	8.0	6.1
86 Maldives	0.6	..	2,082	..	..	2.5 c	..	..	6.3	0.6
87 Turkmenistan	6.0	23.5	1,097	4,320	-6.6 c	-6.1	7,626	1988	..	..
88 Georgia	3.1	13.5	594	2,560	-5.5	-5.5	8,404	1985	20.6 c	4.6
89 Azerbaijan	5.6	25.1	688	3,090	..	-1.3 c	4,036	1992	134.5 c	1.5
90 Jordan	8.8	19.5	1,755	3,870	0.3	0.9	4,698	1986	3.3	1.8
91 Tunisia	20.0	61.9	2,066	6,390	2.0	3.1	6,390	2001	4.2	1.9
92 Guyana	0.7	3.6	912	4,690	0.5	4.4	4,749	1999	6.0 c	2.6
93 Grenada	0.4	0.7	3,965	6,740	3.8 c	2.9	7,173	2000	2.3 c	..
94 Dominican Republic	21.2	59.7	2,494	7,020	1.8	4.2	7,020	2001	8.5	8.9
95 Albania	4.1	11.6	1,300	3,680	-0.5 c	4.3	3,680	2001	24.2 c	3.1
96 Turkey	147.7	390.3	2,230	5,890	2.0	1.7	6,495	1998	77.9	54.4
97 Ecuador	18.0	42.3	1,396	3,280	0.2	-0.3	3,517	1997	38.7	37.7
98 Occupied Palestinian Territories	4.0	..	1,286	..	..	-3.0 c	..	..	.:	..
99 Sri Lanka	15.9	59.6	849	3,180	3.4	3.6	3,273	2000	9.9	14.2
100 Armenia	2.1	10.1	556	2,650	..	-1.3	3,828	1990	55.8 c	3.1

Table 2.5 (*continued*)

HDI rank	GDP US$ billions 2001	GDP PPP US$ billions 2001	GDP per capita US$ 2001	GDP per capita PPP US$ 2001	GDP per capita annual growth rate (%) 1975-2001	GDP per capita annual growth rate (%) 1990-2001	GDP per capita Highest value during 1975-2001 (PPP US$)	Year of highest value	Average annual change in consumer price index (%) 1990-2001	Average annual change in consumer price index (%) 2000-01
101 Uzbekistan	11.3	61.6	450	2,460	-1.9 c	-1.5	2,950	1989	..	..
102 Kyrgyzstan	1.5	13.6	308	2,750	-4.1 c	-3.9	4,392	1990	21.2 c	6.9
103 Cape Verde	0.6	2.5 b	1,317	5,570 b	3.0 c	3.5	5,570	2001	5.2	3.7
104 China	1,159.0	5,111.2	911	4,020	8.2	8.8	4,020	2001	7.6	0.3
105 El Salvador	13.7	33.7	2,147	5,260	0.1	2.4	5,850	1978	7.8	3.8
106 Iran, Islamic Rep. of	114.1	387.2	1,767	6,000	-0.6	2.0	7,808	1976	24.7	11.3
107 Algeria	54.7	187.9 b	1,773	6,090 b	-0.2	0.1	6,836	1985	15.5	4.2
108 Moldova, Rep. of	1.5	9.2	346	2,150	-5.6 c	-8.2	5,764	1989	19.3 c	9.8
109 Viet Nam	32.7	164.5	411	2,070	4.9 c	6.0	2,070	2001	3.2 c	-0.4
110 Syrian Arab Republic	19.5	54.4	1,175	3,280	0.9	1.9	3,487	1998	5.9	0.4
111 South Africa	113.3	488.2 b	2,620	11,290 b	-0.7	0.2	13,510	1981	8.3	4.8
112 Indonesia	145.3	615.2	695	2,940	4.3	2.3	3,267	1997	13.9	11.5
113 Tajikistan	1.1	7.3	169	1,170	-9.9 c	-9.9	3,731	1988	..	..
114 Bolivia	8.0	19.6	936	2,300	-0.4	1.4	2,613	1978	8.1	1.6
115 Honduras	6.4	18.6	970	2,830	0.1	0.3	3,002	1979	18.0	9.7
116 Equatorial Guinea	1.8	..	3,935	..	11.1 c	18.8	..	..	..	..
117 Mongolia	1.0	4.2	433	1,740	-0.3 c	(.)	2,067	1989	39.0 c	8.0
118 Gabon	4.3	7.6	3,437	5,990	-1.5	-0.1	11,633	1976	4.6	..
119 Guatemala	20.5	51.4	1,754	4,400	0.1	1.4	4,522	1980	9.7	7.6
120 Egypt	98.5	229.4	1,511	3,520	2.8	2.5	3,520	2001	8.1	2.3
121 Nicaragua	..	..	..	..	-4.0 c	-0.1 c	..	..	35.1 c	..
122 São Tomé and Principe	(.)	..	311	..	-0.8 c	-0.6	..	..	..	..
123 Solomon Islands	0.3	0.8 b	614	1,910 b	2.1	-1.4	2,766	1996	10.8 c	..
124 Namibia	3.1	12.8 b	1,730	7,120 b	-0.1 c	2.2	7,378	1980	9.5	9.5
125 Botswana	5.2	13.3	3,066	7,820	5.3	2.5	7,820	2001	10.0	6.6
126 Morocco	34.2	105.0	1,173	3,600	1.3	0.7	3,600	2001	3.5	0.6
127 India	477.3	2,930.0	462	2,840	3.2	4.0	2,840	2001	8.7	3.7
128 Vanuatu	0.2	0.6 b	1,058	3,190 b	(.) c	-1.1	3,817	1991	2.7	3.7
129 Ghana	5.3	44.3 b	269	2,250 b	0.2	1.9	2,250	2001	28.1	32.9
130 Cambodia	3.4	22.8	278	1,860	2.1 c	2.2	1,860	2001	5.3 c	-0.6
131 Myanmar	..	..	..	..	1.8	5.7	..	..	25.0	21.1
132 Papua New Guinea	3.0	13.5 b	563	2,570 b	0.5	1.0	3,108	1994	9.7	9.3
133 Swaziland	1.3	4.6	1,175	4,330	1.9	0.1	4,367	1999	9.3	5.9
134 Comoros	0.2	1.1 b	386	1,870 b	-1.0 c	-1.4	2,359	1984	..	..
135 Lao People's Dem. Rep.	1.8	8.8 b	326	1,620 b	3.3 c	3.9	1,620	2001	29.8	7.8
136 Bhutan	0.5	..	644	..	4.0 c	3.5	..	..	9.6 c	..
137 Lesotho	0.8	5.0 b	386	2,420 b	3.0	2.1	2,452	1997	8.8 c	-9.6
138 Sudan	12.5	62.3	395	1,970	0.8	3.2	1,970	2001	66.8 c	..
139 Bangladesh	46.7	214.1	350	1,610	2.3	3.1	1,610	2001	5.1	1.1
140 Congo	2.8	3.0	886	970	0.3	-1.6	1,382	1984	8.5 c	0.1
141 Togo	1.3	7.7	270	1,650	-1.2	-0.6	2,387	1980	7.8	3.9
Low human development										
142 Cameroon	8.5	25.6	559	1,680	-0.6	-0.3	2,463	1986	5.9	4.5
143 Nepal	5.6	30.9	236	1,310	2.2	2.4	1,310	2001	8.1	2.8
144 Pakistan	58.7	266.7	415	1,890	2.7	1.2	1,890	2001	9.1	3.1
145 Zimbabwe	9.1	29.3	706	2,280	0.2	-0.2	2,780	1998	31.8	76.7
146 Kenya	11.4	30.1	371	980	0.3	-0.6	1,079	1990	14.5	5.7
147 Uganda	5.7	33.9 b	249	1,490 b	2.6 c	3.6	1,490	2001	9.5	2.0
148 Yemen	9.3	14.3	514	790	..	2.4	790	2001	32.6 c	..
149 Madagascar	4.6	13.3	288	830	-1.6	-0.6	1,195	1975	17.5	6.9
150 Haiti	3.7	15.1 b	460	1,860 b	-2.0	-2.5	3,194	1980	20.8	14.2
151 Gambia	0.4	2.7 b	291	2,050 b	-0.2	0.1	2,105	1984	4.0	..

Table 2.5 (*continued*)

HDI rank	GDP US$ billions 2001	GDP PPP US$ billions 2001	GDP per capita US$ 2001	GDP per capita PPP US$ 2001	GDP per capita annual growth rate (%) 1975-2001	GDP per capita annual growth rate (%) 1990-2001	GDP per capita Highest value during 1975-2001 (PPP US$)	Year of highest value	Average annual change in consumer price index (%) 1990-2001	Average annual change in consumer price index (%) 2000-01
152 Nigeria	41.4	110.6	319	850	-0.7	-0.3	1,084	1977	30.0	13.0
153 Djibouti	0.6	1.5	894	2,370	-4.6 c	-3.6	4,436	1987	..	..
154 Mauritania	1.0	5.5 b	366	1,990 b	(.)	1.2	2,010	1976	5.9	4.7
155 Eritrea	0.7	4.3	164	1,030	..	2.5 c	1,149	1998	..	..
156 Senegal	4.6	14.7	476	1,500	-0.1	1.1	1,525	1976	5.0	3.1
157 Guinea	3.0	14.8	394	1,960	1.4 c	1.6	1,960	2001	..	..
158 Rwanda	1.7	10.9	196	1,250	-1.2	-1.3	1,643	1983	14.7 c	3.3
159 Benin	2.4	6.3	368	980	0.5	1.9	980	2001	7.9 c	4.0
160 Tanzania, U. Rep. of	9.3	18.0	271	520	0.3 c	0.4	520	2001	19.3	5.1
161 CÙte dêlvoire	10.4	24.4	634	1,490	-2.0	0.1	2,581	1978	6.7	4.3
162 Malawi	1.7	6.0	166	570	0.2	1.5	593	1999	33.5	27.2
163 Zambia	3.6	8.0	354	780	-2.2	-1.7	1,345	1976	80.8 c	..
164 Angola	9.5	27.5 b	701	2,040 b	-2.3 c	-1.1	2,694	1988	633.2	152.6
165 Chad	1.6	8.5 b	202	1,070 b	0.1	-0.5	1,194	1977	7.9	12.4
166 Guinea-Bissau	0.2	1.2	162	970	0.3	-1.3	1,265	1997	30.6	3.3
167 Congo, Dem. Rep. of the	5.2	35.8 b	99	680 b	-5.2	-7.7	2,804	1975	813.4	357.3
168 Central African Republic	1.0	4.9 b	257	1,300 b	-1.5	-0.3	1,825	1977	4.9	3.8
169 Ethiopia	6.2	53.3	95	810	0.1 c	2.4	811	1983	4.7	-8.1
170 Mozambique	3.6	20.6 b	200	1,140 b	1.8 c	4.3	1,140	2001	28.8	9.1
171 Burundi	0.7	4.8 b	99	690 b	-0.8	-4.3	1,034	1991	15.9	9.2
172 Mali	2.6	9.0	239	810	-0.4	1.6	907	1979	4.8	5.2
173 Burkina Faso	2.5	13.0 b	215	1,120 b	1.3	2.0	1,120	2001	5.2	5.0
174 Niger	2.0	9.9 b	175	890 b	-2.0	-0.9	1,473	1979	5.7	4.0
175 Sierra Leone	0.7	2.4	146	470	-3.3	-6.6	1,070	1982	27.0	2.1
Developing countries	6,110.3 T	18,579.4 T	1,270	3,850	2.3	2.9	..	..	..	..
Least developed countries	194.6 T	859.3 T	280	1,274	0.4 c	1.2	..	..	..	..
Arab States	706.5 T	1,424.5 T	2,341	5,038	0.3	0.7	..	..	..	..
East Asia and the Pacific	2,337.3 T	7,962.5 T	1,267	4,233	5.9	5.5	..	..	..	..
Latin America and the Caribbean	1,905.2 T	3,666.7 T	3,752	7,050	0.7	1.5	..	..	..	..
South Asia	727.8 T	3,937.6 T	508	2,730	2.4	3.2	..	..	..	..
Sub-Saharan Africa	300.9 T	1,159.1 T	475	1,831	-0.9	-0.1	..	..	..	..
Central & Eastern Europe & CIS	864.0 T	2,706.9 T	2,094	6,598	-2.5 c	-1.6	..	..	..	..
OECD	25,124.2 T	26,501.8 T	22,149	23,363	2.0	1.7	..	..	..	..
High-income OECD	24,053.3 T	24,567.1 T	26,601	27,169	2.1	1.8	..	..	..	..
High human development	25,935.7 T	27,530.2 T	22,005	23,135	2.0	1.7	..	..	..	..
Medium human development	4,443.6 T	16,505.9 T	1,102	4,053	1.7	2.1	..	..	..	..
Low human development	233.1 T	878.0 T	315	1,186	0.1	0.3	..	..	..	..
High income	24,583.9 T	25,180.8 T	26,395	26,989	2.1	1.7	..	..	..	..
Middle income	5,155.7 T	14,720.0 T	1,928	5,519	1.6	2.2	..	..	..	..
Low income	1,082.1 T	5,587.4 T	432	2,230	1.6	1.4	..	..	..	..
World	30,720.9 T	44,995.3 T	5,133	7,376	1.2	1.2	..	..	..	..

a. In theory, for the United States the value of GDP in PPP US dollars should be the same as that in US dollars, but practical issues arising in the calculation of the PPP US dollar GDP prevent this.

b. Estimate based on regression.

c. Data refer to a period shorter than that specified.

d. Data refer to 2000.

Source: United Nations Development Programme. (2003). *Human Development Report 2003*. Table 12. "International Economic Performance (278–281)." New York: Oxford University Press. Retrieved from http://www.undp.org/hdr2003/pdf/hdr03_complete.pdf. Copyright 2003 by the United Nations Development Programme. Used by permission of Oxford University Press, Inc.

Table 2.6
CPI for Sixteen Countries: 1950 to 2000

(Indexes: 1982-84=100)

Year	United States [1]	Canada [2]	Japan [3]	Australia [4]	Austria	Belgium [5]	Denmark [6]	France [7]
1950	24.1	21.6	14.8	12.6	-	24.0	12.3	11.1
1955	26.8	24.4	20.2	18.9	-	26.8	15.0	14.5
1960	29.6	26.9	21.8	22.1	32.6	29.1	16.7	19.4
1961	29.9	27.1	23.0	22.6	33.8	29.3	17.4	20.0
1962	30.2	27.4	24.6	22.6	35.3	29.8	18.8	21.0
1963	30.6	27.9	26.4	22.7	36.2	30.4	19.8	22.0
1964	31.0	28.4	27.4	23.2	37.6	31.7	20.5	22.7
1965	31.5	29.1	29.5	24.1	39.5	32.9	21.8	23.3
1966	32.4	30.2	31.0	24.9	40.3	34.3	23.3	23.9
1967	33.4	31.3	32.3	25.7	41.9	35.3	25.0	24.6
1968	34.8	32.5	34.0	26.3	43.1	36.3	27.0	25.7
1969	36.7	34.0	35.8	27.1	44.4	37.6	27.9	27.3
1970	38.8	35.1	38.5	28.2	46.4	39.1	29.8	28.8
1971	40.5	36.2	40.9	29.9	48.5	40.8	31.5	30.3
1972	41.8	37.9	42.9	31.6	51.6	43.0	33.6	32.2
1973	44.4	40.7	47.9	34.6	55.5	46.0	36.7	34.6
1974	49.3	45.2	59.1	39.9	60.8	51.9	42.3	39.3
1975	53.8	50.1	66.0	45.9	65.9	58.5	46.4	43.9
1976	56.9	53.8	72.2	52.1	70.8	63.8	50.5	48.2
1977	60.6	58.1	78.1	58.5	74.6	68.4	56.1	52.7
1978	65.2	63.3	81.4	63.1	77.3	71.4	61.8	57.5
1979	72.6	69.1	84.4	68.8	80.2	74.6	67.7	63.6
1980	82.4	76.1	90.9	75.8	85.3	79.6	76.1	72.3
1981	90.9	85.6	95.4	83.2	91.1	85.6	85.0	82.0
1982	96.5	94.9	98.0	92.4	96.0	93.1	93.6	91.6
1983	99.6	100.4	99.8	101.8	99.2	100.3	100.0	100.5
1984	103.9	104.7	102.1	105.8	104.8	106.6	106.4	107.9
1985	107.6	108.9	104.2	112.9	108.2	111.8	111.4	114.2
1986	109.6	113.4	104.8	123.2	110.0	113.3	115.4	117.2
1987	113.6	118.4	104.9	133.7	111.6	115.0	120.0	120.9
1988	118.3	123.2	105.7	142.9	113.8	116.4	125.5	124.2
1989	124.0	129.3	108.1	154.1	116.6	120.0	131.5	128.6
1990	130.7	135.5	111.4	165.3	120.5	124.1	135.0	133.0
1991	136.2	143.1	115.1	170.7	124.4	128.1	138.2	137.2
1992	140.3	145.3	117.0	172.4	129.5	131.2	141.1	140.6
1993	144.5	147.9	118.5	175.5	134.1	134.8	142.9	143.5
1994	148.2	148.2	119.3	178.8	138.2	138.0	145.8	145.9
1995	152.4	151.4	119.2	187.1	141.3	140.1	148.8	148.4
1996	156.9	153.8	119.3	192.0	143.9	142.9	151.9	151.3
1997	160.5	156.2	121.5	192.5	145.8	145.3	155.3	153.2
1998	163.0	157.7	122.2	194.1	147.1	146.7	158.2	154.3
1999	166.6	160.5	121.8	197.0	147.9	148.3	162.0	155.0
2000	172.2	164.8	121.0	205.8	151.4	152.1	166.8	157.7

I=All Households Index, II=Worker Households Index.

1. All urban households from 1978; urban worker households prior to 1978.

2. All households from January 1995; all urban households from September 1978 to December 1994; and middle income urban households prior to September 1978.

3. Excluding agricultural and single person households.

4. Urban worker households prior to September 1998.

5. Excluding rent and several other services prior to 1976.

6. Excluding rent prior to 1964.

7. All households from 1991; urban worker households from 1962 to 1990; worker households in Paris only prior to 1962.

Table 2.6 (*continued*)

Year	Unified Germany I	West Germany I[8]	Italy I[9]	Netherlands I[10]	Norway I[11]	Spain II[12]	Sweden I	Switzerland I[13]	United Kingdom I[14]
1950		33.9	8.9	21.2	13.6	5.5	13.4	33.2	9.8
1955		37.3	10.9	24.9	18.4	6.3	17.5	36.0	12.9
1960		40.9	11.9	28.3	21.1	9.1	21.0	38.2	14.6
1961		41.9	12.2	28.6	21.6	9.2	21.5	38.9	15.1
1962		43.1	12.7	29.3	22.8	9.7	22.5	40.6	15.8
1963		44.4	13.7	30.3	23.4	10.6	23.2	42.0	16.1
1964		45.4	14.5	32.0	24.7	11.3	23.9	43.3	16.6
1965		46.9	15.2	33.3	25.7	12.8	25.1	44.8	17.4
1966		48.6	15.5	35.2	26.6	13.6	26.8	46.9	18.1
1967		49.4	16.1	36.4	27.8	14.5	27.9	48.8	18.5
1968		50.2	16.3	37.8	28.7	15.2	28.4	50.0	19.4
1969		51.1	16.7	40.6	29.6	15.5	29.2	51.3	20.5
1970		52.8	17.5	42.1	32.8	16.4	31.3	53.1	21.8
1971		55.6	18.4	45.3	34.8	17.7	33.6	56.6	23.8
1972		58.7	19.4	48.9	37.3	19.2	35.6	60.4	25.5
1973		62.8	21.6	52.9	40.1	21.4	38.0	65.7	27.9
1974		67.2	25.7	58.1	43.8	24.8	41.7	72.1	32.3
1975		71.2	30.0	63.8	49.0	29.0	45.8	76.9	40.1
1976		74.2	35.1	69.6	53.5	34.1	50.5	78.2	46.8
1977		77.0	41.0	74.1	58.3	42.4	56.3	79.2	54.2
1978		79.0	46.0	77.2	63.1	50.8	61.9	80.1	58.7
1979		82.3	52.8	80.5	66.1	58.8	66.4	83.0	66.6
1980		86.7	64.0	86.1	73.3	67.9	75.5	86.3	78.5
1981		92.2	75.4	91.9	83.3	77.8	84.6	91.9	87.9
1982		97.1	87.8	97.2	92.7	89.0	91.9	97.1	95.4
1983		100.3	100.7	99.8	100.5	99.9	100.0	100.0	99.8
1984		102.7	111.5	103.0	106.8	111.1	108.1	102.9	104.8
1985		104.8	121.8	105.3	112.9	120.9	116.0	106.4	111.1
1986		104.7	129.0	105.6	121.0	131.5	121.0	107.2	114.9
1987		104.9	135.1	105.1	131.6	138.5	126.1	108.8	119.7
1988		106.3	141.9	106.1	140.4	145.1	133.4	110.8	125.6
1989		109.2	150.8	107.1	146.8	155.0	142.0	114.3	135.4
1990		112.1	160.5	109.9	152.8	165.4	156.7	120.5	148.2
1991	100.0	116.2	170.6	113.3	158.0	175.2	171.5	127.5	156.9
1992	105.1	120.9	179.4	116.9	161.7	185.6	175.6	132.7	162.7
1993	109.8	125.2	187.5	120.0	165.4	194.1	183.9	137.0	165.3
1994	112.8	128.6	195.0	123.3	167.7	203.3	187.8	138.3	169.3
1995	114.7	130.7	205.1	125.7	171.8	212.8	192.4	140.8	175.2
1996	116.3	132.4	213.4	128.2	174.0	220.3	193.5	141.9	179.4
1997	118.5	134.8	217.7	131.0	178.5	224.8	194.8	142.5	185.1
1998	119.7	136.0	222.0	133.6	182.5	228.8	194.2	142.7	191.4
1999	120.3	136.9	225.7	136.5	186.7	234.2	195.1	143.8	194.3
2000	122.6	139.7	231.4	140.0	192.5	242.1	196.9	146.0	200.1

8. Refers to the former West Germany Middle income worker households prior to 1962.
9. Middle income worker households prior to 1953.
10. Middle income worker households prior to 1969.
11. Urban worker households prior to 1960.
12. Middle income worker households.
13. Urban worker households prior to May 1993.
14. Excluding pensioner and high income households.

Source: U.S. Department of Labor. (2001). *Report on the American Workforce.* Washington, D.C.: Government Printing Office. Retrieved from http://www.bls.gov/opub/rtaw/pdf/appendix.pdf.

Table 2.7
Producer Price Index by Stage of Processing: 1980 to 2001

[**1982=100.** Minus sign (-) indicates decline.]

Year	Crude materials				Interme-diate materials, supplies, and com-ponents	Finished goods		Finished consumer foods		Finished consumer goods excl. food
	Total	Food-stuffs and feed-stuffs	Fuel	Crude nonfood materials except fuel		Con-sumer goods	Capital equip-ment	Crude	Pro-cessed	
1980.........	95.3	104.6	69.4	91.8	90.3	88.6	85.8	93.9	92.3	87.1
1985.........	95.8	94.8	102.7	94.3	102.7	103.8	107.5	102.9	104.8	103.3
1986.........	87.7	93.2	92.2	76.0	99.1	101.4	109.7	105.6	107.4	98.5
1987.........	93.7	96.2	84.1	88.5	101.5	103.6	111.7	107.1	109.6	100.7
1988.........	96.0	106.1	82.1	85.9	107.1	106.2	114.3	109.8	112.7	103.1
1989.........	103.1	111.2	85.3	95.8	112.0	112.1	118.8	119.6	118.6	108.9
1990.........	108.9	113.1	84.8	107.3	114.5	118.2	122.9	123.0	124.4	115.3
1991.........	101.2	105.5	82.9	97.5	114.4	120.5	126.7	119.3	124.4	118.7
1992.........	100.4	105.1	84.0	94.2	114.7	121.7	129.1	107.6	124.4	120.8
1993.........	102.4	108.4	87.1	94.1	116.2	123.0	131.4	114.4	126.5	121.7
1994.........	101.8	106.5	82.4	97.0	118.5	123.3	134.1	111.3	127.9	121.6
1995.........	102.7	105.8	72.1	105.8	124.9	125.6	136.7	118.8	129.8	124.0
1996.........	113.8	121.5	92.6	105.7	125.7	129.5	138.3	129.2	133.8	127.6
1997.........	111.1	112.2	101.3	103.5	125.6	130.2	138.2	126.6	135.1	128.2
1998.........	96.8	103.9	86.7	84.5	123.0	128.9	137.6	127.2	134.8	126.4
1999.........	98.2	98.7	91.2	91.1	123.2	132.0	137.6	125.5	135.9	130.5
2000.........	120.6	100.2	136.9	118.0	129.2	138.2	138.8	123.5	138.3	138.4
2001.........	121.3	106.2	152.1	101.8	129.7	141.5	139.7	127.6	142.4	141.4
PERCENT CHANGE [1]										
1980.........	10.9	4.6	21.1	22.0	15.2	14.3	10.7	1.7	6.3	18.5
1985.........	-7.4	-9.5	-2.3	2.2	-0.4	0.5	2.2	-7.6	-0.1	1.1
1986.........	-8.5	-1.7	-10.2	-6.6	-3.5	-2.3	2.0	2.6	2.5	-4.6
1987.........	6.8	3.2	-8.8	-19.4	2.4	2.2	1.8	1.4	2.0	2.2
1988.........	2.5	10.3	-2.4	16.4	5.5	2.5	2.3	2.5	2.8	2.4
1989.........	7.4	4.8	3.9	-2.9	4.6	5.6	3.9	8.9	5.2	5.6
1990.........	5.6	1.7	-0.6	12.0	2.2	5.4	3.5	2.8	4.9	5.9
1991.........	-7.1	-6.7	-2.2	-9.1	-0.1	1.9	3.1	-3.0	-	2.9
1992.........	-0.8	-0.4	1.3	-3.4	0.3	1.0	1.9	-9.8	-	1.8
1993.........	2.0	3.1	3.7	-0.1	1.3	1.1	1.8	6.3	1.7	0.7
1994.........	-0.6	-1.8	-5.4	3.1	2.0	0.2	2.1	-2.7	1.1	-0.1
1995.........	0.9	-0.7	-12.5	9.1	5.4	1.9	1.9	6.7	1.5	2.0
1996.........	10.8	14.8	28.4	-0.1	0.6	3.1	1.2	8.8	3.1	2.9
1997.........	-2.4	-7.7	9.4	-2.1	-0.1	0.5	-0.1	-2.0	1.0	0.5
1998.........	-12.9	-7.4	-14.4	-18.4	-2.1	-1.0	-0.4	0.5	-0.2	-1.4
1999.........	1.4	-5.0	5.2	7.8	0.2	2.4	0.6	-1.3	0.8	3.2
2000.........	22.8	1.5	50.1	29.5	4.9	4.7	0.9	-1.6	1.8	6.1
2001.........	0.6	6.0	11.1	-13.7	0.4	2.4	0.6	3.3	3.0	2.2

-. Represents or rounds to zero.

1. Change from immediate prior year.

Source: United States Census Bureau. (2002). *Statistical Abstract of the United States 2002.* Washington, D.C.: Government Printing Office. Retrieved from http://www.census.gov/prod/2003pubs/02statab/prices.pdf.

Table 2.8
Federal Budget—Receipts, Outlays, and Debt: 1960 to 2002

[**In billions of dollars (92.5 represents $92,500,000,000), except percent.** The Balanced Budget and Emergency Deficit Control Act of 1985 put all the previously off-budget federal entities into the budget and moved social security off-budget. Minus sign(-) indicates deficit or decrease.]

Year	Receipts	Outlays	Surplus or deficit(-)	Outlays as percent of GDP [1]	Gross federal debt		Held by the public		
					Total	Federal gov't account	Total	Federal Reserve System	As percent of GDP [1]
1960	92.5	92.2	0.3	17.8	290.5	53.7	236.8	26.5	56.0
1965	116.8	118.2	-1.4	17.2	322.3	61.5	260.8	39.1	46.9
1970	192.8	195.6	-2.8	19.3	380.9	97.7	283.2	57.7	37.6
1975	279.1	332.3	-53.2	21.3	541.9	147.2	394.7	85.0	34.7
1976	298.1	371.8	-73.7	21.4	629.0	151.6	477.4	94.7	36.2
TQ [2]	81.2	96.0	-14.7	21.1	643.6	148.1	495.5	96.7	35.4
1977	355.6	409.2	-53.7	20.8	706.4	157.3	549.1	105.0	35.8
1978	399.6	458.7	-59.2	20.7	776.6	169.5	607.1	115.5	35.0
1979	463.3	504.0	-40.7	20.1	829.5	189.2	640.3	115.6	33.1
1980	517.1	590.9	-73.8	21.6	909.1	197.1	711.9	120.8	33.3
1981	599.3	678.2	-79.0	22.2	994.8	205.4	789.4	124.5	32.5
1982	617.8	745.8	-128.0	23.1	1,137.3	212.7	924.6	134.5	35.2
1983	600.6	808.4	-207.8	23.5	1,371.7	234.4	1,137.3	155.5	39.9
1984	666.5	851.9	-185.4	22.2	1,564.7	257.6	1,307.0	155.1	40.8
1985	734.1	946.4	-212.3	22.9	1,817.5	310.2	1,507.4	169.8	43.9
1986	769.2	990.5	-221.2	22.5	2,120.6	379.9	1,740.8	190.9	48.2
1987	854.4	1,004.1	-149.8	21.6	2,346.1	456.2	1,889.9	212.0	50.5
1988	909.3	1,064.5	-155.2	21.2	2,601.3	549.5	2,051.8	229.2	51.9
1989	991.2	1,143.7	-152.5	21.2	2,868.0	677.1	2,191.0	220.1	53.1
1990	1,032.0	1,253.2	-221.2	21.8	3,206.6	794.7	2,411.8	234.4	55.9
1991	1,055.0	1,324.4	-269.4	22.3	3,598.5	909.2	2,689.3	258.6	60.7
1992	1,091.3	1,381.7	-290.4	22.2	4,002.1	1,002.1	3,000.1	296.4	64.4
1993	1,154.4	1,409.5	-255.1	21.5	4,351.4	1,102.6	3,248.8	325.7	66.3
1994	1,258.6	1,461.9	-203.3	21.1	4,643.7	1,210.2	3,433.4	355.2	66.9
1995	1,351.8	1,515.8	-164.0	20.7	4,921.0	1,316.2	3,604.8	374.1	67.2
1996	1,453.1	1,560.6	-107.5	20.3	5,181.9	1,447.4	3,734.5	390.9	67.3
1997	1,579.3	1,601.3	-22.0	19.6	5,369.7	1,596.9	3,772.8	424.5	65.6
1998	1,721.8	1,652.6	69.2	19.1	5,478.7	1,757.1	3,721.6	458.2	63.2
1999	1,827.5	1,701.9	125.5	18.7	5,606.1	1,973.2	3,632.9	496.6	61.4
2000	2,025.2	1,788.8	236.4	18.4	5,629.0	2,218.9	3,410.1	511.4	57.8
2001	1,991.0	1,863.9	127.1	18.4	5,770.3	2,450.3	3,320.0	534.1	56.8
2002, est.	1,946.1	2,052.3	-106.2	19.8	6,137.1	2,659.6	3,477.5	(NA)	59.2

NA. Not available.

1. Gross domestic product as of fiscal year.

2. Prior to fiscal year 1977 the federal fiscal years began on July 1 and ended on June 30. In calendar year 1976 the July-September period was a separate accounting period (known as the transition quarter or TQ) to bridge the period required to shift to the new fiscal year.

Source: United States Census Bureau. (2002). *Statistical Abstract of the United States 2002.* Washington, D.C.: Government Printing Office. Retrieved from http://www.census.gov/prod/2003pubs/02statab/fedgov.pdf.

Table 2.9
Federal Budget Outlays—Defense, Human and Physical Resources, and Net Interest
Payments: 1980 to 2002

[In billions of dollars (590.9 represents $590,900,000,000). For fiscal year ending in year shown. Minus sign (-) indicates offsets.]

Outlays	1980	1990	1995	1998	1999	2000	2001	2002, est.
Federal outlays, total	590.9	1,253.2	1,515.8	1,652.6	1,701.9	1,788.8	1,863.9	2,052.3
National defense.	134.0	299.3	272.1	268.5	274.9	294.5	308.5	348.0
Human resources	313.4	619.3	923.8	1,033.4	1,057.7	1,115.4	1,196.1	1,315.3
Education, training, employment and social services.	31.8	37.2	51.0	50.5	50.6	53.8	57.3	71.7
Health	23.2	57.7	115.4	131.4	141.1	154.5	172.6	195.2
Medicare	32.1	98.1	159.9	192.8	190.4	197.1	217.5	226.4
Income security.	86.6	148.7	223.7	237.7	242.4	253.5	269.8	310.7
Social security.	118.5	248.6	335.8	379.2	390.0	409.4	433.1	459.7
Veterans benefits and services.	21.2	29.1	37.9	41.8	43.2	47.1	45.8	51.5
Physical resources	66.0	126.0	59.1	74.7	81.9	84.7	99.7	112.1
Energy.	10.2	3.3	4.9	1.3	0.9	-1.1	0.1	0.6
Natural resources and environment. . .	13.9	17.1	21.9	22.3	24.0	25.0	26.3	30.2
Commerce and housing credit	9.4	67.6	-17.8	1.0	2.6	3.2	6.0	3.8
Transportation.	21.3	29.5	39.4	40.3	42.5	46.9	55.2	62.1
Community and regional development .	11.3	8.5	10.7	9.8	11.9	10.6	12.0	15.4
Net interest	52.5	184.4	232.2	241.2	229.8	223.0	206.2	178.4
International affairs.	12.7	13.8	16.4	13.1	15.2	17.2	16.6	23.5
Agriculture	8.8	12.0	9.8	12.2	23.0	36.6	26.6	28.8
Administration of justice	4.6	10.0	16.2	22.9	26.1	28.0	30.4	34.4
General government.	13.0	10.6	14.0	15.6	15.6	13.3	15.2	18.3
Undistributed offsetting receipts	-19.9	-36.6	-44.5	-47.2	-40.4	-42.6	-55.2	-55.2

Source: United States Census Bureau. (2002). *Statistical Abstract of the United States 2002*. Washington, D.C.: Government Printing Office. Retrieved from http://www.census.gov/prod/2003pubs/02statab/fedgov.pdf.

Table 2.10
Priorities in Public Spending for the Different Nations

HDI rank		Public expenditure on education (as % of GDP) [a]		Public expenditure on health (as % of GDP)		Military expenditure (as % of GDP) [b]		Total debt service (as % of GDP)	
		1990 [c]	1998-2000 [d]	1990	2000	1990	2001	1990	2001
High human development									
1	Norway	7.1	6.8 [e]	6.4	6.6	2.9	1.8	..	..
2	Iceland	5.4	..	6.8	7.5	0.0	0.0	..	..
3	Sweden	7.4	7.8 [e]	7.6	6.5	2.7	2.0	..	..
4	Australia	5.1	4.7 [e,f]	5.3	6.0	2.2	1.7	..	..
5	Netherlands	6.0	4.8 [e]	5.7	5.5	2.5	1.6	..	..
6	Belgium	5.0	5.9 [e]	6.6	6.2	2.4	1.3	..	..
7	United States	5.2	4.8 [e]	4.7	5.8	5.3	3.1	..	..
8	Canada	6.5	5.5 [e]	6.8	6.6	2.0	1.2	..	..
9	Japan	..	3.5 [e]	4.6	6.0	0.9	1.0	..	..
10	Switzerland	5.1	5.5 [e]	5.7	5.9	1.8	1.1	..	..
11	Denmark	..	8.2 [e]	7.0	6.8	2.0	1.6	..	..
12	Ireland	5.2	4.4	4.8	5.1	1.2	0.7	..	..
13	United Kingdom	4.9	4.5 [e]	5.1	5.9	3.9	2.5	..	..
14	Finland	5.6	6.1	6.4	5.0	1.6	1.2	..	..
15	Luxembourg	3.0	3.7 [e,f]	5.7	5.3	0.9	0.8	..	..
16	Austria	5.4	5.8 [e]	5.2	5.6	1.0	0.8	..	..
17	France	5.4	5.8 [e]	6.7	7.2	3.5	2.5	..	..
18	Germany	..	4.6	5.9	8.0	2.8 [g]	1.5	..	..
19	Spain	4.4	4.5 [e]	5.2	5.4	1.8	1.2	..	..
20	New Zealand	6.2	6.1 [e]	5.8	6.2	1.9	1.2	..	..
21	Italy	3.1	4.5 [e]	6.3	6.0	(.)	2.0	..	..
22	Israel	6.3	7.3	3.8	8.3	12.2	7.7	..	..
23	Portugal	4.2	5.8 [e]	4.1	5.8	2.7	2.1	..	..
24	Greece	2.5	3.8	4.7	4.6	4.7	4.6	..	..
25	Cyprus	3.5 [h]	5.4 [j]	..	4.3	5.0	3.1	..	..
26	Hong Kong, China (SAR)	..	..	1.6	..	..	..	..	..
27	Barbados	7.8	7.1	5.0	4.1	..	..	8.2	2.5
28	Singapore	..	3.7	1.0	1.2	4.8	5.0	..	..
29	Slovenia	..	..	..	6.8	..	1.4	..	..
30	Korea, Rep. of	3.5	3.8 [e]	1.8	2.6	3.7	2.8	3.3	6.2
31	Brunei Darussalam	..	4.8	1.6	2.5	6.7 [i]	6.1 [j]	..	..
32	Czech Republic	..	4.4 [e]	4.8	6.6	..	2.1	3.0	8.4
33	Malta	4.3	4.9 [f]	..	6.0	0.9	0.8	2.0	3.8
34	Argentina	1.1	4.0 [e]	4.2	4.7	1.3	1.4	4.4	9.0
35	Poland	..	5.0 [e]	4.8	4.2	2.7	1.9	1.6	8.7
36	Seychelles	7.8	7.6 [f]	3.6	4.1	4.0	1.8	5.9	2.4
37	Bahrain	4.2	3.0	..	2.8	5.1	4.1	..	..
38	Hungary	5.8	5.0 [e]	..	5.1	2.8	1.8	12.8	26.4
39	Slovakia	5.1	4.2 [e]	5.0	5.3	..	1.9	2.1	12.8
40	Uruguay	3.0	2.8 [e]	2.0	5.1	2.1	1.3	10.6	8.0
41	Estonia	..	7.5	1.9	4.7	..	1.7	..	6.9
42	Costa Rica	4.4	4.4	6.7	4.4	0.0	0.0	8.8	4.3
43	Chile	2.5	4.2 [e]	2.2	3.1	3.7	2.9	9.1	10.0
44	Qatar	3.5	3.6 [k]	..	2.5	..	..	..	..
45	Lithuania	4.6	6.4	3.0	4.3	..	1.8	..	16.1
46	Kuwait	4.8	..	4.0	2.6	48.5	11.3	..	..
47	Croatia	..	4.2 [f]	9.5	8.0	..	2.6	..	14.6
48	United Arab Emirates	1.9	1.9	0.8	2.5	4.7	2.5	..	..
49	Bahamas	4.0	..	2.8	4.4	..	..	..	..
50	Latvia	3.8	5.9	2.7	3.5	..	1.2	..	6.8

Table 2.10 (*continued*)

HDI rank	Public expenditure on education (as % of GDP)[a]		Public expenditure on health (as % of GDP)		Military expenditure (as % of GDP)[b]		Total debt service (as % of GDP)	
	1990[c]	1998-2000[d]	1990	2000	1990	2001	1990	2001
51 Saint Kitts and Nevis	2.7	2.9 [f]	2.7	3.1	..	..	1.9	6.0
52 Cuba	..	8.5	4.9	6.1	..	..[*]	..	..
53 Belarus	4.9	6.0	2.5	4.7	..	1.4	..	1.9
54 Trinidad and Tobago	3.6	4.0 [f]	2.5	2.6	..	..	8.9	2.6
55 Mexico	3.6	4.4 [e]	1.8	2.5	0.4	0.5	4.3	7.9
Medium human development								
56 Antigua and Barbuda	..	3.2	2.8	3.3	..	..	..	..
57 Bulgaria	5.2	3.4	4.1	3.0	3.5	2.7	6.6	10.1
58 Malaysia	5.2	6.2 [e]	1.5	1.5	2.6	2.2	9.8	7.1
59 Panama	4.7	5.9	4.6	5.3	1.4	1.2 [l]	6.5	11.6
60 Macedonia, TFYR	..	..	9.2	5.1	..	7.0	..	5.7
61 Libyan Arab Jamahiriya	..	..	..	1.6	..	..	..	..
62 Mauritius	3.5	3.5	..	1.9	0.3	0.2	6.5	4.5
63 Russian Federation	3.5	4.4	2.5	3.8	12.3 [m]	3.8	2.0 [n]	5.6
64 Colombia	2.5	..	1.2	5.4	2.2	3.8	9.7	7.6
65 Brazil	..	4.7	3.0	3.4	1.9	1.5	1.8	10.8
66 Bosnia and Herzegovina	..	..	..	3.1	..	9.5	..	6.3
67 Belize	4.7	6.2	2.2	2.1	1.2	..	5.0	12.1
68 Dominica	..	5.1 [f]	3.9	4.3	..	..	3.5	6.0
69 Venezuela	3.0	..	2.5	2.7	1.8 [i]	1.5	10.3	6.0
70 Samoa (Western)	3.4	4.2 [f]	2.8	3.9	..	..	2.7	2.9
71 Saint Lucia	..	5.8	2.1	2.7	..	..	1.6	3.7
72 Romania	2.8	3.5 [f]	2.8	1.9	4.6	2.5	(.)	6.7
73 Saudi Arabia	6.5	9.5	..	4.2	12.8	11.3	..	..
74 Thailand	3.5	5.4 [e]	0.9	2.1	2.3	1.4	6.2	17.5
75 Ukraine	5.2	4.4	3.0	2.9	..	2.7	..	6.0
76 Kazakhstan	3.2	..	3.2	2.7	..	1.0	..	14.9
77 Suriname	8.1	..	3.5	5.5	..	..	..	..
78 Jamaica	4.7	6.3 [e]	2.6	2.6	..	..	14.4	8.3
79 Oman	3.1	3.9	2.0	2.3	18.3	12.2	7.0	4.4 [j]
80 St. Vincent & the Grenadines	6.4	9.3	4.4	4.1	..	..	2.2	3.9
81 Fiji	4.6	5.2 [f]	2.0	2.5	2.3	2.2	7.7	1.5
82 Peru	2.2	3.3 [e]	1.3	2.8	2.4	1.7	1.8	4.1
83 Lebanon	..	3.0	..	..	7.6	5.5	3.5	8.7
84 Paraguay	1.1	5.0	0.7	3.0	1.2	0.9	6.2	5.0
85 Philippines	2.9	4.2 [e]	1.5	1.6	1.4	1.0	8.1	10.9
86 Maldives	4.0	3.9 [f]	3.6	6.3	..	..	4.1	3.7
87 Turkmenistan	4.3	..	4.0	4.6	..	3.8 [j]	..	7.6
88 Georgia	..	..	3.0	0.7	..	0.7	..	2.5
89 Azerbaijan	..	4.2	2.7	0.6	..	2.6	..	2.4
90 Jordan	8.4	5.0 [e]	3.6	4.2	9.9	8.6	15.6	7.6
91 Tunisia	6.0	6.8 [e]	3.0	..	2.0	1.6	11.6	6.8
92 Guyana	3.4	4.1 [f]	2.9	4.2	0.9	..	74.5	6.3
93 Grenada	5.1	4.2 [f]	3.3	3.4	..	..	1.5	4.1
94 Dominican Republic	..	2.5	1.6	1.8	..	..	3.3	2.9
95 Albania	5.8	..	3.3	2.1	5.9	1.2	0.1	0.9
96 Turkey	2.2	3.5 [e]	2.2	3.6	3.5	4.9	4.9	15.2
97 Ecuador	2.8	1.6	1.5	1.2	1.9	2.1 [l]	10.1	8.6
98 Occupied Palestinian Territories	..	..	..	..	..	..	..	..
99 Sri Lanka	2.6	3.1	1.5	1.8	2.1	3.9	4.8	4.5
100 Armenia	7.0	2.9	..	3.2	..	3.1	..	2.6

Table 2.10 (*continued*)

HDI rank	Public expenditure on education (as % of GDP)[a]		Public expenditure on health (as % of GDP)		Military expenditure (as % of GDP)[b]		Total debt service (as % of GDP)	
	1990[c]	1998-2000[d]	1990	2000	1990	2001	1990	2001
101 Uzbekistan	..	..	4.6	2.6	..	1.1	..	7.4
102 Kyrgyzstan	8.3	5.4	4.7	2.2	..	1.7	..	11.6
103 Cape Verde	..	4.4 [f]	..	1.8	..	0.8	1.7	2.4
104 China	2.3	2.1	2.2	1.9	2.7	2.3	2.0	2.1
105 El Salvador	1.9	2.3 [f]	1.4	3.8	2.7	0.8	4.3	2.8
106 Iran, Islamic Rep. of	4.1	4.4	1.5	2.5	2.7	4.8	0.5	1.1
107 Algeria	5.3	..	3.0	3.0	1.5	3.5 [j]	14.2	8.0
108 Moldova, Rep. of	..	4.0	4.4	2.9	..	0.4	..	12.8
109 Viet Nam	..	..	0.9	1.3	7.9	..	2.7	3.7
110 Syrian Arab Republic	4.1	4.1	0.4	1.6	6.9	6.2	9.7	1.4
111 South Africa	6.2	5.5	3.1	3.7	3.8	1.6	..	3.8
112 Indonesia	1.0	..	0.6	0.6	1.8	1.1	8.7	10.7
113 Tajikistan	9.7	2.1	4.9	0.9	..	1.2	..	7.6
114 Bolivia	2.3	5.5	2.1	4.9	2.4	1.6	7.9	6.8
115 Honduras	..	4.0 [f]	3.3	4.3	..	..	12.8	5.3
116 Equatorial Guinea	..	0.6	1.0	2.3	..	..	3.9	0.2
117 Mongolia	12.1	2.3	6.4	4.6	5.7	2.3	..	4.3
118 Gabon	..	3.9 [f]	2.0	2.1	..	..	3.0	10.5
119 Guatemala	1.4	1.7	1.8	2.3	1.5	1.0	2.8	2.2
120 Egypt	3.7	..	1.8	1.8	3.9	2.6	7.1	2.0
121 Nicaragua	3.4	5.0	7.0	2.3	2.1	1.1	1.6	..
122 São Tomé and Principe	..	..	..	1.6	..	..	4.9	8.5
123 Solomon Islands	..	3.6	5.0	5.6	..	..	5.5	2.7
124 Namibia	7.6	8.1	3.7	4.2	5.6 [i]	2.8	..	..
125 Botswana	6.7	8.6 [f]	1.7	3.8	4.1	3.5	2.8	1.0
126 Morocco	5.3	5.5 [f]	0.9	1.3	4.1	4.1	6.9	7.7
127 India	3.9	4.1 [e]	0.9	0.9	2.7	2.5	2.6	1.9
128 Vanuatu	4.6	7.3 [f]	2.6	2.4	..	..	1.6	0.8
129 Ghana	3.2	4.1 [f]	1.3	2.2	0.4	0.6	6.3	6.0
130 Cambodia	..	1.9	..	2.0	3.1	3.0	2.7	0.6
131 Myanmar	..	0.5	1.0	0.4	3.4	2.3 [j]	..	..
132 Papua New Guinea	..	2.3 [f]	3.1	3.6	2.1	0.8 [i]	17.2	9.1
133 Swaziland	5.7	1.5	1.9	3.0	1.5	1.5	5.3	2.2
134 Comoros	..	3.8	2.9	3.2	..	..	0.4	1.0
135 Lao People's Dem. Rep.	..	2.3	0.0	1.3	..	2.1	1.1	2.5
136 Bhutan	..	5.2	1.7	3.7	..	..	1.8	1.2
137 Lesotho	6.1	10.1	2.6	5.2	3.9	3.1 [j]	3.7	8.6
138 Sudan	0.9	..	0.7	1.0	3.6	3.0 [j]	0.4	0.4
139 Bangladesh	1.5	2.5	0.7	1.4	1.0	1.3	2.5	1.4
140 Congo	5.0	4.2	1.5	1.5	..	..	19.0	3.4
141 Togo	5.5	4.8	1.4	1.5	3.2	..	5.3	2.6
Low human development								
142 Cameroon	3.2	3.2	0.9	1.1	1.5	1.4	4.7	4.0
143 Nepal	2.0	3.7	0.8	0.9	0.9	1.1	1.9	1.6
144 Pakistan	2.6	1.8 [f]	1.1	0.9	5.8	4.5	4.8	5.0
145 Zimbabwe	..	10.4 [e, f]	3.2	3.1	4.5	3.2	5.4	1.5
146 Kenya	6.7	6.4	2.4	1.8	2.9	1.8	9.3	4.1
147 Uganda	1.5	2.3 [f]	..	1.5	3.0	2.1	3.4	0.9
148 Yemen	..	10.0	1.1	..	8.5	6.1	3.5	3.1
149 Madagascar	2.1	3.2	..	2.5	1.2	1.2 [i]	7.2	1.5
150 Haiti	1.4	1.1 [f]	1.2	2.4	..	..	1.2	0.7
151 Gambia	3.8	2.7 [f]	2.2	3.4	1.1	1.0	11.9	2.7

Table 2.10 (*continued*)

HDI rank		Public expenditure on education (as % of GDP)[a]		Public expenditure on health (as % of GDP)		Military expenditure (as % of GDP)[b]		Total debt service (as % of GDP)	
		1990[e]	1998-2000[d]	1990	2000	1990	2001	1990	2001
152	Nigeria	0.9	..	1.0	0.5	0.9	1.1	11.7	6.2
153	Djibouti	..	3.5 [f]	..	..	6.3	..	3.6	1.8
154	Mauritania	..	3.0 [f]	..	3.4	3.8	2.1 [l]	14.3	8.9
155	Eritrea	..	4.8	..	2.8	..	27.5 [l]	..	1.0
156	Senegal	3.9	3.2 [f]	0.7	2.6	2.0	1.5	5.7	4.6
157	Guinea	..	1.9 [f]	2.0	1.9	2.4 [i]	1.7	6.0	3.5
158	Rwanda	..	2.8 [f]	1.7	2.7	3.7	3.9	0.8	1.1
159	Benin	..	3.2 [f]	1.6	1.6	1.8	..	2.1	2.1
160	Tanzania, U. Rep. of	3.2	2.1 [f]	1.6	2.8	2.0 [i]	1.3 [l]	4.2 [o]	1.6 [o]
161	Côte d'Ivoire	..	4.6	1.5	1.0	1.5	..	11.7	5.9
162	Malawi	3.3	4.1 [f]	..	3.6	1.3	0.8	7.1	2.2
163	Zambia	2.4	2.3	2.6	3.5	3.7	0.6 [i]	6.2	3.6
164	Angola	3.9	2.7	1.4	2.0	5.8	3.1	3.2	19.7
165	Chad	..	2.0 [f]	..	2.5	..	1.5	0.7	1.5
166	Guinea-Bissau	..	2.1	1.1	2.6	..	3.1	3.4	11.7
167	Congo, Dem. Rep. of the	..	..	..	1.1	..	..	3.7	0.3
168	Central African Republic	2.2	1.9	..	1.4	1.6 [i]	..	2.0	1.4
169	Ethiopia	3.4	4.8	0.9	1.8	8.5	6.2	3.4	2.9
170	Mozambique	3.9	2.4 [f]	3.6	2.7	10.1	2.3	3.2	2.4
171	Burundi	3.4	3.4	1.1	1.6	3.4	8.1	3.7	3.3
172	Mali	..	2.8 [f]	1.6	2.2	2.1	2.0	2.8	3.0
173	Burkina Faso	2.7	..	1.0	3.0	3.0	1.6	1.2	1.5
174	Niger	3.2	2.7 [f]	..	1.8	..	1.1 [i]	4.0	1.3
175	Sierra Leone	..	1.0	..	2.6	0.9	3.6 [i]	3.3	12.8

a. Data refer to total public expenditure on education, including current and capital expenditure.

b. As a result of limitations in the data, comparisons of military expenditure data over time and across countries should be made with caution.

c. Data may not be comparable between countries as a result of differences in methods of data collection.

d. Data refer to the most recent year available during the period specified.

e. Preliminary UNESCO Institute for Statistics estimate, subject to further revision.

f. Data refer to a UNESCO Institute for Statistics estimate where no national estimate is available.

g. Data refer to the Federal Republic of Germany before reunification.

h. Data refer to the Office of Greek Education only.

i. Data refer to 1991.

j. Data refer to 2000.

k. Data refer to a national estimate.

l. Data refer to 1999.

m. Data refer to the former Soviet Union.

n. Data refer to the debt of the former Soviet Union on the assumption that 100% of all outstanding external debt as of December 1991 has become a liability of the Russian Federation.

o. Data refer to mainland Tanzania only.

Source: United Nations Development Programme. (2003). *Human Development Report 2003.* Table 17. "Priorites in Public Spending (295–8)." New York: Oxford University Press. Retrieved from http://www.undp.org/hdr2003/pdf/hdr03_complete.pdf. Copyright 2003 by the United Nations Development Programme. Used by permission of Oxford University Press, Inc.

Table 2.11
United States Gross Domestic Product and Social Welfare Expenditures under Public Programs, Fiscal Years: 1965 to 1995[1]

Item	1965	1970	1975	1980	1985	1990 [2]	1992 [2]	1993 [2]	1994 [2]	1995
	Amount (in millions)									
Gross domestic product	$701,000	$1,023,100	$1,590,800	$2,718,900	$4,108,000	$5,682,900	$6,149,300	$6,476,600	$6,837,100	$7,186,900
Total social welfare expenditures [3]	77,084	145,979	288,967	492,213	731,840	1,048,951	1,266,504	1,366,743	1,435,714	1,505,136
Social insurance	28,123	54,691	123,013	229,754	369,595	513,822	618,938	659,210	683,779	705,483
Public aid	6,283	16,488	41,447	72,703	98,362	146,811	207,953	221,000	238,025	253,530
Health and medical programs	6,155	10,030	16,535	26,762	38,643	61,684	70,143	74,706	80,130	85,507
Veterans' programs	6,031	9,078	17,019	21,466	27,042	30,916	35,642	36,378	37,895	39,072
Education	28,108	50,846	80,834	121,050	172,048	258,332	292,145	331,997	344,091	365,625
Housing	318	701	3,172	6,879	12,598	19,468	20,151	20,782	27,032	29,361
Other social welfare	2,066	4,145	6,947	13,599	13,552	17,918	21,532	22,670	24,762	26,558
All health and medical care [4]	9,302	24,801	51,022	99,145	170,665	274,472	353,174	381,710	408,780	435,075
	As percent of gross domestic product									
Gross domestic product	100.0	100.0	100.0	100.0	100.0	100.0	100.0	100.0	100.0	100.0
Total social welfare expenditures	11.0	14.3	18.2	18.1	17.8	18.5	20.6	21.1	21.0	20.9
Social insurance	4.0	5.3	7.7	8.5	9.0	9.0	10.1	10.2	10.0	9.8
Public aid	.9	1.6	2.6	2.7	2.4	2.6	3.4	3.4	3.5	3.5
Health and medical programs	.9	1.0	1.0	1.0	.9	1.1	1.1	1.2	1.2	1.2
Veteransí programs	.9	.9	1.1	.8	.7	.5	.6	.6	.6	.5
Education	4.0	5.0	5.1	4.5	4.2	4.5	4.8	5.1	5.0	5.1
Housing	(5)	.1	.2	.3	.3	.3	.3	.3	.4	.4
Other social welfare	.3	.4	.4	.5	.3	.3	.4	.4	.4	.4
All health and medical care	1.3	2.4	3.2	3.6	4.2	4.8	5.7	5.9	6.0	6.1

1. Through 1976, fiscal year ended June 30 for federal government, most states, and some localities. Beginning in 1977, federal fiscal year ended September 30.

2. Revised data.

3. Represents program and administrative expenditures from federal, state and local public revenues and trust funds under public law. Includes workers' compensation and temporary disability insurance payments made through private carriers and self-insures. Includes capital outlay and some expenditures abroad.

4. Combines "health and medical programs" with medical services provided in connection with social insurance, public aid, veterans', and "other social welfare" categories.

5. Less than 0.05 percent.

Source: Social Security Administration. (2001). *Annual Statistical Supplement, 2001 to the Social Security Bulletin.* Baltimore: Social Security Administration, Office of Policy. Retrieved from http://www.ssa.gov/policy/docs/statcomps/supplement/2001/supp01.pdf.

Table 2.12
Social Welfare Expenditures under Public Programs in the United States: 1965 to 1995[1]

Item	1965	1970	1975	1980	1985	1990[2]	1992[2]	1993[2]	1994[2]	1995
Total	$77,058.0	$145,979.2	$288,966.0	$492,212.7	$731,840.1	$1,048,950.8	$1,266,502.8	$1,366,743.1	$1,435,714.3	$1,505,136.4
Social insurance	28,122.8	54,691.2	123,013.1	229,754.4	369,595.2	513,821.8	618,938.1	659,209.9	683,778.7	705,483.3
OASDHI [3]	16,997.5	36,835.4	78,429.9	152,110.4	257,535.1	355,264.5	416,564.0	449,276.8	477,339.7	496,355.8
Health Insurance (Medicare) [4]	...	7,149.0	14,781.4	34,991.5	71,384.3	109,709.0	132,246.3	148,093.5	161,392.7	164,713.3
Railroad Retirement [3]	1,128.1	1,609.9	3,085.1	4,768.7	6,275.6	7,229.9	7,737.1	7,920.6	8,025.2	8,106.2
Public employee retirement [5]	4,528.5	8,658.7	20,118.6	39,490.2	63,044.0	90,391.2	103,698.7	112,559.5	119,253.1	128,001.8
Unemployment insurance and employment service [6]	3,002.6	3,819.5	13,835.9	18,326.4	18,343.8	19,973.7	41,166.0	40,720.8	31,251.1	26,302.0
Railroad unemployment insurance	76.7	38.5	41.6	155.4	138.4	64.6	67.4	60.3	53.5	48.4
Railroad temporary disability insurance	46.5	61.1	32.9	68.7	50.6	40.3	27.5	25.9	29.3	30.0
State temporary disability insurance [7]	483.5	717.7	990.0	1,377.4	1,944.1	3,224.2	4,009.4	3,316.0	3,200.8	3,189.1
Workers' compensation [8]	1,859.4	2,950.4	6,479.1	13,457.2	22,263.6	37,633.4	45,668.0	45,330.0	44,626.0	43,450.0
Public aid	6,283.5	16,487.8	41,446.6	72,703.1	98,361.8	146,811.1	207,953.0	220,999.8	238,025.3	253,530.0
Public assistance [9]	5,874.9	14,433.5	27,409.4	45,064.3	66,170.2	105,093.8	152,018.2	160,625.0	171,755.1	187,219.0
Supplemental Security Income [10]	...	...	6,091.6	8,226.5	11,840.0	17,230.4	23,423.2	26,506.2	30,085.5	30,138.0
Food Stamps	35.6	577.0	4,693.9	9,083.3	12,512.7	16,254.5	23,232.9	24,496.7	25,273.6	25,319.0
Other [11]	373.0	1,477.3	3,251.7	10,329.0	7,838.9	8,232.4	9,278.7	9,371.9	10,911.1	10,854.0
Health and medical programs [12]	6,129.0	10,030.0	16,535.0	26,762.0	38,643.0	61,684.0	70,143.0	74,706.0	80,130.0	85,507.0
Hospital and medical care [13]	3,391.0	5,407.0	8,729.0	12,286.0	16,373.0	25,971.0	28,697.0	30,617.0	31,562.0	31,904.0
Maternal and child health program [14]	239.0	450.0	567.0	870.0	1,222.0	1,865.0	2,106.0	2,185.0	2,272.0	2,348.0
Medical research	1,227.0	1,684.0	2,648.0	4,924.0	6,903.0	10,848.0	12,599.0	12,779.0	13,988.0	14,982.0
School health (education agencies)	140.0	247.0	352.0	575.0	790.0	1,113.0	1,230.0	1,309.0	1,384.0	1,667.0
Other public health activities	614.0	1,312.0	2,727.0	6,484.0	11,223.0	19,354.0	22,976.0	24,772.0	27,685.0	30,808.0
Medical facilities construction	518.0	930.0	1,512.0	1,623.0	2,132.0	2,533.0	2,535.0	3,044.0	3,239.0	3,798.0
Veterans' programs	6,031.1	9,078.1	17,018.9	21,465.5	27,042.3	30,916.2	35,642.0	36,378.3	37,894.8	39,072.0
Pensions and compensation [15]	4,141.4	5,393.8	7,578.5	11,306.0	14,333.0	15,792.6	16,539.3	17,205.2	17,481.0	18,070.4
Health and medical programs	1,228.7	1,784.1	3,516.8	6,203.9	9,493.2	12,004.1	15,442.0	15,410.5	16,231.4	16,654.4
Education	40.9	1,018.5	4,433.8	2,400.7	1,170.8	522.8	772.0	937.7	1,098.3	1,118.2
Life insurance [16]	434.3	502.3	556.1	664.5	795.5	1,037.8	1,113.7	904.7	971.5	946.3
Welfare and other	185.8	379.4	933.7	890.4	1,249.8	1,558.9	1,775.0	1,920.2	2,112.6	2,282.7
Education	28,107.8	50,845.5	80,834.1	121,049.6	172,047.5	258,331.6	292,144.6	331,996.8	344,091.0	365,625.3
Housing	318.1	701.2	3,171.7	6,879.0	12,598.5	19,468.5	20,150.6	20,782.3	27,032.0	29,361.1
Other social welfare	2,065.7	4,145.4	6,946.6	13,599.1	13,551.8	17,917.6	21,531.5	22,670.0	24,762.5	26,557.7
Vocational rehabilitation [17]	210.5	703.8	1,036.4	1,251.1	1,536.7	2,126.6	2,446.8	2,379.1	2,560.1	2,630.3
Institutional care [18]	789.5	201.8	296.1	482.4	379.6	629.4	684.4	721.5	783.1	874.0
Child nutrition programs [19]	617.4	896.0	2,517.6	4,852.3	5,308.5	7,165.4	8,775.8	9,392.4	10,099.1	10,653.4
Child welfare [20]	354.3	585.4	597.0	800.0	200.0	252.6	273.9	294.6	294.6	292.0
Special OEO and ACTION programs [21]	51.7	752.8	638.3	2,302.7	503.8	169.4	193.8	208.3	204.4	222.0
Social welfare, not elsewhere classified [22]	42.3	1,005.6	1,861.2	3,910.6	5,623.2	7,574.2	9,156.8	9,674.1	10,821.2	11,886.0

1. Expenditures from federal, state, and local revenues and trust funds under public law; includes capital outlays and administrative expenditures unless otherwise noted. Includes some payments abroad. Through 1976, fiscal year ended June 30 for federal government, most states, and some localities: for federal government, beginning in 1977, fiscal year ends Sept. 30.

2. Revised data.

3. Excludes financial interchange between OASDI and Railroad Retirement.

4. Hospital Insurance and Supplementary Medical Insurance. Included in total shown directly above.

5. Excludes refunds of employee contributions; includes payments to retired military personnel and survivors. Administrative expenses for federal noncontributory retirement not available.

6. Includes unemployment compensation under state programs, programs for federal military and civilian employees and trade adjustment and cash training allowances, and payments under extended, emergency, disaster, and special unemployment insurance programs.

7. Cash and medical benefits in five areas: includes private plans where applicable and state costs of administering state plans and supervising private plans. Administrative expenses of private plans and all data for Hawaii not available.

8. Cash and medical benefits paid under federal and state laws by private insurance carriers, state funds, and self-insurers. Beginning in 1956–1960, includes Alaska and Hawaii. Administrative costs of private carriers and self-insures not available. Beginning in 1969–1970, includes federal "black lung" benefit program.

9. Categorical cash and medical payments under the Social Security Act, and general assistance from state and local funds. Beginning in 1968–1969, includes work-incentive activities.

10. Income-maintenance payments began in January 1974.

11. Work relief, other emergency aid, surplus food for the needy, repatriate and refugee assistance, and work-experience training programs. Beginning 1974 includes WIC program. Beginning in 1981, includes Low-income Home Energy Assistance.

Table 2.12 (*continued*)

12. Excludes state and local expenditures for domicilliary care in institutions other than mental and tuberculosis, and services in connection with OASDI, state temporary disability insurance, workers' compensation, public assistance, vocational rehabilitation, and veterans' programs which are included in expenditures for these programs.

13. Civilian and Department of Defense programs (including medical care provided to military dependents).

14. Includes services fro disabled children.

15. Includes burial awards. Beginning in 1964–1965, includes special allowances for survivors of veterans who did not qualify under OASDI. Beginning in 1973–1974, subsistence payments to disabled veterans undergoing training shifted from the pensions and compensation to the education subgroup.

16. Excludes the service persons' group life insurance program.

17. Beginning in 1973–1974, excludes administrative expenses.

18. Federal expenditures represent primarily surplus food for institutions.

19. Surplus food for schools and programs under National School Lunch and Child Nutrition Acts.

20. Represents primarily child welfare services under the Social Security Act. Beginning in 1968–1969, excludes administrative expenses.

21. Includes domestic programs consolidated in 1971–1972 under ACTION and special Office of Economic Opportunity programs. Beginning 1988, represents ACTION funds only.

22. Federal expenditures include administrative and related expenses of the Secretary of health and Human Services; Indian welfare and guidance, aging and juvenile delinquency, and certain manpower and human development activities. State and local expenditures include amounts for antipoverty and manpower programs, day care, child placement and adoption services, foster cars, legal assistance, care of transients, and other unspecified welfare services; before 1969–1970, these amounts were included with institutional care.

Source: Social Security Administration. (2001). *Annual Statistical Supplement, 2001 to the Social Security Bulletin.* Baltimore: Social Security Administration, Office of Policy. Retrieved from http://www.ssa.gov/policy/docs/statcomps/supplement/2001/supp01.pdf.

Table 2.13
U.S. Private Social Welfare Expenditures by Category and Percent of GDP: 1980 to 1994

	[in millions]								
Category	1980	1987	1988	1989	1990	1991	1992	1993	1994
Private social welfare expenditures	$251,938	$549,423	$606,377	$676,424	$729,989	$774,096	$840,192	$887,555	$924,994
Health [1]	142,463	292,965	333,128	369,844	413,145	440,978	477,024	505,086	528,600
Personal health care	130,026	273,030	307,110	336,005	373,691	399,617	431,456	452,346	469,900
Income maintenance	53,519	143,359	148,533	166,885	164,397	170,307	186,655	194,119	204,736
Private pension payments	37,560	120,442	124,546	140,911	137,739	142,924	158,487	165,097	174,452
Life insurance	5,075	8,166	8,418	9,063	9,278	9,472	9,866	10,276	11,229
Short-term sickness and disability benefits	8,630	11,822	12,789	13,616	13,680	13,787	14,566	15,389	15,901
Long-term disability	1,282	2,293	2,295	2,892	2,926	3,172	3,143	2,900	2,895
Supplemental unemployment	972	636	485	403	774	952	593	457	259
Education [2]	33,180	65,498	72,137	80,383	87,864	93,813	100,491	107,451	105,361
Welfare and other services	22,776	47,601	52,579	59,312	64,583	68,998	76,022	80,899	86,297
Social welfare expenditures as a percent of GDP:									
Total [3]	27.4	29.1	29.2	29.6	31.3	32.9	34.3	34.8	34.5
Public [4]	18.6	18.7	18.5	18.5	18.5	19.8	20.6	21.1	21.8
Private [5]	9.3	11.7	12.0	12.4	12.8	13.2	13.6	13.7	13.5

1. Includes program administration and net cost of health insurance, research, and construction of medical facilities.

2. Includes construction.

3. Represents sum of public and private expenditures as a percent of GDP, after adjustment for elimination of overlap. The overlap occurs when payments received under public or private income-maintenance programs are used to purchases medical care, educational services, or residential care.

4. Represents fiscal year expenditures as a percent of federal fiscal year GDP.

5. Represents calendar year expenditures as a percent of calendar year GDP.

Source: Social Security Administration. (2001). *Annual Statistical Supplement, 2001 to the Social Security Bulletin.* Baltimore: Social Security Administration, Office of Policy. Retrieved from http://www.ssa.gov/policy/docs/statcomps/supplement/2001/supp01.pdf.

Table 2.14
Income Tax (Percentage of Gross Wages), 1979
to 1999—Single Individual

	1979	1985	1991	1993	1994	1995	1996	1997	1998	1999[1]
Australia	21.9	21.9	21.5	21.6	22.1	22.5	22.7	23.3	23.9	
Austria	9.3	10.2	7.5	8.6	7.5	8.9	9.2	10.2	10.5	10.9
Belgium	15.2	26.4	25.9	26.1	26.1	27.2	27.4	27.6	27.8	28.0
Canada	18.3	19.4	20.4	21.1	21.5	21.7	22.2	22.1	21.8	21.5
Czech Republic	–	–	–	8.5	9.4	10.0	10.0	10.4	10.3	10.2
Denmark	35.7	40.0	44.2	44.4	38.3	37.4	36.0	35.1	33.7	33.5
Finland	26.7	30.5	28.3	28.6	28.5	29.3	29.5	28.0	27.8	27.3
France	8.5	7.4	8.1	8.5	8.7	8.8	8.9	10.5	14.1	14.2
Germany	16.0	18.1	18.4	18.3	18.8	20.8	21.0	21.2	21.1	21.2
Greece	1.4	3.2	3.6	1.7	1.4	1.7	1.9	2.0	2.4	2.9
Hungary	–	–	–	–	–	16.4	18.1	17.8	17.4	17.3
Iceland	–	14.5	17.9	19.7	20.5	20.4	21.5	21.2	21.4	22.0
Ireland	23.7	26.8	24.7	23.9	23.1	22.4	22.3	20.5	19.7	19.4
Italy[2]	11.6	18.4	16.3	15.8	16.7	17.5	18.1	18.8	19.9	20.2
Japan	7.6	8.8	8.5	8.4	8.7	6.4	6.7	8.0	6.8	6.5
Korea	–	–	–	–	–	2.5	1.9	1.7	1.6	1.2
Luxembourg	17.4	16.7	11.8	12.7	12.9	13.1	13.4	13.8	11.6	11.5
Mexico	–	–	6.1	6.5	7.1	2.5	0.0	-1.2	0.0	0.1
Netherlands	14.8	11.3	11.5	12.2	7.8	6.7	5.8	6.5	7.2	6.7
New Zealand	26.0	27.9	23.8	24.0	24.3	24.5	22.3	21.6	20.0	19.4
Norway	25.7	22.7	24.4	20.9	21.0	21.8	21.9	21.7	21.8	21.6
Poland	–	–	–	17.2	–	18.1	18.0	16.9	15.8	15.5
Portugal	4.4	6.9	5.9	6.8	7.0	7.0	7.1	7.2	7.1	6.6
Spain	10.1	10.6	11.3	12.3	12.9	13.2	13.5	13.8	13.8	11.7
Sweden	36.5	35.6	28.0	28.5	28.8	28.7	28.8	28.5	27.5	27.2
Switzerland	10.6	11.2	9.6	11.1	11.1	11.0	10.8	10.3	10.4	10.1
Turkey	42.0	22.9	27.1	27.4	25.0	25.2	23.8	23.9	23.8	14.8
United Kingdom	23.2	22.3	18.7	18.0	18.1	18.2	17.4	16.7	16.7	16.5
United States	20.6	21.8	18.4	18.3	18.2	18.1	18.2	18.2	18.1	18.2

1. Estimates.
2. As from 1990 on, data on wages have been revised to include only production workers (excluding employees).

Source: Organization of Economic Co-operation and Development. (2003). OECD Statistics at OECD Web site. Retrieved from http://www.oecdwash.org/DATA/STATS/incometaxrates.pdf. OECD Copyright. Reproduced by permission of the OECD.

Table 2.15
Income Tax (Percentage of Gross Wages), 1979 to 1999—
One-Earner Family with Two Children

	1979	1985	1991	1993	1994	1995	1996	1997	1998	1999[1]
Australia	16.8	16.8	16.8	17.0	17.8	22.5	21.5	20.8	21.6	
Austria	6.5	7.6	3.8	2.8	1.9	3.5	4.0	5.0	5.4	5.0
Belgium	8.0	19.3	15.0	15.5	15.3	16.1	16.3	16.5	16.8	17.1
Canada	9.7	10.3	12.1	10.3	10.8	11.2	12.1	12.6	12.6	12.1
Czech Republic	–	–	–	2.5	3.8	4.5	5.4	5.2	4.7	4.3
Denmark	30.3	34.3	36.0	36.2	29.9	29.4	28.8	27.8	26.6	26.7
Finland	20.9	25.3	21.8	23.3	28.5	29.3	29.5	28.0	27.8	27.3
France	0.4	0.0	1.0	1.7	1.8	1.9	2.7	3.7	7.6	7.6
Germany	9.9	10.9	8.7	7.9	8.3	9.6	1.6	1.0	1.3	0.1
Greece	0.0	0.0	0.5	0.5	0.4	0.8	1.1	2.5	2.8	3.3
Hungary	–	–	–	–	–	16.4	18.1	17.8	17.4	11.5
Iceland	–	6.4	0.3	2.5	3.3	3.6	5.9	6.8	8.5	10.1
Ireland	11.5	16.2	16.2	15.9	15.5	15.4	15.4	14.1	12.9	10.1
Italy[2]	9.4	16.2	12.7	11.9	13.0	14.0	14.4	15.3	15.7	16.1
Japan	1.8	2.8	2.4	2.8	3.0	1.6	2.0	2.6	0.7	1.5
Korea	–	–	–	–	–	1.5	0.8	0.9	0.7	0.4
Luxembourg	3.4	2.2	0.0	0.0	0.0	0.0	0.0	0.0	0.0	0.0
Mexico	–	–	6.1	6.5	7.1	2.5	0.0	−1.2	0.0	0.1
Netherlands	12.5	8.4	10.1	9.5	5.1	4.4	4.4	3.5	5.9	4.8
New Zealand	17.0	24.8	20.8	22.2	24.3	22.4	18.8	16.2	14.8	15.0
Norway	17.5	15.0	17.8	15.9	16.1	17.0	17.1	17.1	17.4	17.4
Poland	–	–	–	15.3	–	16.1	15.9	14.7	13.5	13.1
Portugal	4.0	6.0	1.2	1.1	3.3	3.3	3.5	3.1	3.0	2.5
Spain	6.1	5.9	6.4	5.6	6.1	6.4	6.6	6.8	6.4	2.5
Sweden	33.7	33.9	28.0	28.5	28.8	28.7	28.8	28.5	27.5	27.2
Switzerland	6.3	6.4	5.4	5.7	5.7	5.7	5.6	5.1	5.2	4.8
Turkey	42.0	22.9	27.1	27.4	25.0	25.2	23.8	23.9	23.8	14.8
United Kingdom	19.3	17.9	15.4	15.0	15.7	16.6	15.7	15.1	15.1	15.4
United States	11.6	14.5	11.3	11.3	11.3	11.0	10.4	10.7	10.2	11.0

1. Estimates.

2. As from 1990 on, data on wages have been revised to include only production workers (excluding employees).

Source: Organization of Economic Co-operation and Development. (2003). OECD Statistics at OECD Web site. Retrieved from http://www.oecdwash.org/DATA/STATS/incometaxrates.pdf. OECD Copyright. Reproduced by permission of the OECD.

Table 2.16
Taxation Schemes in OECD Countries: 2000

| | Tax Structures as % of total tax receipts | | | | | | | Highest rates of income taxes[1] | | Disposable Income of average production worker as % of gross pay[2] | |
| | Total tax receipts % of GDP | Personal income tax | Corporate income tax | Social Security Contributions | | Taxes on goods and services | Other taxes | Personal income tax % | Corporate income tax % | Single person | Married with two children[3] |
				Employees	Employers						
Australia	31.5	36.7	20.6	0.0	0.0	27.5	15.2	48.5	30.0	76.4	85.3
Austria	43.7	22.1	4.7	14.0	16.4	28.4	14.4	50.0	34.0	71.4	91.0
Belgium	45.6	31.0	8.1	9.7	18.6	25.4	7.2	56.2	40.2	58.6	78.4
Canada	35.8	36.8	11.1	5.7	8.2	24.4	13.8	43.4	38.6	74.3	84.9
Czech Republic	39.4	12.7	9.8	10.0	28.3	32.0	7.2	32.0	31.0	76.3	96.3
Denmark	48.8	52.6	4.9	3.9	0.7	32.5	5.4	59.7	30.0	56.9	69.5
Finland	46.9	30.8	11.8	4.7	18.8	29.1	4.8	53.8	29.0	68.3	76.8
France	45.3	18.0	7.0	8.9	24.9	25.8	15.4	60.4	..	73.5	85.8
Germany	37.9	25.3	4.8	17.2	19.2	28.1	5.4	51.2	38.9	58.8	81.4
Greece	37.8	13.5	11.6	16.4	13.7	36.1	8.7	40.0	..	83.5	83.0
Hungary	39.1	18.6	5.7	5.4	23.6	40.5	6.2	40.0	18.0	70.9	92.2
Iceland	37.3	34.4	3.3	0.2	7.5	45.0	9.6	45.5	18.0	78.0	103.2
Ireland	31.1	30.8	12.1	4.2	8.6	37.2	7.1	42.0	16.0	83.6	100.8
Italy	42.0	25.7	7.5	5.4	19.8	28.4	13.2	45.9	36.0	71.9	87.8
Japan	27.1	20.6	13.5	14.2	18.6	18.9	14.2	50.0	40.9	83.8	88.1
Korea	26.1	14.6	14.1	9.3	7.5	38.3	16.2	39.6	29.7	91.3	91.9
Luxembourg	41.7	18.3	17.7	11.3	11.4	27.3	14.0	39.0	30.4	77.9	103.6
Mexico	18.5	27.3[a]	..	16.4[b]	..	53.1	3.2	35.0	35.0	96.4	96.4
Netherlands	41.4	14.9	10.1	19.5	11.4	29.0	15.1	52.0	34.5	71.3	82.8
New Zealand	35.1	42.8	11.7	0.0	0.0	34.5	11.0	39.0	33.0	80.0	81.8
Norway	40.3	25.6	15.2	7.7	13.3	34.4	3.8	47.5	28.0	71.2	82.1
Poland	34.1	23.2	6.9	0.0	29.4	36.6	3.9	40.0	..	69.0	75.0
Portugal	34.5	17.5	12.2	9.5	14.7	39.9	6.2	40.0	33.0	83.5	94.8
Slovak Republic	35.8	10.0	8.3	7.7	24.2	35.9	13.9	38.0	25.0	80.7	96.9
Spain	35.2	18.7	8.6	5.5	24.3	29.8	13.1	48.0	35.0	80.8	89.6
Sweden	54.2	35.6	7.5	5.5	22.0	20.7	8.7	55.5	28.0	69.6	79.0
Switzerland	35.7	30.6	7.9	11.0	10.8	19.7	20.0	42.7	25.0	78.5	91.4
Turkey	33.4	21.5	7.0	6.5	8.7	40.7	15.6	40.6	33.0	70.0	70.0
United Kingdom	37.4	29.2	9.8	6.7	9.4	32.3	12.6	40.0	30.0	76.7	89.2
United States	29.6	42.4	8.5	10.2	11.9	15.7	11.3	45.4	45.2	75.7	88.7
EU Average[4]	41.6	25.6	9.2	9.5	15.6	30.0	10.1	48.9	31.9	72.4	86.2
OECD Average[4]	37.4	26.0	9.7	7.9	14.7	31.6	10.1	45.4	31.3	75.3	87.3

Notes: ..—not available.

1. 2002. International comparisons also have to take into account differences between countries in the width of tax brackets, the amount of tax reliefs, and rates of social security contribution. The highest rate of income taxes includes temporary special surcharges. All rates include (average) rates of state and local income taxes as reported in the OECD Tax Data Base.

2. 2002. This percentage is influenced both by the overall tax level and the relative weight of personal income taxes and employees' social security contributions in national tax mixes.

3. One-earner family. Takes account of family allowances and/or tax reliefs.

4. Unweighted.

a. Includes personal and corporate incomes not available separately.

b. Includes employees and employers social security contributions not available separately.

Source: Columbia University. (2003). *Taxation Scheme in OECD Countries 1999*. The International Clearinghouse on International Developments in Child, Youth and Family Policies Web site. Retrieved from http://www.childpolicyintl.org/contexttablespublicsector/table222.pdf.

Table 2.17
**Social Protection Expenditures in Europe as a Percent of
the GDP and Per Capita (In Euros)**

	1991		1995		2000	
	As % of GDP	Per capita In Euros	As % of GDP	Per capita In Euros	As % of GDP	Per capita In Euros
Austria	27.0	4,653	29.6	6,506	28.7	7,345
Belgium	27.1	4,420	28.1	5,867	26.7*	6,477*
Denmark	29.7	6,252	32.2	8,488	28.8	9,384
Finland	29.8	5,938	31.8	6,159	25.2 [p]	6,389 [p]
France	28.4	4,803	30.7	6,131	29.7 [p]	6,954 [p]
Germany	26.1	4,682	28.9	6,646	29.5 [p]	7,291 [p]
Greece	21.6	1,537	22.3	1,917	26.4 [p]	3,073 [p]
Iceland	17.7	3,752	19.0	3,797	19.5	6,437
Ireland	19.6	2,144	18.9	2,674	14.1	3,828
Italy	25.2	4,166	24.8	3,631	25.2 [p]	5,082 [p]
Luxembourg	22.5	5,516	23.7	7,998	21.0	9,785
Netherlands	32.6	5,068	30.9	6,340	27.4 [p]	6,928 [p]
Norway	27.3	6,092	26.9	6,927	25.4	9,911
Portugal	17.2	1,140	22.1	1,824	22.7 [p]	2,553 [p]
Spain	21.2	2,392	22.1	2,516	20.1 [p]	3,069 [p]
Sweden	34.3	7,702	35.5	7,376	32.3 [p]	9,055 [p]
United Kingdom	25.7	3,724	28.2	4,183	26.8 [p]	7,004 [p]

Notes: *. Estimated data.
p. Provisional data.

Source: Columbia University. (2003). *Social Protection Expenditures in Europe as a Percent of the GDP and Per Capita (In Euros) 1991–2000.* The International Clearinghouse on International Developments in Child, Youth and Family Policies Web Site. Retrieved from http://www.childpolicyintl.org/contexttablespublicsector/table243.pdf.

Table 2.18
Gross National Product by Country: 1990 and 2000

[61 represents $61,000,000,000]

Country	Gross national product [1]				GNP on purchasing power parity basis			
	Total (bil. dol.)		Per capita (dol.)		Total (bil. dol.)		Per capita (dol.)	
	1990	2000	1990	2000	1990	2000	1990	2000
Algeria	61	48	2,440	1,580	109	153	4,350	5,040
Argentina	104	276	3,190	7,460	240	446	7,380	12,050
Australia	300	388	17,590	20,240	280	479	16,430	24,970
Bangladesh.	31	48	280	370	110	209	1,000	1,590
Belarus.	35	29	3,460	2,870	72	76	7,030	7,550
Belgium	183	252	18,340	24,540	192	282	19,270	27,470
Brazil.	411	610	2,780	3,580	801	1,243	5,410	7,300
Bulgaria	20	12	2,260	1,520	47	45	5,340	5,560
Canada	550	650	19,790	21,130	539	836	19,400	27,170
Chile	29	70	2,190	4,590	61	138	4,690	9,100
China	368	1,063	320	840	1,587	4,951	1,400	3,920
Colombia	41	85	1,180	2,020	239	256	6,820	6,060
Congo (Kinshasa) .	8	(NA)	230	(NA)	44	(NA)	1,180	(NA)
Costa Rica	5	15	1,790	3,810	15	30	5,050	7,980
Cote dílvoire	9	10	780	600	16	24	1,320	1,500
Croatia.	(NA)	20	(NA)	4,620	34	35	7,080	7,960
Czech Republic	(NA)	54	(NA)	5,250	119	142	11,500	13,780
Denmark.	120	172	23,430	32,280	97	145	18,930	27,250
Ecuador	10	15	970	1,210	26	37	2,540	2,910
Egypt.	42	95	810	1,490	128	235	2,450	3,670
El Salvador	5	13	940	2,000	15	28	2,920	4,410
Ethiopia	8	7	160	100	25	43	480	660
Finland.	124	130	24,890	25,130	86	127	17,310	24,570
France	[2]1,142	[2]1,438	19,860	24,090	1,015	1,438	17,900	24,420
Germany	1,612	2,064	20,290	25,120	1,459	2,047	18,370	24,920
Greece.	79	126	7,770	11,960	120	178	11,770	16,860
Guatemala	8	19	970	1,680	24	43	2,770	3,770
Hong Kong	72	176	12,680	25,920	95	174	16,730	25,590
Hungary	30	47	2,880	4,710	94	120	9,030	11,990
India	332	455	390	450	1,175	2,375	1,380	2,340
Indonesia	111	120	620	570	332	596	1,860	2,830
Iran	141	107	2,590	1,680	212	376	3,890	5,910
Ireland	42	86	11,960	22,660	41	97	11,680	25,520
Israel	51	104	10,860	16,710	61	121	13,130	19,330
Italy	988	1,163	17,420	20,160	974	1,354	17,170	23,470
Japan	3,348	4,519	27,100	35,620	2,509	3,436	20,310	27,080
Kazakhstan.	(NA)	19	(NA)	1,260	99	82	6,100	5,490
Korea, South.	246	421	5,740	8,910	381	818	8,880	17,300
Lebanon	(NA)	17	(NA)	4,010	8	20	2,280	4,550
Luxembourg	12	18	31,350	42,060	10	20	24,900	45,470
Malaysia.	43	79	2,380	3,380	83	194	4,540	8,330
Mexico.	236	497	2,830	5,070	514	861	6,170	8,790
Morocco	25	34	1,030	1,180	67	99	2,780	3,450
Netherlands	285	398	19,070	24,970	263	412	17,560	25,850
New Zealand.	43	50	12,410	12,990	46	71	13,360	18,530
Nigeria	26	33	270	260	66	102	690	800
Norway.	108	155	25,490	34,530	80	133	18,950	29,630
Pakistan	43	61	390	440	147	257	1,360	1,860
Peru	17	53	780	2,080	68	120	3,150	4,660
Philippines	45	79	740	1,040	202	319	3,310	4,220
Poland	(NA)	162	(NA)	4,190	204	348	5,360	9,000
Portugal	64	111	6,420	11,120	110	170	11,110	16,990
Romania.	40	37	1,720	1,670	145	143	6,240	6,360
Russia	(NA)	241	(NA)	1,660	1,492	1,165	10,060	8,010
Saudi Arabia	105	150	6,620	7,230	160	236	10,120	11,390
Singapore.	36	99	11,740	24,740	40	100	13,130	24,910
Slovakia	18	20	3,340	3,700	48	60	9,040	11,040
Slovenia	(NA)	20	(NA)	10,050	24	34	12,070	17,310
South Africa	102	129	2,890	3,020	280	392	7,950	9,160
Spain	458	595	11,790	15,080	498	760	12,810	19,260
Sri Lanka	8	16	470	850	34	67	1,990	3,460
Sweden	214	241	25,050	27,140	151	213	17,610	23,970
Switzerland	225	274	33,510	38,140	169	219	25,190	30,450
Syria	11	15	940	940	26	54	2,150	3,340
Thailand	84	122	1,520	2,000	211	384	3,790	6,320
Turkey	128	202	2,280	3,100	274	459	4,890	7,030
Ukraine	83	35	1,600	700	355	183	6,850	3,700
United Arab Emirates	37	(NA)	19,930	(NA)	40	(NA)	21,520	(NA)
United Kingdom	934	1,459	16,220	24,430	952	1,407	16,540	23,550
United States	**5,846**	**9,602**	**23,440**	**34,100**	**5,847**	**9,601**	**23,440**	**34,100**
Uruguay	9	20	2,870	6,000	18	30	5,950	8,880
Uzbekistan	(NA)	9	(NA)	360	51	58	2,510	2,360
Venezuela.	52	104	2,650	4,310	96	139	4,900	5,740
Vietnam	(NA)	30	(NA)	390	64	157	970	2,000

NA. Not available.

1. Gross national product calculated using the World Bank Atlas method.

2. GNP and GNP per capita estimates include the French overseas departments of French Guians, Guadeloupe, Martinique, and Reunion.

Source: United States Census Bureau. (2002). *Statistical Abstract of the United States 2002.* Washington, D.C.: Government Printing Office. Retrieved from http://www.census.gov/prod/2003pubs/02statab/intlstat.pdf.

Table 2.19
Statistical Leading Indicators by Country: 1980 to 2000

[**Average annual percent change from previous year; derived from indexes with base 1990=100.** The coincident index changes are for calendar years and the leading index changes are for years ending June 30 because they lead the coincident indexes by about 6 months, on average. The G-7 countries are United States, Canada, France, Germany, Italy, United Kingdom, and Japan. Minus sign (-) indicates decrease.]

Country	1980	1985	1990	1992	1993	1994	1995	1996	1997	1998	1999	2000
LEADING INDEX												
Total, 13 countries	2.9	2.9	2.7	-1.1	-0.9	3.9	6.9	-0.6	3.0	2.2	-0.4	6.2
12 countries, excluding U.S.	7.7	5.5	4.4	-3.2	-3.3	3.7	6.1	-0.7	1.5	0.5	-1.6	5.3
G-7 countries	2.9	2.0	2.6	-1.6	-1.4	3.5	7.3	-0.6	3.2	2.4	-0.5	6.2
North America	-2.7	-0.4	-0.5	2.3	3.2	4.5	8.3	-0.4	5.1	4.5	1.1	7.4
United States	-3.1	-0.7	-0.4	2.6	3.1	4.2	8.2	-0.4	5.1	4.5	1.1	7.3
Canada	2.0	3.2	-2.6	-1.1	4.5	8.5	10.0	-0.9	5.3	4.6	0.7	9.4
Four European countries	3.1	2.8	1.5	0.3	-1.3	4.1	6.2	-2.3	0.1	5.4	-0.1	1.6
France	3.2	0.8	-1.0	2.7	-0.3	4.7	3.5	-3.4	1.3	3.1	-1.4	-2.0
Germany	2.0	2.1	4.4	-1.1	-4.5	2.0	8.8	-3.5	1.7	7.3	1.3	1.9
Italy	6.1	6.5	1.0	-0.9	-1.0	7.1	9.9	-0.9	-4.4	10.9	-0.6	5.6
United Kingdom	2.5	3.5	0.4	0.8	2.8	4.1	2.3	-	0.1	0.3	-0.5	1.6
Seven Pacific region countries	16.3	9.4	8.0	-6.6	-6.0	2.9	5.5	1.0	2.6	-5.3	-3.7	9.1
Australia	5.7	7.6	0.3	4.9	5.9	7.1	11.3	6.0	3.1	5.9	7.6	7.6
Taiwan	2.6	5.6	6.1	8.4	4.0	8.1	3.1	-1.6	4.2	3.8	-	4.1
Thailand	4.0	7.1	14.4	7.5	9.2	12.0	5.7	2.0	-3.3	-6.0	-1.6	5.9
Japan	19.8	10.3	8.7	-9.7	-9.3	0.6	6.5	1.5	3.5	-6.9	-5.4	10.6
Korea, South	0.4	6.9	7.1	7.0	6.3	13.1	3.1	-0.7	-2.2	-5.3	1.8	8.5
Malaysia	4.9	-1.0	2.0	-1.2	0.7	7.6	1.5	0.2	0.9	-1.0	-1.1	3.8
New Zealand	2.3	6.0	1.8	3.5	4.5	2.7	0.9	-	2.3	1.2	0.1	7.0
COINCIDENT INDEX												
Total, 13 countries	-	3.5	4.0	0.3	-0.9	2.6	5.4	5.5	6.2	4.6	8.1	7.4
12 countries, excluding U.S.	1.9	3.4	6.5	-0.4	-2.6	1.5	4.6	5.3	4.8	2.2	8.8	7.5
G-7 countries	-0.2	3.4	3.9	-	-1.3	2.2	5.2	5.7	6.3	5.2	8.3	7.4
North America	-2.5	3.7	-	1.2	2.1	4.7	8.2	9.5	9.8	7.7	12.0	6.6
United States	-2.9	3.5	-	1.4	2.1	4.7	6.7	6.1	8.4	8.5	7.3	7.4
Canada	2.2	6.3	-0.1	-0.2	1.9	5.1	13.3	20.3	13.9	5.5	24.7	4.9
Four European countries	0.6	2.3	5.4	-1.6	-5.2	1.3	4.2	1.4	4.1	9.1	9.3	13.9
France	-2.3	-1.6	6.0	-2.6	-8.6	1.0	9.0	2.7	7.9	15.8	16.8	21.3
Germany	1.9	3.1	7.3	-0.7	-4.0	1.0	3.9	-1.2	0.5	8.0	7.8	12.3
Italy	6.9	4.1	6.4	-0.9	-8.4	-1.2	-1.5	3.5	5.4	7.1	9.3	16.8
United Kingdom	-2.1	4.1	0.9	-2.7	-	4.3	3.0	2.8	5.0	3.5	0.9	1.9
Seven Pacific region countries	3.5	4.3	8.4	0.7	-0.6	1.3	2.0	2.8	1.3	-5.3	-0.8	2.3
Australia	4.2	7.2	0.6	-2.0	1.3	9.2	8.8	3.8	4.3	6.7	8.0	6.4
Taiwan	8.5	3.2	5.2	8.4	6.9	7.1	2.6	0.2	4.6	3.0	2.6	3.9
Thailand	4.2	3.3	13.0	7.1	11.8	10.2	4.5	1.6	-6.2	-12.3	6.7	3.8
Japan	4.0	4.4	9.1	-0.1	-2.2	-1.0	0.5	2.3	0.7	-5.4	-3.7	-0.1
Korea, South	-7.1	6.7	11.5	5.0	4.5	11.5	7.8	6.4	3.0	-16.9	12.4	14.9
Malaysia	-2.7	-8.2	-0.3	3.1	4.7	4.8	10.7	8.5	6.1	-5.1	5.7	10.8
New Zealand	1.4	1.3	0.6	0.8	3.3	5.4	10.6	10.3	5.5	0.6	8.4	4.6

-. Represents or rounds to zero.

Source: United States Census Bureau. (2002). *Statistical Abstract of the United States 2002.* Washington, D.C.: Government Printing Office. Retrieved from http://www.census.gov/prod/2003pubs/02statab/intlstat.pdf.

Table 2.20
Index of Industrial Production by Country: 1980 to 2001

[Annual averages of monthly data. Industrial production index measures output in the manufacturing, mining, and electric, gas and water utilities industries. Minus sign (-) indicates decrease.]

Country	Index (1995=100)								Annual percent change				
	1980	1985	1990	1994	1998	1999	2000	2001	1996-97	1997-98	1998-99	1999-00	2000-01
OECD, total.	(NA)	(NA)	(NA)	(NA)	110.6	114.4	120.8	117.7	5.0	2.2	3.4	5.6	-2.6
Canada	71.8	83.0	88.4	95.7	108.3	116.7	123.2	119.6	5.5	0.9	7.8	5.6	-2.9
Mexico [1]	80.3	85.0	95.7	108.5	127.9	133.3	141.5	136.5	9.3	6.3	4.2	6.2	-3.5
Australia	70.1	77.8	92.9	99.5	107.7	112.5	118.5	118.0	1.6	2.1	4.5	5.3	-0.4
Japan [2]	69.9	82.8	103.2	96.8	99.0	99.8	105.4	97.8	3.6	-6.6	0.8	5.6	-7.2
Korea, South [2]	22.0	36.2	66.4	89.3	106.2	131.9	154.0	156.7	5.3	-7.2	24.2	16.8	1.8
New Zealand	74.0	85.0	87.0	96.0	105.0	101.0	105.0	104.0	1.9	-	-3.8	4.0	-1.0
Austria	70.2	76.6	92.3	95.3	116.2	123.2	134.1	134.3	5.9	8.6	6.0	8.8	0.1
Belgium [2]	83.4	86.8	99.3	93.9	108.8	109.7	115.6	114.8	4.7	3.4	0.8	5.4	-0.7
Czech Republic [2] . . .	(X)	(X)	144.9	100.7	108.3	104.8	110.5	118.0	4.4	1.7	-3.2	5.4	6.8
Denmark	63.0	77.0	86.0	96.0	110.0	113.0	120.0	122.0	5.9	1.9	2.7	6.2	1.7
Finland	66.4	76.7	86.9	94.1	122.5	129.0	143.9	142.2	9.3	8.1	5.3	11.6	-1.2
France	89.5	89.5	100.4	98.0	110.0	112.4	116.3	117.3	3.9	5.7	2.2	3.5	0.9
Germany	85.6	88.3	103.2	98.8	108.5	110.4	117.2	117.9	3.5	4.2	1.8	6.2	0.6
Greece	92.6	99.2	101.9	98.2	109.8	114.1	114.7	(NA)	1.3	7.1	3.9	0.5	(NA)
Hungary [2]	116.7	128.1	113.8	95.5	129.1	142.4	168.3	175.2	11.1	12.5	10.3	18.2	4.1
Ireland	34.2	43.9	63.2	84.1	142.3	174.6	201.5	221.0	15.3	14.3	22.7	15.4	9.7
Italy	77.2	73.9	93.2	95.2	102.9	102.9	107.8	106.5	3.8	1.1	-	4.8	-1.2
Luxembourg	71.0	79.8	97.1	98.0	105.8	118.0	123.0	125.2	5.8	-0.1	11.5	4.2	1.8
Netherlands	78.7	83.1	90.6	95.4	105.1	106.8	110.9	109.9	2.6	-1.3	1.6	3.8	-0.9
Norway	50.6	61.5	78.6	94.4	108.4	108.1	111.2	111.0	3.4	-0.6	-0.3	2.9	-0.2
Poland	(X)	107.3	87.7	90.4	127.4	133.5	143.5	144.1	11.2	4.7	4.8	7.5	0.4
Portugal	62.1	71.7	97.0	89.6	114.1	117.6	118.1	120.9	2.6	5.6	3.1	0.4	2.4
Spain	80.1	82.7	96.6	95.4	111.4	114.2	119.2	117.5	7.0	5.5	2.5	4.4	-1.4
Sweden [3,4]	73.0	80.5	88.0	91.1	112.1	115.6	125.3	123.2	6.5	4.2	3.1	8.4	-1.7
Switzerland	77.0	80.0	96.0	98.0	108.0	112.0	122.0	125.0	5.0	2.9	3.7	8.9	2.5
Turkey	38.2	57.2	81.3	88.7	120.5	116.0	123.0	112.4	10.7	1.3	-3.7	6.0	-8.6
United Kingdom	76.8	83.0	94.1	98.2	102.8	104.1	105.8	103.5	1.1	0.7	1.3	1.6	-2.2
United States	**69.6**	**76.9**	**86.4**	**95.3**	**117.2**	**121.9**	**127.4**	**122.5**	**6.0**	**5.8**	**4.0**	**4.5**	**-3.8**

-. Represents or rounds to zero.

NA. Not available.

X. Not applicable.

1. Including construction.

2. Not adjusted for unequal number of working days in the month.

3. Mining and manufacturing.

4. Annual figures correspond to official annual figures and differ from the average of the monthly figures.

Source: United States Census Bureau. (2002). *Statistical Abstract of the United States 2002.* Washington, D.C.: Government Printing Office. Retrieved from http://www.census.gov/prod/2003pubs/02statab/intlstat.pdf.

Table 2.21
Labor Productivity and Hours Worked by Country: 1990 to 2001

[**Annual percent change for period shown**. Data are derived from an annual database supported by the source. The Groningen Growth and Development Centre at the University of Groningen, Netherlands, maintains the database. For OECD countries and Eastern Europe, estimates are based on gross domestic product per hour worked, converted at purchasing power parities for 1996. Hence, estimates expressed in U.S. dollars at the price level of 1996 are corrected for differences in relative price levels. Minus sign (-) indicates decrease.]

Country	Labor productivity		Total hours worked	
	1990-1995	1995-2001	1990-1995	1995-2001
OECD, total	**1.8**	**1.8**	**0.2**	**1.0**
OECD, excl. United States	1.9	1.6	-0.2	0.8
European Union	2.5	1.3	-1.0	1.2
Australia	2.4	2.3	1.0	1.7
Austria	1.8	2.6	0.3	-0.3
Belgium	2.2	2.1	-0.7	0.4
Canada	1.3	0.9	0.2	2.2
Czech Republic	-0.6	1.6	-0.3	-0.5
Denmark	2.4	1.2	-0.4	1.3
Finland	2.8	2.5	-3.4	1.8
France	1.5	1.0	-0.4	1.4
Germany	3.2	1.5	-1.5	0.1
Greece	0.6	2.6	0.7	0.8
Hungary	3.0	2.4	-5.2	1.5
Ireland	3.5	5.1	1.1	3.6
Italy	3.1	0.7	-1.8	1.1
Japan	1.8	1.8	-0.4	-0.6
Mexico	-1.1	1.9	2.7	2.6
Netherlands	1.1	0.9	1.0	2.3
New Zealand	0.9	0.7	2.1	1.7
Norway	3.4	1.7	0.3	1.2
Poland	4.9	4.7	-2.6	-0.1
Portugal	3.6	2.0	-1.8	1.3
South Korea	5.1	3.7	2.2	0.6
Spain	2.3	0.1	-1.0	3.5
Sweden	1.9	1.6	-1.3	1.0
Switzerland	0.6	1.3	-0.6	0.5
Turkey	1.7	1.7	1.5	0.3
United Kingdom	2.5	1.7	-0.9	1.0
United States	**1.1**	**2.0**	**1.2**	**1.6**

Source: United States Census Bureau. (2002). *Statistical Abstract of the United States 2002*. Washington, D.C.: Government Printing Office. Retrieved from http://www.census.gov/prod/2003pubs/02statab/intlstat.pdf.

Table 2.22
Wage and Salaried Workers Paid Hourly Rates with Earnings at or below the Prevailing Federal Minimum Wage by Sex: United States, 1979–2002 Annual Averages

(Numbers in thousands)

Year and sex	Total wage and salary workers	Workers paid hourly rates				Total at or below prevailing Federal minimum wage	
		Total	Percent of total wage and salary workers	Below prevailing Federal minimum wage	At prevailing Federal minimum wage	Number	Percent of hourly paid workers
BOTH SEXES							
1979	87,529	51,721	59.1	2,916	3,997	6,912	13.4
1980	87,644	51,335	58.6	3,087	4,686	7,773	15.1
1981	88,516	51,869	58.6	3,513	4,311	7,824	15.1
1982	87,368	50,846	58.2	2,348	4,148	6,496	12.8
1983	88,290	51,820	58.7	2,077	4,261	6,338	12.2
1984	92,194	54,143	58.7	1,838	4,125	5,963	11.0
1985	94,521	55,762	59.0	1,639	3,899	5,538	9.9
1986[1]	96,903	57,529	59.4	1,599	3,461	5,060	8.8
1987	99,303	59,552	60.0	1,468	3,229	4,698	7.9
1988	101,407	60,878	60.0	1,319	2,608	3,927	6.5
1989	103,480	62,389	60.3	1,372	1,790	3,162	5.1
1990[1]	104,876	63,172	60.2	[2]2,132	[2]1,096	[2]3,228	[2]5.1
1991	103,723	62,627	60.4	[2]2,377	[2]2,906	[2]5,283	[2]8.4
1992	104,668	63,610	60.8	1,939	2,982	4,921	7.7
1993	106,101	64,274	60.6	1,707	2,625	4,332	6.7
1994[1]	107,989	66,549	61.6	1,995	2,132	4,128	6.2
1995	110,038	68,354	62.1	1,699	1,956	3,656	5.3
1996	111,960	69,255	61.9	[2]1,863	[2]1,861	[2]3,724	[2]5.4
1997[1]	114,533	70,735	61.8	[2]2,990	[2]1,764	[2]4,754	[2]6.7
1998[1]	116,730	71,440	61.2	2,834	1,593	4,427	6.2
1999[1]	118,963	72,306	60.8	2,194	1,146	3,340	4.6
2000[1]	122,292	73,638	60.2	1,853	870	2,724	3.7
2001	122,401	73,467	60.0	1,615	638	2,253	3.1
2002	122,009	72,720	59.6	1,598	570	2,168	3.0
MEN							
1979	49,400	28,392	57.5	846	1,353	2,199	7.7
1980	48,700	27,709	56.9	983	1,696	2,678	9.7
1981	48,844	27,576	56.5	1,119	1,533	2,652	9.6
1982	47,591	26,481	55.6	697	1,587	2,284	8.6
1983	47,856	26,831	56.1	585	1,658	2,243	8.4
1984	50,022	28,140	56.3	490	1,626	2,116	7.5
1985	51,015	28,893	56.6	440	1,544	1,984	6.9
1986[1]	51,942	29,666	57.1	408	1,336	1,743	5.9
1987	52,938	30,474	57.6	364	1,283	1,647	5.4
1988	53,912	31,058	57.6	311	1,066	1,377	4.4
1989	54,789	31,687	57.8	379	733	1,112	3.5
1990[1]	55,553	32,104	57.8	[2]712	[2]385	[2]1,097	[2]3.4
1991	54,618	31,639	57.9	[2]795	[2]1,114	[2]1,909	[2]6.0
1992	54,826	32,155	58.6	653	1,231	1,885	5.9
1993	55,475	32,337	58.3	573	1,091	1,664	5.1
1994[1]	56,570	33,528	59.3	674	891	1,565	4.7
1995	57,669	34,420	59.7	542	796	1,338	3.9
1996	58,473	34,838	59.6	[2]619	[2]755	[2]1,374	[2]3.9
1997[1]	59,825	35,521	59.4	[2]1,147	[2]673	[2]1,820	[2]5.1
1998[1]	60,973	35,761	58.7	1,039	628	1,667	4.7
1999[1]	61,914	36,073	58.3	768	446	1,214	3.4
2000[1]	63,752	36,771	57.7	638	324	962	2.6
2001	63,706	36,649	57.5	530	250	780	2.1
2002	63,384	36,135	57.0	582	218	800	2.2

Table 2.22 (*continued*)

(Numbers in thousands)

Year and sex	Total wage and salary workers	Workers paid hourly rates					Total at or below prevailing Federal minimum wage	
		Total	Percent of total wage and salary workers	Below prevailing Federal minimum wage	At prevailing Federal minimum wage		Number	Percent of hourly paid workers
WOMEN								
1979......................	38,129	23,329	61.2	2,070	2,644		4,714	20.2
1980......................	38,944	23,626	60.7	2,104	2,990		5,095	21.6
1981......................	39,672	24,294	61.2	2,394	2,778		5,172	21.3
1982......................	39,777	24,365	61.3	1,651	2,561		4,212	17.3
1983......................	40,433	24,989	61.8	1,492	2,603		4,095	16.4
1984......................	42,172	26,003	61.7	1,348	2,499		3,847	14.8
1985......................	43,506	26,869	61.8	1,198	2,356		3,554	13.2
1986......................	44,961	27,863	62.0	1,192	2,125		3,317	11.9
1987......................	46,365	29,078	62.7	1,105	1,946		3,051	10.5
1988......................	47,495	29,820	62.8	1,008	1,542		2,550	8.6
1989......................	48,691	30,702	63.1	994	1,056		2,050	6.7
1990......................	49,323	31,069	63.0	[2]1,420	[2]711		[2]2,131	[2]6.9
1991......................	49,105	30,988	63.1	[2]1,582	[2]1,792		[2]3,374	[2]10.9
1992......................	49,842	31,454	63.1	1,286	1,751		3,036	9.7
1993......................	50,626	31,937	63.1	1,133	1,534		2,667	8.4
1994......................	51,419	33,021	64.2	1,322	1,241		2,563	7.8
1995......................	52,369	33,934	64.8	1,157	1,161		2,318	6.8
1996......................	53,488	34,418	64.3	[2]1,244	[2]1,106		[2]2,350	[2]6.8
1997......................	54,708	35,214	64.4	[2]1,843	[2]1,092		[2]2,935	[2]8.3
1998......................	55,757	35,680	64.0	1,794	965		2,760	7.7
1999......................	57,050	36,233	63.5	1,426	700		2,126	5.9
2000......................	58,540	36,867	63.0	1,215	547		1,762	4.8
2001......................	58,695	36,818	62.7	1,085	388		1,473	4.0
2002......................	58,625	36,585	62.4	1,016	352		1,368	3.7

1. The comparability of historical labor force data has been affected at various times by methodological and conceptual changes in the Current Population Survey (CPS). For an explanation, see the Explanatory Notes and Estimates of Error section of the February 2003 and subsequent issues of *Employment and Earnings*, a monthly BLS periodical.

2. Data for 1990–1991 and 1996–1997 reflect changes in the minimum wage that took place in those years.

Note: The prevailing Federal minimum wage was $2.90 in 1979, $3.10 in 1980, and $3.35 in 1981–1989. The minimum wage rose to $3.80 in April 1990, to $4.25 in April 1991, to $4.75 in October 1996, and to $5.15 in September 1997. Data exclude the incorporated self-employed. Also note that the presence of a sizable number of workers with reported wages below the minimum does not necessarily indicate violations of the Fair Labor Standards Act, as there are numerous exemptions to the minimum wage provisions of the law. Indeed, the relatively large number of workers with reported wages below the minimum in 1998–2002 includes some hourly-paid workers reported as earning exactly $5.00 per hour (about 1.4 million in 1998, about 900,000 in 1999, about 600,000 in 2000, about 500,000 in 2001 and almost 500,000 in 2002); to some extent, this may reflect rounding on the part of survey respondents.

Source: U.S. Department of Labor. (2003). *Characteristics of Minimum Wages Workers: 2002*. Washington, D.C.: Bureau of Labor Statistics. Retrieved from http://www.bls.gov/cps/minwage2002pdf.pdf.

Table 2.23
Average Hourly Earnings of Production Workers on Private Nonfarm Payrolls by Major Industry Division, Annual Averages: United States, 1947 to 2000

(In current dollars)

Year	Total private	Mining	Construc-tion	Manu-facturing	Trans-portation and public utilities	Wholesale trade	Retail trade	Finance, insur-ance and real estate	Services
1947	$1.13	$1.46	$1.54	$1.21	–	$1.21	$0.83	$1.14	–
1948	1.22	1.66	1.71	1.32	–	1.30	.90	1.20	–
1949	1.27	1.71	1.79	1.37	–	1.35	.95	1.26	–
1950	1.33	1.77	1.86	1.43	–	1.35	.98	1.26	–
1951	1.45	1.93	2.02	1.56	–	1.52	1.06	1.45	–
1952	1.52	2.01	2.13	1.64	–	1.61	1.09	1.51	–
1953	1.61	2.14	2.28	1.74	–	1.69	1.16	1.58	–
1954	1.65	2.14	2.38	1.78	–	1.76	1.20	1.65	–
1955	1.71	2.20	2.45	1.85	–	1.83	1.25	1.70	–
1956	1.80	2.33	2.57	1.95	–	1.93	1.30	1.78	–
1957	1.89	2.45	2.71	2.04	–	2.02	1.37	1.84	–
1958	1.95	2.47	2.82	2.10	–	2.09	1.42	1.89	–
1959	2.02	2.56	2.93	2.19	–	2.18	1.47	1.95	–
1960	2.09	2.60	3.07	2.26	–	2.24	1.52	2.02	–
1961	2.14	2.64	3.20	2.32	–	2.31	1.56	2.09	–
1962	2.22	2.70	3.31	2.39	–	2.37	1.63	2.17	–
1963	2.28	2.75	3.41	2.45	–	2.45	1.68	2.25	–
1964	2.36	2.81	3.55	2.53	$2.89	2.52	1.75	2.30	$1.94
1965	2.46	2.92	3.70	2.61	3.03	2.60	1.82	2.39	2.05
1966	2.56	3.05	3.89	2.71	3.11	2.73	1.91	2.47	2.17
1967	2.68	3.19	4.11	2.82	3.23	2.87	2.01	2.58	2.29
1968	2.85	3.35	4.41	3.01	3.42	3.04	2.16	2.75	2.42
1969	3.04	3.60	4.79	3.19	3.63	3.23	2.30	2.93	2.61
1970	3.23	3.85	5.24	3.35	3.85	3.43	2.44	3.07	2.81
1971	3.45	4.06	5.69	3.57	4.21	3.64	2.60	3.22	3.04
1972	3.70	4.44	6.06	3.82	4.65	3.85	2.75	3.36	3.27
1973	3.94	4.75	6.41	4.09	5.02	4.07	2.91	3.53	3.47
1974	4.24	5.23	6.81	4.42	5.41	4.38	3.14	3.77	3.75
1975	4.53	5.95	7.31	4.83	5.88	4.72	3.36	4.06	4.02
1976	4.86	6.46	7.71	5.22	6.45	5.02	3.57	4.27	4.31
1977	5.25	6.94	8.10	5.68	6.99	5.39	3.85	4.54	4.65
1978	5.69	7.67	8.66	6.17	7.57	5.88	4.20	4.89	4.99
1979	6.16	8.49	9.27	6.70	8.16	6.39	4.53	5.27	5.36
1980	6.66	9.17	9.94	7.27	8.87	6.95	4.88	5.79	5.85
1981	7.25	10.04	10.82	7.99	9.70	7.55	5.25	6.31	6.41
1982	7.68	10.77	11.63	8.49	10.32	8.08	5.48	6.78	6.92
1983	8.02	11.28	11.94	8.83	10.79	8.54	5.74	7.29	7.31
1984	8.32	11.63	12.13	9.19	11.12	8.88	5.85	7.63	7.59
1985	8.57	11.98	12.32	9.54	11.40	9.15	5.94	7.94	7.90
1986	8.76	12.46	12.48	9.73	11.70	9.34	6.03	8.36	8.18
1987	8.98	12.54	12.71	9.91	12.03	9.59	6.12	8.73	8.49
1988	9.28	12.80	13.08	10.19	12.24	9.98	6.31	9.06	8.88
1989	9.66	13.26	13.54	10.48	12.57	10.39	6.53	9.53	9.38
1990	10.01	13.68	13.77	10.83	12.92	10.79	6.75	9.97	9.83
1991	10.32	14.19	14.00	11.18	13.20	11.15	6.94	10.39	10.23
1992	10.57	14.54	14.15	11.46	13.43	11.39	7.12	10.82	10.54
1993	10.83	14.60	14.38	11.74	13.55	11.74	7.29	11.35	10.78
1994	11.12	14.88	14.73	12.07	13.78	12.06	7.49	11.83	11.04
1995	11.43	15.30	15.09	12.37	14.13	12.43	7.69	12.32	11.39
1996	11.82	15.62	15.47	12.77	14.45	12.87	7.99	12.80	11.79
1997	12.28	16.15	16.04	13.17	14.92	13.45	8.33	13.34	12.28
1998	12.78	16.91	16.61	13.49	15.31	14.07	8.74	14.07	12.84
1999	13.24	17.05	17.19	13.90	15.69	14.59	9.09	14.62	13.37
2000	13.75	17.24	17.88	14.38	16.22	15.20	9.46	15.07	13.91

Note: Dash indicates data not available.

Current estimates are projected from March 2000 benchmark levels.

Source: U.S. Department of Labor. (2001). *Report on the American Workforce.* Washington, D.C.: Government Printing Office. Retrieved from http://www.bls.gov/epub/rtaw/pdf/appendix.pdf.

Table 2.24
Hourly Compensation Costs in U.S. Dollars for Production Workers in Manufacturing in Twenty-nine Countries or Areas: 1975 to 1999

Year	United States	Canada	Mexico	Australia[1]	Hong Kong SAR[2]	Israel	Japan	Korea	New Zealand	Singapore
1975	$6.36	$5.96	$1.47	$5.62	$0.76	$2.25	$3.00	$0.32	$3.15	$0.84
1976	6.92	7.06	1.64	6.22	.87	2.38	3.25	.42	2.94	.86
1977	7.59	7.34	1.34	6.29	1.03	2.68	3.96	.56	3.30	.91
1978	8.28	7.42	1.62	7.00	1.18	2.57	5.45	.76	4.06	1.05
1979	9.04	7.87	1.91	7.47	1.31	3.30	5.40	1.01	4.62	1.26
1980	9.87	8.67	2.21	8.47	1.51	3.79	5.52	.96	5.22	1.49
1981	10.87	9.57	2.82	9.80	1.55	4.18	6.08	1.02	5.59	1.80
1982	11.68	10.45	1.97	9.98	1.66	4.43	5.60	1.09	5.51	1.96
1983	12.14	11.16	1.42	9.31	1.51	4.88	6.03	1.15	5.09	2.21
1984	12.55	11.15	1.56	9.83	1.58	4.65	6.23	1.20	4.56	2.46
1985	13.01	10.95	1.59	8.20	1.73	4.06	6.34	1.23	4.38	2.47
1986	13.26	11.07	1.09	8.54	1.88	5.20	9.22	1.31	5.39	2.23
1987	13.52	12.02	1.04	9.46	2.09	6.34	10.79	1.59	6.64	2.31
1988	13.91	13.47	1.25	11.35	2.40	7.67	12.63	2.20	8.02	2.67
1989	14.32	14.72	1.43	12.41	2.79	7.69	12.53	3.17	7.65	3.15
1990	14.91	15.94	1.58	13.07	3.20	8.55	12.80	3.71	8.17	3.78
1991	15.58	17.28	1.84	13.53	3.58	8.79	14.67	4.61	8.20	4.35
1992	16.09	17.17	2.17	13.02	3.92	9.09	16.38	5.22	7.76	4.95
1993	16.51	16.55	2.40	12.49	4.29	8.82	19.21	5.64	8.85	5.25
1994	16.87	15.88	2.47	14.12	4.61	9.19	21.35	6.40	8.76	6.29
1995	17.19	16.10	1.51	15.27	4.82	10.54	23.82	7.29	9.91	7.33
1996	17.70	16.64	1.54	16.88	5.14	11.32	21.00	8.22	10.81	8.32
1997	18.27	16.47	1.78	16.58	5.42	12.04	19.54	7.86	10.81	8.24
1998	18.66	15.60	1.84	14.92	5.47	12.02	18.29	5.39	9.01	7.77
1999	19.20	15.60	2.12	15.89	5.44	11.91	20.89	6.71	9.14	7.18

Year	Sri Lanka	Taiwan	Austria[3]	Belgium	Denmark	Finland[4]	France	Germany[5]	Greece	Ireland
1975	$0.28	$0.40	$4.51	$6.41	$6.28	$4.61	$4.52	$6.31	$1.69	$3.03
1976	.24	.46	4.78	6.90	6.63	5.19	4.70	6.68	1.92	2.86
1977	.32	.53	5.67	8.29	7.25	5.58	5.21	7.81	2.29	3.12
1978	.26	.62	6.91	10.14	8.98	5.88	6.43	9.58	2.84	3.97
1979	.23	.79	7.96	11.82	10.53	7.51	7.69	11.21	3.37	4.85
1980	.22	1.00	8.88	13.11	10.83	8.24	8.94	12.25	3.73	5.95
1981	.21	1.21	7.78	11.31	9.41	8.04	8.02	10.45	3.66	5.59
1982	.24	1.24	7.78	9.49	8.87	8.03	7.85	10.28	4.12	5.71
1983	.25	1.29	7.81	9.08	8.69	7.54	7.74	10.19	3.78	5.67
1984	.25	1.42	7.35	8.63	8.03	7.77	7.29	9.37	3.74	5.59
1985	.28	1.50	7.58	8.97	8.13	8.16	7.52	9.53	3.66	5.92
1986	.29	1.73	10.73	12.43	11.07	10.71	10.28	13.34	4.07	8.02
1987	.30	2.26	13.67	15.25	14.61	13.44	12.29	16.91	4.61	9.31
1988	.31	2.81	14.52	15.82	15.19	15.70	12.95	18.16	5.22	10.00
1989	.31	3.52	14.16	15.48	14.53	16.85	12.65	17.66	5.49	9.61
1990	.35	3.93	17.75	19.17	18.04	21.03	15.49	21.88	6.76	11.66
1991	.40	4.36	18.09	19.75	18.39	21.25	15.65	22.63	6.95	11.91
1992	.40	5.09	20.29	22.05	20.20	19.92	17.47	25.38	7.60	13.12
1993	.42	5.24	20.16	21.44	19.11	16.63	16.79	25.19	7.23	11.90
1994	.45	5.56	21.55	23.07	20.30	19.06	17.63	26.70	7.73	12.42
1995	.48	5.94	25.32	26.65	24.07	24.10	20.01	31.58	9.17	13.61
1996	.48	5.95	24.80	25.97	24.11	23.41	19.93	31.20	9.59	13.91
1997	.46	5.90	21.97	22.88	22.03	21.32	17.99	27.68	9.20	13.61
1998	.47	5.27	22.21	23.20	22.69	21.66	18.28	27.52	8.91	13.39
1999	–	5.62	21.83	22.82	22.96	21.10	17.98	26.93	–	13.57

Table 2.24 (*continued*)

Year	Italy	Luxem-bourg	Nether-lands	Norway	Portugal	Spain	Sweden	Switzer-land	United King-dom
1975	$4.67	$6.50	$6.58	$6.77	$1.58	$2.53	$7.18	$6.09	$3.37
1976	4.34	6.99	6.90	7.52	1.66	2.86	8.25	6.45	3.21
1977	4.99	8.06	8.02	8.56	1.58	3.18	8.88	6.88	3.45
1978	5.83	9.86	9.98	9.51	1.63	3.88	9.65	9.59	4.41
1979	7.06	11.12	11.41	10.28	1.68	5.31	11.33	10.56	5.70
1980	8.15	12.03	12.06	11.59	2.06	5.89	12.51	11.09	7.56
1981	7.57	9.85	9.91	11.01	2.04	5.55	11.80	10.14	7.31
1982	7.44	8.61	9.78	10.83	1.88	5.28	10.07	10.42	6.92
1983	7.70	8.15	9.49	10.32	1.62	4.56	8.89	10.46	6.49
1984	7.35	7.79	8.70	10.07	1.45	4.47	9.17	9.64	6.04
1985	7.63	7.81	8.75	10.37	1.53	4.66	9.66	9.66	6.27
1986	10.47	10.86	12.22	13.24	2.08	6.25	12.43	13.76	7.66
1987	13.02	13.35	15.14	16.79	2.52	7.63	15.12	17.08	9.09
1988	13.98	14.22	15.83	18.45	2.78	8.55	16.82	18.01	10.61
1989	14.40	13.92	15.00	18.29	2.97	8.96	17.52	16.73	10.56
1990	17.45	16.74	18.06	21.47	3.77	11.38	20.93	20.86	12.70
1991	18.32	17.14	18.13	21.63	4.24	12.29	22.15	21.69	13.74
1992	19.35	19.10	20.10	23.03	5.17	13.50	24.59	23.23	14.37
1993	15.80	18.74	19.94	20.21	4.50	11.62	17.59	22.63	12.41
1994	15.89	20.33	20.73	20.97	4.60	11.54	18.62	24.91	12.80
1995	16.22	23.35	24.12	24.38	5.37	12.88	21.44	29.30	13.67
1996	17.75	22.55	23.22	25.05	5.58	13.51	24.37	28.34	14.09
1997	17.57	19.02	20.98	23.72	5.38	12.24	22.22	24.19	15.47
1998	17.11	18.74	21.17	23.50	5.48	12.14	22.02	24.38	16.43
1999	16.60	–	20.94	23.91	–	12.11	21.58	23.56	16.56

1. Production and nonproduction workers other than those in managerial, executive, professional, and higher supervisory positions.

2. Hong Kong Special Administrative Region of China. Average of selected manufacturing industries.

3. Excludes handicraft manufacturers, printing and publishing, and miscellaneous manufacturing.

4. Including mining and electrical power plants.

5. Former West Germany. Excluding handicraft manufacturers.

  Dash indicates data not available.

Source: U.S. Department of Labor. (2001). *Report on the American Workforce.* Washington, D.C.: Government Printing Office. Retrieved from http://www.bls.gov/epub/rtaw/pdf/appendix.pdf.

Table 2.25
Index of Hourly Compensation Costs for Production Workers in Manufacturing by Country: 1980 to 2000

[**United States=100.** Compensation costs include pay for time worked, other direct pay (including holiday and vacation pay, bonuses, other direct payments, and the cost of pay in kind), employer expenditures for legally required insurance programs and contractual and private benefit plans, and for some countries, other labor taxes. Data adjusted for exchange rates. Area averages are trade-weighted to account for difference in countriesí relative importance to U.S. trade in manufactured goods. The trade weights used are the sum of U.S. imports of manufactured products for consumption (customs value) and U.S. exports of domestic manufactured products (f.a.s. value) in 1992.]

Area or country	1980	1985	1990	1995	1999	2000	Area or country	1980	1985	1990	1995	1999	2000
United States	100	100	100	100	100	100	Austria [6]	90	58	119	147	114	98
Total [1]	67	52	83	95	80	76	Belgium	133	69	129	161	125	106
OECD [2]	74	57	90	103	86	82	Denmark	110	63	121	140	120	103
Europe	100	61	116	128	107	93	Finland [7]	84	63	141	140	112	98
Asian newly industrial-							France	91	58	104	116	94	83
izing economies [3]	12	13	25	37	33	34	Germany [6,8]	124	73	146	184	140	121
Canada	88	84	107	94	82	81	Greece	38	28	45	53	(NA)	(NA)
Mexico	22	12	11	9	11	12	Ireland	61	46	79	80	71	63
Australia [4]	86	63	88	89	82	71	Italy	83	59	117	94	87	74
Hong Kong [5]	15	13	22	28	29	28	Luxembourg	122	60	112	132	98	84
Israel	38	31	57	61	62	65	Netherlands	122	67	121	140	112	96
Japan	56	49	86	139	109	111	Norway	117	80	144	142	125	111
Korea, South	10	10	25	42	37	41	Portugal	21	12	25	31	28	24
New Zealand	53	34	55	58	48	41	Spain	60	36	76	75	63	55
Singapore	15	19	25	43	37	37	Sweden	127	74	140	125	113	101
Sri Lanka	2	2	2	3	2	(NA)	Switzerland	112	74	140	170	123	107
Taiwan	10	12	26	35	29	30	United Kingdom	77	48	85	80	86	80

NA. Not available.

1. The 28 foreign economies shown below.

2. Organization for Economic Cooperation and Development.

3. Hong Kong, South Korea, Singapore, and Taiwan.

4. Includes nonproduction workers, except in managerial, executive, professional, and higher supervisory positions.

5. Average of selected manufacturing industries.

6. Excludes workers in establishments considered handicraft manufactures (including all printing and publishing and miscellaneous manufacturing in Austria).

7. Includes workers in mining and electrical power plants.

8. Former West Germany.

Source: United States Census Bureau. (2002). *Statistical Abstract of the United States 2002*. Washington, D.C.: Government Printing Office. Retrieved from http://www.census.gov/prod/2003pubs/02statab/intlstat.pdf.

Table 2.26
Gross Public Debt, Expenditures, and Receipts by Country: 1990 to 2001

[**Percent of nominal gross domestic product. 2001 data estimated.** Expenditures cover current outlays plus net capital outlays. Receipts cover current receipts but exclude capital receipts. Nontax current receipts include operating surpluses of public enterprises, property income, fees, charges, fines, etc.]

Country	Gross debt			Expenditures			Receipts		
	1990	1995	2001	1990	1995	2001	1990	1995	2001
United States [1]	**66.6**	**74.5**	**54.6**	**33.6**	**32.9**	**29.0**	**29.3**	**29.8**	**31.6**
Australia	22.6	42.9	24.3	33.0	35.4	31.0	31.8	31.7	31.7
Austria	56.9	69.1	62.4	48.5	52.4	48.1	46.1	47.3	47.3
Belgium	124.9	129.8	105.4	50.8	50.3	45.8	44.1	46.0	46.1
Canada [2]	93.3	120.6	100.5	46.0	45.3	37.4	40.1	40.0	39.5
Czech Republic	(X)	(NA)	(NA)	(X)	(NA)	47.1	(X)	(NA)	40.6
Denmark	65.8	73.9	46.2	53.6	56.6	50.6	52.5	54.3	53.5
Finland	14.3	57.2	39.7	44.4	54.3	43.1	49.6	50.6	48.0
France	39.5	59.3	63.6	49.6	53.6	49.4	47.4	48.0	49.3
Germany [3]	42.0	57.1	57.8	43.8	46.3	44.5	41.8	43.0	42.8
Greece	89.0	108.7	99.7	47.8	46.6	43.0	31.7	36.4	42.6
Hungary	(NA)	(NA)	(NA)	(NA)	51.2	43.0	(NA)	43.6	39.5
Iceland	36.7	60.1	33.4	39.0	39.2	38.6	35.8	36.2	41.0
Ireland	92.4	80.0	26.7	39.5	37.6	26.7	36.7	35.4	33.2
Italy	103.7	123.1	108.3	53.1	52.3	47.1	42.1	44.7	46.0
Japan [4]	61.5	76.2	118.6	31.3	35.6	38.3	34.2	32.0	32.3
Korea, South	8.2	6.3	9.7	18.3	19.3	23.4	21.8	23.5	28.1
Netherlands	75.6	75.5	53.1	49.4	47.7	40.1	43.7	43.6	41.1
New Zealand	(NA)	(NA)	(NA)	48.8	38.8	40.2	44.0	41.9	41.2
Norway	29.5	35.4	25.6	49.7	47.6	38.8	52.3	51.1	53.7
Portugal	(NA)	64.2	53.8	(NA)	41.2	42.4	(NA)	36.6	41.0
Spain	48.5	71.7	66.5	41.4	44.0	38.2	37.2	37.4	38.4
Sweden	42.7	76.9	48.6	55.8	62.1	53.1	59.8	54.2	56.4
United Kingdom	44.5	61.1	50.7	41.9	44.4	38.8	40.4	38.6	40.9

NA. Not available.

X. Not applicable.

1. Includes funded part of central government employee pension liabilities amounting to 8.3 percent of GDP in 1999. Expenditures data includes outlays net of surpluses of public enterprises. Receipts exclude the operating surpluses of public enterprises.

2. Includes funded government employee pension liabilities amounting to 19 percent of GDP in 1999. This overstates the Canadian debt position relative to countries that have large unfunded liabilities for such pensions which are not counted in those countries' debt figures.

3. Debt data include accounts of the Inherited Debt Fund from 1995 on. The 1995 outlays are net of the debt taken on this year from the inherited Debt funds.

4. Debt data include debt of the Japan Railway Settlement Corporation and the National Forest Special Account from 1998 on. The 1998 expenditure would have risen by 5.4 percentage points of GDP if account were taken of the assumption by the central government of the debt of these two entities.

Source: United States Census Bureau. (2002). *Statistical Abstract of the United States 2002*. Washington, D.C.: Government Printing Office. Retrieved from http://www.census.gov/prod/2003pubs/02statab/intlstat.pdf.

Table 2.27
Percent Distribution of Tax Receipts by Country: 1980 to 1999

Country	Income and profits taxes [2]				Social security contributions			Taxes on goods and services [5]		
	Total [1]	Total [3]	Individual	Corporate	Total [4]	Employees	Employers	Total [3]	General consumption taxes [6]	Taxes on specific goods, services [7]
United States: 1980	100.0	49.8	39.1	10.8	21.9	9.2	11.9	17.6	7.0	8.3
1990	100.0	45.4	37.7	7.7	25.9	11.0	13.4	17.3	8.0	7.1
1999	100.0	49.1	40.7	8.3	23.9	10.5	12.2	16.4	7.6	6.8
Canada: 1980	100.0	46.6	34.1	11.6	10.5	3.7	6.6	32.6	11.5	13.0
1990	100.0	48.5	40.8	7.0	12.1	4.3	7.5	26.0	14.1	10.3
1999	100.0	48.9	38.1	9.8	13.6	5.3	8.0	24.7	14.3	8.7
France: 1980.	100.0	16.8	11.6	5.1	42.7	11.1	28.4	30.4	21.1	8.4
1990.	100.0	16.1	10.7	5.3	44.1	13.2	27.2	28.4	18.8	8.7
1999.	100.0	24.0	17.6	6.4	36.1	8.8	25.0	26.8	17.3	8.6
Germany: 1980 [8]	100.0	35.1	29.6	5.5	34.3	15.3	18.4	27.1	16.6	9.3
1990	100.0	32.4	27.6	4.8	37.5	16.2	19.1	26.7	16.6	9.2
1999	100.0	29.8	25.1	4.8	39.3	17.3	19.3	28.0	18.4	8.7
Italy: 1980.	100.0	31.1	23.1	7.8	38.0	6.9	28.4	26.5	15.6	9.7
1990	100.0	36.5	26.3	10.0	32.9	6.3	23.6	28.0	14.7	10.6
1999	100.0	34.0	26.4	7.7	28.5	5.5	20.0	27.5	13.7	11.2
Japan: 1980	100.0	46.1	24.3	21.8	29.1	10.2	14.8	16.3	-	14.1
1990	100.0	48.5	26.8	21.6	29.0	11.0	15.0	13.2	4.3	7.3
1999	100.0	31.4	18.5	12.9	37.2	14.4	19.1	20.1	9.6	8.2
Netherlands: 1980	100.0	32.8	26.3	6.6	38.1	15.7	17.8	25.2	15.8	7.3
1990	100.0	32.2	24.7	7.5	37.4	23.1	7.5	26.4	16.5	7.5
1999	100.0	25.3	15.2	10.1	40.0	-	11.6	28.0	16.9	8.7
Sweden: 1980	100.0	43.5	41.0	2.5	28.8	0.1	27.6	24.0	13.4	9.2
1990.	100.0	41.6	38.5	3.1	27.2	0.1	26.0	25.0	14.9	9.2
1999.	100.0	41.6	35.6	6.0	25.3	5.8	19.1	21.4	13.8	7.0
United Kingdom: 1980. . .	100.0	37.8	29.4	8.4	16.7	6.4	10.1	29.1	14.7	13.3
1990 . .	100.0	39.5	27.9	11.6	17.2	6.6	10.0	31.1	17.0	12.7
1999 . .	100.0	39.2	28.8	10.4	17.1	7.3	9.7	32.3	18.8	11.9

-. Represents zero.

1. Includes property taxes, employer payroll taxes other than social security contributions, and miscellaneous taxes, not shown separately.

2. Includes taxes on capital gains.

3. Includes other taxes not shown separately.

4. Includes contributions of self-employed not shown separately.

5. Taxes on the production, sales, transfer, leasing, and delivery of goods and services and rendering of services.

6. Primary value-added and sales taxes.

7. For sample, excise taxes on alcohol, tobacco, and gasoline.

8. Data are for former West Germany.

Source: United States Census Bureau. (2002). *Statistical Abstract of the United States 2002.* Washington, D.C.: Government Printing Office. Retrieved from http://www.census.gov/prod/2003pubs/02statab/intlstat.pdf.

Table 2.28
Tax Freedom Day and Total Effective Tax Rates by Level of Government in the United States: Calendar Years 1900 to 2004

Year	All Governments			Federal Government		State-Local Governments	
	Tax Freedom Day	Days Spent Working to Pay Taxes	Total Effective Tax Rate	Days Spent Working to Pay Taxes	Effective Tax Rate	Days Spent Working to Pay Taxes	Effective Tax Rate
1900	January 21	21	5.9%	8	2.1%	13	3.8%
1901	January 21	21	5.8%	7	2.0%	13	3.8%
1902*	January 21	21	5.6%	6	1.7%	14	3.9%
1903*	January 20	20	5.3%	5	1.3%	14	4.0%
1904*	January 20	20	5.7%	5	1.4%	15	4.3%
1905	January 20	20	5.4%	4	1.2%	15	4.2%
1906	January 19	19	5.1%	4	1.2%	14	3.9%
1907*	January 19	19	5.1%	4	1.2%	14	3.9%
1908*	January 20	20	5.7%	4	1.2%	16	4.5%
1909	January 19	19	4.9%	4	1.0%	14	4.0%
1910*	January 19	19	5.0%	4	1.1%	14	3.9%
1911*	January 20	20	5.3%	5	1.2%	14	4.1%
1912*	January 18	18	5.0%	4	1.1%	14	3.9%
1913*	January 19	19	5.2%	4	1.2%	14	4.0%
1914*	January 23	23	6.1%	5	1.3%	17	4.8%
1915	January 25	25	6.7%	5	1.4%	19	5.3%
1916	January 23	23	6.3%	5	1.4%	18	4.9%
1917	January 23	23	6.2%	6	1.8%	16	4.4%
1918*	February 07	38	10.2%	24	6.4%	13	3.8%
1919*	February 06	37	9.9%	23	6.1%	13	3.8%
1920*	February 11	42	11.6%	29	7.9%	13	3.8%
1921*	February 21	52	14.1%	32	8.8%	19	5.3%
1922	February 10	41	11.1%	21	5.7%	19	5.4%
1923*	February 03	34	9.2%	15	4.1%	18	5.1%
1924*	February 05	36	10.0%	16	4.4%	20	5.7%
1925	February 03	34	9.3%	13	3.7%	20	5.6%
1926*	February 05	36	9.7%	14	3.9%	21	5.8%
1927*	February 07	38	10.4%	14	4.0%	23	6.3%
1928	February 07	38	10.5%	14	3.8%	24	6.6%
1929*	February 07	38	10.4%	14	3.8%	24	6.6%
1930*	February 10	41	11.2%	13	3.4%	28	7.9%
1931*	February 12	43	12.0%	9	2.6%	34	9.4%
1932*	February 24	55	15.1%	12	3.1%	43	12.0%
1933*	March 02	62	17.2%	19	5.3%	43	11.9%
1934	February 26	57	15.7%	21	5.6%	36	10.1%
1935	February 24	55	15.3%	20	5.4%	35	9.8%
1936	February 24	55	15.2%	21	5.9%	34	9.3%
1937*	February 29	60	16.6%	28	7.8%	32	8.9%
1938*	March 04	63	17.3%	28	7.6%	35	9.7%
1939	March 02	61	16.7%	28	7.5%	33	9.2%
1940	March 05	64	17.6%	32	8.8%	32	8.8%
	The Revenue Act of 1940 (+1.3%); Second Revenue Act of 1940 (+1.0%)						
1941	March 13	72	19.9%	46	12.6%	26	7.3%
	The Revenue Act of 1941 (+3.1%)						
1942	March 16	75	20.7%	54	14.9%	21	5.8%
	The Revenue Act of 1942 (+6.7%)						
1943	April 04	94	25.8%	77	20.9%	17	4.9%
	The Revenue Act of 1943 (0.5%) and Current Tax Payment Act of 1943 (+1.4%)						
1944	March 29	88	24.3%	72	19.8%	16	4.5%
	The Individual Income Tax Act of 1944 (-0.3%)						
1945*	April 01	91	25.0%	74	20.3%	17	4.7%

Table 2.28 (*continued*)

Year	Tax Freedom Day	All Governments		Federal Government		State-Local Governments	
		Days Spent Working to Pay Taxes	Total Effective Tax Rate	Days Spent Working to Pay Taxes	Effective Tax Rate	Days Spent Working to Pay Taxes	Effective Tax Rate
The Revenue Act of 1945 (-2.9%)							
1946	April 01	91	25.0%	72	19.6%	19	5.4%
1947	April 01	91	25.0%	71	19.5%	20	5.6%
1948*	March 25	84	23.1%	64	17.4%	20	5.7%
The Revenue Act of 1948 (-2.1%)							
1949*	March 21	80	22.0%	57	15.7%	23	6.3%
1950	March 30	89	24.6%	67	18.3%	22	6.3%
The Revenue Act of 1950 (+1.7%); Excess Profits Tax Act of 1950 (+1.2%)							
1951	April 06	96	26.3%	75	20.4%	21	6.0%
The Revenue Act of 1951 (+1.8%)							
1952	April 06	96	26.3%	74	20.2%	22	6.1%
1953*	April 05	95	26.1%	73	19.9%	22	6.2%
1954*	March 31	90	24.8%	66	18.2%	24	6.6%
Internal Revenue Code of 1954 (-0.1%); Excise Tax Reduction Act of 1954 (-0.3%)							
1955	April 02	92	25.5%	68	18.9%	24	6.6%
1956	April 05	95	26.1%	70	19.1%	25	7.0%
1957*	April 05	95	26.1%	70	19.0%	25	7.1%
1958*	April 03	93	25.6%	66	18.1%	27	7.4%
1959	April 06	96	26.5%	69	19.0%	27	7.5%
1960*	April 09	99	27.4%	71	19.5%	28	7.9%
1961*	April 09	99	27.3%	70	19.1%	29	8.2%
1962	April 09	99	27.4%	70	19.2%	29	8.2%
The Revenue Act of 1962 (0.0%)							
1963	April 11	101	27.9%	71	19.6%	30	8.3%
1964	April 06	96	26.5%	66	18.1%	30	8.4%
The Revenue Act of 1964 (-1.9%)							
1965	April 06	96	26.4%	66	18.1%	30	8.4%
1966	April 09	99	27.2%	69	18.8%	30	8.3%
Tax Adjustment Act of 1966 (+0.7%)							
1967	April 10	100	27.6%	69	19.0%	31	8.6%
1968	April 16	106	29.2%	74	20.2%	32	9.0%
Revenue and Expenditure Control Act of 1968 (+1.9%)							
1969*	April 21	111	30.5%	77	21.2%	34	9.4%
Tax Reform Act of 1969 (+0.4%)							
1970*	April 17	107	29.4%	72	19.5%	35	9.8%
1971	April 14	104	28.6%	68	18.5%	36	10.1%
Revenue Act of 1971 (-0.4%)							
1972	April 18	108	29.7%	70	19.3%	38	10.4%
1973*	April 18	108	29.9%	71	19.7%	37	10.2%
1974*	April 21	111	30.6%	74	20.4%	37	10.2%
Employee Retirement Income Security Act of 1974 (0.0%)							
1975*	April 15	105	28.9%	68	18.8%	37	10.2%
Tax Reduction Act of 1975 (-0.7%)							
1976	April 18	108	29.6%	71	19.4%	37	10.3%
Tax Reform Act of 1976 (-0.9%)							
1977	April 19	109	29.9%	72	19.6%	37	10.2%
Tax Reduction and Simplification Act of 1977 (-1.0%)							
1978	April 19	109	30.0%	74	20.2%	35	9.8%
Revenue Act of 1978 (-0.6%)							
1979	April 19	109	30.1%	75	20.7%	34	9.4%

Table 2.28 (*continued*)

Year	Tax Freedom Day	All Governments Days Spent Working to Pay Taxes	Total Effective Tax Rate	Federal Government Days Spent Working to Pay Taxes	Effective Tax Rate	State-Local Governments Days Spent Working to Pay Taxes	Effective Tax Rate
1980*	April 20	110	30.3%	76	20.9%	34	9.4%
Crude Oil Windfall Profit Tax of 1980 (+0.5%)							
1981*	April 23	113	31.0%	79	21.6%	34	9.4%
Economic Recovery Tax Act of 1981 (-1.4%)							
1982*	April 20	110	30.3%	75	20.7%	35	9.7%
Tax Equity and Fiscal Responsibility Act of 1982 (+0.6%);							
Highway Revenue Act of 1982 (+0.1%)							
1983	April 17	107	29.4%	72	19.7%	35	9.7%
Social Security Amendments of 1983 (+0.2%); Interest and Dividend Tax							
Compliance Act of 1983 (-0.1%)							
1984	April 16	106	29.2%	71	19.4%	35	9.8%
Deficit Reducation Act of 1984 (+0.3%)							
1985	April 17	107	29.6%	72	19.7%	35	9.9%
Consolidated Omnibus Budget Reconciliation Act of 1985 (+0.0%)							
1986	April 18	108	29.7%	72	19.7%	36	10.0%
Tax Reform Act of 1986 (+0.5%)							
1987	April 22	112	30.7%	75	20.5%	37	10.2%
Omnibus Budget Reconciliation Act of 1987 (+0.2%)							
1988	April 21	111	30.5%	74	20.3%	37	10.2%
1989	April 22	112	30.7%	75	20.5%	37	10.2%
Omnibus Reconciliation Act of 1989 (+0.1%)							
1990*	April 21	111	30.5%	74	20.2%	37	10.3%
Omnibus Budget Reconciliation Act of 1990 (+0.5%)							
1991*	April 20	110	30.4%	72	19.9%	38	10.5%
1992	April 20	110	30.2%	72	19.6%	38	10.6%
1993	April 20	110	30.4%	72	19.9%	38	10.5%
Omnibus Budget Reconciliation Act of 1993 (+0.4%)							
1994	April 22	112	30.9%	74	20.4%	38	10.5%
1995	April 24	114	31.3%	76	20.8%	38	10.5%
1996	April 25	115	31.7%	77	21.3%	38	10.4%
1997	April 27	117	32.2%	80	21.8%	37	10.3%
Taxpayer Relief Act of 1997 (-0.1%)							
1998	April 29	119	32.8%	82	22.4%	37	10.4%
1999	April 30	120	32.9%	83	22.5%	37	10.4%
2000	May 02	122	33.6%	84	23.1%	38	10.4%
2001*	April 29	119	32.7%	81	22.2%	38	10.5%
Economic Growth and Tax Reform Reconciliation Act of 2001 (-0.8%)							
2002*	April 19	109	29.9%	72	19.7%	37	10.2%
The Job Creation and Worker Assistance Act of 2002 (-0.6%)							
2003	April 14	104	28.5%	68	18.5%	36	10.1%
Job Growth and Tax Relief Reconciliation Act of 2003 (-0.6%)							
2004	April 11	101	27.8%	65	17.9%	36	10.0%

Notes: Leap day is omitted to make dates comparable over time. Positive and negative percentages in parentheses after legislation indicate the first-year fiscal impact of the bill, measured as a percentage of NNP.

*Year with at least one quarter in which GDP shrank.

Source: Moody, J. S. (April 2004). America celebrates Tax Freedom Day. *Special Report*, vol. 129. Washington, D.C.: Tax Foundation. Retrieved from http://www.taxfoundation.org/SR129.pdf.

Figure 2.1
Time Americans Work to Pay Taxes in Relation to Other Expenses: 2004

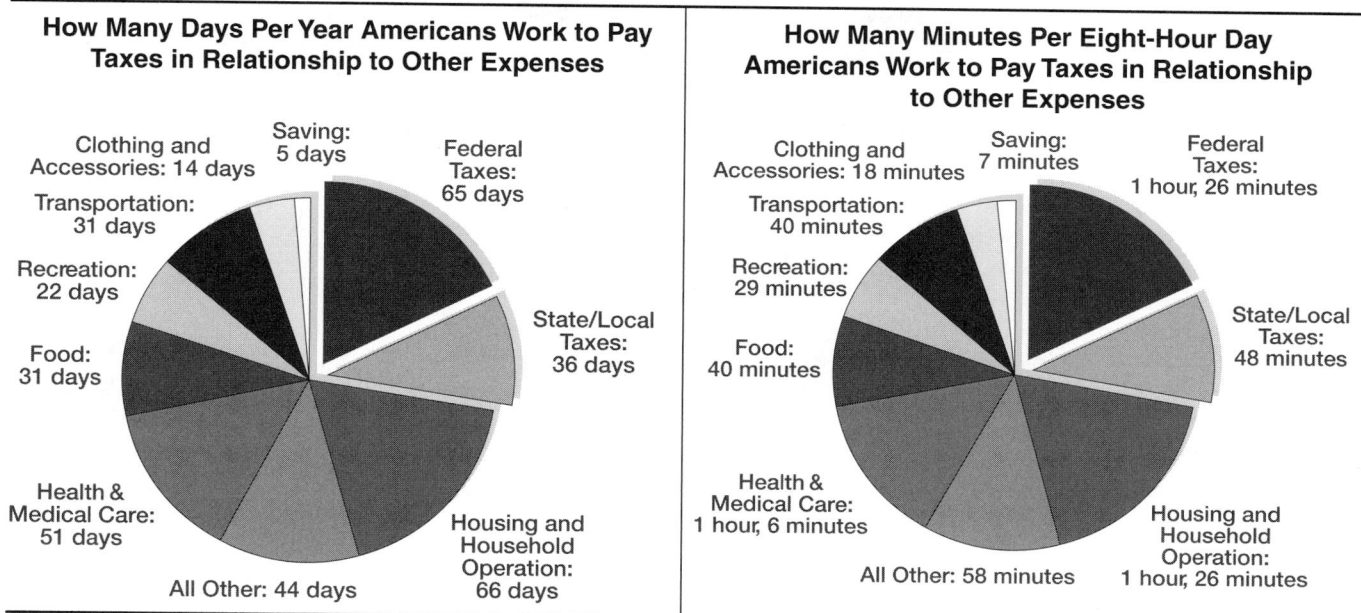

How Many Days Per Year Americans Work to Pay Taxes in Relationship to Other Expenses

Clothing and Accessories: 14 days
Saving: 5 days
Federal Taxes: 65 days
Transportation: 31 days
Recreation: 22 days
State/Local Taxes: 36 days
Food: 31 days
Health & Medical Care: 51 days
All Other: 44 days
Housing and Household Operation: 66 days

How Many Minutes Per Eight-Hour Day Americans Work to Pay Taxes in Relationship to Other Expenses

Clothing and Accessories: 18 minutes
Saving: 7 minutes
Federal Taxes: 1 hour, 26 minutes
Transportation: 40 minutes
Recreation: 29 minutes
State/Local Taxes: 48 minutes
Food: 40 minutes
Health & Medical Care: 1 hour, 6 minutes
All Other: 58 minutes
Housing and Household Operation: 1 hour, 26 minutes

Source: Moody, J. S. (April 2004). America celebrates Tax Freedom Day. *Special Report*, vol. 129. Washington. D.C.: Tax Foundation. Retrieved from http://www.taxfoundation.org/SR129.pdf.

Table 2.29
Total Tax Revenue as Percentage of GDP at Market Prices[1]

	1980	1985	1990	1992	1993	1994	1995	1996	1997*
Denmark	45.5	49.0	48.7	49.2	50.4	51.9	51.4	52.2	
Sweden	48.8	50.0	55.6	51.0	50.1	50.8	49.5	52.0	53.3
Finland	36.9	40.8	45.4	46.8	45.4	47.6	46.1	48.2	47.3
Belgium	43.7	46.9	44.0	44.3	44.9	46.0	46.0	46.0	46.5
France	41.7	44.5	43.7	43.7	43.9	44.1	44.5	45.7	46.1
Luxembourg	42.0	46.7	43.4	41.8	43.9	44.3	44.1	44.7	45.6
Austria	40.3	42.4	41.0	43.0	43.4	43.3	42.3	44.0	44.4
Netherlands	45.2	44.1	44.6	46.8	47.5	44.7	43.8	43.3	43.4
Italy	30.4	34.5	39.2	42.1	43.8	41.7	41.3	43.2	44.9
Poland (2)				38.2	42.4	43.2	42.7	42.1	41
Norway	42.7	43.3	41.8	41.0	40.1	41.3	41.5	41.1	42.5
Greece	29.4	35.1	37.1	39.0	39.5	40.2	40.8	40.6	
Czech Republic (2)					43.7	42.8	41.5	40.5	39
Hungary (2)				45.9	45.8	44.7	43.3	40.3	39
Germany (3)	38.2	38.1	36.7	38.9	39.0	39.2	39.2	38.1	37.5
Canada	32.0	33.1	36.0	36.2	35.6	35.9	36.0	36.8	
United Kingdom	35.1	37.5	36.5	35.1	33.5	34.5	35.6	36.0	35.3
New Zealand	33.0	33.6	38.0	36.9	36.9	37.3	37.9	35.8	36.4
Portugal	25.1	27.6	30.9	34.4	32.4	33.8	34.9	34.9	34.5
Switzerland	29.1	30.8	30.9	31.2	32.2	33.0	33.5	34.7	34.6
Spain	23.9	28.5	34.2	35.6	34.7	34.7	34.0	33.7	35.3
Ireland	32.6	36.4	34.8	35.4	35.4	36.1	33.8	33.7	34.8
Iceland	29.2	28.4	31.4	32.2	31.2	30.9	31.2	32.3	32.0
Australia	28.4	30.0	30.6	28.4	28.5	29.6	30.4	31.1	30.3
United States	26.9	26.0	26.7	26.7	27.0	27.5	27.9	28.5	
Japan	25.4	27.6	31.3	29.2	29.1	27.8	28.5	28.4	
Turkey	17.9	15.4	20.0	22.4	22.7	22.2	22.6	25.4	27.7
Korea	17.5	16.8	19.0	19.8	20.7	21.5	22.3	23.2	
Mexico	16.2	17.0	17.3	17.6	17.7	17.2	16.6	16.3	16.9
Unweighted average:									
OECD Total	33.0	34.8	36.1	36.9	37.3	37.5	37.3	37.7	
OECD America	25.0	25.4	26.7	26.8	26.8	26.9	26.8	27.2	
OECD Pacifi	26	27.0	29.7	28.6	28.8	29.1	29.	29.6	
OECD Europe	35.7	37.9	38.9	39.9	40.3	40.5	40.2	40.6	
EU 15	37.2	40.2	41.0	41.8	41.9	42.2	41.8	42.4	

*. Provisional.

1. Ranked by the 1996 figures.

2. The Czech Republic, Hungary and Poland joined the OECD in 1995/1996. Data for earliers years than included here are not available.

3. United Germany beginning in 1991.

Source: Organization of Economic Co-operation and Development (1998). News Release on *Revenue Statistics of OECD Countries 1965–1997*. Retrieved from http://wwwl.oecd.org/media/publish/PB98-33A.pdf. OECD Copyright. Reproduced by permission of the OECD.

3. The Government's Definition of Poverty

Arbitrary: 1. not fixed by rules but left to one's own judgment or choice; discretionary (arbitrary decision, arbitrary judgment) 2. based on one's preference, notion, whim, etc.; capricious 3. absolute; despotic—SYN. see DICTATORIAL

Webster's New World Dictionary

An additional point worth noting about the word "arbitrary" is that it has several distinct connotations, including: 1) depending on judgment, choice, or discretion (used in particular of decision of a judge as contrasted to a decision or sentence specified in a statute); 2) random or capricious. (Fisher, 1997, 9/72)

MEANS-TESTS AS A PROGRAM CONDITION IN SOCIAL SAFETY NET PROGRAMS

The presence of **means-tests** to determine program eligibility requires a detailed discussion of how governments define poverty. However, prior to delving on the definition of poverty, the discussion needs to first focus on means-testing itself.

Basically, means-tests are assessments that determine if one is able to qualify for benefits from the social safety net at the national, state, or local levels, or if one makes or has too much to qualify. In a sense, they are the most common "gatekeepers" determining access to the safety net in many programs in the United States as well as in many other countries. Their effect is to ration access to these programs, as well as to limit the amount of benefits and services provided under safety net provisions. As a manner of enacting policies, these tests are controversial in the sense that professionals in the field find them onerous to those who need the services, while for politicians and other interest groups, they are a means of providing accountability. The expectation is that only those that merit the aid receive it, and not those who are out there to abuse the system. This is why Chatterjee (1999) reminds students of the welfare state that one important responsibility of

a national government is to protect citizens from external and internal predators.

As will be seen later in this chapter and others in this book, there are significant complications when using means-tests. For example, how is "earned" income measured? What is the difference between "earned" and "unearned" income? How is an in-kind correlation determined? What is the equivalent value that is placed on a service in relationship to income received? Finally and foremost, how is poverty vis-à-vis eligibility defined and acknowledged?

There is no way around the minor detail that defining poverty is a political activity (DiNitto and Dye, 1987). The process itself, from the approach toward making a definition to the means-test utilized, is an example of the political conflict over poverty and what to do about it.[1]

THE FORMULA APPROACH TOWARD DEFINING AND MEASURING POVERTY

The United States has an official measure of poverty. This measure is created by experts through combining objective measures with a degree of subjective judgment to formulate underlying assumptions that then place the measures into a useable frame of reference. "In the simplest terms, the poverty lines represent the level of income that divides the families of a particular size, place, and time into the poor and nonpoor" (Watts, 1977, 28). The U.S. Census Bureau is responsible for collecting poverty data, the Bureau of Labor Statistics performs the analysis of the data, and administrative use of data is the responsibility of the U.S. Department of Health and Human Services. In a sense, there are two principal incantations of this poverty measure resulting from the action of these three federal government entities. **Poverty thresholds** are primarily utilized for statistical analysis. **Poverty guidelines** are used for determining eligibility requirements for a number of programs in the social safety net (Fisher, 1997; United States Department of Health and Human Services, 2000). The best way to look at the difference is, according to the U.S. Department of Health and Human Services (2000), that "the poverty guidelines are a simplified version of the . . . poverty thresholds" (7556). In 1995, more than twenty-five agencies were dependent on the eligibility criteria created from the thresholds (Citro & Michael, 1995). At present, there are about eighty programs that are dependent on the poverty guidelines. Specific examples of these programs include (Institute for Research on Poverty, 2000):

- In the Department of Health and Human Services: Community Services Block Grant, Head Start, Low-Income Home Energy Assistance, Children's Health Insurance Program
- In the Department of Agriculture: Food Stamps, Special Supplemental Nutrition Program for Women, Infants, and Children (WIC), the National School Lunch and School Breakfast programs
- In the Department of Energy: Weatherization Assistance
- In the Department of Labor: Job Corps, Senior Community Service Employment Program, National Farmworker Jobs Program
- In the Legal Services Corporation: Legal services for the poor

In addition, certain relatively recent provisions of Medicaid use the poverty guidelines; however, the rest of that program (accounting for roughly three-quarters of Medicaid eligibility determinations) does not use the guidelines. On the other hand, major means-tested programs that do not use the poverty guidelines in determining eligibility include Temporary Assistance for Needy Families (or its predecessor, Aid to Families with Dependent Children), Supplemental Security Income, the earned income tax credit program (EITC), the Department of Housing and Urban Development's means-tested housing assistance programs, and the Social Services Block Grant.

There is a long-running controversy toward having such a measure as well as how it is measured—what it includes and what it does not—and its application as a rationing agent because of its use as a critical eligibility criterion. In other words, its very presence makes many uncomfortable. Even the use of certain terms—for example, "low income" instead of "poor" or "poverty"—creates problems. Ideally, as Citro and Michael (1995) state, because of its use by differing interests and the implication its use has on the safety net, "it is critical that the measure provide an accurate picture of trends over time and of differences among groups, such as children, the elderly, minorities, working people, people receiving government assistance, people in cities, and people in rural areas" (18). The 1995 report by the Committee on National Statistics, the Commission on Behavioral and Social Sciences and Education, and the National Research Council points out six important weaknesses that demonstrate the charge of arbitrariness against the current poverty measure given the far-reaching changes in U.S. society, economy, and governmental policies (Citro and Michael, 1995):

- The increased participation of mothers in the workforce requiring more working families who must pay for their childcare. The current indicator does not distinguish between the needs of workers and nonworkers.
- Differences in health status and insurance coverage make the impression that different population groups face significant variations in medical care costs; yet, the current measure does not take this into account.
- Thresholds are national although significant price variations exist (for example, in housing) throughout the country.
- The family size **adjustments** in the thresholds are anomalous because of the changing demographic family characteristics from the time that the indicator was created, underscoring the need to reassess these adjustments.
- Broader changes in the **cost of living standard** challenges the notion of continuing to use the values of the original thresholds by updating them for inflation only.
- The current measure defines family resources as **gross money income.** It "does not reflect the effects of important government policy initiatives that have significantly altered families' disposable income, and, hence, their poverty status" (3). Examples of the impact of government policy changes that add and subtract someone's disposable income include the increase in the social security payroll tax which reduces workers' disposable income and the growth of the food stamp program which raises disposable income for beneficiaries.

Furthermore, the Report goes on to say that poverty, if defined under the rubric of deprivation, has to consider more than a lack of economic resources. There is deprivation from a psychological, or social well-being (for example, status, literacy, education, and skills) perspective, and physical well-being (health and safety) point of view. The federal government should develop and consider "indicators for monitoring trends over time among population groups on all of these different dimensions . . . and the relationship among them" (20).

The poverty thresholds were originally developed in 1963 and 1964 from data culled from the Agriculture Department's 1955 Household Food Consumption Survey. The main person responsible for generating the basis of the current poverty line indicator formula, Mollie Orshansky, indicated that there is a degree of arbitrariness to it, but that it is not unreasonable (Fisher, 1997). Ironically, as Fisher reminds those interested in these things, Orshansky did not want to introduce a new general measure of poverty; she was trying to develop a measure to assess the relative risks of low economic status (or, more broadly, the differentials in opportunity) among different demographic groups of families with children. The normative nature of its approach as still seen in the multipliers used generate assumptions that are questioned by many. The indicator's focus on consumer patterns distresses others. How or whether to include in-kind (non-cash) benefits as income in the formula is a concern as well. Much of the current literature throughout the world suggests other considerations and approaches toward poverty.

For the remainder of this chapter, the discussion will take a look at how the formula used in the United States is derived and then compared to efforts elsewhere by international organizations and other countries. The socioeconomic and political implications of how poverty is defined and the resources that are then put in place to "fight" poverty have a tremendous impact in the definition, implementation, administration, and maintenance of the social safety net. These separate nations in accordance to their social philosophies and available resources to meet self-defined social responsibilities. As will be seen in the data section of this chapter, the definition of poverty impacts, and is the basis of, other data indicators that demonstrate the status of many components of interest in the social safety net.

The best way to look at the poverty measure in the United States (and elsewhere as well) is to remember Aaron Wildavsky's (1974) definition of a calculation, because it reminds one of the behind-the-scenes thinking the measure ultimately represents. He may have been talking about the budgetary process; nevertheless, he is also talking about the effect that any formulaic presentation (and this includes hypothesis testing as well as threshold formulae) with policy repercussions has within the legislative process, especially in the area of social policy.

By "calculation" I mean the series of related factors (manifestly including perceptions of influence relationships) which the participants take into account in determining the choice of competing alternatives. Calculation involves a study of how problems arise, how they are identified as such, how they are broken down into manageable dimensions, how they are related to one another, how determinations are made of what is relevant, and how the actions of others are given into consideration. Special attention is paid to the much neglected problem of complexity. For if there is one thing that participants in budgeting share, it is a concern with the extraordinary complexity of the programs and processes with which they deal. (7)

An example of how Wildavsky's definition works is the presence of the two types of poverty measures. The rationale for the two versions is mainly one of timing. Poverty threshold calculations are derived from the March current population survey (CPS) and then indexed via the consumer price index for all urban consumers (CPI-U). Threshold data comes out in its final form the summer after the calendar year that is analyzed. Poverty guidelines are published in the Federal Register in February. This schedule does not sychronize with the calendar or federal fiscal year. Consequently, using this data on a calendar year basis means that agencies would have to rely on data that can be as much as two years old during the months of January through about July. Another example of Wildavsky's comment is how various federal agencies track **family budget** issues, with the Department of Labor compiling three sets of budgets to determine how a standard family of four budgets for all of its necessities, not just food: the higher family budget, an intermediate family budget, and a lower family budget (Schwartz and Volgy, 1992). This echoes—and at a conceptual level, supports—the two measures that Orshansky had available from the Agriculture Department when developing the threshold indicator. Fisher (1997) describes the developmental process:

At the time she was developing the thresholds, the Agriculture Department had food plans at the following four cost levels (listed here from the most costly to the cheapest): liberal, moderate, low-cost, and economy. . . . Orshansky used the low-cost and economy food plans in developing her two sets of poverty thresholds, describing them as follows: "The low-cost plan, adapted to the food patterns of families in the lowest third of the income range, has for many years been used by welfare agencies as a basis for food allotments for needy families and others who wished to keep food costs down." (4–5)

For the record, the lower indicators were adopted as the ones to be used in generating the poverty indicator.

The official poverty indicator in the United States equates poverty with economic deprivation. It presumes that economic well-being is related to the ability to consume goods and services as measured by income stated in dollar terms (Haveman, 1987). There have been few changes to the poverty index used in this country; indeed, in 1990, it was noted that it had been twenty-five years and not many changes had been made on a formula based on research done in the 1950s and 1960s, whose application to the 1990s may be inappropriate (Fisher, 1997). The poverty indicator formula, according to Orshansky (1976), is based on a number of critical judgments significantly affecting **poverty line** levels in the formula utilized by the federal government:

the level of food plans considered to be adequate,

the multiplier relating total income requirements to the cost of food, and

the appropriateness of before-tax or after-tax income, and which one to use.

At present, the formula is based on an **absolute standard**, referring to fixed points of income versus expenses in constant dollars (i.e., within a specified time frame), thus requiring regular updating for changes in real consumption, but not for real growth in consumption (Citro and Michael, 1995). Thresholds differ by the number of adults and children that make up a family. In some categories, a distinction is also made by the age of the head of the household.

Given the importance of the threshold indicator on the social safety net, it is interesting to note that a detailed description of the formula is hard to find. Even a basic description of the process takes some distillation of the source one uses. But because of its importance, it is worth taking a few words to go through it on an overview basis.

*The basic components of the poverty threshold indicator are an algebraic equation that denotes (a) the income needed to make ends meet, (b) defining "ends meet" based on how much an **average family** spends on food and then developing a multiplier to factor in other costs of basic essentials, and (c) indexing or adjusting annually for inflation by using the CPI-U. The multiplier used is 3, based on the 1955 survey finding that a family spent one-third of its income on food. The formula then has to be differentiated by household size, composition of the household unit and, in some instances, the age of* *the household head.* The following lists describe the overall process of how thresholds are developed and updated (Citro & Michael, 41).

The basis for determining who is poor and who is not is based on the annual family money income (Garfinkel and Haveman, 1977). **Income determination** in the surveys is based on pretax earnings, while costs and acquisition factors are based on after-tax disposable income. Costing itself is based on finding out how much it costs to meet nutritional requirements, instead of the more standard "market basket" approach where a collection of consumer goods and services is identified and tracked in order to determine how much it costs to meet one's needs. For example, one of the key assumptions driving the threshold derivations is the notion that increased nutritional demands of children as they get older add to the family's food cost. This assumption is closely tied with **Engel's law** in economics, which states that as an indicator of living standards, a family's proportion of money spent on food decreases as its income level increases. Chart 3.1 illustrates Engel's law by comparing the costs between a household with two adults and one child and a household with only two adults (Citro and Michael, 1995, 171). Line A represents a two-adult family while line B is for a family with a child. Line B is higher because more food is spent by that family at all levels of income. Y_0 and W_0 represent the level of income and food share of a family prior to having the child, y_1 and W_1 represent income and food share with the addition of a child. The family returns to its original standard of living when its food share returns to

Chart 3.1
Elements of the Current U.S. Poverty Measure

Element of the threshold Development process	Current measure's determination process
Threshold concept	Food times a large multiplier for all other expenses
Threshold adjustments by family type	Update 1963 level each year for price changes
Threshold adjustments by geographical type	None (for 48 contiguous states)
Family resource definition (to compare with threshold to determine poverty status)	Gross (before-tax) money income from all sources
Data source (for estimating income)	March current population survey (CPS)
Time period of measure	Annual
Economic unit of analysis	Families and unrelated individuals

Source: Adapted from Citro & Michael, 1995, p.41.

Chart 3.2
Engel Method for Equivalence Scales

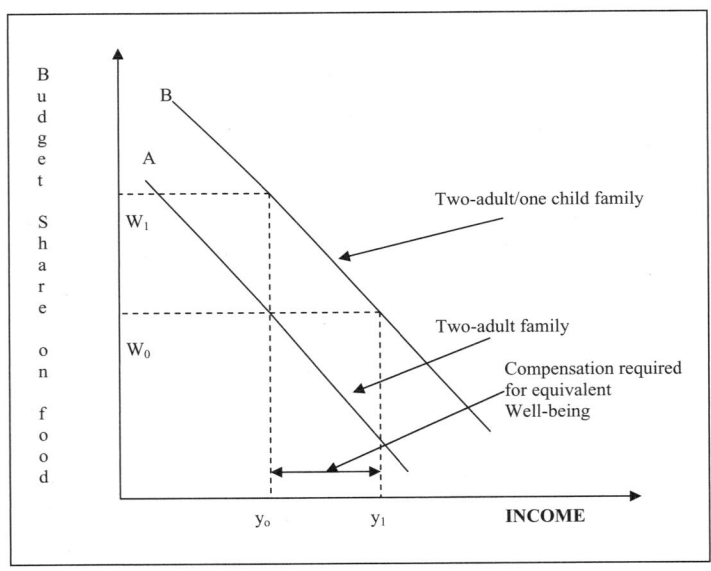

the original value.[2] The challenge to the multiplier is not the assumption that the presence of children influence family spending requirements and choices, it comes from questioning whether or not the formula overstates the consumption needs of children and if it overrepresents the overall consumption patterns in a household.

The basic family unit was defined by Orshansky in 1963 as containing two adults and two children, and this is still the basic landmark for talking about the average family when establishing the poverty threshold indicator; her calculations yielded a multiplier of 3 for this group, although she used 3.7 for a two-person family (corresponding to a 27 percent food share). For single adults, rather than using a multiplier, she set the threshold figure at 80 percent of the two-person family (household). She also identified for threshold determination purposes a total of 124 different family (household) categories, although since 1981 only 48 categories are reported. These represent weighted averages in order to simplify the reporting process. Table 3.1 at the end of the chapter shows the percent of food share in relation to the multiplier generated by the Orshansky method.

Table 3.2 represents the most current scale representing the multiplier effect, calculated by converting the official 1992 two-adult, two-child family threshold for each of the other family types (thresholds for two-adult families and unrelated individuals are for individuals under age 65). Simply multiply the numbers reached for the two-adult, two-child family by this factor and one generates the poverty threshold for the other household types. Table 3.3 provides the official poverty guidelines for 2002. Note that there are three sets, for the forty-eight contiguous states, then one each for Alaska and Hawaii. The federal government recognizes the impact that these two states' different income/cost requirements as a result of their geographical location has on their cost of living standards. Table 3.4 provides a comparison between the official poverty guideline calculation and that of suggested alternatives based on the two-adult, two-child **family unit** for the year 1993. Note that in all instances, regardless of the different approaches to calculating a poverty threshold, the official approach yields the lowest threshold.

The way this narrative is developing, it seems that all members of society are or should be covered by the poverty thresholds and guidelines. However, this is not the case. The Census Bureau does not define poverty for those in military barracks, institutional group quarters, or for unrelated individuals under age 15, such as foster children. These groups are officially excluded from being considered poor. They are not thought of a part of the "poverty universe"—that is they are considered neither as "poor" nor as "nonpoor" (United States Census Bureau, 2002b). These groups do not fit any of the categories originally established by Orshansky and, in two of the three situations, it can be argued that there are societal norms along with practical considerations as to why these groups are excluded (for example, transiency because of the temporariness of the defined group status).

Other countries and international organizations utilize poverty measures, as well. Those that use poverty indicators like the United States position their use based on their definition of social responsibility. Accordingly, the World Bank makes the following statement:

> The most commonly used way to measure poverty is based on incomes or consumption levels. A person is considered poor if his or her consumption or income level falls below some minimum level necessary to meet basic needs. This minimum level is usually called the "poverty line". What is necessary to satisfy basic needs varies across time and societies. Therefore, poverty lines vary in time and place, and each country uses lines which are appropriate to its level of development, societal norms and values. (World Bank, 2002)

As already noted previously in this chapter, poverty indicators have a controversial nature about them. Adding to arguments already presented, there is an additional challenge or opportunity for improvement: the fact that these indicators are dependent on the quality and quantity of data that can be generated. Many countries lack the social infrastructure take care of their citizens and, because of the normative nature of the definition of poverty, measures can be used to undermine the rights and privileges of a significant component of a nation's population to access items such as food and health care.

Two of the central points of social safety nets are defining what the term *poor* means to a society (along with its corollary who the poor are) and how poverty is defined (and its corollary of how the definition is used by that society). As the example of the United States points out, both points have significant administrative, economic, legal, moral, philosophical, political, and social considerations. Loosely, the term *poor* can be defined as those persons that do not and have the resources necessary to meet their basic needs beyond a subsistence level. Who the poor are, as discussed in the Introduction to this book, is defined by the World Bank (1996) to be people "marginalized by virtue of their race and ethnicity as well as those disadvantaged by circumstances beyond their control, such as disabilities and natural or man-made disasters." Poverty is probably best described as a form of deprivation in which individuals within a community do not have access to those resources, goods, and services that allow them to enjoy living conditions that are in accordance to the expectations set by the standards of their community. One of the most important aspects of deprivation is access to food and dietary consumption. Other significant aspects of deprivation are access to healthcare, housing, adequate clothing, education, work, and representation of their interests.

From a comparative perspective, the challenge of thinking of the poor and poverty is the variable (hence, arbitrary) nature of these concepts. Standards of living differ from one country to another, from one region within one country to another. Paradoxically, the more income that individuals can accumulate means that those that are considered to be poor make more money; yet it is still not enough to meet those expectations that their society considers the benefit of living in their community, and this income level still does not allow access to those resources that provide the access to representation, goods, and services that others have as a matter of due course. The line of demarcation between the "haves" and the "have nots" is therefore hard to quantify and judge. This blurry line that traditional notions of poverty presents to those who are interested in such things means that poverty is a difficult item to quantify. It is a laborious task to come up with proper items to include and exclude that experts can agree upon and put into a workable form. One has to think in terms of this simple, yet, elusive question: What level of well-being is enough? Another way of thinking of this question: How much quality does a person have to have in order to lead a "good" life? As Ivan P. Felligi, Canada's Chief Statistician writes:

> In spite of these efforts, there is still no internationally-accepted definition of poverty—unlike measures such as employment, unemployment, gross domestic product, consumer prices, international trade and so on. This is not surprising, perhaps, given the absence of an international consensus on what poverty is and how it should be measured. Such consensus preceded the development of all other international standards.
>
> The lack of an internationally-accepted definition has also reflected indecision as to whether an international standard definition should allow comparisons of well-being across countries compared to some international norm, or whether poverty lines should be established according to the norms within each country. (1997)

"The United States is one of the few developed countries with an official poverty measure . . . , but many countries and international organizations have undertaken poverty measurement" (Citro and Michael, 1995, 126). Australia is an example of how a poverty indicator may have a different perspective, but still utilizes a similar data treatment as that used in the United States. The Henderson Poverty Line (HPL), first developed in the 1960s and utilized as of the 1970s to provide national estimates in Australia on poverty, has a poverty line centered on a two-adult, two-child family set at an income equal to the value of the basic wage plus child endowment payments later called "family allowances" (Saunders, 1996). In this family, there is one adult working, with the spouse and children dependent on this person's earnings. The estimates are updated by the Australian Bureau of Statistics by measuring household income quarterly. Updates have been published on a regular basis from 1979, and since 1981 the updating has been done through a per capita household disposable income (Saunders, 1996). Saunders indicates that for each income unit type, the poverty measure has variances based on "the age, gender and workforce status of each individual member, and according to the total number of individuals living in the income units household." The ensuing equivalency scale gives a single individual a value of 1.0 while a married couple has a factor of 1.7, an implication that the married couple has 70 percent greater needs than a single individual. The living arrangement of the married couple—that they are living together—takes into account the "economy of scale" argument, thus the multiplier less than 2. Nevertheless, as in the United States, the poverty measure is seen as lacking because it lacks other dimensions that influence poverty and

how individuals achieve that status. More to the point, as the Australian Bureau of Statistics (1998) itself tells its users, the use of other poverty measures leads to quite different results in defining poverty in Australia.

Canada has been publishing a series of low-income statistics for a number of years based on a set of low-income cutoffs developed by a hybrid approach to generate the standard (Citro and Michael, 1995). The official bureau of statistics does not endorse the practice of using the current favored measure as an approach to setting poverty lines. According to Phipps and Curtis (2000),

> the most common approach to measuring "low-income" is through the Statistics Canada Low-Income Cutoffs (LICO's). The LICO's are derived using an "Engel methodology" which judges households to be living with low-income if they devote 20 percentage points more than the average Canadian family to the purchase of necessities. While Statistics Canada is very careful to note that the LICO's measure "low income" and not "poverty," public discussion very much treats the LICO's as official poverty lines. (4).

And as Citro and Michael (1995) elaborate:

> The LICOs were developed by first determining the average expenditure of all families on food, shelter, and clothing as a percent of gross income. To this percentage was added an arbitrary 20 percentage points. Then, log-linear curves were fit between food, shelter, and clothing on one side and before-tax income on the other, taking account of variations in family size and urbanization (size of community). . . . Finally, on the basis of these curves, the LICO for each family type that corresponded to the designated proportion of spending on food, shelter, and clothing was determined. (127)

In 1999, the Canadian bureau of statistics, Statistics Canada, made the decision to continue the use of the LICOs as the main and preferred approach to the measurement of low-income in Canada for the time being; however, they are also going to seriously consider an alternate measure, the low income measure (LIM; Statistics Canada, 1999). The low income measure is based on one-half the median income: a fixed percentage (set at 50 percent) of the adjusted median family income, with the adjustment representing the consideration of family needs. The focus of the LIMs is that needs increase as the size of the family increases. Each additional adult is assumed to increase family needs by 40 percent of the needs of the first adult, and the needs of each child are assumed to be 30 percent of the first adult (10). The following list provides the steps for the actual calculation of the LIM (Statistics Canada, 1999, 11).

Actual Calculation of the Canadian Low Income Measure (LIM)

1. For each family, determine "adjusted family size" whereby the first adult is counted as one person and each additional adult as 0.4 of a person, and each child (less than 16 years of age) as 0.3 of a person (except in a family of one adult and children only where the first child is counted as 0.4 of a person);

2. Calculate for each family "adjusted family income" by dividing family income by "adjusted family size";

3. Determine the median "adjusted family income" which is the adjusted family income where 50 percent of families have a smaller adjusted family income and 50 percent have a higher one;

4. The LIM for a family of size one is 50 percent of the median "adjusted family income" and the LIMs for the other types are equal to this value multiplied by "adjusted family size";

5. Repeat the process for each year that LIMs are required.

European countries have a differing approach based on consumption expenditure rather than income, due to the European Union's (EU) declaration that the reduction of poverty is a key objective of future European social policy (Tentschert, Till, and Redl, 2000). Tentschert, Till, and Redl (2000) write that the term *poverty* had meant to refer to income poverty, but now a broader concept of social exclusion and deprivation is being developed as a challenge to the limits that such a view has toward poverty. In consequence, framed by the need to utilize a comparative analysis format because of the unique reporting challenges it faces, the EU uses three approaches to define the income portion of a poverty indicator (Eurostat, 2002):

- *Inequality of income distribution* (income quintile share ratio): The ratio of total income received by the 20 percent of the population with the highest income (top quintile) to that received by the 20 percent of the population with the lowest income (lowest quintile). Income must be understood as equivalent disposable income.

- *Risk-of-poverty rate*: The share of persons with a normalized disposable income below the risk-of-poverty threshold, which is set at 60 percent of the national median equivalised disposable income (after social transfers). This share is calculated before social transfers (original income including pensions but excluding all other social transfers) and after social transfers (total income).

- *Persistent-risk-of-poverty rate*: The share of persons with a normalized disposable income below the risk-of-poverty threshold in the current year and in at least two of the preceding three years. The threshold is set at 60 percent of the national median equivalised disposable income.

The adjustment procedure (equalization or equating to process) works as follows:

The adjusting procedure works as follows: if the equivalence scale says that families of four need two (or three) times as much income or consumption to sustain the same living standard as a single person, then the income (or expenditures) of four-person families would be divided by two (or three) to produce a per capita equivalent amount, and so on for other family sizes. Median or average adjusted income for one-person households would then be produced from the distribution of equivalent per capita amounts. This procedure can be adapted to set a reference threshold for any size family. Thus, for a four-person reference family, income amounts for other families would be converted to four-person equivalent amounts (e.g., the income for a single person would be multiplied by two or three, depending on the ratio of the equivalence scale value for a four-person family to that for a single person). (Citro and Michael, 1995, 126n, 127n).

The considerations underlying this approach are based on the work advocating social indicators to establish a poverty indicator initiated by Peter Townsend as far back as the 1960s. Bradshaw (2001) relates that each EU country's social assistance scale generates lower poverty rates than the relative income method. More to the point, he says that the scales are government determined, or at least government interests influence the standards.[3]

The extent to which the social assistance scales are based on some scientific notion of adequacy, varies from country to country. In some countries the link with science is an old one with the rationale lost in the passage of time (eg France, UK). In others it is more up to date and still formally based on a standard budget (eg Sweden) (Veit Wilson 2000). [Bradshaw, 2001, 6, citations as in source material]

In 2001, the EU's Social Protection Committee came up with a guideline for a poverty measure utilizing social exclusion as an approach to determine poverty. The indicators developed were tiered into primary and secondary indicators, with individual countries able to add a third tier to meet their specific circumstances or assist in interpreting the other two tiers of data. As conceptualized, primary indicators are to consist of a restricted number of lead indicators which cover the broad fields that have been considered the most important elements in leading to social exclusion, while secondary indicators support these lead indicators and describe other dimensions of the problem (Social Protection Committee, 2001, 3).

Primary EU Indicators based on Social Exclusion

1. Low income rate after transfers with low-income threshold set at 60% of median income (with breakdowns by gender, age, most frequent activity status, household type and tenure status; as illustrative examples, the values for typical households)

2. Distribution of income (income quintile ratio)

3. Persistence of low income

4. Median low income gap

5. Regional cohesion

6. Long term unemployment rate

7. People living in jobless households

8. Early school leavers not in further education or training

9. Life expectancy at birth

10. Self perceived health status

Secondary EU Indicators based on Social Exclusion

11. Dispersion around the 60% median low income threshold

12. Low income rate anchored at a point in time

13. Low income rate before transfers

14. Distribution of income (Gini coefficient)

15. Persistence of low income (based on 50% of median income)

16. Long term unemployment share

17. Very long term unemployment rate.

18. Persons with low educational attainment

South Korea provides another example of a nation that has made several attempts at establishing a poverty line measure. As Kwon (1998) indicates, "There is no official poverty line, only a political one in Korea. It can be called a legal poverty line, since low-income people whose income and assets are less than the predetermined level are legally eligible for public assistance benefits" (33; citations as in source material). Kwon goes on to describe the most prevalent methodology used to set the poverty line "has involved constructing a market basket reflecting typical behaviour patterns in the consumption of food items [see Suh et al. 1981; Ahn et al. 1988; Bark et al. 1994]," (32). South Korea's approach nonetheless takes from the United States' practice. Food baskets are an essential component in developing the indicator, non-food items follow Engel's law, and modal household expenditures are used to represent typical costs of living.

"Income thresholds are the ones most commonly used by national governments and international organisations such as the EU or OECD" (Bradshaw, 2001, 3). The World Bank (2002) considers an individual to be poor when this person's consumption or income level falls below some minimum level necessary to meet basic needs. This level they identify as their poverty line. Like with the poverty measures used in many countries, the line of demarcation varies in time and in location, and the definition of need varies in accordance to community norms and values. Information on both consumption and income is generated through survey instruments conducted in a more or less regular manner in most countries, often linking absolute and relative assessments to create a picture of who is impoverished and who is not. In its reporting guidelines, what the World Bank does is to express the result of the varying poverty guidelines in a common unit that can be used as a benchmark mechanism. "Therefore, for the purpose of global aggregation and comparison, the World Bank uses reference lines set at $1 and $2 per day in 1993 Purchasing Power Parity (PPP) terms (where PPPs measure the relative purchasing power of currencies across countries) (World Bank, 2002)." Using these two milestones, they estimate that in 1998 1.2 billion people worldwide (24 percent of the population in the developing world) had consumption levels below $1 per day. The World Bank also calculates for 1998 that 2.8 billion people lived on less than $2 per day.

As already seen in this chapter, poverty can be viewed in two different terms, absolute and relative (Lok-Dessallien, 2002). In attempting to make a measurement of poverty, **absolute poverty** as Lok-Dessallinent writes, points to subsistence below minimum, socially acceptable living conditions (usually based on nutritional requirements and other essential goods). Measuring *relative poverty* is a comparative process where the lower levels of society are compared to the upper segments.

Yamada (2002) argues that there are two ways to examine income under this approach. One way is to look at income quintiles and specific household structures. The second way is to examine low-income cut-off lines. But as he warns, "[s]ince it is possible that many people are clustered around low-income lines, this approach can produce misleading comparisons" (9).

The United Nations takes an approach that seems to fall somewhere between the two forms of poverty measures, although it seems that their approach is more absolute than relative because of their insistence on basic living condition standards. It generates two types of poverty indexes, one for developing countries (HPI-1) and a second for selected Organization for Economic Co-operation and Development (OECD) countries (HPI-2) that reflects a greater availability of data (United Nations Developing Programme, 2002). Both of these indicators focus on the "distribution of progress and measures the backlog of deprivation that still exists" (35). The indicator for developing countries considers deprivation from a three-dimensional perspective: (1) longevity based on the probability at birth of not surviving to age 40, (2) knowledge as measured by the adult illiteracy rate, and (3) overall public and private economic provisioning based on the percentage of people not using improved water sources, and the percentage of children under age 5 that are underweight. An unweighted average of two indicators is used to measure deprivation in a decent standard of living.

Unweighted average = ½ (population not using improved water sources) + ½ (underweight children under 5)

A sample calculation: Central African Republic
Population not using improved water sources = 40%
Underweight children under 5 = 24%

Unweighted average = ½ (40) + ½ (24) = 32%

The formula for calculating the HPI-1 is as follows:

$$HPI = 1 = [1/3 \ (P_1^\alpha + P_2^\alpha + P_3^\alpha)]^{1/\alpha}$$

where:

P_1 = Probability at birth of not surviving to age 40 (times 100)

P_2 = Adult illiteracy rate

P_3 = Unweighted average of population not using improved water sources and underweight children under age 5

$\alpha = 3$

A sample calculation using data from the Central African Republic shows:

$P_1 = 45.3\%$

$P_2 = 53.3\%$

$P_3 = 32.0\%$

HPI-1 = $[1/3 \ (45.3^3 + 53.3^3 + 32.0^3)]^{1/3}$ = 45.2 (United Nations Development Programme, 2002, 254).

The indicator for selected OECD countries has slightly different milestones and adds a fourth dimension to their view of deprivation: (1) longevity based at birth on not surviving to age 60, (2) the adult (ages 16 to 65) illiteracy rate, (3) the percentage of people living below the income poverty line (with disposable household income less than 50 percent of the median), and (4) social exclusion as measured by the long-term (12 months or more) unemployment rate. The formula for calculating the HPI-2 is as follows:

$$\text{HPI-2} = [1/4 \ (P_1^\alpha + P_2^\alpha + P_3^\alpha + P_4^\alpha)]^{1/\alpha}$$

where:

P_1 = Probability at birth of not surviving to age 60 (times 100)

P_2 = Adults lacking functional literacy skills

P_3 = Population below income poverty line (50 percent of median disposable household income)

P_4 = Rate of long-term unemployment (lasting 12 months or more)

$\alpha = 3$

Another sample calculation, this time with data from the United Kingdom, shows

$P_1 = 9.9\%$

$P_2 = 21.8\%$

$P_3 = 13.4\%$

$P_4 = 1.5\%$

$\text{HPI-2} = [1/4(9.9^3 + 21.8^3 + 13.4^3 + 1.5^3)]^{1/3} = 15.1$ (United Nations Development Programme, 2002, 254).

The reason both HPI calculations have an α value (weight) of 3 is to provide a greater emphasis to those areas where the deprivation is greater without making the emphasis on these areas too overwhelming. The factor is a combination of a pragmatic look at available data, differing notions of poverty, and the current trends in the literature about how to go about defining poverty, in particular, the notions on welfare economics delineated by Sen.

The World Bank and the United Nations have a high reliance on a different statistical approach, the Gini coefficient, because of its ability to measures the degree of inequality in the distribution of income in a given society. Used along with Lorenz curves that look at income distribution inequality, the coefficient calculates the average differences to determine the degree of dispersion.

> Lorenz curves are an effective way of showing inequality of income within and between countries. The cumulative percentage of population is plotted along the horizontal axis whilst the cumulative percentage of income is plotted along the vertical axis. The curve shows the actual relationship between the percentage of income recipients and the percentage of income that they did in fact actually receive.

The 45 degree line shows the situation when there is a even distribution of income i.e. 20% of the population earns 20% of the income and 50% of the households earn 50% of the income and so on. This is called the line of absolute equality.

The closer the Lorenz curve of a country is to the 45-degree line the more equal the distribution of income is. In the case of the Lorenz curve in the diagram above 20% of the population earns 5% of the income and 50% of the population earns 20% of the income. The more the Lorenz curve bends away from the 45-degree line of absolute equality, the less equal is the distribution of income.

In reality no country exhibits a totally equitable distribution of income. The ratio between the areas A and B (B being the whole triangle under the line of absolute equality) is called the Gini Coefficient. If a country had a completely even distribution of income the areas A and B would be the same and the Gini Coefficient would be zero. If the income were distributed so unevenly that one person had 100% of all the countries income and the rest of the population had nothing the Gini Coefficient in this case would be one. The closer the Gini Coefficient to one the greater the inequality of income distribution. Countries with Gini Coefficients between 0.5 and 0.7 are regarded as having unequal income distributions whilst countries having Gini Coefficients between 0.2 and 0.35 are considered to have relatively equitable. (Zambia Virtual, 2002)

Sen (1976) challenges the notions of "head counts" when measuring poverty. Quantifying the population may be important, but it ignores other aspects of income distribution in a community, hence the need for a poverty distribution index. The Sen index measures poverty from three perspectives: (1) the number of those living below the poverty line, (2) the income shortfalls of the poor, and (3) the inequality of income among the poor.[4] For Sen, poverty needs are distribution sensitive, expressing how a transfer of income among families below the poverty line influence the poverty index. The use of the Gini coefficient provides the ability to take into account for this potential influence.

Lok (1995) places poverty indicator efforts into five general categories:

means—(income and basic needs),

ends or impact (social),

mixed indices,

poverty-related or proxies, and

process or opportunities (enabling environment and empowerment).

These reference the type of relevance and legitimacy sought by those who use these indicators. But before moving on to the data and subsequent chapters, readers need to consider that the discussion of poverty indicators leads to another topic: quality of life. Much of this book centers on issues that fall under this rubric, not from an overarching principle point-of-view, but from the social responsibility component. The notion of the social safety net is mainly one of how well individuals should live in society. The discussion bifurcates itself into a discussion of those who have the necessary resources to meet their needs and some if not all of their wants, and those who lack the necessary resources—those that are called the poor. From both lines of argumentation, this author suggests that there are some questions that should be kept in the background in discussing the notion of what constitutes quality of life when comparing one nation with another, or when determining how one should specifically focus on defining the poor in order to improve their lot in the community:

1. Is there an improvement of life when economic conditions get better?
2. Is *wealthier* the same as *healthier*?
3. Does greater income correlate to higher quality institutions and inclusionary processes?
4. Does decreased deprivation equal fewer restraints and limitations on personal choice?
5. Are inequities to those traditionally underserved in a community mollified as a result of additional income?
6. Can improved living conditions, improved access, and improved participation repair and/or improve ecological concerns?

Beware of the potential conundrum that forms from the existence of these questions. As Easterly (1999) concludes after performing an analysis of life with per capita income growth, "the evidence that life gets better during growth is surprisingly uneven, while the . . . relationship between income and diverse indicators of the quality of life remain strong" (26).

Although sources for further research are discussed in the Introduction, for those readers interested in delving further into the topic of poverty lines and indicators in the United States, the best place to begin is Citro and Michael's *Measuring Poverty: A New Approach* (1995), the compilation of the report by the Committee on National Statistics, the Commission on Behavioral and Social Sciences and Education, and the National Research Council reviewing the United States' approach to determining the poverty line. Also useful from a historical perspective are the works by Gordon Fisher that are available through the U.S. Census Bureau Web site, http://www.census.gov. For those interested in an alternative perspective toward poverty lines would still be well served to begin their research by reading Schwarz and Volgy's *The Forgotten Americans* published in 1992. When researching in the international arena, one of the first places to begin is the United Nations' *Human Development Report* for 1997 and then more current reports for updated information. A second point of departure for international data is the World Bank PovertyNet site, http://www.worldbank.org/poverty/mission/up2.htm, especially their various technical papers and reports to go alongside the 1996 report, namely *The World Bank Participation Sourcebook* and the *World Development Report 2000/2001: Attacking Poverty*. The reader may then want to follow up with a visit to the OECD site, http://www.oecd.org, to continue research, particularly in the area of income distributions and income insurance programs.

NOTES

1. Means-tests also allude to an important component of the concept of the safety net: There is more to the safety net than access to it. There are also the issues of the ability to remain in the program legitimately and, ultimately, program exit—the ability to move on and return to one's own devices in the community. Recognition of need cannot be the only goal the way most of these programs are defined, authorized, and enacted. There is the second goal of getting people weaned from needing the social safety net when redistribution is not the underlying rationale for the existence of the program in the first place. Incidentally, most providers of services within the social safety net structure will agree with this. Where the controversy lies is in the degree of benefits and services, in the timelines in developing the sought-after self-sufficiency that will ensure beneficiaries will be able to succeed on their own either for the first time or once again.

2. Betson (1996) argues that the present scale implies that the addition of a first child is almost free in comparison to a second child. To illustrate this point more fully, "under the current scale, a spouse adds only 29 percent to family costs; the first child adds almost as much (26 percent), and the second child adds a yet greater amount (40 percent)" (Citro and Michael, 1995, 60).

3. The EU's Social Protection Committee has identified the following methodological principles as appropriate to creating a balanced perspective in regards to measures and outcomes:

> An indicator should capture the essence of the problem and have a clear and accepted normative interpretation;
> an indicator should be robust and statistically validated;
> an indicator should be responsive to policy interventions but not subject to manipulation;
> an indicator should be measurable in a sufficiently comparable way across Member States, and comparable as far as practicable with the standards applied internationally;
> an indicator should be timely and susceptible to revision;
> the measurement of an indicator should not impose too large a burden on Member States, on enterprises, nor on the Union's citizens;
> the portfolio of indicators should be balanced across different dimensions;
> the indicators should be mutually consistent and the weight of single indicators in the portfolio should be proportionate;
> the portfolio of indicators should be as transparent and accessible as possible to the citizens of the European Union. (Social Protection Committee, 2001, 2)

4. The index is derived as follows:

$$S = H[\,I + (1 - I)\,Gp\,(q/q + 1)]$$

where H is the headcount poverty ratio, I is the ratio of the average income shortfall-to-the poverty line (hereafter referred to as the income gap of the poor or poverty gap), Gp is the Gini coefficient of income inequality among the poor, and q is the number of people below the poverty threshold (Formby, Hoover, and Kim, 2001, 5).

PRINCIPAL SOURCES FOR ILLUSTRATIONS

Betson, D.M. (1996). *"Is everything relative?": The role of equivalence scales in poverty measurement.* United States Dept. of Health and Human Services. Retrieved from: http://aspe.hhs.gov/poverty/papers/escale.pdf.

Casey, B. and Yamada, A. (2002). *Getting older, getting poorer? A study of earnings, pensions, assets, and living arrangements of older people in nine countries.* Labour Market and Occasional Papers No. 60. Paris: OECD Directorate for Education, Employment, Labour and Social Affairs. Retrieved from: http://www.olis.oecd.org/OLIS/2002DOC.NSF/LINKTO/ DEELSA-ELSA-WD(2002)4.

Citro, C.F., and Michael, R.T., eds. (1995). *Measuring poverty: A new approach.* Washington, D.C.: National Academy Press. Retrieved from: http://www.census.gov/hhes/img/povmeas/toc.html.

Hoover, G.A., Formby, J.P., and Kim, H. (2001). *Poverty, non-white poverty, and the Sen index.* Tuscaloosa, AL: Culverhouse College of Commerce and Business Administration, Department of Economics, Finance, and Legal Studies Working Paper Series (Working Paper No. 02-04-01). Retrieved from: http://www.cba.ua.edu/pdf/WP02-04-01.pdf.

Smeeding, T.M. (2001). *Income maintenance in old age: What can be learned from cross-national comparisons.* Working Paper for the Center for Retirement Research, No. 2001-11. Chestnut Hill, MA: Boston College. Retrieved from: http://www.bc.edu/centers/ crr/papers/wp_2001-11.pdf.

Social Security Administration. (2001). *Annual Statistical Supplement, 2001 to the Social Security Bulletin.* Baltimore: Social Security Administration, Office of Policy. Retrieved from: http://www.ssa.gov/statistics/Supplement/2001/supp01.pdf.

United Nations Development Programme. (2003). *Human Development Report 2002.* New York: Oxford University Press. Retrieved from: http://www.undp.org/hdr2003/pdf/hdr03_complete.pdf.

United States Census Bureau. (2002). *Statistical abstract of the United States 2002.* Washington, D.C.: Government Printing Office. Retrieved from: http://www.census.gov/statab/www/.

United States Census Bureau. (2003). *Income deficit or surplus of families and unrelated individuals by poverty status: 2001.* United States Census Bureau Web site. Retrieved from: http://www.census.gov/hhes/poverty/poverty01/table6.pdf.

United States Census Bureau. (2003). *Number of Poor and poverty rate: 1959 to 2001.* United States Census Bureau Web site. Retrieved from: http://www.census.gov/hhes/poverty/poverty01/pov01cht.gif.

United States Census Bureau. (2003). *Ratios of family incomes to poverty thresholds by selected characteristics: 2001.* United States Census Bureau Web site. Retrieved from: http://www.census.gov/hhes/poverty/poverty01/table5.pdf.

United States Department of Labor. (2001). *Report on the American workforce.* Washington, D.C.: Government Printing Office. Retrieved from: http://www.bls.gov/opub/rtaw/rtawhome.htm.

United States Government Printing Office. (2002). 2002 Official U.S. Poverty Guidelines. *Federal Registry*, volume 67 (31), p. 6932. Retrieved from: http://opa.osophs.dhhs.gov/titlex/hhs_poverty_guidelines_2002 .pdf.

Yamada, A. (2002). The evolving income retirement package: Trends in adequacy and equality in nine OECD countries. *Labour Market and Occasional Papers—No. 63.* Paris: OECD, Directorate for Education, Employment, Labour and Social Affairs. Retrieved from: http://www.olis.oecd.org/OLIS/2002DOC.NSF/LINKTO/DEELSA-ELSA-WD(2002)7.

BIBLIOGRAPHY

Acs, G., Phillips K.R., and McKenzie, D. (2000). *Playing by the rules but losing the game: America's working poor.* Washington, D.C.: Urban Institute. Retrieved from: http://www.urban.org/workingpoor/playingtherules.html.

Australian Bureau of Statistics. (1998). Income and expenditure—income distribution: Poverty: Different assumptions, different profiles. *Australian Social Trends 1998.* Canberra: Australian Bureau of Statistics. Retrieved from: http://www.abs.gov.au/ausstats/abs@.nsf/94713ad445ff1425ca25682000192af2/5a7b6c246e6f3303ca2569ad000402c2!OpenDocument.

Betson, D.M. (1996). *"Is everything relative?": The role of equivalence scales in poverty measurement.* Washington, D.C.: United States Department of Health and Human Services. Retrieved from: http://aspe.hhs.gov/ poverty/papers/escale.pdf.

Bradshaw, J. (2001). *Methodologies to measure poverty: More than one is best!* Paper for Symposium Poverty: Concepts and Methodologies, Mexico City, March 28–29, 2001. Retrieved from: http://www.bris.ac.uk/poverty/pse/conf_pap/mex01_jrb.pdf.

Burton, M., and Kagan, C. (Forthcoming). Marginalization. In Prilleltensky, I., and Nelson, G. *Community psychology: In pursuit of wellness and liberation.* London: Macmillan/Palgrave. Retrieved from: http://homepages.poptel.org.uk/mark.burton/margibarc.pdf.

Chatterjee, P. (1999). *Repackaging the Welfare State.* Washington, D.C.: National Association of Social Workers.

Citro, C.F., and Michael, R.T., eds. (1995). *Measuring poverty: A new approach.* Washington, D.C.: National Academy Press. Retrieved from: http://www.census.gov/hhes/img/povmeas/toc.html.

City of Scottsdale. (2002). *Fiscal year 2002/2003 budget.* Retrieved August 1, 2003 from https://www.scottsdaleaz.gov/finance/Book/Process_Policies.pdf.

Di Nitto, D.M., and Dye, T.R. (1987). Social Welfare: Politics and public policy. Englewood Cliffs, N.J.: Prentice-Hall, Inc.

Easterly, W. (March 1999). Life during growth: International evidence on quality of life and per capita Income. *Working paper No. 2110.* Washington, D.C.: World Bank. Retrieved from: http://www.econ.worldbank.org/docs/428.pdf.

Eurostat. (2002). Summary methodology. *Eurostat structural indicators.* Retrieved from: http://europa.eu.int/comm/eurostat/newcronos/info/notmeth/en/theme1/strind/socohe_di_sm.htm.

Felligi, I.P. (September 1997). *On poverty and low-income.* Retrieved from: http://www.statcan.ca/english/concepts/poverty/pauv.htm.

Fisher, G.M. (1997), The development of the Orshansky poverty thresholds and their subsequent history as the official U.S. poverty measure. In *Poverty measurement working papers.* Washington, D.C.: U.S. Census Bureau. Retrieved from: http://www.census.gov/hhes/poverty/povmeas/papers/orshansky.html#N_6_.

Food and Agricultural Organization. (1988). Rural Poverty in Latin America and the Caribbean. In *World Conference on Agrarian Reform and Rural Development Ten Years of Follow-up.* Rome, Italy: Author.

Formby, J.P., Hoover, G.A., and Kim, H. (2001). Economic growth and poverty in the United States: Comparisons of estimates based upon official poverty statistics and Sen's index of poverty. *Growth and changes in U.S. Poverty: Working paper no. 00-11-01*. Tuscaloosa, AL: University of Alabama Culverhouse College of Commerce and Business Administration. Retrieved from: http://www.cba.ua.edu/pdf/WP00-11-01.pdf.

Garfinkel, I., and Haveman, R. (1977). Earning capacity, economic status, and poverty. In Moon, M., and Smolensky, E., eds. *Improving measures of economic well-being*. New York: Academic Press, pp. 51–74.

Haveman, R.H. (1987). *Poverty policy and poverty research*. Madison, WI: University of Wisconsin Press.

Innes, J.E. (1990). *Knowledge and public policy: The search for meaningful indicators*. New Brunswick, New Jersey: Transaction Publishers. Quoted in Fisher, G.M. (1997), The development of the Orshansky poverty thresholds and their subsequent history as the official U.S. poverty measure. In *Poverty measurement working papers*. Washington, D.C.: U.S. Census Bureau. Retrieved from: http://www.census.gov/hhes/poverty/povmeas/papers/orshansky.html#N_6_.

Institute for Research on Poverty. (2000). What is the difference between poverty thresholds and poverty guidelines? In *Frequently Asked Questions*. Madison, WI: University of Wisconsin-Madison. Retrieved from: http://www.ssc.wisc.edu/irp/faqs/faq7.htm.

Kwon, S. (1998). The Korean experience of poverty reduction: Lesson and prospects. In *EDAP joint policy studies no. 8: Poverty alleviation*. Seoul: Economic Development Management for Asia and the Pacific, UNDP Regional Project. Retrieved from: http://www.idep.org/pda/8/03koreapoverty.pdf.

Lok, R. (1995). Poverty: Module 1. Poverty indicators. *Technical support document*. New York: United Nations Development Programme. Retrieved from: http://www.undp.org/poverty/publications/tsd/tsd1/tsd1.pdf.

Lok-Dessallien, R. (2002). *Review of poverty concepts and indicators*. New York: United Nations Development Programme Poverty Related Publications. Retrieved from: http://www.undp.org/poverty/publications/pov_red/ Review_of_Poverty-Concepts.pdf.

Majid, N. (2001). The size of the working poor population in developing countries. *Employment paper 2001/16*. Geneva: International Labour Organization. Retrieved from: http://www.ilo.org/public/english/employment/strat/publ/ep01-16.htm.

Phipps, S., and Curtis, L. (2000). *Poverty and child well-being in Canada and the United States: Does it matter how we measure poverty?* Halifax, Nova Scotia: Dalhousie University. Retrieved from: http://labour.ciln.mcmaster.ca/papers/2000/curtisphipps.pdf.

Saunders, P. (1996). Poverty and deprivation in Australia. *Yearbook Australia*, ABS Catalogue No. 1301.0. Canberra: Australian Bureau of Statistics. Retrieved from: http://www.abs.gov.au/Ausstats/abs@.nsf/Lookup/5D709B83B7F7C25ECA2569DE00221C86.

Schwartz, J.E., and Volgy, T.J. (1992). *The forgotten Americans*. New York: W.W. Norton and Company.

Sen, A.K. (1976). Poverty: An Ordinary Approach to Measurement. *Econometrics*, 44, pp. 219–231.

Social Protection Committee. (2001). *Report on indicators in the field of poverty and social exclusion*. Stockholm: European Council.

Retrieved from: http://europa.eu.int/comm/employment_social/news/2002/jan/report_ind_en.pdf.

Statistics Canada. (1999). *Low income measures, low income after tax cut-offs and low income after tax measures*. Ottawa: Statistics Canada. Retrieved from: http://www.statcan.ca/english/freepub/13F0019XIB/0009913F0019.pdf.

Tentschert, U., Till, M., and Redl, J. (2000). *Income poverty and minimum income requirements in the EU 14*. Congress paper prepared for the VIth BIEN Congress, Berlin, October 5, 2000. Retrieved from: http://www.etes.ucl.ac.be/BIEN/Files/Papers/2000TentschertTill.pdf.

United Nations Development Programme. (2002). *Human development report 2002*. New York: Oxford University Press.

United States Census Bureau. (2002a). *Current population survey (CPS)—Definitions and explanations*. Retrieved from: http://www.census.gov/population/www/ cps/cpsdef.html.

United States Census Bureau. (2002b). How the Census Bureau measures poverty. In *Poverty*. Retrieved from: http://www.census.gov/hhes/poverty/povdef.html.

United States Department of Health, Education, and Welfare. (April 1976). *The measure of poverty: A report to Congress as mandated by the Education Amendments of 1974*. Washington, D.C.: U.S. Government Printing Service.

United States Department of Health and Human Services. (February 15, 2000). Notice to provide an update of the HHS poverty guidelines to account for last (calendar) year's increase in prices as measured by the consumer price index. In *Federal Registry*, volume 65 (31), pp. 7555–7557. Retrieved from: http://www.jackson-hertogs.com/misc/Povery.htm.

United States Department of Health and Human Services. (2002a). *The 2002 HHS poverty guidelines: One version of the [U.S.] Federal poverty measure*. Retrieved from: http://aspe.hhs.gov/poverty/02poverty.htm.

United States Department of Health and Human Services. (February 6, 2002b). Annual update on HHS Poverty Guidelines. In *Federal Registry*, volume 65 (31), pp. 7555–7557. Retrieved from: http://aspe.hhs.gov/poverty/02fedreg.htm.

Watts, H.W. (1977). An economic definition of poverty. In Moon, M., and Smolensky, E., eds. *Improving measures of economic well-being*. New York: Academic Press, pp. 19–32.

Wildavsky, A. (1974). *The politics of the budgetary process*. 2nd ed. Boston: Little, Brown and Company.

World Bank. (2002). Measuring poverty at the country level. *PovertyNet: Understanding and responding to poverty*. Retrieved from: http://www.worldbank.org/poverty/mission/up2.htm.

World Bank. (1996). *The World Bank participation sourcebook*. Retrieved from: http://www.worldbank.org/wbi/sourcebook/sb0002.htm.

Yamada, A. (2002). The evolving income retirement package: Trends in adequacy and equality in nine OECD countries. *Labour Market and Occasional Papers—No. 63*. Paris: OECD, Directorate for Education, Employment, Labour and Social Affairs. Retrieved from: http://www.olis.oecd.org/OLIS/2002DOC.NSF/LINKTO/DEELSA-ELSA-WD(2002)7.

Zambia Virtual. (2002). Theories: Lorenz Curves and Gini coefficients. Rural Life and Agriculture. Retrieved from: http://www.bized.ac.uk/virtual/dc/farming/theory/th9.htm.

Table 3.1
Food Shares (θ_i) and Multipliers (M_i) for Different Family Sizes in the United States

Family size of 1		Family size of 2		Family Size of 3 or more	
θ_1 18.5%	M_1 5.42	θ_2 27.0%	M_2 3.70	θ_{3+} 33.3%	M_{3+} 3.00

Source: Adapted from Betson, D.M. (1996). *"Is everything relative?" The Role of Equivalence Scales in Poverty Measurement.* p. 5. U.S. Dept. of Health and Human Services. Retrieved from http://aspe.hhs.gov/poverty/papers/escale.pdf.

Table 3.2
Current Official Equivalency Scale Based on Threshold Multipliers in the United States

Family (household) types	Current official scale
One-person family	0.513
Married couple	0.660
Plus one child	0.794
Plus two children	1.000
Plus three children	1.177
Plus four children	1.318
Plus five children	1.476

Source: Adapted from Citro, C.F., & Michael, R.T. (eds.). (1995). *Measuring Poverty: A New Approach,* pp. 181, 182. Retrieved from http://www.census.gov/hhes/img/povmeas/toc.html.

Table 3.3
2002 Official U.S. Poverty Guidelines

Size of family unit	Poverty guideline for 48 contiguous states and the District of Columbia[a]	Poverty guideline for Alaska[b]	Poverty guideline for Hawaii[c]
1	$8,860	$11,080	$10,200
2	$11,940	$14,930	$13,740
3	$15,020	$18,780	$17,280
4	$18,100	$22,630	$20,820
5	$21,180	$26,480	$24,360
6	$24,260	$30,330	$27,900
7	$27,340	$34,180	$31,440
8	$30,420	$38,030	$34,980

a. For family units with more than 8 members, add $3,080 for each additional member.
b. For family units with more than 8 members, add $3,850 for each additional member.
c. For family units with more than 8 members, add $3,540 for each additional member.

Source: U.S. Government Printing Office. (2002). 2002 Official U.S. Poverty Guidelines. *Federal Registry,* vol. 67 (31), p. 6932. Retrieved from http://opa.osophs.dhhs.gov/titles/hhs_poverty_guidelines_2002.pdf.

Table 3.4

U.S. Poverty Thresholds for Two-Adult/Two-Child (or Four-Person) Families Set by Various Experts Utilizing Different Methods for 1989–1993, in 1992 Dollars (Rounded)

Type and Source of Threshold	Amount
Official Orshansky, 1963: Economy Food Plan times 3.0, updated by the change in the CPI	$14,228
Expert budget threshold: Adaptation by the panel of Orshansky (1963, 1965a) food times a multiplier of 4.4	$20,700
Expert budget threshold: Adaptation by the panel of Ruggles (1990) housing times a multiplier of 3.3	$21,600
Expert budget threshold: Weinberg and Lamas (1993), version A: food plus housing times a multiplier of 2.0	$20,300
Expert budget threshold: Weinberg and Lamas (1993), version B: food plus a higher housing standard times a multiplier of 2.0	$21,800
Expert budget threshold: Adaptation by the panel of Renwick and Bergmann (1993): budget for food, housing and household operations, transportation, healthcare, clothing, childcare, and personal care	$17,600
Expert budget threshold: Schwarz and Volgy (1992): detailed budget for single-earner family	$19,000
Relative threshold: One-half median after-tax four-person family income Extension of series developed by Vaughan (1993)	$18,000
Relative threshold: Adaptation by the panel of Expert Committee on Family Budget Revisions (1980): one-half average expenditures of four-person consumer units	$20,000
Subjective threshold: 1989 Gallup Poll "poverty" line: from Vaughn (1993)	$17,700
Subjective threshold: 1993 General Social Survey "poverty" line	$17,200

Note: All thresholds are after taxes, except that survey respondents to the Gallup Poll and General Social Survey may not have answered the question on the poverty line in after-tax terms.

Source: Citro, C.F., & Michael, R.T. (eds.). (1995). *Measuring Poverty: A New Approach,* p. 47. Retrieved from http://www.census.gov/hhes/img/povmeas/toc.html.

Table 3.5
Persons Below Poverty Level and Below 125 Percent of Poverty Level by Race and Hispanic Origin: United States, 1970 to 2000

[Persons as of March of the following year (25,420 represents 25,420,000). Based on Current Population Survey.]

Year	Number below poverty level (1,000)					Percent below poverty level					Below 125 percent of poverty level	
	All races[1]	White	Black	Asian and Pacific Islander	His-panic[2]	All races[1]	White	Black	Asian and Pacific Islander	His-panic[2]	Num-ber (1,000)	Percent of total popula-tion
1970	25,420	17,484	7,548	(NA)	(NA)	12.6	9.9	33.5	(NA)	(NA)	35,624	17.6
1975	25,877	17,770	7,545	(NA)	2,991	12.3	9.7	31.3	(NA)	26.9	37,182	17.6
1980	29,272	19,699	8,579	(NA)	3,491	13.0	10.2	32.5	(NA)	25.7	40,658	18.1
1981	31,822	21,553	9,173	(NA)	3,713	14.0	11.1	34.2	(NA)	26.5	43,748	19.3
1982 [3]	34,398	23,517	9,697	(NA)	4,301	15.0	12.0	35.6	(NA)	29.9	46,520	20.3
1983 [3]	35,303	23,984	9,882	(NA)	4,633	15.2	12.1	35.7	(NA)	28.0	47,150	20.3
1984	33,700	22,955	9,490	(NA)	4,806	14.4	11.5	33.8	(NA)	28.4	45,288	19.4
1985	33,064	22,860	8,926	(NA)	5,236	14.0	11.4	31.3	(NA)	29.0	44,166	18.7
1986	32,370	22,183	8,983	(NA)	5,117	13.6	11.0	31.1	(NA)	27.3	43,486	18.2
1987 [4]	32,221	21,195	9,520	1,021	5,422	13.4	10.4	32.4	16.1	28.0	43,032	17.9
1988	31,745	20,715	9,356	1,117	5,357	13.0	10.1	31.3	17.3	26.7	42,551	17.5
1989	31,528	20,785	9,302	939	5,430	12.8	10.0	30.7	14.1	26.2	42,653	17.3
1990	33,585	22,326	9,837	858	6,006	13.5	10.7	31.9	12.2	28.1	44,837	18.0
1991	35,708	23,747	10,242	996	6,339	14.2	11.3	32.7	13.8	28.7	47,527	18.9
1992 [5]	38,014	25,259	10,827	985	7,592	14.8	11.9	33.4	12.7	29.6	50,592	19.7
1993	39,265	26,226	10,877	1,134	8,126	15.1	12.2	33.1	15.3	30.6	51,801	20.0
1994	38,059	25,379	10,196	974	8,416	14.5	11.7	30.6	14.6	30.7	50,401	19.3
1995	36,425	24,423	9,872	1,411	8,574	13.8	11.2	29.3	14.6	30.3	48,761	18.5
1996	36,529	24,650	9,694	1,454	8,697	13.7	11.2	28.4	14.5	29.4	49,310	18.5
1997	35,574	24,396	9,116	1,468	8,308	13.3	11.0	26.5	14.0	27.1	47,853	17.8
1998	34,476	23,454	9,091	1,360	8,070	12.7	10.5	26.1	12.5	25.6	46,036	17.0
1999	32,258	21,922	8,360	1,163	7,439	11.8	9.8	23.6	10.7	22.8	44,286	16.2
2000	31,054	21,242	7,862	1,214	7,153	11.3	9.4	22.0	10.7	21.2	43,377	15.7

NA. Not available.

1. Includes other races not shown separately.

2. Persons of Hispanic origin may be of any race.

3. Beginning 1983, data based on revised Hispanic population controls and not directly comparable with prior years.

4. Beginning 1987, data based on revised processing procedures and not directly comparable with prior years.

5. Beginning 1992, based on 1990 population controls.

Source: United States Census Bureau. (2002). *Statistical Abstract of the United States 2002.* Washington, D.C.: Government Printing Office. Retrieved from http://www.census.gov/prod/2003pubs/02statab/income.pdf.

Table 3.6
Children Below Poverty Level by Race and Hispanic Origin: United States, 1970 to 2000

[**Persons as of March of the following year (10,235 represents 10,235,000).** Covers only related children in families under 18 years old. Based on Current Population Survey.]

| Year | Number below poverty level (1,000) | | | | | Percent below poverty level | | | | |
	All races [1]	White	Black	Asian and Pacific Islander	His-panic [2]	All races [1]	White	Black	Asian and Pacific Islander	His-panic [2]
1970	10,235	6,138	3,922	(NA)	(NA)	14.9	10.5	41.5	(NA)	(NA)
1975	10,882	6,748	3,884	(NA)	1,619	16.8	12.5	41.4	(NA)	33.1
1980	11,114	6,817	3,906	(NA)	1,718	17.9	13.4	42.1	(NA)	33.0
1981	12,068	7,429	4,170	(NA)	1,874	19.5	14.7	44.9	(NA)	35.4
1982	13,139	8,282	4,388	(NA)	2,117	21.3	16.5	47.3	(NA)	38.9
1983 [3]	13,427	8,534	4,273	(NA)	2,251	21.8	17.0	46.2	(NA)	37.7
1984	12,929	8,086	4,320	(NA)	2,317	21.0	16.1	46.2	(NA)	38.7
1985	12,483	7,838	4,057	(NA)	2,512	20.1	15.6	43.1	(NA)	39.6
1986	12,257	7,714	4,037	(NA)	2,413	19.8	15.3	42.7	(NA)	37.1
1987 [4]	12,275	7,398	4,234	432	2,606	19.7	14.7	44.4	22.7	38.9
1988	11,935	7,095	4,148	458	2,576	19.0	14.0	42.8	23.5	37.3
1989	12,001	7,164	4,257	368	2,496	19.0	14.1	43.2	18.9	35.5
1990	12,715	7,696	4,412	356	2,750	19.9	15.1	44.2	17.0	37.7
1991	13,658	8,316	4,637	348	2,977	21.1	16.1	45.6	17.1	39.8
1992 [5]	14,521	8,752	5,015	352	3,440	21.6	16.5	46.3	16.0	39.0
1993	14,961	9,123	5,030	358	3,666	22.0	17.0	45.9	17.6	39.9
1994	14,610	8,826	4,787	308	3,956	21.2	16.3	43.3	17.9	41.1
1995	13,999	8,474	4,644	532	3,938	20.2	15.5	41.5	18.6	39.3
1996	13,764	8,488	4,411	553	4,090	19.8	15.5	39.5	19.1	39.9
1997	13,422	8,441	4,116	608	3,865	19.2	15.4	36.8	19.9	36.4
1998	12,845	7,935	4,073	542	3,670	18.3	14.4	36.4	17.5	33.6
1999	11,510	7,123	3,644	348	3,382	16.3	12.9	32.7	11.5	29.9
2000	11,018	6,838	3,417	434	3,173	15.6	12.3	30.4	14.1	27.3

NA. Not available.

1. Includes other races not shown separately.

2. Persons of Hispanic origin may be of any race.

3. Beginning 1983, data based on revised Hispanic population controls and not directly comparable with prior years.

4. Beginning 1987, data based on revised processing procedures and not directly comparable with prior years.

5. Beginning 1992, based on 1990 population controls.

Source: United States Census Bureau. (2002). *Statistical Abstract of the United States 2002.* Washington, D.C.: Government Printing Office. Retrieved from http://www.census.gov/prod/2003pubs/02statab/income.pdf.

Table 3.7
Weighted Average Poverty Thresholds by Size of Unit: United States, 1980 to 2001

[In dollars.]

Size of family unit	1980[1]	1990	1995	1996	1997	1998	1999	2000	2001
One person (unrelated individual) . . .	4,190	6,652	7,763	7,995	8,183	8,316	8,501	8,794	9,044
Under 65 years.	4,290	6,800	7,929	8,163	8,350	8,480	8,667	8,959	9,214
65 years and over	3,949	6,268	7,309	7,525	7,698	7,818	7,990	8,259	8,494
Two persons	5,363	8,509	9,933	10,233	10,473	10,634	10,869	11,239	11,559
Householder under 65 years	5,537	8,794	10,259	10,564	10,805	10,972	11,214	11,590	11,920
Householder 65 years and over . . .	4,983	7,905	9,219	9,491	9,712	9,862	10,075	10,419	10,715
Three persons	6,565	10,419	12,158	12,516	12,802	13,003	13,290	13,738	14,129
Four persons	8,414	13,359	15,569	16,036	16,400	16,660	17,029	17,603	18,104
Five persons	9,966	15,792	18,408	18,952	19,380	19,680	20,127	20,819	21,411
Six persons.	11,269	17,839	20,804	21,389	21,886	22,228	22,727	23,528	24,197
Seven persons.	12,761	20,241	23,552	24,268	24,802	25,257	25,912	26,754	27,514
Eight persons.	14,199	22,582	26,237	27,091	27,593	28,166	28,967	29,701	30,546
Nine or more persons	16,896	26,848	31,280	31,971	32,566	33,339	34,417	35,060	36,058

1. Poverty levels for nonfarm families.

Source: United States Census Bureau. (2002). *Statistical Abstract of the United States 2002*. Washington, D.C.: Government Printing Office. Retrieved from http://www.census.gov/prod/2003pubs/02statab/income.pdf.

Table 3.8
Persons Below Poverty Level by Selected Characteristics: United States, 2000

[**Persons as of March 2001 (31,054 represents 31,054,000).** Based on Current Population Survey.]

Age and region	Number below poverty level (1,000)					Percent below poverty level				
	All races [1]	White	Black	Asian and Pacific Islander	His-panic [2]	All races [1]	White	Black	Asian and Pacific Islander	His-panic [2]
Total	31,054	21,242	7,862	1,214	7,153	11.3	9.4	22.0	10.7	21.2
Male	13,417	9,241	3,267	588	3,287	9.9	8.3	19.6	10.7	19.5
Female.	17,637	12,001	4,595	626	3,866	12.5	10.5	24.1	10.8	22.9
Under 18 years old.	11,553	7,283	3,487	447	3,328	16.1	12.9	30.6	14.4	28.0
18 to 24 years old	3,890	2,709	941	154	896	14.4	12.6	23.6	13.6	21.5
25 to 34 years old	3,892	2,738	882	180	1,080	10.4	9.2	17.1	8.7	19.1
35 to 44 years old	3,678	2,569	896	129	782	8.2	7.0	15.6	6.8	15.5
45 to 54 years old	2,441	1,661	582	131	395	6.4	5.2	13.6	8.8	12.3
55 to 59 years old	1,175	854	253	56	134	8.8	7.5	18.9	12.3	12.8
60 to 64 years old	1,066	828	197	31	184	10.2	9.2	18.6	9.9	22.1
65 years old and over . . .	3,359	2,601	623	86	353	10.2	8.9	22.4	10.3	18.8
65 to 74 years old. . . .	1,592	1,190	317	55	218	8.9	7.6	19.4	11.1	18.9
75 years old and over .	1,767	1,412	306	30	135	11.7	10.4	26.4	9.0	18.5
Northeast	5,363	3,598	1,466	244	1,041	10.3	8.3	22.5	12.9	22.9
Midwest	6,037	4,138	1,627	104	455	9.5	7.5	24.4	8.0	17.7
South.	12,105	7,529	4,184	195	2,422	12.5	10.1	21.7	9.7	20.6
West	7,550	5,978	584	671	3,235	11.9	11.3	18.2	11.0	21.8
Native	26,351	17,716	7,514	414	4,324	10.7	8.6	22.7	9.9	21.2
Foreign born	4,704	3,527	348	800	2,829	15.7	17.6	13.3	11.3	21.2
Naturalized citizen. . . .	1,106	737	59	305	460	9.7	10.8	5.7	8.8	13.2
Not a citizen.	3,597	2,790	289	495	2,369	19.4	21.2	18.1	13.6	24.1

1. Includes other races not shown separately.
2. Persons of Hispanic origin may be of any race.

Source: United States Census Bureau. (2002). *Statistical Abstract of the United States 2002*. Washington, D.C.: Government Printing Office. Retrieved from http://www.census.gov/prod/2003pubs/02statab/income.pdf.

Figure 3.1
Number of Poor and Poverty Rate: United States, 1959 to 2001

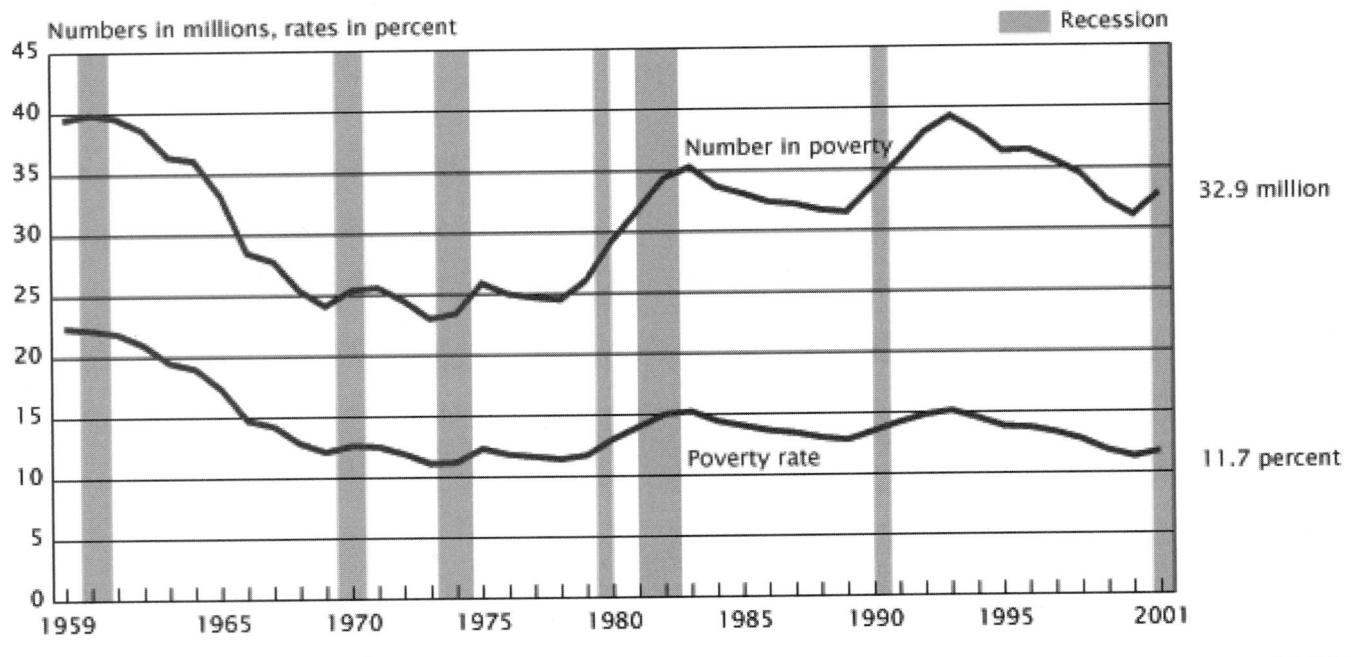

Note: The data points represent the midpoints of the respective years. The latest recession began in March 2001.

Source: United States Census Bureau. (2003). *Number of Poor and Poverty Rate: 1959 to 2001*. U.S. Census Bureau Web site. Retrieved from http://www.census .gov/hhes/poverty/poverty01/pov01cht.gif.

Table 3.9
Percent of People in Poverty by State: 1999, 2000, and 2001

State	3-year average 1999-2001		Average 2000-01		Average 1999-2000		Difference in 2-year moving averages	
	Percent	90-percent C.I. (±)	Percent	90-percent C.I. (±)	Percent	90-percent C.I. (±)	Percent	90-percent C.I. (±)
United States..................	11.6	0.2	11.5	0.2	11.6	0.2	−0.1	0.2
Alabama..........................	14.8	1.5	14.6	1.6	14.3	1.9	0.3	1.8
Alaska...........................	7.9	1.2	8.1	1.2	7.6	1.4	0.5	1.3
Arizona..........................	12.9	1.5	13.2	1.7	11.9	1.8	1.2	1.6
Arkansas	16.3	1.7	17.1	1.9	15.6	2.0	1.6	1.8
California	13.1	0.7	12.6	0.7	13.4	0.8	*−0.7	0.7
Colorado	9.0	1.1	9.2	1.2	9.1	1.4	0.1	1.3
Connecticut......................	7.4	1.1	7.5	1.1	7.4	1.4	0.1	1.3
Delaware	8.5	1.3	7.6	1.3	9.4	1.7	*−1.8	1.5
District of Columbia	16.1	1.8	16.7	1.9	15.0	2.1	1.7	2.0
Florida	12.0	0.8	11.9	0.9	11.7	1.0	0.2	0.9
Georgia	12.6	1.4	12.5	1.5	12.5	1.7	0.1	1.5
Hawaii...........................	10.4	1.4	10.2	1.4	9.9	1.7	0.3	1.6
Idaho............................	12.7	1.5	12.0	1.6	13.3	1.9	−1.3	1.6
Illinois...........................	10.2	0.9	10.4	0.9	10.3	1.0	0.1	0.9
Indiana..........................	7.9	1.1	8.5	1.1	7.6	1.3	0.9	1.2
Iowa	7.7	1.1	7.8	1.2	7.8	1.4	-	1.3
Kansas..........................	10.1	1.3	9.1	1.2	10.1	1.7	−1.1	1.6
Kentucky	12.4	1.4	12.6	1.5	12.3	1.8	0.2	1.6
Louisiana	17.5	1.7	16.7	1.8	18.2	2.2	−1.5	1.9
Maine............................	10.3	1.3	10.2	1.2	10.3	1.7	−0.1	1.6
Maryland	7.3	1.1	7.3	1.1	7.3	1.4	-	1.3
Massachusetts	10.2	1.1	9.4	1.1	10.8	1.4	*−1.4	1.2
Michigan.........................	9.7	0.9	9.6	1.0	9.8	1.1	−0.2	0.9
Minnesota	6.8	1.0	6.5	1.0	6.5	1.3	-	1.2
Mississippi.......................	16.8	1.8	17.1	1.9	15.6	2.1	1.6	1.9
Missouri	10.2	1.3	9.4	1.2	10.4	1.7	−1.0	1.5
Montana.........................	14.4	1.7	13.7	1.8	15.0	2.1	−1.3	1.8
Nebraska	9.7	1.3	9.0	1.3	9.8	1.7	−0.8	1.5
Nevada..........................	9.0	1.2	7.9	1.2	10.0	1.6	*−2.1	1.4
New Hampshire	6.2	1.1	5.5	1.0	6.1	1.4	−0.6	1.4
New Jersey.......................	7.7	0.8	7.7	0.9	7.6	1.0	0.1	0.9
New Mexico......................	18.8	1.9	17.7	2.1	19.2	2.3	−1.5	2.0
New York.........................	14.1	0.8	14.0	0.8	14.0	0.9	-	0.8
North Carolina....................	12.9	1.2	12.5	1.2	13.1	1.4	−0.6	1.2
North Dakota.....................	12.4	1.5	12.1	1.5	11.7	1.8	0.4	1.7
Ohio	10.8	0.9	10.3	1.0	11.0	1.1	−0.7	1.0
Oklahoma	14.3	1.5	15.0	1.7	13.9	1.9	1.1	1.6
Oregon..........................	11.8	1.4	11.3	1.4	11.7	1.8	−0.4	1.6
Pennsylvania.....................	9.2	0.8	9.1	0.8	9.0	1.0	0.1	0.9
Rhode Island.....................	10.0	1.3	9.9	1.2	10.1	1.6	−0.2	1.5
South Carolina	12.7	1.5	13.1	1.5	11.4	1.8	*1.7	1.7
South Dakota	9.0	1.2	9.6	1.3	9.2	1.5	0.3	1.3
Tennessee.......................	13.2	1.5	13.8	1.7	12.7	1.9	1.1	1.7
Texas	15.2	0.9	15.2	1.0	15.4	1.1	−0.2	0.9
Utah	8.0	1.1	9.1	1.3	6.7	1.3	*2.4	1.2
Vermont	9.8	1.3	9.9	1.3	9.8	1.7	-	1.6
Virginia..........................	8.0	1.1	8.1	1.2	8.1	1.4	0.1	1.3
Washington	10.4	1.3	10.8	1.4	10.2	1.6	0.6	1.5
West Virginia.....................	15.6	1.5	15.6	1.6	15.2	1.9	0.4	1.7
Wisconsin	8.6	1.1	8.6	1.1	8.9	1.4	−0.3	1.3
Wyoming	10.3	1.4	9.7	1.4	11.2	1.8	−1.5	1.5

-. Represents zero.
*Statistically significant at the 90-percent confidence level.
For explanation of confidence intervals (C.I.), see "Standard errors and their use" at www.census.gov/hhes/poverty/poverty01/pov01src.pdf.

Source: United States Census Bureau. (2003). *Percent of People in Poverty by State: 1999, 2000, and 2001.* U.S. Census Bureau Web site. Retrieved from http://www.census.gov/hhes/poverty/poverty01/table4.pdf.

Table 3.10
Experimental Poverty Measures by Selected Characteristics: United States, 2001

Characteristic	Official	MSI - NGA	MIT - NGA	CMB - NGA	MSI - GA	MIT - GA	CMB - GA
Total	**11.7**	**12.4**	**12.8**	**13.0**	**12.3**	**12.7**	**12.9**
People in families	**9.9**	**10.5**	**11.0**	**11.1**	**10.5**	**11.1**	**11.1**
People in married-couple families	5.7	6.6	7.1	7.1	6.6	7.1	7.1
People in families with a female householder, no husband present	28.6	26.7	27.9	28.1	27.0	28.1	28.3
People in families with a male householder, no wife present	13.6	15.2	16.2	16.0	15.2	15.6	16.0
Age							
Under 18 years	16.3	14.5	15.7	15.3	14.6	15.8	15.4
18 to 64 years	10.1	10.7	11.4	11.3	10.8	11.5	11.3
65 years and over	10.1	16.1	13.7	17.1	15.5	12.7	16.2
Race and Hispanic Origin							
Non-Hispanic White	7.8	8.9	9.1	9.4	8.4	8.5	8.8
Black	22.7	21.3	22.1	22.2	20.8	21.7	21.8
Hispanic[1]	21.4	21.9	23.4	23.1	24.4	26.3	25.9
Region							
Northeast	10.7	10.5	10.7	11.1	12.9	13.4	13.8
Midwest	9.4	9.9	10.1	10.4	8.7	8.8	9.0
South	13.5	14.7	15.3	15.4	12.5	12.8	13.0
West	12.1	12.7	13.3	13.5	15.1	15.9	16.1

1. Hispanics may be of any race.
Note: While the experimental measures differ among one another in their computation of medical expenses and geographic variations in costs, they are similar in their scaling of thresholds by family size and their treatment of noncash benefits and child care and work-related expenses.
MSI = Medical out-of-pocket expenses (MOOP) subtracted from income
MIT = MOOP included in the threshold
CMB = Combined methods
NGA = No geographic adjustment for housing costs
GA = Geographic adjustment for housing costs

Source: United States Census Bureau. (2003). *Experimental Poverty Measures by Selected Characteristics: 2001.* U.S. Census Bureau Web site. Retrieved from http://www.census.gov/hhes/poverty/poverty01/table8.pdf.

Table 3.11
Ratio of Family Income to Poverty Threshold for People by Selected Characteristics: United States, 2001

(Numbers in thousands)

Characteristic	Total	Under 0.50		Under 1.00		Under 1.25	
		Number	Percent of total	Number	Percent of total	Number	Percent of total
PEOPLE							
Total	281,475	13,440	4.8	32,907	11.7	45,320	16.1
Age							
Under 18 years	72,021	5,107	7.1	11,733	16.3	15,781	21.9
18 to 24 years	27,312	2,100	7.7	4,449	16.3	5,822	21.3
25 to 34 years	38,670	1,896	4.9	4,255	11.0	5,823	15.1
35 to 44 years	44,284	1,590	3.6	3,822	8.6	5,185	11.7
45 to 54 years	39,545	1,112	2.8	2,804	7.1	3,823	9.7
55 to 59 years	14,667	501	3.4	1,274	8.7	1,693	11.5
60 to 64 years	11,208	388	3.5	1,157	10.3	1,594	14.2
65 years and over....................	33,769	746	2.2	3,414	10.1	5,600	16.6
Race[1] and Hispanic Origin							
White................................	229,675	8,703	3.8	22,739	9.9	31,880	13.9
Non-Hispanic.......................	194,538	5,960	3.1	15,271	7.8	21,529	11.1
Black................................	35,871	3,843	10.7	8,136	22.7	10,691	29.8
Other races	15,929	894	5.6	2,032	12.8	2,748	17.3
Asian and Pacific Islander.	12,465	579	4.6	1,275	10.2	1,731	13.9
Hispanic[2]	37,312	3,000	8.0	7,997	21.4	11,034	29.6
FAMILY STATUS							
In families...........................	233,911	9,148	3.9	23,215	9.9	32,601	13.9
Householder........................	74,340	2,754	3.7	6,813	9.2	9,525	12.8
Related children under 18............	70,950	4,699	6.6	11,175	15.8	15,151	21.4
Related children under 6.	23,014	1,859	8.1	4,188	18.2	5,596	24.3
Unrelated individual	46,392	3,999	8.6	9,226	19.9	12,139	26.2
Male................................	22,176	1,881	8.5	3,833	17.3	4,934	22.2
Female	24,216	2,118	8.7	5,393	22.3	7,205	29.8

1. Data for American Indians and Alaska Natives are not shown separately because of the small sample of that population.
2. Hispanics may be of any race.

Source: United States Census Bureau. (2003). *Ratios of Family Incomes to Poverty Threshold for People by Selected Characteristics: 2001.* U.S. Census Bureau Web site. Retrieved from http://www.census.gov/hhes/poverty/poverty01/table5.pdf.

Table 3.12
Income Deficit or Surplus of Families and Unrelated Individuals
by Poverty Status: United States, 2001

(Numbers of families and unrelated individuals in thousands, deficits and surpluses in dollars)

| Characteristic | Total | Size of deficit or surplus | | | | | | | | | | Average deficit or sur-plus- (dollars) | Deficit or surplus per capita (dollars) |
		Under $500	$500 to $999	$1,000 to $1,999	$2,000 to $2,999	$3,000 to $3,999	$4,000 to $4,999	$5,000 to $5,999	$6,000 to $6,999	$7,000 to $7,999	$8,000 or more		
Deficit for Those Below Poverty													
All families............	6,813	368	268	597	596	536	497	517	354	369	2,712	7,231	2,122
Married-couple families..	2,760	154	133	289	268	245	187	200	140	153	991	6,840	1,833
Families with female householders, no husband present	3,470	158	106	256	282	250	261	262	180	189	1,526	7,692	2,378
Unrelated individual.....	9,226	701	633	1,416	1,335	738	630	489	412	401	2,470	4,550	4,550
Male...............	3,833	235	229	491	468	322	300	226	179	164	1,218	4,997	4,997
Female.............	5,393	466	404	925	867	416	331	263	233	237	1,252	4,231	4,231
Surplus for Those Above Poverty													
All families............	67,527	326	369	688	803	902	777	843	892	860	61,067	57,841	18,538
Married-couple families..	53,994	177	172	355	427	580	459	459	568	528	50,269	64,265	20,184
Families with female householders, no husband present	9,676	124	166	274	299	281	250	321	247	248	7,466	29,339	10,125
Unrelated individual.....	37,166	474	927	1,330	1,537	1,216	1,229	1,286	1,062	1,053	27,054	27,589	27,589
Male...............	18,343	189	371	476	629	480	414	547	407	389	14,442	32,318	32,318
Female.............	18,823	285	556	854	908	735	815	739	654	664	12,612	22,980	22,980

Source: United States Census Bureau. (2003). *Income Deficit or Surplus of Families and Unrelated Individuals by Poverty Status: 2001.* U.S. Census Bureau Web site. Retrieved from http://www.census.gov/hhes/poverty/poverty01/table6.pdf.

Table 3.13
Shares of Money Income from Earnings and Other Sources for Aged and Nonaged Families: United States, 1999

(Civilian noninstitutionalized population residing in the 50 states and the District Columbia)

Type of money income received during year [1]	Aged family units						Nonaged family units					
	Individuals aged 65 or older living alone or with nonrelatives only			Multiperson families with householder aged 65 or older			Individuals under age 65 living alone or with nonrelatives only			Multiperson families with householder under age 65		
	Total	Nonpoor	Poor [2]	Total	Nonpoor	Poor [2]	Total	Nonpoor	Poor [2]	Total	Nonpoor	Poor [2]
Number of families and unrelated individuals (in millions)	10.6	8.5	2.1	11.6	11.0	0.6	32.9	26.4	6.5	60.4	54.4	6.1
	Percent receiving income of specified type [3]											
Earnings	14	16	3	45	47	24	84	94	44	95	97	70
Public program payments:												
Social Security [4]	92	94	84	92	93	65	6	5	11	10	10	10
Supplemental Security Income	6	2	21	5	5	13	4	1	12	3	2	11
Other public assistance	2	2	2	4	4	6	10	9	13	12	11	29
Other programs [5]	4	5	3	8	8	4	6	6	3	9	10	7
Other sources:												
Dividends, interest, rent	60	68	26	71	73	28	48	56	17	63	68	15
Employment-related pensions, alimony, annuities, etc	41	49	8	52	54	14	6	6	3	16	16	14
	Percentage distribution of income, by type											
Total percent	100	100	100	100	100	100	100	100	100	100	100	100
Earnings	13	14	(6)	33	33	13	87	88	50	89	89	66
Public program payments:												
Social Security [4]	44	41	83	30	30	64	2	1	18	2	1	8
Supplemental Security Income	1	(6)	10	1	1	9	1	(6)	15	(6)	(6)	7
Other public assistance	(6)	(6)	(6)	(6)	(6)	2	2	2	9	1	1	11
Other programs [5]	1	1	1	1	1	1	1	1	2	1	1	3
Other sources:												
Dividends, interest, rent	20	21	2	17	18	4	6	6	3	5	5	1
Employment-related pensions, alimony, annuities, etc	20	21	3	17	17	7	2	2	3	3	3	4
Median income	$13,809	$16,435	$5,572	$33,131	$34,719	$7,741	$23,365	$28,739	$3,779	$52,593	$56,149	$8,356

1. Household surveys tend to underestimate the number of income recipients with income sources such an interest, dividends, rents, veterans' payments, unemployment compensation, and workers' compensation are more underreported than others. For more detail, see U.S. Census Bureau. *The Value of Noncash Benefits: 1979–1982*, Technical Paper No. 52, Appendix F.

2. Poverty status based on money income of all family members after receipt of OASDI and any other cash transfer payments.

3. Received by individuals or any family member at any time during 1998. Most individuals or families received more than one type of income during the year.

4. Social Security may include more than one type of income during the year.

5. Unemployment insurance, workers' compensation, or veterans' payments.

6. Less than 0.05 percent.

Source: Social Security Administration. (2001). *Annual Statistical Supplement, 2001 to the Social Security Bulletin*. Baltimore: Social Security Administration, Office of Policy. Retrieved from http://www.ssa.gov/policy/docs/statcomps/supplement/2001/supp01.pdf.

Table 3.14
Poverty Guidelines for Families of Specified Size: United States, 1965 to 2001[1,2]

Date of issuance [3]	1 person	2 persons	3 persons	4 persons	5 persons	6 persons	7 persons	8 persons	Increment [4]
December 1965	$1,540	$1,990	$2,440	$3,130	$3,685	$4,135	$4,635	$5,135	$500
August 1967	1,600	2,000	2,500	3,200	3,800	4,200	4,700	5,300	500
September 1968	1,600	2,100	2,600	3,300	3,900	4,400	4,900	5,400	500
September 1969	1,800	2,400	3,000	3,600	4,200	4,800	5,400	6,000	600
December 1970	1,900	2,500	3,100	3,800	4,400	5,000	5,600	6,200	600
November 1971	2,000	2,600	3,300	4,000	4,700	5,300	5,900	6,500	600
October 1972	2,100	2,725	3,450	4,200	4,925	5,550	6,200	6,850	650
March 1973	2,200	2,900	3,600	4,300	5,000	5,700	6,400	7,100	700
May 1974	2,330	3,070	3,810	4,550	5,290	6,030	6,770	7,510	740
March 1975	2,590	3,410	4,230	5,050	5,870	6,690	7,510	8,330	820
April 1976	2,800	3,700	4,600	5,500	6,400	7,300	8,200	9,100	900
April 1977	2,970	3,930	4,890	5,850	6,810	7,770	8,730	9,690	960
April 1978	3,140	4,160	5,180	6,200	7,220	8,240	9,260	10,280	1,020
May 1979	3,400	4,500	5,600	6,700	7,800	8,900	10,000	11,100	1,100
April 1980	3,790	5,010	6,230	7,450	8,670	9,890	11,110	12,330	1,220
March 1981	4,310	5,690	7,070	8,450	9,830	11,210	12,590	13,970	1,380
April 1982	4,680	6,220	7,760	9,300	10,840	12,380	13,920	15,460	1,540
February 1983	4,860	6,540	8,220	9,900	11,580	13,260	14,940	16,620	1,680
February 1984	4,980	6,720	8,460	10,200	11,940	13,680	15,420	17,160	1,740
March 1985	5,250	7,050	8,850	10,650	12,450	14,250	16,050	17,850	1,800
February 1986	5,360	7,240	9,120	11,000	12,880	14,760	16,640	18,520	1,880
February 1987	5,500	7,400	9,300	11,200	13,100	15,000	16,900	18,800	1,900
February 1988	5,770	7,730	9,690	11,650	13,610	15,570	17,530	19,490	1,960
February 1989	5,980	8,020	10,060	12,100	14,140	16,180	18,220	20,260	2,040
February 1990	6,280	8,420	10,560	12,700	14,840	16,980	18,120	21,260	2,140
February 1991	6,620	8,880	11,140	13,400	15,660	17,920	20,180	22,440	2,260
February 1992	6,810	9,190	11,570	13,950	16,330	18,710	21,090	23,470	2,380
February 1993	6,970	9,430	11,890	14,350	16,810	19,270	21,730	24,190	2,460
February 1994	7,360	9,840	12,320	14,800	17,280	19,760	22,240	24,720	2,480
February 1995	7,470	10,030	12,590	15,150	17,710	20,270	22,830	25,390	2,560
March 1996	7,740	10,360	12,980	15,600	18,220	20,840	23,460	26,080	2,620
March 1997	7,890	10,610	13,330	16,050	18,770	21,490	24,210	26,960	2,720
February 1998	8,050	10,850	13,650	16,450	19,250	22,050	24,850	27,650	2,800
March 1999	8,240	11,060	13,880	16,700	19,520	22,340	25,160	27,980	2,820
February 2000	8,350	11,250	14,150	17,050	19,950	22,850	25,750	28,650	2,900
February 2001	8,590	11,610	14,630	17,650	20,670	23,690	26,710	29,730	3,020

1. Except for Alaska and Hawaii. Guidelines for Alaska and Hawaii since 1980 are:

	Alaska		Hawaii	
Year	1 person	Increment	1 person	Increment
1980	$4,760	$1,520	$4,370	$1,400
1981	5,410	1,720	4,980	1,580
1982	5,870	1,920	5,390	1,770
1983	6,080	2,100	5,600	1,930
1984	6,240	2,170	5,730	2,000
1985	6,560	2,250	6,040	2,070
1986	6,700	2,350	6,170	2,160
1987	6,860	2,380	6,310	2,190
1988	7,210	2,450	6,650	2,250
1989	7,480	2,550	6,870	2,350
1990	7,840	2,680	7,230	2,460
1991	8,290	2,820	7,610	2,600
1992	8,500	2,980	7,830	2,740
1993	8,700	3,080	8,040	2,820
1994	9,200	3,100	8,470	2,850
1995	9,340	3,200	8,610	2,940
1996	9,660	3,280	8,910	3,010
1997	9,870	3,400	9,070	3,130
1998	10,070	3,500	9,260	3,220
1999	10,320	3,520	9,490	3,240
2000	10,430	3,630	9,590	3,340
2001	10,730	3,780	9,890	3,470

Separate figures for Alaska and Hawaii reflect Office of Economic Opportunity administrative practice beginning in the 1966–1970 period. The U.S. Census Bureau, producer of the primary version of the poverty measure (the poverty thresholds), does not produce separate figures for Alaska and Hawaii.

2. Before 1983, the guidelines shown are for nonfarm families only.

3. The guidelines are effective from the date of Issuance (unless otherwise specified by a particular program using them).

4. Add this amount for each additional family member. Before 1973, increments between some of the smaller family sizes differed from the increment shown in the table. Beginning in 1973, the increment has been the same between all family sizes in each year's set of guidelines.

Source: Social Security Administration. (2001). *Annual Statistical Supplement, 2001 to the Social Security Bulletin.* Baltimore: Social Security Administration, Office of Policy. Retrieved from http://www.ssa.gov/policy/docs/statcomps/supplement/2001/supp01.pdf.

Table 3.15
Family Net Worth—Mean and Median Net Worth in Constant (1998) Dollars by Selected Family Characteristics: United States, 1992 to 1998

[**Net worth in thousands of constant (1998) dollars (212.7 represents $212,700)**. Constant dollar figures are based on consumer price index for all urban consumers published by U.S. Bureau of Labor Statistics. Families include one-person units and as used in this table are comparable to the Census Bureau household concept. Based on Survey of Consumer Finance.]

Family characteristic	1992			1995			1998		
	Percent of families	Net worth		Percent of families	Net worth		Percent of families	Net worth	
		Mean	Median		Mean	Median		Mean	Median
All families	**100.0**	**212.7**	**56.5**	**100.0**	**224.8**	**60.9**	**100.0**	**282.5**	**71.6**
Age of family head:									
Under 35 years old.	25.8	53.1	10.4	24.8	47.4	12.7	23.3	65.9	9.0
35 to 44 years old	22.8	152.7	50.9	23.0	152.8	54.9	23.3	196.2	63.4
45 to 54 years old	16.2	304.4	89.3	17.9	313.0	100.8	19.2	362.7	105.5
55 to 64 years old	13.2	384.9	130.2	12.5	404.7	122.4	12.8	530.2	127.5
65 to 74 years old	12.6	326.1	112.3	12.0	369.3	117.9	11.2	465.5	146.5
75 years old and over.	9.4	244.4	99.2	9.8	273.8	98.8	10.2	310.2	125.6
Family income in constant (**1998**) dollars:[1]									
Less than $10,000	14.8	32.1	2.9	15.1	46.6	4.8	12.6	40.0	3.6
$10,000 to $24,999	27.0	69.8	27.1	25.4	80.3	31.0	24.8	85.6	24.8
$25,000 to $49,999	29.8	131.4	55.6	31.0	124.0	56.7	28.8	135.4	60.3
$50,000 to $99,999	20.7	245.6	129.9	21.0	258.1	126.6	25.2	275.5	152.0
$100,000 and more	7.6	1,300.8	481.9	7.4	1,411.9	511.4	8.6	1,727.8	510.8

1. Income for year preceding the survey.

Source: United States Census Bureau. (2002). *Statistical Abstract of the United States 2002.* Washington, D.C.: Government Printing Office. Retrieved from http://www.census.gov/prod/2003pubs/02statab/income.pdf.

Table 3.16
Average Annual Expenditures and Percent Distribution of All Consumer Units,
Selected Periods: United States, 1935–1936 to 1998–1999

Item	Averages				Percent of current consumption			
	1935-36	1960-61	1972-73	1998-99	1935-36	1960-61	1972-73	1998-99
Characteristics								
Number of consumer units (in thousands) ..	39,458	55,306	71,220	107,824				
Income before taxes	$1,502	$6,253	$11,726	$42,770				
Income after taxes	-	5,564	10,174	39,489				
Average consumer unit size	3.2	3.2	2.9	2.5				
Percent homeowner	-	61	58	65				
Expenditures								
Current Consumption	$1,273	$5,056	$7,920	$30,778	100.0	100.0	100.0	100.0
Food	428	1,236	1,679	4,861	33.6	24.4	21.2	15.8
Food at home	-	990	1,303	2,848	-	19.6	16.5	9.3
Food away from home	-	246	376	2,013	-	4.9	4.7	6.5
Alcoholic beverages	-	78	82	313	-	1.5	1.0	1.0
Shelter	241	664	1,395	6,796	18.9	13.1	17.6	22.1
Household operations and utilities	134	538	715	2,822	10.5	10.6	9.0	9.2
Housefurnishings	36	266	378	1,435	2.8	5.3	4.8	4.7
Apparel and services	133	519	647	1,649	10.4	10.3	8.2	5.4
Vehicle purchases [1]	96	299	714	3,136	7.5	5.9	9.0	10.2
Vehicle operations	-	393	935	3,246	-	7.8	11.8	10.5
Public transportation	22	77	96	368	1.7	1.5	1.2	1.2
Health care	56	340	429	1,919	4.4	6.7	5.4	6.2
Insurance	-	90	152	918	-	1.8	1.9	3.0
Services	-	168	216	538	-	3.3	2.7	1.7
Drugs	-	69	47	358	-	1.4	.6	1.2
Supplies	-	13	14	105	-	.3	.2	.3
Entertainment	42	200	373	1,710	3.3	4.0	4.7	5.6
Personal care	26	145	101	405	2.0	2.9	1.3	1.3
Tobacco	24	91	128	287	1.9	1.8	1.6	.9
Education	13	54	109	485	1.0	1.1	1.4	1.6
Reading	14	45	48	160	1.1	.9	.6	.5
Other items	8	111	91	1,187	.6	2.2	1.1	3.9

1. Vehicle purchases also includes vehicle operations for 1935–1936 data.
Dash indicates data not available.

Source: U.S. Department of Labor. (2001). *Report on the American Workforce.* Washington, D.C.: Government Printing Office. Retrieved from
http://www.bls.gov/opub/rtaw/pdf/appendix.pdf.

Table 3.17

Shares of Average Annual Expenditures and Characteristics of All Consumer Units Classified by Quintiles of Income before Taxes, Consumer Expenditure Survey: United States, 1989 and 1999

Item	All consumer units	Complete reporting of income						Incomplete reporting of income
		Total complete reporting	Lowest 20 percent	Second 20 percent	Third 20 percent	Fourth 20 percent	Highest 20 percent	
1989								
Number of consumer units (in thousands)	95,818	82,960	16,558	16,584	16,592	16,607	16,620	12,857
Consumer unit characteristics:								
Income before taxes [1]	$31,308	$31,308	$5,720	$13,894	$23,856	$37,524	$75,406	(1)
Age of reference person	47.2	47.1	51.1	50.5	45.5	43.0	45.4	47.7
Average number in consumer unit:								
Persons	2.6	2.5	1.8	2.2	2.6	2.9	3.1	2.7
Children under 18	.7	.7	.5	.5	.7	.9	.8	.7
Persons 65 and over	.3	.3	.5	.5	.3	.2	.1	.3
Earners	1.4	1.4	.7	1.0	1.4	1.8	2.1	1.4
Vehicles	2.0	2.0	.9	1.5	2.0	2.6	3.1	2.0
Percent homeowner	63	62	41	50	60	71	88	66
Average annual expenditures	$27,810	$28,323	$12,119	$17,616	$24,476	$34,231	$53,093	$24,862
Percent distribution:	100.0	100.0	100.0	100.0	100.0	100.0	100.0	100.0
Food	14.9	14.8	18.2	17.6	15.9	14.5	12.8	16.1
Food at home	8.6	8.5	12.5	11.5	9.6	8.1	6.3	9.4
Cereals and bakery products .	1.3	1.3	2.0	1.7	1.4	1.2	.9	1.4
Meats, poultry, fish, and eggs	2.2	2.2	3.2	3.1	2.5	2.0	1.6	2.4
Dairy products	1.1	1.1	1.7	1.5	1.2	1.0	.8	1.2
Fruits and vegetables	1.5	1.4	2.2	2.0	1.6	1.4	1.0	1.7
Other food at home	2.5	2.5	3.4	3.2	2.9	2.5	2.0	2.7
Food away from home	6.3	6.3	5.7	6.1	6.3	6.3	6.5	6.7
Alcoholic beverages	1.0	1.1	1.1	1.1	1.3	1.1	.9	.9
Housing	31.0	30.4	35.2	32.7	30.3	28.7	29.6	35.1
Shelter	17.4	17.0	19.6	17.5	16.5	16.0	17.2	19.7
Owned dwellings	10.2	10.0	6.7	6.1	7.9	9.7	13.3	11.8
Rented dwellings	5.4	5.4	11.8	10.4	7.4	4.8	1.7	5.4
Other lodging	1.7	1.6	1.1	1.0	1.2	1.5	2.2	2.4
Utilities, fuels, and public services	6.6	6.4	9.7	8.5	7.2	5.9	4.9	8.0
Household operations	1.7	1.6	1.2	1.3	1.5	1.5	1.9	2.0
Housekeeping supplies	1.4	1.4	1.5	2.0	1.6	1.3	1.3	1.3
Household furnishings and equipment	3.9	3.9	3.1	3.4	3.6	3.9	4.3	4.2
Apparel and services	5.7	5.7	5.2	5.2	5.7	5.9	5.8	6.0
Transportation	18.7	18.6	16.4	18.2	18.6	21.1	17.7	18.7
Vehicle purchases	8.2	8.3	6.9	7.8	7.7	10.2	7.8	7.7
Gasoline and motor oil	3.5	3.5	3.8	4.0	4.1	3.6	2.9	3.9
Other vehicle expenses	5.9	5.9	4.6	5.6	6.1	6.4	5.8	5.7
Public transportation	1.0	1.0	1.1	.8	.8	.9	1.2	1.3
Health care	5.1	5.0	7.1	7.6	5.6	4.2	3.8	5.6
Entertainment	5.1	5.1	4.2	3.7	4.6	5.1	5.9	5.6
Personal care products and services	1.3	1.3	1.4	1.7	1.4	1.3	1.2	1.3
Reading	.6	.6	.5	.6	.6	.5	.6	.6
Education	1.3	1.2	2.2	.8	.8	.9	1.5	2.1
Tobacco products and smoking supplies	.9	.9	1.5	1.3	1.3	.9	.5	.9
Miscellaneous	2.3	2.4	2.3	2.2	2.7	2.2	2.4	1.8
Cash contributions	3.2	3.3	1.9	2.4	3.0	3.0	4.2	2.8
Personal insurance and pensions	8.9	9.7	2.7	5.0	8.1	10.5	13.2	2.5
Life and other personal insurance	1.2	1.2	.9	1.1	1.1	1.3	1.4	1.3
Pensions and Social Security ..	7.6	8.5	1.7	3.9	7.0	9.2	11.8	1.1

Table 3.17 (*continued*)

Item	All consumer units	Complete reporting of income						Incomplete reporting of income
		Total complete reporting	Lowest 20 percent	Second 20 percent	Third 20 percent	Fourth 20 percent	Highest 20 percent	
1999								
Number of consumer units (in thousands)	108,465	81,692	16,307	16,351	16,332	16,341	16,361	26,773
Consumer unit characteristics:								
Income before taxes [1]	$43,951	$43,951	$7,264	$18,033	$31,876	$52,331	$110,105	(1)
Age of reference person	47.9	47.9	51.6	51.6	46.5	44.1	45.9	47.8
Average number in consumer unit:								
Persons	2.5	2.5	1.8	2.2	2.5	2.8	3.1	2.6
Children under 18	.7	.7	.4	.6	.7	.8	.8	.7
Persons 65 and over	.3	.3	.4	.5	.3	.2	.1	.3
Earners	1.3	1.4	.7	.9	1.3	1.8	2.0	1.3
Vehicles	1.9	2.0	1.0	1.6	2.0	2.4	2.8	1.8
Percent homeowner	65	64	43	55	63	73	88	67
Average annual expenditures	$36,995	$39,143	$16,750	$24,840	$33,029	$45,998	$75,015	$30,787
Percent distribution:	100.0	100.0	100.0	100.0	100.0	100.0	100.0	100.0
Food	13.6	13.3	16.2	15.2	14.5	13.5	11.4	14.9
Food at home	7.9	7.7	10.9	10.0	8.6	7.9	5.7	8.7
Cereals and bakery products	1.2	1.2	1.7	1.5	1.3	1.2	.9	1.4
Meats, poultry, fish, and eggs	2.0	1.9	3.0	2.6	2.2	2.0	1.3	2.4
Dairy products	.9	.9	1.2	1.1	1.0	.9	.7	.9
Fruits and vegetables	1.4	1.3	1.9	1.8	1.5	1.3	1.0	1.5
Other food at home	2.4	2.4	3.1	3.0	2.7	2.5	1.8	2.6
Food away from home	5.7	5.6	5.3	5.2	6.0	5.6	5.7	6.2
Alcoholic beverages	.9	.9	1.0	.9	.8	.8	.9	.8
Housing	32.6	31.5	37.0	34.0	31.6	30.2	30.1	36.8
Shelter	19.0	18.0	21.4	19.0	18.1	17.2	17.5	22.3
Owned dwellings	12.2	11.5	8.1	8.3	10.1	11.5	14.0	14.9
Rented dwellings	5.5	5.3	12.4	9.7	7.2	4.8	1.8	6.0
Other lodging	1.3	1.2	.9	.9	.8	.9	1.7	1.4
Utilities, fuels, and public services	6.4	6.1	9.2	7.9	6.9	5.8	4.5	7.8
Household operations	1.8	1.8	1.5	1.6	1.2	1.6	2.4	1.7
Housekeeping supplies	1.3	1.4	1.5	1.5	1.5	1.5	1.2	1.2
Household furnishings and equipment	4.1	4.1	3.4	3.9	3.9	4.1	4.5	3.8
Apparel and services	4.7	4.8	4.7	5.4	5.3	4.3	4.6	4.6
Transportation	19.0	18.4	16.7	19.1	19.3	19.6	17.6	20.7
Vehicle purchases (net outlay)	8.9	8.7	7.3	9.2	8.8	9.4	8.4	9.7
Gasoline and motor oil	2.9	2.7	3.0	3.1	3.3	2.9	2.2	3.3
Other vehicle expenses	6.1	6.0	5.4	5.9	6.4	6.3	5.7	6.5
Public transportation	1.1	1.0	1.0	1.0	.9	.9	1.2	1.2
Health care	5.3	5.2	7.5	7.7	5.9	4.8	3.8	5.6
Entertainment	5.1	5.1	4.8	4.4	4.7	5.2	5.4	5.3
Personal care products and services	1.1	1.1	1.3	1.2	1.3	1.1	1.0	1.0
Reading	.4	.4	.5	.5	.4	.4	.4	.4
Education	1.7	1.5	2.7	1.1	1.0	1.1	1.8	2.5
Tobacco products and smoking supplies	.8	.8	1.4	1.2	1.0	.8	.4	.8
Miscellaneous	2.3	2.4	2.1	2.3	2.4	2.3	2.5	2.2
Cash contributions	3.2	3.4	1.8	2.6	3.2	3.4	4.2	2.2
Personal insurance and pensions	9.3	11.1	2.4	4.5	8.4	12.3	15.7	2.1
Life and other personal insurance	1.1	1.0	.8	.8	.9	1.0	1.2	1.1
Pensions and Social Security	8.2	10.1	1.6	3.7	7.5	11.3	14.5	

1. Components of income and taxes are derived from "complete income reporters" only.
n.a. Not applicable.

Source: U.S. Department of Labor. (2001). *Report on the American Workforce.* Washington, D.C.: Government Printing Office. Retrieved from http://www.bls.gov/opub/rtaw/pdf/appendix.pdf.

Table 3.18
Human and Income Poverty: OECD, Central and Eastern Europe, and CIS Countries

HDI rank		Human poverty index (HPI-2)[a] Rank	Human poverty index (HPI-2)[a] Value (%)	Probability at birth of not surviving to age 60[A] (% of cohort) 2000-05[b]	People lacking functional literacy skills[A] (% age 16-65) 1994-98[c]	Long-term unemployment[A] (as % of labour force)[d] 2001	Population below income poverty line (%) 50% of median income[e, A] 1990-2000[f]	Population below income poverty line (%) $11 a day 1994-95[f, g]	Population below income poverty line (%) $4 a day 1996-99[f, h]	HPI-2 rank minus income poverty rank[i]
High human development										
1	Norway	2	7.2	8.3	8.5	0.2	6.9	4.3	..	-2
2	Iceland	..	..	7.6	..	0.3	..	..	..	..
3	Sweden	1	6.5	7.3	7.5	1.1	6.6	6.3	..	-2
4	Australia	14	12.9	8.8	17.0	1.4	14.3	17.6	..	-2
5	Netherlands	4	8.4	8.7	10.5	1.6 [j]	8.1	7.1	..	-4
6	Belgium	13	12.4	9.4	18.4 [k]	3.2	8.0	..	..	7
7	United States	17	15.8	12.6	20.7	0.3	17.0	13.6	..	0
8	Canada	12	12.2	8.7	16.6	0.7	12.8	7.4	..	-2
9	Japan	10	11.1	7.5	.. [l]	1.4	11.8 [m]	..	..	-1
10	Switzerland	..	..	9.1	..	0.7	9.3	..	..	..
11	Denmark	5	9.1	11.0	9.6	0.9	9.2	..	..	-4
12	Ireland	16	15.3	9.3	22.6	3.2 [j]	12.3	..	..	4
13	United Kingdom	15	14.8	8.9	21.8	1.3	12.5	15.7	..	2
14	Finland	3	8.4	10.2	10.4	2.4	5.4	4.8	..	1
15	Luxembourg	7	10.3	9.7	.. [l]	0.5 [n]	3.9	0.3	..	6
16	Austria	..	..	9.5	..	0.9	10.6	..	..	..
17	France	8	10.8	10.0	.. [l]	3.3	8.0	9.9	..	2
18	Germany	6	10.2	9.2	14.4	4.2 [o]	7.5	7.3	..	1
19	Spain	9	11.0	8.8	.. [l]	4.6	10.1	..	..	-1
20	New Zealand	..	..	9.8	18.4	0.9	..	..	..	..
21	Italy	11	12.2	8.6	.. [l]	6.1	14.2	..	..	-4
22	Israel	..	..	7.4	..	..	13.5	..	..	..
23	Portugal	..	..	11.7	48.0	1.6	..	..	..	..
24	Greece	..	..	9.1	..	5.5	..	..	..	..
29	Slovenia	..	..	11.8	42.2	..	8.2	..	<1	..
32	Czech Republic	..	..	12.2	15.7	4.3	4.9	..	<1	..
33	Malta	..	..	7.7	..	..	..	..	..	..
35	Poland	..	..	15.6	42.6	8.0	8.6	..	10	..
38	Hungary	..	..	19.6	33.8	2.7	6.7	..	<1	..
39	Slovakia	..	..	15.2	..	9.3	2.1	..	8	..
41	Estonia	..	..	20.4	..	..	12.3	..	18	..
45	Lithuania	..	..	19.5	..	..	..	..	17	..
47	Croatia	..	..	14.5	..	..	..	..	..	..
50	Latvia	..	..	21.4	..	..	..	..	28	..
53	Belarus	..	..	22.8	..	..	..	..	..	..
Medium human development										
57	Bulgaria	..	..	18.6	..	..	..	..	22	..
60	Macedonia, TFYR	..	..	13.3	..	..	..	..	..	..
63	Russian Federation	..	..	28.9	..	..	20.1	..	53	..
66	Bosnia and Herzegovina	..	..	13.7	..	..	..	..	..	..
72	Romania	..	..	20.3	..	..	..	..	23	..
75	Ukraine	..	..	23.0	..	..	..	..	25	..
76	Kazakhstan	..	..	27.0	..	..	..	..	62	..
87	Turkmenistan	..	..	24.8	..	..	..	..	..	..
88	Georgia	..	..	16.2	..	..	..	..	..	..
89	Azerbaijan	..	..	18.5	..	..	..	..	..	..

Table 3.18 (*continued*)

HDI rank		Human poverty index (HPI-2) [a] Rank	Human poverty index (HPI-2) [a] Value (%)	Probability at birth of not surviving to age 60 [Å] (% of cohort) 2000-05 [b]	People lacking functional literacy skills [Å] (% age 16-65) 1994-98 [c]	Long-term unemployment [Å] (as % of labour force) [d] 2001	Population below income poverty line (%) 50% of median income [e, Å] 1990-2000 [f]	Population below income poverty line (%) $11 a day 1994-95 [f, g]	Population below income poverty line (%) $4 a day 1996-99 [f, h]	HPI-2 rank minus income poverty rank [i]
95	Albania	..	..	11.3	..	..	..	..	..	..
100	Armenia	..	..	14.9	..	..	..	..	..	..
101	Uzbekistan	..	..	21.8	..	..	..	..	..	..
102	Kyrgyzstan	..	..	23.7	..	..	..	..	88	..
108	Moldova, Rep. of	..	..	22.8	..	..	..	..	82	..
113	Tajikistan	..	..	22.8	..	..	..	..	..	..

Å. Denotes indicators used to calculate the human poverty index (HPI-2). For further details, see technical note 1.

Note: This table includes Israel and Malta, which are not OECD member countries, but excludes the Republic of Korea, Mexico and Turkey, which are.

a. The human poverty index (HPI-2) is calculated for selected high-income OECD countries only.

b. Data refer to the probability at birth of not surviving to age 60, times 100. They are medium-variant projections for the period specified.

c. Based on scoring at level 1 on the prose literacy scale of the International Adult Literacy Survey. Data refer to the most recent year available during the period specified.

d. Data refer to unemployment lasting 12 months or longer.

e. Poverty line is measured at 50% of the median adjusted household disposable income.

f. Data refer to the most recent year available during the period specified.

g. Based on the US poverty line, $11 (1994 PPP US$) a day per person for a family of three.

h. Poverty line is $4 (1990 PPP US$) a day.

i. Income poverty refers to the percentage of the population living on less than 50% of the median adjusted household disposable income. A positive figure indicates that the country performs better in income poverty than in human poverty, a negative the opposite.

j. Data refer to 1999.

k. Data refer to Flanders.

l. For purposes of calculating the HPI-2, an estimate of 15.1%, the unweighted average for countries with available data, was applied.

m. Smeeding 1997.

n. Data are based on a small sample and should be treated with caution.

o. Data refer to 2000.

Source: United Nations Development Programme. (2003). *Human Development Report 2003*. Table 4. "Human & Income Poverty (248–9)." New York: Oxford University Press. Retrieved from http://www.undp.org/hdr2003/pdf/hdr03_complete.pdf. Copyright 2003 by the United Nations Development Programme. Used by permission of Oxford University Press, Inc.

Table 3.19
Overall Trends in Poverty in Eight Countries

Panel A. Persons with Income Less than Half of Median Income

Country	Years	Final Year Overall Rate	Change in Poverty Rate					
			Overall		Aged		Children	
United States	1979-1997	16.9	+	(1.1)	- - -	(-6.6)	+ +	(1.9)
United Kingdom	1979-1995	13.4	+ + +	(4.2)	- - -	(-7.2)	+ + +	(10.1)
Australia	1981-1994	14.3	+ +	(3.0)	+ + +	(5.4)	+ +	(2.0)
Canada	1981-1997	11.9	0	(-0.5)	- - -	(-16.8)	0	(.9)
Sweden	1975-1995	6.6	0	(.1)	0	(-.2)	0	(.2)
France	1984-1994	8.0	- -	(-3.5)	- - -	(-9.5)	-	(-1.9)
Germany [1]	1984-1994	7.5	+	(1.0)	- -	(-3.3)	+ +	(3.8)
Netherlands	1983-1994	8.1	+ +	(3.8)	+ +	(2.7)	+ + +	(5.4)

Panel B. Trends in Poverty: Persons with Income Less than 40 Percent of the Median (Change in Points)

Country	Year	Final Year Overall Rate	Change in Poverty Rate					
			Overall		Aged		Children	
United States	1979-1997	10.8	0	(.8)	- -	(-3.8)	+	(1.7)
Australia	1981-1994	7.1	+	(1.8)	+ +	(3.9)	0	(.5)
Canada	1981-1997	7.3	0	(-.2)	- - -	(-5.3)	0	(0)
United Kingdom	1979-1995	6.1	+ +	(3.8)	0	(.5)	+ +	(3.8)
Netherlands	1983-1994	4.9	+ +	(2.6)	0	(.5)	+ +	(2.6)
Sweden	1981-1995	4.7	+	(1.7)	0	(.7)	+	(1.7)
Germany [1]	1984-1994	4.1	+	(1.3)	0	(.6)	+	(1.3)
France	1984-1994	3.4	0	(-.8)	-	(-1.9)	0	(-.8)

Note: 1. West Germany only.
Legend of Change from Beginning to End of Period
0 = +/− 1.0 points
+ = increase of 1.0 to 1.9 points
+ + = increase of 2.0 to 3.9 points
+ + + = increase of 4.0 points or more
− = decrease of 1.0 to 1.9 points
− − − = decrease of 2.0 to 3.9 points
− − − − = decrease of 4.0 points or more

Source: Smeeding, T.M. (2001). *Income maintenance in old age: What can be learned from cross-national comparisons.* Working Paper for the Center for Retirement Research, No. 2001–11. Chestnut Hill, MA: Boston College. Retrieved from http://www.bc.edu/centers/crr/papers/wp_2001-11.pdf.

Table 3.20
Ratio of Disposable Income of Older People in
"Retired" Households[a] to Disposable Income of
People Aged 18 to 64

| | Older people in the "retired" housholds | | | | | |
| | single adult, not working | | | two or more adults, no worker | | |
	mid 70s	mid 80s	mid 90s	mid 70s	mid 80s	mid 90s
Canada	33	61	69	40	77	89
Finland	53	60	61	66	79	83
Germany	..	69	70	..	78	85
Italy	..	49	54	..	66	71
Japan	..	38	44	..	58	64
Netherlands	80	75	71	82	83	82
Sweden	56	65	68	66	79	91
United Kingdom	51	53	58	60	64	70
United States	51	61	58	66	80	77

Note: a. The "retired" household means the households with no one in the labor market headed by a person aged 65 and over.

Source: Yamada, A. (2002). The evolving income retirement package: Trends in adequacy and equality in nine OECD countries. *Labour Market and Occasional Papers—No. 63.* Paris: OECD, Directorate for Education, Employment, Labour and Social Affairs. Retrieved from http://www.olis.oecd.org/OLIS/2002DOC.NSF/ LINKTO/DEELSA-ELSA-WD(2002)7. OECD Copyright. Reproduced by permission of the OECD.

Figure 3.2
Mean Disposable Income of the Lowest Income Quintile in Nine OECD Countries

(as a percentage of mean disposable income of people aged 18 to 64 mid-1970s, mid-1980s, and mid-1990s)

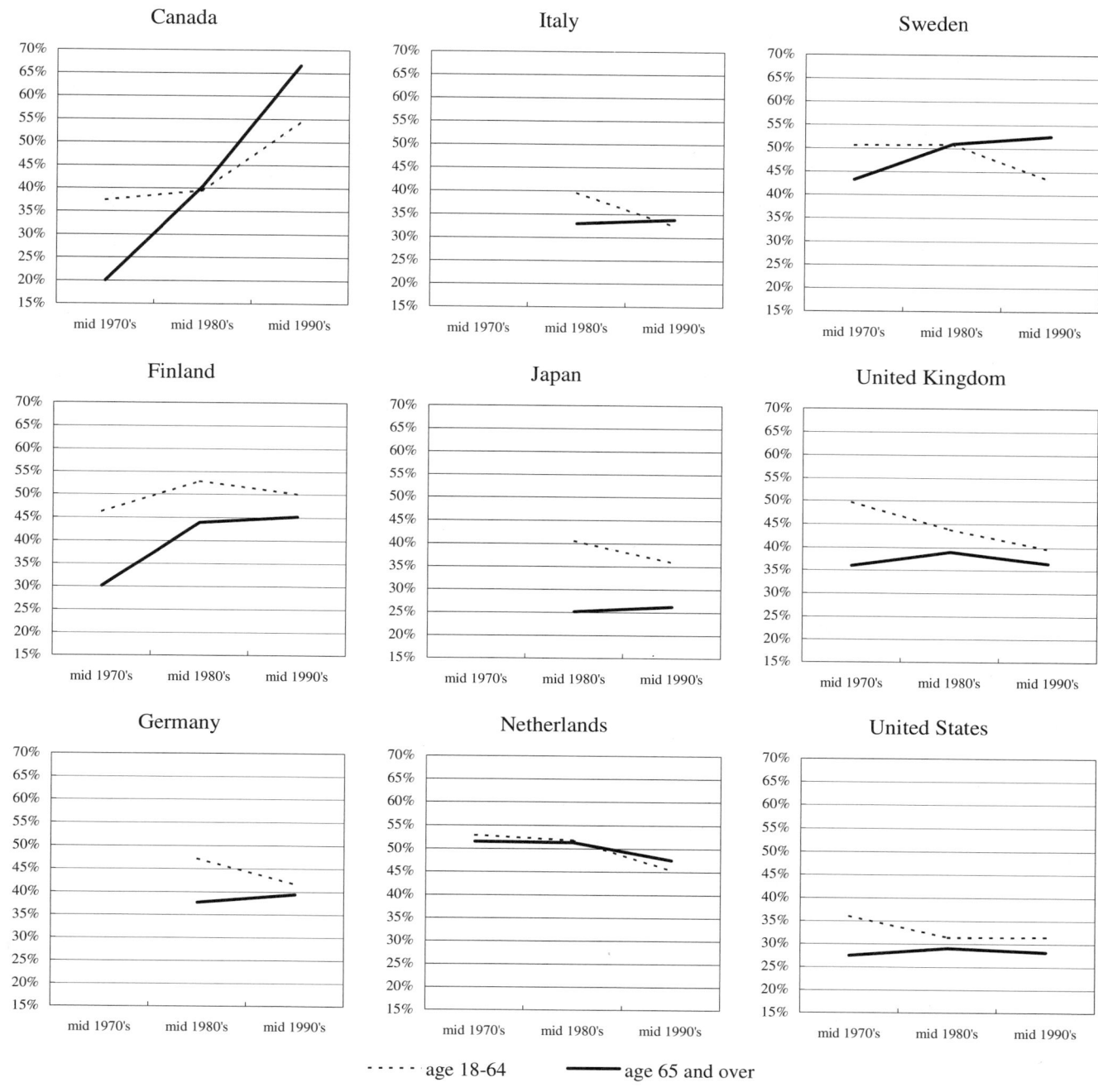

Source: Yamada, A. (2002). The evolving income retirement package: Trends in adequacy and equality in nine OECD countries. *Labour Market and Occasional Papers—No. 63.* Paris: OECD, Directorate for Education, Employment, Labour and Social Affairs. Retrieved from http://www.olis.oecd.org/OLIS/ 2002DOC.NSF/LINKTO/DEELSA-ELSA-WD(2002)7. OECD Copyright. Reproduced by permission of the OECD.

Figure 3.3
Real Income Growth Rates by Age Group in Nine OECD Countries

(mid-1980s and mid-1990s)

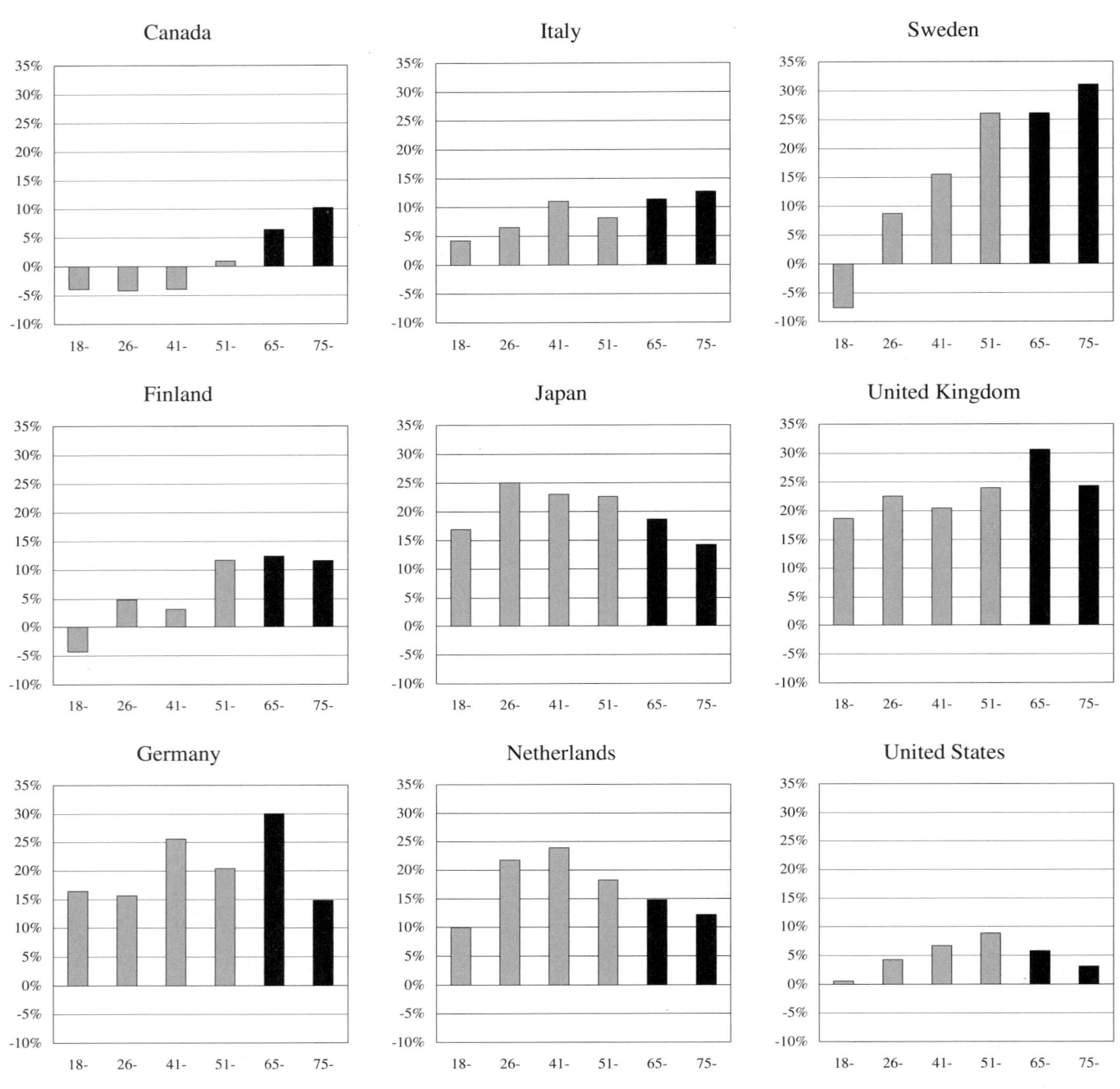

Source: Yamada, A. (2002). The evolving income retirement package: Trends in adequacy and equality in nine OECD countries. *Labour Market and Occasional Papers—No. 63.* Paris. OECD, Directorate for Education, Employment, Labour and Social Affairs. Retrieved from http://www.olis.oecd.org/OLIS/2002DOC .NSF/LINKTO/DEELSA-ELSA-WD(2002)7. OECD Copyright. Reproduced by permission of the OECD.

Figure 3.4
Percentage of Population That Is Below the Low-Income Cut-Off Line[a]
in Nine OECD Countries

(by age group)

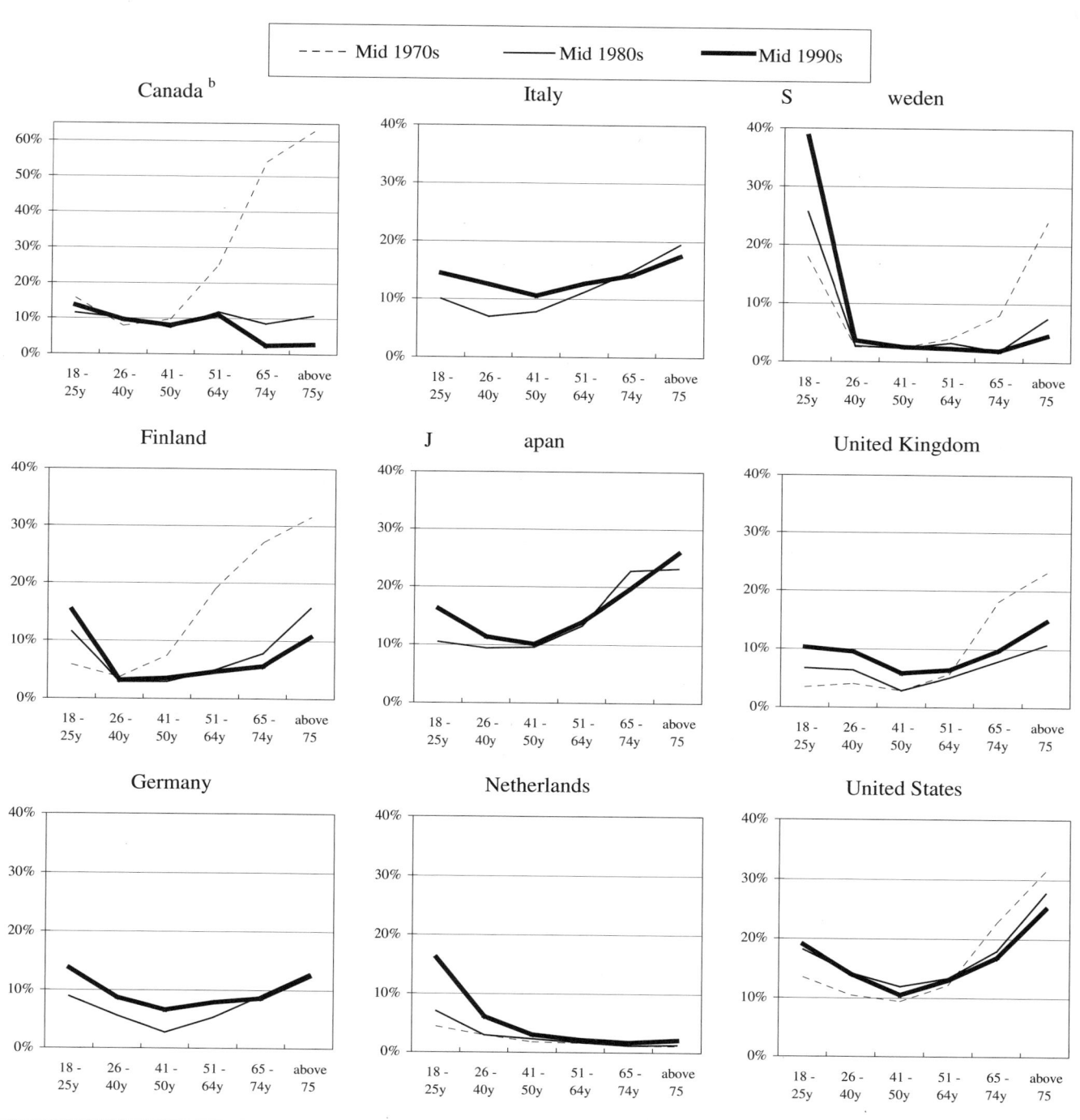

a. Low income cut-off line means 50% of median disposable income of the entire population.
b. Measure of vertical axis is different for Canada.

Source: Yamada, A. (2002). The evolving income retirement package: Trends in adequacy and equality in nine OECD countries. *Labour Market and Occasional Papers—No. 63.* Paris: OECD, Directorate for Education, Employment, Labour and Social Affairs. Retrieved from http://www.olis.oecd.org/OLIS/2002DOC .NSF/LINKTO/DEELSA-ELSA-WD(2002)7. OECD Copyright. Reproduced by permission of the OECD.

Table 3.21
Consumption of Selected Items[a] in Nine OECD Countries

	(1) Food And Non-Alcoholic Beverages					
	Total Spending [b] of Younger Couple = 1.00 unit			Spending Level of Younger Couple for the item = 100 %		
	Older Single [c]	Older Couple [d]	Younger Couple [e]	Older Single [c]	Older Couple [d]	Younger Couple [e]
Canada [f]	0.15	0.18	0.20	73%	89%	100%
Finland	0.14	0.20	0.20	72%	101%	100%
Germany	0.14	0.18	0.17	81%	105%	100%
Italy	0.22	0.26	0.25	87%	103%	100%
Japan	0.12	0.17	0.15	84%	119%	100%
Netherlands	0.12	0.18	0.17	67%	103%	100%
Sweden	0.20	0.26	0.26	77%	99%	100%
United Kingdom	0.12	0.17	0.17	72%	100%	100%
United States	0.08	0.10	0.11	71%	92%	100%

	(2) Transport					
	Total Spending [b] of Younger Couple = 1.00 unit			Spending Level of Younger Couple for the item = 100 %		
	Older Single [c]	Older Couple [d]	Younger Couple [e]	Older Single [c]	Older Couple [d]	Younger Couple [e]
Canada [f]	0.09	0.16	0.23	37%	70%	100%
Finland	0.04	0.12	0.19	19%	65%	100%
Germany	0.07	0.14	0.18	37%	79%	100%
Italy	0.03	0.09	0.15	20%	56%	100%
Japan	0.04	0.07	0.10	39%	67%	100%
Netherlands	0.06	0.11	0.10	53%	103%	100%
Sweden	0.08	0.13	0.17	46%	75%	100%
United Kingdom	0.04	0.12	0.13	29%	92%	100%
United States	0.12	0.21	0.26	45%	81%	100%

	(3) Recreation and Culture					
	Total Spending [b] of Younger Couple = 1.00 unit			Spending Level of Younger Couple for the item = 100 %		
	Older Single [c]	Older Couple [d]	Younger Couple [e]	Older Single [c]	Older Couple [d]	Younger Couple [e]
Canada [f]	0.07	0.11	0.15	51%	74%	100%
Finland	0.07	0.11	0.15	50%	77%	100%
Germany	0.12	0.16	0.14	88%	115%	100%
Italy	0.08	0.07	0.11	74%	69%	100%
Japan	0.12	0.13	0.10	121%	132%	100%
Netherlands	0.11	0.15	0.15	71%	98%	100%
Sweden	0.11	0.14	0.17	65%	85%	100%
United Kingdom	0.08	0.13	0.14	57%	90%	100%
United States	0.05	0.09	0.09	56%	94%	100%

Note:
a. The results here should be treated carefully as not all detailed items are harmonised completely.
b. Excluding housing expenditure, direct tax payments and social security contributions.
c. Single household headed by the person aged 65 and over. For Japan, the household does not include an earner.
d. Two member household headed by the person aged 65 and over. For Japan, the household does not include an earner.
e. For European countries and Japan, couples with two children. For Canada, couples with children but no additional persons. For the U.S., four member households headed by a person aged 35 to 44.
f. In Canadian data, the item "cafes and restaurants" is also covered under the item "food and non-alcoholic beverages."

Source: Casey, B. & Yamada, A. (2002). Getting older, getting poorer? A study of earnings, pensions, assets, and living arrangements of older people in nine countries. OECD's *Labour Market and Occasional Papers No. 60.* Retrieved from http://www.olis.oecd.org/OLIS/2002DOC.NSF/LINKTO/DEELSA-ELSA-WD(2002)4. OECD Copyright. Reproduced by permission of the OECD.

Table 3.22
Inequality in Income or Consumption

| HDI rank | Survey year | Share of income or consumption (%) | | | | Inequality measures | | |
		Poorest 10%	Poorest 20%	Richest 20%	Richest 10%	Richest 10% to poorest 10% [a]	Richest 20% to poorest 20% [a]	Gini index [b]
High human development								
1 Norway	1995 [c]	4.1	9.7	35.8	21.8	5.3	3.7	25.8
2 Iceland	..	..	..	..	..	..	..	..
3 Sweden	1995 [c]	3.4	9.1	34.5	20.1	5.9	3.8	25.0
4 Australia	1994 [c]	2.0	5.9	41.3	25.4	12.5	7.0	35.2
5 Netherlands	1994 [c]	2.8	7.3	40.1	25.1	9.0	5.5	32.6
6 Belgium	1996 [c]	2.9	8.3	37.3	22.6	7.8	4.5	25.0
7 United States	1997 [c]	1.8	5.2	46.4	30.5	16.6	9.0	40.8
8 Canada	1997 [c]	2.7	7.3	39.3	23.9	9.0	5.4	31.5
9 Japan	1993 [c]	4.8	10.6	35.7	21.7	4.5	3.4	24.9
10 Switzerland	1992 [c]	2.6	6.9	40.3	25.2	9.9	5.8	33.1
11 Denmark	1997 [c]	2.6	8.3	35.8	21.3	8.1	4.3	24.7
12 Ireland	1987 [c]	2.5	6.7	42.9	27.4	11.0	6.4	35.9
13 United Kingdom	1995 [c]	2.1	6.1	43.2	27.5	13.4	7.1	36.0
14 Finland	1995 [c]	4.1	10.1	35.0	20.9	5.1	3.5	25.6
15 Luxembourg	1998 [c]	3.2	8.0	39.7	24.7	7.7	4.9	30.8
16 Austria	1995 [c]	2.3	7.0	37.9	22.4	9.8	5.5	30.5
17 France	1995 [c]	2.8	7.2	40.2	25.1	9.1	5.6	32.7
18 Germany	1998 [c]	2.0	5.7	44.7	28.0	14.2	7.9	38.2
19 Spain	1990 [c]	2.8	7.5	40.3	25.2	9.0	5.4	32.5
20 New Zealand	1997 [c]	2.2	6.4	43.8	27.8	12.5	6.8	36.2
21 Italy	1998 [c]	1.9	6.0	42.6	27.4	14.5	7.1	36.0
22 Israel	1997 [c]	2.4	6.9	44.3	28.2	11.7	6.4	35.5
23 Portugal	1997 [c]	2.0	5.8	45.9	29.8	15.0	8.0	38.5
24 Greece	1998 [c]	2.9	7.1	43.6	28.5	10.0	6.2	35.4
25 Cyprus	..	..	..	..	..	..	..	..
26 Hong Kong, China (SAR)	1996 [c]	2.0	5.3	50.7	34.9	17.8	9.7	43.4
27 Barbados	..	..	..	..	..	..	..	..
28 Singapore	1998 [c]	1.9	5.0	49.0	32.8	17.7	9.7	42.5
29 Slovenia	1998 [c]	3.9	9.1	37.7	23.0	5.8	4.1	28.4
30 Korea, Rep. of	1998 [c]	2.9	7.9	37.5	22.5	7.8	4.7	31.6
31 Brunei Darussalam	..	..	..	..	..	..	..	..
32 Czech Republic	1996 [c]	4.3	10.3	35.9	22.4	5.2	3.5	25.4
33 Malta	..	..	..	..	..	..	..	..
34 Argentina	..	..	..	..	..	..	..	..
35 Poland	1998 [d]	3.2	7.8	39.7	24.7	7.8	5.1	31.6
36 Seychelles	..	..	..	..	..	..	..	..
37 Bahrain	..	..	..	..	..	..	..	..
38 Hungary	1998 [d]	4.1	10.0	34.4	20.5	5.0	3.5	24.4
39 Slovakia	1996 [c]	3.1	8.8	34.8	20.9	6.7	4.0	25.8
40 Uruguay [e]	1998 [c]	1.6	4.5	50.4	33.8	21.6	11.2	44.8
41 Estonia	1998 [c]	3.0	7.0	45.1	29.8	10.0	6.5	37.6
42 Costa Rica [f]	1997 [c]	1.7	4.5	51.0	34.6	20.7	11.5	45.9
43 Chile	1998 [c]	1.1	3.2	61.3	45.4	43.2	19.3	57.5
44 Qatar	..	..	..	..	..	..	..	..
45 Lithuania	2000 [d]	3.2	7.9	40.0	24.9	7.9	5.1	36.3
46 Kuwait	..	..	..	..	..	..	..	..
47 Croatia	2001 [d]	3.4	8.3	39.6	24.5	7.3	4.8	29.0
48 United Arab Emirates	..	..	..	..	..	..	..	..
49 Bahamas	..	..	..	..	..	..	..	..
50 Latvia	1998 [c]	2.9	7.6	40.3	25.9	8.9	5.3	32.4

Table 3.22 (*continued*)

HDI rank	Survey year	Share of income or consumption (%) Poorest 10%	Poorest 20%	Richest 20%	Richest 10%	Inequality measures Richest 10% to poorest 10%[a]	Richest 20% to poorest 20%[a]	Gini index[b]
51 Saint Kitts and Nevis	..	..	..	..	..	..	..	..
52 Cuba	..	..	..	..	..	..	..	..
53 Belarus	2000 [d]	3.5	8.4	39.1	24.1	6.9	4.6	30.4
54 Trinidad and Tobago	1992 [c]	2.1	5.5	45.9	29.9	14.4	8.3	40.3
55 Mexico	1998 [c]	1.2	3.4	57.6	41.6	34.6	17.0	51.9
Medium human development								
56 Antigua and Barbuda	..	..	..	..	..	..	..	..
57 Bulgaria	2001 [c]	2.4	6.7	38.9	23.7	9.9	5.8	31.9
58 Malaysia	1997 [c]	1.7	4.4	54.3	38.4	22.1	12.4	49.2
59 Panama	1997 [d]	1.2	3.6	52.8	35.7	29.8	14.7	48.5
60 Macedonia, TFYR	1998 [d]	3.3	8.4	36.7	22.1	6.8	4.4	28.2
61 Libyan Arab Jamahiriya	..	..	..	..	..	..	..	..
62 Mauritius	..	..	..	..	..	..	..	..
63 Russian Federation	2000 [d]	1.8	4.9	51.3	36.0	20.3	10.5	45.6
64 Colombia[f]	1996 [c]	1.1	3.0	60.9	46.1	42.7	20.3	57.1
65 Brazil[f]	1998 [c]	0.7	2.2	64.1	48.0	65.8	29.7	60.7
66 Bosnia and Herzegovina	..	..	..	..	..	..	..	..
67 Belize	..	..	..	..	..	..	..	..
68 Dominica	..	..	..	..	..	..	..	..
69 Venezuela[f]	1998 [c]	0.8	3.0	53.2	36.5	44.0	17.7	49.5
70 Samoa (Western)	..	..	..	..	..	..	..	..
71 Saint Lucia	1995 [c]	2.0	5.2	48.3	32.5	16.2	9.2	42.6
72 Romania	2000 [d]	3.3	8.2	38.4	23.6	7.2	4.7	30.3
73 Saudi Arabia	..	..	..	..	..	..	..	..
74 Thailand	2000 [d]	2.5	6.1	50.0	33.8	13.4	8.3	43.2
75 Ukraine	1999 [d]	3.7	8.8	37.8	23.2	6.4	4.3	29.0
76 Kazakhstan	2001 [d]	3.4	8.2	39.6	24.2	7.1	4.8	31.2
77 Suriname	..	..	..	..	..	..	..	..
78 Jamaica	2000 [d]	2.7	6.7	46.0	30.3	11.4	6.9	37.9
79 Oman	..	..	..	..	..	..	..	..
80 St. Vincent & the Grenadines	..	..	..	..	..	..	..	..
81 Fiji	..	..	..	...	..	.	..	..
82 Peru	1996 [c]	1.6	4.4	51.2	35.4	22.3	11.7	46.2
83 Lebanon	..	..	..	..	..	..	..	..
84 Paraguay	1998 [c]	0.5	1.9	60.7	43.8	91.1	31.8	57.7
85 Philippines	2000 [d]	2.2	5.4	52.3	36.3	16.5	9.7	46.1
86 Maldives	..	..	..	..	..	..	..	..
87 Turkmenistan	1998 [d]	2.6	6.1	47.5	31.7	12.3	7.7	40.8
88 Georgia	2000 [d]	2.2	6.0	45.2	29.3	13.4	7.6	38.9
89 Azerbaijan	2001 [d]	3.1	7.4	44.5	29.5	9.7	6.0	36.5
90 Jordan	1997 [d]	3.3	7.6	44.4	29.8	9.1	5.9	36.4
91 Tunisia	1995 [d]	2.3	5.7	47.9	31.8	13.8	8.5	41.7
92 Guyana	1999 [d]	1.3	4.5	49.7	33.8	25.9	11.1	44.6
93 Grenada	..	..	..	..	..	..	..	..
94 Dominican Republic	1998 [c]	2.1	5.1	53.3	37.9	17.7	10.5	47.4
95 Albania	..	..	..	..	..	..	..	..
96 Turkey	2000 [d]	2.3	6.1	46.7	30.7	13.3	7.7	40.0
97 Ecuador[f]	1995 [d]	2.2	5.4	49.7	33.8	15.4	9.2	43.7
98 Occupied Palestinian Territories	..	..	..	..	..	..	..	..
99 Sri Lanka	1995 [d]	3.5	8.0	42.8	28.0	7.9	5.3	34.4
100 Armenia	1998 [d]	2.6	6.7	45.1	29.7	11.5	6.8	37.9

Table 3.22 (*continued*)

		Share of income or consumption (%)				Inequality measures		
HDI rank	Survey year	Poorest 10%	Poorest 20%	Richest 20%	Richest 10%	Richest 10% to poorest 10% [a]	Richest 20% to poorest 20% [a]	Gini index [b]
101 Uzbekistan	2000 [d]	3.6	9.2	36.3	22.0	6.1	4.0	26.8
102 Kyrgyzstan	2001 [d]	3.9	9.1	38.3	23.3	6.0	4.2	29.0
103 Cape Verde	..	..	..	..	..	..	..	..
104 China	1998 [c]	2.4	5.9	46.6	30.4	12.7	8.0	40.3
105 El Salvador	1998 [c]	1.2	3.3	56.4	39.4	33.6	17.3	50.8
106 Iran, Islamic Rep. of	1998 [d]	2.0	5.1	49.9	33.7	17.2	9.7	43.0
107 Algeria	1995 [d]	2.8	7.0	42.6	26.8	9.6	6.1	35.3
108 Moldova, Rep. of	2001 [d]	2.8	7.1	43.7	28.4	10.2	6.2	36.2
109 Viet Nam	1998 [d]	3.6	8.0	44.5	29.9	8.4	5.6	36.1
110 Syrian Arab Republic	..	..	..	..	..	..	..	..
111 South Africa	1995 [d]	0.7	2.0	66.5	46.9	65.1	33.6	59.3
112 Indonesia	2000 [d]	3.6	8.4	43.3	28.5	7.8	5.2	30.3
113 Tajikistan	1998 [d]	3.2	8.0	40.0	25.2	8.0	5.0	34.7
114 Bolivia	1999 [d]	1.3	4.0	49.1	32.0	24.6	12.3	44.7
115 Honduras	1998 [c]	0.5	2.0	61.0	44.4	91.8	30.3	59.0
116 Equatorial Guinea	..	..	..	..	..	..	..	..
117 Mongolia	1998 [d]	2.1	5.6	51.2	37.0	17.8	9.1	44.0
118 Gabon	..	..	..	..	..	..	..	..
119 Guatemala [f]	1998 [c]	1.6	3.8	60.6	46.0	29.1	15.8	55.8
120 Egypt	1999 [d]	3.7	8.6	43.6	29.5	8.0	5.1	34.4
121 Nicaragua	1998 [d]	0.7	2.3	63.6	48.8	70.7	27.9	60.3
122 São Tomé and Principe	..	..	..	..	..	..	..	..
123 Solomon Islands	..	..	..	..	..	..	..	..
124 Namibia	1993 [c]	0.5	1.4	78.7	64.5	128.8	56.1	70.7
125 Botswana	1993 [d]	0.7	2.2	70.3	56.6	77.6	31.5	63.0
126 Morocco	1998-99 [d]	2.6	6.5	46.6	30.9	11.7	7.2	39.5
127 India	1997 [d]	3.5	8.1	46.1	33.5	9.5	5.7	37.8
128 Vanuatu	..	..	..	..	..	..	..	..
129 Ghana	1999 [d]	2.1	5.6	46.6	30.0	14.1	8.4	39.6
130 Cambodia	1997 [d]	2.9	6.9	47.6	33.8	11.6	6.9	40.4
131 Myanmar	..	..	..	..	..	..	..	..
132 Papua New Guinea	1996 [d]	1.7	4.5	56.5	40.5	23.8	12.6	50.9
133 Swaziland	1994 [c]	1.0	2.7	64.4	50.2	49.7	23.8	60.9
134 Comoros	..	..	..	..	..	..	..	..
135 Lao People's Dem. Rep.	1997 [d]	3.2	7.6	45.0	30.6	9.7	6.0	37.0
136 Bhutan	..	..	..	..	..	..	..	..
137 Lesotho	1995 [d]	0.5	1.4	70.7	53.6	117.8	50.0	56.0
138 Sudan	..	..	..	..	..	..	..	..
139 Bangladesh	2000 [d]	3.9	9.0	41.3	26.7	6.8	4.6	31.8
140 Congo	..	..	..	..	..	..	..	..
141 Togo	..	..	..	..	..	..	..	..
Low human development								
142 Cameroon	1996 [d]	1.8	4.6	53.0	36.5	20.0	11.4	47.7
143 Nepal	1995-96 [d]	3.2	7.6	44.8	29.8	9.3	5.9	36.7
144 Pakistan	1998-99 [d]	3.7	8.8	42.3	28.3	7.6	4.8	33.0
145 Zimbabwe	1995 [d]	1.8	4.6	55.7	40.3	22.0	12.0	56.8
146 Kenya	1997 [d]	2.3	5.6	51.2	36.1	15.6	9.1	44.5
147 Uganda	1996 [d]	3.0	7.1	44.9	29.8	9.9	6.4	37.4
148 Yemen	1998 [d]	3.0	7.4	41.2	25.9	8.6	5.6	33.4
149 Madagascar	1999 [d]	2.5	6.4	44.8	28.6	11.4	7.0	46.0
150 Haiti	..	..	..	..	..	..	..	..
151 Gambia	1998 [d]	1.5	4.0	55.2	38.0	25.4	13.8	47.8

Table 3.22 (*continued*)

HDI rank		Survey year	Share of income or consumption (%)				Inequality measures		
			Poorest 10%	Poorest 20%	Richest 20%	Richest 10%	Richest 10% to poorest 10% [a]	Richest 20% to poorest 20% [a]	Gini index [b]
152	Nigeria	1996-97 [d]	1.6	4.4	55.7	40.8	24.9	12.8	50.6
153	Djibouti	..	..	..	..	..	..	..	..
154	Mauritania	1995 [d]	2.5	6.4	44.1	28.4	11.2	6.9	37.3
155	Eritrea	..	..	..	..	..	..	..	..
156	Senegal	1995 [d]	2.6	6.4	48.2	33.5	12.8	7.5	41.3
157	Guinea	1994 [d]	2.6	6.4	47.2	32.0	12.3	7.3	40.3
158	Rwanda	1983-85 [d]	4.2	9.7	39.1	24.2	5.8	4.0	28.9
159	Benin	..	..	..	..	..	..	..	..
160	Tanzania, U. Rep. of	1993 [d]	2.8	6.8	45.5	30.1	10.8	6.7	38.2
161	Côte d'Ivoire	1995 [d]	3.1	7.1	44.3	28.8	9.4	6.2	36.7
162	Malawi	1997 [d]	1.9	4.9	56.1	42.2	22.7	11.6	50.3
163	Zambia	1998 [d]	1.1	3.3	56.6	41.0	36.6	17.3	52.6
164	Angola	..	..	..	..	..	..	..	..
165	Chad	..	..	..	..	..	..	..	..
166	Guinea-Bissau	1993 [d]	2.1	5.2	53.4	39.3	19.0	10.3	47.0
167	Congo, Dem. Rep. of the	..	..	..	..	..	..	..	..
168	Central African Republic	1993 [d]	0.7	2.0	65.0	47.7	69.2	32.7	61.3
169	Ethiopia	2000 [c]	0.7	2.4	60.8	43.8	59.7	24.8	57.2
170	Mozambique	1996-97 [d]	2.5	6.5	46.5	31.7	12.5	7.2	39.6
171	Burundi	1998 [d]	1.7	5.1	48.0	32.8	19.3	9.5	33.3
172	Mali	1994 [d]	1.8	4.6	56.2	40.4	23.1	12.2	50.5
173	Burkina Faso	1998 [d]	1.8	4.5	60.7	46.3	26.2	13.6	48.2
174	Niger	1995 [d]	0.8	2.6	53.3	35.4	46.0	20.7	50.5
175	Sierra Leone	1989 [d]	0.5	1.1	63.4	43.6	87.2	57.6	62.9

Note: Because the underlying household surveys differ in method and in the type of data collected, the distribution data are not strictly comparable across countries.

a. Data show the ratio of the income or consumption share of the richest group to that of the poorest. Because of rounding, results may differ from ratios calculated using the income or consumption shares in columns 2–5.

b. The Gini index measures inequality over the entire distribution of income or consumption. A value of 0 represents perfect equality, and a value of 100 perfect inequality.

c. Survey based on income.

d. Survey based on consumption.

e. Data refer to urban areas only.

f. World Bank 2002.

Source: United Nations Development Programme. (2003). *Human Development Report 2003*. Table 13. "Inequality in Income or Consumption (282–5)." New York: Oxford University Press. Retrieved from http://www.undp.org/hdr2003/pdf/hdr03_complete.pdf. Copyright 2003 by the United Nations Development Programme. Used by permission of Oxford University Press, Inc.

Table 3.23
Overall Trends in Income Distribution: Summary Results for the Mid-1970s to Mid-1980s, and Mid-1980s to Mid-1990s

| | Relative change [a] of the Gini coefficients | | | | Relative size [b] of the Gini coefficients (working < (>) retirement age population) | | |
| | mid 1970s to 1980s | | mid 1980s to 1990s | | | | |
	the working age population	the retirement age population	the working age population	the retirement age population	mid 1970s	mid 1980s	mid 1990s
Canada	0	- - -	0	- -	<<<	<	>>
Finland	- -	- - -	+++	-	<<<	<	>>
Germnay			++	-		<	>>
Italy			+++	+		>	>>
Japan			+	0	<<<		<<<
Netherlands	++	0	++	+	0	>	>>
Sweden	-	- - -	+++	++	<<	>	>>>
United Kingdom	+++	0	++	++	<<	>>	>>
United States	++	0	0	0	<<<	<<	<

Note: blank—no data available.

a. +++ (−−−) more than 12 per cent increase in the Gini coefficients (decrease in the Gini coefficients)
++ (−−) 7 to 12 per cent increase in the Gini coefficients (decrease in the Gini coefficients)
+ (−) 2 to 7 per cent increase in the Gini coefficients (decrease in the Gini coefficients)
0 −2 to +2 per cent change in the Gini coefficients
b. <<< (>>>) at least 12 per cent larger (smaller) than the Gini coefficients of younger age population
<< (>>) 7 to 12 per cent larger (smaller) than the Gini coefficients of younger age population
< (>) 2 to 7 per cent larger (smaller) than the Gini coefficients of younger age population
0 −2 to 2 per cent difference

Source: Yamada, A. (2002). The evolving income retirement package: Trends in adequacy and equality in nine OECD countries. *Labour Market and Occasional Papers—No. 63.* Paris: OECD, Directorate for Education, Employment, Labour and Social Affairs. Retrieved from http://www.olis.oecd.org/OLIS/2002DOC .NSF/LINKTO/DEELSA-ELSA-WD(2002)7. OECD Copyright. Reproduced by permission of the OECD.

Figure 3.5
Gini Coefficient among the Poor in the United States: 1962 to 1999

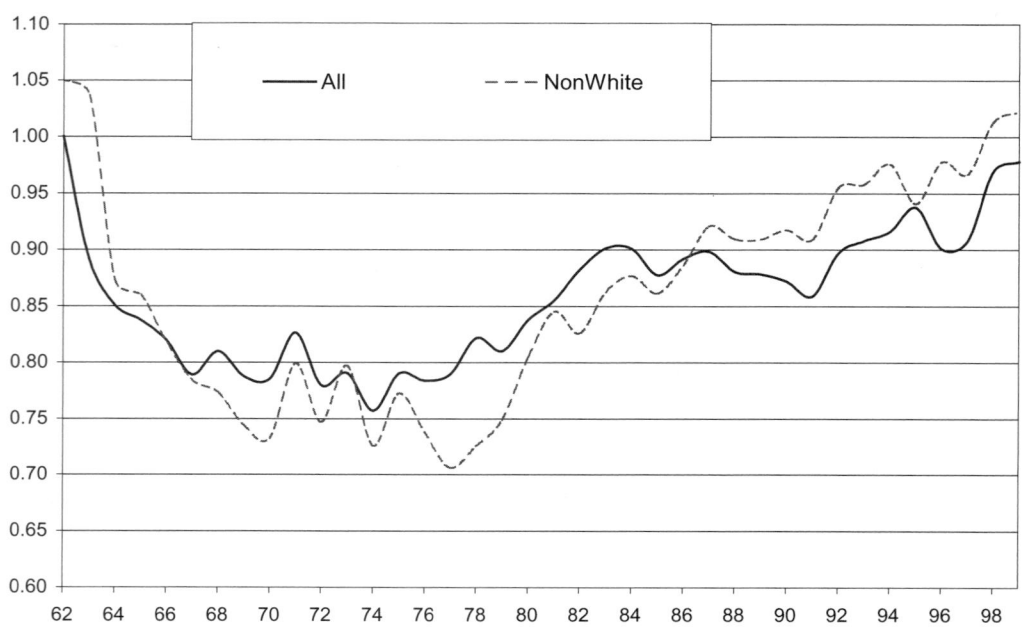

Source: Hoover, G.A., Formby, J.P., & Kim, H. (2001). *Poverty, non-white poverty, and the Sen Index.* Tuscaloosa, A.L.: Culverhouse College of Commerce and Business Administration, Department of Economics, Finance, and Legal Studies Working Paper Series (Working Paper No. 02-04-01). Retrieved from http://www.cha.ua.edu/pdf/WP02-04-01.pdf.

Figure 3.6
U.S. Poverty Using the Sen Index: 1962 to 1999

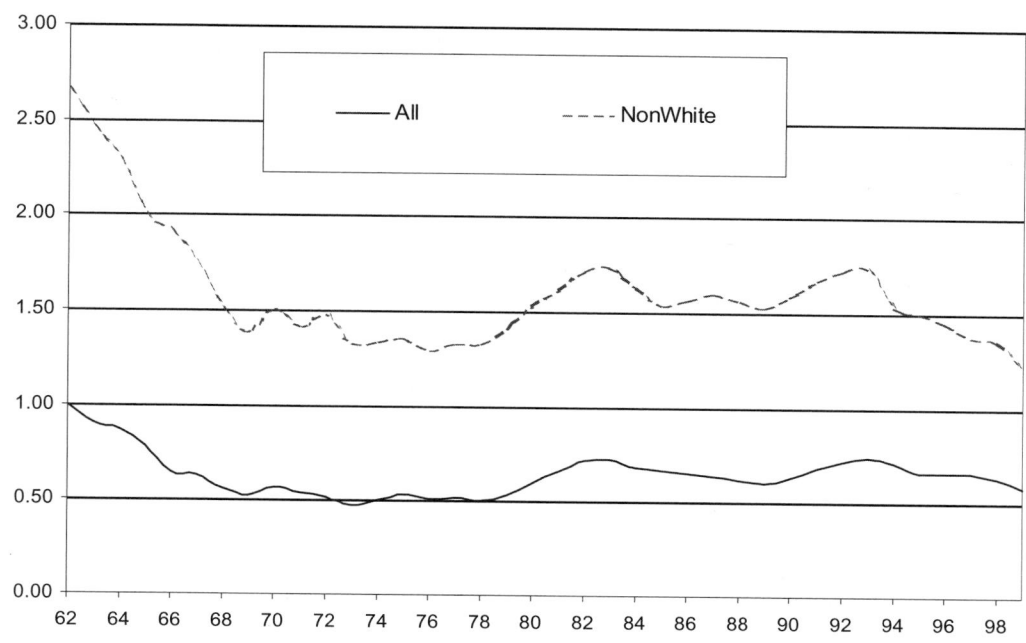

Source: Hoover, G.A., Formby, J.P., & Kim, H. (2001). *Poverty, non-white poverty, and the Sen Index.* Tuscaloosa, AL: Culverhouse College of Commerce and Business Administration, Department of Economics. Finance, and Legal Studies Working Paper Series (Working Paper No. 02-04-01). Retrieved from http://www.cba.ua.edu/pdf/WP02-04-01.pdf.

Table 3.24
Household Size, Mid-1980s and Mid-1990s, and Change

	Average number of household members		Change (percent)
	Entire population		
	Mid 1980s	Mid 1990s	
Canada	2.7	2.6	-5.2
Finland	2.4	2.2	-8.6
Germany	2.6	2.5	-4.6
Italy	3.1	3.0	-3.9
Japan	3.4	2.9	-14.9
Netherlands	2.6	2.3	-11.1
Sweden	1.8	1.8	-1.4
United Kingdom	2.6	2.4	-6.0
United States	2.7	2.7	-1.4

Note: Because the numbers are obtained by income survey data, the numbers could be different from the National Census data.

Source: Yamada, A. (2002). The evolving income retirement package. Trends in adequacy and equality in nine OECD countries. *Labour Market and Occasional Papers—No. 63*. Paris: OECD, Directorate for Education, Employment, Labour and Social Affairs. Retrieved from http://www.olis.oecd.org/ OLIS/2002DOC.NSF/LINKTO/DEELSA-ELSA-WD(2002)7. OECD Copyright. Reproduced by permission of the OECD.

4. Old-Age Insurance: Social Security

Poverty means more than inadequate consumption, education, and health. . . . [It] also means dreading the future—knowing that a crisis may descend at any time, not knowing whether or not one will cope. . . . Poor people are often among the most vulnerable in society because they are the most exposed to a wide array of risks. . . .

Many risks are associated with aging: illness, social isolation, inability to continue working, and uncertainty about whether transfers will provide an adequate living. . . . Consultation with poor people show that income security is a prime concern for the elderly, followed closely by health services, suitable housing, and the quality of family and community life. (World Bank Report, 2001, 135, 137)

This chapter discusses the system of social security as it exists in the United States while also providing some comparisons with other systems presently in use in other countries. What is notable about what in the United States is thought of as social security is that it is a mitigation for the potential vulnerability of an entire class of citizens, the elderly. This chapter focuses only on the income maintenance component of the risks identified by the World Bank.

The purpose of this component of the social safety net is to reduce the risks associated with poverty that senior citizens can face as a result of their inability to continue to work, and to reduce the inherent uncertainty of knowing whether pensions and other retirement incomes will be adequate to meet their needs, especially when facing an unexpected crisis situation. There are two key concepts that one must keep in mind as one pursues an analysis of social security: **insurance** and **income maintenance**, with the former as means of providing a system for the latter. The reasons for these two concepts are more than historical, these are also the practical representation of social preferences based on identified needs and subsequent political will translated into policies at all government levels from national to community levels. Underlying insurance

and income maintenance is the notion of **income redistribution**. The question a nation faces and, ultimately, the safety net structure that is put in place, is based on how a country decides to its satisfaction if its government should be actively involved in establishing an income redistribution system that redistributes national wealth to all members of the community. The first corollary to this question is the degree of government intrusion into individual lives, while the second corollary is the degree of personal choice that individuals have into making lifelong decisions. Then—only then—does one see the set-up of the safety net as a form of **resource allocation**, because a country has to determine what resources it has available, figure out how it is going to collect (usually in the form of taxes) and distribute the resources (money, services, or in-kind contributions), and balance the interest of limits in the resource base against legally established policy (through statutes and **regulatory compliance**).

What is meant by income maintenance? The simplest and broadest answer is the ability to continue receiving a steady flow of income (Dobelstein, 1996). As a policy, it is a government's concern to ensure that all citizens have the ability to continue to receive enough funds in order to be able to live at the least in a minimum accepted quality or standard of life. The normative nature of this accepted standard (often referred to as poverty or as the poverty line) becomes apparent when performing international comparisons, because the notions of what is an appropriate income that must be maintained depend on the costs associated with living in that country. This is why those who are considered poor in the United States can be seen as relatively well-off when compared to standards in developing countries, where poverty is measured and referenced by entities such as the World Bank at $1 or $2 per day (see chapter 3 for a broader discussion in this area).

In the United States, income maintenance is a term of reference for those who receive a specific form of public assistance such as Temporary Assistance for Needy Families (TANF, formerly AFDC), Supplemental Security Income (SSI), Medicaid, and housing assistance. However, this author suggests to expand the use of the term to include other forms of keeping a steady source of income such as retirement plans and unemployment benefits. The basic nature of those two programs is to make sure that retirees, the disabled, and the unemployed are able to maintain a source of funds so that they can make ends meet. Chatterjee (1999) concludes in his book *Repackaging the Welfare State* that the aged are often targets of social redistribution in the form of receiving assistance for housing, health care, pensions, or other similar benefits. Part of the reason for this, as he sees it (supported by the analysis of poverty by the United Nations Programme, the World Bank, the International Monetary Fund and others) is the political influence that elderly people from the middle and upper classes have in the shaping of government policy to meet their needs.

Much of the literature on the subject places income maintenance from the point of view of a philosophical dilemma between **equality** and **equity**. Equality's interest is in that all get their proportional share; equity's raison d'etre is the notion of fairness. This argument echoes the sentiments stated a few paragraphs ago, that nations have to decide what their policy is in regard to people's share of and in the nation's wealth. It is difficult to argue that income is distributed fairly in the United States or elsewhere. Even more difficult to argue is the statement that the distribution of wealth is proportional between classes. In the United States for example, the richest 10 percent of the population has a 30.5 percent share of the income, while the poorest 20 percent of the population has 5.2 percent share of the national income (United Nations Development Programme, 2002, 194). To compare, in Sweden the richest 10 percent have a 20.1 percent share of the national income, while the poorest 20 percent have 9.6 percent share. Canada's top 10 percent account for 23.8 percent of the national wealth, while the poorest 20 percent have a 7.5 percent share in the national wealth. Also, in Germany, the top 10 percent have a 23.7 share; the poorest 20 percent have an 8.2 percent share of the national income. Mexico's richest 10 percent have a 41.7 percent share of the national income, while the lowest 20 percent have a share that only totals 3.5 percent of the national wealth. Some of these countries like Germany and Sweden arguably have an active income redistribution policy in place that drives their social safety nets. Other countries, like the United States, do not support an active income redistribution process as a key part of their fight against poverty. What the comparison bears out is Dobelstein's observation that "equity seems opposed to equality" (1996, 131) because of the continued seeming imbalance in the share of national wealth between those who are "rich" and those that are "poor," even when social redistribution is emphasized in the policies driving the national social safety net. There has to be an awareness that equity and equality issues are enmeshed in distributional concerns, with equality getting a better treatment through government action, while equity works best when distribution choices are closer to the individual user (Dobelstein, 1996). In other words, watch out for the caveat provided by de Jouvenel (1951/1990) that redistribution institutionalizes

poverty rather than alleviates it by creating disincentives for the poor to improve their lot.

Goodin, Headey, Muffels, and Dirven (1999) put the topic of income maintenance in a perspective that balances the philosophical and the sociopolitical practical elements of who should receive what by focusing on income insecurity. Income maintenance needs are based on government's role in stabilizing income sources and levels of income, mainly in the area of salaries and wages. Taking their argument and making a slight adaptation to it, the main point to this line of argument revolves around what happens when there is a disruption in a person's income. What is the role of government in mitigating or eliminating the disruption? How far should the government go to cushion annual fluctuations and make decisions for wage earners in order to protect them from market fluctuations and changes in technology? In other words, what price must the individual and the state pay for stability? Chatterjee (1999) argues that the government's basis for action is to ensure the mitigation of failure: family failure (the nuclear family in particular), market failure and the resulting human suffering such a failure brings, failure resulting from not taking into account and overcoming natural disasters, and failure resulting from an inadequate distribution of income (insufficient purchasing power to make ends meet and market driven wages based on demand for certain occupations and disinterest in others).

Income maintenance programs at times take on the guise of insurance programs. Why insurance programs? The simplest answer is risk aversion and **risk management** by spreading risk among the many. According to the economist Paul Samuelson (1976), "a steady income, equitably divided among individuals instead of arbitrarily apportioned between the lucky and unlucky people . . . , is economically advantageous" (428). More to the point, Chambers (1986) explains the notion of insurance as a means of income maintenance: "The basic idea behind the prior contribution method of establishing entitlement is the same principle that lies behind all private insurance schemes: (1) payment in advance provides for the future and (2) protection against the economic consequences of personal disasters is best done by spreading the risk among a large group of people" (88). The concept of insurance is acceptable—and therefore legitimate to most—because as Daniel Boorstin (1974) contends:

> When communities were local, friends and neighbors were nearby, ready and willing to help in disaster. The church tried to look after widows and orphans. Neighbors who had gathered for a barn raising were likely also to gather and rebuild a barn that had been burned. But the attenuation and stretching of communities created new needs. People who could not confidently rely on their neighbors, people whose relatives had moved to remote parts of the continent, had to find other security. And insurance became a kind of substitute for family, for neighborhood, and for community. Again, insurance handled the problem by creating a centralized source of supply, on which an individual could draw as he needed. . . . By its very nature, insurance—a new kind of consumption community—was a large-scale institution with a democratic reach. (175)

The reason for an insurance scheme as the basis for pension benefits for the elderly is that this system allows—typically requires—the elderly to contribute to their retirement plan while they still work through taxes based on how much they made. The administration of the program generates across-the-board regulations that define eligibility requirements and benefit ceilings. Costs are spread out on an actuarial approach, with the expectation that retirement age and longevity are not too disparate so as to pay off benefits beyond an anticipated period of time.

Insurance acts as a scheme that works on managing risk by reducing the impact a shock has on those that participate within the plan. It does this by estimating and updating benefits received so that these will at least meet or come close to meeting minimum cost requirements needed in order to live. Shock can be defined in many ways. Let it suffice for this instance that shock focuses on the transition from work or an accepted work-capable age to retirement where the incidence of finding work is greatly reduced. Shock is then also seen in terms of occurrences typically faced by the aged such as (a) health-related issues and costs, (b) finding out that accumulated assets are insufficient and that the standard of living that one is accustomed to is now beyond reach, and (c) the accommodations that must be made to cope with the new circumstances. The role of government is crucial because of its oversight and regulatory capabilities based on legislative and administrative functions. Moreover, Samuelson (1976) argues that governments can take care of certain forms of insurance or risk manager because it is in the "business . . . to take losses" (428). Private firms do not have the means, the schemes, and/or infrastructure to provide the ability to spread the costs of risk on their own without themselves getting in trouble financially or in limiting benefits beneath those contracted and paid for by beneficiaries.

Chart 4.1 illustrates the mechanisms individuals, groups, and governments utilize to manage risks formally and informally (World Bank, 2001, 141). Notice the role of insurance schemes in the whole of the process, particularly in the area of mitigating risk. The insurance scheme under this model has as its purpose government's role in protecting individual assets by providing a form of mandated pension systems and forms of crisis insurance (accident, health, and unemployment). It is a mixed model of individual retirement accounts and public assistance infrastructure that seems to be in place on a de facto basis. Individuals and families attempt to form capital in the form of tangible (such as land) and non-tangible (money, for example) assets; however, this may not be enough.

Governments generate policy and create support programs to ensure that individuals and families do not have to completely exhaust their assets—at least in theory—as they manage to meet basic needs at a minimally defined, that is accepted, level or quality of life. Chart 4.2 helps explain the functions of government as a result of its answers to key components that make up the social safety net.

Title II of the Social Security Act of 1935 is responsible for the establishment of government-sponsored old-age pensions in the United States. It is the largest and most comprehensive income maintenance program in the United States (Dobelstein, 1996). Unlike many other income maintenance programs, it is administered directly by the federal government and not by state governments. The creation of the social security system is an example of how a new paradigm comes into being based on understanding the limits of incrementalism as change takes effect. This is important to remember because it helps explains the limitations imposed on the system that is still in use today. Another way of saying the same thing is that the system currently in place in the United States still reflects the times, needs, and biases of the 1920s and 1930s.

The rationale for the creation of the social security system was to provide a social safety net designed to protect displaced workers. The economic downturn that was the basis for unemployment was of such magnitude that the government was forced to change its traditionally held notion of a minimal federal government. The fulcrum to the argument between the old and new paradigms (pre–New Deal and post-1937 when the U.S. Supreme Court allowed Social Security to pass constitutional muster) was the Tenth Amendment to the U.S. Constitution which states that the "powers not delegated to the United States by the Constitution, nor prohibited by it to the States, are reserved to the States respectively, or to the People." The questions that were asked were placed in terms of (1) when are individual rights trumped by the interests of government and (2) how and when should the federal government intervene. In *Lochner v. New York*,[1] the U.S. Supreme Court provided the litmus test that was typical of the old paradigm's approach to government action.

It must, of course, be conceded that there is a limit to the valid exercise of the police power by the State. . . . [The] question necessarily arises: Is this a fair, reasonable and appropriate exercise of police power of the State, or is it an unreasonable, unnecessary and arbitrary interference with the right of the individual to enter into those contracts in support of himself and his family?

It is also urged that it is to the interest of the State that its population should be strong and robust, and therefore any legislation which may be said to tend to make people healthy must be valid as health laws, enacted under police power. If this be a valid argument and a justification for this kind of legislation, it follows that the protection of the Federal Constitution from undue interference with liberty of person and freedom of contract is visionary, wherever the law is sought to be justified as a valid exercise of police power. . . . We do not believe in the soundness of the views which uphold this law. . . .

It is impossible for us to shut our eyes to the fact that many of the laws of this character, while passed under what is claimed to be the police power for the purpose of protecting the public health or welfare, are, in reality, passed from other motives.

And in *Hammer v. Dagenhart*,[2] the Court clearly identified the limit on the extent of federal government intervention:

There is no power vested in Congress to require States to exercise their police powers as to prevent unfair competition. . . .

Chart 4.1
Mechanisms for Managing Risk

	Informal mechanisms		Formal mechanisms	
Objective	**Individual and household**	**Group based**	**Market based**	**Publicly provided**
Reducing risk	• Preventive health practice • Migration • More secure income sources	• Collective action for infrastructure, dikes, terraces • Common poverty resource management		• Sound macroeconomic policy • Environmental policy • Education and training policy • Public health policy • Infrastructure (dams, roads) • Active labor market policies
Mitigating risk				
Diversification	• Crop and plot diversification • Income source diversification • Investment in physical and human capital	• Occupational associations • Rotating savings and credit associations	• Savings account in financial institutions • Microfinance	• Agricultural extension • Liberalized trade • Protection of property rights
Insurance	• Marriage and extended family • Sharecropper tenancy • Buffer stocks	• Investments in social capital (networks, associations, rituals, reciprocal gift giving)	• Old age annuities • Accident, disability and other insurance	• Pension systems • Mandated insurance for unemployment, illness, disability, and other risks
Coping with shocks[a]	• Sale of assets • Loans from money-lenders • Child labor • Reduced food consumption • Seasonal or temporary migration	• Transfers from networks of mutual support	• Sale of financial assets • Loans from financial institutions	• Social assistance • Workfare • Subsidies • Social funds • Cash transfers

a: Publicly provided coping mechanisms can also serve risk-mitigating purposes if they are in place on a permanent basis.
Source: originally adapted from Holtzman, R. and Jorgensen, S. (2000). Social risk management: A new conceptual framework for social protection and beyond. Social Protection Discussion Paper 0006. Washington, D.C.: World Bank, Human Development Network.

Chart 4.2
The Functions of State and the Embedded Welfare Functions
of a Social Safety Net

Functions of the state	Embedded welfare functions within the structure of the social safety net
Sovereign maintenance	Welfare is sometimes provided by a sovereign state, provided that there is a surplus in the national wealth and its production.
Resource procurement by taxation	Taxation leads to answering the question, "Is it progressive or regressive?" The answers come from these perspectives:

- Who is taxed?
- Is taxation proportional to the ability of individuals to pay?
- What activities are taxed?
- What forms of incentives and/or disincentives are created through the taxation process and tax code structure?
- What is the threshold of tolerance, i.e., are people paying too much tax for what they earn?

Protection from:
- external causes (e.g., accident, auto, unemployment insurance)
- internal causes (e.g., life insurance, retirement plans)
- ignorance (e.g., education, training)
- ill health (e.g., health care plan)
- poverty (e.g., welfare programs)

This is a two-tiered system, with the state providing basic protection, while additional protection can be bought at the marketplace.

    Yes

    Yes
    Yes
    Yes

Securing rights
- civil rights
- social rights (right to welfare)
  - based on citizenship
  - based on reciprocity
  - based on community

    Yes

    Yes
    Yes
    Yes

Protecting liberty
- as morality
- as efficiency
- as community

Argument for: Liberty cannot be attained unless basic human needs are met.
Argument against: Liberty is surrendered to the state by having welfare.

Administering justice

A two-tiered system in which the state provides a "basic" level of justice, while "additional" justice can be purchased at the marketplace (e.g., insurance programs, personal retirement annuities, etc.).

- "police powers" to ensure well-being
- distributive (fairness as representing the interests of various groups)
- restitutive (victim/victimization assistance)
- representational (tolerance and acceptance of diversity)

    Yes
    Yes

    Yes
    Yes

Promoting equality
- of opportunity
- of outcome

Argument for: Some equality of outcome is needed for restorative justice.
Argument against: The principle of equality of opportunity is sacrificed.

Representation
- adversarial
- assimilational
- pluralistic

    No
    Conditionally
    Yes

(continued)

Chart 4.2 (*continued*)

Regulation	
• as an approach for standardization	Yes
• as protection	Yes
• as monopoly-prevention	Maybe
Redistribution	Yes, to varying extent. The basic issue here is which form of redistribution should be means-tested and which should be made available on a universalistic basis.
Attainment of full employment	Yes, at least in theory and rhetoric. Chatterjee (1999) identifies two basic issues: (1) whether the state should become the "employer of last resort" and (2) whether and how much productivity should be expected from such programs. However, three additional basic issues come into play as well: (3) whether there is an inherent right to work rather than the providing for an opportunity to work, (4) how the government defines lifetime employment, and (5) the definition used to determine full employment.
Pursuit of equality	
• affirmative action	Debated; at stake is whether or not the interests of redistributive justice override the principle of equality of opportunity.

Source: Adapted from Chatterjee, 1999, pp. 73–74.

The grant of authority over a purely federal matter was not intended to destroy the local power always existing and carefully reserved to the States in the Tenth Amendment to the Constitution. Police regulations relating to internal trade and affairs of the States have been uniformly recognized as within such control.

The plight of the Great Depression and the realization that only the federal government had the ability and means to provide the necessary overhaul in economic, legal, and social infrastructures created a gradual acceptance of the expanded role of government in protecting the rights and the lives of citizens. The understanding that—no matter how bad things were—change was only going to be accepted to a certain point, shaped the process of change. As Leuchtenburg (1963) observed, "Even the most precedent-breaking New Deal projects reflected capitalist thinking and deferred to business sensibilities. Social security was modeled, often irrelevantly, on private insurance systems; relief directors were forbidden to approve projects which interfered with private profit-taking" (165). More to the point, *self-reliance* and *individual choice* were two points that could not and were not challenged.

The gradual—albeit reluctant—acceptance of this new role in government was reflected in how the U.S. Supreme Court disallowed constitutional challenges to the new programs that heretofore it had objected to. The beginning of the new paradigm was reflected in *Nebbia v. New York*,[3] when the Court admitted that government action is warranted as long as it follows due process and is found to be within the parameters of the phrase "affected with public interest," allowing that government can act to create certain controls for the public good. Still, it was not until 1937 that the Court finally relinquished its attempt to curb national programs (it has since deemed critical a number of significant work programs, such

as the National Industrial Recovery Administration and the Agricultural Adjustment Act). The definitive change came in the case *West Coast Hotel v. Parrish*.[4] What the West Coast Hotel case did was reverse the decision rendered in *Adkins v. Children's Hospital*,[5] which stated that "freedom of contract . . . is the general rule and restraint the exception; and the exercise of legislative authority to abridge it can be justified only by the existence of exceptional circumstances. . . ." The new ethos accepted by the Court was that

There is an additional and compelling consideration which recent economic experience has brought into strong light. The exploitation of a class of workers who are in an unequal position with respect to bargaining power and are thus relatively defenseless against the denial of a living wage is not only detrimental to their health and well being but casts a direct burden for their support upon the community.

The principal foci of the New Deal programs were to get individuals back to work and to assure them that they could still make enough money so that they could make ends meet. The federal government did this by restructuring regulatory activities for banks and investments systems, oversight regulations of key businesses and industries, and labor regulations. Three population groups were considered to be particularly vulnerable, the elderly, the disabled, and children. The concerns about the latter were threefold: child labor abuses, access to education, and child welfare.

The Social Security Act created a social safety net for children, the elderly, and the disabled. Children's issues were addressed in Title IV of the Social Security Act that created the Aid to Families with Dependent Children (AFDC) programs. Child labor abuses had been a concern from the inception of the twentieth century, and by the 1930s there had been a series of attempts at regulating child labor. To quote Dobelstein, "[the] child welfare programs created by the Social Security Act . . . established a uniform framework for administration, to which a specified number of existing state programs were required to conform" (1996, 213).[6] Title II of the Social Security Act took care of the elderly and the disabled, while Title III focused on providing unemployment insurance to displaced workers.

The original focus of Title II of the Social Security Act was to provide old-age insurance (Old-age and Survivor Insurance, or OASI) so that retired workers could have sufficient income to make ends meet, and to provide old-age assistance and aid to the blind. The rationale for the old-age component was that the Great Depression had taken away the savings and other assets of many whose employment opportunities were drastically diminished as a result of their age. It was expanded in 1939 to make old-age insurance a family program by adding "benefits for dependents of retired workers and surviving dependents of deceased workers" (United States House of Representatives, Committee on Ways and Means, 2000, 2/75). Then, in 1953, a formal disability insurance (DI) component was added to the program, expanding eligibility to those with disabilities other than blindness. OASI and DI were then formally combined "to show that their purpose is to replace income lost to a family through the retirement, death, or disability of a worker who has earned protection against those risks" (3/75).

The federal government, through the Social Security Administration (SSA), administers social security programs. It is one of the largest and most complex of the programs in the U.S. federal government. It administers the programs authorized under Titles II (Old-Age, Survivors and Disability Insurance, or OASDI) and XVI (Supplementary Security Income, or SSI; see chapter 8). Created in 1946, this agency was made part of what became the U.S. Department of Health and Human Services, but in 1995 it once again became an independent agency whose responsibility is to ensure the day-to-day delivery of services and customer service; the administration of current programs, and the shaping of programs in the future; program solvency and the stewardship of the Social Security trust funds; and public education—awareness, understanding, and confidence. Its mission, through which it defines how it should be looked at and evaluated, is "[to] promote the economic security of the nation's people through compassionate and vigilant leadership in shaping and managing America's social security system" (Social Security Administration, 2000, chapter 1). As an agency, it is guided by five strategic goals it wants to attain that exemplify its previously mentioned responsibilities:

1. To promote valued, strong, and responsive Social Security programs and conduct effective policy development, research, and program evaluation.

2. To deliver customer-responsive, world-class service.

3. To make SSA program management the best in business, with zero tolerance for fraud and abuse.

4. To be an employer that values and invests in each employee.

5. To strengthen public understanding of the Social Security programs.

The way Social Security works, almost all employed persons participate in the retirement program through mandatory contributions by means of payroll taxes that are matched by employers.[7] Still, 6.8 million workers did not have any social security coverage as of 1999.[8] The idea behind it is that Social Security benefits provide an additional source of income to ensure that the elderly and disabled can maintain at least a minimal standard of living. In 2000, the composite breakdown for the sources of income for beneficiaries was 38 percent from Social Security, 23 percent from earnings, 18 percent from pensions,[9] 18 percent from personal asset income (investments), 3 percent from other sources (19).

At the time of this writing, an employed individual contributes 6.2 percent of gross earnings up to a maximum earning level of $80,400 (under the Federal Insurance Contribution Act, or FICA) while the employer pays an additional 6.2 percent. Self-employed individuals pay 12.4 percent of their gross earnings (under the Self-Employed Contribution Act, or SECA). To compensate for the higher rate, self-employed individuals receive a special tax deduction. An employee who exceeds the maximum taxable amount because he or she worked for more than one employer can receive refunds of the excess FICA payments when filing the annual income tax return. Once a retiree begins to receive benefits (whether receiving full benefits because of being 65 or older, or partial benefits for those opting to participate between ages 62 and 64), up to 85 percent of social security benefits may be taxed depending on overall income, marital status, and filing status. The formula utilized to determine the possibility for taxation is the following:[10]

Adjusted gross income before benefits are considered	+	Tax exempt interest income, with further gross income modifications based on some tax provisions of limited applicability among the beneficiary population	+	½ of Social Security and Tier 1 Railroad retirement benefits

Taxes are allocated to a trust fund. The social security trust funds have additional sources of revenue that add to the total assets (and makes them a tempting target of federal officials to pay off excess debt resulting from other areas of government duties and responsibilities): interest accrued on trust fund securities, certain technical transfers, and gifts or bequests (Social Security Administration, 2001). As elaborated on in *The 2000 Green Book*, FICA and SECA taxes go into thousands of depository accounts maintained by the [federal] government with financial institutions across the country. Along with the many other forms of revenues, these Social Security taxes become part of the government's operating cash pool, or what is more commonly referred to as the U.S. Treasury. In effect, once those taxes are received, they become undistinguishable from other moneys the government takes in. They are accounted for separately through the issuance of Federal securities to the Social Security Trust Funds . . . but the trust funds themselves do not hold the money. . . . When more Social Security taxes are received than spent, the money . . . is used to finance other operations of the government. (United States House of Representatives, Committee on Ways and Means, 2000, 5/75)

When the trust funds receive securities from the federal government, they earn interest at the prevailing market rate; however, these are not marketable. These are an obligation because these are seen as granting the trust funds permission to spend—to pay off the beneficiaries as per their calculated benefits. By law, the social security trust funds may only disburse funds for the following reasons:

1. monthly benefits for workers and their families,

2. vocational rehabilitation services for disabled beneficiaries,

3. administrative costs (that are currently less than one percent of expenditures), and

4. lump-sum death payment to eligible survivors.

Given the fact that surpluses in social security taxes can and are usually used for defraying the costs of other areas of government, the questions of financial soundness and solvency have been in the forefront of congressional and presidential scrutiny and the public's concern, especially from the 1980s onward when the first major review occurred under the Reagan administration.[11] The concerns are still there today. The use of the taxes is only one concern. Other concerns are the increasing number of individuals reaching retirement age, a change in the balance between a working and retired workforce (which pays the taxes to continue the scheme), birthrates and increased lifespans, inflation and its impact on poverty levels, eligibility rules, and levels of benefit.

For the short-term, the government assesses the trust funds balances in absolute terms—as a percentage of annual expenditure, whether it is increasing or decreasing. Financial adequacy is equated with the ability to maintain the reserve balance at the end of the first ten-year segment while meeting at least 100 percent of annual expenditures during this time period. This approach is consistent with the **actuarial balance** measure used for long range analysis.

For the long-term, the traditional measure of actuarial balance is defined as the difference between the total summarized income rate—the ratio of the present value of tax income to the present value of taxable payroll over a seventy-five-year period—and the total summarized cost rate—the ratio of the present value of expenditures to the present value of taxable payroll over a seventy-five-year period (United States House of Representatives, Committee on Ways and Means, 2000).[12]

The long-range measure is commonly expressed as a percent of taxable payroll instead of dollar amounts in order to allow for a direct comparison between the tax rate as defined in law and program costs.

An individual can claim **full benefits** when retiring at age 65 (although that is being gradually rolled back to 67 between 2002 and 2027). An individual can, however, pursue the option of claiming for **reduced benefits** between the ages of 62 and 64. To qualify for **fully insured status** after 1991, individuals have to participate in and receive credit for a minimum of forty (40) quarters, or ten (10) years by the time they reach age 62. Prior to 1978, credit for a quarter was given if a worker was paid $50 or more in wages for covered employment, or received $100 in self-employed income; from 1978 onward, crediting is annualized, with one credit (and one can only get up to only 4 credits) equaling $250 of annual earnings reported from covered employment or self-employment.

Benefits received are tied to an annual cost of living adjustment (COLA) tied to the consumer price index for urban wage earners and clerical workers (CPI-W); up to 85 percent may be subject to federal income tax due to the beneficiary's income, marital, and filing status. Beneficiaries under age 65 with earnings over certain exempt amounts may have all or part of their benefits withheld based on an annual earnings test (AET) and established exempt amounts (in set amounts until 2002, thereafter indexed to the growth in average wages), while after the year 2000, beneficiaries over age 65 are no longer bound to the AET. For those under 65, this means a potential withholding rate of $1 for every $2 of earnings above the exempt amount.

Monthly benefits for workers reaching full retirement age or entitled to disability benefits are referred to as the **primary insurance amount (PIA)**.[13] It is also the base figure from which monthly benefits payable to an employee's family members or survivors. The PIA is derived from the worker's annual taxable earnings, averaged over a period encompassing most of that person's adult years. The current measure, used since 1978, is the **average index monthly earnings (AIME)**. The PIA computation is a three-step process:

1. *Indexing of earnings*: annual taxable earnings are updated to reflect the general earnings level in the indexing year (which is the second calendar year before the year in which the worker is first eligible—62), or when death or disability occurs. Earnings in years after indexing are only counted at their actual value.

   a. Indexing for a given year is done by multiplying earnings by an indexing factor.

   b. The index factor is the ratio of the average wage in the national economy for that year that is divided by the corresponding average wage figure for the year to be indexed.

2. *Determining AIME*: the calculation period equals the number of full calendar years elapsing between ages 21 (or 1950, if later) and the first year of eligibility, usually excluding the lowest 5 years. For workers disabled prior to

age 47 have between 0 and 4 excluded years from the computation, with an absolute minimum of 2 years used to compute AIME.

    a. AIME is calculated as the sum of indexed earnings in the computation period that is then divided by the number of months in that period.

3. Computing the PIA: For workers who reach age 62, become disabled, or die in 2001, the PIA equals the sum of:

90% of first $561 of AIME + 32% of next $2,820 of AIME + 15% of AIME over $3,381

    a. The formula used to compute the PIA from AIME is weighted to provide a higher PIA-to-AIME ratio for workers with comparatively low earnings.

    b. The formula applies declining percentages to the AIME brackets.

    c. The dollar amounts defining the AIME brackets are referred to as "bend points." These are updated automatically every year in proportion to increases in the national average wage level.

For a worker to be considered to have full disability benefits depends on the number of quarters of coverage (QC) credited at the time of disability or death, if the worker become disabled or dies before age 62. In the instance a worker dies prior to achieving fully insured status, benefits can still be paid to qualified survivors if the worker was **currently insured** at the time of death, that is, the worker had earned six quarters of coverage in the last thirteen quarters prior to and including the quarter in which death occurred.

To qualify for disability benefits, non-blind workers have to demonstrate recent work activity along with proof that they are fully insured. According to the Social Security Administration (2001),

> Under the test involving recent work experience, a nonblind worker older than 31 must have earned at least 20 QCs among the 40 calendar quarters ending with the quarter in which the disability began. Workers disabled at ages 24 through 30 must have earned QCs in one-half of the calendar quarters elapsing between age 21 and the calendar quarter in which disability began. Workers under age 24 need 6 QCs in the 12-quarter period ending with the quarter of disability onset. Workers who qualify for benefits based on blindness need only be fully insured. (12)

Congress passed the *Ticket to Work and Work Incentive Improvement Act* in 1999 to provide further enhancements to encourage the efforts of the disabled to return to work. The law provided beneficiaries choices in rehabilitation services, and offered expanded healthcare for beneficiaries no longer eligible for cash benefits as a result from returning to work; it even offered extended Medicare coverage for those going back to work, as well as an offers a buy-in for Medicaid coverage (Social Security Administration, 2001). Meanwhile, the Social Security Administration raised the limit for benefit eligibility for those non-blind individuals to be considered as

engaging in substantial gainful activity (SGA) from $500 per month to $700 per month. Earning less than $300 per month demonstrated that beneficiaries were not engaged in SGA, and making a monthly income between $330 and $700 (raised to $740 in 2001) meant that "consideration be given to circumstances related to the work activity" (11) to consider the appropriateness of continued benefits. From 1999 to the present time, eligibility threshold increases have been done via indexing on an annualized basis.

Blind persons receiving Social Security disability benefits get a different definition in the consideration of SGA. Increases in the SGA amount for the blind are tied to increases in the national average wage index and hence, not affected by the rule changes of 1999. To compare, the 2001 SGA limit was $1,240 per month (it was $1,170 per month in 2000).

Widows or widowers of fully insured employees are eligible for unreduced benefits at full retirement age under the same criteria of the employees if they live to claim their benefits. Survivors can also opt to receive reduced benefits at age 60; if disabled, as early as age 50. Survivors need not be married to the deceased at the time of death. Divorced spouses who were married to the deceased for at least ten years and have not remarried before age 60 (or 50 if disabled) can also receive benefits. Benefits are increased if the deceased worker delayed retirement beyond his or her full retirement age. Conversely, if the worker elected early retirement, survivor benefits are limited to the benefits received at age 62; for these individuals, the benefit is the higher of 82.5 percent of the worker's PIA or the amount the worker would have received if he or she was still alive. Disabled widows and widowers between ages 50 and 60 receive the age 60 widow's rate of 71.5 percent regardless of age at the time of eligibility.

Children of deceased workers, as well as the mothers and fathers under full retirement age, are eligible to receive up to 75 percent of the worker's PIA if the worker died while their status qualified as currently insured or fully insured. Children entitled to the worker's benefits are those 16 or under, or those disabled.

There are two categories for the parents of a deceased worker. The first category is the parents that are caring for the qualifying child. The second category is for parents that are dependents of the deceased. A dependent parent aged 62 or older is eligible for monthly benefits that are equal to 82.5 percent of the worker's PIA. If both parents are alive and dependent on the deceased, they can together qualify for up to 75 percent of the worker's PIA. However, "monthly benefits are reduced to conform to the **family maximum benefit**[14] payable on the deceased worker's account" (Social Security Administration, 2001, 16). In this last regard, benefits for a divorced spouse do not enter the equation for the family maximum benefit.

Spouses of eligible employees who are still alive get 50 percent of the worker's PIA if the spouse attained full retirement age when becoming entitled to spousal benefits, regardless of the worker's actual benefit amount. Again, the spouse can elect to receive reduced monthly benefits at age 62, reduced at the rate of $\frac{25}{36}$ of 1 percent a month for the first 36 months immediately preceding the attainment of full retirement age and $\frac{5}{12}$ of 1 percent for each additional month. Spouses that are under age 62 can receive benefits if they care for a worker's entitled child (under 16), up to 50 percent of the worker's PIA.

Children of retired or disabled workers that qualify and are still alive who are under 18 or attending elementary or secondary school on a full-time basis, or adult children under 22 who are themselves disabled, are also eligible to receive benefits. They can receive up to 50 percent of the worker's PIA. As with spouses taking care of a worker's child that is under 16, the monthly benefits children can receive are limited to a family maximum amount.

Social security is also one of the important weapons used in the fight against poverty in the United States. It has had success in terms of an overall reduction in poverty for senior citizens. The Center on Budget and Policy Priorities (1998) Web site points out that "[by] 1996, according to an analysis of U.S. Census data, Social Security reduced the proportion of elderly living in poverty from approximately 50 percent to about 12 percent." By the end of the year 2000, the amount of individuals meeting the poverty criteria while receiving social security benefits was 9 percent, as compared to 48 percent if they did not receive social security benefits—a slight reduction from the 1997 numbers for the elderly who with benefits were not defined poor (11.9 percent)—and 49.1 percent of those who remained poor because they lacked social security or other forms of social insurance benefits (Social Security Administration, 2001; Porter, Larin, and Primus, 1999). Overall, according to a study conducted by Porter, Larin, and Primus at the Center on Budget and Policy Priorities, Social Security has a much larger impact in lifting the elderly out of poverty than all other programs combined because nine of every ten elderly people are lifted from poverty by government benefit programs (including state and local cash assistance programs). To illustrate this point, the study relates how the poverty gap (the amount by which the total income of the poor falls blow the poverty line) went from $70 billion to $10 billion as a result of receiving Social Security benefits.

For the calendar year 2000, overall OASDI payments totaled $407.6 billion (about 4 percent of the national GDP) to 45.4 million individuals (Porter, Larin, and Primus, 1999, xii). Chart 4.3 describes the percent breakdown of beneficiaries and benefits awarded for calendar year 2000 (Social Security Administration, 2001, 20). Trends that were noted and of concern in respect to the fight on poverty vis-à-vis sufficiency of benefits to meet needs and program solvency are implicit in the following data:

- Seventy-one percent of the 28.5 million retired-worker beneficiaries received reduced benefits because of retirement prior to age 65. Relatively more women (75 percent) than men (68 percent) received reduced benefits.

- The number of persons aged 65 or older receiving Social Security benefits rose from 31.4 million in 1995 to 32.7 million

in 2000 (4.0 percent). Beneficiaries aged 85 or older increased at a greater rate during the five-year period (12.8 percent) from 3,576,000 in 1995 to 4,034,000 in 2000. In 2000, 39,500 centenarians were receiving Social Security.

- More than 19 million women aged 65 or older were receiving benefits in December 2000. Seven million (36.4 percent) were entitled solely to a retired-worker benefit, and another 5.5 million (28.9 percent) were dually entitled to a retired-worker benefit and a wife's or widow's benefit. About 6.6 million (34.7 percent) were receiving wife's or widow's benefits only (Social Security Administration, 2001, 2).

One of the significant concerns about social security and poverty is its impact with women. Porter, Larin, and Primus' (1999) study in this area found out that without Social Security benefits, 52.6 percent of elderly women would have been below the poverty line in 1997; however, receiving Social Security benefits meant that only 14.7 percent of elderly women were considered to be below the poverty line. They also found out that states reflected the national norm in this regard.

Women are a special concern not only because of their longer lifespan (and thus outnumber men receiving benefits), but because of (1) legal and benefits issues surrounding marriage status,[15] (2) their earning power is less than men as a result of socialization conditions and type of work historically available, (3) the impact on wage earning by women based on the decision made by many women to stay at home and forgo earnings as an employee for an entire work-life or a significant portion of it, and (4) the impact of divorce on women's asset accumulation over a lifetime. Unfortunately, elderly women are more likely to fall into poverty as they get older; almost 13 percent of women between 65 and 75 remained poor even with social security in 1997; the number remaining in poverty increased to 16.6 percent for those between 75 and 85, and 20.6 percent of women over 85 remained in poverty even after receiving benefits. Moreover,

In 1997, nearly two-thirds of elderly women received a majority of their income from Social Security. For almost one-third of elderly women, Social Security provided at least 90 percent of income. It was the sole source of income for nearly one in five elderly women. For elderly women overall, Social Security benefits provided more than three-fifths of total income. (p. xiii)

Social security also seems to make a difference in fighting poverty within ethnic minority groups, another policy goal that especially emanated from program changes enacted at the federal level in the 1960s. Poverty is a significant issue with these population groups because of the effects of discrimination on access and quality of education, the ability to get work, the quality of work that could be found, and the lower wages that came with most of these jobs. A study commissioned by the International Longevity Center reveals wide disparities between non-Hispanic white households and those of non-Hispanic blacks and Hispanics, signifying the potential for

Chart 4.3
Percent of Beneficiaries and Benefit Award by Type of Benefit for Calendar Year 2000

Category	Beneficiaries by type of benefit	Benefits awarded by type of benefit
Retired-workers	63%	48%
Disabled workers	11%	14%
Wives and husbands	7%	9%
Children	8%	18%
Widows/Widowers and parents	11%	13%

Source: Adapted from Social Security Administration, 2001, p. 20.

significantly lower post-retirement consumption expectations and realities (Honig, 1999). As Porter, Larin, and Primus (1999) document, benefits reduced the number of black elderly poor from 1.6 million to 800,000 and the number of Hispanic elderly poor from 900,000 to 500,000. Even so, a concern is apparently resulting from the fact that

> Much of the difference among racial and ethnic groups in the anti-poverty effects of Social Security is due to differences in wages. Social Security benefit levels are tied to beneficiaries' wages during their working years. Many of those who are old today worked for years before the passage of civil rights laws, when wage differentials between whites and minorities were even larger than they are today. During these periods, black and Hispanic workers often were limited to low-paying occupations. The smaller impact of Social Security on poverty among the Hispanic elderly also reflects the fact that many Hispanic people who are elderly today emigrated to the United States too late in life to amass a sufficient number of years of employment to qualify for substantial Social Security benefits.
>
> For elderly people of all races, Social Security provides a larger share of income than does any other income source. Some 43 percent of the total income of the black elderly, 41 percent of the total income of the Hispanic elderly, and 36 percent of the total income of the white elderly comes from Social Security. The black and Hispanic elderly populations rely on Social Security for somewhat larger shares of their income than the white elderly do because they tend to have less income from other sources. (xvi)

The Center on Budget and Policy Priority's report (1999) also makes the conclusion that 3.7 million adults between the ages of 18 to 64 (mainly disabled) and about 1.0 million children were taken out of poverty (as defined by the poverty line) because of Social Security. The study indicates that the poverty gap was reduced for non-elderly adults by $26.4 billion, closing the gap by 29.2 percent through a combination of Social Security and other social insurance programs. The reduction in the gap is lower for children (a reduction of 15.5 percent, or $6.5 billion), but as Porter, Larin, and Primus (1999) point out, Social Security benefits constitute an important part

of the safety net for children because these lift one million children from poverty about 6 percent of all children who were poor in 1997 before receipt of government benefits—or around one-fifth of children removed from poverty through government assistance programs. In comparison, means-tested cash assistance programs assisted 4.8 percent of children out of poverty who were poor before government benefits; food and housing benefits raised 9.8 percent of these children out of poverty; federal income and payroll taxes, including the earned income tax credit, lifted 8.8 percent of these children from poverty.

However, one area where the policy goal for Social Security does not seem to be met is in the inability for the majority of seniors to have diversified income during their retirement years. Porter, Larin, and Primus find that Social Security is the principal source—about 80 percent—of income earned or received for the poorest fifth of the elderly population in the United States **and** the second poorest fifth in the demographic group. Social Security provides 62 percent of income for those elderly falling in the middle fifth, 41.5 percent for the next-to-highest income fifth, and then it falls to 17 percent for those in the highest income fifth.

Furthermore, Steuerle and Carasso (2001) see three other significant roadblocks in reducing poverty. First, there is a significant demographic increase in divorced and never-married individuals, creating a situation where a larger share of individuals will not be able to qualify for spousal or survivors benefits. This means that funds that are transferred from the general treasury instead of financed through additional contributions through payroll taxes will not be there for individuals who could have need of such funds. Second, the percentage of benefits paid to older retirees is steadily falling relative to benefits paid to younger retirees due to a combination of longer lifespans, earlier retirement, and current laws that schedule higher real levels of benefits resulting from the calculations described earlier in this chapter. As Steuerle and Carasso see it, the impact is that greater benefits are given to those who need it the least, because those who are the oldest may need to rely on social security benefits the most as other assets and income dissipate. Third, the actuarial differences mean that the program has shifted from an old-age program to a middle-age program, due to a reduction in the number of individuals remaining in work and who expect to live at least 16 years beyond retirement—from 80 percent to 35 percent.

A comparison of the United States' Social Security system to other countries can be an exercise in comparing apples and oranges unless there is awareness that social safety nets are inherently influenced by national experience and historical developments. As already stated earlier in this chapter (and in much greater detail elsewhere in this book), differing philosophical underpinnings of society, societal role, and the place government plays in the nation and in individual life have a definite part in the creation, maintenance, and administration of social safety nets. Comparative analyses in this area will not have a simple one-to-one correspondence as a result. These will have to be done by looking at key words and concepts such as old-age pensions (private and public) and retirement programs, old-age insurance schemes, and aging issues. For example, in certain countries, public pension plans similar to Social Security's—a pay as you go scheme that is administered by the government—have been replaced with private pension plans or have a partial pre-funding of public pension liabilities (Yermo, 2002). In other instances, social security plans for government employees have been changed into private pension plans altogether. A second example is how pension funds such as Social Security are administered. The United States, as already described, administers Social Security assets through an autonomous series of trust funds, in other words, through an independent legal entity dedicated exclusively to providing retirement and related benefits. All but four countries belonging to the OECD have this arrangement; only France, Greece, the Slovak Republic, and Turkey do not have autonomous pensions because their laws do not recognize such entities (Yermo and Marossy, 2001).

The OECD is made up of thirty member countries that share a commitment to democratic government and the market economy. Its purpose is to assist governments to ensure the responsiveness of key economic areas through monitoring different geographical areas and to provide help in generating strategic policies by deciphering emerging issues and identifying policies that work. One of its overarching goals is sustainable development, defined in terms of economic growth, social development, and environmental protection. As an organization, it is best known for the statistics and publication it produces. The OECD collects data, performs research, and provides recommendations in about thirty-three areas, ranging from the aging society to trade and transportation. In the area of aging societies, its interests center on the fiscal implications and consequences that older populations have on national resources and individual quality of life. Specific topics of exploration are the economic effects of aging, the characteristics of older workers, pension systems, and the social effects of aging. Historically, the Organization has been at the forefront with these issues at the worldwide level as a result of its work; however, it feels that it needs to take on a more active leadership role in putting into practice what it has been advocating. A concern that some specialists and interested observers have is that the OECD and the countries it represents articulate one specific approach to government, economic development, policy development, and government enaction of programs and citizens. More to the point is that most of these countries are developed countries. Its measuring sticks and approaches reflect the point-of-view of a more highly structured and "rational" approach to issues, an approach that may be difficult to find or implement in developing countries facing the challenges of generating and affording a more crystallized government system that is more responsive in its approach and support of individual rights and national well-being.

For those interested in international comparisons, Table 4.1 provides data of old-age programs found in Europe, two countries from the former Eastern Soviet satellite block (the Czech Republic and Poland), and two countries with a reputation for very advanced forms of socialist regimes in the area of public welfare (Norway and Sweden), along with Germany and the Netherlands. This table also gives information from Australia and three countries in Far East Asia (Japan, South Korea, and Thailand), one of which is not an OECD member nation (Thailand). Some of the data in the table was generated from OECD data; however, the source for a direct comparison came from the Social Security Administration's publication *Social Security Programs Throughout the World 1999* (which is the most complete recent edition available at the time of writing), and it is the latter source that is recommended for a comparative analysis of analogous schemes.

Of interest is the role that private contribution (insurance) schemes play in providing benefits. Most of these countries use them as means of providing added benefits to retirees and qualifying survivors. In at least one instance (Poland), these private schemes seem to provide the basic funds for old-age individuals. Expanding on what was said earlier in this book, privatization is an area of interest because of the potential for increased return on investment and, more importantly, as a means of reducing the burden of cost on governments and taxpayers. Private pension schemes at least seem to provide an additional avenue for income for the elderly and the disabled, improving their quality of life through enhanced affording of choices without overtaxing national resources.

For examining the authorizing legislation and supporting regulations, two excellent sources of information about old-age, survivor, and disability social security system in the United States are the U.S. House of Representatives' Committee on Ways and Means' *Green Book Report 2000* and the *Annual Statistical Supplement to the Social Security Bulletin*. Those individuals requiring current data are encouraged to search through the Social Security Administration Web sites, their regional centers, and state offices. For current or more timely state information, those needing the information should contact (by phone, letter, or by going to their Web site) the desired state's Department of Economic Security or its equivalent.

NOTES

1. 198 U.S. 45, 25 S. Ct. 539, L. Ed. 937 (1905).
2. 247 U.S. 251, 38 S. Ct. 529, L. Ed. 1101 (1918).
3. 291 U.S. 502, 54 S. Ct. 505, 78 L. Ed. 940 (1934).
4. 300 U.S. 379, 57 S. Ct. 578, 81 L. Ed. 703 (1937).
5. 261 U.S. 525, 43 S. Ct. 394, 67 L. Ed. 785 (1918).
6. Please refer to chapter 10 of this text.
7. In 2001, a domestic employee must earn $1,300 from any single employer in a calendar year before FICA is withheld. Most agricultural workers wages are covered if the employer pays more than $2,500 in total wages in a year, or if the individual worker earns over $150 in a year from a single employer. (Social Security Administration, 2001, 11)
8. Those who are excluded from participation are individuals covered under the Railroad Retirement Board; in casual agricultural and domestic employment; limited self-employment with net income below $400; civilian federal employees hired pre-January 1, 1984; and state and local government employees who are not covered under a retirement system. Furthermore, coverage is voluntary for certain state and local government employees (only about 71 percent, or 16.1 million out of 22.6 million) and members of the clergy (Social Security Administration, 2001, 3/75).
9. These include private pensions and annuities, government employee pensions, Railroad Retirement, and individual retirement accounts, Keogh plans, and 401(k) payments to account holders.
10. In 2001, the tax threshold level for a married couple filing jointly was $32,000 per year; any less and no tax was due. For those making between $32,000 and $44,000, the amount of benefits included in the gross income calculation when filing personal income taxes was the lesser of one-half of the income over $32,000. For those making over $44,000, gross income had to be adjusted by adding 85 percent of income over $44,000 plus the lesser of $6,000 or one-half the benefits. The threshold levels for single individuals were $25,000 and $32,000.
11. Prior to 1971, the balances in the trust funds had never fallen below one year's payout of benefits. After 1973, the income began to lag behind payouts, making the amount of funds decline rapidly. Congress had to step in five times in the 1970s and 1980s to keep the social security trust funds from becoming exhausted (U.S. House of Representatives, Committee on Ways and Means, 2000). 1983 was the year when there was a major reform of the program, and a report in 2000 indicated that at the current rate the trust funds would be exhausted in 2037 unless there was another significant reform in the offing.
12. *The Green Book 2000* (United States House of Representatives, Committee on Ways and Means, 2000, 9/75) provides an example of how the formula works for the long range: In case that a 2 percent deficit in taxable income is projected, the current OASDI tax rates in the law would have to be increased by 1 percent for each employee and employer (or a total of 2 percent) to pay for benefits due.

Deficit of 2% of taxable payroll/Projected expenditures of 10% of taxable payrolll=20% of expenditures not covered

In 2000 terms, total taxable payroll was estimated at $3,969 billion; therefore, 2 percent of payroll means about $79 billion. The alternative to raising rates is to reduce benefits, or a combination of both.
13. Workers with low earnings but who have a steady "track record" of employment over most of their adult years may qualify for monthly benefits based on the special minimum PIA computation. The level for the special minimum PIA is the same for workers having the same number of coverage years, regardless of age or year of first eligibility. Persons who receive a pension based on noncovered work after 1956 and social security benefits—such as U.S. Civil Service Retirement System annuities, retirement benefits based on foreign earnings, state and local pensions based on noncovered earnings—are affected by the Windfall Elimination Provision (WEP) that reduces the social security PIA upon which social security benefits are based, affecting all paid on that record except survivors. The WEP reduction amount is never more than one-half of the noncovered pension, and it is generally based on 40 percent of the first bend point instead of 90 percent as with the regular PIA (Social Security Administration, 2001, 14–15).
14. Depending on the year of first eligibility, the benefit level for retired-worker families or survivor families typically ranges from 150 percent to 188 percent of the worker's PIA. The level for disabled-worker families is the smaller of 85 percent of AIME (if larger, 100 percent of the PIA is used instead) or 150 percent of the PIA.
15. Close to three-quarters of elderly women rely on Social Security for a majority of their income. Between 1995 and 1997, Social Security made up 67.6 percent of the total income for elderly widows (Porter, Laris, and Primus, 1999, 29).

PRINCIPAL SOURCES FOR ILLUSTRATIONS

Organization of Economic Co-operation and Development. (2003). *Tables and figures on ageing.* OECD Web site. Retrieved from: http://www.oecd.org/dataoecd/27/44/ 2345400.pdf.

Smeeding, T.M. (2001). *Income maintenance in old age: What can be learned from cross-national comparisons.* Working Paper for the Center for Retirement Research, No. 2001-11. Retrieved from: http://www.bc.edu/centers/crr/papers/wp_2001-11.pdf.

Social Security Administration. (2001). *Annual statistical supplement, 2001 to the Social Security Bulletin.* Baltimore: Social Security Administration, Office of Policy. Retrieved from: http://www.ssa.gov/statistics/Supplement/2001/supp01.pdf.

Social Security Administration. (2002). *Social security programs throughout the world: Europe 2002.* Washington, D.C.: Author. Retrieved from: http://www.ssa.gov/policy/docs/progdesc/ssptw/2002/europe/index.html.

United States Census Bureau. (2002). *Statistical abstract of the United States 2002.* Washington, D.C.: Government Printing Office. Retrieved from: http://www.census.gov/statab/www/.

United States House of Representatives, Committee on Ways and Means. (2000). *The 2000 green book: Background material and data on programs within the jurisdiction of the Committee on Ways and Means.* Retrieved from: http://aspe.hhs.gov/2000gh.

BIBLIOGRAPHY

Boorstin, D.J. (1974). *The Americans: The democratic experience.* New York: Vintage Books.

Center on Budget and Policy Priorities. (1998). News release: Government benefit programs cut poverty nearly in half, analysis finds. In *Strengths of the safety net.* Retrieved from: http://www.cbpp.org/snd98.htm.

Chambers, D.E. (1986). *Social policy and social programs: A method for the practical public policy analyst.* New York: Macmillan Press.

Chatterjee, P. (1999). *Repackaging the welfare state.* Washington, D.C.: National Association of Social Workers.

de Jouvenel, B. (1951/1990). *The ethics of redistribution.* Indianapolis: Liberty Fund.

Dobelstein, A.W. (1996). *Social welfare: Policy and analysis.* 2nd ed. Chicago: Nelson-Hall Publishers.

Dworkin, R. (1977). *Taking rights seriously.* Cambridge, MA: Harvard University Press.

Dworkin, R. (1986). *Law's empire.* Cambridge, MA: Belknap Press.

Goodin, R.E., Headey, B., Muffels, R., and Dirven, H.J. (1999*). The real worlds of welfare capitalism.* Cambridge: Cambridge University Press.

Honig, M. (1999). *Minorities face retirement: Worklife disparities repeated?* New York: International Longevity Center—USA. Retrieved from: http://www.ilcusa.org/_lib/pdf/publications minoritiesface.pdf.

Leuchtenburg, W.E. (1963). *Franklin D. Roosevelt and the New Deal, 1932–1940.* New York: Harper Torchbooks.

Porter, K.H., Larin, K., and Primus, W. (1999). *Social security and poverty among the elderly: A national and state perspective.* Washington, D.C.: Center on Budget and Policy Priorities. Retrived from: http://www.cbpp.org/4-8-99socsec.pdf.

Rawls, J. (1971). *A theory of justice.* Cambridge, MA: Harvard University Press.

Samuelson, P.A. (1976). *Economics.* 10th ed. New York: McGraw-Hill Book Company.

Social Security Administration. (1999). *Social security programs throughout the world.* Baltimore: Social Security Administration. Retrieved from: http://www.ssa.gov/st . . . cs/ssptw/1999/ English.

Social Security Administration. (2000). *Administrative history of SSA 1993–2000.* Baltimore: Social Security Online. Retrieved from: http://www.ssa.gov/history/ssa/ssa.2000 chapter1.html.

Social Security Administration. (2001). *Annual statistical supplement, 2001 to the Social Security Bulletin.* Baltimore: Social Security Administration, Office of Policy. Retrieved from: http://www.ssa.gov/statistics/Supplement/2001/supp01.pdf.

Steuerle, E., and Carasso, A. (October 30, 2001). Social Security: Additional dollars could buy less poverty. *Straight talk on social security and retirement policy: The retirement project, number 33.* Washington, D.C.: The Urban Institute. Retrieved from: http://www.urban.org/UploadedPDF/Straight33.pdf.

United Nations Development Programme. (2002). *Human development report 2002.* New York: Oxford University Press.

United States Census Bureau. (2002). Definitions and explanations. *Current population survey.* Washington, D.C.: U.S. Printing Office. Retrieved from: http://www.census.gov/population/ www/cps/cpsdef.html.

United States House of Representatives, Committee on Ways and Means. (2000). *The 2000 Green book: Background material and data on programs within the jurisdiction of the Committee on Ways and Means.* Retrieved from: http://aspe.hhs.gov/ 2000gh.

World Bank. (2001). *World development report 2000/2001: Attacking poverty.* Oxford: Oxford University Press.

Yermo, J. (October 2002). *Revised taxonomy for pension plans, pension funds, and pension entities.* Washington, D.C.: OECD. Retrieved from: http://www.oecd.org/pdf/M00038096.pdf.

Yermo, J., and Marossy, A. (2001). Pension fund governance. In OECD, *Insurance and private pensions compendium for emerging economies*, Book 2, Part 1:(4)b. Washington, D.C.: OECD. Retrived from: http://www.oecd.org/pdf/ M00024968.pdf.

Table 4.1
Old-Age and Disability Pension Schemes in Eleven Countries

Country	Type of Program	Administrative Organization	Coverage	Source of Funds
United States of America	Social insurance system	Social Security Administration: general administration and administration of cash benefits; Internal Revenue Service: contributions collection	• Coverage for gainfully occupied persons, including self-employed (excluded: casual agricultural and domestic employment, limited self-employment with net income below $400, some federal employees hired pre-1984, and state and local government employees who are not covered under a retirement system) • Voluntary coverage for state and local government employees and clergy	• *From insured:* employed workers at 6.2% of gross earnings earnings up to a maximum earning level of $72,600, for self-employed, 12.4% • *From employer:* 6.2% of payroll
Germany	• Social insurance system • East Germany's and West Germany's systems were merged effective January 1, 1992, at which time Part VI of the Social Act came into force throughout the whole of the united Germany	Federal Ministry of Labor and Social Affairs	• Employed persons (including apprentices), certain self-employed, persons caring for a child under age 3, recipients of social benefits (such as unemployment benefits), and voluntary care workers • Special systems for self-employed persons, miners, public employees (supplementary insurance), and farmers • Voluntary affiliation for all others age 16 or older currently exempt from compulsory insurance, including German citizens residing abroad and resident aliens	• *From insured:* 9.85% of earnings, none if earnings below DM 630/m (DM 102,000 maximum); for self-employed, 19.5% • *From employer:* 9.75% of payroll • *From government:* Subsidy to compensate for cost of benefits not covered by contributions
The Netherlands	Social insurance system	Board of Supervision of Social Insurance: general supervision of contributions and administration of cash benefits; Social Insurance Bank administers old-age pension; National Institute for Social Security collects contributions and implements various Acts; National Revenue Department collects contributions for old-age and survivor pensions and uninsured workers' disability pension	• Old-age pension: all residents • Disability pension: Employed workers, self-employed workers, resident persons disabled since childhood, and students	• *Insured person:* 17.90% of income for old-age pension, 1.25% for survivor pension; self-employed contribute 8.80% to the disability pension • *From employer:* 5.85% of payroll plus variable rate contribution (0.85% average) for disability pension of employed person; a supplement of 2.20% of payroll for up to 159 per day to compensate for part of employee's contribution • *From government:* Funds needed to bring benefits up to social minimum of 721.41 per month for a single individual (1,023.46 for a couple); the cost of pensions for those disabled from childhood; any deficit

Table 4.1 (continued)

Country	Type of Program	Administrative Organization	Coverage	Source of Funds
Czech Republic	Social insurance system	Ministry of Labor and Social Affairs; Czech Social Security Administration	• Employees • Members of assimilated groups (certain students, farmers, artists, unemployed, carers, military personnel, self-employed) • Voluntary coverage available to certain categories of persons, including persons employed abroad	• *From insured:* 6.5% of earnings • *From employer:* 19.5% of payroll • *From government sources:* Any deficit
Poland	Dual social insurance system and mandatory private insurance	Social Insurance Institute (program administration); Pension fund supervision office—UNFE (oversees private pension funds)	• Employees • Members of cooperatives • Self-employed artisans • Home-workers • Attorneys • Clergy • Special systems for independent farmers	• *From insured:* 9.76% of earnings (old-age) and 6.5% of earnings (disability and survivor pensions) • *From employer:* 9.76% of earnings (old-age) and 6.5% of earnings (disability and survivor pensions) • *From government:* Government funds guarantee a minimum pension
Norway	Dual universal and social insurance systems	Ministry of Health and Social Affairs (general supervision); National Insurance Administration and county/local offices (program administration)	• *Universal pension:* All residents; pension income independent of previous income or contributions paid • *Earnings-related pension:* All employees and self-employed earning over base amount (in 2002 @ 51,360 kroner). Special systems for seamen, fishermen, forestry workers, railway employees, and public employees	• Contributions calculated on basis of pensionable income in excess of 22,000 kroner (2002); however, contributions may not exceed 25% of annual income above 2,000 kroner • *From insured:* Employed: 7.8% of income between ages 17–68; self-employed: 10.7% of income up to 12X base amount plus 7.8% of income exceeding 12X base amount • *From employer:* 14.1% of payroll • *From government:* National government meets any deficit
Sweden	• Dual universal and social insurance system (old system) and unified social insurance plus mandatory private accounts (new system) • A new social insurance system plus mandatory private "premium pension" accounts established; there is to be a gradual transition from old system to new for persons born between 1938 and 1953. Persons born in 1954 and later are completely covered under the new system while those born before 1937 will remain entirely within the old system.	National Social Security Board (administration and supervision); Premium Pension Agency (administration of funded portion of new system)	• *Universal old-age pension (old system):* All residents • *Earnings-related pension (old system):* All employees and self-employed earning over increased base amount (set by the government and indexed to the consumer price index—for 2002, base is 37,900 kronor and increased base amount is 38,700 kronor • *Earnings-related pension (new system):* All employed and self-employed residents	• Combined total of insured and employer contributions is 16% to earnings-related component and 2.5% to premium account • *From insured:* Employed:7% of assessable income (up to 7.5X increased base amount); self-employed: 10.21% of assessable earnings • *From employer:* 10.21% of payroll • *From government:* Total cost of the guarantee pension in new system, the universal pension for those who have no earnings-related pensions in the old system, and the partial pension

Country	Type of program	Coverage	Administrative organization	Source of funds
Australia	Dual social security (means-tested) and mandatory occupational pension (earnings-based system)	*Premium pension (new system):* All employed and self-employed residents *Guaranteed pension:* All residents *Social Security:* residents *Mandatory occupational pension:* employed persons earning more than $450 per month; excludes self-employed	Department of Family and Community Services (general supervision); Centerlink (program administration)	• *From insured:* Social security: none; mandatory occupational pension: none required, voluntary contributions encouraged • *From employer:* Social security: none; mandatory occupational pension: 9% of basic wages (2002) • *From government:* Social security: entire cost from general revenue; mandatory occupational pension: none
Japan	Social insurance program that is a two-tiered system: *First tier*—national pension program (flat rate) for all residents *Second tier*—employees' pension insurance or other employment-related programs (earnings related)	*National pension program:* • Residents aged 20–59 • Voluntary coverage for residents 60–64 (65–69 in special cases) • Citizens residing abroad (aged 20–64) *Employees' pension insurance:* • Employees of firms in industry and commerce (including seamen) • Contracting out from employee pension insurance allowed if corporate plan provides equivalent or higher benefits • Other employment-related programs include special systems for public employees, private school teachers and employees, and employees of agricultural, forestry, and fishery cooperative associations	Pension Bureau of the Ministry of health and Welfare (general supervision of both programs); Social Insurance Agency (national program administration)	• Maximum earnings for contributions and benefit purposes: 59,000 yen per month • Minimum earnings for contributions and benefit purposes: 92,000 yen per month *National pension program:* Employed persons and dependent spouses contributions included as part of employee contribution to employment-related programs *Employees' pension insurance:* 8.765% of earnings according to 30 wage classes. • Miners and seamen: 9.575% • Added special premium: 0.5% of bonuses • If contracted out, 8.145% to 8.175% of earnings *National pension program:* Included in employer contribution to employment-related programs *Employees' pension insurance:* Same as for insured person *National pension program:* 33.33% of benefit costs plus administrative costs *Employees' pension insurance:* Cost of administration
South Korea	Social insurance system	• All residents aged 18–59 • Separate systems for public employees, private school teachers, self-employed, and military personnel	Ministry of Health and Welfare (supervision); National Pension Corporation (administration)	• *From insured:* 4.5% of covered monthly earnings; farmers, fishermen, self-employed, and voluntary insured: 3% of monthly covered earnings • *From employer:* 4.5% of payroll • *From government:* Partial cost of administration and of program for farmers and fishermen

Table 4.1 (continued)

Country	Type of Program	Administrative Organization	Coverage	Source of Funds
Thailand	Social insurance system	Ministry of Labor and Social Welfare (general supervision); Social Security Office (administration)	• Employees of firms with 10 or more workers • Voluntary coverage for self-employed • Separate programs for civil servants and private school teachers	• Contributions finance old-age pension and child allowance *From insured:* 1% of employee's wages *From employer:* 1% of employee's wages *From government:* 1% of employee's wages

Country	Qualifying Conditions	Old-Age Benefits	Permanent Disability Benefits	Survivor Benefits
United States of America	*Old-age pension* For age 65 and over, gradually increasing to 67 over period of 2000 to 2007 People aged 62–64 can opt to receive reduced benefits *Disability pension* Defined as inability to engage in substantial gainful activity due to impairment expected to last at least one year or result in death. Minimum coverage based on 1 quarter per year since age 21 up to the year disability began. Maximum coverage is 40 Quarters; also, 20 quarters of coverage in the last 10-year period before disability began. More liberal requirements for the young and the blind. Based on covered earnings from age 21 and indexed for past wage inflation up to the onset of disability (excluding up to 5 years with the lowest earnings) *Survivor pension*	Pension reduced $1 for each $2 of earnings above $9,600 per year. For people under age 65, and reduced $1 for every $3 of earnings above $15,500 for beneficiaries of ages 65–69. Earnings limits adjusted annually based on average wage increases. Benefits tied to COLAs on an annual basis. Dependent's benefit of 50% of worker's pension paid to spouse at any age caring for a child under age 16 or disabled; to each child (or dependent grandchild) under age 18 or age 18–19 and attending elementary or secondary school full-time (no age limit if disabled before age 22). Maximum family pension ranges from 150% to 188% of worker's basic pension. Means-tested allowance payable to needy aged under separate SSI program	Dependent allowance of 50% of worker's pension paid to surviving spouse (or divorced spouse if marriage lasted 10 years) at age 65 (reduced for ages 62–64), or to spouse at any age caring for a child under age 16 or disabled; to each child (or dependent grandchild) under age 18 or age 18–19 and attending elementary or secondary school full time (no age limit if disabled before age 22). Maximum family pension ranges from 100% to 150% of worker's basic pension. Means-tested allowance payable to needy disabled and blind under SSI program	*Widow/widower pension:* Deceased was pensioner or had 1 quarter coverage for each year since age 21 and before the year of death (to a maximum of 40 quarters). Reduced requirements for orphans and non-aged widow with eligible orphan care (6 quarters of coverage in 13 quarters preceding death) Survivor pension is 100% of deceased insured worker's pension at age 65 (reduced for ages 62–64); reduced pension if disabled at age 50–59. Payble to surviving spouse or surviving divorced spouse if the marriage lasted more than 10 years. 75% of worker's pension for surviving spouse or divorced spouse at any age if caring for a child under age 16 or disabled *Orphan's pension:* • Benefits are 75% of worker's pension for each child under age 18 or ages 18–19 if attending elementary or secondary school full time (no age limit if disabled before age 22) Maximum family benefits based on worker's pension. Means-tested allowance payable under federal-state program to needy orphans and relatives with whom they are living

Germany

Old-age pension

- Age 65, with 5 years of contributions
- Early retirement possible from age 63 if have 35 years of coverage, from age 60 if have at least 15 years of contributions and unemployed 1 year after age 58 yrs., 6 months or in part-time work for older employees for at least 24 months before age 60
- For women, age 60 with 0 years of compulsory contributions after age 40
- For severely disabled individuals, age 60 with a minimum of 35 years of coverage
- Partial retirement available for pensioners if under 65 and have partially ceased to work, full pension paid if earnings are less than 325 DM per month and if the amount made is more, the amount of the pension is paid at 2/3, 1/2, or 1/3 depending on the individual's earnin level

Disability pension

- Full reduction in earning capacity (unable to work more than 3 hours per day in any type of employment), or
- Partial reduction in earning capacity (at least 6 hours per day in any form of employment)
- Total of 5 years of contributions and 36 months of compulsory contributions in the last 5-year period

Survivor pension

Deceased had 5 years of contributions or was a pensioner at the time of death

- East Germany's and West Germany's systems were merged effective January 1, 1992, at which time Part VI of the Social Act came into force throughout the whole of the united Germany
- Old age pension: individual annual earnings divided by average earnings of all contributors (periods of incapacity to work, unemployment and schooling are also taken into account)
- Pension value is the monthly benefit for one year's average covered earnings, adjusted for changes in wages
- For delayed retirement age after 65, an added factor of 1.0 plus .005 for each month is used to increase the benefit
- For low-income pensions: people with 35 years of insurance, earning points are adjusted as needed up to the average value to a maximum of 75% of average earnings of all insured
- Annual benefits adjustments for changes in the real value of pensions compared to changes in earnings

- Pension factor same as old-age benefits
- For inability to perform previous employment factor is 0.667; if disability occurs before age 60, period up to age 55 is fully taken into account together with 1/3 of the period from age 55–60 up to a maximum of 20 months
- Annual benefits adjustments for changes in the real value of pensions compared to changes in earnings

Survivor pension is same as old-age pension

- 100% of insured's pension payable for 3 months; thereafter, 60% of pension if age 45, disabled, or caring for at least one child; otherwise, 25%

Orphans pension:

- Pension factor is 0.1 for orphan; 0.2 for full orphan; supplements depend on length of coverage
- Supplements depend on length of coverage; payable in full if net income is less than limit (for those making more, 40% is offset against pension)
- Annual adjustment based on changes in real value of pensions compared to changes in earnings

The Netherlands

Old-age pension

- Age 65
- 50 years of residence for those aged 15 to 64 and, if income earned, contributions for each year from 15–64 to receive a full pension; otherwise, a reduced pension
- 2 persons sharing a household can qualify for couple's pension if both are over 65, or if under 65, the youngest partner satisfies the income test

Survivor pension

- Couple (married or not) receive 1,162.27 guilders per month each singles receive 1,684.70 guilders per month
- Single parent caring for child under 18 receives 2,084.14 guilders per month

- Employed workers receive up to 70% of earnings for at least an 80% disability and 14%–50% of earnings for a disability within the range of 15%–80%
- Maximum earnings by employed workers of 81,000 guilders per year
- Constant-attendance supplement: 30% of full pension

Widow/widower pension:

- Survivor pension for widow/widower or unmarried permanent partner caring for child under 18 (1,830.02 guilders per month)
- Pension benefit reduced by survivor's income from employment exceeding 1,220.53 guilders per month
- Other income deducted in full

Table 4.1 *(continued)*

Country	Qualifying Conditions	Old-Age Benefits	Permanent Disability Benefits	Survivor Benefits
	Disability pension • Full pension: Loss of over 80% of earning capacity in current occupation • Partial pension: 15%–80% for employed worker • Partial pension: 25%–80% for unemployed workers or resident persons disabled from childhood, and students *Survivor pension* • Payable to widow, widower, unmarried permanent partner, or full orphan • Income-tested for survivors born before 1950, or for those with children under 18 and the surviving partner is 45% disabled		• Unemployed workers receive up to 70% of earnings for at least 80% disability and 14%–50% of earnings for a disability ranging from 25%–80% • Maximum earnings: minimum wage (2,350 guilders per month) • Constant-attendance supplement: 30% of full pension • Resident persons disabled from childhood, and students receive up to 70% of minimum wage for at least an 80% disability and payments of 15%–50% of minimum wage for a disability ranging from 25%–80% • Constant-attendance supplement: 30% of full pension • Disability benefits are adjusted automatically 2x per year for changes in the minimum wage	• Dependent child allowance paid until age 18 (18,406.80 guilders per year per child with no income test) *Orphan's pension:* • Receive 585.61 guilders per month for each full orphan under age 10; 878.41 per month for ages 10–16, and 1,171.21 per month if student and aged 16–27 when disability pension becomes payable • adjusted automatically 2x per year for changes in the minimum wage *Death benefit:* • 100% of earnings up to a daily maximum earnings of 310 guilders per day for employed workers, 100% earnings up to minimum wage (2,350 guilders per month) for unemployed workers, both payable for one month for death of disabled person • 100% of pension for death and old-age, payable for one month
Czech Republic	*Old-age pension* • Target for Jan. 1, 2007 is age 62 for men and 57–61 for women depending on number of children • Retirement based on 25 years of insurance • Early retirement possible 3 years prior to full retirement age; all employment must cease *Disability pension* • Total disability (66% loss of earning capacity) or partial disability (33% loss of earning capacity) with 5 years of insurance in last 10 years (up to 4 years if aged under 28) *Survivor pension* • Deceased met pension requirements or was pensioner at time of death	Full benefits calculated from flat-rate basic amount plus earnings-related percentage amount based on personal assessment base and number of years of insurance. Minimum 2002 pension is 2,080 CZK (flat-rate basis for 2002 is 1,310 CZK)	Basic amount plus percentage amount from the personal assessment base of 1.5% for every year of insurance. The anticipated insurance period is credited to the pension from the onset of disability to full retirement age. Minimum 2002 rate is 2,080 CZK; there is no maximum disability pension	*Widow/widower pension:* Basic amount plus 50% of percentage amount of deceased's pension. Payable to all widows/widowers for 1 year; thereafter, only widows aged 55 or widowers who are 58. Payment continues at any age if recipient is disabled, or caring for dependent or disabled child or disabled parent *Orphan's pension:* Basic amount plus 40% of percentage mount of deceased's pension for each dependent child (for full orphans, basic amount is only payable once). Value of pension is increased by 20% of subsistence minimum if orphan is partially disabled, by 40% of predominant incapacity, and by 75% in the case of full disability

Poland

Old-age pension
- Ages 65 (men) and 60 (women) for those insured for 25 years (men) or 20 years (women)
- Full retirement age reduced for dancers, acrobats, miners, underground or unhealthy work, teaching, aviation, and maritime employment
- Pensionable age reduced by 5 years for women with 30 years of insurance, war veterans, and for the disabled

Disability pension
- Determination of meeting total or partial disability definitions and 5 years if employment during the past 10 years (1 to 4 years for those under 30), or if disability occurred while employed or within 18 months of ceasing to work

Survivor pension
- Deceased was a pensioner or met employment requirement for disability or old-age pension at time of death

- Full benefits under old system: 24% ave. natl. salary; 1.3% worker's earning base X number of contribution years; and 0.7% worker's earning base X number of credit years that cannot exceed 1/3 of contribution years

Maximum earnings for benefit purposes: 250% of average national salary

Minimum pension in 2001: 530.26 zlotys per month

- Full benefits under the new system: Total contributions made into old-age scheme taking into account current valuations of contributions per average life expectancy

For both systems:
Total disability—24% ave. natl. salary; 1.3% worker's earning base X number of contribution years; and 0.7% worker's earning base X number of credit years that cannot exceed 1/3 of contribution years

Partial disability—75% of total disability pension amount

Monthly minimum for total disability (2001): 530.26 zlotys
Monthly minimum for partial disability (2001): 407.88 zlotys

Under old system, benefits vary with number of survivors:
1 = 85% deceased's pension value
2 = 90%
3 or more = 95%
If deceased not eligible for old-age pension, then the criteria for total disability pensions is basis for assessment purposes.
Minimum monthly payment (2001): 530.26 zlotys

Under new system, entitlements depend on the type of annuity purchased by the insured

Orphan's pension:
Supplement for full orphans (2001): 255.55 zlotys per month

Norway

Old-age pension
Universal old-age pension and earnings-related old-age pension:
- Age: 67
- 3 years coverage, ages 16 to 66
- Not dependent on ceasing employment
- Earnings test if worker continues to work to age 70: Pension value reduced by 40% of wages exceeding twice wage amount

Disability Pension
Universal disability pension and earnings-related disability pension:
- 3 years coverage immediately preceding claim (in some instances 1 year for universal disability pension)
- Earnings capacity permanently reduced by 50% or more for persons aged 16 to 66

Survivor Pension
Universal disability pension and earnings-related disability pension:

Universal old-age pension:
- Up to 100% of base amount if single, 150% for aged couple
- Full pension for coverage over 40 years, reduced for shorter coverage
- Income-tested supplement:
50% for spouse not drawing old-age pension; 40% base amount for each child under 18; up to 79.33% of base if ineligible for earnings-related pension (79.33% if spouse is a pensioner); 158.66% supporting a spouse 60 or older
Earnings-related old-age pension:
42% current base X insured's average annual number of pension points in the 20 years with most points
- Pension points in 1 year = (worker earnings X year's base amount)/base amount
- Maximum earnings for benefit purposes: 6 X base amount + 1/3 income between 6X and 12X base amount—limit of 7.0 points per year

Universal disability benefits:
- Fully disabled—full base amount, and 40 years of coverage for full pension
- Partial disability—proportionally reduced in relation to the loss of earning capacity
- Income-tested supplement:
50% of pension for spouse 60 or more; 30% of base amount for each child under 18; 533 kroner to 2,668 kroner per month for substantially increased expenses; up to 61.55% of base amount if ineligible for earnings-related pension
Earnings-related disability pension:
- Full disability—Same as earnings-related old-age pension
- Years of coverage credited as if worker to age 67 if certain coverage conditions met
- Partial disability—Reduced proportionally for shorter periods of coverage
Recorded earnings, wage limits, and pensions in force adjusted automatically

Widow/widower pension:
Universal survivor pension:
- Up to 100% of base amount
- Full pension if deceased or spouse have 40 years of coverage (with coverage projected to 66th year)
- If surviving spouse's income exceeds 1/2 base amount, pension equals full pension/40% of excess of spouse income above 1/2 base amount
- Income-tested supplement: Up to 79.33% of base amount if ineligible for earnings-related pension
- Child-care benefit: If survivor or parent is pursuing education or working outside the know and annual income is less than 410,880 kroner

Less than 308,160 kroner—70% of expenses for child care not exceeding 2,571 kroner per month for one child; maximum of 3,801 kroner/month for 3 or more children

Table 4.1 (continued)

Country	Qualifying Conditions	Old-Age Benefits	Permanent Disability Benefits	Survivor Benefits
	• 3 years coverage immediately preceding claim (in some instances 1 year for universal disability pension) • Earnings capacity permanently reduced by 50% or more for persons aged 16 to 66 *Universal survivor pension:* • Deceased has 3 years of coverage immediately preceding death or claim • Surviving spouse married to deceased for 5 or more years or is caring for dependent child(ren). *Earnings-related survivor pension:* • Orphans under 18 • Full orphans under 18 • Under age 20 if student	• Full pension with 20 years of coverage for those born prior 1917, requirement increases year by year to 40 for born later • Recorded earnings, wage limits, and pensions in force adjusted automatically		*Earnings-related survivor pension:* • 55% of earnings-related pension of deceased worker as if worked to age 67 *Transitional grant:* • Surviving spouse temporarily unable to work • Divorced • Separated • Unwed parents (including child-care benefit) *Orphan's pension:* • 40% of base amount for first child, 25% for each additional child under 18 • Full orphans under 18 (20 if student) receive full survivor pension (basic plus earnings-related pension) of parent entitled to highest amount; 40% of base amount paid for second child and 25% for each additional child—divided equally if two or more children
Sweden	*Old-age Pension* Universal old-age pension (old system): • Age 65 (60 to 64 with reductions, deferrals until 70 with increments) • Residence in Sweden, or pension points credit equaling a minimum of 3 years • Full basic pension requires 40 years residency between ages 16–64 inclusive, or 30 years with pension points (pension reduced by 1/40 or 1/30, respectively, for each year that residency or pension points fall short Earnings-related pension (old system): • Age 65 (60 to 64 with reductions, deferrals until 70 with increments) • 3 years coverage • Partial pension—part-time work (aged 61–64), reduced work schedule, fulfilled certain conditions before entitlement, and 10 years earnings-related coverage after age 45	*Universal old-age pension (old system):* 96% current base amount X accrued number of 1/40ths or 1/30ths to a single pensioner (or 78.5% to a married pensioner) • Claimants aged 61–64 receive a permanent reduction of 0.5% per month while those deferring their claim until age 70 get a permanent 0.7% per month increment *Earnings-related pension (old system):* 60% current base amount X insured average annual number of pension points in 15 years with most points Number of pension points in a year equals (worker's covered earnings x year's base amount)/base amount • Limit of 7.5 base amounts (full pension is 30 years of coverage, pension reduced for shorter coverage)	*Universal disability pensions:* • Single person: 90% reduced current base X accrued number of 1/40ths or 1/30ths • Married pensioner: 75% • Supplements: 112.9% reduced base plus accrual (if lineligible for earnings-related pension) • Partial disability: 3/4, 1/2, or 1/4 of full pension *Earnings-related disability pension:* • Same as old-age pension except credit given for years up to age 65 if certain prior coverage requirements met • Partial disability: 3/4, 1/2, or 1/4 of full pension	Transition rules apply to women born prior to 1945. Women born in 1945 or after may also be covered by these transitional rules. *Widow/widower pension:* *Universal survivor pension:* • Adjustment pension payable for 6 months (if at least 5 years of marriage or cohabitation), or payable for as long as living with child under 12 • Maximum pension: 90% of reduced base amount • Special survivor pension paid if illness or unemployment prevents self-support • Transition rules: (a) 90% of current base amount if widow with child under 16, or is 50 and married 5 years at time of husband's death (b) Women aged 36–49 without children, and married for 5 or more years have full pension reduced by 1/15 for each year under age 50

Earnings-related survivor pension:
Earnings-related pensions (new system):
- Flexible retirement age from 61 onwards
- Based on lifetime earnings reported to scheme from age 16
- Must have years with earnings in excess of 24% of base amount (earnings above 7.5X increased base amount excluded)

Premium pension (new system):
- Based on all lifetime earnings reported to scheme from age 16

Guarantee pension:
3 years of residence

Disability pension
Universal disablity pension and earnings-realted disability pension:
- granted in relation to assessed degree of disability at 3/4, 1/2, or 1/4 of a full pension

Survivor Pension
Universal survivor pension:
- Insured was resident in Sweden, or credited with pension points for minimum of 3 years

Earnings-related survivor pension:
Deceased was pensioner or had 3 years of coverage

- Claimants aged 61–64 receive a permanent reduction of 0.5% per month while those deferring their claim until age 70 get a permanent 0.7% per month increment

Earnings-related pension (new system):
- System of notational accounts
- Formula: Annual index base on development of average wages reported to pension system [disability pension payments counted as earnings] plus (annuity factor depending on average life expectancy at time of retirement for appropriate age cohort X "norm" for expected increase of average wages in future years
- Pension payments calculated by: total accrued pension assets/factor generated as described in previous bullet point
- Life expectancy based on most recent average unisex life expectancy statistics over a 5-year period
- "norm" set at 1.6% and used for annual adjustment as well as calculating first year amounts

Premium pension:
Insured contribution plus net returns converted into an annuity (individual, joint, fixed, or variable)

Earnings-related survivor pension:
- Adjustment pension payable for 6 months, up to 40% of deceased's pension
- Transition rules: Widow receives 40% of projected or actual pension of deceased, 35% if she has children

Orphan's pension:
Universal survivor pension:
- 25% reduced rate amount, 50% if full orphan
- Paid to age 18 (20 if student)

Earnings-related survivor pension:
30% of pension of deceased (if more than one child, increased 20% per child)

Australia

- All social security and disability pensions are a means-tested program unless blind

Old-age Pension
Social Security:
- Men: Age 65
- Women: Age 61.5 (gradually increasing to 65 by July 1, 2013)
- Resident and physically present in country
- 10 years continuous residence (5 years if total residence exceeds 10 years)

Mandatory occupational pension:
Age 55 if permanently retired

Disability Pension
Disability pension social security:
- Men: ages 16–65
- Women: ages 16–61

Social security (means-tested):
- Singles: up to A$178.65 per week
- Each member of a couple: A$149.05 per week

Wife pension (means-tested):
- Up to A$149.05 per week
- Benefits for dependent children paid through family allowance scheme

Carer payment (means-tested):
- Up to A$178.65 per week
- A$149.05 if caring for spouse

Rental assistance (means-tested):
- Up to A$49.70 per week in accordance to marital status and level of rent
- Special rules apply to those living in retirement villages

Pharmaceutical assistance:
- A$2.70 per week per family

Social Security (means-tested unless blind):
- Same as for old-age pension for all married pensioners and pensioners 21 and older
- Single, 18–20 and living away from home: up to A$132.35 per week
- Single 18–20 and living at home: A$87.15 per week
- Single disability pensioners under 21 may also be eligible for youth disability supplement of A$37.45 per week
- Mobility allowance (not means-tested): A$28.55 per week
- Wife's pension (means-tested): same as under oldage pension
- Carer's pension (means-tested): same as under old-age pension
- Rental assistance (means-tested): same as under old-age pension

Social security (means-tested):
- Same as single old-age pension
- Rental assistance, concession card: same as old-age pension
- Adjustment: survivor pension adjusted in March and September according to price index

Widow/widower pension:
- Bereavement payment: difference between single and married pension is paid to the surviving partner for 14 weeks after a pensioner's death
- 1 pension payment is credited to the estate of a single pensioner

Orphan's pension:
Orphan payments through family allowances schemes

Table 4.1 (*continued*)

Country	Qualifying Conditions	Old-Age Benefits	Permanent Disability Benefits	Survivor Benefits

	• Minimum 20% impairment level, and
	• Inability to work 30 hours per week at full wages, or be retrained for such work for at least the next 2 years as a result of a physical, intellectual, or psychiatric impairment or permanent blindness
	• Resident and physically present in country. If incapacity happens prior to arrival in Australia, same minimum residence requirements as for old-age pensions. No residency requirement if incapacity happens in Australia
	• Wife pension (means-tested): when both disability pensioner and wife are over 21 unless there are children (no new grants since 1995 except for certain partners of mature age allowance)
	• Mobility allowance (not means tested): disabled person age 16 or more who cannot use public transportation without substantial assitance.
	Mandatory occupational pension: no mandated provision for disability
	Survivor pension
	Survivor pension social security:
	• Widows and widowers with dependent children entitled to parenting payment under family allowances program
	• Widow allowance:
	  • Single women age 50 without children if widowed, separated or divorced after age 40
	  • Resident and physically present in Australia, without recent workforce experience
	  • If widow resides in Australia at time of death, no residency requirement; otherwise, same requirement as for old-age pension
	Mandatory occupational pension: no mandated provision for survivors
		Telephone allowance:
		• A$63.20 per year for telephone subscribers
		Remote area supplement:
		• Single: A$8.75 per week
		• Married: A$15 per week
		• Per child: A$3.50 per week
		• Social security recipients entitled to a concession card which makes available a range of reduced costs on certain federal, state, and local government services
		• Price-indexed adjustments twice per year—single rate of pension maintained as percentage of weekly earnings
		
		Mandatory occupational pension:
		Usually a lump sum of total contributions plan plus interest minus administrative fees and taxes
			• Telephone allowance: same as under old-age pension
			• Remote area supplement: same as under the old-age pension
			• Concession card: same as under old-age pension
			Adjustment: disability pension, carer's pension, and wife's pension adjusted in March and September according to price index	

Japan

Old-age pension

National pension program:

- Age 65, and
- 25 years contribution (including for dependent spouse of employee, years of own coverage plus years married to an employee who is covered by any employment-related programs)
- Pensions payable at ages 60-64 with actuarial reduction
- Pension increased if first paid at age 66 or later.

Employees' pension insurance old-age employees pension:

- Age 60 (55 for seamen and miners)
- 25 years of coverage (including years covered by national pension program)

Disability Pension

National program—disability basic pension:

- Class I—total disability requiring constant attendance
- Class II—disability severely restricting ability in daily living
- Contributions paid or credited during 2/3 of period between age 20 and onset of disability

Employees pension insurance, disability employees pension:

- For Class I and Class II, same as under national pension program

For an additional Class III—incapacity less severe than Class II

Survivor pension

National pension program, survivor basic pension:

- Deceased pensioner at death, or
- Covered at the time of death and had contributions paid or credited during 2/3 of period between ages 20 and death

Employees' pension insurance, survivor employees pension:

- Deceased insured worker or pensioner (old-age or disability) at time of death

- COLA adjustment for both pension programs for old-age pension

National pension program, old-age basic pension:

- Fully insured (480 months of contributions):

804,200 yen per year plus 200 yen for each contribution month if voluntary member

- Benefit actuarially reduced for initial entitlement at ages 60-64 or increased if first paid at age 66 or higher

Employees' pension insurance, old-age insurance pension:

- Formula:

0.75% indexed monthly wages times number of months of coverage

- Ages 60-64 reduced for continued employment—20% if combined total of monthly wage and 80% of pension is under 220,000 yen per month (if combined total is between 220,000 yen per month and 340,000 yen per month, pension is reduced by 1 yen for every 2 yen earned, and if combined total exceed 340,000 yen per month, pension is reduced by 100% of wages over 340,000 yen
- Dependent supplements:

231,400 yen per year for spouse

231,400 yen per year each for 1st and second child

77,100 yen per year for each additional child up to end of the fiscal year the child reaches age 18 or 20 if disabled

National pension program, disability basic pension:

- According to the degree of disability

Class I—1,005,300 yen per year

Class II—804,200 yen per year

- Dependent supplements:

First and second child: 231,400 yen per year

Other children: 77,100 yen per year for each additional child up to end of the fiscal year the child reaches age 18 or 20 if disabled

Employee pension insurance, disability employment pension:

Class I—125% old age pension plus additional benefits for dependents

Class II—100% plus additional benefits for dependents

Class III—100%, with a minimum benefit of 603,100 yen per year

- Lump-sum grant: 200% of old-age pension payable
- Minimum grant: 1,170,000 yen
- Dependent supplements: same as under old-age pension, payable to Class I and Class II disability only

COLA adjustments for both programs

None

Table 4.1 (*continued*)

Country	Qualifying Conditions	Old-Age Benefits	Permanent Disability Benefits	Survivor Benefits
South Korea	*Old-age Pension* Full old-age pension: • Age: 60 • 20 or more years of coverage • No longer engaged in gainful activity Reduced old-age pension: • Age 60 with 10–19 years of coverage • No longer engaged in gainful activity • No retirement test if over 65 Active old-age pension: • Ages 60–64 with 10 or more years of coverage • Still engaged in gainful activity Early old-age pension: • Ages 55–59 with 10 or more years of coverage • Still engaged in gainful activity *Disability Pension* • Disabled as result of disease or injury during insured period, and has paid contributions over 2/3 of insured period, plus period as recipient of disability pension • Exemptions of payment while still insured: students 23 or older, people rearing children under age 3, patients hospitalized for 3 months or more, retirees, unemployed, and others *Survivor Pension* • Payable if insured paid contributions over 2/3 of insured period up to death of the insured • Widows or widower (if latter is 60 or older, or with at least a second degree of disability at any age before eligibility date) • Parents and grandparents (including those of spouse) of insured aged 60 or more, or with at least a second degree of disability	• COLA adjustments • All pensions non-taxable • Basic premium amount (BPA) equals 1.8 times the sum of average covered monthly earnings of all insured persons at the end of the preceding year, and the average monthly covered earnings of the insured person over the entire contribution period • Full old-age pension: BPA plus 5% monthly benefit for each insured year in excess of 20 years • Reduced old-age pension: 47.5% of BPA plus 5% increment of BPA for every year in excess of 10 years of coverage • Active old-age pension: 0.5 to 0.9 times 47.5%BPA [depending on age of pensioner] plus 5% increase of BPA for every insured year in excess of 10 years of coverage • Early old-age pension: 0.75 times 47.5%BPA plus 5% increase of BPA for every year delayed in claiming benefits • Additional benefit for dependents of recipients of full, reduced, or early old-age pension: *Lump-sum refund:* employee and employer contributions paid plus interest	*Full disability pension:* Same as old-age pension *Partial disability benefits:* reduced by up to 40% of BPA depending on degree of incapacity to work First degree = total loss of capacity to work, requiring total attendance Second degree = severe loss of capacity to work Third degree = some loss of capability to work Fourth degree = least severe loss of capability to work	• If insured had 20 or more contribution years: *60% full pension* • If insured had 10–19 contribution years: *50% full pension* • If insured had less than 10 contribution years: *40% full pension* • Lump-sum refund: Employer and employee contributions paid in plus interest • Lump-sum death benefit: Equal amount of deceased person's lump-sum refund maximum: 4x insured person's last monthly covered earnings, or average monthly covered earnings for entire insured period, whichever is highest

• Children and grandchildren under age 18, or at any age if with at least a second degree of disability

Lump-sum death benefit:

• Dependent survivors (siblings and collateral relatives within the fourth degree—e.g., nephews and nieces—not otherwise eligible for survivor benefit or lump-sum refund)

Lump-sum refund:

• If insured is 60 or older: less than 10 years of coverage, or if insured or formerly insured person died without eligibility for a pension, or if insured has less than 10 years of coverage and emigrated (lived outside of Korea and not qualify as Korean national)

Thailand

Old-age Pension

• Age 55
• 180 months of contributions

Disability Pension

• Must have already received cash sickness benefits for period of 1 year
• Cash sickness and medical benefits: 3 months contributions in 15 months before date of treatment

Survivor Pension

• Funeral grant: 1 month contribution in 6 months prior to death; death must have resulted from non-occupational injury or illness

• 15% average wage of last 60 months
• If insured has paid more than 180 months of contributions, rate increases 1% per additional 12 months of contributions in excess of 180 months
• Lump-sum refund: Employee contribution if less than 12 months contributions Employer and employee contributions plus interest if more than 12 months contributions [in case insured person cannot complete 180 months of contributions]

• 50% prior wage payable for whole life
• Maximum: 250 baht/day

Lump sum at amount of 10X of last month old-age pension in case pensioner died within 60 months since the date of entitlement to old-age pension

Source: Adapted from Social Security Administration. (2002). *Social Security Programs throughout the World: Europe 2002.* Washington, D.C.: Author. Retrieved from http://www.ssa.gov/policy/docs/progdesc/ssptw/2002/europe/index.html.

Table 4.2
FICA and Self-Employment Contributions Act (SECA) Tax Rates and Maximum Taxable Earnings, Selected Years 1937 to 2001

(in Percent)

Calendar year	Rate paid by employee and employer					Self-employed rate	Maximum taxable earnings
	OASI	Disability insurance (DI)	OASDI	Hospital insurance (HI)	Total		
1937	1.0	NA	NA	NA	1.0	NA	$3,000
1950	1.5	NA	NA	NA	3.0	NA	3,000
1960	3.0	0.25	2.75	NA	3.0	4.5	4,800
1970	3.65	0.55	4.20	0.60	4.8	6.9	7,800
1980	4.52	0.56	5.08	1.05	6.13	8.1	25,900
1990	5.60	0.60	6.20	1.45	7.65	15.3	51,300
1995	5.26	0.94	6.20	1.45	7.65	15.3[1]	61,200
1999	5.35	0.85	6.20	1.45	7.65	15.3[1]	72,600
2000	5.30	0.90	6.20	1.45	7.65	15.3[1]	76,200
2001 and later	5.30	0.90	6.20	1.45	7.65	15.3[2]	

1. OASDI; no limit (HI).
2. Not yet determined for OASDI; no limit (HI).
NA: Not applicable.
Note: Until 1991 the maximum taxable earnings for HI were the same as for OASDI. In 1991, 1992, and 1993 maximum taxable earnings were $125,000, $130,200, and $135,000 respectively, with no limit after 1993. Only 92.35 percent net self-employment earnings are taxable and half of the SECA taxes so computed is deductible for income tax purposes.

Source: United States House of Representatives, Committee on Ways and Means. (2000). *The 2000 Green Book: Background material and data on programs within the jurisdiction of the Committee on Ways and Means.* Retrieved from http://aspe.hhs.gov/2000gb/sec1.txt.

Table 4.3
OASDI and HI Tax Rates for Self-Employed Individuals, 1980 and Later

(in Percent)

Calendar year	OASI	DI	OASDI	HI	Total (OASDI and HI)
1980	6.2725	0.7775	7.05	1.05	8.10
1981	7.0250	0.9750	8.00	1.30	9.30
1982	6.8125	1.2375	8.05	1.30	9.35
1983	7.1125	0.9375	8.05	1.30	9.35
1984	10.4000	1.0000	11.40	2.60[1]	14.00
1985	10.4000	1.0000	11.40	2.70[1]	14.10
1986–1987	10.4000	1.0000	11.40	2.90[1]	14.30
1988–1989	11.0600	1.0600	12.12	2.90[1]	15.02
1990–1993	11.2000	1.2000	12.40	2.90	15.30
1994–1996	10.5200	1.8800	12.40	2.90	15.30
1997–1999	10.7000	1.7000	12.40	2.90	15.30
2000 and later	10.6000	1.8000	12.40	2.90	15.30

1. Tax credits for the self-employed equaled 2.7 percent in 1984, 2.3 percent in 1985, and 2.0 percent in 1986–1989. The tax rate shown is not reduced for these credits. See text for explanation of change in tax treatment of the self-employed.

Source: United States House of Representatives, Committee on Ways and Means. (2000). *The 2000 Green Book: Background material and data on programs within the jurisdiction of the Committee on Ways and Means.* Retrieved from http://aspe.hhs.gov/2000gb/sec1.txt.

Table 4.4
Social Security (OASDI) Highlights and Trends: 2000

Cost-of-living adjustment for December 2000	3.5 percent
Average monthly benefit, December 2000	
Retired workers	$845
Widows and widowers, nondisabled	810
Disabled workers	786

Employment and Earnings

Workers in OASDI covered employment, 2000	152.9 million
Average earnings, 2000	$31,213
Earnings required in 2001 for—	
1 quarter of coverage	$830
Maximum of 4 quarters of coverage	3,320
Earnings test exempt amounts for 2001	
Under age 65 for entire year	$10,680
For months before attainment of age 65 in 2001	25,000
Beginning with month of attainment of age 65 in 2001	Earnings test eliminated

Program Data

Number of beneficiaries, December 2000	
Old-Age, Survivors, and Disability Insurance	45.4 million
Old-Age Insurance	31.8 million
Retired workers	28.5 million
Survivors Insurance	7.0 million
Widows and widowers, nondisabled	4.7 million
Disability Insurance	6.7 million
Disabled workers	5.0 million
Benefit payments, 2000	
Old-Age, Survivors, and Disability Insurance	$407.6 billion
Old-Age and Survivors Insurance	352.7 billion
Disability Insurance	55.0 billion
Administrative expenses, 2000	
Old-Age and Survivors Insurance	$2.1 billion
As a percent of total benefits paid	0.6 percent
Disability Insurance	$1.6 billion
As a percent of total benefits paid	3.0 percent

Source: Social Security Administration. (2001). *Annual Statistical Supplement, 2001 to the Social Security Bulletin.* Baltimore: Social Security Administration, Office of Policy. Retrieved from http://www.ssa.gov/policy/docs/statcomps/supplement/2001/supp01.pdf.

Table 4.5
Federal Benefit Rates

Act	Living arrangement [1]	Amount [2]		Condition
		Individual	Couple	
1972...............	Own household [3]	$130.00	$195.00	Was to be effective Jan. 1, 1974; superseded by 1973 provision.
1973...............	. . .	140.00	210.00	*Effective Jan. 1, 1974.*
1973...............	. . .	146.00	219.00	*Effective July 1, 1974.*
1974...............	. . .	. . .	. . .	Mechanism established for providing cost-of-living adjustments.
	. . .	157.70	236.60	*Effective July 1, 1975.*
	. . .	167.80	251.80	*Effective July 1, 1976.*
	. . .	177.70	266.70	*Effective July 1, 1977.*
	. . .	189.40	284.10	*Effective July 1, 1978.*
	. . .	208.20	312.30	*Effective July 1, 1979.*
	. . .	238.00	357.00	*Effective July 1, 1980.*
	. . .	264.70	397.00	*Effective July 1, 1981.*
	. . .	284.30	426.40	*Effective July 1, 1982.*
1983...............	. . .	304.30	456.40	*Effective July 1, 1983* (general benefit increase).
	. . .	314.00	472.00	*Effective Jan. 1, 1984.*
	. . .	325.00	488.00	*Effective Jan. 1, 1985.*
	. . .	336.00	504.00	*Effective Jan. 1, 1986.*
	. . .	340.00	510.00	*Effective Jan. 1, 1987.*
	. . .	354.00	532.00	*Effective Jan. 1, 1988.*
	. . .	368.00	553.00	*Effective Jan. 1, 1989.*
	. . .	386.00	579.00	*Effective Jan. 1, 1990.*
	. . .	407.00	610.00	*Effective Jan. 1, 1991.*
	. . .	422.00	633.00	*Effective Jan. 1, 1992.*
	. . .	434.00	652.00	*Effective Jan. 1, 1993.*
	. . .	446.00	669.00	*Effective Jan. 1, 1994.*
	. . .	458.00	687.00	*Effective Jan. 1, 1995.*
	. . .	470.00	705.00	*Effective Jan. 1, 1996.*
	. . .	484.00	726.00	*Effective Jan. 1, 1997.*
	. . .	494.00	741.00	*Effective Jan. 1, 1998.*
	. . .	500.00	751.00	*Effective Jan. 1, 1999.*
	. . .	513.00	769.00	*Effective Jan. 1, 2000.*
	. . .	531.00	796.00	*Effective Jan. 1, 2001.*
1972...............	Receiving institutional care covered by Medicaid	25.00	50.00	*Effective Jan. 1, 1974.* Must be receiving more than 50 percent of the cost of the care from Medicaid (Title XIX of the Social Security Act).
1987...............	. . .	30.00	60.00	*Effective July 1, 1988.* Must be receiving more than 50 percent of the cost of the care from Medicaid (Title XIX of the Social Security Act).

1. For those in another person's household receiving support and maintenance there, the federal benefit rate is reduced by one-third.

2. For those without countable income. These payments are reduced by the amount of countable income of the individual or couple.

3. Includes persons in private institutions whose care is not provided by Medicaid.

Source: Social Security Administration. (2001). *Annual Statistical Supplement, 2001 to the Social Security Bulletin.* Baltimore: Social Security Administration, Office of Policy. Retrieved from http://www.ssa.gov/policy/docs/statcomps/supplement/2001/supp01.pdf.

Table 4.6
Source of Funding from Contributions for Selected Social Insurance Programs: United States, 1965 to 2000

(in Millions)

Program and source	1965	1970	1975	1980	1985	1990	1995	1996	1997	1998	1999	2000
Social Security Trust Funds:												
Old-Age and Survivors Insurance	$16,017	$30,257	$56,815	$103,456	$178,010	$270,507	$309,906	$327,764	$357,104	$380,113	$407,023	$432,977
Employer	7,618	14,489	27,184	49,731	83,682	125,272	143,978	153,388	165,563	176,564	188,461	200,431
Employee	7,440	14,204	26,947	49,436	83,400	124,481	143,335	152,628	164,667	174,786	187,160	198,736
Self-employed	959	1,564	2,684	4,289	7,720	15,906	17,103	15,277	19,448	19,614	20,503	22,216
Taxation of benefits	...	...	...	...	...	3,208	4,848	5,490	6,471	7,426	9,149	10,899	11,594
Disability Insurance	1,188	4,481	7,444	13,255	17,204	28,498	54,695	57,651	56,473	59,485	63,827	71,813
Employer	564	2,154	3,562	6,307	8,119	13,414	25,665	27,299	26,437	28,064	29,936	33,971
Employee	551	2,117	3,530	6,254	8,087	13,338	25,545	27,160	26,279	27,772	29,730	33,701
Self-employed	73	210	352	694	776	1,602	3,144	2,819	3,287	3,091	3,500	3,420
Taxation of benefits	...	...	...	...	222	144	341	373	470	558	661	721
Medicare Trust Funds:												
Hospital Insurance	...	4,880	11,510	23,866	47,173	71,753	103,301	115,853	119,546	130,700	140,306	154,520
Employer	...	2,379	5,578	11,591	22,613	33,850	45,839	52,414	53,345	57,849	61,826	67,526
Employee	...	2,332	5,530	11,518	22,549	33,635	45,852	52,419	53,348	57,849	61,826	67,526
Self-employed	...	169	395	739	1,970	4,146	6,743	5,752	7,976	8,619	8,655	9,299
Voluntarily insured [1]	...	...	7	18	41	122	954	1,199	1,319	1,316	1,447	1,382
Taxation of benefits	...	...	...	...	...	...	3,913	4,069	3,558	5,067	6,552	8,787
Supplementary Medical Insurance [2]	...	1,096	1,917	3,011	5,613	11,319	19,717	18,763	19,289	20,932	18,966	20,556
Aged	...	1,096	1,759	2,707	5,105	10,311	17,651	16,654	17,079	18,594	16,604	17,892
Disabled	...	...	158	304	508	1,008	2,066	2,109	2,210	2,338	2,362	2,664
Railroad Retirement [3]	647	968	1,506	2,630	4,626	4,316	4,032	4,261	4,273	(4)	(4)	(4)
Employer	315	510	1,146	1,722	2,417	2,512	2,592	2,664	2,707	(4)	(4)	(4)
Employee	315	439	356	594	1,110	1,209	1,265	1,316	1,355	(4)	(4)	(4)
Self-employed	17	19	4	313	1,099	595	175	281	211	(4)	(4)	(4)
Federal Civil Service [5]	2,197	3,870	9,507	19,986	27,160	31,869	37,628	38,097	39,745	(4)	(4)	(4)
Employer	1,123	2,001	6,905	16,220	22,472	27,368	33,174	33,720	35,376	(4)	(4)	(4)
Employee	1,073	1,869	2,600	3,766	4,688	4,501	4,454	4,377	4,369	(4)	(4)	(4)
State and local government [6]	4,225	7,895	14,560	25,654	37,455	41,700	59,611	60,898	(4)	(4)	(4)	(4)
Employer	2,525	4,920	9,880	18,776	27,699	29,300	41,011	41,528	(4)	(4)	(4)	(4)
Employee	1,700	2,975	4,680	6,878	9,756	12,400	18,600	19,370	(4)	(4)	(4)	(4)

1. Beginning in July 1973, aged ineligibles may voluntarily enroll for HI.

2. Includes premiums paid on behalf of eligibles by state governments under "buy-in" arrangements.

3. Beginning in 1966, excludes HI contributions and includes employer contributions to supplemental benefit account.

4. Data not available.

5. Employer share represents federal and District of Columbia government contributions: employee share includes voluntary contributions to purchase additional annuity. Beginning in 1960, estimated by the Social Security Administration from fiscal year data.

6. Estimated by Social Security Administration from U.S. Census Bureau fiscal year data. Employer share represents government contribution.

Source: Social Security Administration. (2001). *Annual Statistical Supplement, 2001 to the Social Security Bulletin.* Baltimore: Social Security Administration, Office of Policy. Retrieved from http://www.ssa.gov/policy/docs/statcomps/supplement/2001/supp01.pdf.

Table 4.7
Social Security—Covered Employment, Earnings, and Contribution Rates:
United States, 1980 to 2001

[**140.4 represents 140,400,000.** Includes Puerto Rico, Virgin Islands, American Samoa, and Guam. Represents all reported employment. Data are estimated. OASDHI=Old-age, survivors, disability, and health insurance; SMI=Supplementary medical insurance.]

Item	Unit	1980	1985	1990	1995	1996	1997	1998	1999	2000	2001
Workers with insured status [1]	Million. .	140.4	150.9	164.0	173.2	175.3	177.7	180.0	182.4	184.8	187.3
Male	Million. .	76.6	80.7	86.5	90.2	91.1	92.1	93.0	94.0	95.0	96.1
Female	Million. .	63.8	70.1	77.5	83.0	84.2	85.7	87.1	88.4	89.7	91.1
Under 25 years old	Million. .	25.7	22.0	21.3	18.8	18.8	19.1	19.5	20.0	20.6	21.1
25 to 34 years old	Million. .	36.5	40.1	41.6	39.4	38.9	38.2	37.5	36.9	36.4	36.2
35 to 44 years old	Million. .	23.0	29.9	36.4	40.6	41.2	41.8	42.2	42.5	42.4	42.2
45 to 54 years old	Million. .	18.6	19.2	22.8	29.5	30.8	31.9	33.1	34.4	35.8	36.9
55 to 59 years old	Million. .	9.3	9.0	8.7	9.7	10.2	10.7	11.3	11.8	12.2	13.0
60 to 64 years old	Million. .	8.2	8.8	8.8	8.5	8.5	8.8	8.9	9.2	9.4	9.7
65 to 69 years old	Million. .	7.0	7.5	8.2	8.1	8.1	8.0	7.9	7.9	7.9	8.0
70 years old and over	Million. .	12.1	14.3	16.3	18.5	18.8	19.3	19.6	19.8	20.1	20.2
Workers reported with—											
Taxable earnings [2]	Million. .	113	120	134	141	143	146	149	151	154	153
Maximum earnings [2]	Million. .	10	8	8	8	9	9	9	9	10	10
Earnings in covered employment [2]	Bil. dol..	1,329	1,942	2,704	3,359	3,566	3,847	4,143	4,435	4,786	5,043
Reported taxable [2]	Bil. dol..	1,178	1,725	2,359	2,920	3,074	3,285	3,522	3,745	3,991	4,198
Percent of total	Percent.	88.6	88.8	87.2	86.9	86.2	85.4	85.0	84.4	83.4	83.2
Average per worker:											
Total earnings [2]	Dollars .	11,761	16,125	20,227	23,818	24,869	26,324	27,814	29,289	31,144	32,860
Taxable earnings [2]	Dollars .	10,430	14,326	17,642	20,703	21,432	22,483	23,644	24,733	25,970	27,355
Annual maximum taxable earnings [3]	Dollars .	25,900	39,600	51,300	61,200	62,700	65,400	68,400	72,600	76,200	80,400
Contribution rates for OASDHI: [4]											
Each employer and employee	Percent.	6.13	7.05	7.65	7.65	7.65	7.65	7.65	7.65	7.65	7.65
Self-employed [5]	Percent.	8.10	14.10	15.30	15.30	15.30	15.30	15.30	15.30	15.30	15.30
SMI, monthly premium [6]	Dollars .	9.60	15.50	28.60	46.10	42.50	43.80	43.80	45.50	45.50	50.00

1. Estimated number fully insured for retirement and/or survivor benefits as of end of year.

2. Includes self-employment.

3. Beginning 1994 upper limit on earnings subject to HI taxes was resealed.

4. As of January 1, 2002, each employee and employer pays 7.65 percent and the self-employed pay 15.3 percent.

5. Self-employed pays 11.8 percent in 1985. The additional amount is supplied from general revenues. Beginning 1990, self-employed pays 16.3 percent, and half of the tax is deducible for income tax purposes and for computing self-employment income subject to social security tax.

6. 1980, as of July 1; beginning 1985, as of January 1. As of January 1, 2002, the monthly premium is $54.00.

Source: United States Census Bureau. (2002). *Statistical Abstract of the United States 2002.* Washington, D.C.: Government Printing Office. Retrieved from http://www.census.gov/prod/2003pubs/02statab/socinsur.pdf.

Table 4.8

Social Security (OASDI)—Benefits by Type of Beneficiary: United States, 1980 to 2001

[**35,585 represents 35,585,000**. A person eligible to receive more than one type of benefit is generally classified or counted only once as a retired-worker beneficiary. OASDI=Old-age, survivors, and disability insurance.]

Type of beneficiary	1980	1985	1990	1995	1996	1997	1998	1999	2000	2001
Number of benefits [1] (1,000)	**35,585**	**37,058**	**39,832**	**43,387**	**43,737**	**43,971**	**44,246**	**44,596**	**45,415**	**45,878**
Retired workers [2] (1,000)	19,562	22,432	24,838	26,673	26,898	27,275	27,511	27,775	28,499	28,837
Disabled workers [3] (1,000)	2,859	2,657	3,011	4,185	4,386	4,508	4,698	4,879	5,042	5,274
Wives and husbands [2][4] (1,000)	3,477	3,375	3,367	3,290	3,194	3,129	3,054	2,987	2,963	2,899
Children (1,000)	4,607	3,319	3,187	3,734	3,803	3,772	3,769	3,795	3,803	3,839
Under age 18	3,423	2,699	2,497	2,956	3,010	2,970	2,963	2,970	2,976	2,994
Disabled children [5]	450	526	600	686	697	705	713	721	729	737
Students [6]	733	94	89	92	96	97	93	104	98	109
Of retired workers	639	457	422	442	443	441	439	442	459	467
Of deceased workers	2,610	1,917	1,776	1,884	1,898	1,893	1,884	1,885	1,878	1,890
Of disabled workers	1,358	945	989	1,409	1,463	1,438	1,446	1,468	1,466	1,482
Widowed mothers [7] (1,000)	562	372	304	275	242	230	221	212	203	197
Widows and widowers [2][8] (1,000)	4,411	4,863	5,111	5,226	5,210	5,053	4,990	4,944	4,901	4,828
Parents [2] (1,000)	15	10	6	4	4	4	3	3	3	3
Special benefits [9] (1,000)	93	32	7	1	1	(Z)	(Z)	(Z)	(Z)	(Z)
AVERAGE MONTHLY BENEFIT, CURRENT DOLLARS										
Retired workers [2]	341	479	603	720	745	765	780	804	844	874
Retired worker and wife [2]	567	814	1,027	1,221	1,262	1,295	1,318	1,357	1,420	1,466
Disabled workers [3]	371	484	587	682	704	722	733	754	786	814
Wives and husbands [2][4]	164	236	298	354	369	379	386	398	416	430
Children of retired workers	140	198	259	322	337	349	358	373	395	413
Children of deceased workers	240	331	406	469	487	500	510	526	550	571
Children of disabled workers	110	142	164	183	194	201	208	216	228	238
Widowed mothers [7]	246	332	409	478	515	532	545	566	595	621
Widows and widowers, nondisabled [2]	311	433	556	680	699	731	749	775	810	841
Parents [2]	276	378	482	591	614	636	651	674	704	729
Special benefits [9]	105	138	167	192	197	201	204	209	217	224
AVERAGE MONTHLY BENEFIT, CONSTANT (2001) DOLLARS [10]										
Retired workers [2]	698	774	796	829	830	838	841	844	858	874
Retired worker and wife [2]	1,161	1,316	1,356	1,406	1,406	1,419	1,421	1,425	1,442	1,466
Disabled workers [3]	760	782	775	785	784	791	790	792	799	814
Wives and husbands [2][4]	336	382	394	408	411	415	417	418	423	430
Children of deceased workers	491	535	536	540	543	548	550	552	559	571
Widowed mothers [7]	504	537	540	550	574	583	588	594	604	621
Widows and widowers, nondisabled [2]	637	700	734	783	778	801	807	814	823	841
Number of benefits awarded (1,000)	**4,215**	**3,796**	**3,717**	**3,882**	**3,793**	**3,866**	**3,800**	**3,917**	**4,290**	**4,162**
Retired workers [2]	1,620	1,690	1,665	1,609	1,581	1,719	1,631	1,690	1,961	1,779
Disabled workers [3]	389	377	468	646	624	587	608	620	622	691
Wives and husbands [2][4]	469	440	379	322	302	319	311	322	385	358
Children	1,174	714	695	809	798	757	763	773	777	796
Widowed mothers [7]	108	72	58	52	49	44	42	42	40	41
Widows and widowers [2][8]	452	502	452	445	438	440	444	470	505	496
Parents [2]	1	(Z)	(Z)	(Z)	(Z)	(Z)	(Z)	(Z)	(Z)	(Z)
Special benefits [9]	1	1	(Z)	(Z)	(Z)	(Z)	(Z)	(Z)	(Z)	(Z)

Table 4.8 (*continued*)

BENEFIT PAYMENTS DURING YEAR (bil. dol.)										
Total [11]	120.5	186.2	247.8	332.6	347.1	362.0	375.0	385.8	407.6	431.9
Monthly benefits [12]	120.1	186.0	247.6	332.4	346.9	361.8	374.8	385.6	407.4	431.7
Retired workers [2]	70.4	116.8	156.8	205.3	213.4	223.6	232.3	238.5	253.5	269.0
Disabled workers [3]	12.8	16.5	22.1	36.6	39.6	41.1	43.5	46.5	49.8	54.2
Wives and husbands [2,4]	7.0	11.1	14.5	17.9	18.2	18.6	18.9	18.8	19.4	19.9
Children	10.5	10.7	12.0	16.1	17.1	17.6	18.1	18.6	19.3	20.4
Under age 18	7.4	8.5	9.0	11.9	12.6	13.0	13.3	13.6	14.1	14.8
Disabled children [5]	1.0	1.8	2.5	3.6	3.8	4.0	4.2	4.4	4.6	4.8
Students [6]	2.1	0.4	0.5	0.6	0.6	0.6	0.7	0.7	0.7	0.7
Of retired workers	1.1	1.1	1.3	1.7	1.8	1.9	1.9	2.0	2.1	2.3
Of deceased workers	7.4	7.8	8.6	10.7	11.2	11.7	11.9	12.1	12.5	13.1
Of disabled workers	2.0	1.8	2.2	3.7	4.0	4.1	4.2	4.4	4.7	4.9
Widowed mothers [7]	1.6	1.5	1.4	1.6	1.5	1.5	1.4	1.4	1.4	1.4
Widows and widowers [2,8]	17.6	29.3	40.7	54.8	57.0	59.3	60.5	61.8	63.9	66.8
Parents [2]	0.1	0.1	(Z)	(Z)	(Z)	(Z)	(Z)	(Z)	(Z)	(Z)
Special benefits [9]	0.1	0.1	(Z)	(Z)	(Z)	(Z)	(Z)	(Z)	(Z)	(Z)
Lump sum	0.4	0.2	0.2	0.2	0.2	0.2	0.2	0.2	0.2	0.2

Z. Fewer than 500 or less than $50 million.

1. Number of benefit payments in current-payment status, i.e., actually being made at a specified time with no deductions or with deductions amounting to less than a month's benefit.

2. 62 years and over.

3. Disabled workers under age 65.

4. Includes wife beneficiaries with entitled children in their care and entitled divorced wives.

5. 18 years old and over. Disability began before age 18.

6. Full-time students aged 18–21 through 1984 and aged 18 and 19 beginning 1985.

7. Includes surviving divorced mothers with entitled children in their care and widowed fathers with entitled children in their care.

8. Includes widows aged 60–61, surviving divorced wives aged 60 and over, disabled widows and widowers aged 50 and over; and widowers aged 60–61.

9. Benefits for persons aged 72 and over not insured under regular or transitional provisions of Social Security Act.

10. Constant dollar figures are based on the consumer price index (CPI-U) for December as published by the U.S. Bureau of Labor Statistics.

11. Represents total disbursements of benefit checks by the U.S. Dept. of the Treasury during the years specified.

12. Distribution by type estimated.

Source: United States Census Bureau. (2002). *Statistical Abstract of the United States 2002.* Washington, D.C.: Government Printing Office. Retrieved from http://www.census.gov/prod/2003pubs/02statab/socinsur.pdf.

Table 4.9

Social Security—Beneficiaries, Annual Payments, and Average Monthly Benefit, 1990 to 2001, and by State and Other Areas, 2001

[Number of beneficiaries in current-payment status (**39,832 represents 39,832,000**) and average monthly benefit as of **December.** Data based on 10-percent sample of administrative records.]

Year, state, and other area	Number of beneficiaries (1,000)				Annual payments [2] (mil. dol.)				Average monthly benefit (dol.)		
	Total	Retired workers and dependents [1]	Survivors	Disabled workers and dependents	Total	Retired workers and dependents [1]	Survivors	Disabled workers and dependents	Retired workers [3]	Disabled workers	Widows and widowers [4]
1990	39,832	28,369	7,197	4,266	247,796	172,042	50,951	24,803	603	587	557
1995	43,380	30,139	7,379	5,862	332,581	224,381	67,302	40,898	720	682	680
1998	44,247	30,819	7,091	6,338	374,772	252,659	73,940	48,173	780	734	749
1999	44,599	31,035	7,038	6,526	385,525	258,885	75,309	51,331	804	755	775
2000	45,417	31,761	6,981	6,675	407,431	274,645	77,848	54,938	845	787	810
2001, total [5]	45,874	32,046	6,915	6,913	431,737	290,799	81,359	59,579	875	815	841
United States	44,756	31,354	6,696	6,707	424,880	287,061	79,653	58,167	(NA)	(NA)	(NA)
Alabama	842	522	145	175	7,428	4,467	1,550	1,411	827	784	766
Alaska	57	36	10	11	506	317	101	88	848	796	793
Arizona	813	588	106	119	7,713	5,401	1,260	1,052	888	845	870
Arkansas	521	333	84	104	4,495	2,775	878	843	805	766	745
California	4,247	3,078	591	578	40,358	28,010	7,179	5,169	882	828	873
Colorado	542	382	78	82	5,004	3,365	932	707	852	808	849
Connecticut	580	438	71	72	6,015	4,438	930	647	959	841	931
Delaware	137	98	19	20	1,357	933	239	185	914	843	905
District of Columbia	73	52	12	10	603	403	113	87	741	760	698
Florida	3,235	2,407	413	416	30,455	21,846	4,981	3,629	870	818	867
Georgia	1,125	725	184	216	10,172	6,381	1,967	1,824	844	794	778
Hawaii	189	147	23	19	1,752	1,319	261	171	864	838	811
Idaho	200	144	28	28	1,829	1,263	329	236	854	801	851
Illinois	1,846	1,323	287	236	18,397	12,668	3,614	2,115	915	842	903
Indiana	1,000	699	152	149	9,899	6,698	1,913	1,289	915	824	894
Iowa	541	395	81	65	5,149	3,585	1,012	552	874	788	861
Kansas	441	318	66	57	4,273	2,968	822	484	896	793	891
Kentucky	746	444	128	175	6,578	3,729	1,379	1,470	821	805	757
Louisiana	716	431	153	132	6,248	3,533	1,637	1,077	810	816	771
Maine	254	171	34	49	2,199	1,440	388	371	805	743	797
Maryland	734	525	115	94	7,057	4,835	1,356	867	880	851	851
Massachusetts	1,062	757	138	168	10,161	7,007	1,711	1,444	879	806	872
Michigan	1,658	1,145	259	254	16,827	11,187	3,289	2,351	941	879	902
Minnesota	746	550	106	90	7,048	4,963	1,309	776	867	797	850
Mississippi	523	306	92	125	4,374	2,514	896	964	792	759	714
Missouri	1,013	690	152	171	9,415	6,203	1,773	1,438	863	797	838
Montana	159	112	24	23	1,451	978	278	195	845	800	833
Nebraska	286	209	42	35	2,663	1,866	512	286	856	772	863
Nevada	300	221	36	43	2,869	2,032	435	401	882	873	883
New Hampshire	204	147	26	32	1,970	1,377	325	268	892	816	890
New Jersey	1,356	1,001	185	170	14,221	10,201	2,411	1,609	965	879	931
New Mexico	285	194	46	45	2,451	1,614	474	363	816	783	786
New York	3,015	2,149	410	456	30,142	20,893	5,093	4,156	928	862	893
North Carolina	1,374	922	193	258	12,458	8,193	2,076	2,189	846	789	774
North Dakota	114	82	20	12	1,020	680	239	102	817	765	808
Ohio	1,922	1,337	323	262	18,598	12,289	4,036	2,272	891	811	873
Oklahoma	597	409	99	89	5,429	3,545	1,123	761	835	802	812
Oregon	578	424	77	77	5,536	3,904	957	676	884	812	885
Pennsylvania	2,366	1,704	365	297	23,270	16,036	4,624	2,609	899	831	884
Rhode Island	192	138	22	31	1,821	1,283	274	264	874	797	879
South Carolina	704	457	107	140	6,355	4,041	1,122	1,192	844	803	769
South Dakota	137	98	23	16	1,186	808	251	127	802	742	796
Tennessee	1,011	653	164	194	9,109	5,707	1,787	1,616	842	783	785
Texas	2,673	1,835	477	361	24,367	15,948	5,397	3,021	851	807	816
Utah	246	180	35	31	2,300	1,632	410	257	878	805	892
Vermont	105	73	14	18	973	659	165	149	862	787	843
Virginia	1,053	718	160	175	9,707	6,365	1,831	1,511	852	816	800
Washington	859	626	113	119	8,427	5,918	1,437	1,072	911	823	899
West Virginia	395	235	75	85	3,690	2,054	868	768	862	859	804
Wisconsin	905	669	126	111	8,818	6,274	1,585	959	896	807	884
Wyoming	78	57	10	11	737	516	124	97	872	822	870
Puerto Rico	677	372	120	185	4,231	2,103	869	1,259	577	694	515
Guam	11	7	3	1	71	43	19	8	609	696	593
American Samoa	5	2	1	2	31	9	10	11	522	616	489
Virgin Islands	14	10	2	2	108	76	18	14	739	806	640
Northern Mariana Islands	2	1	1	(Z)	9	5	3	1	478	449	425
Abroad	405	297	92	16	2,381	1,483	782	116	519	701	565

NA. Not available.

Z. Fewer than 500.

1. Includes special benefits for persons aged 72 and over not insured under regular or transitional provisions of Social Security Act.

2. Unnegotiated checks not deducted, 1990 and 1995 include lump-sum payments to survivors of deceased workers.

3. Excludes persons with special benefits.

4. Nondisabled only.

5. Includes those with state or area unknown.

Source: United States Census Bureau. (2002). *Statistical Abstract of the United States 2002.* Washington, D.C.: Government Printing Office. Retrieved from http://www.census.gov/prod/2003pubs/02statab/socinsur.pdf.

Table 4.10
Public Employee Retirement Systems—Participants and Finances: 1980 to 2000

[For fiscal year of retirement system, except data for the Thrift Savings Plan are for calendar year (4,629 represents 4,629,000).]

Retirement plan	Unit	1980	1985	1990	1995	1996	1997	1998	1999	2000, proj.
TOTAL PARTICIPANTS [1]										
Federal retirement systems:										
Defined benefit:										
Civil Service Retirement System	1,000 .	4,629	4,919	4,167	3,731	3,663	3,518	3,423	3,362	(NA)
Federal Employees Retirement System [2]	1,000 .	(X)	(X)	1,180	1,512	1,615	1,679	1,757	1,879	(NA)
Military Service Retirement System [3] . . .	1,000 .	3,380	3,672	3,763	3,387	3,372	3,367	3,368	3,374	(NA)
Thrift Savings Plan [4]	1,000 .	(X)	(X)	1,625	2,195	2,254	2,303	2,300	2,400	(NA)
State and local retirement systems [5] [6]	1,000 .	(NA)	15,234	16,858	14,734	15,153	15,194	16,215	16,195	16,834
ACTIVE PARTICIPANTS										
Federal retirement systems:										
Defined benefit:										
Civil Service Retirement System	1,000 .	2,700	2,800	1,826	1,525	1,343	1,189	1,099	1,042	(NA)
Federal Employees Retirement System [2]	1,000 .	(X)	(X)	1,136	1,318	1,447	1,497	1,547	1,640	(NA)
Military Service Retirement System [3] . . .	1,000 .	2,050	2,192	2,130	1,572	1,525	1,491	1,459	1,438	(NA)
Thrift Savings Plan [4]	1,000 .	(X)	(X)	1,419	1,930	1,987	2,011	1,800	1,900	(NA)
State and local retirement systems [5] [6]	1,000 .	(NA)	10,364	11,345	12,524	13,051	12,817	13,059	13,472	13,917
ASSETS										
Total	Bil. dol..	258	529	1,047	1,655	1,854	2,110	2,403	2,644	2,943
Federal retirement systems	Bil. dol..	73	154	326	537	581	631	686	738	774
Defined benefit	Bil. dol..	73	154	318	502	534	570	608	643	676
Civil Service Retirement System	Bil. dol..	73	142	220	311	329	344	361	376	390
Federal Employees Retirement System [2]	Bil. dol..	(X)	(X)	18	60	70	83	97	111	126
Military Service Retirement System [3] . . .	Bil. dol..	(7)	12	80	131	135	143	150	156	160
Thrift Savings Plan [4]	Bil. dol..	(X)	(X)	8	35	47	61	77	95	98
State and local retirement systems [5]	Bil. dol..	185	374	721	1,118	1,273	1,479	1,717	1,906	2,169
CONTRIBUTIONS										
Total	Bil. dol..	83	106	103	127	129	139	137	142	143
Federal retirement systems	Bil. dol..	19	54	61	67	66	73	73	75	78
Defined benefit	Bil. dol..	19	54	59	61	60	66	65	67	69
Civil Service Retirement System	Bil. dol..	19	27	28	31	32	33	33	33	33
Federal Employees Retirement System [2]	Bil. dol..	(X)	(X)	4	6	6	7	6	8	8
Military Service Retirement System [3] . . .	Bil. dol..	(7)	27	27	24	22	26	26	26	28
Thrift Savings Plan [4]	Bil. dol..	(X)	(X)	2	6	6	7	8	8	9
State and local retirement systems [5]	Bil. dol..	64	52	42	60	63	66	64	67	65
BENEFITS										
Total	Bil. dol..	39	62	89	125	135	142	152	160	172
Federal retirement systems	Bil. dol..	27	40	53	66	70	73	76	78	81
Defined benefit	Bil. dol..	27	40	53	65	69	72	74	76	78
Civil Service Retirement System	Bil. dol..	15	23	31	37	39	41	42	43	44
Federal Employees Retirement System [2]	Bil. dol..	(X)	(X)	(Z)	1	1	1	1	1	1
Military Service Retirement System [3] . . .	Bil. dol..	12	17	22	28	29	30	31	32	33
Thrift Savings Plan [4]	Bil. dol..	(X)	(X)	(Z)	1	1	1	2	2	3
State and local retirement systems [5]	Bil. dol..	12	22	36	59	65	69	76	82	91

NA. Not available.

X. Not applicable.

Z. Less than $500 million.

1. Includes active, separated vested, retired employees, and survivors.

2. The Federal Employees Retirement System was established June 6, 1986.

3. Includes nondisability and disability retirees, surviving families, and all active personnel with the exception of active reserves.

4. The Thrift Savings Plan (a defined contribution plan) was established April 1, 1987.

5. Excludes state and local plans that are fully supported by employee contributions.

6. Not adjusted for double counting of individuals participating in more than one plan.

7. The Military Retirement System was unfunded until October 1, 1984.

Source: United States Census Bureau. (2002). *Statistical Abstract of the United States 2002.* Washington, D.C.: Government Printing Office. Retrieved from http://www.census.gov/prod/2003pubs/02statab/socinsur.pdf.

Table 4.11
Federal Civil Service Retirement: United States, 1980 to 2001

[As of Sept. 30 or for year ending Sept. 30 (2,720 represents 2,720,000). Covers both Civil Service Retirement System and Federal Employees Retirement System.]

Item	Unit	1980	1985	1990	1995	1997	1998	1999	2000	2001
Employees covered [1]	1,000 ..	2,720	2,750	2,945	2,668	2,681	2,658	2,668	2,764	2,655
Annuitants, total	**1,000 ..**	**1,675**	**1,955**	**2,143**	**2,311**	**2,352**	**2,369**	**2,368**	**2,376**	**2,383**
Age and service	1,000 ..	905	1,122	1,288	1,441	1,474	1,488	1,491	1,501	1,509
Disability	1,000 ..	343	332	297	263	257	253	246	242	239
Survivors	1,000 ..	427	501	558	607	621	628	631	633	635
Receipts, total [2]	**Mil. dol.**	**24,389**	**40,790**	**52,689**	**65,684**	**70,227**	**72,156**	**74,522**	**75,967**	**77,949**
Employee contributions	Mil. dol .	3,686	4,679	4,501	4,498	4,358	4,274	4,381	4,637	4,593
Federal government contributions..	Mil. dol .	15,562	22,301	27,368	33,130	35,386	36,188	36,561	37,722	38,442
Disbursements, total [3]	**Mil. dol.**	**14,977**	**23,203**	**31,416**	**38,435**	**41,722**	**43,058**	**43,932**	**45,194**	**47,356**
Age and service annuitants [4]	Mil. dol .	12,639	19,414	26,495	32,070	34,697	35,806	36,492	37,546	39,397
Survivors	Mil. dol .	1,912	3,158	4,366	5,864	6,518	6,763	6,978	7,210	7,533
Average monthly benefit:										
Age and service	Dollars .	992	1,189	1,369	1,643	1,749	1,796	1,830	1,885	1,967
Disability	Dollars .	723	881	1,008	1,164	1,204	1,216	1,221	1,240	1,269
Survivors	Dollars .	392	528	653	819	881	905	923	952	992
Cash and security holdings	Bil. dol. ..	73.7	142.3	238.0	366.2	422.2	451.3	481.3	508.1	542.6

1. Excludes employees in leave without pay status.
2. Includes interest on investments.
3. Includes refunds, death claims, and administration.
4. Includes disability annuitants.

Source: United States Census Bureau. (2002). *Statistical Abstract of the United States 2002.* Washington, D.C.: Government Printing Office. Retrieved from http://www.census.gov/prod/2003pubs/02statab/socinsur.pdf.

Table 4.12
State and Local Government Retirement Systems—Beneficiaries and Finances: United States, 1990 to 2000

[In billions of dollars, except as indicated (4,026 represents 4,026,000). For fiscal years closed during the 12 months ending June 30.]

Year and level of government	Number of beneficiaries (1,000)	Receipts					Benefits and withdrawals			Cash and security holdings
		Total	Employee contributions	Government contributions State	Government contributions Local	Earnings on investments	Total	Benefits	Withdrawals	
1990: All systems	4,026	111.3	13.9	14.0	18.6	64.9	38.4	36.0	2.4	721
State-administered	3,232	89.2	11.6	14.0	11.5	52.0	29.6	27.6	2.0	575
Locally administered	794	22.2	2.2	(Z)	7.0	12.9	8.8	8.4	0.4	145
1995: All systems	4,979	148.8	18.6	16.6	24.4	89.2	61.4	58.8	2.7	1,118
State-administered	4,025	123.3	15.7	16.2	15.4	76.0	48.0	45.8	2.2	914
Locally administered	954	25.5	2.9	0.4	9.0	13.3	13.5	13.0	0.5	204
1999: All systems	5,506	264.3	23.6	17.2	23.4	200.0	85.7	81.8	3.9	1,907
State-administered	4,522	220.7	19.8	16.9	15.4	168.5	67.4	64.3	3.1	1,582
Locally administered	984	43.6	3.8	0.3	8.0	31.5	18.3	17.5	0.8	325
2000: All systems	6,292	297.0	25.0	17.5	22.6	231.9	95.7	91.3	4.4	2,169
State-administered	4,786	247.4	20.7	17.2	16.7	192.8	76.0	72.2	3.8	1,798
Locally administered	1,506	49.7	4.3	0.4	5.9	39.1	19.7	19.1	0.7	371

Z. Less than $50 million.

Source: United States Census Bureau. (2002). *Statistical Abstract of the United States 2002.* Washington, D.C.: Government Printing Office. Retrieved from http://www.census.gov/prod/2003pubs/02statab/socinsur.pdf.

Table 4.13
Private Pension Plans—Summary by Type of Plan: United States, 1990 to 1998

[712.3 represents 712,300. "Pension plan" is defined by the Employee Retirement Income Security Act (ERISA) as "any plan, fund, or program which was heretofore or is hereafter established or maintained by an employer or an employee organization, or by both, to the extent that such plan (a) provides retirement income to employees, or (b) results in a deferral of income by employees for periods extending to the termination of covered employment or beyond, regardless of the method of calculating the contributions made to the plan, the method of calculating the benefits under the plan, or the method of distributing benefits from the plan." A defined benefit plan provides a definite benefit formula for calculating benefit amounts - such as a flat amount per year of service or a percentage of salary times years of service. A defined contribution plan is a pension plan in which the contributions are made to an individual account for each employee. The retirement benefit is dependent upon the account balance at retirement. The balance depends upon amounts contributed, investment experience, and, in the case of profit sharing plans, amounts which may be allocated to the account due to forfeitures by terminating employees. Employee Stock Ownership Plans (ESOP) and 401(k) plans are included among defined contribution plans. Data are based on Form 5500 series reports filed with the Internal Revenue Service.]

Item	Unit	Total				Defined contribution plan				Defined benefit plan			
		1990	1995	1997	1998	1990	1995	1997	1998	1990	1995	1997	1998
Number of plans [1]	1,000. . .	712.3	693.4	720.0	730.0	599.2	623.9	660.5	673.6	113.1	69.5	59.5	56.4
Total participants [2][3] . . .	Million . .	76.9	87.5	95.0	99.5	38.1	47.7	54.6	57.9	38.8	39.7	40.4	41.6
Active participants [2][4] .	Million . .	61.8	66.2	70.7	73.3	35.5	42.7	48.0	50.3	26.3	23.5	22.7	23.0
Contributions [5]	Bil. dol. .	98.8	158.8	177.9	201.9	75.8	117.4	148.1	166.9	23.0	41.4	29.9	35.0
Benefits [6]	Bil. dol. .	129.4	183.0	232.5	273.1	63.0	97.9	135.3	161.9	66.4	85.1	97.2	111.2

1. Excludes all plans covering only one participant.

2. Includes double counting of workers in more than one plan.

3. Total participants include active participants, vested separated workers, and retirees.

4. Any workers currently in employment covered by a plan and who are earning or retaining credited service under a plan. Includes any nonvested former employees who have not yet incurred breaks in service.

5. Includes both employer and employee contributions.

6. Benefits paid directly from trust and premium payments made from plan to insurance carriers. Excludes benefits paid directly by insurance carriers.

Source: United States Census Bureau. (2002). *Statistical Abstract of the United States 2002.* Washington, D.C.: Government Printing Office. Retrieved from http://www.census.gov/prod/2003pubs/02statab/socinsur.pdf.

Table 4.14
401(k) Plans—Summary: 1985 to 1998

[10,339 represents 10,339,000. A 401(k) plan is a qualified retirement plan that allows participants to have a portion of their compensation (otherwise payable in cash) contributed pretax to a retirement account on their behalf.]

Item	1985	1990	1993	1994	1995	1996	1997	1998
Number of plans [1]	29,869	97,614	154,527	174,945	200,813	230,808	265,251	300,593
Active participants [2] (1,000)	10,339	19,548	23,138	26,206	28,061	30,843	33,865	37,114
Assets (bil. dol.)	144	385	616	675	864	1,062	1,264	1,541
Contributions (bil. dol.)	24	49	69	76	87	104	116	135
Benefits (bil. dol.)	16	32	44	51	62	78	93	121
Percentage of all private defined contribution plans:								
Assets	34	54	58	62	65	68	73	74
Contributions	46	65	68	72	74	78	78	81
Benefits	35	51	57	62	64	67	69	75

1. Excludes single-participant plans.

2. May include some employees who are eligible to participate in the plan but have not elected to join. 401(k) participants may participate in one or more additional plans.

Source: United States Census Bureau. (2002). *Statistical Abstract of the United States 2002.* Washington, D.C.: Government Printing Office. Retrieved from http://www.census.gov/prod/2003pubs/02statab/socinsur.pdf.

Table 4.15
Earnings (Retirement) Test for OASDI

Year enacted	Beneficiaries exempt	Earnings subject to test	Amount permitted without reduction in benefits (exempt amount)		Reduction in monthly benefits [1]	Effective year
			Annual earnings	Monthly wages [2]		
			For all beneficiaries			
1935	. . .	Covered	. . .	. . .	Full monthly benefit	. . .
1939	. . .	. . .	. . .	$14.99	. . .	1940
1950	Aged 75 or older	. . .	[3] $600	50.00	. . .	1951
1952	. . .	. . .	[3] 900	75.00	. . .	1953
1954	Aged 72 or older	All [4]	1,200	80.00	One month's full benefit for each $80.00 or fraction thereof	1955
1956	Disabled	. . .	. . .	. . .	. . .	1958
1958	. . .	. . .	. . .	100.00	. . .	1959
1960	. . .	. . .	. . .	. . .	$1 for each $2 of earnings from $1,201–$1,500 $1 for each $1 of earnings above $1,500	1961
1961	. . .	. . .	. . .	. . .	$1 for each $2 of earnings from $1,201–$1,700 $1 for each $1 of earnings above $1,700	1962
1965	. . .	. . .	1,500	125.00	$1 for each $2 of earnings from $1,501–$2,700 $1 for each $1 of earnings above $2,700	1966
1967	. . .	. . .	1,680	140.00	$1 for each $2 of earnings from $1,681–$2,880 $1 for each $1 of earnings above $2,880	1968
1972	. . .	Up to age 72	2,100	175.00	$1 for each $2 of earnings above $2,100	1973
1973	. . .	. . .	2,400	200.00	$1 for each $2 of earnings above $2,400	1974
			[5] 2,520	[5] 210.00	$1 for each $2 of earnings above $2,520	1975
			[5] 2,760	[5] 230.00	$1 for each $2 of earnings above $2,760	1976
			[5] 3,000	[5] 250.00	$1 for each $2 of earnings above $3,000	1977
			For beneficiaries who have not reached full retirement age [6]			
1977	. . .	. . .	[5] $3,240	[5] $270.00	$1 for each $2 of earnings above $3,240	1978
			[5] 3,480	[5] 290.00	$1 for each $2 of earnings above $3,480	1979
			[5] 3,720	[5] 310.00	$1 for each $2 of earnings above $3,720	1980
			[5] 4,080	[5] 340.00	$1 for each $2 of earnings above $4,080	1981
			[5] 4,440	[5] 370.00	$1 for each $2 of earnings above $4,440	1982
			[5] 4,920	[5] 410.00	$1 for each $2 of earnings above $4,920	1983
			[5] 5,160	[5] 430.00	$1 for each $2 of earnings above $5,160	1984
			[5] 5,400	[5] 450.00	$1 for each $2 of earnings above $5,400	1985
			[5] 5,760	[5] 480.00	$1 for each $2 of earnings above $5,760	1986
			[5] 6,000	[5] 500.00	$1 for each $2 of earnings above $6,000	1987
			[5] 6,120	[5] 510.00	$1 for each $2 of earnings above $6,120	1988
			[5] 6,480	[5] 540.00	$1 for each $2 of earnings above $6,480	1989
			[5] 6,840	[5] 570.00	$1 for each $2 of earnings above $6,840	1990
			[5] 7,080	[5] 590.00	$1 for each $2 of earnings above $7,080	1991
			[5] 7,440	[5] 620.00	$1 for each $2 of earnings above $7,440	1992
			[5] 7,680	[5] 640.00	$1 for each $2 of earnings above $7,680	1993
			[5] 8,040	[5] 670.00	$1 for each $2 of earnings above $8,040	1994
			[5] 8,160	[5] 680.00	$1 for each $2 of earnings above $8,160	1995
			[5] 8,280	[5] 690.00	$1 for each $2 of earnings above $8,280	1996
			[5] 8,640	[5] 720.00	$1 for each $2 of earnings above $8,640	1997
			[5] 9,120	[5] 760.00	$1 for each $2 of earnings above $9,120	1998
			[5] 9,600	[5] 800.00	$1 for each $2 of earnings above $9,600	1999

Table 4.15 (*continued*)

Year enacted	Beneficiaries exempt	Earnings subject to test	Amount permitted without reduction in benefits (exempt amount)		Reduction in monthly benefits[1]	Effective year
			Annual earnings	Monthly wages[2]		
			For beneficiaries who have reached full retirement age [6]			
1977	. . .	. . .	[7] $4,000	[7] $333.33	$1 for each $2 of earnings above $4,000	1978
			[7] 4,500	[7] 375.00	$1 for each $2 of earnings above $4,500	1979
			[7] 5,000	[7] 416.66	$1 for each $2 of earnings above $5,000	1980
			[7] 5,500	[7] 458.33	$1 for each $2 of earnings above $5,500	1981
			[7] 6,000	[7] 500.00	$1 for each $2 of earnings above $6,000	1982
1981	Aged 70 or older	Up to age 70	. . .	. . .	. . .	1983
			[5] 6,600	[5] 550.00	$1 for each $2 of earnings above $6,600	1983
			[5] 6,960	[5] 580.00	$1 for each $2 of earnings above $6,960	1984
			[5] 7,320	[5] 610.00	$1 for each $2 of earnings above $7,320	1985
			[5] 7,800	[5] 650.00	$1 for each $2 of earnings above $7,800	1986
			[5] 8,160	[5] 680.00	$1 for each $2 of earnings above $8,160	1987
			[5] 8,400	[5] 700.00	$1 for each $2 of earnings above $8,400	1988
			[5] 8,880	[5] 740.00	$1 for each $2 of earnings above $8,880	1989
1983	. . .	. . .	. . .	. . .	$1 for each $3 of earnings above exempt amount	1990
			[5] 9,360	[5] 780.00	$1 for each $3 of earnings above $9,360	1990
			[5] 9,720	[5] 810.00	$1 for each $3 of earnings above $9,720	1991
			[5] 10,200	[5] 850.00	$1 for each $3 of earnings above $10,200	1992
			[5] 10,560	[5] 880.00	$1 for each $3 of earnings above $10,560	1993
			[5] 11,160	[5] 930.00	$1 for each $3 of earnings above $11,160	1994
			[5] 11,280	[5] 940.00	$1 for each $3 of earnings above $11,280	1995
1996	. . .	. . .	12,500	[8] 1,041.67	$1 for each $3 of earnings above $12,500	1996
			13,500	1,125.00	$1 for each $3 of earnings above $13,500	1997
			14,500	[9] 1,208.33	$1 for each $3 of earnings above $14,500	1998
			15,500	[10] 1,291.67	$1 for each $3 of earnings above $15,500	1999
2000	. . .	. . .	Earnings test eliminated[11]			2000
			For beneficiaries who will not reach full retirement age during year [6]			
2000	. . .	. . .	[5] $10,080	[5] $840	$1 for each $2 of earnings above $10,080	2000
	. . .	. . .	[5] 10,680	[5] 890	$1 for each $2 of earnings above $10,680	2001
			For beneficiaries who will reach full retirement age during year [6]			
2000	. . .	. . .	$17,000	[12] $1,416.67	$1 for each $3 of earnings above $17,000	2000
			25,000	[13] 2,083.33	$1 for each $3 of earnings above $25,000	2001
			30,000	2,500.00	$1 for each $3 of earnings above $30,000	2002

1. Earnings of retired-worker beneficiary affect total monthly family benefit. Earnings of dependent or survivor beneficiary affect only his or her benefit. However, effective January 1985, earnings of retired-worker beneficiary do not affect benefit to divorced spouse who has been divorced at least two years. Effective for benefits after December 1990, the two-year requirement is waived, if the worker was entitled to benefits before the divorce.

2. Monthly test for self-employment income is defined in terms of substantial services. For taxable years beginning after December 31, 1977, monthly test eliminated for both wage and self-employment income except that each individual may use monthly test for one grace year, usually the year of retirement.

3. Applied to self-employment income only.

4. Special provisions for earnings in noncovered employment outside the United States.

5. Became effective due to automatic adjustment provisions mandated by 1972 and 1973 legislation.

6. Age 65 for beneficiaries who attain age 62 (age 60 for widows and widowers) before 2002, gradually increasing to age 67 for beneficiaries who attain age 62 in 2022 or later.

7. Discretionary increase included in 1977 legislation.

8. Actual amount is $1,041.66 ⅔.

9. Actual amount is $1,208.33 ⅓.

10. Actual amount is $1,291.66 ⅔.

11. Public Law 106–182, enacted Apr. 7, 2000, eliminated the earnings test beginning with the month a beneficiary reaches full retirement age (FRA). The annual earnings test that applies in the year of attainment of FRA is based on the annual limits established under P.L. 104–121 (including the $1 for $3 withholding rate). In determining annual earnings for purposes of the annual earnings test under this legislation, only earnings before the month of attainment of FRA will be considered. Public Law 106–182 did not change the annual exempt amount for beneficiaries who are under FRA throughout the year, which continues to be pegged to increases in the average wage.

12. Actual amount is $1,416.66 ⅔.

13. Actual amount is $2,083.33 ⅓.

Source: Social Security Administration. (2001). *Annual Statistical Supplement, 2001 to the Social Security Bulletin.* Baltimore: Social Security Administration, Office of Policy. Retrieved from http://www.ssa.gov/policy/docs/statcomps/supplement/2001/supp01.pdf.

Table 4.16
Earnings Guidelines[1] Regarding Substantial Gainful Activity (SGA): United States, 1961 to 2001

Year	Average monthly amounts of earnings for—		Blind beneficiaries [3]
	Nonblind beneficiaries [2]		
	Maximum	Minimum	
1961–1965	$100	$50	(4)
1966–June 1968	125	75	(4)
July 1968–1973	140	90	(4)
1974–1975	200	130	(4)
1976	230	150	(4)
1977	240	160	(4)
1978	260	170	$334
1979	280	180	375
1980	300	190	417
1981	300	190	459
1982	300	190	500
1983–1989	300	190	(5)
1990	500	300	780
1991	500	300	810
1992	500	300	850
1993	500	300	880
1994	500	300	930
1995	500	300	940
1996	500	300	960
1997	500	300	1,000
1998	500	300	1,050
January–June 1999	500	300	1,110
July 1999	700	300	1,110
January 2000	700	300	1,170
January 2001	[6] 740	300	[7] 1,240

1. Earnings are net of any wage subsidies and impairment-related expenses. SGA guidelines for self-employed individuals differ from the guidelines for wage earners. Self-employment activity is generally examined in terms of time spent and degree of effort, as compared to that of nondisabled self-employed individuals.

2. Earnings above the maximum amount ordinarily demonstrate SGA; earnings below the minimum amount show that SGA has not occurred. When earnings are between the minimum and maximum, other factors are considered.

3. The 1977 amendments provided that, effective 1978, earnings of blind beneficiaries would be evaluated under different SGA guidelines than nonblind beneficiaries.

4. Pre-1978 guidelines are the same as those applicable to nonblind beneficiaries.

5. Annual amounts were determined by automatic adjustments linked to increases in average wage level. The amounts equal the monthly exempt amounts under the earnings test applicable to beneficiaries who have reached full retirement age.

6. Computed as follows: Nonblind SGA amount for 2000, multiplied by the ratio of the 1999 national average wage index to the 1998 index. Rounding is to the nearest multiple of $10. (Had this computation produced a lower SGA level than the 2000 level, the 2000 level would have been used.)

7. Computed as follows: Blind SGA amount for 1994, multiplied by the ratio of the 1999 national average wage index to the 1992 index. Rounding is to the nearest multiple of $10. (Had this computation produced a lower SGA level than the 2000 level, the 2000 level would have been used.)

Source: Social Security Administration. (2001). *Annual Statistical Supplement, 2001 to the Social Security Bulletin*. Baltimore: Social Security Administration, Office of Policy. Retrieved from http://www.ssa.gov/policy/docs/statcomps/supplement/2001/supp01.pdf.

Table 4.17
Minimum and Maximum Monthly Retirement Benefits Payable to Individuals Who Retired at Age 65, United States

Year of attainment of age 65 [1]	Minimum benefit		Maximum benefit			
	Payable at time of retirement	Payable effective December 2000 [2]	Payable at time of retirement		Payable effective December 2000 [2]	
			Men	Women	Men	Women
1940	$10.00	$318.00	$41.20	$41.20	$615.90	$615.90
1941	10.00	318.00	41.60	41.60	615.90	615.90
1942	10.00	318.00	42.00	42.00	623.20	623.20
1943	10.00	318.00	42.40	42.40	623.20	623.20
1944	10.00	318.00	42.80	42.80	623.20	630.00
1945	10.00	318.00	43.20	43.20	630.00	630.00
1946	10.00	318.00	43.60	43.60	637.60	637.60
1947	10.00	318.00	44.00	44.00	643.50	643.50
1948	10.00	318.00	44.40	44.40	643.50	643.50
1949	10.00	318.00	44.80	44.80	649.90	649.90
1950	10.00	318.00	45.20	45.20	658.10	658.10
1951	20.00	318.00	68.50	68.50	658.10	658.10
1952	20.00	318.00	68.50	68.50	658.10	658.10
1953	25.00	318.00	85.00	85.00	726.90	726.90
1954	25.00	318.00	85.00	85.00	726.90	726.90
1955	30.00	318.00	98.50	98.50	726.90	726.90
1956	30.00	318.00	103.50	103.50	768.00	768.00
1957	30.00	318.00	108.50	108.50	802.80	802.80
1958	30.00	318.00	108.50	108.50	802.80	802.80
1959	33.00	318.00	116.00	116.00	802.80	802.80
1960	33.00	318.00	119.00	119.00	822.90	822.90
1961	33.00	318.00	120.00	120.00	829.50	829.50
1962	40.00	318.00	121.00	123.00	837.10	851.20
1963	40.00	318.00	122.00	125.00	843.70	864.10
1964	40.00	318.00	123.00	127.00	851.20	878.40
1965	44.00	318.00	131.70	135.90	851.20	878.40
1966	44.00	318.00	132.70	135.90	857.40	878.40
1967	44.00	318.00	135.90	140.00	878.40	904.30
1968	[3] 55.00	318.00	[3] 156.00	[3] 161.60	891.60	923.90
1969	55.00	318.00	160.50	167.30	917.90	956.40
1970	64.00	318.00	189.80	196.40	943.50	977.10
1971	70.40	318.00	213.10	220.40	962.80	995.10
1972	70.40	318.00	216.10	224.70	977.10	1,015.20
1973	84.50	318.00	266.10	276.40	1,001.80	1,040.80
1974	84.50	318.00	274.60	284.90	1,033.60	1,072.50
1975	93.80	318.00	316.30	333.70	1,072.50	1,131.70
1976	101.40	318.00	364.00	378.80	1,142.20	1,188.90
1977	107.90	318.00	412.70	422.40	1,217.40	1,245.80
1978	114.30	318.00	459.80	459.80	1,280.80	1,280.80
1979	121.80	318.00	503.40	503.40	1,316.50	1,316.50
1980	133.90	318.00	572.00	572.00	1,361.10	1,361.10
1981	153.10	318.00	677.00	677.00	1,409.40	1,409.40
1982	[4] 170.30	318.00	[4] 679.30	[4] 679.30	1,271.10	1,271.10
1983	[4] 166.40	289.30	709.50	709.50	1,236.70	1,236.70
1984	[4] 150.50	252.40	703.60	703.60	1,184.60	1,184.60
1985	(5)	(5)	717.20	717.20	1,167.00	1,167.00
1986	(5)	(5)	760.10	760.10	1,199.50	1,199.50
1987	(5)	(5)	789.20	789.20	1,229.60	1,229.60
1988	(5)	(5)	838.60	838.60	1,254.20	1,254.20
1989	(5)	(5)	899.60	899.60	1,293.40	1,293.40

Table 4.17 (*continued*)

Year of attainment of age 65 [1]	Minimum benefit		Maximum benefit			
	Payable at time of retirement	Payable effective December 2000 [2]	Payable at time of retirement		Payable effective December 2000 [2]	
			Men	Women	Men	Women
1990	(5)	(5)	975.00	975.00	1,339.20	1,339.20
1991	(5)	(5)	1,022.90	1,022.90	1,333.00	1,333.00
1992	(5)	(5)	1,088.70	1,088.70	1,368.20	1,368.20
1993	(5)	(5)	1,128.80	1,128.80	1,377.30	1,377.30
1994	(5)	(5)	1,147.50	1,147.50	1,364.80	1,364.80
1995	(5)	(5)	1,199.10	1,199.10	1,387.30	1,387.30
1996	(5)	(5)	1,248.90	1,248.90	1,408.40	1,408.40
1997	(5)	(5)	1,326.60	1,326.60	1,454.00	1,454.00
1998	(5)	(5)	1,342.80	1,342.80	1,441.50	1,441.50
1999	(5)	(5)	1,373.10	1,373.10	1,455.20	1,455.20
2000	(5)	(5)	1,433.90	1,433.90	1,484.00	1,484.00
2001	(5)	(5)	[6] 1,536.70	[6] 1,536.70	. . .	. . .

1. Assumes the worker began to work at age 22, retired at the beginning of the year, had no earnings after retirement and had no prior period of disability.

2. Final benefit amount payable after Supplementary Medical Insurance (SMI) premium or any other deduction is rounded to next lower $1.

3. Effective for February 1968.

4. Derived from transitional guarantee computation based on 1978 PIA table.

5. Minimum PIA eliminated by 1981 legislation for workers who attain age 62 in 1982 or later. (The minimum is retained until 1991 for members of religious orders who are under a vow of poverty, provided that the order had elected social security coverage before December 29, 1981).

6. The December 1999 cost-of-living adjustment (COLA) was originally determined to be 2.4%, based on the Consumer Price Index (CPI). The underlying CPI was later recomputed by the Bureau of Labor Statistics, a 2.5% COLA would have been consistent with the recomputed CPI. Pursuant to P.L. 106–554, benefits will be calculated and paid in August 2001 and later as if the December 1999 COLA had been 2.5%. Affected beneficiaries will receive a one-time payment to cover the shortfall that occurred before August 2001. The benefit will be adjusted to $1,538.20 to reflect the recomputation of the December 1999 COLA and will be paid retroactivity to January 2001.

Source: Social Security Administration. (2001). *Annual Statistical Supplement, 2001 to the Social Security Bulletin.* Baltimore: Social Security Administration, Office of Policy. Retrieved from http://www.ssa.gov/policy/docs/statcomps/supplement/2001/supp01.pdf.

Table 4.18
Minimum and Maximum Monthly Retirement Benefits Payable to Individuals
Who Retired at Age 62, United States[1]

Year of attainment of age 62 [2]	Minimum benefit		Maximum benefit			
			Payable at time of retirement		Payable effective December 2000 [3]	
	Payable at time of retirement	Payable effective December 2000 [3]	Men	Women	Men	Women
1957	$24.00	$299.50	. . .	$86.80	. . .	$738.10
1958	24.00	299.50	. . .	86.80	. . .	738.10
1959	26.40	299.50	. . .	92.80	. . .	738.10
1960	26.40	298.20	. . .	95.20	. . .	757.20
1961	26.40	296.60	. . .	96.00	. . .	762.60
1962	32.00	295.60	$93.60	96.80	$743.90	769.40
1963	32.00	294.10	94.40	97.60	749.00	774.40
1964	32.00	294.10	95.20	98.40	753.60	779.60
1965	35.20	293.70	102.80	105.40	757.90	777.90
1966	35.20	291.40	102.80	106.20	755.30	780.40
1967	35.20	289.40	105.40	108.80	772.10	796.50
1968	[4] 44.00	285.70	[4] 121.00	[4] 124.80	776.00	801.20
1969	44.00	283.10	124.80	128.40	792.80	815.80
1970	51.20	279.00	146.80	151.90	800.40	828.00
1971	56.40	275.30	163.60	170.50	799.30	833.50
1972	56.40	271.30	167.10	172.90	805.60	833.30
1973	67.60	267.60	207.60	212.90	820.70	842.30
1974	67.60	263.30	217.00	219.70	846.00	856.00
1975	75.10	259.80	253.10	253.10	875.90	875.90
1976	81.20	256.90	285.60	285.60	904.10	904.10
1977	86.40	254.80	319.40	319.40	944.10	944.10
1978	91.50	253.70	354.60	354.60	987.40	987.40
1979	97.60	254.70	[5] 388.90	[5] 388.90	1,016.90	1,016.90
1980	97.60	231.50	[5] 402.80	[5] 402.80	958.30	958.30
1981	97.60	202.20	432.00	432.00	898.70	898.70
1982	[6]	[6]	474.60	474.60	888.30	888.30
1983	[6]	[6]	526.40	526.40	917.00	917.00
1984	[6]	[6]	559.40	559.40	941.60	941.60
1985	[6]	[6]	591.30	591.30	962.10	962.10
1986	[6]	[6]	630.50	630.50	995.00	995.00
1987	[6]	[6]	662.10	662.10	1,031.30	1,031.30
1988	[6]	[6]	686.70	686.70	1,026.70	1,026.70
1989	[6]	[6]	734.00	734.00	1,055.10	1,055.10
1990	[6]	[6]	774.60	774.60	1,063.70	1,063.70
1991	[6]	[6]	810.00	810.00	1,055.40	1,055.40
1992	[6]	[6]	854.10	854.10	1,073.30	1,073.30
1993	[6]	[6]	893.60	893.60	1,090.30	1,090.30
1994	[6]	[6]	948.00	948.00	1,127.50	1,127.50
1995	[6]	[6]	965.90	965.90	1,117.60	1,117.60
1996	[6]	[6]	999.90	999.90	1,127.60	1,127.60
1997	[6]	[6]	1,049.10	1,049.10	1,149.80	1,149.80
1998	[6]	[6]	1,109.60	1,109.60	1,191.10	1,191.10
1999	[6]	[6]	1,183.60	1,183.60	1,254.40	1,254.40
2000	[6]	[6]	1,241.70	1,241.70	1,285.10	1,285.10
2001	[6]	[6]	1,307.30	1,307.30	. . .	. . .

1. Benefit first available at age 62 to female workers effective November 1956 and to male workers effective August 1961.

2. Assumes the worker began to work at age 22, retired at the beginning of the year, had no prior disability, and received the maximum reduction. Through 1999 the assumed reduction was 36 months at ⅚ of 1 percent per month or 20 percent. In 2000, with the increase in the full retirement age to 65 and 2 months, the reduction increased to 20.008333 percent. In 2001 the full retirement age increased to 65 and 4 months for a maximum reduction to 21.666667 percent.

3. Final benefit amount payable after Supplementary Medical Insurance (SMI) premium or any other deduction is rounded to next lower $1.

4. Effective for February 1968.

5. Derived from transitional guarantee computation based on 1978 PIA table.

6. Minimum PIA eliminated by 1981 legislation for workers who attain age 62 in 1982 or later. (The minimum is retained until 1991 for members of religious orders who were under a vow of poverty, provided that the order had elected Social Security coverage before December 29, 1981).

Note: The December 1999 cost-of-living adjustment (COLA) was originally determined to be 2.4 percent, based on the consumer price index (CPI). The underlying CPI was later recomputed by the Bureau of Labor Statistics; a 2.5 percent COLA would have been consistent with the recomputed CPI. Pursuant to P.L. 106–554, benefits will be calculated and paid in August 2001 and later as if the December 1999 COLA had been 2.5 percent. Affected beneficiaries will receive a one-time payment to cover the shortfall that occurred before August 2001.

Source: Social Security Administration. (2001). *Annual Statistical Supplement, 2001 to the Social Security Bulletin.* Baltimore: Social Security Administration, Office of Policy. Retrieved from http://www.ssa.gov/policy/docs/statcomps/supplement/2001/supp01.pdf.

Table 4.19
Amount of Covered Wages Needed to Earn One Quarter of Coverage, Selected Calendar Years 1978 to 2009

1978..	$250
1980..	290
1985..	410
1990..	520
1995..	630
2000..	780
2005..	970[1]
2009..	1,140[1]

1. Based on economic assumptions in the 2000 Annual Report of the Board of Trustees of the Federal OASI and Disability Insurance Trust Funds.

Source: United States House of Representatives, Committee on Ways and Means. (2000). *The 2000 Green Book: Background material and data on programs within the jurisdiction of the Committee on Ways and Means.* Retrieved from http://aspe.hhs.gov/2000gb/sec1.txt.

Table 4.20
Number of Social Security Retired Worker New Benefit Awards and Percent Receiving Reduced Benefits because of Entitlement Before Age 65, Selected Years 1956 to 1999

(in Millions)

Year[1]	Total		Men		Women	
	Number	**Percent**	**Number**	**Percent**	**Number**	**Percent**
1956..	0.9	12	0.6	NA	0.4	31
1960..	1.0	21	0.6	NA	0.4	60
1965..	1.2	49	0.7	43	0.4	60
1970..	1.3	63	0.8	57	0.5	72
1975..	1.5	73	0.9	69	0.6	79
1980..	1.6	76	0.9	73	0.7	80
1985..	1.7	74	1.0	70	0.7	79
1990..	1.7	74	1.0	71	0.7	78
1995..	1.6	72	0.9	69	0.7	75
1999..	1.7	70	0.9	69	0.7	73

1. As of December of given year; data for 1985–1990 based on a 1 percent sample; data for other years based on 100 percent. Includes conversions at age 65 from disability to retirement rolls.
NA—Not applicable.

Source: United States House of Representatives, Committee on Ways and Means. (2000). *The 2000 Green Book: Background material and data on programs within the jurisdiction of the Committee on Ways and Means.* Retrieved from http://aspe.hhs.gov/2000gb/sec1.txt.

Table 4.21
Percentage of Workers Electing Social Security Retirement Benefits at Various Ages, Selected Years: United States, 1940 to 1999[1]

Year	Age 62	Ages 63–64	Age 65	Ages 66 and older	Average age
1940	(2)	(2)	8.3	91.7	68.7
1945	(2)	(2)	17.9	82.1	70.0
1950	(2)	(2)	23.1	76.9	68.5
1955	(2)	(2)	41.2	58.8	68.2
1960	10.0	7.9	35.3	46.7	66.2
1965	23.0	17.7	23.4	35.9	65.9
1970	27.8	23.2	36.9	12.1	64.2
1975	35.7	24.5	31.1	8.7	63.9
1980	40.5	22.2	30.7	6.6	63.7
1985	57.2	21.1	17.7	4.0	63.6
1990	56.6	20.2	16.6	6.7	63.6
1995	58.3	19.5	16.3	6.0	63.6
1999	58.6	18.8	15.6	7.0	63.7

1. The age distribution excludes conversions at age 65 from disability to retirement rolls. Disability conversions are included in the computation of the average age. Age in year of award for 1970–1980. Age in month of award for 1985–1999.

2. Retirement before age 65 was not available.

Source: United States House of Representatives, Committee on Ways and Means. (2000). *The 2000 Green Book: Background material and data on programs within the jurisdiction of the Committee on Ways and Means.* Retrieved from http://aspe.hhs.gov/2000gb/sec1.txt.

Table 4.22
Number of Years to Recover Taxes Plus Interest for Various Workers Retiring at Age 65,[1] Selected Years: United States, 1940 to 2030

Year of retirement	Minimum earner	Average earner	Maximum earner
Illustration 1: Years to recover employee's OASI taxes			
1940..................................	([2])	0.1	0.2
1960..................................	0.5	0.8	1.0
1980..................................	1.5	2.0	2.1
2000..................................	7.2	10.3	11.9
2010..................................	8.9	12.9	18.4
2020..................................	9.4	14.1	22.8
2030..................................	8.5	13.9	24.2
Illustration 2: Years to recover combined employee-employer OASI taxes			
1940..................................	([2])	0.2	0.4
1960..................................	1.0	1.6	2.0
1980..................................	3.0	3.9	4.4
2000..................................	16.6	25.5	38.2
2010..................................	21.1	34.2	61.6
2020..................................	22.5	38.7	131.3
2030..................................	20.0	38.0	([3])
Illustration 3: Years to recover retirement portion of employee's OASI taxes			
1940..................................	([2])	0.1	0.2
1960..................................	0.4	0.6	0.7
1980..................................	1.1	1.4	1.6
2000..................................	5.3	7.4	9.9
2010..................................	6.5	9.3	12.9
2020..................................	7.0	10.3	16.1
2030..................................	6.6	10.5	17.5
Illustration 4: Years to recover retirement portion of combined employee-employer OASI taxes			
1940..................................	([2])	0.2	0.4
1960..................................	0.7	1.1	1.4
1980..................................	2.2	2.8	3.1
2000..................................	11.6	17.1	24.2
2010..................................	14.5	22.1	34.2
2020..................................	15.7	25.2	47.7
2030..................................	14.7	25.9	56.1

1. Under the alternative II assumptions and taking into account benefit increases and continued accrual of interest after retirement but not the taxation of benefits. The retiree is assumed to attain age 65 and retire in January of the designated year. The current law increase in the retirement age is reflected.
2. Less than 0.1 years.
3. Infinite.

Source: United States House of Representatives, Committee on Ways and Means. (2000). *The 2000 Green Book: Background material and data on programs within the jurisdiction of the Committee on Ways and Means.* Retrieved from http://aspe.hhs.gov/2000gb/sec1.txt.

Table 4.23
Poverty Rates for Older Persons, and All Persons in Nineteen Rich Countries During the 1990s

Country	Year	Elderly 40% Level of Poverty Rate	Rank	50% Level of Poverty Rate	Rank	Country	Year	All 40% Level of Poverty Rate	Rank	50% Level of Poverty Rate	Rank
Australia	1994	12.4	1	29.4	1	United States	1997	10.8	1	16.9	1
United States	1997	12.0	2	20.7	2	Italy	1995	9.4	2	14.2	3
Japan	1992	11.4	3	18.4	3	Austria	1995	7.4	3	10.6	7
Israel	1992	11.2	4	17.2	4	Canada	1997	7.3	4	11.9	5
Austria	1995	6.9	5	10.3	11	Australia	1994	7.1	5	14.3	2
Switzerland	1992	4.7	6	8.4	13	Japan	1992	6.9	6	11.8	6
Italy	1995	4.5	7	12.2	7	Switzerland	1992	6.7	7	9.3	10
Belgium	1992	4.2	8	12.1	8	United Kingdom	1995	6.1	8	13.4	4
United Kingdom	1995	4.0	9	13.7	6	Spain	1990	5.2	9	10.1	9
Germany	1994	4.0	9	7.0	14	Israel	1992	5.0	10	10.2	8
Spain	1990	3.9	11	11.3	9	Netherlands	1994	4.9	11	8.1	11
Denmark	1992	3.7	12	11.1	10	Sweden	1995	4.7	12	6.6	16
France	1994	3.4	13	9.8	12	Germany	1994	4.2	13	7.5	13
Netherlands	1994	3.3	14	6.4	16	Denmark	1992	3.8	14	7.2	14
Canada	1997	1.4	15	5.3	17	France	1994	3.4	15	8.0	12
Finland	1995	1.2	16	5.3	17	Norway	1995	3.1	16	6.9	15
Luxembourg	1994	0.9	17	6.7	15	Finland	1995	2.2	17	5.2	17
Norway	1995	0.9	17	14.0	5	Belgium	1992	1.9	18	5.2	17
Sweden	1995	0.8	19	2.7	19	Luxembourg	1994	1.3	19	3.9	19
Overall Average		4.8		11.6		Overall Average		5.4		9.3	

Source: Smeeding, T.M. (2001). *Income maintenance in old age: What can be learned from cross-national comparisons.* Working Paper for the Center for Retirement Research, No. 2001-11. Chestnut Hill, MA: Boston College. Retrieved from http://www.bc.edu/centers/crr/papers/wp_2001-11.pdf.

Table 4.24
Within Decile Gross Income Composition of the Aged[1]

	All Aged			Single Women 65+		
	Decile 1	Decile 5	Decile 10	Decile 1	Decile 5	Decile 10
United States						
Earnings	2.61	9.58	37.90	0.63	1.88	17.17
Capital or Property Income	6.12	9.16	23.16	9.28	5.79	34.64
Occupational Pension	3.68	14.68	20.05	2.65	6.56	21.22
Social Retirement	69.73	65.73	18.75	68.63	84.25	26.75
Safety Net and Other Income	17.87	0.85	0.14	18.81	1.54	0.21
United Kingdom						
Earnings	0.00	1.98	25.30	0.00	0.27	3.14
Capital or Property Income	4.03	7.74	28.62	3.77	2.49	32.57
Occupational Pension	3.37	16.14	30.15	2.98	4.44	37.48
Social Retirement	85.04	65.52	15.32	85.51	64.65	26.75
Safety Net and Other Income	7.56	8.51	0.62	7.74	28.14	0.06
Canada						
Earnings	1.23	5.42	30.22	0.06	0.18	5.97
Capital or Property Income	2.21	8.23	20.37	1.64	6.39	25.39
Occupational Pension	1.66	14.77	27.25	2.72	3.44	32.97
Social Retirement	87.04	68.14	20.07	88.42	85.33	19.92
Safety Net and Other Income	7.85	3.56	2.08	7.15	4.69	1.89
Germany						
Earnings	0.71	5.42	25.29	0.80	1.26	6.16
Capital or Property Income	0.34	8.23	10.47	0.20	0.32	17.24
Occupational Pension	1.02	14.77	28.92	1.01	15.70	31.20
Social Retirement	88.87	68.14	34.09	85.38	80.80	43.29
Safety Net and Other Income	9.07	3.56	1.22	12.61	1.92	2.10
Netherlands						
Earnings	0.21	1.71	11.14	0.00	0.00	0.87
Capital or Property Income	1.89	0.78	14.70	2.25	1.29	16.78
Occupational Pension	5.99	7.97	48.61	5.99	11.96	51.63
Social Retirement	81.54	88.35	24.73	74.91	82.20	30.23
Safety Net and Other Income	10.37	1.19	0.82	16.85	4.55	0.49
Sweden						
Earnings	0.38	1.74	16.46	0.00	0.15	5.09
Capital or Property Income	7.01	7.09	12.37	7.28	12.09	10.65
Social Retirement[2]	76.80	90.58	71.17	78.98	74.66	84.18
Safety Net and Other Income	15.80	0.60	0.00	13.74	13.10	0.08
Australia						
Earnings	1.17	0.95	42.93	0.00	0.00	10.01
Capital or Property Income	16.44	15.63	40.50	23.04	6.15	46.44
Occupational Pension	2.17	2.94	9.56	3.79	1.88	29.55
Social Insurance[3]	75.73	80.47	6.22	64.89	91.97	12.61
Safety Net and Other Income	4.50	0.02	0.78	8.28	0.00	1.40

Notes:

1. Incomes are adjusted for family size using an equivalence elasticity of $E=0.5$ where $EGI=GI/s^E$ and GI is gross income.
2. In Sweden, occupational pensions are included with social retirement.
3. In Australia, social insurance and other income includes small programs for veterans, disabled, and unemployed.

Source: Smeeding, T.M. (2001). *Income maintenance in old age: What can be learned from cross-national comparisons.* Working Paper for the Center for Retirement Research, No. 2001-11. Chestnut Hill, MA: Boston College. Retrieved from http://www.bc.edu/centers/crr/papers/wp_2001-11.pdf.

Figure 4.1
Generosity of the Safety Net: Minimum Old Age Benefit[a] as Percentage of Adjusted Median Income[b] for Single Persons in Eight Nations

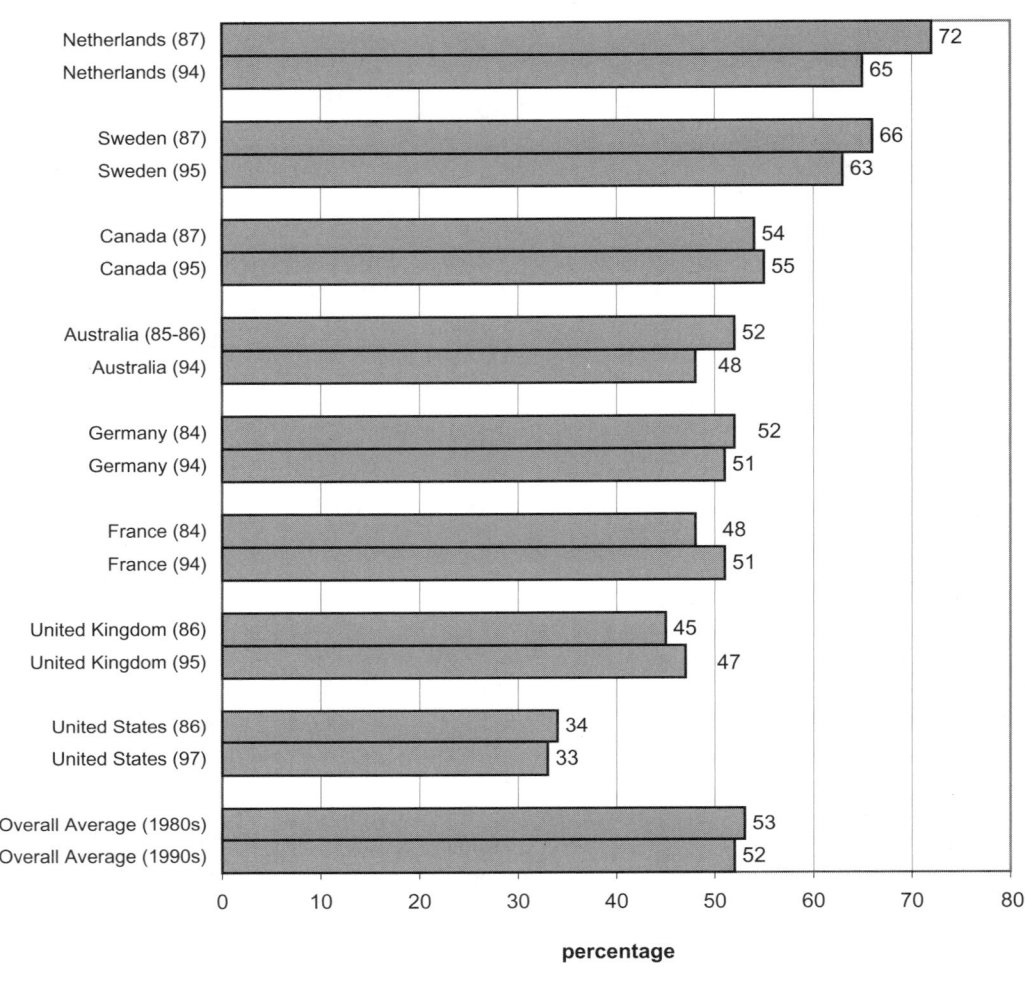

a. Minimum benefits as published by the Organization for Economic Cooperation and Development (OECD) were compared with adjusted median income after adjusting for national price changes using LIS data for the first period. In the second period, updated data was obtained from OECD sources; U.S. Congress (2000), and compared to bunching of incomes for the elderly using LIS data on elderly and overal median incomes.

b. Income is adjusted using the simple equivalence scale that counts the first person as 1.0 and all other persons as 0.5 regardless of age. This is slightly different from the scale where the scale is calculated as S^E and $E = 0.5$. See Burkhauser, Smeeding, and Merz (1996) for more on this topic. Elderly persons are 65 and over.

Source: Smeeding, T.M. (2001). *Income maintenance in old age: What can be learned from cross-national comparisons.* Working Paper for the Center for Retirement Research, No. 2001-11. Chestnut Hill, MA: Boston College. Retrieved from http://www.bc.edu/centers/err/papers/wp_2001-11.pdf.

Table 4.25
Pension Contribution Rates in OECD Countries

	Per cent of average earnings	
	1967	1995
United States	7.1	12.4
Japan	5.5	16.5
Germany	14.0	18.6
France	8.5	19.8
Italy	15.8	29.6
United Kingdom	6.5	13.9
Canada	5.9	5.4
Austria	16.5	22.8
Belgium	12.5	16.4
Denmark	1.0	1.0
Finland	6.5	17.9
Ireland	5.2	15.7
Netherlands	10.2	14.5
Norway	12.8	22.0
Portugal	13.5	13.9
Spain	16.0	28.3
Sweden	6.4	19.8
Switzerland	4.0	8.4

Source: Organization of Economic Co-operation and Development. (2003). *Tables and Figures on Ageing*. OECD Web site. Retrieved from http://www.oecd.org/dataoecd/27/44/2345400.pdf. OECD Copyright. Reproduced by permission of the OECD.

Table 4.26
Tax Concessions for Pension Benefits and Other Income/Savings in OECD Countries

	Concessions for Pensioners of Public Schemes	Other Concessions for Aged People
Australia	Income Tax • Benefits of Age Pension (funded by general taxation) are taxable. • Pensioner Tax Rebate (ensuring that a pensioner does not pay tax until private income exceeds the value of the pension and the income test free area)	Income Tax • Tax-rebate for low-income self-funded retiree phased in to provide same tax concession as for pensioners • Superannuation contributions with tax concessions (though there will be a tax surcharge of up to 15% on contributions by the wealthy) • Savings rebate (from July 1998) will apply to (undeducted) superannuation contributions, or net income receipt from savings and investment, or a combination of both, up to an annual cap of A$3,000. The full rebate will be A$450 a year in 1999-2000 income year. Capital Gains Tax • Concessions from Capital Gains Tax on the income received from selling the small enterprise for the reason of retirement
Austria	Income Tax • Contributions to the scheme are tax deductible (for both employee and employer, including additional voluntary contributions), though benefits are taxed as earned income. • Pensioners Tax Credit of ATS 5,500 per annum • Only 25% of the pension secured by additional voluntary contributions is taxed.	Income Tax • Tax credit for extraordinary costs entailed by physical/mental disability (The elderly people are major beneficiaries of the credit. This credit is not available when the applicant receives such benefits as long-term care benefit (*Pflegegeld*), special, partially lump-sum amounts for expenses for some chronic diseases or for some specific devices (such as wheelchairs) can still be claimed.) Contributions to Social Security Programmes • Retirees only have to pay social security contributions to the health insurance scheme. Moreover, the rates are smaller than those for younger persons.
Belgium	Income Tax • Contributions to the scheme are tax deductible (for both employee and employer), though benefits are taxed as replacement income. • Pensioners are awarded of tax deduction, based on the number of dependants and the level of income. Contributions to Social Security Programmes • Other than "solidarity contributions"(imposed on pension benefits above certain amount), pensioners do not have to pay contributions to the social insurance schemes.	

Table 4.26 (*continued*)

	Concessions for Pensioners of Public Schemes	Other Concessions for Aged People
Canada	Income Tax • Benefit of Old Age Security basic pension (funded by general taxation) is taxable. • Guaranteed Income Supplement and Spouses Allowances are not taxable. (Old Age Security basic pension and Guaranteed Income Supplement are going to be merged, along with the Age and Pension Income Tax Credits, into non-taxable Senior Benefit from January 2001.) • Employer contributions to Canada Pension Plan (CPP) are tax deductible. Employee contributions are not directly deductible, but subject to a tax credit. Benefit of CPP is taxable. • Some provincial income-tested supplements to pensioners are also non-taxable.	Income Tax • Age Credit (deduction of "old age" amount from federal tax payable) -- The amount in full is C$3,482 in 1995. -- There is an income limit for the credit (C$25,921). The excess amount will also be a base for the claim of the credit reduced at a rate of 15%. The credit, or a portion of the credit, may be transferred from one spouse to the other in cases where one spouse does not require the full credit to reduce his/her tax to zero. • Pension Income Credit (Taxfilers with pension income from employer-sponsored pension or Registered Retirement Savings Plan annuity may claim a credit depending on the amount of the income. C$1,000 maximum.) • In case of annuities purchased with no tax-assisted savings, only the portion of investment earnings is taxable.
Czech Republic	Income Tax • Contributions are tax deductible, and benefits are tax free.	
Denmark	Income Tax • Contributions to the ATP scheme are tax deductible (for both employee and employer). Benefits of the old-age pension (*folkepension.* funded by general taxation) and ATP pension are taxed as earned income. Supplementary benefits to pensioners are not taxable.	Property Tax • Tax related to owner-occupier housing is reduced by 50% for persons from age 67

	Concessions for Pensioners of Public Schemes	Other Concessions for Aged People
Finland	Income Tax • Contributions to the scheme are tax deductible (for both employee and employer), though benefits are taxed as earned income with the exceptions of supplements (for a child or spouse, etc.) to the basic pension benefits. [Concession from tax on specific income deriving from pension benefit] • Pension benefit, when below the average amount, is subject to less taxation compared to other source of income of the same size. When above the average, it is subject to more taxation than other source of income of the same size. [Concession from tax on income in general for the reason of being pensioners] • Pension income deduction, in municipal and state taxation, which ensures that no income tax is paid from the pension benefit in case the pensioner has no other taxable income.	Income Tax • Tax allowance for the disabled (A rather large part of pensioners are entitled to this allowance.)
France	Income Tax • Contributions to the scheme are tax deductible (for both employer and employee), though benefits are taxed after deduction of allowances similar to those applied to salary.	Income Tax • Pension benefits from individual plans are normally partially taxed on a fixed scale, based on the pensioner's age.
Germany	Income Tax • Contributions to the scheme are tax deductible (for both employee (up to a certain amount) and employer). • Statutory pension benefits are only taxable for the portion which corresponds to the notional interest for the pension saving. • Civil servants' pensions are fully subject to income tax except for base amount reduction ranging from 40% of the benefits to 6,000DM per calendar year.	Income Tax • Income from sources other than pensions is fully subject to income tax except for base amount reduction ranging from 40% of such income to 3,720DM per calendar year.

Table 4.26 (*continued*)

	Concessions for Pensioners of Public Schemes	Other Concessions for Aged People
Greece	Income Tax • Contributions to the scheme are tax deductible (for both employee and employer), though benefits are taxed as income.	Income Tax • Contributions to private saving schemes are tax-deductible. Maximum tax allowance: 200,000 drs/year or 15% of premium expenditure (whichever lower) • Presumptive taxation provisions do not apply to professionals over the age of 65 who have been practising for at least 10 years.
Hungary	Income Tax • Pension benefit is tax-free, because contributions to the scheme are taxed.	
Iceland	Income Tax • Pension benefits (including supplementary benefits) are taxable income.	
Ireland	Income Tax • Employer contributions to the social security scheme are in general tax deductible, but employee contributions are not. Benefits are usually taxed as earned income. • Employer and employee contributions to occupational and private pension schemes and income from the investment of the contributions are tax deductible up to certain limits. Benefits are taxed, but part of the supplementary pension can be received as a tax free lump-sum payment up to 1.5 times of final salary. • Other social security benefits from public authorities may be exempt from taxes.	Income Tax • Income Tax Age Allowance (£Ir400 for single/widowed persons and £Ir 800 for married couple) • Exemption limits for rent allowances become higher at the age of 55, 65, and 75. Contributions to Social Security Programmes • Those aged 66 or over do not have to pay contributions to the pension scheme, even if they are in employment/self-employment.
Italy	Income Tax • Contributions to the scheme are tax deductible (for both employee and employer). • Benefits are usually taxed, except for disability benefits. Contributions to Social Security Programmes • Pensioners do not have to pay contributions to the Health Care Services out of their pensions.	

	Concessions for Pensioners of Public Schemes	Other Concessions for Aged People
Japan	Income Tax • Contributions to the scheme are tax deductible (for both employee and employer), though benefits are taxed as miscellaneous income. • There are several deductions for pensioners, thus making the majority of pensioners not having to pay taxes.	Contributions to Social Security Programmes • Contribution rules for National Health Insurance (for self-employed people, etc.) are favourable to the elderly
Korea	Income Tax • Public pension benefit is tax-free (though the contribution to the scheme is not exempted from income tax base).	Income Tax • Contributions to private pension schemes are exempted from income tax base.
Luxembourg	Income Tax • Contributions to the scheme are tax deductible (for both employee and employer), though benefits are taxed as income.	
Mexico	Income Tax • Employer contributions to the scheme are tax deductible, but employee contributions are not. Benefits are usually not taxed.	Income Tax • Maximum tax free benefits are established in some cases such as savings funds and social welfare
Netherlands	Income Tax • Contributions to the scheme are tax deductible (for both employee and employer), though benefits are taxed as income.	
New Zealand	Income Tax • Benefits of NZ Superannuation (funded by general taxation) are subject to personal income tax. • Tax base increase test (surcharge) for those receiving NZ Superannuation: removed from April 1998	
Norway	Income Tax • Employer contributions to the scheme are tax deductible, but employee contributions are not. Benefits are taxed as earned income. Supplementary benefits to pensioners are not taxable. Contributions to Social Security Programmes • Old-age pensioners only have to pay contributions to the Health Insurance Scheme.	Income Tax • General tax relief rule (income-tested, includes generally the elderly and some other groups) • Special deduction in taxes due to age

(*continued*)

Table 4.26 (*continued*)

	Concessions for Pensioners of Public Schemes	Other Concessions for Aged People
Poland	Income Tax • Employer contributions to the scheme are tax deductible. (Note: no employee contributions in the current scheme) Benefits are subject to income tax.	
Portugal	Income Tax • Contributions to the scheme are tax deductible (for both employee and employer), though benefits are taxed income. • Retirement pension income follows a different tax processing from that of income tax in general (more advantageous deduction than other category of income). In terms of tax benefits, they are provided when the debtor is disabled. • The social security general system pensions are exempted from the Individual Tax up to a certain amount. (There are further favourable concessions to invalidity pension.)	
Slovak Republic	Income Tax • Contributions are tax deductible, and benefits are tax free.	
Spain	Income Tax • Contributions to the scheme are tax deductible (for both employee and employer), though benefits are usually taxed as earned income. • Disability pensions are tax exempt.	
Sweden	Income Tax • Contributions to the scheme are tax deductible (for both employee and employer), though benefits are taxed as income. • Special basic deduction for those whose basic pension exceeds SEK 6,000 a year → Maximum amount of deduction is equal to the sum of basic pension and pension supplement, reduced if there are other sources of income such as ATP, employment pensions, etc. • Supplementary benefits to pensioners are not taxable, such as means-tested housing supplement.	

	Concessions for Pensioners of Public Schemes	Other Concessions for Aged People
Switzerland	Income Tax • Contributions to the public scheme (AVS, 1st pillar) are tax deductible (for both employee and employer), though benefits are taxed. This is the same as the private compulsory scheme (occupational provident fund, 2nd pillar). • Supplementary AVS (old-age and survivors' insurance) and AI (disability insurance) benefits are non-taxable.	Income Tax • A person who have made a saving under the linked individual provident fund (3rd pillar) benefits form preferential tax treatment (reduced rate at the time of the payment from the funds when the insurance risk occured, and contributions deductible from income). • In some cantons, if retirees are in need of care, they may deduct associated expenses from their taxable income (though there are some restrictions).
Turkey	Income Tax • Contributions to the scheme are tax deductible (for both employee and employer), and benefits are tax free.	Property Tax • Estate duty (tax) on retirees is exempted when they have only one house.
United Kingdom	Income Tax • Employer contributions to the scheme are tax deductible, but employee contributions are not. Benefits are usually taxed as earned income. • Benefits that are more likely to be received by pensioners are subject to different treatment in the tax system (e.g. Some of the disability benefits are not taxable).	Income Tax • Higher personal allowance in income tax for the elderly (£5,220-5,440 against £4,045 as a standard), as well as higher married couples allowance (£3,185-3,225 against £1,830 as a standard) • These age-related allowances can be tapered away at the rate of 50% when income rises above £15,600. Contributions to Social Security Programmes • Elderly do not have to pay the National Insurance Contributions after the state pension age.

United States	Income Tax
	• Employer contributions to the scheme are tax deductible, but employee contributions are not. Benefits are taxed after some favourable adjustment.
	• Some social security benefits are non-taxable. (They are not limited to the elderly, though they are the majority.)
		Income Tax
		• Larger standard deduction for the elderly
		  -- $1,000 for unmarried person, and additional $800 per person aged 65 or older in case of married couple
		  -- However, people rather select itemised specific deductions on various grounds such as home mortgage interest payments and charitable contributions.
		• There is a relatively small program of special tax credit for very low-income elderly and disabled people (most beneficiaries are under age 65).
		Property Tax
		• In many States and local governments, property tax is favourably applied to elderly homeowners.

Source: Organization of Economic Co-operation and Development. (2003). *Tables and Figures on Ageing*. OECD Web site. Retrieved from http://www.oecd.org/dataoecd/27/44/2345400.pdf. OECD Copyright. Reproduced by permission of the OECD.

Table 4.27
Social Expenditures on the Elderly as a Percent of the GDP in OECD Countries[1]

	1980	1981	1982	1983	1984	1985	1986	1987	1988	1989	1990	1991	1992	1993	1994	1995	1996	1997
United States	5.9	6.1	6.4	6.4	6.1	6.0	6.0	5.9	5.8	5.8	5.9	6.1	6.1	6.2	6.1	6.1	6.0	6.0
Japan	4.0	4.3	4.6	4.7	4.8	4.9	5.2	5.3	5.2	5.2	5.1	5.1	5.3	5.6	5.9	6.3	6.4	6.5
Germany	10.5	10.6	10.8	10.7	10.6	10.5	10.4	10.5	10.4	10.2	9.8	9.7	9.9	10.2	10.4	10.7	10.8	10.9
France	9.5	9.8	10.1	10.3	10.5	10.7	10.7	10.7	10.8	10.3	10.9	11.2	11.5	12.0	12.0	12.1	12.3	12.3
Italy	9.0	10.0	10.4	11.2	11.0	11.4	11.7	11.7	11.6	11.8	13.4	13.8	14.9	15.2	15.4	15.2	15.4	15.8
United Kingdom	7.1	7.6	7.7	7.6	7.6	7.3	7.3	7.1	6.6	6.4	7.1	7.6	7.7	7.8	7.6	7.5	7.3	7.1
Canada	3.1	3.2	3.5	3.6	3.7	3.8	3.9	4.1	4.0	4.1	4.3	4.6	4.8	4.9	4.8	4.8	4.8	4.8
Australia[2]	4.0	4.0	4.0	4.1	3.9	3.7	3.6	3.6	3.2	3.1	3.2	3.4	3.4	3.5	3.4	4.7	4.7	4.6
Austria	11.5	..	..	..	..	12.4	..	..	..	..	12.3	12.4	12.4	12.9	13.1	13.1	13.1	12.9
Belgium	9.3	9.8	9.9	10.1	9.9	9.8	9.9	9.7	9.7	9.4	9.4	9.7	9.8	10.1	10.0	10.0	10.1	10.0
Czech Republic	..	..	..	..	..	..	..	..	..	..	..	6.4	6.6	6.4	6.3	6.2	6.4	7.3
Denmark	6.0	6.0	6.0	5.9	5.9	5.8	5.7	5.8	6.0	6.3	6.3	6.5	6.5	6.6	7.6	7.4	7.2	7.0
Finland	5.5	5.8	6.0	6.4	7.2	7.4	7.4	7.6	7.3	7.1	7.4	8.6	9.6	9.5	9.2	8.9	9.1	8.5
Greece	6.0	6.6	8.4	8.5	9.1	9.7	9.8	10.1	9.9	10.3	11.1	10.5	10.5	10.8	10.6	10.8	11.3	11.3
Iceland	..	..	..	..	..	..	..	..	..	..	..	..	..	..	4.1	4.2	4.2	4.2
Ireland	5.3	5.4	5.8	5.9	5.8	5.7	5.7	5.6	5.4	5.0	5.0	5.1	5.1	5.0	4.8	4.5	4.2	3.8
Korea	..	..	..	..	..	..	..	..	..	..	0.8	0.8	0.8	0.9	1.0	1.1	1.0	1.1
Luxembourg	10.2	10.8	10.4	10.2	9.7	9.6	9.4	9.5	9.2	9.0	9.0	9.6	9.7	9.7	9.4	9.7	9.6	9.2
Mexico[3]	..	..	..	..	..	0.3	0.3	0.5	0.5	0.6	0.5	0.6	0.6	0.6	0.6	3.3	3.8	4.6
Netherlands	7.6	7.6	7.9	7.8	7.6	7.6	7.7	7.9	7.9	7.8	8.4	8.3	8.3	8.3	7.8	7.5	7.4	7.3
New Zealand	7.6	7.6	8.3	8.1	7.6	7.9	7.4	7.1	6.9	7.2	7.5	8.0	7.3	6.7	6.2	5.9	5.7	5.6
Norway	5.1	..	..	..	..	5.2	..	..	6.2	6.3	6.3	6.3	6.4	6.4	6.4	6.2	6.0	5.9
Poland	..	..	..	..	..	..	..	..	..	..	5.6	8.7	10.3	10.6	10.6	10.4	10.3	10.6
Portugal	4.1	4.5	4.2	4.7	4.6	4.5	4.7	5.1	5.0	5.0	5.3	5.7	6.1	6.7	6.8	7.3	7.7	8.0
Spain	6.3	6.8	7.0	7.2	7.4	7.6	7.5	7.4	7.4	7.4	7.8	8.0	8.4	8.8	8.8	8.9	9.1	9.0
Sweden	7.2	7.7	7.8	7.9	7.6	7.8	7.9	7.8	7.9	8.0	7.9	8.3	9.0	9.2	9.0	8.6	8.6	8.4
Switzerland	6.1	5.7	6.2	6.1	6.5	6.3	6.3	6.3	6.3	6.0	6.0	6.2	6.5	6.9	6.9	7.1	7.0	7.2
Turkey	1.7	1.7	1.9	2.1	1.9	1.8	1.8	1.8	2.0	2.4	3.2	3.3	3.6	3.6	3.7	3.7	4.3	5.3

1. Includes old age cash benefits plus survivors benefits.
2. Prior to 1995, data on "superannuation pensions" and "superannuation lumpsum" are not available.
3. Prior to 1995, social expenditure were underestimated, particularly with regard to old age cash benefits.

Source: Organization of Economic Co-operation and Development. (2003). *Tables and Figures on Ageing.* OECD Web site. Retrieved from http://www.oecd .org/dataoecd/27/44/2345400.pdf. OECD Copyright. Reproduced by permission of the OECD.

Table 4.28
Longevity Estimates and Projections in OECD Countries

Medium variant estimates and projections for the period shown

	Life expectancy, men			Life expectancy, women			Life expectancy, men and women		
	1960-65	1995-2000	2045-50	1960-65	1995-2000	2045-50	1960-65	1995-2000	2045-50
United States	66.7	73.4	79.0	73.4	80.1	84.6	70.0	76.7	81.8
Japan	66.5	76.8	80.8	71.6	82.9	86.9	69.0	80.0	83.8
Germany	67.4	73.9	79.1	72.9	80.2	84.7	70.3	77.2	81.9
France	67.6	74.2	79.1	74.5	82.0	86.2	71.0	78.1	82.6
Italy	67.4	75.0	79.8	72.6	81.2	85.5	69.9	78.2	82.6
United Kingdom	67.9	74.5	79.4	73.8	79.8	84.6	70.8	77.2	82.0
Canada	68.5	76.1	80.4	74.6	81.8	86.0	71.4	79.0	83.2
Australia	67.8	75.5	80.0	74.2	81.1	85.4	70.9	78.3	82.7
Austria	66.1	73.7	79.0	72.6	80.2	84.7	69.3	77.0	81.7
Belgium	67.9	73.8	79.1	73.9	80.6	85.0	70.8	77.2	82.0
Czech Republic	67.4	70.3	78.1	73.4	77.4	84.3	70.5	73.9	81.2
Denmark	70.3	73.0	77.9	74.4	78.3	83.1	72.3	75.7	80.5
Finland	65.4	73.0	79.6	72.5	80.6	86.0	68.9	76.8	82.7
Greece	67.9	75.6	80.0	71.2	80.7	85.1	69.5	78.1	82.5
Hungary	66.4	66.8	75.8	71.0	74.9	81.5	68.6	70.9	78.7
Iceland	70.8	76.8	81.2	76.1	81.3	85.6	73.4	79.0	83.4
Ireland	68.4	73.6	80.0	72.3	79.2	85.1	70.3	76.4	82.6
Korea	53.6	68.8	76.9	56.9	76.0	82.9	55.2	72.4	79.9
Luxembourg	65.7	73.3	78.9	72.1	79.9	84.7	68.8	76.7	81.8
Mexico	56.4	69.5	76.5	60.6	75.5	82.7	58.3	72.2	78.8
Netherlands	71.1	75.0	79.5	75.8	80.7	85.1	73.4	77.9	82.3
New Zealand	68.3	74.1	79.3	73.9	79.7	84.5	71.0	76.9	81.9
Norway	71.1	75.2	80.8	75.9	81.1	86.7	73.4	78.1	83.7
Poland	65.8	68.2	76.5	71.0	76.9	83.2	68.3	72.5	79.9
Portugal	61.4	71.8	78.1	67.1	78.8	84.1	64.2	75.3	81.1
Spain	67.9	74.5	79.4	72.7	81.5	85.7	70.2	78.0	82.5
Sweden	71.6	76.3	81.4	75.6	80.8	85.9	73.5	78.6	83.6
Switzerland	68.9	75.4	79.9	74.6	81.8	86.0	71.7	78.7	82.9
Turkey	50.5	66.5	76.0	53.7	71.7	81.3	52.1	69.0	78.6

Source: Organization of Economic Co-operation and Development. (2003). *Tables and Figures on Ageing.* OECD Web site. Retrieved from http://www .oecd.org/dataoecd/27/44/2345400.pdf. OECD Copyright. Reproduced by permission of the OECD.

Table 4.29
Social Security Trust Funds: 1980 to 2001

[In billions of dollars (103.5 represents $103,500,000,000).]

Type of trust fund	1980	1990	1995	1996	1997	1998	1999	2000	2001
Old-age and survivors insurance (OASI):									
Net contribution income [1]	103.5	272.4	310.1	328.0	357.4	380.4	407.3	433.0	453.4
Interest received [2]	1.8	16.4	32.8	35.7	39.8	44.5	49.8	57.5	64.7
Benefit payments [3]	105.1	223.0	291.6	302.9	316.3	326.8	334.4	352.7	372.3
Assets, end of year	22.8	214.2	458.5	514.0	589.1	681.6	798.8	931.0	1,071.5
Disability insurance (DI):									
Net contribution income [1]	13.3	28.7	54.7	57.7	56.5	59.5	63.9	71.8	75.7
Interest received [2]	0.5	0.9	2.2	3.0	4.0	4.8	5.7	6.9	8.2
Benefit payments [3]	15.5	24.8	40.9	44.2	45.7	48.2	51.4	55.0	59.6
Assets, end of year	3.6	11.1	37.6	52.9	66.4	80.8	97.3	118.5	141.0

1. Includes deposits by states and deductions for refund of estimated employee-tax overpayment. Beginning in 1990, includes government contributions on deemed wage credits for military service in 1957 and later. Includes taxation of benefits beginning in 1990.

2. In 1990, includes interest on advance tax transfers. Beginning 1990, includes interest on reimbursement for unnegotiated checks.

3. Includes payments for vocational rehabilitation services furnished to disabled persons receiving benefits because of their disabilities. Beginning in 1990, amounts reflect deductions for unnegotiated benefit checks.

Source: United States Census Bureau. (2002). *Statistical Abstract of the United States 2002.* Washington, D.C.: Government Printing Office. Retrieved from http://www.census.gov/prod/2003pubs/02statab/socinsur.pdf.

5. Unemployment and Disability Insurance and Other Worker Benefits

One of the key elements of a social safety net is in the area of worker benefits. In this country, worker benefits include retirement benefits through social security, assistance with medical care coverage via Medicare, unemployment insurance, disability insurance (also through Medicare), fair labor practice laws and regulations, retirement program oversight, and legislated work safety conditions. The focus of this chapter, however, is limited to the unemployment insurance.

Work, especially in the American culture, is one of the key aspects of self-identity as well as the means to engender sufficient wealth to increase personal property and rise in social standing. With increased wealth comes increased participation in social affairs and political influence. Therefore, work has a psychological as well as economic, social, and political meaning. It is the means through which social conformity is reached. To quote from Thorstein Veblen's *Theory of the Leisure Class*, "For the great body of people in any modern community, the proximate ground of expenditure in excess of what is required for physical comfort is not a conscious effort to excel in the expensiveness of their visible consumption, so much as it is a desire to live up to the conventional standard of decency in the amount and grade of goods consumed" (1953, 80).

Unemployment is the limitation of access to work, when there are more individuals seeking work than there are jobs. A better way of viewing this access is that there are more bidders for available positions than there are positions. As discussed in chapter 1, Keynesian economics principles that drive many of the precepts of national economies call for **full employment** as a means of generating increased consumption of the popular classes (see Navarro, 2000); yes, full employment still means that there are some people who remain out of work. New jobs seem to be created, but there still are a number of individuals who are out of work for a number of reasons. The concept of full employment is limited to those who want to work (receiving an appropriate wage for the type of work done), which translates to the belief that about four to five percent of the total population still does not work.[1] This line of reasoning, however, does not take into account individuals who are discouraged from working, those who consider themselves under-employed (actual or perceived), or wage-level adequacy. These form three other important threads in the discussion of labor forces and employment; nonetheless, these threads are outside the scope of this chapter's discussion on unemployment insurance (UI).

Even though some may argue that this approach belongs to the neoliberal economic way of thinking, the image of bidders for jobs is apt because the question that shapes the arguments surrounding the social safety net in this area is one of why persons are unemployed. Is it because they are voluntarily or involuntarily out of work? There are people who want jobs and those that do not. Those who are involuntarily out of work (not as a result of being fired) lost the jobs because, typically, one of these situations occurred:

- Those that have been laid off temporarily or permanently due to lack of demand for their product.

- The downsizing of a firm or merger with another firm or company.

- The shutting down of an entire industry (the downside of job churning, that is, the process of creating new jobs), or industries moving jobs to other countries because of lower labor costs.

- A lack of adequate job skills for the current market.

- Are not physically or mentally able to work (due to documented disability or a result from a job-related injury).

Those who voluntarily are out of work are so because they:

- Seek a better paying and/or "higher" level job (including an interest for a better benefit package).

- Seek a better work opportunity (start up their own business, more interesting job, a position more specific to areas of interest and specialization, better opportunity for recognition, greater potential for self-actualization, ability to move within the next employer's units, eventual promotions).

- Cannot hold a job due to lacking job survival skills (cannot keep a job because they cannot get along with others, follow orders, rules and regulations, and so forth).

- Are not interested in working in a situation that they do not find palatable to their personal wants (and are not necessarily seeking a better job opportunity).

- Do not want to work.

The question of whether unemployment is the result of market conditions or because it is something individuals choose becomes metamorphosed to the corollary of whether the government should provide benefits for those out of work to help them make ends meet. As discussed in chapters 1 and 3, such a view leads directly to the idea that if benefits are to be provided these should be available for those who are deserving of them. Given the polarity of the political spectrum, the political left looks at this issue in terms of dealing with unemployment through an **active labor market policy (ALMP)**, where government impacts a nation's economic market by passing laws emphasizing the social rights of citizens over those of employers (see Janoski, 1990). The political right sees the presence of unemployment insurance as a disincentive to work—it increases unemployment while declining economic performance (Burtless, 1990, 69). "All social benefits, to some extent, provide an incentive for the very circumstances they are established to ameliorate" (Gilbert, Specht, and Terrell, 1993, 76).

In the United States, from the larger social perspective, the combination of the protestant ethic and the views exemplified by social Darwinism are apparent. Those that need help because they have been displaced will be helped. There is an understanding that there is a period in which people find themselves between jobs (see Vedder and Gallaway, 1993). The point is that individuals should not be encouraged to stay between jobs any longer than needed. For those that are disabled, the laws protecting their interests are seen as in place and providing some of their interests in earning sufficient funds so that they may have an acceptable standard of living. Again, there is a belief in restraint, but there is social support for these benefits. The justification is based on the acceptance that individuals should have the ability to enjoy a certain quality of life.

Quality of life is a technical as well as philosophical concept. Philosophically, it comes from the point of view of equity, as discussed in chapter 1, that of avoiding unexpected hardships through the unwavering application of rules. The technical perspective is the application of this approach mainly to identify and analyze the psychological and physical well-being of individuals; however, many parts of society expand the approach to include socioeconomic status and life satisfaction—an individual's standard of living. It is in the extension to the latter that the differences of opinion from the political spectrum come to view. The controversy rests in who should define life satisfaction when it is the government that picks up the tab. Pigou (1932) defines economic welfare as "that part of social welfare that can be brought directly or indirectly into relation with the measuring rod of money" (11). This being the case, should the definition be based on the preferences of those receiving the benefit or that which is observed by the government (see Bliss, 1993)?

The greatest question of all for many individuals and specialists is why is unemployment inevitable. Outside the communist-based economic regime, the issues are to maintain full employment and keeping prices stable. Regardless of the economic theoretical approach espoused (see Vedder and Gallaway, 1993), the complicating element within these issues is productivity—how much can individuals produce for the wages paid? Why hire three people when it only takes one to produce a widget? It may be cheaper for society in terms of taxes to have a firm keep the additional two individuals hired; however, this is done at the expense of the firm itself and the consumer of those goods because the employer will have a lower profit base (if any) and prices for the widget will be higher, possibly lowering demand for the widget. And with lower demand for a product, the pressure to produce the same number is reduced. With this being the case, then it may not prove to be "cheaper" for society because there are fewer products available to buy and the need for state aid and support increases in order to maintain workers employed.

Unemployment compensation (UC) programs are meant to provide a degree of social protection to those who are out of work. Typically, the unemployment rate—the percent of people out of work—and not the employment rate—those that are gainfully employed—measure unemployment.[2] In general, these programs have a complete set of goals: income replacement, medical care, workplace safety, and rehabilitation (Chambers, 1986). Benefits are in the form of cash benefits, social services, and tax breaks (Adema, 2001). Taken to the extent of controlling economic measures to assure social rights, unemployment insurance has the potential for some income transfers as a result of receiving greater amounts of cash or in-kind services than what was contributed into the system (e.g., disability claims). Taxes may have to support the programs along with individual contributions. When the goal is income redistribution, then participation is universal and tax support is a built-in social expectation. When income maintenance assistance is the goal, the need for additional support from the general treasury justifies the potential need to have eligibility requirements (see Bourguignon, 2002).

The U.S. Department of Labor oversees unemployment compensation in the United States; however, each state administers its own program. Established with the passage of the Social Security Act of 1935, "the program has two main objectives: (1) to provide temporary and partial wage replacement to involuntarily unemployed workers who were recently employed; and (2) to help stabilize the economy during recession" (United States House of Representatives, Committee on Ways and Means, 2000, section 4, 1/27). Those eligible to receive this government benefit are otherwise "regularly employed members of the labor force who become involuntarily unemployed and who are able and willing to accept suitable employment" (Social Security Administration, 2001, 63).

The unemployment insurance framework in the United States is funded through a uniform payroll tax of about 6.2 percent: a federal tax of 0.8 percent and a state payroll tax contribution of about 5.4 percent. All contributions collected under state laws are deposited in the unemployment trust fund of the U.S. Treasury Department. Each state has a separate account crediting their collected amounts and interest generated from investment. The fund, though, is invested as a whole. Withdrawals by states is allowed for benefit payments only. At present, private plans cannot substitute for state plans.

UI is a federal and state government partnership. Federal legislation and U.S. Department of Labor regulations provide overall guidelines that states must follow. Each state determines the amount and duration of these benefits, contribution rates for employers and employees, and eligibility and disqualification requirements. The State governments, not the federal government, administer the individual programs, process claims and make eligibility decisions, keep the necessary records, collect the payroll taxes, and pay out the benefits.

Coverage is provided to employees of private employers in business and industry that employ one or more individuals at least one day per week for twenty weeks during the current or preceding year, or if the employer paid more than $1,500 in wages during any calendar quarter during the current or preceding year.[3] Agricultural workers are covered on farms that have a quarterly payroll of $20,000 or more, or farms that employ ten or more individuals in twenty weeks of the year. Domestic workers in private households are covered when the employer pays wages of $1,000 or more in a calendar quarter. Federal civil employees, ex-servicemen from the military branches, railroad workers, state and nonprofit organization employees are participants only from 1976 onwards. Exceptions to coverage are domestic workers who are hired by their families or whose employers are self-employed, agricultural workers not meeting the above definition, employees of religious organizations, and casual employees (temporary workers whose hours fluctuate and are less than part-time as defined under the **Fair Labor Standards Act [FLSA]**).

In the UI scheme, there is no means-test for eligibility. Unemployment compensation is an entitlement because those who paid payroll taxes are only receiving that for which they already paid. Eligibility is first of all based on the amount time employed and contributions into the system. In 75 percent of the states, unemployed individuals qualify for unemployment benefits if they show minimum earnings in the preceding base year[4] equal to a specified multiple of weekly benefits or high-quarter wages, or to a specified total amount (Social Security Administration, 1999). Eight states require a specified number of weeks of employment (for example, 15–20 weeks). The next element of eligibility is that the worker was involuntarily unemployed, is able to work, makes himself or herself available for work, and is actively seeking work. Recipients are required to register at employment service centers and demonstrate that beneficiary is looking for work. The third element of eligibility is that the unemployed worker cannot be responsible for his or her own unemployment—that they were

terminated for cause or quit on their own volition (although being forced to quit as a result of harassment or other illegal behavior on the part of the employer provides a different set of implications that may or may not mitigate denial of benefits). A very important behavior on the part of the claimant must be observed in all fifty states in order to maintain eligibility: the claimant must accept a "suitable job when it is offered."[5]

Eligible individuals receive a maximum of twenty-six weeks of unemployment compensation. Federal law provides for an additional thirteen weeks in states with high unemployment. There is usually a one-week of total unemployment waiting period before benefit can begin in forty-three states.

In all states, the maximum benefit rate is approximately 50 percent of gross reference earnings on a weekly basis, up to specified maximum amounts. In thirty-five states, the maximum is a flexible amount automatically adjusted in accordance to the weekly wages of covered employees. Twelve states provide additional allowances for certain dependents, typically children under 16, 18, or 19 (or older if disabled). Eight of these states also consider the nonworking spouse, while another two states consider dependent relatives as well (Social Security Administration, 2001). Benefits for children and dependent range from $1–$95 per week per dependent, with the average being around $24 per week per dependent.

Extended benefits (EB) come out of a permanent federal-state program created in the 1970s for the purpose of extending benefits to workers who had exhausted their benefits. The federal government and the states pay an equal share into this program. While states develop their own eligibility criteria for this program, the federal government stipulates that a claimant desiring extended benefits must have had twenty weeks in full-time employment or its equivalent in insured wages and must meet special work requirements. The program is not automatic. Under the pre-1992 guidelines, all states have to demonstrate that a set of conditions exists before these funds become available (Social Security Administration, 2001):

1. the weekly unemployment rate among insured workers averages 5 percent or more over a thirteen-week-period, and

2. is at least 20 percent higher than the rate for the same period in the two preceding years.

If the unemployment rate reaches 6 percent, state law may allow a state to disregard the 20-percent requirement for extended benefits to commence. With the passage of PL 102-318 in 1992, the states have the option of following another set of guidelines to provide extended benefits:

1a. the state's seasonally adjusted total unemployment rate for the three most recent months is at least 6.5 percent, and

2a. that the rate is at least 110 percent of the state average total unemployment rate in the corresponding three-month period in either of the two preceding years.

The pre-1992 guidelines stipulate that the total coverage period for a claimant between the regular UC and the EB is thirty-nine weeks. Under the post-1992 option, states can amend their state laws to add an addition seven weeks to the thirteen weeks of extended benefits when:

1b. the total unemployment rate is 8 percent or higher, and

2b. the rate is 110 percent of the state's total unemployment rate for the same three months in either of the two preceding years.

The International Labor Organization (2000) states that as many as 75 percent of the 150 million unemployed throughout the world lack any form of unemployment insurance protection. The program available in the United States is typical of countries belonging to the Organization for Economic Co-operation and Development (OECD) (Adema, 2000), as can be seen in Table 5.1 at the end of this chapter. It has a mandatory component in generating private social benefits, and like Canada and Korea, the United States has additional substantial voluntary social benefits available through the private sector (Adema, 2000). Logically, when compared to other social systems such as those found in social democracies like Germany, the Netherlands, Norway, and Sweden, the United States is at the bottom because the manner in which benefits focus on redistribution of wealth based on a guaranteed standard of living in these countries (Goodin et al., 1999; International Labor Organization, 2000). Australia and Canada also rank at the bottom over redistributive interests based on a guaranteed minimum income, while Sweden and many other European Union countries rank at the top.[6]

In an income compensation system such as the United States has, employee benefits are seen as additional costs of doing business, costs that have to be considered and mitigated in order to keep competitive prices. In nations whose interest is wealth redistribution, the view is that employee benefits are across-the-board benefits that do not change the relative competitive position of firms in the marketplace (see Mitchell and Rojot, 1993). Nevertheless, unemployment reforms are undergoing changes in the European Union, "with the emphasis on curbing expenditure growth and dependency on social protection" (Buti, Franco, and Pench, 1999, 33).

There is a de facto attempt at changing welfare to "workfare" in most OECD countries (see International Labor Organization, 2000). Eligibility criteria are being tightened and tougher sanctions on those refusing a job being but two examples of this reform movement. System abusers have become a concern, and greater emphasis is being placed in reducing the number of those taking advantage of the system.[7] Buti, Franco, and Pench (1999) recommend that the main policy alternative to the current unemployment program in EU countries should be the introduction of a conditional negative income tax and the replacement of unemployment benefits with employment subsidies. The former has analogies in the U.S. social safety net through the earned income tax credit (EITC)—described in chapter 8—while the latter is an example of a direct AMLP approach toward managing employment through market intervention at the national level.

NOTES

1. To look at this phenomenon, many economists still use the Beveridge curve (named after Lord Beveridge, who was the first to identify the relationship between unemployment rates and job availability) to determine the state of labor markets. It is a scatter plot that looks at unemployment rates and job vacancy rates. The curve is also used to look at the reallocation of workers from one job to another, based on the location of the points in the curve.

2. This issue onto itself raises controversies based on what is most appropriate to meet individual and social needs. Being a lagging indicator, it reflects what has already occurred rather than what is happening; therefore, individuals are already in a circumstance of deprivation.

3. Coverage was originally defined by the Federal Unemployment Tax Act (FUTA). A series of laws around 1976 expanded the class of employees that had to participate in the public unemployment insurance scheme.

4. A base period is typically the first four quarters of the last five completed calendar quarters preceding the unemployment benefit claim.

5. The Federal Unemployment Tax Act identifies the exceptions to when a claimant's eligibility will not be jeopardized: (1) if the position is vacant due to a strike, lockout, or dispute; (2) if the wages, hours, or other conditions of work offered are substantially less favorable to the individual than those prevailing for similar work in the locality; if, as a condition of being employed, the individual would be required to join a company union or to resign from or refrain from joining any bona fide labor organization.

6. To illustrate this point, benefit payments, defined as "net wage replacement rates," are 58 percent in Canada and the United States. The rates are lower than the 63 percent provided in Finland and 77 percent given to the unemployed in Spain (International Labor Organization, 2000).

7. Workfare is discussed in chapter 7, when the focus of attention shifts directly to how it has become the new legislated paradigm of the social safety net, replacing in the United States the old Aid to Families with Dependent Children (AFDC) public welfare programs originally set up in 1935 with the new Temporary Aid for Needy Families (TANF).

PRINCIPAL SOURCES FOR ILLUSTRATIONS

Organization for Economic Co-operation and Development. (2002). Statistical Annex. In OECD, *Employment Outlook 2000*, pp. 301–332. Washington, D.C.: Author. Retrieved from: http://www.oecd.org/dataoecd/29/42/1939233.pdf.

Social Security Administration. (2001). *Annual statistical supplement, 2001 to the Social Security Bulletin.* Baltimore: Social Security Administration, Office of Policy. Retrieved from: http://www.ssa.gov/statistics/Supplement/2001/supp01.pdf.

Social Security Administration. (2002). *Social security programs throughout the world: Europe 2002.* Washington, D.C.: Author. Retrieved from: http://www.ssa.gov/policy/docs/progdesc/ssptw/2002/europe/index.html.

United States Census Bureau. (2002). *Statistical abstract of the United States 2002.* Washington, D.C.: Government Printing Office. Retrieved from: http://www.census.gov/statab/www/.

United States Department of Labor. (2001). Report on the American workforce. Washington, D.C.: Government Printing Office. Retrieved from: http://www.bls.gov/opub/rtaw/rtawhome.htm.

BIBLIOGRAPHY

Adema, W. (2001). Labour market and social policy: Occasional papers no. 52. In Organization for Economic Co-operation and Development. *Net social expenditure.* 2nd ed. Retrived from: http://www/oecd.org/olis2001doc.nsf/linkto/DEEKSA-ELSA-WD(2201)5.

Bleakley, H., and Fuhrer, J.C. (September/October1997). Shifts in the Beveridge curve, job matching, and labor market dynamics. *New England Economic Review.* Boston: Federal Reserve Bank of Boston. Retrieved from: http://www.bos.frb.org/economic/neer/neer1997/neer597a.pdf.

Bliss, C. (1993). Life-style and the standard of living. In Nussbaum, M., and Sen, A., eds. *The quality of life.* New York: Oxford University Press, 417–436.

Bourguignon, F. (2002). *Social protection in industrial countries: Which lessons for LAC countries?* World Bank. Retrieved from: http://lnweb18.worldbank.org/External/lac/lac.nsf/92fc607f00e4de4a852568cf00633afd/9491670c24b2801185256aaa00453118/$FILE/lacjune.pdf.

Burtless, G. (1990). Unemployment insurance and labor supply: A survey. In Hansen, W.L. and Byers, J.F., eds. *Unemployment insurance: The second half-century.* Madison: University of Wisconsin Press, 69–107.

Buti, M., Franco, D., and Pench, L.R. (1999). Reconciling the welfare state with sound public finances and high employment. In Buti, M., Franco, D., and Pench, L.R., eds. *The welfare state in Europe: Challenges and reforms.* Cheltenham, UK: Edward Elgar, 3–54.

Chambers, D.E. (1986). *Social policy and social programs: A method for the practical public policy analyst.* New York: Macmillan Press.

Gilbert, N., Specht, H., and Terrell, P. (1993). *Dimensions of social welfare policy.* 3rd ed. Englewood Cliffs, NJ: Prentice Hall.

Goodin, R.E., Headey, B., Muffels, R., and Dirven, H.J. (1999). *The real worlds of welfare capitalism.* Cambridge: Cambridge University Press.

International Labor Organization. (2000). *World labour report 2000: Income security and social protection in a changing world.* Geneva: International Labour Office.

Janoski, T. (1990). *The political economy of unemployment: Active labor market policy in West Germany and the United States.* Berkeley, CA: University of California Press.

Mitchell, J.B., and Rojot, J. (1993). Employee benefits in the single market. In Ulman, L., Eichengreen, B., and Dickens, W.T., eds. *Labor and an integrated Europe.* Washington, D.C.: The Brookings Institution, 128–166.

Navarro, V. (2000). Neoliberalism, "globalization," unemployment, inequalities, and the welfare state. In Navarro, V., ed. *The political economy of social inequalities: Consequences for health and quality of life.* Amityville, NY: Baywood Publishing Company, 33–107.

OECD. (2002) Statistical Annex. In OECD, *Employment outlook 2000.* Washington, D.C.: Author, 301–332. Retrieved from: http://www.oecd.org/dataoecd/29/42/1939233.pdf.

Pigou, A.C. (1932). *The economics of welfare.* London: Macmillan.

Social Security Administration. (1999). *Social security programs throughout the world, 1999.* Baltimore: Social Security Administration, Office of Policy. Retrieved from: http://www.ssa.gov/policy/docs/progdesc/ssptw/1999/.

Social Security Administration. (2001). *Annual statistical supplement, 2001 to the Social Security Bulletin.* Baltimore: Social Security Administration, Office of Policy. Retrieved from: http://www.ssa.gov/statistics/Supplement/2001/supp01.pdf.

United States House of Representatives, Committee on Ways and Means. (2000). *The 2000 Green Book: Background material and data on programs within the jurisdiction of the Committee on Ways and Means.* Retrieved from: http://aspe.hhs.gov/2000gh.

Veblen, T. (1953). *The theory of the leisure class: An economic study of institutions.* New York: The New American Library.

Vedder, R., and Gallaway, L. (1993). *Out of work: Unemployment and government in twentieth-century America.* New York: Holmes and Meier.

Table 5.1
Comparison of Unemployment Compensation and Unemployment Assistance Programs in the United States and Nine OECD Countries

Country	Unemployment Compensation	Unemployment Assistance
United States	• Maximum of 26 weeks of benefits. Federal law provides for an additional 13 weeks in states with high unemployment • Rate is 50% of gross reference earnings • Benefit not means-tested; income from work may reduce benefit to $0 • Overseen by U.S. Department of Labor • Each state administers its own program • Unemployment insurance benefits subject to both state and federal income taxes, but exempt from social security taxes • Exclusions: some agricultural employees, employees of religious organizations, casual employees, family labor, and self-employed • Funding comes from a federal tax 0.8% of taxable payroll (6.2% basic rate less basic rate up to 5.4% state contributions). State program basic rate is about 5.4% • Qualification for unemployment benefits: 75% of states require a minimum earning in preceding base year equal to a specified multiple of weekly benefits or high-quarter wages, or to a specified total amount. Eight states require a specified number of weeks of employment (e.g., 15–20 weeks) • Unemployment benefit recipients are required to register at employment service, and demonstrate that beneficiary is capable of and available for work	None

Germany	• Unemployment benefit:
	About 50% of earnings (according to diversified state formulae)
	Dependent supplements—about 25% of states provide $1–$95 per week per child and sometimes for other dependents
	Payable after a one-week waiting period in most states
	• Unemployment insurance is compulsory (exclusion for negligible employment, however). Contributions must have been made for at least 12 months in order to apply to receive benefits
	  • employed persons
	  • homeworkers
	  • apprentices and trainees
	  • other groups including participants in occupational training schemes
	• Costs:
	  • Insured: 3.25% of covered earnings
	  • Employer: 3.25% of covered earnings
	  • Government: subsidies for employment promotion law and for any deficit; also costs of unemployment assistance
	• Benefits related to previous after-tax income and are augmented when there are dependent children
		• Unemployment assistance benefit is means-tested using income from all sources (family, housing, and child-care benefits are excluded from the income test. Benefits related to previous after-tax income and are augmented when there are dependent children
		• Persons who remain unemployed after exhaustion of their insurance benefits are transferred to unemployment assistance
		• Benefit paid to individual and replacement rate depends on family status. Standard rates:
		  • 53% of worker's previous net earnings
		  • 57% of net earnings for worker with at least one dependent
		  • Net income = gross earnings minus income tax minus deductible social security contributions minus tax allowances for work minus related expenses (NI=GE-IT-SS contributions-tax allowances for expenses)

- Claimants for insurance have to be less than age 65, registered as unemployed, and looking for available work. They must have worked for at least 12 months in the last 3 years to be eligible
- Benefit paid to individual, with replacement rates at 60% of previous earnings net of tax and social contributions; 67% for a worker with at least one dependent child
- Spouses income disregards amounts to the unemployment assistance benefit the spouse would receive in case of unemployment (applicant's benefit is reduced by 47% of spouse's net income exceeding 13,067 DM per year
- Not taxable
- No waiting period
- Duration of payment usually indefinite
- Benefits paid 7 days per week

- People working less than 15 hours per week, and receiving no more than 630 DM per month *do not* qualify for unemployment insurance or pension fund
- Unemployment insurance pays a net benefit; it is not taxable
- No waiting period; duration of payment depends on age and employment record in accordance to a predetermined table
- No special treatment for young persons
- Unemployed people may qualify for retirement at age 60 provided recipient has a 96-month record or alternatively has been unemployed for 12 months
- Benefits often supplemented by former employer to up to 100% of former salary
- Women have the right to full pensions at 60 after 15 years of work
- Anyone who has contributed at least 35 years to a pension fund can retire before normal pension age

The Netherlands
- Unemployment insurance pays 70% of the last earned wage for a period of time dependent on age
  - coverage: employed persons (special system for public employees)
  - Funding sources:
    - insured—average of 6.10% of earnings, according to industry (maximum earnings contributions of 310 guilders per day)
    - employer—average of 4.00% of payroll, according to industry
    - government—none
- Person still unemployed after the earnings-related benefit expired is entitled to the follow-up benefit
- Benefit for 2 years—for older people (57.5 yrs. or older) for up to 3.5 years.
  - persons 57.5 or older at moment they lose job have continued entitlements for follow-up benefit until 65th birthday
- A minimum wage related benefit
  - worked 26 weeks in the last 39 weeks immediately preceding unemployment
  - 70% of minimum wage or 70% of the daily wage if this is less than minimum wage (i.e., part-time work)

Table 5.1 (continued)

- There are three types of benefits (one considered as unemployment assistance program):
  - earnings related benefits (at least half a year up to 5 years)
    - must have worked 26 weeks in last 39 weeks immediately preceding unemployment plus worked at least 52 days or more during 4 of last 5 years
    - calendar years during which person cared for children under age 6 count toward fulfilling requirement (50% for calendar years when taking care of children between ages 6 and 12)
    - benefit paid is 70% of gross earnings lost up to a maximum daily wage of 310.95 guilders per 5-day week)
  - follow-up benefit (see unemployment assistance section)
  - short benefit
    - it is a minimum wage related benefit
    - same as the follow-up benefit
- Unemployment benefits supplemented by the "Supplementary Benefits Act"
  - it is not an entitlement for:
    - unmarried persons under 21 living with parents
    - persons living with a partner (married or not) born after December 31, 1971 who do not have children living at home
  - provides assistance to unemployed or disabled receiving benefits under the unemployment benefit schemes if their income plus that of their partner falls below the minimum guaranteed income (gross level minimum wage divided by 21.75)
  - supplementary benefit will never be more than the difference between daily earnings or basis on which benefit has been calculated and the benefit to recompense for loss of income
  - minimum guaranteed incomes as of July 1, 2001 are:
    - single person @ 70% of minimum wage
    - lone parent @ 90% of minimum wage
    - married persons and couples living together @ 100% of minimum wage
  - term "income" covers all work-related earnings (including most social security benefits) of claimant and partner; property such as private home and capital such as savings are disregarded
  - a maximum of 15% of minimum wage of work-related income is disregarded for up to 2 years
  - maximum supplementary rates are:
    - single person @ 21% of minimum wage
    - lone parent @ 27% of minimum wage
    - married persons/couples living together @ 30% of minimum wage

- must have worked 26 weeks in last 39 weeks immediately preceding unemployment plus worked at least 52 days or more during 4 of last 5 years
- calendar years during which person cared for children under age 6 count toward fulfilling requirement (50% for calendar years when taking care of children between ages 6 and 12)
- benefit paid is 70% of gross earnings lost up to a maximum daily wage of 310.95 guilders per 5-day week)
- Claimant working less than 5 hours per week get gross benefits reduced by 30% of gross earnings; when hours of work exceeding 5 hours per week, total benefit is reduced in proportion to the number of hours worked
- Taxable benefit

Norway

None

- Unemployment insurance scheme is part of the National Insurance Scheme (NIS)
- Social economic assistance may be granted to the individual and may cover all housing costs
- In most cases, the tax unit is the individual
- Precondition for eligibility for daily cash benefits during unemployment: claimant must have had an income from work of at least 1.25 times the basic amount the preceding calendar year, or an income from work which at least equals the basic amount as an average during the three preceding calendar years (income from participation in labor market measures no longer qualifies)
- Benefits calculation:
  - Daily cash benefits based on income from work, income from job creation measures, daily cash benefits during unemployment, sickness, maternity and adoption
  - Calculation basis is the highest of either the income of the last preceding calendar year or the average over the last three preceding calendar years
  - Benefit rate per day = 0.24% of the calculation basis, paid five days a week (an annual compensation of 62.4% of the calculation basis in a typical situation)
  - Maximal benefit basis = 6 times basic amount (maximum amount per week is NOK 3,380)
  - Supplement of NOK 17 per day (NOK 85 per week) given for each dependent child under 18
- Daily cash benefits payable for 5 days a week and granted if claimant has been unemployed three of the last 10 working days while being registered at the employment office as a bona fide applicant for work
- Daily cash benefits related to reduction in working hours on a per week basis, needing to be reduced by at least 40 percent as compared to previous working hours
- Benefits are taxable
- No special treatment for young persons
- For those over 64 are guaranteed three times the basic amount; benefits paid indefinitely until 67
- Benefit period varies depending on earlier income from work
  - Income from work equaling at least 2 times basic amount equals benefit period of 156 weeks (3 years)
  - Income equaling less than 2 times basic amount equals benefit period of 78 weeks (1.5 years)

Table 5.1 (*continued*)

- When initial benefits period expires, a subsequent period may only be granted provided only if the requirement concerning previous income from work during the previous benefit period is met. There are no special conditions concerning a subsequent benefit period

Sweden

- UI consists of a basic assistance scheme and a voluntary income related scheme for those who are members of Unemployment Insurance Societies (typically linked to trade unions)
  - There is an administrative fee for individuals wanting to join these societies who are not trade union members
  - Self-employed are also insured
- Basic assistance scheme is for those who are not members of an Unemployment Insurance Society or do not fulfill the employment criteria
- Low-income wage earners, unemployment benefits recipients, or any other kind of transfer income recipients can claim a means-tested housing benefit
  - Intended for a family with dependent children
  - Also open for low-income households under the age of 29
  - Individuals that have neither income nor assets can claim social assistance
- Taxing unit: the individual (spouses are taxed separately)
- Member of Unemployment Insurance Society must be fit for work and available to work at least 17 hours per week during a 4-week period
- Employees or self-employed individual needs to have been a member of Society for at least 12 months
  - Trade union members have option of payment through part of union fees or paying directly to 1 of 38 Societies or to a 39th society not related to any trade union
- A claimant must have worked at least 6 months, for a minimum of 70 hours per month, or 450 hours during a 6-month period in which the individual worked at least 45 hours each month
- Benefits calculation:
  - Gross replacement rate is 80 percent of previous earnings
  - Minimum daily benefit: SEK 240 (SEK 62,400 per year)
  - Maximum daily benefit: SEK 580 (SEK 150,800 per year)
  - Benefits reduced in proportion to the number of days worked
  - Additional family and housing benefits are available (there are no special family benefits, these are part of available housing benefits)
- Duration of benefits:
  - Payable on a 5-day week basis, for a maximum of 300 days or 60 weeks, after a 5-day waiting period
  - Claimant reaching maximum benefit duration can qualify for a further period after meeting the employment conditions set above
  - It is possible to renew the benefit period by claiming a "job-offer" before the initial period expires, as a means to ensure frequent periods of job training during long-term unemployment (no current restriction on the number of times entitlements can be renewed)

- Basic unemployment insurance is analogous to a form of assistance or minimum guarantee because it is aimed mainly at those not insured, those who do not meet the UI requirements, or individuals who just finished their full-time studies. It is available from the age of 20

Czech Republic

- No special treatment for young persons
- Maximum duration of benefits is 450 days (90 weeks) for those aged between 57 and 64

- Benefits available for up to 6 months
- Gross benefit: 50% first 3 months, 40% in the next 3 months of last earned income net of tax and social security contributions (paid after a 7-day waiting period once per month).
- Eligibility: 12 months of work during the past 3 years plus 6 months of contributions during a 3 year period
- Maximum benefits: 2.5 times the minimum living standard
- Any income from work during this period cancels unemployment benefit
- UI benefit is not taxable
- Treatment of young persons: those meeting eligibility requirements as stated above—time studying is considered the same as time working
- Treatment of older workers: entitlement paid until retirement age, at which time, claimant receives old-age pension benefits

- Retraining subsidies paid directly to education providers administering courses/programs
- Unemployment benefit is 60% of previous earnings while in training program
- Assistance to Disabled Persons
  - Employers with 20 or more employees have the legal duty to have at least 5% of employees be people with a reduced ability to work
  - Employers receive CZK 9,000 per year for a person with a reduced ability to work and CZK 32,000 for a person with a reduced ability to work that has a severe health affliction.
  - Labor Offices provide a one-time contribution to employers creating jobs for persons with disabilities in sheltered workshops or other sheltered workplaces (with a maximum of CZK. 100,000 per year per job and an additional maximum of CZK 40,000 per year per job to cover operational expenses
- Supporting the creation of new jobs
  - Labor Offices provide a range of incentives to employers as encouragement to create "socially purposeful jobs"
  - Stipulation is that position created, the position will be filled by individuals registered with the Labor Offices for at least the first two years
  - Incentive types:
    - repayable interest-free loan
    - bank credit interest subsidy
    - single purpose grant to buy machines and equipment, and to defray other costs of having the job
    - wage subsidy (may fully subsidize pay given participants plus social and health insurance)
  - Maximum amount CZK 80,00 per job
  - Similar conditions apply for grants available to registered job seekers who decide to create new job opportunities by starting their own business
  - Typical public utility work jobs created:
    - maintenance of municipal parks and open public spaces
    - cleaning
    - construction of municipal infrastructure
    - social care

Table 5.1 (*continued*)

- Supporting the employment of the young and those leaving school
  - Labor Office contracts with employer to provide those laving school with work experience
  - Labor Office provides funds to help defray cost of employment
  - Training for lower-level/skill positions provided through this format for those students who failed to meet graduation criteria in secondary or vocational school setting

None

Poland

- Unemployment benefits are available to individuals:
  - who are registered as unemployed;
  - who are able and willing to take employment on a full-time basis in accordance to the working time rate applicable to a particular occupation or service;
  - between the ages of 18–65 (65 for men, 60 for women);
  - cannot own agricultural estates with arable land exceeding 2 hectares;
  - cannot have a monthly income exceeding half the minimum pay; and
  - should not be recipients of a permanent compensatory allowance, guaranteed periodic allowance, or social pension due to other forms of social assistance legislation
- Benefits received after a 7-day waiting period after registration with appropriate district labor office
- Conditions that have to be met to receive UI benefits upon registration:
  - if there are no suitable employment opportunities available;
  - no referral to a subsidized job, public works, or a newly created job; and
  - if the claimant worked for 365 days out of the previous 18 months preceding registration at a pay level at least half of the minimum pay
- Contribution requirements: None
- Benefits calculation based on indexing utilizing the consumer price index (CPI) on a quarterly basis
- Benefits duration:
  - 6 months—while living within the labor office's district, and the district's unemployment rate for the previous year (as of June 30th) prior to the claim is less than the national average
  - 12 months—while living within the labor office's district, and the district's unemployment rate for the previous year (as of June 30th) prior to the claim exceeded the national average (most common case)
  - 18 months—while living within the labor office's district, the district's unemployment rate for the previous year (as of June 30th) prior to the claim is at least twice the national average, and the claimant has at least a 20-year benefit eligibility period, or has a dependent child aged 15 or less and spouse is also unemployed and is willing to forfeit the right to UI benefits due to the expiration of the benefits period
- UI benefits are taxed at 19% of gross benefit (for 1999: gross benefit X 19% - 394.80)

- Youth leaving school that have been referred to training are eligible for a training fellowship equal to 60% of the unemployment benefit during the training period not to exceed 12 months
- An unemployed person the labor office considered threatened by structural unemployment who, within a period of 6 months after being identified as a school-leaver is also potentially eligible for a training fellowship of up to 60% of the UI benefit for up to 12 months if he or she enrolls in a post-primary school for adults
- Older workers meeting eligibility requirements for unemployment and benefits with at least 30 years for women and 30 years for men of eligibility status, or 25 years of women and 30 for men with at least 15 of those years categorized as being under special conditions or special characters are entitled to bridging benefits of up to 120% of UI benefit
  - The benefit increases to 160% if the district labor office considers claimant to be unduly impacted by structural unemployment and termination is the result of a decision by the employer
  - The 160% level is also available to those not considered adversely impacted by structural unemployment if termination occurred after July 1, 1996, if termination is the result of an employer decision creating a one-time reduction in force where at least 100 people have been laid off
- Generally, the amount of the bridging benefit may not exceed 90% of average monthly pay constituting the basis of calculating of social insurance and Labor Fund contributions, and the bridging benefit may not be lower than 120% of unemployment benefits
- Eligibility requirements for bridging benefits:
  - Worked long enough to receive retirement benefits
  - Age 58 for women, 63 for men, or
    - In the calendar year, the employment status is terminated due to employer considerations
    - Age 55 for women, 60 for men, or
    - Employment relationship was terminated because of the reasons on the part of employer have reached the period entitling to the retirement, equal to at least 35 years (women) and 40 years (men), or

Table 5.1 (continued)

- Up until December 31 of the year preceding the termination of the employment relationship, with claimant reaching retirement benefits eligibility, equal to at least 34 years (women) and 39 years (men), and the employment relationship was terminated in connection with employer's insolvency have the right to the pre-retirement allowance equal to 90% of old-age pension amount specified in a decision, which determined the amount of old-age pension
- Bridging benefits and pre-retirement allowances are subject to indexation under the principles laid down for the unemployment benefits
- No supplementary benefits for single parents

Australia   None

- Flat-rate, means-tested unemployment benefits programs
- Administrative determination between long-term and initial benefits, although the distinction does not affect entitlement values
- Benefits are provided at a flat rate; however, rates are dependent on age, marital status, presence of dependent children, and if people are renting from the private market. Categories include:
  - Single, under 18, at home
  - Single, 18–20, at home
  - Single, under 21, away from home
  - Single, under 21, with children
  - Couple, under 21, each without children
  - Couple, under 21, each with children
  - Single, 21 and over, no children
  - Single, 21 and over, with children
  - Single, 60 and over, after 9 months unemployment
  - Couple, each over 21
- There are no restrictions on benefits duration to claimants
- Typically, a one-week payment period after making of claim (ordinary waiting period)
- Exceptions:
  - If a person receives leave entitlements from their previous employment, including annual leave, long service leave, sick leave and maternity leave, they may have to serve an income maintenance period (leave payments are treated as income from the date of payment for the period of leave)
  - If a person has liquid assets beyond a set level on the day they or their partner become unemployed or incapacitated, they may have to serve a liquid assets waiting period
  - If a person or their partner is engaged in high income seasonal or intermittent work in the six months prior to claim, they may have to service a seasonal work preclusion period
  - From 1996, newly arrived migrants must generally serve a two-year waiting period, except where individuals are given refugee or humanitarian status

- Two types of benefits:
  - Activity tested, e.g., Newstart Activity Program (NSA) and Youth Allowance (YA)
  - Non-activity tested
- Newstart Activity Program (NSA): paid to unemployed people aged 21 or over and under age-pension age
- Youth Allowance (YA): paid to unemployed people under 21 years and to full-time students between 15 and 24 (must be studying full-time or, if between 18 and 20 years and unemployed, looking for full-time work or undertaking a combination of activities that make up a full-time load, i.e., part-time study and part-time work)
- Unemployed youth between ages of 16-18 only if an activity agreement is in place or graduated from secondary school
- For young people who are studying, training, or looking for work, allowing them to combine elements of study and work, and assists with the transition from school to work, and encouraging young people to further their education and training
- A parental means is used to measure parental capacity to assist in the education of a youth. It is based on the parents' income, assets, and actual means
- Provides assistance who need to go away from home to study or work (especially from rural areas), providing these beneficiaries with higher allowances in rent assistance, pharmacy allowance, remote area allowance, and fares allowance (to full-time students only)
- Non-activity tested payments requirements:
  - Not required to work or otherwise satisfy the activity test
  - Targeted to unemployed people of workforce age with no recent workforce experience, or with caring responsibilities
- Payment programs:
  - Mature age allowance: for people aged 60 and below pension age (pension age will gradually increase from a 1995 average of 61.5 to 65 in the year 2013)
  - Partner allowance: for partners of income support recipients who have difficulties finding work due to a limited work history (must be born prior to July 1, 1975 and have no dependent children)
  - Widow allowance: paid to widows aged 50 or more who became widowed, divorced, or separated after turning 40 (not available for those born after July 1, 1955)

Table 5.1 (continued)

- Special benefit for those in severe financial need, who have no other form of income and for whom other benefits are not available
- Parenting payment: income support for individuals who are primary carers of children under 16 and who are unable to fully support themselves (only one partner in a couple may receive this payment)
- NSA and YA recipients must be actively seeking work and must be available for and willing to accept suitable work, including part-time and casual employment (exception in certain circumstances such as incapacitation, personal crisis, or caring duties)
- No contribution requirements on the part of individuals
- If both partners in a couple are unemployed, each needs to establish an entitlement right
- Benefits dependent on income and assets tests
  - Spouses each receive half of the total allowance payable to a couple, with the benefits of each means-tested individually
  - Amount disregarded from consideration: A$ 60 per fortnight
  - in 1999, 50% of income up to A$ 503.86 per fortnight is withdrawn after the A$ 60 disregard
  - If the higher earning partner loses all entitlement to benefit when income exceeds A$ 503.86 per fortnight for NSA recipients, the spouse's allowance is reduced by 70% of each dollar his/her partner earns in excess of that amount
  - Other income is not considered in this means-test.
  - YA is subject to both the personal income test and parental means tests
- NSA and YA benefits taxable, but the tax system is structured such that a year-long recipient without other income will pay no tax because of the beneficiary rebate for recipients of allowances
- Total income tax and social security contributions should be zero for a full-year maximum rate NSA recipient with no private income, because of a special "beneficiary rebate"
- Mature age allowance is paid to long-term unemployed people 60 and over and below pension age
- Eligibility:
  - have no recent work experience; and
  - have received an income support payment for at least nine months and be on NSA at the time of the claim; or
  - have received a social security pension, Veteran's Affairs service pension, or a widow, partner, sickness or parenting payment at any time within the 13 weeks immediately before the claim; or
  - have previously received mature age allowance

Japan

None

- Unemployed persons can receive an unemployment insurance benefit for a period varying with claimant's age and employment record
- Claimants can receive UI benefits with a minimum of 6 months of insured work in the last 12 months (working at least 14 days per month)
- Not a means-tested benefit. UI benefits stop when income is earned from work
- Benefits are not taxable
- Benefits paid after a 7-day waiting period
- Gross benefit calculation formula

  $BR = 0.8 + [(0.2 * (4\,290 - DAW)) / (10\,370 - 4\,290)]$

  BR = Benefit Ratio

  DAW = Daily Amount of Wages

- The total basic benefit is calculated from the daily amount of wages, the benefit ratio, and the number of days the basic benefit is paid during the year:
- Duration of benefits 90 to 300 days

Yrs. insured	<29	30–44	45–59	60–64
<1 year	90	90	90	90
1–4 years	90	90	180	240
5–9 years	90	180	210	300
10–19 yrs.	180	210	240	300
20+ years	180	210	300	300

- Maximum benefit: 3,195,000 Yen
- There is also a re-employment benefit: a lump-sum amount is paid to an unemployment benefit recipient who gets steady employment earlier than one third way of the payment duration (or 45 days)
- No particular treatment for youth
- Workers 65 and over who lose their jobs receive benefits in the form of a lump sum

Insured emp. Yrs.	Benefit amount
<1 year	30 × basic benefit
1–4 years	60 × basic benefit
5 years	75 × basic benefit

South Korea

None

- Two kinds of benefits:
- Job-seeking allowance (providing cash payments to maintain a worker's standard of living)
- Employment promotion allowance that is in four parts:
  - Early re-employment allowance
    - To facilitate and encourage the recipients' re-entry into a job, for those who get a steady job earlier than halfway the given benefit duration

Table 5.1 (*continued*)

- Benefit: half of the residual days of basic allowance
- Job abilities development allowance
  - For those who take training from the approved vocational training institutes
- Wide-area jobseeking allowance
  - Paid to those who are seeking jobs 50 kilometers away from their residence referred by the Employment Security Office
  - Moving expenses (for moving expenses to those who move to another place to take jobs or training mandated by the Employment Security Office)
- Voluntarily unemployed individuals are disqualified from receiving benefits
- Benefits eligibility: having worked at least 6 months in the last 18-month period preceding unemployment
- Gross benefit calculation:
  - Basic allowance is 50% of daily wage (calculated by dividing the wage paid in the last three months preceding unemployment by the total number of working days of the same three-month period)
  - Minimum benefit: 90% of the minimum wage (KRW 14,920 as of September 1, 2000)
- Maximum benefit: KRW 900,000
- Benefits stop when beneficiary receives a job and begins to contribute to the Employment Insurance System (EIS), or if claimant works 80 hours or more per month
- Maximum benefits duration: between 2–7 months, depending on claimant's age at the time of job loss and the period of contribution into the EIS

Age	<3yrs. contrib.	3–5 yrs.	5–10yrs.	>10yrs.
<25	60 days	90	120	150
25–30	60	90	120	150
30–50	90	120	150	180
>50	120	150	180	210

- Income disregards: Claimant finding a job can keep part of the benefit (60% of daily job-seeking allowance). This applies if the income earned divided by the number of allowance days to which the beneficiary is entitled exceeds 60 percent of the (daily) job-seeking allowance amount
- Disabled persons, regardless of their age, are entitled to the same number of days of benefits as those over 50 years of age

Source: Adapted from Organization for Economic Co-operation and Development. (1999). Synopsis of Member Nations social programs. Washington, D.C.: Author. Retrieved from http://www.oecd.org; and Social Security Administration. (2002). *Social Security Programs Throughout the World, 1999.* Washington, D.C.: Author. Retrieved from http://www.ssa.gov/policy/docs/progdesc/ssptw/1999/.

Table 5.2
U.S. Unemployment Rates by Industry, 1980 to 2001, and by Sex, 1980 and 2001

[**In percent.** For civilian noninstitutional population 16 years old and over. Annual averages of monthly figures. Rate represents unemployment as a percent of labor force in each specified group. Data for 1985-90 not strictly comparable with other years due to changes in industrial classification.]

Industry	1980	1985	1990	1995	2000	2001	Male 1980	Male 2001	Female 1980	Female 2001
All unemployed [1]	7.1	7.2	5.6	5.6	4.0	4.8	6.9	4.8	7.4	4.7
Industry: [2]										
Agriculture	11.0	13.2	9.8	11.1	7.5	9.7	9.7	9.7	15.1	9.5
Mining	6.4	9.5	4.8	5.2	3.9	4.7	6.7	4.8	4.5	4.0
Construction	14.1	13.1	11.1	11.5	6.4	7.3	14.6	7.5	8.9	5.1
Manufacturing	8.5	7.7	5.8	4.9	3.6	5.2	7.4	4.7	10.8	6.3
Transportation and public utilities	4.9	5.1	3.9	4.5	3.1	4.1	5.1	3.9	4.4	4.5
Wholesale and retail trade	7.4	7.6	6.4	6.5	5.0	5.6	6.6	5.2	8.3	6.1
Finance, insurance, and real estate	3.4	3.5	3.0	3.3	2.3	2.8	3.2	2.7	3.5	2.8
Services	5.9	6.2	5.0	5.4	3.8	4.6	6.3	4.9	5.8	4.3
Government	4.1	3.9	2.7	2.9	2.0	2.1	3.9	2.0	4.3	2.1

1. Includes the self-employed, unpaid family workers, and persons with no previous work experience not shown separately.
2. Covers unemployed wage and salary workers.

Source: United States Census Bureau. (2002). *Statistical Abstract of the United States 2002.* Washington, D.C.: Government Printing Office. Retrieved from http://www.census.gov/prod/2003pubs/02statab/labor.pdf.

Table 5.3
U.S. Unemployment by Occupation, 1990 to 2001, and by Sex, 2001

[**7,047 represents 7,047,000.** For civilian noninstitutional population 16 years old and over. Annual averages of monthly data. Rate represents unemployment as a percent of the labor force for each specified group. Based on Current Population Survey.]

Occupation	Number (1,000) 1990	Number (1,000) 2000	Number (1,000) 2001	Unemployment rate 1990	Unemployment rate 2000	2001 Total	2001 Male	2001 Female
Total [1]	7,047	5,655	6,742	5.6	4.0	4.8	4.8	4.7
Managerial and professional specialty	666	725	973	2.1	1.7	2.3	2.3	2.2
Executive, administrative, and managerial	350	356	491	2.3	1.8	2.4	2.3	2.5
Professional specialty	316	369	482	2.0	1.7	2.2	2.3	2.1
Technical sales, and administrative support	1,641	1,464	1,699	4.3	3.6	4.2	3.9	4.3
Technicians and related support	116	97	133	2.9	2.2	2.9	3.4	2.4
Sales occupations	720	684	794	4.8	4.0	4.7	3.6	5.8
Administrative support, including clerical	804	684	772	4.1	3.5	4.0	4.8	3.8
Service occupations	1,139	1,023	1,150	6.6	5.3	5.9	6.1	5.8
Private household	47	58	53	5.6	6.9	6.9	(B)	6.6
Protective service	74	65	74	3.6	2.6	2.9	2.7	3.9
Service except private household and protective	1,018	900	1,023	7.1	5.6	6.3	7.3	5.8
Precision production, craft, and repair	861	554	711	5.9	3.6	4.6	4.4	6.3
Mechanics and repairers	175	129	153	3.8	2.6	3.1	3.0	4.0
Construction trades	483	312	391	8.5	4.9	5.9	5.8	9.5
Other precision production, craft, and repair	202	113	167	4.7	2.8	4.2	3.6	6.3
Operators, fabricators, and laborers	1,714	1,228	1,481	8.7	6.3	7.7	7.3	8.9
Machine operators, assemblers, inspectors	727	455	573	8.1	5.9	7.8	7.1	9.1
Transportation and material moving occupations	329	253	298	6.3	4.4	5.0	4.9	6.0
Handlers, equipment cleaners, helpers, laborers	657	520	610	11.6	8.7	10.3	10.3	10.1
Construction laborers	177	133	155	18.1	11.6	13.1	13.0	18.0
Farming, forestry, and fishing	237	215	259	6.4	6.0	7.4	6.9	9.1

B. Base less than 35,000.
1. Includes persons with no previous work experience and those whose last job was in the Armed forces.

Source: United States Census Bureau. (2002). *Statistical Abstract of the United States 2002.* Washington, D.C.: Government Printing Office. Retrieved from http://www.census.gov/prod/2003pubs/02statab/labor.pdf.

Table 5.4
U.S. Unemployed and Unemployment Rate by Educational Attainment, Sex, Race, and Hispanic Origin: 1992 to 2001

[6,846 represents 6,846,000. As of March. For the civilian noninstitutional population 25 to 64 years old. Based on Current Population Survey.]

Year, sex, and race	Unemployed (1,000)					Unemployment rate [1]				
	Total	Less than high school diploma	High school gradu-ates, no degree	Less than a bach-elor's degree	College graduate	Total	Less than high school diploma	High school graduate, no degree	Less than a bach-elor's degree	College graduate
Total: [2]										
1992 . . .	6,846	1,693	2,851	1,521	782	6.7	13.5	7.7	5.9	2.9
1995 . . .	5,065	1,150	1,833	1,329	753	4.8	10.0	5.2	4.5	2.5
2000 . .	3,750	883	1,364	966	537	3.3	7.9	3.8	3.0	1.5
2001 . . .	4,072	913	1,516	947	696	3.5	8.1	4.2	2.9	2.0
Male:										
1992	4,207	1,151	1,709	854	493	7.5	14.8	8.8	6.4	3.2
1995	2,925	765	1,064	656	440	5.1	10.9	5.7	4.4	2.6
2000	2,027	475	749	494	308	3.3	7.1	3.9	3.1	1.6
2001	2,281	505	885	521	371	3.7	7.5	4.6	3.2	1.9
Female:										
1992	2,639	542	1,142	666	289	5.7	11.4	6.5	5.3	2.5
1995	2,140	385	770	673	313	4.4	8.6	4.6	4.5	2.4
2000	1,723	407	615	472	229	3.2	9.1	3.6	2.9	1.4
2001	1,792	408	632	427	325	3.3	8.9	3.8	2.6	2.0
White:										
1992	5,247	1,285	2,146	1,176	641	6.0	12.9	6.8	5.3	2.7
1995	3,858	831	1,362	1,054	612	4.3	9.2	4.6	4.2	2.3
2000	2,812	676	1,006	723	407	3.0	7.5	3.3	2.7	1.4
2001	2,995	657	1,066	723	549	3.1	7.2	3.6	2.7	1.8
Black:										
1992	1,353	361	619	291	81	12.4	17.2	14.1	10.7	4.8
1995	905	225	377	218	86	7.7	13.7	8.4	6.3	4.1
2000	717	164	305	179	68	5.4	10.4	6.3	4.3	2.5
2001	890	229	390	183	88	6.5	14.0	7.7	4.3	3.3
Hispanic: [3]										
1992	757	408	224	88	36	9.8	13.6	9.6	5.9	4.2
1995	746	393	211	102	40	8.0	10.9	8.1	5.2	3.7
2000	647	363	159	78	47	5.5	8.3	4.6	3.1	3.2
2001	665	397	145	77	46	5.5	8.9	4.0	3.1	2.9

1. Percent unemployed of the civilian labor force.
2. Includes other races, not shown separately.
3. Persons of Hispanic origin may be of any race.

Source: United States Census Bureau. (2002). *Statistical Abstract of the United States 2002.* Washington, D.C.: Government Printing Office. Retrieved from http://www.census.gov/prod/2003pubs/02statab/labor.pdf.

Table 5.5
U.S. Unemployed Persons by Duration and Reason, Annual Averages:
1948 to 2000

(Numbers in thousands)

Year	Total unem-ployed	Duration of unemployment						Reason for unemployment			
		Less than 5 weeks	5 to14 weeks	15 to 26 weeks	27 weeks and over	Mean dura-tion (weeks)	Median dura-tion (weeks)	Job losers[1]	Job leavers	Reen-trants	New entrants
1948	2,276	1,300	669	193	116	8.6	–	–	–	–	–
1949	3,637	1,756	1,194	428	256	10.0	–	–	–	–	–
1950	3,288	1,450	1,055	425	357	12.1	–	–	–	–	–
1951	2,055	1,177	574	166	137	9.7	–	–	–	–	–
1952	1,883	1,135	516	148	84	8.4	–	–	–	–	–
1953[2]	1,834	1,142	482	132	78	8.0	–	–	–	–	–
1954	3,532	1,605	1,116	495	317	11.8	–	–	–	–	–
1955	2,852	1,335	815	366	336	13.0	–	–	–	–	–
1956	2,750	1,412	805	301	232	11.3	–	–	–	–	–
1957	2,859	1,408	891	321	239	10.5	–	–	–	–	–
1958	4,602	1,753	1,396	785	667	13.9	–	–	–	–	–
1959	3,740	1,585	1,114	469	571	14.4	–	–	–	–	–
1960[2]	3,852	1,719	1,176	503	454	12.8	–	–	–	–	–
1961	4,714	1,806	1,376	728	804	15.6	–	–	–	–	–
1962[2]	3,911	1,663	1,134	534	585	14.7	–	–	–	–	–
1963	4,070	1,751	1,231	535	553	14.0	–	–	–	–	–
1964	3,786	1,697	1,117	491	482	13.3	–	–	–	–	–
1965	3,366	1,628	983	404	351	11.8	–	–	–	–	–
1966	2,875	1,573	779	287	239	10.4	–	–	–	–	–
1967	2,975	1,634	893	271	177	8.7	2.3	1,229	438	945	396
1968	2,817	1,594	810	256	156	8.4	4.5	1,070	431	909	407
1969	2,832	1,629	827	242	133	7.8	4.4	1,017	436	965	413
1970	4,093	2,139	1,290	428	235	8.6	4.9	1,811	550	1,228	504
1971	5,016	2,245	1,585	668	519	11.3	6.3	2,323	590	1,472	630
1972[2]	4,882	2,242	1,472	601	566	12.0	6.2	2,108	641	1,456	677
1973[2]	4,365	2,224	1,314	483	343	10.0	5.2	1,694	683	1,340	649
1974	5,156	2,604	1,597	574	381	9.8	5.2	2,242	768	1,463	681
1975	7,929	2,940	2,484	1,303	1,203	14.2	8.4	4,386	827	1,892	823
1976	7,406	2,844	2,196	1,018	1,348	15.8	8.2	3,679	903	1,928	895
1977	6,991	2,919	2,132	913	1,028	14.3	7.0	3,166	909	1,963	953
1978[2]	6,202	2,865	1,923	766	648	11.9	5.9	2,585	874	1,857	885
1979	6,137	2,950	1,946	706	535	10.8	5.4	2,635	880	1,806	817
1980	7,637	3,295	2,470	1,052	820	11.9	6.5	3,947	891	1,927	872
1981	8,273	3,449	2,539	1,122	1,162	13.7	6.9	4,267	923	2,102	981
1982	10,678	3,883	3,311	1,708	1,776	15.6	8.7	6,268	840	2,384	1,185
1983	10,717	3,570	2,937	1,652	2,559	20.0	10.1	6,258	830	2,412	1,216
1984	8,539	3,350	2,451	1,104	1,634	18.2	7.9	4,421	823	2,184	1,110
1985	8,312	3,498	2,509	1,025	1,280	15.6	6.8	4,139	877	2,256	1,039
1986[2]	8,237	3,448	2,557	1,045	1,187	15.0	6.9	4,033	1,015	2,160	1,029
1987	7,425	3,246	2,196	943	1,040	14.5	6.5	3,566	965	1,974	920
1988	6,701	3,084	2,007	801	809	13.5	5.9	3,092	983	1,809	816
1989	6,528	3,174	1,978	730	646	11.9	4.8	2,983	1,024	1,843	677
1990[2]	7,047	3,265	2,257	822	703	12.0	5.3	3,387	1,041	1,930	688
1991	8,628	3,480	2,791	1,246	1,111	13.7	6.8	4,694	1,004	2,139	792
1992	9,613	3,376	2,830	1,453	1,954	17.7	8.7	5,389	1,002	2,285	937
1993	8,940	3,262	2,584	1,297	1,798	18.0	8.3	4,848	976	2,198	919
1994[2]	7,996	2,728	2,408	1,237	1,623	18.8	9.2	3,815	791	2,786	604
1995	7,404	2,700	2,342	1,085	1,278	16.6	8.3	3,476	824	2,525	579
1996	7,236	2,633	2,287	1,053	1,262	16.7	8.3	3,370	774	2,512	580
1997[2]	6,739	2,538	2,138	995	1,067	15.8	8.0	3,037	795	2,338	569
1998[2]	6,210	2,622	1,950	763	875	14.5	6.7	2,822	734	2,132	520
1999[2]	5,880	2,568	1,832	755	725	13.4	6.4	2,622	783	2,005	469
2000[2]	5,655	2,543	1,803	665	644	12.6	5.9	2,492	775	1,957	431

1. Beginning January 1994 includes persons who completed temporary jobs.
2. The comparability of historical labor force data has been affected at various times by methodological and conceptual changes. For an explanation, see the Explanatory Notes and Estimates of Error section of *Employment and Earnings*, a monthly periodical published by the Bureau of Labor Statistics.
   Dash indicates data not available.

Source: U.S. Department of Labor. (2001). *Report on the American Workforce.* Washington, D.C.: Government Printing Office. Retrieved from http://www.bls.gov/opub/rtaw/pdf/appendix.pdf.

Table 5.6
Total Unemployed and Insured Unemployed by State: 1980 to 2001

[**7,637 represents 7,637,000.** For civilian noninstitutional population 16 years old and over. Annual averages of monthly figures. Total unemployment estimates based on the Current Population Survey. U.S. totals derived by independent population controls; therefore state data may not add to U.S. totals.]

State	Total unemployed								Insured unemployed[2]			
	Number (1,000)				Percent[1]				Number (1,000)		Percent[3]	
	1980	1990	2000	2001	1980	1990	2000	2001	1999	2000	1999	2000
United States . . .	7,637	7,047	5,655	6,742	7.1	5.6	4.0	4.8	[4]2,187.9	[4]2,110	[4]1.8	[4]1.7
Alabama	147	130	99	114	8.8	6.9	4.6	5.3	28.4	29.0	1.6	1.6
Alaska	18	19	21	20	9.7	7.0	6.6	6.3	12.9	12.3	5.1	4.9
Arizona	83	99	91	113	6.7	5.5	3.9	4.7	21.2	20.5	1.0	1.0
Arkansas	76	78	55	63	7.6	7.0	4.4	5.1	24.9	23.9	2.3	2.2
California	790	874	845	927	6.8	5.8	4.9	5.3	367.0	338.5	2.7	2.4
Colorado	88	89	63	85	5.9	5.0	2.7	3.7	15.9	15.0	0.8	0.7
Connecticut	94	95	39	56	5.9	5.2	2.3	3.3	31.2	28.3	1.9	1.7
Delaware	22	19	16	15	7.7	5.2	4.0	3.5	5.5	5.9	1.4	1.5
District of Columbia .	24	22	16	18	7.3	6.6	5.8	6.5	6.5	5.7	1.6	1.3
Florida	251	390	269	365	5.9	6.0	3.6	4.8	73.1	70.8	1.1	1.1
Georgia	163	182	154	165	6.4	5.5	3.7	4.0	32.6	34.5	0.9	0.9
Hawaii	21	16	26	28	4.9	2.9	4.3	4.6	10.7	8.4	2.1	1.7
Idaho	34	29	32	34	7.9	5.9	4.9	5.0	12.5	12.1	2.4	2.3
Illinois	459	369	279	343	8.3	6.2	4.4	5.4	104.0	103.8	1.8	1.8
Indiana	252	149	100	136	9.6	5.3	3.2	4.4	28.6	31.8	1.0	1.1
Iowa	82	62	41	53	5.8	4.3	2.6	3.3	17.9	19.4	1.3	1.4
Kansas	53	57	52	59	4.5	4.5	3.7	4.3	14.7	15.6	1.2	1.2
Kentucky	133	104	82	108	8.0	5.9	4.1	5.5	24.9	25.4	1.5	1.5
Louisiana	121	117	112	122	6.7	6.3	5.5	6.0	25.9	24.0	1.4	1.3
Maine	39	33	24	27	7.8	5.2	3.5	4.0	9.8	8.9	1.8	1.6
Maryland	140	122	108	116	6.5	4.7	3.9	4.1	30.2	28.9	1.4	0.3
Massachusetts	162	195	86	121	5.6	6.0	2.6	3.7	66.2	60.1	2.2	1.9
Michigan	534	350	185	274	12.4	7.6	3.6	5.3	79.7	81.6	1.8	1.8
Minnesota	125	117	90	104	5.9	4.9	3.3	3.7	29.9	31.4	1.2	1.2
Mississippi	79	90	75	72	7.5	7.6	5.7	5.5	18.4	19.7	1.7	1.8
Missouri	167	151	101	140	7.2	5.8	3.5	4.7	40.1	41.8	1.6	1.6
Montana	23	24	24	21	6.1	6.0	4.9	4.6	7.8	7.8	2.2	2.2
Nebraska	31	18	28	29	4.1	2.2	3.0	3.1	7.0	7.3	0.8	0.9
Nevada	27	33	40	55	6.2	4.9	4.1	5.3	18.3	19.5	2.0	2.0
New Hampshire	22	36	19	24	4.7	5.7	2.8	3.5	3.7	3.1	0.7	0.5
New Jersey	260	206	157	176	7.2	5.1	3.8	4.2	91.0	84.8	2.5	2.3
New Mexico	42	46	40	40	7.5	6.5	4.9	4.8	11.0	9.5	1.7	1.4
New York	597	467	408	429	7.5	5.3	4.6	4.9	157.5	146.2	2.0	1.8
North Carolina	187	144	144	221	6.6	4.2	3.6	5.5	51.3	54.3	1.4	1.5
North Dakota	15	13	10	10	5.0	4.0	3.0	2.8	4.1	3.9	1.4	1.3
Ohio	426	310	237	251	8.4	5.7	4.1	4.3	68.1	71.6	1.3	1.3
Oklahoma	66	86	50	64	4.8	5.7	3.0	3.8	14.2	12.2	1.0	0.9
Oregon	107	83	87	114	8.3	5.6	4.9	6.3	42.4	41.2	2.8	2.7
Pennsylvania	425	315	250	287	7.8	5.4	4.2	4.7	136.5	132.4	2.6	2.5
Rhode Island	34	35	21	24	7.2	6.8	4.1	4.7	13.2	12.2	3.0	2.7
South Carolina	96	83	77	106	6.9	4.8	3.9	5.4	25.7	27.1	1.5	1.5
South Dakota	16	13	9	13	4.9	3.9	2.3	3.3	2.1	2.0	0.6	0.6
Tennessee	152	126	110	126	7.3	5.3	3.9	4.5	39.9	42.2	1.6	1.6
Texas	352	544	437	507	5.2	6.3	4.2	4.9	124.6	107.9	1.4	1.2
Utah	40	35	36	49	6.3	4.3	3.2	4.4	10.1	10.5	1.1	1.1
Vermont	16	15	10	12	6.4	5.0	2.9	3.6	5.3	4.8	1.9	1.7
Virginia	128	141	80	127	5.0	4.3	2.9	3.5	22.2	22.2	0.7	0.7
Washington	156	125	158	192	7.9	4.9	5.2	6.4	77.6	70.6	3.1	2.7
West Virginia	74	64	46	41	9.4	8.4	5.5	4.9	16.1	14.1	2.4	2.1
Wisconsin	167	114	104	136	7.2	4.4	3.5	4.6	50.3	53.1	1.9	2.0
Wyoming	9	13	10	11	4.0	5.5	3.9	3.9	3.1	2.9	1.5	1.3

1. Total unemployment as percent of civilian labor force.
2. Source: U.S. Employment and Training Administration, *Unemployment Insurance, Financial Handbook*, annual updates.
3. Insured unemployment as percent of average covered employment in the previous year.
4. Includes 59,100 in Puerto Rico and the Virgin Islands in 1999 and 49,800 in 2000.

Source: United States Census Bureau. (2002). *Statistical Abstract of the United States 2002.* Washington, D.C.: Government Printing Office. Retrieved from http://www.census.gov/prod/2003pubs/02statab/labor.pdf.

Table 5.7
U.S. Unemployment Rates for Selected Demographic Groups, Annual Averages: 1948 to 2000

(Percent)

Year	Total, all workers	Men			Women			White	Black	Married men, spouse present	Women who maintain families
		Total	16 to 19 years	20 years and over	Total	16 to 19 years	20 years and over				
1948	3.8	3.6	9.8	3.2	4.1	8.3	3.6	–	–	–	–
1949	5.9	5.9	14.3	5.4	6.0	12.3	5.3	–	–	–	–
1950	5.3	5.1	12.7	4.7	5.7	11.4	5.1	–	–	–	–
1951	3.3	2.8	8.1	2.5	4.4	8.3	4.0	–	–	–	–
1952	3.0	2.8	8.9	2.4	3.6	8.0	3.2	–	–	–	–
1953[1]	2.9	2.8	7.9	2.5	3.3	7.2	2.9	–	–	–	–
1954	5.5	5.3	13.5	4.9	6.0	11.4	5.5	5.0	–	–	–
1955	4.4	4.2	11.6	3.8	4.9	10.2	4.4	3.9	–	2.6	–
1956	4.1	3.8	11.1	3.4	4.8	11.2	4.2	3.6	–	2.3	–
1957	4.3	4.1	12.4	3.6	4.7	10.6	4.1	3.8	–	2.8	–
1958	6.8	6.8	17.1	6.2	6.8	14.3	6.1	6.1	–	5.1	–
1959	5.5	5.2	15.3	4.7	5.9	13.5	5.2	4.8	–	3.6	–
1960[1]	5.5	5.4	15.3	4.7	5.9	13.9	5.1	5.0	–	3.7	–
1961	6.7	6.4	17.1	5.7	7.2	16.3	6.3	6.0	–	4.6	–
1962[1]	5.5	5.2	14.7	4.6	6.2	14.6	5.4	4.9	–	3.6	–
1963	5.7	5.2	17.2	4.5	6.5	17.2	5.4	5.0	–	3.4	–
1964	5.2	4.6	15.8	3.9	6.2	16.6	5.2	4.6	–	2.8	–
1965	4.5	4.0	14.1	3.2	5.5	15.7	4.5	4.1	–	2.4	–
1966	3.8	3.2	11.7	2.5	4.8	14.1	3.8	3.4	–	1.9	–
1967	3.8	3.1	12.3	2.3	5.2	13.5	4.2	3.4	–	1.8	4.9
1968	3.6	2.9	11.6	2.2	4.8	14.0	3.8	3.2	–	1.6	4.4
1969	3.5	2.8	11.4	2.1	4.7	13.3	3.7	3.1	–	1.5	4.4
1970	4.9	4.4	15.0	3.5	5.9	15.6	4.8	4.5	–	2.6	5.4
1971	5.9	5.3	16.6	4.4	6.9	17.2	5.7	5.4	–	3.2	7.3
1972[1]	5.6	5.0	15.9	4.0	6.6	16.7	5.4	5.1	10.4	2.8	7.2
1973[1]	4.9	4.2	13.9	3.3	6.0	15.3	4.9	4.3	9.4	2.3	7.1
1974	5.6	4.9	15.6	3.8	6.7	16.6	5.5	5.0	10.5	2.7	7.0
1975	8.5	7.9	20.1	6.8	9.3	19.7	8.0	7.8	14.8	5.1	10.0
1976	7.7	7.1	19.2	5.9	8.6	18.7	7.4	7.0	14.0	4.2	10.1
1977	7.1	6.3	17.3	5.2	8.2	18.3	7.0	6.2	14.0	3.6	9.4
1978[1]	6.1	5.3	15.8	4.3	7.2	17.1	6.0	5.2	12.8	2.8	8.5
1979	5.8	5.1	15.9	4.2	6.8	16.4	5.7	5.1	12.3	2.8	8.3
1980	7.1	6.9	18.3	5.9	7.4	17.2	6.4	6.3	14.3	4.2	9.2
1981	7.6	7.4	20.1	6.3	7.9	19.0	6.8	6.7	15.6	4.3	10.4
1982	9.7	9.9	24.4	8.8	9.4	21.9	8.3	8.6	18.9	6.5	11.7
1983	9.6	9.9	23.3	8.9	9.2	21.3	8.1	8.4	19.5	6.5	12.2
1984	7.5	7.4	19.6	6.6	7.6	18.0	6.8	6.5	15.9	4.6	10.3
1985	7.2	7.0	19.5	6.2	7.4	17.6	6.6	6.2	15.1	4.3	10.4
1986[1]	7.0	6.9	19.0	6.1	7.1	17.6	6.2	6.0	14.5	4.4	9.8
1987	6.2	6.2	17.8	5.4	6.2	15.9	5.4	5.3	13.0	3.9	9.2
1988	5.5	5.5	16.0	4.8	5.6	14.4	4.9	4.7	11.7	3.3	8.1
1989	5.3	5.2	15.9	4.5	5.4	14.0	4.7	4.5	11.4	3.0	8.1
1990[1]	5.6	5.7	16.3	5.0	5.5	14.7	4.9	4.8	11.4	3.4	8.3
1991	6.8	7.2	19.8	6.4	6.4	17.5	5.7	6.1	12.5	4.4	9.3
1992	7.5	7.9	21.5	7.1	7.0	18.6	6.3	6.6	14.2	5.1	10.0
1993	6.9	7.2	20.4	6.4	6.6	17.5	5.9	6.1	13.0	4.4	9.7
1994[1]	6.1	6.2	19.0	5.4	6.0	16.2	5.4	5.3	11.5	3.7	8.9
1995	5.6	5.6	18.4	4.8	5.6	16.1	4.9	4.9	10.4	3.3	8.0
1996	5.4	5.4	18.1	4.6	5.4	15.2	4.8	4.7	10.5	3.0	8.2
1997[1]	4.9	4.9	16.9	4.2	5.0	15.0	4.4	4.2	10.0	2.7	8.1
1998[1]	4.5	4.4	16.2	3.7	4.6	12.9	4.1	3.9	8.9	2.4	7.2
1999[1]	4.2	4.1	14.7	3.5	4.3	13.2	3.8	3.7	8.0	2.2	6.4
2000[1]	4.0	3.9	14.0	3.3	4.1	12.1	3.6	3.5	7.6	2.0	5.9

1. The comparability of historical labor force data has been affected at various times by methodological and conceptual changes. For an explanation, see the Explanatory Notes and Estimates of Error section of *Employment and Earnings*, a monthly periodical published by the Bureau of Labor Statistics.

   Dash indicates data not available.

Source: U.S. Department of Labor. (2001). *Report on the American Workforce*. Washington, D.C.: Government Printing Office. Retrieved from http://www.bis.gov/opub/rtaw/pdf/appendix.pdf.

Table 5.8
Civilian Unemployment Rates Approximating U.S. Concepts in Ten Countries: 1959 to 2000

Year	United States	Canada	Australia	Japan	France	Germany (1)	Italy	Nether- lands	Sweden	United Kingdom
1959	5.5	5.6	[2]2.1	2.3	1.6	2.0	4.8	–	[3]1.7	2.8
1960	5.5	6.5	[2]1.6	1.7	1.5	1.1	3.7	–	[3]1.7	2.2
1961	6.7	6.7	[2]3.0	1.5	1.2	.6	3.2	–	1.5	2.0
1962	5.5	5.5	[2]2.9	1.3	1.4	.6	2.8	–	1.5	2.7
1963	5.7	5.2	[2]2.3	1.3	1.6	.5	2.4	–	1.7	3.3
1964	5.2	4.4	1.4	1.2	1.2	.4	2.7	–	1.6	2.5
1965	4.5	3.6	1.3	1.2	1.6	.3	3.5	–	1.2	2.1
1966	3.8	3.4	1.6	1.4	1.6	.3	3.7	–	1.6	2.3
1967	3.8	3.8	1.9	1.3	2.1	1.3	3.4	–	2.1	3.3
1968	3.6	4.5	1.8	1.2	2.7	1.1	3.5	–	2.2	3.2
1969	3.5	4.4	1.8	1.1	2.3	.6	3.5	–	1.9	3.1
1970	4.9	5.7	1.6	1.2	2.5	.5	3.2	–	1.5	3.1
1971	5.9	6.2	1.9	1.3	2.8	.6	3.3	–	2.6	3.9
1972	5.6	6.2	2.6	1.4	2.9	.7	3.8	–	2.7	4.2
1973	4.9	5.5	2.3	1.3	2.8	.7	3.7	3.1	2.5	3.2
1974	5.6	5.3	2.7	1.4	2.9	1.6	3.1	3.6	2.0	3.1
1975	8.5	6.9	4.9	1.9	4.2	3.4	3.4	5.1	1.6	4.6
1976	7.7	[4]6.8	4.8	2.0	4.6	3.4	3.9	5.4	1.6	5.9
1977	7.1	7.8	5.6	2.0	5.2	3.4	4.1	4.9	1.8	6.4
1978	6.1	8.1	6.3	2.3	5.4	3.3	4.1	5.1	2.2	6.3
1979	5.8	7.2	6.3	2.1	6.1	2.9	4.4	5.1	2.1	5.4
1980	7.1	7.2	6.1	2.0	6.5	2.8	4.4	6.0	2.0	7.0
1981	7.6	7.3	5.8	2.2	7.6	4.0	4.9	8.9	2.5	10.5
1982	9.7	10.6	7.2	2.4	8.3	5.6	5.4	10.2	3.1	11.3
1983	9.6	11.5	10.0	2.7	8.6	[4]6.9	5.9	[4]11.4	3.5	11.8
1984	7.5	10.9	9.0	2.8	10.0	7.1	5.9	11.5	3.1	11.7
1985	7.2	10.2	8.3	2.6	10.5	7.2	6.0	9.6	2.8	11.2
1986	7.0	9.2	8.1	2.8	10.6	6.6	[4]7.5	10.0	2.6	11.2
1987	6.2	8.4	8.1	2.9	10.8	6.3	7.9	10.0	[4]2.2	10.3
1988	5.5	7.3	7.2	2.5	10.3	6.3	7.9	[4]7.7	1.9	8.6
1989	5.3	7.0	6.2	2.3	9.6	5.7	7.8	7.0	1.6	7.2
1990	[4]5.6	7.7	6.9	2.1	9.1	5.0	7.0	6.2	1.8	6.9
1991	6.8	9.8	9.6	2.1	9.6	[4]5.6	[4]6.9	5.9	3.1	8.8
1992	7.5	10.6	10.8	2.2	[4]10.4	6.7	7.3	5.6	5.6	10.1
1993	6.9	10.7	10.9	2.5	11.8	7.9	[4]10.2	6.5	9.3	10.5
1994	[4]6.1	9.4	9.7	2.9	12.3	8.5	11.2	7.2	9.6	9.7
1995	5.6	8.5	8.5	3.2	11.8	8.2	11.8	7.1	9.1	8.7
1996	5.4	8.7	8.6	3.4	12.5	8.9	11.7	6.3	9.9	8.2
1997	4.9	8.2	8.6	3.4	12.4	9.9	11.9	5.3	10.1	7.0
1998	4.5	7.5	8.0	4.1	11.8	9.3	12.0	4.0	8.4	6.3
1999	4.2	6.8	7.2	4.7	11.2	8.7	11.5	3.4	7.1	6.1p
2000	4.0	5.8	6.6	4.8	9.7p	8.3p	10.7p	–	5.8	5.5p

1. Former West Germany through 1990, unified Germany thereafter.

2. The Australian labor force survey was initiated in 1964. Unemployment rates for 1959–1963 are estimates made by an Australian researcher.

3. The Swedish labor force survey was initiated in 1961. The figures for 1959-60 are estimates made by the Organization for Economic Cooperation and Development.

4. There are breaks in the series for the United States (1990, 1994), Canada (1976), France (1992), Germany (1983, 1991), Italy (1986, 1991, 1993), the Netherlands (1983, 1988), and Sweden (1987):

The United States (1990): The impact was to raise the unemployment rate by 0.1 percentage point.

The United States (1994): The impact was to raise the unemployment rate by 0.1 percentage point.

Canada (1976): Beginning with 1976, the unemployment rates are adjusted to more closely approximate U.S. concepts. The impact was to lower the unemployment rate 0.4 percentage point in 1976.

France (1992): The impact was to lower the unemployment rate by 0.1 percentage point.

Germany (1983): The impact was to lower the unemployment rate by 0.3 percentage point.

Germany (1991): The impact of including the former East Germany was to increase the 1991 unemployment rate 1.3 percentage points.

Italy (1986): The impact was to raise the unemployment rate by 1.2 percentage points.

Italy (1991): The impact was to raise the unemployment rate by approximately 0.3 percentage point.

Italy (1993): The impact was to raise the unemployment rate by approximately 1.1 percentage points.

Netherlands (1983): The impact was to lower the unemployment rate by about 2 percentage points.

Netherlands (1988): The impact was to lower the unemployment rate by 1.7 percentage points.

Sweden (1987): The net impact of the break and the BLS adjustment for students seeking work lowered the unemployment rate by 0.1 percentage point.

p = preliminary.

Dash indicates data not available.

Source: U.S. Department of Labor. (2001). Report on the American Workforce. Washington, D.C.: Government Printing Office. Retrieved from http://www.bis.gov/opub/rtaw/pdf/appendix.pdf.

Table 5.9
U.S. Unemployment Insurance, Workers' Compensation, Temporary Disability Insurance, and Black Lung Compensation for the Year 2000

Unemployment Insurance

2000	
Total payments	$20.3 billion
Average—	
Weekly benefit amount (regular programs)	$221
Duration of benefits	13.7 weeks
Weekly insured unemployment	2.1 million
Covered employment	127.9 million

Workers' Compensation

1999	
Benefit payments:	
Total	$43.4 billion
Compensation payments	25.3 billion
Medical and hospitalization	18.0 billion
Benefits paid by—	
Private insurance carriers	23.8 billion
State and federal funds	10.2 billion
Employers' self-insurance	9.3 billion
Covered workers per month	123.9 million
Costs as a percent of covered payroll	1.29 percent

Temporary Disability Insurance

Programs in effect in—
California, Hawaii, New Jersey, New York, Rhode Island, Puerto Rico, and the railroad industry.

	Average weekly benefit, 1998	
	State fund	Private plans
California*	$230	$352
New York	$147	$185

*Accounts for half of the workers participating in TDI.

Black Lung

Basic benefit, miner or widow	$500.50
Maximum family benefit	1,001.00
Part B (claims filed before July 1, 1973)	
Number of monthly benefits to miners, widows, and dependents, December 2000	89,400
Average monthly benefit, December 2000	$518.60
Total benefits paid, calendar year 2000	$509.3 million
Part C (claims filed before July 1, 1973 or later)	
Number of monthly benefits to miners and survivors, September 2000	51,700
Total benefits paid, fiscal year 2000	
Disability and survivors benefits	$350.3 million
Medical benefits	75.6 million

Source: Social Security Administration. (2001). *Annual Statistical Supplement, 2001 to the Social Security Bulletin.* Baltimore: Social Security Administration, Office of Policy. Retrieved from http://www.ssa.gov/policy/docs/statcomps/supplement/2001/supp01.pdf.

Table 5.10
Unemployment Insurance Summary Data on State Programs for 1999 and 2000

(Except where noted excludes data for federal employees and for ex-service members; includes data for state and local government employees where covered by state law after 1955.)

State	Covered employment (excludes federal government) Average number of workers (in thousands)	Covered employment Total payroll[6] (in millions)	Insured unemployment as percent of covered employment[1]	Number of first payments	Average weekly benefit for total unemployment Amount[7]	Average weekly benefit Percent of average weekly wages[8]	Average weekly insured unemployment	Average actual duration (in weeks)	Claimants exhausting benefits[2] Number	Claimants exhausting benefits Percent of first payments[2]	Contributions collected (in millions)[3]	Benefits paid (in millions)[4]	Average employer contribution rate (percent)[5]
Total..	125,334	$4,130,377	1.8	6,951,210	$211.75	33.1	2,187,932	14.5	2,300,128	31.4	$19,153.8	$20,270.5	1.8
AL......	1,818	50,209	1.6	127,895	155.55	29.3	28,382	10.1	26,912	19.9	159.1	192.2	1.1
AK	252	8,381	5.1	45,635	181.58	28.4	12,866	14.9	19,252	41.9	105.3	122.8	2.5
AZ	2,104	63,718	1.0	70,638	157.31	27.0	21,228	14.3	22,447	31.8	173.2	150.3	1.1
AR......	1,092	27,408	2.3	76,981	197.20	40.9	24,939	13.0	24,341	29.2	175.6	162.4	2.0
CA......	14,135	528,918	2.6	1,047,526	158.21	22.0	366,976	16.4	412,584	38.2	2,693.0	2,634.5	2.7
CO......	2,051	69,588	.8	55,494	240.96	36.9	15,908	12.1	20,316	36.6	191.3	158.6	1.0
CT	1,630	69,783	1.9	109,049	225.36	27.4	31,248	14.6	27,530	24.2	380.7	372.4	1.8
DE	397	13,901	1.4	22,525	203.70	30.3	5,503	12.6	4,534	19.6	63.7	56.4	2.1
DC	432	20,506	1.5	17,190	235.01	25.7	6,455	19.7	9,425	51.8	88.4	60.1	2.3
FL......	6,720	192,543	1.1	223,361	211.84	38.4	73,090	14.0	94,332	39.8	549.5	670.4	1.2
GA......	3,708	118,993	.9	163,110	198.70	32.2	32,573	9.0	45,919	27.2	154.3	280.7	.5
HI	508	14,728	2.1	30,754	277.63	49.8	10,706	16.4	9,921	28.9	135.7	129.6	1.7
ID	530	13,618	2.4	43,733	200.43	40.5	12,457	12.5	12,536	27.5	79.6	101.5	1.2
IL........	5,756	208,105	1.8	307,325	241.16	34.7	104,015	15.9	92,449	30.2	1,121.8	1,169.0	2.4
IN	2,867	85,648	1.0	111,817	210.31	36.6	28,575	11.3	34,135	26.7	266.5	270.5	1.4
IA.......	1,412	37,820	1.3	80,519	227.05	44.1	17,909	10.8	14,073	17.8	152.5	180.3	1.0
KS	1,273	35,355	1.2	52,947	237.48	44.5	14,680	12.9	15,867	31.1	42.5	158.0	.3
KY	1,696	46,709	1.5	103,664	201.03	38.0	24,945	12.1	18,543	16.9	238.5	240.4	1.8
LA.......	1,812	48,798	1.4	73,959	162.10	31.3	25,930	15.3	21,765	29.3	166.4	186.7	1.5
ME......	560	14,856	1.8	32,599	192.30	37.7	9,816	13.0	13,376	34.6	128.5	81.4	3.6
MD	2,220	74,475	1.4	96,934	204.78	31.7	30,246	13.5	27,069	27.2	284.2	271.0	1.6
MA......	3,133	126,114	2.1	181,671	278.86	36.0	66,242	17.0	59,382	31.3	785.0	822.4	2.3
MI......	4,446	158,447	1.8	323,015	237.88	34.7	79,736	11.5	84,055	21.3	990.2	879.9	2.7
MN	2,517	83,990	1.2	100,147	278.76	43.4	29,944	14.0	26,306	24.8	344.8	356.6	1.1
MS......	1,113	26,744	1.6	54,780	153.30	33.2	18,365	13.7	14,618	25.1	122.6	110.2	1.7
MO	2,588	76,897	1.5	132,136	174.57	30.6	40,110	13.1	35,010	25.7	268.4	293.2	1.4
MT......	358	8,144	2.2	24,517	181.04	41.4	7,830	13.8	7,423	28.6	61.5	56.1	1.3
NE	851	22,450	.8	25,996	177.13	34.9	6,989	12.1	7,811	27.1	32.0	54.8	.6
NV	962	29,838	1.9	65,028	215.61	36.1	18,327	13.8	19,646	31.0	211.8	192.3	1.4
NH......	583	18,664	.6	15,380	208.27	33.8	3,704	9.6	775	4.8	28.1	35.4	.7
NJ......	3,719	151,570	2.4	255,979	277.02	35.3	91,039	17.2	117,080	44.4	1,061.8	1,076.8	1.9
NM	671	17,217	1.6	30,032	178.06	36.1	10,956	16.2	10,915	33.8	83.2	85.7	1.2
NY	8,156	343,441	1.9	416,634	231.93	28.6	157,548	17.7	209,016	45.5	1,485.7	1,639.3	2.7
NC......	3,743	109,645	1.4	215,968	218.71	38.8	51,266	10.0	40,120	18.7	327.0	428.3	.8
ND......	297	6,953	1.4	11,925	201.35	44.7	4,098	14.9	4,455	34.8	31.7	39.9	1.1
OH......	5,368	167,392	1.3	228,265	224.04	37.4	68,074	13.2	46,542	17.8	631.9	687.8	1.5
OK......	1,376	34,703	1.0	44,883	208.67	43.0	14,200	13.9	13,531	26.8	51.7	120.6	.4
OR......	1,547	47,389	2.7	142,505	223.45	37.9	42,374	14.5	39,854	27.1	471.9	429.2	2.1
PA	5,387	174,537	2.5	402,078	250.56	40.2	136,528	15.7	102,613	24.5	1,393.5	1,350.5	3.7
RI	446	13,763	2.9	43,505	245.73	41.4	13,155	13.2	13,562	30.2	159.3	140.6	3.3
SC	1,763	47,453	1.5	96,434	185.48	35.8	25,694	11.3	22,846	22.9	161.9	194.4	1.4
SD	345	8,052	.6	7,657	170.05	37.9	2,115	11.0	815	9.7	12.6	15.9	.6
TN	2,575	75,263	1.6	150,970	183.95	32.7	39,943	11.9	45,392	27.9	269.7	323.0	1.5
TX	8,830	288,791	1.4	358,590	225.36	35.8	124,619	15.9	201,647	54.6	932.4	1,189.4	1.2
UT	987	27,139	1.0	38,217	205.20	38.8	10,108	12.1	11,907	30.5	78.7	97.6	.6
VA	3,176	102,665	.7	92,254	186.91	30.1	22,200	10.2	20,533	20.9	140.5	178.6	.6
VT	282	7,728	1.9	17,836	203.40	38.7	5,276	13.3	2,525	13.8	48.5	45.4	2.5
WA	2,575	91,543	3.0	190,056	275.82	40.3	77,627	18.4	64,095	35.0	864.1	905.7	2.2
WV	659	16,814	2.4	52,317	197.98	40.4	16,090	13.6	10,566	19.4	128.3	128.6	2.9
WI......	2,662	78,482	1.9	209,497	223.46	39.4	50,277	11.8	36,982	17.1	426.8	474.8	1.9
WY	218	5,492	1.4	10,947	200.61	41.4	3,126	13.2	2,914	25.3	22.8	27.1	1.5
Other:													
PR ..	988	17,969	5.2	116,746	102.82	29.4	51,431	19.3	59,225	43.7	170.9	237.2	3.3
VI....	40	1,027	1.2	1,590	172.64	35.3	496	14.7	641	34.2	4.0	3.8	1.6

Table 5.10 (*continued*)

State	Covered employment (excludes federal government) Average number of workers (in thousands)	Total payroll[6] (in millions)	Insured unemployment as percent of covered employment[1]	Number of first payments	Average weekly benefit for total unemployment Amount[7]	Percent of average weekly wages[8]	Average weekly insured unemployment	Average actual duration (in weeks)	Claimants exhausting benefits[2] Number	Percent of first payments[2]	Contributions collected (in millions)[3]	Benefits paid (in millions)[4]	Average employer contribution rate (percent)[5]
Total..	127,858	$4,464,095	1.7	7,033,133	$221.00	32.9	2,110,279	13.7	2,143,989	31.8	$19,899.3	$20,276.9	1.8
AL......	1,824	52,054	1.6	133,933	159.41	29.1	29,046	9.9	26,847	21.5	158.2	202.9	1.1
AK......	259	8,856	4.8	43,557	189.86	28.8	12,290	14.2	16,962	39.2	110.9	110.5	2.7
AZ......	2,173	70,326	.9	69,104	162.51	26.1	20,527	14.0	23,333	33.5	170.9	154.3	1.1
AR......	1,108	28,841	2.2	80,163	210.08	42.0	23,885	11.8	22,722	30.8	175.8	169.6	1.9
CA......	14,615	600,346	2.3	973,333	160.00	20.3	338,454	15.9	370,790	37.1	2,836.8	2,406.7	2.7
CO......	2,132	78,692	.7	51,952	255.86	36.0	15,034	12.0	20,506	39.0	186.1	157.7	.9
CT......	1,653	75,154	1.7	102,837	257.56	29.5	28,347	14.1	24,483	23.3	312.7	348.9	1.5
DE......	403	14,749	1.5	26,978	214.85	30.5	5,870	11.9	4,988	19.9	59.1	74.2	1.8
DC......	453	22,506	1.3	15,164	241.03	25.2	5,705	19.6	8,230	49.6	99.7	61.2	2.3
FL......	6,939	210,178	1.0	224,212	220.21	37.8	70,767	13.3	86,357	39.8	398.3	661.7	.8
GA......	3,798	128,867	.9	177,902	211.89	32.5	34,467	8.7	42,699	27.2	132.3	317.0	.5
HI.......	523	15,544	1.6	25,247	283.67	49.6	8,389	15.4	7,058	25.5	139.6	101.6	1.7
ID	550	15,055	2.2	45,292	209.46	39.8	12,101	11.7	11,219	25.8	90.4	102.8	1.2
IL........	5,840	221,450	1.8	309,386	251.58	34.5	103,824	15.8	91,236	30.7	1,093.1	1,212.2	2.2
IN	2,893	89,263	1.1	129,325	222.19	37.4	31,768	10.7	35,548	32.2	277.1	310.8	1.4
IA.......	1,423	39,507	1.4	84,455	238.42	44.7	19,407	11.2	15,626	19.3	175.7	210.3	1.2
KS......	1,286	37,400	1.2	54,263	247.09	44.2	15,635	13.3	16,641	33.5	143.0	173.9	1.1
KY	1,724	49,322	1.5	111,252	224.78	40.8	25,421	11.5	18,296	18.5	248.9	271.4	1.9
LA......	1,832	50,530	1.3	71,852	182.06	34.3	23,972	14.5	22,561	32.7	117.1	182.0	1.3
ME......	577	15,715	1.5	28,203	202.29	38.6	8,863	14.1	10,569	39.0	150.8	76.6	2.6
MD	2,278	80,643	1.3	92,798	212.51	31.2	28,881	13.4	25,996	27.5	274.6	271.1	1.5
MA......	3,223	142,529	1.9	172,041	293.45	34.5	60,076	16.3	53,639	31.1	821.8	789.7	2.3
MI......	4,527	167,108	1.8	358,509	244.12	34.4	81,550	10.6	80,809	25.5	1,016.5	921.5	2.7
MN	2,572	90,830	1.2	109,278	290.51	42.8	31,385	13.6	26,734	26.6	345.4	397.8	1.0
MS......	1,110	27,530	1.8	60,187	156.62	32.8	19,663	13.6	16,108	29.9	114.9	122.0	1.5
MO......	2,617	81,474	1.6	137,426	186.22	31.1	41,848	13.1	34,663	26.9	237.6	333.5	1.3
MT......	367	8,658	2.1	25,194	187.92	41.4	7,798	13.0	7,216	30.6	55.8	57.8	1.1
NE......	867	23,790	.8	27,838	188.00	35.6	7,323	11.6	8,179	32.2	42.3	59.4	.8
NV......	1,003	32,158	1.9	67,949	222.43	36.1	19,534	13.8	21,190	32.8	213.3	204.3	1.3
NH......	598	20,675	.5	13,595	217.21	32.7	3,108	9.0	817	5.9	30.7	31.1	.8
NJ......	3,811	166,245	2.2	245,606	289.61	34.5	84,750	16.6	109,650	44.4	1,233.3	1,045.8	2.0
NM	687	18,444	1.4	27,492	180.43	34.9	9,475	15.2	8,594	30.6	84.9	72.9	1.2
NY......	8,329	374,357	1.8	424,234	247.48	28.6	146,212	16.0	186,345	46.3	1,870.4	1,602.2	3.2
NC......	3,795	117,380	1.4	256,360	231.21	38.9	54,345	8.9	42,564	18.5	300.5	474.6	.6
ND......	300	7,296	1.3	11,800	210.01	44.8	3,855	14.0	4,282	37.6	37.7	40.2	1.3
OH......	5,428	175,237	1.3	248,223	236.40	38.1	71,623	12.4	48,306	22.0	640.5	742.2	1.5
OK......	1,404	37,032	.9	40,872	214.40	42.3	12,218	13.0	11,846	30.5	47.4	103.7	.4
OR......	1,577	51,368	2.6	147,190	232.62	37.1	41,228	13.7	36,272	25.7	503.9	430.4	2.1
PA	5,446	184,011	2.4	396,227	264.76	40.7	132,350	15.2	96,622	24.8	1,400.3	1,461.6	3.7
RI	457	14,724	2.7	37,798	253.48	40.9	12,159	14.1	12,501	31.9	142.5	224.9	3.4
SC......	1,790	50,058	1.5	101,066	190.18	35.4	27,053	10.9	22,586	24.8	170.7	136.4	3.2
SD......	353	8,592	.6	7,791	180.86	38.6	2,043	10.0	642	9.0	13.5	203.7	1.4
TN	2,614	79,029	1.6	177,875	188.74	32.5	42,216	11.1	45,512	31.2	284.7	15.2	.6
TX	9,101	316,219	1.2	322,307	227.11	34.0	107,906	14.5	165,241	50.4	982.4	363.5	1.5
UT	1,012	29,132	1.0	40,584	213.89	38.6	10,522	11.8	11,571	30.5	61.4	988.7	1.3
VA	3,276	112,668	.7	95,607	203.88	30.8	22,233	9.8	21,975	25.2	149.3	3.0	2.6
VT	290	8,324	1.6	17,593	215.55	39.1	4,789	12.5	2,258	13.6	49.0	44.3	2.4
WA	2,638	97,229	2.7	205,411	280.94	39.6	70,580	16.2	57,301	29.0	919.2	196.9	.6
WV	664	17,491	2.1	48,884	197.53	39.0	14,067	12.6	8,808	19.1	132.1	872.8	2.1
WI......	2,703	82,682	2.0	230,458	233.11	39.6	53,078	11.2	38,121	17.9	440.5	526.3	1.9
WY	223	5,898	1.3	10,833	207.01	40.8	2,867	11.8	2,494	25.2	23.3	26.3	1.4
Other:													
PR ..	1,012	18,666	4.9	114,649	103.91	29.3	49,437	18.7	57,994	48.8	175.7	224.9	3.4
VI....	41	1,120	.8	1,048	183.43	35.2	333	15.4	482	38.3	6.5	3.0	2.6

1. Based on average covered employment in 12-month period.

2. Percentages based on first payments for 12-month period.

3. Contributions, penalties, and interest from employers and contributions from employees in states taxing workers. Adjusted to exclude refunds of contributions and dishonored checks. Excludes state and local government employees covered on reimbursable basis.

4. Adjusted to exclude voided benefit checks and for transfers under interstate combined-wage plan. Excludes Extended Benefits and Emergency Unemployment Compensation.

5. Estimated data. As percent of taxable payroll. Standard contribution rate for most states, 2.7 percent. Excludes state and local jurisdictions covering state and local government employees on a reimbursable basis.

6. Total wages earned in covered employment during all pay periods ended within the year.

7. Includes dependents' allowances for states that provide such benefits.

8. Based on average total weekly wage in current year.

Source: Social Security Administration. (2001). *Annual Statistical Supplement, 2001 to the Social Security Bulletin.* Baltimore: Social Security Administration, Office of Policy. Retrieved from http://www.ssa.gov/policy/docs/statcomps/supplement/2001/supp01.pdf.

Table 5.11
U.S. Workers' Compensation Coverage, Benefits, and Costs: 1940 to 1999[1]

Calendar year	Estimated number of workers covered per month (in millions)	Benefits paid during year (in millions)						Cost of program as a percentage of covered payroll [2]	Benefits as a percentage of covered payroll [3]
		Total	Type of insurance			Type of benefits			
			Insurance losses paid by private carriers [4]	State and federal fund disbursements [5]	Employers' self-insurance payments [6]	Medical and hospitalization	Compensation payments		
1940	24.6	$256	$135	$73	$48	$95	$161	1.19	0.72
1946	32.7	434	270	96	68	140	294	.91	.54
1948	36.0	534	335	121	78	175	359	.96	.51
1949	35.3	566	353	132	81	185	381	.98	.55
1950	36.9	615	381	149	85	200	415	.89	.54
1951	38.7	709	444	170	94	233	476	.90	.54
1952	39.4	785	491	193	101	260	525	.94	.55
1953	40.7	841	524	210	107	280	561	.97	.55
1954	39.8	876	540	225	110	308	568	.98	.57
1955	41.4	916	563	238	115	325	591	.91	.55
1956	43.0	1,002	618	259	125	350	652	.92	.55
1957	43.3	1,062	661	271	130	360	702	.91	.56
1958	42.5	1,112	694	285	132	375	737	.91	.58
1959	44.0	1,210	753	316	141	410	800	.89	.58
1960	44.9	1,295	810	325	160	435	860	.93	.59
1961	45.0	1,374	851	347	176	460	914	.95	.61
1962	46.2	1,489	924	371	194	495	994	.96	.62
1963	47.3	1,582	988	388	207	525	1,057	.99	.62
1964	48.8	1,707	1,070	412	226	565	1,142	1.00	.63
1965	50.8	1,814	1,124	445	244	600	1,214	1.00	.61
1966	53.7	2,000	1,239	486	275	680	1,320	1.02	.61
1967	55.0	2,189	1,363	524	303	750	1,439	1.07	.63
1968	56.8	2,376	1,482	556	338	830	1,546	1.07	.62
1969	59.0	2,634	1,641	607	386	920	1,714	1.08	.62
1970	59.2	3,031	1,843	755	432	1,050	1,981	1.11	.66
1971	59.4	3,563	2,005	1,098	460	1,130	2,433	1.11	.67
1972	62.3	4,061	2,179	1,379	504	1,250	2,811	1.14	.68
1973	66.3	5,103	2,514	1,998	592	1,480	3,623	1.17	.70
1974	68.0	5,781	2,971	2,086	724	1,760	4,021	1.24	.75
1975	67.2	6,598	3,422	2,324	852	2,030	4,568	1.32	.83
1976	69.6	7,584	3,976	2,570	1,039	2,380	5,204	1.49	.87
1977	72.1	8,630	4,629	2,750	1,250	2,680	5,950	1.71	.92
1978	75.6	9,796	5,256	3,043	1,497	2,980	6,816	1.86	.94
1979	78.6	12,027	6,157	4,022	1,848	3,520	8,507	1.95	1.01
1980	78.8	13,618	7,029	4,330	2,259	3,947	9,671	1.96	1.07
1981	78.3	15,054	7,876	4,595	2,583	4,431	10,623	1.85	1.08
1982	77.0	16,407	8,647	4,768	2,993	5,058	11,349	1.75	1.16
1983	78.0	17,575	9,265	5,061	3,249	5,681	11,894	1.67	1.17
1984	81.9	19,685	10,610	5,405	3,671	6,424	13,261	1.66	1.21
1985	84.3	22,217	12,341	5,744	4,132	7,498	14,719	1.82	1.30
1986	86.0	24,613	13,827	6,248	4,538	8,642	15,971	1.99	1.37
1987	88.4	27,318	15,453	6,782	5,082	9,912	17,406	2.07	1.43
1988	91.3	30,733	17,512	7,477	5,744	11,518	19,215	2.16	1.49
1989	93.7	34,316	19,918	7,965	6,433	13,424	20,892	2.04	1.46
1990	95.1	38,238	22,222	8,658	7,358	15,187	23,051	2.13	1.57
1991	93.6	42,169	24,515	9,711	7,944	16,832	25,337	2.16	1.65
1992	94.6	44,660	24,030	10,987	9,643	18,252	26,408	2.13	1.69
1993	96.1	42,925	21,773	11,294	9,857	17,521	25,403	2.17	1.62
1994	109.4	44,586	22,306	10,753	11,527	17,194	27,392	2.05	1.51
1995	112.8	43,373	21,145	10,996	11,232	16,733	26,640	1.83	1.39
1996	114.6	41,836	20,392	10,669	10,775	16,555	25,281	1.67	1.26
1997	117.7	41,147	20,978	10,294	9,875	15,701	25,445	1.47	1.15
1998	120.9	42,312	22,821	10,269	9,222	16,390	25,922	1.37	1.09
1999	123.9	43,371	23,813	10,221	9,337	18,043	25,329	1.29	1.05

1. Beginning in 1959, includes Alaska and Hawaii.

2. Premiums written by private carriers, and state funds and benefits paid by self-insurers increased by 5–11 percent to allow for administrative costs; also includes benefits paid and administrative costs of federal system for government employees.

3. Excludes programs financed from general revenue—most federal Black Lung benefits.

4. Net cash and medical benefits paid during calendar year by private insurance companies under standard workers' compensation policies.

5. Net cash and medical benefits paid by competitive and exclusive state funds and by federal system for government employees and, beginning in 1970, cash benefits paid by federal Black Lung program.

6. Cash and medical benefits paid by self-insurers, plus value of medical benefits paid by employers carrying workers' compensations policies that exclude standard medical coverage.

Source: Social Security Administration. (2001). *Annual Statistical Supplement, 2001 to the Social Security Bulletin.* Baltimore: Social Security Administration, Office of Policy. Retrieved from http://www.ssa.gov/policy/docs/statcomps/supplement/2001/supp01.pdf.

Table 5.12
Workers' Compensation Benefits, by State: 1996 to 1999

[In thousands]

State	1996	1997	1998	1999
Total [1]	$41,835,949	$41,146,574	$42,311,540	$43,371,412
Alabama	525,073	530,230	615,316	596,233
Alaska	121,597	130,045	128,576	137,630
Arizona	458,593	427,885	417,673	427,841
Arkansas	160,328	157,128	163,733	165,854
California	6,829,656	7,073,544	7,374,486	7,856,442
Colorado	679,270	674,035	656,894	702,458
Connecticut	672,241	731,830	711,130	722,156
Delaware	121,154	120,719	118,511	105,436
District of Columbia	89,945	81,696	75,800	82,011
Florida	2,706,603	2,318,086	2,207,984	2,079,830
Georgia	821,952	713,041	807,582	816,249
Hawaii	288,495	254,995	233,491	211,138
Idaho	189,575	212,563	237,444	230,218
Illinois	1,643,487	1,576,695	1,687,070	1,719,617
Indiana	409,901	437,797	482,029	522,237
Iowa	260,628	273,028	292,002	283,983
Kansas	269,507	312,698	318,352	326,196
Kentucky	506,771	380,417	410,003	430,953
Louisiana	557,131	419,777	428,441	428,808
Maine	314,116	271,307	246,145	249,674
Maryland	1,037,957	1,082,280	1,127,128	1,169,386
Massachusetts	700,375	653,327	641,409	633,840
Michigan	1,346,409	1,332,222	1,366,963	1,392,806
Minnesota	739,500	738,100	732,300	744,600
Mississippi	224,341	231,340	234,700	253,532
Missouri	618,911	527,053	589,232	592,993
Montana	149,540	167,812	170,715	145,306
Nebraska	198,923	184,673	181,816	173,149
Nevada	382,873	341,203	334,659	362,971
New Hampshire	188,262	155,397	163,885	170,876
New Jersey	930,724	923,460	954,696	987,378
New Mexico	151,299	119,893	116,819	117,168
New York	2,558,704	2,618,320	2,556,658	2,782,474
North Carolina	500,506	618,426	765,817	710,100
North Dakota	66,819	76,617	81,403	77,236
Ohio	2,146,314	2,030,046	2,068,878	2,018,923
Oklahoma	645,329	547,355	520,181	465,231
Oregon	445,505	417,222	432,825	398,965
Pennsylvania	2,533,788	2,471,021	2,418,072	2,441,255
Rhode Island	135,520	138,211	145,252	152,861
South Carolina	371,724	459,377	483,606	511,735
South Dakota	82,063	73,862	72,722	80,331
Tennessee	432,422	432,662	517,846	514,242
Texas	1,259,647	1,377,393	1,488,896	1,677,824
Utah	224,146	192,381	220,247	219,338
Vermont	74,271	87,488	95,056	103,928
Virginia	560,309	534,350	591,068	581,357
Washington	1,192,926	1,234,495	1,309,371	1,418,255
West Virginia	523,803	616,790	629,480	665,403
Wisconsin	647,520	594,463	621,973	652,281
Wyoming	73,592	68,068	74,469	71,151
Federal programs:				
Civilian employee	1,911,682	1,900,963	1,955,287	2,008,909
Black lung [2]	1,154,222	1,102,798	1,035,450	980,642

1. Calendar year data, except fiscal year data for federal civilian and other programs and for some states with state funds. Payments represent compensation and medical benefits and include insurance losses paid by private insurance carriers (compiled form state workers' compensation agencies and the A.M. Best Company); disbursement of state funds (compiled from the A.M. Best Company, state workers' compensation agencies and U.S. Census Bureau): and self-insurance payments, estimated from available state data. Includes benefit payments under Longshore and Harbor Workers' Compensation Act for states in which such payments are made. For data for years 1990, 1993–95, see U.S. Census Bureau, *Statistical Abstract of the United States; 1999* (119th edition) Washington, DC, 1999, table 630, p. 397.

2. Includes payments by the Social Security Administration and the Department of Labor.

Source: Social Security Administration. (2001). *Annual Statistical Supplement, 2001 to the Social Security Bulletin*. Baltimore: Social Security Administration, Office of Policy. Retrieved from http://www.ssa.gov/policy/docs/statcomps/supplement/2001/supp01.pdf.

Table 5.13
Black Lung Benefits Paid to Miners, Widows, and Dependents:
United States, 1970 to 2000[1]

December	Number				Benefits (in thousands)	
	Total	Miners	Widows	Dependents[2]	Monthly amount	Annual amount
1970	111,976	43,921	24,889	43,166	$12,500	$111,000
1971	231,729	77,213	67,358	87,158	27,200	378,900
1972	298,963	101,802	88,067	109,094	37,800	554,400
1973	461,491	159,837	124,154	177,500	63,700	1,045,200
1974	487,216	169,097	134,700	183,419	71,500	951,300
1975	482,311	165,405	139,407	177,499	75,500	947,700
1976	469,655	158,087	142,495	169,073	77,400	963,300
1977	457,399	148,720	144,543	164,136	80,500	942,200
1978	439,970	138,648	145,829	155,493	82,300	965,100
1979	418,948	129,558	146,527	142,863	86,500	983,100
1980	399,477	120,235	146,603	132,639	91,400	1,032,000
1981	376,505	111,249	146,173	119,083	91,700	1,081,300
1982	354,569	102,234	144,863	107,472	90,800	1,076,000
1983	333,358	93,694	142,967	96,697	86,300	1,055,800
1984	313,822	85,658	140,995	87,169	85,300	1,038,000
1985	294,846	77,836	138,328	78,682	83,700	1,025,000
1986	275,783	70,253	135,033	70,497	78,900	971,000
1987	258,988	63,573	131,561	63,854	76,800	940,000
1988	241,626	56,977	127,322	57,327	73,500	904,000
1989	225,764	51,048	123,220	51,496	72,000	882,000
1990	210,678	45,643	118,705	46,330	70,000	863,400
1991	196,419	40,703	114,046	41,670	68,400	844,400
1992	182,396	35,971	109,091	37,334	66,500	822,500
1993	168,365	31,664	103,334	33,367	64,100	794,300
1994	155,172	27,828	97,414	29,930	60,600	751,900
1995	143,011	24,573	91,517	26,921	56,100	696,700
1996	131,143	21,477	85,559	24,107	52,600	654,600
1997	119,233	18,488	79,238	21,507	49,255	614,888
1998	109,271	15,964	73,420	19,887	46,204	576,389
1999	98,977	13,635	67,359	17,983	43,225	541,200
2000	89,355	11,587	61,542	16,226	40,625	509,290

1. Benefits payable under Part B of the black lung program established by the Federal Coal Mine Health and Safety Act of 1969. Beginning October 1, 1997, responsibility for maintenance and payment of Part B benefits was transferred from the Social Security Administration (SSA) to the Department of Labor (DOL); SSA, however, maintains responsibility for conducting formal hearings necessary to resolve contested issues with regard to Part B claims. Benefits under Part C (generally claims arising July 1, 1973 and later) are also administered by the DOL but are not included here.

2. Includes wives of living miners, divorced wives, children, and dependent brothers and sisters of miners.

Source: Social Security Administration. (2001). *Annual Statistical Supplement, 2001 to the Social Security Bulletin.* Baltimore: Social Security Administration, Office of Policy. Retrieved from http://www.ssa.gov/policy/docs/statcomps/supplement/2001/supp01.pdf.

Table 5.14
Unemployment Rate by Country: 1995 to 2001

[**Annual averages.** The standardized unemployment rates shown here are calculated as the number of unemployed persons as a percentage of the civilian labor force. The unemployed are persons of working age who, in the reference period, are without work, available for work and have taken specific steps to find work.]

Country	1995	1999	2000	2001	Country	1995	1999	2000	2001
OECD, total	7.5	6.8	6.3	6.5	Ireland	12.3	5.6	4.2	3.8
European Union	10.7	9.0	8.1	7.6	Italy	11.9	11.2	10.4	9.5
					Japan	3.1	4.7	4.7	5.0
United States	5.6	4.2	4.0	4.8	Korea, South	(NA)	(NA)	4.3	3.9
Australia	8.6	7.0	6.3	6.7	Luxembourg	2.9	2.4	2.4	2.4
Austria	3.9	4.0	3.7	3.6	Netherlands	6.9	3.2	2.8	2.4
Belgium	9.9	8.6	6.9	6.6	New Zealand	6.3	6.8	6.0	5.3
Canada	9.5	7.6	6.8	7.2	Norway	5.0	3.2	3.5	3.6
Czech Republic	(NA)	8.8	8.9	8.2	Poland	(NA)	(NA)	16.1	18.2
Denmark	7.2	4.8	4.4	4.3	Portugal	7.3	4.5	4.1	4.1
Finland	16.2	10.2	9.7	9.1	Spain	22.9	15.8	14.0	13.0
France	11.7	10.7	9.3	8.6	Sweden	8.8	7.2	5.9	5.1
Germany	8.2	8.6	7.9	7.9	Switzerland	3.5	3.0	2.6	(NA)
Hungary	(NA)	7.1	6.5	5.8	United Kingdom	8.7	5.9	5.4	5.0

NA. Not available.

Source: United States Census Bureau. (2002). *Statistical Abstract of the United States 2002.* Washington, D.C.: Government Printing Office. Retrieved from http://www.census.gov/prod/2003pubs/02statab/intlstat.pdf.

Table 5.15
Civilian Labor Force, Employment, and Unemployment by Country: 1980 to 2001

[106,940 represents 106,940,000. Data based on U.S. labor force definitions except that minimum age for population base varies as follows: United States, Canada, France, Sweden, and United Kingdom, 16 years; Australia, Japan, Netherlands, Germany, and Italy (beginning 1995), 15 years; and Italy (1980 and 1990) 14 years.]

Year	United States	Cana-da	Austra-lia	Japan	France	Ger-many [1]	Italy	Nether-lands	Swe-den	United King-dom
Civilian labor force (1,000):										
1980	106,940	11,707	6,693	55,740	22,930	27,260	21,120	5,870	4,312	26,520
1990	[2]125,840	14,044	8,440	63,050	24,280	29,410	[2]22,670	[2]6,640	[2]4,597	28,730
1995	[2]132,304	14,517	8,995	65,990	[2]24,830	[2]38,980	[2]22,460	7,260	4,460	28,560
1999	[2]139,368	15,536	9,466	67,090	25,830	39,800	23,130	7,900	4,430	29,300
2000	[2]140,863	15,789	9,678	66,990	25,980	39,750	23,340	8,050	4,489	29,450
2001	141,815	16,027	9,817	[3]66,870	(NA)	(NA)	23,540	(NA)	[3]4,537	(NA)
Labor force participation rate: [4]										
1980	63.8	64.9	62.1	62.6	57.5	54.7	48.2	55.4	66.9	62.5
1990	[2]66.5	67.3	64.7	62.6	55.9	55.3	[2]47.2	[2]56.1	[2]67.4	64.1
1995	[2]66.6	64.9	64.6	62.9	[2]55.6	[2]57.1	[2]47.1	59.2	64.1	62.7
1999	[2]67.1	65.8	64.2	62.4	56.4	57.6	47.8	62.8	62.8	63.2
2000	[2]67.2	65.9	64.7	62.0	56.4	57.5	48.1	63.5	63.8	63.3
2001	66.9	66.0	64.7	[3]61.6	(NA)	(NA)	(NA)	(NA)	[3]64.2	(NA)
Civilian employment (1,000):										
1980	99,303	10,857	6,284	54,600	21,440	26,490	20,200	5,520	4,226	24,670
1990	[2]118,793	12,961	7,877	61,710	22,080	27,950	[2]21,080	[2]6,230	[2]4,513	26,740
1995	[2]124,900	13,271	8,256	63,890	21,910	[2]35,780	[2]19,820	6,760	4,056	26,070
1999	[2]133,488	14,456	8,808	63,920	22,940	36,360	20,460	7,640	4,117	27,530
2000	[2]135,208	14,827	9,068	63,790	23,530	36,540	20,840	7,810	4,229	27,830
2001	135,073	14,997	9,157	[3]63,470	(NA)	(NA)	[3]21,280	(NA)	4,309	(NA)
Employment-population ratio: [5]										
1980	59.2	60.2	58.3	61.3	53.8	53.1	46.1	52.1	65.6	58.1
1990	[2]62.8	62.2	60.4	61.3	50.9	52.6	[2]43.9	[2]52.6	[2]66.1	59.6
1995	[2]62.9	59.4	59.2	60.9	49.0	[2]52.4	[2]41.5	55.1	58.3	57.2
1999	[2]64.3	61.3	59.8	59.4	50.1	52.6	42.3	60.8	58.4	59.4
2000	[2]64.5	62.1	60.6	59.0	51.1	52.8	42.9	61.6	60.1	59.8
2001	63.8	61.9	60.3	[3]58.4	(NA)	(NA)	(NA)	(NA)	[3]61.0	(NA)
Unemployment rate:										
1980	7.1	7.3	6.1	2.0	6.5	2.8	4.4	6.0	2.0	7.0
1990	[2]5.6	7.7	6.7	2.1	9.1	5.0	[2]7.0	[2]6.2	[2]1.8	6.9
1995	[2]5.6	8.6	8.2	3.2	[2]11.8	[2]8.2	[2]11.8	6.9	9.1	8.7
1999	[2]4.2	7.0	7.0	4.7	11.2	8.6	11.5	3.4	7.1	6.0
2000	[2]4.0	6.1	6.3	4.8	9.4	8.1	10.7	3.0	5.8	5.5
2001	4.8	6.4	6.7	[3]5.1	[3]8.7	[3]8.0	[3]9.6	(NA)	[3]5.0	(NA)
Under 25 years old	10.6	11.8	(NA)	(NA)	(NA)	(NA)	(NA)	(NA)	(NA)	10.5
Teenagers [6]	14.7	15.4	(NA)	(NA)	(NA)	(NA)	(NA)	(NA)	(NA)	(NA)
20 to 24 years old	8.3	9.6	(NA)	(NA)	(NA)	(NA)	(NA)	(NA)	(NA)	(NA)
25 years old and over	3.7	5.4	(NA)	(NA)	(NA)	(NA)	(NA)	(NA)	(NA)	3.8

NA. Not available.

1. Unified Germany for 1991 onward. Prior to 1991, data relate to the former West Germany.

2. Break in series. Data not comparable with prior years.

3. Preliminary.

4. Civilian labor force as a percent of the civilian working age population. Germany and Japan include the institutionalized population as part of the working age population.

5. Civilian of the working age population.

6. 16- to 19-year-olds in the United States, Canada, France, Sweden, and the United Kingdom; 15- to 19-year-olds in Australia, Japan, Germany, and Italy.

Source: United States Census Bureau. (2002). *Statistical Abstract of the United States 2002.* Washington, D.C.: Government Printing Office. Retrieved from http://www.census.gov/prod/2003pubs/02statab/intlstat.pdf.

Table 5.16
Percent of Persons 15 to 24 Years Old Not Pursuing Education or Entering the Work Force by Age Group and Sex: 1999

[Represents those persons not in education and either unemployed or not in the labor force.]

Country	15 to 19 years old			20 to 24 years old		
	Total	Male	Female	Total	Male	Female
Australia	7.4	7.3	7.5	14.5	10.9	18.3
Belgium	7.0	7.5	6.4	15.9	14.7	17.1
Canada.	6.9	7.7	6.0	11.7	10.8	12.7
Czech Republic	20.9	21.8	20.0	20.6	12.5	29.0
Denmark.	3.4	4.2	2.6	7.6	6.1	8.9
Finland	8.7	12.2	5.2	16.9	17.8	15.9
France	3.3	3.5	3.1	17.5	15.9	19.1
Germany.	4.5	4.2	4.9	16.7	14.5	19.0
Greece	10.1	8.0	12.1	25.7	17.1	33.5
Hungary	10.2	9.7	10.8	21.4	16.8	26.1
Italy	14.8	14.1	15.6	29.9	27.4	32.4
Luxembourg	5.0	3.6	6.3	9.6	6.9	12.5
Mexico	17.9	6.2	29.3	26.2	5.1	45.5
Netherlands.	3.8	3.6	4.0	8.0	5.7	10.4
Poland	4.6	5.2	3.9	27.2	23.4	30.8
Portugal	8.4	6.9	9.8	12.3	8.8	15.7
Spain	13.8	15.6	12.0	18.8	17.3	20.5
Sweden	4.8	6.3	3.3	11.4	11.7	11.1
Switzerland	[1]6.0	8.0	7.1	8.4	7.4	9.4
United States [2].	7.3	6.5	8.2	14.4	9.7	19.0

1. Represents only those not in education and not in labor force.
2. Data for 1998.

Source: United States Census Bureau. (2002). *Statistical Abstract of the United States 2002.* Washington, D.C.: Government Printing Office. Retrieved from http://www.census.gov/prod/2003pubs/02statab/intlstat.pdf.

Table 5.17
Civilian Employment to Population Ratio: 1980 to 2001

[Civilian employment as a percent of the civilian working age population.]

Country	Women					Men				
	1980	1990	1995	2000	2001	1980	1990	1995	2000	2001
United States . .	51.5	[1]57.5	58.9	[1]60.2	60.1	77.4	[1]76.4	75.0	[1]74.7	74.4
Canada	50.8	58.4	57.3	59.4	59.5	79.4	76.6	72.8	72.7	72.6
Australia.	45.5	53.2	54.7	56.0	[2]56.4	79.1	76.4	74.7	73.4	[2]73.1
Japan	46.6	49.1	49.3	48.6	[2]48.5	79.6	77.0	77.5	76.2	[2]75.5
France	44.5	47.0	48.0	49.6	(NA)	72.0	66.0	63.9	64.0	(NA)
Germany [3]	40.3	[1]43.6	47.1	48.7	(NA)	71.3	68.4	68.1	66.9	(NA)
Italy	30.1	[1]32.7	33.4	35.7	(NA)	67.9	63.0	62.1	61.6	(NA)
Netherlands . . .	34.3	42.9	48.3	53.8	(NA)	77.4	69.8	70.4	73.5	(NA)
Sweden	59.3	63.0	59.5	59.3	(NA)	74.9	72.0	68.9	68.6	(NA)
United Kingdom .	47.8	53.2	53.5	55.3	(NA)	78.7	75.9	72.4	71.8	(NA)

NA. Not available.
1. Break in series. Data not comparable with previous years.
2. Preliminary.
3. Unified Germany for 1991 onward. Prior to 1991, data relate to the former West Germany.

Source: United States Census Bureau. (2002). *Statistical Abstract of the United States 2002.* Washington, D.C.: Government Printing Office. Retrieved from http://www.census.gov/prod/2003pubs/02statab/intlstat.pdf.

Table 5.18
Civilian Employment by Industry and Country: 1990 and 2001

[**118,793 represents** 118,793,000. Data based on U.S. labor force definitions except that minimum age for population base varies as follows: United States, Canada, France, Sweden, and United Kingdom, 16 years; Australia, Germany, Italy, Japan, 15 years; and Italy (1990), 14 years. Industries based on International Standard Industrial Classification.]

Industry	United States	Canada	Australia	Japan	France	Germany [1]	Italy	Sweden	United Kingdom
TOTAL EMPLOYMENT (1,000)									
1990, total	**118,793**	**13,084**	**7,877**	**61,710**	**22,082**	**27,952**	**21,080**	**4,501**	**26,818**
Agriculture, forestry, fishing [2] . . .	3,394	559	441	4,270	1,262	965	1,879	178	573
Industry [3]	29,834	3,063	1,879	20,890	6,403	10,875	6,842	1,268	8,128
Manufacturing	21,346	2,053	1,184	15,010	(NA)	8,839	4,755	943	[4]5,971
Services [5]	85,565	9,462	5,557	36,550	14,417	16,112	12,355	3,056	18,117
2001, total	**135,073**	**15,077**	**9,157**	**63,790**[6]	**23,531**[6]	**36,541**[6,7]	**20,843**[6]	**4,217**[6]	**27,677**[6]
Agriculture, forestry, fishing [2] . . .	3,277	435	435	3,080[6]	931[6]	1,036[6,7]	1,113[6]	122[6]	426[6]
Industry [3]	29,118	3,305	1,873	19,710[6]	5,547[6]	12,270[6,7]	6,761[6]	999[6]	6,855[6]
Manufacturing	18,970	2,274	1,113	13,180[6]	(NA)[6]	8,796[6,7]	5,144[6]	761[6]	4,753[6]
Services [5]	102,6,78	11,337	6,849	41,000[6]	17,053[6,7]	23,235[6,7]	12,970[6]	3,096[6]	20,396[6]
PERCENT DISTRIBUTION									
1990, total	**100.0**	**100.0**	**100.0**	**100.0**	**100.0**	**100.0**	**100.0**	**100.0**	**100.0**
Agriculture, forestry, fishing [2] . . .	2.9	4.3	5.6	6.9	5.7	3.5	8.9	4.0	2.1
Industry [3]	25.1	23.4	23.9	33.9	29.0	38.9	32.5	28.2	30.3
Manufacturing	18.0	15.7	15.0	24.3	(NA)	31.6	22.6	20.9	22.3[4]
Services [5]	72.0	72.3	70.5	59.2	65.3	57.6	58.6	67.9	67.6
2001, total	**100.0**	**100.0**	**100.0**	**100.0**	**100.0**	**100.0**	**100.0**	**100.0**	**100.0**
Agriculture, forestry, fishing [2] . . .	2.4	2.9	4.8	4.8[6]	4.0[6]	2.8[6,7]	5.3[6]	2.9[6]	1.5[6]
Industry [3]	21.6	21.9	20.5	30.9[6]	23.6[6,7]	33.6[6,7]	32.4[6]	23.7[6]	24.8[6]
Manufacturing	14.0	15.1	12.2	20.7[6]	(NA)[6]	24.1[6,7]	24.7[6]	18.1[6]	17.2[6]
Services [5]	76.0	75.2	74.8	64.3[6]	72.5[6,7]	63.6[6,7]	62.2[6]	73.4[6]	73.7[6]

NA. Not Available

1. Data for 1990 are for former West Germany (prior to unification); data for 2001 are for unified Germany.

2. Includes hunting.

3. Includes mining and construction.

4. Includes mining.

5. Transportation, communication, public utilities, trade, finance, public administration, private household services, and miscellaneous services.

6. 2000 data.

7. Preliminary.

Source: United States Census Bureau. (2002). *Statistical Abstract of the United States 2002.* Washington, D.C.: Government Printing Office. Retrieved from http://www.census.gov/prod/2003pubs/02statab/intlstat.pdf.

Table 5.19
Employment/Population Ratios, Activity, and Unemployment Rates by Percentages for Both Sexes

		15 to 24					25 to 54					55 to 64				
		1990	1998	1999	2000	2001	1990	1998	1999	2000	2001	1990	1998	1999	2000	2001
Australia	Unemployment rates	13.2	14.5	13.5	12.3	12.7	5.1	6.3	5.4	5.0	5.3	5.4	6.1	5.8	4.0	4.7
	Labour force participation rates	70.4	67.6	68.4	69.0	69.4	79.9	80.0	79.6	80.5	80.6	44.1	46.6	46.9	49.0	48.6
	Employment/population ratios	61.1	57.8	59.2	60.5	60.6	75.8	75.0	75.3	76.5	76.4	41.8	43.7	44.2	47.1	46.3
Austria	Unemployment rates	..	7.5	5.9	6.3	6.0	..	5.0	4.5	4.3	3.6	..	6.4	4.8	6.7	5.6
	Labour force participation rates	..	58.5	58.4	56.1	54.7	..	84.7	85.1	85.3	85.2	..	29.9	30.7	31.4	29.0
	Employment/population ratios	..	54.2	54.9	52.5	51.4	..	80.4	81.3	81.6	82.2	..	28.0	29.2	29.2	27.4
Belgium	Unemployment rates	14.5	20.4	22.6	15.2	15.3	6.5	8.4	7.4	5.8	5.4	3.6	5.3	5.7	3.2	3.0
	Labour force participation rates	35.5	32.6	32.9	35.7	33.6	76.7	81.2	82.5	82.8	80.9	22.2	23.8	26.2	25.9	26.0
	Employment/population ratios	30.4	26.0	25.5	30.3	28.5	71.7	74.4	76.4	77.9	76.6	21.4	22.5	24.7	25.0	25.2
Canada	Unemployment rates	12.4	15.1	14.0	12.6	12.8	7.3	7.1	6.4	5.7	6.2	6.0	6.9	5.9	5.4	5.8
	Labour force participation rates	69.7	61.9	63.5	64.4	64.7	84.2	84.3	84.6	84.8	85.1	49.3	48.6	49.9	51.2	51.3
	Employment/population ratios	61.1	52.5	54.6	56.3	56.4	78.0	78.3	79.2	79.9	79.8	46.3	45.3	46.9	48.4	48.3
Czech Republic	Unemployment rates	..	12.4	17.0	17.0	16.6	..	5.5	7.5	7.7	7.2	..	3.8	4.8	5.2	4.9
	Labour force participation rates	..	49.1	48.3	46.1	43.2	..	88.5	88.6	88.4	88.4	..	38.6	39.4	38.2	39.0
	Employment/population ratios	..	43.0	40.1	38.3	36.1	..	83.7	81.9	81.6	82.1	..	37.1	37.5	36.3	37.1
Denmark	Unemployment rates	11.5	7.2	10.0	6.7	8.3	7.9	4.6	4.3	4.1	3.5	6.1	5.1	4.2	4.0	4.0
	Labour force participation rates	73.5	71.6	73.3	71.9	67.2	91.2	87.5	88.2	87.9	87.5	57.1	53.1	56.6	56.9	58.9
	Employment/population ratios	65.0	66.4	66.0	67.1	61.7	84.0	83.4	84.4	84.3	84.5	53.6	50.4	54.2	54.6	56.6
Finland	Unemployment rates	9.2	23.8	21.5	21.5	19.9	2.1	9.5	8.4	8.0	7.4	2.6	14.0	10.2	9.4	8.9
	Labour force participation rates	57.3	45.8	49.4	50.8	50.4	89.7	87.1	87.7	87.9	88.0	43.7	42.0	43.7	46.6	50.3
	Employment/population ratios	52.1	34.9	38.8	39.8	40.3	87.9	78.9	80.3	80.9	81.5	42.5	36.2	39.2	42.3	45.9
France	Unemployment rates	19.1	25.4	26.5	20.7	18.7	8.0	10.8	10.6	9.2	8.1	6.7	8.7	8.7	7.9	6.1
	Labour force participation rates	36.4	27.8	28.2	29.3	29.9	84.1	86.2	86.2	86.2	86.3	38.1	36.2	37.5	37.3	38.8
	Employment/population ratios	29.5	20.8	20.7	23.2	24.3	77.4	76.8	77.0	78.3	79.3	35.6	33.0	34.2	34.3	36.5
Germany	Unemployment rates	4.5	9.0	8.2	7.7	8.4	4.6	8.4	7.8	7.3	7.5	7.7	14.7	14.4	13.5	11.2
	Labour force participation rates	59.1	51.3	52.0	52.5	52.2	77.1	85.1	85.7	86.5	86.4	39.8	45.0	44.4	44.7	41.5
	Employment/population ratios	56.4	46.7	47.7	48.4	47.8	73.6	78.0	79.0	80.2	80.0	36.8	38.4	38.0	38.6	36.8
Greece	Unemployment rates	23.3	29.7	31.7	29.5	28.0	5.1	9.0	9.8	9.6	8.8	1.6	3.2	4.4	3.8	4.1
	Labour force participation rates	39.4	40.0	39.3	38.1	36.2	72.2	76.8	77.6	77.6	77.2	41.5	40.4	40.2	40.6	39.6
	Employment/population ratios	30.3	28.1	26.8	26.9	26.0	68.5	69.9	70.0	70.2	70.4	40.8	39.1	38.4	39.0	38.0
Hungary	Unemployment rates	..	13.5	12.4	12.1	10.8	..	6.8	6.2	5.6	5.1	..	4.8	2.7	3.0	3.0
	Labour force participation rates	..	40.8	40.7	39.0	36.3	..	75.4	77.1	77.4	77.1	..	17.4	19.9	22.9	24.8
	Employment/population ratios	..	35.3	35.7	34.3	32.4	..	70.3	72.3	73.0	73.1	..	16.6	19.4	22.2	24.1
Iceland[a, b]	Unemployment rates	4.9	6.0	4.4	4.7	4.8	2.2	2.1	1.4	1.7	1.7	2.1	1.6	1.4	1.7	2.0
	Labour force participation rates	59.5	65.5	68.1	71.6	70.2	90.1	90.8	92.1	92.2	92.3	87.2	88.1	87.1	85.7	87.3
	Employment/population ratios	56.6	61.6	65.1	68.2	66.8	88.1	88.9	90.9	90.6	90.7	85.4	86.7	85.9	84.2	85.6

Table 5.19 (*continued*)

		15 to 24					25 to 54					55 to 64				
		1990	1998	1999	2000	2001	1990	1998	1999	2000	2001	1990	1998	1999	2000	2001
Ireland	Unemployment rates	17.7	11.6	8.5	6.4	6.2	12.5	7.3	5.3	4.0	3.2	8.4	5.1	4.3	2.5	2.6
	Labour force participation rates	50.3	48.6	50.7	51.6	50.1	68.5	76.1	77.3	78.5	78.9	42.1	43.8	45.7	46.3	47.9
	Employment/population ratios	41.4	43.0	46.4	48.2	47.0	60.0	70.6	73.2	75.3	76.4	38.6	41.6	43.8	45.2	46.6
Italy[c]	Unemployment rates	31.5	32.1	31.1	29.7	27.0	7.3	9.1	8.9	8.3	7.6	1.8	3.8	4.2	4.1	4.4
	Labour force participation rates	43.5	40.1	39.6	39.5	37.6	70.0	68.8	69.5	70.1	71.0	22.3	19.3	19.0	19.2	19.4
	Employment/population ratios	29.8	27.2	27.3	27.8	27.4	64.9	62.5	63.3	64.3	65.6	21.9	18.6	18.3	18.4	18.6
Japan	Unemployment rates	4.3	7.7	9.3	9.2	9.7	1.6	3.4	4.0	4.1	4.4	2.7	5.0	5.4	5.6	5.7
	Labour force participation rates	44.1	48.3	47.2	47.0	46.5	80.9	82.1	81.9	81.9	82.2	64.7	67.1	67.1	66.5	65.8
	Employment/population ratios	42.2	44.6	42.9	42.7	42.0	79.6	79.2	78.7	78.6	78.6	62.9	63.8	63.4	62.8	62.0
Korea	Unemployment rates	7.0	16.0	14.2	10.2	9.7	1.9	6.3	5.8	3.7	3.4	0.8	4.0	4.5	2.7	2.1
	Labour force participation rates	35.0	31.3	31.3	31.8	32.3	74.6	75.0	74.7	75.2	75.2	62.4	61.5	60.9	59.2	59.2
	Employment/population ratios	32.5	26.3	26.8	28.5	29.1	73.2	70.3	70.4	72.4	72.7	61.9	59.0	58.1	57.6	58.0
Luxembourg	Unemployment rates	3.6	6.4	6.8	6.4	6.7	1.4	2.5	2.0	2.0	1.4	0.6	0.6	1.0	1.4	0.3
	Labour force participation rates	44.8	35.3	34.0	34.0	34.6	72.8	76.7	78.3	79.8	79.8	28.4	25.1	26.5	27.6	24.9
	Employment/population ratios	43.1	33.1	31.7	31.8	32.3	71.8	74.7	76.7	78.2	78.7	28.2	25.0	26.3	27.2	24.8
Mexico[b]	Unemployment rates	5.4	5.3	3.4	4.4	4.1	2.2	2.2	1.8	1.5	1.6	1.0	1.0	0.8	1.2	1.0
	Labour force participation rates	52.2	54.0	52.5	51.8	49.8	65.9	69.8	69.1	69.3	68.9	54.6	54.4	55.7	53.5	52.7
	Employment/population ratios	49.3	51.1	50.8	49.6	47.7	64.4	68.3	67.8	68.3	67.8	54.1	53.9	55.2	52.8	52.1
Netherlands	Unemployment rates	11.1	8.8	7.4	5.3	4.4	7.2	3.7	3.0	2.3	1.7	3.8	2.3	2.7	1.9	1.5
	Labour force participation rates	59.6	66.1	67.7	72.2	73.6	76.0	82.3	83.0	83.6	84.2	30.9	33.8	36.3	39.9	39.9
	Employment/population ratios	53.0	60.3	62.7	68.4	70.4	70.6	79.3	80.6	81.7	82.8	29.7	33.0	35.3	37.9	39.3
New Zealand	Unemployment rates	14.1	14.6	13.8	13.2	11.8	6.0	6.1	5.4	4.5	4.1	4.6	4.6	5.0	4.7	3.5
	Labour force participation rates	67.9	65.2	63.3	63.0	63.5	81.2	81.8	82.1	82.3	82.7	43.8	58.4	59.9	60.0	62.9
	Employment/population ratios	58.3	55.7	54.6	54.7	56.0	76.3	76.8	77.6	78.6	79.3	41.8	55.7	56.9	57.2	60.7
Norway[a]	Unemployment rates	11.8	9.1	9.6	10.2	10.5	4.2	2.4	2.4	2.6	2.6	2.2	1.8	1.1	1.3	1.6
	Labour force participation rates	60.5	63.8	63.9	64.7	63.1	85.9	87.9	87.6	87.6	87.4	63.1	68.4	68.0	68.0	68.5
	Employment/population ratios	53.4	57.9	57.8	58.1	56.5	82.3	85.8	85.5	85.3	85.1	61.7	67.2	67.3	67.1	67.4
Poland	Unemployment rates	..	23.2	30.0	35.2	41.0	..	9.5	10.8	13.9	15.8	..	5.9	7.7	9.4	9.7
	Labour force participation rates	..	37.3	34.7	37.8	37.4	..	82.9	82.6	82.4	82.2	..	34.3	35.2	31.3	32.1
	Employment/population ratios	..	28.6	24.3	24.5	22.1	..	75.0	73.7	70.9	69.3	..	32.3	32.5	28.4	29.0
Portugal	Unemployment rates	9.6	10.2	8.7	8.6	9.2	3.8	4.4	4.0	3.5	3.5	2.1	3.3	3.1	3.2	3.2
	Labour force participation rates	60.7	47.6	47.3	46.7	47.9	81.5	83.9	84.1	84.9	85.3	48.0	51.7	52.4	52.7	52.0
	Employment/population ratios	54.8	42.7	43.2	42.7	43.5	78.4	80.2	80.8	81.9	82.4	47.0	50.0	50.8	51.0	50.3
Slovak Republic	Unemployment rates	..	25.1	33.8	37.0	39.1	..	10.2	13.1	15.5	15.9	..	7.5	9.5	12.3	12.3
	Labour force participation rates	..	46.8	46.8	46.0	45.8	..	87.4	87.6	88.4	88.9	..	24.6	24.6	24.3	25.4
	Employment/population ratios	..	35.0	31.0	29.0	27.9	..	78.5	76.1	74.7	74.8	..	22.8	22.3	21.3	22.3

Table 5.19 (*continued*)

		15 to 24					25 to 54					55 to 64				
		1990	1998	1999	2000	2001	1990	1998	1999	2000	2001	1990	1998	1999	2000	2001
Spain[a]	Unemployment rates	30.1	33.9	28.3	25.3	20.8	13.1	16.6	14.0	12.3	9.3	8.1	10.3	9.7	9.4	6.3
	Labour force participation rates	54.9	46.9	48.0	48.5	46.8	70.3	76.3	76.8	78.0	76.5	40.0	39.2	38.8	40.9	41.9
	Employment/population ratios	38.3	31.0	34.4	36.3	37.1	61.1	63.6	66.1	68.4	69.5	36.8	35.1	35.1	37.0	39.2
Sweden[a]	Unemployment rates	4.5	16.8	14.2	11.9	11.8	1.3	7.6	6.2	4.9	4.1	1.5	6.5	6.7	6.1	4.9
	Labour force participation rates	69.1	50.0	51.1	52.3	54.3	92.8	88.0	88.0	88.1	88.2	70.5	67.5	68.6	69.4	70.4
	Employment/population ratios	66.0	41.6	43.8	46.1	47.9	91.6	81.3	82.6	83.8	84.6	69.4	63.0	64.0	65.1	67.0
Switzerland[b]	Unemployment rates	3.2	5.8	5.6	4.8	5.6	1.6	3.3	2.6	2.3	2.1	1.1	3.1	2.5	2.7	1.7
	Labour force participation rates	71.6	67.2	68.6	68.3	67.8	85.9	87.9	87.5	87.4	87.8	63.8	66.6	66.4	65.1	68.2
	Employment/population ratios	69.3	63.3	64.7	65.0	64.0	84.5	84.9	85.2	85.4	86.0	63.1	64.5	64.7	63.3	67.1
Turkey	Unemployment rates	16.0	14.2	15.2	13.2	19.9	5.4	4.9	5.8	5.0	8.6	3.1	1.8	1.8	2.4	3.5
	Labour force participation rates	54.7	45.1	46.4	41.6	40.0	65.1	62.1	62.1	59.3	58.3	44.1	41.1	41.3	36.2	34.2
	Employment/population ratios	45.9	38.7	39.3	36.1	32.0	61.6	59.0	58.5	56.3	53.3	42.7	40.3	40.6	35.3	32.9
United Kingdom[a]	Unemployment rates	10.1	12.4	12.3	11.8	10.5	5.8	5.0	4.9	4.4	3.9	7.2	5.3	5.1	4.4	3.3
	Labour force participation rates	78.0	69.4	69.2	69.7	61.1	83.9	83.3	83.8	84.1	83.9	53.0	51.0	52.1	52.8	54.0
	Employment/population ratios	70.1	60.8	60.7	61.5	54.7	79.1	79.1	79.7	80.4	80.7	49.2	48.3	49.4	50.5	52.2
United States[a]	Unemployment rates	11.2	10.4	9.9	9.3	10.6	4.6	3.5	3.2	3.1	3.8	3.3	2.6	2.7	2.5	3.1
	Labour force participation rates	67.3	65.9	65.5	65.9	64.6	83.5	84.1	84.1	84.1	83.7	55.9	59.3	59.3	59.2	60.2
	Employment/population ratios	59.8	59.0	59.0	59.8	57.8	79.7	81.1	81.4	81.5	80.6	54.0	57.7	57.7	57.7	58.4
European Union[d]	Unemployment rates	16.1	18.5	17.3	15.4	13.9	6.7	8.7	8.1	7.3	6.5	6.0	9.2	8.9	8.2	6.4
	Labour force participation rates	54.0	47.6	48.0	48.6	47.1	78.3	80.8	81.3	81.8	81.7	41.4	41.1	41.6	42.2	41.9
	Employment/population ratios	45.1	38.8	39.7	41.2	40.6	72.7	73.8	74.7	75.8	76.4	38.1	37.3	37.9	38.7	39.2
OECD Europe[d]	Unemployment rates	16.0	17.7	17.7	16.6	17.1	6.5	8.2	8.0	7.6	7.4	5.6	8.1	7.9	7.6	6.2
	Labour force participation rates	54.3	46.4	46.7	46.3	44.9	77.0	79.2	79.6	79.6	79.4	42.0	40.3	40.8	40.7	40.4
	Employment/population ratios	45.4	38.2	38.4	38.7	37.2	71.7	72.8	73.2	73.6	73.5	39.0	37.0	37.6	37.6	37.9
Total OECD[d]	Unemployment rates	11.7	12.8	12.5	11.8	12.4	4.8	5.9	5.7	5.3	5.5	3.9	5.4	5.4	5.1	4.7
	Labour force participation rates	55.4	52.0	51.9	51.9	50.7	78.7	80.1	80.1	80.2	80.0	50.9	50.7	51.2	50.8	50.8
	Employment/population ratios	48.9	45.3	45.4	45.7	44.4	74.8	75.4	75.6	75.9	75.6	48.6	48.0	48.4	48.2	48.4

a. Age group 15 to 24 refers to 16 to 24.

b. The year 1990 refers to 1991.

c. Age groups 25 to 54 and 55 to 64 refer to age groups 25 to 59 and 60 to 64.

d. For above countries only.

Table 5.20
Employment/Population Ratios, Activity, and Unemployment Rates by Educational Attainment for Persons Aged 25 to 64: 2000

(percentages)

		Both sexes			Men			Women		
		Less than upper secondary education	Upper secondary education	Tertiary education	Less than upper secondary education	Upper secondary education	Tertiary education	Less than upper secondary education	Upper secondary education	Tertiary education
Australia	Unemployment rates	7.5	4.5	3.6	8.0	4.1	3.7	7.0	5.5	3.4
	Labour force participation rates	65.8	80.3	85.9	80.2	88.8	92.3	55.5	65.8	80.3
	Employment/population ratios	60.8	76.7	82.9	73.8	85.2	88.8	51.6	62.2	77.5
Austria	Unemployment rates	6.3	3.0	1.6	6.9	2.8	1.4	5.9	3.2	1.9
	Labour force participation rates	57.4	76.9	88.1	70.9	84.8	90.5	49.3	68.0	84.4
	Employment/population ratios	53.8	74.6	86.7	66.1	82.4	89.2	46.4	65.8	82.8
Belgium	Unemployment rates	9.8	5.3	2.7	7.7	3.9	2.3	13.5	7.0	3.1
	Labour force participation rates	56.0	79.3	87.7	70.8	87.5	92.0	41.2	70.6	83.5
	Employment/population ratios	50.5	75.1	85.3	65.4	84.0	89.9	35.6	65.6	80.9
Canada	Unemployment rates	9.9	5.8	3.8	9.6	5.7	3.7	10.5	6.0	3.9
	Labour force participation rates	61.1	80.8	86.0	73.1	87.7	91.0	48.4	73.3	81.7
	Employment/population ratios	55.0	76.1	82.7	66.1	82.7	87.6	43.3	68.9	78.5
Czech Republic	Unemployment rates	19.3	6.7	2.5	20.8	5.1	2.0	18.4	8.8	3.1
	Labour force participation rates	58.1	81.0	89.0	71.1	88.2	94.6	52.0	73.2	81.5
	Employment/population ratios	46.9	75.5	86.8	56.3	83.7	92.7	42.5	66.7	78.9
Denmark	Unemployment rates	6.3	3.9	2.6	4.9	3.3	2.7	7.8	4.7	2.6
	Labour force participation rates	66.7	84.2	90.8	74.5	87.1	93.1	59.8	80.9	88.7
	Employment/population ratios	62.5	80.9	88.4	70.9	84.2	90.6	55.1	77.1	86.4
Finland	Unemployment rates	12.1	8.9	4.7	11.0	7.9	3.9	13.3	10.1	5.4
	Labour force participation rates	65.2	82.2	88.6	68.9	85.8	91.1	60.8	78.2	86.4
	Employment/population ratios	57.3	74.9	84.4	61.3	79.0	87.6	52.7	70.3	81.8
France	Unemployment rates	13.9	7.9	5.1	11.9	6.1	4.6	16.2	10.2	5.5
	Labour force participation rates	66.2	82.2	87.5	76.9	88.0	91.4	57.2	75.6	84.0
	Employment/population ratios	57.0	75.8	83.1	67.8	82.6	87.1	47.9	67.9	79.4
Germany	Unemployment rates	13.7	7.8	4.0	15.3	7.4	3.6	12.1	8.3	4.7
	Labour force participation rates	58.6	76.3	86.9	75.5	83.2	90.0	48.2	69.4	81.9
	Employment/population ratios	50.6	70.4	83.4	64.0	77.1	86.8	42.4	63.7	78.0
Greece	Unemployment rates	7.9	10.9	7.2	5.3	6.8	4.9	12.5	16.9	10.3
	Labour force participation rates	60.2	72.7	87.1	82.2	89.1	90.0	41.1	57.3	83.6
	Employment/population ratios	55.4	64.7	80.8	77.9	83.0	85.6	36.0	47.6	75.0
Hungary	Unemployment rates	9.9	5.3	1.3	11.8	5.6	1.3	8.0	4.9	1.2
	Labour force participation rates	40.1	76.3	83.6	48.8	83.2	88.8	34.2	68.5	78.9
	Employment/population ratios	36.2	72.2	82.5	43.0	78.5	87.6	31.4	65.1	77.9

Table 5.20 (*continued*)

		Both sexes			Men			Women		
		Less than upper secondary education	Upper secondary education	Tertiary education	Less than upper secondary education	Upper secondary education	Tertiary education	Less than upper secondary education	Upper secondary education	Tertiary education
Iceland	Unemployment rates	2.5	1.5	0.8	1.5	1.0	0.3	3.4	2.4	1.3
	Labour force participation rates	89.0	90.7	95.8	96.1	94.7	98.1	83.8	84.7	93.5
	Employment/population ratios	86.8	89.3	95.0	94.7	93.8	97.8	80.9	82.6	92.3
Ireland	Unemployment rates	6.8	2.5	1.9	7.0	2.4	1.6	6.2	2.7	2.2
	Labour force participation rates	60.7	75.7	86.9	79.7	92.2	94.7	39.7	62.2	79.1
	Employment/population ratios	56.6	73.8	85.2	74.1	90.0	93.1	37.3	60.5	77.4
Italy	Unemployment rates	10.0	7.4	5.9	7.7	4.9	4.0	15.1	10.6	8.1
	Labour force participation rates	53.2	76.6	86.5	74.7	86.0	91.4	32.7	67.0	81.3
	Employment/population ratios	47.9	71.0	81.4	69.0	81.8	87.7	27.7	59.9	74.7
Japan	Unemployment rates	6.0	4.7	3.5	6.6	5.0	3.1	5.0	4.3	4.2
	Labour force participation rates	71.4	77.4	82.4	86.6	95.4	97.6	56.3	61.6	64.3
	Employment/population ratios	67.1	73.8	79.5	80.9	90.7	94.6	53.4	59.0	61.6
Korea	Unemployment rates	3.4	3.8	3.4	4.8	4.2	3.7	2.2	3.0	2.4
	Labour force participation rates	70.2	71.5	78.1	84.7	89.4	91.0	61.3	51.3	55.7
	Employment/population ratios	67.8	68.8	75.5	80.6	85.6	87.6	60.0	49.8	54.4
Luxembourg	Unemployment rates	3.1	1.6	1.0	2.7	1.0	0.7	3.6	2.6	1.4
	Labour force participation rates	59.8	74.3	85.2	77.2	87.4	90.4	45.4	59.7	78.1
	Employment/population ratios	57.9	73.2	84.3	75.1	86.6	89.8	43.7	58.1	77.0
Mexico	Unemployment rates	1.3	1.6	2.0	1.3	1.2	1.8	1.3	1.9	2.5
	Labour force participation rates	64.0	67.0	84.7	94.1	95.7	94.8	37.6	57.8	71.2
	Employment/population ratios	63.2	65.9	83.0	92.9	94.6	93.1	37.1	56.7	69.4
Netherlands	Unemployment rates	3.5	2.1	1.8	2.7	1.6	1.6	4.5	2.9	2.2
	Labour force participation rates	61.8	81.8	88.1	78.8	89.0	91.8	48.0	73.9	82.9
	Employment/population ratios	59.6	80.1	86.5	76.7	87.6	90.4	45.8	71.8	81.1
New Zealand	Unemployment rates	7.8	3.5	3.6	8.6	3.2	3.6	6.8	4.0	3.6
	Labour force participation rates	65.8	83.2	83.8	79.6	91.1	91.0	54.2	74.1	78.0
	Employment/population ratios	60.7	80.3	80.8	72.8	88.2	87.7	50.5	71.1	75.2
Norway	Unemployment rates	2.2	2.6	1.9	2.3	3.0	2.0	2.2	2.2	1.7
	Labour force participation rates	66.8	85.0	91.6	75.1	89.2	93.9	59.0	80.3	89.3
	Employment/population ratios	65.3	82.7	89.9	73.4	86.6	92.0	57.7	78.5	87.8
Poland	Unemployment rates	20.6	13.9	4.3	19.6	11.5	4.0	21.8	16.8	4.5
	Labour force participation rates	53.9	77.3	88.3	64.7	83.5	90.9	45.0	70.8	86.3
	Employment/population ratios	42.8	66.6	84.5	52.0	74.0	87.3	35.2	58.9	82.4

Table 5.20 (*continued*)

		Both sexes			Men			Women		
		Less than upper secondary education	Upper secondary education	Tertiary education	Less than upper secondary education	Upper secondary education	Tertiary education	Less than upper secondary education	Upper secondary education	Tertiary education
Portugal	Unemployment rates	3.6	3.3	2.8	2.9	2.2	2.3	4.3	4.4	3.1
	Labour force participation rates	75.8	86.7	92.9	86.5	88.8	94.8	65.5	84.5	91.5
	Employment/population ratios	73.1	83.8	90.3	84.0	86.8	92.7	62.7	80.7	88.6
Slovak Republic	Unemployment rates	36.3	14.3	4.6	41.7	13.9	5.3	32.2	14.7	3.7
	Labour force participation rates	48.5	82.4	89.7	61.5	88.2	92.9	41.8	76.1	86.4
	Employment/population ratios	30.9	70.6	85.6	35.8	75.9	88.0	28.3	64.9	83.1
Spain	Unemployment rates	13.7	11.0	9.5	9.4	6.4	6.1	21.9	17.4	13.6
	Labour force participation rates	62.4	80.9	87.9	83.9	91.6	92.0	41.9	69.7	83.6
	Employment/population ratios	53.9	72.0	79.5	76.1	85.7	86.4	32.7	57.6	72.2
Sweden	Unemployment rates	8.0	5.3	3.0	7.6	5.7	3.6	8.5	4.9	2.5
	Labour force participation rates	73.9	86.2	89.4	79.4	89.0	90.2	67.3	83.4	88.6
	Employment/population ratios	68.0	81.7	86.7	73.3	83.9	87.0	61.6	79.3	86.4
Switzerland	Unemployment rates	5.0	2.0	1.3	4.9	1.5	1.1	5.2	2.6	1.9
	Labour force participation rates	69.0	83.6	92.2	86.1	93.8	95.6	59.0	75.1	84.0
	Employment/population ratios	65.5	81.9	90.9	81.9	92.4	94.5	56.0	73.2	82.5
Turkey	Unemployment rates	4.7	5.6	3.7	4.9	4.6	3.5	3.9	11.0	4.1
	Labour force participation rates	55.2	65.2	81.5	84.4	87.7	87.3	22.0	25.9	71.1
	Employment/population ratios	52.6	61.6	78.5	80.2	83.6	84.2	21.1	23.1	68.1
United Kingdom	Unemployment rates	8.9	4.5	2.1	11.6	4.8	2.2	6.0	4.1	2.1
	Labour force participation rates	58.9	82.8	89.8	68.0	88.7	92.4	51.6	76.8	86.5
	Employment/population ratios	53.7	79.1	87.8	60.1	84.5	90.4	48.5	73.7	84.7
United States	Unemployment rates	7.9	3.6	1.8	7.1	3.7	1.8	9.1	3.5	1.7
	Labour force participation rates	62.7	79.5	86.5	74.9	86.2	91.7	50.4	73.3	81.5
	Employment/population ratios	57.8	76.7	85.0	69.6	83.1	90.0	45.8	70.7	80.2
European Union [a]	Unemployment rates	10.6	6.5	4.3	8.8	5.6	3.5	13.1	7.6	5.3
	Labour force participation rates	60.3	79.6	87.9	77.0	86.7	91.3	45.7	72.3	84.0
	Employment/population ratios	53.9	74.5	84.2	70.2	81.9	88.1	39.7	66.8	79.6
OECD Europe [a]	Unemployment rates	10.0	7.2	4.1	8.4	6.2	3.4	12.6	8.6	5.0
	Labour force participation rates	58.8	79.1	87.8	77.7	86.5	91.2	41.7	71.2	83.7
	Employment/population ratios	52.9	73.3	84.2	71.2	81.1	88.1	36.4	65.1	79.5
Total OECD [a]	Unemployment rates	7.4	5.6	3.0	6.6	5.2	2.8	8.9	6.1	3.4
	Labour force participation rates	61.7	78.6	85.8	81.1	87.8	92.6	44.3	69.4	78.4
	Employment/population ratios	57.1	74.2	83.2	75.8	83.3	90.0	40.4	65.2	75.8

a. For above countries only.

Source: Organization for Economic Co-operation and Development. (2002). Statistical Annex. In OECD, *Employment Outlook 2000*, pp. 301–332. Washington, D.C.: Author. Retrieved from http://www.oecd.org/dataoecd/29/42/1939233.pdf. OECD Copyright. Reproduced by permission of the OECD.

Table 5.21
Incidence of Long-Term Unemployment as a Percentage of Total Unemployment [a, b, c, d, e]

	1990		1998		1999		2000		2001	
	6 months and over	12 months and over	6 months and over	12 months and over	6 months and over	12 months and over	6 months and over	12 months and over	6 months and over	12 months and over
Australia	41.0	21.6	52.2	33.6	48.4	29.4	43.6	27.9	38.7	21.5
Austria	..	..	44.0	30.3	39.3	25.9	39.7	25.9	36.2	23.5
Belgium	81.4	68.7	76.3	61.7	73.5	60.5	71.8	56.3	66.5	51.7
Canada	20.2	7.2	24.1	13.8	24.1	11.6	19.5	11.2	16.8	9.5
Czech Republic	..	..	54.6	31.2	61.9	37.1	69.9	48.8	71.3	52.7
Denmark	53.2	29.9	41.4	26.9	38.5	20.5	38.1	20.0	38.5	22.2
Finland[f]	32.6	9.2	42.2	27.5	46.4	29.6	46.5	29.0	42.2	26.2
France	55.5	38.0	64.3	44.2	55.6	40.4	62.0	42.6	57.2	37.6
Germany	64.7	46.8	69.6	52.6	67.2	51.7	67.6	51.5	..	..
Greece	71.9	49.8	74.8	54.9	74.3	55.3	73.5	56.4	69.0	52.8
Hungary	..	..	71.0	49.8	70.4	49.5	69.7	48.9	68.1	46.7
Iceland[f]	13.6	6.7	22.9	16.1	20.2	11.7	18.6	11.8	21.1	12.5
Ireland	81.0	66.0	..	..	76.1	55.3	..	..	..	..
Italy	85.2	69.8	77.3	59.6	77.2	61.4	77.6	61.3	77.4	63.4
Japan	39.0	19.1	39.3	20.9	44.5	22.4	46.9	25.5	46.2	26.6
Korea	13.9	2.6	14.7	1.6	18.6	3.8	14.3	2.3	13.0	2.3
Luxembourg[g]	(66.7)	(42.9)	(55.2)	(31.3)	(53.8)	(32.3)	(37.0)	(22.4)	(43.5)	(27.6)
Mexico	..	..	3.3	0.9	6.8	1.7	4.9	1.1	4.1	1.1
Netherlands	63.6	49.3	83.5	47.9	80.7	43.5	..	..	..	..
New Zealand	39.5	20.9	37.9	19.4	39.0	20.8	36.2	19.2	34.0	18.3
Norway	40.8	20.4	20.5	8.2	16.2	6.8	16.3	5.0	16.6	4.9
Poland	..	..	60.4	37.4	57.1	34.8	63.0	37.9	66.1	43.1
Portugal	62.4	44.8	64.5	44.7	63.8	41.2	60.0	42.9	58.0	38.1
Slovak Republic	..	..	68.0	51.3	69.2	47.7	74.4	54.6	67.6	48.2
Spain	70.2	54.0	70.5	54.3	67.8	51.2	64.8	47.6	61.8	44.0
Sweden	22.2	12.1	49.2	33.5	45.2	30.1	41.5	26.4	36.7	22.3
Switzerland[f]	27.5	17.0	49.2	34.8	61.2	39.6	45.7	29.0	47.3	29.9
Turkey	72.6	47.0	60.7	40.1	49.8	28.4	35.9	21.1	37.7	23.1
United Kingdom	50.3	34.4	47.3	32.7	45.4	29.6	43.2	28.0	43.6	27.7
United States	10.0	5.5	14.1	8.0	12.3	6.8	11.4	6.0	11.8	6.1
European Union[h]	65.3	48.6	66.7	49.2	63.7	47.4	63.8	46.9	60.4	43.7
OECD Europe[h]	64.8	46.9	64.5	45.9	61.0	43.2	61.4	43.2	58.2	40.4
Total OECD[h]	44.6	30.9	48.6	33.4	47.2	31.8	46.9	31.6	41.8	27.5

a. While data from labour force surveys make international comparisons easier, compared to a mixture of survey and registration data, it is not perfect. Questionnaire wording and design survey timing, differences actress countries in the age groups covered, and other reasons mean that care is required in interpreting cross-country differences in levels.

b. The duration of unemployment database maintained by the Secretariat is composed of detailed duration categories disaggregated by age and sex. All totals are derived by adding each component. Thus, the total for men is derived by adding the number of unemployed men by each duration and age group category. Because published data are usually rounded to the nearest thousand, this method sometimes results in slight differences between the percentages shown here and those that would be obtained using the available published figures.

c. Data are averages of monthly figures for Canada, Sweden and United States, averages of quarterly figures for the Czech Republic, Hungry, Norway, New Zealand, Poland, the Slovak Republic, and Spain, and averages of semi-annual figures for Turkey. The reference period for the remaining countries is an follows (among EU countries it occasionally varies from year to year): Australia, August; Austria, April; Belgium, April; Denmark, April-May; Finland, autumn prior to 1995, spring between 1995 and 1998, and averages of monthly figures since 1999; France, March; Germany, April; Greece, March-July; Iceland, April; Ireland, May; Italy, April; Japan, February; Luxembourg, April; Mexico, April; the Netherlands, March-May; Portugal, February-April; Switzerland, second quarter: and the United Kingdom, March-May.

d. Data refer to persons aged 15 and over in Australia, Austria, Belgium, Canada, the Czech Republic, Denmark, France, Germany Greece, Ireland, Italy, Japan, Luxembourg, Mexico, the Netherlands, New Zealand, Poland, Portugal, the Slovak Republic, Switzerland and Turkey: and aged 16 and over is Iceland, Spain, the United Kingdom and the United States. Data for Finland refer to persons aged 15-64 (excluding unemployment pensioners). Data for Hungry refer to persons aged 15-74, for Norway to persons aged 16-24 and for Sweden to persons aged 16-64.

e. Persons for whom no duration of unemployment was specified are excluded.

f. Data for 1990 refer to 1991.

g. Data in brackets are based on small sample sizes and, therefore, must be treated with care.

h. For above countries only.

Source: Organization for Economic Co-operation and Development. (2002). Statistical Annex. In OECD, *Employment Outlook 2000*, pp. 301–332. Washington, D.C.: Author. Retrieved from http://www.oecd.org/dataoecd/29/42/1939233.pdf. OECD Copyright. Reproduced by permission of the OECD.

Table 5.22
Civilian Labor Force and Participation Rates, with Projections: United States, 1980 to 2010

[**106.9 represents 106,900,000.** For civilian noninstitutional population 16 years old and over. Annual averages of monthly figures. Rates are based on annual average civilian noninstitutional population of each specified group and represent proportion of each specified group in the civilian labor force. Based on Current Population Survey.]

Race, sex, and age	Civilian labor force (millions)						Participation rate (percent)					
	1980	1990	1995	2000	2001	2010, proj.	1980	1990	1995	2000	2001	2010, proj.
Total [1]	**106.9**	**125.8**	**132.3**	**140.9**	**141.8**	**157.7**	**63.8**	**66.5**	**66.6**	**67.2**	**66.9**	**67.5**
White	93.6	107.4	112.0	117.6	118.1	128.0	64.1	66.9	67.1	67.4	67.2	67.6
Male	54.5	59.6	61.1	63.9	64.1	68.2	78.2	77.1	75.7	75.4	75.1	73.8
Female	39.1	47.8	50.8	53.7	54.0	59.9	51.2	57.4	59.0	59.8	59.7	61.6
Black	10.9	13.7	14.8	16.6	16.7	20.0	61.0	64.0	63.7	65.8	65.4	67.1
Male	5.6	6.8	7.2	7.8	7.9	9.0	70.3	71.0	69.0	69.0	68.5	68.2
Female	5.3	6.9	7.6	8.8	8.9	11.1	53.1	58.3	59.5	63.2	62.9	66.2
Hispanic [2]	6.1	10.7	12.3	15.4	15.8	20.9	64.0	67.4	65.8	68.6	68.1	69.0
Male	3.8	6.5	7.4	8.9	9.1	11.7	81.4	81.4	79.1	80.6	79.8	79.0
Female	2.3	4.2	4.9	6.4	6.7	9.2	47.4	53.1	52.6	56.9	56.8	59.4
Male	61.5	69.0	71.4	75.2	75.7	82.2	77.4	76.4	75.0	74.7	74.4	73.2
16 to 19 years	5.0	4.1	4.0	4.3	4.2	4.7	60.5	55.7	54.8	53.0	50.7	52.3
20 to 24 years	8.6	7.9	7.3	7.6	7.6	8.6	85.9	84.4	83.1	82.6	81.5	81.2
25 to 34 years	17.0	19.9	18.7	17.1	16.8	17.9	95.2	94.1	93.0	93.4	92.7	93.1
35 to 44 years	11.8	17.5	19.2	20.3	20.2	17.8	95.5	94.3	92.3	92.6	92.5	92.3
45 to 54 years	9.9	11.1	13.4	16.0	16.6	18.9	91.2	90.7	88.8	88.6	88.5	87.8
55 to 64 years	7.2	6.6	6.5	7.6	7.9	11.1	72.1	67.8	66.0	67.3	68.1	67.0
65 years and over . .	1.9	2.0	2.2	2.4	2.5	3.1	19.0	16.3	16.8	17.5	17.7	19.5
Female	45.5	56.8	60.9	65.6	66.1	75.5	51.5	57.5	58.9	60.2	60.1	62.2
16 to 19 years	4.4	3.7	3.7	4.1	3.9	4.6	52.9	51.6	52.2	51.3	49.4	52.2
20 to 24 years	7.3	6.8	6.3	6.8	6.9	8.1	68.9	71.3	70.3	73.3	72.9	75.7
25 to 34 years	12.3	16.1	15.5	14.6	14.3	16.3	65.5	73.5	74.9	76.3	75.8	81.4
35 to 44 years	8.6	14.7	16.6	17.5	17.4	16.2	65.5	76.4	77.2	77.3	77.1	80.0
45 to 54 years	7.0	9.1	11.8	14.5	15.0	17.9	59.9	71.2	74.4	76.8	76.4	80.0
55 to 64 years	4.7	4.9	5.4	6.4	6.7	10.1	41.3	45.2	49.2	51.8	53.0	55.2
65 years and over . .	1.2	1.5	1.6	1.8	1.8	2.3	8.1	8.6	8.8	9.4	9.7	11.1

1. Includes other races, not shown separately.
2. Persons of Hispanic origin may be of any race.

Source: United States Census Bureau. (2002). *Statistical Abstract of the United States 2002*. Washington, D.C.: Government Printing Office. Retrieved from http://www.census.gov/prod/2003pubs/02statab/labor.pdf.

Table 5.23
Employment Status of the Civilian Population: United States, 1970 to 2001

[In thousands (137,085 represents 137,085,000), **except as indicated**. Annual averages of monthly figures. For the civilian noninstitutional population 16 years old and over. Based on Current Population Survey.]

Year, sex, race, and Hispanic origin	Civilian noninstitu- tional popula- tion	Civilian labor force			Employ- ment/ popu- lation ratio [1]	Unemployed		Not in labor force	
		Total	Percent of popula- tion	Employed		Number	Percent of labor force	Number	Percent of population
Total: [2]									
1970.	137,085	82,771	60.4	78,678	57.4	4,093	4.9	54,315	39.6
1980.	167,745	106,940	63.8	99,303	59.2	7,637	7.1	60,806	36.2
1985.	178,206	115,461	64.8	107,150	60.1	8,312	7.2	62,744	35.2
1990.	189,164	125,840	66.5	118,793	62.8	7,047	5.6	63,324	33.5
1995.	198,584	132,304	66.6	124,900	62.9	7,404	5.6	66,280	33.4
1999.	207,753	139,368	67.1	133,488	64.3	5,880	4.2	68,385	32.9
2000.	209,699	140,863	67.2	135,208	64.5	5,655	4.0	68,836	32.8
2001.	211,864	141,815	66.9	135,073	63.8	6,742	4.8	70,050	33.1
Male:									
1970.	64,304	51,228	79.7	48,990	76.2	2,238	4.4	13,076	20.3
1980.	79,398	61,453	77.4	57,186	72.0	4,267	6.9	17,945	22.6
1985.	84,469	64,411	76.3	59,891	70.9	4,521	7.0	20,058	23.7
1990.	90,377	69,011	76.4	65,104	72.0	3,906	5.7	21,367	23.6
1995.	95,178	71,360	75.0	67,377	70.8	3,983	5.6	23,818	25.0
1999.	99,722	74,512	74.7	71,446	71.6	3,066	4.1	25,210	25.3
2000.	100,731	75,247	74.7	72,293	71.8	2,954	3.9	25,484	25.3
2001.	101,858	75,743	74.4	72,080	70.8	3,663	4.8	26,114	25.6
Female:									
1970.	72,782	31,543	43.3	29,688	40.8	1,855	5.9	41,239	56.7
1980.	88,348	45,487	51.5	42,117	47.7	3,370	7.4	42,861	48.5
1985.	93,736	51,050	54.5	47,259	50.4	3,791	7.4	42,686	45.5
1990.	98,787	56,829	57.5	53,689	54.3	3,140	5.5	41,957	42.5
1995.	103,406	60,944	58.9	57,523	55.6	3,421	5.6	42,462	41.1
1999.	108,031	64,855	60.0	62,042	57.4	2,814	4.3	43,175	40.0
2000.	108,968	65,616	60.2	62,915	57.7	2,701	4.1	43,352	39.8
2001.	110,007	66,071	60.1	62,992	57.3	3,079	4.7	43,935	39.9
White:									
1970.	122,174	73,556	60.2	70,217	57.5	3,339	4.5	48,618	39.8
1980.	146,122	93,600	64.1	87,715	60.0	5,884	6.3	52,523	35.9
1985.	153,679	99,926	65.0	93,736	61.0	6,191	6.2	53,753	35.0
1990.	160,625	107,447	66.9	102,261	63.7	5,186	4.8	53,178	33.1
1995.	166,914	111,950	67.1	106,490	63.8	5,459	4.9	54,965	32.9
1999.	173,085	116,509	67.3	112,235	64.8	4,273	3.7	56,577	32.7
2000.	174,428	117,574	67.4	113,475	65.1	4,099	3.5	56,854	32.6
2001.	175,888	118,144	67.2	113,220	64.4	4,923	4.2	57,744	32.8
Black:									
1973.	14,917	8,976	60.2	8,128	54.5	846	9.4	5,941	39.8
1980.	17,824	10,865	61.0	9,313	52.2	1,553	14.3	6,959	39.0
1985.	19,664	12,364	62.9	10,501	53.4	1,864	15.1	7,299	37.1
1990.	21,477	13,740	64.0	12,175	56.7	1,565	11.4	7,737	36.0
1995.	23,246	14,817	63.7	13,279	57.1	1,538	10.4	8,429	36.3
1999.	24,855	16,365	65.8	15,056	60.6	1,309	8.0	8,490	34.2
2000.	25,218	16,603	65.8	15,334	60.8	1,269	7.6	8,615	34.2
2001.	25,559	16,719	65.4	15,270	59.7	1,450	8.7	8,840	34.6
Hispanic: [3]									
1980.	9,598	6,146	64.0	5,527	57.6	620	10.1	3,451	36.0
1985.	11,915	7,698	64.6	6,888	57.8	811	10.5	4,217	35.4
1990.	15,904	10,720	67.4	9,845	61.9	876	8.2	5,184	32.6
1995.	18,629	12,267	65.8	11,127	59.7	1,140	9.3	6,362	34.2
1999.	21,650	14,665	67.7	13,720	63.4	945	6.4	6,985	32.3
2000.	22,393	15,368	68.6	14,492	64.7	876	5.7	7,025	31.4
2001.	23,122	15,751	68.1	14,714	63.6	1,037	6.6	7,371	31.9
Mexican:									
1986.	7,377	4,941	67.0	4,387	59.5	555	11.2	2,436	33.0
1990.	9,752	6,707	68.8	6,146	63.0	561	8.4	3,045	31.2
1995.	11,609	7,765	66.9	7,016	60.4	750	9.7	3,844	33.1
1999.	13,582	9,267	68.2	8,656	63.7	611	6.6	4,315	31.8
2000.	14,386	9,955	69.2	9,364	65.1	591	5.9	4,430	30.8
2001.	14,850	10,264	69.1	9,577	64.5	687	6.7	4,586	30.9
Puerto Rican:									
1986.	1,494	804	53.8	691	46.3	113	14.0	690	46.2
1990.	1,718	960	55.9	870	50.6	91	9.5	758	44.1
1995.	1,896	1,098	57.9	974	51.4	123	11.2	798	42.1
1999.	2,058	1,269	61.6	1,165	56.6	104	8.2	789	38.3
2000.	2,025	1,278	63.1	1,196	59.1	82	6.4	747	36.9
2001.	2,164	1,294	59.8	1,193	55.1	101	7.8	871	40.2
Cuban:									
1986.	842	570	67.7	533	63.3	36	6.4	272	32.3
1990.	918	603	65.7	559	60.9	44	7.2	315	34.3
1995.	1,019	613	60.2	568	55.7	45	7.4	406	39.8
1999.	1,141	714	62.6	681	59.7	33	4.6	427	37.4
2000.	1,104	680	61.6	650	58.9	30	4.4	424	38.4
2001.	1,043	608	58.3	568	54.5	40	6.5	435	41.7

1. Civilian employed as a percent of the civilian noninstitutional population.

2. Includes other races, not shown separately.

3. Persons of Hispanic origin may be of any race. Includes persons of other Hispanic origin, not shown separately.

Source: United States Census Bureau. (2002). *Statistical Abstract of the United States 2002*. Washington, D.C.: Government Printing Office. Retrieved from http://www.census.gov/prod/2003pubs/02statab/labor.pdf.

Table 5.24
Civilian Labor Force and Participation Rates by Educational Attainment, Sex, Race, and Hispanic Origin: United States, 1992 to 2001

[**102,387 represents 102,387,000 As of March.** For the civilian noninstitutional population 25 to 64 years of age. Based on Current Population Survey.]

Year, sex, and race	Civilian labor force					Participation rate [1]				
		Percent distribution								
	Total (1,000)	Less than high school diploma	High school graduate, no degree	Less than a bach-elor's degree	College graduate	Total	Less than high school diploma	High school gradu-ates, no degree	Less than a bach-elor's degree	College graduate
Total: [1]										
1992	102,387	12.2	36.2	25.2	26.4	79.0	60.3	78.3	83.5	88.4
1995	106,519	10.8	33.1	27.8	28.3	79.3	59.8	77.3	83.2	88.7
1998	111,857	10.7	32.8	27.4	29.1	80.2	63.0	78.4	83.5	88.0
1999	112,542	10.3	32.3	27.4	30.0	80.0	62.7	78.1	83.0	87.6
2000	114,052	9.8	31.8	27.9	30.4	80.3	62.7	78.4	83.2	87.8
2001	115,073	9.8	31.4	28.1	30.7	80.3	63.5	78.4	83.0	87.0
Male:										
1992 . . .	55,917	13.9	34.7	23.8	27.5	88.6	75.1	89.0	91.8	93.7
1995 . . .	57,454	12.2	32.3	25.7	29.7	87.4	72.0	86.9	90.1	93.8
1998 . . .	59,905	12.3	32.3	25.8	29.6	87.8	75.3	86.7	90.0	93.4
1999 . . .	60,030	11.7	32.0	25.8	30.5	87.5	74.4	86.6	89.4	93.0
2000 . . .	60,510	11.1	31.8	26.1	30.9	87.5	74.9	86.2	88.9	93.3
2001 . . .	61,091	11.0	31.6	26.3	31.1	87.4	75.4	85.8	89.1	92.9
Female:										
1992 . . .	46,469	10.2	37.9	26.9	25.0	70.0	45.6	69.1	76.2	82.2
1995 . . .	49,065	9.1	34.1	30.2	26.6	71.5	47.2	68.9	77.3	82.8
1998 . . .	51,953	8.8	33.3	29.3	28.6	73.0	49.8	70.9	77.8	82.3
1999 . . .	52,512	8.7	32.7	29.2	29.5	72.8	50.5	70.4	77.4	81.9
2000 . . .	53,541	8.4	31.8	30.0	29.8	73.5	50.4	71.2	78.3	82.0
2001 . . .	53,982	8.5	31.1	30.1	30.2	73.9	51.7	71.3	77.7	80.9
White:										
1992 . . .	87,656	11.3	36.1	25.5	27.1	79.8	61.5	78.7	83.8	88.7
1995 . . .	90,192	10.0	32.8	27.8	29.3	80.1	61.6	77.9	83.4	88.8
1998 . . .	93,527	10.2	32.7	27.4	29.8	80.6	63.8	78.6	83.5	88.3
1999 . . .	94,216	9.8	32.2	27.2	30.8	80.6	64.2	78.5	83.3	87.9
2000 . . .	95,073	9.5	31.8	27.7	31.0	80.8	64.2	78.7	83.1	87.9
2001 . . .	95,562	9.5	31.0	28.0	31.4	80.7	64.5	78.7	83.2	87.2
Black:										
1992 . . .	10,936	19.2	40.3	24.9	15.6	74.4	55.4	76.9	83.4	89.1
1995 . . .	11,695	14.1	38.6	29.6	17.7	74.2	51.0	74.5	82.8	90.9
1998 . . .	12,893	14.3	37.3	30.1	18.2	77.7	59.3	77.0	85.0	88.8
1999 . . .	12,945	13.0	37.2	30.4	19.5	76.5	55.1	76.5	82.9	88.6
2000 . . .	13,383	11.8	36.1	31.5	20.7	77.9	55.5	77.0	84.2	90.3
2001 . . .	13,617	12.0	37.1	31.1	19.8	78.1	58.7	76.8	83.0	90.5
Hispanic: [2]										
1992 . . .	7,702	39.1	30.2	19.3	11.4	73.8	64.6	77.5	84.2	87.1
1995 . . .	9,298	38.9	28.2	21.3	11.6	73.2	64.7	75.9	81.9	87.9
1998 . . .	10,922	37.3	29.1	20.3	13.3	75.8	67.9	78.8	82.3	86.9
1999 . . .	11,129	36.5	29.2	21.4	12.9	75.7	67.0	79.0	84.0	85.0
2000 . . .	11,800	37.1	29.4	21.0	12.5	76.9	69.9	78.5	83.5	87.0
2001 . . .	12,149	36.9	29.7	20.4	13.0	77.3	69.1	81.0	84.6	85.2

1. Includes other races, not shown separately.

2. Persons of Hispanic origin may be of any race.

Source: United States Census Bureau. (2002). *Statistical Abstract of the United States 2002.* Washington, D.C.: Government Printing Office. Retrieved from http://www.census.gov/prod/2003pubs/02statab/labor.pdf.

Table 5.25
School Enrollment and Labor Force Status: United States, 1990 and 2001

[**In thousands (31,421 represents 31,421,000), except percent. As of October.** For the civilian noninstitutional population 16 to 24 years old. Based on Current Population Survey.]

Characteristic	Population		Civilian labor force		Employed		Unemployed		
							1990, total	2001	
	1990	2001	1990	2001	1990	2001		Total	Rate [1]
Total, 16 to 24 years [2]	31,421	35,195	20,679	22,458	18,317	19,996	2,363	2,461	11.0
Enrolled in school [2]	15,210	18,949	7,301	9,047	6,527	8,174	774	873	9.6
16 to 19 years	10,118	12,519	4,244	5,109	3,645	4,476	599	632	12.4
20 to 24 years	5,092	6,430	3,057	3,938	2,882	3,698	174	241	6.1
Sex:									
Male	7,704	9,331	3,635	4,202	3,215	3,738	420	464	11.0
Female	7,507	9,617	3,666	4,845	3,312	4,436	353	409	8.4
College level	8,139	9,958	4,542	5,721	4,231	5,311	311	410	7.2
Full-time.	6,810	8,289	3,376	4,219	3,117	3,900	259	319	7.6
Race:									
White	12,308	14,906	6,294	7,531	5,705	6,911	588	619	8.2
Below college	5,535	7,027	2,374	2,862	2,021	2,530	354	332	11.6
College level	6,772	7,879	3,919	4,669	3,685	4,381	234	288	6.2
Black.	2,129	2,759	718	1,009	576	817	142	193	19.1
Below college	1,207	1,480	306	349	212	247	94	102	29.3
College level	922	1,279	411	660	364	570	47	91	13.7
Not enrolled [2]	16,210	16,246	13,379	13,411	11,789	11,822	1,589	1,588	11.8
White	13,317	13,107	11,276	10,995	10,193	9,901	1,083	1,094	9.9
Black	2,441	2,497	1,752	1,898	1,298	1,482	454	416	21.9

1. Percent unemployed of civilian labor force in each category.
2. Includes other races, not shown separately.

Source: United States Census Bureau. (2002). *Statistical Abstract of the United States 2002.* Washington, D.C.: Government Printing Office. Retrieved from http://www.census.gov/prod/2003pubs/02statab/labor.pdf.

Table 5.26
Labor Force Participation Rates by Marital Status, Sex, and Age: United States, 1970 to 2001

[**Annual averages of monthly figures.** Based on Current Population Survey.]

Marital status and year	Male participation rate							Female participation rate						
	Total	16-19 years	20-24 years	25-34 years	35-44 years	45-64 years	65 and over	Total	16-19 years	20-24 years	25-34 years	35-44 years	45-64 years	65 and over
Single:														
1970 . .	65.5	54.6	73.8	87.9	86.2	75.7	25.2	56.8	44.7	73.0	81.4	78.6	73.0	19.7
1980 . .	72.6	59.9	81.3	89.2	82.2	66.9	16.8	64.4	53.6	75.2	83.3	76.9	65.6	13.9
1985 . .	73.8	56.3	81.5	89.4	84.6	65.5	15.6	66.6	52.3	76.3	82.4	80.8	67.9	9.8
1990 . .	74.8	55.1	81.6	89.9	84.5	67.3	15.7	66.7	51.7	74.5	80.9	80.8	66.2	12.1
1995 . .	73.7	54.4	80.3	88.7	81.4	67.0	17.9	66.8	52.2	72.9	80.2	79.5	67.3	11.6
1996 . .	73.3	52.8	79.8	89.1	82.1	67.4	18.2	67.1	51.5	73.3	80.9	79.4	68.5	12.2
1997 . .	73.1	51.9	80.1	89.0	82.1	68.5	14.8	67.9	51.0	75.1	82.3	80.1	70.8	11.5
1998 . .	73.3	52.9	79.7	89.1	82.5	70.2	15.2	68.5	52.4	75.3	83.0	80.9	69.9	9.7
1999 . .	73.4	52.5	79.7	89.5	83.5	70.6	17.3	68.7	51.1	76.1	84.2	80.8	69.6	9.9
2000 . .	73.5	52.7	80.5	89.4	82.8	69.7	17.1	69.0	51.3	76.3	84.1	80.9	70.0	10.8
2001 . .	72.6	50.4	79.5	88.9	83.1	69.9	15.4	68.2	49.5	75.4	83.4	81.1	69.9	12.5
Married: [1]														
1970 . .	86.1	92.3	94.7	98.0	98.1	91.2	29.9	40.5	37.8	47.9	38.8	46.8	44.0	7.3
1980 . .	80.9	91.3	96.9	97.5	97.2	84.3	20.5	49.8	49.3	61.4	58.8	61.8	46.9	7.3
1985 . .	78.7	91.0	95.6	97.4	96.8	81.7	16.8	53.8	49.6	65.7	65.8	68.1	49.4	6.6
1990 . .	78.6	92.1	95.6	96.9	96.7	82.6	17.5	58.4	49.5	66.1	69.6	74.0	56.5	8.5
1995 . .	77.5	89.2	94.9	96.3	95.4	82.4	18.0	61.0	51.6	64.7	72.0	75.7	62.7	9.1
1996 . .	77.6	84.4	94.5	96.4	95.4	83.2	18.3	61.2	48.6	66.0	71.7	75.8	63.7	9.0
1997 . .	77.7	84.6	94.9	96.1	95.7	83.6	18.3	61.6	50.1	66.1	71.9	76.0	64.6	8.9
1998 . .	77.6	83.8	95.0	96.4	95.8	83.7	17.5	61.2	49.8	66.1	71.6	74.5	64.9	8.9
1999 . .	77.5	83.2	93.7	96.5	95.9	83.4	18.3	61.2	49.8	64.5	70.9	74.6	65.3	9.6
2000 . .	77.3	79.6	94.0	96.7	95.8	83.1	19.0	61.3	53.4	64.2	70.5	74.8	65.4	10.1
2001 . .	77.4	79.2	93.8	95.8	95.7	83.8	19.0	61.4	46.0	64.1	70.2	74.5	66.1	10.3
Other: [2]														
1970 . .	60.7	(B)	90.4	93.7	91.1	78.5	19.3	40.3	48.6	60.3	64.6	68.8	61.9	10.0
1980 . .	67.5	(B)	92.6	94.1	91.9	73.3	13.7	43.6	50.0	68.4	76.5	77.1	60.2	8.2
1985 . .	68.7	(B)	95.1	93.7	91.8	72.8	11.4	45.1	51.9	66.2	76.9	81.6	61.0	7.5
1990 . .	68.9	(B)	93.1	93.0	90.7	74.9	12.0	47.2	53.9	65.4	77.0	82.1	65.0	8.4
1995 . .	66.2	(B)	92.7	90.9	88.2	72.4	12.1	47.4	55.8	67.2	77.1	80.7	67.2	8.4
1996 . .	66.4	(B)	90.6	92.0	88.8	73.1	11.5	48.1	42.6	70.7	78.5	82.1	67.7	8.0
1997 . .	67.4	60.8	89.9	92.1	89.6	74.7	13.2	48.6	49.7	70.4	80.2	81.9	68.6	8.1
1998 . .	66.9	66.2	89.1	93.0	89.1	73.7	13.1	48.8	50.4	73.7	81.0	82.8	68.6	8.4
1999 . .	65.9	(B)	90.2	92.3	88.7	73.4	12.3	49.1	45.3	73.6	82.4	83.4	69.1	8.4
2000 . .	66.6	60.4	87.7	93.2	89.8	74.0	12.7	49.4	45.8	74.0	83.2	82.9	69.7	8.7
2001 . .	66.0	58.0	85.7	92.3	89.4	73.6	14.1	49.5	46.0	75.0	81.5	82.7	69.3	9.1

B. Percentage not shown where base is less than 35,000.

1. Spouse present.

2. Widowed divorced, and married (spouse absent).

Source: United States Census Bureau. (2002). *Statistical Abstract of the United States 2002*. Washington, D.C.: Government Printing Office. Retrieved from http://www.census.gov/prod/2003pubs/02statab/labor.pdf.

Table 5.27
Families with Own Children—Employment Status of Parents: United States,
1995 and 2001

[**Annual average of monthly figures (33,544 represents 33,544,000)**. For families with own children. Based on the Current Population Survey.]

Characteristic	Number (1,000)		Percent distribution		Characteristic	Number (1,000)		Percent distribution	
	1995	**2001**	**1995**	**2001**		**1995**	**2001**	**1995**	**2001**
WITH OWN CHILDREN UNDER 18					Father employed, not mother	2,921	3,144	22.5	22.9
					Neither parent employed	517	403	4.0	2.9
Total families	**33,544**	**34,365**	**100.0**	**100.0**					
Parent(s) employed	29,659	31,412	88.4	91.4	Families maintained by women [1]	4,360	4,750	100.0	100.0
No parent employed	3,886	2,953	11.6	8.6	Mother employed	3,142	3,743	72.1	78.8
					Mother not employed	1,219	1,006	27.9	21.2
Married-couple families	24,604	24,810	100.0	100.0					
Parent(s) employed	23,643	24,092	96.1	97.1	Families maintained by men [1]	908	1,114	100.0	100.0
Mother employed	16,629	16,782	67.6	67.6	Father employed	766	944	84.3	84.7
Both parents employed	15,491	15,676	63.0	63.2	Father not employed	143	171	15.7	15.4
Mother employed, not father	1,137	1,105	4.6	4.5	WITH OWN CHILDREN UNDER 6				
Father employed, not mother	7,014	7,311	28.5	29.5	**Total families**	**15,275**	**14,758**	**100.0**	**100.0**
Neither parent employed	962	718	3.9	2.9	Parent(s) employed	13,267	13,386	86.9	90.7
					No parent employed	2,007	1,373	13.1	9.3
Families maintained by women [1]	7,433	7,665	100.0	100.0					
Mother employed	4,755	5,710	64.0	74.5	Married-couple families	11,604	11,067	100.0	100.0
Mother not employed	2,678	1,955	36.0	25.5	Parent(s) employed	11,159	10,753	96.2	97.2
					Mother employed	7,066	6,586	60.9	59.5
Families maintained by men [1]	1,507	1,890	100.0	100.0	Both parents employed	6,646	6,188	57.3	55.9
Father employed	1,261	1,610	83.7	85.2	Mother employed, not father	421	398	3.6	3.6
Father not employed	245	280	16.3	14.8	Father employed, not mother	4,092	4,167	35.3	37.7
WITH OWN CHILDREN 6 to 17					Neither parent employed	445	314	3.8	2.8
Total families	**18,270**	**19,608**	**100.0**	**100.0**					
Parent(s) employed	16,391	18,026	89.7	91.9	Families maintained by women [1]	3,073	2,916	100.0	100.0
No parent employed	1,878	1,580	10.3	8.1	Mother employed	1,613	1,967	52.5	67.5
					Mother not employed	1,460	949	47.5	32.5
Married-couple families	13,001	13,743	100.0	100.0					
Parent(s) employed	12,484	13,339	96.0	97.1	Families maintained by men [1]	598	775	100.0	100.0
Mother employed	9,562	10,196	73.6	74.2	Father employed	496	666	82.8	85.9
Both parents employed	8,846	9,488	68.0	69.0	Father not employed	102	110	17.1	14.2
Mother employed, not father	717	707	5.5	5.1					

1. No spouse present.

Source: United States Census Bureau. (2002). *Statistical Abstract of the United States 2002.* Washington, D.C.: Government Printing Office. Retrieved from http://www.census.gov/prod/2003pubs/02statab/labor.pdf.

Table 5.28
Multiple Jobholders: United States, 2001

[**Annual average of monthly figures (7,319 represents 7,319,000).** For the civilian noninstitutional population 16 years old and over. Multiple jobholders are employed persons who, either 1) had jobs as wage or salary workers with two employers or more; 2) were self-employed and also held a wage and salary job; or 3) were unpaid family workers on their primary jobs but also held wage and salary job. Based on the Current Population Survey.]

Characteristic	Total		Male		Female	
	Number (1,000)	Percent of employed	Number (1,000)	Percent of employed	Number (1,000)	Percent of employed
Total [1]	**7,319**	**5.4**	**3,808**	**5.3**	**3,511**	**5.6**
Age:						
16 to 19 years old	318	4.6	130	3.7	188	5.5
20 to 24 years old	756	5.7	345	5.0	411	6.4
25 to 54 years old	5,412	5.6	2,868	5.6	2,544	5.7
55 to 64 years old	686	4.9	372	4.9	314	4.8
65 years old and over	146	3.5	92	3.8	54	3.0
Race and Hispanic origin:						
White	6,281	5.5	3,275	5.3	3,006	5.8
Black	759	5.0	390	5.5	369	5.2
Hispanic origin [2]	504	3.4	290	3.5	214	3.2
Marital status:						
Married, spouse present	4,028	5.2	2,380	5.8	1,648	4.9
Widowed, divorced, or separated	1,297	6.0	472	5.3	824	6.6
Single, never married	1,994	5.4	956	4.8	1,038	6.6
Full- or part-time status:						
Primary job full time, secondary job part time	3,992	(X)	2,311	(X)	1,681	(X)
Both jobs part time	1,581	(X)	507	(X)	1,073	(X)
Both jobs full time	280	(X)	181	(X)	100	(X)
Hours vary on primary or secondary job	1,425	(X)	787	(X)	639	(X)

X. Not applicable.

1. Includes a small number of persons who work part time on their primary job and full time on their secondary job(s), not shown separately. Includes other races, not shown separately.

2. Persons of Hispanic origin may be of any race.

Source: United States Census Bureau. (2002). *Statistical Abstract of the United States 2002.* Washington, D.C.: Government Printing Office. Retrieved from http://www.census.gov/prod/2003pubs/02statab/labor.pdf.

Table 5.29
Average Number of Jobs Held from Ages 18 to 34: United States, 1978 to 1998

[**In percent.** For persons 33 to 41 in 1998. A job is an uninterrupted period of work with a particular employer. Educational attainment as of 1998. Based on the National Longitudinal Survey of Youth 1978.]

Sex and educational attainment	Number of jobs held by age—			
	Total [1]	Age 18 to 24 years old	Age 25 to 29 years old	Age 30 to 34 years old
Total [2]	**9.2**	**5.6**	**3.0**	**2.4**
Less than a high school diploma	9.3	5.2	3.0	2.4
High school graduates, no college	8.7	5.2	2.8	2.4
Less than a bachelor's degree	9.6	5.8	3.2	2.5
Bachelor's degree or more	9.7	6.3	3.0	2.4
Male	9.6	5.8	3.2	2.6
Less than a high school diploma	10.7	6.1	3.5	2.8
High school graduates, no college	9.1	5.5	3.1	2.5
Less than a bachelor's degree	10.0	6.0	3.4	2.6
Bachelor's degree or more	9.3	6.0	2.9	2.4
Female	8.8	5.4	2.8	2.3
Less than a high school diploma	7.4	4.0	2.2	2.0
High school graduates, no college	8.2	4.8	2.5	2.3
Less than a bachelor's degree	9.2	5.6	3.0	2.4
Bachelor's degree or more	10.1	6.6	3.1	2.3

Table 5.29 (*continued*)

Sex and educational attainment	Total [1]	Number of jobs held by age—		
		Age 18 to 24 years old	Age 25 to 29 years old	Age 30 to 34 years old
White, non-Hispanic	9.4	5.8	3.0	2.4
Less than a high school diploma	9.8	5.6	3.1	2.6
High school graduates, no college	8.7	5.3	2.8	2.4
Less than a bachelor's degree	9.9	6.0	3.2	2.5
Bachelor's degree or more	9.8	6.4	3.0	2.3
Black, non-Hispanic	8.5	4.7	2.9	2.5
Less than a high school diploma	8.0	3.9	2.7	2.2
High school graduates, no college	8.4	4.5	2.9	2.5
Less than a bachelor's degree	8.5	5.0	2.9	2.4
Bachelor's degree or more	9.4	6.0	3.1	2.7
Hispanic origin	8.7	5.0	2.9	2.4
Less than a high school diploma	8.8	4.9	2.8	2.2
High school graduates, no college	8.6	5.0	2.8	2.4
Less than a bachelor's degree	8.6	5.1	3.0	2.3
Bachelor's degree or more	8.9	5.3	2.7	2.6

1. Jobs held in more than one age category were counted in each category, but only once in the total.

2. Includes other races, not shown separately.

Source: United States Census Bureau. (2002). *Statistical Abstract of the United States 2002*. Washington, D.C.: Government Printing Office. Retrieved from http://www.census.gov/prod/2003pubs/02statab/labor.pdf.

Table 5.30
Displaced U.S. Workers by Selected Characteristics: United States, 2000

[**In percent, except total (3,275 represents 3,275,000). As of February.** For persons 20 years old and over with tenure of 3 years or more who lost or left a job between January 1997 and December 1999 because of plant closings or moves, slack work, or the abolishment of their positions. Data revised since originally published. Based on Current Population Survey and subject to sampling error.]

Characteristic	Total (1,000)	Employment status			Reason for job loss		
		Employed	Unemployed	Not in the labor force	Plant or company closed down or moved	Slack work	Position or shift abolished
Total [1]	3,275	73.5	10.4	16.1	49.4	21.6	29.0
20 to 24 years old	100	87.7	3.7	8.7	49.8	29.5	20.7
25 to 54 years old	2,503	79.5	10.3	10.2	48.3	22.1	29.6
55 to 64 years old	517	56.0	13.6	30.4	56.6	15.3	28.1
65 years old and over	155	26.3	5.2	68.6	43.1	29.0	27.9
Males	1,765	78.9	9.6	11.5	47.1	24.0	28.9
20 to 24 years old	75	86.6	4.9	8.4	43.4	36.1	20.5
25 to 54 years old	1,331	85.1	9.1	5.8	46.2	24.0	29.8
55 to 64 years old	279	62.9	13.3	23.8	56.3	17.4	26.3
65 years old and over	80	23.6	10.0	66.4	33.5	34.6	31.9
Females	1,511	67.3	11.3	21.4	52.1	18.7	29.1
20 to 24 years old	25	(2)	(2)	(2)	(2)	(2)	(2)
25 to 54 years old	1,172	73.2	11.7	15.1	50.7	19.9	29.4
55 to 64 years old	238	47.9	14.0	38.1	57.0	12.8	30.2
65 years old and over	75	29.1	-	70.9	53.4	23.0	23.6
White	2,778	74.4	9.9	15.7	48.9	20.9	30.3
Black	363	72.2	12.8	15.0	53.2	26.5	20.3
Hispanic origin [3]	346	69.7	13.0	17.3	50.4	32.1	17.5

-. Represents zero.

1. Includes other races, not shown separately.

2. Data not shown where base is less than 75,000.

3. Persons of Hispanic origin may be of any race.

Source: United States Census Bureau. (2002). *Statistical Abstract of the United States 2002*. Washington, D.C.: Government Printing Office. Retrieved from http://www.census.gov/prod/2003pubs/02statab/labor.pdf.

6. Health Services: Medicare and Medicaid—Services for Old Age, the Mainstream, and for Low-Income Individuals

There are many normative issues making the analysis of health policy difficult, starting with an adequate definition of health and what it represents, and including the affordability of healthcare and access to health insurance (see Dobelstein, 1996), as reflected in the debate of universal health coverage in the United States during the early part of the 1990s. Costs, accessibility, and quality of care were and still are three of the major issues driving the reevaluation process.

A national healthcare plan centered on universal coverage as presented and advocated for by the first Clinton administration arguably failed because it was considered too radical, due to the role that the government would play in the new plan. Regardless of the political preferences on both sides of the discussion, one reason for the failure of such a large scope systems change was that it demanded a paradigm shift from the country's citizens. Franklin Roosevelt did not advocate for a national healthcare system as part of the New Deal because he thought that the public would not accept it. Sixty years later or so, it was still apparent that the majority of United States citizens still had an aversion for what they would consider an inordinate intrusion by the government on individual life and choices. It seemed that the term "quality" of services and benefits did not correlate with the thought of government program intervention.

The healthcare system in the United States reflects the accepted notions of individual choice, voluntarism, entrepreneurship, low taxation, and low government interaction. It is an insurance-based program predicated on whether individuals want to enter into a health insurance group program, or want to set money aside as allowed by law to cover for medical costs on their own. The major challenge with this approach is what happens to those who cannot afford the insurance or cannot qualify to become enrolled because of preexisting conditions or other circumstances.

Most people in the United States get access to healthcare insurance through their employer. Those who are self-employed or are retired and want more than the basic government benefits are also able to shop and get their own. Under the **Employee Retirement Income Security Act of 1974 (ERISA)**,

employers are required to follow a number of regulations defining the standards of coverage. Employers go to various healthcare providers and insurance companies and shop around for a health insurance plan that meets their budgetary realities as well as contractual and legal obligations. In the days of lifetime employment in one company, continued access was not an issue, but in today's workplace where downsizing and mobility mean that the thirty-year employee is becoming the exception rather than the rule, keeping healthcare coverage is a significant issue. Two other issues that are critical in considering healthcare are the ability to continue to receive coverage between jobs and the ability to remain qualified for insurance in spite of preexisting conditions that may have occurred after a person started a group plan but prior to starting with the new coverage. Under the **Consolidated Omnibus Budget Reconciliation Act of 1986 (COBRA)**, workers and their families who lose coverage as a result of job loss or reduction in hours worked are able to continue to get group healthcare coverage up to eighteen months. However, the individual worker or family has to bear the full cost of the coverage (up to 102 percent with administrative costs) during the eighteen months. Meanwhile, the **Health Insurance Portability and Accountability Act of 1996 (HIPAA)** provides rights and protections for participants and beneficiaries by protecting worker coverage from benefit limits resulting from pre-existing medical conditions when changing jobs and discrimination against employees and dependents based on their health status.

Blue Cross was the first private group insurance system developed back in 1929. The idea behind it was to spread the risk of high costs resulting from illness between all of the individuals participating in the program. Under the traditional insurance system, physicians directed the care of their patients. **Health Maintenance Organizations (HMOs)** began providing alternative delivery methods of healthcare based on the notion of managed care, which has the effect of creating a triadic relationship between the patient, the physician, and the insurer behind the program. This relationship shifted the decision-making of patient treatment from only the physician to a shared process between the physician and the payer. HMOs do this through **capitation**, where providers receive a fixed amount of funds on a periodic basis for health services rendered to plan members. The payment of these fees amounts to a prepayment plan. Fees are set by contract on a per person basis, usually adjusted for age, gender, and family size and not the amount of services rendered (Lomotan, 1996). If the amount of services exceeds the capitated fees paid, the medical provider absorbs the extra cost. If services given are less than the capitated fees, then the provider keeps the difference. At the federal level, HMOs are regulated under the Health Maintenance Organization Act of 1973. This law also allowed employers with twenty-five or more employees to provide HMOs to employees as their basic healthcare coverage program. "From 1985 to 1995, the number of Americans enrolled in HMOs increased from 18.9 million to 56 million" (Lomotan, 1996, 10).

Managed healthcare's main purpose is cost reduction through an efficient use of healthcare resources. It attempts to create efficiency by selecting the healthcare providers, regulating clinical choices, and directing medical provider practice patterns. Lomotan (1996) describes these three elements of managed care as follows:

> First, *selecting providers*: Insurers build provider networks, typically within a specified geographic area. Primary care physicians represent the core of managed-care plans, with specialty care channeled to a smaller number of specialty providers.
>
> Second, *regulating clinical choices*: The primary care physician acts as a "gatekeeper" and channels referrals to specialists as needed. Medical care is reviewed before and after treatment and/or hospital admission. If deemed inappropriate, payment is not rendered.
>
> Third, *directing provider practice patterns*: Traditionally this has taken the form of appealing to professional standards, while preserving an individual physician's clinical autonomy. With the advent of practice guidelines, profiling and/or outcomes research can be used to monitor precision of care or compliance with guidelines. Further, there are financial incentives to practice cost efficiency. (10)

HMOs direct provider practice patterns through the process referred to as **utilization review** (UR). This review process determines which practices are "appropriate" or "medically necessary" based on guidelines and profiling on similar cases and procedures. Because of the impact of the approval process this determination has on medical care received, it is controversial. Different HMOs vary in specifics; nevertheless, the process tends to be as follows:

> Essentially, the reviewer goes through all the health-care services and decides whether or not the payer will pay the provider for care. This can be done on a retrospective, concurrent, or prospective basis. Under *retrospective review*, the service has already been provided to the patient. The reviewer decides whether or not to reimburse the provider. *Prospective review* involves coverage decisions being made before the service is rendered—e.g, deciding whether or not hospitalization will be covered before the patient is admitted. *Concurrent review* takes

place throughout the course of treatment. . . . Generally, the reviewers are trained health-care providers themselves (nurses, physicians, etc.) who analyze the appropriateness of medical decisions on a case-by-case basis. (Deng, 1996, 13, italics in original)

Many would argue that a healthcare system's chief objective is to maintain a person's health and overall quality of life through access to medical intervention that is preventive as well as curative. Putting costs ahead of care creates a conflict of interest that is inherent based on one's position in the triad between the patient, healthcare provider, and insurance payer. Critics point out that the United States' system has three underlying problems: (1) its failure to use evidence-based medicine, (2) its inability to put the patient in the center of the system, and (3) the lack of collaboration and communication among professions and organizations (Canadian Medical Journal Association, 2001).

The United States spends more on healthcare than any other country in the world. Interestingly enough, this country also has a reputation for having the most advanced medical technology; however, in terms of mortality rate and other medical indicators it ranks in the middle of a group of other countries of the so-called first world. According to the United Nations Development Programme (2002), The United States ranked sixth overall in human indicators. It spent $4,271 per capita on health expenditures. In terms of the 1998 national gross domestic product (GDP), 5.7 percent of expenditures came from public sources and 7.1 percent from private derivation. Life expectancy was calculated at 77.0 years, and a mortality rate for children under 5 in the year 2000 at 8 per 1,000 live births. This translated to a probability of 85.7 percent for women and 77.4 percent for men surviving from birth to age 65. Table 6.1 at the end of the chapter provides a comparison with the ten countries previously used in this book as examples of how other health care provider systems are made up and what type of programs they contain.

The information in Table 6.1 provides an excellent source for comparative information; however, care must be given not to read too much into the data. There are a number of cultural and extrinsic factors that influence longevity and quality of health demonstrated by the general population. On the other hand, although the level of technical advancement is not part of some of the data, it cannot be denied that the number of deaths of children under 5 in the United States is higher than most other countries in Europe. Whether or not some researchers and policymakers find it inappropriate to have a comparative look at the healthcare delivery structure and access, the data as well as anecdotal evidence (as evinced in many of the current periodicals, magazines, and newspapers) and personal experience do bring up significant questions of the healthcare system and delivery in terms of its effectiveness. A question that lurks near the surface is the degree of positive impact that the effectiveness-efficiency paradox has on current practice and approach in the United States.[1] Also of interest, and to some as controversial (if not more), is the role of private systems and privatization of healthcare programs through insurance schemes.

Table 6.2 provides information on the healthcare systems of several nations. The data generates a comparison base for those who want to pursue research or craft an argument from a comparative analysis point of view. The best sources for comparative information are the United Nations Development Programme *Human Development Reports*, the analyses generated by the OECD through its reports and working papers, and the Social Security Administration in its *Social Security Programs Throughout the World* studies (the most current complete set is from 1999; 2002 data printed out between 2002 and 2004).

The two major health programs run by the federal and state governments are Medicare and Medicaid. The vast majority of the elements in these programs are structured and administered as a partnership between state governments and the federal government, although federal laws, regulations, and administrative requirements are controlling. At the federal level, as of July 1, 2001, both of these programs are administered through the Centers for Medicare and Medicaid Services (CMS), formerly known as the Health Care Financing Administration (HCFA). The agency is organized around three centers: the Center for Medicare Management, concentrating on the management of the traditional fee-for-service Medicare program; the Center for Beneficiary Choices, overseeing the management of the Medicare+Choice plans, consumer research and demonstrations, and grievance and appeals functions along with providing information about Medicare, Medicare Select, Medicare+Choice, and Medigap options; and the Center for Medicaid and State Operations, converging on the oversight of Medicaid, the State Children's Health Insurance Program (SCHIP), insurance regulation functions, survey and certification, and the Clinical Laboratory Improvements Act (CLIA). According to the CMS Web site (2002), the goals of these programs are to:

- protect and improve beneficiary health and satisfaction

- foster appropriate and predictable payments and high quality care

- promote understanding of CMS programs among beneficiaries, the healthcare community, and the public

- promote the fiscal integrity of CMS programs and be an accountable steward of public funds

- foster excellence in the design and administration of CMS programs

- provide leadership in the broader healthcare marketplace to improve health

MEDICARE

Created as one of the key components in the fight against poverty under the Johnson administration in 1965, Medicare (Title XVIII of the Social Security Act) is the United States' principal form of national health insurance. It is designed for senior citizens and qualifying disabled individuals, covering about 95 percent of the country's aged

population along with many others who receive Social Security benefits because of disability (Social Security Administration, 2001). It has two major components: Part A that is a health insurance (HI) program and Part B which provides a supplementary medical insurance (SMI). A third component has been added, Part C, to reflect the coverage options available under Medicare.

Most persons who are 65 or older are automatically entitled to Part A coverage. One can get Part A coverage at age 65 without having to pay premiums if:

- the claimant is already receiving retirement benefits from Social Security or the Railroad Retirement Board;

- is eligible to receive social security or railroad benefits and have yet to file for them; or

- the person seeking coverage or their spouse had Medicare-covered government employment.

Disabled individuals who receive social security benefits are given coverage under Part A after a twenty-four-month waiting period. Most individuals who are in need of a kidney transplant or renal dialysis may also be covered regardless of age.

Most people enrolled in Part A also opt to belong to Part B, the Supplemental Medical Insurance (SMI) program (37 million total in 2000, with 32 million elderly citizens and 5 million disabled individuals). The latter is a purely voluntary program requiring monthly payments from those enrolled in the program. Plan B's purpose is to provide protection against physician's costs and other medical services. Chart 6.1 provides a breakdown of service covered under both programs.

Medicare provides different options to beneficiaries for receiving benefits as defined under Part C. How many choices are available depends on where one lives. These options are referred to as the *Original Medicare Plan* and *Medicare+Choice*.[2] The former is available nationwide while the latter is only available in certain parts of the country. Many beneficiaries who enroll in the Original Medicare Plan also have a medical supplementary insurance called *Medigap* or some form of supplemental insurance provided by their former employer to take care of those healthcare costs not covered by Medicare. Medicare+Choice reflects a privatization element in the program because these programs are made up of private companies that contract with Medicare to offer Medicare health plans. These companies can be managed care programs like HMOs or private fee-for-service plans. Beneficiary payment share is based on the cost-sharing structure of the selected plan (typically having lower deductible and co-insurance amounts than those enrolled in Part A and Part B on a fee-for-service basis).

Part A is financed mainly through a mandatory payroll tax of 1.45 percent of all covered earnings without limit (2.90 percent for self-employed individuals). Employers pay a matching amount for each employee. Almost all working and self-employed individuals pay taxes to support the cost of benefits for the aged and disabled beneficiaries (Social Security

Chart 6.1
Medicare Program Coverage and Length of Coverage for Services

Part A: Hospital Insurance (HI)

- *Inpatient hospital care:*
  - Semiprivate room
  - Meals
  - Regular nursing services
  - Operating and recovery rooms
  - Intensive care
  - Inpatient prescription drugs
  - Laboratory tests
  - X-rays
  - Psychiatric hospitals
  - Inpatient rehabilitation
  - Long-term care hospitalization when necessary
  - All other medical services and supplies provided in the hospital
- *Skilled nursing facility* (SNF) only if it is within 30 days from hospitalization of 3 or more days and is certified as medically necessary
  - Covered services similar to inpatient care
  - Also includes rehabilitation services and appliances
- *Home health agency (HHA):*
  - Costs associated with out-of-hospital care that is not part of SNF covered through SMI
  - HI covers first 100 visits following a 3-day hospital or skilled nursing facility care, SMI covers subsequent visits
  - May be furnished part-time in the residence of a home-bound beneficiary if intermittent or part-time skilled nursing and/or certain other therapy or rehabilitation care is necessary
  - Certain medical supplies and durable medical equipment may also be provided
  - There has to be a treatment plan and periodical review by a physician
- *Hospice care:*
  - Service provided to patients that are terminally ill with life expectations of 6 months or less who elect to forgo standard Medicare benefits to treat their illness and only want to receive hospice care for that illness.
  - Pain relief
  - Supportive medical and social services
  - Physical therapy
  - Nursing services
  - Symptom management
  - Medicare coverage for illnesses not related to terminal illness

Part B: Supplemental Medical Insurance (SMI)

- Physician and surgeon services
- Emergency room services, or outpatient clinic
- Home health not covered under HI
- Laboratory tests, X-rays, and other diagnostic radiology services as well as certain preventive care screening tests
- Ambulatory surgical center services in a Medicare-approved facility
- Most physical and occupational therapy and speech pathology services
- Comprehensive outpatient rehabilitation facility services, and mental healthcare in a partial hospitalization psychiatric program, if a physician certifies that inpatient treatment would be required without it
- Radiation therapy, renal (kidney) dialysis and transplants, heart, lung, heart-lung, liver, pancreas, bone marrow, and intestinal transplants
- Approved durable medical equipment for home use (oxygen equipment, wheelchairs, prosthetic devices, surgical dressings, splints, and casts)
- Drugs and biologicals that cannot be self-administered (hepatitis B vaccines and immunosuppresive drugs, while certain self-administered anticancer drugs are also covered)

Chart 6.1 (*continued*)

Out of pocket costs

- For hospital stay: initial deductible payment plus copayment for all hospital days following day 60 within a benefit period (days 61–90, and, if needed, a nonrenewable "lifetime reserve" of up to a total of 60 additional days)
- Skilled nursing facility (SNF); copayment required for days 21–100
- Hospice care: small copay for drugs and in-patient respite care

Length of Coverage

- Hospital stay:
  - Benefit period consists of when entering the hospital and ends when there is a break of at least 60 consecutive days since inpatient or skill nursing care provided
  - There is no limit to how many benefit periods of up to 90 days a person may have
- Skilled nursing facility:
  - 100 day benefit period

Services not covered (unless part of selected Medicare + Choice program)

- Skilled nursing facility (SNF) if patient does not require skilled nursing or rehabilitation services
- Home health agency (HHA) care does not include full-time nursing care, food, blood, and drugs
- Long-term nursing care
- Custodial care
- Other health-care needs
  - Dentures and dental care
  - Eye-glasses
  - Hearing aids
  - Most prescription drugs

Out of pocket costs

- Deductible
- Co-insurance
- Certain medical services and related care subject to special payment rules
  - deductible for blood
  - maximum approved amounts for Medicare-approved physical, speech, or occupational services performed after 2002 in settings other than hospitals
  - higher cost sharing requirements for outpatient treatment for mental health

Length of Coverage

Not Applicable

Services not covered (unless part of selected Medicare+Choice program)

- Long-term nursing care
- Custodial care
- Other health-care needs
  - Dentures and dental care
  - Eye-glasses
  - Hearing aids
  - Most prescription drugs

Administration, 2001). Additional sources of revenue that go into the HI trust fund include:

1. a portion of the income taxes levied on Social Security benefits paid to high-income beneficiaries,

2. premiums from certain persons not otherwise eligible and voluntarily choose to enroll,

3. reimbursements from the U.S. Treasury general fund for the cost of services given certain aged persons who retired at the time when the HI began and therefore could not earn enough quarters of coverage,

4. interest earnings on invested assets, and

5. other miscellaneous sources.

The Supplemental Medical Insurance (SMI) portion of Medicare Part B, is generally subject to co-insurance and a deductible. SMI is funded through premium payments ($50 per month in 2001 per beneficiary) set at a 25 percent coverage level of average expenditures for aged beneficiaries, and through contributions from the U.S. Treasury general fund. There are gaps, particularly in the SMI program, that are fee-for-service requiring beneficiaries or third parties to pick up these costs. If eligible for Medicaid, Medicaid pays for the service. However, if there is a third party payor, it must meet federally imposed standards for the type of coverage offered. This type of insurance is referred to as Medigap insurance because it is designed to pick up the costs not picked up by the HI or SMI components of Medicare.

MEDICAID

Authorized as Title XIX of the Social Security Act, Medicaid was also established in 1965 as part of the Johnson administration attack on poverty. It is a federal-state matching, means-tested entitlement program that provides medical assistance to low-income individuals who are aged, blind, disabled, members of families with dependent children (traditionally a family in which one parent is absent, incapacitated or unemployed), pregnant women, or children. Also, certain individuals with higher incomes such as those facing large costs for medical care are eligible under the category of "medically needy," and as of the 1980s eligibility was expanded to include certain higher income pregnant women and children under 6 (whose family income is less than 133 percent of the federal poverty income guideline). According to the Centers for Medicare and Medicaid Services (2002):

> Eligibility for the medically needy program does not have to be as extensive as the categorically needy program. However, states which elect to include the medically needy under their plans are required to include certain children under age 18 and pregnant women who, except for income and resources, would be eligible as categorically needy. They may choose to provide coverage to other medically needy persons: aged, blind, and/ or disabled persons; certain relatives of children deprived of parental support and care; and certain other financially eligible children up to age 21. In 1995, there were 40 medically needy programs which provided at least some services to recipients.

In all, federal law recognizes over fifty population groups eligible for coverage; some of these groups require mandatory coverage in all states while coverage for other groups are optional. Chart 6.2 provides specific examples of mandated and optional eligibility groups (Centers for Medicare and Medicaid Services, 2002e). By 1998, the data indicate that 10.2 percent of the total population (excluding institutionalized individuals) is covered by Medicaid, as are 40.3 percent of those whose income is less than the federal poverty line (United States House of Representatives, Committee on Ways and Means, 2000). However, a recent trend is the increase in Medicaid-covered populations as a result of federal mandates, population growth, and an earlier economic recession (prior to the economic slowdown that began in 2000) while the enrollment in Medicaid has somewhat declined (Social Security Administration, 2001).

Eligibility in each state is based on a combination of federal law and state decisions connected with the structuring of Medicaid programs within their jurisdictions. Means-test criteria are determined on a state-by-state basis. To qualify for benefits, individuals must have income and resources that fall within the limits imposed by the states. State criteria themselves must follow the guidelines set by federal law. As the U.S. House of Representatives' Committee on Ways and Means (2000) acknowledges:

> Consequently, income and resource standards vary considerably among States, and different standards apply to different population groups within a State. In general, individuals in similar circumstances may be automatically eligible for coverage in one State, but required to assume a certain portion of their medical expenses before they can obtain coverage in a second State, and not eligible at all in a third State. (Section 15, 27/106)

The passage of the Personal Responsibility and Work Opportunity Reconciliation Act (PRWORA) in 1996 changed the links between Medicaid and welfare programs. Prior to 1996, those individuals receiving cash assistance through Aid to Families with Dependent Children (AFDC) or Supplemental Security Income (SSI) were automatically eligible. So were pregnant women and children who had no ties to welfare but fell under new legislation passed during the period of 1986 to 1991. The creation of Temporary Assistance for Needy Families (TANF) in 1996 as a replacement for AFDC severed the automatic connection between welfare recipients and Medicaid eligibility. Still, individuals who met the AFDC requirements in their states as of July 16, 1996 had their Medicaid entitlement preserved even if they did not meet eligibility criteria under TANF.

Other groups targeted for maintaining their Medicaid eligibility were persons who did not receive AFDC funds because payments would have been less than $10, persons whose benefits were reduced to zero due to the recovery of previous overpayments, certain work supplementation participants, and individuals otherwise ineligible for AFDC because of a requirement that could not be imposed under Medicaid. Another recognized group was those that needed "transitional medical assistance." This group includes individuals who could successfully obtain employment. The rationale behind making this group eligible was that the loss of Medicaid benefits would act as a disincentive to find and keep work.

Interestingly enough, Medicaid is not an insurance program. It may act like one, but states operate Medicaid programs directly or by contracting with private insurance agencies for administrative services (Dobelstein, 1996). Recipients select their own healthcare provider(s) and payment is given to the provider(s) as if it was an insurance program.

Medicaid acts as a supplement to Medicare by providing assistance in paying out-of-pocket expenses for senior citizens who are low-income and/or face high medical expenses. In effect, "there are various benefits available to 'dual eligibles' who are entitled to Medicare and are eligible for some type of Medicaid benefit" (Center for Medicare and Medicaid Services, 2002e). Those who are eligible for full Medicare benefits are provided services and supplies available through the state Medicaid program. Medicare pays the first portion of the services or supplies as per its prescribed limits. Once that threshold is reached, Medicaid pays the difference up to the state limit. "Medicaid also covers additional services (e.g., nursing facility care beyond the 100 day limit covered by Medicare, prescription drugs, eyeglasses, and hearing aids)" (Centers for Medicare and Medicaid Services, 2002e). Please refer to the "Certain Medicare beneficiaries" in Chart 6.1 for specific coverage provided to

Chart 6.2
Mandated and Optional Eligibility Groups Under Medicaid

Mandated Eligibility groups

- Low income families with children, as described in Section 1931 of the Social Security Act, who meet certain of the eligibility requirements in the State's AFDC plan in effect on July 16, 1996
- Supplemental Security Income (SSI) recipients (or in States using more restrictive criteria—aged, blind, and disabled individuals who meet criteria which are more restrictive than those of the SSI program and which were in place in the State's approved Medicaid plan as of January 1, 1972)
- Infants born to Medicaid-eligible pregnant women. Medicaid eligibility must continue throughout the first year of life so long as the infant remains in the mother's household and she remains eligible, or would be eligible if she were still pregnant
- Children under age 6 and pregnant women whose family income is at or below 133 percent of the Federal poverty level. (The minimum mandatory income level for pregnant women and infants in certain States may be higher than 133 percent, if as of certain dates the State had established a higher percentage for covering those groups.) States are required to extend Medicaid eligibility until age 19 to all children born after September 30, 1983 (or such earlier date as the State may choose) in families with incomes at or below the Federal poverty level. . . . Once eligibility is established, pregnant women remain eligible for Medicaid through the end of the calendar month in which the 60th day after the end of the pregnancy falls, regardless of any change in family income. States are not required to have a resource test for these poverty level related groups. However, any resource test imposed can be no more restrictive than that of the AFDC program for infants and children and the SSI program for pregnant women.
- Recipients of adoption assistance and foster care under Title IV-E of the Social Security Act.
- Certain Medicare beneficiaries:

Medicare beneficiaries who have low income and limited resources may receive help paying for their out-of-pocket medical expenses from their State Medicaid program.

Qualified Medicare Beneficiaries (QMBs), With resources at or below twice the standard allowed under the SSI program and income at or below 100% of the Federal poverty level (FPL), do not have to pay their monthly Medicare premiums, deductibles, and co-insurance.

Specified Low-Income Medicare Beneficiaries (SLMBs), with resources at or below twice the standard allowed under the SSI program and income exceeding the QMB level, but less than 120% of the FPL, do not have to pay the monthly Medicare Part B premiums.

Optional Eligibility groups

- Infants up to age one and pregnant women not covered under the mandatory rules whose family income is below 185 percent of the Federal poverty level (the percentage to be set by each State).
- Optional targeted low-income children.

- Certain aged, blind, or disabled adults who have incomes above those requiring mandatory coverage, but below the Federal poverty level.

- Children under age 21 who meet income and resources requirements for AFDC, but who otherwise are not eligible for AFDC.

- Institutionalized individuals with income and resources below specified limits.
- Persons who would be eligible if institutionalized but are receiving care under home and community-based services waivers.

(continued)

Chart 6.2 (*continued*)

Mandated Eligibility groups	Optional Eligibility groups
Qualifying Individuals (QIs), who are not Otherwise eligible for full Medicaid benefits and with resources at or below twice the standard allowed under the SSI program, will get help with all or a small part of their monthly Medicare Part B premiums, depending upon whether their income exceeds the SLMB level, but is less than 135% of the FPL, or their income is at least 135%, but less than 175% of the FPL.	
• Special protected groups who may keep Medicaid for a period of time. Examples are: persons who lose SSI payments due to earnings from work or increased Social Security benefits; and families who are provided 6 to 12 months of Medicaid coverage following loss of eligibility under Section 1931 due to earnings, or 4 months of Medicaid coverage following loss of eligibility under Section 1931 due to an increase in child or spousal support.	• Recipients of State supplementary payments.
	• TB-infected persons who would be financially eligible for Medicaid at the SSI level (only for TB-related ambulatory services and TB drugs)
	• Low-income, uninsured women screened and diagnosed through a Center's for Disease Control and Prevention's Breast and Cervical Cancer Early Detection Program and determined to be in need of treatment for breast or cervical cancer.

Source: Centers for Medicare & Medicaid Services, 2002, *Medicaid eligibility.*

the identified different types of Medicare recipients. In addition:

Individuals who were receiving Medicare due to disability, but have lost entitlement to Medicare benefits because they returned to work, may purchase Part A of Medicare. If the individual has income below 200% of the FPL and resources at or below twice the standard allowed under the SSI program, and they are not otherwise eligible for Medicaid benefits, they may qualify to have Medicaid pay their monthly Medicare Part A premiums as Qualified Disabled and Working Individuals (QDWIs). (Centers for Medicare and Medicaid Services, 2002e)

The following lists illustrate the scope of services under Medicaid. Data for 1998 show payments for services rendered to 21.6 million children (Social Security Administration, 2001, 61). Children constitute around 51 percent of all Medicaid recipients, averaging in 1998 a per payment cost of $1,150 per child. This compares to a per person average of $1,775 per year for 8.6 million adults (circa 21 percent of recipients); $9,700 per person for 4 million elderly adults (approximately 11 percent of all Medicaid recipients); and $8,600 per person for 7.2 million disabled recipients (around 18 percent of all recipients). The 2000 total expenditures for Medicaid was $194.7 billion ($111.1 billion in federal and $83.6 billion in state funds) and they are expected to grow to $334.9 billion in

fiscal year 2006. Overall outlays for Medicaid in 2000 is calculated to be as follows:

Direct payment to providers: $146.4 billion

Payments for various premiums (HMOs, Medicare, etc.): $33.9 billion

Payments to disproportional share hospitals: $14.4 billion

Administrative costs: $10.6 billion

Scope of Medicaid Services

- Inpatient hospital services
- Outpatient hospital services
- Prenatal care
- Vaccines for children
- Physician services
- Nursing facility services for persons aged 21 or older
- Family planning services and supplies
- Rural health clinic services
- Home health care for persons ineligible for skilled nursing services
- Laboratory and X-ray services
- Pediatric and family nurse practitioner services

- Nurse-midwife services
- Federally qualified health center (FQHC) services, and ambulatory services for an FQHC that would be available in other settings
- Early and periodic screening, diagnostic, and treatment (EPSDT) services for children under 21

Most common of 34 currently approved Medicaid services through federal matching funds to states

- Diagnostic services
- Clinical services
- Intermediate care facilities for the mentally retarded (ICFs/MR)
- Prescribed drug and prosthetic devices
- Optometrist services and eyeglasses
- Nursing facility services for children under 21
- Transportation services
- Rehabilitation and physical therapy services
- Home and community-based care to certain persons with chronic impairments

Balanced Budget Amendment sponsored state all-inclusive program for the elderly (PACE)

- Alternative to institutional care for adults 55 or older requiring a nursing facility level of care
- PACE team offers and manages all health, medical and social services and mobilizes other services as needed to provide preventive, rehabilitative, curative, and supportive care
- Care provided in day health centers, homes, hospitals, and nursing homes
- Payment given only through PACE agreement
- Must make available all items and services covered under Titles XVIII (Medicare) and XIX (Medicaid) without limitations as to amount, duration, or scope of services and without application of any deductibles, co-payments, or other cost sharing.

The process used for cost containment by both Medicare and Medicaid has created a significant problem for service providers because the payment plans have not kept up with the rising costs of healthcare. In fact, because of adjustments made and the rollback on fee schedules legislatively mandated for a number of services provided, health service providers of all sorts are protesting and cutting back on services rendered Medicare and Medicaid patients. A component of the Contract with America Advancement Act of 1996 repeals a previous amendment that allowed Medicaid reimbursements to follow the guidelines of reasonableness and adequacy to cover the costs of "efficiently and economically operated" facilities (United States House of Representatives, Committee on Ways and Means, 2000) in favor of fee scheduled amounts.

And one of the provisions in the Balanced Budget Amendment Act of 1997 that passed created a freeze on the dollar amount a hospital may charge beneficiaries along with the amounts the federal government reimburses health service providers for listed approved services. Part of the protest also is the result of a technical correction in the Medicare formula for outpatient services. As indicated in the U.S. House of Representatives' Committee on Ways and Means *Green Book Report 2000* (2000):

> When Medicare paid for hospital outpatient services under the blended rate formula, the program's share of the payment to the hospital was computed as if the beneficiary had paid only 20 percent of the Medicare approved amount . . . instead of 20 percent of the hospital's charges, which generally disregarded the limitations of a fee schedule. Thus, the Medicare formula that assumed the beneficiary had paid the lesser amount resulted in a larger Medicare payment, and, consequently, hospitals were "overpaid" by Medicare. This hospital overpayment situation was referred to as the "formula driven overpayment." (Section 2, 45/85)

Although Medicare and Medicaid are the two major health programs, there are also two other health programs that are made available through the government and administered through the CMS worth noting. One program is the Health Insurance Program targeting children. Another program element is based on the oversight of different aspects of the HIPAA. In addition, CMS also regulates all laboratory testing on humans in the United States except for research purposes under the program that came about by the passage of the Clinical Laboratory Improvement Amendments.

HEALTH INSURANCE PROGRAM (SCHIP)

In 1997, the Balanced Budget Act included a provision that established the Health Insurance Program (SCHIP) under Title XXI of the Social Security Act. Its purpose was to allow states access to funds for coverage of targeted low-income children through group health or other insurance plans. The program was established completely separate of Medicaid; however, it allows states to manage their healthcare assistance for these groups through their Medicaid system while paying for the costs through these independent funds.

The principal notion behind this concept is to insure children from working families that cannot qualify for Medicaid because they make too much money, yet not do not make enough to afford private health insurance through other means. Prior to the reforms instigated by PRWORA in 1996, Medicaid eligibility was linked to welfare. This program allows children to receive Medicaid benefits by reducing some of the barriers faced by many in the low-income categories, especially those families with children that are transitioning from welfare to the workplace. In effect, a critical component of SCHIP is to act as an outreach effort to identify and enroll children that are eligible. (Please refer to chapter 10 for a more detailed discussion on the social safety net for children.)

HEALTH INSURANCE PORTABILITY AND ACCOUNTABILITY ACT (HIPAA)

Passed by Congress in 1996, the purpose of the program authorized under this act is to protect the health insurance coverage for workers and their families when they change or lose their jobs (Tile I of the Act). Under Title I, the emphasis of the program is to protect employees working for smaller firms (firms with less than fifty employees). Eligibility for HIPAA protection is dependent on meeting all of the following criteria:

• You have at least 18 months of creditable coverage without a significant break in coverage—a period of 63 or more days during all of which you had no coverage. If you get coverage by midnight of the 63rd day, you have not incurred a significant break;

• Your most recent coverage must have been through a group health plan (through your or a family member's employer or union);

• You are not eligible for coverage under any other group health plan;

• You are not eligible for Medicare or Medicaid;

• You do not have other health insurance;

• You did not lose your insurance for not paying the premiums or for committing fraud; and

• You accepted and used up your COBRA continuation coverage or similar State coverage if it was offered to you (Centers for Medicare and Medicaid Services, 2000a).

The focus is on ensuring that an individual receives credit for maintaining health coverage and limiting how a new employer may impose limits on healthcare coverage due to preexisting conditions. Under HIPAA,

> creditable coverage can be used to reduce or eliminate preexisting condition exclusions that might be applied to you under a future plan or policy. In general, if you had other health coverage—for example, under another group health plan or under an individual health insurance policy, Medicare, Medicaid, an HMO, or a State high-risk pool—your new plan's preexisting condition exclusion period must be reduced by the period of your other coverage. (Centers for Medicare and Medicaid Services, 2002c)

Administratively, CMS has

> advisory jurisdiction with respect to COBRA as it applies to state and local governmental employers and their group health plans. The Pension and Welfare Benefits Administration, Department of Labor, and the Internal Revenue Service, Department of the Treasury, share jurisdiction with respect to COBRA as it applies to private sector employers and their group health plans. (Centers for Medicare and Medicaid Services, 2002b)

It furthermore establishes national standards for electronic healthcare transactions and generates national identifiers for providers, health plans, and employers (Center for Medicare

and Medicaid Services, 2002d). It also addresses the issues of the security and privacy of health data. The purpose behind these activities is to control and reduce costs associated with the "paper trail" component of healthcare administration.

CLINICAL LABORATORY IMPROVEMENT AMENDMENTS (CLIA)

Passed as the Clinical Laboratory Improvement Amendments in 1988 CLIA is mainly a quality control and assurance system. It establishes "quality standards for all laboratory testing to ensure the accuracy, reliability and timeliness of patient test results regardless of where the test was performed" (Center for Medicare and Medicaid Services, 2002a). It covers approximately 175,000 laboratories. Although it does not have any direct connection with Medicare or Medicaid, it ties in to these programs in the sense that all clinical laboratories must be properly certified to receive payments from Medicare or Medicaid for services rendered.

SOURCES FOR FURTHER RESEARCH

The best sources of extensive statistical information on the Medicare and Medicaid systems (and ancillary programs attached to these) in the United States are the *Statistical Abstract of the United States*, the *Green Book Report 2000*, and the *Annual Statistical Supplement to the Social Security Bulletin*. The *Statistical Abstract* provides the reader with about any statistics one would want that are derived from the U.S. census. The other two sources are reports that focus expressly on many of the components of the national social safety net. As with most of data tables, there is usually a delay of at least one or two years because of the time needed to collect and analyze the data. Consequently, the use of the data is illustrative of levels of service or allocations, of distribution, trends, and historical development. For more timely information, the best sources are the Web sites for each of the individual programs. When international data is desired, the United Nations Human Development Programme is a good place to begin, along with the Web sites for the World Health Organization and the OECD.

NOTES

1. The effectiveness-efficiency paradox refers to how organizations and government agencies attempt to provide products and/or services that meet the needs of those desiring and receiving the products or services (i.e., the level of positive satisfaction) that lead to a perception of effective performance by the organization and/or government agency while still maintaining costs to the minimum possible amount (i.e., being efficient in terms of cost leading to the production or provision of services).

2. Three basic plan formats:

Coordinated Care plans: HMOs, Provider-sponsored organizations (PSOs), PPOs, and other certified coordinated care plans that meet statutory requirements.

Private, unrestricted FFS plan: allow beneficiaries to select certain providers (providers are not put at risk by the plan's payment terms and conditions, nor does it vary rates based on utilization).

Medical Savings Account (MSA): plans that provide benefits after a single high deductible is met. Medicare makes an annual contribution to the MSA, and beneficiary is expected to use the money in the MSA to pay for medical expenses below the annual deductible.

PRINCIPAL SOURCES FOR ILLUSTRATIONS

Organization for Economic Co-operation and Development. (2003). *OECD Health Data 2003*. 2nd ed. Washington, D.C.: Author. Retrieved from: http://www.oecd.org/statisticsdata/0,2643,en_ 2649_37407_1_119656_1_2_37407,00.html.

Organization for Economic Co-operation and Development. (2002). *OECD Health Data 2002*. 4th ed. Washington, D.C.: Author. Retrieved from: http://www.oecd.org/statisticsdata/0,2643,en_ 2649_37407_1_119656_1_2_37407,00.html

Social Security Administration. (2001). *Annual statistical supplement, 2001 to the Social Security Bulletin*. Baltimore: Social Security Administration, Office of Policy. Retrieved from: http://www.ssa.gov/statistics/Supplement/2001/supp01.pdf.

United Nations Development Programme. (2003). *Human development report 2003*. New York: Oxford University Press. Retrieved from: http://www.undp.org/hdr2003/pdf/hdr03_ complete.pdf.

United States House of Representatives, Committee on Ways and Means. (2000). *The 2000 Green Book: Background material and data on programs within the jurisdiction of the Committee on Ways and Means*. Retrieved from: http://aspe.hhs.gov/ 2000gh

World Health Organization. (2002). *World health report 2002: Reducing risks, promoting healthy life*. Geneva: Author. Retrieved from: http://www.who.int/whr/ 2002/en/.

BIBLIOGRAPHY

Canadian Medical Journal Association. (March 13, 2001). US system needs $1 billion overhaul. *eCMAJ NewsDesk*. Retrieved from: http://www.cma.ca/cmaj/cmaj_today/2001/03_13.htm.

Centers for Medicare and Medicaid Services. (2002a): *CLIA, FAQ*. Retrieved from: http://questions.cms.hhs.gov/cgi-bin/cmshhs .cfg/php/enduser/std_adp.php?p_sid=vhR7aSyg&p_lva=& p_faqid=320&p_created=1018900779&p_sp=cF9zcmNoP SZwX2dyaWRzb3J0PSZwX3Jvd19jbnQ9MTEmcF9zZW FyY2hfdGV4dD1DTElBJnBfcGFnZT0x&p_li=.

Centers for Medicare and Medicaid Services. (2002b). *Consolidated Omnibus Reconciliation Act (COBRA)*. Retrieved from: http://cms.hhs.gov/hipaa/hipaa1/cobra/default.asp.

Centers for Medicare and Medicaid Services. (2002c). *Five steps to understanding how HIPAA may affect you*. Retrieved from: http://cms.hhs.gov/hipaa/hipaa1/content/ hipsteps.asp#Step1.

Centers for Medicare and Medicaid Services. (2002d). *The Health Insurance Portability and Accountability Act of 1996 (HIPAA)*. Retrieved from: http://cms.hhs.gov/hipaa/.

Centers for Medicare and Medicaid Services. (2002e). *Medicaid eligibility*. Retrieved from: http://cms.hhs.gov/medicaid/eligibility/criteria.asp.

Centers for Medicare and Medicaid Services. (2002f). *Mission, vision, goals, and objectives*. Retrieved from: http://cms.hhs .gov/about/agency.asp.

Deng, J. (1996). Quality assurance and utilization review. In Nordgren, R., and Deng, J., eds. *The U.S. health system: A primer*. Reston, VA: Legislative Action Committee of the American Medical Student Association, pp. 12–13. Retrieved from: http://www.amsa.org/pdf/ushealthprimer.pdf.

Dobelstein, A.W. (1996). *Social welfare: Policy and analysis*. 2nd ed. Chicago: Nelson-Hall Publishers.

Illinois Academy of Family Physicians. (April, 1997). *Primary care fact sheet*. Retrieved from: http://www.iafp.com/legislative/ pc_fact.html.

Juran, J.M., and Godfrey, A.B. (1999). The quality control process. In *Juran's quality handbook*. 5th ed. New York: McGraw-Hill, pp. 4.1–4.29.

Lomotan, L. (1996). Managed Care. In Nordgren, R., and Deng, J., eds. *The U.S. health system: A primer*. Reston, VA: Legislative Action Committee of the American Medical Student Association, pp. 10–11. Retrieved from: http://www.amsa.org/ pdf/ushealthprimer.pdf.

Social Security Administration. (1999). *Social security programs throughout the World*. Baltimore: Social Security Administration. Retrieved from: http://www.ssa.gov/st . . . cs/ssptw/ 1999/English.

Social Security Administration. (2001). *Annual statistical supplement, 2001 to the Social Security Bulletin*. Baltimore: Social Security Administration, Office of Policy. Retrieved from: http://www.ssa.gov/statistics/Supplement/2001/supp01.pdf.

Social Security Administration. (2002). *Social security programs throughout the World: 2002 Europe*. Baltimore: Social Security Administration. Retrieved from: http://www.ssa.gov/statistics/ ssptw/2002/europe.

United Nations Development Programme. (2002). *Human development report 2002*. New York: Oxford University Press.

United States Code. (1973). *U.S. Code 42—Public Health, Chapter 6A Subchapter XI—Health Maintenance Organizations*. Retrieved from: http://harp.org/hmoa1973 .htm.

United States House of Representatives, Committee on Ways and Means. (2000). *The 2000 Green Book; Background material and data on programs within the jurisdiction of the Committee on Ways and Means*. Retrieved from: http://aspe.hhs.gov/ 2000gh.

Table 6.1
Health Indicators for Ten Countries Used as Benchmarks

Country (Human development indicator rank)	Life expectancy (1995–2000)	Mortality rate for children under 5 (2000)	Probability at birth of surviving to age 65 (% of cohort group 1995–2000)		Percent spent in healthcare in terms of GDP (1998, in US$)
Norway (1)	78	4 per 1,000 live births	Women: Men:	90% 82%	Per capita: $3,182 Public sources: 7.0% Private source: 2.2%
Sweden (2)	80	4 per 1,000 live births	Women: Men:	91% 85%	Per capita: $2,145 Public sources: 6.6% Private source: 1.3%
Australia (5)	79	6 per 1,000 live births	Women: Men:	90% 83%	Per capita: $1,714 Public sources: 6.0% Private source: 2.6%
Netherlands (8)	78	5 per 1,000 live births	Women: Men:	89% 83%	Per capita: $2,173 Public sources: 6.0% Private source: 2.8%
Japan (9)	81	4 per 1,000 live births	Women: Men:	92% 84%	Per capita: $2,243 Public sources: 5.7% Private source: 1.6%
Germany (17)	77	5 per 1,000 live births	Women: Men:	89% 79%	Per capita: $2,697 Public sources: 7.9% Private source: 2.6%
South Korea (27)	74	5 per 1,000 live births	Women: Men:	88% 72%	Per capita: $470 Public sources: 2.4% Private source: 3.0%
Czech Republic (33)	74	5 per 1,000 live births	Women: Men:	87% 72%	Per capita: $380 Public sources: 6.6% Private source: 0.6%
Poland (37)	73	10 per 1,000 live births	Women: Men:	85% 66%	Per capita: $248 Public sources: 4.7% Private source: 1.5%
Thailand (70)	70	29 per 1,000 live births	Women: Men:	79% 67%	Per capita: $112 Public sources: 1.9% Private source: 4.1%

Source: Adapted from United Nations Development Programme. (2002). *Human Development Report 2002*, pp. 166–167, 174–175. New York: Oxford University Press. Retrieved from http://hdr.undp.org/reports/global/2002/en/pdf/complete.pdf.

Table 6.2
Sickness, Maternity, and Worker's Benefits

Country	Type of System	Coverage	Source of Funds	Qualifying Conditions
United States of America	Social insurance system	See text of chapter 6	• Hospital insurance contribution is rated at 1.45% on all gross earnings (no limit on earnings) • Self-employed individuals contribution is 2.9% • Employer contribution is 1.45% of payroll • Federal and state contribute to Medicaid funds • No maximum earnings for contributions purposes toward hospitalization; maximum earnings between $6,900 and $38,000 per year for cash benefits • Six states have cash benefit programs. Contributions to these programs vary • Cash benefits also apply to national system for railroad employees	Hospitalization: Persons eligible for a pension age 65 and over, certain others who qualify at age 65, disability pensioners on roll for more than 2 years, and persons with chronic kidney disease. Other medical services: Available to above group and to all other persons aged 65 or over through voluntary coverage. Federal-state system for medically indigent (Medicaid)
Germany	Social insurance system	• Long-term care: all persons covered by statutory sickness insurance scheme; persons with private sickness insurance schemes must buy equivalent private coverage for long-term care • Coverage: all wage and salary earners making up to 75,600 DM per year; pensioners, students, and disabled persons under certain conditions; • Special system for miners, artists, public employees, and self-employed farmers • Long-term care for all persons covered by statutory sickness insurance scheme and some special groups subject to certain conditions	*From insured:* • 6.9% of covered earnings average • No contributions if earning less than 630 DM per month • Pensioners contribute 6.9% of pension • For long-term care: 0.85% of earnings in all but one state (1.7% in that one) *From employer:* • 6.9% of payroll average • 13.8% for employees earning less than 630 DM per month • For long-term care: 0.85% of earnings in all but one state (0% in that one)	*Cash sickness and medical benefits:* • Membership in sickness fund (no minimum membership period required) *Cash sickness benefit:* • Insured person unable to work, who is hospitalized, or taking care of a sick child younger than age 12 *Long-term care benefit:* Payable at three levels— 1. Substantial need for care with at least 1 daily required procedure 2. Severe need for care with daily required procedures at least 3x per day 3. Critical need for care with round-the-clock care

Table 6.2 (*continued*)

Country	Type of System	Coverage	Source of Funds	Qualifying Conditions
		• Those with private sickness insurance plan must buy equivalent private coverage for long-term care	*From government:* • Maternity benefits • Benefits for unemployed • Benefits for persons in authorized training • Subsidy for pensioned farmers • Subsidy for student health benefits • Pension system contribution toward pensioners' medical coverage • For long-term care: contributions for unemployed, farmers, and students receiving a training allowance • As of 2000, to be eligible, the insured must have at least 5 years coverage in a long-term care fund	
The Netherlands	Social insurance system	*Medical benefits:* • Wage earners, salaried employees earning less than 30,700 guilders per year, and pensioners • Cover extended to partner and children subject to certain conditions • Exceptional Medical Expenses: all residents *Cash benefits:* • Sickness and maternity benefits for all wage earners and salaried employees • Up to 16 weeks of Materinty benefits for unemployed workers • Under the Civil Code, employers must continue to pay up to 70% of wages up to 310 guilders per day during employee's illness for up to 52 weeks	• Premiums paid for general social security schemes not deductible for tax purposes. As of 1990, contributions covering exceptional medical expenses and disability benefits levied to employees and not employers (as of 1998, the contribution for disability benefits abolished) *From insured:* • Flat rate contribution set by the sickness fund (1.55% for earnings for medical benefits, and 10.25% for exceptional medical insurance) • Contribution for sickness and maternity benefits included in contributions for unemployment for employed workers • Contribution for maternity benefits included in contribution for disability benefits for unemployed workers	*Medical benefits:* Registration with approved sickness fund *Sickness benefit:* Inability to perform own work *Maternity benefit:* Employed or unemployed person

From employers:
- 5.85% of payroll for medical benefits
- Contribution for sickness and maternity benefits included in contributions for unemployment for employed workers

From government:
- Annually determines contribution toward the financing of medical benefits
- Maximum earnings for contribution purposes: medical benefits @ 210 guilders per day exceptional medical expenses @ 48,175 guilders per year cash sickness benefits and maternity benefits for unemployed workers @ 84,000 guilders per year (minimum earnings @ 29,000 guilders per year)

Czech Republic — Social insurance system and public health insurance system

Cash benefits:
- Mandatory for all employees, members of industrial production cooperatives, and advanced students
- Voluntary coverage: self-employed

Medical benefits:
All permanent residents in Czech Republic or employees whose employer is resident in Czech Republic

Health insurance:
All permanent residents in Czech Republic or employees whose employer is resident in Czech Republic

From insured:
- Cash sickness and maternity benefits: 1.1% of earnings
- Medical care: 4.5%

From employer:
- Cash sickness and maternity benefits: 3.3% of payroll
- Medical care: 9% of payroll

From government:
- Cash sickness and maternity benefits: any deficit
- Health care: any deficit and full payments for special categories of covered people

Cash sickness benefits:
- Only those earning >400CZK per month or those working more than 7 days/month are insured
- Physician certificate required from the first day of illness onward to prove incapacity
- No minimum period of employment or residence required
- No waiting period

Cash maternity benefits:
- 270 days of insurance in the 2 years preceding childbirth
- loss of earnings
- childbirth or substitute care of a child (may include men)
- medical confirmation of pregnancy

Cash medical benefits:
- currently insured
- no minimum coverage period
- eligibility continued for 6 weeks after coverage ceases

Table 6.2 (continued)

Country	Type of System	Coverage	Source of Funds	Qualifying Conditions
Poland	Social insurance system (cash and medical benefits)	• Employees, members of farmer's cooperatives, artisans, those connected with agricultural circles, self-employed artisans, attorneys, and home-workers • Pensioners and some groups of self-employed persons, including farmers, are covered for medical benefits only • Special systems for farmers, military, and police	*From insured:* • 10.20% of earnings (2.45% for cash sickness, 7.75% for medical benefits) *From employer:* • None *From government:* • Subsidies for medical benefits	• Cash sickness and maternity benefits: currently in insured employment • Medical benefits: currently in insured employment or pensioner
Norway	Social insurance system (cash and medical benefits)	*Cash benefits:* • Employed and self-employed with income no less than ½ the base amount • Income limit does not affect employer's obligation to pay cash benefits for first 16 calendar days *Medical benefits:* • All residents (including resident alien seamen serving on Norwegian ships) Special provisions for seamen, military personnel, and (for cash benefits) fishermen, casual workers, and temporarily unemployed	• No maximum earnings for contribution purposes *From insured:* • Contributions for sickness and maternity benefits taken from contributions made for Old Age, Disability and Survivors program *From employer:* • Contributions for sickness and maternity benefits taken from 14.1% of payroll contribution made for Old Age, Disability and Survivors program • Total cost of cash sickness benefit for first 16 days *From government:* • National government meets any deficit	• Cash sickness benefit: 14 days if employment or self-employment • Cash maternity benefit: 6 months of employment or self-employment during last 10 months (mother, father, or both) • Maternity grant: insured mothers not entitled to cash maternity benefits • Additional grant: widowed, divorced, separated, and unwed mothers with 3 years of insurance immediately preceding the claim
Sweden	Dual social insurance (cash benefits) and universal (medical care) system	*Cash benefits:* • Gainfully occupied persons earning 6,000 kronor per year or more *Medical benefits:* • All residents	*From insured:* *Cash benefits:* • None for employed persons • Self-employed: 8.23% of earnings *Medical care:* • No contribution	*Cash sickness benefits:* • Income from employment unless involuntarily unemployed *Cash maternity benefits (parent's cash benefits):* • Each parent eligible for above guaranteed level (120 kronor/day) if insured for at least 240 days before childbirth

Pregnancy cash benefit:
- For pregnant employee in physically demanding job whose employer is not able to transfer her to less demanding work

From employer:
Cash benefits:
- 7.5% of payroll

Medical care:
No contribution

From government:
Cash benefits:
None, at present

Medical care:
Total cost met by regional councils

Insured person medical benefits:
- 1.5% levy on income above A$22,594 for couples and single parents (increased by A$2,100/child), or A$13,389 for single person without dependents
- Exemption from levy: veterans, war widows, Armed Forces personnel with dependents (1/2 levy if without dependents)

From employer: None

From government:
- Whole cost of cash benefits and assistance towards a wide-range of drugs under pharmaceutical benefits scheme
- Rebates for medical and hospital benefits
- Funding provided for residential and community aged care
- Federal government general revenue grants and Medicare grants to states and territories for public hospital operating costs meets approximately 40% to 50% of funding of medical insurance scheme

Sickness allowance (means-tested):
- Age 21 (25 if full-time student) to pension age
- Resident in country
- Sickness or injury prevents work
- Must have a job to return to or intend to resume full-time studies

Medical benefit:
- Residents

Pharmaceutical benefit:
- Residents

Australia

Dual social assistance (cash benefits) and universal (medical care) systems

- Cash benefits: gainfully employed persons with limited income and others meeting qualifying conditions
- Medical benefits: Residents

Table 6.2 (*continued*)

Country	Type of System	Coverage	Source of Funds	Qualifying Conditions
Japan	Dual social insurance system. National Health Insurance provides medical benefits, Employees Health Insurance provides cash and medical benefits	*National Health Insurance:* • All residents not under employment-related health insurance or special schemes under local government (municipalities, townships, or village) programs • Special National Health Insurance societies provide coverage for self-employed *Employee health insurance:* • Employees of firms in industry and commerce with 5 or more employees (government-managed programs unless member of health insurance society) • Voluntary coverage for other employees • Special systems for persons aged 70 or over, seamen, private school teachers, and public employees	• Maximum basic wage for contribution and benefit purposes: 980,000 yen per month • Minimum basic wage for contribution and benefit purposes: 92,000 yen per month ***From insured:*** *National Health Insurance:* • National health tax or premium fixed by individual carrier according to individual household income and assets, and not to exceed 530,000 yen per year per household • Insurers of municipality-run programs may reduce premiums 30% to 70% for qualifying low-income residents or households • Other insurers may reduce premiums by 20% for low-income individuals or households *Employer Health Insurance:* • 4.25% of basic monthly wage according to 40 wage classes • Insurance society average in 1996 @ 3.658% ***From employer:*** *National health Insurance:* • None *Employee Health Insurance:* • 4.25% of basic monthly wage • Special premium of 0.5% of bonuses of insured • If managed by health insurance society: average in 1996 @ 4.736% ***From government:*** *National Health Plan:* • 50% medical care costs • Cost of administration • Some local subsidies	*National Health Insurance:* • Residence in municipality, township, or village *Employee Health Insurance cash sickness, maternity and medical benefits:* • Covered employment • Sickness and maternity benefits continued for normal duration if beneficiary leaving employment was in covered employment during last 12 months • Medical care provided to same beneficiary up to 5 years from the initial day of treatment

South Korea

Social insurance system (medical care only)

- All permanent residents (including noncitizens residing in Korea of 1 or more years), except for those covered by Medical Aid program

Employee Health Insurance:
- 13% of benefit costs (none if managed by health insurance societies)
- 16.4% health care costs for the aged costs (none if managed by health insurance societies)
- Cost of administration costs (partially if managed by health insurance societies)

From insured:
- Employees in general: 1% to 4% of covered monthly earnings (average: 1.64%)
- Government and private school employees: 2.61%
- Self-employed: rates based on income, assets, age, and gender of insured

From employer:
- 1% to 4% of covered monthly earnings (average: 1.64%)
- Private schools: 1.26%

From government:
- Employees in general: none
- Government employees: 2.1% of covered monthly earnings
- Private school employees: 0.84% of covered monthly earnings
- Self-employed: 30% of contributions
- Minimum earnings for contribution and benefit purposes: 75,000 won per month for employees, 5,000,000 won in taxable annual income for self-employed
- No maximum for contribution and benefit purposes

No minimum qualifying period or contributions to program

Thailand

Social Insurance System

- Employees of firms with 10 or more workers
- Voluntary coverage for self-employed Separate programs for civil servants and private school teachers

- Contributions finance disability and death wage range for contribution purposes between 1,650 to 15,000 baht per month

Cash sickness and medical benefits:
- 3 months of contributions in 15 month before date of treatment

Table 6.2 (continued)

Country	Type of System	Coverage	Source of Funds	Qualifying Conditions
			From insured: • 1% of employees wages *From employer:* • 1% of employees wages *From government:* • 1% of employees wages	*Cash maternity and medical benefits:* • 7 months of contributions in 15 months before treatment • Limited to 2 pregnancies

Country	Sickness Benefit	Worker's medical benefits	Dependent's medical benefits
United States of America	Cash benefits—minimum insurance wages in last year ($300-$6,900), specific weeks of employment in last year (4–20), or combination of conditions. Sickness benefit—percent of earnings as defined by the state providing cash benefit Maternity benefit—same as cash and sickness benefits	Services furnished by providers paid for directly by carriers, or refunds to patients by carriers as part of medical expenses. 　Hospitalization—inpatient care provided for stays up to 90 days; beneficiary responsible for first day deductible amount adjusted each year and, for 60–90 days, 1/4 of first day deductible amount per day. For stays longer than 90 days, coverage available for up to 60 lifetime reserve days with beneficiary responsible for 1/2 first day deductible amount per day. 　Posthospital skilled nursing Facility care for an additional 100 days (patient paying $96 for 21–100 days); laboratory, x-rays for inpatients, and posthospital home health services. 　Other medical services—payment for 80% of reasonable charges above $100 per year. For physician's services, outpatient diagnostic and physical therapy, laboratory services, appliances, and transportation. 100% of reasonable charges for home health services (after paying of $100 deductible). • Persons eligible for both hospitalization and other medical care services under the regular Medicare program except for those with chronic kidney disease can elect to participate in electives available in their area such as *Medicare+Choice.*	Available only if age 65 and satisfies other qualifying requirements or has chronic kidney disease.

Germany	• Cash maternity benefits are 12 weeks of insurance, or continuous employment relationship from tenth month up to the fourth month preceding confinement.
	• Sickness benefit: employer pays full wage or salary for first 6 weeks; thereafter, sickness fund pays 70% of gross earnings (up to 90% of net earnings) for up to 78 weeks in 3 years for the same illness.
	• Maternity benefit: 100% of female worker's net earnings payable 6 weeks before and 8 weeks after confinement.
	  • Max. rate: 25 DM per day
	  • Lump sum of 150 DM payable per birth if insured not eligible for maternity benefit
	• Long-term care: career's allowance payable in cases when the insured provide care themselves.
	  • payoff range from 400 DM, 800 DM, or 1300 DM per month
	  • allowance can also be claimed in-kind
		• Services provided to patient by doctors, hospitals, and druggists under contract
		• Services include comprehensive medical and dental care, preventive examination and treatment, lab tests, maternity care with midwife or doctor, hospitalization, surgery, appliances, and prescribed medicines
		• Copayment required for medicines, appliances, hospitalization, and transportation (not required for particularly disadvantaged cases)
		• Long-term home care benefits (amounts fixed for different services):
		  • various aids and services
		  • appliances
		  • technical assistance such as home modification
		  • day or night care (including services partially provided by a health care establishment)
		  • short-term institutional health care
		  • Institutional care benefits: costs covered up to maximum amounts—insured pay for room and service costs
			• Same as for insured person for medical benefits and long-term care

The Netherlands	• Sickness benefit is 70% of earnings up to a daily maximum earnings of 310, payable up to 52 weeks
	• Maternity benefit is 100% of earnings up to a daily maximum of 310 guilders per day, payable during pregnancy, for a total of 16 weeks and extended up to 52 weeks in case of disability caused by pregnancy or delivery
	• Maternity benefit for unemployed workers receive 100% of earnings with a maximum of the minimum wage (2.350 guilders per month), payable for a total of 16 weeks
		• Workers' medical benefits provided by doctors, hospitals, and druggists under contract with and paid directly by sickness funds. Services include general and specialist care, hospitalization, laboratory services, medicines, limited dental care, maternity care, appliances, rehabilitation, and transportation.
		  • specific cost sharing for long-term hospitalization, artificial limbs, and transportation:
		  • maximum duration: no limit except for physiotherapy
		  • exceptional medical expenses insurance takes over from 366th day
			• Same as for insured person.
			• For maternity care, partner and children of insured man receive same nursing or hospitalization benefit as insured woman
			• Death benefit is 100% of earnings up to a daily maximum of 310 guilders per day, payable for one month

Czech Republic	• First 3 days: 50% of daily assessment base (DAB)
	• Fourth day on: 69% of DAB
	• Daily assessment base: Gross earnings (GE) up to 480CZK: 100% inclusion GE between 480 to 690 CZK: 60% inclusion; GE over 690 CZK: not included
	• Minimum earnings for calculation of sickness benefit is 606 CZK per day
		• Provided free of charge under scope and conditions stipulated by law
		• Care includes:
		  • medical treatment in outpatient and incare patient facilities
		  • emergency and rescue services
		  • preventive care
		  • provision of drugs
		  • medical aid and appliances
			No substitution payments because the Czech health insurance system is based on individual insurance for each person

Table 6.2 (*continued*)

Country	Sickness Benefit	Worker's medical benefits	Dependent's medical benefits

	• Benefit payable from first day of incapacity for up to 1 year, or 2 years if recovery likely
	• Maternity benefit:
	  • 69% of DAB as calculated for cash sickness benefit
	  • Maximum per day: 419 CZK
	  • Payable for 28 weeks (37 weeks for single mother and multiple births) including at least 6 weeks before expected delivery date
		• stomatologic (diseases of the mouth) treatment
		• spa treatment
		• care of children in special medical institutions and convalescent homes
		• preventive care provided in enterprise and factory surgeries
		• transportation of the sick
		• refunding of travel costs
		• medical assessment
		• examination of deceased insured persons and autopsy including the transportation of the dead
		• No duration limit	

Poland	*Sickness benefit:*
	• 80% of earnings averaged over the preceding 6 months
	• If incapacity rises during pregnancy or continues beyond 90 days, entitlement equates to 100% of earnings
	• Benefit payable from first day of incapacity for up to 26 weeks (may be extended to 39 weeks if recovery likely)
	• If recovery likely, entitlement to sickness benefit may be followed by entitlement to rehabilitation benefit for up to 12 months (payable @ 75% of earnings)
	• Employer pays first 35 days
	
	Maternity benefits:
	• 100% earnings payable for 16 weeks for the birth of first child (18 weeks for subsequent births)
	• For multiple births, benefit payable for 26 weeks
	• Maternity benefit followed by maternity leave of 24 months (36 months for single mother) to 72 months if child is disabled
	• Maternity leave payment = 308.80 zlotys per month (491.00 for single mother)
	• Maternity leave benefit adjusted every 3 months
		• Provided directly to patients by private health care providers contracted by health care funds
		• Services include:
		  • general and specialist care
		  • hospitalization
		  • basic prescription drugs (government provides a partial subsidy for these)
		• Patients select physician and hospital
		• No duration limit if employed; if employment ceases, 26 weeks (with possible extension up to 39 weeks)
			• Provided directly to patients by private health care providers contracted by health care funds
			• Services include:
			  • general and specialist care
			  • hospitalization
			  • basic prescription drugs (government provides a partial subsidy for these)
			• Patients select physician and hospital
			• No duration limit if employment ceases, 26 weeks (with possible extension up to 39 weeks)

Norway

- Cash refunds of part or all of medical expenses, or service benefits furnished by providers under contract with funds
- Includes:
  - part of physician fees (patient pays 110 kroner per consultation in most cases)
  - free care in public hospital
  - patient pays 36% of expenses for listed essential medicine (up to 330 kroner per prescription)
  - laboratory services
  - transportation in excess of 90 kroner per trip
- Patient's own expenses (including children aged 7–16) limited in 2002 to 1,350 kroner, with certain exemption for special diseases
- Parliament sets limits for 1 year at a time
- When ceiling reached, patient entitled to free treatment for remainder of year
- Pensions reduced from the second month of institutional care; sickness benefit, from the fourth month
- No duration limit

Insured in their own right because coverage is based on residency

Sickness benefit:
- 100% covered earnings
- Payable from first full day of incapacity for up to 52 weeks (thereafter covered by rehabilitation allowance or disability pension)
- Maximum earnings for benefit purposes: 6x base amount
- Self-employed receive 65% of assessed covered earnings after a 14-day waiting period (may voluntarily insure for 100% of earnings, a shorter waiting period, or both)
- Casual workers and temporarily unemployed: 65% of assessed earnings after 14-day waiting period

Care leave:
- For care for sick child under 12 (mother or father)
- 10 days per year (20 days if single parent)
- More than 2 children: 15 days (30 days for single parent)
- Disabled or chronically ill child under 18: 20 days each (40 days for single parent)
- For sick child under 16, if illness potentially life-threatening: up to 780 days

Maternity benefit:
- 100% covered earnings (self-employed @ 65% of assessed earnings) for 42 weeks, or 80% for 52 weeks to insured parents (mother or father)
- Mother required to take 3 weeks of benefit period prior to expected birth date, and at least 6 weeks immediately after giving birth
- 4 weeks of total maternity cash benefit period reserved for the father ("father quota")
- Reduced work week may count as partial maternity benefit

Maternity grant:
- 32,138 kroner if not receiving maternity benefit (also paid in case of adoption)
- Giving birth at home: 1,765 kroner

Table 6.2 *(continued)*

Country	Sickness Benefit	Worker's medical benefits	Dependent's medical benefits
Sweden	*Sickness benefit:* • 80% of lost income after day 15, based on income up to 7.5x base amount • Payable after day 15 of incapacity for duration of illness, 7 days per week • Pensioners with income from work limited to 180 days • Employer pays days 2 to 14 @ 80% of lost income • Self-employed and other qualifying non-employees receive 80% of income loss from day 2 • Maximum daily benefit: 626 kronor • Benefits subject to taxation *Parents' cash benefit (for childbirth):* • Replaces 80% of income loss for 390 days (guaranteed level of 120 kronor/day), and an additional 90 days @ 60 kronor/day • Benefits payable up to 480 days per child until child is age 8 (both parents combined) • Benefits subject to taxation *Pregnancy cash benefit:* • Same as sickness benefit, payable for 50 days beginning no earlier than 60 days or later than 11 days prior to expected date of birth *Temporary benefit:* • Care of children under 12 (16 if chronically ill or disabled) • Similar to sickness benefit • Payable for 70 days per child per year (both parents combined) on occasions when child or child's carer is sick • Additional 60 days per child (not for sick carer)	• Includes: • physician consultation (patient pays 100 kronor to 260 kronor per visit and an additional 30 to 80 kronor for home visit) • hospitalization in ward, including maternity ward of public hospital (patient pays maximum of 80 kronor per day—reduced for low-income earners) • Partial refund of travel costs • Free dental care for children up to 18 • Fixed subsidies for preventive dental care • High-cost limit for prosthetic treatment • Free insulin • Patients pay full cost of other medicines up to 900 kronor in a 12-month period, partial costs thereafter not to exceed 1,800 kronor per year • Maximum payment for other kinds of medical services: 900 kronor per year • Pensioners pay maximum of 80 kronor per day for hospital care (limited to 1/3 amount of pension received)	Same as for family head
Australia	*Sickness allowance (means-tested):* • Up to A$149.50 per week if partnered and with dependent children • Single person, aged 21 or over, with no dependents: A$161.70 per week	*Medical benefits:* • Patient pays 1.5% of scheduled fee for outpatient ambulatory care, or A$50.10—whichever is less (indexed annually for price changes)	*Medical benefits for dependents:* • Same as medical and hospital benefits as head of family • Family membership in private benefit organization also covers dependents

- Single, 21 or older, with dependents; or over age 60: up to A$174.95 per week
- Children benefits paid under family allowances scheme
- Payable after 7-day waiting period for as long as qualified

Rental assistance, pharmaceutical allowance, remote area supplement:
- Same as under old-age pension (see chapter 3)

Concession card:
- Entitled, which makes available additional health, household and transportation assistance from state and local governments
- Adjusted in March and September according to price index

Pharmaceutical benefit:
- Most prescribed medicines, with a fee up to A$20.30 per prescription
- Pensioners, beneficiaries, and low-income persons pay A$3.20 fee per prescription
- Government pays pharmacist

Hospital benefits:
- Free standard ward accommodations
- Free treatment by staff physicians in public hospitals
- Private benefit organizations pay for private hospital stay, or public hospital charge for those who choose treatment by their own physician in public hospitals

Japan

National Health Insurance:
- No cash benefits provided by law, but all carriers provide lump-sum grant

Employee Health Insurance Sickness Benefit:
- 60% of average daily basic wage, according to wage class
- Payable after 3-day waiting period for up to 1 year and 6 months, or determination of disability
- Health insurance societies may provide more liberal benefits

Maternity benefit:
- 60% of average daily basic wage for 42 days before (98 days in case of multiple birth) and 56 days after confinement
- Payment discontinued or partially reduced if receiving wage or cash sickness benefit
- Lump-sum birth grant of 300,000 yen

National Health Insurance and Employee Health Insurance Medical Benefits:
- Medical care (usually provided by clinics, hospitals, and druggists under contract with and paid by carrier)
- Medical treatment
- Surgery
- Hospitalization
- Nursing
- Dental care
- Maternity care (difficult childbirth only)
- Medicines
- Some carriers provide services directly through own clinics and hospitals

National Health Insurance:
- Insured pays 30% of costs for all care—maximum: 63,000 yen per month for same illness (35,400 yen per month if low-income family)
- Duration: no limit
- Inpatient also pays 760 yen per day for part of food expenses (low-income family pays 650 yen per day up to 90 days and 500 yen per day thereafter)
- Special provisions for those aged 70 or older, or if bedridden, to ages 65–70—

National Health Insurance Medical Benefits:
- Same as for insured

Employee Health Insurance Medical Benefits:
- Same as for insured, but with patient paying 30% of cost (20% if inpatient) up to 63,600 yen per month
- Funeral grant: 100,000 yen

Table 6.2 (*continued*)

Country	Sickness Benefit	Worker's medical benefits	Dependent's medical benefits
		(1) Inpatient pays for part of cost of food expenses @ 760 yen per day; 650 yen per day if qualified low-income aged, and 500 yen per day when hospitalization exceeds 90 days (2) Inpatients pay 300 yen per day and no copayment for hospitalization beyond 2 months for old-age welfare pension recipients *Employee Health Insurance:* • Insured pays 20% of costs for all care • Maximum: 63,600 yen per month for same illness (35,400 yen per month if low-income family) • Maximum after paying monthly maximum for 3 times during last 12 months: 37,200 yen per month (24,600 yen per month for low-income family) • Duration: no time limit • Also pays for part of food expenses @ 760 yen per day (600 yen per day for up to 90 days and then 500 yen per day thereafter if low-income family)	

South Korea	None	• Services provided by designated physicians, clinics, hospitals, and pharmacists.
		• Includes:
		  • Medical treatment
		  • Surgery
		  • Hospitalization
		  • Medicines
		  • Maternity services to insured or dependent, with no limit on number of children—no cash benefit for maternity
		• Insured pays:
		  • 20% of hospitalization costs
		  • 30% to 55% of outpatient care (55% if provided by the General Hospital, 40% if by the regular hospital, and 30% if by a clinic)
		  • Maximum: 500,000 won for each 30-day period for employees in general and their dependents
		  • 1,000,000 won for each 30-day period for government and private school employees and their dependents, and the self-employed
			• Same as for insured
			  • Spouse
			  • Direct lineal descendants of employee and spouse
			  • Direct linear descendants and their spouses
			  • Brothers/sisters chiefly supported by the insured person
			• Funeral grant for both insured workers and dependents—lump-sum payment of 300,000 won for insured person, and 200,000 won for any dependent

Thailand

- Duration of benefits: 330 days per year per insured person—no limit for the aged, disabled, pulmonary tubercular patients, or recipients of national merit awards and medals.

- Includes:
  - Medical examination and treatment
  - Hospitalization
  - Medicines
  - Ambulance fees
  - Rehabilitation
  - Other necessary expenses under the capitation system

Sickness benefit:
- 50% of wages
- Maximum of 250 baht per day
- Payable for up to 90 days for each illness, but not more than 180 days in any calendar year
- For each incidence of chronic disease, payable for no more than 365 days

Maternity benefit:
- 50% of wages payable for up to 90 days for each confinement
- Payable only for female insured person
- Lump sum of 4,000 baht per one confinement

Maternity medical benefits for spouse, lump-sum only

Table 6.3
Medicare and Medicaid Program Activities for 2000

Medicare

Hospital Insurance (Part A):	
Total benefits paid in calendar year 2000	$128.5 billion
Supplementary Medical Insurance (Part B):	
Total benefits paid in calendar year 2000	$88.9 billion
Number of enrollees in July 2000, (one or both of Parts A and B)	39.6 million
Aged	34.3 million
Disabled	5.3 million
Administrative costs, 2000:	
Hospital Insurance	$2.6 billion
As a percent of total benefits paid	2.1 percent
Supplementary Medical Insurance	$1.8 billion
As a percent of total benefits paid	2.0 percent

Medicaid

Medical service expenditures in fiscal year 1998	$142.3 billion
Number of unduplicated recipients, fiscal year 1998	40.7 million
Average 1998 vendor payment per unduplicated recipient:	
Persons aged 65 or older	$10,242
Permanently and totally disabled persons	9,095
Dependent children under age 21	1,203
Average 1998 vendor payment for medical services:	
Nursing facility services	$19,379
Inpatient general hospital care	5,031
Prescribed drugs	699
Physician's services	327

Source: Social Security Administration. (2001). *Annual Statistical Supplement, 2001 to the Social Security Bulletin.* Baltimore: Social Security Administration, Office of Policy. Retrieved from http://www.ssa.gov/policy/docs/statcomps/supplement/2001/supp01.pdf.

Table 6.4
Medicare Outlays, Selected Fiscal Years 1967 to 2010

[in Millions of Dollars]

Fiscal year	Part A	Total Part B	Medicare Medicare outlays	Net premium offsets	Medicare outlays	Percent increase (over prior year)
1967	$2,597	$798	$3,395	-$647	$2,748	NA
1970	4,953	2,196	7,149	-936	6,213	9.1
1972	6,276	2,544	8,820	-1,340	7,480	13.0
1973	6,842	2,637	9,479	-1,427	8,052	7.6
1974	8,065	3,283	11,348	-1,708	9,640	19.7
1975	10,612	4,170	14,782	-1,907	12,875	33.6
1976	12,579	5,200	17,779	-1,945	15,834	23.0
TQ	3,404	1,401	4,805	-541	4,264	NA
1977	15,207	6,342	21,549	-2,204	19,345	NA
1978	17,862	7,350	25,212	-2,443	22,769	17.7
1979	20,343	8,805	29,148	-2,653	26,495	16.4
1980	24,288	10,746	35,034	-2,945	32,089	21.1
1981	29,248	13,240	42,488	-3,340	39,148	22.0
1982	34,864	15,559	50,423	-3,856	46,567	19.0
1983	38,551	18,317	56,868	-4,253	52,615	13.0
1984	42,295	20,374	62,669	-4,942	57,727	9.7
1985	48,667	22,730	71,397	-5,562	65,835	14.0
1986	49,685	26,217	75,902	-5,739	70,163	6.6
1987	50,803	30,837	81,640	-6,520	75,120	7.1
1988	52,730	34,947	87,677	-8,798	78,879	5.0
1989	58,238	38,316	96,554	-11,590	84,964	7.7
1990	66,687	43,022	109,709	-11,607	98,102	15.5
1991	70,742	47,021	117,763	-12,174	105,589	7.6
1992	81,971	50,285	132,256	-13,232	119,024	12.7
1993	91,604	54,254	145,858	-15,305	130,553	9.7
1994	102,770	59,724	162,494	-17,747	144,747	10.9
1995	114,883	65,213	180,096	-20,241	159,855	10.4
1996	127,683	68,946	196,629	-20,088	176,591	10.5
1997	137,884	72,553	210,437	-20,421	190,016	7.6
1998	137,298	76,272	213,570	-20,747	192,823	1.5
1999	131,500	80,518	212,018	-21,561	190,457	-1.2
2000[1]	133,100	88,300	221,300	-21,800	199,500	4.7
2001[1]	140,600	98,800	239,400	-23,300	216,100	8.3
2002[1]	143,600	103,500	247,100	-25,400	221,700	2.6
2003[1]	153,500	114,300	267,800	-28,100	239,800	8.2
2004[1]	163,200	123,800	287,000	-31,100	255,900	6.7
2005[1]	176,800	136,600	313,400	-34,200	279,200	9.1
2006[1]	182,400	141,600	324,000	-37,200	286,700	2.7
2007[1]	198,000	155,300	353,200	-40,300	312,900	9.1
2008[1]	211,300	167,400	378,800	-43,600	335,300	7.2
2009[1]	226,100	181,300	407,500	-47,200	360,200	7.4
2010[1]	241,600	196,800	438,400	-51,000	387,400	7.6

1. Congressional Budget Office projections.

NA. Not applicable.

Note: Totals may not add due to rounding.

TQ. transitional quarter.

Source: United States House of Representatives, Committee on Ways and Means. (2000). *The 2000 Green Book: Background material and data on programs within the jurisdiction of the Committee on Ways and Means.* Retrieved from http://aspe.hhs.gov/2000gb/sec2.txt.

Table 6.5
Part A and Part B Deductible, Coinsurance, and Premiums,[1] Selected Years 1966 to 2000

Calendar year	Inpatient hospital[2]		Skilled nursing reserve days (nonrenewable) coinsurance day[4]	facility 21st-100th day per per day[5]	HI monthly premium[6]			SMI premium		
	First 60 days deductible	60 lifetime 61st-90th day coinsurance per day[3]			Effective coinsurance	Full date	Reduced amount	SMI deductible amount	Effective date	Amount
1966	$40	$10	[7]	[7]	[8]	[8]	NA	$50	7/66	$3.00
1968	40	10	$20	$5.00	[8]	[8]	NA	50	4/68	4.00
1970	52	13	26	6.50	[8]	[8]	NA	50	7/70	5.30
1972	68	17	34	8.50	[8]	[8]	NA	50	7/72	5.80
1973	72	18	36	9.00	7/73	$33	NA	60	9/73[9]	6.30
1974	84	21	42	10.50	7/74	36	NA	60	7/74	6.70
1975	92	23	46	11.50	7/75	40	NA	60	[8]	6.70
1976	104	26	52	13.00	7/76	45	NA	60	7/76	7.20
1977	124	31	62	15.50	7/77	54	NA	60	7/77	7.70
1978	144	36	72	18.00	7/78	63	NA	60	7/78	8.20
1979	160	40	80	20.00	7/79	69	NA	60	7/79	8.70
1980	180	45	90	22.50	7/80	78	NA	60	7/80	9.60
1981	204	51	102	25.50	7/81	89	NA	60	7/81	11.00
1982	260	65	130	32.50	7/82	113	NA	75	7/82	12.20
1983	304	76	152	38.00	[8]	113	NA	75	[8]	12.20
1984	356	89	178	44.50	1/84	155	NA	75	1/84	14.60
1985	400	100	200	50.00	1/85	174	NA	75	1/85	15.50
1986	492	123	246	61.50	1/86	214	NA	75	1/86	15.50
1987	520	130	260	65.00	1/87	226	NA	75	1/87	17.90
1988	540	135	270	67.50	1/88	234	NA	75	1/88	24.80
1989	560[10]	NA	NA	25.50[11]	1/89	156	NA	75	1/89	31.90
1990	592	148	296	74.00	1/90	175	NA	75	1/90	28.60
1991	628	157	314	78.50	1/91	177	NA	100	1/91	29.90
1992	652	163	326	81.50	1/92	192	NA	100	1/92	31.80
1993	676	169	338	84.50	1/93	221	NA	100	1/93	36.60
1994	696	174	348	87.00	1/94	245	$184	100	1/94	41.10
1995	716	179	358	89.50	1/95	261	183	100	1/95	46.10
1996	736	184	368	92.00	1/96	289	188	100	1/96	42.50
1997	760	190	380	95.00	1/97	311	187	100	1/97	43.80
1998	764	191	382	95.50	1/98	309	170	100	1/98	43.80
1999	768	192	384	96.00	1/99	309	170	100	1/99	45.50
2000	776	194	388	97.00	1/00	301	166	100	1/00	45.50

1. For services furnished on or after January 1, 1982, the coinsurance amounts are based on the inpatient hospital deductible for the year in which the services were furnished. For services furnished prior to January 1, 1982, the coinsurance amounts are based on the inpatient hospital deductible applicable for the year in which the individual's benefit period began.

2. For care in psychiatric hospital there is a 190-day lifetime limit.

3. Always equal to one-fourth of inpatient hospital deductible through 1988 and for 1990 and later; eliminated for 1989.

4. Always equal to one-half of inpatient hospital deductible through 1988 and for 1990 and later; eliminated for 1989.

5. Always equal to one-third of inpatient hospital deductible through 1988 and for 1990 and later. For 1989 it was equal to 20 percent of estimated Medicare covered average cost per day.

6. Not applicable prior to July 1973. Applies to aged individuals who are not fully insured, and to certain disabled individuals who have exhausted other entitlement. The reduced amount is available to aged individuals who are not fully insured but who have, or whose spouse has or had, at least 30 quarters of coverage under title II of the Social Security Act. The reduced amount is 75 percent of the full amount in 1994, 70 percent in 1995, 65 percent in 1996, 60 percent in 1997, and 55 percent in 1998 and thereafter.

7. Not covered.

8. Not applicable.

9. For August 1973 the premium was $6.10.

10. In 1989, the HI deductible was applied on an annual basis, not a benefit period basis (unlike the other years).

11. In 1989, the skilled nursing facility coinsurance was on days 1–8 of the 150 days allowed annually; for the other years it is on days 21–100 of 100 days allowed per benefit period.

NA. Not available.

In addition to the deductible and coinsurance amounts shown in the table, the first three pints of blood are not reimbursed by Medicare. Currently there is no deductible or coinsurance on home health benefits. From January 1973 to June 30, 1982, there was a $60 annual deductible and prior to July 1, 1981, benefits were limited to 100 visits per benefit period under part A and 100 visits per calendar year under part B.

Special limits apply to certain benefits: (1) Outpatient physician services for mental illness; 50 percent of approved charges, up to a maximum of $250 in benefits per year, July 1, 1966 through December 31, 1987; $450 in benefits per year, January 1, 1988 through December 31, 1988; $1,100 in benefits per year, January 1, 1989 through December 31, 1989; beginning January 1, 1990, the limit was removed; (2) physical and occupational therapy services furnished by physical therapists in independent practice: maximum annual approved charges July 1, 1973 through December 31, 1981, $80 per year; January 1, 1982 through December 31, 1982, $400 per year; January 1, 1983 through December 31, 1989, $500 per year; January 1, 1990 through December 31, 1993, $750 per year; and January 1, 1994 through December 31, 1998; in 1999 there was an annual $1,500 limit on all physical therapy services (except those provided by a hospital) and an annual $1,500 limit on all occupational therapy services (except those provided by a hospital); and no limit in 2000.

Source: United States House of Representatives, Committee on Ways and Means. (2000). The 2000 Green Book: Background material and data on programs within the jurisdiction of the Committee on Ways and Means. Retrieved from http://aspe.hhs.gov/2000gb/sec2.txt.

Table 6.6
Medicare Savings Attributable to Secondary Payer Provisions by Type of Provision, Fiscal Years 1988 to 1998

[in Millions of Dollars]

Year and Medicare part	Workers' compensation	Working aged	End-stage renal disease	Automobile	Disability	Total
1988:						
Part A	99.4	867.7	75.0	179.6	399.3	1,621.0
Part B	27.5	337.1	25.1	28.2	137.0	554.9
Total	128.2	1,100.5	108.6	171.9	369.0	1,878.2
1989:						
Part A	$110.1	$786.7	$88.4	$149.6	$275.5	$1,410.3
Part B	18.1	313.8	20.2	22.3	93.5	467.9
Total	126.9	1,204.8	100.1	207.8	536.3	2,175.9
1990:						
Part A	120.9	981.6	144.1	220.1	498.4	1,965.1
Part B	21.6	325.8	21.5	26.4	123.2	518.5
Total	142.5	1,307.4	165.6	246.5	621.6	2,483.6
1991:						
Part A	107.4	932.7	144.9	235.6	526.6	1,947.2
Part B	21.2	417.5	40.2	26.6	186.2	691.7
Total	128.6	1,350.2	185.1	262.2	712.8	2,638.9
1992:						
Part A	118.9	1,044.9	140.8	233.9	600.9	2,139.4
Part B	17.3	398.3	37.4	34.5	182.9	670.4
Total	136.2	1,443.2	178.2	268.4	783.8	2,809.8
1993:						
Part A	100.4	1,073.1	133.6	239.6	657.8	2,204.5
Part B	11.3	392.2	32.8	28.9	192.3	657.5
Total	111.7	1,465.3	166.4	268.5	850.1	2,862.0
1994:						
Part A	96.5	1,101.1	130.2	265.9	682.3	2,276.0
Part B	13.0	398.1	31.8	32.7	211.8	687.4
Total	109.5	1,499.2	162.0	298.6	894.1	2,963.4
1995:						
Part A	107.0	1,068.0	142.0	295.5	728.9	2,341.4
Part B	10.5	360.3	39.0	40.2	215.5	665.5
Total	117.5	1,428.3	181.0	335.7	944.4	3,006.9
1996:						
Part A	93.6	1,062.5	133.4	335.0	728.5	2,353.0
Part B	11.1	295.1	34.3	50.1	196.4	586.9
Total	104.7	1,357.6	167.6	385.0	924.9	2,939.9
1997:						
Part A	99.7	1,046.5	114.3	366.8	697.5	2,324.9
Part B	11.8	276.4	32.4	63.7	178.9	563.2
Total	111.5	1,322.9	146.7	430.6	876.3	2,888.0
1998:						
Part A	96.7	1,303.0	108.1	219.2	810.8	2,683.9
Part B	11.6	364.3	35.0	28.0	238.4	707.7
Total	108.3	1,667.3	143.1	247.1	1,049.3	3,391.6

Note: Totals may not add due to rounding.

Source: United States House of Representatives, Committee on Ways and Means. (2000). *The 2000 Green Book: Background material and data on programs within the jurisdiction of the Committee on Ways and Means.* Retrieved from http://aspe.hhs.gov/2000gb/sec2.txt.

Table 6.7
Medicaid Payments and Per Capita Payments by Basis of Eligibility, Selected Fiscal Years 1975 to 1998

Basis of eligibility	Fiscal year						Percent change 1975-98
	1975	1980	1985	1990	1995	1998	
Nominal payments, in millions of dollars							
Payments:							
Age 65 and older.......	$4,358	$8,739	$14,096	$21,508	$36,527	$40,602	831.7
Blind/disabled............	3,145	7,621	13,452	24,403	49,418	60,375	1819.7
Children....................	2,186	3,123	4,414	9,100	17,976	20,459	835.9
Adults.......................	2,062	3,231	4,746	8,590	13,511	14,833	619.4
Other........................	492	596	798	1,051	1,499	6,048	1129.3
Total..........................	12,242	23,311	37,508	64,859	120,140	142,318	1062.5
Per capita payment:							
Age 65 and older......	1,205	2,540	4,605	6,717	8,868	10,242	750.0
Blind/disabled............	2,146	2,619	7,600	11,807	17,678	9,095	323.8
Children....................	228	335	452	811	1,047	1,117	389.9
Adults.......................	455	663	860	1,429	1,777	1,876	312.3
Other........................	273	NR	658	1,062	2,380	1,579	478.4
Total..........................	556	1,079	1,719	2,568	3,311	3,501	529.7
Constant 1998 dollars in millions							
Payments:							
Age 65 and older......	13,684	17,740	21,426	27,100	39,084	40,602	196.7
Blind/disabled............	9,875	15,471	20,447	30,748	52,877	60,375	511.4
Children....................	6,864	6,340	6,709	11,466	19,234	20,459	198.1
Adults.......................	6,475	6,559	7,214	10,823	14,457	14,833	129.1
Other........................	1,545	1,210	1,213	1,324	1,604	6,048	291.5
Total..........................	38,440	47,321	57,012	81,722	128,550	142,318	270.2
Per capita payment:							
Age 65 and older......	3,784	5,156	7,000	8,463	9,489	10,242	170.7
Blind/disabled............	6,738	5,317	31,080	14,877	18,915	9,095	35.0
Children....................	716	680	687	1,022	1,120	1,117	56.0
Adults.......................	1,429	1,346	1,307	1,801	1,901	1,876	31.3
Other........................	857	NR	1,000	1,338	2,547	1,579	84.2
Total..........................	1,746	2,190	2,613	3,236	3,543	3,501	100.5

Note: Totals may not add due to rounding and include other coverage groups and individuals for whom basis of eligibility is unknown. Fiscal year 1975 ended in June; all other fiscal years end in September. Nominal dollars were converted to constant dollars by inflating each year's spending for the cumulative growth in the consumer price index for all urban consumers (CPI-U) (inflation) between that fiscal year and fiscal year 1998. The 1998 data reflect changes in HCFA-2082 reporting forms that affected coverage categories. For fiscal years 1975–1997, a recipient is an individual for whom a fee-for-service claim was paid during the year. For fiscal year 1998 only, a recipient is an individual for whom a fee-for-service claim was paid during the year, or for whom a capitation payment was paid during the year. The fiscal year 1998 dollar figures include payments for capitated delivery systems and fee-for-service delivery systems. Medicaid payments reported on the HCFA-2082 for fiscal year 1998 include payments made for Medicaid claims processed during the year.

Source: United States House of Representatives, Committee on Ways and Means. (2000). *The 2000 Green Book: Background material and data on programs within the jurisdiction of the Committee on Ways and Means.* Retrieved from http://aspe.hhs.gov/2000gb/sec15.txt.

Table 6.8
Medicare Enrollees: 1980 to 2000

[**In millions (28.5 represents 28,500,000). As of July 1.** Includes Puerto Rico and outlying areas and enrollees in foreign countries and unknown place of residence.]

Item	1980	1985	1990	1995	1997	1998	1999	2000
Total	**28.5**	**31.1**	**34.2**	**37.5**	**38.4**	**38.8**	**39.1**	**39.6**
Aged	25.5	28.2	30.9	33.1	33.6	33.8	33.9	34.2
Disabled	3.0	2.9	3.3	4.4	4.8	5.0	5.2	5.4
Hospital insurance	28.1	30.6	33.7	37.1	38.1	38.4	38.7	39.2
Aged	25.1	27.7	30.5	32.7	33.2	33.4	33.5	33.8
Disabled	3.0	2.9	3.3	4.4	4.8	5.0	5.2	5.4
Supplementary medical insurance	27.4	30.0	32.6	35.7	36.5	36.8	37.0	37.4
Aged	24.7	27.3	29.7	31.7	32.2	32.3	32.4	32.6
Disabled	2.7	2.7	2.9	3.9	4.3	4.5	4.6	4.8

Source: United States Census Bureau. (2002) *Statistical Abstract of the United States 2002.* Washington, D.C.: Government Printing Office. Retrieved from http://www.census.gov/prod/2003pubs/02statab/health.pdf.

Table 6.9
Medicare Disbursement by Type of Beneficiary: 1980 to 2000

[**In millions of dollars (35,025 represents $35,025,000,000). For years ending Sept. 30.** Distribution of benefits by type is estimated and subject to change.]

Type of beneficiary	1980	1990	1995	1996	1997	1998	1999	2000
Total disbursements	**35,025**	**109,709**	**180,096**	**194,263**	**210,342**	**213,412**	**211,959**	**219,275**
Hospital insurance disbursements [1]	24,288	66,687	114,883	125,317	137,789	137,140	131,441	130,284
Benefits	23,776	65,721	113,394	123,908	136,007	134,321	129,107	125,992
Aged	20,951	58,503	100,107	109,379	120,239	118,467	113,321	110,142
Disabled	2,825	7,218	13,288	14,529	15,768	15,854	15,786	15,850
Disabled	2,654	6,467	12,320	13,474	14,659	14,791	14,731	14,768
ESRD [2]	171	751	968	1,055	1,109	1,063	1,056	1,082
Peer review activity	14	191	189	180	168	188	177	236
Administrative expenses [3]	497	774	1,300	1,229	1,614	1,653	1,978	2,350
Supplementary medical insurance disbursements [1]	10,737	43,022	65,213	68,946	72,553	76,272	80,518	88,991
Benefits	10,144	41,498	63,490	67,165	71,117	75,782	79,151	88,876
Aged	8,497	36,837	54,830	57,807	60,989	65,118	67,996	76,507
Disabled	1,647	4,661	8,660	9,358	10,128	10,664	11,154	12,369
Disabled	1,256	3,758	7,363	7,943	8,604	9,156	9,668	10,750
ESRD [2]	391	903	1,297	1,415	1,524	1,508	1,486	1,619
Peer review activity	-	-	2	11	16	33	36	43
Administrative expenses	593	1,524	1,722	1,771	1,420	1,435	1,510	1,779

-. Represents zero.

1. Beginning 1998 home health agency transfers are excluded from total supplementary medical insurance disbursements and included in total hospital insurance disbursements.

2. Represents persons entitled because of End Stage Renal Disease only. Benefits for those who have ESRD but would be entitled due to their aged or disabled status are included in aged and disabled benefits.

3. Includes costs of experiments and demonstration projects. Includes costs of the health care fraud and abuse control program.

Source: United States Census Bureau. (2002). *Statistical Abstract of the United States 2002.* Washington, D.C.: Government Printing Office. Retrieved from http://www.census.gov/prod/2003pubs/02statab/health.pdf.

Table 6.10
Medicare Benefits by Type of Provider: 1980 to 2000

[In millions of dollars (23,776 represents $23,776,000,000). For years ending Sept. 30. Distribution of benefits by type is estimated and subject to change.]

Type of provider	1980	1990	1995	1996	1997	1998	1999	2000
Hospital insurance benefits, total. . .	**23,776**	**65,721**	**113,394**	**123,908**	**136,007**	**134,321**	**129,107**	**125,992**
Inpatient hospital.	22,860	57,012	81,095	84,513	88,541	86,942	85,696	86,566
Skilled nursing facility.	392	2,761	8,683	10,416	12,388	13,377	11,488	10,593
Home health agency	524	3,295	15,715	17,157	17,938	14,115	8,994	4,552
Hospice.	(NA)	318	1,854	1,969	2,082	2,080	2,494	2,818
Managed care	(NA)	2,335	6,047	9,853	15,059	17,807	20,435	21,463
Supplementary medical insurance benefits, total.	**10,144**	**41,498**	**63,490**	**67,165**	**71,117**	**75,782**	**79,151**	**88,876**
Physician fee schedule.	(NA)	(NA)	31,110	31,569	31,958	32,338	33,379	35,947
Durable medical equipment.	(NA)	(NA)	3,576	3,785	4,112	4,104	4,278	4,573
Carrier lab [1]	(NA)	(NA)	2,819	2,654	2,414	2,166	2,085	2,201
Other carrier [2]	(NA)	(NA)	4,513	4,883	5,452	5,854	6,400	7,164
Hospital [3].	(NA)	(NA)	8,448	8,683	9,251	8,977	8,473	8,439
Home health.	(NA)	(NA)	223	236	246	189	405	4,570
Intermediary lab [4]	(NA)	(NA)	1,437	1,338	1,419	1,478	1,517	1,622
Other intermediary [5]	(NA)	(NA)	5,110	5,664	6,372	6,543	5,642	6,013
Managed care	(NA)	(NA)	6,253	8,353	9,893	14,132	16,970	18,348

NA. Not available.

1. Lab services paid under the lab fee schedule performed in a physician's office lab or an independent lab.

2. Includes free-standing ambulatory surgical centers facility costs, ambulance, and supplies.

3. Includes the hospital facility costs for Medicare Part B services which are predominantly in the outpatient department. The physician reimbursement associated with these services is included on the "Physician Fee Schedule" line.

4. Lab fee services paid under the lab fee schedule performed in a hospital outpatient department.

5. Includes ESRD free-standing dialysis facility payments and payments to rural health clinics, outpatient rehabilitation facilities, psychiatric hospitals, and federally qualified health centers.

Source: United States Census Bureau. (2002). *Statistical Abstract of the United States 2002.* Washington, D.C.: Government Printing Office. Retrieved from http://www.census.gov/prod/2003pubs/02statab/health.pdf.

Table 6.11
Medicare—Summary by State and Other Areas: 1995 and 2000

[For fiscal year ending in year shown (37,535 represents 37,535,000).]

State and area	Enrollment [1] (1,000)		Payments [2] (mil. dol.)		State and area	Enrollment [1] (1,000)		Payments [2] (mil. dol.)	
	1995	2000	1995	2000		1995	2000	1995	2000
All areas .	37,535	39,140	176,884	214,868	MO	833	854	3,821	4,274
U.S.	36,758	38,286	175,976	213,555	MT........	130	135	489	575
					NE........	249	252	840	1,225
AL........	642	677	3,042	3,885	NV........	194	229	894	1,069
AK........	34	40	133	189	NH........	156	167	597	629
AZ........	602	658	2,717	2,938	NJ........	1,168	1,195	5,603	6,767
AR........	423	436	1,638	2,083	NM........	211	229	710	854
CA........	3,633	3,837	20,406	23,621	NY........	2,630	2,694	13,904	18,653
CO........	421	458	1,835	2,338	NC........	1,027	1,111	4,276	5,942
CT........	502	512	2,584	3,291	ND........	103	103	412	501
DE........	101	110	445	430	OH........	1,666	1,692	7,262	9,310
DC........	78	76	1,164	784	OK........	488	504	2,178	2,137
FL........	2,628	2,771	14,828	19,221	OR........	469	484	1,685	1,853
GA........	833	898	4,090	4,111	PA........	2,071	2,088	10,796	13,257
HI........	149	162	580	622	RI	168	170	772	1,075
ID........	150	161	463	639	SC........	509	555	1,926	2,947
IL........	1,617	1,629	7,276	7,309	SD........	117	119	563	564
IN	823	845	3,491	4,720	TN........	771	815	4,083	4,907
IA	474	476	1,527	1,453	TX........	2,080	2,223	11,504	14,538
KS........	383	389	1,545	1,915	UT........	187	201	708	918
KY........	586	615	2,401	3,153	VT........	83	88	284	315
LA........	581	597	3,448	4,383	VA........	818	876	2,979	4,038
ME........	201	213	707	793	WA	688	725	2,603	2,843
MD........	602	635	2,868	3,998	WV	330	336	1,208	1,656
MA........	933	954	5,496	5,466	WI	762	777	2,673	3,498
MI........	1,347	1,389	6,237	6,269	WY	60	64	180	247
MN........	631	648	2,378	3,109	PR	477	525	875	1,224
MS........	397	414	1,723	2,248	Other areas .	300	330	33	89

1. Hospital and/or medical insurance enrollment for 1995 as of July and for 2000 as of September.
2. Distribution of benefit payments by state is based on a methodology which considered actual payments to health maintenance organizations and estimated payments for other providers of medicare services.

Source: United States Census Bureau. (2002). *Statistical Abstract of the United States 2002.* Washington, D.C.: Government Printing Office. Retrieved from http://www.census.gov/prod/2003pubs/02statab/health.pdf.

Table 6.12
Medicaid—Selected Utilization Measures: 1980 to 1998

[In thousands (2,255 represents 2,255,000). For year ending September 30. Includes Virgin Islands.]

Measure	1980	1985	1990	1994	1995	1996	1997	1998
General hospitals:								
Recipients discharged	2,255	2,390	3,261	3,890	3,743	3,300	3,135	2,793
Total days of care	24,089	29,562	27,471	28,941	25,711	23,072	21,532	19,091
Nursing facilities: [1]								
Total recipients	1,395	1,375	1,461	1,639	1,667	1,594	1,497	1,555
Total days of care	273,497	277,996	360,044	400,785	400,123	409,663	388,985	384,549
Intermediate care facilities: [2]								
Total recipients	121	147	146	159	151	140	146	124
Total days of care	250,124	47,324	49,730	54,105	56,878	56,625	62,423	50,636

1. Includes skilled nursing facilities and intermediate care facilities for all other than the mentally retarded.
2. Mentally retarded.

Source: United States Census Bureau. (2002). *Statistical Abstract of the United States 2002.* Washington, D.C.: Government Printing Office. Retrieved from http://www.census.gov/prod/2003pubs/02statab/health.pdf.

Table 6.13
Medicaid—Recipients and Payments: 1990 to 1998

[For year ending September 30 (25,255 represents 25,255,000). Includes Puerto Rico and outlying areas. Medical vendor payments are those made directly to suppliers of medical care.]

Basis of eligibility and type of service	Recipients (1,000)					Payments (mil. dol.)				
	1990	1995	1996	1997	1998	1990	1995	1996	1997	1998
Total [1].............	25,255	36,282	36,118	34,872	40,649	64,859	120,141	121,685	124,430	142,318
Age 65 and over	3,202	4,119	4,285	3,955	3,964	21,508	36,527	36,947	37,721	40,602
Blindness..............	83	92	95	(NA)	(NA)	434	848	869	(NA)	(NA)
Disabled [2]..............	3,635	5,767	6,126	6,129	6,638	23,969	48,570	51,196	54,130	60,375
AFDC [3] program	17,230	24,767	23,866	22,594	26,872	17,690	31,487	29,819	29,851	37,639
Other and unknown	1,105	1,537	1,746	2,195	3,176	1,257	2,708	2,853	2,727	3,702
Inpatient services inó General hospital........	4,593	5,561	5,362	4,746	4,273	16,674	26,331	25,176	23,143	21,499
Mental hospital........	92	84	93	87	135	1,714	2,511	2,040	2,009	2,801
Intermediate care facilities, mentally retarded	147	151	140	136	126	7,354	10,383	9,555	9,798	9,482
Nursing facility services [4]....	1,461	1,667	1,594	1,603	1,646	17,693	29,052	29,630	30,504	31,892
Physicians	17,078	23,789	22,861	21,170	18,555	4,018	7,360	7,238	7,041	6,070
Dental	4,552	6,383	6,208	5,935	4,965	593	1,019	1,028	1,036	901
Other practitioner	3,873	5,528	5,343	5,142	4,342	372	986	1,094	979	587
Outpatient hospital	12,370	16,712	15,905	13,632	12,158	3,324	6,627	6,504	6,169	5,759
Clinic...............	2,804	5,322	5,070	4,713	5,285	1,688	4,280	4,222	4,252	3,921
Laboratory [5]	8,959	13,064	12,607	11,074	9,381	721	1,180	1,208	1,033	939
Home health [6]	719	1,639	1,727	1,861	1,225	3,404	9,406	10,868	12,237	2,702
Prescribed drugs	17,294	23,723	22,585	20,954	19,338	4,420	9,791	10,697	11,972	13,522
Family planning	1,752	2,501	2,366	2,091	2,011	265	514	474	418	449
Prepaid health care	(NA)	(NA)	(NA)	(NA)	20,203	(NA)	(NA)	(NA)	(NA)	19,296

NA. Not available.

1. Recipient data do not add due to small number of recipients that are reported in more than one category. Includes recipients of, and payments for, other care not shown separately.

2. Permanently and totally. Beginning 1997, includes blind.

3. Aid to families with dependent children includes children, adults, and foster care.

4. Nursing facility services includes skilled nursing facility services and intermediate care facility services for all other than the mentally retarded.

5. Includes radiological services.

6. Data for 1998 not comparable with earlier years.

Source: United States Census Bureau. (2002). *Statistical Abstract of the United States 2002.* Washington, D.C.: Government Printing Office. Retrieved from http://www.census.gov/prod/2003pubs/02statab/health.pdf.

Table 6.14
Medicaid—Summary by State and Other Areas: 1995 and 1999

[**For year ending September 30 (36,282 represents 36,282,000).** Data for 1999 includes managed care recipients and capitation payments.]

State and area	Recipients [1] (1,000)		Payments [2] (mil. dol.)		State and area	Recipients [1] (1,000)		Payments [2] (mil. dol.)	
	1995	1999	1995	1999		1995	1999	1995	1999
All areas .	**36,282**	**(NA)**	**120,141**	**(NA)**	MO	695	877	2,039	2,798
U.S.	**35,210**	**40,844**	**119,885**	**152,629**	MT	99	96	326	365
					NE	168	223	608	876
AL	539	650	1,455	1,695	NV	105	153	350	459
AK	68	99	252	398	NH	97	105	473	527
AZ	494	644	218	1,878	NJ	790	841	3,813	4,386
AR	353	483	1,376	1,365	NM	287	370	714	1,123
CA	5,017	6,217	10,521	15,440	NY	3,035	3,327	22,086	25,357
CO	294	352	1,063	1,641	NC	1,084	1,182	3,175	4,266
CT	380	410	2,125	2,671	ND	61	62	297	346
DE	79	113	324	462	OH	1,533	1,390	5,585	6,329
DC	138	145	532	759	OK	394	525	1,055	1,434
FL	1,735	2,116	4,802	6,440	OR	452	534	1,327	1,596
GA	1,147	1,237	3,076	3,232	PA	1,230	1,773	4,633	6,133
HI	52	(NA)	258	(NA)	RI	135	155	673	881
ID	115	94	360	520	SC	496	725	1,438	2,459
IL	1,552	1,696	5,600	6,339	SD	74	92	305	369
IN	559	668	1,878	2,750	TN	1,466	1,533	2,772	3,285
IA	304	313	1,036	1,364	TX	2,562	2,676	6,565	8,126
KS	256	260	831	1,096	UT	160	198	464	797
KY	641	677	1,945	2,598	VT	100	139	320	421
LA	785	775	2,708	2,534	VA	681	691	1,833	2,207
ME	153	201	760	1,206	WA	639	895	1,461	2,575
MD	414	628	2,019	3,044	WV	389	377	1,169	1,344
MA	728	1,043	3,972	4,953	WI	460	563	1,894	2,246
MI	1,168	1,335	3,409	4,707	WY	51	52	171	199
MN	473	587	2,550	3,038	PR	1,055	(NA)	244	(NA)
MS	520	545	1,266	1,600	VI	17	(NA)	12	(NA)

NA. Not available.

1. Persons who had payments made on their behalf at any time during the fiscal year.

2. Payments are for fiscal year and reflect federal and state contribution payments. Data exclude disproportionate hospital share payments. Disproportionate share hospitals receive higher medicaid reimbursement than other hospitals because they treat a disproportionate share of medicaid patients.

Source: United States Census Bureau. (2002). *Statistical Abstract of the United States 2002.* Washington, D.C.: Government Printing Office. Retrieved from http://www.census.gov/prod/2003pubs/02statab/health.pdf.

Table 6.15
Medicaid Managed Care Enrollment by State and Other Areas: 1995 to 2000

[For year ending June 30 (33,373 represents 33,373,000).]

State and area	Total medi-caid (1,000)	Managed care enrollment		State and area	Total medi-caid (1,000)	Managed care enrollment		State and area	Total medi-caid (1,000)	Managed care enrollment	
		Number (1,000)	Percent of total			Number (1,000)	Percent of total			Number (1,000)	Percent of total
1995	33,373	9,800	29.4	IL.	1,392	138	9.9	NC.	876	599	68.3
1999	31,940	17,757	55.6	IN	563	376	66.8	ND.	43	24	55.1
				IA	202	182	90.3	OH.	1,121	239	21.4
2000,				KS.	192	108	56.3	OK.	404	279	69.1
total . .	**33,690**	**18,786**	**55.8**	KY.	575	464	80.7	OR.	376	312	83.1
				LA	772	49	6.3	PA	1,343	975	72.6
U.S.. . . .	**32,720**	**17,958**	**54.9**	ME.	162	57	35.4	RI	151	104	68.7
AL	543	325	59.9	MD.	479	386	80.5	SC	538	32	6.0
AK.	81	-	-	MA.	911	583	64.0	SD.	73	68	92.7
AZ.	479	442	92.4	MI	1,064	1,064	100.0	TN	1,323	1,323	100.0
AR.	389	222	57.1	MN.	466	291	62.5	TX	1,789	606	33.9
CA.	5,037	2,525	50.1	MS.	559	218	39.1	UT	133	119	89.5
CO.	282	254	90.2	MO	754	304	40.4	VT	119	56	46.7
CT.	321	230	71.7	MT.	69	42	61.1	VA	479	281	58.6
DE.	95	76	79.4	NE.	183	140	76.7	WA	800	800	100.0
DC.	119	79	66.2	NV.	96	38	39.5	WV	262	91	34.6
FL	1,701	1,017	59.8	NH.	79	4	5.6	WI	479	210	43.9
GA.	842	806	95.7	NJ	628	372	59.2	WY	37	-	-
HI	164	122	73.9	NM.	312	199	63.8	PR	951	828	87.1
ID	108	32	29.9	NY.	2,751	691	25.1	VI.	19	-	-

-. Represents zero.

Source: United States Census Bureau. (2002). *Statistical Abstract of the United States 2002.* Washington, D.C.: Government Printing Office. Retrieved from http://www.census.gov/prod/2003pubs/02statab/health.pdf.

Table 6.16
Unduplicated Number of Medicaid Recipients, Total Vendor Payments, and Average Amounts, by Type of Medical Service, Fiscal Years 1972 to 1998[1,2]

Fiscal year	Total	Inpatient services inó: General hospital	Mental hospital	Intermediate-care facility (ICF) services foró: Mentally retarded	All other	Nursing facility[3]	Physicians	Dental	Other practitioner	Outpatient hosptal	Clinic	Laboratory and radiological	Home health	Prescribed drugs	Family planning	Other
Number (in thousands)																
1972	17,606	2,832	40	...	...	552	12,282	2,397	1,600	5,215	501	3,523	105	11,139	...	2,531
1975	22,007	3,432	67	69	682	630	15,198	3,944	2,673	7,437	1,086	4,738	343	14,155	1,217	2,911
1980	21,605	3,680	66	121	789	606	13,765	4,652	3,234	9,705	1,531	3,212	392	13,707	1,129	2,563
1985	21,814	3,434	60	147	828	547	14,387	4,672	3,357	10,072	2,121	6,354	535	13,921	1,636	5,371
1986	22,515	3,544	53	145	828	571	14,894	5,161	3,451	10,702	2,027	7,123	593	14,704	1,732	5,573
1987	23,109	3,767	57	149	849	572	15,373	5,131	3,542	10,979	2,183	7,596	609	15,083	1,652	5,957
1988	22,907	3,832	60	145	866	579	15,265	5,072	3,480	10,533	2,256	7,579	569	15,323	1,525	6,601
1989	23,511	4,170	90	148	888	564	15,686	4,214	3,555	11,344	2,391	7,759	609	15,916	1,564	7,278
1990	25,255	4,593	92	147	860	601	17,078	4,552	3,873	12,370	2,804	8,959	719	17,294	1,752	8,302
1991	28,280	5,072	65	146	(3)	1,500	19,321	5,209	4,282	14,137	3,511	10,505	813	19,602	2,185	10,319
1992	30,926	5,768	77	151	(3)	1,573	21,627	5,700	4,711	15,120	4,115	11,804	925	22,030	2,550	12,427
1993	33,432	5,894	75	149	(3)	1,610	23,746	6,174	5,229	16,436	4,839	12,970	1,067	23,901	2,538	15,035
1994	35,053	5,866	85	159	...	1,639	24,267	6,352	5,409	16,567	5,258	13,412	1,293	24,471	2,566	17,321
1995	36,282	5,561	84	151	...	1,667	23,789	6,383	5,528	16,712	5,322	13,064	1,639	23,723	2,501	19,277
1996	36,118	5,362	93	140	...	1,594	22,861	6,208	5,343	15,905	5,070	12,607	1,727	22,585	2,366	21,104
1997	34,873	4,746	87	136	...	1,603	21,170	5,935	5,142	13,632	4,713	11,074	1,861	20,954	2,091	20,284
1998	40,649	4,273	135	126	...	1,646	18,555	4,965	4,342	12,158	5,285	9,381	1,225	19,338	2,011	34,820
Amount (in millions)																
1972	$6,300	$2,557	$113	...	...	$1,471	$794	$170	$59	$365	$41	$81	$24	$512	...	$112
1975	12,242	3,374	405	$380	$1,885	2,434	1,225	339	127	373	389	126	70	815	$67	233
1980	23,311	6,412	775	1,989	4,202	3,685	1,875	462	198	1,101	320	121	332	1,318	81	440
1985	37,508	9,453	1,192	4,731	6,516	5,071	2,346	458	251	1,789	714	337	1,120	2,315	195	1,020
1986	41,005	10,364	1,113	5,072	6,773	5,660	2,547	531	252	1,980	807	424	1,352	2,692	226	1,212
1987	45,050	11,302	1,409	5,591	7,280	5,967	2,776	541	263	2,226	963	475	1,690	2,988	228	1,349
1988	48,710	12,076	1,375	6,022	7,923	6,354	2,953	577	284	2,413	1,105	543	2,015	3,294	206	1,569
1989	54,500	13,378	1,470	6,649	8,871	6,660	3,408	498	317	2,837	1,249	590	2,572	3,689	227	2,085
1990	64,859	16,674	1,714	7,354	9,667	8,026	4,018	593	372	3,324	1,688	721	3,404	4,420	265	2,618
1991	77,048	19,891	2,010	7,680	...	20,709	4,952	710	437	4,283	2,211	897	4,101	5,424	359	3,384
1992	90,814	23,503	2,196	8,550	...	23,544	6,102	851	538	5,279	2,818	1,035	4,886	6,765	500	4,243
1993	101,709	25,734	2,161	8,831	...	25,431	6,952	961	937	6,215	3,457	1,137	5,601	7,970	538	5,784
1994	108,270	26,180	2,057	8,347	...	27,095	7,189	969	1,040	6,342	3,747	1,176	7,042	8,875	516	7,695
1995	120,141	26,331	2,511	10,383	...	29,052	7,360	1,019	986	6,627	4,280	1,180	9,406	9,791	514	10,700
1996	121,685	25,176	2,040	9,555	...	29,630	7,238	1,028	1,094	6,504	4,222	1,208	10,868	10,697	474	11,948
1997	124,429	23,143	2,009	9,798	...	30,504	7,041	1,036	979	6,169	4,252	1,033	12,237	11,972	418	12,958
1998	142,318	21,499	2,801	9,482	...	31,892	6,070	901	587	5,759	3,921	939	2,702	13,522	449	38,747
Average amount																
1972	$358	$903	$2,825	...	...	$2,665	$65	$71	$37	$70	$82	$23	$229	$46	...	$44
1975	556	983	6,017	$5,538	$2,764	3,865	81	86	48	50	358	27	204	58	$55	80
1980	1,079	1,742	11,697	16,439	5,322	6,079	136	99	61	113	113	38	846	96	72	172
1985	1,719	2,753	20,021	32,238	7,868	9,278	163	98	75	178	337	53	2,092	166	119	190
1986	1,821	2,924	20,952	35,089	8,182	9,910	171	103	73	185	398	60	2,278	183	130	217
1987	1,949	3,000	24,714	37,490	8,571	10,432	181	105	74	203	441	63	2,777	198	138	227
1988	2,126	3,151	22,956	41,413	9,153	10,971	193	114	82	229	490	72	3,542	215	135	238
1989	2,318	3,208	16,397	44,999	9,994	11,809	217	118	89	250	523	76	4,225	232	145	286
1990	2,568	3,630	18,548	50,048	11,236	13,356	235	130	96	269	602	80	4,733	256	151	315
1991	2,725	3,922	30,948	52,750	...	13,811	256	136	102	303	630	85	5,048	277	164	328
1992	2,936	4,075	28,364	56,502	...	14,965	282	149	114	349	685	88	5,283	307	196	342
1993	3,042	4,366	28,948	59,156	...	15,798	293	156	179	378	714	88	5,250	333	212	385
1994	3,089	4,463	24,120	52,571	...	16,533	296	153	192	383	713	88	5,445	363	201	444
1995	3,311	4,735	29,847	68,613	...	17,424	309	160	178	397	804	90	5,740	413	206	555
1996	3,369	4,696	21,873	68,232	...	18,589	317	166	205	409	833	96	6,293	474	200	566
1997	3,568	4,877	22,990	72,033	...	19,029	333	275	190	453	902	93	6,575	571	200	639
1998	3,501	5,031	20,701	74,960	...	19,379	327	182	135	474	742	100	2,206	699	223	1,113

1. Fiscal year 1977 began in October 1976 and was the first year of the new federal fiscal cycle. Before 1977, the fiscal year began in July.

2. Beginning in fiscal year 1980, recipients' categories do not add to unduplicated total because of the small number of recipients that are in more than one category during the year.

3. Beginning in fiscal year 1991, "Nursing facility services" category combines "ICF, All other" and "Skilled nursing facility services," which were previously separate. Data under "Nursing facility services" prior to 1991, reflect "Skilled nursing facility services."

Source: Social Security Administration. (2001). *Annual Statistical Supplement, 2001 to the Social Security Bulletin.* Baltimore: Social Security Administration, Office of Policy. Retrieved from http://www.ssa.gov/policy/docs/statcomps/supplement/2001/supp01.pdf.

Table 6.17
Unduplicated Number of Medicaid Recipients, Total Vendor Payments, and Average Amounts, by Type of Eligibility Category, Fiscal Years 1972 to 1998[1,2]

Fiscal year	Total	Aged 65 or older	Blind	Permanent and total disability	Dependent children under age 21	Adults in families with dependent children	Other
			Number (in thousands)				
1972	17,606	3,318	108	1,625	7,841	3,137	1,576
1975	22,007	3,615	109	2,355	9,598	4,529	1,800
1980	21,605	3,440	92	2,819	9,333	4,877	1,499
1985	21,814	3,061	80	2,937	9,757	5,518	1,214
1986	22,515	3,140	82	3,100	10,029	5,647	1,362
1987	23,109	3,224	85	3,296	10,168	5,599	1,418
1988	22,907	3,159	86	3,401	10,037	5,503	1,343
1989	23,511	3,132	95	3,496	10,318	5,717	1,175
1990	25,255	3,202	83	3,635	11,220	6,010	1,105
1991	28,280	3,359	85	3,983	13,415	6,778	658
1992	30,926	3,742	84	4,378	15,104	6,954	664
1993	33,432	3,863	84	4,932	16,285	7,505	763
1994	35,053	4,035	87	5,372	17,194	7,586	779
1995	36,282	4,119	92	5,767	17,164	7,604	1,537
1996	36,118	4,285	95	6,126	16,739	7,127	1,746
1997	34,872	3,955	...	6,129	15,791	6,803	2,195
1998	40,649	3,964	...	6,638	18,964	7,908	3,176
			Amount (in millions)				
1972	$6,300	$1,925	$45	$1,354	$1,139	$962	$875
1975	12,242	4,358	93	3,052	2,186	2,062	492
1980	23,311	8,739	124	7,497	3,123	3,231	596
1985	37,508	14,096	249	13,203	4,414	4,746	798
1986	41,005	15,097	277	14,635	5,135	4,880	980
1987	45,050	16,037	309	16,507	5,508	5,592	1,078
1988	48,710	17,135	344	18,250	5,848	5,883	1,198
1989	54,500	18,558	409	20,476	6,892	6,897	1,268
1990	64,859	21,508	434	23,969	9,100	8,590	1,257
1991	77,048	25,453	475	27,798	11,690	10,439	1,193
1992	90,814	29,078	530	33,326	14,491	12,185	1,204
1993	101,709	31,554	589	38,065	16,504	13,605	1,391
1994	108,270	33,618	644	41,654	17,302	13,585	1,467
1995	120,141	36,527	848	48,570	17,976	13,511	2,708
1996	121,685	36,947	869	51,196	17,544	12,275	2,853
1997	124,430	37,721	...	54,130	17,544	12,307	2,727
1998	142,318	40,602	...	60,375	22,806	14,833	3,702
			Average amount				
1972	$358	$580	$417	$833	$145	$307	$555
1975	556	1,205	850	1,296	228	455	273
1980	1,079	2,540	1,358	2,659	335	663	398
1985	1,719	4,605	3,104	4,496	452	860	658
1986	1,821	4,808	3,401	4,721	512	864	719
1987	1,949	4,975	3,644	5,008	542	999	761
1988	2,126	5,425	4,005	5,366	583	1,069	891
1989	2,318	5,926	4,317	5,858	668	1,206	1,079
1990	2,568	6,717	5,212	6,595	811	1,429	1,138
1991	2,725	7,577	5,572	6,979	871	1,540	1,813
1992	2,936	7,770	6,298	7,612	959	1,752	1,813
1993	3,042	8,168	7,036	7,717	1,013	1,813	1,824
1994	3,089	8,331	7,412	7,755	1,006	1,791	1,884
1995	3,311	8,868	9,256	8,422	1,047	1,777	1,762
1996	3,369	8,622	9,143	8,357	1,048	1,722	1,635
1997	3,568	9,538	...	8,832	1,111	1,809	3,597
1998	3,501	10,242	...	9,095	1,203	1,876	1,166

1. Fiscal year 1977 began in October 1976 and was the first year of the new federal fiscal cycle. Before 1977, the fiscal year began in July.

2. Beginning in fiscal year 1980, recipients' categories do not add to unduplicated total because of the small number of recipients that are in more than one category during the year.

Source: Social Security Administration. (2001). *Annual Statistical Supplement, 2001 to the Social Security Bulletin.* Baltimore: Social Security Administration, Office of Policy. Retrieved from http://www.ssa.gov/policy/docs/statcomps/supplement/2001/supp01.pdf.

Table 6.18
Commitment to Health: Access, Services, and Resources

HDI rank	Population with access to improved sanitation (%) 2000	Population with sustainable access to an improved water source (%) 2000	Population with sustainable access to affordable essential drugs (%)[a] 1999	One-year-olds fully immunized Against tuberculosis (%) 2001	Against measles (%) 2001	Oral rehydration therapy use rate (%) 1994-2000[b]	Contra-ceptive prevalence rate (%)[c] 1995-2001[b]	Births attended by skilled health personnel (%) 1995-2001[b]	Physicians (per 100,000 people) 1990-2002[b]	Health expenditure Public (as % of GDP) 2000	Private (as % of GDP) 2000	Per capita (PPP US$) 2000
High human development												
1 Norway	..	100	95-100	92	93	..	..	..	413	6.5	1.1	2,769
2 Iceland	..	..	95-100	..	88	..	..	..	326	7.6	1.4	2,642
3 Sweden	100	100	95-100	..	94	..	..	..	311	6.2	1.8	2,108
4 Australia	100	100	95-100	..	93	..	..	100	260	6.0	2.3	2,213
5 Netherlands	100	100	95-100	..	96	..	..	100	251	5.5	2.6	2,216
6 Belgium	..	..	95-100	..	83	..	..	..	395	6.2	2.5	2,306
7 United States	100	100	95-100	..	91	..	76	99	276	5.8	7.3	4,499
8 Canada	100	100	95-100	..	96	..	75	98	186	6.5	2.5	2,534
9 Japan	..	..	95-100	..	96	..	..	100	197	5.9	1.8	2,009
10 Switzerland	100	100	95-100	..	81	..	82	..	336	6.0	4.7	3,161
11 Denmark	..	100	95-100	..	94	..	..	..	339	6.8	1.5	2,434
12 Ireland	..	..	95-100	90 [d]	73	..	..	..	226	5.1	1.6	1,908
13 United Kingdom	100	100	95-100	..	85	..	..	99	164	5.9	1.4	1,804
14 Finland	100	100	95-100	99	96	..	..	..	306	5.0	1.7	1,698
15 Luxembourg	..	..	95-100	..	91	..	..	..	253	5.3	0.5	2,785
16 Austria	100	100	95-100	..	79	..	51	..	302	5.6	2.4	2,245
17 France	..	..	95-100	84	84	..	..	..	303	7.2	2.3	2,380
18 Germany	..	..	95-100	..	89	..	..	..	354	8.0	2.6	2,768
19 Spain	..	..	95-100	..	94	..	81	..	436	5.4	2.3	1,547
20 New Zealand	..	..	95-100	..	85	..	75	100	226	6.2	1.8	1,646
21 Italy	..	..	95-100	..	70	..	60	..	567	5.9	2.1	2,028
22 Israel	..	..	95-100	..	94	..	..	..	378	8.1	2.6	2,338
23 Portugal	..	..	95-100	82	87	..	..	100	312	5.8	2.4	1,397
24 Greece	..	..	95-100	88	88	..	..	..	392	4.6	3.7	1,349
25 Cyprus	100	100	95-100	..	86 [d]	..	..	..	269	3.9	4.1	904
26 Hong Kong, China (SAR)	..	..	..	..	..	..	..	..	..	..	..	..
27 Barbados	100	100	95-100	..	92	..	..	91	121	4.2	2.2	909
28 Singapore	100	100	95-100	97	89	..	..	100	135	1.3	2.3	913
29 Slovenia	..	100	95-100	96	98	..	..	..	215	6.8	1.8	1,463
30 Korea, Rep. of	63	92	95-100	89	97	..	81	100	173	2.6	3.3	899
31 Brunei Darussalam	..	..	95-100	99	99	..	..	99	85	2.5	0.6	618
32 Czech Republic	..	..	80-94	98 [d]	..	..	72	..	308	6.5	0.6	1,031
33 Malta	100	100	95-100	..	65	..	..	..	263	6.1	2.8	803
34 Argentina	..	..	50-79	99	94	..	..	98	294	4.7	3.9	1,091
35 Poland	..	..	80-94	95	97	..	..	..	233	4.2	1.8	575
36 Seychelles	..	..	80-94	99	95	..	..	..	132	3.9	2.0	749
37 Bahrain	..	..	95-100	..	98	..	62	98	169	2.8	1.3	641
38 Hungary	99	99	95-100	99	99	..	..	..	361	5.1	1.6	838
39 Slovakia	100	100	95-100	93	99	..	..	..	322	5.2	0.6	653
40 Uruguay	94	98	50-79	99	94	..	..	99	375	5.1	5.8	1,007
41 Estonia	..	..	95-100	99	95	..	..	..	307	4.5	1.4	540
42 Costa Rica	93	95	95-100	92	82	..	..	98	178	4.7	2.1	474
43 Chile	96	93	80-94	97	97	..	..	100	115	3.1	4.2	697
44 Qatar	..	..	95-100	99	92	..	43	..	220	2.5	0.7	849
45 Lithuania	..	..	80-94	99	97	..	47	..	394	4.4	1.8	430
46 Kuwait	..	..	95-100	.. [d]	99	..	50	98	160	2.7	0.4	538
47 Croatia	..	..	95-100	97	94	..	..	..	229	7.5	1.6	665
48 United Arab Emirates	..	..	95-100	98	94	..	28	99	177	2.5	0.7	762
49 Bahamas	100	97	80-94	..	93	..	..	99 [e]	106	4.4	3.4	1,111
50 Latvia	..	..	80-94	99	98	..	48	100	313	3.5	2.3	406

Table 6.18 (*continued*)

HDI rank		Population with access to improved sanitation (%) 2000	Population with sustainable access to an improved water source (%) 2000	Population with sustainable access to affordable essential drugs (%)ᵃ 1999	One-year-olds fully immunized Against tuberculosis (%) 2001	One-year-olds fully immunized Against measles (%) 2001	Oral rehydration therapy use rate (%) 1994-2000ᵇ	Contra-ceptive prevalence rate (%)ᶜ 1995-2001ᵇ	Births attended by skilled health personnel (%) 1995-2001ᵇ	Physicians (per 100,000 people) 1990-2002ᵇ	Health expenditure Public (as % of GDP) 2000	Private (as % of GDP) 2000	Per capita (PPP US$) 2000
51	Saint Kitts and Nevis	96	98	50-79	97	94	..	..	100	117	3.1	2.1	658
52	Cuba	98	91	95-100	99	99	..	..	100	590	6.1	1.0	193
53	Belarus	..	100	50-79	99	99	..	50	..	457	4.9	0.1	389
54	Trinidad and Tobago	99	90	50-79	..	91	17 ᵉ	..	99	79	2.3	2.2	468
55	Mexico	74	88	80-94	99	97	..	67	86	130	2.5	2.8	477
Medium human development													
56	Antigua and Barbuda	95	91	50-79	..	97	..	..	100 ᵉ	17	3.3	2.2	629
57	Bulgaria	100	100	80-94	98	90	..	42	..	344	2.9	0.8	225
58	Malaysia	..	..	50-79	99	92	..	..	96	68	1.8	1.6	310
59	Panama	92	90	80-94	99	97	7	..	90	117	4.8	2.1	464
60	Macedonia, TFYR	..	..	50-79	97	92	..	..	..	300	5.1	0.9	301
61	Libyan Arab Jamahiriya	97	72	95-100	99	93	..	40	94	120	1.5	1.4	370
62	Mauritius	99	100	95-100	89	90	..	..	..	85	2.1	1.2	315
63	Russian Federation	..	99	50-79	97	98	..	73 ᶠ	..	423	3.7	1.4	405
64	Colombia	86	91	80-94	86	75	..	77	86	109	5.3	4.0	612
65	Brazil	76	87	0-49	99	99	18	77	88	158	3.4	4.9	631
66	Bosnia and Herzegovina	..	..	80-94	95	92	11	48	100	140	3.1	4.7	259
67	Belize	50	92	80-94	95	96	..	..	77 ᵉ	55	2.1	2.5	273
68	Dominica	83	97	80-94	99	99	..	..	100	49	4.3	1.8	340
69	Venezuela	68	83	80-94	94	49	..	..	95	203	2.7	2.0	280
70	Samoa (Western)	99	99	95-100	98	92	..	..	100	70	5.0	1.7	227
71	Saint Lucia	89	98	50-79	99	89	..	..	100	518	2.6	1.6	272
72	Romania	53	58	80-94	99	98	..	64	98	191	1.9	1.1	190
73	Saudi Arabia	100	95	95-100	94	94	..	32	91	153	3.5	1.0	641
74	Thailand	96	84	95-100	99	94	..	72	85	24	2.1	1.6	237
75	Ukraine	99	98	50-79	98	99	..	68	99	299	2.9	1.2	152
76	Kazakhstan	99	91	50-79	96	96	20	66	99	339	2.8	1.0	211
77	Suriname	93	82	95-100	..	90	24	..	85	45	5.5	4.3	424
78	Jamaica	99	92	95-100	96	85	..	66	95	140	2.6	2.9	208
79	Oman	92	39	80-94	98	99	88	24	91	137	2.0	0.5	388
80	St. Vincent & the Grenadines	96	93	80-94	99	98	..	..	100 ᵉ	88	4.1	2.2	374
81	Fiji	43	47	95-100	99	90	..	..	100	36	2.6	1.4	194
82	Peru	71	80	50-79	88	97	29	69	59	117	2.8	2.0	238
83	Lebanon	99	100	80-94	..	94	30	61	88	274	3.7	8.5	719
84	Paraguay	94	78	0-49	51	77	..	57	58	117	3.0	4.9	323
85	Philippines	83	86	50-79	45	75	28	47	56	124	1.5	1.8	167
86	Maldives	56	100	50-79	99	99	..	..	70	40	6.3	1.3	254
87	Turkmenistan	..	..	50-79	99	98	31	62	97	300	4.6	0.8	267
88	Georgia	100	79	0-49	97	73	33	41	96	487	0.7	6.3	197
89	Azerbaijan	81	78	50-79	98	99	27	55	88	357	0.9	1.2	57
90	Jordan	99	96	95-100	..	99	..	53	97	205	4.3	3.8	341
91	Tunisia	84	80	50-79	97	92	..	..	90	70	5.5	1.5	472
92	Guyana	87	94	0-49	95	92	7	..	95	48	4.2	0.9	198
93	Grenada	97	95	95-100	..	96	..	..	100 ᵉ	50	3.4	1.4	351
94	Dominican Republic	67	86	50-79	96	98	22	64	96	216	1.8	4.6	357
95	Albania	91	97	50-79	93	95	48	58	99	133	2.1	1.3	129
96	Turkey	90	82	95-100	89	90	15	64	81	127	3.6	1.4	315
97	Ecuador	86	85	0-49	99	99	..	66	69	138	1.2	1.2	78
98	Occupied Palestinian Territories	100	86	..	..	..	43	..	..	..	..	..	..
99	Sri Lanka	94	77	95-100	99	99	..	..	97	41	1.8	1.9	120
100	Armenia	..	..	0-49	97	93	30	61	97	305	3.2	4.4	192

Table 6.18 (*continued*)

HDI rank		Population with access to improved sanitation (%) 2000	Population with sustainable access to an improved water source (%) 2000	Population with sustainable access to affordable essential drugs (%)[a] 1999	One-year-olds fully immunized Against tuberculosis (%) 2001	One-year-olds fully immunized Against measles (%) 2001	Oral rehydration therapy use rate (%) 1994-2000[b]	Contra-ceptive prevalence rate (%)[c] 1995-2001[b]	Births attended by skilled health personnel (%) 1995-2001[b]	Physicians (per 100,000 people) 1990-2002[b]	Health expenditure Public (as % of GDP) 2000	Health expenditure Private (as % of GDP) 2000	Health expenditure Per capita (PPP US$) 2000
101	Uzbekistan	89	85	50-79	98	99	19	67	96	300	2.8	0.8	86
102	Kyrgyzstan	100	77	50-79	99	99	13	60	98	288	3.5	2.2	145
103	Cape Verde	71	74	80-94	84	72	..	53	53	17	1.9	0.7	106
104	China	40	75	80-94	77	79	29	84	89	167	2.0	3.4	205
105	El Salvador	82	77	80-94	99	97	..	60	51	121	3.8	5.0	391
106	Iran, Islamic Rep. of	83	92	80-94	93	96	..	73	..	110	2.7	3.3	356
107	Algeria	92	89	95-100	97	83	62	64	92	85	3.0	0.6	142
108	Moldova, Rep. of	99	92	50-79	98	81	19	62	99	325	2.9	0.7	65
109	Viet Nam	47	77	80-94	99	97	20	75	70	52	1.4	3.9	130
110	Syrian Arab Republic	90	80	80-94	99	93	..	..	76 [e]	142	1.6	0.9	51
111	South Africa	87	86	80-94	87	72	..	56	84	443	3.7	5.1	663
112	Indonesia	55	78	80-94	65	59	18	57	56	16	0.6	2.1	84
113	Tajikistan	90	60	0-49	97	86	20	34	77	207	2.0	0.5	29
114	Bolivia	70	83	50-79	94	79	40	53	59	130	4.3	1.8	145
115	Honduras	75	88	0-49	99	95	..	50	54	83	4.3	2.5	165
116	Equatorial Guinea	53	44	0-49	34	19	..	..	..	25	1.0	2.2	168
117	Mongolia	30	60	50-79	98	95	32	60	97	254	4.7	2.0	120
118	Gabon	53	86	0-49	89	55	..	33	86	..	2.0	0.9	171
119	Guatemala	81	92	50-79	92	90	15	38	41	90	2.3	2.5	192
120	Egypt	98	97	80-94	98	97	..	56	61	218	1.8	2.3	143
121	Nicaragua	85	77	0-49	98	99	18	60	65	61	2.3	2.1	108
122	São Tomé and Principe	..	..	0-49	81	69	25	..	86 [e]	47	1.6	0.8	23
123	Solomon Islands	34	71	80-94	85	..	..	..	85	13	5.5	0.3	97
124	Namibia	41	77	80-94	69	58	..	..	78	29	4.2	2.9	366
125	Botswana	66	95	80-94	99	83	..	40	99	26	3.7	2.2	358
126	Morocco	68	80	50-79	93	96	..	50	40	49	1.6	3.1	174
127	India	28	84	0-49	73	56	..	48 [g]	43	48	0.9	4.0	71
128	Vanuatu	100	88	..	90	94	..	..	89	12	2.3	1.5	119
129	Ghana	72	73	0-49	91	81	22	22	44	6	2.2	1.9	51
130	Cambodia	17	30	0-49	64	59	..	24	32	30	1.0	6.1	97
131	Myanmar	64	72	50-79	70	73	24	33	..	30	0.4	1.8	24
132	Papua New Guinea	82	42	80-94	74	58	..	26	53	7	3.8	0.4	145
133	Swaziland	..	..	95-100	95	72	7	..	70	15	2.7	1.2	195
134	Comoros	98	96	80-94	90	70	22	21	62	7	3.1	1.2	35
135	Lao People's Dem. Rep.	30	37	50-79	60	50	20	32	21	61	1.3	2.1	52
136	Bhutan	70	62	80-94	81	78	..	..	15 [e]	16	3.7	0.4	64
137	Lesotho	49	78	80-94	92	77	..	30	60	7	5.2	1.1	100
138	Sudan	62	75	0-49	51	67	21	..	86 [e]	16	0.9	2.1	43
139	Bangladesh	48	97	50-79	94	76	..	54	12	20	1.5	2.6	47
140	Congo	..	51	50-79	53	35	13	..	..	25	1.5	0.5	23
141	Togo	34	54	50-79	84	58	23	24	49	8	1.5	1.4	35
Low human development													
142	Cameroon	79	58	50-79	77	62	23	19	56	7	1.0	2.9	55
143	Nepal	28	88	0-49	84	71	11	39	11	4	1.6	3.6	64
144	Pakistan	62	90	50-79	78	54	19	28	20	68	0.9	3.2	76
145	Zimbabwe	62	83	50-79	80	68	50	54	73	14	3.7	3.6	170
146	Kenya	87	57	0-49	91	76	30	39	44	14	2.4	6.4	123
147	Uganda	79	52	50-79	81	61	..	23	39	5	1.6	2.4	38
148	Yemen	38	69	50-79	73	79	..	21	22	22	1.5	3.4	69
149	Madagascar	42	47	50-79	72	55	16	19	47	11	2.6	1.0	33
150	Haiti	28	46	0-49	71	53	..	27	24	25	2.4	2.4	56
151	Gambia	37	62	80-94	99	90	26	10	51	4	3.0	0.6	51

Table 6.18 (*continued*)

HDI rank	Population with access to improved sanitation (%) 2000	Population with sustainable access to an improved water source (%) 2000	Population with sustainable access to affordable essential drugs (%)[a] 1999	One-year-olds fully immunized Against tuberculosis (%) 2001	One-year-olds fully immunized Against measles (%) 2001	Oral rehydration therapy use rate (%) 1994-2000[b]	Contraceptive prevalence rate (%)[c] 1995-2001[b]	Births attended by skilled health personnel (%) 1995-2001[b]	Physicians (per 100,000 people) 1990-2002[b]	Health expenditure Public (as % of GDP) 2000	Health expenditure Private (as % of GDP) 2000	Per capita (PPP US$) 2000
152 Nigeria	54	62	0-49	54	40	24	15	42	19	0.5	1.2	15
153 Djibouti	91	100	80-94	38	49	..	..	..	13	2.4	2.5	63
154 Mauritania	33	37	50-79	70	58	..	8	53	14	3.4	0.9	52
155 Eritrea	13	46	50-79	98	88	..	5	21	5	2.9	1.5	24
156 Senegal	70	78	50-79	89	48	4	13	51	10	2.6	2.0	56
157 Guinea	58	48	80-94	71	52	21	6	35	13	1.9	1.4	56
158 Rwanda	8	41	0-49	74	78	4	13	31	..	2.6	2.5	40
159 Benin	23	63	50-79	94	65	18	19	66	10	1.8	1.4	28
160 Tanzania, U. Rep. of	90	68	50-79	89	83	21	25	36	4	2.2	2.5	27
161 Côte d'Ivoire	52	81	80-94	72	61	25	15	47	9	1.0	1.8	45
162 Malawi	76	57	0-49	93	82	..	31	56	..	3.6	4.0	38
163 Zambia	78	64	50-79	92	85	8	25	47	7	3.5	2.1	49
164 Angola	44	38	0-49	74	72	..	8	23	5	2.0	1.6	52
165 Chad	29	27	0-49	44	36	36	8	16	3	2.3	0.5	16
166 Guinea-Bissau	56	56	0-49	70	48	13	8	35	17	1.8	0.4	12
167 Congo, Dem. Rep. of the	21	45	..	57	46	..	..	61	7	0.3	2.7	..
168 Central African Republic	25	70	50-79	38	29	34	15	44	4	1.4	1.0	31
169 Ethiopia	12	24	50-79	76	52	..	8	6	3	1.1	2.7	14
170 Mozambique	43	57	50-79	97	92	27	6	44	6	2.8	1.6	30
171 Burundi	88	78	0-49	84	75	10	..	25	1	1.7	1.5	16
172 Mali	69	65	50-79	68	37	22	8	24	5	2.2	2.7	32
173 Burkina Faso	29	42	50-79	72	46	37	12	31	3	3.0	1.2	37
174 Niger	20	59	50-79	49	51	38	14	16	4	1.5	1.8	22
175 Sierra Leone	66	57	0-49	74	37	28	4	42	9	2.0	1.7	24
Developing countries	51	78	..	78	69	..	..	56	..	..	..	..
Least developed countries	44	62	..	77	63	..	..	31	..	..	..	..
Arab States	83	86	..	85	84	..	..	67	..	..	..	..
East Asia and the Pacific	48	76	..	75	77	..	..	80	..	..	..	..
Latin America and the Caribbean	77	86	..	95	91	..	..	82	..	..	..	..
South Asia	37	85	..	77	60	..	..	36	..	..	..	..
Sub-Saharan Africa	53	57	..	73	58	..	..	38	..	..	..	..
Central & Eastern Europe & CIS	..	93	..	97	97	..	..	96	..	..	..	..
OECD	..	..	..	..	91	..	..	94	..	..	..	..
High-income OECD	..	..	..	..	90	..	..	99	..	..	..	..
High human development	..	..	..	..	91	..	..	96	..	..	..	..
Medium human development	51	82	..	80	74	..	..	64	..	..	..	..
Low human development	51	62	..	73	57	..	..	31	..	..	..	..
High income	..	..	..	..	89	..	..	99	..	..	..	..
Middle income	60	82	..	85	86	..	..	84	..	..	..	..
Low income	44	76	..	75	60	..	..	40	..	..	..	..
World	61 [h]	82 [h]	..	79	72	..	..	60	..	..	..	..

a. The data on access to essential drugs are based on statistical estimates received from World Health Organization (WHO) country and regional offices and regional advisers and through the World Drug Situation Survey carried out in 1998–99. These estimates represent the best information available to the WHO Department of Essential Drugs and Medicines Policy to date and are currently being validated by WHO member states. The department assigns the estimates to four groupings: very low access (0–49%), low access (50–79%), medium access (80–94%) and good access (95–100%). These groupings, used here in presenting the data, are often employed by the WHO in interpreting the data, as the actual estimates may suggest a higher level of accuracy than the data afford.

b. Data refer to the most recent year available during the period specified.

c. Data usually refer to married women aged 15–49; the actual age range covered may vary across countries.

d. WHO 2003d.

e. Data refer to a year or period other than that specified, differ from the standard definition or refer to only part of the country.

f. Data refer to the cities of Ivanovo, Perm and Yekaterinburg.

g. Excluding the state of Tripura.

h. Data refer to the world aggregate according to UNICEF 2003b.

Source: United Nations Development Programme. (2003). *Human Development Report 2003.* Table 6. "Commitment to Health (254–7)." New York: Oxford University Press. Retrieved from http://www.undp.org/hdr2003/pdf/hdr03_complete.pdf. Copyright 2003 by the United Nations Development Programme. Used by permission of Oxford University Press, Inc.

Table 6.19
Selected National Health Accounts Indicators for All Member States, Estimates for 1995 to 2000[a]

These figures were produced by WHO using the best available evidence. They are not necessarily the official statistics of Member States.

	Member State	Total expenditure on health as % of GDP						Private expenditure on health as % of total expenditure on health						General government expenditure on health as % of total expenditure on health					
		1995	1996	1997	1998	1999	2000	1995	1996	1997	1998	1999	2000	1995	1996	1997	1998	1999	2000
1	Afghanistan	1.3	1.3	1.4	1.6	1.5	1	50	50	47.4	42.3	43.1	36.5	50	50	52.6	57.7	56.9	63.5
2	Albania	3.3	3.6	3.2	3.3	3.4	3.4	23	32	36.2	36.4	35.8	37.9	77	68	63.8	63.6	64.2	62.1
3	Algeria	4.8	4.4	4.1	4.4	4.2	3.6	21.2	19.2	20.2	19.8	18.7	17.8	78.8	80.8	79.8	80.2	81.3	82.2
4	Andorra	9.6	8.7	9.3	10.6	8.1	7.9	13.3	13.3	13.4	11	13.2	13.5	86.7	86.7	86.6	89	86.8	86.5
5	Angola	4.8	3.9	3.9	3.5	3.3	3.6	50.5	48.5	54.8	60.2	55.8	44.1	49.5	51.5	45.2	39.8	44.2	55.9
6	Antigua and Barbuda	5.7	5.7	5.4	5.3	5.3	5.5	36.4	38.2	38.1	37.5	38.7	40.1	63.6	61.8	61.9	62.5	61.3	59.9
7	Argentina	8.2	7.9	7.8	8	8.5	8.6	39.1	41.3	43.6	44.7	44.3	45	60.9	58.7	56.4	55.3	55.7	55
8	Armenia	7.8	7.8	7.8	7.3	7.6	7.5	60.3	56.6	58.5	57.1	58.7	57.7	39.7	43.4	41.5	42.9	41.3	42.3
9	Australia	8.2	8.3	8.4	8.5	8.4	8.3	32.9	33.4	31.5	30.2	28.9	27.6	67.1	66.6	68.5	69.8	71.1	72.4
10	Austria	8.6	8.7	8	8	8.1	8	28.2	29.4	29.1	28.6	30	30.3	71.8	70.6	70.9	71.4	70	69.7
11	Azerbaijan	2.7	2.2	2.2	2.3	2.4	2.1	22.3	28	26.6	26.9	51.1	55.8	77.7	72	73.4	73.1	48.9	44.2
12	Bahamas	5.8	6.6	6.7	7.3	7.7	8	43.7	41.2	44.4	42.4	43.7	44.5	56.3	58.8	55.6	57.6	56.3	55.5
13	Bahrain	4.5	4.4	4.8	5	4.8	4.1	29.7	31.1	29.5	30.3	30.7	30.9	70.3	68.9	70.5	69.7	69.3	69.1
14	Bangladesh	3.5	4	3.9	3.8	4	3.8	66.1	64.2	63.9	63.5	63.3	63.6	33.9	35.8	36.1	36.5	36.7	36.4
15	Barbados	6.2	6.1	5.9	5.6	5.8	6.4	32.5	31.9	35.1	36.2	36	35.2	67.5	68.1	64.9	63.8	64	64.8
16	Belarus	5.7	5.5	6.2	5.4	5.7	5.7	15.2	15.1	12.5	14.8	17.5	17.2	84.8	84.9	87.5	85.2	82.5	82.8
17	Belgium	8.7	8.8	8.5	8.5	8.7	8.7	30.4	28.2	29.5	29.4	28.9	28.8	69.6	71.8	70.5	70.6	71.1	71.2
18	Belize	3.8	3.7	4	4.3	4.7	4.6	57.8	59.1	57.1	54.1	55.2	54.5	42.2	40.9	42.9	45.9	44.8	45.5
19	Benin	3.1	3.2	3.1	3.3	3.2	3.2	48.9	50.4	51.5	50.6	50.3	50	51.1	49.6	48.5	49.4	49.7	50
20	Bhutan	2.9	3.4	3.6	3.8	3.7	4.1	9.7	11.7	9.6	9.7	10.4	9.4	90.3	88.3	90.4	90.3	89.6	90.6
21	Bolivia	4.4	4.6	4.5	5	5.2	6.7	34.9	32.4	32.6	34.4	33.9	27.6	65.1	67.6	67.4	65.6	66.1	72.4
22	Bosnia and Herzegovina	4.6	4.1	3.4	3.8	4	4.5	53.8	47.1	44.6	42.9	37.3	31	46.2	52.9	55.4	57.1	62.7	69
23	Botswana	5.4	5.6	5.4	5.3	5.8	6	47.8	48.2	43.4	42	40.7	36.9	52.2	51.8	56.6	58	59.3	63.1
24	Brazil	7.2	7.4	7.5	7.5	7.9	8.3	57.3	59.6	56.5	56	57.2	59.2	42.7	40.4	43.5	44	42.8	40.8
25	Brunei Darussalam	2.6	2.6	2.8	3	3.2	3.1	20	19.4	20.6	18.7	20.6	20	80	80.6	79.4	81.3	79.4	80
26	Bulgaria	4.4	3.8	4.3	4	4.1	3.9	18.1	19.2	18.9	20.6	21.1	22.4	81.9	80.8	81.1	79.4	78.9	77.6
27	Burkina Faso	3.1	3.7	3.9	3.9	4.3	4.2	39	33.7	31.6	31	28.4	29.3	61	66.3	68.4	69	71.6	70.7
28	Burundi	3.5	3.2	2.5	2.8	2.6	3.1	52.1	47	48.5	47.6	47.3	46.9	47.9	53	51.5	52.4	52.7	53.1
29	Cambodia	6.7	7.5	8.3	8.4	8.1	8.1	79	76.7	77	76.5	76.2	75.5	21	23.3	23	23.5	23.8	24.5
30	Cameroon	4.1	4.1	4.1	4.2	4.3	4.3	79.2	79.4	79	78.1	76.2	75.3	20.8	20.6	21	21.9	23.8	24.7
31	Canada	9.1	8.9	8.9	9.1	9.2	9.1	28.6	29.2	29.8	29.2	29.2	28	71.4	70.8	70.2	70.8	70.8	72
32	Cape Verde	2.4	2.5	2.4	2.6	2.6	2.6	22.2	28.6	30.7	31	31.1	31.5	77.8	71.4	69.3	69	68.9	68.5
33	Central African Republic	2.1	2	2.4	2.5	2.8	2.9	46.9	51.3	49.6	50.6	53.8	51.6	53.1	48.7	50.4	49.4	46.2	48.4
34	Chad	3	3.1	3.1	2.9	2.9	3.1	20.7	20	20.7	21.4	21.4	20.2	79.3	80	79.3	78.6	78.6	79.8
35	Chile	6.7	6.9	7.2	7.5	7.3	7.2	64.4	63.3	62.1	60.4	59.2	57.4	35.6	36.7	37.9	39.6	40.8	42.6
36	China	3.9	4.2	4.5	4.7	5.1	5.3	53.3	57.8	60	61	62	63.4	46.7	42.2	40	39	38	36.6
37	Colombia	7.4	8.8	9.3	9.3	9.9	9.6	42.4	40.8	42.4	45.2	46.3	44.2	57.6	59.2	57.6	54.8	53.7	55.8
38	Comoros	4.8	4.6	4.5	4.5	4.4	4.4	32.6	31.6	31.8	28.2	28.3	28.4	67.4	68.4	68.2	71.8	71.7	71.6
39	Congo	3.3	2.8	2.8	3.5	2.9	2.2	31.9	31.8	35.4	43.7	32.7	29.8	68.1	68.2	64.6	56.3	67.3	70.2
40	Cook Islands	6.1	5	5.3	5.3	4.9	4.7	21.1	33.3	32.9	31.7	36.6	37.2	78.9	66.7	67.1	68.3	63.4	62.8
41	Costa Rica	6.3	6.2	6.3	6.5	6.4	6.4	31.6	32.8	33.2	33.5	31.3	31.6	68.4	67.2	66.8	66.5	68.7	68.4
42	Côte d'Ivoire	2.9	2.9	2.8	2.7	2.6	2.7	56.3	58.8	59.1	58.1	63.7	63.1	43.7	41.2	40.9	41.9	36.3	36.9
43	Croatia	8.6	8.9	8.1	8.8	8.6	8.6	19.1	18.2	19.5	18.2	17.2	15.4	80.9	81.8	80.5	81.8	82.8	84.6
44	Cuba	5.7	5.8	6.3	6.4	6.9	6.8	9.8	10.5	12.5	12.4	11.4	10.8	90.2	89.5	87.5	87.6	88.6	89.2
45	Cyprus	7	7.7	8.2	7.9	7.8	7.9	44.6	48	48.7	46.9	46.7	46.2	55.4	52	51.3	53.1	53.3	53.8
46	Czech Republic	7.3	7.1	7.1	7.1	7.2	7.2	7.3	7.5	8.3	8.1	8.5	8.6	92.7	92.5	91.7	91.9	91.5	91.4
47	Democratic People's Republic of Korea	3.1	3	3	3	2.6	2.1	20.1	19.5	16.5	16.5	17.6	22.7	79.9	80.5	83.5	83.5	82.4	77.3
48	Democratic Republic of the Congo	1.8	1.7	1.6	1.7	1.6	1.5	35.7	30	25.9	25.9	26.2	26.3	64.3	70	74.1	74.1	73.8	73.7
49	Denmark	8.2	8.3	8.2	8.4	8.5	8.3	17.5	17.6	17.7	18.1	17.8	17.9	82.5	82.4	82.3	81.9	82.2	82.1
50	Djibouti	4.8	5	4.6	4.9	5	5	49.4	50.8	55.6	53.7	51.6	51.3	50.6	49.2	44.4	46.3	48.4	48.7
51	Dominica	6.1	6.2	6.3	6.1	6.4	6.1	32.3	31.9	28.8	29	29.2	29.1	67.7	68.1	71.2	71	70.8	70.9
52	Dominican Republic	4.9	5.1	6.4	6.5	6.4	6.3	73.5	73.4	70.9	71.7	69.4	72	26.5	26.6	29.1	28.3	30.6	28
53	Ecuador	4.6	5.1	4.6	4.3	3.9	2.4	44.6	37.8	39.5	44.4	51	49.6	55.4	62.2	60.5	55.6	49	50.4
54	Egypt	3.7	3.8	3.9	4	3.9	3.8	56.1	55.4	54.1	54	53.6	53.9	43.9	44.6	45.9	46	46.4	46.1
55	El Salvador	6.6	7.6	8.1	8.3	8.5	8.8	59.2	58.9	61.3	57.5	57.8	57	40.8	41.1	38.7	42.5	42.2	43

Table 6.19 (*continued*)

		General government expenditure on health as % of total general government expenditure						External resources for health as % of general government expenditure on health						Social security expenditure on health as % of general government expenditure on health					
		1995	1996	1997	1998	1999	2000	1995	1996	1997	1998	1999	2000	1995	1996	1997	1998	1999	2000
1	Afghanistan	3.2	3.3	3.6	4.2	3.7	2.9	6	13.7	10.1	6	6.7	5.9	0	0	0	0	0	0
2	Albania	7.6	7.8	6.9	6.9	6.8	6.7	11.9	11.2	17.4	11.9	8.3	12.6	7	18.5	23.3	24.3	24.1	26.1
3	Algeria	12.1	12.1	11.6	11.3	11.5	10.2	0.1	0	0	0	0	0	61.1	64	65.2	65.2	63.2	63.5
4	Andorra	20.9	20.7	22.1	24.8	19.2	18.8	0	0	0	0	0	0	89	89.8	84.8	66.1	90.4	88.3
5	Angola	7.6	6.1	5.4	3.4	2.4	3.6	6	5.5	6.9	11.9	13.2	8	0	0	0	0	0	0
6	Antigua and Barbuda	14.3	14.6	14.2	14.5	13.9	14.1	4.2	3.9	3.8	5.5	5.3	5.3	0	0	0	0	0	0
7	Argentina	27.7	26.8	20.1	20	21.3	21.3	0.3	0.4	0.5	0.5	0.6	0.6	62	61.4	60.2	59.5	58.6	58.6
8	Armenia	7	12.6	12.2	13	11.1	11.6	9.1	9.5	9.8	11.7	5.6	4.9	0	0	0	0	0	0
9	Australia	14.2	14.7	15.7	16.3	16.6	16.2	0	0	0	0	0	0	0	0	0	0	0	0
10	Austria	10.7	10.8	10.4	10.6	10.4	10.6	0	0	0	0	0	0	68.6	68.5	59.8	59.8	60.6	61
11	Azerbaijan	9.9	5.6	7.6	6.5	4.6	4	2.5	3.3	2	2.3	4.1	8.8	0	0	0	0	0	0
12	Bahamas	14.2	15.3	13.7	15.9	15.1	16.2	0	0	0	0	0	0	0	0	0	0	0	0
13	Bahrain	11.2	11.2	11.4	11.2	11.4	11.6	0	0	0	0	0	0	0.4	0.4	0.4	0.4	0.4	0.4
14	Bangladesh	5.3	6.1	6.2	6.9	7.4	7.1	34.2	23.5	13	22.3	27.4	41.1	0	0	0	0	0	0
15	Barbados	14	12.5	11.5	10.8	11.1	11.9	8.1	7.7	7.6	7.5	6.9	6.1	0	0	0	0	0	0
16	Belarus	10.9	11.5	11.9	11	11.2	13.1	0	0.1	0.1	0.1	0.1	0.1	0	0	0	0	0	0
17	Belgium	11.4	12	11.7	11.9	12.3	12.6	0	0	0	0	0	0	89.6	85.3	89.5	89.3	86.7	82.1
18	Belize	5	5	5.4	5.9	5.7	5.5	16.8	17.4	15	8.7	7.5	6.8	0	0	0	0	0	0
19	Benin	7.1	7.1	6	6.3	6.3	6.3	46.6	45.3	32.5	38.8	22.1	26.1	0	0	0	0	0	0
20	Bhutan	7.1	8.5	10.1	12.2	8.3	9.2	21.4	17.2	35.6	33.9	32.6	46.4	0	0	0	0	0	0
21	Bolivia	9.3	10.1	9.1	10	10.4	14.2	10.8	7.7	9.4	7.9	14.5	13.1	57.5	64	65.3	64.8	62	48.3
22	Bosnia and Herzegovina	5	6	6.2	6.4	7.2	9.1	1.2	14.6	23.8	14.4	19.5	20	0	0	0	0	0	0
23	Botswana	6.6	6.4	7.1	6.4	6.5	7.4	3.5	3.5	5.8	2.2	2	1.7	0	0	0	0	0	0
24	Brazil	8.3	8.3	9.1	9	9.3	8.4	0.4	0.4	0.8	1.2	1.2	1	0	0	0	0	0	0
25	Brunei Darussalam	4.2	4.5	4.5	5.1	5.3	5.4	0	0	0	0	0	0	0	0	0	0	0	0
26	Bulgaria	6.9	5	8.9	8.1	7.7	6.8	0	8.5	0.1	0	0.3	18	17.4	23.1	10.5	14.3	15.1	16
27	Burkina Faso	9	10.9	10.6	10.6	10.6	10.6	39.8	33.4	36.5	31.8	29.6	31.1	0	0	0	0	0	0
28	Burundi	6.4	5.8	5.8	6.1	6.2	5.7	35.4	40.3	52.4	57.8	63.6	59.9	0	0	0	0	0	0
29	Cambodia	14.5	18.4	20.2	20.4	19.9	20.5	75.4	70.1	65.4	70.1	66.1	49.1	0	0	0	0	0	0
30	Cameroon	6.4	6.5	6.6	6.5	6.4	6.7	14.5	14.6	15.8	15.1	14.5	18.3	0	0	0	0	0	0
31	Canada	13.3	13.4	13.9	14.4	15.1	15.5	0	0	0	0	0	0	1.4	1.4	1.6	1.7	1.8	1.9
32	Cape Verde	3.6	3.9	4.2	4.3	5	3.4	4.6	4.6	11.6	15.6	19.5	22	0	0	0	0	0	0
33	Central African Republic	4.1	3.7	3.8	3.9	4.2	4.6	20.8	13.2	21.2	28.6	28.9	34.8	0	0	0	0	0	0
34	Chad	13.1	13.4	13.6	15	13.5	13.5	39.1	62.4	70.6	53.1	67.1	58.5	0	0	0	0	0	0
35	Chile	10.8	10.8	12.1	12.4	11.8	11.9	1.7	1.5	1.3	1.2	1.3	1.2	89.2	89.1	83.6	75.7	77.3	71.8
36	China	15.5	15.2	14.7	13.7	12	11	0.8	0.7	0.7	0.5	0.7	0.6	62.1	60	58	53	51.4	50.7
37	Colombia	17.5	17.7	18.2	17.4	18.1	18.3	0.2	0.5	0.5	0.5	0.6	0.4	39.8	40.7	40.3	38.4	37	36.5
38	Comoros	7.6	7.5	8.7	9.4	10	10.3	33.1	30.2	55.6	72.9	43.9	49.3	0	0	0	0	0	0
39	Congo	6.9	6.4	4.8	4.6	5.7	5.6	9.7	9.7	10.4	5.2	2.3	2.2	0	0	0	0	0	0
40	Cook Islands	9	8.8	10.3	10.6	9.2	9.2	0.2	0.3	0.3	25.9	31.1	29.8	0	0	0	0	0	0
41	Costa Rica	16.2	17.7	17.2	17.1	17.1	18.2	1.7	1.6	2.8	2.6	2.4	1.8	93.5	93.3	93.8	94.1	94	94.4
42	Côte d'Ivoire	4.7	4.7	4.7	5	4.3	5.1	13.7	11.7	11.8	12	15.3	14.4	0	0	0	0	0	0
43	Croatia	14.3	14.5	13.2	13.7	12.2	12.6	0.3	0.3	0.3	0.3	0.5	0.4	94.6	92.4	92.6	86.1	94.3	96.5
44	Cuba	8	9.3	10	10.3	11.8	13.5	0.1	0	0.2	0.1	0.3	0.2	17.7	13	20.9	19.4	11	10.6
45	Cyprus	12	11.4	11.4	11.4	11.6	11.6	0	0	0	0	0	0	48	46.8	44.7	44.6	44.2	44.2
46	Czech Republic	11.2	12.9	14	13.6	13.9	13.9	0	0	0	0	0	0	83.8	87.7	89.5	90.2	89.4	89.4
47	Democratic People's Republic of Korea	5.6	5.5	5.5	5.5	4.7	5.7	0	0	0	0.2	0.2	0.1	0	0	0	0	0	0
48	Democratic Republic of the Congo	13.7	10.4	12.3	11.1	10.6	9.9	8.6	1.4	1	1.3	0	0	0	0	0	0	0	0
49	Denmark	11.2	11.4	11.7	11.9	12.5	12.7	0	0	0	0	0	0	0	0	0	0	0	0
50	Djibouti	6.4	7.1	5.7	5.9	6.1	6.1	11.4	7.9	35.6	18.6	22.7	26.6	0	0	0	0	0	0
51	Dominica	11.7	11.4	11.8	11.8	12.8	12.8	2.3	2.1	4.2	3.1	2.8	1.6	0	0	0	0	0	0
52	Dominican Republic	9.9	10.2	10.5	10.2	10.9	10.9	4	4.9	4.6	10.3	9.2	8.4	28.4	24.7	26.8	21.4	19.1	19.1
53	Ecuador	9.6	12.2	10.4	9.8	7.2	9.2	1.4	1	1.9	2.3	6.3	9.9	38.1	30.8	32.8	30.6	30.4	28.8
54	Egypt	4.8	5.2	5.9	6.5	6.2	6.5	5.7	5.8	4.2	4.5	3.8	3.8	27.9	28.3	28	28.4	29.5	29.5
55	El Salvador	19.1	19.9	21.1	22	25.8	26.2	7.7	8.4	5	4.4	5.9	5.4	44.4	42.9	43.3	41.7	41	41.4

Table 6.19 (*continued*)

	Member State	Total expenditure on health as % of GDP						Private expenditure on health as % of total expenditure on health						General government expenditure on health as % of total expenditure on health					
		1995	1996	1997	1998	1999	2000	1995	1996	1997	1998	1999	2000	1995	1996	1997	1998	1999	2000
56	Equatorial Guinea	4.2	4.7	3.6	4.2	3.4	3.4	34.8	44.4	44	40.6	32.4	32.4	65.2	55.6	56	59.4	67.6	67.6
57	Eritrea	3.4	3.9	4.4	5.4	4.1	4.3	14.9	12.9	34.2	33.9	35.7	34.4	85.1	87.1	65.8	66.1	64.3	65.6
58	Estonia	8.6	7.2	6.3	6	6.6	6.1	8.6	10.2	11.5	13.7	19.6	23.3	91.4	89.8	88.5	86.3	80.4	76.7
59	Ethiopia	3.8	3.8	4.4	4.9	4.6	4.6	62.7	60.8	62.1	57.1	60.2	60.6	37.3	39.2	37.9	42.9	39.8	39.4
60	Fiji	3.8	3.9	3.9	4.1	3.7	3.9	35	33.8	33.3	34.6	34.8	34.8	65	66.2	66.7	65.4	65.2	65.2
61	Finland	7.5	7.7	7.3	6.9	6.9	6.6	24.5	24.2	23.9	23.7	24.7	24.9	75.5	75.8	76.1	76.3	75.3	75.1
62	France	9.6	9.6	9.4	9.3	9.4	9.5	23.9	23.9	23.8	24	23.9	24	76.1	76.1	76.2	76	76.1	76
63	Gabon	3.1	3	2.9	3.2	3.3	3	33.8	33.7	33.5	36.5	38.8	31.4	66.2	66.3	66.5	63.5	61.2	68.6
64	Gambia	3.9	3.6	3.5	3.8	4.2	4.1	18.6	18.6	18.2	17.9	17.1	17.6	81.4	81.4	81.8	82.1	82.9	82.4
65	Georgia	4.6	6.9	6.9	7.1	6.9	7.1	87.1	86.1	85.3	86.7	89.8	89.5	12.9	13.9	14.7	13.3	10.2	10.5
66	Germany	10.6	10.9	10.7	10.6	10.7	10.6	23.3	23.2	24.7	25.2	25.2	24.9	76.7	76.8	75.3	74.8	74.8	75.1
67	Ghana	4.2	4.1	3.9	4.1	4.2	4.2	56.6	56	55.2	48.5	48.1	46.5	43.4	44	44.8	51.5	51.9	53.5
68	Greece	8.9	8.9	8.7	8.7	8.7	8.3	45.5	44.8	44.8	45.6	45.7	44.5	54.5	55.2	55.2	54.4	54.3	55.5
69	Grenada	4.4	4.8	4.7	4.8	4.8	4.8	33.4	31.7	33.9	34.2	30.3	29.9	66.6	68.3	66.1	65.8	69.7	70.1
70	Guatemala	4.1	4.1	4.3	4.5	4.7	4.7	56.2	57.6	55.1	52.9	51.7	52.1	43.8	42.4	44.9	47.1	48.3	47.9
71	Guinea	3.5	3.5	3.6	3.6	3.8	3.4	45.7	45.6	42.8	39.6	37.5	42.9	54.3	54.4	57.2	60.4	62.5	57.1
72	Guinea-Bissau	3.6	4.3	3.9	4	3.9	3.9	37.9	36.1	36	34.9	34.2	34.6	62.1	63.9	64	65.1	65.8	65.4
73	Guyana	4.7	4.5	4.8	4.8	5	5.1	17.6	17.5	16.5	16.6	16	17.3	82.4	82.5	83.5	83.4	84	82.7
74	Haiti	5.8	5.1	4.9	5.1	4.9	4.9	43.2	47.7	48.3	50.1	49	50.7	56.8	52.3	51.7	49.9	51	49.3
75	Honduras	6.8	6.8	6.1	6.6	6.3	6.8	47.5	45.5	42.4	35	38.4	36.9	52.5	54.5	57.6	65	61.6	63.1
76	Hungary	7.5	7.2	7	6.9	6.8	6.8	16	18.4	18.7	20.4	21.8	24.3	84	81.6	81.3	79.6	78.2	75.7
77	Iceland	8.2	8.2	8	8.3	8.7	8.9	15.5	16.1	16.3	16.1	15.2	15.6	84.5	83.9	83.7	83.9	84.8	84.4
78	India	5	5.2	5.3	5	5.1	4.9	83.8	84.4	84.3	81.6	82.1	82.2	16.2	15.6	15.7	18.4	17.9	17.8
79	Indonesia	1.7	2.3	2.4	2.5	2.6	2.7	62.7	72.1	76.3	72.8	72	76.3	37.3	27.9	23.7	27.2	28	23.7
80	Iran, Islamic Republic of	5.6	5.4	5.7	5.6	5.4	5.5	54.4	51.8	54	54.5	53.8	53.7	45.6	48.2	46	45.5	46.2	46.3
81	Iraq	4.9	4.6	5	4.4	3.7	3.7	40.7	41.8	41.1	40.9	40	40.1	59.3	58.2	58.9	59.1	60	59.9
82	Ireland	7.3	7	6.9	6.8	6.8	6.7	27.5	26.7	24.1	23.8	23.7	24.2	72.5	73.3	75.9	76.2	76.3	75.8
83	Israel	9.9	10.2	10.1	10	10.9	10.9	25.6	21.4	21.3	23	22.3	24.1	74.4	78.6	78.7	77	77.7	75.9
84	Italy	7.4	7.5	7.7	7.7	7.8	8.1	27.8	28.2	27.8	28	27.7	26.3	72.2	71.8	72.2	72	72.3	73.7
85	Jamaica	4.5	4.5	4.9	5.3	5.8	5.5	53.8	53.4	52.1	50.2	50.2	53	46.2	46.6	47.9	49.8	49.8	47
86	Japan[b]	7	7	7.2	7.1	7.4	7.8	21.8	19.7	20.5	22.6	22	23.3	78.2	80.3	79.5	77.4	78	76.7
87	Jordan	9.6	9.9	8.8	8.8	8	8.1	50.2	49.8	43.1	43.1	44.7	48.2	49.8	50.2	56.9	56.9	55.3	51.8
88	Kazakhstan	6	6	6.2	5.1	4.2	3.7	18.2	23.7	23.6	29.4	29.1	26.8	81.8	76.3	76.4	70.6	70.9	73.2
89	Kenya	8.1	8.1	8.3	8.4	8.4	8.3	73.4	72.7	73.8	73.8	73.5	77.8	26.6	27.3	26.2	26.2	26.5	22.2
90	Kiribati	9	8.8	9	8.4	8.3	8.1	0.9	0.9	0.9	0.8	0.8	1.3	99.1	99.1	99.1	99.2	99.2	98.7
91	Kuwait	3.6	3.1	3.3	3.9	3.5	3	10	13	12.6	12.9	13.2	12.8	90	87	87.4	87.1	86.8	87.2
92	Kyrgyzstan	7.8	6.7	6.4	6.8	6.1	6	11.9	19.2	20.3	28.1	33.4	38.3	88.1	80.8	79.7	71.9	66.6	61.7
93	Lao People's Democratic Republic	2.8	2.9	3.5	3.3	3.4	3.4	52.9	58	61.5	64	63	62	47.1	42	38.5	36	37	38
94	Latvia	6.5	6.3	6.2	6.6	6.4	5.9	34.6	36.9	38.2	38.9	37.1	40	65.4	63.1	61.8	61.1	62.9	60
95	Lebanon	10.8	10.9	11.3	11.6	11.7	11.8	72	71.6	72.3	72.5	72.5	72.2	28	28.4	27.7	27.5	27.5	27.8
96	Lesotho	6.2	5.6	5.3	5.9	6.4	6.3	21.3	22	24	21.7	18.8	17.7	78.7	78	76	78.3	81.2	82.3
97	Liberia	2.9	3	3.2	3.5	3.9	4	31.1	32.1	30.9	26.6	23.5	23.8	68.9	67.9	69.1	73.4	76.5	76.2
98	Libyan Arab Jamahiriya	3.6	3.6	3.5	3.7	3.3	3.3	59.5	58.1	50	50	50.9	51.4	40.5	41.9	50	50	49.1	48.6
99	Lithuania	5.2	5.5	5.9	6.3	6.1	6	13.7	23.1	22.3	23.3	24.9	27.6	86.3	76.9	77.7	76.7	75.1	72.4
100	Luxembourg	6.4	6.4	5.9	5.8	6	5.8	7.6	7.2	7.6	7.6	7.1	8.1	92.4	92.8	92.4	92.4	92.9	91.9
101	Madagascar	2.7	2.7	2	2.8	3	3.5	40.4	39.1	19.3	38.1	34.6	28.2	59.6	60.9	80.7	61.9	65.4	71.8
102	Malawi	6.1	6.5	7.3	6.8	6.9	7.6	50.6	54.8	49.4	49.7	50.2	52.2	49.4	45.2	50.6	50.3	49.8	47.8
103	Malaysia	2.2	2.3	2.3	2.5	2.5	2.5	43.9	41.7	42.4	42.3	40.2	41.2	56.1	58.3	57.6	57.7	59.8	58.8
104	Maldives	5.9	6.4	6.5	6.4	6.8	7.6	16.2	15.5	18.1	18.2	17.5	16.6	83.8	84.5	81.8	81.8	82.5	83.4
105	Mali	3.2	3.3	4.2	4.5	4.7	4.9	46.9	50.4	54.2	53.5	53.2	54.5	53.1	49.6	45.8	46.5	46.8	45.5
106	Malta	8.3	8.4	8.6	8.4	8.4	8.8	28.6	30	32.1	30.7	32.5	31.5	71.4	70	67.9	69.3	67.5	68.5
107	Marshall Islands	7.8	8.8	9.2	9.5	9.8	9.4	38.8	38.3	38.1	38.4	38.9	38.6	61.2	61.7	61.9	61.6	61.1	61.4
108	Mauritania	3.2	3.2	3.3	3.8	4.2	4.3	25.5	24	26.7	27.2	24.1	20.7	74.5	76	73.3	72.8	75.9	79.3
109	Mauritius	3.6	3.6	3.5	3.4	3.6	3.4	45.9	47	46.7	46.2	43.3	43.7	54.1	53	53.3	53.8	56.7	56.3
110	Mexico	5.6	5.3	5.3	5.3	5.4	5.4	58.5	57.5	56.7	52	52.7	53.6	41.5	42.5	43.3	48	47.3	46.4

Table 6.19 (*continued*)

		General government expenditure on health as % of total general government expenditure						External resources for health as % of general government expenditure on health						Social security expenditure on health as % of general government expenditure on health					
		1995	1996	1997	1998	1999	2000	1995	1996	1997	1998	1999	2000	1995	1996	1997	1998	1999	2000
56	Equatorial Guinea	11.2	10.4	7.9	8.3	11.6	14.3	10.4	10.2	19	24.2	23.6	19.6	0	0	0	0	0	0
57	Eritrea	4.1	5.3	5.3	4.5	3.9	4	32.8	24.7	63.3	31.7	46.2	60.7	0	0	0	0	0	0
58	Estonia	18.8	15.9	14.6	13.3	12.7	12.4	0.6	0.9	1.1	1.7	4.4	0.5	68.8	70.6	72.2	77.1	82.1	86
59	Ethiopia	5.8	6.2	6.9	8.2	5.9	5.5	17.9	21.7	16.9	22.3	29.4	35.6	0.6	0.6	0.6	0.5	0.6	0.6
60	Fiji	8.5	8.1	7.4	6.9	6.9	7.5	7.2	6.5	6.4	19.1	18.3	19.4	0	0	0	0	0	0
61	Finland	9.5	9.7	9.8	9.9	10	10.2	0	0	0	0	0	0	17.7	18.3	18.7	19.4	19.8	20.4
62	France	13.2	13.1	13.1	13.2	13.3	13.5	0	0	0	0	0	0	96.9	96.9	96.8	96.8	96.7	96.8
63	Gabon	6.4	6.4	6.2	6.4	6.4	8.9	3.7	3.8	6.1	4.6	5.7	5.8	0	0	0	0	0	0
64	Gambia	13.7	12.7	14.3	14.7	12.1	12.1	31.5	23.2	29.3	35.1	41.1	37.5	0	0	0	0	0	0
65	Georgia	1.6	4.6	4.8	4.5	3.3	3.4	11.9	8.5	9.4	14.2	11.1	9.7	11.3	10.3	15.6	15	20.2	14.6
66	Germany	14.5	16.6	16.3	16.3	16.3	17.3	0	0	0	0	0	0	86.3	88.1	90.7	91.4	91.5	91.7
67	Ghana	8.3	8.1	8.4	8.2	8.1	7.9	15.8	14.3	17.1	14.6	14.7	24.1	0	0	0	0	0	0
68	Greece	9.5	9.8	9.9	9.8	9.6	9.2	0	0	0	0	0	0	23.6	25.2	28	38.6	38.4	36.9
69	Grenada	10.4	10	10.6	11.3	12.3	12.3	5.6	4.8	1.5	1.3	0	0	0	0	0	0	0	0
70	Guatemala	17.2	16.9	15.5	14	15.5	16.4	6.5	6.4	6.4	11.4	10.9	9.5	58.6	55.6	57.7	55.3	54.8	56.7
71	Guinea	9.2	9.2	9.7	12.9	11.9	11.9	5.3	7.4	8.5	9.6	9	16.2	0	0	0	0	0	0
72	Guinea-Bissau	9.6	10.1	10.4	13.9	11.1	8.4	11.3	13.3	36	33.1	33	39.3	0	0	0	0	0	0
73	Guyana	9.6	9.2	9.3	9.3	9.1	9.3	4.8	4.3	5.6	4.4	4.8	3.8	0	0	0	0	0	0
74	Haiti	28.1	19.8	19.6	19	20.9	22.1	40.4	45.7	29.3	41.3	46.1	67	0	0	0	0	0	0
75	Honduras	17.3	18.1	17	20.8	18.2	18.3	11.9	20.3	18.5	13.5	14.7	12.1	9.7	9.6	9.7	8.9	9.8	10.2
76	Hungary	11.3	11.4	11.4	10.2	11.5	11.8	0	0	0	0	0	0	80	82.4	82.8	82.8	83.5	83.2
77	Iceland	17.5	17.6	18.9	21	20.3	20.4	0	0	0	0	0	0	34.9	35.7	31.5	29.8	28.7	28.8
78	India	4.7	4.7	4.7	5.6	5.7	5.3	13.2	12.8	14.8	13.1	12.5	12.4	0	0	0	0	0	0
79	Indonesia	3.6	3.5	2.8	3.2	3.2	3.1	3.2	3.7	15	30.7	30.1	28.5	11.4	10.6	14.1	9	7.3	7.5
80	Iran, Islamic Republic of	10.5	12.3	10.5	10.9	11.3	11.8	0	0	0	0	0	1	40.2	37.4	36.9	39.1	39.5	39.3
81	Iraq	10.7	10.5	12.5	13.5	15.2	15.1	0	0	0	0	0	0	0	0	0	0	0	0
82	Ireland	12.8	12.9	14	14.8	14.8	16	0	0	0	0	0	0	9.7	9.2	8.3	9	11.7	12.9
83	Israel	15.7	16.8	14.6	14.3	15.9	15.7	0	0	0	0	0.3	0.4	23.8	24.9	25.6	26.3	24.3	25.8
84	Italy	10	10.1	10.9	11.1	11.6	12.7	0	0	0	0	0	0	0.4	0.4	0.4	0.1	0.1	0.1
85	Jamaica	8	5.8	7.2	7.5	7.6	7	7.9	5.5	6.1	5.8	5	4.4	0	0	0	0	0	0
86	Japan[b]	15.1	15.2	16.2	13.2	15.3	15.4	0	0	0	0	0	0	84.7	84.4	89	84.8	84	89.1
87	Jordan	12.2	12.3	12.3	12.3	12.3	12.4	2	2.1	3.6	4.1	4.2	4.3	0	0	0	0	0	0
88	Kazakhstan	15	16.1	17.4	13.4	13.4	12.3	0.4	0.3	0.3	0.4	9.3	2.4	10.2	9.5	26.9	28.3	28.7	26.4
89	Kenya	6.6	7.2	8	8.1	8.1	8.1	32.3	26.1	26.9	29.8	32.3	38.3	13.4	13	13.3	13.1	12.8	15.2
90	Kiribati	16.4	14.5	14.5	14	13.8	13.2	1.6	1.5	1.5	1.7	0.5	0.5	0	0	0	0	0	0
91	Kuwait	6.8	7.9	8.4	8	8.2	8.9	0	0	0	0	0	0	0	0	0	0	0	0
92	Kyrgyzstan	21.5	23.7	21.8	21.3	20.2	18.8	1.5	4.7	6.7	8.5	15.5	20.4	0	0	0.3	2.5	4.9	5.8
93	Lao People's Democratic Republic	6.3	5.1	5.9	4.9	4.6	5	29.4	29	33.2	46.8	72.9	73.7	0.7	0.8	0.7	0.8	0.4	0.4
94	Latvia	11	10.3	10.1	10.3	9.9	9.7	0.1	0.1	0.1	0.7	0.6	0.7	51.4	48.6	49.9	50.5	57.1	65.4
95	Lebanon	8.5	8.1	7.3	9.8	9.9	9.8	2.2	2.3	2	1.7	1.6	1.6	48	47.6	49.7	45.6	45.9	45.5
96	Lesotho	9.6	8.6	8.1	9.3	10.4	10.8	5.5	6.3	10.4	7.9	5.9	6.8	0	0	0	0	0	0
97	Liberia	9.5	9	9.3	10.1	10.8	10.7	31.4	48.3	39	37.3	36.8	40.5	0	0	0	0	0	0
98	Libyan Arab Jamahiriya	2.2	2.3	2.6	2.7	2.4	2.4	0	0	0	0	0	0	0	0	0	0	0	0
99	Lithuania	12.1	12.3	13.6	14.8	11.7	13.9	0	0	0	0	0	0	17.2	19	82.7	89.9	92.2	90.7
100	Luxembourg	13	13.1	12.5	12.7	13.3	13.3	0	0	0	0	0	0	83.4	84.3	86	82.7	88.5	90.9
101	Madagascar	9.2	9.6	10.3	10.3	11.2	15.1	36.3	29.3	30.6	36.9	37	26.9	0	0	0	0	0	0
102	Malawi	11.3	11.7	14.6	14.5	14.6	14.6	50.2	42.2	42.7	74.4	71.8	86.7	0	0	0	0	0	0
103	Malaysia	5	5.7	5.6	6	5.8	5.8	2.2	1.7	1.8	2.3	2	1.8	0	0	0	0	0	0
104	Maldives	9.2	11.3	10.9	10.1	10.4	10.2	8.5	7	6.3	7.5	6.5	6.6	0	0	0	0	0	0
105	Mali	6.9	6.6	7.8	8.3	8.3	8.3	39.6	44.1	32.4	33.6	26.4	27.3	0	0	0	0	0	0
106	Malta	13	12.3	11.7	11.9	11.8	13.2	0	0	0	0	0	0	61.5	56.5	64.5	68.9	68	59.9
107	Marshall Islands	8	7.5	9.7	10	10.6	10.8	26.4	25	24	23.6	63.6	64.8	0	0	0	0	0	0
108	Mauritania	9.5	9.9	9.3	12.5	14.6	16.3	23.7	28.6	29	33.6	43	46.6	0	0	0	0	0	0
109	Mauritius	8.9	8.4	7.9	8.3	8.4	8.4	3.4	2.6	3	3	2.6	2.5	0	0	0	0	0	0
110	Mexico	11.3	11.5	11.6	13.6	16.5	15.6	0.8	0.8	0.6	1.8	1.6	1.4	77.9	73	73.6	70.4	72.4	71.1

Table 6.19 (*continued*)

	Member State	Total expenditure on health as % of GDP						Private expenditure on health as % of total expenditure on health						General government expenditure on health as % of total expenditure on health					
		1995	1996	1997	1998	1999	2000	1995	1996	1997	1998	1999	2000	1995	1996	1997	1998	1999	2000
111	Micronesia, Federated States of	12.1	11.4	11.4	11.2	10.9	10.5	42.9	44	43.3	44.7	45.4	46.3	57.1	56	56.7	55.3	54.6	53.7
112	Monaco	7.1	7.3	7	7.2	7.4	7.4	50	50	50	50.7	51.4	51.9	50	50	50	49.3	48.6	48.1
113	Mongolia	4.2	5.2	5	6.2	6.1	6.6	31	36.9	37.3	34.6	33.5	29.7	69	63.1	62.7	65.4	66.5	70.3
114	Morocco	4.6	4.5	4.4	4.3	4.4	4.5	71.3	71	70.5	71.8	70.6	70.4	28.7	29	29.5	28.2	29.4	29.6
115	Mozambique	4.9	5	4.6	4.3	4.1	4.3	38.9	37.2	37	37.2	38.1	36.6	61.1	62.8	63	62.8	61.9	63.4
116	Myanmar	2.1	2.2	2.1	2	2	2.2	81	82.7	85.7	89.4	88.3	82.9	19	17.3	14.3	10.6	11.7	17.1
117	Namibia	8.2	7.4	7.4	7.6	7.3	7.1	43	49	48.4	48.3	40.8	40.7	57	51	51.6	51.7	59.2	59.3
118	Nauru	10	10.6	11.7	11.8	11.4	11.3	1.1	1.1	1.1	1.1	1.1	1.1	98.9	98.9	98.9	98.9	98.9	98.9
119	Nepal	5.1	5.2	5.5	5.7	5.5	5.4	73.6	74	69.4	67.4	71.1	70.7	26.4	26	30.6	32.6	28.9	29.3
120	Netherlands	8.4	8.3	8.2	8.1	8.2	8.1	29	33.8	32.2	32.2	33.5	32.5	71	66.2	67.8	67.8	66.5	67.5
121	New Zealand	7.2	7.2	7.5	7.9	7.9	8	22.8	23.3	22.7	23	22.5	22	77.2	76.7	77.3	77	77.5	78
122	Nicaragua	6.4	6	5.2	4.8	4.7	4.4	21.7	25.6	46.2	39.7	47.2	48.3	78.3	74.4	53.8	60.3	52.8	51.7
123	Niger	3.8	3.8	3.8	3.9	3.8	3.9	54.9	57.2	56.3	55.3	54.6	55.1	45.1	42.8	43.7	44.7	45.4	44.9
124	Nigeria	2.8	2.6	2.4	2.5	2.4	2.2	85.5	88.3	86.4	81.1	77.1	79.2	14.5	11.7	13.6	18.9	22.9	20.8
125	Niue	7.4	7.9	7.6	6.7	8.2	7.6	3.2	2.6	2.7	3.3	2.9	3.8	96.8	97.4	97.3	96.7	97.1	96.2
126	Norway	8	8	7.9	8.6	8.8	7.8	15.8	15.8	15.7	15.3	14.8	14.8	84.2	84.2	84.3	84.7	85.2	85.2
127	Oman	3	2.9	2.7	3.1	2.9	2.8	20.5	19.9	21.2	21.7	20.5	17.1	79.5	80.1	78.8	78.3	79.5	82.9
128	Pakistan	4.2	4	4	4	4.1	4.1	75.2	77	77.1	76.4	78.1	77.1	24.8	23	22.9	23.6	21.9	22.9
129	Palau	7.5	6.5	6.1	6.4	6.5	6.4	11.4	12.3	12.5	12	11.8	11.5	88.6	87.7	87.5	88	88.2	88.5
130	Panama	7.8	8	7.4	7.4	7.6	7.6	29.8	29	31.6	29.7	30.1	30.8	70.2	71	68.4	70.3	69.9	69.2
131	Papua New Guinea	2.9	2.7	3.2	3.9	4.2	4.1	8.4	10.1	10.6	9.1	10.1	11.4	91.6	89.9	89.4	90.9	89.9	88.6
132	Paraguay	7.8	7.2	7.6	7.3	7.9	7.9	72.5	64	67.2	62.6	60.6	61.7	27.5	36	32.8	37.4	39.4	38.3
133	Peru	4.6	4.5	4.5	4.7	4.9	4.8	44.1	41.7	42.6	42.3	40.4	40.8	55.9	58.3	57.4	57.7	59.6	59.2
134	Philippines	3.4	3.5	3.6	3.6	3.6	3.4	60.1	58.6	56.6	57.6	53.5	54.3	39.9	41.4	43.4	42.4	46.5	45.7
135	Poland	6	6.4	6.1	6.4	6.2	6	27.1	26.6	28	34.6	28.9	30.3	72.9	73.4	72	65.4	71.1	69.7
136	Portugal	8.3	8.5	8.6	8.3	8.4	8.2	38.3	35.3	35.2	32.5	29.3	28.8	61.7	64.7	64.8	67.5	70.7	71.2
137	Qatar	4.8	4.8	4	4.5	4.1	3.2	26.1	23.4	23.7	23.4	22.7	22.5	73.9	76.6	76.3	76.6	77.3	77.5
138	Republic of Korea	4.7	4.9	5	5.1	5.6	6	63.5	61.2	59	53.8	56.9	55.9	36.5	38.8	41	46.2	43.1	44.1
139	Republic of Moldova	6.2	7.1	6.4	4.7	3.4	3.5	7.2	5.7	6.3	9.2	15.2	17.6	92.8	94.3	93.7	90.8	84.8	82.4
140	Romania	2.8	4.5	4	3.5	3.3	2.9	34	27.8	37.1	43.1	40.7	36.2	66	72.2	62.9	56.9	59.3	63.8
141	Russian Federation	5.5	5.4	5.8	5.9	5.6	5.3	18.5	21.9	27.1	31.1	35.3	27.5	81.5	78.1	72.9	68.9	64.7	72.5
142	Rwanda	6.2	6.1	5.5	5	5.4	5.2	52.4	50.1	52.1	48.7	46.6	48.7	47.6	49.9	47.9	51.3	53.4	51.3
143	Saint Kitts and Nevis	4.7	5.1	4.7	4.7	4.9	5.2	33.9	33.9	32.5	31.9	36.5	40.8	66.1	66.1	67.5	68.1	63.5	59.2
144	Saint Lucia	3.8	4	4.2	4.3	4.1	4.3	38.8	36.9	37.7	34.4	34.7	37.9	61.2	63.1	62.3	65.6	65.3	62.1
145	Saint Vincent and the Grenadines	5.8	5.7	6.1	5.9	6.1	6.3	34	32.9	36.2	37.5	38.5	34.6	66	67.1	63.8	62.5	61.5	65.4
146	Samoa	5.3	5.6	5.4	5.7	6.4	6.6	24.8	24.5	24.1	24.3	23.6	23.8	75.2	75.5	75.9	75.7	76.4	76.2
147	San Marino	10.8	10.9	10.9	11.9	11.6	11.7	14.3	15.4	15.6	14	14.2	14.3	85.7	84.6	84.4	86	85.8	85.7
148	Sao Tome and Principe	3.3	3.5	3	2.9	2.3	2.3	30.6	28.6	33.3	32.1	32.1	32.2	69.4	71.4	66.7	67.9	67.9	67.8
149	Saudi Arabia	5.3	5.1	5.1	5.7	5.4	5.3	21.3	22	21.5	20.9	20.7	20.9	78.7	78	78.5	79.1	79.3	79.1
150	Senegal	4.7	4.9	4.9	4.7	4.7	4.6	47.1	46.8	46.6	44	43.9	43.4	52.9	53.2	53.4	56	56.1	56.6
151	Seychelles	6.2	6.4	6.6	6.7	6.5	6.2	31.5	30.9	27.9	30.6	31.2	33.1	68.5	69.1	72.1	69.4	68.8	66.9
152	Sierra Leone	2.8	2.6	2.8	3	3.5	4.3	59	59	61	58	50	40	41	41	39	42	50	60
153	Singapore	3.7	3.7	3.6	4.1	4	3.5	58.2	59.8	60.5	58	61.2	64.3	41.8	40.2	39.5	42	38.8	35.7
154	Slovakia	7	7.5	6.1	5.9	5.8	5.9	17.9	18.8	8.3	8.4	10.6	10.4	82.1	81.2	91.7	91.6	89.4	89.6
155	Slovenia	9.1	8.8	8.9	8.7	8.7	8.6	21.9	20.6	20.7	21.3	21.4	21.1	78.1	79.4	79.3	78.7	78.6	78.9
156	Solomon Islands	4.3	4.2	4.6	5.3	5.6	5.9	3.8	3.8	4.7	4.2	2.7	5.5	96.2	96.2	95.3	95.8	97.3	94.5
157	Somalia	2.6	2.3	2.4	2	1.6	1.3	57.1	54.6	37.5	37.6	21.1	28.6	42.9	45.4	62.5	62.4	78.9	71.4
158	South Africa	8.4	9.2	9	8.7	8.8	8.8	51.3	53.1	53.9	57.6	57.4	57.8	48.7	46.9	46.1	42.4	42.6	42.2
159	Spain	7.7	7.7	7.6	7.6	7.7	7.7	29.1	28.9	28.9	29.5	29.8	30.1	70.9	71.1	71.1	70.5	70.2	69.9
160	Sri Lanka	3.4	3.3	3.2	3.4	3.6	3.6	51.9	50.4	50.8	49	51.3	51	48.1	49.6	49.2	51	48.7	49
161	Sudan	3.8	3.5	3.3	4.2	4.2	4.7	71.4	71.4	79.1	75.9	75.9	78.8	28.6	28.6	20.9	24.1	24.1	21.2
162	Suriname	8.3	8.8	9.1	9.9	9.7	9.8	23.8	28.9	35.4	38.4	39.3	43.9	76.2	71.1	64.6	61.6	60.7	56.1
163	Swaziland	3.3	3.9	3.3	3.7	4	4.2	27.2	27	28.4	28	30.1	27.9	72.8	73	71.6	72	69.9	72.1
164	Sweden	8.1	8.4	8.1	7.9	8.6	8.4	14.8	15.2	15.7	16.2	22.2	22.7	85.2	84.8	84.3	83.8	77.8	77.3
165	Switzerland	10	10.4	10.4	10.6	10.7	10.7	46.2	45.3	44.8	45.1	44.7	44.4	53.8	54.7	55.2	54.9	55.3	55.6

Table 6.19 (*continued*)

		General government expenditure on health as % of total general government expenditure						External resources for health as % of general government expenditure on health						Social security expenditure on health as % of general government expenditure on health					
		1995	1996	1997	1998	1999	2000	1995	1996	1997	1998	1999	2000	1995	1996	1997	1998	1999	2000
111	Micronesia, Federated States of	9.8	10.2	10.9	10.4	10.4	10.5	7.3	0	0	0	17.9	17.9	0	0	0	0	0	0
112	Monaco	17.6	17.8	17.8	17.9	18.4	18.5	0	0	0	0	0	0	93.3	93.8	93.8	94.1	94.4	94.6
113	Mongolia	16.3	17.4	13.4	14.7	15.2	14	10.9	5.8	6.6	13.8	28.4	24.4	17.8	14.3	36.8	39.9	39.3	40.2
114	Morocco	3.9	4.4	4.3	3.9	4	3.9	6.4	8.8	9.3	8.7	6.7	7.7	9.1	8.2	8.4	9.2	9.1	9.3
115	Mozambique	12.4	17.3	14.8	13.8	13	13.7	55.5	69.7	69.9	68.7	66.8	68.5	0	0	0	0	0	0
116	Myanmar	2.9	2.8	3.2	3.6	4.2	6.5	0.2	3.2	2.5	4.2	2.9	2.3	0.9	1.4	3.1	0.9	1.8	1.8
117	Namibia	12.9	10.2	10.3	10.4	11.3	11.1	3.7	4.4	4.2	5.2	5.7	5.7	0	0	0	0	0	0
118	Nauru	27.1	27.5	27.6	28.6	28.2	29.5	0	0	0	0	0	0	0	0	0	0	0	0
119	Nepal	7.6	7.2	9.3	9.9	9	9	37.1	36	33.9	29.8	34.4	27.5	0	0	0	0	0	0
120	Netherlands	10.6	11.1	11.5	11.7	11.5	12.1	0	0	0	0	0	0	93.6	93.7	93.6	93.8	93.8	94.1
121	New Zealand	12.2	11.5	12.7	13.5	13.9	14.5	0	0	0	0	0	0	0	0	0	0	0	0
122	Nicaragua	28.9	26.6	17	17.9	12.6	10.3	11.9	21.1	19.6	26.5	30.3	30.5	14.4	15.4	24.3	23	27.9	29.7
123	Niger	5	6.4	6.5	6.6	6.5	6.6	30.1	34	40	33.5	34.9	36.7	5.3	4.3	4.5	3.7	4	4
124	Nigeria	1.7	1.3	2.1	2.9	3.2	3	22.4	23	12	37.8	39.6	32.2	0	0	0	0	0	0
125	Niue	12	13.3	13	12.6	15.9	15.6	0	0	0	0	0	0	0	0	0	0	0	0
126	Norway	13.2	13.8	14.3	14.7	15.3	15.8	0	0	0	0	0	0	0	0	0	0	0	0
127	Oman	5.3	6	5.6	5.9	6.1	6.7	0	0	0	0	0	0	0	0	0	0	0	0
128	Pakistan	4.3	3.6	3.8	4.1	4	4	8.8	10.7	10.7	8.1	9.7	8.2	55.1	55	55.1	55.2	55.2	50
129	Palau	8.4	9.3	8.9	9.1	9.3	9.6	20	19.7	21.4	26.2	22.9	22.3	0	0	0	0	0	0
130	Panama	16.9	15.7	18.7	18.5	18.5	18.4	2.1	2	2.1	1.9	1.8	1.7	70.1	69.5	60.6	66.2	58.9	66.4
131	Papua New Guinea	8.7	8.7	9.6	12.3	13.3	12.9	15.2	24.9	30.1	31.9	20.5	24.6	0	0	0	0	0	0
132	Paraguay	11.8	14.9	13.6	14.9	17.4	16.8	0.3	4.8	5	5.1	4.9	5.1	42.1	39	47.8	44.9	46.7	48.3
133	Peru	10.9	11.6	11.7	11.9	12	11.7	3.5	3.2	3.1	3.1	3.7	3.7	42.6	45.4	44	43.5	43.9	44
134	Philippines	6.3	6.5	6.7	6.6	7.1	6.7	6.9	4	3.1	7.6	5.3	6.9	11.4	12.2	11.8	8.8	9	9.9
135	Poland	9.1	10	9.5	9.4	10.6	10.2	0	0	0	0	0	0	0	0	0	0	0	0
136	Portugal	11.4	12	12.5	12.9	13.1	13.1	0	0	0	0	0	0	7.2	6.6	6.7	7.7	7	7.2
137	Qatar	7.8	7.4	7.6	7.8	8.3	6.6	0	0	0	0	0	0	0	0	0	0	0	0
138	Republic of Korea	8.6	9.1	9.4	9.6	10.2	11.2	0	0	0	0	0	0	69.6	71	71.9	74.5	75.2	77.3
139	Republic of Moldova	15.8	18.4	14.9	13	10.2	11	0.4	0.5	0.5	1.7	7.5	13.9	0	0	0	0	0	0
140	Romania	5.3	9.6	7.5	5.5	5.1	5	0.1	0.1	1	0.9	1.5	1.1	30.7	14.5	18.7	21.6	17.5	13.3
141	Russian Federation	11.7	10.4	10.6	12.3	11.9	14.5	0.3	0.4	0.5	1.7	5.8	4.4	28.1	31.5	33.8	36.3	36.9	24.5
142	Rwanda	14	13.3	13.3	13.5	12.9	12.9	29.9	41.4	60.8	53.8	54.2	48.2	0.8	0.7	0.6	0.6	0.7	0.8
143	Saint Kitts and Nevis	9.7	9.7	10.9	10.9	10.6	10.6	13.1	11.4	10.8	10.3	10.1	9.3	0	0	0	0	0	0
144	Saint Lucia	8	8.9	9	8.8	7.9	7.8	1.2	1	1	0.8	0.8	0.8	0	0	0	0	0	0
145	Saint Vincent and the Grenadines	13.1	12.1	9.2	8.7	9	9.7	3.1	3	2.8	2.7	2.5	2.2	0	0	0	0	0	0
146	Samoa	16.4	16.9	18.2	19.7	19.5	19.3	14.2	10.8	9.5	13.6	15	32.2	0	0	0	0	0	0
147	San Marino	24.2	24.2	22.7	26.4	25.6	26.2	0	0	0	0	0	0	25.1	26	26.5	25.2	26.5	27
148	Sao Tome and Principe	2.9	3.7	2.9	3.6	3.6	3.6	44.9	36.4	71.3	75.1	89.8	71.8	0	0	0	0	0	0
149	Saudi Arabia	13.3	14	12.2	11.1	13.9	14.6	0	0	0	0	0	0	0	0	0	0	0	0
150	Senegal	13.1	13.2	13.1	13.1	13.1	13	18.4	10.8	11.8	10.7	13.3	14.3	0	0	0	0	0	0
151	Seychelles	8.2	7.8	8.7	7.9	8	6.8	1.3	1.3	4.9	5.6	5.7	5.7	0	0	0	0	0	0
152	Sierra Leone	7.1	7.2	6.5	9	8.3	9.2	19.8	23.6	19.1	27.9	22	26.7	0	0	0	0	0	0
153	Singapore	9.4	6.9	6.7	8.7	8.2	6.7	0	0	0	0	0	0	19.1	19.6	20.2	17.5	19.1	23.3
154	Slovakia	15.8	18.2	18.3	18.6	18.5	19.4	0	0	0	0.1	0	0	87.9	96.9	96.7	96.6	96.7	96.8
155	Slovenia	16.4	16.5	16.3	15.6	15.4	15.4	0	0	0	0	0	0.8	74.5	76.8	77	80.7	79.8	82
156	Solomon Islands	8.9	9	11.4	11.4	11.1	11.4	12.5	11.6	7.7	8.3	7.6	17.7	0	0	0	0	0	0
157	Somalia	4.1	3.8	5.6	4.5	4.4	3.3	22.5	14.7	7.4	10.5	5.1	1.3	0	0	0	0	0	0
158	South Africa	12.6	12.6	12.4	11.3	11.1	11.2	0.1	0.2	0.2	0.2	0.2	0.2	0	0	0	0	0	0
159	Spain	12.2	12.6	12.9	12.9	13.2	13.5	0	0	0	0	0	0	23.8	20.2	13.5	11.6	9.2	0
160	Sri Lanka	5.4	5.7	6	5.8	5.7	6.1	4.6	6.7	6.4	5.5	5.6	5.5	0	0	0	0	0	0
161	Sudan	5	4.4	3	4.2	4.2	4.2	2.6	2.5	4.2	4.5	6.8	6	0	0	0	0	0	0
162	Suriname	19.4	19	20.3	18.2	17.6	16.5	20.6	14.4	11.4	18.6	42.7	25.2	24	28.9	25.8	25	24.4	22.7
163	Swaziland	8	7.9	7.9	8.1	8	8.6	5.5	4.7	6.6	6.3	3.7	3.4	0	0	0	0	0	0
164	Sweden	10.2	10.8	10.8	10.9	11	11.3	0	0	0	0	0	0	0	0	0	0	0	0
165	Switzerland	14.5	15.2	15.3	15.4	11.9	12.7	0	0	0	0	0	0	70	70.5	71.6	72.3	72.1	72.7

Table 6.19 (*continued*)

	Member State	Total expenditure on health as % of GDP						Private expenditure on health as % of total expenditure on health						General government expenditure on health as % of total expenditure on health					
		1995	1996	1997	1998	1999	2000	1995	1996	1997	1998	1999	2000	1995	1996	1997	1998	1999	2000
166	Syrian Arab Republic	2	2	2.1	2.3	2.5	2.5	23.9	28.1	31.2	33.4	35.2	36.6	76.1	71.9	68.8	66.6	64.8	63.4
167	Tajikistan	2	2.9	3	2.5	2.8	2.5	39.5	36.9	34	35	15.4	19.2	60.5	63.1	66	65	84.6	80.8
168	Thailand	3.4	3.6	3.7	3.9	3.7	3.7	51.1	48.9	42.8	38.6	41.7	42.6	48.9	51.1	57.2	61.4	58.3	57.4
169	The former Yugoslav Republic of Macedonia	5.2	5.8	6.1	7.6	5.9	6	9.4	13	16.1	12.9	15.9	15.5	90.6	87	83.9	87.1	84.1	84.5
170	Togo	2.9	2.6	3.1	2.7	2.7	2.8	52.4	58.4	51.5	44.8	42.9	45.7	47.6	41.6	48.5	55.2	57.1	54.3
171	Tonga	7.5	7.3	7.9	7.7	7.8	7.5	56.7	56.7	53.2	53.9	54.1	53.2	43.3	43.3	46.8	46.1	45.9	46.8
172	Trinidad and Tobago	4.5	4.6	4.8	5.3	5.3	5.2	49.5	51.2	52.5	49.1	49	49.3	50.5	48.8	47.5	50.9	51	50.7
173	Tunisia	6.8	6.6	6.4	6.8	7	7	43.9	32.5	22.3	20.9	21.2	21.8	56.1	67.5	77.7	79.1	78.8	78.2
174	Turkey	3.4	3.9	4.2	4.8	4.9	5	29.7	30.8	28.4	28.1	28.9	28.9	70.3	69.2	71.6	71.9	71.1	71.1
175	Turkmenistan	2.4	2.8	4	5	5.3	5.4	22.9	18.6	25.5	18.9	17.4	15.1	77.1	81.4	74.5	81.1	82.6	84.9
176	Tuvalu	8.9	8.3	8.4	8.6	8.8	7.8	29.1	31.3	30.2	29.3	29.3	28.6	70.9	68.8	69.8	70.7	70.7	71.4
177	Uganda	3.5	3.4	3.4	3.7	4	3.9	60.5	56.7	54.8	62	58.1	62	39.5	43.3	45.2	38	41.9	38
178	Ukraine	5.8	5	5.4	5.1	4.3	4.1	16	20.4	25	28.9	31.9	29.9	84	79.6	75	71.1	68.1	70.1
179	United Arab Emirates	3.4	3.2	3.7	4.1	3.7	3.2	20.1	20.6	20.7	20.3	21.4	22.3	79.9	79.4	79.3	79.7	78.6	77.7
180	United Kingdom	7	7	6.8	6.8	7.1	7.3	16.1	17.1	20.1	20.1	19.8	19	83.9	82.9	79.9	79.9	80.2	81
181	United Republic of Tanzania	5.3	5.1	5.2	5	5.5	5.9	44.6	51.2	51.9	51.3	56.6	53	55.4	48.8	48.1	48.7	43.4	47
182	United States of America	13.3	13.2	13	12.9	13	13	54.7	54.5	54.8	55.5	55.7	55.7	45.3	45.5	45.2	44.5	44.3	44.3
183	Uruguay	9.2	9.6	10	10.2	10.8	10.9	50.5	53	54.1	53.6	51.3	53.5	49.5	47	45.9	46.4	48.7	46.5
184	Uzbekistan	4.8	4.8	4.5	3.9	3.9	3.7	22.7	17.5	17.9	15.3	21.2	22.5	77.3	82.5	82.1	84.7	78.8	77.5
185	Vanuatu	3.3	2.8	3.3	3.5	3.9	3.9	33.9	42.4	35.8	34.6	39.7	39.1	66.1	57.6	64.2	65.4	60.3	60.9
186	Venezuela, Bolivarian Republic of	4.6	3.9	4.3	5	4.6	4.7	47.7	47.7	45.4	48.4	47.4	42.6	52.3	52.3	54.6	51.6	52.6	57.4
187	Viet Nam	3.9	4.6	4.5	4.7	5.5	5.2	59.6	65.2	68.8	70.9	75.6	74.2	40.4	34.8	31.2	29.1	24.4	25.8
188	Yemen	5.1	4.4	4.6	5.2	5	5	77.7	71.6	69.8	64	67.8	68	22.3	28.4	30.2	36	32.2	32
189	Yugoslavia	6.5	7.1	6.7	5.6	5.6	5.6	42.1	42.6	41.4	49.1	49.1	49	57.9	57.4	58.6	50.9	50.9	51
190	Zambia	5.2	5.8	6	5.6	5.2	5.6	46.9	46.8	44.9	43.1	40.7	37.9	53.1	53.2	55.1	56.9	59.3	62.1
191	Zimbabwe	7.1	7.5	9.3	11.4	8.1	7.3	49	45.4	40.9	44.1	51.1	57.4	51	54.6	59.1	55.9	48.9	42.6

Table 6.19 (*continued*)

		General government expenditure on health as % of total general government expenditure						External resources for health as % of general government expenditure on health						Social security expenditure on health as % of general government expenditure on health					
		1995	1996	1997	1998	1999	2000	1995	1996	1997	1998	1999	2000	1995	1996	1997	1998	1999	2000
166	Syrian Arab Republic	5.4	5.2	5.2	5.1	5.2	6	0.7	0.5	1.1	0.8	0.5	0.4	0	0	0	0	0	0
167	Tajikistan	4.9	10.1	9.4	9.6	11.4	11.3	28.1	10.3	11.3	13.7	4.4	19.5	0	0	0	0	0	0
168	Thailand	8.1	9.6	10.9	13.3	11.4	11.4	0.2	0.6	0.5	0.7	0.9	0.9	26.5	27.9	30.2	25.8	26.3	26.4
169	The former Yugoslav Republic of Macedonia	12.6	13.6	14.5	19	14.8	15.6	1.4	2.8	3.1	3	3.4	3.7	98	95.1	96.3	96.8	93.8	87.5
170	Togo	4.9	3.8	5.4	5.3	5.7	5.2	31.9	39.8	27.5	30.9	25.6	28	0	0	0	0	0	0
171	Tonga	12	12.2	13.1	14.2	14.2	14	2.9	2.8	9.3	9.2	8.2	16.8	0	0	0	0	0	0
172	Trinidad and Tobago	7.9	8	7.9	8	8.1	8	0.1	0.1	10.1	8.2	7.9	7.6	16.7	16.9	16.8	16.6	16.6	16.7
173	Tunisia	11.5	13.5	15.7	16.9	17.3	17.2	1.2	0.9	0.9	0.7	0.6	0.7	37.2	42.2	45.3	47.1	47.8	47.6
174	Turkey	10.7	10	10.8	11.5	9.1	9	0.9	0.9	0.6	0.5	0.1	0.1	33.8	29.7	38.8	43.8	28.4	28.4
175	Turkmenistan	7.9	13.9	11.7	16.7	19.5	20.2	0.8	1.7	3.3	3.2	1.9	0.8	8.4	6.3	9.9	14	21.1	18.9
176	Tuvalu	12.6	13.4	5.6	6.5	7.9	6.8	6.5	5.6	5.4	5.9	5.3	5.5	0	0	0	0	0	0
177	Uganda	9.2	9.2	9.2	9.2	10.8	9.5	84	80.4	81.9	49	75.1	96	0	0	0	0	0	0
178	Ukraine	11.4	9.8	9.3	8	8.3	7.6	0.3	0.4	0.8	0.5	0.2	0	0	0	0	0	0	0
179	United Arab Emirates	6.5	7.2	7.9	7.4	7.2	6.3	0	0	0	0	0	0	0	0	0	0	0	0
180	United Kingdom	13.1	13.5	13.2	13.7	14.6	14.9	0	0	0	0	0	0	11.3	11.3	11.9	12.2	11.6	11.2
181	United Republic of Tanzania	14.7	15.1	15.5	12.5	12.2	11.4	31.7	34.4	39.2	44.2	48.5	41.9	0	0	0	0	0	0
182	United States of America	16.8	17	17.2	16.8	16.7	16.7	0	0	0	0	0	0	32.1	32.8	32.2	33.4	33.3	33.7
183	Uruguay	14.8	15.3	13.7	14.2	15.1	14.8	1.9	1.5	1.3	1.3	1.3	1	70.1	63.6	51.7	53	36.9	34.8
184	Uzbekistan	9.7	9.5	11.1	10	9.9	9.6	0.7	0.8	1.2	1.5	1.7	1.3	0	0	0	0	0	0
185	Vanuatu	8	6.3	8.8	7.3	9.3	9.4	32.3	41.8	32.2	46.6	45.1	46.8	0	0	0	0	0	0
186	Venezuela, Bolivarian Republic of	10.7	10	9.4	10.9	10.9	10.9	4.3	4.1	3	2.4	2.4	0.9	18.6	33.1	27.7	28.6	31.4	31.3
187	Viet Nam	6.6	6.7	6.2	6.8	6.4	6.5	6.6	10.8	13.7	15.6	12.5	12.3	0.8	1	1.2	1.3	1.6	1.5
188	Yemen	5	4.1	4.1	4.8	5.4	5.4	6.1	8.9	8.1	7.8	9.1	8.1	0	0	0	0	0	0
189	Yugoslavia	18.3	13	13.8	10.5	10.5	10.5	0	0	0	0.2	0.8	6.2	0	0	0	0	0	0
190	Zambia	11.5	14.6	13.1	12.5	12.3	11.2	22	34.7	40.3	43.2	21.3	24.8	0	0	0	0	0	0
191	Zimbabwe	10.1	11.6	15.4	17.9	10	6.3	16.4	13.4	8.6	6.8	12	17.4	0	0	0	0	0	0

a. A zero does not always mean "not applicable"; when no information has been collated to estimate an entry, say private insurance and other prepaid plans, that entry is shown as zero.

b. There is a break in the series for Japan between 1997 and 1998. Since 1998, data have been based on new Japanese national health accounts, estimated as a pilot implementation of the ORD manual *A System of Health Accounts*. Consequently, the comparability of data over time is limited. In addition, the data for the year 2000 have been largely developed by WHO and are not endorsed by the Government of Japan.

Source: World Health Organization. (2002). *World Health Report 2002: Reducing risks, promoting healthy life.* Geneva: Author. Retrieved from http://www.who.int/whr/2002/en/.

Table 6.20
Selected National Health Accounts Indicators for All Member States,
Estimates for 1995 to 2000[a]—Second Set of Indicators

These figures were produced by WHO using the best available evidence. They are not necessarily the official statistics of Member States.

Member State	Out-of-pocket expenditure % of total expenditure on health						Prepaid plans as % of private expenditure on health						Per capita total expenditure on health at average exchange rate (US$)					
	1995	1996	1997	1998	1999	2000	1995	1996	1997	1998	1999	2000	1995	1996	1997	1998	1999	2000
1 Afghanistan	50	50	47.4	42.3	43.1	36.5	0	0	0	0	0	0	13	5	6	8	9	8
2 Albania	19.6	17.8	20.2	21.1	21.2	23.8	12.8	43.2	43.1	41.1	40	36.4	26	31	23	33	40	41
3 Algeria	20.7	18.8	19.7	19.3	18.3	17.4	0	0	0	0	0	0	73	73	69	72	69	64
4 Andorra	13.3	13.3	13.4	11	13.2	13.5	0	0	0	0	0	0	1330	1246	1218	1434	1120	953
5 Angola	50.5	48.5	54.8	60.2	55.8	44.1	0	0	0	0	0	0	22	22	25	18	16	24
6 Antigua and Barbuda	36.4	38.2	38.1	37.5	38.7	40.1	0	0	0	0	0	0	438	477	484	506	533	562
7 Argentina	28.3	30.2	32.3	33.5	33.4	34.1	27.8	27	26	25.1	24.6	24.2	610	612	643	662	656	658
8 Armenia	60.3	56.6	58.5	57.1	58.7	57.7	0	0	0	0	0	0	27	33	34	37	37	38
9 Australia	15.9	16.5	16	18.4	17.6	16.8	32.7	31.9	29.9	27	26.3	25.9	1686	1884	1879	1683	1796	1698
10 Austria	14.6	15.2	17.3	16.8	18.2	18.6	28.1	25.1	26.6	25.6	23.8	23.2	2508	2489	2016	2096	2085	1872
11 Azerbaijan	22.3	28	26.6	26.9	51.1	55.8	0	0	0	0	0	0	9	9	11	13	14	14
12 Bahamas	43.7	41.2	44.4	42.4	43.7	44.5	0	0	0	0	0	0	587	650	701	752	790	880
13 Bahrain	21.2	22	20.9	21.2	21.5	21.6	24.2	25.2	25.4	26.2	26	26.3	464	462	502	501	504	512
14 Bangladesh	66.1	62.1	60.7	59.7	59.6	59.7	0	0	0	0	0	0	9	11	11	12	13	14
15 Barbados	24.6	24.2	26.6	27.7	27.7	27.1	24.2	24.2	24.2	23.7	23	23	445	462	489	504	542	606
16 Belarus	15.2	15.1	12.5	14.8	17.5	17.2	0	0	0	0	0	0	58	77	85	80	68	57
17 Belgium	13.4	13.5	13.7	13.9	13.6	16	6	7	6.8	6.9	6.9	6.8	2368	2341	2034	2095	2120	1936
18 Belize	57.8	59.1	57.1	54.1	55.2	54.5	0	0	0	0	0	0	111	108	118	126	147	158
19 Benin	48.8	50.4	51.4	50.5	50.2	50	0	0	0	0	0	0	11	12	11	12	12	11
20 Bhutan	9.7	11.7	9.6	9.7	10.4	9.4	0	0	0	0	0	0	5	6	7	8	8	9
21 Bolivia	26.3	24.5	27.2	29.5	29	22.7	13.2	13.3	9.1	7.8	8.1	9.5	40	45	46	53	53	67
22 Bosnia and Herzegovina	53.8	47.1	44.6	42.9	37.3	31	0	0	0	0	0	0	27	33	37	43	47	50
23 Botswana	12.6	13.1	11.4	12.1	12.1	11	29.3	24.9	24.1	23.8	22.8	21.6	168	164	177	168	176	191
24 Brazil	39	40.9	37.8	37.5	38.3	38.5	32	31.4	33.1	33.1	32.9	35.1	319	355	365	351	248	267
25 Brunei Darussalam	20	19.4	20.6	18.7	20.6	20	0	0	0	0	0	0	459	475	432	467	490	490
26 Bulgaria	18.1	19.2	18.9	20.6	21.1	22.4	0	0	0	0	0	0	69	46	54	60	63	59
27 Burkina Faso	39	33.7	31.6	31	28.4	29.3	0	0	0	0	0	0	7	9	8	9	9	8
28 Burundi	52.1	47	48.5	47.6	47.3	46.9	0	0	0	0	0	0	6	5	4	4	3	3
29 Cambodia	79	76.7	77	76.5	76.2	75.5	0	0	0	0	0	0	18	20	21	19	19	19
30 Cameroon	70.4	70.3	69.7	68.7	67	66.3	0	0	0	0	0	0	27	28	26	29	25	24
31 Canada	15.8	16.1	16.8	16.2	16.1	15.5	71.9	73.1	73.7	77.2	76.4	70.7	1821	1831	1868	1839	1939	2058
32 Cape Verde	22.2	28.6	30.7	31	31.1	31.5	0	0	0	0	0	0	31	33	31	35	34	30
33 Central African Republic	39	39.9	38.3	39.5	43.4	41.6	0	0	0	0	0	0	7	6	7	7	8	8
34 Chad	20.7	20	20.7	21.4	21.4	20.2	0	0	0	0	0	0	6	7	7	7	6	6
35 Chile	42.7	41.9	41.2	40	38.8	34.3	33.8	33.8	33.7	33.8	34.5	40.2	307	329	371	369	331	336
36 China	50.2	54.3	56.5	57.3	58.9	60.4	0	0	0.4	0.6	0.4	0.4	22	28	33	36	40	45
37 Colombia	32.3	28	25.9	27.7	28.4	29	23.8	31.5	38.9	38.6	38.6	34.4	178	218	247	226	202	186
38 Comoros	32.6	31.6	31.8	28.2	28.3	28.4	0	0	0	0	0	0	17	16	13	15	15	13
39 Congo	31.9	31.8	35.4	43.7	32.7	29.8	0	0	0	0	0	0	27	26	24	24	22	22
40 Cook Islands	21.1	33.3	32.9	31.7	36.6	37.2	0	0	0	0	0	0	329	270	273	237	208	188
41 Costa Rica	26.6	27.6	28.4	28.9	26.8	27.5	8	7.7	6.9	6.4	6.9	6.3	206	200	214	236	246	273
42 Côte d'Ivoire	45.8	49.3	50.3	50	55.5	55	18.6	16	14.9	14	12.9	12.9	20	21	19	20	19	16
43 Croatia	19.1	18.2	19.5	18.2	17.2	15.4	0	0	0	0	0	0	348	382	354	408	369	353
44 Cuba	9.8	10.5	12.5	12.4	11.4	10.8	0	0	0	0	0	0	112	121	131	138	157	169
45 Cyprus	44.6	48	48.7	46.9	46.7	46.2	0	0	0	0	0	0	839	911	913	933	925	888
46 Czech Republic	7.3	7.5	8.3	8.1	8.5	8.6	0	0	0	0	0	0	367	395	364	392	380	358
47 Democratic People's Republic of Korea	20.1	19.5	16.5	16.5	17.6	22.7	0	0	0	0	0	0	8	14	14	14	14	18
48 Democratic Republic of the Congo	35.7	30	25.9	25.9	26.2	26.3	0	0	0	0	0	0	11	9	26	14	19	9
49 Denmark	16.3	16.2	16.3	16.6	16.2	16.4	6.7	7.7	7.9	8.2	8.8	8.9	2830	2885	2639	2737	2791	2512
50 Djibouti	14.9	15	16.5	16	15.4	15.6	0	0	0	0	0	0	45	44	39	41	42	41
51 Dominica	26.9	26.6	23.7	24.1	24.5	24.4	16.7	16.7	17.6	16.7	16.1	16.1	194	207	216	221	246	247
52 Dominican Republic	57	55.9	54.7	54.6	53.6	55.6	12.7	14.2	13.1	14.2	13	12.8	98	111	122	126	134	151
53 Ecuador	32.6	28.9	25.8	29	36.5	37.5	14.1	12.4	10.5	10.5	9.4	8.5	72	83	77	70	43	26
54 Egypt	51	50.4	49.5	49.5	49.3	49.6	0.4	0.5	0.5	0.6	0.5	0.5	36	41	46	48	52	51
55 El Salvador	58.3	57.6	59.5	55.5	56.2	55.4	1.2	2	2.7	3.3	2.7	2.7	111	135	153	164	172	184

Table 6.20 (*continued*)

		Per capita total expenditure on health in international dollars						Per capita government expenditure on health at average exchange rate (US$)						Per capita government expenditure on health in international dollars					
		1995	1996	1997	1998	1999	2000	1995	1996	1997	1998	1999	2000	1995	1996	1997	1998	1999	2000
1	Afghanistan	17	8	8	10	10	9	6	3	3	5	5	5	9	4	4	6	6	5
2	Albania	89	108	91	104	117	129	20	21	15	21	26	26	68	73	58	66	75	80
3	Algeria	158	149	146	163	162	142	58	59	55	58	56	53	125	121	117	131	132	117
4	Andorra	1915	1725	1874	2143	1654	1639	1154	1081	1055	1277	973	824	1661	1496	1622	1908	1436	1418
5	Angola	58	52	55	49	46	52	11	11	11	7	7	13	29	27	25	19	21	29
6	Antigua and Barbuda	480	513	523	540	578	629	279	295	300	316	327	337	305	317	324	338	354	377
7	Argentina	886	906	977	1037	1067	1091	372	359	363	366	365	362	539	532	551	574	595	600
8	Armenia	142	154	161	164	178	192	11	14	14	16	15	16	56	67	67	70	74	81
9	Australia	1765	1855	1951	2059	2141	2213	1132	1255	1287	1175	1277	1229	1185	1236	1336	1437	1523	1601
10	Austria	1831	1936	1869	1965	2063	2171	1801	1756	1430	1497	1460	1305	1315	1366	1326	1404	1445	1513
11	Azerbaijan	49	41	44	51	57	57	7	6	8	9	7	6	38	29	33	37	28	25
12	Bahamas	677	772	828	921	1033	1137	331	382	389	434	445	488	381	454	460	531	582	631
13	Bahrain	683	686	728	747	705	641	326	318	354	350	349	354	480	473	513	521	488	443
14	Bangladesh	34	40	42	42	46	47	3	4	4	4	5	5	11	14	15	15	17	17
15	Barbados	782	760	765	741	795	915	300	314	317	321	347	393	528	517	496	472	509	593
16	Belarus	290	297	380	363	405	430	49	66	74	68	56	47	246	252	332	309	334	356
17	Belgium	1900	1981	2011	2006	2142	2269	1648	1682	1435	1480	1507	1379	1322	1423	1419	1417	1524	1616
18	Belize	188	184	207	223	254	273	47	44	50	58	66	72	79	75	89	102	114	124
19	Benin	21	22	23	25	26	27	6	6	6	6	6	6	11	11	11	12	13	14
20	Bhutan	34	42	48	52	54	64	4	5	7	7	7	8	31	38	43	47	48	58
21	Bolivia	94	104	99	115	120	158	26	31	31	35	35	48	61	70	67	75	79	114
22	Bosnia and Herzegovina	109	127	156	230	271	319	12	18	20	25	30	34	50	67	86	131	170	221
23	Botswana	245	269	272	276	315	358	88	85	100	98	104	120	128	139	154	160	187	226
24	Brazil	476	503	531	533	566	631	136	143	159	154	106	109	203	203	231	234	243	257
25	Brunei Darussalam	461	480	529	576	615	618	367	383	343	380	389	392	369	387	420	468	488	495
26	Bulgaria	241	191	204	192	196	198	56	37	43	48	49	46	197	154	165	153	155	154
27	Burkina Faso	22	27	30	31	37	37	4	6	6	6	7	6	13	18	21	22	26	26
28	Burundi	17	14	12	14	13	16	3	2	2	2	2	2	8	8	6	7	7	8
29	Cambodia	79	93	105	105	105	111	4	5	5	4	5	5	16	22	24	25	25	27
30	Cameroon	46	48	50	49	52	55	6	6	6	6	6	6	9	10	11	11	12	13
31	Canada	2114	2092	2184	2287	2428	2534	1299	1296	1312	1302	1373	1483	1509	1482	1535	1619	1719	1826
32	Cape Verde	63	69	70	81	87	92	24	23	21	24	23	20	49	49	49	56	60	63
33	Central African Republic	23	21	27	29	34	37	4	3	3	4	4	4	12	10	13	14	16	18
34	Chad	18	19	19	19	18	19	5	6	5	5	5	4	14	15	15	15	14	15
35	Chile	507	566	640	687	670	697	109	121	141	146	135	143	180	208	242	272	274	297
36	China	94	113	135	153	177	205	10	12	13	14	15	17	44	48	54	60	67	75
37	Colombia	452	547	598	600	610	616	103	129	142	124	109	104	260	324	344	329	328	344
38	Comoros	41	39	37	37	35	35	11	11	9	11	10	9	27	27	25	27	25	25
39	Congo	39	31	30	39	31	25	18	18	15	14	15	15	26	21	20	22	21	18
40	Cook Islands	482	400	436	447	432	426	260	180	183	162	132	118	380	267	293	305	274	267
41	Costa Rica	385	378	403	445	466	481	141	134	143	157	169	187	263	254	269	296	320	329
42	Côte d'Ivoire	40	42	43	44	44	45	9	9	8	9	7	6	17	17	18	18	16	16
43	Croatia	487	547	539	606	597	638	282	313	285	334	305	299	394	447	434	495	494	540
44	Cuba	125	141	158	165	181	186	101	108	114	121	139	150	112	126	139	144	161	166
45	Cyprus	987	1106	1217	1242	1292	1415	465	474	468	495	493	478	547	575	624	659	689	762
46	Czech Republic	902	917	930	944	972	1031	340	366	334	360	347	327	836	848	853	867	889	942
47	Democratic People's Republic of Korea	32	33	37	40	38	33	6	12	12	11	12	14	25	27	31	33	31	26
48	Democratic Republic of the Congo	32	31	27	28	24	21	7	7	19	10	14	6	21	22	20	21	18	16
49	Denmark	1882	2009	2106	2247	2364	2428	2335	2378	2171	2242	2295	2061	1553	1656	1733	1841	1944	1992
50	Djibouti	63	62	58	60	62	63	23	22	18	19	20	20	32	30	26	28	30	31
51	Dominica	281	297	312	321	347	340	131	141	154	157	174	175	190	202	222	228	246	241
52	Dominican Republic	187	212	289	309	331	357	26	30	35	36	41	42	49	57	84	87	101	100
53	Ecuador	148	167	157	145	122	78	40	52	46	39	21	13	82	104	95	81	60	39
54	Egypt	100	110	121	127	133	138	16	18	21	22	24	24	44	49	55	58	61	64
55	El Salvador	255	296	331	346	367	388	45	55	59	70	72	79	104	121	128	147	155	167

Table 6.20 (*continued*)

#	Member State	Out-of-pocket expenditure % of total expenditure on health						Prepaid plans as % of private expenditure on health						Per capita total expenditure on health at average exchange rate (US$)					
		1995	1996	1997	1998	1999	2000	1995	1996	1997	1998	1999	2000	1995	1996	1997	1998	1999	2000
56	Equatorial Guinea	34.8	44.4	44	40.6	32.4	32.4	0	0	0	0	0	0	18	29	41	46	50	54
57	Eritrea	14.9	12.9	34.2	33.9	35.7	34.4	0	0	0	0	0	0	6	7	9	10	9	9
58	Estonia	8.6	10	11.3	13.2	14	19.7	0	0	0	0	4.1	4.1	206	215	203	218	239	218
59	Ethiopia	57	52.7	54.4	49.1	51.5	51.6	0	0	0	0	0	0	4	4	5	5	5	5
60	Fiji	35	33.8	33.3	34.6	34.8	34.8	0	0	0	0	0	0	98	106	106	82	85	80
61	Finland	20.5	20.3	19.9	19.6	20.4	20.6	11.7	11.8	12.2	12.5	12	12	1919	1912	1745	1733	1710	1559
62	France	11.1	10.6	10.5	10.4	10.3	10.2	49.5	51.5	51.7	52.3	52.7	53.1	2566	2545	2260	2303	2282	2057
63	Gabon	33.8	33.7	33.5	36.5	38.8	31.4	0	0	0	0	0	0	140	152	138	128	122	120
64	Gambia	18.6	18.6	18.2	17.9	17.1	17.6	0	0	0	0	0	0	13	12	13	14	11	10
65	Georgia	87.1	86.1	85.3	86.7	89.8	89.5	0	0	0	0	0	0	26	40	46	49	36	41
66	Germany	10	10.1	10.8	11.2	10.9	10.6	51.6	50.4	49.8	48.8	49.7	50.3	3194	3162	2775	2773	2729	2422
67	Ghana	56.6	56	55.2	48.5	48.1	46.5	0	0	0	0	0	0	16	16	15	17	17	11
68	Greece	35.2	38.6	36.9	36.6	35.7	37.4	4.8	4.9	4.9	4.7	4.6	4.9	998	1044	1006	1002	1034	884
69	Grenada	33.4	31.7	33.9	34.2	30.3	29.9	0	0	0	0	0	0	132	152	159	180	196	212
70	Guatemala	51.9	53.2	50.9	48.7	44.3	44.8	3.8	3.7	3.8	4.4	5.4	5.2	60	64	73	79	78	79
71	Guinea	45.7	45.6	42.8	39.6	37.5	42.9	0	0	0	0	0	0	18	18	18	17	17	13
72	Guinea-Bissau	37.9	36.1	36	34.9	34.2	34.6	0	0	0	0	0	0	15	12	9	10	10	9
73	Guyana	17.6	17.5	16.5	16.6	16	17.3	0	0	0	0	0	0	39	43	48	48	44	48
74	Haiti	18.7	20.3	20.8	20.1	21.2	22	0	0	0	0	0	0	18	18	20	23	24	21
75	Honduras	47.4	45.5	42.4	34.9	38.4	36.8	0.2	0.1	0.2	0.2	0.2	0.2	48	48	49	57	54	62
76	Hungary	16	18.4	18.7	17.4	18.8	21.2	0	0	0	0.2	0.5	0.8	327	320	314	323	328	315
77	Iceland	15.5	16.1	16.3	16.1	15.2	15.6	0	0	0	0	0	0	2139	2199	2162	2476	2705	2729
78	India	83.8	84.4	84.3	81.6	82.1	82.2	0	0	0	0	0	0	20	21	23	22	23	23
79	Indonesia	43.8	58.1	73	67.9	64.5	70.1	30.1	19.5	4.3	6.7	10.4	8.2	17	26	26	11	17	19
80	Iran, Islamic Republic of	52.1	49.2	51.6	51.6	50.4	50.9	1.3	1.4	1.3	1.8	1.9	1.9	92	117	139	160	211	258
81	Iraq	40.7	41.8	41.1	40.9	40	40.1	0	0	0	0	0	0	147	163	242	286	348	375
82	Ireland	15.6	13.5	13	12.1	11.7	11	24	25.6	26.4	27.1	24.5	23.8	1354	1394	1500	1587	1707	1692
83	Israel	22.2	21.4	21.3	23	22.3	24.1	0	0	0	0	0	0	1653	1823	1819	1767	1888	2021
84	Italy	24.4	24.2	24.1	24.5	24	22.9	3.5	3.6	3.6	3.3	3.4	3.4	1415	1605	1571	1599	1605	1498
85	Jamaica	35.5	35.9	35.2	33.8	34.6	36.6	34	32.7	32.6	32.6	31	31	104	116	142	155	171	165
86	Japan[b]	20.8	19.8	16.2	17.7	17.1	19.3	0	0	0	1.3	1.3	1.4	2950	2594	2467	2213	2631	2908
87	Jordan	42.1	41.6	33.7	33.5	34.4	37.6	4.1	4.3	5.8	5.9	6.2	6.1	148	149	135	137	137	137
88	Kazakhstan	18.2	23.7	23.6	29.4	29.1	26.8	0	0	0	0	0	0	63	72	81	66	46	44
89	Kenya	52	51.5	52.8	53.1	52.8	56.4	4.5	4.5	4.6	4.5	4.4	4.5	27	27	31	33	29	28
90	Kiribati	0.9	0.9	0.9	0.8	0.8	1.3	0	0	0	0	0	0	53	56	55	47	49	44
91	Kuwait	10	13	12.6	12.9	13.2	12.8	0	0	0	0	0	0	563	571	580	564	557	586
92	Kyrgyzstan	11.9	19.2	20.3	28.1	33.4	38.3	0	0	0	0	0	0	26	26	24	23	16	16
93	Lao People's Democratic Republic	52.9	58	61.5	64	63	62	0	0	0	0	0	0	11	11	13	8	10	11
94	Latvia	34.6	36.9	38.2	38.9	37.1	40	0	0	0	0	0	0	115	129	142	164	176	174
95	Lebanon	58.1	57.9	58.5	59.6	59.3	58.6	16.6	16.5	16.7	15.4	15.8	16.4	375	431	504	534	590	590
96	Lesotho	21.3	22	24	21.7	18.8	17.7	0	0	0	0	0	0	31	28	28	27	29	28
97	Liberia	26.7	27.7	26.6	23.3	20.8	20	0	0	0	0	0	0	1	1	1	1	2	2
98	Libyan Arab Jamahiriya	59.5	58.1	50	50	50.9	51.4	0	0	0	0	0	0	334	352	328	327	241	246
99	Lithuania	13.7	23.1	22.3	23.3	24.9	27.6	0	0	0	0	0	0	84	116	154	183	176	185
100	Luxembourg	6.2	7.2	7.4	7.6	7	6.7	18.8	20.3	21.4	21.3	20.3	17.5	2812	2792	2454	2573	2732	2514
101	Madagascar	36.5	35.3	14.1	34.4	31.1	25.3	9.6	9.8	26.8	9.7	10.3	10.3	6	8	5	7	7	9
102	Malawi	10.5	19.4	17.5	17	17.6	23	2	1.6	1.6	2.2	2.2	1.8	9	15	18	12	11	11
103	Malaysia	43.9	41.7	42.4	42.3	40.2	41.2	0	0	0	0	0	0	99	116	110	84	90	101
104	Maldives	16.2	15.5	18.1	18.2	17.5	16.6	0	0	0	0	0	0	64	74	83	85	95	100
105	Mali	42.3	43.6	48.7	46.7	46.6	48.3	0	0	0	0	0	0	8	8	10	11	11	10
106	Malta	28.6	30	32.1	30.7	32.5	31.5	0	0	0	0	0	0	714	739	747	761	782	807
107	Marshall Islands	38.8	38.3	38.1	38.4	38.9	38.6	0	0	0	0	0	0	162	167	171	173	178	172
108	Mauritania	25.5	24	26.7	27.2	24.1	20.7	0	0	0	0	0	0	15	15	14	14	15	14
109	Mauritius	45.9	47	46.7	46.2	43.3	43.7	0	0	0	0	0	0	128	137	127	122	131	134
110	Mexico	55.2	54.2	53.2	47.9	48.8	49.5	2.7	2.7	2.7	4	3.8	3.8	177	189	227	234	267	311

Table 6.20 (*continued*)

		Per capita total expenditure on health in international dollars						Per capita government expenditure on health at average exchange rate (US$)						Per capita government expenditure on health in international dollars					
		1995	1996	1997	1998	1999	2000	1995	1996	1997	1998	1999	2000	1995	1996	1997	1998	1999	2000
56	Equatorial Guinea	48	68	67	95	89	103	11	16	23	27	34	37	31	38	38	56	60	70
57	Eritrea	17	21	26	33	25	25	5	6	6	7	6	6	15	19	17	22	16	16
58	Estonia	531	481	483	487	541	556	188	193	179	188	192	167	485	432	427	420	435	426
59	Ethiopia	11	12	15	16	16	17	1	2	2	2	2	2	4	5	6	7	6	7
60	Fiji	174	187	187	189	184	194	64	70	70	54	56	52	113	124	125	124	120	126
61	Finland	1415	1487	1549	1529	1607	1667	1450	1449	1328	1321	1288	1171	1069	1127	1179	1166	1211	1252
62	France	1970	1985	2032	2094	2211	2335	1954	1937	1722	1751	1736	1563	1500	1511	1548	1592	1683	1775
63	Gabon	175	178	185	203	196	171	93	101	92	81	75	82	116	118	123	129	120	117
64	Gambia	36	34	34	39	45	46	11	10	10	11	9	9	29	28	28	32	37	38
65	Georgia	87	149	168	181	184	199	3	6	7	6	4	4	11	21	25	24	19	21
66	Germany	2264	2341	2466	2520	2618	2754	2449	2430	2089	2075	2042	1819	1736	1799	1857	1886	1959	2067
67	Ghana	42	43	42	47	49	51	7	7	7	9	9	6	18	19	19	24	25	27
68	Greece	1131	1176	1220	1301	1368	1390	544	576	555	545	561	491	616	649	673	708	742	772
69	Grenada	223	251	264	291	324	351	88	104	105	119	137	149	148	172	175	192	226	246
70	Guatemala	143	148	159	171	187	192	26	27	33	37	38	38	62	63	72	81	90	92
71	Guinea	49	51	54	57	62	56	10	10	10	11	11	7	27	28	31	35	39	32
72	Guinea-Bissau	28	35	33	24	26	28	10	8	6	6	7	6	17	22	21	16	17	18
73	Guyana	146	155	177	175	189	197	32	35	40	40	37	40	120	127	148	146	159	163
74	Haiti	56	51	51	53	52	54	10	10	10	11	12	10	32	27	26	27	27	27
75	Honduras	149	153	144	158	146	165	25	26	28	37	33	39	78	83	83	103	90	104
76	Hungary	678	672	696	754	790	846	274	261	255	257	256	238	569	548	565	600	618	640
77	Iceland	1823	1904	1978	2196	2410	2626	1806	1845	1810	2078	2295	2304	1540	1598	1656	1843	2044	2217
78	India	54	60	65	64	71	71	3	3	4	4	4	4	9	9	10	12	13	13
79	Indonesia	50	73	81	72	75	84	6	7	6	3	5	5	18	20	19	20	21	20
80	Iran, Islamic Republic of	281	286	318	317	310	336	42	56	64	73	98	119	128	138	146	144	143	156
81	Iraq	287	295	363	410	497	573	87	95	143	169	209	225	170	172	214	243	298	344
82	Ireland	1320	1312	1518	1569	1744	1944	981	1022	1139	1209	1302	1283	957	962	1153	1196	1330	1474
83	Israel	1777	1921	1941	1966	2188	2338	1229	1432	1431	1361	1467	1534	1321	1510	1527	1515	1699	1776
84	Italy	1486	1566	1685	1776	1886	2040	1022	1153	1133	1151	1161	1103	1073	1125	1216	1279	1364	1503
85	Jamaica	166	166	179	192	213	208	48	54	68	77	85	78	77	78	86	96	106	98
86	Japan[b]	1632	1700	1831	1735	1850	2009	2308	2083	1961	1713	2053	2230	1277	1365	1455	1343	1443	1540
87	Jordan	361	370	338	341	320	325	74	75	77	78	76	71	180	186	193	194	177	168
88	Kazakhstan	268	251	275	225	212	211	51	55	62	47	32	32	219	192	210	159	154	154
89	Kenya	106	110	114	117	117	115	7	7	8	9	8	6	28	30	30	31	31	26
90	Kiribati	134	136	144	143	146	140	53	56	54	47	49	44	132	135	143	141	144	138
91	Kuwait	577	562	620	745	628	542	506	497	507	491	483	511	519	489	542	648	545	473
92	Kyrgyzstan	150	138	147	157	147	145	23	21	19	17	11	10	132	112	117	113	98	90
93	Lao People's Democratic Republic	33	36	47	45	49	52	5	5	5	3	4	4	16	15	18	16	18	20
94	Latvia	310	317	352	394	397	398	75	82	88	100	111	104	203	200	218	241	249	239
95	Lebanon	537	560	604	590	684	696	105	123	140	147	162	164	150	159	167	162	188	193
96	Lesotho	82	81	83	87	97	100	24	22	21	21	24	23	65	63	63	68	79	82
97	Liberia	2	2	2	3	3	3	1	1	1	1	1	1	1	1	2	2	2	2
98	Libyan Arab Jamahiriya	406	407	402	422	375	392	135	147	164	164	118	119	165	170	201	211	184	190
99	Lithuania	277	314	374	423	400	420	72	89	120	140	133	134	239	241	291	324	301	304
100	Luxembourg	2138	2194	2206	2363	2620	2740	2598	2592	2267	2378	2537	2310	1976	2037	2038	2184	2434	2518
101	Madagascar	22	23	17	25	27	33	4	5	4	4	5	6	13	14	14	15	18	24
102	Malawi	26	30	35	32	34	38	4	7	9	6	6	5	13	13	18	16	17	18
103	Malaysia	166	192	201	199	213	234	55	67	63	48	54	60	93	112	116	115	127	138
104	Maldives	141	163	180	190	219	254	53	63	68	70	78	84	118	138	147	155	181	212
105	Mali	17	18	24	26	29	32	4	4	5	5	5	5	9	9	11	12	13	14
106	Malta	720	740	739	758	780	803	510	517	507	527	528	553	514	518	502	525	527	550
107	Marshall Islands	338	323	306	307	321	312	99	103	106	107	109	106	207	199	189	189	196	191
108	Mauritania	33	35	36	43	49	52	11	11	10	10	11	11	25	27	27	31	37	42
109	Mauritius	258	275	290	299	326	330	69	73	68	66	74	75	140	146	155	161	185	186
110	Mexico	384	379	410	430	453	483	74	80	98	112	126	144	160	161	177	206	214	224

Table 6.20 (*continued*)

Member State	Out-of-pocket expenditure % of total expenditure on health						Prepaid plans as % of private expenditure on health						Per capita total expenditure on health at average exchange rate (US$)					
	1995	1996	1997	1998	1999	2000	1995	1996	1997	1998	1999	2000	1995	1996	1997	1998	1999	2000
111 Micronesia, Federated States of	14.3	14.7	14.4	14.9	15.1	16.5	0	0	0	0	0	0	228	218	210	202	199	197
112 Monaco	50	50	50	50.7	51.4	51.9	0	0	0	0	0	0	1893	1949	1690	1784	1816	1837
113 Mongolia	19.8	27.4	27.4	25.8	24.8	21.9	0	0	0	0	0	0	21	25	22	24	21	23
114 Morocco	56.3	54.9	53.2	54.3	53.5	53.6	19.6	21.2	23	22.9	22.9	22.4	55	59	53	54	53	50
115 Mozambique	15.8	14.5	15.2	15.5	15.5	15	0	0	0	0	0	0	7	9	9	9	9	9
116 Myanmar	81	82.2	85.4	89.2	88.1	82.6	0	0	0	0	0	0	51	63	80	104	140	153
117 Namibia	5.3	5.9	6.2	6	6.2	6.5	81.1	82.3	82.1	82.4	79.2	78.9	182	160	163	152	143	136
118 Nauru	1.1	1.1	1.1	1.1	1.1	1.1	0	0	0	0	0	0	376	394	385	328	339	313
119 Nepal	67	67.3	63.1	61.3	64.4	64	0	0	0	0	0	0	11	11	12	12	12	12
120 Netherlands	9.6	8.1	7.7	8.5	8.6	8.6	74	79.2	80.3	77.2	74.3	76.7	2253	2193	1977	2038	2059	1900
121 New Zealand	16.2	16.3	15.6	16.3	15.7	15.4	27.9	28.8	29.8	27.7	27.9	28.5	1203	1294	1310	1132	1163	1062
122 Nicaragua	20.7	24.5	44.9	38.5	44.4	45.4	2.5	2.3	1.5	1.7	4.8	4.8	52	52	45	44	43	43
123 Niger	50.8	49.4	49.2	47.5	46.6	47.5	0	0	0	0	0	0	7	7	6	7	6	5
124 Nigeria	85.5	88.3	86.4	81.1	77.1	79.2	0	0	0	0	0	0	5	6	6	7	7	8
125 Niue	3.2	2.6	2.7	3.3	2.9	3.8	0	0	0	0	0	0	329	400	394	303	357	297
126 Norway	15.2	15.3	15.2	14.8	14.3	14.3	0	0	0	0	0	0	2689	2860	2798	2868	3033	2832
127 Oman	10	9.8	10.6	11.1	10.2	8.4	0	0	0	0	0	0	287	284	256	249	251	295
128 Pakistan	75.2	77	77.1	76.4	78.1	77.1	0	0	0	0	0	0	20	18	18	18	18	18
129 Palau	11.4	12.3	12.5	12	11.8	11.5	0	0	0	0	0	0	342	361	332	296	264	263
130 Panama	24.3	23.7	26.2	24.4	24.7	25	18.5	18.4	17.2	18	18.2	18.7	235	245	236	250	260	268
131 Papua New Guinea	7.6	9.1	9.3	7.9	8.4	9.8	0	0	2.1	4.8	9.4	8.3	31	33	35	32	31	31
132 Paraguay	55.1	44.9	45.9	47.8	44.1	44.8	24	29.8	31.6	23.7	27.1	27.3	145	139	143	121	115	112
133 Peru	34.6	31.7	32.3	32	30.8	30.9	17.9	20.8	21.2	21.7	21	21.7	104	105	108	107	101	100
134 Philippines	50.4	48.7	46.9	48	44.7	45.1	16.2	16.9	17.1	16.8	16.5	16.9	37	42	41	32	37	33
135 Poland	24.3	23.8	28	34.6	24.9	25.9	0	0	0	0	0	0	198	238	228	264	249	246
136 Portugal	21.4	20.4	19.5	20.5	21	19.6	3.4	3.9	4.3	4.9	5.7	5.5	902	959	922	941	962	862
137 Qatar	6.7	5.7	5.8	5.7	6.1	6.2	0	0	0	0	0	0	762	830	836	842	895	940
138 Republic of Korea	51.1	49.1	46.1	41.6	43	41	9.2	10.2	11.3	12.9	13.6	16.6	508	568	523	354	486	584
139 Republic of Moldova	5.4	5.7	6.3	9.2	15.2	17.6	0	0	0	0	0	0	21	28	29	19	9	11
140 Romania	34	27.8	37.1	43.1	40.7	36.2	0	0	0	0	0	0	44	70	63	65	52	48
141 Russian Federation	15.2	17.4	21.1	25.1	29.9	23.4	5.1	7.3	6.7	5.6	4.6	4.3	126	153	167	112	71	92
142 Rwanda	38.1	37.5	38.3	32.6	28.9	29.5	0.4	0.3	0.3	0.3	0.3	0.3	16	16	18	16	14	12
143 Saint Kitts and Nevis	33.9	33.9	32.5	31.9	36.5	40.8	0	0	0	0	0	0	273	317	329	346	382	447
144 Saint Lucia	38.8	36.9	37.7	34.4	34.7	37.9	0	0	0	0	0	0	150	163	169	186	190	202
145 Saint Vincent and the Grenadines	34	32.9	36.2	37.5	38.5	34.6	0	0	0	0	0	0	139	143	161	168	180	190
146 Samoa	21.8	21.8	21.2	21.6	21	20.9	0	0	0	0	0	0	64	76	81	79	77	81
147 San Marino	14.3	15.4	15.6	14	14.2	14.3	0	0	0	0	0	0	2065	2338	2208	2456	2373	2127
148 Sao Tome and Principe	30.6	28.6	33.3	32.1	32.1	32.2	0	0	0	0	0	0	12	12	10	9	8	8
149 Saudi Arabia	4.7	4.5	4.3	6.2	4.1	3.8	7.4	7.1	7.3	7.8	8.3	7.4	397	408	411	387	394	448
150 Senegal	43	42.7	42.5	39.9	40.1	39.6	8.5	8.7	8.7	9.4	8.8	8.7	26	27	24	24	24	22
151 Seychelles	24.3	23.5	21.7	23	23.4	24.7	0	0	0	0	0	0	416	424	481	493	484	440
152 Sierra Leone	59	59	61	58	50	40	0	0	0	0	0	0	6	6	6	5	5	6
153 Singapore	56.9	59	60.1	57.5	60.7	63.7	0	0	0	0	0	0	881	930	923	890	840	814
154 Slovakia	17.9	18.8	8.3	8.4	10.6	10.4	0	0	0	0	0	0	239	277	230	235	213	210
155 Slovenia	13.2	11	10.7	10.8	10.9	10.8	39.5	46.8	48.1	49.1	48.9	48.9	853	834	811	852	873	788
156 Solomon Islands	0.4	0.4	0.3	0.3	0.2	3.2	0	0	0	0	0	0	36	38	43	38	39	38
157 Somalia	57.1	54.6	37.5	37.6	21.1	28.6	0	0	0	0	0	0	4	4	5	4	11	19
158 South Africa	12.3	11.3	10.6	12.6	12.5	12.6	71.7	76.3	78.3	76.4	76.7	76.6	318	324	322	275	269	255
159 Spain	26.1	25.7	25.7	26.2	26.4	26.6	10.1	10.8	11	11.3	11.5	11.7	1137	1190	1074	1123	1158	1073
160 Sri Lanka	50.7	49.3	49.7	48	50.2	50	1	1	1	1	1	1.1	24	25	26	29	30	31
161 Sudan	71.4	71.4	79.1	75.9	75.9	78.8	0	0	0	0	0	0	10	10	12	12	11	13
162 Suriname	6.3	7.7	13.7	14.8	13.5	14.9	2	2.6	1.7	1.4	0.6	0.2	106	161	199	196	104	186
163 Swaziland	27.2	27	28.4	28	30.1	27.9	0	0	0	0	0	0	50	56	50	51	54	56
164 Sweden	14.8	15.2	15.7	16.2	22.2	22.7	0	0	0	0	0	0	2214	2473	2193	2144	2346	2179
165 Switzerland	33	31.4	32.3	32.8	33.3	32.8	48.7	51.7	47.7	44.2	42.2	42.4	4305	4278	3724	3876	3866	3573

Table 6.20 (*continued*)

		Per capita total expenditure on health in international dollars						Per capita government expenditure on health at average exchange rate (US$)						Per capita government expenditure on health in international dollars					
		1995	1996	1997	1998	1999	2000	1995	1996	1997	1998	1999	2000	1995	1996	1997	1998	1999	2000
111	Micronesia, Federated States of	432	406	388	367	355	343	130	122	119	112	109	106	247	227	220	203	194	184
112	Monaco	1503	1583	1567	1668	1791	1877	946	974	845	879	883	883	752	792	783	822	871	902
113	Mongolia	63	80	83	105	109	120	15	16	14	16	14	16	44	51	52	68	72	85
114	Morocco	142	155	152	156	157	166	16	17	16	15	15	15	41	45	45	44	46	49
115	Mozambique	24	26	27	28	28	30	4	5	6	6	6	6	15	16	17	17	17	19
116	Myanmar	19	20	21	20	21	24	10	11	11	11	16	26	4	4	3	2	2	4
117	Namibia	373	344	353	366	362	366	104	82	84	79	85	80	213	175	182	189	214	217
118	Nauru	584	579	586	576	539	525	372	389	380	324	335	310	578	572	580	570	533	519
119	Nepal	51	54	60	63	63	66	3	3	4	4	3	4	13	14	18	21	18	19
120	Netherlands	1787	1816	1955	2038	2175	2255	1600	1451	1341	1381	1370	1283	1270	1202	1326	1381	1447	1523
121	New Zealand	1244	1267	1364	1450	1526	1623	929	992	1012	872	901	829	960	972	1054	1117	1183	1266
122	Nicaragua	133	130	117	110	111	108	40	39	24	27	23	22	104	96	63	67	59	56
123	Niger	20	21	21	23	22	22	3	3	3	3	3	2	9	9	9	10	10	10
124	Nigeria	23	21	20	22	20	20	1	1	1	1	2	2	3	3	3	4	5	4
125	Niue	833	997	1000	874	1092	1111	319	390	384	294	346	286	806	971	972	846	1060	1068
126	Norway	1865	2025	2193	2441	2558	2373	2265	2407	2358	2429	2584	2412	1571	1705	1848	2067	2179	2022
127	Oman	431	422	419	484	440	448	228	228	202	195	199	245	343	338	330	379	350	371
128	Pakistan	68	67	68	69	72	76	5	4	4	4	4	4	17	15	15	16	16	17
129	Palau	540	503	452	453	474	482	303	317	290	260	233	233	478	441	395	399	418	427
130	Panama	396	420	407	422	446	464	165	174	161	175	181	186	278	298	278	296	312	321
131	Papua New Guinea	105	106	118	135	153	147	29	29	31	29	28	27	96	95	105	123	137	130
132	Paraguay	320	296	320	304	324	323	40	50	47	45	45	43	88	106	105	114	128	124
133	Peru	197	200	212	220	236	238	58	61	62	62	60	59	110	116	122	127	141	141
134	Philippines	144	156	168	165	172	167	15	17	18	14	17	15	57	64	73	70	80	76
135	Poland	420	469	461	543	558	578	144	175	164	173	177	171	306	344	332	355	397	403
136	Portugal	1146	1210	1359	1344	1413	1469	556	620	597	635	681	614	707	782	880	907	1000	1045
137	Qatar	809	847	867	1034	964	849	563	636	638	645	693	729	598	648	661	792	746	658
138	Republic of Korea	536	614	661	635	766	909	185	221	215	164	210	258	196	238	271	294	330	401
139	Republic of Moldova	115	126	119	83	59	64	19	26	27	17	8	9	107	119	111	75	50	53
140	Romania	176	299	257	215	203	190	29	51	40	37	31	31	116	216	162	122	121	121
141	Russian Federation	369	355	390	382	379	405	103	119	122	77	46	66	300	277	284	263	245	293
142	Rwanda	42	46	44	39	41	40	8	8	9	8	8	6	20	23	21	20	22	20
143	Saint Kitts and Nevis	419	493	501	528	577	658	181	209	222	235	243	265	277	326	338	359	366	390
144	Saint Lucia	203	225	240	256	252	272	92	103	105	122	124	125	124	142	149	168	165	169
145	Saint Vincent and the Grenadines	269	271	307	315	344	374	92	96	103	105	111	124	178	182	196	196	212	244
146	Samoa	146	168	168	182	194	221	48	58	62	60	59	62	110	127	128	138	148	168
147	San Marino	2349	2410	2470	2723	2707	2805	1769	1978	1863	2111	2037	1822	2012	2039	2084	2341	2324	2402
148	Sao Tome and Principe	29	32	28	27	23	23	8	9	7	6	6	5	20	23	18	18	15	16
149	Saudi Arabia	681	649	652	729	683	684	312	318	322	306	313	354	536	506	512	576	542	541
150	Senegal	46	49	51	51	54	56	14	14	13	14	14	12	24	26	27	29	30	32
151	Seychelles	528	565	714	776	775	758	285	293	346	342	333	294	362	390	515	539	533	507
152	Sierra Leone	22	22	20	21	22	28	2	2	2	2	3	4	9	9	8	9	11	17
153	Singapore	737	780	824	915	936	913	368	374	364	374	326	290	308	314	325	385	363	326
154	Slovakia	596	695	608	641	649	690	196	225	211	215	191	188	489	564	558	587	580	618
155	Slovenia	1135	1163	1249	1282	1368	1462	667	662	643	671	687	621	887	923	991	1010	1076	1154
156	Solomon Islands	89	89	95	106	110	97	35	37	41	36	38	36	86	86	91	102	107	92
157	Somalia	15	13	13	11	9	7	2	2	3	3	8	13	6	6	8	7	7	5
158	South Africa	557	632	637	620	638	663	155	152	148	116	115	108	271	296	294	262	272	280
159	Spain	1168	1222	1278	1366	1451	1539	806	846	764	792	813	750	828	869	909	963	1019	1076
160	Sri Lanka	84	85	90	101	110	120	12	12	13	15	14	15	41	42	44	52	54	59
161	Sudan	30	29	29	39	41	51	3	3	3	3	3	3	9	8	6	9	10	11
162	Suriname	255	310	358	408	400	424	80	114	129	121	63	104	194	220	231	251	243	238
163	Swaziland	145	177	158	179	195	210	36	41	36	37	38	40	105	129	113	129	137	151
164	Sweden	1622	1714	1767	1746	2010	2097	1885	2096	1848	1797	1826	1685	1382	1453	1489	1464	1565	1622
165	Switzerland	2527	2588	2812	2927	3069	3229	2315	2339	2054	2127	2140	1988	1359	1415	1551	1606	1698	1796

Table 6.20 (*continued*)

	Member State	Out-of-pocket expenditure % of total expenditure on health						Prepaid plans as % of private expenditure on health						Per capita total expenditure on health at average exchange rate (US$)					
		1995	1996	1997	1998	1999	2000	1995	1996	1997	1998	1999	2000	1995	1996	1997	1998	1999	2000
166	Syrian Arab Republic	23.9	28.1	31.2	33.4	35.2	36.6	0	0	0	0	0	0	18	21	24	26	28	30
167	Tajikistan	39.5	36.9	34	35	15.4	19.2	0	0	0	0	0	0	2	5	5	6	5	4
168	Thailand	44.7	42.6	36.9	32.7	35.3	36.2	7.6	7.8	8.6	9.7	9.7	9.6	97	110	93	71	73	71
169	The former Yugoslav Republic of Macedonia	9.4	13	16.1	12.9	15.9	15.5	0	0	0	0	0	0	119	129	114	135	107	106
170	Togo	52.4	58.4	51.5	44.8	42.9	45.7	0	0	0	0	0	0	10	9	11	10	9	8
171	Tonga	56.7	56.7	53.2	53.9	54.1	53.2	0	0	0	0	0	0	129	138	143	123	117	108
172	Trinidad and Tobago	43	44.4	45.6	42.6	42.4	42.7	6.4	6.3	6.5	6.6	6.5	6.5	189	207	220	250	259	268
173	Tunisia	38.1	27.1	17.3	16.3	16.8	17.6	13.2	16.6	22.8	21.9	20.5	19.5	137	142	133	145	155	145
174	Turkey	29.7	30.8	28.3	28	28.8	28.8	0.3	0.2	0.2	0.2	0.2	0.1	93	113	126	150	138	150
175	Turkmenistan	22.9	18.6	25.5	18.9	18.3	15.1	0	0	0	0	0	0	33	15	24	32	38	52
176	Tuvalu	29.1	31.3	30.2	29.3	29.3	28.6	0	0	0	0	0	0	110	130	131	117	127	120
177	Uganda	36.2	34.9	32.3	33.5	32.9	34.5	0.5	0.5	0.6	0.5	0.5	0.5	11	10	11	11	11	10
178	Ukraine	16	20.4	25	28.9	31.9	29.9	0	0	0	0	0	0	42	43	54	42	27	26
179	United Arab Emirates	13.1	13.4	13.7	13.1	14	15	19.5	19.2	19	19.9	19	18.3	619	631	729	752	758	767
180	United Kingdom	10.9	11	10.7	11	10.7	10.6	19.8	19.2	17	17.1	16.5	16.9	1357	1422	1531	1657	1753	1747
181	United Republic of Tanzania	36.7	43.3	44.5	44.4	47.2	44.1	0	0	0	0	4.5	4.2	7	9	10	10	11	12
182	United States of America	15.1	14.9	15.1	15.5	15.5	15.3	62	61.9	61.2	61.1	61.6	62.5	3621	3762	3905	4068	4252	4499
183	Uruguay	22.2	21.1	19.8	19.4	17	16.7	56.1	60.2	63.3	63.7	66.8	68.8	552	606	662	697	682	653
184	Uzbekistan	22.7	17.5	17.9	15.3	21.2	22.5	0	0	0	0	0	0	21	28	26	24	27	30
185	Vanuatu	33.9	42.4	35.8	34.6	39.7	39.1	0	0	0	0	0	0	47	40	46	43	47	44
186	Venezuela, Bolivarian Republic of	45.4	45	42.9	46	45	40.4	5	5.6	5.6	4.9	5.2	5.2	162	122	166	205	201	233
187	Viet Nam	55.2	60.3	63.5	65.6	70.1	68.7	0	0	0	0	0	0	11	15	16	17	21	21
188	Yemen	70.8	63.8	62.3	57.3	60.9	61.1	0	0	0	0	0	0	41	21	19	18	19	21
189	Yugoslavia	42.1	42.6	41.4	49.1	49.1	49	0	0	0	0	0	0	57	108	125	87	97	50
190	Zambia	32.3	33	31.9	31.9	30.5	28.6	0	0	0	0	0	0	20	20	24	20	18	18
191	Zimbabwe	30.9	30.1	27.4	33.2	23	22.2	23.4	20.9	21	16.4	39.6	46.5	44	54	67	60	36	43

Table 6.20 (*continued*)

		Per capita total expenditure on health in international dollars						Per capita government expenditure on health at average exchange rate (US$)						Per capita government expenditure on health in international dollars					
		1995	1996	1997	1998	1999	2000	1995	1996	1997	1998	1999	2000	1995	1996	1997	1998	1999	2000
166	Syrian Arab Republic	43	39	43	47	51	51	14	15	16	17	18	19	33	28	30	31	33	32
167	Tajikistan	22	27	28	25	29	29	1	3	3	4	4	3	14	17	19	17	25	23
168	Thailand	210	237	242	227	228	237	47	56	53	44	43	41	103	121	138	140	133	136
169	The former Yugoslav Republic of Macedonia	213	242	263	339	277	300	108	112	95	118	90	90	193	210	220	295	233	254
170	Togo	34	31	39	35	36	36	5	4	5	5	5	4	16	13	19	20	20	19
171	Tonga	284	277	286	281	298	312	56	60	67	57	54	51	123	120	134	130	137	146
172	Trinidad and Tobago	298	320	352	409	440	468	95	101	104	127	132	136	150	156	167	208	225	237
173	Tunisia	332	347	361	400	442	472	77	96	103	115	122	113	186	234	280	316	348	369
174	Turkey	190	235	273	304	292	323	65	78	90	108	98	107	134	162	196	218	208	230
175	Turkmenistan	92	114	145	193	204	286	26	12	18	26	31	44	71	93	108	157	169	243
176	Tuvalu	725	839	885	918	924	860	78	90	91	83	90	86	514	577	617	648	654	614
177	Uganda	27	27	29	32	36	36	4	4	5	4	5	4	11	12	13	12	15	14
178	Ukraine	208	164	179	167	146	152	35	34	40	30	19	18	175	131	134	119	99	107
179	United Arab Emirates	663	651	783	816	769	761	495	502	578	600	596	596	530	518	621	651	604	591
180	United Kingdom	1315	1422	1482	1530	1672	1774	1138	1179	1223	1324	1405	1415	1103	1179	1184	1223	1340	1437
181	United Republic of Tanzania	20	20	21	21	24	27	4	4	5	5	5	6	11	10	10	10	10	13
182	United States of America	3621	3762	3905	4068	4252	4499	1639	1714	1767	1810	1883	1992	1639	1714	1767	1810	1883	1992
183	Uruguay	726	807	894	966	997	1005	273	285	304	324	332	304	359	379	411	449	486	468
184	Uzbekistan	95	95	94	86	88	86	16	23	21	21	22	24	74	79	77	73	70	66
185	Vanuatu	97	84	99	106	115	119	31	23	29	28	28	27	64	48	64	69	69	72
186	Venezuela, Bolivarian Republic of	270	228	267	310	266	280	84	64	91	106	106	134	141	119	146	160	140	160
187	Viet Nam	68	87	93	104	128	129	5	5	5	5	5	5	28	30	29	30	31	33
188	Yemen	62	54	60	69	68	70	9	6	6	6	6	7	14	15	18	25	22	22
189	Yugoslavia	205	243	251	217	228	237	33	62	73	45	49	26	119	140	147	111	116	121
190	Zambia	41	48	51	46	44	49	10	11	13	12	11	11	22	25	28	26	26	30
191	Zimbabwe	155	174	225	279	197	171	22	30	40	33	17	18	79	95	133	156	97	73

a. A zero does not always mean "not applicable"; when no information has been collated to estimate an entry, say private insurance and other prepaid plans, that entry is shown as zero.

b. There is a break in the series for Japan between 1997 and 1998. Since 1998, data have been based on new Japanese national health accounts, estimated as a pilot implementation of the ORD manual *A System of Health Accounts*. Consequently, the comparability of data over time is limited. In addition, the data for the year 2000 have been largely developed by WHO and are not endorsed by the Government of Japan.

Source: World Health Organization. (2002). *World Health Report 2002: Reducing risks, promoting healthy life.* Geneva: Author. Retrieved from http://www.who.int/whr/2002/en/.

Table 6.21
Healthy Life Expectancy (HALE) in All Member States, Estimates for 2000 and 2001

These figures were produced by WHO using the best available evidence. They are not necessarily the official statistics of Member States.

	Member State	Total population At birth 2000	Total population At birth 2001	Males 2001 At birth	Males 2001 Uncertainty interval	Males 2001 At age 60	Males 2001 Uncertainty interval	Females 2001 At birth	Females 2001 Uncertainty interval	Females 2001 At age 60	Females 2001 Uncertainty interval	Expectation of lost healthy years at birth (years) Males 2001	Expectation of lost healthy years at birth (years) Females 2001	Percentage of total life expectancy lost Males 2001	Percentage of total life expectancy lost Females 2001
1	Afghanistan	33.8	33.4	31.1	24.9 - 37.6	4.9	3.2 - 6.8	35.7	27.4 - 44.6	8.7	6.9 - 10.7	10.0	8.1	24.4	18.4
2	Albania	58.6	58.7	55.9	55.0 - 58.4	8.8	8.3 - 9.9	61.5	60.5 - 63.2	12.7	12.0 - 14.1	10.4	11.7	15.7	16.0
3	Algeria	57.5	57.8	55.8	54.2 - 58.5	10.3	9.3 - 11.9	59.9	58.7 - 62.1	12.2	11.5 - 13.5	11.9	11.2	17.6	15.8
4	Andorra	70.8	70.9	68.8	67.9 - 70.3	15.8	15.2 - 17.0	73.0	69.7 - 76.8	18.5	16.3 - 21.2	7.4	10.0	9.8	12.0
5	Angola	28.9	28.7	25.7	19.8 - 31.9	5.8	2.9 - 8.4	31.7	24.5 - 38.2	9.2	7.4 - 11.1	8.4	6.5	24.8	17.1
6	Antigua and Barbuda	59.7	59.7	56.9	55.4 - 60.0	10.3	9.4 - 11.4	62.6	61.9 - 64.6	13.4	13.0 - 14.1	11.8	10.9	17.2	14.8
7	Argentina	62.9	63.1	60.6	59.6 - 62.2	11.9	11.3 - 12.9	65.7	64.8 - 67.6	15.1	14.6 - 16.3	9.5	12.0	13.6	15.5
8	Armenia	57.9	58.3	55.4	54.1 - 57.3	9.2	8.5 - 10.2	61.1	59.6 - 63.5	12.2	11.6 - 13.3	10.8	11.9	16.3	16.3
9	Australia	71.4	71.6	70.1	69.4 - 71.2	16.4	15.8 - 17.3	73.2	72.5 - 74.4	18.8	18.4 - 19.6	7.3	9.5	9.4	11.4
10	Austria	70.7	71.0	68.9	68.5 - 69.7	15.7	15.4 - 16.3	73.0	72.4 - 74.2	18.5	18.3 - 19.0	7.0	8.8	9.3	10.7
11	Azerbaijan	51.7	52.8	50.3	49.2 - 52.6	8.5	7.9 - 9.9	55.4	54.1 - 57.4	11.0	10.3 - 12.3	10.4	11.2	17.2	16.8
12	Bahamas	58.4	58.6	54.7	53.0 - 57.6	11.1	9.9 - 13.2	62.5	61.3 - 64.9	14.7	14 - 16.2	14.1	12.5	20.5	16.7
13	Bahrain	61.9	61.8	62.3	61.4 - 63.6	10.5	9.5 - 11.6	61.3	60.6 - 63.0	9.4	8.9 - 10.2	9.9	12.2	13.7	16.6
14	Bangladesh	52.0	52.1	51.7	50.0 - 54.1	9.4	8.8 - 10.5	52.6	51.5 - 54.4	10.9	10.3 - 11.7	10.2	9.2	16.5	14.9
15	Barbados	63.9	64.3	61.0	59.9 - 63.1	12.3	11.6 - 13.3	67.6	66.7 - 69.5	16.4	15.8 - 17.7	9.5	10.6	13.5	13.5
16	Belarus	58.8	58.4	53.9	53.0 - 55.7	9.5	9.1 - 10.2	62.8	61.6 - 64.8	13.0	12.3 - 14.3	9.0	11.4	14.3	15.4
17	Belgium	69.6	69.7	67.7	67.2 - 68.7	14.8	14.4 - 15.5	71.8	71.1 - 73.0	17.8	17.6 - 18.3	7.1	9.4	9.5	11.6
18	Belize	58.7	58.9	56.3	54.9 - 58.5	10.4	9.7 - 11.4	61.5	60.1 - 63.8	12.9	12.0 - 14.4	11.4	11.3	16.8	15.5
19	Benin	42.1	42.1	40.1	34.4 - 46.7	7.1	4.8 - 9.3	44.1	38.5 - 51.7	9.5	6.7 - 12.3	10.9	9.2	21.4	17.3
20	Bhutan	51.2	51.4	50.0	43.8 - 57.2	9.2	7.4 - 11.3	52.9	46.0 - 61.3	11.1	8.6 - 13.9	10.5	9.9	17.3	15.7
21	Bolivia	50.4	50.8	48.0	41.2 - 55.2	8.4	6.4 - 10.6	53.6	46.6 - 62.7	11.0	9.1 - 13.7	13.1	10.7	21.4	16.7
22	Bosnia and Herzegovina	62.3	62.5	60.0	59.2 - 61.7	11.3	10.8 - 12.3	64.9	63.7 - 66.7	14.3	13.6 - 15.7	9.3	11.5	13.4	15.0
23	Botswana	34.4	32.9	33.0	29.7 - 36.3	9.1	7.1 - 11.2	32.7	29.7 - 35.8	12.2	8.6 - 15.7	6.4	5.9	16.2	15.2
24	Brazil[b]	56.3	56.7	52.2	50.0 - 55.1	9.4	8.3 - 10.8	61.1	59.5 - 63.5	13.0	12.2 - 14.9	13.3	11.0	20.2	15.2
25	Brunei Darussalam	62.0	62.0	60.4	59.5 - 62.3	10.5	10.0 - 11.8	63.7	62.1 - 65.9	12.8	12.3 - 13.7	12.8	12.2	17.4	16.1
26	Bulgaria	63.1	63.0	60.8	60.2 - 62.1	11.5	11.2 - 12.1	65.2	64.5 - 66.7	13.9	13.4 - 15.1	7.5	9.6	11.0	12.8
27	Burkina Faso	35.0	35.1	33.9	29.0 - 39.8	7.0	5.1 - 9.2	36.3	31.3 - 42.7	9.4	7.1 - 11.8	8.3	7.2	19.6	16.5
28	Burundi	33.9	33.7	31.7	27.6 - 36.7	6.8	4.9 - 8.6	35.7	30.1 - 41.3	9.6	7.7 - 11.8	6.8	6.6	17.6	15.6
29	Cambodia	45.9	46.4	43.0	37.7 - 48.7	7.6	6.0 - 9.4	49.9	44.0 - 59.0	10.5	8.6 - 13.6	10.3	9.1	19.3	15.4
30	Cameroon	41.0	40.4	38.8	33.8 - 45.2	7.3	4.7 - 10.3	42.0	36.7 - 48.4	9.9	8.0 - 12.5	10.1	8.4	20.6	16.7
31	Canada	69.7	69.9	68.2	67.6 - 69.1	15.3	15.0 - 16.0	71.6	70.9 - 72.7	17.9	17.6 - 18.6	8.4	10.4	11.0	12.6
32	Cape Verde	56.3	56.5	52.2	49.3 - 55.3	9.2	8.0 - 10.4	60.8	57.0 - 64.6	12.3	10.2 - 14.5	13.6	11.3	20.6	15.6
33	Central African Republic	34.0	34.0	32.3	26.9 - 38.1	6.0	3.7 - 8.3	35.6	30.3 - 42.0	9.2	7.3 - 11.2	9.7	7.7	23.1	17.7
34	Chad	38.5	38.7	35.9	29.4 - 43.8	6.3	3.8 - 8.9	41.5	35.5 - 49.0	9.3	7.1 - 11.8	11.1	8.7	23.7	17.3
35	Chile	65.8	66.1	64.4	63.4 - 65.8	13.3	12.8 - 14.2	67.8	66.8 - 69.6	15.5	15.0 - 16.4	8.7	11.7	12.0	14.7
36	China	62.8	63.2	62.0	61.5 - 63.0	12.7	12.4 - 13.2	64.3	63.4 - 66.0	14.2	14.0 - 14.6	7.7	8.4	11.1	11.6
37	Colombia	58.6	58.7	55.3	54.0 - 57.4	10.7	10.0 - 12.0	62.1	60.5 - 64.5	12.9	12.6 - 13.8	11.4	12.7	17.1	16.9
38	Comoros	49.7	49.9	47.0	40.7 - 54.9	7.6	5.7 - 9.7	52.8	46.6 - 61.6	10.2	8.2 - 13.0	12.8	11.0	21.4	17.2
39	Congo	42.9	43.0	40.9	34.9 - 47.4	7.7	5.2 - 10.4	45.2	39.2 - 51.7	10.6	8.1 - 13.5	10.9	8.7	21.1	16.1
40	Cook Islands	60.4	60.5	58.3	57.1 - 60.5	10.2	9.6 - 11.0	62.6	60.8 - 64.9	12.7	11.9 - 14.0	11.6	11.4	16.6	15.5
41	Costa Rica	65.0	64.8	62.6	61.6 - 64.7	12.9	12.0 - 14.3	67.0	66.0 - 69.2	15.3	14.9 - 16.3	11.1	11.6	15.1	14.7
42	Côte d'Ivoire	38.0	37.8	36.3	31.2 - 42.7	7.3	5.4 - 9.4	39.3	34.2 - 45.1	9.7	7.3 - 12.2	8.7	7.7	19.3	16.4
43	Croatia	63.1	63.3	59.7	59.2 - 60.5	10.1	9.9 - 10.6	66.9	66.1 - 68.2	14.4	14.2 - 14.8	9.2	10.2	13.3	13.3
44	Cuba[b]	66.6	66.6	64.7	64.0 - 66.2	14.4	14.0 - 15.3	68.5	67.6 - 69.9	16.6	16.0 - 17.6	10.0	10.8	13.4	13.6
45	Cyprus	66.2	66.2	65.3	64.4 - 66.9	13.2	12.5 - 14.7	67.2	66.4 - 69.2	14.5	14.1 - 15.6	9.4	12.0	12.5	15.1
46	Czech Republic	66.4	66.6	63.8	63.2 - 64.7	12.8	12.4 - 13.4	69.5	68.6 - 70.8	16.0	15.7 - 16.4	8.1	9.3	11.3	11.8
47	Democratic People's Republic of Korea	55.8	55.8	53.5	52.5 - 56.4	10.7	10.4 - 11.5	58.1	57.0 - 60.3	13.2	12.5 - 14.1	10.5	10.3	16.5	15.0
48	Democratic Republic of the Congo	34.9	34.8	32.3	26.2 - 40.1	6.3	4.5 - 8.1	37.3	30.3 - 45.9	9.2	7.4 - 11.3	9.8	8.2	23.3	18.0
49	Denmark	69.8	70.1	69.3	68.8 - 70.4	15.5	15.1 - 16.1	70.8	70.2 - 72.1	16.7	16.4 - 17.3	5.5	8.7	7.3	10.9
50	Djibouti	39.9	40.1	37.9	31.7 - 44.5	6.9	4.6 - 9.0	42.3	36.2 - 49.4	9.6	8.1 - 11.7	10.0	8.1	20.9	16.1
51	Dominica	62.0	62.1	59.4	57.4 - 62.3	13.0	12.4 - 14.3	64.8	63.6 - 66.6	15.0	14.4 - 16.0	12.2	11.2	17.1	14.7
52	Dominican Republic	56.0	56.4	53.0	51.9 - 55.8	9.7	9.2 - 10.7	59.8	58.7 - 62.2	13.1	12.5 - 14.2	11.1	10.7	17.2	15.1
53	Ecuador	59.0	59.5	56.6	54.9 - 59.0	11.6	11.0 - 12.6	62.4	61.2 - 64.4	14.2	13.4 - 15.6	11.1	10.8	16.4	14.7

Table 6.21 (*continued*)

	Member State	Total population At birth 2000	2001	Males 2001 At birth	Uncertainty interval	At age 60	Uncertainty interval	Females 2001 At birth	Uncertainty interval	At age 60	Uncertainty interval	Expectation of lost healthy years at birth (years) Males 2001	Females	Percentage of total life expectancy lost Males 2001	Females
54	Egypt	56.4	56.7	56.4	55.8 - 57.6	9.4	8.8 - 10.4	57.0	55.9 - 58.9	9.2	8.9 - 10.0	8.9	10.8	13.7	16.0
55	El Salvador	56.8	57.4	53.7	52.3 - 56.5	11.2	10.5 - 12.4	61.2	59.9 - 63.4	13.5	12.6 - 15.1	12.7	11.5	19.1	15.8
56	Equatorial Guinea	43.6	43.8	41.7	35.7 - 48.5	7.7	6.0 - 9.5	45.9	38.9 - 53.9	10.0	7.7 - 12.5	10.6	9.2	20.2	16.7
57	Eritrea	37.5	44.1	42.3	37.5 - 48.4	8.0	5.9 - 10.6	45.9	39.9 - 53.6	10.3	8.0 - 12.9	9.9	9.1	19.0	16.5
58	Estonia	61.9	62.0	58.0	57.4 - 59.0	11.1	10.9 - 11.6	66.1	64.9 - 67.8	15.0	14.7 - 15.6	7.7	10.4	11.7	13.6
59	Ethiopia	38.5	38.8	36.9	30.2 - 43.5	7.0	4.6 - 9.6	40.7	33.8 - 48.0	9.4	7.0 - 11.7	10.0	8.5	21.3	17.2
60	Fiji	58.7	58.8	56.8	55.5 - 59.2	10.0	9.4 - 11.4	60.8	59.2 - 63.3	12.3	11.6 - 13.7	11.0	11.0	16.2	15.3
61	Finland	69.9	70.1	67.7	67.3 - 68.4	15.2	14.9 - 15.6	72.5	72.1 - 73.3	18.1	18 - 18.5	6.8	8.8	9.1	10.8
62	France	71.1	71.3	69.0	68.7 - 69.7	16.1	15.8 - 16.5	73.5	72.9 - 74.3	19.1	18.9 - 19.5	6.6	9.5	8.7	11.4
63	Gabon	49.7	49.9	48.2	43.1 - 54.0	9.1	7.4 - 11.4	51.5	45.7 - 60.0	11.0	9.4 - 13.8	9.8	9.0	16.9	14.9
64	Gambia	47.8	48.0	45.1	43.7 - 47.5	7.8	7.0 - 9.4	51.0	49.4 - 53.2	10.3	9.5 - 11.5	11.1	10.1	19.7	16.5
65	Georgia	59.7	59.8	57.5	56.7 - 58.6	10.3	10 - 10.8	62.2	61.3 - 64.0	12.1	11.8 - 12.8	7.9	10.2	12.1	14.1
66	Germany	70.1	70.2	68.3	67.7 - 69.1	15.0	14.6 - 15.6	72.2	71.7 - 73.5	17.7	17.5 - 18.2	6.8	8.9	9.1	10.9
67	Ghana	47.7	47.8	45.8	40.3 - 52.8	8.4	6.2 - 10.9	49.7	43.0 - 57.3	10.6	8.3 - 13.4	10.0	9.2	17.9	15.6
68	Greece	70.4	70.4	69.0	68.6 - 69.8	15.7	15.4 - 16.2	71.9	71.3 - 73.2	17.1	16.9 - 17.5	6.5	8.9	8.6	11.0
69	Grenada	57.3	57.5	56.0	54.8 - 58.1	10.1	9.5 - 11.0	59.0	57.7 - 61.2	12.1	11.4 - 13.3	9.7	9.7	14.8	14.1
70	Guatemala	54.0	54.3	51.4	49.4 - 54.9	10.4	9.4 - 12.1	57.2	55.6 - 59.8	11.6	11.1 - 12.8	12.2	11.9	19.2	17.2
71	Guinea	42.0	42.4	40.0	33.9 - 46.7	7.3	5.3 - 9.3	44.7	37.9 - 52.6	9.6	7.3 - 12.4	10.1	9.1	20.1	16.9
72	Guinea-Bissau	38.3	38.3	36.1	30.7 - 42.4	6.9	4.2 - 9.6	40.6	34.3 - 47.9	9.4	7.1 - 11.9	9.8	8.2	21.4	16.7
73	Guyana	53.5	54.1	51.6	50.3 - 54.2	9.4	9.0 - 10.2	56.7	55.2 - 59.9	12.1	11.3 - 13.0	9.7	10.0	15.9	14.9
74	Haiti	45.1	42.9	38.5	34.4 - 42.9	8.4	6.6 - 10.3	47.3	40.9 - 53.9	11.2	7.5 - 15.0	7.1	7.4	15.5	13.6
75	Honduras	55.7	55.9	52.1	49.0 - 55.6	9.3	8.0 - 10.7	59.6	55.6 - 64.2	12.6	10.9 - 14.7	12.3	10.7	19.1	15.2
76	Hungary	61.6	61.8	58.0	57.3 - 58.9	10.4	10.0 - 11.1	65.5	64.7 - 67.2	14.4	14.2 - 15.0	9.3	10.5	13.8	13.9
77	Iceland	71.3	71.2	70.5	70.0 - 71.6	16.8	16.5 - 17.6	71.9	71.2 - 73.5	17.6	17.2 - 18.1	7.6	9.4	9.8	11.6
78	India	51.2	51.4	51.5	50.7 - 52.9	9.7	9.1 - 10.5	51.3	50.0 - 53.2	10.2	9.8 - 11.1	8.4	10.4	14.1	16.9
79	Indonesia	56.2	56.7	56.1	55.7 - 57.1	10.6	10.3 - 11.4	57.2	56.3 - 59.2	11.1	10.7 - 11.6	8.3	10.1	12.9	15.1
80	Iran, Islamic Republic of	56.5	56.7	55.5	54.5 - 57.7	9.8	8.8 - 11.3	57.9	55.9 - 60.7	11.4	10.6 - 12.6	10.9	13.2	16.5	18.5
81	Iraq	50.4	50.5	47.7	45.5 - 51.6	8.1	6.9 - 10.4	53.3	51.7 - 56.5	11.0	10.3 - 12.4	11.0	9.6	18.7	15.3
82	Ireland	68.9	69.0	67.6	67.0 - 68.6	13.9	13.6 - 14.6	70.4	69.7 - 71.5	16.1	15.8 - 16.6	6.1	8.9	8.3	11.2
83	Israel	69.4	69.4	68.0	67.2 - 69.3	15.8	15.4 - 16.7	70.8	70.1 - 72.4	16.9	16.4 - 17.8	8.1	10.0	10.6	12.4
84	Italy	70.9	71.0	69.2	68.8 - 70.2	15.5	15.2 - 16.2	72.9	72.4 - 74.0	18.2	18.0 - 18.6	7.0	9.3	9.2	11.3
85	Jamaica	62.9	62.8	61.1	60.1 - 63.3	11.8	11.4 - 12.5	64.5	63.7 - 66.4	13.9	13.3 - 15.2	9.9	10.0	13.9	13.4
86	Japan[b]	73.5	73.6	71.4	70.8 - 72.3	17.1	16.7 - 17.8	75.8	75.2 - 77.1	20.7	20.2 - 21.6	6.5	8.9	8.3	10.6
87	Jordan	58.5	58.5	57.2	56.5 - 58.8	9.9	9.2 - 10.8	59.9	58.7 - 61.6	11.5	11.0 - 12.4	11.4	13.6	16.7	18.5
88	Kazakhstan	52.1	52.4	49.0	47.6 - 51.3	8.7	8.1 - 10.6	55.8	54.9 - 57.6	10.8	10.1 - 11.8	9.8	11.3	16.7	16.9
89	Kenya	41.4	40.8	39.5	35.1 - 44.5	8.1	6.3 - 10.2	42.1	37.8 - 47.7	10.7	9.1 - 12.8	8.7	7.5	18.1	15.1
90	Kiribati	52.9	53.2	51.1	49.9 - 54.2	8.7	7.9 - 10.3	55.4	54.3 - 58.1	10.8	9.9 - 12.3	10.6	10.5	17.1	15.9
91	Kuwait	65.1	64.9	64.1	63.3 - 65.9	12.2	11.5 - 13.3	65.8	64.7 - 68.2	13.0	12.2 - 14.8	10.8	10.2	14.4	13.4
92	Kyrgyzstan	51.4	51.5	47.7	46.5 - 50.5	6.9	5.5 - 9.4	55.4	53.8 - 57.9	10.4	9.7 - 12.0	12.5	12.8	20.8	18.8
93	Lao People's Democratic Republic	44.2	44.2	42.4	40.0 - 45.6	7.5	6.9 - 8.8	46.0	44.2 - 48.5	9.8	9.2 - 11.2	11.1	9.6	20.7	17.2
94	Latvia	59.9	60.0	55.2	54.5 - 56.7	10.0	9.6 - 10.4	64.9	63.9 - 66.7	14.4	14.1 - 15.1	10.1	11.1	15.4	14.6
95	Lebanon	59.2	59.4	56.5	55.4 - 58.8	10.0	9.2 - 11.5	62.2	61.4 - 64.2	12.9	12.3 - 14.0	11.1	9.8	16.4	13.8
96	Lesotho	34.9	33.4	33.2	29.3 - 37.6	8.4	6.3 - 11.0	33.6	29.0 - 38.1	10.6	8.3 - 13.4	6.9	6.3	17.2	15.7
97	Liberia	37.0	37.5	35.3	28.7 - 41.5	6.6	5.3 - 8.2	39.6	33.5 - 46.0	9.1	7.3 - 11.2	9.3	8.3	20.9	17.4
98	Libyan Arab Jamahiriya	59.3	59.6	56.8	54.1 - 59.7	9.8	8.3 - 11.5	62.4	58.6 - 66.4	12.9	10.4 - 15.3	11.4	10.8	16.7	14.7
99	Lithuania	60.8	61.1	56.9	56.3 - 58.0	11.0	10.7 - 11.5	65.4	64.5 - 67.0	14.8	14.5 - 15.4	10.8	12.6	16.0	16.1
100	Luxembourg	70.3	70.6	68.6	68.2 - 69.4	15.1	14.7 - 15.7	72.7	72.0 - 74.0	18.3	18.0 - 18.9	6.4	9.0	8.5	11.1
101	Madagascar	44.4	44.5	42.2	36.6 - 48.7	7.4	5.7 - 9.4	46.7	39.5 - 55.4	9.8	7.4 - 12.7	11.1	9.7	20.8	17.1
102	Malawi	30.1	29.8	29.0	24.8 - 34.0	7.2	5.4 - 9.1	30.7	25.5 - 36.4	9.5	7.5 - 12.0	6.7	6.3	18.7	17.0
103	Malaysia	60.5	60.4	57.6	56.4 - 59.8	9.2	8.2 - 10.9	63.2	61.9 - 65.1	12.0	11.5 - 13.1	11.7	11.2	16.8	15.1
104	Maldives	51.1	51.9	49.6	47.7 - 53.1	5.7	4.5 - 7.6	54.3	53.3 - 56.5	7.5	6.8 - 8.7	14.3	10.1	22.4	15.6
105	Mali	35.6	35.7	33.7	27.5 - 41.1	6.5	4.8 - 8.4	37.7	29.9 - 45.8	9.2	7.0 - 11.3	10.5	8.5	23.8	18.3
106	Malta	69.2	69.2	67.6	66.9 - 68.6	14.3	13.9 - 15.0	70.9	70.2 - 72.2	16.5	16.2 - 16.9	8.2	9.5	10.9	11.8
107	Marshall Islands	52.3	52.6	50.4	49.1 - 53.3	7.9	7.0 - 9.8	54.7	53.6 - 56.7	10.3	9.6 - 11.9	10.3	9.6	17.0	14.9

Table 6.21 (*continued*)

	Member State	Total population At birth 2000	2001	Males 2001 At birth	Uncertainty interval	At age 60	Uncertainty interval	Females 2001 At birth	Uncertainty interval	At age 60	Uncertainty interval	Expectation of lost healthy years at birth (years) Males 2001	Females 2001	Percentage of total life expectancy lost Males 2001	Females 2001
108	Mauritania	41.5	41.6	39.6	32.6 - 48.1	6.9	4.7 - 9.3	43.6	36.6 - 51.6	9.4	7.1 - 11.7	11.4	9.5	22.3	17.9
109	Mauritius	57.2	57.1	56.4	55.1 - 59.0	9.4	8.5 - 10.7	57.7	55.0 - 61.5	11.2	10.0 - 13.5	11.0	17.2	16.4	22.9
110	Mexico	63.8	63.8	62.6	61.6 - 64.4	14.5	13.9 - 15.6	65.0	63.5 - 67.0	14.9	14.4 - 16.0	9.0	11.8	12.6	15.3
111	Micronesia, Federated States of	55.5	55.8	54.0	52.5 - 56.4	9.3	8.6 - 10.7	57.5	56.1 - 59.7	11.2	10.6 - 12.3	10.6	10.3	16.4	15.2
112	Monaco	70.8	71.3	69.0	68.4 - 70.5	16.3	15.8 - 17.5	73.5	72.2 - 76.0	19.4	18.6 - 21.8	7.5	10.5	9.8	12.5
113	Mongolia	53.7	53.9	49.9	48.2 - 52.5	9.7	9.0 - 11.0	58.0	57.1 - 59.9	12.7	11.9 - 14.1	11.4	10.3	18.6	15.0
114	Morocco	55.3	55.4	54.9	54.1 - 56.5	9.2	8.5 - 10.7	55.9	54.8 - 57.7	10.0	9.4 - 11	12.6	15.5	18.7	21.7
115	Mozambique	36.3	36.0	34.4	28.4 - 40.4	6.9	4.1 - 9.4	37.7	31.8 - 43.5	9.5	7.7 - 11.2	9.3	8.3	21.4	18.0
116	Myanmar[b]	48.9	48.9	46.5	39.8 - 53.5	9.0	7.2 - 11v	51.4	43.8 - 61.1	11.0	8.9 - 13.9	8.2	8.5	15.0	14.3
117	Namibia	41.8	40.4	39.8	34.7 - 45.7	8.7	6.9 - 11.4	41.1	36.8 - 47.3	10.9	8.8 - 14.1	8.6	8.0	17.8	16.2
118	Nauru	52.5	52.7	48.8	46.9 - 53.0	6.8	6.2 - 8.3	56.6	55.0 - 60.1	10.4	9.4 - 12.3	9.9	9.6	16.9	14.5
119	Nepal	48.7	48.9	48.7	47.5 - 50.9	8.9	8.3 - 10.0	49.1	47.6 - 51.7	10.5	9.9 - 11.9	9.9	8.8	16.8	15.2
120	Netherlands[b]	69.7	69.9	68.7	68.2 - 69.4	15.0	14.8 - 15.6	71.1	70.7 - 72.1	17.3	17.1 - 17.7	7.1	9.6	9.4	11.9
121	New Zealand	70.1	70.3	69.1	68.5 - 70.2	15.9	15.4 - 16.7	71.5	70.8 - 72.7	17.7	17.3 - 18.4	6.9	9.4	9.1	11.6
122	Nicaragua	57.7	57.8	54.4	53.0 - 58.0	10.7	10.0 - 12.1	61.3	60.1 - 63.5	13.7	13.1 - 15	12.7	10.7	18.9	14.9
123	Niger	33.1	33.2	31.7	25.3 - 39.3	6.1	3.2 - 8.6	34.7	27.0 - 42.5	8.6	6.8 - 10.4	10.2	8.5	24.3	19.6
124	Nigeria	41.9	41.9	40.0	34.6 - 46.2	7.0	5.1 - 9.4	43.8	37.1 - 50.6	9.5	7.9 - 11.5	10.6	8.9	20.9	16.8
125	Niue	59.2	59.1	56.4	54.5 - 59.6	10.0	9.2 - 11.6	61.9	60.5 - 64.1	13.0	12.1 - 14.7	11.3	11.6	16.7	15.8
126	Norway	70.7	70.8	69.3	68.8 - 70.4	15.6	15.3 - 16.4	72.2	71.2 - 73.6	17.9	17.4 - 18.8	6.8	9.3	8.9	11.4
127	Oman	60.4	60.4	59.0	57.0 - 61.2	10.4	8.9 - 12.0	61.7	58.0 - 64.7	12.3	10.8 - 13.9	10.4	12.9	15.0	17.3
128	Pakistan	50.9	50.9	50.4	48.9 - 53.3	9.3	8.6 - 10.3	51.5	50.0 - 53.9	10.8	10.0 - 12.3	10.7	10.0	17.5	16.3
129	Palau	57.4	57.7	55.5	54.6 - 57.5	9.2	8.5 - 10.1	59.9	58.5 - 62.3	11.7	11.0 - 13.0	11.4	10.7	17.1	15.1
130	Panama	63.9	64.1	61.2	59.9 - 63.5	13.6	12.9 - 14.7	66.9	65.7 - 68.8	16.4	15.6 - 17.7	10.8	11.1	15.0	14.2
131	Papua New Guinea	49.6	49.8	47.9	41.9 - 54.7	8.2	6.4 - 10.2	51.8	44.9 - 59.0	10.4	8.4 - 12.9	10.5	9.5	18.0	15.5
132	Paraguay	58.4	58.7	55.4	53.6 - 58.1	9.6	8.8 - 11.3	61.9	60.6 - 63.8	12.9	12.3 - 13.8	12.9	11.0	18.9	15.0
133	Peru	57.1	57.4	54.7	53.6 - 57.0	10.7	9.9 - 12.2	60.1	59.2 - 62.0	13.2	12.5 - 14.5	11.5	10.8	17.4	15.3
134	Philippines	55.2	55.5	51.1	49.8 - 53.7	8.0	7.3 - 9.5	59.8	58.8 - 62.4	11.9	10.9 - 13.7	13.1	11.7	20.3	16.4
135	Poland	64.3	64.3	62.1	61.7 - 62.8	11.9	11.7 - 12.4	66.6	65.6 - 68.0	14.6	14.3 - 15.1	7.8	11.5	11.1	14.7
136	Portugal	66.8	66.8	64.3	63.6 - 65.3	13.4	13.0 - 14.0	69.4	68.6 - 70.7	16.2	15.9 - 16.7	8.5	10.7	11.7	13.4
137	Qatar	61.2	61.2	59.2	57.6 - 61.5	9.4	8.5 - 11.1	63.1	62.0 - 65.1	12.7	12.3 - 13.8	11.5	11.2	16.2	15.1
138	Republic of Korea	67.2	67.4	64.5	63.8 - 65.6	12.9	12.6 - 13.5	70.3	69.6 - 71.8	16.6	16.4 - 17.1	6.7	8.4	9.4	10.6
139	Republic of Moldova	57.3	57.5	54.2	53.1 - 56.6	9.3	8.7 - 10.6	60.8	59.7 - 62.8	11.7	11.1 - 13.0	10.0	10.9	15.6	15.2
140	Romania	61.0	60.9	58.6	57.6 - 60.5	11.1	10.4 - 12.1	63.3	62.2 - 65.3	13.5	12.7 - 14.6	9.2	11.2	13.6	15.1
141	Russian Federation	56.6	56.7	51.5	50.9 - 52.7	8.5	7.4 - 10.3	61.9	61.0 - 63.8	12.7	12.5 - 13.3	7.4	10.4	12.6	14.4
142	Rwanda	34.1	33.8	31.7	27.1 - 36.1	6.7	4.1 - 9.5	36.0	31.1 - 41.3	9.6	7.8 - 11.2	7.3	6.8	18.7	15.9
143	Saint Kitts and Nevis	60.7	60.8	58.8	57.3 - 61.2	11.1	10.6 - 11.8	62.8	61.3 - 64.8	13.5	12.8 - 14.7	10.2	10.0	14.8	13.7
144	Saint Lucia	60.4	60.6	58.9	57.7 - 61.0	11.0	10.5 - 12v	62.4	61.1 - 64.4	13.5	12.8 - 14.8	10.7	10.6	15.3	14.5
145	Saint Vincent and the Grenadines	59.8	59.8	57.5	56.1 - 59.7	11.3	10.7 - 12.4	62.2	61.6 - 64.3	14.0	13.4 - 15.3	10.3	10.2	15.1	14.1
146	Samoa	57.8	57.7	56.0	54.6 - 58.0	9.3	8.6 - 10.6	59.5	58.7 - 61.2	11.6	10.9 - 12.8	11.0	10.4	16.5	14.9
147	San Marino	72.1	72.2	70.4	69.7 - 71.7	16.3	15.9 - 17.2	74.0	73.3 - 75.5	19.1	18.6 - 20.2	7.2	9.8	9.3	11.7
148	Sao Tome and Principe	51.2	51.4	48.1	42.5 - 54.6	8.2	6.1 - 10.7	54.7	47.8 - 64.9	10.8	9.2 - 13.6	14.8	10.3	23.5	15.8
149	Saudi Arabia	59.8	60.0	57.4	54.1 - 60.0	10.0	8.1 - 11.8	62.5	58.2 - 66.9	13.0	10.5 - 15.2	10.9	11.0	16.0	15.0
150	Senegal	45.3	45.4	43.1	37.8 - 49.1	7.4	5.5 - 9.2	47.7	40.9 - 54.9	9.8	7.2 - 12.4	11.3	9.5	20.8	16.6
151	Seychelles	59.0	59.1	55.4	53.9 - 57.6	8.6	7.7 - 10.2	62.9	62.0 - 65.3	13.1	12.2 - 14.5	11.3	13.6	17.0	17.8
152	Sierra Leone	25.8	26.5	24.0	17.3 - 30.8	5.5	3.2 - 7.7	29.0	21.8 - 36.2	8.5	6.0 - 10.3	8.6	6.9	26.4	19.3
153	Singapore	68.5	68.7	67.9	67.3 - 69.5	14.5	13.8 - 15.4	69.5	68.3 - 71.4	15.8	15.1 - 17.1	8.6	11.6	11.2	14.3
154	Slovakia	64.1	64.1	61.6	61.1 - 62.3	11.5	11.2 - 12.0	66.6	65.8 - 68.1	14.6	14.3 - 15.0	7.7	10.7	11.1	13.9
155	Slovenia	67.5	67.7	65.1	64.3 - 66.6	13.3	13.1 - 13.9	70.3	69.5 - 72.0	16.6	16.1 - 17.6	7.0	9.2	9.7	11.6
156	Solomon Islands	54.6	54.8	52.6	51.1 - 55.9	8.7	7.6 - 11.2	56.9	55.7 - 60.0	11.0	10.4 - 12.4	12.0	11.5	18.6	16.8
157	Somalia	35.1	35.0	32.5	28.0 - 37.8	6.3	3.8 - 8.8	37.4	31.6 - 44.2	8.8	6.4 - 11.6	8.5	7.9	20.7	17.5
158	South Africa	43.0	41.3	40.0	38.2 - 41.8	8.9	7.6 - 10.1	42.7	39.9 - 45.7	11.4	9.7 - 13.5	7.7	7.6	16.2	15.1
159	Spain	70.7	70.9	68.7	68.0 - 69.7	15.2	14.8 - 16.0	73.0	72.5 - 74.2	18.2	17.9 - 18.7	6.6	9.6	8.8	11.6
160	Sri Lanka	58.3	58.9	55.2	53.7 - 57.8	8.8	8.0 - 10.5	62.6	61.6 - 64.3	12.7	11.8 - 13.9	11.5	11.4	17.2	15.4

Table 6.21 (*continued*)

	Member State	Total population At birth 2000	2001	Males 2001 At birth	Uncertainty interval	At age 60	Uncertainty interval	Females 2001 At birth	Uncertainty interval	At age 60	Uncertainty interval	Expectation of lost healthy years at birth (years) Males 2001	Females 2001	Percentage of total life expectancy lost Males 2001	Females 2001
161	Sudan	45.9	45.5	42.9	37.3 – 49.0	7.4	5.4 – 9.7	48.1	41.1 – 56.1	9.9	8.1 – 11.9	11.2	9.8	20.7	16.9
162	Suriname	57.2	57.5	54.2	53.1 – 56.4	9.4	8.7 – 10.5	60.7	59.9 – 62.5	12.6	12.1 – 13.7	10.0	10.0	15.6	14.1
163	Swaziland	35.4	33.9	33.8	29.5 – 38.3	9.0	6.9 – 11.3	34.1	29.4 – 38.4	11.0	8.6 – 13.6	6.4	6.1	16.0	15.1
164	Sweden	71.6	71.8	70.5	70.0 – 71.5	16.5	16.1 – 17.2	73.2	72.6 – 74.5	18.5	18.3 – 19.1	7.2	9.1	9.2	11.1
165	Switzerland	72.5	72.8	71.1	70.6 – 72.2	16.9	16.5 – 17.7	74.4	73.7 – 75.6	19.4	19.1 – 19.9	6.2	8.4	8.0	10.2
166	Syrian Arab Republic[b]	59.0	59.2	58.0	56.9 – 60.3	10.0	8.9 – 11.6	60.5	59.3 – 62.6	11.5	10.5 – 13.0	10.7	12.7	15.6	17.4
167	Tajikistan	49.4	50.1	47.0	44.8 – 51.2	8.4	7.5 – 10.3	53.2	51.3 – 56.8	11.8	10.7 – 14.0	12.8	13.7	21.4	20.5
168	Thailand	58.6	58.6	56.4	55.7 – 58.0	12.0	11.4 – 13.0	60.8	59.5 – 63.2	12.6	12.2 – 13.3	9.3	11.5	14.1	15.9
169	The former Yugoslav Republic of Macedonia	62.3	62.2	60.4	59.7 – 61.9	11.4	10.8 – 12.2	63.9	62.9 – 65.5	13.0	12.5 – 14.0	8.5	11.0	12.4	14.7
170	Togo	42.8	42.7	40.6	35.6 – 46.6	7.6	5.3 – 10.4	44.9	39.6 – 50.3	10.2	8.2 – 12.4	9.7	8.2	19.3	15.5
171	Tonga	59.0	58.8	57.1	56.1 – 59.0	10.0	9.2 – 11.3	60.4	59.1 – 62.4	11.9	11.5 – 12.9	11.0	10.5	16.1	14.8
172	Trinidad and Tobago	60.4	60.4	58.9	58.1 – 60.6	11.5	10.9 – 12.4	62.0	60.9 – 64.2	12.8	12.3 – 13.7	8.4	10.6	12.5	14.6
173	Tunisia	61.1	61.3	58.9	57.9 – 60.4	10.8	10.3 – 11.4	63.7	62.8 – 65.5	13.4	12.9 – 14.6	10.1	9.8	14.7	13.3
174	Turkey	59.7	59.8	58.5	57.9 – 59.3	11.2	10.9 – 11.7	61.1	60.2 – 62.7	12.4	12.1 – 12.9	8.5	10.1	12.7	14.2
175	Turkmenistan	50.2	50.3	46.7	45.3 – 49.6	6.8	5.9 – 8.6	53.8	52.3 – 56.2	9.7	9.0 – 11.1	12.1	12.7	20.6	19.1
176	Tuvalu	53.9	53.9	52.0	51.1 – 54.2	8.8	8.3 – 10.0	55.7	54.5 – 58.0	11.0	10.2 – 12.8	9.9	9.7	16.0	14.8
177	Uganda	37.5	38.0	36.2	33.3 – 39.6	6.9	5.5 – 8.3	39.8	35.2 – 44.8	9.4	6.3 – 12.8	9.0	7.9	20.0	16.6
178	Ukraine	57.5	57.4	52.9	52.4 – 53.8	8.8	8.4 – 9.3	61.8	60.9 – 63.8	12.2	12.0 – 12.6	9.3	11.5	14.9	15.6
179	United Arab Emirates	62.4	62.5	61.7	61.0 – 63.1	10.6	10.0 – 11.6	63.3	62.2 – 65.2	12.3	11.9 – 13.2	9.0	11.5	12.8	15.4
180	United Kingdom[b]	69.2	69.6	68.4	68.0 – 69.4	15.0	14.7 – 15.6	70.9	70.1 – 72.4	16.9	16.5 – 17.4	6.6	9.0	8.8	11.3
181	United Republic of Tanzania	37.8	37.8	36.3	34.5 – 39.3	6.8	5.9 – 8.8	39.3	38.3 – 41.3	9.5	8.7 – 11.0	9.5	7.9	20.7	16.8
182	United States of America[b]	67.4	67.6	66.4	65.8 – 67.5	14.9	14.5 – 15.7	68.8	67.9 – 70.2	16.6	16.2 – 17.3	8.0	10.7	10.8	13.5
183	Uruguay	64.7	64.7	61.2	60.3 – 63.4	12.3	12.0 – 13.2	68.3	67.2 – 70.2	16.8	16.2 – 18.2	9.7	10.9	13.7	13.7
184	Uzbekistan	53.4	53.5	50.9	49.3 – 54.6	8.2	6.9 – 10.2	56.1	54.8 – 59.3	10.8	9.9 – 12.4	11.7	12.4	18.7	18.2
185	Vanuatu	54.6	54.9	53.4	48.0 – 59.9	8.9	6.9 – 11.6	56.3	49.1 – 63.4	10.8	8.7 – 13.4	11.0	10.8	17.1	16.1
186	Venezuela, Bolivarian Republic of	60.9	61.1	57.1	55.5 – 59.9	11.6	10.3 – 13.4	65.0	63.7 – 67.5	15.0	14.5 – 15.9	13.7	11.5	19.3	15.0
187	Viet Nam	58.5	58.6	55.9	54.5 – 58.2	9.9	9.2 – 10.9	61.4	60.5 – 63.6	12.5	11.6 – 14.0	11.0	10.4	16.5	14.5
188	Yemen	47.9	48.4	45.5	39.8 – 52.4	7.0	4.6 – 9.4	51.2	44.1 – 58.9	10.4	8.3 – 12.7	12.9	10.2	22.0	16.6
189	Yugoslavia	62.0	62.1	60.7	60.1 – 62.0	11.0	10.5 – 11.7	63.6	62.6 – 65.4	12.8	12.1 – 13.9	9.0	11.2	13.0	15.0
190	Zambia	31.1	30.9	30.5	26.7 – 34.3	7.5	5.9 – 9.3	31.4	27.8 – 35.3	10.0	7.7 – 12.3	6.2	5.6	17.0	15.2
191	Zimbabwe	32.0	31.3	31.6	29.8 – 33.3	8.6	7.2 – 10.0	31.0	28.3 – 33.7	10.7	8.8 – 12.6	5.6	5.5	15.0	15.0

a. Healthy life expectancy estimates published have are not directly comparable to those published in The World Health Airport 2001, because of improvements in survey methodology and the use of new epidemiological data for some diseases and revisions of the tables for 2000 for many Member States to take new data into account see Statistical Annexexplanatory notes. The figures reported in the Table along with the data collection and estimation methods have been largely developed by WHO and do not necessarily reflect official statistics of Member States. Further development in collaboration with Member States is underway for improved data collection and estimation methods.

b. Figures not endorsed by Member State as official statistics.

Source: World Health Organization. (2002). *World Health Report 2002: Reducing risks, promoting healthy life.* Geneva: Author. Retrieved from http://www.who.int/whr/2002/en/.

Table 6.22
Social Security Schemes—Percent of Total Health Expenditures

	1960	1970	1980	1985	1990	1991	1992	1993	1994	1995	1996	1997	1998	1999	2000	2001	2002
Australia	0		0	0	0	0	0	0	0	0	0	0	0	0	0	0	
Austria										66.2	66.4	56.6	56.6	57.3	58	59.2	58.9
Belgium																	
Canada			1.4	1.5	1.4	1.5	1.5	1.4	1.4	1.5	1.6	1.8	1.8	1.9	2	2	2.1
Czech Republic								81.2	83	83.8	87.7	89.5	90.2	89.4	89.4	90.4	89.2
Denmark			0	0	0	0	0	0	0	0	0	0	0	0	0	0	0
Finland		14.3	15.8	13	13.1	13.7	14	16	17.3	17.7	18.3	18.7	19.4	19.8	20.4	20.7	21
France	84	91.2	94.7	95.5	97	97.2	97.3	97.3	97	96.9	96.8	96.8	96.8	96.7	96.6	96.5	96.8
Germany		80.1	85.1	85.5	85.8		81.7	80.7	81.4	82.2	84	86.3	87	87.2	87.3	87.1	87.4
Greece																	
Hungary						81.9	78.8	78.7	77.7	80	82.4	82.8	83.4	83.8	83.9	83.3	81.3
Iceland	61.1	102.8	63.9	57	39.1	37.9	36.9	33.9	34.6	34.9	35.7	30.7	29.8	26.8	29.2	28	
Ireland					1.1	1.1	1.1	1.3	1.3	1.3	1.2	1.1	1.1	1.1	1.2	0.9	0.8
Italy						0.4	0.4	0.4	0.4	0.4	0.4	0.4	0.1	0.1	0.1	0.3	0.1
Japan										81.7	82.4	82	80.9	81.2	80.9	80.5	
Korea				79	77.9	76.8	76.3	76.9	76.5	74.5	75.4	75.7	76.9	74.7	76.7	80	
Luxembourg									83.8	83.4	84.3	86	82.7	93	94	94.4	94.1
Mexico					81	81.3	81.1	80.6	80.5	79.3	76.5	72.9	72.4	69.2	67.7	66.5	66
Netherlands			92.3	94	93	92.5	93.1	93.2	93.7	93.6	93.7	93.6					
New Zealand		0	0	0	0	0	0	0	0	0	0	0	0	0	0	0	0
Norway																	
Poland																	
Portugal														83.5	82.6	83.8	87.4
Slovak Republic												96.7	96.6	94.2	94.4	95.1	96.4
Spain						28.1	28.4	29.3	29	23.6	20.1	13.4	11.8	9.4	9.6	9.2	6.8
Sweden																	
Switzerland				64	63.5	63.6	65.1	67.8	69	70	70.5	71.6	72.3	72.1	72.6	70.4	69.1
Turkey														53	55.5		
United Kingdom	0	0	0	0	0	0	0	0	0	0	0	0	0			0	0
United States	10.2	29.3	32.8	37.5	37.4	35.5	34.2	32.2	33	32.1	32.8	32.1	33.4	33.1	33.7	32.8	30.8

Source: Organization for Economic Co-operation and Development. (2004). *OECD Health Data 2004.* (1st ed.). Washington, D.C.: Author. Retrieved from http://www.oecd.org/dataoecd/13/8/31963527.xls. OECD Copyright. Reproduced by permission of the OECD.

Table 6.23
Private Insurance—Percent of Total Health Expenditures

	1960	1970	1980	1990	1991	1992	1993	1994	1995	1996	1997	1998	1999	2000	2001	2002
Australia	10.3		15.7	11.4	11.6	11.5	11.2	10.9	10.7	10.5	9	7.6	6.6	7.3	7.8	
Austria	6.8	8.1	7.6	9	9	8.9	8.8	8.6	8.3	7.7	8.1	7.6	7.3	7.2	7.4	7.3
Belgium																
Canada				8.1	8.4	8.9	9.5	9.8	10.3	10.7	10.9	11.3	11.1	11.4		
Czech Republic																
Denmark			0.8	1.3	1.2	1.2	1	1.1	1.2	1.4	1.4	1.4	1.7	1.6	1.6	
Finland	2.4	1.7	1.4	2.1	1.9	2.4	2.5	2.5	2.4	2.4	2.6	2.6	2.7	2.6	2.5	
France			11	11	11	11.2	12	11.9	12.4	12.4	12.6	12.6	12.7	12.7		
Germany		7.5	5.9	7.2		11.8	12.3	12.1	12	11.7	12.3	12.3	12.5	12.6	12.6	
Greece																
Hungary												0	0.1	0.2	0.3	
Iceland																
Ireland				9.1	9	8.6	8.9	9.2	9.1	9.2	8.7	8.9	8	7.6	6.8	
Italy				0.6	0.7	0.8	0.9	0.9	1	1	1	0.9	0.9	0.9	0.9	0.9
Japan									0.4	0.3	0.3	0.3	0.3	0.3	0.3	
Korea				4.8	5.3	5.1	5.9	5.9	5.8	6.2	6.7	7	7.7	8.7		
Luxembourg													1.5	1.6		
Mexico				1.2	1.7	1.7	1.8	1.8	1.7	2	2.2	2.2	2.2	2.6	2.8	
Netherlands											15.5	15.7	15.2	15.5		
New Zealand			1.1	2.8	3.6	4.8	5.2	6.1	6.4	6.7	6.8	6.4	6.2	6.3	6.3	5.9
Norway																
Poland																
Portugal				0.8	0.9	1.2	1.3	1.4	1.3	1.4	1.5					
Slovak Republic											0	0				
Spain		3.3	3.2	3.7	2.9	3	3.2	3.4	3.4	3.5	3.5	3.7	3.8	3.9	4	
Sweden																
Switzerland				11	10.7	10.9	11.5	11.7	12.2	12.9	11.5	11.4	10.4	10.5	10.2	
Turkey					0.1			0.7								
United Kingdom		0.9	1.3	3.3	3.4	3.4	3.4	3.3	3.2	3.3						
United States	22.5	21.9	28.4	34.2	33.9	33.7	34.2	33.9	33.8	33.7	33.5	33.8	34.4	35.1	35.6	

Source: Organization for Economic Co-operation and Development. (2004). *OECD Health Data 2003.* (3rd ed.). Washington, D.C.: Author. Retrieved from http://www.oecd.org/dataoecd/12/53/2957435.xls. OECD Copyright. Reproduced by permission of the OECD.

Table 6.24
Life Expectancy in Years and by Sex: 1960 to 2002

	1960		1970		1980	
	Females at birth	Males at birth	Females at birth	Males at birth	Females at birth	Males at birth
Australia	73.9	67.9	74.2	67.4	78.1	71
Austria	71.9	65.4	73.4	66.5	76.1	69
Belgium	73.5	67.7	74.2	67.8	76.8	70
Canada					78.9	71.7
Czech Republic	73.4	67.9	73	66.1	73.9	66.8
Denmark	74.4	70.4	75.9	70.7	77.3	71.2
Finland	72.5	65.5	75	66.5	77.6	69.2
France	73.6	67	75.9	68.4	78.4	70.2
Germany	72.4	66.9	73.6	67.2	76.1	69.6
Greece	72.4	67.3	73.8	70.1	76.8	72.2
Hungary	70.1	65.9	72.1	66.3	72.7	65.5
Iceland	75	70.7	77.3	71.2	79.7	73.7
Ireland	71.9	68.1	73.5	68.8	75.6	70.1
Italy					77.4	70.6
Japan	70.2	65.3	74.7	69.3	78.8	73.4
Korea	53.7	51.1				
Luxembourg	72.2	66.5	73.4	67.1	75.9	69.1
Mexico	59.2	55.8	63.2	58.5	70.2	64.1
Netherlands	75.4	71.5	76.5	70.8	79.2	72.5
New Zealand	73.9	68.7	74.6	68.3	76.3	70
Norway	75.8	71.3	77.3	71	79.2	72.3
Poland	70.6	64.9	73.3	66.6	74.4	66
Portugal	66.8	61.2	70.8	64.2	75.2	67.7
Slovak Republic	72.7	68.4	72.9	66.7	74.3	66.8
Spain	72.2	67.4	74.8	69.2	78.6	72.5
Sweden	74.9	71.2	77.1	72.2	78.8	72.8
Switzerland	74.5	68.7	76.9	70.7	79.6	72.8
Turkey	50.3	46.3	56.3	52	60.3	55.8
United Kingdom	73.7	67.9	75	68.7	76.2	70.2
United States	73.1	66.6	74.7	67.1	77.4	70

	1990		1995		2000	
	Females at birth	Males at birth	Females at birth	Males at birth	Females at birth	Males at birth
Australia	80.1	73.9	80.8	75	82	76.6
Austria	78.8	72.2	79.9	73.3	81.1	75.1
Belgium	79.4	72.7	80.2	73.4	80.8	74.6
Canada	80.8	74.4	81.1	75.1	82	76.7
Czech Republic	75.4	67.6	76.6	69.7	78.4	71.7
Denmark	77.7	72	77.8	72.7	79.3	74.5
Finland	78.9	70.9	80.2	72.8	81	74.2
France	80.9	72.8	81.8	73.9	82.7	75.3
Germany	78.4	72	79.7	73.3	81	75
Greece	79.5	74.6	80.3	75	80.6	75.5
Hungary	73.7	65.1	74.5	65.3	75.9	67.4
Iceland	80.5	75.4	80	75.9	81.4	78
Ireland	77.6	72.1	78.4	72.9	79.1	73.9
Italy	80.1	73.6	81.3	74.9	82.5	76.6
Japan	81.9	75.9	82.9	76.4	84.6	77.7
Korea			77.4	69.6		
Luxembourg	78.5	72.3	80.2	73	81.1	74.8
Mexico	74.1	68.3	75.3	70	76.5	71.6
Netherlands	80.9	73.8	80.4	74.6	80.5	75.5
New Zealand	78.3	72.4	79.5	74.2	80.9	76
Norway	79.8	73.4	80.8	74.8	81.4	76
Poland	76.3	66.7	76.4	67.6	77.9	69.7
Portugal	77.4	70.4	78.7	71.6	80	73.2
Slovak Republic	75.4	66.6	76.3	68.4	77.4	69.2
Spain	80.3	73.3	81.5	74.3	82.5	75.7
Sweden	80.4	74.8	81.4	76.2	82	77.4
Switzerland	80.7	74	81.7	75.3	82.6	76.9
Turkey	68.7	64.2	69.4	64.9	70.4	65.8
United Kingdom	78.5	72.9	79.2	74	80.2	75.5
United States	78.8	71.8	78.9	72.5	79.5	74.1

Table 6.24 (*continued*)

	2001		2002	
	Females at birth	**Males at birth**	**Females at birth**	**Males at birth**
Australia	82.4	77	82.6	77.4
Austria	81.5	75.6	81.7	75.8
Belgium	81.1	74.9	81.1	75.1
Canada	82.2	77.1		
Czech Republic	78.5	72.1	78.7	72.1
Denmark	79.3	74.7	79.5	74.8
Finland	81.5	74.6	81.5	74.9
France	82.9	75.5	82.9	75.6
Germany	81.3	75.6		
Greece	80.7	75.4	80.7	75.4
Hungary	76.4	68.1	76.7	68.4
Iceland	82.2	78.3	82.3	78.5
Ireland	79.7	74.7	80.3	75.2
Italy	82.8	76.7	82.9	76.8
Japan	84.9	78.1	85.2	78.3
Korea	80	72.8		
Luxembourg	80.7	75.2	81.5	74.9
Mexico	76.8	71.9	77.1	72.1
Netherlands	80.7	75.8	80.7	76
New Zealand	80.9	76		
Norway	81.5	76.2	81.5	76.4
Poland	78.3	70.2	78.7	70.4
Portugal	80.3	73.5	80.5	73.8
Slovak Republic	77.7	69.6	77.8	69.9
Spain	82.9	75.6	83.1	75.7
Sweden	82.1	77.6	82.1	77.7
Switzerland	83	77.4	83	77.8
Turkey	70.6	66	70.9	66.2
United Kingdom	80.4	75.7		
United States	79.8	74.4		

Source: Organization for Economic Co-operation and Development. (2004). *OECD Health Data 2004.* (1st ed.). Washington, D.C.: Author. Retrieved from http://www.oecd.org/dataoecd/13/41/31963112.xls. OECD Copyright. Reproduced by permission of the OECD.

Table 6.25
Out-of-Pocket Payments—Per Capita, in U.S. Dollars PPP: 1960 to 2002

	1960	1970	1980	1985	1990	1991	1992	1993	1994	1995	1996	1997	1998	1999	2000	2001	2002
Australia	34		110	142	216	237	252	269	286	287	317	337	381	403	450	483	
Austria										277	309	325	349	377	400	397	388
Belgium																	
Canada					247	264	279	299	314	324	329	358	373	392	404	419	445
Czech Republic					14	17	25	39	50	64	68	76	75	80	84	94	96
Denmark		55	107	173	249	245	259	286	306	300	316	331	354	369	373	399	396
Finland	27	45	107	175	220	242	255	285	285	293	307	311	312	333	346	371	389
France	21	36	89	159	177	196	202	211	214	218	220	223	231	238	254	263	268
Germany		37	99	154	192	193	201	213	225	242	262	277	279	278	290	292	
Greece																	
Hungary																	
Iceland	21	55	82	146	214	223	254	289	293	298	329	329	382	410	419	451	450
Ireland				95	131	145	154	157	167	188	185	191	159	227	240	245	311
Italy			86	145	214	232	271	303	343	372	388	411	440	446	454	425	439
Japan										234	256	284	305	313	330	342	
Korea				102	177	199	221	235	243	261	288	292	254	306	335	347	
Luxembourg			46	84	84	90	98	104	130	127	153	159	174	201	200	219	364
Mexico					169	181	205	217	220	213	206	213	221	232	252	281	288
Netherlands													206	222	233	253	266
New Zealand			51	67	143	144	174	198	190	200	205	212	234	243	247	290	298
Norway					202	231	240	251	263	288	315	331	342	367	399	421	439
Poland					25	87	89	101	104	115	131	142	195	165	173	177	180
Portugal																	
Slovak Republic												45	47	60	63	68	76
Spain						177	194	210	225	281	290	297	319	342	353	372	388
Sweden																	
Switzerland				554	728	789	804	791	813	843	833	908	972	993	1023	1042	1085
Turkey						59	63	55	55	71				114	123		
United Kingdom			41		104	121	131	133	148	152	161						
United States	71	122	256	401	550	562	569	565	546	550	564	594	635	661	682	703	737

Source: Organization for Economic Co-operation and Development. (2004). *OECD Health Data 2004.* (1st ed.). Washington, D.C.: Author. Retrieved from http://www.oecd.org/dataoecd/13/31/31963545.xls. OECD Copyright. Reproduced by permission of the OECD.

Table 6.26
Total Expenditure on In-Patient Care—Percent of Total Expenditure on Health: 1960 to 2003

	1960	1970	1980	1985	1990	1991	1992	1993	1994	1995
Australia	43		51.6	48.8	46.5	46.1	44.5	43.2	43.1	43.1
Austria										44.7
Belgium		25.7	33.1	34	32.8	33.6	34	35.1	35.7	33.5
Canada	43.7	52.6	53.8	51.6	49.1	48.9	48.5	47.4	45.8	44.6
Czech Republic										29.6
Denmark			61.6	60.4	56.7	56.4	55.9	55.3	55.4	55
Finland	39.9	46.4	46.3	46	44.7	44.4	43.9	43.1	42.2	42
France	38.6	40.6	50.2	48.7	45.7	44.9	44.7	44.6	45	45.1
Germany		30.8	33.2	34.1	34.7		35.8	37.4	37.6	36.9
Greece										
Hungary						65.2	62.6	59.1	55.8	54.8
Iceland	37	50.9	59.1	56.5	54.7	54.8	53.6	54.1	54	54.4
Ireland			58.8							
Italy					42.7	43.9	44	45.2	45.9	44.8
Japan	34.1	26.4	30.9	32.8	33	32.1	32.8	32.2	31	36.8
Korea				19.2	23.3	23.5	24.1	23.6	22.9	23.4
Luxembourg			31.3	27.4	26.4	26.7	26.9	28	27.7	31.3
Mexico										
Netherlands			54.6	54.1	49.2	49.8	49.7	49.8	49.7	49.1
New Zealand			72.2	76.2	60.4	59.1	56.5	59.1		
Norway	38.1	68.2	63.9	64.8	61.7					
Poland										
Portugal			28.7	26.4	32.3	33	35	36.5	36.8	33.9
Slovak Republic										
Spain			54.1	55.7	44.1	47.3	47.6	48.1	47.5	31
Sweden								49	47.8	49
Switzerland	35.7	44.4	47.5	46.7	47.9	49.9	49.8	49.9	49.1	47.9
Turkey					33.4	35.1	25.3	25.9	26.9	28.7
United Kingdom										
United States	35.6	41.1	44.1	40.4	36.1	35.7	35	34.1	33.1	32.2

	1996	1997	1998	1999	2000	2001	2002	2003
Australia	42.9	43.3	43.1	41.9	40.7	40.2		
Austria	43.6	39.6	38.6	38.5	38.3	38	38.2	
Belgium	34.5	34.6						
Canada	44	43.2	42.5	30	30	29.1	28.8	28.8
Czech Republic	33.8	35.6	35.4	33.9	34.6	36.6	37.8	
Denmark	55.3	54.7	54.5	54.4	53.2	51.9	51.1	
Finland	41.7	41.3	41.1	40.5	39.9	39.3	39.2	
France	45.2	45	44.3	43.2	42.3	41.7	41.3	
Germany	36.3	36.4	36.7	36.5	36.6	36.1	36.1	
Greece								
Hungary	52.4		29.3	29.3	29.3	28.1	29	
Iceland	54.7	54.8	54.9	53.6	55.2	54.6		
Ireland								
Italy	41.7	42.5	41.4	41.8	41.4	41.5	41.5	41.8
Japan	37	37.7	38.3	38.5	39	38.9		
Korea	24.3	25.3	25.8	27	25.5	22.9		
Luxembourg	32.4	36	30.7	40.2	41.2	39.5	40.3	
Mexico				36	37.3	41.6	33	
Netherlands	49.6	49.9	40.1	39.9	39.8	40.5	40.8	
New Zealand								
Norway								
Poland								
Portugal								
Slovak Republic				30.7	26.4	28.7	35	
Spain	30.8	30	29.3	28.8	28.2	27.9	27.6	
Sweden	47.7	47.2	42.6	40.8	46.3	31.6	31.2	
Switzerland	48	47.8	47.2	46.8	46.8	47.3	48.1	
Turkey	28.2	28.8	29.3	21.3	19.9			
United Kingdom								
United States	31.6	30.9	30.2	29.1	28.4	28	27.6	

Source: Organization for Economic Co-operation and Development. (2004). *OECD Health Data 2004.* (1st ed.). Washington, D.C.: Author. Retrieved from http://www.oecd.org/dataoecd/13/10/31963499.xls. OECD Copyright. Reproduced by permission of the OECD.

Table 6.27

Total Expenditure on Pharmaceuticals—Percent of Total Expenditure on Health: 1960 to 2003

	1960	1970	1980	1985	1990	1991	1992	1993	1994	1995
Australia	22.6		8	8.1	9	9.5	9.9	10.4	11	11.2
Austria										11.1
Belgium		28.1	17.4	15.7	15.5	15.6	16.3	17.4	17.5	16.3
Canada	12.9	11.3	8.5	9.6	11.5	11.8	12.4	13	13.1	13.8
Czech Republic					21	18.4	21.1	19.4	24.7	25.6
Denmark			6	6.6	7.5	8	7.9	8.5	8.8	9.1
Finland	17.1	12.6	10.7	9.7	9.4	9.9	10.8	12.3	13.4	14.1
France	23.5	23.8	16	16.2	16.9	17.2	17.1	17.5	17.4	17.6
Germany			16.2	13.4	13.8	14.3	14.7	13.2	12.9	12.7
Greece		25.5	18.8		14.3	16.3	17	16.6	16.1	15.7
Hungary						27.6	26.5	28.4	28	25
Iceland	18.5	17.1	15.9	16.6	13.5	12.3	13	12.4	13.1	13.4
Ireland		22.2	10.9	9.9	12.2	11.6	11.1	10.7	10.6	10.4
Italy					21.2	20.4	20.4	19.9	19.9	20.9
Japan			21.2	18	21.4	22.9	22	22.3	21.1	22.3
Korea				27.1	24.5	25.6	23.5	22.9	21.4	21
Luxembourg		19.7	14.5	14.7	14.9	15				
Mexico									12.2	12
Netherlands			8	9.3	9.6	9.6	10.5	11	10.9	11
New Zealand			11.9	13.3	13.8	14.1	14.2	14.9	15.8	14.8
Norway		7.8	8.7	9.1	7.2	7.3	7.5	9.6	8.8	9
Poland										
Portugal		13.4	19.9	25.4	24.9	24.3	24.7	25.6	25.2	23.6
Slovak Republic										
Spain			21	20.3	17.8					19.2
Sweden		6.6	6.5	7	8	8.7	9.7	10.9	11.9	12.5
Switzerland				11.3	10.2	9.8	9.4	9.7	9.8	10
Turkey				13.2	20.5				31.6	
Unitek Kingdom		14.7	12.8	14.1	13.5	13.8	14.2	14.8	15.1	15.3
United States	16.6	12.4	9.1	9	9.2	9.1	8.8	8.6	8.6	8.9

	1996	1997	1998	1999	2000	2001	2002	2003
Australia	11.5	11.7	11.9	12.4	13.4	13.8		
Austria	11.2	13.1	14	14.6	15.4	15.8	16.1	
Belgium	15.5	16.2						
Canada	14	14.8	15.2	15.5	16	16.3	16.6	16.7
Czech Republic	25.5	25.3	23.2	22.7	22	21.9	22.6	
Denmark	8.9	9	9	8.7	8.7	8.8	9.2	
Finland	14.4	14.8	14.6	15.1	15.5	15.7	15.9	
France	17.6	18	18.6	19.5	20.3	20.9	20.8	
Germany	12.8	12.9	13.4	13.5	13.6	14.3	14.5	
Greece	16.1	16.2	13.9	14.4	15.4	15.6	15.3	
Hungary	26	25.9				28.5	27.6	
Iceland	14	13.6	13.6	14.1	14.1	14		
Ireland	10.5	10.2	10.4	10.5	10.6	10.3	11	
Italy	21.1	21.3	21.8	22.3	22.3	22.4	22.4	21.9
Japan	21.6	20.6	18.9	18.4	18.7	18.8		
Korea	19	16.3	13.4	13.5	16	22.4		
Luxembourg	11.5	12.6	12.3	11.9	12	12	11.6	
Mexico				18.6	19.5	19.9	21.6	
Netherlands	11	11	10.2	10.6	10.8	10.6	10.4	
New Zealand	14.5	14.4						
Norway	9.1	9.2						
Poland								
Portugal	23.8	23.8	23.4					
Slovak Republic				34	34	34	37.3	
Spain	19.8	20.8	21	21.5	21.3	21.2	21.5	
Sweden	13.7	12.5	13.8	14	13.9	13.3	13.1	
Switzerland	10	10.3	10.2	10.5	10.7	10.6	10.3	
Turkey				24.3	24.8			
Unitek Kingdom	15.6	15.8						
United States	9.2	9.6	10.3	11.2	11.9	12.4	12.8	

Source: Organization for Economic Co-operation and Development. (2004). *OECD Health Data 2004.* (1st ed.). Washington, D.C.: Author. Retrieved from http://www.oecd.org/dataoecd/13/9/31963517.xls. OECD Copyright. Reproduced by permission of the OECD.

Table 6.28
Average Length of Stay: Acute Care, Days

	1960	1970	1980	1985	1990	1991	1992	1993	1994	1995
Australia	11.5	8.7	7.7	7.4		6.5	6.6	6.4	6.4	6.5
Austria			14.5	10.8	9.3	8.8	8.5	8.2	8	7.9
Belgium								9.8	9.6	9.4
Canada			10	10.4	10.3	10.2	10	9.9	7.4	7.2
Czech Republic	15	15	13.6	13.1	12	11.9	11.6	11.2	10.8	10.2
Denmark		12.5	8.5	7.8	6.4	6.3	6.1	6	4.1	4.1
Finland	12.5	12.8	8.8	8	7	7	6.1	5.7	5.6	5.5
France			10.2	8.6	7	6.7	6.5	6.4	6.4	6.2
Germany		24.6	19.6	18	16.7	16.2	15.6	15	14.7	14.2
Greece			10.2	8.9	7.5	7.2	7.1	6.6	6.7	6.4
Hungary	11.3	11.2	11.2	10.6	9.9	9.7	9.5		9.8	9.2
Iceland					7	6.6	6.4	6.4	6.3	5.9
Ireland			8.5	7.4	6.7	6.7	6.8	6.7	6.7	6.6
Italy						9.5	9.3	9.2	9	8.4
Japan										
Korea			10	11	12	11	11	11	11	11
Luxembourg			13	11.9	11	10.8	10.3	10.2	9.9	9.8
Mexico					4.2	4.3	4.3	4.2	3.8	3.7
Netherlands	20.1	18.8	14	12.5	11.2	10.9	10.6	10.4	10.1	9.9
New Zealand										
Norway		14.8	10.9	9.6	7.8	7.4	6.9	6.8	6.6	6.5
Poland										
Portugal		15.3	11.4	11.1	8.4	8.3	7.9	7.7	7.7	7.9
Slovak Republic										
Spain				10.1	9.6	9.3	9.2	9.1	9	8.8
Sweden		11	8.5	7.5	6.5	6.2	5.8	5.5	5.3	5.2
Switzerland			15.5	14.7	13.4	13	12.1	12.1	12	12
Turkey			6.3	6.2	6	6	6	5.9	5.8	5.7
United Kingdom			8.7	8.1	5.9	5.9	5.7	5.6	5.4	7
United States	7.6	8.2	7.6	7.1	7.3	7.2	7.1	7	6.8	6.5

	1996	1997	1998	1999	2000	2001	2002
Australia	6.4	6.2	6.1	6.2	6.1	6.1	
Austria	7.6	7.1	6.8	6.5	6.3	6.2	6
Belgium	9.2	8.8	8.7	8			
Canada	7.1	7	7	7.1	7.2	7.3	
Czech Republic	9.6	9.1	8.8	8.6	8.7	8.5	8.3
Denmark	4.1	4	3.9	3.9	3.8	3.8	3.7
Finland	5.3	5	4.7	4.5	4.4	4.4	4.3
France	6.1	5.9	5.8	5.5	5.6	5.7	
Germany	13.5	12.5	12.3	12	11.9	11.6	
Greece	6.5	6.3	6.3	6.3			
Hungary	8.6	8.2	7.8	7.5	7.1	7	6.9
Iceland			5.7				
Ireland	6.5	6.5	6.5	6.5	6.4	6.4	6.5
Italy	8	7.3	7.2	7.1	7	6.9	
Japan							
Korea	11	11	11	10	11	11	11
Luxembourg	9.8		8	7.9	7.7	7.6	7.6
Mexico	3.6	3.5	3.7	3.7	3.6	3.5	3.5
Netherlands	9.8	9.6	9.5	9.2	9	8.6	
New Zealand		5.5	4.9				
Norway	6.3	6.4	6.2	6.1	6	5.8	5.7
Poland							
Portugal	7.9	7.5	7.3	7.3	7.7	7.3	
Slovak Republic	10.6	10.2	9.4	8.7	8.6	8.3	7.8
Spain	8	7.6	7.5		7.1		
Sweden	5	5.1	5.1	5	5	5	4.8
Switzerland	12	10.5	9.9	9.8	9.3	9.2	9.2
Turkey	5.6	5.5	5.4	5.4	5.4	5.4	5.2
United Kingdom	7.1	7.1	6.8	6.8	6.9	6.9	6.9
United States	6.2	6.1	6	5.9	5.8	5.8	5.7

Source: Organization for Economic Co-operation and Development. (2004). *OECD Health Data 2004.* (1st ed.). Washington, D.C.: Author. Retrieved from http://www.oecd.org/dataoecd/13/57/31963371.xls. OECD Copyright. Reproduced by permission of the OECD.

Table 6.29
Hospital Insurance: 1966 to 2000

Calendar year	Receipts Total	Payroll taxes	Income from taxation of benefits	Transfers from Railroad Retirement account	Reimbursements from general revenues for6 Uninsured persons	Military wage credits	Premiums from voluntary enrollees	Interest on investments and other income1	Expenditures Total	Benefit payments2	Administrative expenses Amount3	Percentage of benefit payments	Trust fund assets at end of year
1966	$1,943	$1,858	. . .	$16	$26	$11	. . .	$32	$999	$891	$108	12.1	$944
1967	3,559	3,152	. . .	44	301	11	. . .	51	3,430	3,353	77	2.3	1,073
1968	5,287	4,116	. . .	54	1,022	22	. . .	74	4,277	4,179	99	2.4	2,083
1969	5,279	4,473	. . .	64	617	11	. . .	113	4,857	4,739	118	2.5	2,505
1970	5,979	4,881	. . .	66	863	11	. . .	158	5,281	5,124	157	3.1	3,202
1971	5,732	4,921	. . .	66	503	48	. . .	193	5,900	5,751	150	2.6	3,034
1972	6,403	5,731	. . .	63	381	48	. . .	180	6,503	6,318	185	2.9	2,935
1973	10,821	9,944	. . .	99	451	48	$2	278	7,289	7,057	232	3.3	6,467
1974	12,024	10,844	. . .	132	471	48	5	523	9,372	9,099	272	3.0	9,119
1975	12,980	11,502	. . .	138	621	48	7	664	11,581	11,315	266	2.4	10,517
1976	13,766	12,727	. . .	143	(4)	141	9	746	13,679	13,340	339	2.5	10,605
1977	15,856	14,114	. . .	(5)	4 803	6 143	12	784	16,019	15,737	283	1.8	10,442
1978	19,213	17,324	. . .	5 214	688	141	13	834	18,178	17,682	496	2.8	11,477
1979	22,825	20,768	. . .	191	734	141	16	975	21,073	20,623	450	2.2	13,228
1980	26,097	23,848	. . .	244	697	141	18	1,149	25,577	25,064	512	2.0	13,749
1981	35,725	32,959	. . .	276	659	207	22	1,603	30,726	30,342	384	1.3	18,748
1982	37,998	34,586	. . .	351	808	207	24	2,022	36,144	35,631	513	1.4	7 8,164
1983	44,570	37,259	. . .	358	878	8 3,456	27	2,593	39,877	39,337	540	1.4	12,858
1984	46,720	42,288	. . .	351	752	250	33	3,046	43,887	43,257	629	1.5	15,691
1985	51,397	47,576	. . .	371	766	9 -719	41	3,362	48,414	47,580	834	1.8	7 20,499
1986	59,267	54,583	. . .	364	566	91	43	3,619	50,422	49,758	664	1.3	7 39,957
1987	64,064	58,648	. . .	368	447	94	38	4,469	50,289	49,496	793	1.6	53,732
1988	69,239	62,449	. . .	364	475	80	41	5,830	53,331	52,517	815	1.6	69,640
1989	76,721	68,369	. . .	379	515	86	55	7,317	60,803	60,011	792	1.3	85,558
1990	80,372	72,013	. . .	367	413	10 -993	122	8,451	66,997	66,239	758	1.1	98,933
1991	88,839	77,851	. . .	352	605	89	432	9,510	72,570	71,549	1,021	1.4	115,202
1992	93,836	81,745	. . .	374	621	86	522	10,487	85,015	83,895	1,121	1.3	124,022
1993	98,187	84,133	. . .	400	367	81	675	11 12,531	94,391	93,487	904	1.0	127,818
1994	109,570	95,280	$1,639	413	506	80	907	10,745	104,545	103,282	1,263	1.2	132,844
1995	115,027	98,421	3,913	396	462	61	954	10,820	117,604	116,368	1,236	1.1	130,267
1996	124,603	110,585	4,069	401	419	12 -2,293	1,199	10,222	129,929	128,632	1,297	1.0	124,942
1997	130,154	114,670	3,558	419	481	70	1,319	9,637	139,452	137,762	1,690	1.2	115,643
1998	140,547	124,317	5,067	419	34	67	1,316	9,327	135,771	13 133,990	1,782	1.3	120,419
1999	151,597	132,306	6,552	430	652	71	1,447	10,139	130,632	13 128,766	1,866	1.4	141,385
2000	167,185	144,351	8,787	465	470	2	1,382	11,729	131,095	13 128,458	2,636	2.1	177,475

1. Other income includes recoveries of amounts reimbursed from the trust fund which are not obligations of the trust fund, receipts from the fraud and abuse control program, and a small amount of miscellaneous income.

2. Includes costs of Peer Review Organizations (beginning with the implementation of the Prospective Payment System on Oct. 1, 1983).

3. Includes costs of experiments and demonstration projects. Beginning in 1997, includes fraud and abuse control expenses, as provided for by P.L. 104–91.

4. No transfer was made in 1976 because of the change in transfer dates from December to March. The 1977 transfer was for benefits and administrative expenses during the 15-month period beginning July 1976 and ending September 1977.

5. No transfer was made in 1977 because of the change in transfer dates from August to June. The 1978 transfer was for contributions during the 15-month period beginning July 1976 and ending September 1977.

6. Includes $2 million in reimbursements from general revenues from costs arising from the granting of deemed wage credits to persons of Japanese ancestry who were interned during World War II.

7. For 1982, assets exclude $12,437 million loaned to the OASI trust fund under the interfund borrowing provisions of the law. Repayments of $1,824 million and $10,613 million were made in 1985 and 1986, respectively.

8. The lump-sum general revenue transfer, as provided for by section 151 of P.L. 98–21.

9. Includes the lump-sum general revenue adjustment of-$805 million, as provided for by section 151 of P.L. 98–21.

10. Includes the lump-sum general revenue adjustment of-$1,100 million, as provided for by section 151 of P.L. 98–21.

11. Includes $1,805 million transfer from the Supplementary Medical Insurance (SMI) catastrophic coverage reserve fund, as provided for by P.L. 102–394.

12. Includes the lump-sum general revenue adjustment of-$2,366 million, as provided for by section 151 of P.L. 98–21.

13. Includes monies transferred to the SMI trust fund for home health agency costs, as provided for by P.L. 105–33.

Note: Totals do not necessarily equal the sums of rounded components.

Source: Social Security Administration. (2001). *Annual Statistical Supplement, 2001 to the Social Security Bulletin.* Baltimore: Social Security Administration, Office of Policy. Retrieved from http://www.ssa.gov/policy/docs/statcomps/supplement/2001/supp01.pdf.

Table 6.30
Historical Projections of HI Trust Fund
Insolvency: United States, 1970 to 2000

Year of Trustees' Report	Projected year of insolvency	Projected number of years until insolvency
1970	1972	2
1971	1973	2
1972	1976	4
1973	none indicated	NA
1974	none indicated	NA
1975	late 1990s	NA
1976	early 1990s	NA
1977	late 1980s	NA
1978	1990	12
1979	1992	13
1980	1994	14
1981	1991	10
1982	1987	5
1983	1990	7
1984	1991	7
1985	1998	13
1986	1996	10
1986 amended	1998	12
1987	2002	15
1988	2005	17
1989	([1])	NA
1990	2003	13
1991	2005	14
1992	2002	10
1993	1999	6
1994	2001	7
1995	2002	7
1996	2001	5
1997	2001	4
1998	2008	10
1999	2015	16
2000[2]	2025	25

1. Contained no long range projections
2. As amended
NA. Not available.

Source: United States House of Representatives, Committee on Ways and Means. (2000). *The 2000 Green Book: Background material and data on programs within the jurisdiction of the Committee on Ways and Means.* Retrieved from http://aspe .hhs.gov/2000gb/sec2.txt.

7. Welfare Programs: Temporary Assistance for Needy Families (TANF)— From Welfare to Workfare

American culture values the traits of independence and self-sufficiency. However, the country has established a social compact to provide a safety net for its citizens facing special needs. In fiscal year 1998, the federal government spent about $325 billion on these safety net programs, including programs designed to provide income support, health services, housing assistance, and food assistance to more than 30 million low-income Americans, including children, the elderly, the homeless, and the disabled. (General Accounting Office, 2002)

Welfare programs underwent a major paradigm shift in the United States in 1996. The Personal Responsibility and Work Opportunity Reconciliation Act of 1996 (PRWORA) converted the former Aid to Families with Dependent Children (AFDC) program into block grants to states, giving individual states greater control over the shape of their welfare programs. Along with this change came a different emphasis in how to provide a social safety net to those needing assistance. What became identified as a dependency of qualifying population groups on public assistance now is seen as a means to getting people back to work. The Federal government defines this redirection: "The transition of the nation's human services from income maintenance to self-sufficiency requires a system-wide paradigm shift that affects people, culture, processes procedures, information, and information systems" (United States Department of Human and Health Services, Welfare, 2000).

Limited budgets, particularly in times of economic upheaval, require governments to make difficult choices about how to spend available funds. One of the most difficult decisions is whether to put obtainable funds into economic growth activity or into direct assistance for the poor. During economic boom times, more moneys are available to provide direct assistance and, unfortunately, the opposite is the case when tax revenue and other economic output factors are down. Therefore, the question becomes one of how are the poor best

served in order to minimize the impact that a bad economy has on them.

Since the end of 1932, five principles or rules have been in place which determine the administration of public welfare relief in the United States (Brownlow, 1958, 274):

1. The major responsibility rests with the government. This responsibility can only be met adequately by the active participation of the federal, state, and local governments. All participating agencies should establish effective means for the development and maintenance of efficient standards of administration.

2. An effective administrative unit should be established for the direction and supervision of the expenditure of all state and federal funds appropriated for relief purposes. Funds should be made available to local units on a needs basis rather than population or wealth. In most of the states, the county is the smallest practical administrative unit. Unification of state and county welfare services is necessary to secure efficient and economical administration.

3. Public funds should be administered only by regularly established public agencies.

4. In any appropriations, a definite allocation of funds for administrative purposes should be included in order to insure proper standards of administration.

5. Public welfare administration is a technical function of government and includes types of services which require properly prepared, qualified personnel. Personnel standards are a primary concern to all state and local welfare systems, and can be best attained by stressing education and experience rather than residence.

The public welfare system, in particular the AFDC programs, was already beset by many critics from both sides of the political spectrum by the mid 1960s. The primary critiques were economics-oriented, focusing on incentives, and efficiency. Other critiques centered on the equity of public assistance, other legal and social analyses of the operations, and administration of these programs and how they dealt with recipients (Haveman, 1987). Studies at the time, according to Haveman, drew attention to several characteristics of the income support system and the potentially serious and adverse economic and social impacts (83–84):

1. Inadequate levels of benefit payments.

2. Inequities in the eligibility criteria applied to various groups of individuals and by geographic region, attributed to the categorical nature of the system, and in states' administration of programs and determination of benefit levels.

3. Administrative discretion that resulted in arbitrariness and inequity.

4. High costs of the system, and the extent to which benefit levels nevertheless failed to aid the most needy.

5. Incentives implicit in the programs, especially those that encouraged reduction in work efforts, increases in family and marital instability, and geographic mobility.

6. The overlapping nature of the programs and the opportunity for multiple-benefit recipients.

7. Inefficiencies due to the presence of in-kind (choice constraining) rather than cash benefits.

8. Administrative inefficiencies due to multiple agencies and multiple and inconsistent eligibility rules, income definitions, means tests, and work requirements.

By the 1990s, according to the Republican Party, these characteristics "promoted welfare programs which encourage illegitimacy, discourage work, mock marriage, and require dependence, consigning generations to hopelessness and despair" (Ashcroft, 1995). As a result of their takeover of Congress in 1996, one of the Republicans key planks from their "Contract with America" means that welfare programs underwent a major paradigm shift. PRWORA converted the former AFDC program into block grants to states, under what is now known as Temporary Assistance for Needy Families (TANF).

The change in programs reflects the following views that Republican policymakers are arguably placing as amendments to what Brownlow and the group of welfare professionals and administrators generated, over three generations ago.

• End welfare as an entitlement.

• "Radically limit Washington's intermeddling, micromanaging, counterproductive control of welfare." For the past 30 years, the view was that Washington knows best, prescribing a one size fits all approach that does not work. What has happened is that Washington's oversight created a situation where "the bureaucracy has levied a sort of tax upon the poor, taking up money and preventing it from reaching those in need."

• Encourage a national debate on illegitimacy while simultaneously ensuring that illegitimacy is reduced. "Most of the

problems surrounding welfare can be tied, in one form or another, to illegitimacy."

• Not to fall into the trap of believing that laws by themselves will solve welfare problems. Private and religious charitable organizations should become part of the process because they "have a character entirely different from that of governmental entitlement" in that their services are predicated on a character of concern and compassion, whereas the government's approach is one of sterile indifference.

• Come to understand and realize that unanimous reform is seldom real reform. "These are enormously difficult and divisive issues; genuine efforts at solution do not lend themselves to unanimity." (Ashcroft, 1995)

The change in the paradigm from welfare to workfare is based on the notion that work reduces dependence on other types of **unearned income**, such as entitlements. Some of the reasons for this, according to Rector and Youssef (1999) of the Heritage Foundation are:

1. *The elimination of fraud* because a work requirement, coupled with a full-check sanction for non-compliance, means that "phantom" recipients can no longer receive benefits.

2. *Uncovering unreported earnings* through serious work requirements, making it more difficult for recipients to receive benefits "and simultaneously work at unreported jobs." The expectation is to force beneficiaries to make a choice between the work income or the benefits they receive. "Many simply will leave welfare and begin to rely more fully on employment for support."

3. *Reducing incentives for idleness* because a serious work requirement creates a two-way contribution instead of the traditional "one-way handout" that used to exist under the AFDC entitlement system. Now, "aid is given, but in exchange the recipient is expected to perform community service work or to undertake other significant steps toward self-sufficiency, such as a supervised job search or on-the-job training."

4. *Preparing beneficiaries for the real world of employment* creates an environment that will prepare the recipient for the real world of work through the requirement of community service work or other constructive activity. "Under such a system, recipients are held accountable for their own actions and thus learn the habits of self-control, responsibility, and persistence, which are the hallmarks of eventual self-sufficiency."

5. *Sending a positive symbolic message* to "welfare recipients and potential recipients that society expects them to engage in work and to strive for self-sufficiency."

Yet, the change into a workfare system has to be cognizant of the limitations that job churning imposes on job availability and ability to get that available job. "*Churning*, the phenomenon of employment expansion occurring alongside employment contraction, seems to be a reality of the contemporary economy" (Minnesota Department of Economic Security, 1998, 1). The addition of jobs or their deletion is predicated on the employer's willingness to make changes to its workforce based on a number of key performance decisions, ranging from demand to changes in the technology or other concerns such as "product obsolescence stagnant management or a more competitive marketplace" (4). Technology changes and product obsolescence imply the need to adapt to the preferences and newer technology of current markets and, in turn, this generates a significant impact on the skill level of the employees and those seeking to work in these areas. Putting in new technology and putting it to work often requires significant amount of capital in terms of equipment, infrastructure, and salaries (see United States Department of Labor, 2001, 5).

In sum, "[the] impact of any welfare-to-work [workfare] program depends on diverse factors, such as the amount and use of resources, the mix of services provided, the message that is communicated to participants, and the quality of implementation" (Brown, 1997, 6). Case management under these circumstances means that there is a need to focus on a series of items that are not always easily related. On the one hand, there is the need to provide assistance to the family in need. Then there is the situation of identifying and assisting the beneficiaries with job search and/or education or training requirements. Third, then, while job training and/or searches are happening, the case manager has to determine eligibility and access to support issues such as transportation or child care. Fourth, to complicate matters, depending on the household type, beneficiaries are still required to hold a job (whether as a form of voluntary community service or actual paid employment) even while undergoing education or training activities, the combination of which should total about forty hours per week. Fifth, there is a need to monitor the length of time of benefit duration, because many of the provisions under TANF impose a lifetime limit of five years. Sixth, one of the chief goals of TANF is to reduce the caseload—the number of beneficiaries; therefore, the pressure of trying to find a proper situation for beneficiaries (a living wage that may mean a definite and permanent exit from benefit dependency) contradicts the attempt reduce the caseload as soon as it is plausible to do so. This last consideration creates a conundrum for the program's overall effectiveness because, as the Center for Women Policy Studies (2002) found,

TANF's much-touted success—defined solely as reductions in the welfare rolls—hides a tragic reality. Even though states report decreased numbers of TANF recipients, many of those who left TANF for work are not employed in jobs that will lead to economic stability for themselves and their families and instead remain in poverty. In fact, a national study of recipients who left TANF in 1997 and 1999 found that half (52 percent) of women who left welfare in 1999 remained in poverty. Further, 22 percent of women who left TANF returned to cash assistance and the former TANF recipients who were employed earned a median hourly wage of $7.15 (Loprest, 2001). (7; citation as in source material)

AID TO FAMILIES WITH DEPENDENT CHILDREN (AFDC)—WHAT WAS, AND ITS CURRENT LEGACY

AFDC was established in 1935 as an original component to the Social Security Act of 1935 under Title IV. Its purpose was to provide transitional financial assistance to families. It was a federal program that was a partnership with states who shared in its cost as well as program administration, program formulation, and benefit determination. The federal role was to provide matching funds (50 percent for administrative and training costs, while benefits matches were based on a formula taking into account the state's per capita income, a range of between 50 percent and 83 percent) and the broad guidelines and program requirements that states had to follow. Eligibility was based on a family having a dependent child who was (a) 18 or younger (with states having the option to consider a child up to 19 if a full-time student and expected to graduate at that time); (b) deprived by a parent's death, incapacity, continued absence, or unemployment of the main breadwinner in a two-parent household under the AFDC-Unemployed Parent program; (c) living at home with parents or specified close relatives; (d) being a resident of the state; and (e) being a U.S. citizen or resident alien. Each state established its own payment standard to determine the assistance unit's benefit amount by considering the countable income of all persons included in the assistance unit and applying it against the state's payment standard. The AFDC benefit package more or less included the following (each state had its own variation on what benefits were allowed to eligible recipients):

1. A cash benefit based on the number and age of dependent children.

2. A medical card providing Medicaid payments to children and parents for hospital benefits, physician care, and medical procedures.

3. Women, Infants and Children (WIC) nutritional benefits (special nutrition allowances for pregnant women and children under age 3). Eligibility for special vocational training through the work incentive (WIN) aspect of the program.

4. Eligibility for family planning services (counseling, appliances, and/or pharmaceuticals).

5. Vendor payments to providers of counseling services for AFDC families and children.

6. Payments for temporary foster care when ordinary caretakers or parents were disabled.

7. Many AFDC recipients either automatically were eligible for food stamps or meet the AFDC's more stringent criteria, making it virtually automatic for them to establish eligibility for food stamps (adapted from Chambers 1986, 81, 157–158).

States also determined eligibility requirements, using income-based means-tests to determine need. It was a two-step process:

1. Determining the gross income after applicable disregards (the first $50 per month of child support, and optional earned income disregards for certain students), could not exceed 185 percent of the state-determined need standard; and

2. Family income was compared to the state's need standard, with a disregard for the earned income tax credit (EITC) and (a) $90 per month for work expenses for individuals employed full- or part-time; (b) actual expenses for dependent care up to $175 per month for each dependent child who is at least age 2 or each incapacitated adult, and up to $200 per month for each dependent child who is under age 2 for full-time workers (states may opt to pay less for part-time workers); (c) for those receiving AFDC benefits in one of the last four months, all of the monthly earned income of a child who is a full-time student or who was a part-time student and not employed full-time, $30 and one-third of such person's remaining income for the first four consecutive months, and $30 for each of the eight subsequent months.

In 1988, the Family Support Act established the jobs opportunities and basic skills (JOBS) training program along with revamping the requirements for the state-run welfare-to-work programs that were already in place. Unless exempt, recipients under AFDC had to then participate in this program as a condition of eligibility.

TEMPORARY ASSISTANCE FOR NEEDY FAMILIES (TANF)

The gravamen of the change from AFDC to TANF in 1996 was to promote work as the means of reducing the dependency of the poor on the benefits made available through the U.S. social safety net. The purposes behind TANF are to:

- Assist needy families so children can be cared for in their own homes.

- Reduce the parents' dependency on welfare benefits by promoting job preparation, work, and marriage.

- Prevent out-of-wedlock pregnancies.

- Encourage the formation and maintenance of two-parent families.

As written in the *Annual Statistical Supplement, 2001 to the Social Security Bulletin* (Social Security Administration 2001), "The law marks the end of federal entitlement to assistance. In TANF, states and territories operate programs, and Indian tribes have the option to run their own programs. States, territories, and tribes each receive a block grant allocation, and states must maintain a historical level of state spending known as maintenance of effort" (74). Jobs can be created by using money that is currently used for giving welfare checks, and by channeling the funds for making community service jobs, providing income subsidies, or giving hiring incentives to potential employers. In an interesting twist on normal budgeting practice, states may carry over any excess funds from one fiscal year to the next; however, the carryover amount can only be used for assistance purposes.[1]

The paradigm shift in PRWORA represents the perceived differences between income maintenance and self-sufficiency. The premise is that there is a significant change in primary goals as well as the level of expectations from participants and the system providing the service. Moreover, there is a distinct feeling that the income-maintenance approach toward helping people provided a low-risk environment, whereby people did what they had to do in order to get by rather than taking the necessary opportunities and inherent risks available in order to be able to be the best that they can be without the need of assistance from others. Chart 7.1 provides some of the differences in thinking that the two approaches toward the social safety net represent (adapted from United States Department of Health and Human Services, 2000, table 1).

States must present a plan for approval detailing the elements and provisions in their program.[2] Key TANF provisions that the federal government requires and a brief general description of these are provided in Chart 7.2. It seems as if there is a price that states pay for their increased decision-making latitude provided by the program. The two most important provisions are the lifetime five-year limit imposed on receiving family assistance and the **maintenance of effort (MOE) requirements** that define minimum state expenditures. There are performance bonuses built-in to TANF for those states who have a high rate of success in moving individuals from welfare to work situations and those states who reduce the out-of-wedlock birth rates while also reducing their abortion rate. States accrue penalties in the form of block grant–amount reductions when they fail to do any of the following (Social Security Administration, 2001, 75), although the maximum penalty in a given year cannot exceed 25 percent of the state's block grant allotment:[3]

- Satisfy work requirements. A penalty of 5 percent accrues in the first year. The penalty amount increases 2 percent per year for each consecutive failure. The penalty is adjusted based on degree of failure. The maximum penalty is 21 percent.

- Comply with 5-year limit on assistance. Failure to comply results in a 5 percent penalty.

- Meet the state's basic maintenance of effort requirements. The penalty is based on the amount of the state's underspending. The state also loses its Welfare-to-Work funds.

- Meet the State's Contingency Fund MOE requirement. The penalty is a reduction of the State's Federal TANF grant by the amount of Contingency Funds received and not remitted.

- Reduce recipient grants for refusing to participate in work activities without good cause. A penalty of between

1 percent and 5 percent is assessed based on the degree of noncompliance. Maintain assistance when a single custodial parent with a child under six cannot obtain child care. Failure to comply results in a penalty of 5 percent.

- Submit required data reports. A penalty of 4 percent accrues.
- Comply with paternity establishment and child support enforcement requirements. Failure to comply results in a penalty of up to 5 percent.
- Participate in the Income and Eligibility Verification System. A penalty of up to 2 percent accrues.
- Repay a federal loan on time. The penalty will be based on the amount unpaid.
- Use funds appropriately. Misuse of funds can result in states being penalized for the amount misused. If this misuse is

found to be intentional, an additional penalty of 5 percent will be assessed.

- Replace federal penalty reductions with additional state funds. This provision results in a penalty of up to 2 percent and requires states to contribute state funds to make up for any reductions in federal funds due to penalties.

TANF has changed the tenor of the relationship that family benefits under its auspices have with other major components of the social safety net in this country. Chart 7.3 provides an overview of the new relationships that are now in place as a result of the transition from AFDC to TANF. As part of the changeover from AFDC, states are allowed to privatize some of their program by administering and providing program services through contracted charitable, religious, or private organizations.

Chart 7.1
Characteristics of Income Maintenance and Self-Sufficiency Programs

Income Maintenance Program

Primary goal—Timely and accurate benefits.

Rule-based decisions—Eligibility decisions are based in rules. There is a "right answer" in any given decision. Individuals are held accountable for getting the answer right.

Process focus—How things must be done is very clear in the program.

Managers know the answers—Management structure needs to minimize mistakes in the program and ensure consistency.

Error avoidance—Individuals are extensively trained to avoid costly errors, resulting in a focus on what can't be done. Individuals try to operate as much as possible in "black and white" clarity in decision-making in order to reduce problems in the program.

Limited expectations—Focus is on certifying client needs and lack of resources as part of the eligibility process. Program is geared to help people by providing for their basic needs because they have demonstrated in the eligibility process that they are not doing so for themselves.

Services provided for or to clients—Staff have ultimate authority and expertise to get clients benefits.

Entitlement system—All who are eligible must receive all benefits for which they are eligible and to which they are entitled.

Self-Sufficiency Program

Primary goal—Decreasing dependence on public assistance through work and other resources.

Principle-based decisions—Self-sufficiency service decisions are based on principles, outcomes, and an assessment of the individual situation. There is not one "right answer." Individuals are held accountable for making decisions that reflect principles/outcomes.

Outcome focus—What must be achieved is very clear in the program. Principles guide the how.

Managers know how to get people to ask good questions—Management structure needs to facilitate experimentation, keep focus on outcomes and principles, and move good decision-making to the front-line level.

Experiment—Individuals are extensively trained to experiment with the best ways to reach outcomes, resulting in a focus on what can be done. Individuals operate primarily in areas of many shades of gray. New leadership and team structures result from this focus on service outcomes and experimentation.

High expectations—Focus is on discovering client strengths and resources. There are high expectations of the client. There is a social contract in which the basic support services are provided in exchange for participation in actitivies leading to self-sufficiency.

Services provided with clients—Staff can't "make" clients self-sufficient. Staff can only work with clients on process, taking part in process, not controlling it.

Temporary assistance—Wide range of choices made at state, local, and worker level that influences the type of benefits provided.

Source: Adapted from U.S. Department of Health and Human Services, 2000, Table 1.

Chart 7.2
Key Provisions and Explanation of their Requirements Under TANF

Key Provision	General Overview
Work Requirements	• Recipients must work as soon as a job is ready for them, or no later than 2 years after the commencement of benefits
	• By 2002, states had to certify that 50 percent of all families in the state were participating in work activities (for two-parent families the minimum participation rate was 75 percent and was to increase to 90 percent).
	• Unmarried underaged parents must participate in educational and training activities while living with a responsible adult or in an adult-supervised settings as conditions for receiving assistance.
	• Single parent participation in work activities (by 2000): 30 hours per week
	• Two-parent participation: 35 hours per week or 55 hours per week, depending on circumstances
	• Non-participation in work requirement may lead to the reduction or termination of benefits to the family. The exception is if a single parent of a child under the age of 6 who cannot find childcare (states can opt to not count these individuals for up to 12 months in their reports).
Work Activities	• States can count as part of participation rate the following kinds of work:
	• Unsubsidized employment
	• Subsidized employment
	• on-the-job training
	• work experience
	• community service
	• job search (no more than 6 total weeks of job search, no more than 4 consecutive weeks of job search counted)
	• vocational training (no more than 12 months counted)
	• jobs skills training related to work
	• education directly related to work
	• satisfactory secondary school attendance
	• providing childcare services to individuals participating in community service
	• As of FY2000, only 30 percent of those said to meet participation rates can be included due to participation in vocational training or attending secondary school due to their being a teen parent.
Five-year Time Limit	• Families can only receive a total of five (5) years of benefits under TANF. Those already receiving benefits for this amount of time or longer are no longer eligible for federal funds.
	• States have the option of increasing benefits beyond the five year limit for up to 20 percent of their caseloads, provide benefits from the state-only funds or through social services block grants.
State Maintenance of Effort (MOE) Requirements	• States are required to spend a certain minimum of their own funds each fiscal year on programs that will benefit eligible families under the TANF provisions.
	• The required MOE amount is based on an applicable percentage of the state's (non-federal) expenditures on AFDC and the AFDC-related programs in 1994. Applicable percentage is based on whether the state is able to meet its minimum participation rates. States meeting the participation rates are required to spend 75 percent of their 1994 AFDC expenditures, those not meeting the participation rates are required to spend 80 percent of their 1994 AFDC expenditures.
	• Needy states with economic problems can ask for funds from the Contingency Fund to augment their TANF grant funds.[4]

Source: Author's findings from various government sources.

Chart 7.3
Relationship between TANF and other Federal Social Safety Net Agencies

Agency	Relationship between TANF and agency
Medicaid	• All TANF recipients (adults and children) must receive Medicaid. States may refuse benefits to adults who do not take part of work program, but must continue Medicaid benefits to the children. All children born after September 30, 1983 are eligible to receive Medicaid benefits if their family fell below the federal poverty guideline. • States must provide Medicaid coverage and benefits to children and family members who would have been eligible for AFDC as it existed on July 16, 1996. States could increase by the percentage increase in the CPI-U (for all urban users) or decrease AFDC income and resource standards to those in effect on May 1, 1988. • The law requires the continuance of up to 12 months of medical assistance to children and adults who lose TANF eligibility because of earnings that lift counted income above the July 16, 1996, AFDC eligibility limit.
Food stamps	• TANF recipients living alone (and not with others) are eligible for food stamps. • States have the option of running a simplified form of food stamps in which they can apply many of the TANF rules, but only as long as the costs of running the program do not increase federal costs. • TANF recipients who lose benefits may also be disqualified from receiving food stamps. • If TANF recipient's cash benefits are reduced for noncompliance with TANF rules, the state may also reduce its food stamp allotment to that household by 25 percent. The state is not allowed to offset the loss of cash benefits by increasing the food stamp benefits (United States House of Representatives, Committee on Ways and Means, 2000, section 7).
Earned income tax credit (EITC)	• States have the option to determine if they want to count earned income tax credits as income in the eligibility determination formula. • There is a limitation, however: prohibits EITC payments for TANF recipients whose earnings are derived from work experience or community service.
Free and Reduced-cost Lunch Program	• As under AFDC, TANF children automatically eligible.
Women, Infants, and Children's Program (WIC)	• As under AFDC, women, infants, and children receiving TANF benefits automatically qualify for the Supplemental Nutrition Program.

Source: Author's findings from various government sources.

WELFARE-TO-WORK (WTW)

Welfare-to-work (WtW) is a block grant program created by the Balanced Budget Act of 1997. The intent of this program is to provide states and local communities funds to create additional job opportunities for the hardest-to-employ welfare recipients and non-custodial parents.[5] It provides states with two kinds of grants: formula-based grants to states and competitive grants to local communities. $100 million of the funds is set aside for performance bonuses to states that have successful programs based on a formula that considers (but is not limited to) job placement, duration of placement, and increased earnings.

WtW is part of the TANF system housed in the U.S. Department of Health and Human Services; however, it is administered through the U.S. Department of Labor. States and direct grant recipients administer the grants; however, the key administrative element is the Workforce Investment Board, the policy-making arm of the **one-stop centers** that are set up under the Workforce Investment Act programs (see next section).

Workforce Investment Boards (WIBs) are free to determine the barriers to employment and those that lead to long-term dependence on welfare as they exist in that locality to better address those specific issues in order to get people back to work. These identified barriers to employment work alongside those that have been identified at the federal level, ostensibly to provide a comprehensive approach at getting the hard to employ into a meaningful work situation. An example of such a barrier is substance abuse. The federal government has identified this as a barrier to gainful employment.[6] The local WIB is free to identify this as a barrier and to utilize some of the funds received under the grants sponsored by WtW to address this specific issue.

Seventy-five percent of the funds are reserved to the states based on a formula that takes into account in equal proportions the state's share of the nation's total number of poor individuals and the number of adult TANF benefit recipients. Eighty-five percent of state formula funds have to be passed on to the Workforce Investment Boards, with the other 15 percent to be used for discretionary welfare-to-work projects.[7] States are required to match every $2 received from federal funds with a $1 contribution of their own. States must submit an administrative plan that has to pass federal muster, with the burden of administration of funds and coordination of efforts falling on the states' governors.

The remaining 25 percent of the funds are directly available from the federal government to local governments, WIBs, and appropriate agencies[8] that partnered with one or more WIBs. Applicants that receive special considerations because of their potential to meet the program's goals based on their demographics are rural areas and cities with large concentrations of poverty.

Targeted groups under the WtW program are long-term TANF benefit recipients who meet two of three identified barriers to employment,[9] and non-custodial parents who meet the barriers and whose children are long-term TANF recipients.[10] At least 70 percent of the funds are expected to provide services to these two groups. Based on changes made by the Welfare-to-Work Amendments of 1999, the remaining 30 percent of the funds go to TANF recipients whose profile indicates long-term dependency, youth who have formerly received foster care services, custodial parents with incomes below the poverty line, and TANF recipients who face barriers to self-sufficiency under criteria established by the local WIB. Activities that are funded for these groups focus on helping move eligible individuals into long-term unsubsidized jobs. These activities include programs that support the following strategies:

- job creation through short-term public or private sector wage subsidies;
- on-the-job training;
- contracts with public or private providers of job readiness, job placement, and post-employment services;
- job vouchers for similar services (except for grantees which are not WIBs which may provide these services directly);
- community service or work experience;

- job retention and supportive services (if such services are not otherwise available); or
- six months of preemployment job training or vocational educational training.

WORKFORCE INVESTMENT ACT

In 2000 the Workforce Investment Act of 1998 (WIA) replaced the Job Training Partnership Act of 1982 (JTPA), which provided for training assistance to disadvantaged youth and adults that met its eligibility requirement. JTPA was a block grant program that supported three kinds of programs: adult training, summer youth training and employment for those in the ages between 16 and 24 (Job Corps), and year-round youth training. In 1997, nearly 36 percent of participants in the adult training program received cash welfare benefits, most of which came from TANF (United States House of Representatives, Committee on Ways and Means, 2000, section 15). Eighty-six percent of the cash benefit recipients were women. The JTPA's adult program's results included the following findings: "Sixty-eight percent of cash welfare recipients entered employment in program year 1997, compared with 73 percent for those II-A terminees who did not receive cash welfare payments. The average hourly starting wage for cash welfare recipients entering employment was $7.88, compared with $8.46 for nonrecipients" (86/106). For its year-round youth training program,

of the youth participants in year-round services who terminated during program year 1997, 38 percent were white, 33 percent were black, and 24 percent were Hispanic. Of the title II-C participants who terminated, 48 percent entered employment, and the average hourly wage for terminees who entered employment was $6.52.

Among the 26 percent of title II-C (youth) participants receiving cash welfare payments in program year 1997, 48 percent entered employment, compared with 48 percent of II-C participants who did not receive cash welfare payments. The average hourly starting wage for cash welfare recipients was $6.55, compared with $6.51 for nonrecipients. Among the 53 percent of II-C terminees who had either dropped out of school or were behind in grade level, the average entered employment rate in program year 1997 was 40 percent as compared with 57 percent for those not in this legislatively defined hard-to-serve category. The average hourly starting wage for youths who had dropped out of school or were behind in their grade level was $6.13 compared with $6.83 for those not in this category. (86/106, 88/106)

For the Job Corps program, the results for the programming year 1997 were:

[of the] nearly 66,000 new students enrolled in Job Corps Centers, 60 percent of whom were male. In that same year, 50 percent of new students were African-American, 28 percent were white, 16 percent were Hispanic, 4 percent were Native Americans, and 2 percent were Asian or Pacific Islanders. Seventy-eight percent of new students had dropped out of high school and 63 percent had never worked full time. Thirty-three percent of new students in program year 1997 came from families on public assistance. The average length of stay in Job Corps in

Chart 7.4
WIA Core Indicators of Performance for the Two Key Target Population Groups

Core performance indicators under WIA	
Adults (18 years of age and over)	**Youth aged 14–17**
1. Entry into unsubsidized employment;	1. Attainment of basic skills and, as appropriate, work readiness or occupational skills;
2. Retention in unsubsidized employment 6 months after entry into employment;	2. Attainment of secondary school diplomas and their recognized equivalents; and
3. Earnings received in unsubsidized employment 6 months after entry into the employment; and	3. Placement and retention in postsecondary education or advanced training, or placement and retention in military service, or employment—including qualified apprenticeship.
4. Attainment of a recognized credential relating to achievement of educational or occupational skills for individuals who enter employment. (For youth age 19–21, educational and skill attainment is measured for all individuals who enter postsecondary education, advanced training, or employment.)	

Source: Adapted from U.S. Department of Labor, 1998 White Paper Web site.

program year 1997 was 7.3 months. The Labor Department estimates that 70 percent of terminees entered employment after leaving the program, while another 10 percent either continued their education or entered another training program, for a total positive termination rate in 1997 of 80 percent. (88/106)

The purpose of WIA is to coordinate the various training programs available to those who receive benefits in order to be able to go out and get work. The changes are seen as a response to the need for employers to have access to more and better-qualified workers and provide a means by which to streamline the transition process from welfare to work. It is seen as a means of increasing and improving choices for individuals, employers, and the community. Core performance indicators for adults and for youth aged from 14 to 18 years old are provided in Chart 7.4 (United States Department of Labor, 1998).

The mainstay of the WIA is the creation of the *one-stop center* where core services are provided, with core services defined as job search assistance, comprehensive assessments, and job training.[11] They also provide what they refer to as "intensive services."[12] Under WIA requirements, there are nineteen mandated partners that provide services through the one-stop center. Two of these partners are the state's employment services and welfare-to-work.[13] A local workforce investment board with the agreement of the locality's mayor creates the one-stop centers.[14] In situations where WIA funds are limited, priority is to be given to those receiving public assistance and others that meet the low-income criteria. Overall, the major differences between WIA and the replaced JTPA are:

- The creation of the one-stop center to coordinate training activities and other needed services to help people get assistance for which they are eligible as well as jobs.

- There are no income eligibility requirements to use the one-stop center for adults over age 18; instead, eligibility under WIA requires the individual to be unemployed. In addition, to receive comprehensive assessments and other "intense" services, the person has to be unable to obtain employment through core services, or employed but in need of intensive services to obtain or retain employment that allows for self-sufficiency. For job training, the adult has to have met the eligibility for intensive service and been unable to obtain employment through those services.

- Under WIA, training is done through individual training accounts that allows individuals the opportunity to select training courses and providers from identified and eligible providers while JTPA provided training for groups of individuals.

- Under WIA, the Summer Youth Employment and Training Program is eliminated as a separately funded program; still, localities are required to provide summer employment opportunities under youth activities for low-income youth (as under JTPA). WIA adds the requirement that youth have to be placed in centers closest to their homes (for the reasons of strengthening linkages between the one-stop centers and local communities along with the establishment of performance measures and expected performance levels).

As an element in the transition from welfare to workfare and the reduction of dependence on public assistance benefits, the federal government sees the WIA in the following terms:

Working with the hardest to serve is a major challenge in welfare reform despite reduced caseloads. This Act aims to reduce welfare dependency and provide the tools to do so through the One-Stop system that includes the Welfare-to-Work program, and is able to integrate TANF and other programs that serve the welfare customer—in order to invest in the employment and job retention of the hardest to serve. In areas where adult funding is limited, welfare recipients and other low wage individuals will receive priority for intensive and training services. Collaboration between the workforce investment and welfare systems is important for several reasons. Both systems now focus on helping clients become employed. In addition, the two systems serve many of the same customers. Common customers also include employers who hire clients of the two systems. Finally, given scarce resources, strong collaboration will ensure that efforts are not duplicated. (United States Department of Labor, 1998)

Any discussion in the collection of welfare data in the United States has to begin with a basic discussion of the significant philosophical and programmatic changes that occurred during the 1990s. The changes are more than the results of early parallel efforts and studies focusing on work as the means for welfare reform in the 1960s, 1970s, 1980s, and 1990s by various states as well as the federal government. The changes tracked by the U.S. Bureau of the Census between 1994 and 2000 reflect the trend that work levels have increased between 1993 and 1999 (U.S. Bureau of the Census, 1994–2000). The changes are based on a completely different approach the role and scope of government intervention in personal life and personal responsibility in a person's day-to-day choices. It is therefore critical to understand how the program changes not only vary the focus of services and eligibility factors available, but how the data are collected, analyzed, reported, and utilized. Accountability and performance information are seen in new ways, requiring an understanding of what these changes mean in terms of philosophies and requirements. Chart 7.5 provides the government's point of view about how the data base indicators have to change (United States House of Representatives, Committee on Ways and Means, 2000, Table 2).

Making program performance data more difficult to address is the fact that the only comprehensive data on TANF comes from the pilot study performed in Minnesota through the Minnesota Family Incentive Program (MFIP). Theirs is the only longitudinal data just recently available at the time of this writing that provides specific numbers at the programmatic level. The information in this section, therefore, only provides a compilation of federal and state level information on the welfare component of the social safety net. The data is suggestive of budgets, percent of eligible populations participating in the programs, and the basic identification of programs at the state level. Most of the data will focus on what happened under the old income-maintenance system and although the new paradigm that TANF represents has been in effect, the information that is available, as already stated, does not have sufficient time to have a track record and, although the data may be similar, even by government thinking the analyses are different. Nevertheless, the sources of information for

TANF that are easily accessed are those from the *Social Security Statistical Supplement*, the *Green Book Report 2000*, and the congressional reports provided annually by TANF.

Table 7.1 at the end of this chapter provides a comparison of basic social and family benefits structures of the social safety nets in the United States and seven OECD countries. This is not a simple comparison to do because the workfare provision is not something that seems to be echoed in these systems. The programs used for comparison purposes are still mainly entrenched in the income maintenance mode. Privatization of benefits and services is not something that is present in these components of national social safety nets elsewhere. But what is still shared by many of these systems, including in the United States, is the notion of means-tested eligibility requirements. (Please note that part of Chart 7.4 can also be used for comparative purposes for child-based benefits and services as discussed later on in chapter 10.)

Readers interested in pursuing more immediate information for their research or personal interest purposes are going to find materials on TANF difficult to find, as befits new programs under a recently created paradigm. The challenges to welfare have been around for a long time as can be surmised here and elsewhere throughout this book; however, the transition is only a handful of years old. Most of the current information on public welfare, especially from books and articles written prior to 1996 are from the AFDC programs. Much of the data on TANF programs are still based on pilot projects in different states. The caveat here is to be aware that the information in the databases may seem similar but, because of new paradigm definitions, the reader may be facing disparate sets of data. One state that provides much of the early information is Minnesota; go to their ISEEK Web site that was created to serve as a one-stop database link with many of the efforts supported by current legislation. Minnesota's Department of Economic Security and other state agency Web sites dealing with WtW and One-Stop Centers may prove of some benefit. Other states' Department of Economic Security (or equivalent agency) Web sites may also be of assistance, and for state level information, these sites are as good source of data as is currently available.

At the national level, begin with the *Green Book Report 2000*, or its most current edition in order to find information on TANF itself and key data points that seem to be hard to find elsewhere at this time. There are many non-profit organizations such as the Urban Institute and the Center for Budget and Policy Priorities whose Web sites are excellent sources to use as well (a number of these organizations' Web sites can be reached from the Department of Health and Human Services site). Much more data seems to be available from these external fonts of information than from government sources. The *Statistical Abstract of the United States* is at present the source of basic TANF statistical data at the federal level. Analysis of U.S. Census data through its Web site, which allows for specific queries based on their information, is probably the best source of information at this time.

For those with international comparative data interests, first remember that the paradigm in the United States is

Chart 7.5
Official Perspective on Database Changes due to Paradigm Shift in Providing of Services within the Social Safety Net

Characteristics of Information in an Income Maintenance System

Self-contained—Information is held internally. Information needs are met almost exclusively through internal systems and processes.

Consistent user needs—Information required to issue timely and accurate benefits is clear and well-documented, resulting in relatively straight-forward user needs analysis and action by IT. Specific information changes over time, but overall purpose and scope of information gathering remains tied to timely and accurate benefits.

Standardized information—Goal of timely and accurate benefits requires standardized information from all applicants. Application information stays the same from client to client. Eligibility data elements are universally collected and reported.

Centralized—IT modifications and improvements are generally made centrally to a self-contained system. Even in more decentralized structures, there is a single overarching agency identity.

Client service process is data-based—Majority of contact with client is carefully structured to collect and report standardized eligibility information in order to ensure timely and accurate benefits.

Narrow audience—While overall interest in welfare dynamics may be high, the audience for information collected and reported related to timely and accurate benefits is generally narrow. There are well-defined purposes and uses for the information, many of which are federally driven.

Characteristics of Information in a Self-Sufficiency System

Dispersed—Information is held both internally and externally with other service providers. Information needs are met through a complicated, changing, and wide-reaching network of internal and external IT systems.

Variable user needs—Information required to effectively move clients to self-sufficiency is complex and variable, resulting in complicated and difficult process for user-needs analysis and action by IT. Scope of information and specific data needed will vary from client to client, depending on intensity of services required. Overall expansion to purpose of program means much greater depth and breadth in information needs.

Individualized information—Goal of self-sufficiency requires individualized client information to develop service plan. Information gathering will vary widely from client to client. It is difficult to determine which of these "new" data elements should be universally collected and reported in order to learn what elements are tied to what types of outcomes.

Decentralized—IT modifications and improvements must be made across many systems to ensure needed data collection and reporting. There are many separate organizations involved.

Client service process is outcome-based—Majority of contact with client is structured around activities designed to reach employment and training goals. Information collected varies across activities carried out in support of each client.

Expanding audience—As more information is available on the movement of clients to self-sufficiency, a much broader audience has interest in both reviewing and influencing the information being collected. There are multiple purposes and uses for information about program activities.

Source: Adapted from U.S. House of Representatives, 2000, Table 2.

significantly different from elsewhere, although, as stated in chapter 1, other countries seem to be going in the direction of shifting from a welfare model to a workfare prototype. Begin by accessing information from the *Social Security Programs Throughout the World* reports available through the Social Security Administration Web site. The OECD Web site, publications, and reports are an excellent as a next step, as are the United Nations Development Programme, the World Bank, European Union Social Indicator (EUSI) Web sites. For a number of countries, their national statistical office Web sites are recommended. Please refer back to the Introduction of this volume for suggestions in this regard.

NOTES

1. The federal government has defined assistance in the following terms:

- Payments "directed at ongoing, basic needs—even when individuals are participating in community service and work experience (or other work activities) as a condition of receiving payments that address their basic needs."
- Excluded are "non-recurrent, short-term benefits designed to deal with individual crisis situations rather than ongoing need. These benefits cannot provide for needs that will extend beyond 4 months. The definition also excludes child care, transportation and supports provided to employed families, Individual Development Account (IDA) benefits, refundable earned income

tax credits, work subsidies to employers, and services such as education and training, case management, job search, and counseling." (U.S. Department of Health and Human Services, 1999)

2. "To be eligible for a family assistance grant, States must submit each 2 years a TANF plan that contains required elements. The plan must outline how the State intends to: (1) conduct a program that provides cash assistance to needy families and that provides parents with work and support services; (2) require a parent or caretaker recipients to engage in work, as defined by the State, after a maximum of 24 months; (3) comply with the requirement for participation in creditable work activities by certain percentages of adult recipients; (4) take steps to restrict the use and disclosure of information about TANF recipients; (5) establish goals and take action to prevent and reduce the incidence of nonmarital pregnancies; and (6) conduct a program providing education and training on the problem of statutory rape. Also, the document must indicate whether the State intends to treat families moving into the State differently from State residents, whether it intends to provide aid to noncitizens, and if so, provide an overview of the aid. The plan must contain certain certifications, including that the State will operate a Child Support Enforcement Program and a Foster Care and Adoption Program, that it will provide equitable access to TANF for Indians who are not eligible for aid under a tribal plan, and that it has established and is enforcing standards and procedures against program fraud and abuse. The plan may certify that the State has established and is enforcing standards and procedures to screen and identify recipients with a history of domestic violence and will refer them to services and waive some program requirements for them in certain cases." (United States House of Representatives, Committee on Ways and Means, 2000, section 7, 11/72–12/72)

3. The exception to penalties is if the states can demonstrate reasonable cause for not meeting the requirements, or they develop a corrective compliance plan that is approved and removes the deficiencies.

4. There was a contingency fund of $2 billion available over the first 5 years for states that were experiencing economic downturns. There was also an additional $800 million over 4 years of supplemental grants for states with historically low welfare participation experiencing high population growth. In addition, there was another $1.7 billion set aside as a federal loan fund.

5. The emphasis on non-custodial parents is because most of the children receiving welfare benefits live with the custodial parent in a single-parent household and only 20 percent of these households receive child support from the non-custodial parent. According to the U.S. Department of Labor (2002), the vast majority of these non-custodial parents, especially the fathers, are unemployed, or earn low wages, or only work on an intermittent basis.

6. "WtW has identified the need for substance abuse treatment as one eligibility factor and recognizes non-medical treatment as an example of an allowable job retention service. Using Federal WtW funds for non-medical substance abuse treatment is programmatically sound since it addresses the need of a particular target group and can help individuals make successful transitions to work" (United States Department of Labor, 2002).

7. Funds are distributed to localities through a formula, with at least half of the funds having to go through the local Workforce Investment Boards (WIBs) or alternate administering agencies. The formula is a poverty formula, i.e., the number of poor individuals in excess of 7.5 percent of the total population. Not more than half of the funds may be distributed based on two additional factors: (1) the number of adults receiving TANF assistance for 30 months or more, and (2) the number of unemployed in the area.

8. Types of entities that can seek funds as a partner with a WIB include community development corporations and community-based organizations, community action agencies, and other private organizations.

9. TANF recipient eligibility is based on meeting two of these three conditions: (1) they received assistance for at least 30 months, (2) if they are within 12 months of reaching their TANF time limit, or (3) if they have exhausted their receipt of TANF due to time limits.

10. Eligibility requirements for non-custodial parents is based on the following criteria: (1) unemployed, underemployed, or having difficulty making child support payments; (2) their minor children are eligible for or receiving TANF benefits, received TANF benefits during the preceding year, or are eligible for or receiving food stamps, SSI, Medicaid, or Children's Health Insurance Program benefits; and (3) they agree to enter into a personal responsibility contract agreeing to commit to cooperate in establishing paternity, paying child support, and participating in services to increase their employment and earnings to enable them to support their children.

11. Specifically, core services are the following:

- Determination of eligibility of services
- Outreach, intake (which may include worker profiling), and orientation to the one-stop system
- Initial assessment
- Job search and placement assistance, and career counseling
- Provision of labor market information
- Provision of information on eligible training providers, local performance outcomes, one-stop activities, filing claims for unemployment insurance, and supportive services
- Assistance in establishing eligibility for Welfare-to-Work and financial aid assistance
- Follow-up services

12. Intensive services are defined to include the following:

- Comprehensive and specialized assessments of skill levels (i.e. diagnostic testing)
- Development of an individual employment plan
- Group counseling
- Individual counseling and career planning
- Case management
- Short-term prevocational services

13. "Partners must enter into written agreements with the local boards regarding services to be provided, the funding of the services and operating costs of the system, and methods of referring individuals among partners. A one-stop operator, which could be a single entity or a consortium of entities (e.g., a postsecondary education institution, an employment service agency, a private nonprofit organization, and a government agency) must be designated by the board through a competitive process or through an agreement between the board and a consortium of at least three partners" (U.S. House of Representatives, 2000, Section 15, p. 90/106).

14. Workforce Investment Boards are certified by the state's governor. The board's responsibility centers on the setting local workforce investment policy; its makeup is similar to the JTPA's Private Industry Council.

PRINCIPAL SOURCES FOR ILLUSTRATIONS

De Jong, A., and Broeckman, R. (July 2000). *National and regional trends in the labor force in the European Union 1985–2050.* Luxembourg: Office for Official Publications of the

European Communities, 2003. Retrieved from: http://europa
.eu.int/comm/eurostat/Public/datashop/print-product/EN?
catalogue=Eurostat&product=KS-AP-01-035-_-I-EN&mode=
download.

Parrott, S., and Wu, N. (June 3, 2003). *States are cutting TANF and child-care programs: Supports for low-income working families and welfare-to-work programs are particularly hit hard.* Washington, D.C.: Center on Budget and Policy Priorities. Retrieved from: http://www.cbpp.org/6-3-03tanf.pdf.

Savings, J.S. (2000). The effect of welfare reform and technological change on unemployment. *Journal of Economic and Financial Review*, number 2, pp. 26–34. Retrieved from: http://www.dallasfed.org/research/efr/2000/efr0002c.pdf.

Social Security Administration. (2001). *Annual statistical supplement, 2001 to the Social Security Bulletin.* Baltimore: Social Security Administration, Office of Policy. Retrieved from: http://www.ssa.gov/statistics/Supplement/2001/supp01.pdf.

Social Security Administration. (2002). *Social security programs throughout the world: Europe 2002.* Washington, D.C.: Author. Retrieved from: http://www.ssa.gov/policy/docs/progdesc/ssptw/2002/europe/index.html.

United Nations Development Programme. (2003). *Human development report 2003.* New York: Oxford University Press. Retrieved from: http://www.undp.org/hdr2003/pdf/hdr03_complete.pdf.

United States Census Bureau. (2002). *Statistical abstract of the United States 2002.* Washington, D.C.: Government Printing Office. Retrieved from: http://www.census.gov/statab/www/.

United States Department of Labor. (2001). *Report on the American workforce.* Washington, D.C.: Government Printing Office. Retrieved from: http://www.bls.gov/opub/rtaw/rtawhome.htm.

United States House of Representatives, Committee on Ways and Means. (2000). *The 2000 Green Book: Background material and data on programs within the jurisdiction of the Committee on Ways and Means.* Retrieved from: http://aspe.hhs.gov/2000gh.

Zedlewski, S.R., and Holland, J. (August 21, 2003). Work activities of current welfare recipients. In Urban Institute, *Snapshot of America's family III.* (Paper Numer 4). Washington, D.C.: Urban Institute. Retrieved from: http://www.urban.org/url.cfm?ID=310835.

BIBLIOGRAPHY

Ashcroft, J. (1995). *Which will survive: The welfare state or the Republican revolution?* Heritage Foundation Lecture #539. Retrieved from: http://www.heritage.org/Research/Welfare/index.cfm.

Brown, A. (March 1997). *ReWORKing welfare technical assistance for states and localities: A how-to guide.* Washington, D.C.: Manpower Demonstration Research Corporation. Retrieved from: http://aspe.os.dhhs.gov/hsp/isp/work1st/frontm.htm.

Brownlow, L. (1958). *A passion for anonymity: The autobiography of Louis Brownlow, the second half.* Chicago: University of Chicago Press.

Center for Women Policy Studies. (2002). *From poverty to self-sufficiency: The role of postsecondary education in welfare reform.* Washington, D.C.: Center for Women Policy Studies. Retrieved from: http://www.centerwomenpolicy.org/pubfiles/20021223fptss.pdf.

Chambers, D.E. (1986). *Social policy and social programs: A method for the practical public policy analyst.* New York: Macmillan Press.

General Accounting Office. (2002). The social safety net for Americans in need. In *Social safety net: Strategic objective plan 2000–2002.* Retrieved from: http://www.gao.gov/sp/glsocial.pdf.

Haveman, R.H. (1987). *Poverty policy and poverty research.* Madison, WI: University of Wisconsin Press.

Minnesota Department of Economic Security. (September 1998). *The Dynamics of employment expansion and contraction: Behind the scenes of job churning.* St. Paul, MN: Department of Economic Security, Research and Statistics Office. Retrieved from: http://www.mnwfc.org/lmi/pub1/churn.pdf.

Organization for Economic Cooperation and Development. (1999). Benefit Systems and Work Incentives 1999 Country Chapters. *OECD 1999 Synopsis of Member Nations Social Programs.* Washington, D.C.: OECD. Retrieved from: http://www.oecd.org/EN/document/0, EN-document-211-5-no-1-31684-211,00.html.

Rector, R.E., and Youssef, S.E. (1999). *The determinants of welfare caseload decline: Center for Data Analysis report #99-04.* Washington, D.C.: Heritage Foundation. Retrieved from: http://www.heritage.org/Research/Welfare/index.cfm.

Social Security Administration. (2001). *Annual statistical supplement, 2001 to the Social Security Bulletin.* Baltimore: Social Security Administration, Office of Policy. Retrieved from: http://www.ssa.gov/statistics/Supplement/2001/supp01.pdf.

United States Department of Health and Human Services. (1999). Executive Summary. *TANF Final Rules.* Washington, D.C.: Administration for Families and Change Web site. Retrieved from: http://www.acf.hhs.gov/programs/ofa/exsumcl.htm.

United States Department of Human and Health Services, Welfare. (October 2000). *Reform information technology: A study of issues in implementing information systems for the Temporary Assistance for Needy Families (TANF) program, overarching issue.* Washington, D.C. Administration for Families and Change. Retrieved from: http://www.acf.dhhs.gov/programs/oss/WRITReport/WRIT-body.htm#background.

United States Department of Labor. (1998). *White Paper: Implementing the Workforce Investment Act of 1998.* Washington, D.C.: U.S. Deparment of Labor Employment and Training Administration Web site. Retrieved from: http://www.doleta.gov/usworkforce/documents/misc/wpaper3.asp.

United States Department of Labor. (2001). *Report on the American workforce.* Washington, D.C.: U.S. Printing Office. Retrieved from: http://www.bls.gov/opub/rtaw/pdf/rtaw2001.pdf.

United States Department of Labor. (2002a). *Welfare to Work: Noncustodial Parents.* U.S. Department of Labor Employment and Training Administration Web site. Retrieved from: http://wtw.doleta.gov/resources/fact-noncustodial.pdf.

United States Department of Labor. (2002b). *Welfare to Work and Substance Abuse.* U.S. Department of Labor Employment and Training Administration Web site. Retrieved from: http://wtw.doleta.gov/resources/fact-substance.pdf.

United States House of Representatives, Committee on Ways and Means. (2000). *The 2000 Green Book: Background material and data on programs within the jurisdiction of the Committee on Ways and Means.* Retrieved from: http://aspe.hhs.gov/2000gh.

Table 7.1
Comparisons of Social and Family Benefits in the United States and Seven OECD Countries

Country	Social Benefit	Family Benefit

United States of America	• SSI (see next chapter) means-tested monthly cash payments in accordance with uniform, nationwide eligibility requirements to needy aged, blind and disabled
	• Food Stamps
	  means-tested based on income tests (basic gross income at no more than 130% of poverty and net monthly income must not exceed 100% of poverty guideline)
	  able-bodied adults without dependants eligible for 3 months within a 36-month period unless they meet a work requirement of 20 hours per week or more, or participate in a qualifying work activity expectations
	  behind benefit calculation is that families expected to spend 30% of income on food
	  not taxable
	  not part of means-tests for other programs
		• TANF replaced AFDC and JTPA in 1996 ending federal entitlement to assistance. States determine eligibility and benefit levels and services provided to needy families
		• Most TANF benefits also qualify for Medicaid benefits
		  Medicaid is a federal-state program of medical assistance for low-income persons who are aged, blind, disabled, members of families with dependent children, and certain other pregnant women and children
		  transitional Medicaid benefits may be available up to 12 months after loss of TANF benefits due to employment
		• Under AFDC guidelines, program designed to assist mothers without a spouse to support them to take care of their children at home. Under TANF, the program expects recipients to work and become self-sufficient within the state's time limit, but no longer than 60 months
		• Benefits not taxable
		• Federal funding for TANF benefits is limited to 60 months for each family; the 60 months do not have to be consecutive, but it is a lifetime limit. Some states have opted to shorten the limit
		• States have flexibility to give special treatment to victims of domestic violence (referrals to counseling and other support services, waiving time limits, residency requirements, child support cooperation requirements, and family cap provisions)

Germany	• Social assistance guarantees a minimum income level and is also available to working people whose income threshold is lower than the minimum income level
	• Two forms:
	  • Cost-of-living assistance (food, clothing, everyday necessities)
	  • Assistance in special circumstances
	  Cost-of-living assistance may be received by people who cannot cover their cost of living at all or only inadequately through their own capabilities or resources (particularly income and assets)
	  • Granted to people living in private households
	  • No general threshold to determine qualification
	  • Formula: Standard basic rate of head-of-household or person living alone plus standard rates for any other household member plus any extra allowances for additional needs plus rent and utilities and heating costs=Social assistance need – Net Income=Actual cost-of-living assistance to be paid
	  • Federal government defines what the standards need to include, the Länder decide the actual amount of the standard rates on the basis of annual federal definition
		• Family benefits take on the form of tax credits and allowances
		• The Kindergeld (family care) program is in the form of a monthly tax refund
		  • coverage: residents who are subject to income tax with 1 or more children
		  • whole cost borne by government without contributions from an insurance fund
		  • paid to all children up to age 18
		  • payments prolonged up to age 27 for children undergoing training, and up to age 21 for children without a job
		  • ages adjusted for military service
		  • children over 18 with an income of their own exceeding 13,020 DM generally not eligible for family allowance
		  • not income related, awarded in the form of a monthly tax refund—in some cases where parents not subject to income tax liability are paid as a monthly social security benefit staggered by the number of children (in January 1999 it was DM 250 per month for first and second children, 300 DM for the third child, and 350 DM for fourth and subsequent children)

- family allowance usually paid out by private and public employers (small and medium sized businesses can be exempted); otherwise, by the local family office
- Mothers or fathers taking care of their own newly-born children themselves, receive a child-raising allowance of up to DM 600 per month up to the end of the twenty-fourth month of life. While receiving this stipend, they are entitled to work up to 19 hours per week
- income dependent
- single parents making over 75,000 DM and married couples making over 100,000 DM do not qualify for program
- single parents making less than 23,700 DM and married couple earning less than 29,400 DM receive allowances that are gradually reduced (income ceiling rises by 4,200 DM in both cases with each additional child)
- child-raising allowance generally reduced by the amount of maternity allowance paid following childbirth

- All children under 18 qualify got child benefits
- Cost wholly borne by the government. Benefits are not income related (and are not included in any means test)
- Family allowances range from 321.92 guilders per quarter for families with one child under age 6 to 641.69 guilders per quarter per child for families with six children between ages 12 to 17
- As of January 5, 1997, parents of handicapped children aged 3 to 18 can get a supplementary benefit as a partial compensation of the extra costs (TOG-agreement)
- benefit for parents of multihandicapped children (mental and physical): 389 guilders per quarter
- benefit for children that are seriously physically handicapped or chronologically ill: 260 guilders per quarter
- Adjustments occur twice per year on basis of price index changes
- Non-taxable benefit

- Disabled people and persons who are alone living with and caring for a child under 7 or two children under 16 get an additional 40% of the basic benefit rate. A single parent taking care of 4 or more children, parent receives an increased need allowance of 60% of the basic benefit rate
- Even in cases where costs exceed a level reasonable for the specific features of the individual situation, the costs of rent, utilities and heating are fully covered as long as it is impossible or unreasonable for the assistance recipient to reduce his expenses by changing residences.
- A "lower rank principle" of the social assistance system dictates that the assistance seeker must first utilize personal income and assets, with assistance stepping in if these resources do not cover the costs of living (at all or only in part)

The Netherlands

- National Assistance Act guarantees a minimum income to any Dutch citizen who does not have sufficient means of existence
- beneficiaries mainly those no longer entitled to benefits under social insurance schemes, persons without a work history, and persons who unexpectedly lose income
- entitlement in dependent on claimant seeking employment and registered with local employment exchange
- general assistance benefit duration is for as long as there is a need
- additional allowances have a duration that is also for as long as there is a need
- Payments intended to cover normal costs of living (food, housing, heating, furniture, and recreation)
- Three benefit rates related to family composition:
- couples—100% proportion of subsistence minimum (23,991 guilders)
- lone parent families—90% proportion of subsistence minimum (21,592 guilders)
- single 23 or older—70% proportion of subsistence minimum (16,794 guilders)
- One-to-one income-test using household income; savings and assets over 9,850 guilders (19,700 for couples) are taken into account; family benefits and individual housing benefits are excluded from income-test; claimant dwelling disregarded only up to a certain amount (value of house – mortgage = more than minimum) at which point recipient can receive social assistance as a loan
- Taxable; however general assistance is defined on net value because a net income level is guaranteed. Income taxes on social assistance benefit not paid by the recipient, but transferred to the tax inspector by the municipality administering the benefit

Table 7.1 (continued)

Country	Social Benefit	Family Benefit

	• Persons receiving social assistance that are 57.5 years old or older are not required to look for work
	• Lone parents must start looking for work if youngest child is 5 years of age or older
	• Individuals aged 18–21 are deemed to be in work, education or in the WIW (Law Involving Unemployment); parents are supposed to provide support to these young adults until age 21, thus, municipalities only obliged to provide benefits to applicants in this age group that demonstrate exceptional circumstances
	  • >21 years of age with children and single parent receives monthly allowance of 745.28 guilders
	  • married couple in which one parent is greater than 21 yrs. of age and the other is less than 21 yrs. of age and have children receives a monthly allowance of 1744.89 guilders
	  • married couple that are both are older than 21 and have children receive a monthly allowance of 1090.71 guilders
	  • <21 yrs. of age and single receives a monthly allowance of 345.43 guilders
	  • married couple that are both less than 21 yrs. of age without children receive a monthly allowance of 690.86 guilders
	  • married couple, one greater than 21 yrs. of age and the other less than 21 years of age without children receive a monthly allowance of 1345.04 guilders	

Czech Republic	• Objective: prevent social exclusion and deprivation due to poverty • The main criterion on which social assistance benefits and allowances are based is the existence of social need • Lump sum benefit: designed to cover the citizen's needs in emergency and similar situations • Ongoing payments: supplement an insufficient income or to cover increased living costs caused by disabilities or illness and, by their nature, are not time limited and are provided as long as the contingency and the need to supplement income exists • Grants and allowances are means-tested (necessary to distinguish between the benefits to supplement income to reach the minimum living standard (MLS) and benefits designed to remedy individual problems and impact of various health handicaps) – permanent residence, impossibility to obtain an increased income by using own efforts, in particular by gainful activities, and impossibility to use the persons' property to remedy his or her present situation. In case of unemployment, the unemployed has to be registered with the public employment service (not required from old age and invalidity pensioners, persons over 65, parents caring for children meeting other prescribed conditions, and other relates circumstances	• Child allowance, and family benefits • Family benefits consist of: 1. the benefits related to family income (child allowance, social allowance, housing benefit, transportation benefit), and 2. the benefits provided irrespective of income (parental allowance, maintenance benefit, foster care allowances, birth grant, funeral grant) • Eligibility criteria: Each child under 15 years old (until the end of compulsory education), or under 26 years old (if in full-time education, vocational training or disabled) is entitled to the child allowance. The family has to meet certain income criteria • Child benefit allowance determination (is the basic long-term allowance provided to a dependent child aged 15 to 26 years of age with the objective to contribute to the coverage of costs incurred in upbringing and sustenance) • Child allowance is provided at three levels depending on last year's family income • Allowance calculation:

1. at the increased rate, i.e. the child personal needs amount multiplied by a coefficient of 0.32, if the decisive family income does not exceed the family minimum living standard multiplied by a coefficient of 1.10;
2. at the basic rate, i.e. the child personal needs amount multiplied by a coefficient of 0.28, if the decisive family income exceeds the family minimum living standard multiplied by a coefficient of 1.10 but does not exceed the family minimum living standard multiplied by a coefficient of 1.80;
3. at the reduced rate, i.e. the child personal needs amount multiplied by a coefficient of 0.14, if the decisive family income exceeds the family minimum living standard multiplied by a coefficient of 1.80 but does not exceed the family minimum living standard multiplied by a coefficient of 3.00

• Benefit is not taxable

• Benefit is nontaxable

Poland

• Eligibility:
1. To have insufficient means of living under income criteria and to meet social criteria. Income criteria differ depending on kind of benefit and demographic composition of a family
2. Social criteria: Poverty, orphanage, homelessness, protection of maternity, unemployment, disability, permanent illness, alcohol and drug addiction, difficulties in adjustment to life after imprisonment, natural ecological disaster, inability to provide for the care of children or a household, especially in a large or incomplete families

• Income based means-tested program
• Benefit is not taxable

• Claimant must have a dependent child aged under 16, or under 20 if still in education. A dependent wife aged over 60 or husband aged over 65 or when this person have a child who is eligible for nursing benefit or is disabled also qualifies. Benefit given on a per household member basis
• Gross benefit calculation(1998–1999)
1. 35.3 PLN for the first and second child (each),
2. 43.7 PLN for the third child,
3. 54.6 PLN for the fourth and next child (each)
• Benefit ceases if the total gross income per each household member, in a calendar year preceding a period of collecting benefit, exceeds 50% of the national average wage for the same calendar year. Benefit is granted for a period of 12 months, thus the right to benefit is tested once a year
• Benefit is not taxable

Norway

• Social Economic Assistance (SEA) is an individual complementary benefit. The benefit unit is always the individual, but the resource unit is the dependent family. The Ministry of Health and Social Affairs does not set any fixed national payment rates, assistance is granted according to the local social workers' discretion (based on national guidelines on what kind of expenses the beneficiary should be able to cover). Many municipalities have their own guidelines
• Eligibility: SEA is a means-tested benefit. Only legal residents in Norway are entitled to SEA. The assistance may be conditional requirement to work for the municipality, active job search, participation in labor market training, etc.
• Calculation of benefit amount performed at the local level, with the average annual benefit as:
Average benefit,
One-person family: 81,500 kroner per year

• Family benefits are paid only to families with dependent children. Each child aged 16 or under qualifies
• Child benefits increase with the number of children in the household. Lone parents receive benefits for the number of children plus one more

1st child: 11,110 kroner per year
2nd child: 11,110 kroner per year
3rd child: 13,090 kroner per year
4th and subsequent
child: 13,090 kroner per year
• Family benefits are not taxable

Table 7.1 (*continued*)

Country	Social Benefit	Family Benefit
	Average benefit, Lone parent with children Under 18: 95,500 kroner per year Couple without children: 101,100 kroner per year Couple with children Under 18: 142,300 kroner per year • Exclusion from income eligibility determination: none. SEA is withdrawn 100% against all income (including family benefits) • Benefit duration: expected to be temporary relief; however, there is no set time limit • Benefit is not taxable	
Sweden	• Social Welfare Allowance, which is municipally administered • Eligibility: It is an income and assets-tested benefit, based on the obligation to exhaust all other means of support, and to be actively seeking employment. Social assistance is, according to the legislation, a right to a certain standard of living if no other means of income can be obtained; topping-up net incomes that fall below this standard is usually not possible • Benefit calculation: The National Board of Health and Welfare (NBHW) works out a national guideline norm for social assistance. The norm is calculated annually and has an individual part that depends on the age of the child and a household part that depends on the size of the household. For 1999 the norm is as shown in the table below. For children below the age of 7 attending day care institutions the rate is slightly lower • Social assistance recipients receive a supplementary element that covers any reasonable housing costs, after housing benefit from the state system has been received. Social workers may add extra payments for special purposes like medical or dental expenses and child-care costs but usually there can be an addition for local transportation expenses and union dues • Maximum assistance benefit is reduced with 100% of net income. Net income is defined as earned and taxable social security income after income tax and social security contribution and including housing benefit, family allowance, maintenance advance that are not taxed • Benefit duration: indefinite as long as eligibility conditions are met • Benefit is not taxable	• Child benefit: eligibility is for each child aged 16 or under (or until 20 if still at school) qualifies the family for child benefit. Not subjected to any means-test • Gross benefit calculation: the annual amount is SEK 9,000 per child (SEK 750 per month), with a supplement of SEK 2,400 for the third child, SEK 7,200 for the fourth child, and SEK 9,000 for the fifth and each subsequent child • Benefit is not taxable

Australia

- Special Benefit serves as a benefit of last resort. It is paid to people in severe financial need, who have no other means of support and for whom no other benefit is available. The benefit is not payable when the available funds and liquid assets of the person are A$ 5,000.00 or more. Payment rates are at the discretion of the Secretary of the Department of Family and Community Services (FaCS) but cannot exceed the maximum NSA, YA or Austudy payment rates that would otherwise be payable to the person. In practice, the policy is to pay the rate that most closely resembles the person's circumstances. (For example, a person under 21 years is paid at the YA rate.) The benefit is means tested against any income with a 100% withdrawal rate. Any amount of in-kind income support, such as free board and lodgings, also reduces the rate of payment

- Australia also has an emergency relief program which pays funds to community based centers that help families in crises

- Family benefits consist of the Family Allowance (FA), the Family Tax Initiative (Family Tax Assistance—FTA), maternity allowances and double orphan pensions. FA is an allowance paid to help parents and guardians with the cost of raising children. FTI provides extra assistance to families with dependent children either in the form of reduced taxes or as a regular fortnightly payment. Maternity allowance (MA) is a lump sum payment that helps families with the extra costs incurred at the time of having a new baby. Maternity Immunization Allowance is a one off lump sum payment paid for a child at age 18 months if the child has been immunized or has gained an exception to the immunization requirements

- Eligibility: parents and guardians with the cost of raising children. FTI provides extra assistance to families with dependent children either in the form of reduced taxes or as a regular fortnightly payment. Maternity allowance (MA) is a lump sum payment that helps families with the extra costs incurred at the time of having a new baby. Maternity Immunization Allowance is a one off lump sum payment paid for a child at age 18 months if the child has been immunized or has gained an exception to the immunization requirements

- It is available to all families with dependent children subject to an income test. Families can receive their assistance through the tax system or as a fortnightly payment (Family Tax Payment) if their income is such that they would not receive the full benefit through the tax system. FTI has two parts:

  - Part A provides one parent with a A$ 1,000 per year increase in their tax free threshold for each dependent child (an increase in disposable income of A$ 7.70 per fortnight for each child); and

  - Part B provides one parent in families with at least one child under 5 years with an additional A$ 2,500 increase in their tax free threshold (A$ 9.24 per fortnight)

- Benefit calculation: The benefit amounts are differentiated into four age groups for children aged under 13, 13–15, 16–18, and 18–24

- Maternity allowance is a one off payment of A$ 750.00. Maternity Immunization Allowance is a one off lump sum payment of $200.00

- Income and asset tested determination for eligibility

- Income includes taxable income, foreign income, certain employer provided fringe benefits and net rental property

- Family Allowance is reduced by 50 cents per dollar income above A$ 23,550 a year plus A$ 624 for each additional child after the first. Above certain limits, only minimum FA is paid (A$ 27,466 plus A$ 4,540 for each additional child under 13, or A$ 29,016 plus A$ 6,089 for each additional child 13–15). All FA ceases when family income exceeds A$ 66,403 plus A$ 3,322 for each additional child after the first

- There are two parts to the Family Tax Assistance. Families may be entitled to one or both parts depending on their family circumstances

Table 7.1 (*continued*)

Country	Social Benefit	Family Benefit
		• Eligibility for Part A benefit is based upon the combined taxable incomes of the parents. The income ceiling of A$ 70,000 upon which eligibility is measured increases by A$ 3,000 for the second and additional children • Eligibility for Part B benefit is contingent upon the main income earner and their spouse meeting separate income tests and the existence of at least one dependant child under the age of five. The income ceiling of A$ 65,000 for the main income earner increases by A$ 3,000 for the second and additional dependent children irrespective of their age(s). The spouse income test is the same as the cut-off for basic parenting payment (A$ 178.86 per fortnight) • Family benefits are not taxable
Japan	• Social assistance consists of seven parts or aids, provided for those who are unable to provide minimum living standards. These are livelihood aid, housing aid, medical aid, occupational aid, education aid, maternity aid, and funeral aid. Only livelihood aid and housing aid are considered here. The selected rates are classified as Grade 1-1, as paid in Osaka and Tokyo • Means-tested against income • 2 types of livelihood benefit: personal expenses based on the age of each family member (Category 1) and household expenses based on the number of family members (Category 2). The maximum amount of livelihood aid is calculated by summing up amounts of Category 1 for each family member and amounts of Category 2. A housing aid is also available, it covers housing costs up to 13,000 yen per month • Earnings net of tax and social security contributions up to 8,340 yen per month are disregarded. From this level, social assistance is reduced by earnings net of tax and social security contributions exceeding a threshold which increases with earnings. The monthly disregard is assumed to increase proportionally with gross earnings. The monthly amounts are as follows for the same region (Grade 1-1) as for personal expenses: Monthly Gross earnings X (JPY) Monthly Threshold Y (JPY) 0–8,340 0–8,340 8,340–92,000 8,340–22,570 92,000–248,000 22,570–33,560 248,000+ 33,560 • Benefit is not taxable	• The benefit is income-tested. It is paid for a child under 3 years old • Gross benefit calculation: The benefit is income-tested. It is paid for a child under 3 years old • It is paid if the annual gross income minus the employment income deduction is lower than 1,700,000 yen plus 380,000 yen per child • Benefit is not taxable
South Korea	• Livelihood protection programmes (LPPs) distinguish between two broad types of support	None

1. First, there is *livelihood aid* for households where no-one is able to work due to disability, old age (over age 65) or pregnancy. Recipients of LPP aid are categorized as either necessitating *institutional care* or requiring *home care support*

2. Second, for the other cases, there exists *self-support care*. Recipients of self-support care have a greater ability to work than those protected by livelihood aid

   • Eligibility: satisfying the conditions regarding income support and other conditions relating to work ability, or satisfying the income and property standard. For the latter, the income limit is KRW 230,000 per month and the property limit is KRW 29 million

   • Calculation of benefit: Livelihood aid (payments of living cost) is paid to recipients of self-support only for 6 months during the winter period. Recipients of self-support care may receive as well medical, educational and maternity aid. Only livelihood aid has been included in the calculations. The benefit level varies according to the number of household members of recipients

   • Benefits not taxable

Source: Adapted from Organization for Economic Co-operation and Development. (1999). Synopsis of Member Nations social programs. Washington, D.C.: Author. Retrieved from http://www.oecd.org.

Table 7.2
Summary of U.S. Government Transfer Payments to Individuals: 1970 to 2000

[In billions of dollars (69.3 represents $69,300,000,000).]

Year	Total	Retirement & disability insurance benefits	Medical payments	Income maintenance benefits	Unemployment insurance benefits	Veterans benefits	Federal education & training assistance payments	Other
1970	69.3	34.3	13.0	9.9	4.2	7.5	0.4	0.1
1975	159.3	72.0	30.7	21.5	18.2	14.0	1.0	1.9
1980	262.7	128.8	62.0	34.3	18.7	14.7	4.1	0.2
1985	394.7	197.2	114.6	44.4	15.9	16.6	5.5	0.6
1990	561.4	263.9	189.1	63.5	18.2	17.7	7.3	1.8
1991	635.7	285.7	223.5	72.5	26.9	18.1	7.3	1.8
1992	714.8	304.7	257.3	84.6	39.7	18.6	8.0	2.0
1993	760.6	320.8	284.7	90.3	34.9	19.4	9.1	1.4
1994	792.8	334.8	308.3	95.6	24.1	19.7	8.6	1.8
1995	841.0	350.0	337.5	100.4	21.9	20.5	9.0	1.6
1996	883.0	364.6	361.3	102.5	22.5	21.4	8.6	2.1
1997	914.9	379.4	379.6	100.3	20.3	22.2	11.5	1.7
1998	935.1	392.0	386.3	100.7	19.9	23.2	11.2	1.9
1999	965.2	403.0	399.6	104.4	20.7	24.1	11.4	2.1
2000	1,013.4	425.3	423.2	106.4	20.7	24.9	10.7	2.1

1. Excludes veterans. Consists largely of federal fellowship payments (National Science Foundation fellowships and traineeships, subsistence payments to state maritime academy cadets, and other federal fellowships), interest subsidy on higher education loans, basic educational opportunity grants, and Job Corps payments.

2. Consists largely of Bureau of Indian Affairs payments, education exchange payments, Alaska Permanent Fund dividend payments, compensation of survivors of public safety officers, compensation of victims of crime, disaster relief payments, compensation for Japanese internment, and other special payments to individuals.

Source: United States Census Bureau. (2002). *Statistical Abstract of the United States 2002.* Washington, D.C.: Government Printing Office. Retrieved from http://www.census.gov/prod/2003pubs/02statab/socinsur.pdf.

Table 7.3
U.S. Government Transfer Payments to Individuals by Type: 1990 to 2000

[In millions of dollars (561,399 represents $561,399,000,000).]

Item	1990	1995	1996	1997	1998	1999	2000
Total	561,399	841,041	883,042	914,942	935,058	965,206	1,013,424
Retirement & disability insurance benefit payments	263,854	350,027	364,623	379,415	391,987	402,990	425,333
Old age, survivors, & disability insurance	244,135	327,667	341,987	356,602	369,347	379,895	401,408
Railroad retirement and disability	7,221	8,028	8,085	8,193	8,225	8,203	8,265
Workerís compensation payments (federal & state)	8,618	10,530	10,795	10,606	10,344	10,560	11,111
Other government disability insurance & retirement [1]	3,880	3,802	3,756	4,014	4,071	4,332	4,549
Medical payments	189,099	337,532	361,342	379,557	386,273	399,597	423,180
Medicare	107,929	180,283	195,581	209,198	208,755	208,126	215,882
Public assistance medical care [2]	78,176	155,017	163,629	168,288	175,475	189,464	205,281
Military medical insurance [3]	2,994	2,232	2,132	2,071	2,043	2,007	2,017
Income maintenance benefit payments	63,481	100,444	102,494	100,288	100,694	104,421	106,421
Supplemental Security Income (SSI)	16,670	27,726	28,903	29,154	30,322	31,023	31,675
Family assistance [4]	19,187	22,637	20,325	17,717	17,026	17,683	18,277
Food stamps	14,741	22,447	21,955	18,732	16,465	15,473	14,939
Other income maintenance [5]	12,883	27,634	31,311	34,685	36,881	40,242	41,530
Unemployment insurance benefit payments	18,208	21,864	22,480	20,299	19,859	20,724	20,707
State unemployment insurance compensation	17,644	20,975	21,614	19,469	19,154	20,010	19,938
Unemployment compensation for federal civilian employees	215	339	326	281	236	206	227
Unemployment compensation for railroad employees	89	62	65	72	61	65	81
Unemployment compensation for veterans	144	320	279	259	211	201	182
Other unemployment compensation [6]	116	168	196	218	197	242	279
Veterans benefit payments	17,687	20,545	21,430	22,233	23,168	24,058	24,939
Veterans pension and disability	15,550	17,565	18,286	19,061	20,049	20,904	21,885
Veterans readjustment [7]	257	1,086	1,138	1,234	1,220	1,323	1,331
Veterans life insurance benefits	1,868	1,883	1,997	1,929	1,891	1,823	1,714
Other assistance to veterans [8]	12	11	9	9	8	8	9
Federal education & training assistance payments [9]	7,300	9,007	8,568	11,481	11,189	11,366	10,729
Other payments to individuals [10]	1,770	1,622	2,105	1,669	1,888	2,050	2,115

1. Consists largely of temporary disability payments, pension benefit guaranty payments, and black lung payments.

2. Consists of medicaid and other medical vendor payments.

3. Consists of payments made under the TriCare Management Program (formerly called CHAMPUS) for the medical care of dependents of active duty military personnel and of retired military personnel and their dependents at nonmilitary medical facilities.

4. Through 1995, consists of emergency assistance and aid to families with dependent children. Beginning with 1998, consists of benefits—generally known as temporary assistance for needy families—provided under the Personal Responsibility and Work Opportunity Reconciliation Act of 1996. For 1996–97, consists of payments under all three of these programs.

5. Consists largely of general assistance, expenditures for food under the supplemental program for women, infants, and children; refugee assistance; foster home care and adoption assistance; earned income tax credits; and energy assistance.

6. Consists of trade readjustment allowance payments. Redwood Park benefit payments, public service employment benefit payments, and transitional benefit payments.

7. Consists largely of veterans' readjustment benefit payments, educational assistance to spouses and children of disabled or deceased veterans, payments to paraplegics, and payments for autos and conveyances for disabled veterans.

8. Consists largely of state and local government payments to veterans.

9. Excludes veterans. Consists largely of federal fellowship payments (National Science Foundation fellowships and traineeships, subsistence payments to state maritime academy cadets, and other federal fellowships), interest subsidy on higher education loans, basic educational opportunity grants, and Job Corps payments.

10. Consists largely of Bureau of Indian Affairs payments, education exchange payments, Alaska Permanent Fund divided payments, compensation of survivors of public safety officers, compensation of victims of crime, disaster relief payments, comparison for Japanese internment, and other special payments to individuals.

Source: United States Census Bureau. (2002). *Statistical Abstract of the United States 2002*. Washington, D.C.: Government Printing Office. Retrieved from http://www.census.gov/prod/2003pubs/02statab/socinsur.pdf.

Table 7.4
U.S. Government Transfer Payments to Individuals by State: 1990 to 2000

[In millions of dollars (561,399 represents $561,399,000,000).]

State	1990, total	1995, total	2000 Total	Retirement & disability insurance benefits	Medical payments	Income maintenance benefits	Unemployment insurance benefits	Veterans benefits	Federal education & training assistance payments [1]	Other [2]
U.S.	561,399	841,041	1,013,424	425,333	423,180	106,421	20,707	24,939	10,729	2,115
AL.	8,738	13,395	16,701	7,187	6,619	1,857	237	569	220	12
AK.	1,294	1,860	2,908	482	725	292	111	85	13	1,198
AZ.	7,864	12,653	15,802	7,560	5,771	1,426	182	554	230	80
AR.	5,459	8,063	9,841	4,429	3,636	1,049	199	422	102	4
CA.	65,912	96,576	113,693	42,244	45,834	19,407	2,509	2,115	1,471	113
CO	5,796	9,273	11,058	4,872	4,453	990	153	434	141	17
CT.	8,121	12,470	14,325	5,941	6,516	1,238	340	200	84	5
DE.	1,364	2,148	2,725	1,310	1,036	213	71	67	26	1
DC	1,676	2,318	2,676	611	1,471	429	58	61	42	4
FL.	33,029	52,572	64,371	29,533	26,597	5,058	709	1,916	524	34
GA	11,843	19,042	23,485	9,813	9,468	2,773	338	820	258	14
HI	2,139	3,480	3,893	1,655	1,341	618	108	128	40	3
ID	1,849	2,836	3,729	1,882	1,260	287	113	128	54	5
IL	25,216	36,032	41,461	18,211	16,694	4,256	1,231	601	419	48
IN	11,363	16,191	20,278	9,696	7,975	1,681	305	382	229	11
IA	6,065	8,215	9,823	5,054	3,518	699	214	214	116	7
KS.	5,264	7,298	8,810	4,300	3,331	650	178	233	109	9
KY.	8,343	12,503	15,891	6,840	6,387	1,789	293	426	150	6
LA.	9,284	15,257	16,901	6,074	7,741	2,231	179	456	213	8
ME	2,814	4,203	5,155	2,141	2,137	523	86	221	44	3
MD	9,168	13,513	16,641	7,069	7,075	1,614	279	429	164	11
MA	16,490	23,068	26,888	9,889	13,144	2,221	798	582	243	11
MI	22,351	29,984	36,271	16,234	14,486	3,723	918	569	326	15
MN	9,469	13,241	15,774	7,021	6,472	1,336	399	378	153	15
MS	5,609	8,648	10,745	4,221	4,436	1,440	128	342	166	13
MO	11,277	17,029	21,186	9,241	9,079	1,808	331	502	214	11
MT	1,893	2,636	3,092	1,546	1,052	255	71	119	39	10
NE.	3,141	4,425	5,561	2,702	2,168	384	55	188	62	3
NV.	2,479	4,217	5,695	2,924	1,923	397	200	197	47	7
NH	2,013	3,461	3,931	1,915	1,580	238	27	139	30	1
NJ.	18,376	27,593	32,139	14,321	13,695	2,269	1,079	490	270	15
NM	2,786	4,586	5,906	2,406	2,202	792	86	265	91	63
NY.	54,178	82,755	95,679	30,796	49,214	11,837	1,595	1,140	1,058	39
NC	12,658	21,054	27,349	11,887	11,209	2,599	504	881	251	17
ND	1,510	1,940	2,366	1,132	932	157	33	61	29	22
OH	26,578	36,753	42,829	20,116	16,891	3,862	724	840	372	24
OK	6,615	9,937	11,954	5,418	4,496	1,141	125	607	152	15
OR	6,374	9,529	11,936	5,793	4,168	1,011	415	391	142	17
PA.	32,238	45,821	55,208	23,385	24,427	4,521	1,454	990	414	18
RI	2,776	4,027	4,793	1,880	2,136	461	151	109	50	6
SC.	6,724	10,621	13,800	6,151	5,380	1,429	211	467	150	13
SD.	1,445	2,061	2,489	1,152	949	194	16	98	40	40
TN.	10,814	17,338	22,243	8,820	10,150	2,094	387	603	175	13
TX.	29,214	49,155	60,798	23,617	26,450	6,756	1,107	2,040	766	62
UT.	2,594	3,892	4,919	2,362	1,781	408	119	130	109	10
VT.	1,163	1,743	2,179	939	877	235	45	57	25	1
VA.	10,174	15,539	19,352	9,518	6,877	1,709	197	812	227	11
WA	10,973	16,608	20,336	9,344	7,306	1,724	967	743	221	32
WV	5,125	7,426	8,627	4,318	3,012	829	120	268	77	3
WI	10,941	14,829	17,714	8,552	6,642	1,403	525	417	160	16
WY	819	1,225	1,495	823	462	110	28	52	18	2

1. Excludes veterans. Consists largely of federal fellowship payments (National Science Foundation, fellowships and traineeships, subsistence payments to state maritime academy cadets, and other federal fellowships), interest subsidy on higher education loans, basic educational opportunity grants, and Job Corps payments.
2. Consists largely of Bureau of Indian Affairs payments, education exchange payments, Alaska Permanent Fund dividend payments, compensation of survivors of public safety officers, compensation of victims of crime, disaster relief payments, compensation for Japanese internment, and other special payments to individuals.

Source: United States Census Bureau. (2002). *Statistical Abstract of the United States 2002.* Washington, D.C.: Government Printing Office. Retrieved from http://www.census.gov/prod/2003pubs/02statab/socinsur.pdf.

Table 7.5
Temporary Assistance for Needy Families (TANF)—Families and Recipients:
1980 to 2001

[In thousands (3,712 represents 3,712,000). **Average monthly families and recipients for calendar year, except 2001 for Jan.-Sept. period.** Prior to TANF, the cash assistance program to families was called Aid to Families with Dependent Children (1980-1996). Under the new welfare law (Personal Responsibility and Work Opportunity Reconciliation Act of 1996), the program became TANF. Includes Puerto Rico, Guam, and Virgin Islands.]

Year	Families	Recipients	Year	Families	Recipients	Year	Families	Recipients
1980	3,712	10,774	1988	3,749	10,915	1996	4,434	12,321
1981	3,835	11,079	1989	3,799	10,993	1997	3,740	10,376
1982	3,542	10,258	1990	4,057	11,695	1998	3,050	8,347
1983	3,686	10,761	1991	4,467	12,930	1999	2,554	6,828
1984	3,714	10,831	1992	4,829	13,773	2000	2,219	5,790
1985	3,701	10,855	1993	5,012	14,205	2001	2,110	5,420
1986	3,763	11,038	1994	5,033	14,161			
1987	3,776	11,027	1995	4,791	13,418			

Source: United States Census Bureau. (2002). *Statistical Abstract of the United States 2002*. Washington, D.C.: Government Printing Office. Retrieved from http://www.census.gov/prod/2003pubs/02statab/socinsur.pdf.

Table 7.6
TANF—Recipients by State and Other Areas: 1995 to 2001

[In thousands (4,791 represents 4,791,000). **Average monthly families and recipients for calendar year, except as noted.**]

State or other area	Families 1995	Families 2000	Families 2001 [1]	Recipients 1995	Recipients 2000	Recipients 2001 [1]	State or other area	Families 1995	Families 2000	Families 2001 [1]	Recipients 1995	Recipients 2000	Recipients 2001 [1]
Total .	4,791	2,219	2,110	13,418	5,790	5,420	MT.	11	5	5	33	13	14
U.S.	4,734	2,186	2,080	13,242	5,690	5,334	NE.	15	9	10	41	24	24
AL	45	19	18	114	45	43	NV.	16	6	8	41	16	20
AK	12	7	6	36	22	17	NH.	10	6	6	27	14	14
AZ	68	33	34	185	84	84	NJ.	110	50	45	310	125	112
AR	24	12	12	62	29	28	NM.	34	23	18	103	69	53
CA	916	492	471	2,675	1,283	1,219	NY.	452	250	223	1,241	695	600
CO	38	11	11	106	28	27	NC.	123	45	42	305	97	90
CT	61	27	26	169	64	59	ND.	5	3	3	14	8	9
DE	11	6	5	24	12	12	OH.	222	95	84	592	235	195
DC	26	17	16	72	46	43	OK.	44	14	14	120	35	34
FL	224	65	57	606	143	121	OR.	38	18	19	101	41	43
GA	138	52	50	378	125	119	PA.	201	88	82	582	232	213
HI	22	15	13	66	42	41	RI.	22	16	15	60	44	41
ID	9	1	1	24	2	2	SC.	48	16	17	127	37	41
IL	233	78	60	684	234	175	SD.	6	3	3	17	7	6
IN	62	37	42	177	101	118	TN.	102	57	60	271	148	156
IA	35	20	20	97	53	55	TX.	269	129	130	730	347	346
KS	28	13	13	77	32	33	UT.	16	8	7	44	22	22
KY	74	38	36	184	87	81	VT.	10	6	5	27	16	15
LA	77	27	25	251	71	64	VA.	70	31	29	179	69	64
ME.	21	11	10	59	28	26	WA	101	56	54	283	148	141
MD.	80	29	28	220	72	67	WV	38	13	15	102	33	40
MA.	97	43	42	263	100	99	WI	71	17	18	202	38	40
MI.	195	72	72	578	199	197	WY	5	1	1	14	1	1
MN.	61	39	39	178	114	113	PR	54	32	26	164	88	74
MS.	51	15	16	140	34	36	GU	2	3	3	8	10	10
MO	88	47	45	249	125	121	VI.	1	1	1	5	3	2

1. January–September period only.

Source: United States Census Bureau. (2002). *Statistical Abstract of the United States 2002*. Washington, D.C.: Government Printing Office. Retrieved from http://www.census.gov/prod/2003pubs/02stab/socinsur.pdf.

Table 7.7
TANF—Expenditures by State: 1999 and 2000

[**In millions of dollars (22,585 represents $22,585,000,000), except as indicated**. Represents federal and state funds expended in fiscal year.]

| State | 1999, total | 2000 | | | State | 1999, total | 2000 | | |
		Total [1]	Percent federal funds	Expenditures on assistance			Total [1]	Percent federal funds	Expenditures on assistance
U.S. . . .	**22,585**	**23,590**	**53**	**13,323**	MO	317	321	54	189
AL	91	93	58	39	MT	41	44	65	24
AK	88	93	46	67	NE	116	77	63	48
AZ	240	265	65	118	NV	65	56	51	23
AR	72	112	79	31	NH	60	73	56	42
CA	6,252	6,228	53	4,761	NJ	450	322	7	226
CO	160	205	42	51	NM	130	149	73	113
CT	385	436	56	171	NY	3,652	3,498	43	2,126
DE	59	55	56	24	NC	394	435	59	140
DC	128	134	42	72	ND	33	33	72	25
FL	484	765	51	265	OH	656	987	60	394
GA	410	383	55	251	OK	151	134	54	85
HI	168	161	52	141	OR	286	256	64	128
ID	27	44	70	4	PA	1,038	891	54	496
IL	840	880	50	280	RI	164	167	51	111
IN	188	342	65	113	SC	107	124	71	29
IA	175	165	63	80	SD	22	21	59	21
KS	176	151	51	174	TN	209	273	68	160
KY	208	205	65	108	TX	591	743	66	315
LA	128	126	55	86	UT	80	91	72	45
ME	109	108	52	94	VT	65	59	54	44
MD	328	333	47	196	VA	258	222	42	100
MA	632	587	39	255	WA	504	531	49	311
MI	1,034	1,198	61	384	WV	58	134	71	72
MN	377	382	50	193	WI	322	419	60	55
MS	44	62	63	37	WY	14	16	30	7

1. Includes other items not shown separately.

Source: United States Census Bureau. (2002). *Statistical Abstract of the United States 2002.* Washington, D.C.: Government Printing Office. Retrieved from http://www.census.gov/prod/2003pubs/02statab/socinsur.pdf.

Table 7.8
Average Number of Monthly Recipients, Total Amount of Cash Payments, and Average Monthly Payment for AFDC/TANF 1936 to 1999

(Includes nonmedical vendor payments. Includes Alaska and Hawaii, beginning in 1943; Puerto Rico and the Virgin Islands, beginning in October 1950, and Guam, beginning in July 1959)

	Temporary Assistance for Needy Families/ Aid to Families with Dependent Children [1]						Emergency Assistance [2]		
	Average monthly number (in thousands)			Amount in payments [3]					
		Recipients			Monthly average per—		Average monthly number of families (in thousands)	Total assistance payments during year (in thousands)	Average monthly payment per family
Year	Families	Total	Children	Total (in thousands)	Family	Recipient			
1936	147	534	361	$49,678	$28.15	$7.75	. . .	. . .	. . .
1940	349	1,182	840	133,770	31.98	9.43	. . .	. . .	. . .
1945	259	907	656	149,667	48.18	13.75	. . .	. . .	. . .
1950	644	2,205	1,637	551,653	71.33	17.64	. . .	. . .	. . .
1955	612	2,214	1,673	617,841	84.17	23.26	. . .	. . .	. . .
1960	787	3,005	2,314	1,000,784	105.75	27.75	. . .	. . .	. . .
1961	869	3,354	2,587	1,156,769	110.97	28.74	. . .	. . .	. . .
1962	931	3,676	2,818	1,298,774	116.30	29.44	. . .	. . .	. . .
1963	947	3,876	2,909	1,365,851	120.19	29.36	. . .	. . .	. . .
1964	992	4,118	3,091	1,510,352	126.88	30.57	. . .	. . .	. . .
1965	1,039	4,329	3,256	1,660,186	133.20	31.96	. . .	. . .	. . .
1966	1,088	4,513	3,411	1,863,925	142.83	34.42	. . .	. . .	. . .
1967	1,217	5,014	3,771	2,266,400	155.19	37.67	. . .	. . .	. . .
1968	1,410	5,705	4,275	2,849,298	168.41	41.62	. . .	. . .	. . .
1969	1,698	6,706	4,985	3,563,427	174.89	44.28	7.5	$6,699	$117.23
1970	2,208	8,466	6,214	4,852,964	183.13	47.77	7.5	11,396	126.14
1971	2,762	10,241	7,434	6,203,528	187.16	50.48	11.1	19,843	148.54
1972	3,049	10,947	7,905	6,909,260	188.87	52.60	19.9	44,180	184.91
1973	3,148	10,949	7,902	7,212,035	190.91	54.89	18.8	39,265	174.05
1974	3,230	10,864	7,822	7,916,563	204.27	60.72	31.3	64,031	170.38
1975	3,498	11,346	8,095	9,210,995	219.44	67.65	38.3	77,516	168.85
1976	3,579	11,304	8,001	10,140,543	236.10	74.75	27.5	55,673	168.43
1977	3,588	11,050	7,773	10,603,820	246.27	79.97	32.8	66,132	168.05
1978	3,522	10,570	7,402	10,730,415	253.89	84.60	34.5	80,919	195.24
1979	3,509	10,312	7,179	11,068,864	262.86	89.45	35.7	84,043	195.92
1980	3,712	10,774	7,419	12,475,245	280.03	96.49	48.6	113,238	194.29
1981	3,835	10,079	7,527	12,981,115	282.04	97.64	49.1	123,467	209.51
1982	3,542	10,258	6,903	12,877,906	303.02	103.60	27.5	102,344	4 278.54
1983	3,686	10,761	7,098	13,837,228	312.82	107.16	30.0	125,246	4 283.15
1984	3,714	10,831	7,144	14,503,710	325.44	111.60	32.1	141,137	4 276.97
1985	3,701	10,855	7,198	15,195,835	342.15	116.65	32.6	157,304	4 312.98
1986	3,763	11,038	7,334	16,033,074	355.04	121.05	34.8	178,824	4 362.45
1987	3,776	11,027	7,366	16,372,535	361.37	123.73	42.4	213,903	4 358.29
1988	3,749	10,915	7,329	16,826,794	374.07	128.47	48.8	278,906	4 420.89
1989	3,799	10,993	7,420	17,465,943	383.14	132.40	48.7	296,841	4 461.45
1990	4,057	11,695	7,917	19,066,541	391.67	135.86	56.0	348,986	4 476.50
1991	4,467	12,930	8,715	20,930,600	390.44	134.89	59.7	302,894	4 422.07
1992	4,829	13,773	9,303	21,655,881	373.71	131.03	52.7	272,853	4 431.41
1993	5,012	14,205	9,574	22,688,016	377.24	133.10	56.8	387,113	4 568.17
1994	5,035	14,164	9,570	22,827,399	377.78	134.30	60.5	802,258	4 1,105.95
1995	4,791	13,418	9,135	21,608,686	375.31	134.21	84.1	3,447,361	4 3,415.93
1996	4,434	12,321	8,469	20,614,437	386.68	139.44	69.8	2,708,401	4 3,235.10
1997	3,740	10,376	7,042	22,031,399	490.01	176.95	81.8	403,138	4 410.74
1998	3,050	8,347	6,034	19,328,429	528.04	192.96	. . .	. . .	. . .
1999	2,555	6,835	5,130	22,759,897	742.45	277.48	. . .	. . .	. . .

1. Thirty-four states had converted to TANF as of January 1, 1997; eight phased in over the next 5 months; the remaining 12 waited until July 1, 1997.

2. Reporting initiated July 1969. Number of states with program: 1969–1970, 23; 1971, 24; 1972, 27; 1973–1975, 29; 1976–1978, 26; 1979, 24; 1980–1984, 27; 1985–1986, 28; 1987, 29; 1988, 30; 1989, 31; 1990, 33; 1991, 34; 1992, 34; 1993, 35; 1994, 49; 1995, 50; 1996, 51; and 1997, 34. Program ended June 30, 1997.

3. TANF expenditures include services as well as cash payments.

4. Excludes family count and expenditures for states providing only partial data.

Source: Social Security Administration. (2001). *Annual Statistical Supplement, 2001 to the Social Security Bulletin.* Baltimore: Social Security Administration, Office of Policy. Retrieved from http://www.ssa.gov/policy/docs/statcomps/supplement/2001/supp01.pdf.

Table 7.9
Family Assistance Grants and Required State Spending under TANF

[In thousands of dollars]

State	Family assistance grant	75 percent of historic State spending[1]	80 percent of historic State spending[1]	Maximum child care spending that can be ``double-counted'' toward both the CCDF and TANF MOE	Minimum spending on needy families that cannot be double counted for MOEs of both CCDF and TANF
Alabama	$93,315	$39,214	$41,828	$6,896	$32,318
Alaska	63,609	48,942	52,205	3,545	45,398
Arizona	222,420	95,028	101,363	10,033	84,995
Arkansas	56,733	20,839	22,228	1,887	18,952
California	3,733,818	2,732,406	2,914,566	85,593	2,646,813
Colorado	136,057	82,871	88,396	8,986	73,885
Connecticut	266,788	183,421	195,649	18,738	164,683
Delaware	32,291	21,771	23,222	5,179	16,592
District of Columbia	92,610	70,449	75,146	4,567	65,882
Florida	562,340	370,919	395,647	33,416	337,503
Georgia	330,742	173,369	184,926	22,183	151,186
Hawaii	98,905	72,981	77,847	4,972	68,010
Idaho	31,938	13,679	14,591	1,176	12,503
Illinois	585,057	429,021	457,622	56,874	372,147
Indiana	206,799	113,525	121,093	15,357	98,168
Iowa	131,525	61,963	66,094	5,079	56,885
Kansas	101,931	61,750	65,866	6,673	55,077
Kentucky	181,288	67,418	71,913	7,275	60,144
Louisiana	163,972	55,415	59,109	5,219	50,196
Maine	78,121	37,778	40,296	1,750	36,028
Maryland	229,098	176,965	188,763	23,301	153,664
Massachusetts	459,371	358,948	382,877	44,973	313,974
Michigan	775,353	468,518	499,753	24,411	444,107
Minnesota	267,985	179,745	191,728	19,690	160,055
Mississippi	86,768	21,724	23,173	1,715	20,009
Missouri	217,052	120,121	128,129	16,549	103,572
Montana	45,534	15,689	16,735	1,314	14,375
Nebraska	58,029	28,971	30,903	6,499	22,472
Nevada	43,977	25,489	27,188	2,580	22,908
New Hampshire	38,521	32,115	34,256	4,582	27,533
New Jersey	404,035	303,956	324,219	26,374	277,581
New Mexico	126,103	37,450	39,947	2,895	34,555
New York	2,442,931	1,710,795	1,824,848	101,984	1,608,811
North Carolina	302,240	154,176	164,454	37,927	116,248
North Dakota	26,400	9,069	9,674	1,017	8,052
Ohio	727,968	390,551	416,588	45,404	345,147
Oklahoma	148,014	61,250	65,334	10,630	50,620
Oregon	167,925	92,255	98,405	11,715	80,540
Pennsylvania	719,499	407,126	434,267	46,629	360,497
Rhode Island	95,022	60,367	64,392	5,321	55,046
South Carolina	99,968	35,839	38,229	4,085	31,754
South Dakota	21,894	8,774	9,359	803	7,971
Tennessee	191,524	82,810	88,331	18,976	63,834
Texas	486,257	235,725	251,440	34,681	201,043
Utah	76,829	25,291	26,977	4,475	20,816
Vermont	47,353	25,653	27,364	2,666	22,987
Virginia	158,285	128,173	136,718	21,329	106,844
Washington	404,332	272,061	290,198	38,708	233,353
West Virginia	110,176	32,701	34,881	2,971	29,730
Wisconsin	318,188	169,229	180,511	16,449	152,779
Wyoming	21,781	10,665	11,376	1,554	9,112
Total	16,488,667	10,434,961	11,130,625	887,607	9,547,354

1. Fiscal year 1994 spending on AFDC, EA, JOBS, and AFDC-related child care.

Source: United States House of Representatives, Committee on Ways and Means. (2000). *The 2000 Green Book: Background material and data on programs within the jurisdiction of the Committee on Ways and Means.* Retrieved from http://aspe.hhs.gov/2000gb/see7.txt.

Table 7.10
Summary Table of Enacted and Proposed Cuts in TANF-Funded and Childcare Programs at the State Level

Program Area	States In Which Cuts Have Been Enacted or Proposed by the Governor[1]
Welfare-to-Work Programs (includes job training, education, job search, and other employment services programs)	Arizona, California, Connecticut, D.C., Indiana, Iowa, Louisiana, Massachusetts, Missouri, Montana, Oregon, Rhode Island, Tennessee, Washington, Wisconsin
TANF Cash Assistance Programs (includes cuts to basic benefit levels, cash benefits for working TANF recipients, cash benefits for grandparents and other relatives caring for children, and limitations on access to cash benefits through changes to time limit policies or asset-eligibility rules being made for budgetary reasons)	California, Connecticut, Indiana, Minnesota, Montana, Nevada, Oregon, Texas, Washington, West Virginia
TANF-Funded Transportation Programs	Arizona, Arkansas, Missouri, Montana, Tennessee, Washington, West Virginia, Wisconsin
TANF-Funded Services for Very Disadvantaged Families (includes TANF-funded domestic violence services, substance abuse treatment, homelessness programs, programs that provide emergency assistance such as payments to avoid eviction, services for families that have been sanctioned for failing to meet program requirements, and other families with serious barriers to employment)	Arizona, Connecticut, D.C., Illinois, Iowa, Massachusetts, Nevada, North Carolina, Oregon, Washington, Wisconsin
TANF-Funded Teen Pregnancy Prevention and Teen Parent Programs	D.C., Massachusetts, North Carolina, Tennessee
Child Care Programs (includes funding reductions, new eligibility restrictions, cuts in provider payments, and cuts in quality initiatives)	Alabama, Alaska, Arizona, California, Colorado, Connecticut, D.C., Georgia, Idaho, Illinois, Indiana, Kansas, Kentucky, Louisiana, Maryland, Massachusetts, Michigan, Minnesota, Montana, Nebraska, New Jersey, New Mexico, North Carolina, Ohio, Oklahoma, Oregon, Rhode Island, South Carolina, Tennessee, Texas, Washington, Wisconsin

1. Enacted cuts include cuts that were made in SFY 2002, 2003 or will be made in 2004. Proposed cuts are cuts being proposed for SFY 2004 and/or SFY 2005. Cuts that were included in a governor's budget proposal but not included in enacted budget legislation this year have not been included.

Source: Parrott, S., & Wu, N. (June 3, 2003). States are cutting TANF and Child-care programs: Supports for low-income working families and Welfare-to-Work programs are particularly hit hard. Washington, D.C.: Center on Budget and Policy Priorities. Retrieved from http://www.cbpp.org/6-3-03tanf.pdf.

Table 7.11
Social Security and Selected Public Assistance Programs—Average Monthly Amounts in Current and 2000 Dollars: United States, 1950 to 2000

Period	Consumer Price Index, all items [1] (1982-84 = 100)	Average monthly Social Security benefit in current-payment status				Average monthly amount per recipient under6			
		Retired workers		Widowed mother or father and 2 children		Old-Age Assistance/ Supplemental Security Income [2]		Temporary Assistance for Needy Families [3]	
		Current dollars	2000 dollars	Current dollars	2000 dollars	Current dollars	2000 dollars	Current dollars	2000 dollars
December:									
1950	25.0	$43.86	$305.27	$93.90	$653.54	$43.05	$299.63	$20.85	$145.12
1951	26.5	42.14	276.69	93.80	615.89	44.55	292.52	22.00	144.45
1952	26.7	49.25	320.96	106.00	690.79	48.80	318.02	23.45	152.82
1953	26.9	51.10	330.54	111.90	723.81	48.90	316.30	23.20	150.07
1954	26.7	59.14	385.41	130.50	850.45	48.70	317.37	23.25	151.52
1955	26.8	61.90	401.89	135.40	879.09	50.05	324.95	23.50	152.57
1956	27.6	63.09	397.74	141.00	888.91	53.25	335.71	24.80	156.35
1957	28.4	64.58	395.67	146.30	896.35	55.50	340.04	25.40	155.62
1958	28.9	66.35	399.48	151.70	913.35	56.95	342.88	26.65	160.45
1959	29.4	72.78	430.74	170.70	1010.27	56.70	335.57	27.30	161.57
1960	29.8	74.04	432.31	188.00	1,097.72	58.90	343.91	28.35	165.53
1961	30.0	75.65	438.77	189.30	1,097.94	57.60	334.08	29.45	170.81
1962	30.4	76.19	436.09	190.70	1,091.51	61.55	352.29	29.30	167.70
1963	30.9	76.88	432.92	192.50	1,083.98	62.80	353.63	29.70	167.24
1964	31.2	77.57	432.60	193.40	1,078.58	63.65	354.97	31.50	175.67
1965	31.8	83.92	459.18	219.80	1,202.68	63.10	345.26	32.85	179.75
1966	32.9	84.35	446.11	221.90	1,173.57	68.05	359.90	36.25	191.72
1967	33.9	85.37	438.18	224.40	1,151.79	70.15	360.06	39.50	202.74
1968	35.5	98.86	484.55	257.10	1,260.15	69.55	340.89	44.75	219.34
1969	37.7	100.40	463.38	255.80	1,180.62	73.90	341.08	45.15	208.38
1970	39.8	118.10	516.32	291.10	1,272.65	77.65	339.47	50.30	219.90
1971	41.1	132.17	559.55	320.00	1,354.74	77.50	328.10	52.30	221.42
1972	42.5	162.35	664.68	383.10	1,568.46	79.95	327.32	54.10	221.49
1973	46.2	166.42	626.78	391.00	1,472.60	76.15	286.80	56.95	214.49
1974	51.9	188.21	630.99	438.40	1,469.78	91.06	305.29	63.37	212.45
1975	55.5	207.18	649.54	468.60	1,469.12	90.93	285.08	69.69	218.49
1976	58.2	224.86	672.26	503.40	1,505.01	94.37	282.14	75.20	224.82
1977	62.1	243.00	680.87	546.60	1,531.54	96.62	270.72	80.08	224.38
1978	67.7	263.20	676.47	591.90	1,521.28	100.43	258.12	83.60	214.87
1979	76.7	294.30	667.64	655.00	1,485.92	122.67	278.29	90.34	204.94
1980	86.3	341.40	688.34	759.20	1,530.72	128.20	258.48	97.10	195.78
1981	94.0	385.97	714.46	858.00	1,588.21	137.81	255.10	103.15	190.94
1982	97.6	419.30	747.52	885.50	1,578.66	145.69	259.73	106.33	189.56
1983	101.3	440.77	757.10	923.00	1,585.41	157.89	271.20	109.93	188.82
1984	105.3	460.57	761.06	948.30	1,566.99	157.88	260.88	114.72	189.57
1985	109.3	478.62	761.94	981.50	1,562.50	164.26	261.49	118.17	188.12
1986	110.5	488.44	769.13	994.00	1,565.21	173.66	273.46	122.09	192.25
1987	115.4	512.65	772.97	1,032.30	1,556.50	180.64	272.37	125.19	188.76
1988	120.5	536.77	775.09	1,070.40	1,545.64	188.23	271.80	130.30	188.15
1989	126.1	566.85	782.17	1,120.04	1,545.50	198.81	274.33	131.89	181.99
1990	133.8	602.56	783.60	1,177.70	1,531.54	212.66	276.55	135.96	176.81
1991	137.9	629.32	794.07	1,216.76	1,535.29	221.30	279.23	134.98	170.32
1992	141.9	652.64	800.28	1,252.40	1,535.71	227.39	278.83	132.92	162.99
1993	145.8	674.06	804.43	1,282.60	1,530.67	236.52	282.27	132.87	158.57
1994	149.7	697.34	810.54	1,328.40	1,544.03	242.54	281.91	133.71	155.41
1995	153.5	719.80	815.93	1,365.50	1,547.86	250.65	284.12	134.35	152.29
1996	158.6	744.96	817.30	1,450.60	1,591.45	260.75	286.07	133.53	146.50
1997	161.3	774.84	835.85	1,502.60	1,620.91	268.46	289.60	170.71	184.15
1998	163.9	779.69	827.74	1,537.70	1,632.46	277.45	294.55	197.80	209.99
1999	168.3	804.30	831.54	1,590.40	1,644.26	289.19	298.98	236.16	244.16
2000	174.0	844.48	844.48	1,675.40	1,675.40	299.69	299.69	[4]147.78	147.78

1. Data from Bureau of Labor Statistics, consumer price index for all urban consumers (CPI-U).
2. Beginning in 1974, represents payments to the aged under the SSI program.
3. Effective July 1, 1997, the Temporary Assistance for Needy Families (TANF) block grant program replaced the Aid to Families with Dependent Children (AFDC) program. Beginning in 1997, payments include services.
4. Preliminary data.

Source: Social Security Administration. (2001). *Annual Statistical Supplement, 2001 to the Social Security Bulletin.* Baltimore: Social Security Administration, Office of Policy. Retrieved from http://www.ssa.gov/policy/docs/statcomps/supplement/2001/supp01.pdf.

Table 7.12
Average Monthly Benefits for AFDC/TANF Families, Fiscal Years 1994 to 1998

State	1994	1995	1996	1997	1998
Alabama	$148.48	$146.13	$144.21	$142.10	$139.58
Alaska	805.26	822.90	769.01	NA	669.00
Arizona	299.27	299.57	291.11	290.03	278.76
Arkansas	177.71	177.65	169.70	170.92	166.68
California	551.72	558.16	538.51	526.25	NA
Colorado	315.20	313.97	302.36	304.10	300.48
Connecticut	563.73	515.32	463.10	465.67	462.35
Delaware	297.41	296.00	304.35	280.74	270.52
District of Columbia	393.86	392.48	384.00	350.80	345.68
Florida	254.20	255.50	250.42	229.89	228.45
Georgia	245.56	244.63	242.62	242.74	236.82
Guam	504.77	494.60	548.80	527.29	502.30
Hawaii	665.54	671.64	668.11	613.17	519.78
Idaho	282.16	269.75	265.88	287.74	256.78
Illinois	314.82	306.12	295.17	289.18	280.74
Indiana	257.29	255.46	244.52	233.00	229.34
Iowa	359.21	340.97	336.95	326.52	329.62
Kansas	345.68	335.91	319.59	311.40	296.90
Kentucky	207.58	202.97	222.90	223.19	219.64
Louisiana	163.28	159.62	153.10	157.20	159.13
Maine	418.28	403.84	393.79	390.97	367.95
Maryland	315.53	315.76	309.46	303.14	310.60
Massachusetts	544.42	531.80	523.65	473.84	504.94
Michigan	429.23	415.58	405.87	396.30	357.37
Minnesota	477.69	479.75	470.28	477.85	NA
Mississippi	119.72	123.00	116.95	117.51	101.15
Missouri	261.37	260.71	257.45	251.67	243.68
Montana	343.80	344.00	349.25	348.29	367.84
Nebraska	319.39	308.88	310.58	320.13	323.14
Nevada	283.83	284.82	279.38	274.23	288.09
New Hampshire	467.30	467.82	466.26	459.14	417.12
New Jersey	361.01	355.41	345.61	332.28	342.72
New Mexico	325.21	343.13	352.13	342.24	382.99
New York	495.43	494.04	487.14	478.50	479.85
North Carolina	229.37	226.97	222.86	218.72	219.56
North Dakota	355.43	352.73	353.23	355.62	338.29
Ohio	308.46	305.18	301.91	291.52	306.25
Oklahoma	292.14	279.85	258.36	252.62	217.22
Oregon	394.67	394.49	339.51	401.37	380.99
Pennsylvania	379.69	379.48	373.71	372.95	364.83
Puerto Rico	101.79	100.47	99.69	101.95	98.33
Rhode Island	495.11	510.40	485.89	490.56	477.20
South Carolina	175.31	180.34	176.45	162.21	157.60
South Dakota	293.10	292.58	301.72	285.44	294.23
Tennessee	168.65	170.71	172.35	163.74	169.91
Texas	162.50	157.60	155.95	159.96	164.49
Utah	341.60	356.51	347.66	346.16	354.40
Vermont	525.63	502.31	450.18	442.75	460.60
Virginia	259.33	251.29	248.18	247.18	245.74
Virgin Islands	264.51	268.23	256.91	285.65	334.15
Washington	492.65	498.13	489.02	476.38	464.08
Wisconsin	463.01	457.28	432.54	422.37	565.70
Wyoming	300.01	299.47	286.91	263.06	218.50

NA. Not available.

Source: United States House of Representatives, Committee on Ways and Means. (2000). *The 2000 Green Book: Background material and data on programs within the jurisdiction of the Committee on Ways and Means.* Retrieved from http://aspe.hhs.gov/2000gb/sec7.txt.

Table 7.13
Maximum Combined AFDC/TANF Benefit for a Family of Three (Parent with Two Children), July 1994 to January 2000

State	July 1994	July 1996	July 1998	January 2000	change from July 1994-January 2000
Alabama	$164	$164	$164	$164	-10.7
Alaska	923	923	923	923	-10.7
Arizona	347	347	347	347	-10.7
Arkansas	204	204	204	204	-10.7
California	607	596	565	626	-7.9
Colorado	356	356	356	357	-10.5
Connecticut	680	636	636	636	-16.5
Delaware	338	338	338	338	-10.7
District of Columbia	420	415	379	379	-19.5
Florida	303	303	303	303	-10.7
Georgia	280	280	280	280	-10.7
Guam	330	673	673	673	82.0
Hawaii:					
Work exempt	712	712	712	712	-10.7
Nonexempt	712	712	570	570	-28.5
Idaho	317	317	276	293	-17.5
Illinois	377	377	377	377	-10.7
Indiana	288	288	288	288	-10.7
Iowa	426	426	426	426	-10.7
Kansas	429	429	429	429	-10.7
Kentucky	228	262	262	262	2.6
Louisiana	190	190	190	190	-10.7
Maine	418	418	439	461	-1.6
Maryland	373	373	388	417	-0.2
Massachusetts:					
Work exempt	579	579	579	579	-10.7
Nonexempt	579	565	565	565	-12.9
Michigan:					
Washtenaw County	489	489	489	489	-10.7
Wayne County	459	459	459	459	-10.7
Minnesota	532	532	532	532	-10.7
Mississippi	120	120	120	170	26.5
Missouri	292	292	292	292	-10.7
Montana	416	438	461	469	0.6
Nebraska	364	364	364	364	-10.7
Nevada	348	348	348	348	-10.7
New Hampshire	550	550	550	575	-6.7
New Jersey	424	424	424	424	-10.7
New Mexico	381	389	489	439	2.8
New York:					
New York City	577	577	577	577	-10.7
Suffolk County	703	703	703	703	-10.7
North Carolina	272	272	272	272	-10.7
North Dakota	431	431	440	457	-5.4
Ohio	341	341	362	373	-2.4
Oklahoma	324	307	292	292	-19.6
Oregon	460	460	460	460	-10.7
Pennsylvannia	421	421	421	421	-10.7
Puerto Rico	180	180	180	180	-10.7
Rhode Island	554	554	554	554	-10.7
South Carolina	200	200	201	204	-9.1
South Dakota	430	430	430	430	-10.7
Tennessee	185	185	185	185	-10.7
Texas	188	188	188	201	-4.6
Utah	414	416	451	451	-2.8
Vermont	650	633	656	708	-2.8
Virgin Islands	240	240	240	240	-10.7
Virginia	354	354	354	354	-10.7
Washington	546	546	546	546	-10.7
West Virginia	253	253	253	328	15.7
Wisconsin:					
Community service	517	517	673	673	16.2
W2 transition	517	517	628	628	8.4
Wyoming	360	360	340	340	-15.7
Median State	381	415	421	421	-10.5

Note: The Consumer Price Index for All Urban Consumers inflation adjustment factor for converting July 1994 dollars to January 2000 dollars is 1.1203.

Source: United States House of Representatives, Committee on Ways and Means. (2000). *The 2000 Green Book: Background material and data on programs within the jurisdiction of the Committee on Ways and Means.* Retrieved from http://aspe.hhs.gov/2000gb/sec7.txt.

Table 7.14
AFDC/TANF Maximum Benefit for a Three-Person Family
by State, Selected Years 1970 to 2000

State	July 1970[1]	July 1975	July 1980	July 1985	January 1990[2]	January 1995[2]	January 2000[2]	Percent change in real value, 1970-2000[3]
Alabama	$65	$108	$118	$118	$118	$164	$164	-42
Alaska	328	350	457	719	846	923	923	-35
Arizona	138	163	202	233	293	347	347	-42
Arkansas	89	125	161	192	204	204	204	-47
California	186	293	473	587	694	607	626[4]	-22
Colorado	193	217	290	346	356	356	356	-57
Connecticut	283	346	475	569	649	680	636	-48
Delaware	160	221	266	287	333	338	338	-51
District of Columbia	195	243	286	327	409	420	379	-55
Florida	114	144	195	240	294	303	303	-39
Georgia	107	123	164	223	273	280	280	-40
Guam	NA	NA	261	265	330	330	673	NA
Hawaii	226	428	468	468	602	712	712[5]	-27
Idaho	211	300	323	304	317	317	293	-68
Illinois	232	261	288	341	367	377	377	-62
Indiana	120	200	255	256	288	288	288	-45
Iowa	201	294	360	360	410	426	426	-51
Kansas	222	321	345	391	409	429	429	-55
Kentucky	147	185	188	197	228	228	262	-59
Louisiana	88	128	152	190	190	190	190	-50
Maine	135	176	280	370	453	418	461	-21
Maryland	162	200	270	329	396	373	417	-40
Massachusetts	268	259	379	432	539	579	579[5]	-50
Michigan:								
Washtenaw County	NA	NA	NA	447	546	489	489	NA
Wayne County	219	333	425	417	516	459	459	-52
Minnesota	256	330	417	528	532	532	532	-52
Mississippi	56	48	96	96	120	120	170	-30
Missouri	104	120	248	274	289	292	292	-35
Montana	202	201	259	354	359	416	469	-46
Nebraska	171	210	310	350	364	364	364	-51
Nevada	121	195	262	285	330	348	348	-34
New Hampshire	262	308	346	389	506	550	575	-49
New Jersey	302	310	360	404	424	424	424	-68
New Mexico	149	169	220	258	264	381	439	-32
New York:								
New York City	279	332	394	474	577	577	577	-52
Suffolk County	NA	NA	NA	579	703	703	703	NA
North Carolina	145	183	192	246	272	272	272	-57
North Dakota	213	283	334	371	386	431	457	-50
Ohio	161	204	263	290	334	341	373	-46
Oklahoma	152	217	282	282	325	324	292	-56
Oregon	184	337	282	386	432	460	460	-42
Pennsylvania	265	296	332	364	421	421	421	-63
Puerto Rico	43	43	44	90	90	180	180	-3
Rhode Island	229	278	340	409	543	554	554	-44
South Carolina	85	96	129	187	206	200	204	-45
South Dakota	264	289	321	329	377	430	430	-62
Tennessee	112	115	122	153	184	185	185	-62
Texas	148	116	116	167	184	188	201	-69
Utah	175	252	360	376	387	426	451	-40
Vermont	267	322	492	583	662	650	708	-39
Virgin Islands	NA	131	209	171	240	240	240	NA
Virginia	225	268	310	354	354	354	354	-64
Washington	258	315	458	476	501	546	546	-51
West Virginia	114	206	206	249	249	253	328	-33
Wisconsin	184	342	444	533	517	517	628[6]	-21
Wyoming	213	235	315	360	360	360	340	-63
Median State[7]	184	235	288	332	364	377	421	-47

1. Data on three-person families were not published or reported before 1975. Thus, the 1970 data were derived by reducing the reported four-person maximum benefit amount by the proportional difference between three- and four-person AFDC maximum benefit as shown in the July 1975 reports of the (then) Department of Health, Education and Welfare.

2. Congressional Research Service Survey data.

3. Real percentage change. The Consumer Price Index for All Urban Consumers inflation adjustment factor used for converting July 1970 dollars to January 2000 dollars was 4.3256.

4. Benefits for region 1.

5. Benefits for persons exempt from work.

6. Benefits for persons in W-2 transitions (work preparation activities).

7. Among the 50 States and the District of Columbia.

Source: United States House of Representatives, Committee on Ways and Means. (2000). *The 2000 Green Book: Background material and data on programs within the jurisdiction of the Committee on Ways and Means.* Retrieved from http://aspe.hhs.gov/2000gb/sec7.txt.

Table 7.15

Annualized Earnings and Income from Selected Major Benefit Programs for Single Parent with Two Children Working Half-Time at Minimum Wage in Month 13 of Employment, January 1, 2000

	Net earnings	EIC	TANF	Food stamps	Combined total	As a percent of 1999 poverty threshold				
						Net earnings	EIC	TANF	Food stamps	Combined total
Alabama	$4,946	$2,142	0	$3,216	$10,305	36.8	16.0	0.0	24.0	76.8
Alaska	5,426	2,350	$11,076	0	18,853	40.4	17.5	82.5	0.0	140.5
Arizona	4,946	2,142	1,171	2,856	11,115	36.8	16.0	8.7	21.3	82.8
Arkansas	4,946	2,142	1,224	4,020	12,333	36.8	16.0	9.1	29.9	91.9
California:										
Region 1	5,523	2,392	5,872	1,296	15,083	41.1	17.8	43.7	9.7	112.4
Region 2	5,523	2,392	5,512	1,404	14,831	41.1	17.8	41.1	10.5	110.5
Colorado[1]	4,946	2,142	658	3,012	10,758	36.8	16.0	4.9	22.4	80.1
Connecticut	5,907	2,558	7,632	2,208	18,305	44.0	19.1	56.9	16.4	136.4
Delaware	5,426	2,350	2,804	2,244	12,825	40.4	17.5	20.9	16.7	95.5
District of Columbia	5,907	2,558	1,950	2,376	12,791	44.0	19.1	14.5	17.7	95.3
Florida	4,946	2,142	2,158	2,568	11,815	36.8	16.0	16.1	19.1	88.0
Georgia	4,946	2,142	812	2,964	10,865	36.8	16.0	6.0	22.1	80.9
Guam[2]	4,946	2,142	3,800	3,228	14,117	36.8	16.0	28.3	24.0	105.2
Hawaii:										
Work exempt	5,042	2,184	7,284	3,252	17,763	37.6	16.3	54.3	24.2	132.3
Nonexempt	5,042	2,184	5,580	3,768	16,575	37.6	16.3	41.6	28.1	123.5
Idaho	4,946	2,142	1,370	2,796	11,255	36.8	16.0	10.2	20.8	83.8
Illinois	4,946	2,142	2,739	2,388	12,215	36.8	16.0	20.4	17.8	91.0
Indiana	4,946	2,142	0	3,216	10,305	36.8	16.0	0.0	24.0	76.8
Iowa[1]	4,946	2,142	2,970	2,316	12,374	36.8	16.0	22.1	17.3	92.2
Kansas[1]	4,946	2,142	2,582	2,436	12,107	36.8	16.0	19.2	18.1	90.2
Kentucky	4,946	2,142	0	3,216	10,305	36.8	16.0	0.0	24.0	76.8
Louisiana	4,946	2,142	0	3,216	10,305	36.8	16.0	0.0	24.0	76.8
Maine	4,946	2,142	5,122	1,680	13,891	36.8	16.0	38.2	12.5	103.5
Maryland[1]	4,946	2,142	1,523	2,760	11,371	36.8	16.0	11.3	20.6	84.7
Massachusetts:[1]										
Work exempt	5,763	2,496	1,788	2,460	12,507	42.9	18.6	13.3	18.3	93.2
Nonexempt	5,763	2,496	1,620	2,508	12,387	42.9	18.6	12.1	18.7	92.3
Michigan:										
Washtenaw County	4,946	2,142	3,503	2,160	12,752	36.8	16.0	26.1	16.1	95.0
Wayne County	4,946	2,142	3,143	2,268	12,500	36.8	16.0	23.4	16.9	93.1
Minnesota[1]	4,946	2,142	4,011	3,084	14,184	36.8	16.0	29.9	23.0	105.7
Mississippi	4,946	2,142	0	3,216	10,305	36.8	16.0	0.0	24.0	76.8
Missouri	4,946	2,142	0	3,216	10,305	36.8	16.0	0.0	24.0	76.8
Montana	4,946	2,142	3,411	2,184	12,684	36.8	16.0	25.4	16.3	94.5
Nebraska	4,946	2,142	0	3,216	10,305	36.8	16.0	0.0	24.0	76.8
Nevada	4,946	2,142	0	3,216	10,305	36.8	16.0	0.0	24.0	76.8
New Hampshire	4,946	2,142	4,222	1,944	13,255	36.8	16.0	31.5	14.5	98.7
New Jersey	4,946	2,142	2,410	2,484	11,983	36.8	16.0	18.0	18.5	89.3
New Mexico	4,979	2,157	3,493	2,160	12,789	37.1	16.1	26.0	16.1	95.3
New York:[1]										
New York City	4,946	2,142	4,615	1,824	13,528	36.8	16.0	34.4	13.6	100.8
Suffolk County	4,946	2,142	6,127	1,368	14,584	36.8	16.0	45.6	10.2	108.6
North Carolina	4,946	2,142	0	3,216	10,305	36.8	16.0	0.0	24.0	76.8
North Dakota	4,946	2,142	1,574	2,736	11,399	36.8	16.0	11.7	20.4	84.9
Ohio	4,946	2,142	3,298	2,220	12,607	36.8	16.0	24.6	16.5	93.9
Oklahoma	4,946	2,142	1,546	2,748	11,383	36.8	16.0	11.5	20.5	84.8
Oregon[1]	6,243	2,704	2,140	2,232	13,319	46.5	20.1	15.9	16.6	99.2
Pennsylvania	4,946	2,142	2,374	2,496	11,959	36.8	16.0	17.7	18.6	89.1
Rhode Island[1]	5,426	2,350	4,730	1,668	14,175	40.4	17.5	35.2	12.4	105.6
South Carolina	4,946	2,142	979	2,916	10,984	36.8	16.0	7.3	21.7	81.8
South Dakota	4,946	2,142	1,739	2,688	11,516	36.8	16.0	13.0	20.0	85.8
Tennessee	4,946	2,142	2,220	2,544	11,853	36.8	16.0	16.5	19.0	88.3
Texas	4,946	2,142	0	3,216	10,305	36.8	16.0	0.0	24.0	76.8
Utah	4,946	2,142	3,334	2,208	12,631	36.8	16.0	24.8	16.4	94.1
Vermont[1]	5,523	2,392	3,596	1,980	13,491	41.1	17.8	26.8	14.8	100.5
Virginia	4,946	2,142	4,248	1,932	13,269	36.8	16.0	31.6	14.4	98.9
Virgin Islands[2]	4,946	2,142	0	5,136	12,225	36.8	16.0	0.0	38.3	91.1
Washington	6,243	2,704	3,172	1,920	14,039	46.5	20.1	23.6	14.3	104.6
West Virginia	4,946	2,142	1,794	2,676	11,558	36.8	16.0	13.4	19.9	86.1
Wisconsin:[1]										
Community service	4,946	2,142	2,760	2,388	12,237	36.8	16.0	20.6	17.8	91.2
W2 transition	NA	NA	NA	NA	NA	NA	NA	NA	NA	NA
Wyoming	4,946	2,142	1,124	2,868	11,081	36.8	16.0	8.4	21.4	82.5

1. These states have their own earned income credits (generally circulated as a percentage of the Federal EIC) but they are not shown in this table.

2. Guam and the Virgin Islands have territorial tax systems that mirror the Internal Revenue Code, including the earned income credit (EIC). However, revenues foregone and refunds paid under their EICs affect their own territorial treasuries, not the U.S. Treasury.

NA. Not applicable. (Persons with jobs are not eligible for the Wisconsin program of transitional aid.)

Note: Puerto Rico is omitted from this table. It is not covered by the federal income tax and has no EIC. A half-time minimum wage worker in Puerto Rico would be ineligible for Temporary Assistance for Needy Families (TANF).

Source: United States House of Representatives, Committee on Ways and Means. (2000). *The 2000 Green Book: Background material and data on programs within the jurisdiction of the Committee on Ways and Means.* Retrieved from http://aspe.hhs.gov/2000gb/sec7.txt.

Table 7.16

Earnings and Income from Selected Major Benefit Programs for Single Parent with Two Children Working Full-Time at Minimum Wage, Working in Month 13, Annualized, January 1, 2000

	Net earnings	EIC	TANF	Food stamps	Combined total earnings	As a percent of poverty threshold Net EIC	EIC	TANF	Food	Combined
Alabama	$9,893	$3,888	0	$1,920	$15,701	73.7	29.0	0.0	14.3	117.0
Alaska	10,853	3,888	$7,440	0	22,181	80.9	29.0	55.4	0.0	165.2
Arizona	9,893	3,888	0	1,920	15,701	73.7	29.0	0.0	14.3	117.0
Arkansas	9,893	3,888	0	1,920	15,701	73.7	29.0	0.0	14.3	117.0
California:										
Region 1	11,045	3,888	2,882	756	18,571	82.3	29.0	21.5	5.6	138.4
Region 2	11,045	3,888	2,522	864	18,319	82.3	29.0	18.8	6.4	136.5
Colorado[1]	9,893	3,888	0	1,920	15,701	73.7	29.0	0.0	14.3	117.0
Connecticut	11,813	3,867	7,632	2,208	25,520	88.0	28.8	56.9	16.4	190.1
Delaware	10,853	3,888	0	1,680	16,421	80.9	29.0	0.0	12.5	122.3
District of Columbia	11,813	3,867	0	1,428	17,108	88.0	28.8	0.0	10.6	127.5
Florida	9,893	3,888	0	1,920	15,701	73.7	29.0	0.0	14.3	117.0
Georgia	9,893	3,888	0	1,920	15,701	73.7	29.0	0.0	14.3	117.0
Guam[2]	9,893	3,888	0	3,072	16,853	73.7	29.0	0.0	22.9	125.5
Hawaii:										
Work exempt	10,085	3,888	4,489	2,784	21,246	75.1	29.0	33.4	20.7	158.3
Nonexempt	10,085	3,888	2,785	3,300	20,058	75.1	29.0	20.7	24.6	149.4
Idaho	9,893	3,888	0	1,920	15,701	73.7	29.0	0.0	14.3	117.0
Illinois	9,893	3,888	953	1,644	16,378	73.7	29.0	7.1	12.2	122.0
Indiana	9,893	3,888	0	1,920	15,701	73.7	29.0	0.0	14.3	117.0
Iowa[1]	9,893	3,888	827	1,680	16,288	73.7	29.0	6.2	12.5	121.3
Kansas[1]	9,893	3,888	0	1,920	15,701	73.7	29.0	0.0	14.3	117.0
Kentucky	9,893	3,888	0	1,920	15,701	73.7	29.0	0.0	14.3	117.0
Louisiana	9,893	3,888	0	1,920	15,701	73.7	29.0	0.0	14.3	117.0
Maine	9,893	3,888	2,444	1,188	17,413	73.7	29.0	18.2	8.9	129.7
Maryland[1]	9,893	3,888	0	1,920	15,701	73.7	29.0	0.0	14.3	117.0
Massachusetts:[1]										
Work exempt	11,525	3,888	0	1,500	16,913	85.9	29.0	0.0	11.2	126.0
Nonexempt	11,525	3,888	0	1,500	16,913	85.9	29.0	0.0	11.2	126.0
Michigan:										
Washtenaw County	9,893	3,888	0	1,920	15,701	73.7	29.0	0.0	14.3	117.0
Wayne County	9,893	3,888	0	1,920	15,701	73.7	29.0	0.0	14.3	117.0
Minnesota[1]	9,893	3,888	691	3,084	17,555	73.7	29.0	5.1	23.8	130.8
Mississippi	9,893	3,888	0	1,920	15,701	73.7	29.0	0.0	14.3	117.0
Missouri	9,893	3,888	0	1,920	15,701	73.7	29.0	0.0	14.3	117.0
Montana	9,893	3,888	0	1,920	15,701	73.7	29.0	0.0	14.3	117.0
Nebraska	9,893	3,888	0	1,920	15,701	73.7	29.0	0.0	14.3	117.0
Nevada	9,893	3,888	0	1,920	15,701	73.7	29.0	0.0	14.3	117.0
New Hampshire	9,893	3,888	1,544	1,464	16,789	73.7	29.0	11.5	10.9	125.1
New Jersey	9,893	3,888	0	1,920	15,701	73.7	29.0	0.0	14.3	117.0
New Mexico	9,896	3,888	0	1,920	15,704	73.7	29.0	0.0	14.3	117.0
New York:[1]										
New York City	9,893	3,888	1,723	1,404	16,907	73.7	29.0	12.8	10.5	126.0
Suffolk County	9,893	3,888	3,235	960	17,975	73.7	29.0	24.1	7.2	133.9
North Carolina	9,893	3,888	0	1,920	15,701	73.7	29.0	0.0	14.3	117.0
North Dakota	9,893	3,888	0	1,920	15,701	73.7	29.0	0.0	14.3	117.0
Ohio	9,893	3,888	620	1,740	16,141	73.7	29.0	4.6	13.0	120.2
Oklahoma	9,893	3,888	0	1,920	15,701	73.7	29.0	0.0	14.3	117.0
Oregon[1]	12,486	3,713	0	1,248	17,447	93.0	27.7	0.0	9.3	130.0
Pennsylvania	9,893	3,888	0	1,920	15,701	73.7	29.0	0.0	14.3	117.0
Rhode Island[1]	10,853	3,888	1,792	1,140	17,673	80.9	29.0	13.4	8.5	131.7
South Carolina	9,893	3,888	0	1,920	15,701	73.7	29.0	0.0	14.3	117.0
South Dakota	9,893	3,888	0	1,920	15,701	73.7	29.0	0.0	14.3	117.0
Tennessee	9,893	3,888	676	1,728	16,185	73.7	29.0	5.0	12.9	120.6
Texas	9,893	3,888	0	1,920	15,701	73.7	29.0	0.0	14.3	117.0
Utah	9,893	3,888	656	1,728	16,165	73.7	29.0	4.9	12.9	120.4
Vermont[1]	11,045	3,888	0	1,632	16,565	82.3	29.0	0.0	12.2	123.4
Virginia	9,893	3,888	4,248	648	18,677	73.7	29.0	31.6	4.8	139.1
Virgin Islands[2]	9,893	3,888	0	3,840	17,621	73.7	29.0	0.0	28.6	131.3
Washington	12,486	3,713	0	1,248	17,447	93.0	27.7	0.0	9.3	130.0
West Virginia	9,893	3,888	0	1,920	15,701	73.7	29.0	0.0	14.3	117.0
Wisconsin:[1]										
Community service[3]	9,893	3,888	0	1,920	15,701	73.7	29.0	0.0	14.3	117.0
W2 transition	NA	NA	NA	NA	NA	NA	NA	NA	NA	NA
Wyoming	9,893	3,888	0	1,920	15,701	73.7	29.0	0.0	14.3	117.0

1. These states have their own earned income credits (generally calculated as a percentage of the Federal EIC) but they are not shown in this table.

2. Guam and the Virgin Islands have territorial tax systems that mirror the Internal Revenue Code, including the EIC. However, revenues foregone and refunds paid under their EICs affect their own territorial treasuries, not the U.S. Treasury.

3. This entry applies to a person who has moved from community service to a full-time unsubsidized job (and thus is no longer eligible for a community service payment).

NA. Not applicable. (Persons with jobs are not eligible for the Wisconsin program of transitional aid.)

Note: Puerto Rico is omitted from this table. It is not covered by the federal income tax and has no EIC. A full-time minimum wage worker in Puerto Rico would be ineligible for TANF.

Source: United States House of Representatives, Committee on Ways and Means. (2000). *The 2000 Green Book: Background material and data on programs within the jurisdiction of the Committee on Ways and Means.* Retrieved from http://aspe.hhs.gov/2000gb/sec7.txt.

Figure 7.1
Work Activity Among the TANF Caseload: 1997 to 2002

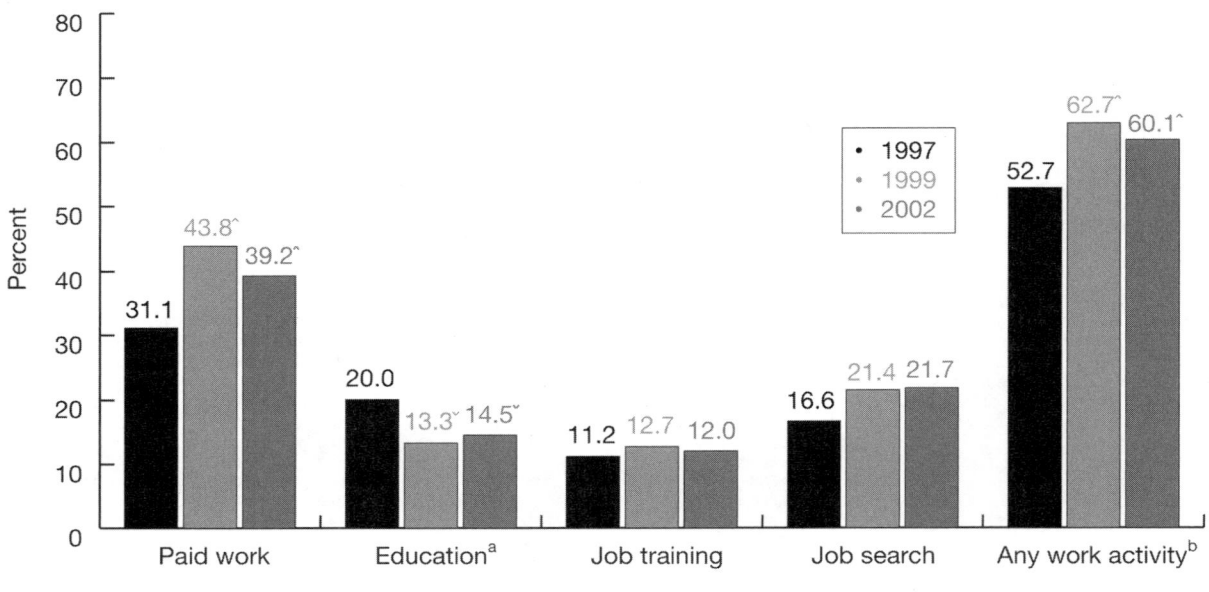

a. Does not include individuals who worked on and completed a high school diploma or GED in the year before the interview. In 2002, an additional 2 percent reported taking classes toward and completing their diplomas or GEDs during the previous year. Comparable data are not available for 1997 and 1999.
b. Percentage engaged in at least one activity.
^. Increase from 1997 is significant at the 0.10 level.
v. Decrease from 1997 is significant at the 0.10 level.

Source: Zedlewski, S.R., & Holland, J. (August 21, 2003). Work activities of current welfare recipients. In Urban Institute, *Snapshot of America's Family III*, (Paper Number 4). Washington, D.C.: Urban Institute. Retrieved from: http://www.urban.org/UploadedPDF/3108355_snapshots3_no4.pdf.

Table 7. 17
Work Barriers of Current Caseload: 1999
and 2002 (Percentage)

	1999	2002
Barriers		
Very poor mental or physical health	35.7	34.6
Education less than high school	44.1	41.8
Last worked three or more years ago	27.7	29.5
Has an infant[a]	17.1	18.9
Has a child on Supplemental Security Income	5.7	8.2
Spanish interview	5.0	9.7^
Number of Barriers		
Zero	19.7	22.9
One	39.8	33.3
Two or more	40.6	43.8

Note: Includes adults likely to be subject to work requirements.
a. An infant is a child under the age of one.
^. Increase from 1999 is significant at the 0.10 level.

Source: Zedlewski, S.R., & Holland, J. (August 21, 2003). Work and barriers to work among welfare recipients in 2002. In Urban Institute, *Snapshot of America's Family III* (Paper Number 3). Washington, D.C.: Urban Institute. Retrieved from: http://www.urban.org/UploadedPDF/310836_snapshots3_no3.pdf.

Table 7.18
Barriers to Work by Length of Time on Welfare: 2002 (Percentage)

	Entrants	Cyclers	Stayers
Share of Total Caseload			
1999	25.9	23.7	47.4
2002	33.8^	23.9	37.9
Barriers			
Very poor mental or physical health	28.2	47.2*	34.8
Education less than high school	34.4	44.0	44.5
Last worked three or more years ago	24.0*	24.0*	38.8
Has an infant[a]	23.8*	19.2	14.4^
Has a child on Supplemental Security Income	8.8	8.0	7.5
Spanish interview	4.5*	3.8*	17.9^
Number of Barriers			
Zero	25.9	19.0	23.1
One	36.7^	35.1	27.3
Two or more	37.5*	45.9	49.6

Notes: Includes adults receiving TANF and likely to be subject to work requirements. Entrants first entered welfare in the past two years. Cyclers first received welfare more than two years ago but have received it only intermittently over the past two years. Stayers first received welfare more than two years ago and have been on welfare continuously for the past two years.
a. An infant is a child under the age of one.
^. Increase from 1999 is significant at the 0.10 level.
*. Estimate is significantly different from estimate for stayers at the 0.10 level.

Source: Zedlewski, S.R., & Holland, J. (August 21, 2003). Work and barriers to work among welfare recipients in 2002. In Urban Institute, *Snapshot of America's Family III* (Paper Number 3). Washington, D.C.: Urban Institute. Retrieved from: http://www.urban.org/UploadedPDF/310836_snapshots3_no3.pdf.

Figure 7.2
Relationship of Length of Time on Welfare to Current Work Status: 1999 and 2002

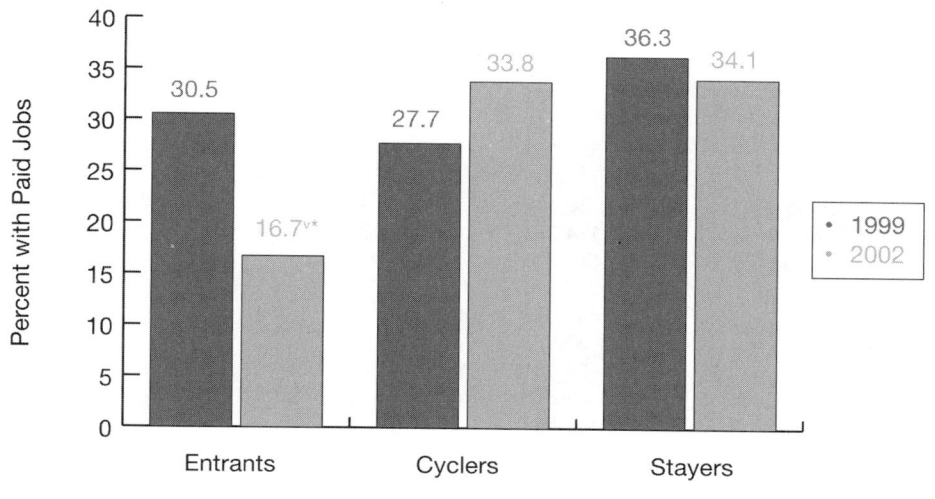

Note: Includes adults receiving TANF and likely to be subject to work requirements.
*. Decrease from 1999 is significant at the 0.10 level.
˘. Estimate for 2002 entrants is significantly different from estimate for 2002 stayers at the 0.10 level.

Source: Zedlewski, S.R., & Holland, J. (August 21, 2003). Work and barriers to work among welfare recipients in 2002. In Urban Institute, *Snapshot of America's Family III* (Paper Number 3). Washington, D.C.: Urban Institute. Retrieved from: http://www.urban.org/UploadedPDF/310836_snapshots3_no3.pdf.

Table 7.19
Number of Welfare Recipients Declines

	August 1996	September 1999	Percent change
Alabama	100,662	46,086	−54
Alaska	35,544	22,546	−37
Arizona	169,442	88,485	−48
Arkansas	56,343	29,707	−47
California	2,581,948	1,668,173	−35
Colorado	95,788	32,507	−66
Connecticut	159,246	79,071	−50
Delaware	23,654	15,515	−34
District of Columbia	69,292	48,576	−30
Florida	533,801	174,588	−67
Georgia	330,302	140,558	−57
Guam	8,314	9,497	14
Hawaii	66,482	42,713	−36
Idaho	21,780	2,222	−90
Illinois	642,644	321,999	−50
Indiana	142,604	111,842	−22
Iowa	86,146	56,302	−35
Kansas	63,783	32,199	−50
Kentucky	172,193	92,415	−46
Louisiana	228,115	86,470	−62
Maine	53,873	33,474	−38
Maryland	194,127	76,504	−61
Massachusetts	226,030	121,586	−46
Michigan	502,354	234,262	−53
Minnesota	169,744	116,623	−31
Mississippi	123,828	33,911	−73
Missouri	222,820	124,519	−44
Montana	29,130	13,191	−55
Nebraska	38,592	29,378	−24
Nevada	34,261	17,032	−50
New Hampshire	22,937	14,677	−36
New Jersey	275,637	152,535	−45
New Mexico	99,661	76,300	−23
New York	1,143,962	763,648	−33
North Carolina	267,326	108,179	−60
North Dakota	13,146	8,064	−39
Ohio	549,312	247,798	−55
Oklahoma	96,201	39,200	−59
Oregon	78,419	43,204	−45
Pennsylvania	531,059	269,515	−49
Puerto Rico	151,023	99,022	−34
Rhode Island	56,560	47,942	−15
South Carolina	114,273	39,847	−65
South Dakota	15,896	6,932	−56
Tennessee	254,818	149,005	−42
Texas	649,018	287,296	−56
Utah	39,073	23,427	−40
Vermont	24,331	17,403	−28
Virgin Islands	4,898	3,387	−31
Virginia	152,845	86,279	−44
Washington	268,927	160,471	−40
West Virginia	89,039	32,238	−64
Wisconsin	148,888	23,892	−84
Wyoming	11,398	1,395	−88
U.S. Total	12,241,489	6,603,607	−46

Source: Savings, J.S. (2000). The effect of welfare reform and technological change on unemployment. *Journal of Economic and Financial Review*, Number 2, pp. 26–34. Retrieved from www.dallasfed.org/research/efr/2000/efr0002c.pdf.

Table 7.20
Commitment to Education: Public Spending

| HDI rank | Public expenditure on education [a] | | | | Public expenditure on education by level (as % of all levels) [b] | | | | | |
| | As % of GDP | | As % of total government expenditure | | Pre-primary and primary | | Secondary | | Tertiary | |
	1990 [c]	1998-2000 [d]	1990 [c]	1998-2000 [d]	1990 [c]	1998-2000 [d]	1990 [c]	1998-2000 [d]	1990 [c]	1998-2000 [d]
High human development										
1 Norway [e]	7.1	6.8	14.6	16.2	39.5	..	24.7	..	15.2	..
2 Iceland [e]	5.4	..	..	..	59.5	..	25.6	..	14.9	..
3 Sweden [e]	7.4	7.8	13.8	13.4	47.7	..	19.6	..	13.2	..
4 Australia [e]	5.1	4.7 [f]	14.8	..	2.2	33.1	57.4	39.3	32.0	26.0
5 Netherlands [e]	6.0	4.8	14.8	10.7	21.5	..	37.7	..	32.1	..
6 Belgium [e]	5.0	5.9	..	11.6	23.3	..	42.9	..	16.5	..
7 United States [e]	5.2	4.8	12.3	..	..	..	..	..	..	..
8 Canada [e]	6.5	5.5	14.2	..	..	..	62.2	..	28.6	..
9 Japan [e]	..	3.5	..	9.3	..	..	..	..	..	..
10 Switzerland [e]	5.1	5.5	18.7	15.2	49.9	..	25.1	..	19.7	..
11 Denmark [e]	..	8.2	..	15.3	..	..	..	..	..	..
12 Ireland	5.2	4.4	10.2	13.2	37.8	..	40.1	..	20.4	..
13 United Kingdom [e]	4.9	4.5	..	11.4	29.7	33.2	43.8	46.7	19.6	20.1
14 Finland	5.6	6.1	11.9	12.5	27.9	26.7	39.4	39.5	23.9	33.8
15 Luxembourg [e]	3.0	3.7 [f]	10.4	8.5 [f]	..	..	..	..	..	..
16 Austria [e]	5.4	5.8	7.6	12.4	23.7	27.3	46.6	44.1	19.1	26.2
17 France [e]	5.4	5.8	..	11.5	27.3	..	40.7	..	13.8	..
18 Germany	..	4.6	..	9.7	..	..	..	..	..	..
19 Spain [e]	4.4	4.5	9.4	11.3	29.3	33.9	45.0	46.0	15.4	20.1
20 New Zealand [e]	6.2	6.1	..	..	30.5	..	25.3	..	37.4	..
21 Italy [e]	3.1	4.5	..	9.5	33.0	..	63.2	..	..	..
22 Israel	6.3	7.3	11.3	..	43.0	..	31.3	..	16.2	..
23 Portugal [e]	4.2	5.8	..	13.1	44.6	..	32.5	..	16.3	..
24 Greece	2.5	3.8	..	7.0	34.1	..	45.1	..	19.5	..
25 Cyprus [g]	3.5	5.4	11.3	..	38.5	34.7	50.3	50.6	3.8	14.8
26 Hong Kong, China (SAR)	..	..	..	..	26.6	..	38.8	..	30.8	..
27 Barbados	7.8	7.1	22.2	18.5	37.5	35.9 [f]	37.6	32.8	19.2	29.1
28 Singapore	..	3.7	..	23.6 [f]	29.6	27.1 [f]	36.5	28.1 [f]	29.3	26.0 [f]
29 Slovenia	..	..	..	..	..	..	..	..	..	..
30 Korea, Rep. of [e]	3.5	3.8	22.4	17.4	44.4	..	34.1	..	7.4	..
31 Brunei Darussalam	..	4.8	..	9.1 [f]	24.1	..	26.1	..	9.5	..
32 Czech Republic [e]	..	4.4	..	9.7	..	..	..	..	..	..
33 Malta	4.3	4.9 [f]	8.3	..	25.1	28.9	44.7	42.8	14.6	18.2
34 Argentina [e]	1.1	4.0	10.9	11.8	3.4	42.8	44.9	36.9	46.7	17.1
35 Poland [e]	..	5.0	..	11.4	42.8	..	17.5	..	22.0	..
36 Seychelles	7.8	7.6 [f]	14.8	10.7	28.2	23.1	40.7	40.8	9.5	8.1
37 Bahrain	4.2	3.0	14.6	11.4	..	30.1	45.8	34.5	..	0.0
38 Hungary [e]	5.8	5.0	7.8	14.1	55.4	..	23.9	..	15.2	..
39 Slovakia [e]	5.1	4.2	..	13.8	..	..	..	..	..	..
40 Uruguay [e]	3.0	2.8	15.9	..	37.5	..	30.3	..	22.6	..
41 Estonia	..	7.5	..	..	..	44.5	..	34.1	..	16.8
42 Costa Rica	4.4	4.4	20.8	..	..	51.8	..	28.0	..	19.4
43 Chile [e]	2.5	4.2	10.4	17.5	60.1	50.2	17.3	33.3	20.3	16.5
44 Qatar	3.5	3.6 [h]	..	..	..	..	..	..	..	..
45 Lithuania	4.6	6.4	13.8	..	..	..	..	..	..	..
46 Kuwait	4.8	..	3.4	..	53.4	..	13.6	..	16.0	..
47 Croatia	..	4.2 [f]	..	10.4 [f]	..	..	..	..	..	..
48 United Arab Emirates	1.9	1.9	14.6	..	..	53.3	..	45.1	..	0.0
49 Bahamas	4.0	..	17.8	..	..	..	..	..	..	..
50 Latvia	3.8	5.9	10.8	..	11.2	33.3	56.3	48.7	11.6	16.3

Table 7.20 (*continued*)

		Public expenditure on education [a]				Public expenditure on education by level (as % of all levels) [b]					
		As % of GDP		As % of total government expenditure		Pre-primary and primary		Secondary		Tertiary	
HDI rank		1990 [c]	1998-2000 [d]	1990 [c]	1998-2000 [d]	1990 [c]	1998-2000 [d]	1990 [c]	1998-2000 [d]	1990 [c]	1998-2000 [d]
51	Saint Kitts and Nevis	2.7	2.9 [f]	..	16.4 [f]	..	59.8 [f]	..	32.3 [f]	..	..
52	Cuba	..	8.5	12.3	15.1	25.7	44.5 [f]	39.0	36.7 [f]	14.4	18.5 [f]
53	Belarus	4.9	6.0	..	..	57.7	..	16.2	..	14.4	..
54	Trinidad and Tobago	3.6	4.0 [f]	11.6	16.7 [f]	42.5	59.6 [f]	36.8	32.3 [f]	11.9	3.7 [f]
55	Mexico [e]	3.6	4.4	12.8	22.6	32.3	..	29.6	..	16.5	..
Medium human development											
56	Antigua and Barbuda	..	3.2	..	..	..	36.9 [f]	..	37.3 [f]	..	15.1 [f]
57	Bulgaria	5.2	3.4	..	..	70.7	41.7	..	43.9	13.9	14.4
58	Malaysia [e]	5.2	6.2	18.3	26.7	34.3	31.8	34.4	32.9	19.9	31.9
59	Panama	4.7	5.9	20.9	..	37.0	40.8 [f]	23.3	33.9 [f]	21.3	25.3 [f]
60	Macedonia, TFYR	..	..	..	..	..	..	..	..	..	..
61	Libyan Arab Jamahiriya	..	..	..	..	..	..	..	..	..	..
62	Mauritius	3.5	3.5	11.8	12.1	37.7	..	36.4	..	16.6	..
63	Russian Federation	3.5	4.4	..	..	..	..	..	..	..	..
64	Colombia	2.5	..	16.0	..	39.3	..	30.9	..	20.7	..
65	Brazil	..	4.7	..	12.9	..	41.0	..	37.6	..	21.4
66	Bosnia and Herzegovina	..	..	..	..	..	..	..	..	..	..
67	Belize	4.7	6.2	18.5	20.9	61.0	46.7 [f]	20.2	36.5 [f]	8.1	4.9 [f]
68	Dominica	..	5.1 [f]	..	..	..	64.4 [f]	..	30.1 [f]	..	0.0
69	Venezuela	3.0	..	12.0	..	23.5	..	4.5	..	40.7	..
70	Samoa (Western)	3.4	4.2 [f]	10.7	13.3 [f]	52.6	..	25.2	..	0.0	..
71	Saint Lucia	..	5.8	..	16.9	48.2	40.1 [f]	23.3	28.9 [f]	12.8	11.6 [f]
72	Romania	2.8	3.5 [f]	7.3	..	52.1	..	22.1	..	9.6	..
73	Saudi Arabia	6.5	9.5	17.8	..	78.8	..	..	..	21.2	..
74	Thailand [e]	3.5	5.4	20.0	31.0	56.2	36.0	21.6	27.1	14.6	24.1
75	Ukraine	5.2	4.4	19.7	15.7	54.9	14.4	15.0	53.1	15.1	19.9
76	Kazakhstan	3.2	..	17.6	..	..	..	..	..	..	..
77	Suriname	8.1	..	..	..	60.5	..	14.5	..	8.8	..
78	Jamaica [e]	4.7	6.3	12.8	11.1	37.4	40.4	33.2	40.0	21.1	18.8
79	Oman	3.1	3.9	11.1	..	54.1	39.1	37.0	50.7	7.4	1.6
80	St. Vincent & the Grenadines	6.4	9.3	13.8	..	..	56.6 [f]	..	29.5 [f]	..	6.0 [f]
81	Fiji	4.6	5.2 [f]	..	17.0 [f]	..	53.4 [f]	..	43.9 [f]	..	2.5 [f]
82	Peru [e]	2.2	3.3	..	21.1	..	41.3	..	26.6	..	20.4
83	Lebanon	..	3.0	..	11.1	..	..	..	..	..	..
84	Paraguay	1.1	5.0	9.1	11.2 [f]	..	..	22.6	..	25.8	..
85	Philippines [e]	2.9	4.2	10.1	20.6	..	..	..	..	..	..
86	Maldives	4.0	3.9 [f]	10.0	11.2 [f]	..	..	..	..	..	..
87	Turkmenistan	4.3	..	21.0	..	..	..	..	..	..	..
88	Georgia	..	..	..	..	..	..	..	..	..	..
89	Azerbaijan	..	4.2	23.5	24.4	..	..	..	..	..	..
90	Jordan [e]	8.4	5.0	17.1	5.0	..	32.9 [f]	62.4	31.5 [f]	35.1	33.0 [f]
91	Tunisia [e]	6.0	6.8	13.5	17.4	39.8	..	36.4	..	18.5	..
92	Guyana	3.4	4.1 [f]	4.4	..	..	..	..	..	..	..
93	Grenada	5.1	4.2 [f]	13.2	..	64.1	72.3 [f]	31.7	23.8 [f]	0.0	0.0
94	Dominican Republic	..	2.5	..	15.7	..	..	..	..	..	..
95	Albania	5.8	..	..	..	..	..	..	..	..	..
96	Turkey [e]	2.2	3.5	..	..	58.1	52.5	29.4	19.6	..	27.9
97	Ecuador	2.8	1.6	17.2	8.0	34.4	49.4 [f]	34.2	42.7 [f]	18.3	6.9 [f]
98	Occupied Palestinian Territories	..	..	..	..	..	..	..	..	..	..
99	Sri Lanka	2.6	3.1	8.1	..	..	..	84.3	..	13.4	..
100	Armenia	7.0	2.9	20.5	..	..	7.2 [f]	..	78.1	..	11.1

Table 7.20 (*continued*)

		Public expenditure on education [a]			Public expenditure on education by level (as % of all levels) [b]					
	As % of GDP		As % of total government expenditure		Pre-primary and primary		Secondary		Tertiary	
HDI rank	1990 [c]	1998-2000 [d]	1990 [c]	1998-2000 [d]	1990 [c]	1998-2000 [d]	1990 [c]	1998-2000 [d]	1990 [c]	1998-2000 [d]
101 Uzbekistan	..	..	20.4	..	..	..	..	..	..	..
102 Kyrgyzstan	8.3	5.4	22.5	..	8.5	..	57.9	..	10.0	..
103 Cape Verde	..	4.4 [f]	..	..	..	..	..	..	..	..
104 China	2.3	2.1	12.8	..	..	37.4	..	32.2	..	15.6
105 El Salvador	1.9	2.3 [f]	16.6	13.4 [f]	..	15.9 [f]	..	75.1 [f]	..	8.8 [f]
106 Iran, Islamic Rep. of	4.1	4.4	22.4	20.4	33.2	26.7 [f]	39.2	34.8	13.6	19.4
107 Algeria	5.3	..	21.1	..	..	..	..	..	..	..
108 Moldova, Rep. of	..	4.0	..	15.0	..	19.5	..	69.0	..	11.6
109 Viet Nam	..	..	7.5	..	..	..	..	..	..	..
110 Syrian Arab Republic	4.1	4.1	17.3	11.1	38.5	..	28.2	..	21.3	..
111 South Africa	6.2	5.5	..	25.8	75.6	47.2	..	31.3	21.5	14.5
112 Indonesia [e]	1.0	..	..	..	..	..	..	..	..	..
113 Tajikistan	9.7	2.1	24.7	11.8	6.9	..	57.0	..	9.1	..
114 Bolivia	2.3	5.5	..	23.1	..	52.3 [f]	..	22.9 f	..	23.8 [f]
115 Honduras	..	4.0 [f]	..	..	..	..	..	..	..	..
116 Equatorial Guinea	..	0.6	..	..	..	39.1 [f]	..	30.7 [f]	..	30.1 [f]
117 Mongolia	12.1	2.3	17.6	2.2	13.9	22.0	48.8	60.1	14.5	18.0
118 Gabon	..	3.9 [f]	..	..	..	35.6 [f]	..	38.9 [f]	..	25.5 [f]
119 Guatemala	1.4	1.7	11.8	11.4	31.1	67.2 [f]	12.9	32.8 [f]	21.2	0.0
120 Egypt	3.7	..	..	..	..	..	..	..	..	..
121 Nicaragua	3.4	5.0	9.7	13.8	..	..	..	..	..	..
122 São Tomé and Principe	..	..	..	..	..	..	..	..	..	..
123 Solomon Islands	..	3.6 [f]	..	15.4 [f]	..	..	..	..	..	..
124 Namibia	7.6	8.1	..	..	..	58.5	..	27.3	..	12.0
125 Botswana	6.7	8.6 [f]	17.0	..	..	53.2	..	23.8	..	18.6
126 Morocco	5.3	5.5 [f]	26.1	26.1	34.8	48.2 [f]	48.9	50.5 [f]	16.2	0.4 [f]
127 India [e]	3.9	4.1	12.2	12.7	38.9	39.4 [f]	27.0	40.5 [f]	14.9	20.1 [f]
128 Vanuatu	4.6	7.3 [f]	..	17.4 [f]	59.8	34.6 [f]	26.6	57.7 [f]	3.4	6.8 [f]
129 Ghana	3.2	4.1 [f]	24.3	..	29.2	..	34.3	..	11.0	..
130 Cambodia	..	1.9	..	10.1	..	65.2 [f]	..	23.6 [f]	..	4.9
131 Myanmar	..	0.5	..	9.0 [f]	..	35.6	..	19.7	..	34.3
132 Papua New Guinea	..	2.3 [f]	..	17.5 [f]	..	71.4 [f]	..	24.3 [f]	..	4.3 [f]
133 Swaziland	5.7	1.5	19.5	..	31.2	33.2	24.5	26.9	26.0	32.1
134 Comoros	..	3.8	..	..	42.4	41.6	28.2	41.2	17.3	3.3
135 Lao People's Dem. Rep.	..	2.3	..	8.8	..	47.3 [f]	..	20.5 [f]	..	19.8 [f]
136 Bhutan	..	5.2	..	12.9	..	26.9 [f]	..	47.9 [f]	..	19.6 [f]
137 Lesotho	6.1	10.1	12.2	18.5	..	48.6	..	27.7	..	16.7
138 Sudan	0.9	..	2.8	..	..	..	..	..	..	..
139 Bangladesh	1.5	2.5	10.3	15.7	45.6	46.7 [f]	42.2	43.0 [f]	8.7	10.1
140 Congo	5.0	4.2	14.4	12.6	..	..	..	..	..	..
141 Togo	5.5	4.8	26.4	23.2	30.4	51.0 [f]	25.8	30.8 [f]	29.0	18.2 [f]
Low human development										
142 Cameroon	3.2	3.2	19.6	12.5	70.5	..	..	..	29.5	..
143 Nepal	2.0	3.7	8.5	14.1	48.2	60.0 [i]	15.7	24.6	23.3	11.9
144 Pakistan	2.6	1.8 [f]	7.4	7.8 [f]	..	..	..	..	..	..
145 Zimbabwe [e]	..	10.4 [f]	..	..	54.1	56.1 [f]	28.6	29.2 [f]	12.3	14.8 [f]
146 Kenya	6.7	6.4	17.0	22.5	50.3	1.4 [h]	18.8	0.7 [h]	21.6	11.5 [h]
147 Uganda	1.5	2.3 [f]	11.5	..	..	..	..	..	..	..
148 Yemen	..	10.0	..	32.8	..	..	..	..	..	..
149 Madagascar	2.1	3.2	..	10.2	49.1	..	35.6	..	..	..
150 Haiti	1.4	1.1 [f]	20.0	10.9 [f]	53.1	38.3 [f]	19.0	61.0 [f]	9.1	0.8 [f]
151 Gambia	3.8	2.7 [f]	14.6	14.2 [f]	41.6	..	21.2	..	17.8	..

Table 7.20 (*continued*)

HDI rank	Public expenditure on education [a] As % of GDP 1990[c]	Public expenditure on education [a] As % of GDP 1998-2000[d]	Public expenditure on education [a] As % of total government expenditure 1990[c]	Public expenditure on education [a] As % of total government expenditure 1998-2000[d]	Pre-primary and primary 1990[c]	Pre-primary and primary 1998-2000[d]	Secondary 1990[c]	Secondary 1998-2000[d]	Tertiary 1990[c]	Tertiary 1998-2000[d]
152 Nigeria	0.9	..	..	..	..	..	..	..	..	..
153 Djibouti	..	3.5 [f]	10.5	..	58.0	65.9 [f,i]	21.7	..	11.5	..
154 Mauritania	..	3.0 [f]	..	18.9	33.3	..	37.7	..	24.9	..
155 Eritrea	..	4.8	..	..	..	..	..	..	..	..
156 Senegal	3.9	3.2 [f]	26.9	..	43.9	42.5 [h]	25.7	25.3 [h]	24.0	23.1 [h]
157 Guinea	..	1.9 [f]	..	25.6 [f]	..	..	..	..	..	..
158 Rwanda	..	2.8 [f]	..	..	..	..	..	..	..	..
159 Benin	..	3.2 [f]	..	..	..	55.1 [f]	..	26.9 [f]	..	18.0 [f]
160 Tanzania, U. Rep. of	3.2	2.1 [f]	11.4	..	..	..	..	..	..	..
161 Côte d'Ivoire	..	4.6	..	21.5	..	42.4 [f]	..	32.5 [f]	..	25.1 [f]
162 Malawi	3.3	4.1 [f]	11.1	24.6	44.7	..	13.1	..	20.2	..
163 Zambia	2.4	2.3	8.7	17.6	..	..	..	..	..	..
164 Angola	3.9	2.7	10.7	..	96.3	..	..	..	3.7	..
165 Chad	..	2.0 [f]	..	..	..	57.5 [f]	..	25.9 [f]	..	16.6 [f]
166 Guinea-Bissau	..	2.1	..	4.8	..	..	..	..	..	..
167 Congo, Dem. Rep. of the	..	..	..	..	..	..	..	..	..	..
168 Central African Republic	2.2	1.9	..	..	..	..	..	..	..	..
169 Ethiopia	3.4	4.8	9.4	13.8	53.9	..	28.1	..	12.1	..
170 Mozambique	3.9	2.4 [f]	12.0	12.3 [f]	49.8	..	15.7	..	9.9	..
171 Burundi	3.4	3.4	16.7	..	46.8	38.0	29.1	35.0	22.0	26.9
172 Mali	..	2.8 [f]	..	..	..	45.7 [f]	..	39.7 [f]	..	14.6 [f]
173 Burkina Faso	2.7	..	..	..	..	..	..	..	..	..
174 Niger	3.2	2.7 [f]	18.6	..	..	51.6 [f]	..	28.6 [f]	..	19.9
175 Sierra Leone	..	1.0	..	..	..	39.5	..	23.6	..	28.1

Note: As a result of limitations in the data and methodological changes, comparisons of education expenditure data across countries and over time must be made with caution. For detailed notes on the data, see UNESCO 1999 and http://www.uis.unesco.org/.

a. Data refer to total public expenditure on education, including current and capital expenditure.

b. Data refer to current public expenditure on education. Data may not be strictly comparable between 1990 and 1998–2000 as a result of methodological changes. Expenditures by level may not sum of 100% as a result of rounding or the omission of the categories expenditures in postsecondary and expenditures not allocated by level.

c. Data may not be comparable between countries as a result of differences in methods of data collection.

d. Data refer to the most recent year available during the period specified.

e. All 1998–2000 data are preliminary UNESCO Institute for Statistics estimates, subject to further revision.

f. Data refer to a UNESCO Institute for Statistics estimate where no national estimate is available.

g. Data refer to the Office of Greek Education only.

h. Data refer to a national estimate.

i. Data refer to primary school expenditure only.

Source: United Nations Development Programme. (2003). *Human Development Report 2003.* Table 9. "Commitment to Education (266–9)." New York: Oxford University Press. Retrieved from http:www.undp.org/hdr2003/pdf/hdr03_complete.pdf. Copyright 2003 by the United Nations Development Programme. Used by permission of Oxford University Press, Inc.

Table 7.21
Literacy and Enrollment

HDI rank	Adult literacy rate (% age 15 and above)		Youth literacy rate (% age 15-24)		Net primary enrolment ratio (%)[a]		Net secondary enrolment ratio (%)[a,b]		Children reaching grade 5 (%)	Tertiary students in science, math and engineering (as % of all tertiary students)
	1990	2001	1990	2001	1990-91	2000-01[c]	1990-91	2000-01[c]	1999-2000[c,d]	1994-97[e]
High human development										
1 Norway	..	..	..	..	100	101[f]	88	95[f]	..	18
2 Iceland	..	..	..	..	..	102[f]	..	83[f]	..	20
3 Sweden	..	..	..	..	100	102[f]	85	96[d,f]	..	31
4 Australia	..	..	..	..	99	96[f]	79	90[f]	..	32
5 Netherlands	..	..	..	..	95	100[f]	84	90[f]	..	20
6 Belgium	..	..	..	..	97	101[f]	88	..	..	..
7 United States	..	..	..	..	96	95[f]	86	88[f]	..	..
8 Canada	..	..	..	..	97	99[d,f]	89	98[d,f]	..	..
9 Japan	..	..	..	..	100	101[f]	97	101[f]	..	23
10 Switzerland	..	..	..	..	84	99[f]	80	88[f]	101[f]	31
11 Denmark	..	..	..	..	98	99[d,f]	87	89[d,f]	..	21
12 Ireland	..	..	..	..	91	90[d,f]	80	..	98[f]	30
13 United Kingdom	..	..	..	..	97	99[f]	79	94[f]	..	29
14 Finland	..	..	..	..	99[g]	100[f]	93	95[f]	100[f]	37
15 Luxembourg	..	..	..	..	..	97[f]	..	78[f]	99[f]	..
16 Austria	..	..	..	..	90[g]	91[f]	..	89[f]	..	28
17 France	..	..	..	..	101	100[f]	..	92[f]	..	25
18 Germany	..	..	..	..	84[g]	87[d,f]	..	88[d,f]	..	31
19 Spain	96.3	97.7	99.6	99.8	103	102[f]	..	94[f]	..	31
20 New Zealand	..	..	..	..	101	99[f]	85	92[f]	..	21
21 Italy	97.7	98.5	99.8	99.8	..	100[f]	..	91[f]	..	28
22 Israel	91.4	95.1	98.7	99.5	..	101	..	88	..	..
23 Portugal	87.2	92.5	99.5	99.8	102	..	..	85[f]	..	31
24 Greece	94.9	97.3	99.5	99.8	94	97[f]	83	87[f]	..	..
25 Cyprus	94.3	97.2	99.7	99.8	87	95	..	88	99	17
26 Hong Kong, China (SAR)	89.7	93.5	98.2	99.4	..	..	..	..	..	..
27 Barbados	99.4	99.7	99.8	99.8	78[h]	105	..	85	..	21
28 Singapore	88.8	92.5	99.0	99.8	..	..	..	..	..	..
29 Slovenia	99.6	99.6	99.8	99.8	..	93	..	..	..	29
30 Korea, Rep. of	95.9	97.9	99.8	99.8	104	99[f]	86	91[f]	..	34
31 Brunei Darussalam	85.5	91.6	97.9	99.4	91[h]	..	..	..	92	6
32 Czech Republic	..	..	..	..	..	90[f]	..	..	..	34
33 Malta	88.4	92.3	97.5	98.6	99	99[d]	80	79[i]	100[i]	13
34 Argentina	95.7	96.9	98.2	98.6	..	107[f]	..	79[f]	90[f]	30
35 Poland	99.6	99.7	99.8	99.8	97	98[f]	76	91[f]	99[f]	..
36 Seychelles	..	..	..	..	..	..	..	..	..	..
37 Bahrain	82.1	87.9	95.6	98.5	99	96	85	92	101	..
38 Hungary	99.1	99.3	99.7	99.8	91	90[f]	75	87[d,f]	..	32
39 Slovakia	..	..	..	..	..	89[f]	..	75[f]	..	43
40 Uruguay	96.5	97.6	98.7	99.1	91[h]	90[f]	..	70[f]	91[f]	24
41 Estonia	99.8	99.8	99.8	99.7	..	98	..	83	99	32
42 Costa Rica	93.9	95.7	97.4	98.3	86	91	36	49	80	18
43 Chile	94.0	95.9	98.1	98.9	88	89[f]	55	75[f]	101[f]	43
44 Qatar	77.0	81.7	90.3	95.0	87	95[i]	67	78[i]	..	..
45 Lithuania	99.3	99.6	99.8	99.8	..	95	..	89	..	38
46 Kuwait	76.7	82.4	87.5	92.7	45[h]	66[d]	..	50[i]	..	23
47 Croatia	96.9	98.4	99.6	99.8	79	..	63	..	..	38
48 United Arab Emirates	71.0	76.7	84.7	91.0	94	87	59	67	98	27
49 Bahamas	94.4	95.5	96.5	97.3	96[h]	83[d]	..	72[d]	..	..
50 Latvia	99.8	99.8	99.8	99.8	83[g]	92	..	74	..	29

Table 7.21 (*continued*)

HDI rank	Adult literacy rate (% age 15 and above) 1990	Adult literacy rate (% age 15 and above) 2001	Youth literacy rate (% age 15-24) 1990	Youth literacy rate (% age 15-24) 2001	Net primary enrolment ratio (%)[a] 1990-91	Net primary enrolment ratio (%)[a] 2000-01[c]	Net secondary enrolment ratio (%)[a, b] 1990-91	Net secondary enrolment ratio (%)[a, b] 2000-01[c]	Children reaching grade 5 (%) 1999-2000[c, d]	Tertiary students in science, math and engineering (as % of all tertiary students) 1994-97[e]
51 Saint Kitts and Nevis	..	..	..	..	..	..	..	..	..	..
52 Cuba	95.1	96.8	99.3	99.8	92	97	69	82	95	21
53 Belarus	99.5	99.7	99.8	99.8	..	108	..	76	..	33
54 Trinidad and Tobago	96.8	98.4	99.6	99.8	91	92	..	71	100	41
55 Mexico	87.3	91.4	95.2	97.2	100	103 [f]	45	60 [f]	88 [f]	31
Medium human development										
56 Antigua and Barbuda	..	..	..	..	..	..	..	..	..	..
57 Bulgaria	97.2	98.5	99.4	99.7	86	94	63	88	..	25
58 Malaysia	80.7	87.9	94.8	97.7	..	98 [f]	..	70 [f]	..	..
59 Panama	89.0	92.1	95.3	96.9	91	100	51	62	92	27
60 Macedonia, TFYR	..	..	..	..	94	92	..	81 [d]	..	38
61 Libyan Arab Jamahiriya	68.1	80.8	91.0	96.7	97 [g]	..	..	..	..	..
62 Mauritius	79.8	84.8	91.1	94.0	95	95	..	64	..	17
63 Russian Federation	99.2	99.6	99.8	99.8	..	..	..	..	..	49
64 Colombia	88.4	91.9	94.9	97.0	..	89	..	57	..	31
65 Brazil	82.0	87.3	91.8	95.5	86	97 [f]	15	71 [f]	..	23
66 Bosnia and Herzegovina	..	..	..	..	..	..	..	..	..	..
67 Belize	89.1	93.4	96.0	98.1	98 [h]	100	29	63	..	..
68 Dominica	..	..	..	..	..	..	..	..	86	..
69 Venezuela	88.9	92.8	96.0	98.1	88	88	19	50	91 [i]	..
70 Samoa (Western)	98.0	98.7	99.0	99.4	..	97	..	68	83 [i]	..
71 Saint Lucia	..	..	..	..	..	100	..	80	..	..
72 Romania	97.1	98.2	99.3	99.6	77 [g]	93	..	80	..	32
73 Saudi Arabia	66.2	77.1	85.4	93.1	59	58	31	51	94	18
74 Thailand	92.4	95.7	98.1	99.0	..	85 [f]	..	..	97 [f, i]	21
75 Ukraine	99.4	99.6	99.8	99.9	..	72 [i]	..	..	..	..
76 Kazakhstan	98.8	99.4	99.8	99.8	..	89	..	83	..	42
77 Suriname	..	..	..	..	..	92	..	43	..	..
78 Jamaica	82.2	87.3	91.2	94.3	96	95 [f]	64	74 [f]	89 [f]	20
79 Oman	54.7	73.0	85.6	98.2	70	65	..	59	96	31
80 St. Vincent & the Grenadines	..	..	..	..	..	..	..	..	..	..
81 Fiji	88.6	93.2	97.8	99.2	101 [h]	99 [i]	..	..	88 [f, i]	..
82 Peru	85.5	90.2	94.5	96.9	..	104 [d, f]	..	61 [f, i]	97	17
83 Lebanon	80.3	86.5	92.1	95.4	..	74	..	70 [i]	76 [f]	22
84 Paraguay	90.3	93.5	95.6	97.2	93	92 [f]	26	47 [f]	..	..
85 Philippines	91.7	95.1	97.3	98.8	98 [h]	93 [f]	..	53 [f]	..	..
86 Maldives	94.8	97.0	98.1	99.1	..	99	..	31 [d]	..	..
87 Turkmenistan	..	..	..	..	..	..	..	..	..	48
88 Georgia	..	..	..	..	..	95	..	73 [i]	..	..
89 Azerbaijan	..	..	..	..	..	91 [d]	..	78 [i]	..	..
90 Jordan	81.5	90.3	96.7	99.3	66	94 [d, f]	..	76 [d, f]	98 [f, i]	27
91 Tunisia	59.1	72.1	84.1	93.8	94	99 [f]	..	70 [f]	93 [f]	27
92 Guyana	97.2	98.6	99.8	99.8	93	98 [d]	71	..	..	25
93 Grenada	..	..	..	..	..	84	..	46	..	..
94 Dominican Republic	79.4	84.0	87.5	91.4	..	93	..	40	75 [i]	25
95 Albania	77.0	85.3	94.8	98.0	..	98	..	74	..	22
96 Turkey	77.9	85.5	92.7	96.7	89	..	41	..	..	22
97 Ecuador	87.6	91.8	95.5	97.3	..	99	..	48	78	..
98 Occupied Palestinian Territories	..	..	..	..	..	97	..	78	..	10
99 Sri Lanka	88.7	91.9	95.1	96.9	..	97 [f, i]	..	..	..	29
100 Armenia	97.5	98.5	99.5	99.8	..	69	..	64	..	33

Table 7.21 (*continued*)

HDI rank		Adult literacy rate (% age 15 and above)		Youth literacy rate (% age 15-24)		Net primary enrolment ratio (%)[a]		Net secondary enrolment ratio (%)[a, b]		Children reaching grade 5 (%)	Tertiary students in science, math and engineering (as % of all tertiary students)
		1990	2001	1990	2001	1990-91	2000-01[c]	1990-91	2000-01[c]	1999-2000[c, d]	1994-97[e]
101	Uzbekistan	98.7	99.2	99.6	99.7	..	..	..	..	..	..
102	Kyrgyzstan	..	..	..	..	..	82	..	..	..	..
103	Cape Verde	63.8	74.9	81.5	88.6	..	99 [i]	..	..	..	..
104	China	78.3	85.8	95.3	97.9	97	93 [d, f]	..	..	..	53
105	El Salvador	72.4	79.2	83.8	88.5	75 [g]	81 [d]	..	39 [i]	71 [i]	20
106	Iran, Islamic Rep. of	63.2	77.1	86.3	94.2	..	74	..	..	..	36
107	Algeria	52.9	67.8	77.3	89.2	93	98	54	62	97	50
108	Moldova, Rep. of	97.5	99.0	99.8	99.8	..	78	..	68	..	44
109	Viet Nam	90.4	92.7	94.1	95.4	..	95	..	62	..	..
110	Syrian Arab Republic	64.8	75.3	79.9	87.7	98	96	46	39	..	31
111	South Africa	81.2	85.6	88.5	91.5	103 [h]	89	..	57	65	18
112	Indonesia	79.5	87.3	95.0	97.9	98	92 [f]	38	48 [d, f]	97 [f]	28
113	Tajikistan	98.2	99.3	99.8	99.8	..	103	..	76	..	23
114	Bolivia	78.1	86.0	92.6	96.1	91	97	29	68	83	..
115	Honduras	68.1	75.6	79.7	85.5	89 [h]	88	..	..	..	26
116	Equatorial Guinea	73.3	84.2	92.7	97.2	..	72	..	26 [i]	..	..
117	Mongolia	97.8	98.5	98.9	99.1	..	89	..	58	..	25
118	Gabon	..	..	..	..	..	88	..	..	..	..
119	Guatemala	61.0	69.2	73.4	79.6	..	84	..	26	..	..
120	Egypt	47.1	56.1	61.3	70.5	..	93 [f]	..	79 [f]	..	15
121	Nicaragua	62.7	66.8	68.2	72.0	72	81	..	36	48	31
122	São Tomé and Principe	..	..	..	..	..	..	..	..	..	..
123	Solomon Islands	..	..	..	..	..	..	..	..	..	..
124	Namibia	74.9	82.7	87.4	91.9	89 [g]	82	..	38	92	4
125	Botswana	68.1	78.1	83.3	88.7	93	84	34	70	87	27
126	Morocco	38.7	49.8	55.3	68.4	58	78	..	30 [d]	80	29
127	India	49.3	58.0	64.3	73.3	..	..	..	68 [f, i]	..	25
128	Vanuatu	..	..	..	..	..	96	..	23 [i]	101 [i]	..
129	Ghana	58.5	72.7	81.8	91.6	..	58	..	31	66	..
130	Cambodia	62.0	68.7	73.5	79.7	..	95	..	17	63	23
131	Myanmar	80.7	85.0	88.2	91.2	..	83	..	37	..	37
132	Papua New Guinea	56.6	64.6	68.6	76.3	..	84 [d]	..	21 [d]	..	..
133	Swaziland	71.6	80.3	85.1	90.8	88	93	..	44 [d]	84	22
134	Comoros	53.8	56.0	56.7	58.8	..	56	..	..	77	..
135	Lao People's Dem. Rep.	56.5	65.6	70.1	78.6	..	81	..	30	..	..
136	Bhutan	..	..	..	..	..	..	..	..	90	..
137	Lesotho	78.0	83.9	87.2	90.8	73	78	..	21	75	13
138	Sudan	45.8	58.8	65.0	78.1	..	46 [d]	..	..	87 [i]	..
139	Bangladesh	34.2	40.6	42.0	49.1	64	89	18	43	..	..
140	Congo	67.1	81.8	92.5	97.6	..	..	..	..	..	..
141	Togo	44.2	58.4	63.5	76.5	75	92	18	23 [i]	74	11
Low human development											
142	Cameroon	57.9	72.4	81.1	90.5	..	..	..	..	81 [i]	..
143	Nepal	30.4	42.9	46.6	61.6	..	72	..	..	..	14
144	Pakistan	35.4	44.0	47.4	57.8	..	66	..	..	..	..
145	Zimbabwe	80.7	89.3	93.9	97.4	..	80 [f]	..	40 [f]	..	23
146	Kenya	70.8	83.3	89.8	95.5	..	69	..	23	71 [i]	..
147	Uganda	56.1	68.0	70.1	79.4	..	109	..	12 [d]	..	15
148	Yemen	32.7	47.7	50.0	66.5	..	67	..	37 [i]	..	6
149	Madagascar	58.0	67.3	72.2	80.8	..	68	..	11 [i]	..	20
150	Haiti	39.7	50.8	54.8	65.3	22	..	..	..	..	..
151	Gambia	25.6	37.8	42.2	58.6	51 [h]	69	..	35	69 [i]	..

Table 7.21 (*continued*)

HDI rank	Adult literacy rate (% age 15 and above)		Youth literacy rate (% age 15-24)		Net primary enrolment ratio (%)[a]		Net secondary enrolment ratio (%)[a, b]		Children reaching grade 5 (%)	Tertiary students in science, math and engineering (as % of all tertiary students)
	1990	2001	1990	2001	1990-91	2000-01[c]	1990-91	2000-01[c]	1999-2000[c, d]	1994-97[e]
152 Nigeria	48.7	65.4	73.6	87.8	..	..	..	..	..	41
153 Djibouti	53.0	65.5	73.2	84.9	32	33	..	..	77 [i]	..
154 Mauritania	34.8	40.7	45.8	49.3	..	64	..	14	61	..
155 Eritrea	46.4	56.7	60.9	71.1	..	41	..	22	..	..
156 Senegal	28.4	38.3	40.1	51.8	48 [h]	63	..	..	72	..
157 Guinea	..	..	..	..	..	47	..	12 [i]	84	42
158 Rwanda	53.3	68.0	72.7	84.2	66	97 [d]	7	..	39	..
159 Benin	26.4	38.6	40.4	54.3	49 [h]	70 [d]	..	17 [d]	84	18
160 Tanzania, U. Rep. of	62.9	76.0	83.1	91.1	51	47	..	5	82	39
161 Côte d'Ivoire	38.5	49.7	52.6	62.4	47	64	..	..	91	..
162 Malawi	51.8	61.0	63.2	71.8	50	101	..	25	49	..
163 Zambia	68.2	79.0	81.2	88.7	..	66	..	19	81	..
164 Angola	..	..	..	..	..	37	..	..	..	..
165 Chad	27.7	44.2	48.0	68.3	..	58	..	8 [d]	54	14
166 Guinea-Bissau	27.2	39.6	44.1	59.5	..	54 [d]	..	..	38 [i]	..
167 Congo, Dem. Rep. of the	47.5	62.7	68.9	82.7	54	33 [i]	..	12 [i]	..	..
168 Central African Republic	33.2	48.2	52.1	68.7	53	55	..	..	..	..
169 Ethiopia	28.6	40.3	43.0	56.2	..	47	..	13	64	36
170 Mozambique	33.5	45.2	48.8	61.7	47	54	..	9	..	46
171 Burundi	37.0	49.2	51.6	65.1	52 [g]	54	..	..	58	..
172 Mali	18.8	26.4	27.6	37.1	21	43 [i]	5	..	95	..
173 Burkina Faso	16.3	24.8	24.9	35.8	27	36	..	8	69	19
174 Niger	11.4	16.5	17.0	23.8	25	30	6	5	74	..
175 Sierra Leone	..	..	..	..	..	..	..	26	..	..
Developing countries	67.2	74.5	81.1	84.8	80	82	..	..	..	..
Least developed countries	43.7	53.3	56.5	66.3	54	60	..	..	..	..
Arab States	50.0	60.8	66.5	76.7	73	77	..	..	..	..
East Asia and the Pacific	80.2	87.1	95.2	97.4	96	93	..	..	..	..
Latin America and the Caribbean	85.0	89.2	92.7	95.2	87	97	..	..	..	..
South Asia	47.7	56.3	61.7	70.6	73	79	..	..	..	..
Sub-Saharan Africa	50.3	62.4	67.4	77.9	56	59	..	..	..	..
Central & Eastern Europe & CIS	98.8	99.3	99.7	99.8	88	91	..	..	..	..
OECD	..	..	..	..	97	98	..	..	..	..
High-income OECD	..	..	..	..	97	97	..	..	..	..
High human development	..	..	..	..	97	98	..	..	..	..
Medium human development	71.8	78.1	84.5	87.8	86	88	..	..	..	..
Low human development	42.8	55.0	59.8	71.5	50	59	..	..	..	..
High income	..	..	..	..	97	97	..	..	..	..
Middle income	80.9	86.6	93.1	95.4	92	93	..	..	..	..
Low income	54.8	63.0	68.0	75.9	69	74	..	..	..	..
World	..	..	..	..	82	84	..	..	..	..

a. Data refer to the 1990/91 or 2000/01 school year. The net enrolment ratio is the ratio of enrolled children of the official age for the education level indicated to the total population of that age. Net enrolment ratios exceeding 100% reflect discrepancies between these two data sets.

b. Enrolment ratios are based on the new International Standard Classification of Education, adopted in 1997 (UNESCO 1997), and so may not be strictly comparable with those for earlier years.

c. Data for some countries may refer to national or UNESCO Institute for Statistics estimates. For details, see http://www.uis.unesco.org/. Because data are from different sources, comparisons across countries should be made with caution.

d. Data refer to the 1999/2000 school year.

e. Data refer to the most recent year available during the period specified.

f. Preliminary UNESCO Institute for Statistics estimate, subject to further revision.

g. Data refer to the 1992/93 school year.

h. Data refer to the 1991/92 school year.

i. Data refer to the 1998/99 school year.

Source: United Nations Development Programme. (2003). *Human Development Report 2003.* Table 10. "Literacy and Enrollment (270–3)." New York: Oxford University Press. Retrieved from http:www.undp.org/hdr2003/pdf/hdr03_complete.pdf. Copyright 2003 by the United Nations Development Programme. Used by permission of Oxford University Press, Inc.

Table 7.22
Labor Force Participation of Age Group 15 to 24,[1] in Selected Countries:
1995 and 2020

	Observed 1995		Low scenario 2020		High scenario 2020		Baseline scenario 2020	
	MALES	FEMALES	MALES	FEMALES	MALES	FEMALES	MALES	FEMALES
Austria	65.1	59.3	56.5	48.9	77.9	71.7	68.8	62.7
Belgium	36.5	31.7	26.3	24.0	48.7	47.1	32.7	33.9
Denmark	75.4	68.2	65.0	60.2	80.5	79.3	72.8	68.7
Finland	52.2	48.2	37.6	42.8	59.8	59.9	48.2	47.9
France	38.9	33.7	23.3	33.8	53.5	57.8	43.3	45.6
Germany	56.2	50.8	48.8	44.8	62.3	62.6	58.2	50.9
Greece	43.7	33.7	38.3	30.7	60.8	52.4	47.4	38.4
Ireland	49.0	41.9	42.9	39.4	68.7	61.5	56.1	50.6
Italy	44.5	34.4	37.3	25.4	64.7	49.0	44.6	39.8
Luxembourg	42.5	40.9	38.1	39.4	64.3	57.5	50.7	46.6
Netherlands	62.4	61.9	59.6	59.6	76.2	75.2	67.9	67.5
Portugal	48.3	39.5	33.5	37.3	55.8	49.4	43.9	45.0
Spain	49.6	42.8	43.7	37.4	59.0	49.0	47.0	44.7
Sweden	49.0	52.7	42.6	42.2	62.1	66.1	49.5	52.7
United Kingdom	75.9	66.0	64.0	59.3	75.5	73.1	70.0	67.0

1. Active persons as a percentage of total number of people aged 15–75.

Source: De Jong, A., & Broeckman, R. (July 2000). *National and regional trends in the labor force in the European Union 1985–2050.* Luxembourg: Office for Official Publications of the European Communities, 2003. Retrieved from http://europa.eu.int./comm/eurostat/Public/datashop/print-product/EN?catalogue= Eurostat&product=KS-AP-01-035-_-1-EN&mode=download.

Table 7.23
Labor Force Participation of Age Group 25 to 49,[1] in Selected Countries:
1995 and 2020

	Observed 1995		Low scenario 2020		High scenario 2020		Baseline scenario 2020	
	MALES	FEMALES	MALES	FEMALES	MALES	FEMALES	MALES	FEMALES
Austria	94.3	75.8	88.4	77.4	97.3	90.4	92.2	83.7
Belgium	93.7	72.0	87.4	75.3	95.5	88.6	91.4	80.9
Denmark	92.4	83.9	88.2	82.3	96.9	92.9	92.1	89.0
Finland	89.2	82.8	85.5	78.5	94.6	92.0	91.2	85.9
France	95.8	78.5	88.0	79.5	96.7	92.6	93.8	86.0
Germany	93.3	74.2	89.9	79.3	95.0	91.4	91.8	83.8
Greece	95.5	57.9	88.5	61.2	96.6	78.7	91.3	67.1
Ireland	91.9	57.6	86.4	56.9	96.4	80.3	93.2	66.5
Italy	91.3	56.9	85.4	60.0	96.6	60.0	90.1	66.0
Luxembourg	94.6	55.8	88.8	56.3	96.4	80.4	93.5	67.4
Netherlands	93.6	68.2	87.5	73.6	96.7	88.8	92.7	79.7
Portugal	94.7	77.0	85.2	76.6	96.3	90.3	90.1	83.1
Spain	93.5	59.4	86.7	57.6	96.6	79.1	91.0	67.7
Sweden	93.4	88.3	85.7	80.8	94.3	91.8	90.3	86.2
United Kingdom	93.6	74.6	88.4	77.3	97.3	91.2	91.3	83.1

1. Active persons aged 25–49 as a percentage of total number of persons aged 25–49.

Source: De Jong, A., & Broeckman, R. (July 2000). *National and regional trends in the labor force in the European Union 1985–2050.* Luxembourg: Office for Official Publications of the European Communities, 2003. Retrieved from http://europa.eu.int./comm/eurostat/Public/datashop/print-product/EN?catalogue= Eurostat&product=KS-AP-01-035-_-1-EN&mode=download.

Table 7.24
Labor Force Participation of Age Group 50 and Older,[1] in Selected Countries:
1995 and 2020

	1995		Low scenario 2020		High scenario 2020		Baseline scenario 2020	
	MALES	FEMALES	MALES	FEMALES	MALES	FEMALES	MALES	FEMALES
Austria	43.8	22.1	43.8	28.5	56.7	49.6	47.1	39.7
Belgium	33.6	13.8	29.8	17.4	44.4	35.3	37.7	24.9
Denmark	53.5	34.0	47.2	35.1	63.6	49.7	55.1	41.6
Finland	40.5	33.4	36.5	28.7	46.1	44.4	40.8	35.9
France	35.6	24.1	28.3	22.9	52.3	42.0	41.7	32.4
Germany	49.6	28.2	44.5	31.2	58.6	46.1	52.6	38.7
Greece	51.4	20.3	44.5	19.9	60.8	37.0	54.1	25.9
Ireland	54.7	17.9	42.7	12.1	59.8	34.4	52.4	22.4
Italy	39.4	13.7	35.0	15.0	56.5	33.1	47.2	22.5
Luxembourg	38.4	12.6	30.7	11.8	47.9	27.1	38.9	21.4
Netherlands	41.9	18.8	31.9	23.0	54.8	41.3	44.5	31.7
Portugal	54.9	30.9	51.9	34.0	66.8	52.8	57.5	40.8
Spain	43.9	15.8	41.0	16.8	59.5	32.7	51.0	22.1
Sweden	55.6	46.1	42.1	33.8	57.6	54.8	50.1	43.0
United Kingdom	49.6	32.8	45.2	32.4	63.0	52.3	53.4	43.8

1. Active persons aged 50–75 as a percentage of total number of persons aged 50–75.

Source: De Jong, A., & Broeckman, R. (July 2000). *National and regional trends in the labor force in the European Union 1985–2050.* Luxembourg: Office for Official Publications of the European Communities, 2003. Retrieved from http://europa.eu.int./comm/eurostat/Public/datashop/print-product/EN?catalogue= Eurostat&product=KS-AP-01-035-_-1-EN&mode=download.

Table 7.25
Percent of AFDC/TANF Adults Engaged in Work
or Job Preparation Activity: Fiscal Years 1994
to 1998

	1994	1995	1996	1997	1998
Some activity	19.2	20.4	22.4	24.7	35.3
Unsubsidized employment	8.3	9.3	11.3	13.3	22.8
Subsidized employment	1.4	1.2	1.7	2.4	5.5
Job search	4.0	4.1	4.7	5.3	5.1
Education	3.6	3.9	3.5	3.0	5.0
Other[1]	2.7	2.8	2.4	2.3	1.2

1. Includes activities that States conduct under pre-TANF waivers from AFDC/ JOBS rules.

Source: United States House of Representatives, Committee on Ways and Means. (2000). *The 2000 Green Book: Background material and data on programs within the jurisdiction of the Committee on Ways and Means.* Retrieved from http://aspe .hhs.gov/2000gb/sec7.txt.

Table 7.26
Number of Earners in Families by Type of Family, Selected Years: United States, 1989 to 1999

(In thousands.)

Characteristic	1989	1993	1994	1995	1996	1997	1998	1999
Total, all families	66,623	69,211	69,971	70,174	70,840	71,443	72,056	72,574
Married-couple families	52,385	53,246	53,927	53,621	53,654	54,361	54,829	55,352
No earners	6,812	7,280	7,227	7,278	7,148	7,289	7,257	7,163
One earner	11,748	11,842	11,772	11,739	11,556	11,728	12,279	12,328
Husband	9,212	8,745	8,719	8,821	8,671	8,792	9,198	9,093
Wife	1,840	2,411	2,372	2,253	2,214	2,302	2,419	2,595
Other family member	695	687	681	664	671	634	662	640
Two earners	26,011	26,957	27,472	27,361	27,474	27,935	27,801	28,254
Husband and wife	23,929	24,806	25,377	25,478	25,536	25,959	25,928	26,401
Husband and other family member	1,657	1,540	1,533	1,365	1,443	1,412	1,288	1,307
Husband is not an earner	425	612	562	518	496	564	586	546
Three earners or more	7,815	7,166	7,455	7,243	7,476	7,409	7,492	7,607
Husband and wife	6,950	6,496	6,748	6,582	6,870	6,805	6,883	6,959
Husband is an earner, not wife	716	511	516	514	456	441	438	509
Families maintained by women[1]	11,309	12,974	12,768	12,998	13,269	13,112	13,198	13,148
No earner	2,510	3,111	2,855	2,679	2,586	2,342	2,156	1,889
One earner	5,530	6,495	6,581	6,868	7,112	7,146	7,433	7,515
Householder	4,468	5,367	5,495	5,657	5,906	5,903	6,253	6,207
Other family member	1,063	1,128	1,086	1,211	1,205	1,243	1,180	1,308
Two earners or more	3,268	3,368	3,332	3,452	3,572	3,623	3,609	3,744
Householder and other family member(s)	2,903	3,049	3,044	3,156	3,341	3,332	3,313	3,420
Householder is not an earner	365	319	289	296	230	291	296	324
Families maintained by men[1]	2,929	2,992	3,276	3,555	3,916	3,970	4,030	4,074
No earner	281	332	382	357	359	346	387	377
One earner	1,376	1,615	1,705	1,821	1,982	2,106	2,039	2,076
Householder	1,127	1,372	1,437	1,568	1,683	1,806	1,751	1,758
Other family member	249	242	268	253	298	301	288	318
Two earners or more	1,272	1,045	1,189	1,377	1,576	1,518	1,604	1,621
Householder and other family member(s)	1,201	983	1,118	1,278	1,454	1,413	1,506	1,481
Householder is not an earner	72	63	71	98	122	105	99	139

1. Families maintained by widowed, divorced, separated, or single persons.
Note: Data on the number and type of families are collected in March of the subsequent year. Earner status refers to the preceding calendar year. The comparability of historical labor force data has been affected at various times by methodological and conceptual changes. For an explanation, see the Explanatory Notes and Estimates of Error section of *Employment and Earnings*, a monthly periodical published by the Bureau of Labor Statistics.

Source: U.S. Department of Labor. (2001). *Report on the American Workforce.* Washington, D.C.: Government Printing Office. Retrieved from http://www.bls.gov/opub/rtaw/pdf/appendix.pdf.

Table 7.27

Employed Persons by Usual Full- and Part-Time Status and Sex, Annual Averages: United States, 1970 to 2000

(In thousands.)

Year	Total employed	Full time	Part time	Economic part time[1]
TOTAL				
1970	78,678	66,753	11,925	2,446
1971	79,367	66,973	12,393	2,688
1972[2]	82,153	69,214	12,939	2,648
1973[2]	85,064	71,803	13,262	2,554
1974	86,794	73,093	13,701	2,988
1975	85,846	71,586	14,260	3,804
1976	88,752	73,964	14,788	3,607
1977	92,017	76,625	15,391	3,608
1978[2]	96,048	80,193	15,855	3,516
1979	98,824	82,654	16,171	3,577
1980	99,303	82,562	16,740	4,321
1981	100,397	83,243	17,154	4,768
1982	99,526	81,421	18,106	6,170
1983	100,834	82,322	18,511	6,266
1984	105,005	86,544	18,462	5,744
1985	107,150	88,534	18,615	5,590
1986[2]	109,597	90,529	19,069	5,588
1987	112,440	92,957	19,483	5,401
1988	114,968	95,214	19,754	5,206
1989	117,342	97,369	19,973	4,894
1990[2]	118,793	98,666	20,128	5,204
1991	117,718	97,190	20,528	6,161
1992	118,492	97,664	20,828	6,520
1993	120,259	99,114	21,145	6,481
1994[2]	123,060	99,772	23,288	4,625
1995	124,900	101,679	23,220	4,473
1996	126,708	103,537	23,170	4,315
1997[2]	129,558	106,334	23,224	4,068
1998[2]	131,463	108,202	23,261	3,665
1999[2]	133,488	110,302	23,186	3,357
2000[2]	135,208	112,291	22,917	3,190
Men				
1970	48,990	44,825	4,166	1,298
1971	49,390	45,023	4,367	1,395
1972[2]	50,896	46,373	4,523	1,347
1973[2]	52,349	47,843	4,507	1,279
1974	53,024	48,378	4,646	1,519
1975	51,857	46,988	4,870	1,973
1976	53,138	48,150	4,988	1,825
1977	54,728	49,551	5,178	1,749
1978[2]	56,479	51,281	5,198	1,638
1979	57,607	52,427	5,180	1,645
1980	57,186	51,717	5,471	2,107
1981	57,397	51,906	5,492	2,285
1982	56,271	50,334	5,937	3,030
1983	56,787	50,643	6,145	2,966
1984	59,091	53,070	6,020	2,651
1985	59,891	53,862	6,028	2,572
1986[2]	60,892	54,685	6,207	2,590
1987	62,107	55,746	6,360	2,513
1988	63,273	56,816	6,457	2,474
1989	64,315	57,885	6,430	2,287
1990[2]	65,104	58,501	6,604	2,519
1991	64,223	57,407	6,815	3,104
1992	64,440	57,363	7,077	3,230
1993	65,349	58,123	7,226	3,124
1994[2]	66,450	58,832	7,617	2,299
1995	67,377	59,936	7,441	2,210
1996	68,207	60,762	7,445	2,106
1997[2]	69,685	62,258	7,427	1,988
1998[2]	70,693	63,189	7,504	1,796
1999[2]	71,446	63,930	7,516	1,634
2000[2]	72,293	64,938	7,355	1,571

Table 7.27 (*continued*)

Year	Total employed	Full time	Part time	Economic part time[1]
Women				
1970	29,688	21,929	7,758	1,148
1971	29,976	21,950	8,026	1,293
1972[2]	31,257	22,842	8,416	1,300
1973[2]	32,715	23,960	8,756	1,274
1974	33,769	24,714	9,055	1,468
1975	33,989	24,598	9,391	1,832
1976	35,615	25,814	9,799	1,782
1977	37,289	27,076	10,213	1,859
1978[2]	39,569	28,912	10,658	1,879
1979	41,217	30,227	10,990	1,932
1980	42,117	30,845	11,270	2,215
1981	43,000	31,337	11,664	2,484
1982	43,256	31,086	12,170	3,140
1983	44,047	31,679	12,367	3,300
1984	45,915	33,473	12,441	3,091
1985	47,259	34,672	12,587	3,018
1986[2]	48,706	35,845	12,862	2,999
1987	50,334	37,210	13,124	2,889
1988	51,696	38,398	13,298	2,733
1989	53,027	39,484	13,544	2,607
1990[2]	53,689	40,165	13,524	2,685
1991	53,496	39,783	13,713	3,057
1992	54,052	40,301	13,751	3,290
1993	54,910	40,991	13,919	3,357
1994[2]	56,610	40,940	15,670	2,325
1995	57,523	41,743	15,779	2,263
1996	58,501	42,776	15,725	2,210
1997[2]	59,873	44,076	15,797	2,080
1998[2]	60,771	45,014	15,757	1,869
1999[2]	62,042	46,372	15,670	1,723
2000[2]	62,915	47,353	15,562	1,619

1. Includes some persons who usually work full time.
2. The comparability of historical labor force data has been affected at various times by methodological and conceptual changes. For an explanation, see the Explanatory Notes and Estimates of Error section of *Employment and Earnings,* a monthly periodical published by the Bureau of Labour Statistics.

Source: U.S. Department of Labor. (2001). *Report on the American Workforce.* Washington, D.C.: Government Printing Office. Retrieved from http://www.bls.gov/opub/rtaw/pdf/appendix.pdf.

Table 7.28
U.S. Policy Changes Under Welfare Reform

Asset limit increase	Set countable asset limit above the $1,000 of AFDC law and/or permit recipients to have a vehicle of greater value than allowed by AFDC law ($1,500 in equity value).
Child support liberalization	Disregard more than $50 monthly of child support.
Earnings disregard enhancement	Disregard more earnings than AFDC law allowed (after 4 months of work, the AFDC disregard was $120 monthly).
Education-focused programs	Require participation in a program of education and training.
Employment-focused program	Require participation in an employment-focused program, such as job search.
Family cap	Deny increase in family benefit (or pay less than full benefit) for new baby conceived or born to mother already on welfare.
Food stamp benefit combined with cash grant	Combine cash aid and food stamps into one cash grant.
Mixed employment/education program	Assign recipients to either an employment-focused or education/training program.
Personal responsibility sanctions	Penalize family for failure to meet personal responsibility rules like assuring school attendance or taking the child for immunizations.
Time limit	End family benefits when adult has received assistance for a specified period.
Time limit (adult only)	Reduce family benefits (end adult share) when adult has received assistance for a specified period.
Transitional benefits extension	Extend transitional Medicaid and/or child care beyond the 12 months required by AFDC law (for those who lose eligibility for cash aid due to increased earnings).
Two-parent family eligibility	End special eligibility rules for two-parent families.
Wage supplementation	Use welfare benefit to subsidize wages of recipients.
Work requirements: younger child	Require mothers with children younger than age 3 to participate in work/training (AFDC required work if youngest child was 3, but permitted states to lower this to age 1).
Work sanctions	Penalize work failure more severely than AFDC/Job Opportunities and Basic Skills (JOBS) law allowed (e.g., loss of adult benefit and use of protective payee).
Work-trigger time limit	Require work as a condition of continued eligibility for assistance after being on the rolls for a specified period.

Source: United States House of Representatives, Committee on Ways and Means. (2000). *The 2000 Green Book: Background material and data on programs within the jurisdiction of the Committee on Ways and Means.* Retrieved from http://aspe.hhs.gov/2000gb/appnl.txt.

8. Public Assistance, Tax Deferment, and Exclusion Programs in the Social Safety Net Available to Low- and Moderate-Income Able and Disabled Families and Individuals

Rather than making sweeping changes in our system of social welfare, citizens and elected officials have been content to live with a variety of piecemeal programs geared toward different needs and to different segments of the population and reflecting different principles and values (Gilbert, Specht, and Terrell, 1993, 82).

According to Dobelstein (1996), the development of income maintenance provides a classic example of incremental policy formation. There are different aspects to these programs, some seemingly contradictory, but from a Gestaltist perspective they still represent a normative consistency. Some key aspects of the social safety net in the United States are based on a very limited notion of guaranteed income as a means of income maintenance. It can be argued to a further extent that guaranteed-income programs are based on the notion that is referred to as a negative income tax. As a revolutionary way to change the present social safety net system it failed; however, there are enough tax-based programs available to individuals at all income levels to suggest that the basic idea behind the negative income tax does make up a part of the current social safety net. Its approach is limited, but it is helping to further specific areas of social policy through the use of the existing tax structure and codes.

The concept of the negative income tax was originally developed by Milton Friedman back in 1962 in his book *Capitalism and Freedom*. Friedman's idea was that the national tax system could be an instrument whereby if an individual's income fell below the sum of allowable deductions and exemptions that the taxpayer would receive a government subsidy on some portion of the difference between what the taxpayer earned and an identified minimal standard (the poverty line). "In Friedman's view, adoption of a NIT [negative tax income] would enable numerous existing categorical transfer programs to be eliminated—including AFDC [now TANF], Aid to the Aged, Blind, and Totally Disabled [now SSI], and a variety of in-kind assistance programs, such as

social services" (Haveman, 1987, 99). Therefore, for the more conservative policymakers,

> In its purest form a NIT promised a revolution in American social policy. Gone would be the intrusive and costly welfare bureaucracy, the pernicious distinctions between "worthy" and "unworthy" recipients, the perverse disincentives for work effort and family formation. The needy would, like everyone else, simply file annual—or perhaps quarterly—income returns with the Internal Revenue Service. . . . The NIT would thus be a mirror image of the regular tax system. Instead of tax liabilities varying positively with income according to a tax rate schedule, benefits would vary inversely with income according to a negative tax rate (or benefit-reduction) schedule. (Allen, 2002, 1)

While Friedman envisioned the replacement of all existing programs in the social safety net, U.S. policy is going in the diametrically opposite direction (Moffitt, 2002). Means-tested transfer programs grew significantly from 1968 to 2000 as a result of increasing expenditures on the aged and the disabled, along with the extension of benefits to additional classes of low-income individuals. The resulting categorization demonstrates the voting public's interest to "divide the population into different boxes according to characteristics that are presumed to proxy different types of need, and with a different program for each" (19). A reading of the *Green Book Report 2000* identifies a number of the tax credits and exclusions that support Moffit's conclusion that the built-in incentives available through tinkering with the tax system are working even though it may represent the antithesis of what the negative income tax was meant to be.

In this chapter, the initial focus is on categorical programs, most of which the strong defenders of the negative income tax wanted—and still want—to replace. These income maintenance programs, nevertheless, reflect through their eligibility requirements a reliance on demonstrating poverty through the deprivation of income, and the need for the public treasury to mitigate this deprivation so that eligible beneficiaries are at least able to meet minimal dietary, housing, and quality of life standards. The second part of the narrative in this chapter then goes on to describe and present how some of the tax-based programs work.

SUPPLEMENTARY SECURITY INCOME (SSI)

A form of public assistance through income maintenance provided through the existing Social Security Administration programs established in 1974, Title XVI of the Social Security Act authorizes the Supplementary Security Income (SSI) program to provide income to help individuals who are 65 or older, blind or disabled adults, and blind or disabled children. It is a federally administered program that replaced the federal-state programs of Old-Age Assistance and Aid to the Blind established under the original Social Security Act of 1935, and the program of Aid to the Permanently Disabled created under the Social Security Amendments of 1950. SSI provides assistance in the form of monthly cash payments in compliance with uniform, nationwide eligibility requirements. States have the option of supplementing the SSI cash allowance for all or selected categories of persons regardless of previous state program eligibility. In addition, the Social Security Act section 1615(d) requires the Social Security Administration (SSA)—which administers the program—to reimburse state vocational rehabilitation agencies for the reasonable and necessary costs of services resulting in disabled SSI recipients being successfully rehabilitated (defined as the ability to perform a substantial gainful activity for a continuous period of nine months). An emergency advance payment is available for those needing a cash advance prior to the commencement of payments, the advance of which is withheld from the first check. In addition, payments can begin six months prior to the determination of disability once the determination is made.

"Since its inception SSI has been viewed as 'program of last resort'" (United States House of Representatives, Committee on Ways and Means, 2000, section 3, 12/54). SSI is a means-tested program; monthly payments to eligible recipients are based on a statutory federal benefits rate. These rates are indexed for annual increases in the same manner as the OASDI programs under the Social Security system. Individuals are not generally eligible for SSI if their resources exceed $2,000 ($3,000 for a couple). However, the following assets are not included in the determination process:

home

automobile used for essential transportation

household goods and personal insurance of reasonable value

burial plots and spaces

life insurance

The federal payment is based on the person's **counted income**. SSI excludes in its calculations $65 of monthly earnings plus one-half of any earnings above $65. It also does not count the first $20 monthly in OASDI benefits or other earned or unearned monthly income.

Individuals and couples become eligible for SSI if their incomes fall below the federal maximum monthly SSI benefit.[1,2] To qualify, an individual has to be 65 or older, or meet the criteria for blindness (20/200 vision with corrective lenses, or less than a 20-degree field of vision) or disability (those unable to engage in any substantial gainful activity). Substantial gainful activity is defined in the year 2000 as earning $700 per month in counted income minus impairment-related expenses. To be considered under the disability category, "[generally], the individual must be unable to do any kind of work that exists in the national economy, talking into account age, education, and work experience" (United States House of Representatives, Committee on Ways and Means, 2000, section 3, 5/54). Children may qualify if they are under age 18 (or 22 if a full-time student) and are unmarried, meet the applicable SSI definition of blindness or disability, and meet the applicable SSI definition for income and resource requirements.

If an individual or couple live as part of another household and receive food and shelter from that other individual, family, or group, the federal benefit is reduced by one-third in lieu of having to determine the actual dollar value of the third party's in-kind contribution. Payments made to institutionalized persons depend on the type of institutions. For example, in most cases (with only few exceptions), inmates at public institutions[3] are not eligible (Social Security Administration, 2001). For those institutionalized for a complete calendar month, the maximum federal SSI payment is $30 per month, but it applies where "(1) the institution receives a substantial part of the cost of the person's care from the Medicaid program, or (2) recipients' under age 18 have private health insurance making payments to the institution" (22). Other eligible persons in an institution may still be able to receive up to the full federal benefit rate.

Prior to 1997, drug addiction and alcoholism were qualifying medical impairments under SSI and the disability insurance (DI) portion of social security; however, Congress passed a law in 1996 terminating drug and alcohol addiction as qualifying conditions for SSI. This meant the termination of benefits for 59.6 percent (124,746) of beneficiaries identified as having a drug or alcohol addiction (United States House of Representatives, Committee on Ways and Means, 2000, section 3, 34/54). It continued benefits for the remainder based on another disability.

As of December 1999, 36.3 percent of all SSI recipients also received social security benefits (60 percent of this group were elderly, 30 percent disabled, and 35 percent blind; United States House of Representatives, Committee on Ways and Means, 2000, section 3, 12/54). In terms of recipients seeking other forms of aid, states have three options on how to treat SSI recipients when it comes to establishing Medicaid eligibility.[4] Except in California, SSI recipients may be eligible to receive food stamps; beneficiaries living alone or in a household where all other members of the household receive or are applying for SSI benefits can file for food stamps at an SSA office. Table 8.1 at the end of this chapter provides data about overall program costs for the year 2000.

VETERAN'S BENEFITS AND SERVICES

Veteran's benefits and services are offered by the Department of Veterans Affairs (VA), in the amount of $44 billion in fiscal year 1999 (United States House of Representatives, Committee on Ways and Means, 2000, section 13, 98/106). These benefits ostensibly are for the veterans who are eligible for these benefits and services, members of their families, and survivors of deceased veterans. Programs include:

veterans compensation and pensions

readjustment benefits

medical care

housing and loan guarantee programs

Also made available through VA auspices are life insurance, burial benefits, and special counseling and outreach programs. The VA also provides education and training for military personnel meeting the designated eligibility criteria, as well as vocational rehabilitation services to disabled veterans (this last program cost the VA close to $1 billion in 1999).

Service-connected compensation is given to disabled veterans who became disabled as a result of injuries and/or illnesses directly attributable to a period of active-duty military service. The amount of the monthly benefit is determined by disability ratings. These ratings are based on the presumed average reductions in earning capacities caused by the disability or disabilities.[5] In some instances the disability may be deemed to be service-connected, yet, receive a rating of 0 percent. For the fiscal year 1999, it is calculated that 2.3 million disabled veterans and 324,000 survivors received around $18 billion in compensation (United States House of Representatives, Committee on Ways and Means, 2000, section 13, 99/106).

Veterans benefits are means-tested cash benefits to war veterans who are recognized as partially or totally disabled from non-service-related causes and to their survivors. The benefit is based on family size, with the pension providing the income floor: in 1999, about 304,000 persons received close to $3.1 billion in pension payments (United States House of Representatives, Committee on Ways and Means, 2000).

The Veterans Administration provides a "Comprehensive array of inpatient and outpatient medical services through 172 medical centers, 134 nursing homes, 40 domiciliaries, 527 ambulatory clinics, and 206 readjustment counseling centers (Vet centers)" (United States House of Representatives, Committee on Ways and Means, 2000, 100/106). Current eligibility rules require the VA to provide free in-patient and out-patient medical care for service-connected conditions and to low-income veterans[6] (at a cost in 1999 of $18 billion for 3.6 million separate applicants that led to 752,000 in-patient and 38 million interactions).

FOOD STAMPS

A traditional public assistance program formally established as a full program by the Food Stamp Act of 1964, the food stamps program is designed to increase the buying power for food by eligible low-income households. Specifically, the program's interest is for low-income individuals to be able to consume a nutritionally adequate low-cost diet. Eligible single persons and individuals living in households receive coupons or electronic benefit transfers (EBTs) redeemable for consumable food as well as for getting garden seeds and plants; these are accepted at most retail food stores. Special provisions allow the homeless, drug addicts, alcoholics, blind or disabled residents in certain group living arrangements, residents of shelters for battered spouses and children, and persons who are 60 or older to use their coupons for meals prepared at a nonprofit facility (Social Security Administration, 2001, 77).[7] Food stamps are not taxed as income, sales tax cannot be charged for purchases made with food stamps, and the benefit does not directly affect other assistance available to low-income households. Participation for the fiscal year 2000 is estimated at 17.2 million individual per month, with an average per person benefit of $72.79 per month and a total value of benefits issued at $15 billion (at a total cost to the federal government of $17.1 billion).

The program is administered by the U.S. Department of Agriculture's (USDA) agency for Food and Nutritional Services (FNS); however, the food stamps themselves are provided to recipients by state and local agencies. Those that qualify receive an allotment of stamps based on income, family size, and deductible expenses. Food stamps are given in order to make up the expected difference between what individuals and families can contribute to feeding themselves and the actual cost of eating a nutritious diet. Participating households are supposed to devote 30 percent of their monthly earnings to food, and food stamps make up for what that 30 percent does not provide in terms of foodstuffs. Households determined to be without income[8] receive an amount that is equal to 100 percent of the June monthly cost of the Thrifty Food Plan (a nutritionally adequate diet), adjusted for size and economy-of-scale possibilities as compared to the baseline indicator family as well as annually (in October) to account for increases in the cost of food. In 2000, the benefit equated to $434 per month for a baseline indicator of a family of four. Households deemed to have income receive food stamps valued at the difference between the maximum allotment and 30 percent of their income (after certain allowable deductions). As indicated in the Social Security Administration's *Annual Statistical Supplement 2001*:

To qualify for the program, a household must have (1) less than $2,000 in disposable assets ($3,000, if one member is aged 60 or older), (2) gross income below 130 percent of the poverty guidelines for the household size, and (3) net income [after subtracting the six deductions listed in note 8], of less than 100 percent of the poverty guidelines. Households with a person aged 60 or older or a disabled person receiving either

Supplemental Security Income (SSI), Social Security (OASDI), state general assistance, or veterans' disability benefits (or interim disability assistance pending approval of any of the above programs) may have gross income exceeding 130 percent of the poverty guide-lines, if, after subtracting the deductions listed in note 8, the income is lower than 100 percent of the poverty guidelines. One- and two-person households that meet the applicable standard receive at least $10 a month in food stamps. All households in which all members receive Temporary Assistance to Needy Families (TANF) or SSI are categorically eligible for food stamps without meeting these income or resource criteria. (2001, 77)

Households are certified to receive food stamps for different lengths of time based on individual sources of income and circumstances. This certification has to be done at least on an annual basis. When SSI payments or Social Security benefits are the sole source of income, certification is for an entire year. Furthermore, households have to report changes in income or expenses that are at least $25, along with any other circumstance changes that may impact eligibility. Those households who lose income or food as a result of natural disasters may be eligible for food stamps for up to one month if they meet the special disaster income and asset limit (Social Security Administration, 2001).

TANF, SSI, and state government assistance (GA) programs recipients tend to automatically be eligible for food stamps if the household is made up entirely of TANF, SSI, and GA beneficiaries. In fact, the food stamps program is intertwined with TANF, SSI, and GA programs administratively, as well as linked because most beneficiaries are also part of the other programs.

States have the primary responsibility for day-to-day program administration. They determine eligibility, calculate benefits, and issue food stamp allotments. In their determination, states have a number of options they can pursue that allow them to vary from federal rules (especially for those recipients that also receive state welfare benefits). States also have a major role to play in carrying out employment and training programs for food stamp recipients.

The Food Stamp Act provides 100 percent funding of food stamp benefits, with the exception of those states that elect to "buy-into" the program and pay for issuing food stamp benefits to ineligible non-citizens or those made ineligible by the new work rules under new regulations (United States House of Representatives, Committee on Ways and Means, 2000, section 15). The federal government is responsible for meeting its own administrative expenses and for covering 50 percent to 60 percent of a state's welfare agency' administration. Along with sharing in the cost of employment and training programs for recipients. The federal share is formula-based, considering a pool of funds and basic operating costs. States can receive the higher percentage of federal support if they have a low rate of improperly issued benefits, and they can retain a portion of those improper benefits they are able to recover (35 percent in fraud cases, 20 percent for other instances).

Most able-bodied adults have to do the following to gain or retain eligibility (United States House of Representatives, Committee on Ways and Means, 2000, 12/106):

1. register for work (typically at a one-stop center or with a welfare agency or state employment service office);
2. accept a suitable job if offered one;
3. fulfill any work, job search, or training requirements established by administering welfare agencies;
4. provide the administering welfare agency with sufficient information to allow a determination with respect to the job availability; and
5. not voluntarily quit a job without good cause or reduce work effort below thirty hours per week.

Program components that agencies may require from eligible beneficiaries include supervised job search or training for a job search, workfare, job experience or training programs, education programs to improve basic skills, or any other employment or training activity approved by the Department of Agriculture. Recipients who participate in employment or training activity cannot be required to work more than the minimum wage equivalent of their household's benefit (total hours of participation cannot exceed 120 hours per month). While engaged in these activities, agencies must, in turn, provide support for costs directly associated with their participation such as transportation and childcare, although this support may be limited to $25 per participant per month for costs other than childcare and childcare costs to local market rates.

If a head of the household does not fulfill any one of these requirements, at the discretion of the state, the entire household could be disqualified up to 180 days and not receive benefits during that time. If it happens more than once, the disqualification period can increase up to the maximum amount of six months. The law, however, exempts the following class of individuals:

- Those physically or mentally unfit for work
- Individuals under the age of 16 or over 59
- Individuals between the ages of 16 and 18 if they are not a head of a household or are attending school or a training program
- Persons working at least 30 hours per week or earning the minimum wage equivalent
- Persons caring for dependents who are disabled or children under the age of 6
- Those caring for children between the ages of 6 and 12 if adequate child-care is not available
- Individuals already subject to and complying with another assistance program's work, training, or job search
- Otherwise eligible post-secondary students
- Residents of drug addiction and alcoholic treatment programs

The Personal Responsibility and Work Opportunity Reconciliation Act of 1996 also made changes to the food stamps program, particularly in the area of adding restrictions on eligibility of certain low-income groups. To quote from the Social Security Administration's *Supplement* (2001):

- Legal immigrants became ineligible for benefits, unless they met one of the following criteria: were naturalized citizens, had worked and paid taxes in the country for 40 quarters (or were the spouse or minor child of someone who had met the work requirement), had served in the U.S. Armed Forces (or were the spouse or child or a veteran) or were refugees, asylees, or persons granted a stay of deportation when admitted and have lived in the United States for less than 5 years. Legal immigrants currently receiving benefits were allowed to receive benefits until their first recertification after April 1, 1997, or until August 22, 1997, whichever date came first.

- Time limits were imposed for childless unemployed adults aged 18–50. Those who are not disabled are limited to receiving 3 months of benefits in any 36-month period, unless they are working 20 hours per week, participating in a work training program for at least 20 hours per week, or participating in work fare. States may request waivers for areas with at least 10-percent unemployment or insufficient jobs. (79)

FEDERAL HOUSING ASSISTANCE

The rationale for the need of federal assistance in housing is best exemplified by the quote below taken from Schwartz and Volgy's book, *The Forgotten Americans* (1992):

> Housing expenses are so high that most Americans who live at the top end of the economy budget—155 percent of the official poverty line—cannot pay their present housing costs without scrimping on food, clothing, health care, or other necessities. The Economic Policy Institute's detailed analysis of the American Housing Surveys reveals that about 90 percent of the families of four living at this income level in 1987 (equivalent then to about $18,000 for a family of four) did not, after spending only the minimal amounts allotted for food, medical, clothing, and other items on the economy budget, have enough money left to cover the rent or mortgage and utilities they had to pay for the shelter in which they lived. (47–48)

Andrew Dobelstein (1996) asserts that there are three normative issues surrounding housing: (1) standards, (2) supply, and (3) housing subsidies and their distribution. However, Schwartz and Volgy's comments bring out a fourth and critical normative issue that is inherent in two of Dobelstein's three issues: cost. The fiscal year 2003 budget echoes these four concerns by funding the following six considerations:

1. Expanding homeownership
2. Ensuring affordable rental housing opportunities
3. Helping individuals achieve self-sufficiency
4. Supporting community and economic development
5. Protecting vulnerable populations
6. Enforcing fair housing laws

The current forms of housing assistance were first developed in 1937 with the passage of the Housing Act and the creation of the Federal Housing Administration (FHA). In 1978, Congress reshuffled and recreated the U.S. Department of Housing and Urban Development (HUD), making the FHA and other housing programs part of HUD. HUD itself did not come into being as a cabinet-level agency until 1965 through the passage of the Department of Housing and Urban Development Act. Even with the administrative rearrangement, the FHA "continued its core mission of contributing to the building and maintenance of healthy, prosperous neighborhoods and expanding opportunities for affordable home ownership, rental housing and healthcare" (United States Department of Housing and Urban Development, 2002).

HUD offers a series of programs with the purpose of enacting a coordinated and comprehensive response to meet the overall housing needs of those residing in the United States.[9] Among the key activities it generates are:

- insurance of loans for first-time and low-income homebuyers to increase access to the benefits of homeownership

- providing grants to communities to help meet locally defined needs for housing, economic development, and infrastructure

- supporting the nation's public housing authorities so they can provide housing for poor and disadvantaged families

- enforcing fair housing laws to ensure equal opportunity in homeownership and rental housing

- providing grants to community-based organizations and local governments to support a full range of assistance to people who are homeless so they can move to permanent housing

- helping families and individuals make progress towards self-sufficiency by providing housing assistance, job training, and other supportive services

- providing housing vouchers that give families access to safe and decent housing in communities with lower poverty rates and greater economic opportunity

- insuring loans for owners of multifamily housing to increase the availability of affordable rental housing

- establishing and monitoring affordable housing goals for Fannie Mae and Freddie Mac to assure homeownership opportunities for lower-income families and for underserved neighborhoods

- providing housing-related assistance for the elderly, persons with disabilities, and people with HIV/AIDS

- providing grants to communities to remove lead based paint hazards (United States Department of Housing and Urban Development, 2000a, 2)

In terms of the number of eligible recipients, over 4.5 million low-income, elderly and formerly homeless households and persons with disabilities currently receive HUD rental assistance.

Following what HUD identifies as trends impacting the housing situation in the United States, students, researchers, and individuals looking at these benefits of the public assistance component of this agency need to consider:

1. the impact of a fluctuating economy based on the longest economic expansion in U.S. history, followed by recessionary trends exacerbated by the post-September 11, 2001, fears of conflict with terrorist groups and Iraq;

2. the inherent contradiction that an economic expansion meant that the average income share of the poorest one-fifth of families has decreased, making their ability to find, compete, and receive housing more difficult;

3. the creation of a situation where an inverse relationship exists in that the number of affordable housing units for people who have an **extremely low income** has decreased while the number of individuals meeting the definition for extremely low income has increased;

4. shortages in affordable housing constrain employment opportunities for extremely-low-income families;

5. the monthly rate on rents continues to increase, making people have to pay a greater percentage of their income on shelter which may force more people into homelessness;

6. demographic shifts adding to the need of more housing opportunities because of increasing populations and a reduction in the number of people living in one household;

7. an increasing need for housing for the elderly and disabled individuals, two population groups anticipated to increase in size from 13 percent to 20 percent by the year 2030, with the fastest growing group being individuals aged 85 or older;

8. the changes in welfare laws from 1996 may mean decreased income and increased costs of housing subsidies for some subsets of the welfare population if economic conditions do not support entry-level jobs;

9. a recent U.S. Supreme Court decision mandating states to place persons with disabilities in community settings rather than institutions when treatment professionals determine that community placement is appropriate;[10]

10. the continued demographic shift from the inner cities to the suburbs, the impact that middle-class flight has on the inner city, and older but closer suburbs infrastructure spending patterns;

11. the impact of new building technologies making for more energy-efficient housing and lower material, construction, and processing costs; and

12. increased demands as these relate to increased pressures to place housing in coastal areas, flood zones, former farm land, and forested areas (see United States Department of Housing and Urban development, 2000a, 9–10).

Assistance programs take on the form of two approaches. The first approach is helping people own a home and keep it. The second approach is to provide rental subsidies. House ownership is the holy grail of FHA programs and activities. FHA provides loan insurance guarantees to individuals and developers under Section 202 (housing for the elderly), Section 235 (middle-income housing subsidies), and Farmer Home Loans (Dobelstein, 1996). Chart 8.1 explains who benefits from the housing subsidies, mainly focusing on house ownership (and some tenantship benefits for owners).

Home ownership is not a viable option for everyone. HUD recognizes this and, therefore, also focuses on providing help in the area of rental assistance. HUD's best-known rental assistance programs are public housing and Section 8 (low-income rent subsidies). In addition, as a result of the U.S. Supreme Court decision in the *Olmestead v. L.C.* case, Section 811 (housing for persons with disabilities) is becoming a significant rent assistance program in itself.

Public housing is a different concept than Section 8 assistance. It includes low-income assistance in the form of rent subsidies under the local supervision of local housing authorities and assistance in the construction of low-income public housing. Large building projects have given way to smaller units or single-family dwellings. There are approximately 1.3 million households living in public housing units managed by some 3,300 local housing authorities (HAs; United States Department of Housing and Urban Development, 2000b). Eligibility is determined by the local housing authority based on annual gross income, if an applicant qualifies as an elderly person or one having a disability, and citizenship or eligible immigration status. The amount of rent needed is based on the applicant's anticipated gross annual income minus deductions, if any.[11] Duration of stay is at least for as long as the duration of the lease. Under public housing assistance also falls the Community Development Block Grant providing financial support to states to help redevelopment of an aging housing infrastructure.

The basic premise of the Section 8 program is providing very low-income beneficiaries with housing choice vouchers that allow them to find, select, and lease or purchase safe, decent, and affordable privately-owned rental housing. The program has different types of vouchers that are available to beneficiaries:

• Conversion vouchers: (1) to assist with relocation or replacement housing needs resulting from the demolition, disposition, or mandatory conversion of public housing units; (2) assistance to families living in Section 8 projects where the owner is opting out of the program, situations in which HUD is taking enforcement action against the owners, and when the owner is prepaying the mortgage.

• Family unification vouchers: for families for whom the lack of adequate housing is a primary factor in the separation, or threat of imminent separation, of children from their families or in the prevention of reunifying the children with their families.

Chart 8.1
Who Benefits from Housing Subsidies

Federal housing subsidies and their recipients		
Form of subsidy	**Direct beneficiary**	**Present source of policy (section numbers refer to specific portion of the Federal Housing Act)**
Reduction of interest rate	Developer/tenants	sections 235, 238
Increased loan coverage	Developer	section 221
Payment of principal and interest on housing costs	Tenant/owner	section 2, public housing
Payment of capital grant to developer	Developer	———
Housing allowances to tenants	Tenant	———
Housing allowance to owners	Owner	———
Allocating housing for general income maintenance	Low-income tenants	———
Allocating housing in public assistance	Low-income tenants	TANF (AFDC elements) and other assistance programs
Tax deduction of mortgage interest and property taxes	Owner/developer	Tax codes (see tax break section below)
Accelerated depreciation	Developer	Section 236, tax codes (see tax break section below)
Reduction of local property taxes	Owner/tenant	Section 2 (see tax break section below)
Reduction of land costs	Developers/owners	Community Block Grant (Housing Act)

Source: Dobelstein, 1996, p. 197.

- Homeownership voucher: assist first-time homeowners with their monthly homeownership expenses of a home that has passed appropriate inspections prior to purchase by designated agents.

- Project-based vouchers: public housing authorities may attach up to 20 percent of its voucher assistance to specific housing units if the owner agrees to either rehabilitate (requiring at least $1,000 per unit of repairs or upgrades) or construct the units, or the owner agrees to set-aside a portion of the units in an existing development.

- Tenant-based vouchers: allows recipients to find, select, choose, and lease safe, decent, and affordable privately-owned rental housing.

- Vouchers for people with disabilities: there are three types, (1) mainstream vouchers for elderly and non-elderly households that have a person who is disabled, enabling them to lease affordable housing of their choice, (2) designated housing vouchers for non-elderly households who could be eligible for public housing if it was not limited to the elderly (allowing them to find an affordable place of their choice), and (3) certain development vouchers for non-elderly households with a person that has a disability who currently do not receive any type of housing assistance, in certain developments where owners establish preferences for, or restrict occupancy to, elderly families so that they may obtain affordable housing.

- Welfare-to-Work vouchers: approximately an additional 50,000 housing choice vouchers targeting families who have a critical need for housing in order to obtain or retain viable employment.

It is important to understand that federal housing assistance has never been provided as an entitlement to those who qualify; nevertheless, the federal government traditionally provides direct aid for housing to low-income families in the form of rental and mortgage interest subsidies. It does this in conjunction with public and private partners. Partners from the public side are the local public housing authorities (PHAs) established under state laws to develop, own, and operate low-rent public housing using HUD subsidies (United States Department of Housing and Urban Development, 2000b). HUD also relies on other partnerships from the public sector to help ensure fair housing opportunities; partners from the private sector includes mortgage banks. "FHA mortgage insurance enables lenders to reduce interest rates, and Ginnie Mae facilitates investment in mortgages by packaging them in pools for resale to private investors" (14). Other partners from the private sector include nonprofit community and faith-based organizations and many institutions of higher education, either as administrators for particular community programs in the case of the former organizations, or as matching resource partners providing neighborhood revitalization programs such as training and providing technical assistance

(United States Department of Housing and Urban Development, 2000b).

Housing costs expectations and formulas are based on the notion that households should spend about 25 percent to 30 percent of their income on housing, with 30 percent being a ceiling limit. Individuals and families who spend more than this amount are considered to have a serious impediment to being able to maintain an affordable overall lifestyle and standards of living. Assistance for those that need help is a means-tested process in which income limits determine eligibility. Income limits can be summarized as follows:

- Low-income families are defined as families whose incomes do not exceed 80 percent of the median family income for the area.

- Very low-income families are defined as families whose incomes do not exceed 50 percent of the median family income for the area.

- The 1998 amendments to the U.S. Housing Act of 1937 establish a 30 percent of median family income program targeting standard.

- Income limits for nonmetropolitan areas may not be less than limits based on the State nonmetropolitan median family income level.

- Income limits are adjusted for family size.

- Income limits are adjusted for areas with unusually high or low family income or housing-cost-to-income relationships.

- The Secretary of Agriculture is to be consulted prior to establishing income limits for rural areas, since these limits also apply to certain rural housing and community development service programs (United States Department of Housing and Urban Development, 2003, 1).

The actual formulas for income limits are legislatively mandated in the U.S. Housing Act of 1937, section 3, as amended, partly because other income limits are linked to their calculation.[12] As spelled out in HUD's *FY 2003 Income Limits Briefing Materials* (2003):

> Because there are currently several legislated income limit standards (e.g., 30%, 50%, 60%, 65%, 80%, 95%, 100%, 115%, 125%) which were intended to have progressive relationships, the very low income limits have been used as the basis for deriving other income limits (e.g., otherwise low-income limits would be less than very low income limits in areas where very low income limits had been adjusted upward by more than 60 percent because of unusually low area median family incomes). (4)

The Department of Health and Human Services manages a block grant under the title of Low-Income Home Energy Assistance Program (LIHEAP). The Administration of Children and Families' Office of Community Services directly administers the program. The purpose is to provide grants for states to assist eligible households to meet the costs of home energy.[13] Funds for this program provide payments to eligible households for heating or cooling costs and for home energy

crises; up to 15 percent of available funds can be used for low-cost weatherization or other energy-related home repair. States are given the widest discretion in the running of this program.

HUD programs are of significant scope and variety, to say the least; therefore, in concluding this discussion on housing, Chatterjee's (1999) comments provide a counterpoint for reflection about the role of government in providing assistance to those who need some form of help in getting housing.

> The state should not be in the housing business. More often than not, state-erected housing units create ghettos rather than communities. . . . Instead it should create a tax policy encouraging private parties to build and acquire housing on an asset-acquisition plan. Ownership should be encouraged and supported by tax and lending policy. Housing policy should encourage community building rather than simply the construction of spatial units. In effect, housing should be privatized, and the state's regulatory and taxation powers should be used to make housing available to all social groups. (185)

For the remainder of this chapter, the discussion takes from Dobelstein's (1996) perspective in considering tax-based credits and exemptions as elements for an analysis of policy considerations pertaining to the social safety net. The discussion, however, believes that tax-based credits and their built-in incentives in themselves do constitute one aspect of the social safety net, one that is normally not seen in relationship to the other aspects of benefit provisions for those who live in the United States legally. Nevertheless, this approach seems to be consistent with the OECD analysis of national welfare structures. What makes the consideration difficult for some analysts is that the benefits of the tax-based programs go to those who are able to generate sufficient resources to be able to declare and file taxes. This means that, to a certain extent—more than is comfortable for many—it is those in the middle and higher class brackets that receive the greater amount of returns from taking the tax deductions and exemptions. It also means that those individuals who enter the country illegally and are not capable of filing without fear of exposing themselves to deportation typically cannot access these benefits, and this is one class of individuals in the United States that as a whole seems to have a greater need of these benefits.

Table 8.2 describes housing programs that are part of nine other countries' social safety nets. Only two of these countries provide more than one type of benefit (Australia and Sweden) while for most of the remaining countries, the housing benefit is an additional benefit. In Japan, however, the structure is one where the benefit is part of the overall umbrella of services provided to those who require assistance from their social safety net.

EARNED INCOME TAX CREDIT (EITC)

The earned income tax credit (EITC) is a tax break for low- and moderate-income working families. It is a program administered by the federal government through the Internal

Revenue Service (IRS). The credit is a tax relief that is identified and credited by filing federal income taxes. For those who qualify, the EITC acts as a wage supplement; therefore, it is a form of income maintenance. An increasing number of states also have their own earned income tax credits, most of which are based on the federal credit. The estimated 2003 cost for the program is $34.2 billion which compares to actual claims made through EITC of $31.46 billion.

Originally enacted in 1975 primarily for the purpose of tax relief, the EITC grew into a visible tax-transfer system that became a significant element of the antipoverty component of the social safety net. The program was significantly expanded four times from the mid-1980s onward: 1986, 1990, 1993, and most recently in 2001. "Through these expansions, the EITC became a central element of federal efforts to boost income from work and lessen poverty among families with children, a set of goals often called the 'make work pay' strategy" (Johnson, 2001, 3). At first it was an attractive program to politicians from both sides of the political spectrum because of its income-based approach—it was a work-oriented alternative to existing welfare programs. However, the program did not remain in favor with many individuals because as Ventry (2001) indicates,

> By the 1990s, the same political forces that had nurtured the EITC threatened to eliminate it. The EITC was now part of the problem; it had begun to look more like a welfare subsidy (replete with work disincentives, poor targeting, and high costs), and less like a tax offset. It had become simply another federal handout, a welfare program administered through the tax system. (1)

The federal EITC has the effect of offsetting some of the income taxes paid by low- and moderate-income taxpayers and by offsetting part or all of the federal payroll taxes that finance Social Security and Medicare (Johnson, 2001). Although some fear that it would be a disincentive for work, studies have typically indicated the opposite, the expansions of the EITC in the 1980s have been a major factor behind the trend toward greater participation in the workforce; so too in the states that have enacted their own EITC programs (Johnson, 2001; Ventry, 2001). As Ventry points out, "[the] credit provides unambiguous incentives for single workers to participate in the labor force" (2001, 41). Ventry goes on to say that studies demonstrate that EITC

- only has a slight impact in reducing the total number of hours worked by those already in the workforce,
- raises the workforce participation rates of single women who might otherwise choose welfare over work, and
- raises workforce participation among married men.

Data from the Center on Budget and Policy Priorities show that the federal EITC lifts more children out of poverty than any other government program (Johnson, Llobera, and Zahradnik, 2003). Out of about 4.8 million people that are identified as being removed from poverty due to the federal credit, 2.6 million are children.

The states are happy with the EITC approach because it is seen as a way to continue fighting child poverty, assists low-income families who enter or remain in the workforce by providing them with additional funds (understanding that minimum wage jobs are often not enough to lift a family out of poverty), and it is a way to ensure in times of tax cuts followed by needed tax increases that low-income individuals do not bear most of the brunt of new taxes (this is especially important "because most state tax systems rely heavily on regressive sales, excise, and property taxes" [Johnson, 2001, 7], not to mention that nearly half of the states impose an income tax on working-poor families).[14]

The EITC can be broken down into three distinct ranges based on the amount of income earned: a *subsidy range* (each additional dollar of income is supplemented by the credit), a *flat range* (when increased earnings do not change the amount of credit received), and the *phase-out range* (when credit is gradually reduced or phased out as the worker's earnings increase; California Legislative Analyst Office, 1997). Johnson, Llobera, and Zahradnik (2003) explain that the way the federal EITC works is that it goes only to households with earnings. The size of the credit increases as earnings increase, but only to a certain point. The credit is capped at $4,204 for a family with two children and $2,547 for a family with one child. The federal credit then phases out gradually at a slightly higher income level for married couple families than for other family types. Families with two children may qualify with incomes up to $34,692. Low-income workers without a qualifying child can also receive a federal credit, but the maximum credit for individuals or couples without children was only $382 in 2003.

State EITC programs are similarly structured, however, at a concomitant lower scale, and paid from the states' general funds. Fifteen of the seventeen states with programs (and the District of Columbia) align themselves closely with the federal program, utilizing the same eligibility rules for families with children, even stating their credit as a specified percentage of the federal credit. States provide the credit in a refundable format—the family receives a refund check if the credit is higher than the tax they have to pay—or nonrefundable format where the family's tax liability would be eliminated. Chart 8.2 is an example of how the EITC works at the federal level and two typical state refund levels.

TAX PROVISIONS RELATED TO RETIREMENT, HEALTH, POVERTY, EMPLOYMENT, DISABILITY AND OTHER SOCIAL ISSUES

> Analyzing the effectiveness of tax provisions at achieving their policy goals often involves examining the distribution of benefits from the provisions allocated by the income class of those who take advantage of the provisions. (United States House of Representatives, Committee on Ways and Means, 2000, section 13, 2/55)

In keeping with the analysis of the tax system, it is worth noting what other impacts the income tax structure has on

Chart 8.2
Earned Income Tax Credit Levels for Federal and State Credits in 2003

Earned Income Tax Credit Amounts by Family Income Levels, 2003[15]				
	Gross earnings	**Federal EITC**	**25% State EITC**	**15 State EITC**
Family of four with two children				
• Half-time minimum wage	$5,350	$2,140	$535	$321
• Full-time minimum wage	$10,700	$4,204	$1,051	$631
• Wages equal federal poverty line	$18,800	$3,347	$837	$502
• Wages equal 150% of poverty line	$28,200	$1,367	$342	$205
Family of three with one child				
• Half-time minimum wage	$5,350	$1,819	$455	$273
• Full-time minimum wage	$10,700	$2,547	$637	$382
• Wages equal federal poverty line	$14,600	$2,547	$637	$382
• Wages equal 150% of poverty line	$21,900	$1,401	$350	$210

Source: Adapted from Johnson, Llobera, & Zahradnik, 2003, p. 4.

social safety net issues. Although not specific programmatic components in the U.S. social safety net, there are certain redistributive and income-maintaining elements within the tax code that have a positive impact in helping those who need assistance (although the argument can be made that the benefits are not well distributed because of the regressive factor—the lower the income, the less the tax code benefit an individual, family, or household can receive).

One of the older forms of tax relief and redistribution through deferrals is profit sharing and stock bonus plans that qualify under the IRS code. These programs benefit those who have worked a significant amount of time in a somewhat uninterrupted circumstance; consequently, those benefiting the most are those from moderate to higher income brackets. The basic form of these programs is defined and carefully regulated under the Employee Retirement Income Security Act of 1974 (ERISA). The most popular plan under this type of program is the 401(k), an employer-sponsored program where employees can elect to receive cash or have their employers contribute a portion of their earnings to a qualified profit sharing, stock bonus, or a pension plan (these plans also favor those who work for firms employing more than ten workers). Tax relief and income maintenance are components of this tax-based instrument because it is what is termed a deferred compensation plan, meaning that the income generated from these plans is not taxed until it is taken out under the guidelines set forth by law (such as minimum and maximum amount of contributions, minimum age requirement for withdrawal, approach to withdrawal, and amount requirements). Noncompliance with these regulations leads to significant penalties to contributors and participants. Two potential advantages are discernible. There is the ability to earn tax-free

returns to savings; the participant is able to earn a higher rate of return through a pension plan rather than through a full-taxed savings plan. There is also the expectation that the participant's tax rate will be lower during retirement, the expected time of life for the withdrawal of the funds.

Another popular plan is the individual retirement account (IRA). In these accounts, a qualifying individual or couple can currently put away up to $3,500 per any one year and have the amount deducted from their income tax returns (in their 1040 forms). However, the IRA deduction is phased out as a filing individual or couple increases their earnings beyond stipulated levels. The investment income is not taxed until it is withdrawn in accordance to regulations. A variation of the IRA is the Roth IRA in which an individual may make a nondeductible contribution, again currently of up to $3,500 per year. Earnings accumulate on a tax-free basis. Both types of IRAs incur penalties of 10 percent for early withdrawal unless:

1. the owner of the account reaches the age of 59 1/2 or dies; or

2. the owner becomes disabled prior to age 59 1/2; or

3. withdrawal is one of a series of substantially equal periodic payments made at least annually over the life or life expectancy of the owner (and owner and beneficiary); or

4. withdrawal is used to pay medical expenses in excess of 7.5 percent of the adjusted gross income (AGI) or for insurance premiums while owner is unemployed; or

5. withdrawal is used by a first-home buyer to cover expenses (there is a $10,000 lifetime cap) or for qualified higher education expenses.

Continuing the breakdown of tax incentives as identified in the U.S. House of Representatives' Committee on Ways and Means' *Green Book Report 2000*, about one-third of Social Security recipients pay taxes on their benefits because they earn more than allowable limits. The rationale for the tiered structure is to minimize the amount of additional benefits that higher-earning individuals receive. In addition, this approach ensures that more of the funds are given to those who have a greater need for the money.

Employer contributions to group health insurance policies are not taxable to employees. The idea of this policy is to encourage compensation to employees in the form of health coverage rather than a cash subsidy. The impact of this form of tax relief is that the exclusion has allowed for a majority of the population to receive health insurance as a consequence of their own employment or that of a family member. "[Nearly] 75% of all workers under age 65 [are] covered by employment-based health insurance" (United States House of Representatives, Committee on Ways and Means, 2000, section 13, 16/54).

Self-employed individuals are currently able to deduct 60 percent of their health insurance expenses incurred for themselves, spouses, and dependents. According to the Committee on Ways and Means, the "exclusion from income of Medicare benefits has never been expressly established by statute" (2000, section 13, 24/55), indicating that IRS rulings and regulations are the ones that allow for Part A and Part B benefits to be excluded. The effect of the exclusion is to attempt to not allow the erosion of benefits for those who are dependent on the benefits because of what could be termed, through the means-tests, the receiving of higher income.

Individuals are also allowed an itemized deduction for unreimbursed medical expenses above a specified minimum (7.5 percent as of 1987); however, nonprescription drugs are ineligible. Eligible costs include (1) health insurance; (2) diagnosis, treatment, or disease prevention, or for purpose of affecting any structure or function of the body; (3) transportation mainly for and essential to medical care; (4) lodging away from home primarily for and essential to medical care (up to $50 per night in 2000); and (5) prescription drugs and insulin. As far as a policy to help equity, unfortunately, those in the higher tax rates reap the greater benefits from each deductible dollar spent on medical expenses than those in the lower rates. "However, because the floor automatically rises with a taxpayer's income, higher income taxpayers are able to deduct a smaller amount (if any) of medical expenses above their floor than are low-income taxpayers incurring the same aggregate amount of medical expenses" (United States House of Representatives, Committee on Ways and Means, 2000, section 13, 26/55).

According to the *Green Book Report 2000*, other exclusions of social safety net benefits from taxes resulting from IRS rulings include those for SSI and for TANF (formerly AFDC public assistance benefit programs). In addition, there are a number of specific tax credits made available to those who qualify. These credits include:

dependent care tax credit

hope credit and lifetime learning credit

qualified state tuition programs and education IRAs

student loan interest

employer-provided dependent care exclusion

work opportunity tax credit

welfare-to-work tax credit

worker's compensation and special benefits for disabled coal miners

additional standard deduction for the elderly and the blind

tax credits for the elderly and certain disabled individuals

owner-occupied housing expense tax deductions

low-income housing credit

adoption expenses tax credits and deductions

child tax credit

For a basic explanation of what these programs are, please refer to the glossary of this volume. These tax credits and exemptions work by meeting eligibility criteria, and they impact the total amounts of the taxpayer's adjusted gross income. Credit for the deductions are graduated, typically reducing the credit amount as the taxpayer's adjusted gross income increases.

It is difficult to provide a one-to-one program comparison of the programs described in this chapter and those that make up the social safety net in other countries. The SSI component is only one part of benefits families receive. For example, a comparative analysis is better served by bundling SSI and food stamps data with data on TANF and other closely related programs. What can be compared to some extent are the housing assistance programs and the role that tax-rate structure deductions and exemptions have in forming part of the social safety net structure. Table 8.3 attempts to provide a basic comparison of tax treatments in nine OECD countries to see how they use their taxing structure to assist in the pursuit of their social policy and how these may interact with the existing social safety net framework.[16]

The best source of information for the programs in this chapter is the *Green Book Report 2000* written for the U.S. House of Representatives' Committee on Ways and Means, because it has relatively current data on all of these programs, the purpose of which is to provide legislators with program analysis to assist in their policy-making and resource allotment activities. The second best source, mainly for the SSI program, is the Social Security Administration's *Annual Statistical Supplement 2001*. More current information is available at the appropriate SSI Web site. For housing issues, refer to the HUD Web site and follow the many links available through that site. The *Statistical Abstract of the United States* provides a basic statistical source of information. The U.S. Census Web site can provide data that the reader can message in order to provide a more detailed set of data for communities within the state.

Needless to say, much of the information on tax incentives and structures requires knowledge of policy as well as output measures. These are not easily found in any one area and approaches are influenced by political persuasion. The sources found in this bibliography should be able to assist readers interested in entering this maze for whatever their reason or reasons.

International information sources such as those provided by the OECD, the International Monetary Fund (IMF), and the World Bank Web sites are useful, particularly their research data and working papers. For European data, the European Union Social Indicator Web sites provide an excellent introduction to sources and materials, although most of these will not be immediately accessible due to cost considerations and the need to navigate their Web sites with a priori full knowledge of the subject matter. The United Nations Statistical Office and the United Nations Development Programme also provide a staging area for further information. Still, the reader interested in international data may have to go through individual national Web sites to find information on these supplemental programs that make up part of the social safety net in any country.

NOTES

1. "If only one member of the couple qualifies for SSI, part of the ineligible spouse's income is considered to be that of the eligible spouse (this procedure is called "deeming"). If a couple separates, each person is treated as an individual in the month following the month of separation." "If an unmarried child living at home is under age 18, some of the parent's income is deemed to that child. If an immigrant is sponsored into the United States, some of the sponsor's and the sponsor's spouse income may be deemed to that immigrant" (United States House of Representatives, Committee on Ways and Means, 2000, section 3, 6/54).

2. The maximum monthly SSI benefit is $512 per month for an individual, $769 per month for a couple in 2000.

3. Public institutions are prisons, hospitals, nursing homes, or any institution that is operated or administered by a governmental unit (U.S. House of Representatives, Committee on Ways and Means, 2000, section 3, 11/54).

4. State options for Medicare eligibility as defined by the U.S. House of Representatives' Committee on Ways and Means (2000, section 3, 12/54–13/54) are:

Option 1: Current law allows the Social Security Administration to enter into agreements with states to cover all SSI recipients with Medicaid eligibility; therefore, SSI recipients are not required to make a separate application for Medicaid. Thirty-two states and the District of Columbia exercise this option as of January 1, 2000.

Option 2: States provide Medicaid eligibility, but only if the recipient completes a separate application with the state's administering agency. Seven states pursue this option (Alaska, Idaho, Kansas, Nebraska, Nevada, Oregon, and Utah).

Option 3: States may impose more restrictive criteria than SSI's, as long as the criteria chosen are no more restrictive than the state's approved Medicaid state plan in January 1972. Eleven states use this option (Connecticut, Hawaii, Illinois, Indiana, Minnesota, Missouri, New Hampshire, North Dakota, Ohio, Oklahoma, and Virginia).

5. Disability ranges usually go from 10 percent to 100 percent, in 10 percent intervals.

6. In 2000, the eligibility requirement to meet the low-income criterion was (U.S. House of Representatives, 2000, section 13, 100/106):

Married with one dependent—$27,468 or less in income ($1,532 for each additional dependent)
Single—$22,887 or less in income

7. The elderly and homeless may also use food stamps to use concession-priced means from authorized restaurants.

8. Net income is computed by deducting the following from monthly gross income:

1. Twenty percent of earned income.
2. A standard deduction of $134 for fiscal year 2000.
3. The amount paid for dependent care (up to $200 a month per child under age 2 and $175 for all other dependents) while the dependent's caretaker is working or looking for work.
4. Any out-of-pocket medical expenses in excess of a $35 deductible for a person aged 60 or older or a disabled person. If more than one person in the household is aged or disabled, $35 is subtracted once before deducting combined medical expenses.
5. A child-support deduction for legally obligated child support paid for a nonhousehold member.
6. An excess shelter deduction, which is total shelter costs including utilities minus 50 percent of income after all the above deductions have been sub-tracted. Effective October 1, 2000, the limit was $300. For households whose certification period began after March 1, 2001, the limit rose to $340. Households with an aged or disabled person do not have a limit on this deduction. (Social Security Administration, 2001, 77)

9. HUD programs include the following (see General Service Administration, 2002):

Interest Reduction Payments Rental and Cooperative Housing for Lower Income Families
Rehabilitation Mortgage Insurance
Manufactured Home Loan Insurance Financing Purchase of Manufactured Homes as Principal Residences of Borrowers
Mortgage Insurance for Construction or Substantial Rehabilitation of Condominium Projects
Mortgage Insurance: Homes
Mortgage Insurance: Homes for Disaster Victims
Mortgage Insurance: Homes in Outlying Areas
Mortgage Insurance: Homes in Urban Renewal Areas
Mortgage Insurance: Housing in Older, Declining Areas
Mortgage Insurance: Cooperative Projects
Mortgage Insurance: Manufactured Home Parks
Mortgage Insurance: Hospitals
Mortgage Insurance: Nursing Homes, Intermediate Care Facilities, Board and Care Homes and Assisted Living Facilities
Mortgage Insurance: Purchase of Sales-Type Cooperative Housing Units
Mortgage Insurance: Purchase of Units in Condominiums
Mortgage Insurance: Rental Housing
Mortgage Insurance: Rental and Cooperative Housing for Moderate Income Families and Elderly, Market Interest Rate
Mortgage Insurance: Rental Housing for the Elderly
Mortgage Insurance: Rental Housing in Urban Renewal Areas
Property Improvement Loan Insurance for Improving All Existing Structures and Building of New Nonresidential Structures

Rent Supplements: Rental Housing for Lower Income Families

Supplemental Loan Insurance: Multifamily Rental Housing

Mortgage Insurance for the Purchase or Refinancing of Existing Multifamily Housing Projects

Supportive Housing for the Elderly

Section 245 Graduated Payment Mortgage Program

Mortgage Insurance: Combination and Manufactured Home Lot Loans

Mortgage Insurance: Single Family Cooperative Housing

Operating Assistance for Troubled Multifamily Housing Projects

Mortgage Insurance: Homes in Military Impacted Areas

Mortgage Insurance: Two Year Operating Loss Loans, Section 223(d)

Land Sales: Certain Subdivided Land

Housing Counseling Assistance Program

Manufactured Home Construction and Safety Standards

Mortgage Insurance: Growing Equity Mortgages

Adjustable Rate Mortgages

Supportive Housing for Persons with Disabilities

Home Equity Conversion Mortgages

Mortgages Insurance for Single Room Occupancy (SRO) Projects

Housing Finance Agencies (HFA) Risk Sharing

Qualified Participating Entities (QPE) Risk Sharing

Multifamily Housing Service Coordinators

Federally Assisted Low-Income Housing Drug Elimination

Section 8 Housing Assistance Payments Program: Special Allocations

Multifamily Assisted Housing Reform and Affordability Act

Officer Next Door Sales Program

Multifamily Property Disposition

Community Development Block Grants/Entitlement Grants

Community Development Block Grants/Small Cities Program

Community Development Block Grants/Special Purpose Grants/Insular Areas

Community Development Block Grants/Special Purpose Grants/Technical Assistance Program

Community Development Block Grants/State's Program

Emergency Shelter Grants Program

Supportive Housing Program

Shelter Plus Care

HOME Investment Partnerships Program

Housing Opportunities for Persons with AIDS

Opportunities for Youth: Youthbuild Program

Empowerment Zones Program

Community Development Block Grants/Economic Development Initiative

Self-Help Homeownership Opportunity Program

Community Development Block Grants/Section 108 Loan Guarantees

Section 8 Moderate Rehabilitation Single Room Occupancy

Rural Housing and Economic Development

Teacher Next Door Initiative

Single Family Property Disposition

New Approach Anti-Drug Grants

Dollar Home Sales

Assisted Living Conversion for Eligible Multifamily Housing Projects

Equal Opportunity in Housing

Fair Housing Assistance Program: State and Local

Non-Discrimination in Federally-Assisted Programs (On the Basis of Age)

Non-Discrimination in Federally Assisted and Conducted Programs (On the Basis of Disability)

Non-Discrimination in Federally Assisted Programs (On the Basis of Race, Color, or National Origin)

Non-Discrimination in the Community Development Block Grant Program (On the Basis of Race, Color, National Origin, Religion, or Sex)

Architectural Barriers Act Enforcement

Fair Housing Initiatives and Administrative Enforcement Initiative Program

Fair Housing Initiatives Program (FHIP) Education and Outreach Initiative

Fair Housing Initiatives Program (FHIP) Private Enforcement Initiative

Employment Opportunities for Lower Income Persons and Businesses

Fair Housing Initiatives and Fair Housing Organizations Initiative Program

Non-Discrimination on the Basis of Disability by Public Entities

Non-Discrimination on the Basis of Sex in Education Programs and Activities Receiving Federal Financial Assistance

General Research and Technology Activity

Community Outreach Partnership Center Program

Community Development Work-Study Program

Hispanic-Serving Institutions Assisting Communities

Alaska Native/Native Hawaiian Institutions Assisting Communities

Doctoral Dissertation Research Grants

Early Doctoral Student Research Grants

HUD Urban Scholars Fellowship Grants

Tribal Colleges and Universities Program

Historically Black Colleges and Universities Program

Public and Indian Housing

Lower Income Housing Assistance Program: Section 8 Moderate Rehabilitation

Indian Community Development Block Grant Program

Public and Indian Housing: Indian Loan Guarantee Program

Demolition and Revitalization of Severely Distressed Public Housing

Indian Housing Block Grants

Title VI Federal Guarantees for Financing Tribal Housing Activities

Resident Opportunity and Supportive Services

Section 8 Housing Choice Vouchers

Public Housing Capital Fund

Lead-Based Paint Hazard Control in Privately-Owned Housing

Healthy Homes Initiative Grants

10. *Olmstead v. L.C.*, 525 U.S. 1062; 119 S. Ct. 633; 142 L. Ed. 2d 571 (1998).

11. Exclusions to gross income exclude the following: $480 for each dependent; $400 for any elderly family, or a person with a disability; and some medical deductions for families headed by an elderly person or a person with disabilities. (United States Department of Housing and Urban Development, 2000b)

12. The formula for the *very low-income limit* for a four-person family is calculated as follows:

1. 50 percent of the area median family income is calculated and set as the preliminary four-person family income limit,

2. if it is lower, the four-person income limit is increased to the amount at which 35 percent of it equals 85 percent of the

annualized two-bedroom Section 8 FMR (this adjusts income limits upward for areas where rental housing costs are unusually high in relation to the median income);

3. if it is higher, the four-person income limit is reduced to the greater of the amount at which 30 percent of it equals 100 percent of the two-bedroom FMR or 80 percent of the U.S. median family income level (this adjusts income limits downward for areas of unusually high median family incomes);

4. to minimize program management problems, income limits are held at FY 2002 levels for areas where lower income limits would result because of FMR reductions; and,

5. in no instance are income limits less than if based on the state nonmetropolitan median family income level.

The formula for the *low-income limit* is calculated as:

1. setting the four-person low-income limit at (i.e., 80%/50%) times the relevant four-person very low-income limit;

2. the only exception is that the resulting income limit family income may not exceed the U.S. median family level ($50,056 for FY 2003) except when justified by high housing costs.

13. Also receiving grants in:

- fiscal year 1997—6 insular areas and 121 Indian tribes or tribal organizations;
- fiscal year 1998—6 insular areas and 128 Indian tribes or tribal organizations; and
- fiscal year 1999—5 insular areas and 130 Indian tribes or tribal organizations. (Social Security Administration, 2001, 81)

14. "In 19 of 42 states with a personal income tax, working poor families with children may pay income taxes. For a two-parent family of four in the states that taxed the poor in 2001, the average income tax threshold the point at which families began owing tax was $12,900, some $5,000 below the poverty line for a family of four. The average tax on a family with income at the poverty line was $244.

"In addition, most states rely heavily on sales, excise, and property taxes, with the result that state tax systems are quire regressive. In 2002, the average state and local tax burden on the poorest fifth of married, non-elderly families was 11.4 percent of income. By contrast, the average burden on the wealthiest one percent of such families was 7.3 percent of income" (Johnson, Llobera, and Zahradnik, 2003, 2).

15. In 2001, the percent of federal credit refunded by states breaks down as follows (Johnson, 2001, 9):

Refundable credits: Colorado is 10%. District of Columbia is 25%. Kansas is 10%. Maryland is 15% (also offers non-refundable EITC set at 50% of the credit; low- and moderate-income taxpayers may claim one or other, not both). Massachusetts is 15%. Minnesota is 25%–45% depending on earnings. New Jersey is 15% (20%, increase slated for 2003)—to families with incomes less than $20,000. New York is 25% (30%, increase slated for 2003). Oklahoma is 5%. Vermont is 32%. Wisconsin is 4% (one child), 14% (two children), 43% (three children).

Non-refundable credits: Illinois is 5%. Iowa is 6.5%. Maine is 5%. Oregon is 5%. Rhode Island is 25%.

16. Please refer to the analysis in chapters 5 and 6 to provide a correlation of some of the terms and how these programs may link.

PRINCIPAL SOURCES FOR ILLUSTRATIONS

Adema, W. (2001). *Labour market and social policy: Net social expenditures.* 2nd ed. Paris: OECD, Directorate for Education,
Employment, Labour and Social Affairs Committee (Occasional Working Paper No. 52). Retrieved from: http://www.olis.oecd.org/OLIS/2001DOC.NSF/LINKTO/DEELSA-ELSA-WD(2001)5.

Johnson, N. (December 2001). *A hand up: How state earned income tax credits help working families escape poverty in 2001.* Washington, D.C.: Center on Budget and Policy Priorities. Retrieved from: http://www.cbpp.org/12-27-01sfp.pdf.

Organization for Economic Co-operation and Development. (1999). *Synopsis of member nations social programs.* Washington, D.C.: Author. Retrieved from: http://www.oecd.org.

Social Security Administration. (2001). *Annual statistical supplement, 2001 to the Social Security Bulletin.* Baltimore: Social Security Administration, Office of Policy. Retrieved from: http://www.ssa.gov/statistics/Supplement/2001/supp01.pdf.

United States Census Bureau. (2002). *Statistical abstract of the United States 2002.* Washington, D.C.: Government Printing Office. Retrieved from: http://www.census.gov/statab/www/.

United States Department of Agriculture. (July 2003). *Characteristics of food stamp households: Fiscal year 2002 (Advanced Report).* Washington, D.C.: Office of Analysis, Nutrition, and Evaluation. Retrieved from: http://www.fns.usda.gov/oane/MENU/Published/FSP/FILES/Participation/2002AdvRpt.pdf.

United States Department of Agriculture, Food and Nutrition Service. (2003). Characteristics of food stamp households in FY 2001. In *Applicant and recipients,* Food and Nutrition Services Web site. Retrieved from: http://www.fns.usda.gov/fsp/rules/Memo/Support/03/2001-characteristics.htm.

United States House of Representatives, Committee on Ways and Means. (2000). *The 2000 green book: Background material and data on programs within the jurisdiction of the Committee on Ways and Means.* Retrieved from: http://aspe.hhs.gov/2000gh.

BIBLIOGRAPHY

Allen, J.T. (2002). Negative income tax. Henderson, D.R., ed. *The concise encyclopedia of economics.* Indianapolis: Liberty Fund, Inc. Retrieved from: http://www.econlib.org/library/Enc/NegativeIncomeTax.html.

California Legislative Analyst Office. (1997). *Earned income tax credit.* Sacramento: Legislative Analyst Office. Retrieved from: http://www.loa.ca.gov/part5b_earned_income_tax_credit_pi97.html.

Chatterjee, P. (1999). *Repackaging the welfare state.* Washington, D.C.: National Association of Social Workers.

Dobelstein, A.W. (1996). *Social welfare: Policy and analysis.* Chicago: Nelson-Hall Publishers.

Friedman, M. (1962). *Capitalism and freedom.* Chicago: University of Chicago Press.

General Service Administration. (2002). *Programs for Department of Housing and Urban Development.* The Catalog of Federal Domestic Assistance Web site. Retrieved from: http://www.cfda.gov/public/browse_agy.asp?agy_id=14&st=1.

Gilbert, N., Specht, H., and Terrell. (1993). *Dimensions of social welfare policy.* 3rd ed. Englewood Cliffs, NJ: Prentice Hall.

Haveman, R.H. (1987). *Poverty policy and poverty research.* Madison, WI: University of Wisconsin Press.

Johnson, N. (December 2001). *A hand up: How state earned income tax credits help working families escape poverty in 2001.*

Washington, D.C.: Center on Budget and Policy Priorities. Retrieved from: http://www.cbpp.org/12-27-01sfp.pdf.

Johnson, N., Llobera, J., and Zahradnik, B. (March 2003). *A hand up: How state earned income tax credits help working families escape poverty in 2003*. Washington, D.C.: Center on Budget and Policy Priorities. Retrieved from: http://www.cbpp.org/3-3-03sfp.htm.

Moffitt, R.A. (2002). *Milton Friedman, the negative income tax, and the evolution of U.S. welfare policy*. First draft. Retrieved from: http://www.econ.jhu.edu/People/Moffitt/friedman_v1.pdf.

Moneychimp. (2002). Adjusted Gross Income. *Glossary of terms*. Retrieved from: http://www.moneychimp.com/glossary/agi.htm.

Organization for Economic Cooperation and Development. (1999). Benefit Systems and Work Incentives 1999 Country Chapters. *OECD 1999 synopsis of member nations social programs*. Washington, D.C.: OECD. Retrieved from: http://www.oecd.org/EN/document/0,,EN-document-211-5-no-1-31684-211,00.html.

Schwartz, J.E., and Volgy, T.J. (1992). *The forgotten Americans*. New York: W.W. Norton and Company.

Social Security Administration. (2001). *Annual statistical supplement, 2001 to the Social Security Bulletin*. Baltimore: Social Security Administration, Office of Policy. Retrieved from: http://www.ssa.gov/statistics/Supplement/2001/supp01.pdf.

United States Department of Housing and Urban Development. (2000a). *FY 2000–FY 2006 strategic plan*. Washington, D.C.: HUD. Retrieved from: http://www.hud.gov/reform/strategicplan.pdf.

United States Department of Housing and Urban Development. (2000b). Renting: HUD's public housing Program. *Home and Communities* Web site. Retrieved from: http://www.hud.gov/renting/phprog.cfm.

United States Department of Housing and Urban Development. (2002). About Housing. *Home and Community* Web site. Retrieved from: http://www.hud.gov/offices/hsg/hsgabout.cfm.

United States Department of Housing and Urban Development. (2003). *FY 2003 HUD income limits briefing materials*. Washington, D.C.: Office of Policy Development and Research. Retrieved from: http://www.huduser.org/datasets/il/fmr03/BRIEFING-MATERIAL-2-19-03.pdf.

United States House of Representatives, Committee on Ways and Means. (2000). *The 2000 Green Book: Background material and data on programs within the jurisdiction of the Committee on Ways and Means*. Retrieved from: http://aspe.hhs.gov/2000gh.

Ventry, D.J., Jr. (2001). *The collision of tax and welfare politics: The political history of the earned income tax credit, 1969–1999*. JCPR Working Paper #149. Chicago: Joint Center for Poverty Research, Northwestern University/ University of Chicago. Retrieved from: http://www.jcpr.org/wpfiles/ventry_eitc99_update.PDF.

Table 8.1
Costs of Supplemental Security Income in 2000

Federal benefit rate change, effective January 2001	
Cost-of-living adjustment	3.5 percent
Monthly amount for—	
Individual living in his or her own household	$531
Couple with both members eligible	$796

Program Data

Total:	
Benefits paid in 2000	$31.6 billion
Number of recipients, December 2000	6.7 million
Average benefit, December 2000	$385.52
Federally administered payments:	
Benefits paid in 2000	$30.7 billion
Number of recipients, December 2000	6.6 million
Average benefit, December 2000	$378.82
Federal SSI payments:	
Benefits paid in 2000	$27.3 billion
Number of recipients, December 2000	6.3 million
Average benefit, December 2000	$351.48
Federally administered state supplementation:	
Benefits paid in 2000	$3.4 billion
Number of recipients, December 2000	[1]2.5 million
Average benefit, December 2000	$112.16
State-administered supplementation:	
Benefits paid in 2000	$0.9 billion
Number of recipients, December 2000	[2]0.7 million
Average benefit, December 2000	$110.95

1. Includes 2.2 million persons receiving federal SSI and state supplementation and 0.3 million persons receiving state supplementation only.
2. Includes 83,500 persons receiving state supplementation only.

Source: Social Security Administration. (2001). *Annual Statistical Supplement, 2001 to the Social Security Bulletin.* Baltimore: Social Security Administration, Office of Policy. Retrieved from http://www.ssa.gov/policy/docs/statcomps/supplement/2001/supp01.pdf.

Table 8.2
Housing Programs in the United States and Nine OECD Countries

Country	Housing program

United States of America	• Federal government provides low-income housing assistance through three mechanisms:
	  1. Low-rent public housing administered by state public housing authorities (PHAs)
	  2. Housing choice vouchers to subsidize private-market rentals (also administered by PHAs)
	  3. Direct contact with some 20,000 owners of certain private projects
	• Not entitlements, access to assistance rationed through waiting lists
	• Gross annual income of participants have to be less than 80% of area median income.
	• Assistance is generally about 30% of the tenant's adjusted income
	• Primary adjustments of $480 per child per year. And $400 per adult per year; medical expenses more than 3% of gross income also deducted, but only if the household has an elderly or disabled head or spouse
	• Not taxable
	• No statutory limit on duration of assistance
	• Benefits prorated to households with undocumented non-citizens

Germany	• Anyone with low income and high rent or high financial obligations resulting from own dwelling may be eligible • Housing allowance granted to as a tabulated housing allowance and also, since 1991, as a lump-sum housing allowance for tenant households whose members receive social assistance payments or war victim's support. Tabulation calculated as percentage of differences between rent or financial obligation eligible for assistance and a contribution covered by the tenant or owner occupier • Owner occupied housing may entitle owner to a housing allowance as a home-ownership subsidy • Tabulated housing benefit depends on the number of persons in the household, family income and the rent or burden from financial obligations (up to ceilings differentiated according to regional cost level, quality and age of dwelling, household size) • Recipients of social assistance payments or war victims' support receive a housing allowance equal to 100% of rent. Rent amounts for those under social assistance is estimated in accordance to published statistics • Housing assistance benefit based on an assessable earnings definition (gross earnings of all household members, family benefits, and unemployment benefits). No additional income tests are required • Not taxable

The Netherlands	• All children under 18 qualify for child benefits
	• Cost wholly borne by the government. Benefits are not income related (and are not included in any means test)
	• Family allowances range from 321.92 guilders per quarter for families with one child under age 6 to 641.69 guilders per quarter per child for families with six children between ages 12 to 17
	• As of January 5, 1997, parents of handicapped children aged 3 to 18 can get a supplementary benefit as a partial compensation of the extra costs (TOG-agreement)
	  • benefit for parents of multihandicapped children (mental and physical): 389 guilders per quarter
	  • benefit for children that are seriously physically handicapped or chronologically ill: 260 guilders per quarter

(continued)

Table 8.2 (*continued*)

Country	Housing program
	• Adjustments occur twice per year on basis of price index changes • Nontaxable benefit
Czech Republic	• Housing contribution towards household costs constitutes a part of minimum living standard (MLS). The benefit is designed to assist low-income families and individuals in covering expenditure connected with housing • Benefit is differentiated by the income situation of the family and the number of persons in the household. Housing benefits are provided irrespective of the type of housing—whether it is a community or co-operative flat, privately owned flat or privately owned house—and actual cost of housing. • Entitlement to housing benefits belongs to the owner or tenant of a flat, who is registered as a permanent resident, if the family income does not exceed the amount of the family minimum living standard multiplied by a coefficient of 1.60 • Formula: Housing = family's household - (fam. Household amt. x rel. fam. inc.) benefit amount min. fam. living std. x 1.60
Poland	• Housing benefits are paid by local authorities to low income households. Benefit is outside the social assistance system • Low-income formula: under income guidelines -minimum pension per capita • Gross benefit formula: difference between costs of rent and standard cost provided by the legislation.
Norway	• There is a special government housing benefit (housing allowance) for persons with a combination of low income and high housing costs. Eligible groups in 1999 were: • recipients of pensions or allowances from the National Insurance Scheme (NIS) or comparable pension benefits • recipients of Social Economic Assistance (SEA) • elderly persons (from the age of 65) • households with children under the age of 18 • Formula for housing allowance is 70% of the difference between the actual and a standard ("reasonable") housing expense. The standard is calculated on the basis of an increasing percentage above a specified income level. Households w/o children = 15% of income up to 65,000 (0.003 percentage point is added for every additional NOK 1,000 in income) Families w/Children—2-person household = 15% of income up to 65,000 (0.003 percentage point is added for every additional NOK 1,000 in income) Families w/Children—3-person household = 15% of income up to 80,000 (0.003 percentage point is added for every additional NOK 1,000 in income) Families w/Children—4+ person household = 15% of income up to 90,000 (0.003 percentage point is added for every additional NOK 1,000 in income)
Sweden	• 3 main forms of housing assistance: • the income-tested housing allowance, it varies according to age, the income, the housing cost, and the number of children;

Table 8.2 (*continued*)

Country	Housing program
	• rent is fully covered for social assistance claimants, with a supplement to the housing allowance; • an income-tested housing supplement (BTP) also exists for pensioners • Total housing costs are divided in brackets; 50 to 75 per cent per bracket is added to a flat benefit. The size of each bracket and the flat benefit rate depend on age and family situation. Benefit is calculated on a monthly basis according to the expected income during the calendar year but the benefit received during a year is provisional and will be checked against the final income assessment. Capital income is also considered • The housing benefit is income-tested. Reduction rates and disregards depend on age and family situation • Subsidy rate for means-test: Single, less than 29, with no children = 33% Lone parents = 20% Families with no children = 33% Families w/ 1 or more children = 20%
Australia	• There are 2 types of housing assistance available for those who qualify: 1. Rent assistance (RA): a non-taxable income supplement paid to Department of Family and Community clients who rent in the private rental market and pay rent above the applicable rent threshold 2. Public housing: provided by state governments to low income households through a joint Commonwealth-State Housing Agreement • RA is paid at the rate of 75 cents for every dollar of rent paid above the specified minimum rent threshold until the maximum rate is reached • Maximum rates and thresholds vary according to a customer's family situation, the number of children they have and for singles without children whether accommodation is shared with others • Rent thresholds and maximum rates are indexed in March and September each year to reflect CPI increases • RA is added to family payments for abatement purposes in the case of single parents and couples with children. For families with children RA is withdrawn at the rate of 30 cents in the dollar. RA is added to the basic benefit for people without children and withdrawn at the rate of 70 cents in the dollar after basic benefit under the benefits abatement regime • Public housing rents are set by state governments at levels that ensure tenants pay no more than 20–25 percent of their income in housing costs • Housing benefits nontaxable
Japan	• Social assistance consist of seven parts or aids, provided for those who are unable to provide minimum living standards: (1) livelihood aid, (2) housing aid, (3) medical aid, (4) occupational aid, (5) education aid, (6) maternity aid, and (7) funeral aid. • All seven types of assistance are means-tested against gross earnings. Earnings net of tax and social security contributions up to 8,340 yen per month are disregarded (monthly disregard is assumed to increase proportionally with gross earnings)

(*continued*)

Table 8.2 (*continued*)

Country	Housing program
	• Household expenses (Category 2) are related to the number of family members:
	Korea

	Number of family members			
	1	2	3	4 + X
Basic amount (in yen per month)	43,780	48,460	53,720	58,450 + 440 X

• Benefits are not taxable
• Duration is for as long as needed

Korea — None

Source: Adapted from Organization for Economic Co-operation and Development. (1999). Synopsis of Member Nations social programs. Washington, D.C.: Author. Retrieved from http://www.oecd.org.

Table 8.3
Taxing Structures in the United States and Nine OECD Countries

Country	Taxing structures supporting the social safety net
United States of America	• Basic relief is $7,200 for married couple filing jointly; $6,350 for single heads of household, or $4,300 for single individuals • Exemption per person is $2,750, reduced $0.02 for each $2,500 taxpayer income exceeds $189,950 for couple; $158,300 for heads of households; or $126,600 for individuals • Taxpayer entitled to a dependency exemption of $2,750 per each child claimed as a dependent • For each child under 17 claimed as a dependent, taxpayer entitled to a credit of $500, reduced by $50 for each $1000 of gross income over $110,000 for couples and $75,000 for heads of households and individuals

Germany	• 5 different general tax allowances exist apart from the 0 rate bracket:
	  • child tax allowance per dependent child (DM 6,912)
	  • lone parents' allowances (Haushaltsfreibetrag) (DM 5,616)
	  • work related tax allowances—fixed for all working levels (DM 2,000 for each person in work)
	  • tax allowances for social security contributions:
	    • 6,000/12,000 DM (single/couple), lowered by 16% of gross wage to correct for employer's contribution
	    • social security contributions exceeding those amounts deductible up to 1,305/2,610 DM (single/couple)
	    • of remaining expenses in excess of 2,610/5,220 DM (single/couple) are deductible up to 1,305/2,610 DM (single/couple)
	    • church tax is completely deductible
	• Solidarity surcharge of 5.5% of the income tax liability is paid if the calculated income tax is higher than 1,838/3,672 DM (single/couple)
	• Spouses assessed jointly using the splitting method, but have the option to separate tax assessments. Tax liability for a couple utilizes a formula calculated with respect to half of the joint taxable income. The resulting amount is doubled to arrive at the income tax liability of the couple (splitting method)
	• Employee social security contribution schedule;
	  • pension fund: 9.85% of gross earnings up to 102,000 DM
	  • unemployment insurance: 3.25% of gross earnings up to 102,000 DM
	  • sickness: 6.8% of gross earnings up to 76,500 DM
	  • home care insurance: 0.85% of gross earnings up to 76,500 DM

The Netherlands	• All taxpayers are in principle entitled to a basic allowance of 8,799 guilders
	  • if one spouse/partner has noincome or income < 8,380 guilders, 8,380 guilders can be transferred and claimed by the other spouse/partner
	• Additional personal allowances:
	  • single parent supplement: 6,704 guilders for any single parent with dependent children under age 27
	  • extra single parent supplement (see lone-parent benefits section)
	• Supplement eligibility or to use partner's basic allowance requires the taxpayer to meet relevant conditions for at least six months in that year
	• Social security contribution relief:
	  • employee: deductible with exception of health insurance contribution
	  • employers pay employees a "compensation allowance" for exceptional medical expenses that is taxable to the employee
	• Work-related expenses:
	  • as of 1990, commuter travel expenses of < 10km. no longer deductible
	  • other work-related expenses may always (without proof) be deducted at 12% of annual wage (minimum of 258 guilders, maximum of 3,174 guilders)
	• Level of means-tested benefits is fixed as a net value. The benefit supplier is responsible to pay taxes of which levels are based in accordance to family type

(continued)

Table 8.3 (*continued*)

Country	Taxing structures supporting the social safety net
Czech Republic	• Taxable income definition: gross earnings minus the defined tax allowances. • Tax allowances: • Basic = 34,920 CZK per year (1999) • Marital Status = 19,884 CZK if married or living in a common household with a partner who earns no more than 34,920 • Dependent child = 21,600 CZK per child under 18 (or under 26 if in full-time education or disabled) • Social Security Contributions = All • Tax unit = the individual
Poland	• Taxable income = Gross income minus tax allowances • Tax allowances: • Relief for work related expenses (standard deductions depend on the number of workplaces and on whether dwelling place and work place are the same or not • Basic tax credit of PLN 394.80 given as part of tax calculation for those earning < PLN 29,624 • Tax unit = the individual (couples have option of filing joint return)
Norway	• Two definitions of taxable income: (1) personal income, income from work and/or pensions with no deductions, social security tax and surtax are levied on personal income; and (2) ordinary income, taxable income of all type after deductions • Tax credit for stimulating house purchases is in place • Tax allowances/credits (ordinary income): • For tax on ordinary income a flat allowance exists depending on the marriage status (NOK 26,300 class 1, NOK 52,600 class 2) • Basic relief of 21% of personal income, relief bound by a minimum of NOK 3,900 and a maximum of NOK 34,900 • If the family can provide evidence of child-care expenses for children younger than 12 years the couple will get a deduction up to NOK 25,000 for one child and NOK 30,000 for two or more children. The allowance applied to the spouse with the lowest income; the allowance applies also to lone parents • Refundable tax credit for dependent children: NOK 1,820 if aged under 16, NOK 2,540 if aged between 16 and 18 • Lone parents receiving the transitional benefit only (and pensioners receiving the comparable benefit) are exempt from taxation, the ceiling being NOK 90886. When additional income results in the ceiling being exceeded, a special "tax liability limitation schedule" applies • Tax unit: Class 1 = individual (in most cases) Class 2 = joint taxation (for couples, most desirable) When spouse has little or no income
Sweden	• Tax allowances: • Social Security contributions (paid up to 8.06 of the entitlement base amount (8.06 × 37,200), and rounded to the nearest multiple of 100.) • Earned income allowances • if gross earnings are under 1.86 times BA, the allowance is 24% of BA; • if gross earnings are between 1.86 and 2.89 times BA, the allowance is 24% of BA raised with 25 per cent of earnings above 1.86 times BA; • if gross earnings are between 2.89 and 3.04 times BA, the allowance has its maximum value (24% of BA raised with 25% of BA); • if gross earnings are exceeding 3.04 times BA, the maximum value of the allowance is decreased with 10 per cent of the earnings above 3.04 times BA.

Table 8.3 (*continued*)

Country	Taxing structures supporting the social safety net
	Note: The allowance is rounded down to a Multiple of 100. This allowance is also valid on transfer income, but not social assistance. • Each individual (adult) in the household is taxed separately
Australia	• No tax allowances • Tax credits • Standard marital status relief: A taxpayer may claim a tax credit where he or she contributes to the maintenance of a dependent spouse (legal or de facto). The credit is A\$ 1,340 for a dependent spouse and A\$ 1,452 where there are dependent children. The credit is reduced by A\$ 1 for every A\$ 4 by which the spouse's separate net income exceeds A\$ 282 • Relief for low-income earners: an A\$ 150 tax credit is available for taxpayers whose taxable income was less than A\$ 20,700. This credit is reduced by four cents for every A\$ 1 by which the taxpayer's taxable income exceeds this amount, and no tax credit is available once the taxpayer's taxable income exceeds A\$ 24,450 • To contribute towards the cost of basic medical and hospital care a Medicare Levy is imposed on the taxable incomes of resident taxpayers. In 1999–2000 the levy applied at the rate of 1.5 per cent of the taxable income of an individual, a single taxpayer was exempt from the levy where the taxable income was less than or equal to A\$ 13,550. Where a taxpayer was married or was entitled to a child-housekeeper, housekeeper or sole parent rebate no levy was payable if the taxable family income did not exceed A\$ 22,865, the threshold increasing by A\$ 2,100 for each dependent child
Japan	• No tax credits • Tax allowances: • basic exemption: 380,000 yen; • spouse exemption: 380,000 yen if dependent spouse; • special spouse exemption: 380,000 yen; • dependent exemption: 480,000 yen per dependent child under 16; • social security contributions; • employment income deduction (regressive with gross annual earnings) • Taxable income: gross income minus the above tax allowances • Tax unit: the individual; couples are taxed separately
Korea	• Standard reliefs: • *Employment income deduction* Up to KRW 5,000,000 = Total amount KRW 5,000,000 to KRW 15000 000 = KRW 5 000 000 plus 40% of the salary over KRW 5,000,000 Over KRW 15,000,000 = KRW 9,000,000 + 10% of salary over KRW 15,000,000 (limit : KRW 12,000,000) • *Basic allowance*: up to 1,000,000 per qualifying persons: • taxpayer himself/herself • spouse whose taxable income is less than KRW 1,000,000 • taxpayer's (including the spouse's) dependents (parents, siblings, children) within the same household whose taxable income is under KRW 1,000,000—male parents @ 60 or more, female parents @ 55 or more, brother @ 60 or older/20 or under, sister @ 55 or older/20 or under, children under 20 • *Additional allowance*: a taxpayer can deduct KRW 500 000 from his/her gross income when the taxpayer or his/her dependents fall into the following categories: person 65 or older, disabled person prescribed by Presidential decree, female wage-earner who is head of household, female wage earner with a spouse, child under 6 years of age (permitted only for a female wage earner or a male wage earner without a spouse)

(*continued*)

Table 8.3 (*continued*)

Country	Taxing structures supporting the social safety net
	• *Extra tax allowance*: for a single income earner without a spouse or any other dependents (KRW 1,000,000 from gross income), a single income earner with a dependent (e.g., spouse, child) (KRW 1,000,000 from gross income) • *Tax credits*:

Calculated tax	Tax credit amt.
Up to KRW 500.000 Over KRW 500 000	45% of calculated tax KRW 225,000 + 30% Of calculated tax over KRW 500,000 (limit: KRW 600,000)

- Non-standard tax relief:
  - Lump-sum tax relief: Any taxpayer whose total deductible expenses listed is not over KRW 600,000 may deduct KRW 600 000 from their gross income as a lump-sum tax relief: insurance premiums, medical expenses, educational expenses, saving/payments for housing, charities and credit card purchases (all of them up to specific limits)
- Each individual is taxed for his/her own income. Exception: married couple receiving rental income from real estate property or interest and dividend income (only if more than KRW 40 million combined), the income from both spouses is combined to determine their taxable income

Source: Adapted from Organization for Economic Co-operation and Development. (1999). Synopsis of Member Nations social programs. Washington, D.C.: Author. Retrieved from http://www.oecd.org.

Table 8.4
Overview of U.S. Veterans' Benefits, Food Stamps, and Low-Income Energy Assistance, with Poverty Thresholds for 2000

Veterans' Benefits

Disability compensation or pension, 2000

Number of veterans with—
Service-connected disability	2,308,000
Non-service-connected disability	364,000

Monthly payment in 2001 for —
Service-connected disability
10 percent disability	$101
Total disability	2,107

Non-service-connected disability (maximum payment)
Without dependent	775
With one dependent and in need of aid and attendance	1,533

Food Stamps

Monthly benefits, beginning Oct. 1, 2000:
Four-person household with no income	$434
Standard deduction	134

Fiscal year 2000
Average number of participants	17.2 million
Total benefits	$15.0 billion

Low-Income Home Energy Assistance

In fiscal year 1999 the Department of Health and Human Services issued—
- $1.06 billion in block grants to the 50 states and the District of Columbia;
- $9.6 million in direct block grants to 130 Indian tribes and tribal organizations;
- $1.5 million in block grants to the Commonwealth of Puerto Rico, Virgin Islands, America Samoa, Guam, and the Commonwealth of the Northern Mariana Islands; and
- $20.6 million in leveraging incentive awards to 33 states, 23 tribes;
- $5.6 million for Residential Emergency Assistance Challenge (REACH) program awards to 5 states; $681,000 to 6 Indian tribes and tribal organizations; $124,000 to 1 insular area; and $512,000 for states' second and third year REACH administrative costs;
- $174.6 million in emergency contingency funds to 26 states and $699,000 to 18 Indian tribes and tribal organizations.

Poverty

2000 weighted average poverty thresholds:
Individual, aged 65 or older	$8,259
Couple, householder aged 65 or older	10,414
Family of four	17,601

Percent of population with income below poverty level, 1999:
All ages	11.8 percent
Children under age 18 living in families	16.3 percent
Persons aged 65 or older	9.7 percent

Source: Social Security Administration. (2001). *Annual Statistical Supplement, 2001 to the Social Security Bulletin.* Baltimore: Social Security Administration, Office of Policy. Retrieved from http://www.ssa.gov/policy/docs/statcomps/supplement/2001/supp01.pdf.

Table 8.5
Number of Persons Receiving Payments, by Source and Category: United States, 1974 to 2000

Month and year	Total	Federally administered	Federal SSI	State supplementation Total	Federally administered Total	Federally administered Only	State administered Total	State administered Only
				All persons				
January 1974	3,248,949	3,215,632	2,955,959	1,838,602	1,480,309	259,673	358,293	33,317
December:								
1975	4,359,625	4,314,275	3,893,419	1,987,409	1,684,018	420,856	303,391	45,350
1980	4,194,100	4,142,017	3,682,411	1,934,239	1,684,765	459,606	249,474	52,083
1985	4,200,177	4,138,021	3,799,092	1,915,503	1,660,847	338,929	254,656	62,156
1990	4,888,180	4,817,127	4,412,131	2,343,803	2,058,273	404,996	285,530	71,053
1995	6,575,753	6,514,134	6,194,493	2,817,408	2,517,805	319,641	299,603	61,619
1996	6,676,729	6,613,718	6,325,531	2,731,681	2,421,470	288,187	310,211	63,011
1997	6,564,613	6,494,985	6,211,867	3,029,449	2,372,479	283,118	656,970	69,628
1998	6,649,465	6,566,069	6,289,070	3,072,392	2,411,707	276,999	660,685	83,396
1999	6,641,256	6,556,634	6,274,707	3,116,309	2,441,482	281,927	674,827	84,622
2000	6,685,169	6,601,686	6,319,907	3,163,504	2,480,637	281,779	682,867	83,483
				Aged				
January 1974	1,889,898	1,865,109	1,690,496	1,022,244	770,318	174,613	251,926	24,789
December:								
1975	2,333,685	2,307,105	2,024,765	1,028,596	843,917	282,340	184,679	26,580
1980	1,838,381	1,807,776	1,533,366	837,318	702,763	274,410	134,555	30,605
1985	1,529,674	1,504,469	1,322,292	698,634	583,913	182,177	114,721	25,205
1990	1,484,160	1,454,041	1,256,623	765,420	649,530	197,418	115,890	30,119
1995	1,479,415	1,446,122	1,314,720	777,841	663,390	131,402	114,451	33,293
1996	1,446,321	1,412,632	1,296,462	752,760	638,173	116,170	114,587	33,689
1997	1,395,845	1,362,350	1,251,374	750,168	619,516	110,976	130,652	33,495
1998	1,369,206	1,331,782	1,225,578	756,209	617,984	106,204	138,225	37,424
1999	1,346,771	1,308,062	1,203,056	759,681	620,261	105,006	139,420	38,709
2000	1,327,567	1,289,339	1,186,309	767,312	622,668	103,030	144,644	38,228
				Blind				
January 1974	73,850	72,390	55,680	45,828	37,326	16,710	8,502	1,460
December:								
1975	75,315	74,489	68,375	36,309	31,376	6,114	4,933	826
1980	79,139	78,401	68,945	39,863	36,214	9,456	3,649	738
1985	82,622	82,220	73,817	41,323	38,291	8,403	3,032	402
1990	84,109	83,686	74,781	43,376	40,334	8,905	3,042	423
1995	84,273	83,545	77,064	42,272	38,695	6,481	3,577	728
1996	82,815	82,137	76,180	40,173	36,759	5,957	3,414	678
1997	81,449	80,778	74,926	40,593	36,050	5,852	4,543	671
1998	81,029	80,243	74,623	40,828	36,193	5,620	4,635	786
1999	80,097	79,291	73,579	40,765	36,118	5,712	4,647	806
2000	79,295	78,511	72,931	40,585	35,940	5,580	4,645	784
				Disabled				
January 1974	1,285,201	1,278,122	1,209,783	769,501	672,575	68,350	96,926	7,068
December:								
1975	1,950,625	1,932,681	1,800,279	922,229	808,725	132,402	113,504	17,944
1980	2,276,130	2,255,840	2,080,100	1,050,155	945,788	175,740	104,367	20,290
1985	2,586,741	2,551,332	2,402,983	1,167,326	1,038,643	148,349	128,683	35,409
1990	3,319,911	3,279,400	3,080,727	1,535,007	1,368,409	198,673	166,598	40,511
1995	5,010,326	4,984,467	4,802,709	1,995,262	1,815,720	181,758	179,542	25,859
1996	5,145,850	5,118,949	4,952,889	1,933,493	1,746,538	166,060	186,955	26,901
1997	5,078,995	5,051,857	4,885,567	1,998,187	1,716,913	166,290	281,274	27,138
1998	5,190,815	5,154,044	4,988,869	2,067,530	1,757,530	165,175	310,000	36,771
1999	5,205,997	5,169,281	4,998,072	2,107,982	1,785,103	171,209	322,879	36,716
2000	5,270,126	5,233,836	5,060,667	2,147,945	1,822,029	173,169	325,916	36,290

Source: Social Security Administration. (2001). *Annual Statistical Supplement, 2001 to the Social Security Bulletin.* Baltimore: Social Security Administration, Office of Policy. Retrieved from http://www.ssa.gov/policy/docs/statcomps/supplement/2001/supp01.pdf.

Table 8.6
Total Annual Amount of Payments, by Source and Category: United States, 1974 to 2000

[In thousands]

Calendar year	Total[1]	Federal SSI[1]	State supplementation Federally administered	State administered[1]
All persons				
1974	$5,245,719	$3,833,161	$1,263,652	$148,906
1975	5,878,224	4,313,538	1,402,534	162,152
1980	7,940,734	5,866,354	1,848,286	226,094
1985	11,060,476	8,777,341	1,972,597	310,538
1990	16,598,680	12,893,805	3,239,154	465,721
1992	22,232,503	18,246,934	3,435,476	550,093
1993	24,556,867	20,721,613	3,269,540	565,714
1994	25,876,571	22,175,233	3,115,854	585,483
1995	27,627,658	23,919,430	3,117,850	590,378
1996	28,791,924	25,264,878	2,987,596	539,450
1997	29,052,089	25,457,387	2,913,181	681,521
1998	30,216,345	26,404,793	3,003,415	808,137
1999	30,959,475	26,805,156	3,300,976	853,343
2000	31,564,439	27,290,248	3,381,451	892,740
Aged				
1974	$2,503,407	$1,782,742	$631,292	$89,373
1975	2,604,792	1,842,980	673,535	88,277
1980	2,734,270	1,860,194	756,829	117,247
1985	3,034,596	2,202,557	694,114	137,925
1990	3,736,104	2,521,382	1,038,006	176,716
1992	4,139,612	2,901,063	1,023,030	215,519
1993	4,250,092	3,097,616	933,852	218,624
1994	4,366,528	3,265,711	876,053	224,764
1995	4,467,146	3,374,772	864,450	227,924
1996	4,507,202	3,449,407	833,091	224,705
1997	4,531,973	3,479,948	823,581	228,444
1998	4,424,877	3,327,856	838,375	258,646
1999	4,724,748	3,514,689	921,332	271,003
2000	4,811,048	3,595,384	942,530	283,073
Blind				
1974	$130,195	$91,308	$34,483	$4,404
1975	130,936	92,427	34,813	3,696
1980	190,075	131,506	54,321	4,248
1985	264,162	195,183	64,657	4,322
1990	334,120	238,415	90,534	5,171
1992	370,769	275,606	87,783	7,380
1993	374,998	287,754	79,479	7,765
1994	372,461	292,102	72,596	7,763
1995	375,512	298,238	69,203	8,071
1996	371,869	298,897	65,894	7,077
1997	374,857	302,656	65,189	7,012
1998	366,452	291,050	67,137	8,265
1999	391,181	308,556	73,028	8,557
2000	394,484	312,144	73,688	8,636
Disabled				
1974	$2,601,936	$1,959,112	$597,876	$44,948
1975	3,142,476	2,378,131	694,186	70,159
1980	5,013,948	3,874,655	1,037,137	102,156
1985	7,754,588	6,379,601	1,213,826	161,161
1990	12,520,568	10,134,007	2,110,615	275,946
1992	17,710,514	15,070,265	2,324,664	315,585
1993	19,925,929	17,336,243	2,256,209	333,477
1994	21,131,001	18,617,421	2,167,205	346,375
1995	22,778,547	20,246,415	2,184,197	347,935
1996	23,905,578	21,516,579	2,088,610	300,389
1997	24,006,254	21,685,421	2,024,410	296,423
1998	25,304,721	22,785,879	2,097,903	420,939
1999	25,722,400	22,598,270	2,306,616	452,640
2000	26,198,350	23,399,442	2,365,233	479,635

1. Includes data not distributed by category.

Source: Social Security Administration. (2001). *Annual Statistical Supplement, 2001 to the Social Security Bulletin.* Baltimore: Social Security Administration, Office of Policy. Retrieved from http://www.ssa.gov/policy/docs/statcomps/supplement/2001/supp01.pdf.

Table 8.7
Average Monthly Amount,[1] by Source of Payment and Category: United States, 1975 to 2000

December	Total	Federally administered	Federal SSI	State supplementation Total	State supplementation Federally administered	State supplementation State administered[2]
				Total		
1975	$108.46	$106.33	$90.59	$57.55	$61.72	$38.69
1980	164.66	161.92	138.14	93.44	95.17	81.57
1985	220.70	218.09	193.77	99.37	99.39	99.21
1990	279.91	276.45	241.52	128.24	127.83	131.32
1995	338.73	335.45	312.83	103.23	98.66	142.59
1996	347.62	343.88	322.11	104.82	98.80	152.91
1997	356.96	350.58	327.53	101.46	101.92	99.82
1998	365.28	359.45	336.06	102.47	102.33	102.97
1999	374.96	368.53	341.86	110.44	110.92	108.70
2000	385.52	378.82	351.48	112.16	112.50	110.95
				Aged		
1975	$88.91	$86.72	$73.77	$50.61	$57.38	$28.68
1980	130.28	126.66	105.69	92.64	95.60	77.55
1985	168.16	164.01	141.41	101.25	103.58	89.91
1990	213.40	208.26	170.74	133.62	136.31	118.82
1995	256.66	250.27	220.15	116.26	109.62	153.94
1996	267.69	260.27	228.25	120.53	111.74	168.66
1997	275.83	268.46	235.45	120.11	114.35	147.09
1998	285.95	277.45	243.28	123.29	115.29	158.80
1999	298.23	289.19	249.36	133.51	125.90	167.17
2000	309.40	299.69	258.12	135.88	128.46	167.49
				Blind		
1975	$140.20	$137.58	$112.69	$68.81	$78.57	$35.40
1980	195.60	192.51	163.36	109.79	111.41	97.56
1985	263.86	260.25	224.31	121.76	122.15	118.07
1990	323.31	319.03	267.34	165.57	167.29	148.26
1995	360.61	355.24	317.06	143.65	138.31	188.15
1996	366.59	362.07	326.16	141.92	138.18	171.65
1997	385.42	381.65	337.79	149.55	152.83	123.70
1998	395.20	390.19	344.77	154.21	154.33	153.18
1999	407.19	401.99	350.72	166.66	167.64	159.15
2000	418.14	413.22	360.51	168.91	171.01	154.79
				Disabled		
1975	$130.59	$128.49	$108.55	$65.63	$65.68	$65.20
1980	190.96	188.70	160.78	93.57	94.38	86.19
1985	248.36	246.50	219.61	97.73	96.63	107.06
1990	305.82	302.78	266.84	125.01	123.36	139.70
1995	360.99	358.18	336.39	97.76	94.26	134.44
1996	368.65	365.49	345.36	98.32	93.63	142.92
1997	375.45	372.52	351.28	95.09	96.29	87.88
1998	384.67	380.46	359.07	99.32	96.63	114.30
1999	393.18	388.29	364.24	107.06	104.52	120.92
2000	402.93	397.92	373.41	108.66	105.86	124.09

1. Excludes retroactive payments.
2. Includes data not distributed by category.

Source: Social Security Administration. (2001). *Annual Statistical Supplement, 2001 to the Social Security Bulletin*. Baltimore: Social Security Administration, Office of Policy. Retrieved from http://www.ssa.gov/policy/docs/statcomps/supplement/2001/supp01.pdf.

Table 8.8
Number of Persons Receiving Federally Administered SSI Payments and Total Annual Amounts, by Category: 2000

State	Number, December				Amount of payments, calendar year (in thousands)			
	Total	Aged	Blind [1]	Disabled [2]	Total	Aged	Blind	Disabled
Total [3]	6,601,686	1,289,339	78,511	5,233,836	$30,671,699	$4,540,045	$385,927	$25,745,710
Alabama	159,343	26,534	1,152	131,657	658,648	52,344	4,514	601,791
Alaska	8,636	1,453	123	7,060	36,717	3,907	514	32,296
Arizona	81,278	13,194	959	67,125	355,074	39,084	4,333	311,656
Arkansas	85,310	14,206	943	70,161	332,628	25,114	3,871	303,644
California	1,087,614	333,892	21,949	731,773	6,385,553	1,729,632	140,135	4,515,786
Colorado	53,694	8,985	553	44,156	228,481	26,795	2,378	199,307
Connecticut	48,731	7,115	510	41,106	215,865	23,658	2,262	189,946
Delaware	11,961	1,387	117	10,457	50,172	3,388	490	46,294
District of Columbia	20,073	2,524	190	17,359	92,673	6,987	885	84,801
Florida	376,555	94,038	3,109	279,408	1,620,866	312,575	13,286	1,295,005
Georgia	196,780	34,112	2,264	160,404	785,363	73,308	9,454	702,601
Hawaii	21,009	7,047	168	13,794	103,603	29,248	841	73,514
Idaho	18,347	1,839	182	16,326	76,065	3,908	730	71,426
Illinois	248,833	32,541	2,374	213,918	1,174,336	113,997	10,613	1,049,727
Indiana	88,017	7,309	1,045	79,663	381,786	16,396	4,317	361,073
Iowa	40,298	4,477	827	34,994	157,905	9,595	3,174	145,135
Kansas	36,277	3,784	376	32,117	151,084	9,224	1,630	140,230
Kentucky	174,346	18,753	1,442	154,151	740,790	38,492	6,117	696,181
Louisiana	165,525	24,563	1,894	139,068	715,106	53,293	7,911	653,902
Maine	29,705	3,298	234	26,173	115,902	5,584	909	109,410
Maryland	88,073	15,726	745	71,602	400,089	49,697	3,241	347,151
Massachusetts	167,784	45,959	4,251	117,574	807,328	171,146	21,946	614,235
Michigan	209,608	19,413	1,892	188,303	988,272	57,019	8,602	922,651
Minnesota	64,084	10,152	721	53,211	271,952	30,256	3,071	238,625
Mississippi	128,791	22,440	1,257	105,094	512,112	43,535	4,921	463,656
Missouri	112,230	12,877	987	98,366	470,986	27,929	3,977	439,079
Montana	13,845	1,342	125	12,378	57,334	2,695	522	54,117
Nebraska	21,221	2,382	239	18,600	85,105	5,284	965	78,855
Nevada	25,405	6,972	644	17,789	108,413	21,989	3,168	83,256
New Hampshire	11,577	1,006	119	10,452	48,825	2,380	490	45,956
New Jersey	146,350	34,048	1,080	111,222	672,255	124,176	4,692	543,387
New Mexico	46,662	8,930	566	37,166	193,252	22,370	2,465	168,417
New York	617,167	138,971	3,370	474,826	3,197,466	572,354	16,009	2,609,104
North Carolina	191,053	33,990	2,093	154,970	731,568	68,029	8,273	655,266
North Dakota	8,167	1,351	80	6,736	29,797	2,815	325	26,656
Ohio	239,911	17,526	2,248	220,137	1,114,044	47,524	9,668	1,056,852
Oklahoma	72,140	10,782	866	60,492	302,057	23,276	3,623	275,157
Oregon	51,936	7,238	634	44,064	228,109	21,400	2,757	203,952
Pennsylvania	283,969	36,547	2,457	244,965	1,367,077	109,264	11,256	1,246,556
Rhode Island	27,778	4,606	226	22,946	130,379	14,977	991	114,411
South Carolina	107,469	17,162	1,583	88,724	428,933	34,925	6,501	387,507
South Dakota	12,642	1,999	110	10,533	48,363	3,936	426	44,001
Tennessee	164,202	23,118	1,663	139,421	664,461	45,861	6,992	611,607
Texas	409,162	115,402	5,725	288,035	1,574,945	294,276	23,571	1,257,098
Utah	20,130	2,096	270	17,764	87,074	6,769	1,201	79,104
Vermont	12,525	1,567	115	10,843	51,487	3,216	507	47,765
Virginia	131,942	24,530	1,455	105,957	535,180	65,276	6,092	463,811
Washington	100,761	14,148	949	85,664	484,345	54,941	4,424	424,979
West Virginia	71,420	5,527	589	65,304	318,198	10,983	2,555	304,661
Wisconsin	84,887	9,771	969	74,147	357,084	23,598	4,033	329,454
Wyoming	5,798	559	53	5,186	23,444	988	209	22,247
Other: Northern Mariana Islands	665	151	19	495	3,174	643	90	2,440

1. Includes approximately 18,800 blind persons aged 65 or older.
2. Includes approximately 702,700 disabled persons aged 65 or older.
3. Includes data not distributed by state.

Source: Social Security Administration. (2001). *Annual Statistical Supplement, 2001 to the Social Security Bulletin.* Baltimore: Social Security Administration, Office of Policy. Retrieved from http://www.ssa.gov/policy/docs/statcomps/supplement/2001/supp01.pdf.

Table 8.9
Number of Persons Receiving Federally Administered SSI Payments and Average Monthly Amount: December 2000

State	Total		Federal SSI		State supplementation		Number with—		
	Number	Average monthly amount	Number	Average monthly amount	Number	Average monthly amount	Federal SSI only	Federal SSI and state supple- mentation	State supple- mentation only
Total [1]	6,601,686	$378.82	6,319,907	$351.48	2,480,637	$112.50	4,121,049	2,198,858	281,779
Alabama	159,343	327.13	159,343	327.13	. . .	307.00	159,342	. . .	. . .
Alaska	8,636	344.48	8,636	344.47	. . .	22.90	8,636	. . .	. . .
Arizona	81,278	359.68	81,278	359.67	. . .	173.50	81,278	. . .	. . .
Arkansas	85,310	309.82	85,310	309.82	8	53.16	85,302	8	. . .
California	1,087,614	484.97	906,163	367.62	1,086,919	178.41	695	905,468	181,451
Colorado	53,694	340.70	53,694	340.69	. . .	. . .	53,694	. . .	. . .
Connecticut	48,731	360.83	48,731	360.84	. . .	. . .	48,730	. . .	. . .
Delaware	11,961	344.43	11,839	340.97	643	126.83	11,318	521	122
District of Columbia	20,073	377.32	19,932	365.82	1,720	163.05	18,353	1,579	141
Florida	376,555	352.51	376,555	352.51	7	36.55	376,548	7	. . .
Georgia	196,780	322.96	196,779	322.97	15	26.98	196,765	14	1
Hawaii	21,009	397.72	20,212	361.97	19,522	53.37	1,487	18,725	797
Idaho	18,347	336.26	18,347	336.26	. . .	. . .	18,346	. . .	. . .
Illinois	248,833	386.16	248,833	386.16	. . .	. . .	248,831	. . .	. . .
Indiana	88,017	352.31	88,017	352.31	. . .	. . .	88,017	. . .	. . .
Iowa	40,298	324.34	40,031	321.10	1,647	132.93	38,651	1,380	267
Kansas	36,277	340.81	36,276	340.80	14	51.24	36,263	13	1
Kentucky	174,346	349.35	174,346	349.35	. . .	. . .	174,346	. . .	. . .
Louisiana	165,525	345.13	165,523	345.13	22	16.81	165,503	20	2
Maine	29,705	316.10	29,705	316.10	. . .	. . .	29,703	. . .	. . .
Maryland	88,073	363.51	88,072	363.50	38	42.43	88,035	37	1
Massachusetts	167,784	394.68	147,625	355.72	167,563	81.59	221	147,404	20,159
Michigan	209,608	383.65	205,247	380.69	19,191	119.03	190,417	14,830	4,361
Minnesota	64,084	349.96	64,084	349.96	. . .	. . .	64,084	. . .	. . .
Mississippi	128,791	321.61	128,789	321.61	19	21.84	128,772	17	2
Missouri	112,230	341.86	112,230	341.86	. . .	. . .	112,230	. . .	. . .
Montana	13,845	336.15	13,747	333.72	895	76.50	12,950	797	98
Nebraska	21,221	325.85	21,221	325.85	. . .	. . .	21,221	. . .	. . .
Nevada	25,405	349.15	24,576	344.34	7,481	53.63	17,924	6,652	829
New Hampshire	11,577	332.61	11,577	332.59	. . .	. . .	11,577	. . .	. . .
New Jersey	146,350	373.04	138,729	347.97	145,733	44.09	617	138,112	7,621
New Mexico	46,662	336.37	46,662	336.37	. . .	. . .	46,662	. . .	. . .
New York	617,167	420.79	569,928	376.50	612,031	73.84	5,136	564,792	47,239
North Carolina	191,053	310.83	191,053	310.83	. . .	. . .	191,053	. . .	. . .
North Dakota	8,167	298.15	8,167	298.15	. . .	. . .	8,167	. . .	. . .
Ohio	239,911	377.49	239,910	377.48	30	30.00	239,881	29	1
Oklahoma	72,140	332.77	72,140	332.77	. . .	. . .	72,139	. . .	. . .
Oregon	51,936	354.57	51,936	354.57	. . .	. . .	51,935	. . .	. . .
Pennsylvania	283,969	390.24	271,391	369.62	278,797	37.96	5,172	266,219	12,578
Rhode Island	27,778	383.58	25,019	349.50	27,740	68.96	38	24,981	2,759
South Carolina	107,469	324.23	107,469	324.22	. . .	. . .	107,468	. . .	. . .
South Dakota	12,642	314.92	12,642	314.89	12	34.68	12,630	12	. . .
Tennessee	164,202	331.89	164,201	331.89	8	21.94	164,194	7	1
Texas	409,162	312.36	409,160	312.36	. . .	. . .	409,156	. . .	. . .
Utah	20,130	354.05	20,127	353.93	1,514	2.77	18,616	1,511	3
Vermont	12,525	340.87	11,214	313.89	12,478	60.27	47	11,167	1,311
Virginia	131,942	329.45	131,942	329.44	. . .	. . .	131,942	. . .	. . .
Washington	100,761	388.04	98,729	376.47	96,573	20.18	4,188	94,541	2,032
West Virginia	71,420	359.87	71,420	359.87	. . .	. . .	71,420	. . .	. . .
Wisconsin	84,887	345.39	84,887	345.39	. . .	. . .	84,886	. . .	. . .
Wyoming	5,798	329.30	5,798	329.30	. . .	. . .	5,798	. . .	. . .
Other: Northern Mariana Islands	665	412.39	665	412.39	. . .	. . .	665	. . .	. . .

1. Includes data not distributed by state.

Source: Social Security Administration. (2001). *Annual Statistical Supplement, 2001 to the Social Security Bulletin.* Baltimore: Social Security Administration, Office of Policy. Retrieved from http://www.ssa.gov/policy/docs/statcomps/supplement/2001/supp01.pdf.

Table 8.10
Percent of Persons Receiving Both Federally Administered Payments and Social Security Benefits, Average Monthly Amount of Benefits, by Age, Sex, and State: December 2000

| | Percent with Social Security benefits | | | | | | | Average monthly Social Security benefit | | | | | | |
| | | Category | | | Age | | | | Category | | | Age | | |
State	Total	Aged	Blind	Dis-abled	Under 18	18–64	65 or older	Total	Aged	Blind	Disabled	Under 18	18–64	65 or older
Total [1]	36.1	59.1	34.5	30.5	7.2	30.3	59.1	$399.44	$398.87	$412.92	$399.49	$181.85	$416.84	$394.07
Alabama	43.6	87.0	42.4	34.9	9.8	34.3	80.3	380.60	384.75	369.89	378.62	176.18	399.15	377.71
Alaska	31.1	43.0	35.0	28.5	6.9	29.9	44.8	376.52	330.05	367.65	391.12	156.77	411.57	328.97
Arizona	33.6	61.2	25.4	28.3	7.0	28.2	60.2	368.64	355.25	345.45	374.64	174.64	399.24	350.10
Arkansas	45.6	89.7	36.7	36.8	9.9	36.3	83.3	381.97	394.30	360.92	376.17	176.89	394.90	384.74
California	37.5	46.5	36.6	33.3	5.4	32.4	48.6	456.77	434.65	486.83	469.86	212.15	486.79	439.20
Colorado	36.6	58.2	28.6	32.3	7.1	32.7	59.8	385.35	386.22	373.03	385.16	179.35	399.34	378.89
Connecticut	30.7	44.4	24.9	28.3	7.9	28.2	47.4	376.62	360.30	347.46	381.37	168.94	396.63	361.85
Delaware	34.6	68.6	33.3	30.1	7.3	33.0	67.0	400.51	398.41	383.82	401.35	185.40	422.44	393.93
District of Columbia	28.3	66.8	26.3	22.8	5.9	20.6	61.5	380.95	376.74	394.40	382.57	212.67	405.33	371.74
Florida	34.8	52.4	32.6	28.8	7.8	31.6	52.1	375.15	370.34	373.46	378.11	182.08	399.85	368.97
Georgia	41.6	78.3	34.6	33.8	7.3	32.5	74.1	388.70	393.95	371.20	386.38	188.46	403.36	385.65
Hawaii	31.6	38.5	28.6	28.1	5.0	27.4	40.3	405.71	374.02	456.54	427.20	196.69	444.91	376.51
Idaho	36.8	80.0	29.7	32.1	7.9	34.3	77.2	385.01	397.48	376.59	381.59	170.47	394.25	391.37
Illinois	23.7	41.9	24.3	20.9	5.8	20.7	43.4	371.61	369.19	370.16	372.36	178.77	387.95	368.17
Indiana	32.6	76.0	30.2	28.6	7.3	30.9	70.7	377.73	390.00	379.24	374.73	164.26	389.38	383.38
Iowa	39.6	74.3	40.0	35.2	7.6	36.9	72.3	394.48	404.19	379.91	392.25	164.69	402.99	396.68
Kansas	36.3	67.2	30.3	32.7	8.3	34.9	65.3	385.81	395.89	357.07	383.68	168.53	397.75	388.10
Kentucky	35.9	83.9	33.6	30.1	9.4	28.3	75.1	369.91	378.24	351.14	367.29	162.77	384.81	368.50
Louisiana	36.2	81.1	35.5	28.2	7.8	26.9	74.0	368.31	377.63	354.23	363.83	186.99	380.93	370.28
Maine	45.4	88.0	42.3	40.1	12.1	39.1	82.8	393.24	410.38	377.84	388.64	146.90	399.79	399.66
Maryland	29.5	47.3	30.1	25.6	6.2	25.7	49.6	383.14	377.14	390.79	385.48	207.01	402.21	375.06
Massachusetts	38.4	59.7	42.2	29.9	9.5	32.9	58.8	441.10	445.55	459.59	436.69	181.79	448.29	446.14
Michigan	30.2	60.3	31.0	27.0	7.1	27.5	60.8	396.59	402.53	388.65	395.32	174.91	409.71	397.75
Minnesota	33.1	54.9	26.6	29.0	6.6	30.8	53.6	378.64	384.33	353.01	376.90	169.05	387.99	378.79
Mississippi	44.6	88.7	41.6	35.2	9.4	33.8	80.6	375.05	381.56	357.22	371.79	175.36	392.64	372.74
Missouri	38.6	77.9	37.1	33.4	8.6	34.0	73.1	379.59	391.44	371.32	376.06	165.27	390.36	381.46
Montana	39.6	80.3	36.0	35.2	7.9	35.7	76.5	392.48	402.39	345.13	390.52	180.65	403.32	388.66
Nebraska	40.4	74.6	35.6	36.0	7.8	38.9	70.9	394.05	403.06	369.92	391.97	166.47	405.63	392.94
Nevada	34.5	60.3	36.3	24.4	5.7	29.5	59.6	421.29	426.12	447.64	415.18	183.20	429.06	425.71
New Hampshire	38.1	69.7	33.6	35.2	12.0	36.0	69.4	390.47	375.34	370.65	393.57	151.14	410.39	380.03
New Jersey	32.9	43.9	35.6	29.5	7.2	30.4	46.6	400.51	389.14	394.44	405.75	201.63	423.47	389.45
New Mexico	40.1	73.5	30.2	32.2	7.1	30.0	69.2	365.83	360.33	353.90	369.02	195.23	388.01	355.56
New York	31.9	45.5	36.7	27.8	6.4	26.9	47.0	426.41	417.95	424.79	430.48	187.03	453.75	412.45
North Carolina	45.6	85.4	36.2	37.0	8.5	37.1	79.0	380.49	387.88	368.19	376.92	177.20	397.41	377.31
North Dakota	46.7	80.9	37.5	39.9	7.4	40.7	74.7	375.85	386.50	307.27	372.29	165.95	382.25	376.22
Ohio	27.0	62.8	27.8	24.2	6.6	24.3	61.2	368.27	378.84	367.66	366.09	168.59	378.67	373.56
Oklahoma	39.0	80.3	31.8	31.7	7.0	31.0	73.9	376.95	389.17	363.19	371.64	185.64	384.73	379.11
Oregon	35.4	57.6	31.4	31.9	6.1	33.2	58.5	390.27	395.20	345.60	389.44	186.38	399.24	387.22
Pennsylvania	32.7	66.5	33.4	27.7	7.2	27.3	63.2	407.47	428.70	399.88	399.94	176.68	416.55	412.85
Rhode Island	40.9	65.7	43.8	35.9	8.1	36.7	64.1	431.11	448.78	404.95	424.94	174.11	439.76	433.82
South Carolina	42.0	86.4	36.6	33.5	7.9	32.8	78.7	377.62	382.06	359.58	375.76	190.16	393.53	375.03
South Dakota	42.3	75.1	35.5	36.1	7.9	38.7	70.4	373.23	400.50	361.10	362.60	153.86	376.86	383.43
Tennessee	40.8	85.4	32.4	33.6	8.1	31.9	76.8	378.28	385.68	355.85	375.42	177.18	391.38	375.66
Texas	42.9	69.7	31.8	32.4	5.5	30.5	64.1	368.54	364.38	354.92	372.40	203.34	390.13	360.73
Utah	30.0	50.1	22.2	27.7	5.5	30.4	50.8	378.11	370.63	310.22	380.54	185.03	391.52	367.87
Vermont	50.4	89.0	50.4	44.8	10.5	44.1	83.4	424.73	436.40	400.71	421.66	162.98	433.78	424.64
Virginia	39.1	64.8	33.6	33.3	7.9	33.8	64.4	379.40	384.65	369.57	377.16	173.85	393.70	377.65
Washington	28.9	36.9	27.6	27.6	6.0	28.0	42.1	400.57	392.44	382.51	402.57	181.11	416.36	386.29
West Virginia	32.7	82.4	29.7	28.5	9.7	26.4	70.2	371.75	387.26	358.32	368.09	160.39	381.34	374.12
Wisconsin	35.4	69.5	29.9	30.9	6.7	33.1	66.8	386.38	396.57	382.78	383.41	172.54	394.41	391.95
Wyoming	39.0	82.3	37.7	34.3	8.4	36.5	78.5	387.48	410.34	412.75	381.28	182.82	392.41	398.35
Other: Northern Mariana Islands	28.3	51.7	26.3	21.2	0.7	29.0	47.0	265.04	243.05	221.00	283.47	374.00	288.83	240.34

1. Includes recipients not distributed by state.

Source: Social Security Administration. (2001). *Annual Statistical Supplement, 2001 to the Social Security Bulletin.* Baltimore: Social Security Administration, Office of Policy. Retrieved from http://www.ssa.gov/policy/docs/statcomps/supplement/2001/supp01.pdf.

Table 8.11
Number of Noncitizens Receiving Federally Administered Payments
as a Percent of SSI Recipients, by Category: 1982 to 2000

December	Total		Aged		Blind and disabled	
	Noncitizens	Percent of total SSI	Noncitizens	Percent of total SSI	Noncitizens	Percent of total SSI
1982	127,900	3.3	91,900	5.9	36,000	1.6
1985	210,800	5.1	146,500	9.7	64,300	2.4
1986	244,300	5.7	165,300	11.2	79,000	2.8
1987	282,500	6.4	188,000	12.9	94,500	3.2
1988	320,300	7.2	213,900	14.9	106,400	3.5
1989	370,300	8.1	245,700	17.1	124,600	4.0
1990	435,600	9.0	282,400	19.4	153,200	4.6
1991	519,660	10.2	329,690	22.5	189,970	5.2
1992	601,430	10.8	372,930	25.4	228,500	5.6
1993	683,150	11.4	416,420	28.2	266,730	5.9
1994	738,140	11.7	440,000	30.0	298,140	6.2
1995	785,410	12.1	459,220	31.8	326,190	6.3
1996	724,990	11.0	417,360	29.5	307,630	5.9
1997	650,830	10.0	367,200	27.0	283,630	5.5
1998	669,630	10.2	364,980	27.4	304,650	5.8
1999	684,930	10.4	368,330	28.2	316,600	6.0
2000	692,590	10.5	364,470	28.3	328,120	6.2

Source: Social Security Administration. (2001). *Annual Statistical Supplement, 2001 to the Social Security Bulletin.* Baltimore: Social Security Administration, Office of Policy. Retrieved from http://www.ssa.gov/policy/docs/statcomps/supplement/2001/supp01.pdf.

Table 8.12

Number of Persons Receiving Special SSI Payments and Extended Medicaid Coverage, for Selected Months: 1982 to 2000

Reporting month	Special SSI cash payments (section 1619(a))		Continuation of Medicaid coverage only (section 1619(b)) [1]	
	Number	Percentage change over prior report month	Number	Percentage change over prior report month
December: [2]				
1982	287	. . .	5,515	. . .
1983	392	. . .	5,165	. . .
1987	14,559	. . .	15,632	. . .
1988	19,920	36.8	15,625	. . .
1989	25,655	28.8	18,254	16.8
1990	13,994	-45.5	23,517	28.8
1991	15,531	11.0	27,264	15.9
1992	17,603	13.3	31,649	16.1
1993	20,028	13.8	35,299	11.5
1994	24,315	21.4	40,683	15.3
1995	28,060	15.4	47,002	15.5
1996	31,085	10.8	51,905	10.4
1997	34,673	11.5	57,089	10.0
1998	37,271	7.5	59,542	4.3
1999	25,528	-31.5	69,265	16.3
2000	27,542	7.9	83,572	20.7
1998				
March	34,637	-.1	54,639	-4.3
June	35,528	2.6	55,761	2.1
September	37,216	4.8	58,183	4.3
December	37,271	.1	59,542	2.3
1999				
March	39,457	5.9	63,431	6.5
June	23,304	-40.9	66,939	5.5
September	23,914	2.6	70,580	5.4
December	25,528	6.7	69,265	-1.9
2000				
March	25,055	-1.9	69,545	.4
June	25,837	3.1	77,782	11.8
September	26,180	1.3	84,199	8.2
December	27,542	5.2	83,572	-.7

1. Includes blind participants. For December 2000, of the 83,572 participants, 1,488 were blind.

2. Data not available for December 1984, 1985, 1986.

Note: In January 1990, the SGA level was raised from $300 to $500 and section 1619(a) participants with earnings below $500 became eligible for regular SSI benefits rather than the special cash payments under section 1619(a). This is reflected in the decrease shown for 1990. In July 1999, the SGA level was further increased to $700, resulting in the decrease shown for June 1999.

Source: Social Security Administration. (2001). *Annual Statistical Supplement, 2001 to the Social Security Bulletin.* Baltimore: Social Security Administration, Office of Policy. Retrieved from http://www.ssa.gov/policy/docs/statcomps/supplement/2001/supp01.pdf.

Table 8.13
Veterans' Benefits—Number of Payments, by Type of Payment and Age: United States, 1940 to 2000

[In thousands]

Period	Total [1]	Disability compensation or pension									
		Service-connected							Non-service-connected		
			Under age 65			Aged 65 or older					
				Disability rating [2]			Disability rating [2]				
		All ages	Total	Less than 70 percent	70–100 percent	Total	Less than 70 percent	70–100 percent	All ages	Under age 65	Aged 65 or older
As of June 30:											
1940	610	385	. . .	. . .	. . .	. . .	. . .	. . .	189	. . .	. . .
1945	1,144	912	. . .	. . .	. . .	. . .	. . .	. . .	159	. . .	. . .
1950	2,368	1,990	. . .	. . .	. . .	. . .	. . .	. . .	290	. . .	. . .
1955	2,669	2,076	. . .	. . .	. . .	. . .	. . .	. . .	531	. . .	. . .
1956	2,739	2,083	2,026	1,841	185	57	43	14	597	319	278
As of June 20:											
1957	2,797	2,074	2,004	1,825	179	70	53	17	670	304	366
1958	2,850	2,064	1,980	1,807	173	84	65	19	741	279	462
1959	2,934	2,053	1,952	1,781	171	101	78	23	841	257	584
1960	3,009	2,027	1,908	1,746	162	119	93	26	947	219	728
1961	3,107	2,000	1,868	1,711	158	131	104	27	1,077	182	895
1962	3,150	1,987	1,849	1,693	156	138	109	29	1,138	166	972
1963	3,181	1,989	1,844	1,686	158	145	115	30	1,170	165	1,005
1964	3,197	1,993	1,846	1,684	162	147	117	30	1,186	176	1,010
1965	3,217	1,992	1,846	1,679	167	146	117	29	1,210	197	1,013
1966	3,201	1,993	1,850	1,677	173	143	115	28	1,196	221	975
1967	3,182	1,999	1,858	1,683	175	141	114	27	1,173	243	930
1968	3,164	2,011	1,873	1,696	177	138	112	26	1,145	265	880
1969	3,160	2,039	1,904	1,712	192	135	110	25	1,114	286	828
1970	3,181	2,091	1,950	1,754	196	141	116	25	1,086	310	776
1971	3,222	2,146	1,995	1,780	215	151	128	23	1,073	335	738
1972	3,269	2,183	2,022	1,804	218	161	135	26	1,086	381	705
1973	3,257	2,204	2,028	1,806	222	176	150	26	1,053	402	651
1974	3,241	2,211	2,018	1,796	222	193	165	28	1,030	410	620
1975	3,227	2,220	2,006	1,784	222	214	185	29	1,006	430	576
1976	3,236	2,232	1,996	1,767	229	236	209	27	1,003	456	547
As of September 30:											
1977	3,280	2,248	1,989	1,759	230	258	226	32	1,032	505	527
1978	3,284	2,259	1,971	1,741	230	288	254	34	1,025	516	509
1979	3,241	2,267	1,944	1,717	227	323	285	38	974	500	474
1980	3,196	2,274	1,912	1,689	223	362	320	42	922	467	455
1981	3,154	2,279	1,873	1,656	217	406	359	47	875	438	437
1982	3,096	2,274	1,818	1,606	210	456	404	52	824	406	418
1983	3,044	2,263	1,744	1,544	200	519	461	58	781	373	408
1984	2,980	2,251	1,666	1,476	190	585	520	65	729	339	390
1985	2,931	2,240	1,589	1,408	181	651	579	72	690	306	384
1986	2,883	2,225	1,505	1,335	169	720	641	79	658	274	384
1987	2,844	2,212	1,428	1,268	160	784	698	86	631	244	387
1988	2,804	2,199	1,361	1,209	153	838	746	92	606	219	387
1989	2,776	2,192	1,302	1,156	146	890	792	98	584	196	388
1990	2,746	2,184	1,253	1,113	140	931	828	102	562	175	387
1991	2,709	2,179	1,238	1,098	140	941	838	103	530	156	375
1992	2,674	2,181	1,245	1,104	141	936	833	103	493	138	354
1993	2,660	2,198	1,265	1,122	143	932	828	104	462	128	335
1994	2,659	2,218	1,290	1,144	146	928	824	104	441	122	319
1995	2,669	2,236	1,310	1,158	152	926	819	107	433	120	313
1996	2,671	2,253	1,330	1,171	158	923	814	109	418	116	302
1997	2,667	2,263	1,346	1,178	168	917	805	112	404	112	292
1998	2,668	2,277	1,372	1,191	180	905	790	115	391	110	281
1999	2,673	2,294	1,404	1,209	195	890	771	119	379	113	266
2000	2,672	2,308	1,435	1,224	211	874	751	123	364	115	249

1. Persons receiving payments under special acts and as retired emergency and reserve officers included in total but excluded from distribution.
2. Disability rated by the Department of Veterans Affairs according to average impairment of earning capacity, graduated in intervals from 10–100 percent.

Source: Social Security Administration. (2001). *Annual Statistical Supplement, 2001 to the Social Security Bulletin.* Baltimore: Social Security Administration, Office of Policy. Retrieved from http://www.ssa.gov/policy/docs/statcomps/supplement/2001/supp01.pdf.

Table 8.14
Disabled Veterans Receiving Compensation by Period of Service: United States, 1980 to 2001

[In thousands (2,274 represents 2,274,000), except as indicated. **As of end of fiscal year.** Represents veterans receiving compensation for service-connected disabilities. Totally disabled refers to veterans with any disability, mental or physical, deemed to be total and permanent which prevents the individual from maintaining a livelihood and are rated for disability at 100 percent.]

Period of service	1980	1990	1994	1995	1996	1997	1998	1999	2000	2001
Disabled, all periods [1]	2,274	2,184	2,218	2,236	2,253	2,263	2,277	2,294	2,308	2,321
Peace time [1]	262	444	492	514	529	539	550	561	567	569
World War I [1]	30	3	1	1	(Z)	(Z)	(Z)	(Z)	(Z)	(Z)
World War II	1,193	876	731	692	655	616	578	541	505	470
Korea	236	209	195	191	187	182	179	175	171	166
Vietnam	553	652	694	705	714	724	729	736	741	750
Persian Gulf	(X)	(X)	106	134	168	202	241	282	325	366
Compensation (mil. dol.)	6,104	9,284	11,056	11,644	11,072	13,004	13,791	14,542	15,489	16,529

X. Not applicable.

Z. Less than 500.

1. Includes Spanish-American War and Mexican Border service, not shown separately.

Source: United States Census Bureau. (2002). *Statistical Abstract of the United States 2002*. Washington, D.C.: Government Printing Office. Retrieved from http://www.census.gov/prod/2003pubs/02statab/defense.pdf.

Table 8.15
Federal Food Programs: United States, 1990 to 2001

[20.1 represents 20,100,000. For years ending Sept. 30. Program data include Puerto Rico, Virgin Islands, Guam, American Samoa, Northern Marianas, and the former Trust Territory when a federal food program was operated in these areas. Participation data are average monthly figures except as noted. Participants are not reported for the commodity distribution programs. Cost data are direct federal benefits to recipients; they exclude Federal administrative payments and applicable state and local contributions. Federal costs for commodities and cash-in-lieu of commodities are shown separately from direct cash benefits for those programs receiving both.]

Program	Unit	1990	1995	1996	1997	1998	1999	2000	2001
Food Stamp:									
Participants	Million . .	20.1	26.6	25.5	22.9	19.8	18.2	17.2	17.3
Federal cost	Mil. dol. .	14,187	22,765	22,441	19,550	16,889	15,755	14,985	15,535
Monthly average coupon value per recipient	Dollars . .	58.92	71.26	73.21	71.27	71.12	72.21	72.78	74.76
Nutrition assistance program for Puerto Rico:									
Federal cost	Mil. dol. .	937	1,131	1,143	1,174	1,204	1,236	1,268	1,296
National school lunch program (NSLP):									
Free lunches served	Million . .	1,662	2,090	2,128	2,194	2,198	2,207	2,205	2,183
Reduced-price lunches served	Million . .	273	309	326	347	362	392	409	424
Children participating [1]	Million . .	24.1	25.7	25.9	26.3	26.6	26.9	27.2	27.5
Federal cost	Mil. dol. .	3,214	4,466	4,662	4,934	5,102	5,314	5,493	5,613
School breakfast (SB):									
Children participating [1]	Million . .	4.1	6.3	6.6	6.9	7.1	7.4	7.6	7.8
Federal cost	Mil. dol. .	596	1,049	1,119	1,214	1,272	1,345	1,393	1,448
Special supplemental food program (WIC): [2]									
Participants	Million . .	4.5	6.9	7.2	7.4	7.4	7.3	7.2	7.3
Federal cost	Mil. dol. .	1,637	2,517	2,690	2,815	2,808	2,853	2,852	3,008
Child and adult care (CC): [3]									
Participants [4]	Million . .	1.5	2.4	2.4	2.5	2.6	2.7	2.7	2.7
Federal cost	Mil. dol. .	720	1,296	1,360	1,393	1,372	1,438	1,501	1,548
Federal cost of commodities donated to— [5]									
Child nutrition (NSLP, CC, SF [6], and SB)	Mil. dol. .	646	733	734	661	774	754	704	917
Emergency feeding [7]	Mil. dol. .	286	100	52	152	190	225	181	332

1. Average monthly participation (excluding summer months of June through August). Includes children in public and private elementary and secondary schools and in residential childcare institutes.

2. WIC serves pregnant and postpartum women, infants, and children up to age five.

3. Program provides year-round subsidies to feed preschool children in child care centers and family day care homes. Certain care centers serving disabled or elderly adults also receive meal subsidies.

4. Average quarterly daily attendance at participating institutions.

5. Includes the Federal cost of commodity entitlements, cash-in-lieu of commodities, and bonus foods.

6. Summer Feeding (SF) program provides free meals to children in poor areas during summer months.

7. Provides free commodities to needy persons for home consumption through food banks, hunger centers, soup kitchens, and similar nonprofit agencies. Includes the Emergency Food Assistance Program, the commodity purchases for soup kitchens/food banks program, and commodity disaster relief.

Source: United States Census Bureau. (2002). *Statistical Abstract of the United States 2002.* Washington, D.C.: Government Printing Office. Retrieved from http://www.census.gov/prod/2003pubs/02statab/socinsur.pdf.

Table 8.16
Federal Food Stamp Program, by State: 1995 to 2001

[**Participation data are average monthly number (26,619 represents 26,619,000). For years ending Sept. 30.** Food stamp costs are for benefits only and exclude administrative expenditures.]

State	Persons (1,000)			Benefits (mil. dol.)			State	Persons (1,000)			Benefits (mil. dol.)		
	1995	2000	2001	1995	2000	2001		1995	2000	2001	1995	2000	2001
Total [1] ..	26,619	17,158	17,316	22,765	14,985	15,535	MS	480	276	298	383	226	254
U.S. ...	26,579	17,120	17,280	22,714	14,928	15,480	MO	576	423	454	488	358	395
							MT	71	59	62	57	51	54
AL.......	525	396	411	441	344	365	NE.......	105	82	81	77	61	63
AK.......	45	38	38	50	46	47	NV.......	99	61	69	91	57	65
AZ.......	480	259	291	414	240	280	NH	58	36	36	44	28	28
AR.......	272	247	256	212	206	223							
CA.......	3,175	1,832	1,668	2,473	1,639	1,582	NJ	551	345	318	506	304	292
CO	252	156	154	217	127	131	NM	239	169	163	196	140	137
CT.......	226	165	157	169	138	136	NY.......	2,183	1,439	1,354	2,065	1,361	1,365
DE.......	57	32	32	47	31	32	NC	614	488	494	495	403	425
DC	94	81	73	93	77	70	ND	41	32	38	32	25	27
FL.......	1,395	882	887	1,307	773	771	OH	1,155	610	641	1,017	520	573
							OK	375	253	271	315	208	236
GA	816	559	574	700	489	515	OR	289	234	281	254	198	238
HI	125	118	108	177	166	150	PA.......	1,173	777	748	1,006	656	639
ID	80	58	60	59	46	47	RI	93	74	71	82	59	59
IL	1,151	779	825	1,056	777	810							
IN	470	300	347	382	268	306	SC.......	364	295	316	297	249	269
IA	184	123	126	141	100	107	SD.......	50	43	45	40	37	39
KS.......	184	117	124	144	83	92	TN.......	662	496	522	554	415	454
KY.......	520	403	413	413	337	350	TX.......	2,558	1,333	1,366	2,246	1,215	1,270
LA.......	711	500	518	629	448	483	UT.......	119	82	80	90	68	67
ME	132	102	104	112	81	86	VT.......	59	41	39	46	32	31
							VA.......	546	336	332	450	263	263
MD	399	219	208	365	199	191	WA	476	295	309	417	241	261
MA	410	232	219	315	182	173	WV	309	227	221	253	185	178
MI	971	603	641	806	457	504	WI	320	193	216	220	129	152
MN	308	196	198	240	165	172	WY	34	22	23	28	19	19

1. Includes Guam and the Virgin Islands. Several outlying areas receive nutrition assistance grants in lieu of food stamp assistance (e.g., Puerto Rico, American Samoa and the Northern Marianas).

Source: United States Census Bureau. (2002). *Statistical Abstract of the United States 2002.* Washington, D.C.: Government Printing Office. Retrieved from http://www.census.gov/prod/2003pubs/02statab/socinsur.pdf.

Table 8.17
Selected Characteristics of Food Stamp Households and Participants: United States, 1990 to 1998

[**For years ending September 30.** Data for 1990–1992 exclude Guam and the Virgin Islands. Based on a sample of households from the Food Stamp Quality Control System.]

Year	Households				Participants		
	Total (1,000)	Percent of total			Total (1,000)	Percent of total	
		With children	With elderly [1]	With disabled [2]		Children	Elderly [1]
1990	7,803	60.3	18.1	8.9	20,411	49.6	7.7
1991	8,855	60.4	16.4	9.0	22,963	52.0	7.0
1992	10,049	62.2	15.4	9.5	25,743	51.9	6.6
1993	10.791	62.1	15.5	10.7	27,595	51.5	6.8
1994	11,091	61.1	15.8	12.5	28,009	51.4	7.0
1995	10,883	59.7	16.0	18.9	26,955	51.5	7.1
1996	10,552	59.5	16.2	20.2	25,926	51.0	7.3
1997	9,452	58.3	17.6	22.3	23,117	51.4	7.9
1998	8,246	58.3	18.2	24.4	19,969	52.8	8.2

1. Persons 60 years old and over.
2. Beginning 1995, disabled households are defined as households with at least one member under age 65 who received SSI, or at least one member age 18 to 61 who received Social Security, veterans benefits, or other government benefits as a result of a disability. For years prior to 1995, disabled households are defined as households with SSI but no members over age 59. The substantial increase in the percentage of households with a disabled member between 1994 and 1995 is due in part to the change in the definition of disabled households. Using the previous definition, 13.3 percent of households included a disabled person in fiscal year 1995.

Source: United States Census Bureau. (2002). *Statistical Abstract of the United States 2002.* Washington, D.C.: Government Printing Office. Retrieved from http://www.census.gov/prod/2003pubs/02statab/socinsur.pdf.

Table 8.18
Characteristics of Food Stamp Households in the United States in Fiscal Year 2001

Household income and resources	• 27% of households have earnings ($753 on average) • 23% have TANF income ($375 on average) • 32% have SSI income ($422 on average) • 25% have Social Security income ($528 on average) • 9% have no gross income • 34% have income at 50% or less of the poverty guideline • 11% have income above the poverty guideline • Average monthly gross income was $624 • Average countable resources was $148 • 68% of households have no countable resources
Average monthly deductions	• Average total deductions for all households was $311 • 27% of households received the earned income deduction, with an average deduction of $150 • 4% received the dependent care deduction, with an average deduction of $119 • 60% received the excess shelter deduction, with an average deduction of $205 • 4% of households received medical deduction, with an average deduction of $123 • 1% received the child support deduction, with an average deduction of $166
Household size	• Average household has 2.3 persons • Average household with children has 3.4 persons • Average household with elderly has 1.3 persons • Average household with disabled has 2.0 persons
Average monthly benefits	• $163 for all households • $242 for households with children • $58 for households with elderly • $101 for households with disabled • $182 for households with noncitizens • 11% of households received the minimum benefit • 22% received the maximum benefit
Gender and racial characteristics	• 60% of participants are female • 41% are White • 35% are African-American • 18% are Hispanic • 3% are Asian • 2% are Native American • 1% are of unknown race
Age and disability status	• 51% of recipients are children • 10% are elderly • 13% are disabled • 5% are non-elderly, non-disabled, childless adults
Citizenship	• 93% of recipients are U.S.-born citizens • 3% are naturalized citizens • 3% are legal permanent resident aliens • 1% are refugees • 6% are citizen children living with noncitizens

Source: U.S. Department of Agriculture, Food and Nutrition Service. (2003). Characteristics of Food Stamp Households in FY 2001. In *Applicant and Recipients*, Food and Nutrition Service Web site. Retrieved from http://www.fns.usda.gov/fsp/rules/Memo/Support/03/2001-characteristics.htm.

Figure 8.1
Food Stamp Program Participants, Unemployed Individuals and Individuals in Poverty:
United States, 1985 to 2002

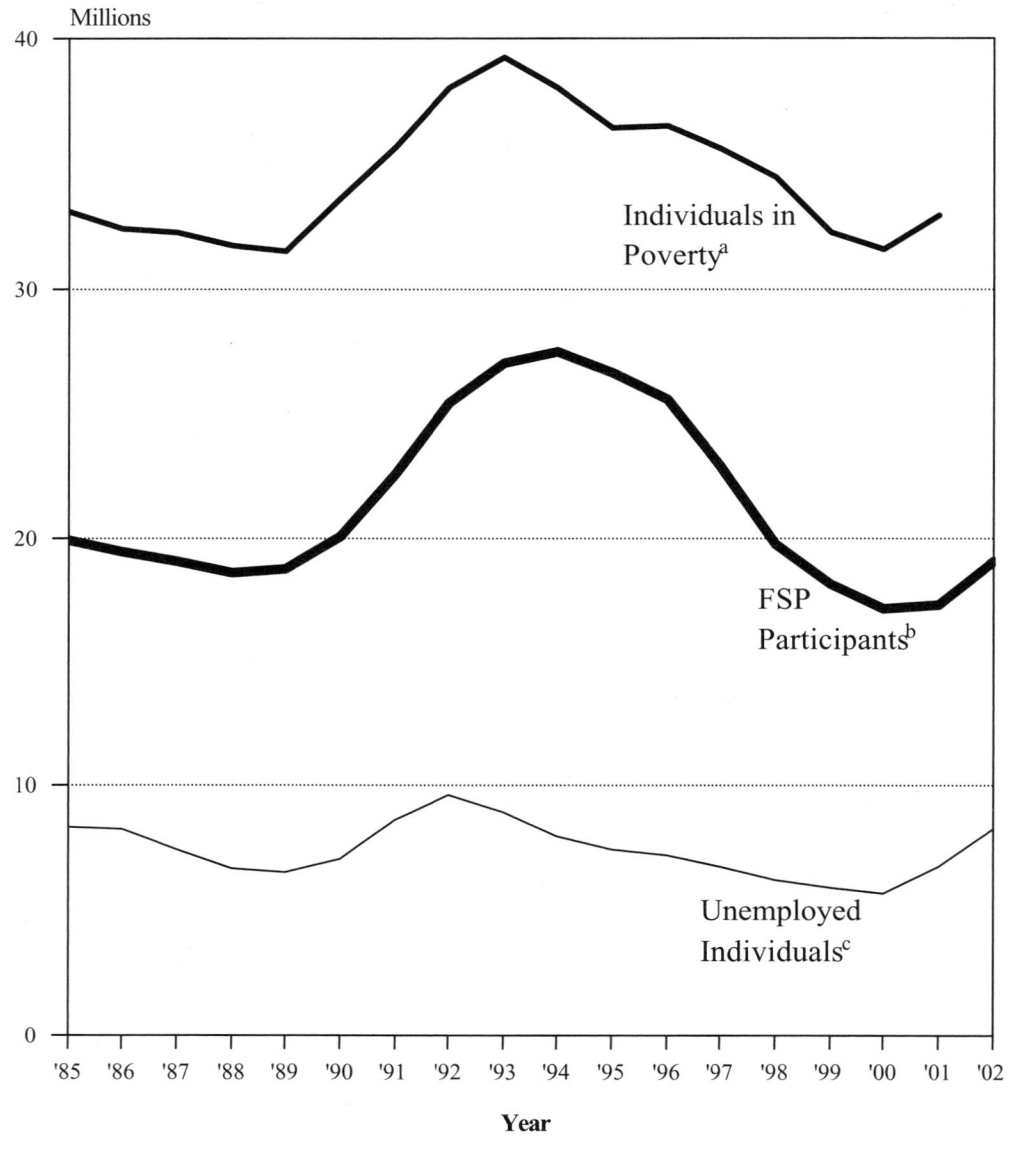

a. Annual values. The number of individuals in poverty in Fiscal Year 2002 was not available when this report went to print.

b. Average monthly values.

c. Average monthly values.

Source: U.S. Department of Agriculture. (July 2003). *Characteristics of Food Stamp Households: Fiscal Year 2002 (Advanced Report)*. Washington, D.C.: Office of Analysis, Nutrition, and Evaluation. Retrieved from http://www.fns.usda.gov/oane/MENU/Published/FSP/FILES/Participation/2002AdvRpt.pdf.

Table 8.19
Sources of Income Among Food Stamp Households: United States, Fiscal Year 1989 to Fiscal Year 2002

Fiscal Year	Earned Income		AFDC/TANF		GA		SSI[a]		Social Security		No Income	
	Number (thousands)	Percent	Number (thousands)	Percent	Number (thousands)	Percent	Number (thousands)	Percent	Number (thousands)	Percent	Number (thousands)	Percent
2002	2,303	28.1	1,714	20.9	438	5.3	2,417	29.5	1,995	24.3	865	10.5
2001	1,993	26.7	1,714	23.0	415	5.6	2,379	31.9	1,887	25.3	704	9.5
2000	1,993	27.2	1,891	25.8	395	5.4	2,324	31.7	1,870	25.5	617	8.4
1999	2,058	26.8	2,096	27.3	435	5.7	2,315	30.2	1,897	24.7	649	8.5
1998	2,167	26.3	2,591	31.4	486	5.9	2,263	27.4	1,924	23.3	724	8.8
1997	2,284	24.2	3,270	34.6	588	6.2	2,460	26.0	1,999	21.1	868	9.2
1996	2,379	22.5	3,866	36.6	677	6.4	2,538	24.1	2,034	19.3	1,078	10.2
1995	2,329	21.4	4,171	38.3	786	7.2	2,461	22.6	2,019	18.6	1,053	9.7
1994	2,374	21.4	4,225	38.1	769	6.9	2,371	21.4	1,998	18.0	1,132	10.2
1993	2,226	20.6	4,253	39.4	809	7.5	2,097	19.4	1,908	17.7	1,047	9.7
1992	2,035	20.2	3,972	39.5	871	8.7	1,847	18.4	1,748	17.4	963	9.6
1991	1,757	19.8	3,590	40.5	916	10.3	1,646	18.6	1,585	17.9	733	8.3
1990	1,484	19.0	3,278	42.0	830	10.6	1,530	19.6	1,483	19.0	577	7.4
1989	1,416	19.6	3,023	41.9	727	10.1	1,489	20.6	1,448	20.1	515	7.1

a. A portion of the difference in the proportion of households with SSI from 1996 through 1999 is likely due to changes in the identification of SSI recipients.

Source: U.S. Department of Agriculture. (July 2003). *Characteristics of Food Stamp Households: Fiscal Year 2002 (Advanced Report).* Washington, D.C.: Office of Analysis, Nutrition, and Evaluation. Retrieved from http://www.fns.usda.gov/oane/MENU/Published/FSP/FILES/Participation/2002AdvRpt.pdf.

Table 8.20
Cash and Noncash Benefits for Persons with Limited Income: United States, 1999 and 2000

[For years ending September 30, except as noted (408,405 represents $408,405,000,000). Programs covered provide cash, goods, or services to persons who make no payment and render no service in return. In case of many programs, including family cash welfare, food and housing programs, job and training programs and some educational programs, some recipients must work or study. Most of the programs base eligibility on individual, household, or family income, but some use group or area income tests; and a few offer help on the basis of presumed need.]

Program	Average monthly recipients (1,000)		Expenditures (mil. dol.)					
			Total		Federal		State and local	
	1999	2000	1999	2000	1999	2000	1999	2000
Total	(X)	(X)	408,405	436,985	291,022	306,520	117,383	130,465
Medical care [1]	(X)	(X)	207,042	225,858	119,674	131,468	87,368	94,390
Medicaid [2,3]	42,020	(NA)	190,443	207,195	107,819	117,684	82,624	89,511
Veterans [4,5]	114	123	6,781	7,420	6,781	7,420	-	-
General assistance [5]	(NA)	(NA)	4,052	3,898	-	-	4,052	3,898
State children's health insurance program	1,980	3,300	1,182	2,474	922	1,929	260	545
Indian health services [2,3]	1,500+	1,500+	2,240	2,391	2,240	2,391	-	-
Maternal and child health services	27,097	(NA)	1,131	1,144	699	708	432	436
Consolidated health centers [2]	9,150	9,600	925	1,018	925	1,018	-	-
Cash aid [1]	(X)	(X)	93,603	91,703	74,364	72,516	19,239	19,187
Supplemental security income [3,6]	6,595	6,609	34,838	35,066	30,616	30,718	4,222	4,348
Temporary assistance for needy families (TANF) [7]	7,203	6,035	15,741	14,490	7,882	6,852	7,859	7,638
Earned income tax credit (refunded portion) [8] ..	57,300	55,320	27,344	25,800	27,344	25,800	-	-
Foster care	302	312	7,585	7,941	4,012	4,237	3,573	3,704
General assistance [8]	(NA)	(NA)	2,867	2,649	-	-	2,867	2,649
Pensions for needy veterans [9,10]	671	635	3,084	2,953	3,084	2,953	-	-
Food benefits [1]	(X)	(X)	34,618	34,347	32,583	32,182	2,035	2,165
Food stamps [3,11]	19,300	18,200	20,984	20,341	19,022	18,255	1,962	2,086
School lunch program [12,13]	15,382	15,389	5,507	5,629	5,507	5,629	(NA)	(NA)
Women, infants and children [3,14]	7,300	7,200	3,927	3,944	3,927	3,944	-	-
Child and adult care food program [15]	1,900	1,900	1,468	1,557	1,468	1,557	-	-
School breakfast [12]	6,275	6,339	1,299	1,349	1,299	1,349	-	-
Housing benefits [1]	(X)	(X)	28,929	34,906	28,929	29,261	(NA)	5,645
Low-income housing asst. (Sec. 8) [16]	2,985	3,196	5,652	15,972	15,652	15,972	-	-
Low-rent public housing [16,17]	1,274	1,267	5,956	6,526	5,956	6,526	(NA)	(NA)
Rural housing loans [18,19]	54	46	3,944	3,291	3,944	3,291	-	-
Home investment partnerships [3,19,20]	76	86	1,600	7,275	1,600	1,636	(NA)	5,639
Education aid [1]	(X)	(X)	18,471	20,385	17,281	19,043	1,190	1,342
Pell grants [21,22]	3,838	3,810	7,345	7,704	7,345	7,704	-	-
Head Start	826	858	5,823	6,583	4,658	5,266	1,165	1,317
Stafford loans [21]	5,388	5,354	2,673	3,332	2,673	3,332	-	-
Federal Work-Study Program [21,22]	892	930	830	870	830	870	-	-
Services [1]	(X)	(X)	18,697	20,724	12,105	14,201	6,592	6,523
Social services (Title 20) [23]	(NA)	(NA)	6,149	5,623	3,171	2,854	2,978	2,769
Child care for TANF recipients and ex-recipients [24]	(NA)	(NA)	1,139	2,308	604	1,411	535	897
Child care and development block grant [25]	1,875	1,800	6,236	6,934	4,640	5,059	1,596	1,875
TANF services	(NA)	(NA)	3,095	3,687	1,612	2,705	1,483	982
Jobs and training [1]	(X)	(X)	5,651	7,348	4,777	6,219	874	1,128
TANF work activities	(X)	(X)	1,654	2,272	1,125	1,515	529	757
Training for disadvantaged adults and youth [26]	513	(NA)	1,084	1,950	1,084	1,950	-	-
Job Corps	71	70	1,307	1,357	1,307	1,357	-	-
Energy assistance [1]	(X)	(X)	1,394	1,715	1,309	1,630	85	85
Low-income energy assistance [3,27]	4,400	4,100	1,176	1,495	1,176	1,495	(NA)	(NA)

-. Represents zero.

NA. Not available.

X. Not applicable.

1. Includes other programs not shown separately.

2. Recipient data represent unduplicated annual number.

3. Expenditures include administrative expenses.

Table 8.20 (*continued*)

4. Medical care for veterans with a nonservice-connected disability.
5. Estimated expenditures.
6. Includes state-administered SSI supplements.
7. Excludes data for child support operations.
8. Estimated recipients.
9. Estimated recipients as of September.
10. Includes dependents and survivors.
11. Includes Puerto Rico's nutritional assistance program.
12. Free and reduced-price segments.
13. Includes estimate of commodity assistance.
14. Special supplemental food program for women, infants and children.
15. Recipient data are numbers of children receiving free or reduced price meals and snacks in child care centers and estimates of children in family day care homes with incomes below 185 percent of poverty.
16. Recipient data represent units eligible for payment at end of year.
17. Includes operating subsidies, capital grants, and HUD-administered Indian housing.
18. Recipient data represent total families or dwelling units during year.
19. Expenditure data represent amounts obligated.
20. Recipient data are housing units provided or rehabilitated.
21. Recipient data are total numbers for the school year ending in year shown.
22. Expenditure data are appropriations available for school year ending the fiscal year named.
23. Nonfederal expenditure data are rough estimates.
24. P.L. 104–193, which created TANF established a mandatory block grant for TANF-related childcare.
25. Recipient data are estimated number of children served.
26. Recipient data are total number of participants.
27. Households served during the year with heating and winter crisis aid. Federal funds include amounts transferred to other programs serving the needy.

Source: United States Census Bureau. (2002). *Statistical Abstract of the United States 2002*. Washington, D.C.: Government Printing Office. Retrieved from http://www.census.gov/prod/2003pubs/02statab/socinsur.pdf.

Table 8.21
Number of Households Receiving Home Energy Assistance, by Type of Assistance and State: Fiscal Years 1997 to 1999

State	Heating	Cooling	Energy crisis intervention		Low-cost residential weatherization/energy-related home repair
			Winter	Summer	
			Number of households assisted: 1997 [1]		
Total	[2] 4,069,409	[3] 129,184	769,154	19,121	82,931
Alabama	44,261	. . .	8,784	13,180	445
Alaska	11,947	. . .	419	. . .	1,310
Arizona	[2] 17,713	(3)	3,141	. . .	560
Arkansas	42,964	. . .	12,692	. . .	556
California	[2] 171,574	(3)	18,949	. . .	16,373
Colorado	59,566	. . .	1,091	. . .	1,999
Connecticut	59,586	. . .	15,356	. . .	. . .
Delaware	10,958	. . .	534	. . .	263
District of Columbia	11,147	. . .	2,664	. . .	285
Florida	[2] 69,999	(3)	21,826	. . .	1,116
Georgia	80,060	. . .	. . .	. . .	786
Hawaii	[2] 5,703	(3)	. . .	1,655	. . .
Idaho	21,186	. . .	2,148	. . .	1,527
Illinois	192,337	. . .	10,509	. . .	524
Indiana	104,945	5,469	23,122	. . .	1,617
Iowa	67,993	. . .	5,194	. . .	1,029
Kansas	21,015	. . .	6,481	. . .	401
Kentucky	98,544	. . .	58,597	. . .	3,087
Louisiana	15,016	28,291	103	. . .	1,204
Maine	43,561	. . .	786	. . .	1,006
Maryland	73,404	. . .	3,299	. . .	. . .
Massachusetts	119,017	. . .	8,478	. . .	4,861
Michigan	305,634	. . .	73,968	. . .	4,090
Minnesota	88,650	. . .	17,909	. . .	562
Mississippi	27,262	10,220	1,376	580	. . .
Missouri	105,010	. . .	28,261	. . .	. . .
Montana	17,025	. . .	187	. . .	480
Nebraska	27,071	5,149	30,902	360	693
Nevada	8,076	4,316	. . .	124	. . .
New Hampshire	19,074	. . .	2,505	. . .	354
New Jersey	139,567	15,320	7,046	. . .	1,298
New Mexico	65,564	. . .	3,577	547	151
New York	659,270	. . .	90,026	. . .	2,818
North Carolina	163,161	. . .	44,325	. . .	1,747
North Dakota	13,303	105	1,213	. . .	1,321
Ohio	226,464	. . .	119,843	364	7,498
Oklahoma	62,322	. . .	5,397	. . .	305
Oregon	45,469	. . .	213	. . .	1,960
Pennsylvania	234,577	. . .	63,259	. . .	5,059
Rhode Island	17,602	. . .	2,535	. . .	409
South Carolina	50,247	. . .	2,818	1,613	675
South Dakota	14,874	. . .	707	. . .	760
Tennessee	62,709	7,056	20,142	. . .	1,707
Texas	29,722	48,177	6,350	. . .	1,051
Utah	25,573	5,081	584	. . .	646
Vermont	13,691	. . .	5,683	698	1,146
Virginia	95,970	. . .	1,769	. . .	768
Washington	55,157	. . .	920	. . .	2,902
West Virginia	42,895	. . .	13,141	. . .	555
Wisconsin	103,534	. . .	19,148	. . .	4,851
Wyoming	7,440	. . .	1,177	. . .	176

Table 8.21 (*continued*)

State	Heating	Cooling	Energy crisis intervention		Low-cost residential weatherization/energy-related home repair
			Winter	Summer	
			Number of households assisted: 1998 [1]		
Total	[2] 3,641,836	[3] 316,764	704,640	154,708	85,708
Alabama	36,389	. . .	6,705	44,743	570
Alaska	10,729	. . .	573	. . .	1,036
Arizona	[2]17,316	(3)	3,041	. . .	495
Arkansas	39,030	19,850	16,640	5,436	607
California	[2]121,161	(3)	22,916	. . .	16,983
Colorado	57,802	. . .	1,245	. . .	1,569
Connecticut	56,602	. . .	10,945	. . .	. . .
Delaware	10,517	. . .	777	. . .	246
District of Columbia	10,842	. . .	2,502	. . .	350
Florida	33,770	48,054	14,421	51,368	783
Georgia	64,189	48,334	. . .	. . .	875
Hawaii	[2]5,298	(3)	. . .	1,550	. . .
Idaho	21,803	. . .	2,739	. . .	1,178
Illinois	152,497	. . .	8,544	. . .	2,841
Indiana	105,380	22,269	24,574	. . .	1,668
Iowa	64,039	. . .	4,894	. . .	970
Kansas	18,721	. . .	5,181	. . .	385
Kentucky	92,642	. . .	48,778	. . .	1,874
Louisiana	14,687	29,375	. . .	. . .	383
Maine	36,604		852	40,273	251
Maryland	68,733	. . .	16,554	2,278	42
Massachusetts	112,593	. . .	8,259	. . .	6,800
Michigan	299,787	. . .	49,469	. . .	3,133
Minnesota	81,486	. . .	10,317	. . .	466
Mississippi	21,265	18,914	2,370	5,873	. . .
Missouri	93,143	. . .	26,917	. . .	. . .
Montana	15,211	. . .	189	. . .	301
Nebraska	23,064	5,333	10,947	. . .	519
Nevada	8,257	4,343	. . .	. . .	. . .
New Hampshire	17,598	. . .	2,606	. . .	219
New Jersey	120,656	19,441	7,726	. . .	964
New Mexico	11,543	3,372	7,220	1,275	93
New York	563,883	. . .	9,580	. . .	9,590
North Carolina	216,539	. . .	84,719	. . .	2,301
North Dakota	11,007	275	1,004	. . .	1,093
Ohio	207,951	. . .	108,942	362	6,022
Oklahoma	56,841	37,383	6,087	. . .	291
Oregon	42,781	. . .	117	. . .	1,960
Pennsylvania	231,740	. . .	65,324	. . .	4,150
Rhode Island	16,288	. . .	2,351	127	456
South Carolina	48,909	. . .	1,839	1,332	675
South Dakota	13,134	. . .	469	. . .	702
Tennessee	50,746	28,671	13,941	. . .	2,172
Texas	19,034	31,150	53,464	. . .	1,946
Utah	26,037	. . .	662	. . .	782
Vermont	14,140	. . .	4,600	91	1,192
Virginia	91,275	. . .	3,320	. . .	736
Washington	46,214	. . .	904	. . .	3,257
West Virginia	43,131	. . .	11,737	. . .	516
Wisconsin	92,271	. . .	17,074	. . .	2,071
Wyoming	6,561	. . .	605	. . .	195

Table 8.21 (*continued*)

State	Heating	Cooling	Energy crisis intervention		Low-cost residential weatherization/energy-related home repair
			Winter	Summer	
	Number of households assisted: 1999 [1]				
Total	2 3,338,720	3 532,619	757,410	315,470	84,106
Alabama	43,785	. . .	5,980	23,378	407
Alaska	8,226	. . .	343	. . .	985
Arizona	2 16,484	(3)	2,711	. . .	473
Arkansas	35,600	. . .	16,338	5,329	395
California	2 06,338	(3)	27,363	. . .	15,377
Colorado	48,656	. . .	979	. . .	1,536
Connecticut	52,587	. . .	7,375	32,919	. . .
Delaware	9,716	2,620	676	. . .	181
District of Columbia	14,046	. . .	3,710	. . .	119
Florida	34,701	36,425	12,617	63,638	1,346
Georgia	62,881	. . .	. . .	. . .	1,457
Hawaii	2 5,509	(3)	. . .	1,442	. . .
Idaho	21,229	. . .	1,691	. . .	1,004
Illinois	84,334	27,417	6,358	. . .	1,987
Indiana	84,469	31,226	12,394	. . .	1,487
Iowa	60,159	60,159	1,718	568	2,058
Kansas	20,500	. . .	4,699	. . .	448
Kentucky	84,469	44,127	51,804	. . .	802
Louisiana	3,457	17,285	. . .	. . .	321
Maine	35,696	31,816	814	. . .	326
Maryland	64,773	64,773	5,319	2,415	. . .
Massachusetts	105,665	95,056	7,453	. . .	6,763
Michigan	289,878	. . .	34,331	. . .	1,212
Minnesota	89,924	. . .	19,479	. . .	498
Mississippi	21,855	15,985	2,714	580	. . .
Missouri	88,498	. . .	43,830	. . .	. . .
Montana	13,984	. . .	348	348	553
Nebraska	21,472	5,607	27,508	575	557
Nevada	8,001	4,363	. . .	9	. . .
New Hampshire	17,051	5,823	2,193	. . .	151
New Jersey	113,086	19,983	8,846	28,723	1,826
New Mexico	18,856	. . .	3,343	. . .	441
New York	547,246	. . .	90,712	. . .	8,579
North Carolina	117,052	. . .	65,156	. . .	1,993
North Dakota	10,983	3	955	. . .	471
Ohio	195,272	. . .	102,487	43,734	4,453
Oklahoma	57,316	. . .	10,745	. . .	338
Oregon	46,082	. . .	151	. . .	1,960
Pennsylvania	215,876	. . .	42,696	84,490	4,347
Rhode Island	15,886	. . .	2,220	13,626	195
South Carolina	52,222	. . .	2,690	2,488	1,181
South Dakota	12,038	. . .	398	. . .	664
Tennessee	45,390	16,003	12,953	. . .	2,380
Texas	18,176	28,895	65,609	. . .	3,867
Utah	17,363	. . .	391	. . .	675
Vermont	13,165	12,717	4,504	940	1,000
Virginia	82,988	7,533	4,063	. . .	1,700
Washington	50,507	. . .	1,417	. . .	3,257
West Virginia	39,216	. . .	13,156	. . .	974
Wisconsin	87,002	. . .	23,414	11,196	3,257
Wyoming	6,317	. . .	759	. . .	105

1. An unduplicated total of households assisted cannot be derived from these data because the same households may be included under more than one type of assistance.

2. Totals include households that received combined heating and cooling assistance in Arizona, California, and Florida; households that received energy assistance in Hawaii with no differentiation made between heating and cooling assistance.

3. Excludes households that received combined heating and cooling assistance in Arizona, California, and Florida; households that received energy assistance in Hawaii with no differentiation made between heating and cooling assistance.

Source: Social Security Administration. (2001). *Annual Statistical Supplement, 2001 to the Social Security Bulletin.* Baltimore: Social Security Administration, Office of Policy. Retrieved from http://www.ssa.gov/policy/docs/statcomps/supplement/2001/supp01.pdf.

Table 8.22
Number of Households Receiving Home Energy Assistance, by Type of Assistance: United States, Fiscal Years 1982 to 1999

Fiscal year	Number of households assisted [1]				
	Heating	Cooling	Energy crisis intervention		Low-cost residential weatherization/energy-related home repair
			Winter	Summer	
1982	5,990,176	1,075,061	707,123	. . .	430,830
1983	6,414,448	529,036	972,894	25,342	482,620
1984	6,443,637	537,598	963,743	28,841	180,748
1985	6,545,616	511,333	857,809	27,196	217,864
1986	6,359,924	535,553	951,945	114,194	191,316
1987	6,495,409	366,721	1,060,425	60,797	172,372
1988	5,827,481	309,044	981,775	57,750	156,770
1989	5,595,268	126,977	890,616	20,384	142,584
1990	5,459,631	358,823	1,058,067	37,340	148,104
1991	5,769,346	374,483	1,004,634	39,399	127,587
1992	5,906,292	384,468	950,275	25,570	106,066
1993	5,282,993	143,279	956,435	47,169	111,295
1994	5,663,040	145,684	1,127,832	24,532	126,086
1995	5,147,619	341,041	932,263	77,915	102,817
1996	4,069,409	129,184	769,154	29,121	82,931
1997	4,069,409	129,184	769,154	19,121	82,931
1998	3,641,836	316,764	704,640	154,708	85,708
1999	3,338,720	532,619	757,410	315,470	84,106

1. An unduplicated total of households assisted cannot be derived from these data because the same households may be included under more than one type of assistance. Totals include households that received combined heating and cooling assistance in Arizona, California, and Florida; households that received energy assistance in Hawaii with no differentiation made between heating and cooling assistance.

Source: Social Security Administration. (2001). *Annual Statistical Supplement, 2001 to the Social Security Bulletin.* Baltimore: Social Security Administration, Office of Policy. Retrieved from http://www.ssa.gov/policy/docs/statcomps/supplement/2001/supp01.pdf.

Table 8.23
Estimated Home Energy Assistance Obligations, by Type of Assistance and State: Fiscal Years 1997 to 1999

State	Heating assistance benefits	Cooling assistance benefits	Crisis assistance benefits	Weatherization assistance benefits
	Estimated Amount: 1997[1]			
Total	[2] $749,704,757	[3] $18,755,118	$176,095,176	$153,589,045
Alabama	5,830,577	. . .	2,711,801	495,000
Alaska	3,733,663	. . .	74,937	[4] 7,181,255
Arizona	[2] 3,032,890	(3)	457,388	885,780
Arkansas	3,517,192	. . .	1,806,598	1,365,425
California	[2] 26,260,573	(3)	8,502,595	15,074,072
Colorado	17,563,743	. . .	370,053	2,858,896
Connecticut	21,793,624	. . .	4,096,647	. . .
Delaware	2,500,632	. . .	102,629	308,129
District of Columbia	2,420,434	. . .	427,254	640,881
Florida	[2] 8,682,322	(3)	3,938,698	2,763,264
Georgia	9,920,230	. . .	. . .	1,864,701
Hawaii	[2] 854,660	(3)	271,548	. . .
Idaho	3,720,628	. . .	1,143,912	1,237,160
Illinois	52,811,770	. . .	5,241,395	9,576,402
Indiana	24,701,779	. . .	3,068,010	3,360,745
Iowa	17,484,616	306,982	1,151,621	3,686,382
Kansas	7,282,063	. . .	1,790,955	1,332,912
Kentucky	8,701,462	. . .	4,648,157	2,445,353
Louisiana	3,239,607	. . .	. . .	1,372,070
Maine	11,696,873	4,535,452	304,139	2,273,881
Maryland	14,269,602	. . .	504,532	. . .
Massachusetts	38,627,195	. . .	(5)	2,835,936
Michigan	39,192,409	. . .	13,743,248	4,459,098
Minnesota	44,803,997	. . .	7,937,324	2,383,352
Mississippi	4,764,167	. . .	333,166	. . .
Missouri	18,991,968	1,787,925	8,100,000	. . .
Montana	5,838,126	. . .	46,839	1,259,347
Nebraska	4,307,321	. . .	4,225,859	1,336,863
Nevada	1,502,034	417,705	19,267	. . .
New Hampshire	6,794,957	452,624	730,883	800,000
New Jersey	35,651,367	. . .	1,910,000	3,108,217
New Mexico	4,103,392	1,726,000	300,449	835,194
New York	80,597,313	. . .	32,655,454	21,905,111
North Carolina	5,216,233	. . .	10,754,869	4,078,042
North Dakota	6,282,228	. . .	201,856	2,955,558
Ohio	24,776,680	50,000	22,442,499	8,297,287
Oklahoma	6,316,555	. . .	653,008	757,935
Oregon	9,429,185	. . .	72,808	3,089,276
Pennsylvania	49,008,836	. . .	13,796,209	11,845,623
Rhode Island	5,503,616	. . .	253,450	1,200,000
South Carolina	6,081,943	. . .	590,167	1,174,735
South Dakota	6,120,498	. . .	59,584	1,332,649
Tennessee	9,401,925	. . .	2,593,634	1,296,817
Texas	6,728,436	648,409	3,656,759	4,303,632
Utah	5,310,753	7,898,599	165,019	1,988,030
Vermont	5,389,829	. . .	838,206	100,000
Virginia	17,229,067	. . .	159,248	1,695,865
Washington	16,266,212	931,422	355,096	3,471,957
West Virginia	4,966,029	. . .	2,227,212	1,593,612
Wisconsin	28,242,562	. . .	6,660,111	5,898,056
Wyoming	2,240,984	. . .	83	864,545

Table 8.23 (*continued*)

State	Heating assistance benefits	Cooling assistance benefits	Crisis assistance benefits	Weatherization assistance benefits
		Estimated Amount: 1998[1]		
Total..................................	[2] $633,618,243	[3] $62,178,981	$212,043,081	$138,217,577
Alabama..	4,581,398	. . .	9,967,400	980,000
Alaska	3,357,402	. . .	104,718	[4] 4,388,936
Arizona...	[2] 2,408,314	(3)	701,667	749,212
Arkansas.......................................	2,897,999	2,303,058	2,747,241	1,849,949
California	[2] 20,822,171	(3)	9,739,868	10,954,643
Colorado	20,359,208	. . .	458,966	2,720,074
Connecticut	18,875,502	. . .	2,175,354	. . .
Delaware..	1,949,425	. . .	114,996	391,774
District of Columbia.......................	2,083,376	. . .	448,222	561,914
Florida	[2] 2,654,265	[3] 4,631,367	23,377,490	4,313,680
Georgia	8,701,308	10,278,329	. . .	2,837,834
Hawaii	[2] 713,922	(3)	237,412	. . .
Idaho...	2,961,477	. . .	535,659	1,351,840
Illinois...	35,809,968	. . .	2,629,540	6,985,646
Indiana..	21,327,410	1,171,767	2,640,346	3,314,931
Iowa..	12,424,215	. . .	1,011,528	2,721,582
Kansas..	5,646,619	. . .	1,605,023	1,123,011
Kentucky..	7,749,812	. . .	3,866,113	2,101,637
Louisiana	2,728,416	3,819,781	8,670,206	1,155,565
Maine	8,636,320	. . .	345,408	2,260,132
Maryland	14,079,929	. . .	389,740	140,000
Massachusetts...............................	33,380,601	. . .	(5)	4,280,040
Michigan	40,200,000	. . .	7,450,480	1,000,000
Minnesota	26,279,401	. . .	6,512,473	1,933,770
Mississippi	6,071,094	3,241,433	487,434	. . .
Missouri	16,855,027	. . .	3,907,051	. . .
Montana...	4,871,979	. . .	45,423	794,140
Nebraska	3,756,483	448,704	2,710,555	1,076,736
Nevada	1,313,888	464,426	. . .	. . .
New Hampshire	5,480,092	. . .	630,321	600,000
New Jersey.....................................	27,556,443	1,944,000	2,576,000	5,384,083
New Mexico	1,467,599	389,211	1,425,051	703,342
New York	70,199,073	. . .	26,760,128	18,758,021
North Carolina................................	6,284,055	. . .	15,953,653	4,128,478
North Dakota	4,008,468	120,000	581,435	1,643,000
Ohio..	25,435,321	. . .	15,348,595	6,843,754
Oklahoma	5,488,400	4,977,000	556,499	637,354
Oregon	7,234,289	. . .	32,501	2,652,169
Pennsylvania	44,486,068	. . .	13,865,771	9,980,000
Rhode Island..................................	5,395,945	. . .	260,433	1,000,000
South Carolina...............................	4,670,204	. . .	5,596,320	997,350
South Dakota	4,357,788	. . .	60,327	779,667
Tennessee	8,651,281	7,401,714	2,528,666	1,431,370
Texas	10,000,000	20,988,191	23,208,715	11,521,720
Utah..	6,016,932	. . .	160,772	352,641
Vermont	4,620,455	. . .	1,189,736	190,588
Virginia	15,229,395	. . .	434,428	1,152,767
Washington....................................	13,865,140	. . .	356,139	2,980,286
West Virginia..................................	5,225,630	. . .	2,085,614	793,530
Wisconsin	22,684,505	. . .	5,421,833	4,972,011
Wyoming..	1,764,231	. . .	129,831	728,400

Table 8.23 (*continued*)

State	Heating assistance benefits	Cooling assistance benefits	Crisis assistance benefits	Weatherization assistance benefits
	Estimated Amount: 1999[1]			
Total..................................	[2] $684,600,568	[3]$72,294,009	$210,175,301	$145,039,987
Alabama...........................	4,334,898	. . .	3,408,034	389,354
Alaska	[2] 5,469,575	. . .	77,382	[4]4,387,304
Arizona	2,992,307	(2)	493,402	837,500
Arkansas.........................	3,482,832	. . .	2,524,724	1,756,131
California	[2]17,567,157	(3)	12,534,928	13,382,930
Colorado	14,401,728	. . .	384,150	2,652,610
Connecticut	17,441,272	. . .	4,117,901	. . .
Delaware.........................	2,005,539	565,800	87,880	551,423
District of Columbia...........	2,871,554	. . .	565,445	548,169
Florida.............................	[2] 2,890,935	[3]3,578,319	7,530,433	2,010,114
Georgia...........................	8,475,954	. . .	. . .	1,557,999
Hawaii.............................	[2] 829,208	(3)	215,713	. . .
Idaho...............................	4,565,299	. . .	452,023	838,385
Illinois.............................	43,530,070	17,166,080	5,423,791	. . .
Indiana............................	24,167,415	2,538,447	1,676,326	4,211,300
Iowa	12,494,831	. . .	1,168,487	3,173,847
Kansas............................	8,022,490	. . .	1,329,902	1,870,478
Kentucky	7,061,323	6,104,255	4,744,602	3,084,467
Louisiana	1,623,315	4,869,918	721,470	1,414,648
Maine	10,523,168	636,320	523,398	2,405,855
Maryland	16,491,111	2,845,348	570,448	150,000
Massachusetts.................	33,934,032	6,748,300	. . .	4,299,600
Michigan	41,140,699	(5)	6,736,217	9,122,344
Minnesota	25,739,080	. . .	9,853,994	1,957,328
Mississippi	5,133,471	1,414,186	336,654	. . .
Missouri	17,556,313	. . .	8,987,271	. . .
Montana	4,644,676	. . .	214,331	1,037,889
Nebraska.........................	3,533,812	469,013	4,945,637	1,491,260
Nevada............................	1,238,286	499,171	1,416	. . .
New Hampshire	5,679,162	696,656	809,221	800,000
New Jersey......................	31,305,717	2,000,000	10,727,985	3,607,000
New Mexico......................	3,097,853	. . .	546,679	773,404
New York	85,498,591	. . .	29,581,769	25,098,238
North Carolina..................	11,794,326	. . .	24,484,664	2,720,435
North Dakota	4,603,413	. . .	888,835	1,070,640
Ohio................................	27,347,922	. . .	22,350,627	9,275,584
Oklahoma........................	7,035,173	. . .	397,548	703,185
Oregon	8,951,696	. . .	51,227	2,984,502
Pennsylvania	50,132,354	. . .	19,925,770	10,411,788
Rhode Island....................	5,118,275	. . .	1,763,431	1,383,293
South Carolina	5,509,527	. . .	845,304	1,267,956
South Dakota	4,640,124	. . .	49,796	857,249
Tennessee	5,492,190	4,146,141	1,567,313	1,460,309
Texas	2,885,363	12,390,089	1,697,272	3,635,058
Utah	6,237,673	. . .	101,850	681,729
Vermont...........................	4,331,310	318,900	1,313,192	. . .
Virginia............................	19,477,808	2,866,295	1,389,647	3,364,719
Washington......................	15,035,740	. . .	689,240	3,227,870
West Virginia....................	5,053,136	. . .	4,532,380	1,701,927
Wisconsin	28,831,369	. . .	7,493,380	6,083,208
Wyoming..........................	1,570,275	. . .	151,433	800,958

1. Includes federal LIHEAP appropriated funds and non-federal funds operated through the LIHEAP program.

2. Includes funds for households that received combined heating and cooling assistance in Arizona, California, and Florida; households that received energy assistance in Hawaii with no differentiation made between heating and cooling assistance.

3. Excludes funds for households that received combined heating and cooling assistance in Arizona, California, and Florida; households that received energy assistance in Hawaii with no differentiation made between heating and cooling assistance.

4. Includes $6.2 million in state funds.

5. Excludes funds for households that received expedited heating assistance for winter crisis situations.

Source: Social Security Administration. (2001). *Annual Statistical Supplement, 2001 to the Social Security Bulletin.* Baltimore: Social Security Administration, Office of Policy. Retrieved from http://www.ssa.gov/policy/docs/statcomps/supplement/2001/supp01.pdf.

Table 8.24
Estimated Home Energy Assistance Obligations, by Type of Assistance: United States, Fiscal Years 1982 to 1999

Fiscal year	Estimated amount[1]			
	Heating assistance benefits	Cooling assistance benefits	Crisis assistance benefits	Weatherization assistance benefits
1982	$1,124,476,630	$51,498,572	$138,941,133	$136,195,046
1983	1,343,267,155	33,020,830	191,771,756	195,463,612
1984	1,372,772,591	32,374,067	225,795,893	186,662,906
1985	1,466,721,924	29,135,118	191,407,205	227,096,051
1986	1,351,903,078	35,620,945	199,178,003	193,420,839
1987	1,280,302,113	29,581,262	197,719,071	220,419,633
1988	1,145,560,993	21,151,405	190,046,023	170,292,505
1989	1,017,024,757	12,341,113	187,442,779	147,952,928
1990	1,030,150,903	25,007,676	188,844,316	133,479,484
1991	1,098,583,280	27,416,776	220,795,517	129,279,737
1992	990,903,081	22,645,002	197,218,623	134,816,010
1993	948,596,196	22,274,975	183,189,522	146,444,590
1994	1,062,552,111	24,862,635	225,583,805	214,342,289
1995	884,846,144	43,883,481	212,713,182	159,076,150
1996	696,801,144	17,597,204	167,622,219	135,835,358
1997	749,704,757	18,755,118	176,095,176	153,589,045
1998	633,618,243	62,178,981	212,043,081	138,217,577
1999	684,600,568	72,294,009	210,175,301	145,039,987

1. Includes federal LIHEAP appropriated funds and non-federal funds operated through the LIHEAP program.

Source: Social Security Administration. (2001). *Annual Statistical Supplement, 2001 to the Social Security Bulletin.* Baltimore: Social Security Administration, Office of Policy. Retrieved from http://www.ssa.gov/policy/docs/statcomps/supplement/2001/supp01.pdf.

Table 8.25
Net New Commitments for Renters and Home
Buyers Receiving Direct Housing Assistance
Administered by HUD, by Type of Subsidy: United States,
Selected Years 1977 to 2000

Fiscal year	Net new commitments for renters			Net new commitments for home buyers[3]
	Existing housing[1]	New construction[2]	Total	
1977...	12,7581	226,832	354,413	4,719
1980...	58,402	129,490	187,892	58,907
1981...	83,520	75,365	158,885	5,102
1982...	37,818	18,018	55,836	4,754
1983...	54,071	-339	53,732	2,630
1984...	78,648	9,619	88,267	930
1985...	85,741	16,980	102,721	4,586
1986...	85,476	13,109	98,585	5
1987...	72,788	20,192	92,980	60
1988...	64,270	19,991	84,261	0
1989...	67,653	14,053	81,706	0
1990...	61,309	7,428	68,737	0
1991[4].....................................	55,900	13,082	68,982	0
1992[4].....................................	62,008	23,537	85,545	0
1993[4].....................................	50,162	18,715	68,877	0
1994[4].....................................	47,807	17,652	65,459	0
1995[4].....................................	16,904	16,587	33,491	0
1996[4].....................................	7,055	1,438	8,493	0
1997[4].....................................	9,229	12,449	21,678	0
1998[4].....................................	18,376	17,675	36,051	0
1999[4].....................................	16,225	11,060	27,285	0
2000 est.[4]...............................	126,000	9,556	135,556	0

1. Includes units assisted through section 8 certificates and vouchers, loan management set-aside (LMSA), PD, and Moderate Rehabilitation Programs.
2. Includes units assisted through the section 8 New Construction and Substantial Rehabilitation Program, section 202/811 Housing for the Elderly and the Disabled, section 236, and Public and Indian Housing Programs. Excludes units constructed under the Indian Housing Block Grant Program.
3. Includes units assisted through the various section 235 programs.
4. Figures are no longer adjusted for units for which funds were deobligated because data were unavailable.
Note: Because reliable data are not readily available, this table excludes substantial numbers of commitments made through the various programs for the homeless (including HOPWA) and other block grant programs such as the HOME Investment Partnerships Program.

Source: United States House of Representatives, Committee on Ways and Means. (2000). *The 2000 Green Book: Background material and data on programs within the jurisdiction of the Committee on Ways and Means.* Retrieved from http://aspe.hhs.gov/2000gb/sec15.txt.

Table 8.26
Total Households Receiving Direct Housing Assistance Administered by HUD, by Type of Subsidy: United States, 1977 to 2000

(in Thousands of Households)

Start of fiscal year	Existing housing			New construction[3]	Total assisted renters[4]	Total assisted homeowners[5]	Total assisted renters and homeowners[4]
	Household-based[1]	Project-based[2]	Subtotal existing housing				
1977	162	105	268	1,799	2,067	331	2,398
1978	297	126	423	1,928	2,350	293	2,643
1979	427	175	602	1,978	2,580	262	2,842
1980	521	185	707	2,090	2,797	235	3,032
1981	599	221	820	2,228	3,212	219	3,431
1982	651	194	844	2,373	3,379	241	3,619
1983	691	265	955	2,485	3,615	242	3,857
1984	728	357	1,086	2,589	3,851	230	4,081
1985	749	431	1,180	2,657	4,015	210	4,225
1986	797	456	1,253	2,686	4,135	200	4,336
1987	893	473	1,366	2,721	4,279	182	4,461
1988	956	490	1,446	2,736	4,371	159	4,530
1989	1,025	509	1,534	2,748	4,485	148	4,632
1990	1,090	527	1,616	2,755	4,569	141	4,710
1991	1,137	540	1,678	2,778	4,656	130	4,786
1992	1,166	554	1,721	2,786	4,705	125	4,830
1993	1,326	574	1,900	2,762	4,861	98	4,959
1994	1,392	593	1,985	2,764	4,939	95	5,035
1995	1,474	607	2,081	2,778	5,049	80	5,130
1996	1,413	608	2,021	2,817	5,028	76	5,104
1997	1,465	586	2,051	2,822	5,063	68	5,132
1998	1,481	564	2,045	2,786	5,021	60	5,082
1999	1,613	542	2,154	2,757	5,101	53	5,154
2000	1,621	522	2,143	2,728	5,061	43	5,104

1. Includes units assisted through section 8 certificates and vouchers.

2. Includes units assisted through the section 8 loan management set-aside (LMSA), PD, conversion (from rent supplement and section 236 Rental Assistance Program), and Moderate Rehabilitation Programs.

3. Includes units assisted through the section 8 New Construction and Substantial Rehabilitation Program, section 236, Rent Supplement, and Public Housing Programs, including Indian units originally constructed under the Public Housing Program but currently assisted through the section 8 loan management set-aside (LMSA), PD, conversion (from rest supplement and section 236 Rental Assistance Program), and Moderate Rehabilitation Programs.

4. Figures for total assisted renters have been adjusted since 1980 to avoid double-counting households receiving more than one subsidy. Therefore, the total is less than the sum of the components.

5. Includes units assisted through the various section 235 programs.

Note: Because reliable data are not readily available, this table excludes substantial numbers of households receiving aid through the various programs.

Source: United States House of Representatives, Committee on Ways and Means. (2000). *The 2000 Green Book: Background material and data on programs within the jurisdiction of the Committee on Ways and Means.* Retrieved from http://aspe.hhs.gov/2000gb/sec15.txt.

Table 8.27
Net Budget Authority Appropriated for Housing Assistance Administered by HUD, by Broad Program Categories: United States, 1977 to 2000

(in Millions of Current and 2000 Dollars)

Fiscal year	Direct housing assistance[1] in current dollars	Homeless programs[2] in current dollars	Other housing block grants[3] in current dollars	Total net budget authority Current dollars	Total net budget authority 2000 dollars
1977	$28,579	0	0	$28,579	$77,944
1978	32,193	0	0	32,193	82,470
1979	25,123	0	0	25,123	59,100
1980	27,435	0	0	27,435	58,075
1981	26,021	0	0	26,021	50,057
1982	14,766	0	0	14,766	26,544
1983	10,001	0	0	10,001	17,214
1984	10,810	0	$615	11,425	18,867
1985	11,071	0	0	11,071	17,633
1986	9,888	0	144	10,032	15,591
1987	8,645	$195	300	9,140	13,806
1988	8,353	107	204	8,664	12,570
1989	8,664	172	170	9,006	12,476
1990	10,331	284	152	10,767	14,206
1991	19,029	339	105	19,473	24,457
1992	16,730	498	1,861	19,089	23,277
1993	18,280	672	1,485	20,437	24,181
1994	18,107	979	1,173	20,259	23,358
1995	11,676	1,291	1,462	14,429	16,182
1996	13,218	994	1,400	15,612	17,036
1997	8,672	1,019	1,370	11,061	11,753
1998	14,175	1,027	1,500	16,702	17,463
1999	16,544	1,200	1,600	19,344	19,846
2000	17,459	1,252	1,600	20,311	20,311

1. Includes the following programs: section 8 Low-Income Housing Assistance, section 202/811 Housing for the Elderly and the Disabled, section 236 Rental Housing Assistance, Rent Supplement, section 235 Homeownership Assistance, Public Housing Capital, Public Housing Operating Subsidies, Public Housing Drug Elimination Grants, Revitalization of Severely Distressed Public Housing, Low-Rent Public Housing Loan Fund, Indian Housing Block Grants.

2. Includes the following programs: Housing Opportunities for Persons with AIDS (HOPWA), Homeless Assistance Grants, Supplemental Assistance for Facilities to Assist the Homeless, Emergency Shelter Grants, Supportive Housing, Shelter Plus Care Program, section 8 Moderate Rehabilitation for Single Room Occupancy Dwellings, Innovative Homeless Initiatives Demonstration Program.

3. Includes the following programs: HOME Investment Partnerships Program, Nehemiah Housing Opportunity Grant Program, Rental Housing Development Grants (HoDAG), Rental Rehabilitations Block Grant Program.

Note: All figures are not of funding rescissions, exclude reappropriations of funds, and include supplemental appropriations. Figures exclude budget authority for HUD's section 202 loan fund.

Source: United States House of Representatives, Committee on Ways and Means. (2000). *The 2000 Green Book: Background material and data on programs within the jurisdiction of the Committee on Ways and Means.* Retrieved from http://aspe.hhs.gov/2000gb/sec15.txt.

Table 8.28
Outlays for Housing Assistance Administered by HUD, by Broad Program Categories: United States, 1977 to 2000

(in Millions of Current and 2000 Dollars)

Fiscal year	Direct housing assistance in current dollars)			Homeless programs[3] (in current dollars)	Other housing block grants[4] (in current dollars)	Total outlays	
	Section 8 and other assisted housing[1]	Public housing[2]	Subtotal assisted housing			Current dollars	2000 dollars
1977	$1,331	$1,564	$2,895	0	0	$5,790	$15,791
1978	1,824	1,779	3,603	0	0	7,206	18,460
1979	2,374	1,815	4,189	0	0	8,378	19,709
1980	3,146	2,218	5,364	0	0	10,728	22,709
1981	4,254	2,478	6,732	0	0	13,464	25,901
1982	5,293	2,553	7,846	0	0	15,692	28,208
1983	6,102	3,318	9,420	0	0	18,840	32,428
1984	7,068	3,932	11,000	0	0	22,000	36,331
1985	7,771	17,261	25,032	0	$15	50,079	79,760
1986	8,320	3,859	12,179	0	142	24,500	38,075
1987	8,993	3,517	12,510	$2	165	25,187	38,046
1988	9,985	3,699	13,684	37	180	27,585	40,020
1989	10,689	3,774	14,463	72	275	29,273	40,553
1990	11,357	4,331	15,688	85	276	31,737	41,875
1991	12,107	4,786	16,893	125	168	34,079	42,802
1992	13,052	5,182	18,234	150	35	36,653	44,694
1993	14,032	6,447	20,479	180	276	41,414	49,002
1994	15,289	6,857	22,146	225	862	45,379	52,321
1995[5]	16,448	7,505	23,953	359	1,259	49,524	55,542
1996[5]	17,496	7,668	25,164	616	1,273	52,217	56,979
1997	17,131	7,809	24,940	718	1,263	51,861	55,104
1998[5]	16,975	8,028	25,003	916	1,316	52,238	54,617
1999[5]	17,171	7,805	24,976	1,032	1,367	52,351	53,710
2000 est.[5]	17,443	8,094	25,537	1,174	1,456	53,704	53,704

1. Includes the following programs: section 8 Low-Income Housing Assistance, section 202/811 Housing for the Elderly and the Disabled, section 236 Rental Housing Assistance, Rent Supplement, section 235 Homeownership Assistance.

2. Includes the following programs: Public Housing Capital, Public Housing Operating Subsidies, Public Housing Drug Elimination Grants, Revitalization of Severely Distressed Public Housing, Low-Rent Public Housing Loan Fund, Indian Housing Block Grants.

3. Includes the following programs: Housing Opportunities for Persons with AIDS (HOPWA), Homeless Assistance Grants, Supplemental Assistance for Facilities to Assist the Homeless, Emergency Shelter Grants, Supportive Housing, Shelter Plus Care Program, section 8 Moderate Rehabilitation for Single Room Occupancy Dwellings Program, Innovative Homeless Initiatives Demonstration Program.

4. Includes the following programs: HOME Investment Partnerships Program, Nehemiah Housing Opportunity Grant Program, Rental Housing Development Grants (HoDAG), Rental Rehabilitations Block Grant Program.

5. In order to reflect trends more accurately, figures have been adjusted to account for advance spending in certain years. In 1995, $1.2 billion of spending occurred that should have occurred in 1996. In 1998, $680 million of spending occurred that should have occurred in 1999. The Congressional Budget Office also expects that $680 million of spending will occur in 2000 that should occur in 2001.

Source: United States House of Representatives, Committee on Ways and Means. (2000). *The 2000 Green Book: Background material and data on programs within the jurisdiction of the Committee on Ways and Means.* Retrieved from http://aspe.hhs.gov/2000gb/sec15.txt.

Table 8.29
Per Unit Outlays for Housing Aid Administered by HUD: United States, 1977 to 1997

(in Current and 1997 Dollars)

	Per unit outlays	
Fiscal year	Current dollars	1997 dollars
1977......................................	$1,160	$2,980
1978......................................	1,310	3,160
1979......................................	1,430	3,160
1980......................................	1,750	3,480
1981......................................	2,100	3,810
1982......................................	2,310	3,900
1983......................................	2,600	4,220
1984......................................	2,900	4,500
1985......................................	6,420	9,620
1986......................................	3,040	4,440
1987......................................	3,040	4,320
1988......................................	3,270	4,460
1989......................................	3,390	4,420
1990......................................	3,610	4,480
1991......................................	3,830	4,530
1992......................................	4,060	4,670
1993......................................	4,450	4,960
1994......................................	4,720	5,120
1995......................................	5,080	5,360
1996......................................	5,350	5,490
1997 (estimate).......................	5,490	5,490

Note: The peak in outlays per unit in 1985 of $6,420 is attributable to the bulge in 1985 expenditures associated with the change in the method for financing public housing. Without this change, outlays per unit would have amounted to around $2,860.

Source: United States House of Representatives, Committee on Ways and Means. (2000). *The 2000 Green Book: Background material and data on programs within the jurisdiction of the Committee on Ways and Means.* Retrieved from http://aspe.hhs.gov/2000gb/sec15.txt.

Table 8.30
Estimated Tax Base Exceptions and Credits Under the Present Income Tax for Various Items[1]: United States, Calendar Years 2001 to 2005

(in Billions of Dollars)

Item	Year					Total 2001-5
	2001	2002	2003	2004	2005	
I. Tax base exceptions related to: Retirement:						
Net exclusion of pension contributions and earnings........	$372.9	$361.5	$344.9	$341.3	$344.3	$1,764.8
Keogh plans.........................	20.1	20.4	20.6	21.9	23.7	106.8
Individual retirement plans.........	55.5	62.9	67.6	73.3	76.7	336.1
Exclusion of Social Security and railroad retirement benefits in excess of employee share of payroll tax[2]...........................	269.7	279.3	288.4	298.8	307.1	1,443.3
Health:						
Exclusions of employer contributions for medical care, health insurance premiums and long-term care insurance premiums[3]...........	359.5	384.5	407.1	431.9	458.9	2,042.0
Exclusion of Medicare benefits:						
Medicare part A.................	131.7	138.3	145.4	153.8	164.8	734.0
Medicare part B.................	81.7	88.0	96.3	103.2	111.9	481.1
Deductibility of medical expenses[4]......	29.5	32.3	33.9	35.5	36.5	167.7
Deductibility of health insurance expenses of the self-employed[5]..	7.2	9.0	14.1	14.9	15.8	60.9
Exclusion of accelerated death benefits...........................	2.1	2.5	2.9	3.5	3.9	14.8
Poverty:						
Exclusion of public assistance and SSI cash benefits..................	54.7	57.4	60.4	63.4	69.8	305.8
Employment:						
Exclusion of employer-provided dependent care[6].................	0.7	0.7	0.7	0.8	0.8	3.6
Employee stock ownership plans......	13.5	14.0	14.6	15.2	15.8	73.1
Exclusion for benefits provided under cafeteria plans[7]........	45.7	48.9	51.8	55.0	58.5	259.9
Elderly and disabled:						
Exclusion of workers' compensation and special benefits for disabled coal miners:						
Workers' compensation...........	32.1	33.7	34.6	35.3	37.2	172.8
Special benefits for disabled coal miners...................	0.3	0.3	0.3	0.3	0.3	1.6
Additional standard deduction for elderly and blind.................	12.1	12.5	13.0	13.5	14.4	65.5
Housing:						
Deductibility of mortgage interest..	239.4	250.9	261.7	273.4	285.8	1,311.2
Deductibility of property tax on owner-occupied housing............	85.4	89.5	93.8	98.2	102.6	469.5
Exclusion of interest on State and local government bonds for owner-occupied housing...................	3.3	3.3	3.3	3.4	3.4	16.8
Depreciation of rental housing in excess of alternative depreciation system............................	6.7	7.6	8.2	9.3	10.6	42.4
Exclusion of interest on State and local government bonds for rental housing...........................	0.7	0.7	0.7	0.8	0.8	3.6
Families:						
Qualified State tuition programs and education IRAs....................	0.1	0.2	0.2	0.2	0.2	0.9
Student loan interest deduction.....	0.4	0.4	0.4	0.5	0.5	2.2
Employer-provided adoption expenses	(8)	(8)	(8)	(8)	(8)	(8)

Table 8.30 (*continued*)

II. Tax credits related to:						
Poverty:						
Earned income credit:						
Nonrefundable portion...........	4.3	4.3	4.4	4.5	4.6	22.0
Refundable portion[9].........	26.4	26.7	27.2	27.8	28.4	136.5
Employment:						
Dependent care credit..............	2.4	2.3	2.3	2.3	2.1	11.5
Work opportunity tax credit.........	0.3	0.3	0.2	0.1	([8])	0.8
Welfare-to-work tax credit.........	0.1	0.1	([8])	([8])	([8])	0.2
Elderly and disabled:						
Tax credit for elderly and disabled.	([8])	([8])	([8])	([8])	([8])	0.1
Housing:						
Low-income housing tax credit.......	3.7	3.9	4.0	4.1	4.2	19.7
Child tax credit: Families:						
Nonrefundable portion..........	19.1	18.5	18.3	17.8	17.2	90.9
Refundable portion.............	0.8	0.8	0.8	0.8	0.8	4.0
HOPE credit and lifetime learning credit............................	4.6	4.2	4.3	4.3	4.3	21.6
Adoption credit....................	0.3	0.1	0.1	0.1	0.1	0.5

1. Estimates of exclusions and deductions represent changes in the tax base; they do not measure changes in tax liability. Tax effects of provisions are not comparable.

2. In addition to OASDI: benefits for retired workers, these figures also include disability insurance benefits and benefits for dependents and survivors.

3. Estimate includes employer-provided health insurance purchased through cafeteria plans and health care spending through flexible spending accounts.

4. Amounts reported on tax returns in excess of the medical deductions floor (7.5 percent of adjusted gross income).

5. Amounts deductible from gross income (60 percent of health insurance expenses in 2001, 70 percent in 2002, and 100 percent in 2003–5).

6. Estimate includes employer-provided child care purchased through dependent care flexible spending accounts.

7. Estimate includes amounts of employer-provided health insurance purchased through cafeteria plans and employer-provided child care purchased through dependent care flexible spending accounts. These amounts are also included in other line items in this table.

8. Less than $50 million.

9. Estimate provided by the Congressional Budget Office.

Note: Details may not add to totals due to rounding.

Source: United States House of Representatives, Committee on Ways and Means. (2000). *The 2000 Green Book: Background material and data on programs within the jurisdiction of the Committee on Ways and Means.* Retrieved from http://aspe.hhs.gov/2000gb/sec13.txt.

Table 8.31
Use of Deductible Individual Retirement Accounts: United States, 1980 to 1997

Year	Number of tax returns deducting IRA contributions (millions)	Total IRA deductions (billions)
1980	2.6	$3.4
1981	3.4	4.8
1982	12.0	28.3
1983	13.6	32.1
1984	15.2	35.4
1985	16.2	38.2
1986	15.5	37.8
1987	7.3	14.1
1988	6.4	11.9
1989	5.8	10.8
1990	5.2	9.9
1991	4.7	9.0
1992	4.5	8.7
1993	4.4	8.5
1994	4.3	8.4
1995	4.1	8.3
1996	4.4	8.6
1997	4.1	8.7

Source: United States House of Representatives, Committee on Ways and Means. (2000). *The 2000 Green Book: Background material and data on programs within the jurisdiction of the Committee on Ways and Means*. Retrieved from http://aspe.hhs.gov/2000gb/sec13.txt.

Table 8.32
Dependent Care Tax Credit: Number
of Families and Amount of Credit: United States,
1976 to 1998

Year	Number of returns claiming dependent credit (thousands)	Aggregate amount of credit claimed (millions)	Average credit claimed per return
1976	2,660	$548	$206
1977	2,910	521	179
1978	3,431	654	191
1979	3,833	793	207
1980	4,231	956	226
1981	4,578	1,148	251
1982	5,004	1,501	300
1983	6,367	2,051	322
1984	7,456	2,649	351
1985	8,417	3,127	372
1986	8,950	3,398	380
1987	8,520	3,438	404
1988	9,023	3,813	423
1989	6,028	2,440	405
1990	6,144	2,549	415
1991	5,896	2,521	427
1992	5,980	2,527	433
1993	6,090	2,559	419
1994	6,012	2,526	420
1995	5,964	2,518	445
1996	6,003	2,663	444
1997	5,796	2,464	425
1998[1]	6,120	2,649	433

1. Preliminary.

Source: United States House of Representatives, Committee on Ways and Means. (2000). *The 2000 Green Book: Background material and data on programs within the jurisdiction of the Committee on Ways and Means.* Retrieved from http://aspe.hhs.gov/2000gb/sec13.txt.

Table 8.33
Credit for the Elderly and Disabled: United States, 1976 to 1997

Year	Number of families that received credit (thousands)	Total amount of credit (millions)	Average credit per return
1976	1,011	$206	$204
1977	569	93	163
1978	689	145	210
1979	607	132	217
1980	562	135	240
1981	474	124	262
1982	483	131	271
1983	423	116	275
1984	475	107	225
1985	460	106	230
1986	430	86	200
1987	354	67	189
1988	357	69	193
1989	320	65	202
1990	342	63	183
1991	285	57	200
1992	240	51	213
1993	223	49	220
1994	222	47	210
1995	252	48	191
1996	168	32	189
1997	190	41	217

Source: United States House of Representatives, Committee on Ways and Means. (2000). *The 2000 Green Book: Background material and data on programs within the jurisdiction of the Committee on Ways and Means.* Retrieved from http://aspe.hhs.gov/2000gb/sec13.txt.

Figure 8.2
The U.S. Federal Earned Income Tax Credit in Tax Year 2001

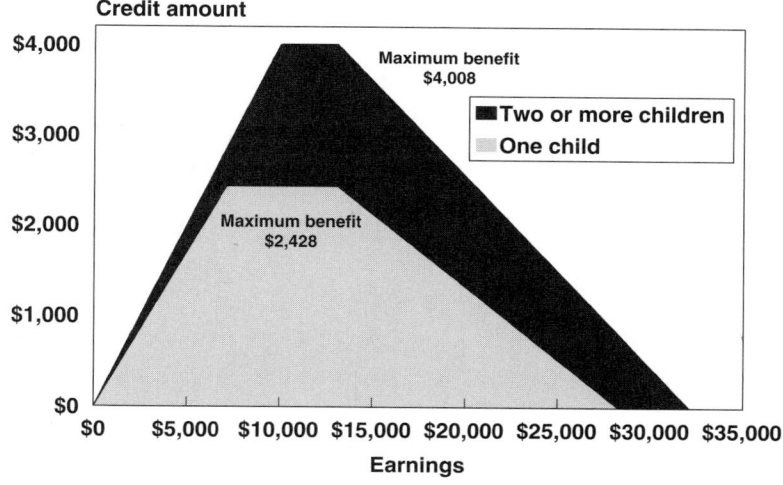

Source: Johnson, N. (December 2001). *A Hand Up: How State Earned Income Tax Credits help working families escape poverty in 2001.* Washington, D.C.: Center on Budget and Policy Priorities. Retrieved from http://www.cbpp.org/12-27-01sfp.pdf.

Table 8.34
Earned Income Credit Parameters: United States,
1975 to 1999

(Dollar Amounts Unadjusted for Inflation)

Calendar year	Credit rate (percent)	Mininum income for maximum credit	Maximum credit	Phaseout rate (percent)	Phaseout range	
					Beginning income	Ending income
1975-78....................................	10.00	$4,000	$400	10.00	$4,000	$8,000
1979-84....................................	10.00	5,000	500	12.50	6,000	10,000
1985-86....................................	14.00	5,000	550	12.22	6,500	11,000
1987..	14.00	6,080	851	10.00	6,920	15,432
1988..	14.00	6,240	874	10.00	9,840	18,576
1989..	14.00	6,500	910	10.00	10,240	19,340
1990..	14.00	6,810	953	10.00	10,730	20,264
1991:						
One child....................................	16.70	7,140	1,192	11.93	11,250	21,250
Two children................................	17.30	7,140	1,235	12.36	11,250	21,250
1992:						
One child....................................	17.60	7,520	1,324	12.57	11,840	22,370
Two children................................	18.40	7,520	1,384	13.14	11,840	22,370
1993:						
One child....................................	18.50	7,750	1,434	13.21	12,200	23,050
Two children................................	19.50	7,750	1,511	13.93	12,200	23,050
1994:						
No children..................................	7.65	4,000	306	7.65	5,000	9,000
One child....................................	26.30	7,750	2,038	15.98	11,000	23,755
Two children................................	30.00	8,425	2,528	17.68	11,000	25,296
1995:						
No children..................................	7.65	4,100	314	7.65	5,130	9,230
One child....................................	34.00	6,160	2,094	15.98	11,290	24,396
Two children................................	36.00	8,640	3,110	20.22	11,290	26,673

Source: United States House of Representatives, Committee on Ways and Means. (2000). *The 2000 Green Book: Background material and data on programs within the jurisdiction of the Committee on Ways and Means.* Retrieved from http://aspe.hhs.gov/2000gb/sec13.txt.

Table 8.35
Number of Families and Individuals that Received the EITC for
Tax Year 1999, by State

State	EITC Recipients	State	EITC Recipients
Alabama	440,060	Montana	64,829
Alaska	30,374	Nebraska	91,694
Arizona	336,523	Nevada	125,638
Arkansas	246,868	New Hampshire	53,250
California	2,334,947	New Jersey	441,288
Colorado	227,264	New Mexico	178,869
Connecticut	144,554	New York	1,307,617
Delaware	48,760	North Carolina	639,219
District of Columbia	51,685	North Dakota	35,544
Florida	1,289,189	Ohio	673,191
Georgia	704,750	Oklahoma	274,500
Hawaii	66,632	Oregon	194,030
Idaho	82,080	Pennsylvania	680,246
Illinois	752,237	Rhode Island	58,233
Indiana	356,503	South Carolina	372,035
Iowa	143,521	South Dakota	47,174
Kansas	143,887	Tennessee	474,954
Kentucky	298,718	Texas	1,867,016
Louisiana	480,221	Utah	107,749
Maine	77,245	Vermont	34,207
Maryland	315,447	Virginia	430,833
Massachusetts	272,091	Washington	303,384
Michigan	547,783	West Virginia	134,908
Minnesota	210,724	Wisconsin	242,492
Mississippi	343,389	Wyoming	31,185
Missouri	379,333		

Source: Johnson, N. (December 2001). *A Hand Up: How State Earned Income Tax Credits help working families escape poverty in 2001*. Washington, D.C.: Center on Budget and Policy Priorities. Retrieved from http://www.cbpp.org/12-27-01sfp.pdf.

Table 8.36
State Income Tax Thresholds for Two-Parent Families of Four: 2000

Poverty line (estimated): $17,601

Rank	State	Threshold	Rank	State	Threshold
1	Alabama	$4,600	20	District of Columbia	$18,600
2	Kentucky	5,400	21	Nebraska	18,900
3	Indiana	9,500	22	North Dakota	19,000
3	Montana	9,500	23	Mississippi	19,600
5	West Virginia	10,000	24	New Jersey	20,000
6	Hawaii	11,000	25	Idaho	20,100
7	Ohio	12,700	26	Delaware	20,300
8	Michigan	12,800	27	Massachusetts	20,600
9	Louisiana	13,000	28	Wisconsin	20,700
9	Oklahoma	13,000	29	New Mexico	21,000
11	Illinois	14,000	30	Kansas	21,100
12	Missouri	14,100	31	South Carolina	21,400
13	Oregon	14,800	32	Maine	23,100
14	Georgia	15,300	33	Arizona	23,600
15	Arkansas	15,600	34	New York	23,800
16	Utah	15,800	35	Connecticut	24,100
17	North Carolina	17,000	36	Maryland	25,200
18	Virginia	17,100	37	Rhode Island	25,900
19	Iowa	17,400	38	Minnesota	26,800
			38	Vermont	26,800
			40	Colorado	27,900
			41	Pennsylvania	28,000
			42	California	36,800
Average Threshold 2000		**$12,768**	**Average Threshold 2000**		**$23,187**
Amount Below Poverty		**$4,833**	**Amount Above Poverty**		**$5,586**

Note: A threshold is the lowest income level at which a family has state income tax liability. In this table thresholds are rounded to the nearest $100. The 2000 poverty line is a Census Bureau estimate based on the actual 1999 line adjusted for inflation. The threshold calculations include earned income tax credits, other general tax credits, exemptions, and standard deductions. Credits that are intended to offset the effects of taxes other than the income tax or that are not available to all low-income families are not taken into account.

Source: Johnson, N. (December 2001). *A Hand Up: How State Earned Income Tax Credits help working families escape poverty in 2001*. Washington, D.C.: Center on Budget and Policy Priorities. Retrieved from http://www .cbpp.org/12-27-01sfp.pdf.

Table 8.37
Taxes and Social Spending in Sixteen Selected Countries as Percent of GDP Factor Costs: 1995 and 1997

	Australia		Austria		Belgium			Canada	
	1995	1997	1995	1997	1993	1995	1997	1995	1997
1 Gross public social expenditure	19.2	18.7	30.0	28.5	30.5	30.0	30.4	22.5	20.7
− Direct taxes and social contributions	0.3	0.3	2.6	2.5	1.7	1.9	1.8	1.8	1.7
2 Net cash public social expenditure	18.9	18.4	27.3	26.0	28.9	28.1	28.6	20.7	19.0
− Indirect taxes	0.8	0.8	3.2	3.0	2.7	2.8	2.8	1.4	1.3
3 Net direct public social expenditure	18.0	17.6	24.1	23.0	26.2	25.4	25.8	19.3	17.8
+ T1 TBSPs similar to cash benefits	0.3	0.2	0.4	0.4	0.6	0.6	0.6	0.7	0.6
− Indirect taxes	0.0	0.0	0.1	0.1	0.1	0.1	0.1	0.1	0.1
4 Net TBSPs similar to cash benefits	0.3	0.2	0.4	0.3	0.5	0.5	0.5	0.6	0.6
+ T2 TBSPs towards current private benefits	0.0	0.0	0.1	0.1	0.0	0.0	0.0	0.4	0.4
5 Net TBSPs (not including pensions)	0.3	0.3	0.5	0.4	0.5	0.5	0.5	1.0	0.9
6 Net current public social expenditure	18.3	17.9	24.6	23.4	26.7	25.9	26.3	20.4	18.7
7 Gross mandatory private soc. exp.	1.2	1.2	1.0	0.9	1.8	1.7	1.7	0.0	0.0
− Direct taxes and social contributions	0.2	0.2	0.3	0.3	0.1	0.1	0.1	0.0	0.0
− Indirect taxes	0.1	0.1	0.1	0.1	0.2	0.2	0.2	0.0	0.0
8 Net current mand. private soc. exp.	0.9	0.9	0.6	0.5	1.5	1.3	1.3	0.0	0.0
9 Net publicly mandated soc. exp. (6+8)	19.2	18.8	25.1	23.9	28.1	27.2	27.5	20.4	18.7
10 Gross voluntary private soc. exp.	3.0	3.4	0.9	0.9	0.8	1.0	1.0	5.3	4.8
− Direct taxes and social contributions	0.1	0.1	0.0	0.0	0.0	0.0	0.0	1.2	1.1
− Indirect taxes	0.1	0.2	0.0	0.0	0.0	0.0	0.0	0.3	0.3
11 Net current voluntary private soc. exp.	2.8	3.1	0.8	0.8	0.8	0.9	0.9	3.8	3.5
12 Net current private soc. exp. (8+11)	3.7	4.1	1.4	1.3	2.2	2.2	2.2	3.8	3.5
13 Net total social expenditure (6+12-T2)	22.0	21.9	26.0	24.6	28.9	28.1	28.5	24.1	21.8
Memorandum item									
TBSPS towards pensions	1.6	1.6	0.0	0.0	..	..	..	2.7	2.5
Selected items related to GDP mp									
Gross public social expenditure	17.7	17.4	29.3	25.4	27.5	27.0	27.2	19.5	17.9
Gross total social expenditure	21.6	21.7	31.2	27.0	29.8	29.4	29.5	23.2	22.1
Net current public social expenditure	16.9	16.6	24.4	20.9	24.0	23.3	23.5	17.5	16.2
Net current mand. private soc. exp.	0.9	0.9	0.6	0.5	1.3	1.2	1.1	0.0	0.0
Net current voluntary private soc. exp.	2.6	2.9	0.9	0.7	0.7	0.8	0.8	3.4	3.0
Net total social expenditure (6+12-T2)	20.3	20.4	25.7	22.0	26.0	25.3	25.4	20.6	18.9

Table 8.37 (*continued*)

		Czech Republic			Denmark			Finland		Germany		
		1993	1995	1997	1993	1995	1997	1995	1997	1993	1995	1997
	1 Gross public social expenditure	21.5	21.0	21.7	37.1	37.7	35.9	35.9	33.3	33.1	29.5	29.2
-	Direct taxes and social contributions	0.0	0.0	0.0	4.4	5.5	5.1	5.1	4.4	1.5	1.3	1.3
	2 Net cash public social expenditure	21.5	21.0	21.7	32.7	32.2	30.8	30.8	28.9	31.6	28.2	27.8
-	Indirect taxes	2.3	2.3	2.5	4.6	4.5	4.1	4.6	4.2	2.6	2.4	2.3
	3 Net direct public social expenditure	19.2	18.8	19.3	28.0	27.7	26.7	26.2	24.8	29.0	25.8	25.5
+ T1	TBSPs similar to cash benefits	..	..	..	0.1	0.1	0.0	0.0	0.0	2.2	0.9	1.9
-	Indirect taxes	..	..	..	0.0	0.0	0.0	0.0	0.0	0.3	0.1	0.3
	4 Net TBSPs similar to cash benefits	..	..	..	0.1	0.0	0.0	0.0	0.0	..	..	..
+ T2	TBSPs towards current private benefits	..	..	..	0.0	0.0	0.0	0.0	0.0	0.0	0.0	0.0
	5 Net TBSPs (not including pensions)	..	..	..	0.1	0.0	0.0	0.0	0.0	..	..	..
	6 Net current public social expenditure	19.2	18.8	19.3	28.1	27.7	26.7	26.2	24.8	29.0	25.8	25.5
	7 Gross mandatory private soc. exp.	..	..	..	0.5	0.5	0.4	0.2	0.2	1.5	1.7	1.3
-	Direct taxes and social contributions	0.0	0.0	0.0	0.2	0.2	0.2	0.0	0.0	0.5	0.6	0.5
-	Indirect taxes	0.0	0.0	0.0	0.1	0.1	0.1	0.0	0.0	0.1	0.2	0.1
	8 Net current mand. private soc. exp.	..	..	..	0.2	0.2	0.2	0.1	0.1	0.8	1.0	0.7
	9 Net publicly mandated soc. exp. (6+8)	..	..	..	28.3	28.0	26.9	26.2	24.8	29.8	26.8	26.3
	10 Gross voluntary private soc. exp.	..	..	..	0.7	0.9	1.1	1.3	1.3	1.3	1.2	1.1
-	Direct taxes and social contributions	..	..	..	0.2	0.3	0.3	0.3	0.3	0.1	0.1	0.1
-	Indirect taxes	..	..	..	0.1	0.1	0.1	0.2	0.2	0.1	0.1	0.1
	11 Net current voluntary private soc. exp.	..	..	..	0.4	0.5	0.6	0.8	0.8	1.1	0.9	0.9
	12 Net current private soc. exp. (8+11)	..	..	..	0.6	0.7	0.8	0.9	0.9	1.9	1.9	1.6
	13 Net total social expenditure (6+12-T2)	19.2	18.8	19.3	28.7	28.4	27.5	27.0	25.6	30.9	27.7	27.2

Memorandum item
TBSPS towards pensions

TBSPS towards pensions	..	..	..	..	..	..	..	..	0.1	0.1	0.1	

Selected items related to GDP mp

	1993	1995	1997	1993	1995	1997	1995	1997	1993	1995	1997
Gross public social expenditure	19.0	18.6	19.4	32.3	32.5	30.7	31.2	28.7	26.3	26.6	26.4
Gross total social expenditure	19.0	18.6	19.4	33.3	33.7	32.0	32.5	30.0	28.8	29.2	28.6
Net current public social expenditure	17.0	16.6	17.2	24.5	23.9	22.9	22.8	21.4	23.7	24.0	24.6
Net current mand. private soc. exp.	0.0	0.0	0.0	0.2	0.2	0.2	0.1	0.1	0.9	0.9	0.6
Net current voluntary private soc. exp.	0.0	0.0	0.0	0.3	0.4	0.5	0.7	0.7	0.8	0.8	0.8
Net total social expenditure (6+12-T2)	17.0	16.6	17.2	25.0	24.5	23.5	23.6	22.1	25.5	25.7	26.1

Table 8.37 (*continued*)

	Ireland		Italy		Korea		Netherlands		
	1995	1997	1995	1997	1995	1997	1993	1995	1997
1 Gross public social expenditure	21.3	19.6	28.7	29.4	3.8	4.4	32.0	28.8	27.1
− Direct taxes and social contributions	0.4	0.3	2.7	2.9	0.0	0.0	6.0	4.9	4.4
2 Net cash public social expenditure	20.9	19.3	26.0	26.6	3.8	4.4	25.9	23.9	22.7
− Indirect taxes	2.8	2.5	2.4	2.4	0.2	0.2	2.8	2.5	2.4
3 Net direct public social expenditure	18.1	16.7	23.6	24.1	3.6	4.2	23.2	21.4	20.2
+ T1 TBSPs similar to cash benefits	0.3	0.3	..	..	0.3	0.4	0.1	0.0	0.0
− Indirect taxes	0.1	0.1	..	..	0.0	0.0	0.0	0.0	0.0
4 Net TBSPs similar to cash benefits	0.2	0.2	..	..	0.3	0.4	0.1	0.0	0.0
+ T2 TBSPs towards current private benefits	0.2	0.2	..	..	0.0	0.0	0.1	0.0	0.1
5 Net TBSPs (not including pensions)	0.4	0.4	..	..	0.3	0.4	0.2	0.0	0.1
6 Net current public social expenditure	18.6	17.1	23.6	24.1	3.9	4.6	23.3	21.5	20.3
7 Gross mandatory private soc. Exp.	0.0	0.0	1.6	1.5	1.6	2.5	0.4	0.8	0.8
− Direct taxes and social contributions	0.0	0.0	0.2	0.2	0.0	0.1	0.1	0.3	0.3
− Indirect taxes	0.0	0.0	0.2	0.2	0.2	0.3	0.0	0.1	0.1
8 Net current mand. private soc. exp.	0.0	0.0	1.2	1.1	1.4	2.1	0.2	0.4	0.5
9 Net publicly mandated soc. exp. (6+8)	18.6	17.1	24.8	25.2	5.3	6.7	23.5	21.9	20.8
10 Gross voluntary private soc. exp.	2.0	1.8	0.1	0.1	0.6	1.9	4.3	4.4	4.7
− Direct taxes and social contributions	0.1	0.1	0.0	0.0	0.0	0.0	1.0	0.9	0.9
− Indirect taxes	0.2	0.2	0.0	0.0	0.0	0.0	0.4	0.4	0.4
11 Net current voluntary private soc. exp.	1.6	1.5	0.1	0.1	0.6	1.9	3.0	3.1	3.3
12 Net current private soc. exp. (8+11)	1.6	1.5	1.3	1.2	2.0	4.0	3.2	3.5	3.8
13 Net total social expenditure (6+12-T2)	20.1	18.4	24.9	25.3	5.9	8.6	26.5	25.0	24.0
Memorandum item									
TBSPS towards pensions	0.0	2.7	..	..	0.0	0.0	..	0.6	1.2
Selected items related to GDP mp									
Gross public social expenditure	19.2	17.6		26.4	3.7	4.3	28.6	26.0	24.2
Gross total social expenditure	20.9	19.2		27.8	5.8	8.4	33.0	30.7	29.1
Net current public social expenditure	16.7	15.4		21.6	3.8	4.4	21.0	19.4	18.2
Net current mand. private soc. exp.	0.0	0.0		1.0	1.4	2.1	0.2	0.4	0.4
Net current voluntary private soc. exp.	1.4	1.3		0.1	0.6	1.8	2.7	2.8	3.0
Net total social expenditure (6+12-T2)	17.9	16.5		22.7	5.7	8.3	23.8	22.5	21.5

Table 8.37 (*continued*)

	Norway		Sweden			UK			US		
	1995	1997	1993	1995	1997	1993	1995	1997	1993	1995	1997
1 Gross public social expenditure	32.0	30.2	41.9	37.3	35.7	21.1	25.6	23.8	16.4	16.4	15.8
- Direct taxes and social contributions	2.7	2.6	5.7	5.1	4.4	0.3	0.4	0.4	0.3	0.3	0.4
2 Net cash public social expenditure	29.3	27.6	36.3	32.2	31.3	23.4	25.1	23.4	16.1	16.1	15.5
- Indirect taxes	3.6	3.2	3.5	3.0	2.8	2.0	2.4	2.3	0.5	0.5	0.4
3 Net direct public social expenditure	25.8	24.4	32.8	29.2	28.5	21.1	22.7	21.1	15.6	15.6	15.0
+ T1 TBSPs similar to cash benefits	0.0	0.0	..	..	..	0.3	0.4	0.3	0.3	0.3	0.3
- Indirect taxes	0.0	0.0	..	..	..	0.0	0.1	0.1	0.0	0.0	0.0
4 Net TBSPs similar to cash benefits	0.0	0.0	..	..	..	0.3	0.3	0.3	0.2	0.2	0.2
+ T2 TBSPs towards current private benefits	0.0	0.0	..	..	..	0.1	0.2	0.2	1.0	1.2	1.2
5 Net TBSPs (not including pensions)	0.0	0.0	..	..	..	0.5	0.5	0.5	1.3	1.5	1.4
6 Net current public social expenditure	25.8	24.4	32.8	29.2	28.5	21.6	23.2	21.6	16.9	17.1	16.4
7 Gross mandatory private soc. exp.	1.1	1.2	0.6	0.4	0.4	0.3	0.3	0.4	0.5	0.5	0.4
- Direct taxes and social contributions	0.3	0.3	0.2	0.1	0.1	0.0	0.1	0.1	0.1	0.1	0.1
- Indirect taxes	0.2	0.2	0.1	0.0	0.0	0.0	0.0	0.1	0.0	0.0	0.0
8 Net current mand. private soc. exp.	0.6	0.7	0.3	0.2	0.2	0.3	0.2	0.3	0.5	0.4	0.3
9 Net publicly mandated soc. exp. (6+8)	26.4	25.1	33.1	29.4	28.7	21.9	23.4	21.9	17.3	17.5	16.8
10 Gross voluntary private soc. exp.	..	..	3.4	3.3	3.0	3.2	3.9	3.8	8.4	8.3	8.4
- Direct taxes and social contributions	..	..	0.7	0.6	0.7	0.4	0.5	0.5	0.3	0.3	0.4
- Indirect taxes	..	..	0.4	0.4	0.3	0.4	0.5	0.5	0.2	0.2	0.2
11 Net current voluntary private soc. exp.	..	..	2.3	2.3	1.9	2.9	2.9	2.9	7.9	7.8	7.8
12 Net current private soc. exp. (8+11)	..	..	2.7	2.6	2.2	3.2	3.2	3.2	8.4	8.2	8.1
13 Net total social expenditure (6+12-T2)	26.4	25.1	35.5	31.7	30.6	24.6	26.4	24.6	25.3	25.3	23.4
Memorandum item											
TBSPS towards pensions	0.0	0.0	..	..	..	3.0	2.7	2.7	1.0	0.9	1.1
Selected items related to GDP mp											
Gross public social expenditure	27.6	26.1	36.7	33.0	31.8	23.6	22.8	21.2	15.2	15.2	14.7
Gross total social expenditure	28.6	27.2	40.1	36.3	34.8	27.5	26.5	24.9	23.5	23.4	22.9
Net current public social expenditure	22.2	21.1	28.7	25.8	25.4	21.4	20.6	19.2	15.6	15.9	15.3
Net current mand. private soc. exp.	0.5	0.6	0.3	0.2	0.2	0.2	0.2	0.3	0.4	0.4	0.3
Net current voluntary private soc. exp.	0.0	..	2.0	2.1	1.7	2.8	2.6	2.5	7.4	7.3	7.3
Net total social expenditure (6+12-T2)	22.8	21.7	31.0	28.1	27.3	24.3	23.3	21.8	22.4	22.4	21.8

Source: Adema, W. (2001). *Labour market and social policy: Net social expenditure.* (2nd ed.). Paris: OECD, Directorate for Education, Employment, Labour and Social Affairs Committee (Occasional Working Paper No. 52). Retrieved from http://www.olis.oecd.org/OLIS/2001DOC.NSF/LINKTO/DEELSA-ELSA-WD(2001)5. OECD Copyright. Reproduced by permission of the OECD.

Table 8.38
Average Indirect Tax Rates in Eighteen Countries: 1997

Item [1,2]	Australia	Austria	Belgium	Canada	Czech republic	Denmark	Finland	Germany	Ireland	Italy	Japan	Korea	Netherlands	New Zealand	Norway	Sweden	United Kingdom	United States
1 Private final consumption expenditure	338	1437	4484	489	771	551	312	2002	26	1181	298	255	355	62	516	893	497	5309
2 Private consumption plus Government consumption minus Government wages	380	1620	5313	556	1000	662	362	2401	30	1325	318	266	448	68	588	1074	587	5724
3 General consumption taxes plus excise duties (5110+5121)	29	276	823	62	182	169	84	338	6	165	20	30	73	11	148	192	87	295
General consumption taxes -- 5110	14	207	609	45	118	109	54	241	4	111	10	19	49	9	96	128	56	178
Excises -- 5121 [3]	14	69	214	17	64	59	30	97	2	54	10	11	24	2	52	65	32	117
4 Taxes on production sale transfer (5100)	37	299	1	75	197	174	88	364	6	196	21	42	79	12	167	203	95	335
5 Taxes on Goods and Services (5000)	46	314	1045	80	211	182	91	378	7	227	24	44	87	12	172	209	99	383
6 Implicit average indirect tax rate on consumption out of benefit income [3/2]	7.5%	17.0%	15.5%	11.2%	18.2%	25.5%	23.1%	14.1%	20.7%	12.4%	6.2%	11.4%	16.3%	15.6%	25.1%	17.9%	14.9%	5.2%
7 Implicit average tax rate using a broad concept of the indirect tax base [5/2]	12.2%	19.4%	19.7%	14.4%	21.1%	27.5%	25.0%	15.8%	22.7%	17.2%	7.6%	16.5%	19.3%	18.2%	29.2%	19.5%	16.9%	6.7%

1. All totals in line 1 to 5 are in billions of national currency, except for Belgium, Italy and Japan.
2. The 4-digit codes in the second column refer to the categorisation used in the OECD *Revenue Statistics.*
3. Excises for Norway (5121) do not include excises on oil and gas products, while Excises for Korea the special excise tax (e.g., on jewellery) has not been included.

Source: Adema, W. (2001). *Labour market and social policy: Net social expenditures.* (2nd ed.). Paris: OECD, Directorate for Education, Employment, Labour and Social Affairs Committee (Occasional Working Paper No. 52). Retrieved from http://www.olis.oecd.org/OLIS/2001DOC.NSF/LINKTO/DEELSA-ELSA-WD(2001)5. OECD Copyright. Reproduced by permission of the OECD.

Table 8.39
Tax Breaks for Social Purposes in Twelve Countries
as Percent of GDP: 1997[1,2,3,4]

Items	Australia	Austria	Belgium	Canada	Germany	Ireland
TBSPs similar to cash benefits	0.2	0.4	0.5	0.5	1.7	0.2
TBSPs towards current private social benefits	0.0	0.1	0.0	0.3	0.0	0.2
Total TBSPs	0.3	0.4	0.5	0.9	1.7	0.4
Memorandum item						
TBSPs towards pensions.	1.5	..	..	2.1	0.1	2.4

Items	Japan	Korea	Netherlands	New Zealand	United Kingdom	United States
TBSPs similar to cash benefits	0.4	0.4	0.0	0.0	0.3	0.2
TBSPs towards current private social benefits	0.0	0.0	0.1	0.1	0.1	1.1
Total TBSPs	0.0	0.4	0.1	0.1	0.4	1.3
Memorandum item						
TBSPs towards pensions.	0.8	0.0	1.0	0.0	2.4	1.0

1. There is no international, or sometimes national, consensus on how to demarcate fiscal measures used as social expenditure instruments. Therefore, the results presented here are therefore only indicative and provisional.

2. "0.0" item does not exist or, when it concerns tax benefits similar to cash benefits, that relevant tax advantages have been accounted when calculating the adjustment for direct taxation: ".."; information not available.

3. Data on Italy is not available. Information on Finland, Norway and Sweden has not been included as it concerns very small items: less than 0.05% of GDP.

4. TBSPs similar to cash benefits and towards current private social benefits are recorded on basis of revenue foregone—cash basis.

Source: Adema, W. (2001). *Labour market and social policy: Net social expenditures.* (2nd ed.). Paris: OECD, Directorate for Education, Employment, Labour and Social Affairs Committee (Occasional Working Paper No. 52). Retrieved from http://www.olis.oecd.org/OLIS/2001DOC.NSF/ LINKTO/DEELSA-ELSA-WD(2001)5. OECD Copyright. Reproduced by permission of the OECD.

9. Women and the Social Safety Net

Poor women face a double disadvantage in access to resources and voice—they are poor, and they are women. Poor people have much less access to education and health care than the nonpoor, and the gender gap in these services is larger among poor people. (World Bank, 2001, 118)

A discussion of benefits for women has to start with acknowledging that most benefits women receive are not for them, they are for the household in general and, often times, for children. Poor women who require assistance are able to receive them only in relation to their work experience or potential unless they are a part of a household, or heading it. Unfortunately, given the historical record of women in work, this means that the social safety net structure is built in such a way that prior discriminatory practices based on previously accepted social norms about women translates to lower benefit amounts. Women are, in effect, unnamed beneficiaries or indirect receivers (or surrogates) of assistance programs. Usually, this means that women receive the benefits and oversee their distribution in accordance to program need,[1] then, actual recipient needs, and finally, maybe, their own needs based on their assessment of their immediate and surrounding circumstances.

The reason for the inequity is that the entry of women into the workforce in the United States in significant numbers began only in the 1970s; prior to this time period, women were discouraged to participate in the workforce and to remain in the home. This also meant a reduced expectation for women to continue their education beyond high school (and in instances, graduating from high school was belayed because of marriage). Even in school, women were encouraged to follow a less difficult track that focused on homemaking skills. If women had to work, the expectation was that they were the second income in the household; women were not supposed to be the main breadwinners for the family. The net impact was and continues to be a wage discrepancy when compared to men, due to lower level jobs and increased difficulty in accessing jobs that are traditionally reserved for men.

Under the traditional nuclear family set-up, the woman either did not work, worked part-time, or in a job that was considered expendable in relation to the needs of the household. This meant that her Social Security benefits were actually tied to her spouse. The retirement programs in the United States and in many parts of the world (as can be seen in the comparative information and tables provided in chapter 3) were designed for the wife to be able to enter into the system earlier at reduced benefits. More to the point, the credited amounts for the individual benefit the wife would receive were lower in the proportion of the lower income she was able to generate throughout her work life. If the husband died, then she would be placed in a vulnerable situation because the benefits she was to receive would be based on the lower amount, and, in some instances, some of the potential benefits to which she would be eligible would run out as a result of the time limits in receiving these benefits, whether they be in the form of cash assistance on in-kind services.[2]

Demographic shifts during the second half of the twentieth century meant that women have had to increasingly shoulder the responsibility of maintaining a household with children. The increase in the divorce rate has added to the number of families with stepchildren and single families headed by a single parent, typically a woman. This exacerbates possibilities for assistance for poor women because it has been poor women, particularly women of color, who have the disproportionate share of needing assistance not just for them but also for their children. Complicating matters is the expectation that women

presumably expect their monetary needs to be met through the family system, so they work in the household, without earning wages or pension rights. Their problem is that this expectation of their youth may not be realized when they grow old. . . .

The absence of labor force participation and asset ownership among women was part of a traditional family system in which husbands participated in the formal markets and wives worked in the home. Women provided non-monetized services, especially when young, while their monetary needs were supposed to be covered by their spouses and eventually their children. But in many cases this system fails, especially in old age, when women are at the receiving end of the lifetime contract. Marriages break up and the husband is the one with the formal income. Husbands die earlier than wives, with their retirement benefits used up, and often do not leave adequate resources to support the surviving spouse. . . . Children move away or have income problems of their own. In these cases, the monetary support that the family was supposed to provide is not forthcoming and the low personal income of women becomes a social problem. (James, 1999, 5, 16)

Extrapolating from her article on the ethics of social policy legislation, Weinberg (1992) asserts that the benefit provisions for those in need by the various elements of the social safety net have always had a significant impact on the autonomy of both young and older women. One of the basic reasons why there is a significant impact is motherhood and the primary role women play in the reproductive process. Motherhood substantially impacts a woman's ability to enter and remain in the workforce over the course of her life (see Gray and McDonald, 2002). Like Gray and McDonald write, this is due to the role-conflict of rewards and costs. These authors focus on education, well-being, and previous experience as positive influences in getting women to return to the workforce faster in Australia (and presumably elsewhere); notwithstanding this theoretical perspective, consideration should be given to the psychological as well as social expectations of childcare and family dynamics—the conflicting emotions of wanting to be near a child (particularly after childbirth and the period immediately after), and the emotions surrounding the best interests of the family economically and psychologically, compounded by those individuous feelings of what women want for themselves and what society expects from women. Another way of looking at the inherent conflict is the application of the notion of fairness to women's decision-making processes.

The role of women in many societies (including that of the United States) benefits from an analysis through the lens of social exclusion as a definition for poverty. In many countries, women—as a result of policy decisions, social constructs, or inadvertent happenstance such as those Streeten illustrates (1998)—may have adequate incomes and food, but they may still be deprived because of the resulting workload from the dual responsibilities of employment and taking care of the household (plus the children, if there are any). Dollar and Kraay's (2000) report, although controversial in some circles, suggests that economic growth means an increase in income. This suggests that an argument can be made that access to these activities and programs becomes an essential element of maintaining economic and social well-being.[3] Social integration depends on the ability of any one individual to transition from a sense of capability to function in an enactive[4] circumstance. As Kakwani and Pernia (2000) point out, capability is only the sense of an ability to achieve, whereas functioning is achieving. Otherwise, women are kept dependent and with minimal autonomy in making decisions for self and/or the

household (unless they are a single head of household in which case their ability to function as an equal member of the community adds additional pressures and obstacles to achieving as defined in their own terms).

The social integration perspective toward poverty and relating it to the role of women in societies throughout the world is why the United Nations equates the eradication of poverty with human rights (United Nations Development Programme, 2000). This perspective equates a decent standard of living, adequate nutrition, healthcare, education, decent work, and protection against calamities as quintessential components of an individual's human rights. Without these, individuals and the societies in which they live are not capable of developing to their full potential. The liability to achieve these capabilities act as an impeding barrier that are not only in the way but actually detract from the possibility of being a full-fledged member of a community. Individuals are deprived from reaching a status that can be recognized as equal and above the negative economic and psychological circumstances that are part of what poverty is all about.

Goodin, Headey, Muffels, and Dirven's (1999) comparison of Germany, the Netherlands, and the United States finds that these three countries were in the midst of something of a social revolution during the 1980s and 1990s in terms of labor force participation. What they conclude is that

this revolution in female labour participation hit first in the US, where at the beginning of our period [of analysis] the median non-head's labour income was 30 per cent of that of the head of household. By the middle year it had risen to over 40 per cent and by the tenth year to over 50 per cent. In Germany, the median non-head's labour income was 9 per cent at the beginning of our study, rising to over 20 per cent in the middle year, and rising again to over 35 per cent in the tenth year. In the Netherlands, in contrast, the median non-head's labour income was literally zero (and hence zero per cent of the head's) in the first and middle year of our study, and only negligible in the final year. (222)

Following up on this finding is Orloff's (1998) analysis which concludes that:

The U.S. welfare state was made formally gender-neutral in the 1960s and 1970s, but women who do not have the typical male worker's pattern of uninterrupted, full-time work are still at greater risk of poverty if single or widowed. Civil rights laws invalidated protective legislation and discriminatory hiring practices for women only. But labor market and family "failures" are still covered by different programs. Wage earners are treated differently from those who do primarily unpaid domestic work; thus, men's and women's different locations within the labor force and the household division of labor mean they are not treated equivalently. (2)

It was suggested at the beginning of this chapter, and as the preponderance of the literature suggests, that social institutions are still predominantly based on dated notions of the role of men and women in society. Institutions are slowly tackling the need to revise and update these notions. As the discussion in chapter 3 of this book points out, the determination of the official poverty line in the United States does not account for the demographic shifts of an increased number of women head of households, women working in greater number, the increase in the divorce rate and many of the issues surrounding parenthood. These changes are not comfortable for some members of the community and, in some instances, there is moral disapproval heaped on the practical end results of some of these demographic changes. A particular example of this in the United States were the accusations levied at single mothers who were welfare recipients—the so-called welfare mothers—under the old AFDC programs because pregnancy and childbirth meant additional funds. Yet, although there were and are instances of system abuse, for women with low potential earnings it was and continues to be logical that welfare payments are attractive because they are competitive with minimum wage income (see Chambré, 1977).

The Australian Agency for International Development (2002) has developed guidelines to use in assessing gender-related issues that are part of development programs. Within these guidelines, the document asks key questions to determine the scope of participation and support given to women at policy and programmatic levels in government and its sponsoring society. Some of those questions that assist in identifying how women are able to access appropriate benefits and services are provided in Chart 9.1. The approach of these questions is adapted to reflect the concerns and existing social understanding and expectations of countries such as the United States rather than the original approach to providing a system for analyzing developing countries. The questions included are, therefore, those from the original suggested set that fit the perspective in this book as presented in chapter 1.

An area that exemplifies the difficulty women have in creating upper mobility for themselves by increasing independence while decreasing reliance on the social safety net is the level of education they receive. Education provides the capacity for individuals to become literate—read and write, use basic arithmetical computation skills, and acquire some life skills (see United Nations Development Programme, 2000). In many parts of the world, girls are deprived of the ability to access primary education, as reflected in data from 1990 indicating that two-thirds of the 948 million adults who were illiterate were women, and 77 million of the estimated 132 million out-of-school children were girls (United Nations Children's Fund, 1995). The lack of access to education has a negative impact because the more education an individual receives can be equated with higher personal returns on an investment in education. Women tend to receive higher returns on their schooling investments the higher up the educational system they are able to proceed. On an overall basis, the average rate of return to a partaking of an additional year of school is 10 percent (Psacharopoulos and Patrinos, 2002). Yet, in the United States, the changes engendered by welfare reform signify that for all of the positive evidence that education, especially higher (tertiary) education, is an asset, women are not encouraged to pursue this avenue out of poverty and benefit dependence yet, as a study sponsored by the Center for Women Policy Studies (2002) finds

women who earn four year college degrees increase their annual incomes most significantly—a trend that should benefit women moving from poverty and welfare to upward mobility in the workplace. In 2001, Latinas with bachelor's degrees earned a median weekly income of $676, compared to $467 with an associate's degree and $406 with a high school

Chart 9.1
Economic Guideline and Program Access Questions

Key Areas of Concern	Guiding Question
Government policy context	• Is there a national policy, plan of action, or aspects of the national development plan that specifically address the status or development of women?
Government institutional context	• What other institutions and NGOs are dedicated to promoting gender equality, and what capacity do they have for economic analysis?
Gender division of labor	• What do wage statistics reveal about the position of women in the economy relative to men? (Indicate whether women/men are concentrated/underrepresented in particular levels, and how this relates to educational attainment and gender stereotyping of occupations.) • How will men and women in the informal sector be affected by economic trends, development policies, and programs?

(continued)

Chart 9.1 (*continued*)

Key Areas of Concern	Guiding Question
Access and control of resources for economic advancement (natural resources)	• How is women's and men's access to these resources affected by economic trends, policies, and programs? • Are there legal impediments to women and men utilizing these resources on an equal basis, and do legal provisions affect/impact on men and women differently in their use of these resources?
Access and control of resources for economic advancement (credit, capital, and training)	• Are there legal impediments to women and men utilizing these resources on an equal basis, and do legal provisions affect/impact on men and women differently in their use of these resources?
Access and control of resources for economic advancement (education)	• What trends and differences emerge between boys and girls at different educational levels and in different regions of the country? • How are these differences related to human resource development problems and needs in different sectors of the economy? • What factors constrain equal access and outcomes from education? (Consider how pressure on women's labor in different sectors of the economy or regions of the country may impact on girls' educational opportunities.)
Access and control of resources for economic advancement (social policies and practices)	• What policies and practices exist regarding childcare and parental leave? • Are provisions in place to support primary carers of children? (consider flexible working practices such as flexible hours, part-time work, job sharing.) • Do current wage levels make it possible for women or men to take up flexible working practices? • What sectors of the economy are taking a lead in this area (public sector, private sector, NGOs)?
Access and control of resources for economic advancement (health, distribution of poverty)	• Have demographic factors such as the incidence of female-headed households, regional differences, permanent and seasonal migration patterns, and overseas remittances been taken into account in analyses of the distribution of poverty and disadvantaged groups?
Social, cultural, religious, economic, and demographic factors and trends	• What major social and cultural attitudes about gender roles and relations impinge on economic planning and performance? • What legal impediments exist to equal participation in economic activities for women and men? (Consider legal and traditional rights to land and property, access to credit, use of assets)

Source: Adapted from Australian Agency for International Development, 2002, pp. 38/93–41/93.

diploma. African American women with bachelor's degrees earned a median weekly income of $692, compared to $502 with an associate's degree and $395 with a high school diploma. White women with bachelor's degrees earned $744 weekly, compared to $579 with an associate's degree and $453 with a high school diploma (United States Department of Labor, Bureau of Labor Statistics, 2002).

Three significant areas of concern for the care of children are based on providing assistance to mothers in feeding their children a nutritious diet. The first area of concern is on issues surrounding birth. The Women's, Infants, and Children Nutrition Program (WIC) addresses these concerns for eligible mothers. The second area of concern is providing a balanced meal to children as they are growing up. Schools are enlisted to assist in this regard through the provision of school-based breakfasts and lunches. There is an additional federal entitlement to continue providing nutrition to children in childcare centers and afterschool centers. Finally, the third area of concern is childcare itself. Childcare is becoming a significant issue to the U.S. public because of the increased need on the part of many two-earner household families, not just the increase in the number of poor, single head-of-household mothers. As Congress admits in the *Green Book Report 2000*:

> Concerns that child care may be in short supply, not of good enough quality, or too expensive for many families escalated during the late 1980s into a national debate over the nature and extent of the Nation's child care problems and what, if any, Federal interventions would be appropriate. The debate culminated in the enactment of legislation in 1990 that expanded Federal support for child care by establishing two new State child care grant programs. The programs—the Child Care and Development Block Grant (CCDBG) and the At-Risk Child Care Program—were enacted as part of the Omnibus Budget Reconciliation Act of 1990 (Public Law 101-508). (United States House of Representatives, Committee on Ways and Means, 2000, section 9, 1/47)

Yet, for all of these concerns, available information indicates that, nationally, only 12 percent of all families making up to 85 percent of the state median income receive government assistance (Murray, Serafini, and Twohey, 2001).

Childcare quality is also a major concern to public and government officials due to research findings linking quality of care to child development in cognitive and affective domain areas such as awareness, intellectual development, and socialization. The Carnegie Corporation's (1994) study of early childcare programs finds that close to half of the infants and young children start life at a disadvantage and do not have the supports necessary to grow and thrive. The study goes to identify significant challenges due to:

- inadequate prenatal care,
- the isolation of parents as a result of divorce,
- substandard childcare based on the mother's return to the workforce within a year of birth,
- poverty (about 25 percent of families with children under the age of 3 live in poverty), and
- insufficient attention (only about one-half of the parents routinely take time to read to their children, with many not paying attention to their intellectual development).[5]

The overall perspective of these studies can be summed up by Howard Gardner, the author of *Multiple Intelligences*:

> In the first years of life, young children the world over develop powerful theories and conceptions of how the world works—the physical world and the world of other people. They also develop at least a first-draft level of competence with the basic human symbol systems—language, number, music, two-dimensional depiction, and the like. What is striking about these acquisitions is that they do not depend on explicit tutelage. Children develop these symbolic skills and these theoretical conceptions largely by the dint of their own spontaneous interactions with the world in which they live. This is not to deny that specific cultures exert specific effects, but rather to make the assertion that the kinds of capacities that evolve would be difficult to thwart, given any reasonably rich and supportive environment. (Gardner, 1993, 56)

WOMEN'S, INFANTS, AND CHILDREN'S NUTRITION PROGRAM (WIC)

In short, this is a program that provides an extra food allowance for children who are under 5 years of age, pregnant women, and postpartum women and their infants (United States House of Representatives, Committee on Ways and Means, 2000, section 15). It is a federal program, but it is administered by state and local agencies—in 1999, the program provided $3.956 billion in benefits to a monthly average of 7.3 million recipients (23 percent women, 26 percent infants, and 51 percent children).

As can be seen, the "program has categorical, income, and nutritional risk requirements for eligibility" (81/106). Its purpose is to enhance the nutritional consumption of low-income women, infants, and young children. The program also provides nutrition risk screening, and related services such as nutrition education and breastfeeding support. According to the *Green Book Report 2000*:

> Beneficiaries of the WIC Program receive supplemental foods each month in the form of actual food items or, more commonly, vouchers for purchases of specific items in retail stores. The law requires that the WIC Program provide foods containing protein, iron, calcium, vitamin A, and vitamin C, and allows Federal limits on the foods that may be provided by the WIC Program. Among the items that may be included in a food package are milk, cheese, eggs, infant formula, cereals, and fruit or vegetable juices. U.S. Department of Agriculture regulations require tailored food packages that provide specified types and amounts of food appropriate for six categories of participants: (1) infants from birth to 3 months; (2) infants from 4 to 12 months; (3) women and children with special dietary needs; (4) children from 1 to 5 years of age; (5) pregnant and nursing mothers; and (6) postpartum nonnursing mothers. In addition to food benefits, recipients also must receive nutrition education and breast feeding support (where called for). (81/106)

Receiving eligibility requires the applicant to have a healthcare professional certify the presence of medically verifiable evidence of health or nutrition risk. The applicant's income must be below the 185 percent mark of the currently published poverty guidelines (states can set even more stringent standards but seldom do). Benefits last for a period of up to six months after birth (with benefits beginning during the pregnancy). Nursing mothers need to be recertified every six months until the child attains its first birthday.

SCHOOL LUNCH AND BREAKFAST PROGRAM

This program provides federal cash along with federal food surpluses for the purpose of providing free or reduced-cost breakfast and lunch at schools and residential childcare institutions that opt to be enrolled in this plan. This is an entitlement program for eligible low-income children. Meals must meet the federal nutritional guidelines. Subsidies for breakfasts tend to be about twenty cents higher per meal than lunches served. As written in the *Green Book Report 2000*:

> Each program has a three-tiered system for per-meal Federal reimbursements to schools and RCCIs that: (1) allows children to receive free meals if they have family income below 130 percent of the Federal poverty guidelines (about $21,700 for a four-person family in the 1999–2000 school year); (2) permits children to receive reduced-price meals (no more than 40 cents for a lunch or 30 cents for a breakfast) if their family income is between 130 and 185 percent of the poverty guidelines (between about $21,700 and $30,900 for a four-person family in the 1999–2000 school year); and (3) provides a small per-meal subsidy for "full-price" meals (the price is set by the school or RCCI) served to children whose families do not apply, or whose family income does not qualify them for free or reduced-price meals. Children in Temporary Assistance for Needy Families (TANF) and food stamp households may automatically qualify for free school meals without an income application, and the majority actually receive them. (U.S. House of Representatives, Committee on Ways and Means, 2000, section 15, 78/106–79/106)

The lunch program is the larger of the two, serving approximately 4.5 billion meals in 1999, which translates to about 57 percent of students enrolled at participating schools and residential childcare institutions (48 percent ate free lunches and 9 percent ate reduced rate lunches) at an overall cost of $6 billion. In contrast, the breakfast program only served 1.3 billion meals, with an average participation rate of about 21 percent of enrolled students. Seventy-seven percent received free meals while 8 percent purchased breakfast at the reduced rate.

In addition to the two programs, the National School Lunch Act (under section 17), authorizes another permanent federal government entitlement to provide subsidies for breakfasts, lunches, suppers, and snacks at participating nonresidential childcare centers[6] and family or group daycare homes; it also provides for snacks offered in out-of-school programs. The Child and Adult Care Food Program (CACFP) is mainly given federal assistance in the form of cash subsidies based on the number of meals/snacks served or paid for administration. The U.S. Department of Agriculture's Food and Nutritional Services (FNS) administers the program.

CHILD CARE AND DEVELOPMENT BLOCK GRANT (CCDBG)

Authorized under the Omnibus Reconciliation Act of 1990, the current incarnation of this block grant program is designed to achieve several purposes:

- as a component of welfare reform, childcare is a part of the support element provided to promote self-sufficiency through work; and

- outside the context of welfare reform, the program attempts to address concerns over childcare effectiveness and program efficiency by streamlining of the federal role through the reduction of the number of programs and their conflicting rules (United States House of Representatives, Committee on Ways and Means, 2000, section 9).[7]

Chart 9.2 illustrates the program as it existed prior to 1996 and the changes in approach that currently represent the thinking on providing childcare support.

The program is funded from 1996 onwards through a combination of discretionary and entitlement amounts, with the combined funds sometimes referred to as the Child Care and Development Fund (CCDF). The discretionary component is authorized at $1 billion per year, with the funds allocated to the states—which are not required to match this amount—based on a formula that takes into account (1) the state's share of children under age 5, (2) the state's share of children receiving free or reduced-priced lunches, and (3) the state's per capita income. The entitlement amounts are established on an annual basis, ranging from $1.967 billion in fiscal year 1997 to $2.717 billion in fiscal year 2002 (United States House of Representatives, Committee on Ways and Means, 2000, section 9, 27/47). Entitlement allocations are based on the following criteria:

- 1 percent to 2 percent reserved for payment to Native American tribes and tribal organizations;

- each state receives a fixed annual amount equal to the funding the state would have received under the three child care programs previously authorized under the 1994 or 1995 levels of no longer existing AFDC structure, or the average of fiscal years 1992 through 1994, whichever is greater (approximately $1.2 billion each year);

- after guaranteed amounts (see previous bullet) are distributed, the remainder of the entitlement funds are distributed in accordance to the state's share of children under the age of 13—for these funds, states have to meet maintenance-of-effort and matching requirements; also,

- states may also transfer up to 30 percent of their TANF block grant allocation into their CCDBG or Social Services Block Grant programs, with these funds having to be spent in accordance to CCDBG rules.[8]

Program eligibility is for those whose family income does not exceed the 85 percent of the state's median income, although states may opt to set more stringent eligibility income requirements. Childcare is not considered an entitlement for individuals; therefore, states are not required to provide assistance to families even if their incomes fall below the eligibility levels. "Federal law does require States to give priority to families defined in their plans as very-low income" (United States House of Representatives, Committee on Ways and Means, 2000, section 9, 28/47). For those families seeking assistance,

- their children must be less than 13 years old and be living with parents who are working or enrolled in training, or
- children need to be in need of protective services.

States are required to give parents the maximum amount of choices in selecting the care provider. Parents are given the option of enrolling their children in an approved program or receive a voucher to purchase services for their child(ren) at an eligible provider of their choice.

There may be a slight confusion between the CCDBG and the CCDF programs, especially when looking for funding data throughout the various statistical databases describing childcare support programs in the United States. As Gish (2002) indicates, the terms tend to be used interchangeably, but this is technically inappropriate. The term CCDF does not appear in statutory language, it is in essence a funding term. Following Gish's (2002) description, the technical difference between the two is that CCDF seems to relate more to the money that states are entitled for childcare purposes (as part of entitlement funding activity), while CCDBG is the discretionary funds allotted through the annual appropriation process. The distinction is almost moot because all CCDF funds go to the CCBDG; however, it explains why most of the available data refers to CCDF and not CCDBG.

HEAD START

Head Start is a federal comprehensive child development program established in 1965 that serves eligible children from birth to age 5, pregnant women, and their families. The services provided are child-focused, and have the overall goal of increasing the school readiness of young children in low-income families. The eligibility guideline is the official poverty guideline as identified for the various household types (refer to chapter 3 for a more detailed discussion); in June 1999, 30 percent of participating children came from families receiving TANF. At least ten (10) percent of available openings in the program must be reserved for children with disabilities. The programs provided by Head Start include the following:

- Early Head Start: promotes healthy prenatal outcomes, enhances the development of infants and toddlers, and promotes healthy family functioning
- Migrant and Seasonal Program: consistent and high quality services in support of healthy child development across the nation
- American Indian-Alaska Native Program: "provides American Indian and Alaska Native children and families nationally with comprehensive health, educational, nutritional, socialization and other developmental services promoting school readiness. These services are directed primarily toward economically disadvantaged preschool children (ages 3 to 5) and infants and toddlers (birth through age 3)" (Head Start Bureau, 2002)

Getting data of any type by gender is a difficult proposition at the national and international comparison levels, even in the United States. A major reason for this difficulty is that economic reports tend to be prescriptive, making it very arduous to determine the distribution of benefits of policy prescriptions, research that is impossible without a sound sex-disaggregated database, which also differentiates population groups according to other key factors such as regional location where relevant, socioeconomic and/or ethnic groupings (Australian Agency for International Development, 2002). Illustration 9.1 at the end of this chapter provides a comparison of childcare benefit programs that can be found in nine OECD

Chart 9.2
Components of Child Care System Prior to 1996 Changes

- **AFDC Childcare**—Free childcare for AFDC recipients. Guaranteed care limited to children under 13.
- **Transitional Childcare**—12 months of entitlement for families needing subsidized childcare to accept/retain job and no longer on AFDC due to income level.
- **At-Risk Childcare**—Childcare for low-income families not on AFDC but at-risk of being eligible without subsidized care.

- Mandatory funds
- 3 programs,
- 3 sets of rules,
- 3 target populations
- Committee Jurisdiction
  - Ways and Means
  - Finance

- **CCDBG of 1990**—Childcare subsidized on a sliding fee scale for children under age 13 (with exceptions) whose working family income coes not exceed 75% of state median income.

- Discretionary funds
- Committee Jurisdiction
  - Education and Workforce
  - HELP Committee

Source: Adapted from Gish, M. (2002). *Child care funding and spending under federal block grants*, Figure 1, p. 3.

member nations. However, the Carnegie Corporation report titled *Starting Points: Meeting the Needs of Our Youngest Children* (1994) provides the backdrop of where the United States is in relationship to other programs that is worth looking at before looking at these national elements of different social safety nets.

The United States:

- Is not one of 150 nations that have signed or ratified the UN Convention on the Rights of the Child (Cambodia, Iran, Iraq, Libya, and South Africa have also not signed).

- Is not one of 127 nations that permit employees to take paid parental leave after the birth of a baby (as do Canada, France, Germany, and Japan, among others).

- Has a worse low-birthweight rate than 30 other nations.

- Has a smaller proportion of babies immunized against polio than 16 other nations.

- Has one of the highest adolescent pregnancy rates in the developed world—twice as high as England and seven times as high as the Netherlands.

Our policies contrast sharply with those of most other industrialized countries, particularly those in Europe. European child care for children under age three varies significantly from country to country, but generally speaking, the Europeans are moving toward paid leaves for new parents and a range of subsidized child care options for toddlers.

Here are some examples of countries that offer job protection and paid leaves to employed parents (usually, but not always, mothers) who have sufficient work histories:

- In Germany, a new parent can receive modest financial support while staying at home for up to one and a half years, or she can work part-time at her previous workplace.

- In France, she can count on modest compensation at home for as long as three years, or she can go back to work and take advantage of subsidized child care.

- In Sweden, she receives full pay while staying at home with a new baby for a year and a half, or she can opt to work part-time for a longer period and receive full pay.

- In Finland, she can stay home until her child is three, knowing that her job (or a comparable job) will be waiting for her when she returns. She receives her full salary for one year and a lesser amount for the next two years. Or she can take advantage of subsidized child care.

- In Austria, she can stay at home throughout her child's first two years, or work part-time until the child's third birthday, while receiving financial support equivalent to the wage of an unskilled worker. (from abridged report, Carnegie Corporation of New York Web site)

Sources of information at the international level that will shed light to the overall situation of women and poverty are the World Bank's *World Development Report* for various years and the United Nations Development Programme's (UNDP) *Human Development* reports, particularly the 2003 report, and the United Nations Economic Commission for Europe Web site on gender issues. Begin, though, by reading the United Nations report titled *The World's Women 2000:*

Trends and Statistics. Although not included in this chapter's tables because of the difficulties it presents readers to download the information free of cost, The European Union Social Indicators' (EUSI) Web site (http://www.gesis .org/en/social_monitoring/social_indicators/EU_Reporting/ subpubl.htm) has a significant amount of information that is useful to the reader in the area of women and their participation in society and the workforce, especially because it does provide comparative data between European countries and some other countries (mainly OECD), including the United States.

For information about the United States, begin at the U.S. Department of Labor's Women's Bureau Web site. There are some statistics, other information, and links that are a good place to begin. Also, it is suggested that the reader go to the National Child Care Information Center's Web address to look for more extensive information through links for data on programs described in this chapter. Another recommendation for more of an analysis geared toward child-focused issues is the U.S. Department of Health and Human Services report with the title of *Trends in the Well-Being of America's Children and Youth 2000.*

The *Statistical Abstract of the United States* provides only some data for these programs. The Web sites for programs such as Head Start are good places to begin basic research on these programs. The *Green Book Report 2000* is a good source of information about the costing and programmatic policies of programs impacting women, especially those with children and is also recommended as a good source for initiating more detailed research. In addition, the U.S. Department of Labor's *Report on the American Workforce* gives information that is of particular use when looking at women as part of the working class.

NOTES

1. As a positive example of women controlling some of the benefits received:

> Because food is often seen as the domain of women, women in a household are likely to have control over the use of transfers of food, and of cash-like instruments tied to food. The fact that women control food-related transfers is one possible explanation of the fact, widely documented, that transfers in the form of food or tied to food are more likely to increase households' net food consumption than are equivalent cash transfers. (Rogers and Coates, 2002, Abstract)

2. In Canada and a number of other European countries the data suggests that in countries where private pensions are important, women who reach retirement pension age lose a portion to most (if not all) of their source of income upon the death of their spouse (Casey and Yamada, 2002).

3. "This applies to the range of resources and benefits where women experience discrimination, including access to education and training, access to new technology, political representation, gender stereotyping in employment opportunities, and ownership of

assets." (Australian Agency for International Development, 2002, 64/93)

4. Most of the literature would refer to this concept as empowerment; however, this author is of the opinion that the inherent abilities and interest are there and those are what must be tapped, rather than providing skills that help find those inherent abilities and then decide whether or not to act.

5. These are some of the key points in the Carnegie Corporation of New York's report (1994) on young children in the United States. What they term "the Quiet Crisis" is the result of the following:

Of the 12 million children under the age of three in the United States today, a staggering number are affected by one or more risk factors that make healthy development more difficult.

Changes In Family Structure Are Troubling

- In 1960, only 5 percent of all births in the United States were to unmarried mothers; by 1988, the proportion had risen to 26 percent.
- About every minute, an American adolescent has a baby; every year, about 1 million adolescents become pregnant.
- Divorce rates are rising: In 1960, less than one percent of children experienced their parents' divorce each year; by 1986, the percentage had more than doubled, and by 1993 almost half of all children could expect to experience a divorce during childhood and to live an average of five years in a single-parent family.
- Children are increasingly likely to live with just one parent, usually the mother: In 1960, fewer than 10 percent of all children under the age of eighteen lived with one parent; by 1989 almost a quarter of all children lived with one parent. Fathers are increasingly absent from the home.

Many Young Children Live In Poverty

- One in four infants and toddlers under the age of three (nearly 3 million children) live in families with incomes below the federal poverty level.
- While the number of children under six increased by less than 10 percent between 1971 and 1991, the number of poor children under six increased by more than 60 percent.

More Children Live In Foster Homes

- In a mere five years, from 1987 to 1991, the number of children in foster care jumped by more than 50 percent—from 300,000 in 1987 to 460,000 in 1991.
- Babies under the age of one are the fastest growing category of children entering foster care, according to a study conducted in New York and Illinois.

Infants And Toddlers Are Spending Less Time With Their Parents

- Pressures on both parents to work mean that they have less time with their young children; more than half of mothers of infants now work outside the home.
- More than 5 million children under the age of three are in the care of other adults while their parents work. Much child care for infants and toddlers is of substandard quality, whether it is provided by centers, family child care homes, or relatives.

Health Data Are Discouraging

- In the United States, nine out of every thousand infants die before age one—a mortality rate higher than that of 19 other nations.

- The mortality rate is higher for infants born in minority families: African American babies are twice as likely to die within the first year of life as white babies.
- In 1992, rates of immunization against common childhood diseases among two-year-olds were only 0 percent in some states; in most states, they were below 60 percent.

Physical Abuse, Neglect, And Unintentional Injury Are Common

- One in three victims of physical abuse is a baby—less than a year old. In 1990, more one-year-olds were maltreated than in any previous year for which we have data.
- Almost 90 percent of children who died of abuse and neglect in 1990 were under the age of five; 53 percent were less than a year old.
- The leading cause of death among children aged one to four is unintentional injury.

6. These include homeless shelters, Head Start centers, and afterschool care centers.

7. To further quote from the *Green Book Report 2000*, the United States House of Representatives, Committee on Ways and Means (2000) is on record saying that:

Despite this increase in Federal resources, concerns persist about the adequacy and quality of child care in the era of welfare reform. Although welfare caseloads have declined, freeing up potential funds from the Temporary Assistance for Needy Families Block Grant for use for child care, the Administration for Children and Families (ACF) estimates that in an average month in 1998 only 15 percent of children eligible for Child Care and Development Fund (CCDF) subsidies received them, raising questions of whether total child care funding is adequate (CCDF or otherwise). (Section 9, 27/47)

8. States need to spend at least 70 percent of their total entitlement funds to provide childcare services for TANF families and those that are at-risk of becoming dependent on public assistance.

PRIMARY SOURCES FOR ILLUSTRATIONS

Bartlett, S., Brown-Lyons, M., Moore, D., and Estacion, A. (1998). *WIC participant and program characteristics 1998.* (Nutritional Assistance Program Report Series, Number WIC-00-PC) Washington, D.C.: U.S. Department of Agriculture, Food and Nutrition Service, Office of Analysis, Nutrition, and Evaluation. Retrieved from: http://www.abtassoc.com/reports/ES-20006343640181.pdf.

Gish, M. (March 19, 2002). *Child care funding and spending under federal block grants.* (CRS Report for Congress received through the CRS Web, Number RL31274). Washington, D.C.: Library of Congress, Congressional Research Service. Retrieved from: http://www.nccic.org/pubs/crsreport/crsreport.pdf.

Grogger, J., Karoly, L.A., and Klerman, J.A. (2002). *Consequences of welfare reform: A research synthesis.* (Report #: DRU-2676-DHHS). Washington, D.C.: Administration for Children and Families. Retrieved from: http://www.acf.dhhs.gov/programs/opre/welfare_reform/rand_report.pdf.

Guttman, B., and Hamilton, J. (2000). *Trends in the well-being of America's children and youth 2000.* Washington, D.C.: United States Department of Health and Human Services,

Office of the Assistant Secretary for Planning and Evaluation. Retrieved from: http://aspe.hhs.gov/hsp/00trends/contents.htm#ES.

Head Start Bureau. (2003). *Head Start Program fact sheet 2003*. United States Department of Health and Human Services, Administration for Children and Families Web site. Retrieved from: http://www2.acf.hhs.gov/programs/hsb/research/factsheets.htm.

International Labor Organization (2003). National Statistics for Equal Opportunities Web site. Retrieved from: http://www.ilo.org/public/english/employment/gems/eeo/stat/main.htm.

Organization for Economic Co-operation and Development. (1999). *Synopsis of member nations social programs*. Washington, D.C.: Author. Retrieved from: http://www.oecd.org.

United Nations. (2000). *The world's women 2000: Trends and statistics*. New York: United Nations Publications. Retrieved from: http://unstats.un.org/unsd/demographic/ww2000/table5g.htm.

United Nations Development Programme. (2003). *Human development report 2003*. New York: Oxford University Press. Retrieved from: http://www.undp.org/hdr2003/pdf/hdr03_complete.pdf.

United States Census Bureau. (2002). *Statistical abstract of the United States 2002*. Washington, D.C.: Government Printing Office. Retrieved from: http://www.census.gov/statab/www/.

United States Department of Labor. (2001). *Report on the American workforce*. Washington, D.C.: Government Printing Office. Retrieved from: http://www.bls.gov/opub/rtaw/rtawhome.htm.

United States Department of Labor Women's Bureau. (2003). *Twenty leading indicators of employed women: 2002*. United States Department of Labor Women's Bureau Web site. http://www.dol.gov/wb/stats/main.htm.

United States House of Representatives, Committee on Ways and Means. (2000). *The 2000 Green Book: Background material and data on programs within the jurisdiction of the Committee on Ways and Means*. Retrieved from: http://aspe.hhs.gov/2000gh.

BIBLIOGRAPHY

Australian Agency for International Development. (2002). Human rights framework. *Guide to gender and development*. Canberra: Australian Agency for International Development. Retrieved from: http://www.ausaid.gov.au/publications/pdf/guidetogenderanddevelopment.pdf.

Carnegie Corporation of New York. (1994). *Starting points: Meeting the needs of our youngest children*. New York: Carnegie Corporation. Abridged version available at http://www.carnegie.org/starting_points/startpt1.html.

Casey, B., and Yamada, A. (2002). Getting older, getting poorer? A study of earnings, pensions, assets, and living arrangements of older people in nine countries. *Labour Market and Social Policy—Occasional Papers no. 60*. Paris: OECD Directorate for Education, Employment, Labour and Social Affairs. Retrieved from: http://www.olis.oecd.org/OLIS/2002DOC.NSF/LINKTO/DEELSA-ELSA-WD(2002)4.

Center for Women Policy Studies. (2002). *From poverty to self-sufficiency: The role of postsecondary education in welfare reform*. Washington, D.C.: Center for Women Policy Studies. Retrieved from: http://www.centerwomenpolicy.org/pubfiles/20021223fptss.pdf.

Chambré, S.M. (March 1977). Welfare work and family structure. *Social Work* 22(2), pp. 103–108.

Dollar, D., and Kraay, A. (2000). *Growth IS good for the poor*. Washington, D.C.: World Bank. Retrieved from: http://www.worldbank.org/research/growth/pdfiles/growthgoodforpoor.pdf.

Gardner, H. (1993). *Multiple intelligences: The theory in practice*. New York: Basic Books.

Gish, M. (March 19, 2002). *Child care funding and spending under federal block grants*. (CRS Report for Congress received through the CRS Web, Number RL31274). Washington, D.C.: Library of Congress, Congressional Research Service. Retrieved from: http://www.nccic.org/pubs/crsreport/crsreport.pdf.

Goodin, R.E., Headey, B., Muffels, R., and Dirven, H.J. (1999). *The real worlds of welfare capitalism*. Cambridge: Cambridge University Press.

Gray, E., and McDonald, P. (October 2002). The relationship between personal, family, resource and work factors and maternal employment in Australia. *Labour Market and Social Policy—Occasional Papers no. 62*. Paris: OECD, Directorate for Education, Employment, Labour and Social Affairs. Retrieved from: http://www.olis.oecd.org/OLIS/2002DOC.NSF/43bb6130e5e86e5fc12569fa005d004c/169eabb40f45e72dc1256c61004ba0c3/$FILE/JT00134287.PDF.

Head Start Bureau. (2002). *Programs and Services*. Author's Web site. Retrieved from: http://www2.acf.dhhs.gov/programs/hsb/programs/index.htm.

James, E. (1999). *Coverage under old age security programs and protection for the uninsured—What are the issues?* Paper presented at Inter-American Development Bank Conference on Social Protection, Feb. 4–5, 1999. Retrieved from: http://econ.worldbank.org/docs/885.pdf.

Kakwani, N., and Pernia, E.M. (October 2000). *Pro-poor growth and income inequality*. New York: United Nations Development Programme. Retrieved from: http://hdr.undp.org/docs/events/global_forum/2000/pernia.pdf.

Murray, M., Serafini, M.W., and Twohey, M. (March 10, 2001). Untested safety net. *National Journal*, vol. 33 (10), pp. 684–694.

Orloff, A.S. (1998). Welfare State. *Reader's companion to U.S. women's history Web site*. New York: Houghton Mifflin College Division. Retrieved from: http://college.hmco.com/history/readerscomp/women/html/wh_039100_welfarestate.htm.

Psacharopoulos, G., and Patrinos, H.A. (September 2002). Returns to investment in education: A further update. *Policy Research Working Paper No. 2881*. Washington, D.C.: World Bank. Retrieved from: http://www-wds.worldbank.org/servlet/WDSContentServer/WDSP/IB/2002/09/27/000094946_02091705491654/Rendered/PDF/multi0page.pdf.

Rogers, B.L., and Coates, J. (June 2002). *Food-based safety nets and related programs*. Washington, D.C.: World Bank, Social Safety Net Primer Series. Retrieved from: http://poverty.worldbank.org/files/12993_primer_foodbased_sn.pdf.

Streeten, P. (1998). Beyond the six veils: Conceptualizing and measuring poverty. *Journal of International Affairs*, vol. 52 (1), pp. 1–31.

United Nations. (2000). *The world's women 2000: Trends and statistics*. New York: United Nations Publications.

United Nations Children's Fund (April 1995). *UNICEF strategies in basic education*. New York: UNICEF Web site. Retrieved from: http://www.unicef.org/pdeduc/education/board95.htm.

United Nations Development Programme. (2000). *Human development report 2000*. New York: Oxford University Press.

United States Department of Health and Human Services. (1993). *The at-risk child care program*. Washington, D.C.: Health and Human Services, Office of the Inspector General. Retrieved from: http://oig.hhs.gov/oei/reports/oei-02-92-00140 .pdf.

United States Department of Health and Human Services. (2002). *Head Start Bureau* Web site. Retrieved from: http://www.acf .hhs.gov/programs/hsb/programs/index.htm.

United States House of Representatives, Committee on Ways and Means. (2000). *The 2000 green book: Background material and data on programs within the jurisdiction of the Committee on Ways and Means*. Retrieved from: http://aspe.hhs.gov/2000gh.

Weinberg, J.K. (1992). Poverty, reproduction, and autonomy in the welfare state: Some thoughts on the ethics of social policy legislation. *Columbia Journal of Gender and Law*, vol. 3 (1), pp. 375–401.

World Bank. (2001). *World development report 2000/2001: Attacking poverty*. Oxford: Oxford University Press.

Table 9.1
Basic Childcare Structures in the United States and Nine OECD Countries

Country	Child care programs
United States of America	• Federal funding through the Child Care Development Fund (CCDF) • CCDF requires states to serve families through a single, integrated childcare system • Subsidized childcare available to eligible parents through certificates or contracted programs • Subsidies are for families receiving, leaving, or at risk of dependency on TANF as well as low-income working families • Majority of funds for direct assistance for children under age 13 • State administer programs; however, federal law mandates maximum level for eligibility to be 85% of state's median income and requires states to give priority to "very low income" families • Benefit amounts set by state and vary by income and number of children • Not treated as taxable • No statutory time limit on assistance; families lose assistance if they no longer meet eligibility standards
Germany	• General payments to subsidize or reduce costs of childcare do not exist • Day care and related services offered by local youth agencies and mostly publicly funded • Parents may be asked to contribute, with these contributions deductible as expenses from taxable income
The Netherlands	• Three forms of formal childcare: • care in centers supervised by the local government • spaces in childcare centers rented by employers • unsubsidized private childcare • Monthly feel for subsidized childcare is a function of parents pooled net income, i.e., gross earnings plus taxable benefits minus income and social security taxes • 1st child: parents pay fixed amount (103 guilders) plus 25% of difference between net income and social minimum (basic social assistance payment rate for relevant family type): maximum payment is 1,133 guilders • 2nd child: parents pay a fee equal to 30% of their contribution for the first child • amounts are for full day care (5 days per week) for children up to age 4; after school care (5 days per week) for children ages 4–12 cost 50% of day care
Czech Republic	• *Parental allowance:* to assist parents who personally provide full-time regular care for a small child, have no gainful income of their own, or their capacity to earn such income is greatly reduced • Condition for receiving benefit: 1. Parent is entitled to parental allowance when personally provides full-time and regular care for at least one child up to the age of 4 years, or up to the age of 7 years in a case of child suffering from a long-term incapacity or severe long-term incapacity 2. Parent who has a low income from gainful activity. The limit placed on such income is that the parent's net income from gainful activity does not exceed the MLS amount for personal needs of the parent concerned. Also other conditions have to be met (a child can be placed in the kindergarten but only for certain number of days in a month, etc.) • Gross benefit calculation: The amount of parental allowance for a calendar month is determined as the entitled parent personal needs amount of MLS multiplied by a coefficient 1.10 • Benefit is not taxable.
Poland	• Who may qualify: families or single parents raising child or children under 6 years • Maximum benefit duration: 3 years • Benefit amount as of 1999: PLN 264.90 and PLN 421.30 for lone parent

Norway	• Income tested (means-test) on a per member of the family basis (309.87 zlotys maximum earnings allowed) • Benefit not taxed
	• A tax allowance available if: • If the family can provide evidence of childcare expenses for children younger than 12 years the couple will get a deduction up to NOK 25,000 for one child and NOK 30,000 for two or more children. The allowance applied to the spouse with the lowest income; the allowance applies also to lone parents • Refundable tax credit for dependent children: NOK 1,820 if aged under 16, NOK 2,540 if aged between 16 and 18 • Lone parents receiving the transitional benefit only (and pensioners receiving the comparable benefit) are exempt from taxation, the ceiling being NOK 90,886. When additional income results in the ceiling being exceeded, a special "tax liability limitation schedule" applies
Sweden	• Childcare is heavily subsidized by state and local governments. Parents pay a certain share in childcare fees varying by municipality (approximately 17 per cent)
Australia	Two kinds of child welfare assistance (as of 1 July 2000, Child Care Benefit (CCB) will replace both the Childcare Assistance and Childcare Rebate): • Childcare Assistance (CA) • Childcare Rebate (CR) • Eligibility • Assistance (CA): families with low to middle incomes whose children are in approved child-care services. Families are eligible for some CA if their incomes are less than A\$ 1,277 a week before tax—for families with one dependent child in care or A\$ 1,498 a week before tax (for families with two or more dependent children in care), or A\$ 1,828 a week for three or more dependent children in care • Childcare Rebate (CR): payable regardless of family income, but a lower rebate percentage applies to family incomes higher than A\$ 70,000 plus A\$ 3,000 for each additional child • Approved childcare services receive childcare payments from the government on behalf of the families to reduce their fees • Benefit calculation: • Childcare Assistance (CA): The maximum fee or ceiling on which CA will be paid in approved long day care, family day care and some occasional care services is A\$ 2.34 an hour for non-school children and A\$ 1.99 for school children. This is a maximum of A\$ 117.00 for a non-school child and A\$ 99.50 for a school child using 50 hours of care • Childcare Rebate (CR): The maximum weekly childcare expenses on which families can claim is A\$ 117.00 per week for one child in care; or A\$ 234.00 per week per child for two or more children in care. Families can claim up to 30 percent of their weekly childcare costs, after paying the first A\$ 20.50 and deducting any CA paid. The maximum weekly rebate is A\$ 28.95 per week for one child in care or A\$ 64.05 per week for two or more children in care • Both programs are not taxable
Japan	• No childcare benefit. Instead, an income-based system exists that is related to childcare costs • Qualifying condition: having a child under 5 years of age. The cost/contribution is income related: it increases with local and central income tax (the more income tax a family pays, the bigger the contribution to the childcare costs) • This is an implicit benefit; yet, it is not taxed
Korea	Not yet installed

Source: Adapted from Organization for Economic Co-operation and Development. (1999). Synopsis of Member Nations social programs. Washington, D.C.: Author. Retrieved from http://www.oecd.org.

Table 9.2
Gender Inequality in Education

HDI rank		Adult literacy		Youth literacy		Net primary enrolment [a, b]		Net secondary enrolment [a, b]		Gross tertiary enrolment [b, c]	
		Female rate (% age 15 and above) 2001	Female rate as % of male rate 2001	Female rate (% age 15-24) 2001	Female rate as % of male rate 2001	Female ratio (%) 2000-01	Ratio of females to males [d] 2000-01	Female ratio (%) 2000-01	Ratio of females to males [d] 2000-01	Female ratio (%) 2000-01	Ratio of females to males [d] 2000-01
High human development											
1	Norway	..	..	..	..	102 [e]	1.00 [e]	95 [e]	1.01 [e]	85 [e]	1.52 [e]
2	Iceland	..	..	..	..	102 [e]	1.00 [e]	86 [e]	1.05 [e]	62 [e]	1.74 [e]
3	Sweden	..	..	..	..	102 [e]	0.99 [e]	98 [e, f]	1.04 [e, f]	85 [e]	1.52 [e]
4	Australia	..	..	..	..	96 [e]	1.01 [e]	91 [e]	1.03 [e]	70 [e]	1.24 [e]
5	Netherlands	..	..	..	..	99 [e]	0.99 [e]	90 [e]	1.00 [e]	57 [e]	1.07 [e]
6	Belgium	..	..	..	..	100 [e]	1.00 [e]	..	..	61 [e, f]	1.13 [e, f]
7	United States	..	..	..	..	96 [e]	1.01 [e]	89 [e]	1.02 [e]	83 [e]	1.32 [e]
8	Canada	..	..	..	..	99 [e, f]	1.00 [e, f]	98 [e, f]	1.01 [e, f]	69 [e, f]	1.33 [e, f]
9	Japan	..	..	..	..	101 [e]	1.00 [e]	101 [e, f]	1.01 [e, f]	44 [e]	0.85 [e]
10	Switzerland	..	..	..	..	99 [e]	0.99 [e]	85 [e]	0.95 [e]	37 [e]	0.78 [e]
11	Denmark	..	..	..	..	99 [e, f]	1.00 [e, f]	91 [e, f]	1.03 [e, f]	68 [e]	1.35 [e]
12	Ireland	..	..	..	..	90 [e, f]	1.00 [e, f]	..	..	53 [e]	1.27 [e]
13	United Kingdom	..	..	..	..	99 [e]	1.00 [e]	95 [e]	1.02 [e]	67 [e]	1.27 [e]
14	Finland	..	..	..	..	100 [e]	1.00 [e]	95 [e]	1.02 [e]	..	..
15	Luxembourg	..	..	..	..	97 [e]	1.01 [e]	81 [e]	1.08 [e]	10 [e, f, g]	1.24 [e, f, g]
16	Austria	..	..	..	..	92 [e]	1.01 [e]	88 [e]	0.99 [e]	62 [e]	1.14 [e]
17	France	..	..	..	..	100 [e]	1.00 [e]	93 [e]	1.02 [e]	59 [e]	1.23 [e]
18	Germany	..	..	..	..	87 [e, f]	1.02 [e, f]	88 [e, f]	1.01 [e, f]	45 [e, h]	0.96 [e, h]
19	Spain	96.9	98	99.8	100	103 [e]	1.01 [e]	95 [e]	1.03 [e]	64 [e]	1.15 [e]
20	New Zealand	..	..	..	..	99 [e]	1.00 [e]	93 [e]	1.02 [e]	84 [e]	1.52 [e]
21	Italy	98.1	99	99.8	100	100 [e]	1.00 [e]	91 [e]	1.01 [e]	57 [e]	1.32 [e]
22	Israel	93.1	96	99.3	100	101	1.00	89	1.01	62	1.39
23	Portugal	90.3	95	99.8	100	..	..	89 [e]	1.08 [e]	58 [e]	1.37 [e]
24	Greece	96.1	97	99.8	100	97 [e]	1.00 [e]	89 [e]	1.03 [e]	..	..
25	Cyprus	95.7	97	99.8	100	95	1.01	89	1.02	22 [f, i]	1.29 [f, i]
26	Hong Kong, China (SAR)	89.6	92	99.8	101	..	..	..	..	..	..
27	Barbados	99.7	100	99.8	100	105	1.01	84	0.97	55	2.45
28	Singapore	88.7	92	99.8	100	..	..	..	..	..	..
29	Slovenia	99.6	100	99.8	100	93	0.99	..	..	70	1.35
30	Korea, Rep. of	96.6	97	99.8	100	100 [e]	1.01 [e]	91 [e]	1.00 [e]	57 [e]	0.59 [e]
31	Brunei Darussalam	88.1	93	99.8	101	..	..	..	..	19	1.96
32	Czech Republic	..	..	..	..	90 [e]	1.00 [e]	..	..	31 [e]	1.05 [e]
33	Malta	93.0	102	99.8	102	100 [f]	1.02 [f]	77 [h]	0.95 [h]	24 [f]	1.22 [f]
34	Argentina	96.9	100	98.8	100	107 [e]	0.99 [e]	82 [e]	1.06 [e]	60 [e, f]	1.64 [e, f]
35	Poland	99.7	100	99.8	100	98 [e]	1.00 [e]	92 [e]	1.03 [e]	66 [e]	1.44 [e]
36	Seychelles	..	..	..	..	..	..	..	..	..	..
37	Bahrain	83.2	91	98.7	100	97	1.01	95	1.07	31 [h]	1.59 [h]
38	Hungary	99.2	100	99.8	100	90 [e]	0.99 [e]	88 [e, f]	1.01 [e, f]	45 [e]	1.27 [e]
39	Slovakia	..	..	..	..	90 [e]	1.01 [e]	75 [e]	1.01 [e]	32 [e]	1.09 [e]
40	Uruguay	98.1	101	99.4	101	91 [e]	1.01 [e]	74 [e]	1.11 [e]	47 [e]	1.83 [e]
41	Estonia	99.8	100	99.8	100	97	0.98	84	1.03	70	1.55
42	Costa Rica	95.8	100	98.6	101	91	1.00	52	1.11	18	1.21
43	Chile	95.7	100	99.1	100	88 [e]	0.99 [e]	64 [e]	0.76 [e]	36 [e]	0.92 [e]
44	Qatar	83.7	104	97.3	105	96 [h]	1.01 [h]	82 [h]	1.10 [h]	38	2.97
45	Lithuania	99.5	100	99.8	100	94	0.99	89	1.01	63	1.51
46	Kuwait	80.3	95	93.6	102	65 [f]	0.95 [f]	50 [h]	1.02 [h]	30 [h]	2.31 [h]
47	Croatia	97.4	98	99.8	100	..	..	..	..	..	..
48	United Arab Emirates	79.8	106	94.7	108	87	1.02	72	1.13	..	..
49	Bahamas	96.3	102	98.3	102	79 [f]	0.92 [f]	71 [f]	0.99 [f]	..	..
50	Latvia	99.8	100	99.8	100	92	1.00	77	1.08	79	1.65

Table 9.2 (*continued*)

	Adult literacy		Youth literacy		Net primary enrolment [a, b]		Net secondary enrolment [a, b]		Gross tertiary enrolment [b, c]	
HDI rank	Female rate (% age 15 and above) 2001	Female rate as % of male rate 2001	Female rate (% age 15-24) 2001	Female rate as % of male rate 2001	Female ratio (%) 2000-01	Ratio of females to males [d] 2000-01	Female ratio (%) 2000-01	Ratio of females to males [d] 2000-01	Female ratio (%) 2000-01	Ratio of females to males [d] 2000-01
51　Saint Kitts and Nevis	..	..	..	..					..	..
52　Cuba	96.7	100	99.8	100	97	0.99	84	1.05	26	1.16
53　Belarus	99.6	100	99.8	100	107	0.99	76	1.01	63	1.29
54　Trinidad and Tobago	97.8	99	99.8	100	92	1.00	73	1.07	8	1.53
55　Mexico	89.5	96	96.8	99	104 [e]	1.01 [e]	62 [e]	1.08 [e]	20 [e]	0.96 [e]
Medium human development										
56　Antigua and Barbuda	..	..	..	..			..	..	..	..
57　Bulgaria	98.0	99	99.6	100	93	0.98	87	0.98	47	1.35
58　Malaysia	84.0	92	97.8	100	99 [e]	1.00 [e]	74 [e]	1.11 [e]	29 [e]	1.08 [e]
59　Panama	91.4	99	96.5	99	100	1.00	65	1.09	44 [f]	1.67 [f]
60　Macedonia, TFYR	..	..	..	..	92	1.00	80 [f]	0.98 [f]	28	1.32
61　Libyan Arab Jamahiriya	69.3	76	93.5	94	..	..			48	0.96
62　Mauritius	81.7	93	94.5	101	95	1.00	65	1.04	13	1.36
63　Russian Federation	99.4	100	99.8	100	..	..	..	..	..	..
64　Colombia	91.9	100	97.7	101	88	1.00	59	1.10	24	1.09
65　Brazil	87.2	100	96.9	103	94 [e]	0.93 [e]	74 [e]	1.08 [e]	19 [e]	1.29 [e]
66　Bosnia and Herzegovina	..	..	..	..			..	..		
67　Belize	93.3	100	98.8	101	102	1.04	66	1.07	..	..
68　Dominica	..	..	..	..	..	..	..	..	..	..
69　Venezuela	92.4	99	98.8	101	89	1.02	55	1.20	34	1.45
70　Samoa (Western)	98.4	99	99.5	100	95	0.97	71	1.08	11	1.05
71　Saint Lucia	..	..	..	..	100	1.01	90	1.28	24 [h]	0.87 [h]
72　Romania	97.4	98	99.7	100	93	0.99	81	1.02	30	1.20
73　Saudi Arabia	68.2	82	91.0	96	56	0.92	50	0.95	25 [f]	1.29 [f]
74　Thailand	94.1	97	98.4	99	84 [e]	0.97 [e]	..	..	32 [e]	0.82 [e]
75　Ukraine	99.5	100	99.9	100	71 [h]	0.99 [h]	..	..	46 [h]	1.14 [h]
76　Kazakhstan	99.2	100	99.8	100	88	0.99	82	0.98	34	1.19
77　Suriname	..	..	..	..	90	0.96	46	1.13	..	..
78　Jamaica	91.0	109	97.6	107	95 [e]	1.00 [e]	76 [e]	1.04 [e]	22 [e]	1.89 [e]
79　Oman	63.5	78	96.8	97	64	0.99	60	1.01	10	1.40
80　St. Vincent & the Grenadines	..	..	..	..	..	..	..	..	..	..
81　Fiji	91.2	96	99.1	100	100 [h]	1.00 [h]	..	..	..	..
82　Peru	85.7	90	95.5	97	104 [e, f]	1.00 [e, f]	61 [e, h]	0.98 [e, h]	15 [e, h]	0.34 [e, h]
83　Lebanon	81.0	88	93.3	96	74	1.00	73 [h]	1.09 [h]	44	1.09
84　Paraguay	92.5	98	97.2	100	92 [e]	1.01 [e]	48 [e]	1.06 [e]	..	..
85　Philippines	95.0	100	99.0	100	93 [e]	1.01 [e]	57 [e]	1.18 [e]	33 [e]	1.10 [e]
86　Maldives	96.9	100	99.2	100	99	1.01	33 [f]	1.13 [f]	..	..
87　Turkmenistan	..	..	..	..	..	..	..	..	..	..
88　Georgia	..	..	..	..	95	1.00	73 [h]	1.02 [h]	34	0.99
89　Azerbaijan	..	..	..	..	93 [f]	1.03 [f]	78 [h]	1.01 [h]	21 [f]	0.93 [f]
90　Jordan	85.1	89	99.4	100	94 [e, f]	1.01 [e, f]	78 [e, f]	1.07 [e, f]	31 [e, f]	1.14 [e, f]
91　Tunisia	61.9	75	89.8	92	99 [e]	0.99 [e]	72 [e]	1.05 [e]	21 [e]	0.97 [e]
92　Guyana	98.2	99	99.8	100	97 [f]	0.97 [f]	..	..	..	..
93　Grenada	..	..	..	..	..	..	..	..	..	..
94　Dominican Republic	84.0	100	92.2	102	93	1.02	45	1.28	..	..
95　Albania	77.8	84	96.7	97	97	1.00	75	1.03	19	1.69
96　Turkey	77.2	82	94.4	95	..	..	..	..	12 [e, f]	0.70 [e, f]
97　Ecuador	90.3	97	97.1	99	100	1.01	49	1.04	..	..
98　Occupied Palestinian Territories	..	..	..	..	98	1.02	81	1.08	28	0.96
99　Sri Lanka	89.3	94	96.8	100	97 [e, h]	1.00 [e, h]	..	..	..	..
100　Armenia	97.8	98	99.7	100	70	1.02	65	1.06	22	1.25

Table 9.2 (*continued*)

HDI rank		Adult literacy		Youth literacy		Net primary enrolment [a, b]		Net secondary enrolment [a, b]		Gross tertiary enrolment [b, c]	
		Female rate (% age 15 and above) 2001	Female rate as % of male rate 2001	Female rate (% age 15-24) 2001	Female rate as % of male rate 2001	Female ratio (%) 2000-01	Ratio of females to males [d] 2000-01	Female ratio (%) 2000-01	Ratio of females to males [d] 2000-01	Female ratio (%) 2000-01	Ratio of females to males [d] 2000-01
101	Uzbekistan	98.9	99	99.6	100	..	..	..	..	..	..
102	Kyrgyzstan	..	..	..	..	81	0.97	..	..	42	1.04
103	Cape Verde	67.0	79	85.5	93	99 [h]	1.01 [h]	..	..	..	..
104	China	78.7	85	96.9	98	95 [e, f]	1.03 [e, f]	..	..	..	..
105	El Salvador	76.6	93	87.7	98	87 [f]	1.17 [f]	39 [h]	0.99 [h]	19	1.24
106	Iran, Islamic Rep. of	70.2	84	91.9	95	73	0.98	..	..	10	0.93
107	Algeria	58.3	76	84.6	90	97	0.97	63	1.05	..	..
108	Moldova, Rep. of	98.4	99	99.8	100	78	1.00	69	1.03	31	1.29
109	Viet Nam	90.9	96	95.6	101	92	0.94	..	..	8	0.74
110	Syrian Arab Republic	61.6	69	79.7	83	94	0.95	37	0.90	..	..
111	South Africa	85.0	98	91.5	100	88	0.98	60	1.12	17	1.23
112	Indonesia	82.6	90	97.3	99	92 [e]	0.99 [e]	46 [e, f]	0.96 [e, f]	13 [e]	0.77 [e]
113	Tajikistan	98.9	99	99.8	100	98	0.92	69	0.84	7	0.32
114	Bolivia	79.9	87	94.0	96	97	1.00	67	0.98	..	..
115	Honduras	75.7	100	87.1	104	88	1.02	..	..	17	1.31
116	Equatorial Guinea	76.0	82	95.7	97	68	0.89	14 [h]	0.36 [h]	2 [f]	0.43 [f]
117	Mongolia	98.3	100	99.4	101	91	1.04	64	1.21	42	1.74
118	Gabon	..	..	..	..	87	0.98	..	..	6 [h]	0.55 [h]
119	Guatemala	61.8	81	73.2	85	82	0.95	25	0.94	..	..
120	Egypt	44.8	67	63.7	83	90 [e]	0.95 [e]	77 [e]	0.96 [e]	..	..
121	Nicaragua	67.1	101	72.6	102	81	1.01	38	1.18	..	..
122	São Tomé and Principe	..	..	..	..	..	..	..	..	..	..
123	Solomon Islands	..	..	..	..	..	..	..	..	..	..
124	Namibia	81.9	98	93.7	104	84	1.07	44	1.38	7 [f]	1.24 [f]
125	Botswana	80.6	107	92.4	109	86	1.04	74	1.14	4	0.89
126	Morocco	37.2	59	59.7	78	74	0.91	27 [f]	0.83 [f]	9	0.80
127	India	46.4	67	65.8	82	..	..	..	..	8 [e, f]	0.66 [e, f]
128	Vanuatu	..	..	..	..	100	1.10	25 [h]	1.20 [h]	(.) [h]	0.62 [h]
129	Ghana	64.5	80	89.4	95	57	0.95	28	0.86	2	0.40
130	Cambodia	58.2	72	75.2	89	90	0.90	12	0.59	2	0.38
131	Myanmar	81.0	91	90.8	99	83	0.99	35	0.95	15	1.75
132	Papua New Guinea	57.7	81	72.1	90	80 [f]	0.91 [f]	18 [f]	0.77 [f]	2 [h]	0.66 [h]
133	Swaziland	79.4	98	91.6	102	94	1.02	47 [f]	1.17 [f]	5	0.87
134	Comoros	48.8	77	52.0	79	52	0.87	..	..	1 [f]	0.73 [f]
135	Lao People's Dem. Rep.	54.4	71	71.8	84	78	0.92	27	0.81	2	0.59
136	Bhutan	..	..	..	..	..	..	..	..	..	..
137	Lesotho	93.9	128	98.6	119	82	1.09	25	1.54	3	1.76
138	Sudan	47.7	68	72.9	87	42 [f]	0.83 [f]	..	..	7 [h]	0.92 [h]
139	Bangladesh	30.8	62	40.4	71	90	1.02	44	1.05	5	0.55
140	Congo	75.9	86	97.0	99	..	..	..	..	1	0.13
141	Togo	44.0	60	65.2	74	83	0.82	14 [h]	0.44 [h]	1 [f]	0.20 [f]
Low human development											
142	Cameroon	65.1	82	88.7	96	..	..	..	..	1 [f]	0.17 [f]
143	Nepal	25.2	42	44.4	57	67	0.87	..	..	2	0.27
144	Pakistan	28.8	49	43.1	60	56	0.74	..	..	..	..
145	Zimbabwe	85.5	92	96.0	97	80 [e]	1.00 [e]	39 [e]	0.92 [e]	3 [e]	0.60 [e]
146	Kenya	77.3	86	94.7	98	69	1.02	23	0.97	3	0.77
147	Uganda	58.0	74	73.0	85	106	0.94	10 [f]	0.72 [f]	2	0.52
148	Yemen	26.9	39	48.5	58	49	0.58	21 [h]	0.40 [h]	5 [h]	0.28 [h]
149	Madagascar	60.6	82	77.4	92	68	1.01	12 [h]	1.03 [h]	2	0.84
150	Haiti	48.9	93	65.5	101	..	..	..	..	..	..
151	Gambia	30.9	69	50.8	76	66	0.93	29	0.70	..	..

Table 9.2 (*continued*)

HDI rank		Adult literacy		Youth literacy		Net primary enrolment[a,b]		Net secondary enrolment[a,b]		Gross tertiary enrolment[b,c]	
		Female rate (% age 15 and above) 2001	Female rate as % of male rate 2001	Female rate (% age 15-24) 2001	Female rate as % of male rate 2001	Female ratio (%) 2000-01	Ratio of females to males[d] 2000-01	Female ratio (%) 2000-01	Ratio of females to males[d] 2000-01	Female ratio (%) 2000-01	Ratio of females to males[d] 2000-01
152	Nigeria	57.7	79	85.4	95	..		..	..	..	..
153	Djibouti	55.5	73	80.6	90	28	0.77	..	..	1	0.70
154	Mauritania	30.7	60	41.2	72	62	0.93	13	0.78	1	0.20
155	Eritrea	45.6	67	61.5	76	38	0.86	19	0.74	(.)	0.15
156	Senegal	28.7	60	43.2	71	60	0.90	..	..	..	..
157	Guinea	..	..	..	..	41	0.79	6 [h]	0.38 [h]	..	..
158	Rwanda	61.9	83	82.6	96	97 [f]	1.00 [f]	..	..	1	0.50
159	Benin	24.6	46	37.3	52	57 [f]	0.69 [f]	11 [f]	0.46 [f]	1 [f]	0.24 [f]
160	Tanzania, U. Rep. of	67.9	80	88.6	95	48	1.04	5	0.94	(.)	0.31
161	Côte d'Ivoire	38.4	64	53.6	75	55	0.75	..	..	4 [h]	0.36 [h]
162	Malawi	47.6	63	61.9	76	104	1.07	23	0.85	(.) [h]	0.39 [h]
163	Zambia	72.7	85	86.2	95	65	0.99	18	0.87	2	0.47
164	Angola	..	..	..	..	35	0.91	..	..	1 [f]	0.63 [f]
165	Chad	35.8	67	62.0	83	47	0.67	4 [f]	0.31 [f]	(.) [f]	0.17 [f]
166	Guinea-Bissau	24.7	45	45.5	62	45 [f]	0.71 [f]	..	..	(.) [f]	0.18 [f]
167	Congo, Dem. Rep. of the	51.8	70	76.4	86	32 [h]	0.95 [h]	9 [h]	0.58 [h]	..	..
168	Central African Republic	36.6	60	60.8	79	45	0.70	..	..	1 [f]	0.19 [f]
169	Ethiopia	32.4	67	50.2	81	41	0.77	10	0.68	1	0.27
170	Mozambique	30.0	49	47.7	63	50	0.85	8	0.68	(.)	0.79
171	Burundi	42.0	74	63.6	96	49	0.83	..	..	1	0.36
172	Mali	16.6	45	26.0	54	36 [h]	0.71 [h]	..	..	..	..
173	Burkina Faso	14.9	43	24.5	52	29	0.71	6	0.65	..	..
174	Niger	8.9	36	14.5	44	24	0.67	4	0.67	1	0.34
175	Sierra Leone	..	..	..	..	..	..	24	0.83	1	0.40
Developing countries		67.1	82	80.9	91	79	0.93	..	..	..	..
Least developed countries		43.8	70	59.3	81	57	0.90	..	..	..	..
Arab States		48.8	68	69.6	83	73	0.90	..	..	..	..
East Asia and the Pacific		81.3	88	96.6	98	93	1.01	..	..	..	..
Latin America and the Caribbean		88.2	98	95.4	101	96	0.99	..	..	..	..
South Asia		44.8	67	62.4	80	72	0.84	..	..	..	..
Sub-Saharan Africa		54.5	77	73.2	89	56	0.92	..	..	..	..
Central & Eastern Europe & CIS		99.1	99	99.8	100	91	1.02	..	..	..	..
OECD		..	..	..	..	98	1.00	..	..	..	..
High-income OECD		..	..	..	..	98	1.01	..	..	..	..
High human development		..	..	..	..	98	1.01	..	..	..	..
Medium human development		71.6	85	84.8	94	85	0.95	..	..	..	..
Low human development		44.4	68	63.9	81	54	0.86	..	..	..	..
High income		..	..	..	..	97	1.01	..	..	..	..
Middle income		81.8	90	94.9	98	93	1.00	..	..	..	..
Low income		53.9	75	69.8	85	69	0.87	..	..	..	..
World		..	..	..	..	81	0.94	..	..	..	..

a. The net enrolment ratio is the ratio of enrolled children of the official age for the education level indicated to the total population of that age. Net enrolment ratios exceeding 100% reflect discrepancies between these two data sets.

b. Data refers to the 2000–2001 school year. Data for some countries may refer to national or UNESCO Institute for Statistics estimates. For details, see http://www.uis.unesco.org/. Because data is from different sources, comparisons across countries should be made with caution.

c. Tertiary enrolment is generally calculated as a gross ratio.

d. Calculated as the ratio of the female enrolment ratio to the male enrolment ratio.

e. Preliminary UNESCO Institute for Statistics estimate, subject to further revision.

f. Data refers to the 1998/99 school year.

g. The ratio is an underestimate, as many students pursue their studies in nearby countries.

h. Data refer to the 1999–2000 school year.

i. Excludes Turkish students.

Source: United Nations Development Programme. (2003). *Human Development Report 2003.* Table 24. "Gender Inequality in Education (318–321)." New York: Oxford University Press. Retrieved from http://www.undp.org/hdr2003/pdf/hdr03_complete.pdf. Copyright 2003 by the United Nations Development Programme. Used by permission of Oxford University Press, Inc.

Table 9.3
Gender Inequality in Economic Activity

		Female economic activity rate (age 15 and above)			Employment by economic activity (%)						Contributing family workers	
					Agriculture		Industry		Services		Female (as % of total)	Male (as % of total)
		Rate (%)	Index (1990 = 100)	As % of male rate	Female	Male	Female	Male	Female	Male		
HDI rank		2001	2001	2001	1995-2001[a]	1995-2001[a]	1995-2001[a]	1995-2001[a]	1995-2001[a]	1995-2001[a]	1995-2000[a]	1995-2000[a]
High human development												
1	Norway	59.5	109	85	2	6	9	33	88	61	63	38
2	Iceland	66.7	101	83	5	12	15	34	80	53	67	33
3	Sweden	62.6	102	89	1	4	12	38	87	59	54	46
4	Australia	56.1	107	77	3	6	10	31	86	63	59	41
5	Netherlands	45.6	106	67	2	4	9	31	84	63	78	22
6	Belgium	39.9	106	66	2	3	13	37	86	60	85	15
7	United States	59.1	106	82	1	4	12	32	86	64	62	38
8	Canada	60.3	104	82	2	5	11	32	87	63	69	31
9	Japan	50.9	103	67	6	5	22	38	73	57	82	18
10	Switzerland	50.8	104	66	4	5	13	36	83	59	..	..
11	Denmark	61.7	100	84	2	5	15	37	83	58	..	..
12	Ireland	37.5	117	53	2	12	15	38	83	50	59	41
13	United Kingdom	53.0	105	74	1	2	12	36	87	61	66	34
14	Finland	56.9	98	87	4	8	14	40	82	52	47	53
15	Luxembourg	38.1	104	58	..	..	..	..	..	..	..	..
16	Austria	44.0	102	65	7	6	14	43	79	52	67	33
17	France	48.8	107	77	..	2	13	35	86	63	..	..
18	Germany	47.9	100	70	2	3	19	46	79	50	75	25
19	Spain	37.8	112	57	5	8	14	41	81	51	64	36
20	New Zealand	57.6	109	80	6	11	12	32	81	56	68	32
21	Italy	38.6	107	59	5	6	21	39	74	55	55	45
22	Israel	48.8	114	68	1	3	13	35	86	61	77	23
23	Portugal	51.4	105	72	14	11	24	44	62	45	66	34
24	Greece	38.2	108	59	20	16	12	29	67	54	69	31
25	Cyprus	49.1	103	62	10	11	18	30	71	58	87	13
26	Hong Kong, China (SAR)	50.9	105	65	..	..	12	28	88	71	..	..
27	Barbados	62.0	107	79	3	5	11	31	85	64	..	..
28	Singapore	50.1	99	64	..	..	23	33	77	67	70	30
29	Slovenia	54.5	98	81	11	11	28	46	61	42	63	37
30	Korea, Rep. of	53.6	111	70	13	10	19	34	68	56	88	12
31	Brunei Darussalam	50.4	112	63	..	..	..	..	..	..	..	..
32	Czech Republic	61.2	100	83	4	6	28	49	69	48	78	22
33	Malta	26.1	112	37	..	..	..	..	..	..	..	..
34	Argentina	36.2	124	47	..	1	10	34	89	65	64	36
35	Poland	57.1	100	80	19	19	21	41	60	39	60	40
36	Seychelles	..	..	..	..	..	..	..	..	..	..	..
37	Bahrain	33.8	119	39	..	..	..	..	..	..	..	..
38	Hungary	48.5	102	71	4	9	25	42	71	48	67	33
39	Slovakia	62.7	99	84	5	10	26	49	69	42	68	32
40	Uruguay	48.3	109	67	1	6	14	34	85	61	68	32
41	Estonia	60.7	95	82	7	11	23	40	70	49	59	41
42	Costa Rica	37.4	113	46	4	22	17	27	79	51	41	59
43	Chile	38.1	119	49	5	19	14	31	82	49	..	..
44	Qatar	41.6	126	46	..	..	..	..	..	..	..	..
45	Lithuania	57.6	97	80	16	24	40	33	63	43	61	39
46	Kuwait	36.5	96	48	..	..	..	..	..	..	..	..
47	Croatia	48.8	102	73	17	16	22	38	61	46	76	24
48	United Arab Emirates	31.8	109	37	..	..	..	..	..	..	..	..
49	Bahamas	66.8	104	84	1	6	5	24	93	69	..	..
50	Latvia	59.6	95	80	14	17	18	35	69	49	52	48

Table 9.3 (*continued*)

HDI rank	Female economic activity rate (age 15 and above)			Employment by economic activity (%)						Contributing family workers	
				Agriculture		Industry		Services		Female (as % of total)	Male (as % of total)
	Rate (%) 2001	Index (1990 = 100) 2001	As % of male rate 2001	Female 1995-2001[a]	Male 1995-2001[a]	Female 1995-2001[a]	Male 1995-2001[a]	Female 1995-2001[a]	Male 1995-2001[a]	1995-2000[a]	1995-2000[a]
51 Saint Kitts and Nevis	..	..	..	..	..	..	..	..	..	..	..
52 Cuba	50.2	119	65	..	..	..	..	..	..	..	..
53 Belarus	59.2	98	82	..	..	..	..	..	..	..	..
54 Trinidad and Tobago	44.5	114	59	3	11	13	37	83	52	70	30
55 Mexico	39.8	117	48	7	23	22	29	71	47	49	51
Medium human development											
56 Antigua and Barbuda	..	..	..	..	..	..	..	..	..	..	..
57 Bulgaria	56.4	94	86	..	..	..	..	..	..	..	..
58 Malaysia	48.7	109	61	13	21	29	33	58	46	..	..
59 Panama	43.7	113	55	2	25	10	22	88	52	27	73
60 Macedonia, TFYR	49.8	103	72	..	..	..	..	..	..	..	..
61 Libyan Arab Jamahiriya	25.3	123	34	..	..	..	..	..	..	..	..
62 Mauritius	38.2	110	48	13	15	43	39	45	46	..	..
63 Russian Federation	59.2	98	82	8	15	23	36	69	49	42	58
64 Colombia	48.5	114	61	..	2	20	30	80	68	69	31
65 Brazil	43.8	98	52	19	26	10	27	71	47	..	..
66 Bosnia and Herzegovina	43.1	99	60	..	..	..	..	..	..	..	..
67 Belize	27.3	114	32	6	37	12	19	81	44	30	70
68 Dominica	..	..	..	14	31	10	24	72	40	..	..
69 Venezuela	43.5	115	54	2	16	13	29	85	55	..	..
70 Samoa (Western)	..	..	..	..	..	..	..	..	..	..	..
71 Saint Lucia	..	..	..	16	27	14	24	71	49	..	..
72 Romania	50.6	97	76	45	39	22	33	33	29	71	29
73 Saudi Arabia	21.6	145	28	..	..	..	..	..	..	..	..
74 Thailand	73.1	98	85	47	50	17	20	36	31	66	34
75 Ukraine	55.5	98	80	..	..	..	..	..	..	64	36
76 Kazakhstan	61.1	101	82	..	..	..	..	..	..	..	..
77 Suriname	36.6	123	49	3	7	10	32	86	56	..	..
78 Jamaica	67.2	101	86	10	30	9	26	81	45	66	34
79 Oman	19.6	154	26	..	..	..	..	..	..	..	..
80 St. Vincent & the Grenadines	..	..	..	..	..	..	..	..	..	..	..
81 Fiji	37.9	143	46	..	..	..	..	..	..	..	..
82 Peru	34.9	119	44	3	8	11	25	86	67	62	38
83 Lebanon	29.9	123	39	..	..	..	..	..	..	..	..
84 Paraguay	37.1	110	43	3	7	10	31	87	62	..	..
85 Philippines	49.7	106	61	27	47	13	18	61	36	..	..
86 Maldives	65.4	100	80	..	..	..	..	..	..	57	43
87 Turkmenistan	62.3	105	81	..	..	..	..	..	..	..	..
88 Georgia	55.7	100	78	..	..	..	..	..	..	60	40
89 Azerbaijan	54.8	106	75	..	..	..	..	..	..	..	..
90 Jordan	27.1	160	35	..	..	..	..	..	..	..	..
91 Tunisia	37.2	113	48	..	..	..	..	..	..	..	..
92 Guyana	41.1	115	50	..	..	..	..	..	..	..	..
93 Grenada	..	..	..	10	17	12	32	77	46	..	..
94 Dominican Republic	40.4	118	48	3	24	20	27	77	49	23	77
95 Albania	59.9	103	73	..	..	..	..	..	..	..	..
96 Turkey	50.3	115	62	72	34	10	25	18	41	65	35
97 Ecuador	33.0	119	39	2	11	14	26	84	63	66	34
98 Occupied Palestinian Territories	9.3	148	13	..	..	..	..	..	..	54	46
99 Sri Lanka	43.1	107	55	49	38	22	23	27	37	56	44
100 Armenia	62.4	100	88	..	..	..	..	..	..	..	..

Table 9.3 (*continued*)

HDI rank		Female economic activity rate (age 15 and above)			Employment by economic activity (%)						Contributing family workers	
		Rate (%) 2001	Index (1990 = 100) 2001	As % of male rate 2001	Agriculture		Industry		Services		Female (as % of total) 1995-2000[a]	Male (as % of total) 1995-2000[a]
					Female 1995-2001[a]	Male 1995-2001[a]	Female 1995-2001[a]	Male 1995-2001[a]	Female 1995-2001[a]	Male 1995-2001[a]		
101	Uzbekistan	62.5	106	85	..	..	..	..	..	..	..	..
102	Kyrgyzstan	61.0	104	84	53	52	8	14	38	34	..	..
103	Cape Verde	46.4	109	53	..	..	..	..	..	..	..	..
104	China	72.6	98	86	..	..	..	..	..	..	..	..
105	El Salvador	46.5	125	55	6	37	25	24	69	38	42	58
106	Iran, Islamic Rep. of	29.5	137	38	..	..	..	..	..	..	..	..
107	Algeria	30.2	158	40	..	..	..	..	..	..	..	..
108	Moldova, Rep. of	60.3	98	84	..	..	..	..	..	..	62	38
109	Viet Nam	73.7	96	91	..	..	..	..	..	..	..	..
110	Syrian Arab Republic	28.9	122	37	..	..	..	..	..	..	..	..
111	South Africa	47.2	102	59	..	..	..	..	..	..	..	..
112	Indonesia	55.6	110	68	42	41	16	21	42	39	..	..
113	Tajikistan	58.1	112	80	..	..	..	..	..	..	..	..
114	Bolivia	48.2	106	58	2	2	16	40	82	58	63	37
115	Honduras	40.8	120	48	9	50	25	21	67	30	40	60
116	Equatorial Guinea	45.7	101	52	..	..	..	..	..	..	..	..
117	Mongolia	73.6	103	88	..	..	..	..	..	..	..	..
118	Gabon	63.2	101	76	..	..	..	..	..	..	..	..
119	Guatemala	36.6	131	42	14	37	19	26	68	38	..	..
120	Egypt	35.4	117	45	35	29	9	25	56	46	43	57
121	Nicaragua	47.7	118	56	..	..	..	..	..	..	..	..
122	São Tomé and Principe	..	..	..	..	..	..	..	..	..	..	..
123	Solomon Islands	81.1	97	92	..	..	..	..	..	..	..	..
124	Namibia	53.7	101	67	39	38	8	19	52	43	..	..
125	Botswana	62.8	96	77	..	..	..	..	..	..	45	55
126	Morocco	41.6	107	52	6	6	40	32	54	63	22	78
127	India	42.2	105	50	..	..	..	..	..	..	..	..
128	Vanuatu	..	..	..	..	..	..	..	..	..	..	..
129	Ghana	80.0	98	98	..	..	..	..	..	..	..	..
130	Cambodia	80.3	98	97	..	..	..	..	..	..	71	29
131	Myanmar	65.8	100	75	..	..	..	..	..	..	..	..
132	Papua New Guinea	67.6	100	79	..	..	..	..	..	..	..	..
133	Swaziland	41.7	106	52	..	..	..	..	..	..	..	..
134	Comoros	62.4	99	73	..	..	..	..	..	..	..	..
135	Lao People's Dem. Rep.	74.5	101	85	..	..	..	..	..	..	..	..
136	Bhutan	57.1	100	65	..	..	..	..	..	..	..	..
137	Lesotho	47.5	102	56	..	..	..	..	..	..	..	..
138	Sudan	35.1	114	41	..	..	..	..	..	..	..	..
139	Bangladesh	66.4	101	76	78	54	8	11	11	34	81	19
140	Congo	58.4	100	71	..	..	..	..	..	..	..	..
141	Togo	53.5	101	62	..	..	..	..	..	..	..	..
Low human development												
142	Cameroon	49.4	105	58	..	..	..	..	..	..	..	..
143	Nepal	56.8	101	66	..	..	..	..	..	..	..	..
144	Pakistan	35.8	125	43	66	41	11	20	23	39	33	67
145	Zimbabwe	65.1	98	78	..	..	..	..	..	..	..	..
146	Kenya	74.7	100	85	16	20	10	23	75	57	..	..
147	Uganda	79.4	98	88	..	..	..	..	..	..	..	..
148	Yemen	30.6	109	37	..	..	..	..	..	..	26	74
149	Madagascar	69.0	99	78	..	..	..	..	..	..	..	..
150	Haiti	55.9	97	70	..	..	..	..	..	..	..	..
151	Gambia	69.7	101	78	..	..	..	..	..	..	..	..

Table 9.3 (*continued*)

HDI rank	Female economic activity rate (age 15 and above)			Employment by economic activity (%)						Contributing family workers	
	Rate (%) 2001	Index (1990 = 100) 2001	As % of male rate 2001	Agriculture		Industry		Services		Female (as % of total)	Male (as % of total)
				Female 1995-2001[a]	Male 1995-2001[a]	Female 1995-2001[a]	Male 1995-2001[a]	Female 1995-2001[a]	Male 1995-2001[a]	1995-2000[a]	1995-2000[a]
152 Nigeria	47.7	102	56	2	4	11	30	87	67	..	..
153 Djibouti	..	..	..	..	..	..	..	..	..	..	..
154 Mauritania	63.3	98	74	..	..	..	..	..	..	..	..
155 Eritrea	74.6	99	87	..	..	..	..	..	..	..	..
156 Senegal	61.7	101	72	..	..	..	..	..	..	..	..
157 Guinea	77.2	98	89	..	..	..	..	..	..	..	..
158 Rwanda	82.5	99	88	..	..	..	..	..	..	..	..
159 Benin	73.4	96	90	..	..	..	..	..	..	..	..
160 Tanzania, U. Rep. of	81.6	98	93	..	..	..	..	..	..	..	..
161 Côte d'Ivoire	43.9	102	51	..	..	..	..	..	..	..	..
162 Malawi	77.8	98	90	..	..	..	..	..	..	..	..
163 Zambia	64.1	98	75	..	..	..	..	..	..	..	..
164 Angola	72.7	98	82	..	..	..	..	..	..	..	..
165 Chad	67.3	101	77	..	..	..	..	..	..	..	..
166 Guinea-Bissau	57.0	100	63	..	..	..	..	..	..	..	..
167 Congo, Dem. Rep. of the	60.5	97	72	..	..	..	..	..	..	..	..
168 Central African Republic	67.5	96	79	..	..	..	..	..	..	..	..
169 Ethiopia	57.3	98	67	88	89	2	2	11	9	..	..
170 Mozambique	82.7	99	92	..	..	..	..	..	..	..	..
171 Burundi	81.9	99	89	..	..	..	..	..	..	..	..
172 Mali	69.9	97	79	..	..	..	..	..	..	..	..
173 Burkina Faso	74.8	97	85	..	..	..	..	..	..	..	..
174 Niger	69.4	99	75	..	..	..	..	..	..	..	..
175 Sierra Leone	44.8	106	54	..	..	..	..	..	..	..	..
Developing countries	55.7	101	67	..	..	..	..	..	..	..	..
Least developed countries	64.2	99	74	..	..	..	..	..	..	..	..
Arab States	32.7	117	41	..	..	..	..	..	..	..	..
East Asia and the Pacific	68.8	99	82	..	..	..	..	..	..	..	..
Latin America and the Caribbean	42.2	109	52	..	..	..	..	..	..	..	..
South Asia	43.6	106	52	..	..	..	..	..	..	..	..
Sub-Saharan Africa	62.2	99	73	..	..	..	..	..	..	..	..
Central & Eastern Europe & CIS	57.5	99	81	..	..	..	..	..	..	..	..
OECD	51.3	106	71	..	..	..	..	..	..	..	..
High-income OECD	52.0	106	73	..	..	..	..	..	..	..	..
High human development	50.7	106	70	..	..	..	..	..	..	..	..
Medium human development	56.7	100	69	..	..	..	..	..	..	..	..
Low human development	56.7	102	66	..	..	..	..	..	..	..	..
High income	51.9	106	73	..	..	..	..	..	..	..	..
Middle income	59.1	100	73	..	..	..	..	..	..	..	..
Low income	51.9	103	62	..	..	..	..	..	..	..	..
World	55.2	102	68	..	..	..	..	..	..	..	..

Note: As a result of limitations in the data, comparisons of labour statistics over time and across countries should be made with caution. The percentage shares of employment by economic activity may not sum to 100 because of rounding or the omission of activities not classified.
a. Data refer to the most recent year available during the period specified.

Source: United Nations Development Programme. (2003). *Human Development Report 2003*. Table 25. "Gender Inequality in Economic Activity (322–5)." New York: Oxford University Press. Retrieved from http://www.undp.org/hdr2003/pdf/hdr03_complete.pdf. Copyright 2003 by the United Nations Development Programme. Used by permission of Oxford University Press, Inc.

Table 9.4
Gender, Work Burden and Time Allocation

| | | Burden of work | | | Time allocation (%) | | | | | |
| | | Total work time (minutes per day) | | Female work time as % of male | Total work time | | Time spent by females | | Time spent by males | |
	Year	Females	Males		Market activities	Non-market activities	Market activities	Non-market activities	Market activities	Non-market activities
Selected developing countries										
Urban areas										
Colombia	1983	399	356	112	49	51	24	76	77	23
Indonesia	1992	398	366	109	60	40	35	65	86	14
Kenya	1986	590	572	103	46	54	41	59	79	21
Nepal	1978	579	554	105	58	42	25	75	67	33
Venezuela	1983	440	416	106	59	41	30	70	87	13
Average [a]	--	481	453	107	54	46	31	69	79	21
Rural areas										
Bangladesh	1990	545	496	110	52	48	35	65	70	30
Guatemala	1977	678	579	117	59	41	37	63	84	16
Kenya	1988	676	500	135	56	44	42	58	76	24
Nepal	1978	641	547	117	56	44	46	54	67	33
Highlands	1978	692	586	118	59	41	52	48	66	34
Mountains	1978	649	534	122	56	44	48	52	65	35
Rural hills	1978	583	520	112	52	48	37	63	70	30
Philippines	1975-77	546	452	121	73	27	29	71	84	16
Average [a]	--	617	515	120	59	41	38	62	76	24
National [b]										
India	2000	457	391	117	61	39	35	65	92	8
Mongolia	2000	545	501	109	61	39	49	51	75	25
South Africa	2000	332	273	122	51	49	35	65	70	30
Average [a]	--	445	388	116	58	42	40	60	79	21
Selected OECD countries [c]										
Australia	1997	435	418	104	46	54	30	70	62	38
Austria [d]	1992	438	393	111	49	51	31	69	71	29
Canada	1998	420	429	98	53	47	41	59	65	35
Denmark [d]	1987	449	458	98	68	32	58	42	79	21
Finland [d]	1987-88	430	410	105	51	49	39	61	64	36
France	1999	391	363	108	46	54	33	67	60	40
Germany [d]	1991-92	440	441	100	44	56	30	70	61	39
Hungary	1999	432	445	97	51	49	41	59	60	40
Israel [d]	1991-92	375	377	99	51	49	29	71	74	26
Italy [d]	1988-89	470	367	128	45	55	22	78	77	23
Japan	1996	393	363	108	66	34	43	57	93	7
Korea, Rep. of	1999	431	373	116	64	36	45	55	88	12
Latvia	1996	535	481	111	46	54	35	65	58	42
Netherlands	1995	308	315	98	48	52	27	73	69	31
New Zealand	1999	420	417	101	46	54	32	68	60	40
Norway [d]	1990-91	445	412	108	50	50	38	62	64	36
United Kingdom [d]	1985	413	411	100	51	49	37	63	68	32
United States [d]	1985	453	428	106	50	50	37	63	63	37
Average [e]	--	423	403	105	52	48	37	64	69	31

Note: Data are estimates based on time use surveys available in time for publication. Time use data are also being collected in other countries, including Benin, Chad, Cuba, the Dominican Republic, Ecuador, Guatemala, the Lao People's Democratic Republic, Mali, Mexico, Morocco, Nepal, Nicaragua, Nigeria, Oman, the Philippines, Thailand and Viet Nam. Market activities refer to market-oriented production activities as defined by the 1993 revised UN System of National Accounts; surveys before 1993 are not strictly comparable with those for later years.

a. Refers to the unweighted average for the countries or areas shown above.

b. Classifications of market and non-market activities are not strictly base on the 1993 revised UN System of National Accounts, so comparisons between countries and areas must be made with caution.

c. Israel and Latvia are included here, although they are not OECD countries.

d. Harvey 1995.

e. Refers to the unweighted average for the OECD countries shown above (that is, excluding Israel and Latvia).

Source: United Nations Development Programme. (2003). *Human Development Report 2003.* Table 26. "Gender—Work Burden & Time Allocation (326)." New York: Oxford University Press. Retrieved from http://www.undp.org/hdr2003/pdf/hdr03_complete.pdf. Copyright 2003 by the United Nations Development Programme. Used by permission of Oxford University Press, Inc.

Table 9.5
Gender-Related Development Index

HDI rank	Gender-related development index (GDI) Rank	Gender-related development index (GDI) Value	Life expectancy at birth (years) 2001 Female	Life expectancy at birth (years) 2001 Male	Adult literacy rate (% age 15 and above) 2001 Female	Adult literacy rate (% age 15 and above) 2001 Male	Combined primary, secondary and tertiary gross enrolment ratio (%) 2000-01[a] Female	Combined primary, secondary and tertiary gross enrolment ratio (%) 2000-01[a] Male	Estimated earned income (PPP US$) 2001[b] Female	Estimated earned income (PPP US$) 2001[b] Male	HDI rank minus GDI rank[c]
High human development											
1 Norway	1	0.941	81.7	75.8	.. [d]	.. [d]	102 [e,f]	94 [f]	23,317 [g]	36,043 [g]	0
2 Iceland	2	0.940	81.8	77.5	.. [d]	.. [d]	96 [f]	87 [f]	23,130	36,799	0
3 Sweden	3	0.940	82.4	77.4	.. [d]	.. [d]	123 [e,f]	103 [e,f]	19,636 [g]	28,817 [g]	0
4 Australia	4	0.938	81.9	76.3	.. [d]	.. [d]	117 [e,f]	112 [e,f]	20,830	29,945	0
5 Netherlands	7	0.934	80.9	75.5	.. [d]	.. [d]	99 [f]	100 [e,f]	18,846	35,675	-2
6 Belgium	8	0.931	81.7	75.4	.. [d]	.. [d]	111 [e,f,h]	104 [e,f,h]	15,835	35,601	-2
7 United States	5	0.935	79.7	74.0	.. [d]	.. [d]	97 [f]	90 [f]	26,389 [g]	42,540 [g]	2
8 Canada	6	0.934	81.8	76.5	.. [d]	.. [d]	96 [f,h]	91 [f,h]	20,990 [g]	33,391 [g]	2
9 Japan	13	0.926	84.7	77.7	.. [d]	.. [d]	82 [f]	84 [f]	15,617	35,061	-4
10 Switzerland	12	0.927	82.2	75.8	.. [d]	.. [d]	86 [f]	90 [f]	18,782	37,619	-2
11 Denmark	9	0.928	78.9	74.0	.. [d]	.. [d]	102 [e,f]	95 [f]	24,086	34,011	2
12 Ireland	16	0.923	79.4	74.1	.. [d]	.. [d]	93 [i]	89 [i]	18,701 [g]	46,280 [g]	-4
13 United Kingdom	11	0.928	80.4	75.4	.. [d]	.. [d]	119 [e,f]	105 [e,f]	18,180	30,476	2
14 Finland	10	0.928	81.3	74.1	.. [d]	.. [d]	108 [e,i]	99 [i]	20,234	28,831	4
15 Luxembourg	18	0.920	81.2	74.8	.. [d]	.. [d]	74 [f,h,j]	72 [f,h,j]	29,569	78,723 [k]	-3
16 Austria	14	0.924	81.3	75.1	.. [d]	.. [d]	93 [f]	91 [f]	17,940 [g]	35,923 [g]	2
17 France	17	0.923	82.6	74.9	.. [d]	.. [d]	93 [f]	90 [f]	18,607	29,657	0
18 Germany	15	0.924	81.0	74.9	.. [d]	.. [d]	93 [i]	95 [i]	18,474	32,557	3
19 Spain	20	0.912	82.6	75.6	96.9 [d]	98.6 [d]	95 [f]	90 [f]	12,331 [g]	28,275 [g]	-1
20 New Zealand	19	0.914	80.6	75.6	.. [d]	.. [d]	104 [e,f]	94 [f]	15,524	22,900	1
21 Italy	21	0.910	81.8	75.4	98.1 [d]	98.9 [d]	84 [f]	81 [f]	15,452 [g]	34,460 [g]	0
22 Israel	22	0.900	80.8	76.9	93.1	97.1	92	88	13,726 [g]	26,011 [g]	0
23 Portugal	23	0.892	79.4	72.3	90.3 [d]	95.0 [d]	97 [f]	90 [f]	12,782	23,940	0
24 Greece	24	0.886	80.8	75.6	96.1 [d]	98.5 [d]	81 [i]	80 [i]	10,833 [g]	24,235 [g]	0
25 Cyprus	25	0.886	80.4	75.8	95.7	98.8	75 [h]	74 [h]	13,513	28,899	0
26 Hong Kong, China (SAR)	26	0.886	82.6	77.1	89.6	96.9	66 [i]	61 [i]	18,028	31,883	0
27 Barbados	27	0.885	79.3	74.3	99.7 [d]	99.7 [d]	94	84	11,852 [g]	19,496 [g]	0
28 Singapore	28	0.880	80.0	75.7	88.7	96.4	75 [i]	76 [i]	14,992	30,262	0
29 Slovenia	29	0.879	79.5	72.2	99.6 [d]	99.7 [d]	85 [i]	80 [i]	13,152 [g]	21,338 [g]	0
30 Korea, Rep. of	30	0.873	79.0	71.4	96.6 [d]	99.2 [d]	84 [f]	97 [f]	9,529	20,578	0
31 Brunei Darussalam	31	0.867	78.7	74.0	88.1	94.6	84	81	11,716 [g,l]	26,122 [g,l]	0
32 Czech Republic	32	0.857	78.4	71.7	.. [d]	.. [d]	77 [f]	76 [f]	10,555	19,113	0
33 Malta	33	0.844	80.4	75.6	93.0	91.5	76 [h]	75 [h]	6,787	19,647	0
34 Argentina	34	0.839	77.4	70.3	96.9	96.9	94 [f,h]	85 [f,h]	6,064 [g]	16,786 [g]	0
35 Poland	35	0.839	77.8	69.4	99.7 [d]	99.8 [d]	91 [f]	86 [f]	7,253 [g]	11,777 [g]	0
36 Seychelles	..	..	..	..	..	..	..	..	..	..	..
37 Bahrain	40	0.829	75.7	72.1	83.2	91.1	84 [m]	78 [m]	7,578	22,305	-4
38 Hungary	36	0.834	75.7	67.3	99.2 [d]	99.5 [d]	83 [f,h]	80 [f,h]	9,183	15,803	1
39 Slovakia	37	0.834	77.2	69.3	.. [d]	.. [d]	74 [f]	72 [f]	9,468 [g]	14,595 [g]	1
40 Uruguay	39	0.830	78.6	71.3	98.1	97.2	89 [f]	79 [f]	5,774 [g]	11,190 [g]	0
41 Estonia	38	0.831	76.5	65.9	99.8 [d]	99.8 [d]	93	85	7,993 [g]	12,720 [g]	2
42 Costa Rica	41	0.824	80.3	75.6	95.8	95.6	66	65	5,189	13,589	0
43 Chile	43	0.821	78.8	72.8	95.7	96.1	71 [f]	81 [f]	5,055 [g]	13,409 [g]	-1
44 Qatar	..	..	75.0	70.1	83.7	80.8	85	78	..	..	..
45 Lithuania	42	0.823	77.3	67.1	99.5 [d]	99.7 [d]	88	83	6,843	10,326	1
46 Kuwait	45	0.813	78.8	74.7	80.3	84.3	57 [m]	52 [m]	8,605 [g]	25,333 [g]	-1
47 Croatia	44	0.814	77.9	70.0	97.4	99.4 [d]	69 [i]	68 [i]	6,612 [g]	11,929 [g]	1
48 United Arab Emirates	49	0.802	77.1	73.0	79.8	75.2	74 [f]	64 [f]	6,041 [g,l]	28,223 [g,l]	-3
49 Bahamas	46	0.811	70.6	63.8	96.3	94.6	77 [i]	72 [i]	12,783 [g,n]	19,857 [g,n]	1
50 Latvia	47	0.810	75.8	65.0	99.8 [d]	99.8 [d]	91	82	6,470	9,215	1

Table 9.5 (*continued*)

HDI rank	Gender-related development index (GDI) Rank	Value	Life expectancy at birth (years) 2001 Female	Male	Adult literacy rate (% age 15 and above) 2001 Female	Male	Combined primary, secondary and tertiary gross enrolment ratio (%) 2000-01[a] Female	Male	Estimated earned income (PPP US$) 2001[b] Female	Male	HDI rank minus GDI rank[c]
51 Saint Kitts and Nevis	..	..	..	..	..	..	..	..	..	..	..
52 Cuba	..	..	78.5	74.6	96.7	96.9	77	75	..	..	..
53 Belarus	48	0.803	75.0	64.3	99.6 [d]	99.8 [d]	87	84	6,084 [g]	9,358 [g]	1
54 Trinidad and Tobago	50	0.796	74.6	68.6	97.8	99.0	68	65	5,645 [g]	12,614 [g]	0
55 Mexico	52	0.790	76.1	70.1	89.5	93.5	74 [f]	74 [f]	4,637	12,358	-1
Medium human development											
56 Antigua and Barbuda	..	..	..	..	..	..	..	..	..	..	..
57 Bulgaria	51	0.794	74.6	67.4	98.0	99.0 [d]	79	76	5,484	8,378	1
58 Malaysia	53	0.784	75.3	70.4	84.0	91.7	74 [f]	71 [f]	5,557 [g]	11,845 [g]	0
59 Panama	54	0.781	77.1	72.0	91.4	92.7	78 [h]	73 [h]	3,399 [g]	8,056 [g]	0
60 Macedonia, TFYR	..	..	75.5	71.2	..	..	70	70	..	..	..
61 Libyan Arab Jamahiriya	..	..	75.0	70.4	69.3	91.3	91 [f]	87 [f]	..	..	..
62 Mauritius	59	0.770	75.5	68.0	81.7	88.0	68	70	5,273 [g]	14,497 [g]	-4
63 Russian Federation	56	0.774	72.9	60.6	99.4 [d]	99.7 [d]	82 [i]	75 [i]	5,609 [g]	8,795 [g]	0
64 Colombia	55	0.774	75.0	68.6	91.9	91.9	72	69	4,534 [g]	9,608 [g]	2
65 Brazil	58	0.770	72.3	63.7	87.2	87.4	97 [f]	93 [f]	4,391	10,410	0
66 Bosnia and Herzegovina	..	..	76.5	71.1	..	..	..	..	..	..	..
67 Belize	64	0.756	73.4	70.2	93.3	93.6	76 [f]	75 [f]	2,188 [g]	9,100 [g]	-5
68 Dominica	..	..	..	..	..	..	..	..	..	..	..
69 Venezuela	60	0.767	76.4	70.6	92.4	93.3	70	65	3,288 [g]	8,021 [g]	0
70 Samoa (Western)	..	..	73.0	66.5	98.4	98.9	72	70	..	..	..
71 Saint Lucia	..	..	73.8	70.5	..	..	81 [m]	83 [m]	..	..	..
72 Romania	57	0.771	74.2	67.0	97.4	99.1 [d]	70	67	4,313 [g]	7,416 [g]	4
73 Saudi Arabia	68	0.743	73.3	70.7	68.2	83.5	57 [h]	60 [h]	4,222 [g]	21,141 [g]	-6
74 Thailand	61	0.766	73.2	64.9	94.1	97.3	69 [f]	75 [f]	4,875	7,975	2
75 Ukraine	63	0.761	74.4	64.1	99.5 [d]	99.8 [d]	79 [m]	83 [m]	3,071	5,826	1
76 Kazakhstan	62	0.763	71.5	60.3	99.2 [d]	99.7 [d]	78	77	5,039	8,077	3
77 Suriname	..	..	73.4	68.2	..	..	79 [f]	75 [f]	..	..	..
78 Jamaica	65	0.750	77.5	73.5	91.0	83.4	71 [f,h]	67 [f,h]	2,969 [g]	4,492 [g]	1
79 Oman	71	0.736	74.1	70.8	63.5	80.9	56 [m]	59 [m]	3,919 [g,n]	17,960 [g,n]	-4
80 St. Vincent & the Grenadines	..	..	75.3	72.4	..	..	..	..	..	..	..
81 Fiji	67	0.743	71.1	67.7	91.2	95.2	75 [f,m]	77 [f,m]	2,507 [g]	7,113 [g]	1
82 Peru	72	0.734	72.0	66.9	85.7	94.8	78 [f,m]	89 [f,m]	1,903	7,206	-3
83 Lebanon	70	0.737	74.8	71.7	81.0	92.4	77	75	1,963 [g]	6,472 [g]	0
84 Paraguay	69	0.739	72.8	68.3	92.5	94.5	64 [i]	64 [i]	2,548	7,832	2
85 Philippines	66	0.748	71.6	67.6	95.0	95.3	81 [f]	79 [f]	2,838	4,829	6
86 Maldives	..	..	66.3	67.4	96.9	97.1	79	78	..	..	..
87 Turkmenistan	..	..	70.0	63.3	..	..	81 [i]	81 [i]	..	..	..
88 Georgia	..	..	77.4	69.2	..	..	70	69	1,507	3,712	..
89 Azerbaijan	..	..	75.2	68.3	..	..	69 [h]	69 [h]	..	..	..
90 Jordan	75	0.729	72.1	69.3	85.1	95.2	78 [f,h]	76 [f,h]	1,771	5,800	-2
91 Tunisia	76	0.727	74.5	70.5	61.9	82.3	76 [f]	76 [f]	3,377 [g]	9,359 [g]	-2
92 Guyana	74	0.730	66.5	60.1	98.2	99.0	84 [f,h]	85 [f,h]	2,658 [g]	6,844 [g]	1
93 Grenada	..	..	..	..	..	..	..	..	..	..	..
94 Dominican Republic	77	0.727	69.3	64.4	84.0	84.0	77 [f]	71 [f]	3,663 [g]	10,278 [g]	-1
95 Albania	73	0.732	76.5	70.6	77.8	92.5	70	67	2,608 [g]	4,705 [g]	4
96 Turkey	81	0.726	72.8	67.6	77.2	93.7	54 [f,h]	65 [f,h]	3,717 [g]	8,028 [g]	-3
97 Ecuador	84	0.716	73.2	68.0	90.3	93.4	71 [f]	73 [f]	1,504 [g]	5,040 [g]	-5
98 Occupied Palestinian Territories	..	..	73.7	70.5	..	..	78 [h]	76 [h]	..	..	..
99 Sri Lanka	80	0.726	75.5	69.6	89.3	94.5	64 [f,m]	63 [f,m]	2,095	4,189	0
100 Armenia	78	0.727	75.3	68.7	97.8	99.3 [d]	63	57	2,175 [g]	3,152 [g]	3

Table 9.5 (*continued*)

HDI rank	Gender-related development index (GDI)		Life expectancy at birth (years) 2001		Adult literacy rate (% age 15 and above) 2001		Combined primary, secondary and tertiary gross enrolment ratio (%) 2000-01[a]		Estimated earned income (PPP US$) 2001[b]		HDI rank minus GDI rank[c]
	Rank	Value	Female	Male	Female	Male	Female	Male	Female	Male	
101 Uzbekistan	79	0.727	72.1	66.4	98.9	99.6 d	74 i	79 i	1,951 g	2,976 g	3
102 Kyrgyzstan	..	..	71.9	64.2	..	..	80	79	..	..	..
103 Cape Verde	82	0.719	72.4	66.6	67.0	84.9	79 f	80 f	3,557 g	7,781 g	1
104 China	83	0.718	72.9	68.6	78.7	92.5	62 f,h	65 f,h	3,169 g	4,825 g	1
105 El Salvador	85	0.707	73.3	67.3	76.6	81.9	63 m	63 m	2,771	7,846	0
106 Iran, Islamic Rep. of	86	0.702	71.3	68.5	70.2	83.8	63	66	2,599 g	9,301 g	0
107 Algeria	88	0.687	70.7	67.7	58.3	77.1	69 f	73 f	2,784 g	9,329 g	-1
108 Moldova, Rep. of	87	0.697	71.8	64.9	98.4	99.6 d	63	60	1,714 g	2,626 g	1
109 Viet Nam	89	0.687	71.0	66.3	90.9	94.5	61	67	1,696 g	2,447 g	0
110 Syrian Arab Republic	93	0.668	72.7	70.2	61.6	88.8	61 i	65 i	1,423 g	5,109 g	-3
111 South Africa	90	0.678	54.4	47.7	85.0	86.3	78	78	7,047 g	15,712 g	1
112 Indonesia	91	0.677	68.2	64.3	82.6	92.1	63 f	65 f	1,987 g	3,893 g	1
113 Tajikistan	92	0.673	71.0	65.6	98.9	99.6 d	65	78	891 g	1,451 g	1
114 Bolivia	94	0.663	65.4	61.3	79.9	92.3	80 f	88 f	1,427 g	3,181 g	0
115 Honduras	96	0.656	71.3	66.4	75.7	75.4	61 f	64 f	1,509 g	4,131 g	-1
116 Equatorial Guinea	..	..	50.4	47.6	76.0	92.8	49 h	68 h	..	..	..
117 Mongolia	95	0.659	65.3	61.3	98.3	98.6	69	58	1,398 g	2,082 g	1
118 Gabon	..	..	57.7	55.6	..	..	81 f	85 f	..	..	..
119 Guatemala	97	0.638	68.4	62.5	61.8	76.6	54 f	61 f	2,144 g	6,620 g	0
120 Egypt	99	0.634	70.4	66.3	44.8	67.2	72 i	80 i	1,970	5,075	-1
121 Nicaragua	98	0.636	71.5	66.8	67.1	66.5	66 f,h	63 f,h	1,494 g,l	3,415 g,l	1
122 São Tomé and Principe	..	..	72.4	66.6	..	..	..	..	..	..	..
123 Solomon Islands	..	..	70.1	67.5	..	..	..	..	..	..	..
124 Namibia	100	0.622	49.2	45.5	81.9	83.4	75 h	72 h	4,833 g	9,511 g	0
125 Botswana	101	0.611	46.0	43.3	80.6	75.3	81	79	5,888 g	9,826 g	0
126 Morocco	102	0.590	69.9	66.2	37.2	62.6	46 h	56 h	2,057 g	5,139 g	0
127 India	103	0.574	64.0	62.8	46.4	69.0	49 f,h	63 f,h	1,531 g	4,070 g	0
128 Vanuatu	..	..	70.1	67.1	..	..	54 m	54 m	..	..	..
129 Ghana	104	0.564	59.3	56.2	64.5	81.1	42	49	1,924 g	2,579 g	0
130 Cambodia	105	0.551	59.4	55.2	58.2	80.5	49	60	1,621 g	2,113 g	0
131 Myanmar	..	..	59.8	54.4	81.0	89.1	48	47	..	..	..
132 Papua New Guinea	106	0.544	58.1	56.2	57.7	71.1	39 m	43 m	1,865 g	3,231 g	0
133 Swaziland	107	0.536	39.9	36.5	79.4	81.3	75 h	78 h	2,395 g	6,453 g	0
134 Comoros	108	0.521	61.6	58.8	48.8	63.3	36 h	44 h	1,340 g	2,395 g	0
135 Lao People's Dem. Rep.	109	0.518	55.2	52.7	54.4	76.8	51	63	1,278 g	1,962 g	0
136 Bhutan	..	..	63.8	61.3	..	..	..	..	..	..	..
137 Lesotho	110	0.497	41.7	35.4	93.9	73.3	65	61	1,375 g	3,620 g	0
138 Sudan	116	0.483	56.9	54.0	47.7	70.0	32 m	36 m	935 g	2,992 g	-5
139 Bangladesh	112	0.495	60.9	60.1	30.8	49.9	54	54	1,153 g	2,044 g	0
140 Congo	111	0.496	50.3	46.7	75.9	88.2	53 f	61 f	695 g	1,253 g	2
141 Togo	118	0.483	52.0	48.6	44.0	73.4	53 m	80 m	1,058 g	2,254 g	-4
Low human development											
142 Cameroon	114	0.488	49.4	46.6	65.1	79.9	43 f,h	52 f,h	1,032 g	2,338 g	1
143 Nepal	119	0.479	58.9	59.4	25.2	60.5	57	70	867 g	1,734 g	-3
144 Pakistan	120	0.469	60.3	60.6	28.8	58.2	27 f	45 f	909 g	2,824 g	-3
145 Zimbabwe	113	0.489	35.4	35.5	85.5	93.3	58 f,h	62 f,h	1,667 g	2,905 g	5
146 Kenya	115	0.488	47.9	44.9	77.3	89.5	52	53	930	1,031	4
147 Uganda	117	0.483	45.4	43.9	58.0	78.1	66	75	1,185 g	1,799 g	3
148 Yemen	127	0.424	60.5	58.3	26.9	68.5	34 m	70 m	365 g	1,201 g	-6
149 Madagascar	121	0.467	54.2	51.9	60.6	74.2	43 f	45 f	616 g	1,046 g	1
150 Haiti	122	0.462	49.8	48.5	48.9	52.9	51 i	53 i	1,339 g	2,396 g	1
151 Gambia	123	0.457	55.2	52.2	30.9	45.0	43 f	51 f	1,530 g	2,581 g	1

Table 9.5 (*continued*)

HDI rank		Gender-related development index (GDI)		Life expectancy at birth (years) 2001		Adult literacy rate (% age 15 and above) 2001		Combined primary, secondary and tertiary gross enrolment ratio (%) 2000-01[a]		Estimated earned income (PPP US$) 2001[b]		HDI rank minus GDI rank[c]
		Rank	Value	Female	Male	Female	Male	Female	Male	Female	Male	
152	Nigeria	124	0.450	52.3	51.3	57.7	73.3	41 [i]	49 [i]	505 [g]	1,191 [g]	1
153	Djibouti	..	..	47.3	44.9	55.5	76.1	19 [h]	23 [h]	..	..	..
154	Mauritania	125	0.445	53.5	50.3	30.7	51.1	40	45	1,429 [g]	2,566 [g]	1
155	Eritrea	126	0.434	54.1	50.9	45.6	68.2	29	38	703	1,361	1
156	Senegal	128	0.420	54.5	50.2	28.7	48.1	34 [f]	41 [f]	1,065 [g]	1,941 [g]	0
157	Guinea	..	..	48.9	48.1	..	..	26 [f]	41 [f]	965 [g]	1,567 [g]	..
158	Rwanda	129	0.416	38.7	37.6	61.9	74.5	51 [f]	52 [f]	965 [g]	1,567 [g]	0
159	Benin	131	0.395	53.2	48.6	24.6	53.5	38 [f]	60 [f]	803 [g]	1,163 [g]	-1
160	Tanzania, U. Rep. of	130	0.396	45.0	43.0	67.9	84.5	31	31	432 [g]	610 [g]	1
161	Côte d'Ivoire	134	0.376	42.1	41.2	38.4	60.3	31 [m]	46 [m]	792 [g]	2,160 [g]	-2
162	Malawi	132	0.378	39.1	37.9	47.6	75.0	70 [f]	74 [f]	464 [g]	679 [g]	1
163	Zambia	133	0.376	33.4	33.3	72.7	85.8	43	47	554 [g]	1,009 [g]	1
164	Angola	..	..	41.6	38.8	..	..	26 [h]	31 [h]	..	..	..
165	Chad	135	0.366	45.7	43.5	35.8	53.0	24 [h]	43 [h]	796 [g]	1,350 [g]	0
166	Guinea-Bissau	137	0.353	46.7	43.5	24.7	55.2	34 [h]	52 [h]	636 [g]	1,313 [g]	-1
167	Congo, Dem. Rep. of the	136	0.353	41.7	39.6	51.8	74.2	24 [f,m]	30 [f,m]	486 [g]	879 [g]	1
168	Central African Republic	138	0.352	41.8	39.1	36.6	60.8	20 [i]	29 [i]	987 [g]	1,632 [g]	0
169	Ethiopia	139	0.347	46.7	44.6	32.4	48.1	27	41	550 [g]	1,074 [g]	0
170	Mozambique	140	0.341	40.9	37.4	30.0	61.2	32	42	916 [g]	1,382 [g]	0
171	Burundi	141	0.331	41.0	39.9	42.0	56.9	28	35	573 [g]	814 [g]	0
172	Mali	142	0.327	48.9	47.8	16.6	36.7	26 [f]	38 [f]	615 [g]	1,009 [g]	0
173	Burkina Faso	143	0.317	46.4	45.0	14.9	34.9	18 [f]	27 [f]	927 [g]	1,323 [g]	0
174	Niger	144	0.279	45.9	45.3	8.9	24.4	14	21	646 [g]	1,129 [g]	0
175	Sierra Leone	..	..	35.8	33.2	..	..	44	57	..	..	..

a. Data refers to the 2000–2001 school year. Data for some countries may refer to national or UNESCO Institute for Statistics estimates. For details, see http://www.uis.unesco.org/. Because data is from different sources, comparisons across countries should be made with caution.

b. Because of the lack of gender-disaggregated income data, female and male earned income are crudely estimated on the basis of data on the ratio of the female nonagricultural wage to the male nonagricultural wage, the female and male shares of the economically active population, the total female and male population and GDP per capita (PPP US$). Unless otherwise specified, estimates are based on data for the most recent year available during 1991–2000.

c. The HDI ranks used in this column are those recalculated for the 144 countries with a GDI value. A positive figure indicates that the GDI rank is higher than the HDI rank, a negative the opposite.

d. For purposes of calculating the GDI, a value of 99% was applied.

e. For purposes of calculating the GDI, value of 100% was applied.

f. Preliminary UNESCO Institute for Statistics estimate, subject to further revision.

g. No wage data available. For purposes of calculating the estimated female and male earned income, an estimate of 75% was used for the ratio of the female nonagricultural wage to the male nonagricultural wage.

h. Data refers to the 1999–2000 school year.

i. Data refers to the 1999–2000 school year. They were provided by the UNESCO Institute for Statistics for *Human Development Report 2001*.

j. The ratio is an underestimate, as many secondary and tertiary students pursue their studies in nearby countries.

k. For purposes of calculating the GDI, a value of $40,000 (PPP US$) was applied.

l. Calculated on the basis of GDP per capita (PPP US$) for 1998.

m. Data refers to the 1998–1999 school year.

n. Calculated on the basis of GDP per capita (PPP US$) for 2000.

Source: United Nations Development Programme. (2003). *Human Development Report 2003*. Table 22. "Gender-Related Development Index (310–3)." New York: Oxford University Press. Retrieved from http://www.undp.org/hdr2003/pdf/hdr03_complete.pdf. Copyright 2003 by the United Nations Development Programme. Used by permission of Oxford University Press, Inc.

Table 9.6
Population and Labor Force

	Population						Labor force							
	Total Millions		Avg. annual growth rate (%)		Ages 15–64 Millions		Total Millions		Avg. annual growth rate (%)		Female % of labor force		Children ages 10–14 % of age group	
Economy	1980	1999	1980–90	1990–99	1980	1999	1980	1999	1980–90	1990–99	1980	1999	1980	1999
Albania	2.7	3.4	2.1	0.3	2	2	1	2	2.7	0.8	39	41	4	1
Algeria	18.7	30.5	2.9	2.2	9	18	5	10	3.7	4.0	21	27	7	1
Angola	7.0	12.4	2.7	3.2	4	6	3	6	2.3	3.0	47	46	30	26
Argentina	28.1	36.6	1.5	1.3	17	23	11	15	1.5	1.9	28	33	8	3
Armenia	3.1	3.8	1.4	0.8	2	3	1	2	1.6	1.3	48	48	0	0
Australia	14.7	19.0	1.5	1.2	10	13	7	10	2.3	1.4	37	43	0	0
Austria	7.6	8.1	0.2	0.5	5	6	3	4	0.4	0.7	41	40	0	0
Azerbaijan	6.2	8.0	1.5	1.2	4	5	3	4	1.0	1.7	48	44	0	0
Bangladesh	86.7	127.7	2.4	1.6	44	74	41	66	2.2	3.0	42	42	35	29
Belarus	9.6	10.2	0.6	–0.1	6	7	5	5	0.4	–0.1	50	49	0	0
Belgium	9.8	10.2	0.1	0.3	6	7	4	4	0.1	0.8	34	41	0	0
Benin	3.5	6.1	3.1	2.8	2	3	2	3	2.5	2.8	47	48	30	27
Bolivia	5.4	8.1	2.0	2.4	3	5	2	3	2.6	2.6	33	38	19	13
Botswana	0.9	1.6	3.4	2.4	0	1	0	1	3.4	2.4	50	45	26	15
Brazil	121.7	168.1	2.0	1.4	70	110	47	79	3.2	2.2	28	35	19	15
Bulgaria	8.9	8.2	–0.2	–0.7	6	6	5	4	–0.4	–0.7	45	48	0	0
Burkina Faso	7.0	11.0	2.4	2.4	3	6	4	5	1.9	1.9	48	47	71	47
Burundi	4.1	6.7	2.8	2.2	2	3	2	4	2.6	2.2	50	49	50	49
Cambodia	6.8	11.8	2.9	2.8	4	6	4	6	2.6	2.8	55	52	27	24
Cameroon	8.7	14.7	2.8	2.7	5	8	4	6	2.3	3.0	37	38	34	24
Canada	24.6	30.6	1.2	1.1	17	21	12	17	1.8	1.3	40	46	0	0
Central African Republic	2.3	3.5	2.4	2.1	1	2	..	..	..	..	..	..	..	..
Chad	4.5	7.5	2.5	2.9	2	3	2	4	2.1	2.9	43	45	42	37
Chile	11.1	15.0	1.6	1.5	7	10	4	6	2.7	2.4	26	33	0	0
China	981.2	1,249.7	1.5	1.1	586	844	540	750	2.2	1.3	43	45	30	9
Hong Kong, China	5.0	6.9	1.2	2.1	3	5	2	4	1.6	2.5	34	37	6	0
Colombia	28.4	41.5	2.1	1.9	16	26	9	18	4.0	2.7	26	38	12	6
Congo, Dem. Rep.	27.0	49.8	3.2	3.2	14	25	12	20	2.8	2.9	45	43	33	29
Congo, Rep.	1.7	2.9	2.9	2.8	1	1	1	1	2.9	2.5	42	43	27	26
Costa Rica	2.3	3.6	2.7	2.0	1	2	1	1	3.5	2.6	21	31	10	5
Côte d'Ivoire	8.2	14.7	3.5	2.6	4	8	3	6	3.0	3.2	32	33	28	19
Croatia	4.6	4.5	0.4	–0.8	3	3	2	2	0.4	–0.8	40	44	0	0
Czech Republic	10.2	10.3	0.1	–0.1	6	7	5	6	0.3	0.5	47	47	0	0
Denmark	5.1	5.3	0.0	0.4	3	4	3	3	0.8	0.0	44	46	0	0
Dominican Republic	5.7	8.4	2.2	1.9	3	5	2	4	3.0	2.9	25	30	25	14
Ecuador	8.0	12.4	2.5	2.1	4	8	3	5	3.4	3.3	20	28	9	5
Egypt, Arab Rep.	40.9	62.4	2.5	1.9	23	38	14	24	2.5	2.9	27	30	18	10
El Salvador	4.6	6.2	1.1	2.1	2	4	2	3	2.2	3.5	27	36	17	14
Eritrea	2.4	4.0	2.8	2.7	..	2	1	2	2.6	2.7	47	47	44	39
Estonia	1.5	1.4	0.6	–0.9	1	1	1	1	0.4	–0.7	51	49	0	0
Ethiopia	37.7	62.8	3.1	2.8	20	32	17	27	3.1	1.8	42	41	46	42
Finland	4.8	5.2	0.4	0.4	3	3	2	3	0.8	0.0	47	48	0	0
France	53.9	59.1	0.5	0.5	34	39	24	27	0.5	0.7	40	45	0	0
Georgia	5.1	5.5	0.7	0.0	3	4	3	3	0.5	0.0	49	47	0	0
Germany	78.3	82.0	0.1	0.4	52	56	38	41	0.6	0.4	40	42	0	0
Ghana	10.7	18.9	3.3	2.7	6	10	5	9	3.3	2.7	51	51	16	13
Greece	9.6	10.5	0.5	0.4	6	7	4	5	1.0	0.9	28	38	5	0
Guatemala	6.8	11.1	2.5	2.6	3	6	2	4	2.8	3.2	22	28	19	15
Guinea	4.5	7.2	2.5	2.6	2	4	2	3	2.1	2.1	47	47	41	32
Haiti	5.4	7.8	1.9	2.1	3	4	3	3	1.5	1.8	45	43	33	24
Honduras	3.6	6.3	3.1	2.9	2	3	1	2	3.1	3.8	25	31	14	8
Hungary	10.7	10.1	–0.3	–0.3	7	7	5	5	–0.8	0.1	43	45	0	0
India	687.3	997.5	2.1	1.8	394	609	302	439	1.7	2.3	34	32	21	13
Indonesia	148.3	207.0	1.8	1.7	83	133	58	99	3.0	2.6	35	41	13	9
Iran, Islamic Rep.	39.1	63.0	3.3	1.6	20	38	12	20	3.0	2.4	20	27	14	3
Ireland	3.4	3.7	0.3	0.7	2	2	1	2	0.3	2.1	28	34	1	0
Israel	3.9	6.1	1.8	3.0	2	4	1	3	2.4	4.1	34	41	0	0
Italy	56.4	57.6	0.1	0.2	36	39	23	26	0.8	0.7	33	38	2	0
Jamaica	2.1	2.6	1.2	0.9	1	2	1	1	2.0	1.5	46	46	0	0
Japan	116.8	126.6	0.6	0.3	79	87	57	68	1.2	0.7	38	41	0	0
Jordan	2.2	4.7	3.7	4.4	1	3	1	1	4.9	5.2	15	24	4	0
Kazakhstan	14.9	15.4	0.9	–0.6	9	10	7	8	0.9	–0.2	48	47	0	0
Kenya	16.6	30.0	3.5	2.7	8	16	8	15	3.7	3.3	46	46	45	40
Korea, Rep.	38.1	46.8	1.2	1.0	24	33	16	24	2.3	2.1	39	41	0	0
Kuwait	1.4	1.9	4.4	–1.1	1	1	0	1	5.9	–1.6	13	31	0	0
Kyrgyz Republic	3.6	4.7	1.9	0.8	2	3	2	2	1.4	1.4	48	47	0	0
Lao PDR	3.2	5.1	2.3	2.6	2	3	..	..	..	..	..	..	31	26
Latvia	2.5	2.4	0.5	–1.0	2	2	1	1	0.3	–1.0	51	50	0	0
Lebanon	3.0	4.3	1.9	1.8	2	3	1	1	2.9	3.1	23	29	5	0
Lesotho	1.3	2.1	2.5	2.2	1	1	1	1	2.0	2.5	38	37	28	21
Lithuania	3.4	3.7	0.9	–0.1	2	2	2	2	0.7	–0.1	50	48	0	0
Macedonia, FYR	1.9	2.0	0.1	0.7	1	1	1	1	0.5	1.2	36	42	1	0
Madagascar	8.9	15.1	2.7	2.9	5	8	4	7	2.3	2.9	45	45	40	35
Malawi	6.2	10.8	3.2	2.6	3	6	3	5	3.0	2.4	51	49	45	33
Malaysia	13.8	22.7	2.8	2.5	8	14	5	9	3.1	3.0	34	38	8	3

Table 9.6 (*continued*)

| | Population | | | | | | Labor force | | | | | | | |
| | Total Millions | | Avg. annual growth rate (%) | | Ages 15–64 Millions | | Total Millions | | Avg. annual growth rate (%) | | Female % of labor force | | Children ages 10–14 % of age group | |
Economy	1980	1999	1980–90	1990–99	1980	1999	1980	1999	1980–90	1990–99	1980	1999	1980	1999
Mali	6.6	10.9	2.5	2.8	3	5	3	5	2.3	2.6	47	46	61	52
Mauritania	1.6	2.6	2.7	2.8	1	1	1	1	2.0	3.0	45	44	30	23
Mexico	67.6	97.4	2.1	1.8	35	60	22	40	3.2	2.9	27	33	9	6
Moldova	4.0	4.3	0.9	-0.2	3	3	2	2	0.3	0.0	50	49	3	0
Mongolia	1.7	2.6	2.9	1.9	1	2	1	1	2.9	2.8	46	47	4	2
Morocco	19.4	28.2	2.2	1.8	10	18	7	11	2.4	2.7	34	35	21	3
Mozambique	12.1	17.3	1.6	2.2	6	9	7	9	1.2	2.0	49	48	39	33
Myanmar	33.8	45.0	1.8	1.2	19	30	17	24	1.8	1.6	44	43	28	24
Namibia	1.0	1.7	2.7	2.6	1	1	0	1	2.5	2.3	40	41	34	19
Nepal	14.5	23.4	2.6	2.4	8	13	7	11	2.2	2.4	39	40	56	43
Netherlands	14.2	15.8	0.6	0.6	9	11	6	7	1.9	0.9	32	40	0	0
New Zealand	3.1	3.8	1.0	1.2	2	2	1	2	2.3	1.6	34	45	0	0
Nicaragua	2.9	4.9	2.7	2.8	1	3	1	2	3.3	4.0	28	35	19	13
Niger	5.6	10.5	3.2	3.4	3	5	3	5	3.0	2.9	45	44	48	44
Nigeria	71.1	123.9	3.0	2.8	36	66	29	50	2.8	2.8	36	36	29	25
Norway	4.1	4.5	0.4	0.5	3	3	2	2	0.8	1.0	41	46	0	0
Pakistan	82.7	134.8	2.7	2.5	44	74	29	50	2.9	2.8	23	28	23	16
Panama	2.0	2.8	2.1	1.8	1	2	1	1	3.2	2.6	30	35	6	3
Papua New Guinea	3.1	4.7	2.2	2.3	2	3	2	2	2.2	2.3	42	42	28	18
Paraguay	3.1	5.4	3.0	2.7	2	3	1	2	2.8	3.3	27	30	15	7
Peru	17.3	25.2	2.2	1.7	9	15	5	9	3.1	2.7	24	31	4	2
Philippines	48.3	76.8	2.6	2.3	27	46	19	32	2.8	2.8	35	38	14	6
Poland	35.6	38.7	0.7	0.2	23	26	19	20	0.1	0.6	45	46	0	0
Portugal	9.8	10.0	0.1	0.1	6	7	5	5	0.5	0.5	39	44	8	1
Romania	22.2	22.5	0.4	-0.4	14	15	11	11	-0.2	0.1	46	44	0	0
Russian Federation	139.0	146.5	0.6	-0.1	95	101	76	78	0.1	0.1	49	49	0	0
Rwanda	5.2	8.3	3.0	2.0	3	4	3	4	3.2	2.4	49	49	43	41
Saudi Arabia	9.4	21.4	5.2	3.4	5	12	3	7	6.5	3.1	8	15	5	0
Senegal	5.5	9.3	2.8	2.6	3	5	3	4	2.6	2.6	42	43	43	29
Sierra Leone	3.2	4.9	2.1	2.4	2	3	1	2	1.6	2.4	36	37	19	15
Singapore	2.3	3.2	1.7	1.9	2	2	1	2	2.7	1.7	35	39	2	0
Slovak Republic	5.0	5.4	0.6	0.2	3	4	2	3	0.8	0.9	45	48	0	0
Slovenia	1.9	2.0	0.5	-0.1	1	1	1	1	0.3	0.3	46	46	0	0
South Africa	27.6	42.1	2.4	2.0	16	26	10	17	2.7	2.3	35	38	1	0
Spain	37.4	39.4	0.4	0.2	23	27	14	17	1.4	0.9	28	37	0	0
Sri Lanka	14.7	19.0	1.4	1.2	9	13	5	8	2.2	2.0	27	36	4	2
Sweden	8.3	8.9	0.3	0.4	5	6	4	5	0.9	0.4	44	48	0	0
Switzerland	6.3	7.1	0.6	0.7	4	5	3	4	1.6	0.9	37	40	0	0
Syrian Arab Republic	8.7	15.7	3.3	2.8	4	9	2	5	3.3	4.0	24	27	14	4
Tajikistan	4.0	6.2	2.9	1.8	2	3	2	2	2.1	2.7	47	45	0	0
Tanzania	18.6	32.9	3.2	2.9	9	17	9	17	3.3	2.6	50	49	43	38
Thailand	46.7	61.7	1.7	1.2	26	42	24	37	2.7	1.7	47	46	25	14
Togo	2.6	4.6	2.9	2.9	1	2	1	2	2.5	2.7	39	40	36	28
Tunisia	6.4	9.5	2.4	1.6	3	6	2	4	2.7	2.8	29	31	6	0
Turkey	44.5	64.4	2.3	1.5	25	43	19	31	2.6	2.8	36	37	21	9
Turkmenistan	2.9	4.8	2.5	2.9	2	3	1	2	2.5	3.5	47	46	0	0
Uganda	12.8	21.5	2.4	3.0	6	11	7	11	2.2	2.6	48	48	49	44
Ukraine	50.0	49.9	0.4	-0.4	33	34	27	25	-0.2	-0.2	50	49	0	0
United Kingdom	56.3	59.1	0.2	0.3	36	39	27	30	0.6	0.3	39	44	0	0
United States	227.2	272.9	0.9	1.0	151	179	109	139	1.3	1.2	41	46	0	0
Uruguay	2.9	3.3	0.6	0.7	2	2	1	2	1.6	1.2	31	42	4	1
Uzbekistan	16.0	24.5	2.5	2.0	9	14	6	10	2.3	2.8	48	47	0	0
Venezuela, RB	15.1	23.7	2.6	2.2	8	15	5	9	3.4	3.0	27	34	4	0
Vietnam	53.7	77.5	2.1	1.8	28	48	26	40	2.7	1.8	48	49	22	7
Yemen, Rep.	8.5	17.0	3.3	4.0	4	8	2	5	3.6	4.7	33	28	26	19
Zambia	5.7	9.9	3.0	2.7	3	5	2	4	2.8	2.9	45	45	19	16
Zimbabwe	7.0	11.9	3.3	2.2	3	7	3	5	3.5	2.2	44	44	37	28
World	**4,430.2 s**	**5,974.7 s**	**1.7 w**	**1.0 w**	**2,595 s**	**3,761 s**	**2,035 s**	**2,892 s**	**1.9 w**	**1.7 w**	**39 w**	**41 w**	**20 w**	**12 w**
Low income	1,612.9	2,417.0	2.3	2.0	890	1,417	709	1,085	2.1	2.4	38	38	24	19
Middle income	2,027.9	2,666.8	1.7	1.2	1,199	1,748	970	1,374	2.1	1.5	40	42	21	7
Lower middle income	1,607.9	2,093.7	1.6	1.1	955	1,379	805	1,121	2.0	1.4	42	43	24	7
Upper middle income	419.9	573.1	1.8	1.4	245	369	165	253	2.4	2.1	33	36	9	6
Low and middle income	3,641.0	5,083.8	1.9	1.6	2,090	3,166	1,679	2,459	2.1	1.9	39	40	23	13
East Asia & Pacific	1,397.8	1,836.9	1.6	1.3	820	1,220	719	1,038	2.3	1.5	43	45	26	9
Europe & Central Asia	425.8	475.3	0.9	0.2	274	318	214	238	0.5	0.6	47	46	3	1
Latin America & Caribbean	360.3	509.2	2.0	1.7	201	319	130	219	3.0	2.5	28	35	13	9
Middle East & North Africa	174.0	290.9	3.1	2.2	91	171	54	97	3.1	3.1	24	27	14	5
South Asia	902.6	1,329.3	2.2	1.9	508	797	392	585	1.8	2.5	34	33	23	16
Sub-Saharan Africa	380.5	642.3	2.9	2.6	195	340	170	282	2.7	2.6	42	42	35	30
High income	789.1	890.9	0.6	0.6	505	596	357	433	1.1	0.9	38	43	0	0

Note: Figures in italics are for years other than those specified.

Source: The World Bank. (2001). *World Development Report 2000/2001: Attacking Poverty.* Washington, D.C.: Author. Retrieved from http://www.worldbank.org/poverty/wdrpoverty/report/tab3.pdf.

Figure 9.1
Percentage of Part-Time Workers Based on
Overall Employment, by Gender

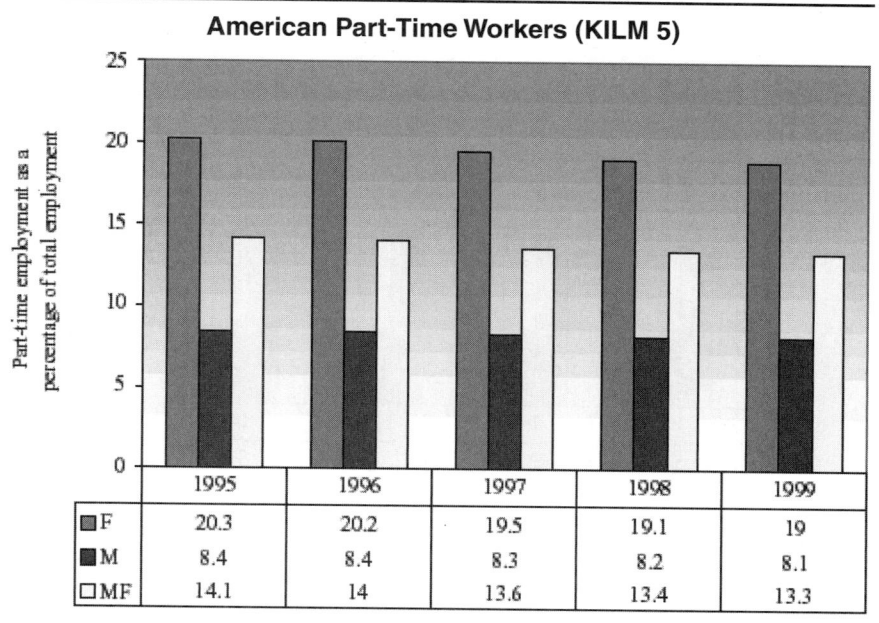

American Part-Time Workers (KILM 5)

	1995	1996	1997	1998	1999
F	20.3	20.2	19.5	19.1	19
M	8.4	8.4	8.3	8.2	8.1
MF	14.1	14	13.6	13.4	13.3

In the late 1990s, part-time work represented on average 13.7 percent of total employment in the economy. Around one-fifth of employed women worked part-time compared to around one twelfth of employed men. During the above years, the average female share of part-time employment was 68.4 percent.

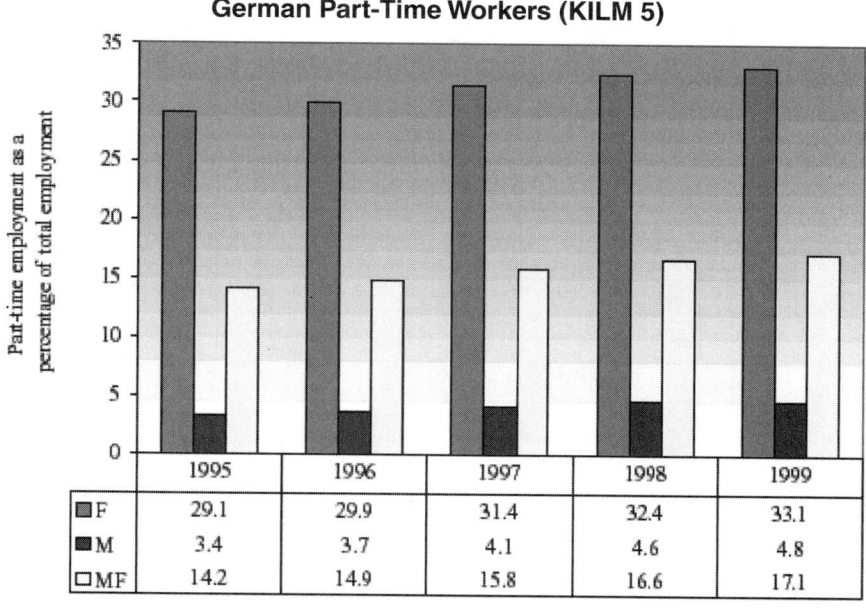

German Part-Time Workers (KILM 5)

	1995	1996	1997	1998	1999
F	29.1	29.9	31.4	32.4	33.1
M	3.4	3.7	4.1	4.6	4.8
MF	14.2	14.9	15.8	16.6	17.1

During the late 1990s, the total share of part-time to total employment increased nearly 3 percentage points. The difference between men and women in part-time work is substantial. While less than 5 percent of employed men work part-time, nearly a third of working women are part-timers.

Figure 9.1 (*continued*)

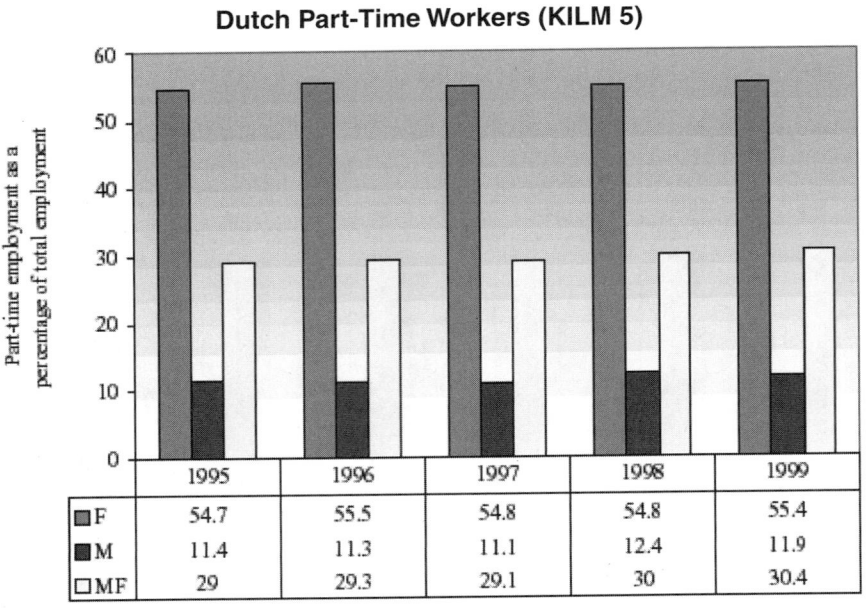

Dutch Part-Time Workers (KILM 5)

	1995	1996	1997	1998	1999
F	54.7	55.5	54.8	54.8	55.4
M	11.4	11.3	11.1	12.4	11.9
MF	29	29.3	29.1	30	30.4

Part-time employment represented an average of 29.6 percent of total employment from 1995 to 1999. During this time, the average female share of part-time work was 77 percent. Over one half of working women were part-time employees.

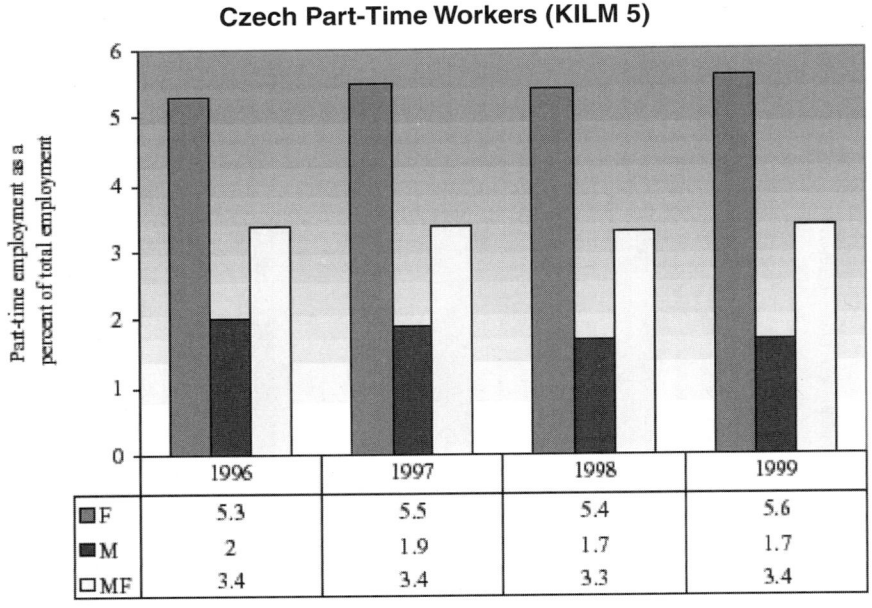

Czech Part-Time Workers (KILM 5)

	1996	1997	1998	1999
F	5.3	5.5	5.4	5.6
M	2	1.9	1.7	1.7
MF	3.4	3.4	3.3	3.4

Part-time work accounted for less than 4 percent of total employment in the late 1990s. Within this small population of part-time workers, there were more women than men.

Figure 9.1 (*continued*)

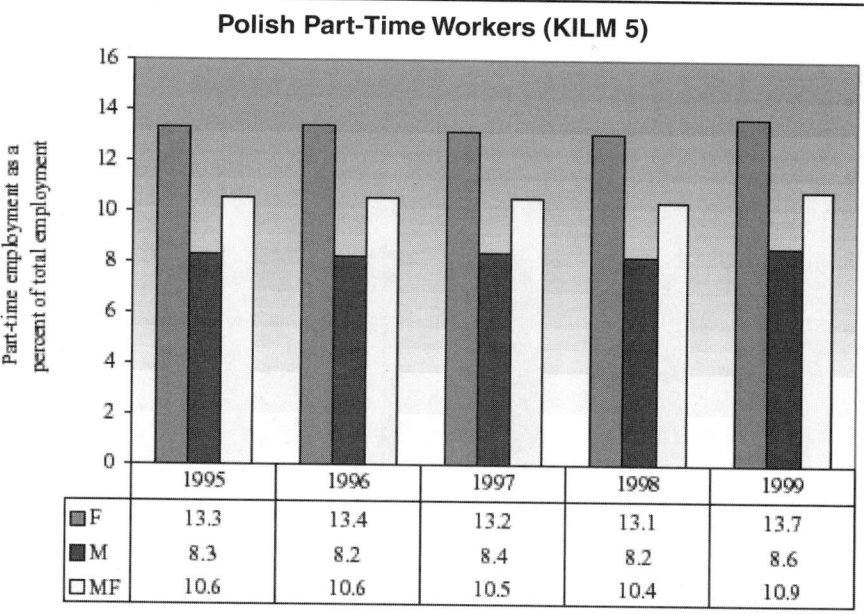

Polish Part-Time Workers (KILM 5)

	1995	1996	1997	1998	1999
■F	13.3	13.4	13.2	13.1	13.7
■M	8.3	8.2	8.4	8.2	8.6
□MF	10.6	10.6	10.5	10.4	10.9

Part-time work in Poland represented near 11 percent of total employment, this rate did not fluctuate much in the late 1990s. Women were more likely than men to work parttime but the difference is relatively small compared to another countries. From 1995 to 1999, the average female share of part-time employment was near 57 percent.

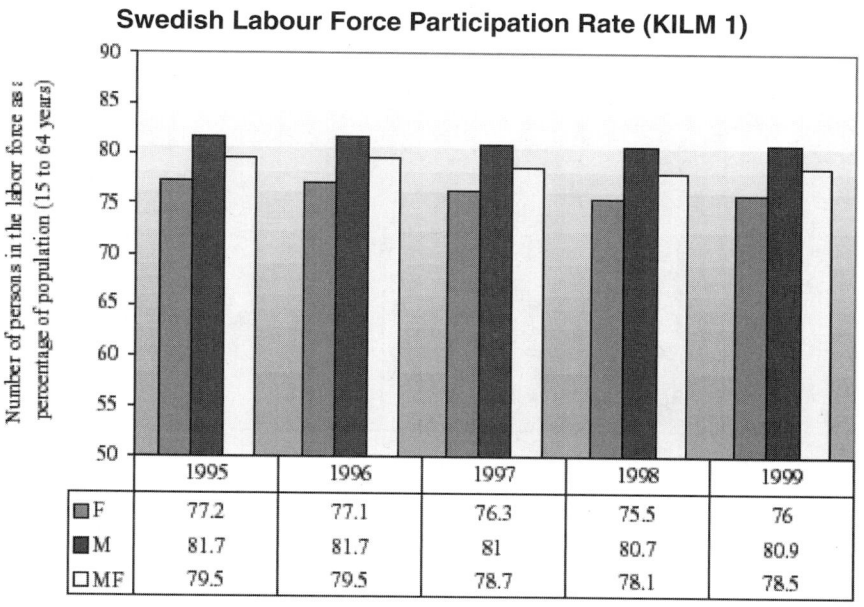

Swedish Labour Force Participation Rate (KILM 1)

	1995	1996	1997	1998	1999
■F	77.2	77.1	76.3	75.5	76
■M	81.7	81.7	81	80.7	80.9
□MF	79.5	79.5	78.7	78.1	78.5

There was little variation in Sweden's labor force participation rate during the late 1990s. Both sexes maintained high levels of participation and while men were more likely than women to be considered economically active; the sex differential was very small relative to other countries.

Figure 9.1 (*continued*)

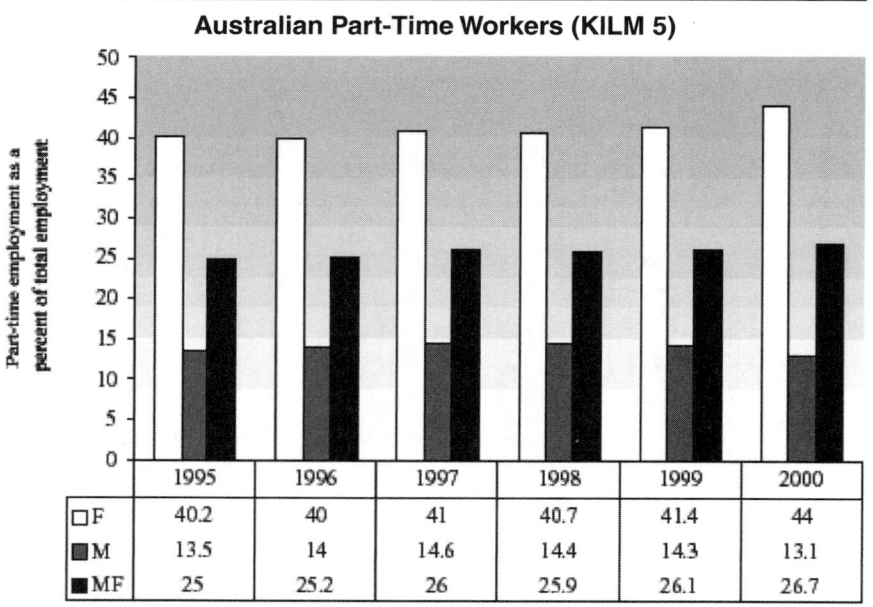

Australian Part-Time Workers (KILM 5)

	1995	1996	1997	1998	1999	2000
☐ F	40.2	40	41	40.7	41.4	44
■ M	13.5	14	14.6	14.4	14.3	13.1
■ MF	25	25.2	26	25.9	26.1	26.7

Women consistently made up a substantially greater proportion of the overall parttime labour force than men. The female share of part-time employment ranged from 69.2 percent in 1995 to 72.7 percent in 2000.

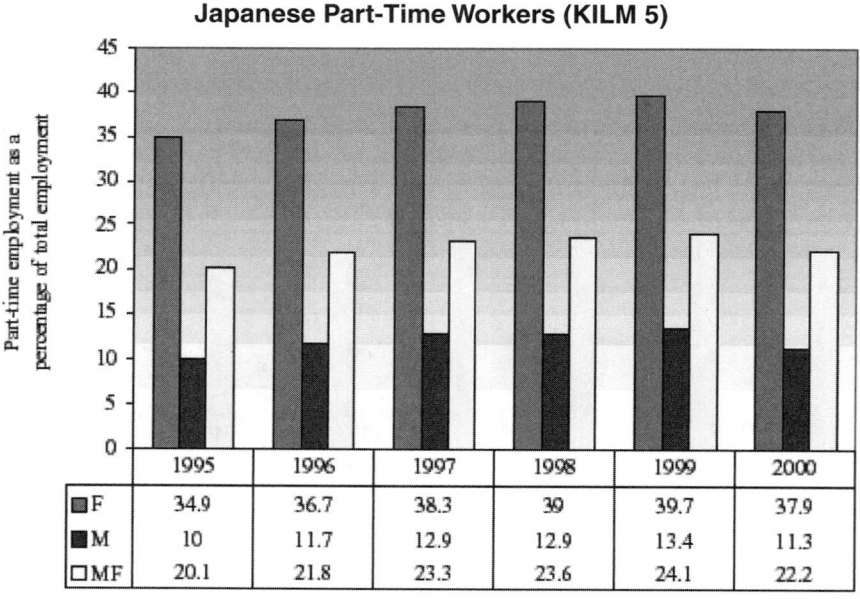

Japanese Part-Time Workers (KILM 5)

	1995	1996	1997	1998	1999	2000
■ F	34.9	36.7	38.3	39	39.7	37.9
■ M	10	11.7	12.9	12.9	13.4	11.3
☐ MF	20.1	21.8	23.3	23.6	24.1	22.2

Over one-fifth of employment in Japan is part-time work. Women are more likely than men to hold part-time positions, near two-fifths compared to over one-tenth respectively. From 1995 to 2000, the female share of part-time employment averaged over 68 percent.

Figure 9.1 (*continued*)

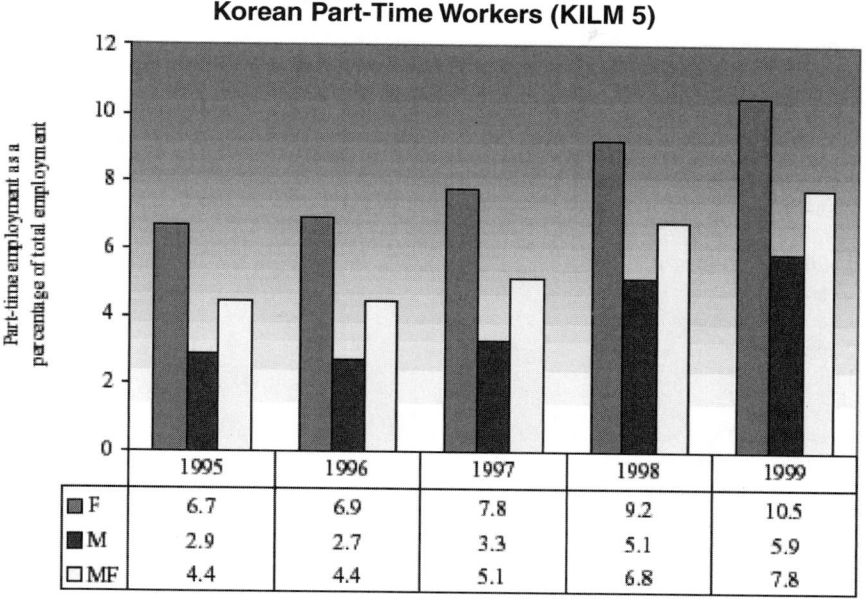

Part-time employment as a share of total employment increased in the late 1990s. In 1999, near 5.9 percent of working men were part-timers compared to 10.5 percent of working women. The female average share of part-time employment in the years above was 59.4 percent.

Source: Adapted from International Labor Organization. (2003). National Statistics for Equal Opportunities Web site. Retrieved from http://www.ilo.org/public/english/employment/gems/eeo/stat/main.htm.

Table 9.7
Women's Wages Relative to Men's

Country or area	1990	1995/2001
Africa/Botswana	. .	52[a]
Egypt	68	75
Eritrea	. .	66
Kenya	73	123
Swaziland	73	63[b]
Zambia	73	. .
Latin America/Brazil	54	61
Costa Rica	74	83
El Salvador	94	79
Mexico	50	70
Panama	. .	93
Paraguay	66	44
Asia/Bahrain	62	42[c]
Bangladesh	49	. .
Cyprus	58	54[d]
China, Hong Kong SAR	69	66
China, Macao SAR	67	54
Georgia	. .	62
Jordan	57	58
Kazakstan	. .	79
Malaysia	49	63
Myanmar	106	112
Occupied Palestinian Territory[e]	. .	48
Philippines	. .	80
Republic of Korea	50	58
Singapore	55	59
Sri Lanka	88	82
Thailand	64	68
Turkey	81	97
Developed regions Australia	82	84[f]
Austria	. .	68
Belgium	75	72
Bulgaria	. .	70
Czech Republic	. .	65
Denmark	85	84
Finland	77	80[g]
France	79	78
Germany	73	74
Greece	78	82
Hungary	70	73[g]
Ireland	69	74
Italy	83	. .
Japan	41	59[c]
Latvia	84	84
Lithuania	. .	77[g]
Luxembourg	62	72
Malta	. .	83
Netherlands	77	78.
New Zealand	74	81
Norway	86	88[g]
Portugal	69	65

Table 9.7 (*continued*)

Country or area	1990	1995/2001
Spain	72	. .
Sweden	89	91
Switzerland	68	72
United Kingdom[h]	68	77
United States	68	. .

Source: Prepared by the Statistics Division of the United Nations Secretariat from ILO, Yearbook of Labour Statistics (Geneva, various years up to 2002), Table 5B.

a. Citizens only.

b. Skilled wage earners.

c. Private sector.

d. Including family allowances and the value of payments in kind.

e. West Bank and Gaza Strip only.

f. Full-time adult non-managerial employees.

g. Full-time employees.

h. Excluding Northern Ireland.

Technical notes:

The indicator presented in this table is the ratio of female wages to male wages in manufacturing, expressed as a percentage. The statistics of wages from which the ratio is computed are, in general, average earnings per wage-earner (regardless of age) or in some cases wage rates. The data on average earnings are usually derived from payroll data supplied by a sample of establishments often also furnishing data on hours of work and on employment. In a few cases, average earnings are compiled from social insurance statistics.

International comparisons of wage ratios presented here must be made with great caution. As indicated above, the coverage, definitions and methods of compiling wage statistics differ significantly from country to country. Disaggregation of statistics by sex is available for only a few countries and may be based on a narrow segment of the population. Furthermore, earnings are very much dependent on the number of hours worked, and where female workers generally work a much smaller number of hours than male workers, this factor must be kept in mind when interpreting the wage ratio.

Source: United Nations. (2000). *The World's Women 2000: Trends and Statistics.* New York: United Nations Publications. Retrieved from http://unstats.un.org/unsd/demographic/ww2000/table5g.htm.

Table 9.8

Percent Distribution of All Hours Worked by Women in the Private Business Sector by Years of Completed Schooling: United States, 1948 to 1999

Year	Years of completed schooling						
	0-4	5-8	9-11	12	13-15	16	17+
1948	4.8	29.5	18.8	36.3	6.8	2.5	1.3
1949	4.5	25.4	20.5	35.5	9.2	3.2	1.6
1950	4.5	25.4	20.3	35.7	9.2	3.2	1.6
1951	4.6	25.8	20.1	36.4	8.4	3.2	1.6
1952	4.6	26.2	19.8	37.0	7.6	3.2	1.6
1953	4.3	25.5	19.9	37.9	7.7	3.2	1.6
1954	4.1	24.7	19.8	38.8	7.8	3.3	1.6
1955	3.7	24.1	19.8	39.6	7.8	3.3	1.6
1956	3.4	23.4	19.9	40.4	7.9	3.4	1.6
1957	3.1	22.5	19.8	41.3	8.0	3.5	1.7
1958	3.0	22.3	20.6	40.2	8.8	3.4	1.6
1959	2.9	22.5	21.7	38.7	9.5	3.2	1.5
1960	2.7	21.7	22.2	38.0	10.6	3.3	1.5
1961	2.5	20.5	20.8	40.3	10.5	4.1	1.2
1962	2.3	18.9	19.4	43.0	10.6	4.8	1.0
1963	2.2	18.5	19.4	44.2	10.1	4.4	1.2
1964	2.1	18.2	19.4	45.2	9.7	4.0	1.4
1965	2.0	17.4	19.2	45.9	9.7	4.2	1.6
1966	1.6	16.7	19.1	47.4	10.3	3.5	1.5
1967	1.3	15.2	18.9	48.0	12.0	3.5	1.1
1968	1.4	13.5	18.6	50.1	11.7	3.3	1.3
1969	1.1	12.4	17.7	50.6	12.3	4.1	1.7
1970	1.1	11.7	17.2	50.3	13.2	4.4	2.1
1971	1.2	10.5	16.9	51.3	13.6	4.8	1.6
1972	1.1	9.5	16.0	52.5	14.2	4.8	1.8
1973	1.0	8.9	15.5	50.8	15.9	5.6	2.2
1974	.8	8.3	14.9	50.8	16.1	6.3	2.8
1975	.8	7.7	15.1	50.3	16.4	6.9	2.8
1976	.9	7.3	14.9	50.4	16.8	7.1	2.7
1977	.8	6.9	14.4	50.1	17.6	7.3	2.8
1978	.8	6.0	13.2	50.4	18.5	7.7	3.4
1979	.7	5.7	12.4	50.2	18.8	8.6	3.6
1980	.6	5.2	11.9	50.0	19.7	8.9	3.6
1981	.7	4.9	11.3	49.8	19.7	9.3	4.4
1982	.6	4.4	10.4	48.7	20.6	10.4	4.9
1983	.6	3.9	9.9	48.5	21.0	11.0	5.2
1984	.6	3.7	9.7	47.3	22.0	11.7	5.1
1985	.5	3.4	9.1	47.0	22.6	12.2	5.2
1986	.4	3.3	8.9	46.8	22.7	12.3	5.5
1987	.7	3.0	9.3	46.0	23.0	12.5	5.5
1988	.7	2.8	9.0	45.6	22.8	13.2	5.9
1989	.6	2.7	8.5	45.0	23.3	13.5	6.3
1990	.6	2.7	8.4	44.4	23.4	14.1	6.3
1991[1]	.5	2.2	6.6	41.1	29.5	15.2	4.9
1992[2]	.5	2.1	6.2	39.8	30.4	15.7	5.2
1993[2]	.5	2.2	6.6	37.4	32.2	15.8	5.2
1994	.5	2.2	6.6	36.5	32.4	16.2	5.6
1995	.5	2.2	6.8	36.1	31.8	16.9	5.7
1996	.4	2.1	6.5	36.7	31.2	17.4	5.7
1997	.5	2.1	6.3	35.8	31.5	17.6	6.2
1998	.5	2.0	6.6	35.3	31.7	17.8	6.0
1999	.5	2.1	6.4	34.5	32.2	18.2	6.2

1. March 1992 Current Population Survey used in measuring 1991 data revised questions on educational attainment. Data prior to 1991 are not strictly comparable.

2. May not be strictly comparable before 1993 data due to comprehensive revisions in the CPS questionnaire.

Note: Rows may not sum to 100.0 due to rounding.

Source: U.S. Department of Labor. (2001). *Report on the American Workforce*. Washington, D.C.: Government Printing Office. Retrieved from http://www.bls.gov/opub/rtaw/pdf/appendix.pdf.

Table 9.9

Percent Distribution of the Labor Force of Women by Presence and Age of Children: United States, March 1980 to 2000

(Percent)

Year	Total women	With no children under 18	With children under 18				
			Total	6 to 17 years	With children under 6		
					Total	3 to 5 years	Under 3 years
1980	100.0	60.4	39.6	25.0	14.6	6.6	7.9
1981	100.0	60.3	39.7	24.8	14.9	6.7	8.2
1982	100.0	60.2	39.8	24.2	15.6	6.9	8.8
1983	100.0	60.4	39.6	23.7	15.9	7.0	8.9
1984	100.0	60.3	39.7	23.4	16.3	7.3	8.9
1985	100.0	60.6	39.4	23.2	16.1	7.1	9.0
1986	100.0	60.1	39.9	23.3	16.5	7.3	9.3
1987	100.0	59.6	40.4	23.5	17.0	7.4	9.6
1988	100.0	60.1	39.9	23.5	16.4	7.2	9.2
1989	100.0	60.3	39.7	23.2	16.6	7.4	9.2
1990	100.0	60.5	39.5	22.8	16.7	7.4	9.3
1991	100.0	60.4	39.6	22.5	17.1	7.5	9.6
1992	100.0	60.2	39.8	23.0	16.7	7.4	9.3
1993	100.0	59.9	40.1	23.4	16.7	7.4	9.3
1994[1]	100.0	59.4	40.6	23.2	17.3	7.7	9.6
1995	100.0	59.2	40.8	23.6	17.2	7.8	9.3
1996	100.0	59.6	40.4	23.6	16.8	7.6	9.2
1997[1]	100.0	59.3	40.7	23.8	16.9	7.6	9.3
1998[1]	100.0	59.9	40.1	23.5	16.6	7.4	9.2
1999[1]	100.0	60.7	39.3	23.4	15.9	7.2	8.7
2000[1]	100.0	60.9	39.1	23.5	15.6	7.0	8.6

1. The comparability of historical labor force data has been affected at various times by methodological and conceptual changes. For an explanation, see the Explanatory Notes and Estimates of Error section of *Employment and Earnings*, a monthly periodical published by the Bureau of Labor Statistics.

Note: Data refer to single, married, spouse present, and widowed, divorced, and separated women.

Source: U.S. Department of Labor. (2001). *Report on the American Workforce.* Washington, D.C.: Government Printing Office. Retrieved from http://www.bls.gov/opub/rtaw/pdf/appendix.pdf.

Table 9.10
Median Usual Weekly Earnings[1] of Full-Time[2] Wage and Salary Workers,[3] by Sex, Race, and Hispanic Origin, Annual Averages: United States, 1986–2000

Characteristic	Year														
	1986	1987	1988	1989	1990	1991	1992	1993	1994	1995	1996	1997	1998	1999	2000
Black															
Both sexes	$291	$301	$314	$319	$329	$348	$357	$369	$371	$383	$387	$400	$426	$445	$468
Men	318	326	347	348	361	375	380	392	400	411	412	432	468	488	503
Women	263	275	288	301	308	323	335	348	346	355	362	375	400	409	429
Hispanic origin															
Both sexes	277	284	290	298	304	312	322	331	324	329	339	351	370	385	396
Men	299	306	307	315	318	323	339	346	343	350	356	371	390	406	414
Women	241	251	260	269	278	292	302	313	305	305	316	318	337	348	364
White															
Both sexes	370	383	394	409	424	442	458	475	484	494	506	519	545	573	591
Men	433	450	465	482	494	506	514	524	547	566	580	595	615	638	669
Women	294	307	318	334	353	373	387	401	408	415	428	444	468	483	500
EARNINGS RATIOS															
Black to white	78.6	78.6	79.7	78.0	77.6	78.7	77.9	77.7	76.7	77.5	76.5	77.1	78.2	77.7	79.2
Black men to white men	73.4	72.4	74.6	72.2	73.1	74.1	73.9	74.8	73.1	72.6	71.0	72.6	76.1	76.5	75.2
Black women to white women ...	89.5	89.6	90.6	90.1	87.3	86.6	86.6	86.8	84.8	85.5	84.6	84.5	85.5	84.7	85.8
Hispanic to white	74.9	74.2	73.6	72.9	71.7	70.6	70.3	69.7	66.9	66.6	67.0	67.6	67.9	67.2	67.0
Hispanic men to white men	69.1	68.0	66.0	65.4	64.4	63.8	66.0	66.0	62.7	61.8	61.4	62.4	63.4	63.6	61.9
Hispanic women to white women	82.0	81.8	81.8	80.5	78.8	78.3	78.0	78.1	74.8	73.5	73.8	71.6	72.0	72.0	72.8

1. Earnings are expressed in nominal dollars.
2. Full-time workers include persons who usually work 35 hours or more a week on their sole, or principal, job.
3. Wage and salary workers exclude self-employed persons whether or not their businesses are incorporated.

Source: U.S. Department of Labor. (2001). *Report on the American Workforce.* Washington, D.C.: Government Printing Office. Retrieved from http://www.bls.gov/opub/rtaw/pdf/chapter1.pdf.

Table 9.11
Fertility, Death Rate, and Life Expectancy Assumptions: United States, Selected Years 1940 to 2075

Calendar year	Total fertility rate[1] (per woman)	Age-sex-adjusted death rate[2] (per 100,000)	Life expectancy at birth[3]		Life expectancy at age 65[3]	
			Male	Female	Male	Female
1940	2.23	1,672.6	61.4	65.7	11.9	13.4
1945	2.42	1,488.6	62.9	68.4	12.6	14.4
1950	3.03	1,339.9	65.6	71.1	12.8	15.1
1955	3.50	1,243.0	66.7	72.8	13.1	15.6
1960	3.61	1,237.9	66.7	73.2	12.9	15.9
1965	2.88	1,210.8	66.8	73.8	12.9	16.3
1970	2.43	1,138.4	67.1	74.9	13.1	17.1
1975	1.77	1,020.9	68.7	76.6	13.7	18.0
1980	1.85	961.1	69.9	77.5	14.0	18.4
1985	1.84	912.3	71.1	78.2	14.4	18.6
1990	2.07	865.8	71.8	78.9	15.0	19.0
1991	2.07	854.8	71.9	79.0	15.1	19.1
1992	2.06	843.7	72.2	79.2	15.2	19.2
1993	2.04	863.5	72.0	78.9	15.1	19.0
1994	2.04	852.5	72.2	79.0	15.3	19.0
1995	2.02	850.1	72.4	79.0	15.3	19.0
1996	2.03	837.1	72.8	79.1	15.4	19.0
1997	2.04	822.6	73.3	79.3	15.5	19.1
1998	2.06	796.1	73.9	79.4	16.0	19.1
1999	2.06	803.0	73.7	79.5	15.8	19.1
2000	2.05	796.3	73.9	79.6	15.9	19.2
2005	2.03	767.0	74.7	80.0	16.1	19.3
2010	2.01	744.2	75.4	80.4	16.4	19.4
2015	1.99	720.1	75.9	80.7	16.6	19.6
2020	1.97	692.7	76.4	81.1	16.9	19.8
2025	1.95	665.9	76.9	81.6	17.2	20.1
2030	1.95	640.6	77.4	82.0	17.5	20.4
2035	1.95	617.0	77.9	82.4	17.8	20.7
2040	1.95	594.8	78.3	82.7	18.1	21.0
2045	1.95	574.0	78.7	83.1	18.3	21.2
2050	1.95	554.5	79.1	83.5	18.6	21.5
2055	1.95	536.1	79.5	83.8	18.9	21.8
2060	1.95	518.7	79.9	84.1	19.1	22.0
2065	1.95	502.3	80.3	84.5	19.4	22.3
2070	1.95	486.9	80.7	84.8	19.6	22.5
2075	1.95	472.2	81.0	85.1	19.9	22.7

1. The total fertility rate for any year is the average number of children who would be born to a woman in her lifetime if she were to experience the birth rates by age observed in, or assumed for, the selected year, and if she were to survive the entire childbearing period.

2. The age-sex-adjusted death rate is the crude rate that would occur in the enumerated total population as of April 1, 1990, if that population were to experience the death rates by age and sex observed in, or assumed for, the selected year.

3. The period life expectancy for any year is the average number of years of life remaining for a group of persons if that group were to experience the death rates by age observed in, or assumed for, the selected year.

Source: United States House of Representatives, Committee on Ways and Means. (2000). *The 2000 Green Book: Background material and data on programs within the jurisdiction of the Committee on Ways and Means.* Retrieved from http://aspe.hhs.gov/2000gb/sec1.txt.

Table 9.12
Twenty Leading Occupations of Employed Women,
Full-Time Wage and Salary Workers: United States,
2002 Annual Average

(Employment in thousands)

Occupation	Total Employed Women	Total Employed (Men and Women)	Percent Women	Women's Median Usual Weekly Earnings
Total, 16 years and older (all employed women, full time wage and salary workers)	43,773	100,204	43.7	$530
Retail and personal sales workers, including cashiers	1,907	3,519	54.1	326
Secretaries	1,709	1,732	98.7	496
Elementary school teachers	1,677	2,039	82.2	750
Registered nurses	1,597	1,737	91.9	870
Nursing aides, orderlies, and attendants	1,434	1,603	89.5	367
Sales supervisors and proprietors	1,313	3,301	39.8	507
Cashiers	1,036	1,387	74.7	307
Bookkeepers, accounting, and auditing clerks	928	1,011	91.8	500
Accountants and auditors	851	1,424	59.8	734
Investigators and adjusters, except insurance	723	972	74.4	495
Receptionists	688	709	97.0	429
Secondary school teachers	639	1,135	56.3	767
Managers, medicine and health	549	714	76.9	750
Social workers	553	753	73.4	632
Managers, food serving and lodging establishments	487	1,031	47.2	517
Cooks, except short order	486	1,395	34.8	303
General office clerks	486	579	83.4	474
Janitors and cleaners	471	1,548	30.4	336
Administrators, education and related fields	453	727	62.3	832
Waiters and waitresses	441	624	70.7	311

Note: Median not available where base in less than 50,000 male workers.

Source: U.S. Department of Labor Women's Bureau. (2003). *20 leading indicators of employed women: 2002.* U.S. Department of Labor Women's Bureau Web site. Retrieved from http://www.dol.gov/wb/factsheets/20lead2002.pdf.

Figure 9.2
Percentage of Distribution of Childcare Arrangements of Children under Age 5 in the United States with Employed Mothers, by Mother's Employment Status: United States, Selected Years 1965 to 1994

	1965[a,b]	1977[b]	1982[b]	1984-85	1986	1987	1988	1991	1993	1994
Mother employed full-time										
Day care center or preschool	8	15	20	30	26	28	31	28	34	34
Nonrelative care in provider's home	20	27	25	27	26	25	27	21	18	18
Grandparent/other relative in relative's home	18	21	21	16	18	14	14	14	17	17
Father in child's home	10	11	11	10	11	10	8	15	11	13
Other care in child's home[c]	37	18	16	13	15	15	13	15	15	13
Other care outside child's home[d]	7	8	7	4	5	8	7	7	5	5
Mother employed part-time										
Day care center or preschool	3	9	8	17	16	18	17	15	23	22
Nonrelative care in provider's home	8	16	19	14	21	18	17	13	14	10
Grandparent/other relative in relative's home	9	13	16	16	14	13	11	11	13	13
Father in child's home	23	23	21	22	21	25	27	29	25	28
Other care in child's home[c]	24	20	20	18	14	15	14	17	15	17
Other care outside child's home[d]	33	19	26	13	13	13	14	15	10	10

a. Data for 1965 are for children under 6 years old.

b. Data for 1982 and earlier are based on survey questions that asked about care arrangements for the youngest child in the family. Percentages for 1982 and earlier have been recalculated after removal of cases in "don't know" category.

c. Includes care by relatives and nonrelatives.

d. Includes children who are cared for by their mother at work or in kindergarten or school-based activities.

Source: Guttman, B., & Hamilton, J. (2000). *Trends in the well-being of America's children & youth 2000.* Washington, D.C.: U.S. Department of Health and Human Services, Office of the Assistant Secretary for Planning and Evaluation. Retrieved from http://aspe.hhs.gov/hsp/00trends/ES3.pdf.

Table 9.13
Childcare Arrangements of Preschool Children, by Type of Arrangement: United States, 1991 to 1999

[**In percent, except as indicated (8,428 represents 8,428,000).** Estimates are based on children 3 to 5 years old who have not entered kindergarten. Based on interviews from a sample survey of the civilian, noninstitutional population in households with telephones.]

Characteristic	Children		Type of nonparental arrangement [1]			
	Number (1,000)	Percent distribution	In relative care	In nonrela- tive care	In center- based pro- gram [2]	With parental care only
1991, total	8,428	100.0	16.9	14.8	52.8	31.0
1995, total	9,232	100.0	19.4	16.9	55.1	25.9
1999, total	**8,549**	**100.0**	**23.3**	**15.9**	**59.3**	**23.3**
Age:						
3 years old	3,827	44.8	25.1	16.5	45.6	30.7
4 years old	3,722	43.5	22.3	15.3	68.9	18.3
5 years old	1,001	11.7	20.3	16.2	76.1	13.5
Race-ethnicity:						
White, non-Hispanic	5,296	61.9	18.8	19.3	59.4	23.6
Black, non-Hispanic.	1,258	14.7	36.0	8.0	72.5	13.1
Hispanic	1,421	16.6	25.9	12.7	44.4	33.6
Other	574	6.7	31.0	9.9	66.0	17.5
Household income:						
Less than $10,001	1,126	13.2	28.9	12.8	56.6	26.6
$10,001 to $20,000	1,395	16.3	29.5	12.9	51.1	28.1
$20,001 to $30,000	1,327	15.5	27.7	12.2	50.8	29.6
$30,001 to $40,000	1,050	12.3	23.3	14.9	54.5	25.3
$40,001 to $50,000	792	9.3	20.9	14.2	59.7	23.1
$50,001 to $75,000	1,351	15.8	17.3	20.5	65.5	19.0
$75,001 or more	1,509	17.7	16.2	21.9	74.0	13.4

1. Columns do not add to 100.0 because some children participated in more than one type of nonparental arrangement.

2. Center-based programs include day care centers, head start programs, preschools, prekindergarten, and nursery schools.

Source: United States Census Bureau. (2002). *Statistical Abstract of the United States 2002.* Washington, D.C.: Government Printing Office. Retrieved from http://www.census.gov/prod/2003pubs/02statab/socinsur.pdf.

Table 9.14
CCDF Appropriations (Mandatory and Discretionary):
United States, Fiscal Years 1997 to 2002

(in Millions of Dollars)

Fiscal year	Discretionary Funding			Mandatory ("Entitlement") funding	Total
	Advance appropriation from prior year	Same year's appropriation	All available funds for FY		
1997	0[a]	19[a]	19[a]	1,967	**1,986[a]**
1998	937	66	1,003	2,067	**3,070**
1999	1,000	0	1,000	2,167	**3,167**
2000	1,183	0	1,183	2,367	**3,550**
2001	1,183	817	2,000	2,567	**4,567**
2002	0	2,100	2,100	2,717	**4,817**

a. What appears above to be limited discretionary CCDF funding in FY 1997, and consequently, in total funding, actually reflects a shift to advance appropriating of funds for the following fiscal year. The FY 1997 appropriation law provided $956 million for CCDBG, with only $19 million available immediately during FY 1997, and the remainder available on October 1, 1997 (the first day of FY 1998). In earlier years the funds appropriated for CCDBG became available for obligation only in the last month of the given fiscal year, and therefore most of the appropriation for a given year ($935 million in FY 1996) was actually obligated in the following fiscal year.

Source: Gish, M. (March 19, 2002). *Child care funding and spending under federal block grants.* (CRS Report for Congress received through the CRS Web, Number RL31274). Washington, D.C.: Library of Congress, Congressional Research Service. Retrieved from http://www.nccic.org/pubs/crsreport/crsreport.pdf.

Table 9.15
Total CCDF Expenditures by Funding Sources: United States,
Fiscal Years 1992 to 2000

(in Millions of Dollars)

Fiscal year	Federal CCDF funds			State CCDF funds		Total CCDF spending
	Discretionary funds[a]	Mandatory "guaranteed" funds[b]	Matching federal share	MOE	Matching state share	
1992	332	801	—	616	—	1,749
1993	675	890	—	662	—	2,227
1994	835	1,055	—	798	—	2,688
1995	832	1,235	—	950	—	3,017
1996	850	1,280	—	994	—	3,125
1997	1,009	986	552	945	416	3,909
1998	1,486	1,169	867	1,031	715	5,268
1999	2,583	1,165	882	1,018	636	6,283
2000	3,064	1,127	1,095	1,049	887	7,222

Notes: Child care expenditures in the territories are excluded. Totals may not add due to rounding.

a. Discretionary fund expenditures include spending from TANF transfers to CCDF.

b. Expenditures made in FY1992–FY1996 from the federal share of AFDC-related child care matching funds are included in the same column as the mandatory CCDF expenditures because these expenditures were the basis for determining mandatory "guaranteed" funding levels for the CCDF. Similarly, the FY1992–FY1996 expenditures made from the state share of AFDC-related child care matching funds appear in the same column showing CCDF MOE expenditures (for FY1997–FY2000) because they formed the basis of determining the MOE requirement level.

Source: Gish, M. (March 19, 2002). *Child care funding and spending under federal block grants.* (CRS Report for Congress received through the CRS Web, Number RL31274). Washington, D.C.: Library of Congress, Congressional Research Service. Retrieved from http://www.nccic.org/pubs/crsreport/crsreport.pdf.

Table 9.16
Total CCDF Expenditures by State: Fiscal Years 1992 to 2000

(in Millions of Dollars)

State	1992	1993	1994	1995	1996	1997	1998	1999	2000	Percentage change: FY1996-FY2000
Alabama	31.9	39.8	40.8	47.0	48.6	52.4	60.7	74.4	103.6	113.0
Alaska	6.6	7.6	7.5	10.0	7.2	13.1	17.3	31.7	27.0	273.2
Arizona	32.6	35.8	41.0	47.1	53.9	61.2	81.9	107.9	105.6	95.9
Arkansas	8.1	14.1	13.7	13.8	17.0	23.2	16.5	34.2	44.1	159.9
California	206.5	152.3	335.2	285.1	330.8	368.8	586.1	796.8	956.6	189.2
Colorado	16.6	26.1	33.2	32.7	27.2	32.9	51.2	66.7	53.0	95.1
Connecticut	23.1	27.5	30.6	49.5	59.0	58.7	72.2	143.2	158.5	168.5
Delaware	6.7	8.7	10.3	12.3	12.2	17.5	24.4	24.7	34.1	180.6
Dist. of Columbia	8.5	9.1	9.4	10.9	10.6	13.6	20.2	27.6	45.1	327.3
Florida	98.7	104.0	109.0	129.1	147.4	157.3	232.7	350.0	327.5	122.2
Georgia	58.2	73.6	82.8	88.2	105.2	132.4	162.1	145.5	177.9	69.1
Hawaii	2.1	6.1	9.3	13.1	12.8	20.5	30.6	34.6	25.2	97.2
Idaho	4.1	7.2	12.4	6.1	6.0	9.1	16.1	24.6	25.7	330.7
Illinois	51.6	90.4	105.4	164.7	191.9	236.0	300.8	354.8	387.8	102.1
Indiana	6.3	27.9	50.3	63.2	66.9	78.3	138.6	92.2	146.7	119.5
Iowa	17.5	17.7	16.6	23.0	21.5	20.1	49.3	47.2	86.2	300.5
Kansas	27.6	21.6	27.8	25.2	28.6	35.1	45.7	49.9	61.1	113.3
Kentucky	22.9	42.7	39.8	41.7	43.6	51.6	60.6	62.8	75.2	72.5
Louisiana	13.0	31.7	33.8	39.6	40.5	47.4	62.3	120.1	134.0	230.6
Maine	3.1	9.3	8.0	5.7	12.3	15.4	19.0	24.7	23.4	90.2
Maryland	44.4	52.7	61.2	60.4	58.6	58.4	104.8	101.3	147.9	152.3
Massachusetts	69.2	80.6	91.8	93.6	116.8	243.1	216.5	244.1	227.9	95.2
Michigan	48.9	75.3	66.0	86.8	65.1	122.0	295.7	178.9	94.4	45.0
Minnesota	35.4	44.8	51.2	56.8	62.4	69.6	68.9	91.0	127.0	103.4
Mississippi	7.7	5.6	36.4	11.4	17.8	48.4	32.5	43.3	65.3	266.8
Missouri	37.5	48.2	52.4	59.4	62.8	79.9	89.3	114.6	133.2	112.0
Montana	4.7	5.7	7.3	7.1	8.4	8.3	14.1	18.9	20.2	140.4
Nebraska	19.2	17.1	28.9	21.6	19.3	27.3	40.9	51.6	60.9	215.7

Table 9.16 (*continued*)

State	1992	1993	1994	1995	1996	1997	1998	1999	2000	Percentage change: FY1996– FY2000
Nevada	4.9	8.1	7.3	9.4	8.7	13.0	18.4	20.3	22.1	153.9
New Hampshire	9.3	9.8	8.8	14.1	11.1	16.2	20.5	18.9	24.4	118.9
New Jersey	61.8	55.7	77.3	111.2	114.3	108.7	134.0	86.3	218.0	90.7
New Mexico	9.1	18.3	23.1	14.3	21.5	28.8	39.5	46.6	52.8	145.6
New York	137.3	193.7	188.5	261.5	201.4	236.2	393.1	502.2	608.1	201.9
North Carolina	43.5	93.7	141.1	136.3	100.1	169.5	224.5	274.1	250.0	149.7
North Dakota	4.3	6.3	5.8	5.3	4.1	7.5	5.4	10.1	9.1	123.4
Ohio	83.8	119.7	120.6	143.4	144.8	191.3	226.8	219.2	317.0	119.0
Oklahoma	41.7	42.8	46.3	50.5	52.8	57.6	71.5	110.5	92.6	75.4
Oregon	21.7	34.0	39.9	41.6	51.7	53.3	56.3	60.2	64.0	23.8
Pennsylvania	79.3	95.4	112.2	134.1	139.8	192.8	170.3	281.3	297.3	112.7
Rhode Island	9.7	11.3	13.3	14.6	15.3	18.7	25.8	33.8	52.7	245.3
South Carolina	11.5	19.7	18.8	31.5	38.2	28.5	67.0	59.5	59.7	56.3
South Dakota	3.0	4.6	5.6	6.0	2.8	6.3	10.7	11.7	13.2	366.1
Tennessee	26.0	45.1	67.8	77.5	82.8	107.9	136.7	155.6	170.6	106.0
Texas	125.0	172.5	167.8	192.0	198.6	218.0	274.7	356.0	421.4	112.2
Utah	17.5	18.0	30.9	25.8	29.7	28.4	39.6	46.2	44.3	49.1
Vermont	5.5	6.5	9.0	10.6	10.6	15.5	17.5	19.1	19.8	87.7
Virginia	37.5	55.5	41.9	56.5	55.8	85.6	79.2	136.3	134.0	140.0
Washington	57.1	66.1	81.2	95.1	100.8	116.6	172.4	216.3	283.9	181.7
West Virginia	7.7	15.2	18.5	17.7	15.9	24.1	41.1	17.2	44.2	178.6
Wisconsin	35.1	46.5	44.2	56.9	63.3	76.9	123.7	137.3	139.0	119.7
Wyoming	4.1	5.3	5.6	6.2	6.0	5.7	8.1	7.6	7.8	29.0
Total	**1,749.0**	**2,227.0**	**2,687.7**	**3,017.1**	**3,124.6**	**3,908.8**	**5,268.0**	**6,283.5**	**7,221.2**	**131.1**

Note: Included in these amounts are any expenditures made from funds transferred from TANF.

Source: Gish, M. (March 19, 2002). *Child care funding and spending under federal block grants.* (CRS Report for Congress received through the CRS Web, Number RL31274). Washington, D.C.: Library of Congress, Congressional Research Service. Retrieved from http://www.nccic.org/pubs/crsreport/crsreport.pdf.

Table 9.17
Transfers from TANF to CCDF, Cumulatively (Fiscal Years 1997 to 2000) and for FY2000, by State, with Percentages of Cumulative Grants and FY2000 TANF Grant

State	Total cumulative TANF grants awarded FY1997-FY2000	Cumulative TANF grants (FY1997-FY2000) transferred to CCDF	Percent of cumulative TANF grants (FY1997-FY2000)	FY2000 TANF grants transferred to CCDF in FY2000	Percent of FY2000 TANF grant transferred to CCDF in FY2000
Alabama	418,753,154	73,248,632	17.5%	20,306,319	17%
Alaska	214,505,299	33,375,162	15.6%	13,134,900	20%
Arizona	937,872,629	102,214,710	10.9%	51,734,178	20%
Arkansas	199,270,696	5,000,000	2.5%	5,000,000	8%
California	14,458,958,043	877,615,000	6.1%	520,315,000	14%
Colorado	469,438,218	65,194,150	13.9%	29,221,458	20%
Connecticut	1,069,529,232	-	0.0%	-	0%
Delaware	118,424,438	5,849,500	4.9%	4,849,500	14%
D.C.	382,790,488	48,043,926	12.6%	18,521,963	16%
Florida	2,344,950,569	264,631,372	11.3%	117,613,943	19%
Georgia	1,307,877,397	95,750,125	7.3%	51,700,000	14%
Hawaii	325,524,819	20,213,506	6.2%	915,000	1%
Idaho	111,118,345	13,235,039	11.9%	6,624,947	20%
Illinois	1,985,575,708	242,337,170	12.2%	125,325,778	20%
Indiana	835,988,658	195,476,822	23.4%	41,359,822	19%
Iowa	497,634,166	42,034,454	8.4%	26,404,972	20%
Kansas	407,724,244	28,490,335	7.0%	15,336,680	15%
Kentucky	713,081,419	115,760,032	16.2%	36,240,000	20%
Louisiana	653,707,831	156,210,354	23.9%	54,106,043	30%
Maine	306,839,541	23,190,837	7.6%	7,336,003	9%
Maryland	877,685,860	137,458,818	15.7%	45,819,606	20%
Massachusetts	1,868,046,687	383,787,077	20.5%	91,874,224	20%
Michigan	3,143,942,863	281,798,590	9.0%	9,363,210	1%
Minnesota	915,479,748	72,292,367	7.9%	17,098,100	6%
Mississippi	360,344,979	42,645,514	11.8%	18,691,998	20%
Missouri	838,993,744	64,123,032	7.6%	20,712,684	10%
Montana	169,642,404	25,769,908	15.2%	7,612,239	17%
Nebraska	223,426,590	9,000,000	4.0%	4,000,000	7%
Nevada	175,273,137	-	0.0%	-	0%

Table 9.17 (*continued*)

State	Total cumulative TANF grants awarded FY1997-FY2000	Cumulative TANF grants (FY1997-FY2000) transferred to CCDF	Percent of cumulative TANF grants (FY1997-FY2000)	FY2000 TANF grants transferred to CCDF in FY2000	Percent of FY2000 TANF grant transferred to CCDF in FY2000
New Hampshire	154,085,043	-	0.0%	-	0%
New Jersey	1,514,263,411	301,852,683	19.9%	79,795,989	20%
New Mexico	455,187,418	46,521,342	10.2%	19,528,227	15%
New York	9,319,061,424	761,600,000	8.2%	437,000,000	18%
North Carolina	1,180,040,646	157,833,798	13.4%	65,880,426	20%
North Dakota	88,876,489	500,000	0.6%	500,000	2%
Ohio	2,911,873,040	77,453,492	2.7%	77,453,492	11%
Oklahoma	594,451,025	118,890,206	20.0%	30,199,871	20%
Oregon	668,204,335	-	0.0%	-	0%
Pennsylvania	2,629,891,350	194,091,000	7.4%	67,122,000	9%
Rhode Island	334,962,828	17,730,261	5.3%	4,085,057	4%
South Carolina	394,967,259	10,175,262	2.6%	1,046,630	1%
South Dakota	82,536,526	5,963,361	7.2%	4,363,361	20%
Tennessee	804,213,896	133,444,177	16.6%	50,402,091	24%
Texas	2,005,877,272	168,653,815	8.4%	38,292,192	7%
Utah	322,686,833	3,740,480	1.2%	-	0%
Vermont	189,412,724	25,889,490	13.7%	7,729,551	16%
Virginia	592,469,414	88,984,715	15.0%	27,699,905	17%
Washington	1,510,874,418	250,005,775	16.5%	100,037,747	24%
West Virginia	415,166,588	15,353,655	3.7%	-	0%
Wisconsin	1,270,217,409	176,429,520	13.9%	63,500,000	20%
Wyoming	82,230,508	9,100,000	11.1%	-	0%
Total	**63,853,950,762**	**5,988,959,464**	**9.4%**	**2,435,855,106**	**14%**

Source: Gish, M. (March 19, 2002). *Child care funding and spending under federal block grants.* (CRS Report for Congress received through the CRS Web, Number RL31274). Washington, D.C.: Library of Congress, Congressional Research Service. Retrieved from http://www.nccic.org/pubs/crsreprot/crsreport.pdf.

Table 9.18
Head Start Program by State/Region, Allocations and Enrollments in FY2002

STATE	2002 FUNDING	ENROLLMENT
Alabama	$100,154,494	16,529
Alaska	$12,104,386	1,839
Arizona	$96,912,656	13,297
Arkansas	$61,023,626	10,930
California	$801,429,541	98,687
Colorado	$65,716,131	9,872
Connecticut	$49,984,520	7,224
Delaware	$12,286,428	2,231
District of Columbia	$24,090,814	3,403
Florida	$252,369,803	35,610
Georgia	$161,740,120	23,414
Hawaii	$21,977,038	3,073
Idaho	$21,662,707	3,347
Illinois	$259,780,216	39,619
Indiana	$88,666,972	14,145
Iowa	$49,494,840	7,620
Kansas	$47,909,093	8,013
Kentucky	$103,472,617	16,190
Louisiana	$135,048,223	22,136
Maine	$26,661,319	4,002
Maryland	$74,928,894	10,527
Massachusetts	$104,182,066	13,040
Michigan	$225,290,497	35,269
Minnesota	$69,643,329	10,331
Mississippi	$155,259,338	26,742
Missouri	$113,255,841	17,646
Montana	$20,117,436	2,982
Nebraska	$34,580,417	5,252
Nevada	$19,785,629	2,754
New Hampshire	$12,860,678	1,632
New Jersey	$125,175,590	15,262
New Mexico	$49,185,413	7,749
New York	$418,238,532	49,493
North Carolina	$132,667,143	19,202
North Dakota	$16,036,018	2,307
Ohio	$236,999,439	38,081
Oklahoma	$76,909,804	13,460
Oregon	$57,105,005	9,199
Pennsylvania	$219,114,506	30,986
Rhode Island	$21,184,290	3,150
South Carolina	$78,506,579	12,248
South Dakota	$18,078,512	2,827
Tennessee	$112,343,511	16,507
Texas	$454,292,444	67,664
Utah	$36,270,290	5,527
Vermont	$13,022,989	1,573
Virginia	$95,366,343	13,772
Washington	$97,246,982	11,167
West Virginia	$48,624,566	7,650
Wisconsin	$86,940,813	13,489
Wyoming	$11,882,457	1,803
Native Americans	$181,794,159	23,837
Migrant Programs	$257,814,769	33,850
Outer Pacific	$14,942,945	6,209
Puerto Rico	$234,303,518	36,920
Virgin Islands	$9,878,464	1,161

Source: Head Start Bureau. (2003). *Head Start Program Fact Sheet 2003.* U.S. Department of Health and Human Services, Administration for Children and Families Web site. Retrieved from http://www2.acf.hhs.gov/programs/hsb/research/factsheets.htm.

Table 9.19
Head Start—Summary: 1980 to 2001

[For years ending September 30 (376 represents 376,000).]

Year	Enrollment (1,000)	Appropria- tion (mil. dol.)	Age and race	Enrollment, 2001 (percent)	Item	Number
1980 . . .	376	735	Under 3 years old	7	Average cost per child (dollars):	
1985 . . .	452	1,075	3 years old.	35	1995.	4,534
1990 . . .	541	1,552	4 years old.	54	2000.	5,951
1992 . . .	621	2,202	5 years old and over . . .	4	2001.	6,633
1993 . . .	714	2,776				
1994 . . .	740	3,326			Paid staff (1,000):	
1995 . . .	751	3,534	White	30	1995.	147
1996 . . .	752	3,569	Black	34	2000.	180
1997 . . .	794	3,981	Hispanic	30	2001.	195
1998 . . .	822	4,347	American Indian	4	Volunteers (1,000):	
1999 . . .	826	4,658	Asian	2	1995.	1,235
2000 . . .	858	5,267	Hawaiian/		2000.	1,252
2001 . . .	905	6,200	Pacific Islander	1	2001.	1,345

Source: United States Census Bureau. (2002). *Statistical Abstract of the United States 2002.* Washington, D.C.: Government Printing Office. Retrieved from http://www.census.gov/prod/2003pubs/02statab/socinsur.pdf.

Figure 9.3
Income, Earnings, Welfare, and Poverty for Female-Headed Families: United States, 1990 to 1999

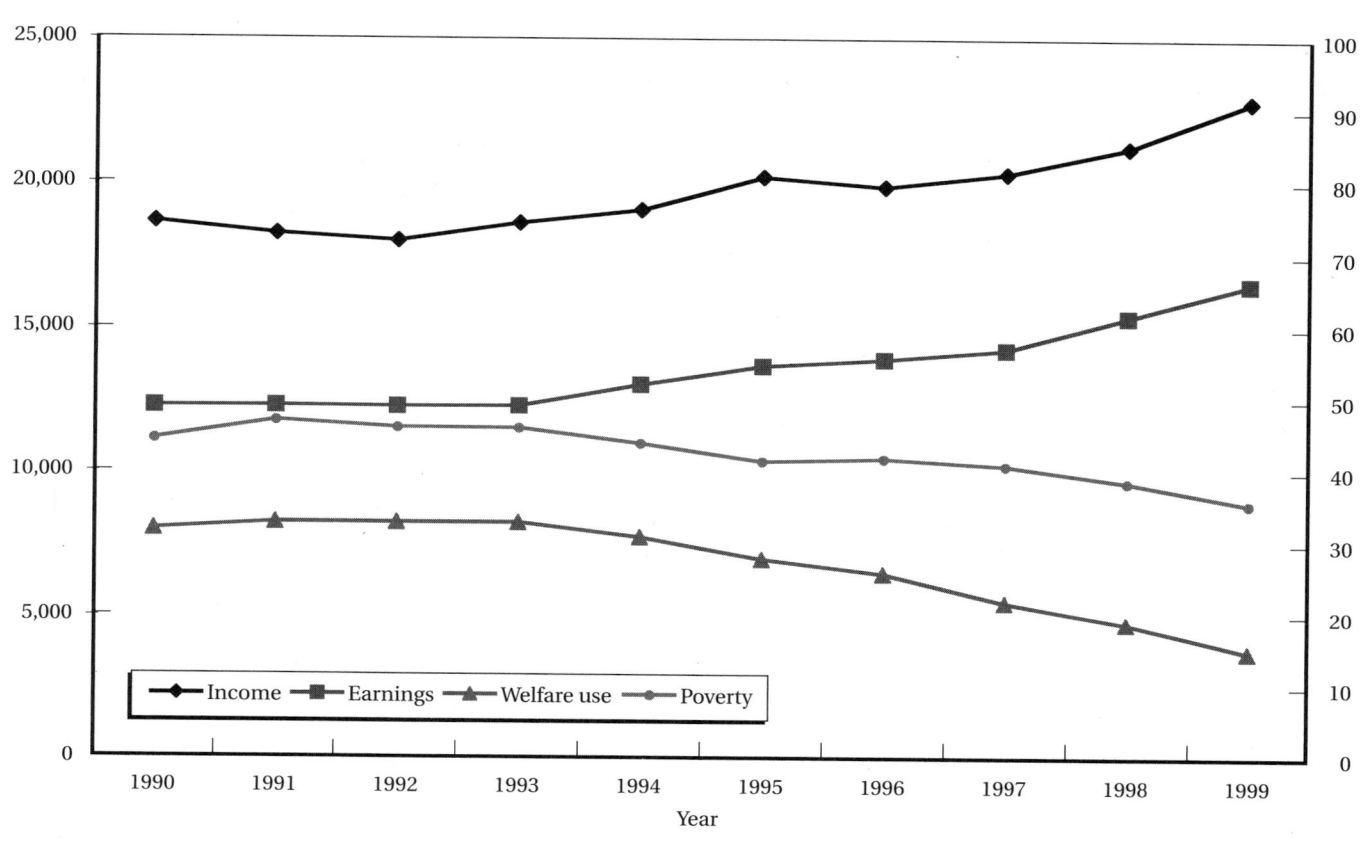

Source: Grogger, J., Karoly, L.A., & Klerman, J.A. (2002). *Consequences of welfare reform: A research synthesis.* (Report #: DRU-2676-DHHS). Washington, D.C.: Administration for Children and Families. Retrieved from http://www.acf.dhhs.gov/programs/opre/welfare_reform/rand_report.pdf.

Figure 9.4
Percentage of Children Living with Two Parents: United States, 1968 to 2000

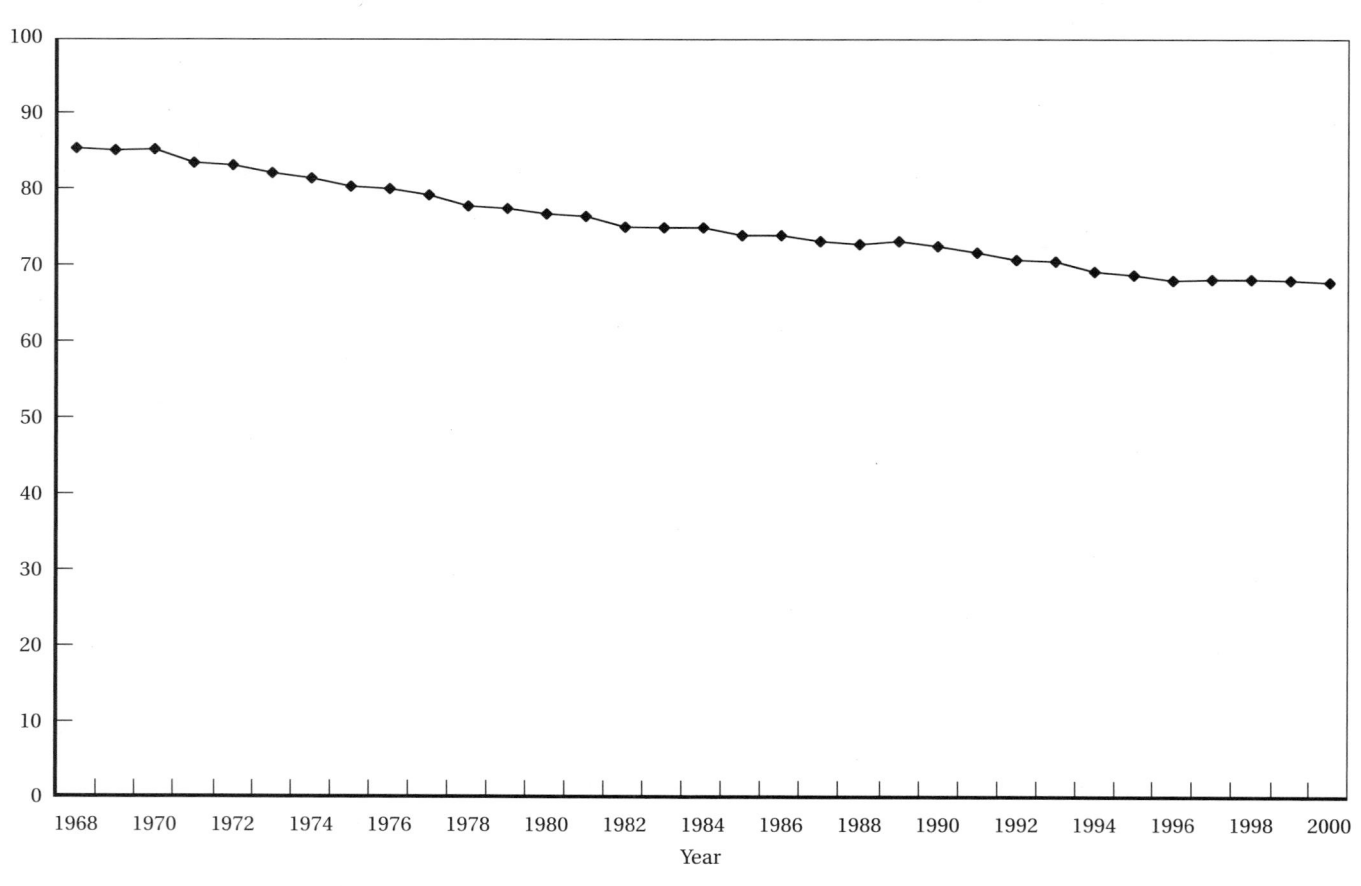

Source: Grogger, J., Karoly, L.A., & Klerman, J.A. (2002). *Consequences of welfare reform: A research synthesis.* (Report #: DRU-2676-DHHS). Washington, D.C.: Administration for Children and Families. Retrieved from http://www.acf.dhhs.gov/programs/opre/welfare_reform/rand_report.pdf.

Figure 9.5
Percentage of Births to Unmarried Women: United States, 1950 to 2000

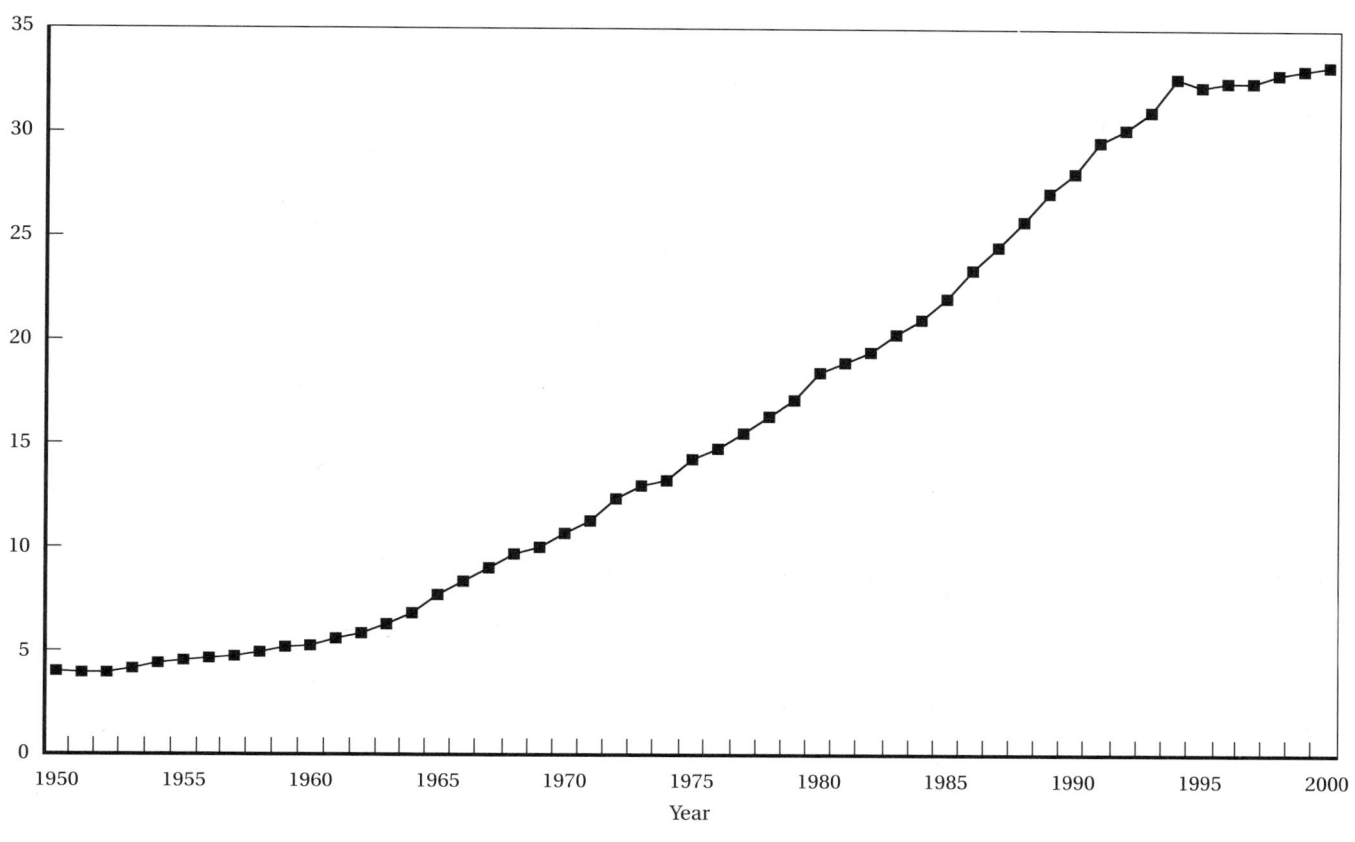

Source: Grogger, J., Karoly, L.A., & Klerman, J.A. (2002). *Consequences of welfare reform: A research synthesis.* (Report #: DRU-2676-DHHS). Washington, D.C.: Administration for Children and Families. Retrieved from http://www.acf.dhhs.gov/programs/opre/welfare_reform/rand_report.pdf.

Figure 9.6
The Welfare Caseload, Unemployment, and Statewide Reform: United States, 1970 to 2000

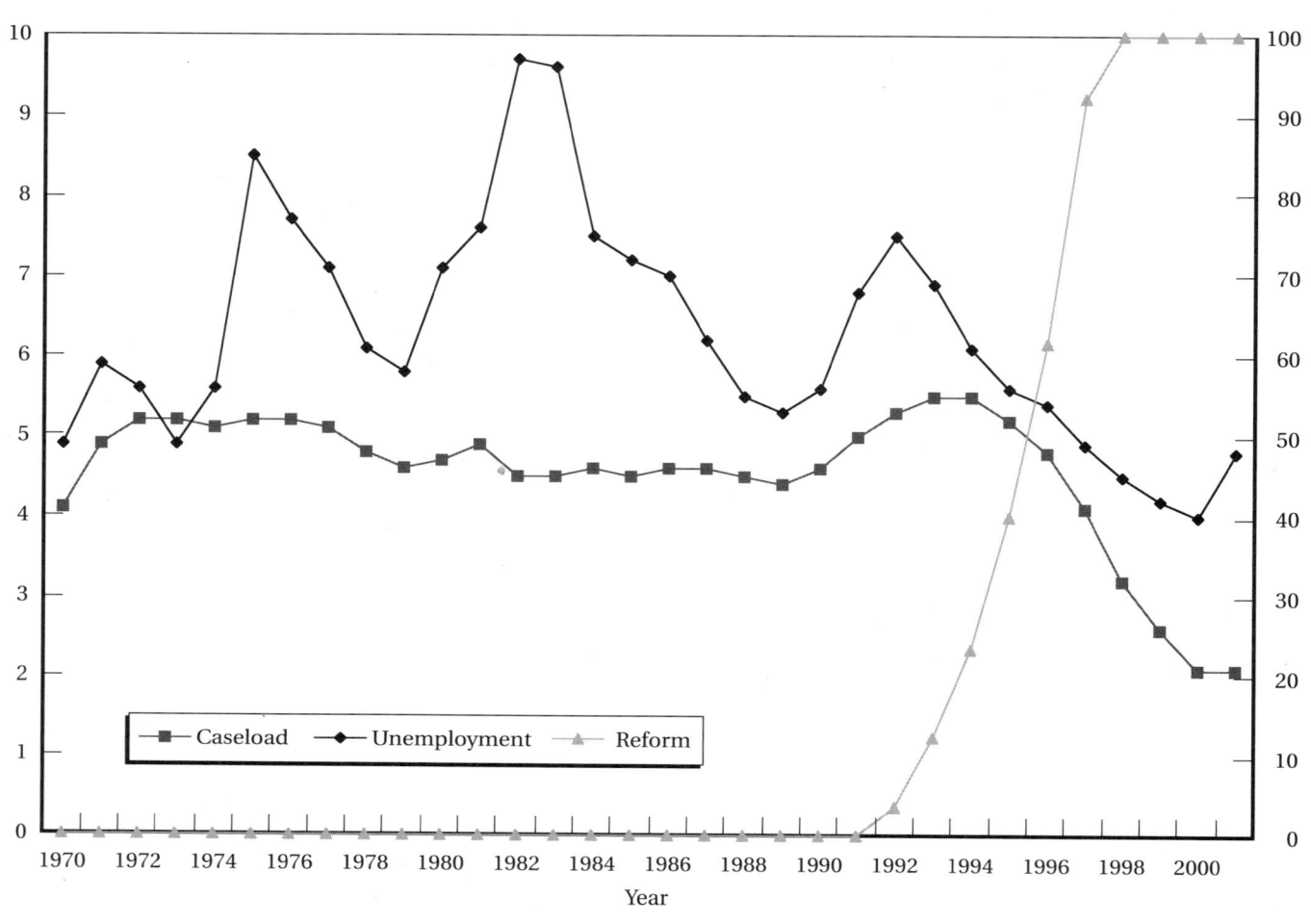

Source: Grogger, J., Karoly, L.A., & Klerman, J.A. (2002). *Consequences of welfare reform: A research synthesis.* (Report #: DRU-2676-DHHS). Washington, D.C.: Administration for Children and Families. Retrieved from http://www.acf.dhhs.gov/programs/opre/welfare_reform/rand_report.pdf.

Table 9.20
Households and Persons Having Problems with Access to Food: United States, 1995 to 2000

[**100,445 represents 100,445,000.** Food secure means that a household had access at all times to enough food for an active healthy life, with no need for recourse to emergency food sources or other extraordinary coping behaviors to meet their basic food needs. A food insecure household did not have this same access to enough food to fully meet basic needs at all times. Food insecure households with hunger were those with one or more household members who were hungry at least sometime during the period due to inadequate resources for food. The omission of homeless persons may be a cause of underreporting. The Federal food security measure was developed through a collaborative process between private non-government experts, academic researchers, and a Federal interagency working group, with leadership from the U.S. Dept. of Agriculture and the U.S. Dept. of Health and Human Services. The severity of food insecurity and hunger in households is measured through a series of questions about experiences and behaviors known to characterize households that are having difficulty meeting basic food needs. These experiences and behaviors generally occur in an ordered sequence as the severity of food insecurity increases. As resources become more constrained, adults in typical households first worry about having enough food, then they stretch household resources and juggle other necessities, then decrease the quality and variety of household membersí diets, then decrease the frequency and quantity of adultsí food intake, and finally decrease the frequency and quantity of childrenís food intake. All questions refer to the previous 12 months and include a qualifying phrase reminding respondents to report only those occurrences that resulted from inadequate financial resources. Restrictions to food intake due to dieting or busy schedules are excluded. Data are from the Food Security Supplement to the Current Population Survey (CPS).]

Household food security level	Number (1,000)				Percent distribution			
	1995	1998 [1]	1998 [2]	2000	1995	1998 [1]	1998 [2]	2000
Households, total.	**100,445**	**103,480**	**103,309**	**106,043**	**100.0**	**100.0**	**100.0**	**100.0**
Food secure	90,097	92,972	91,121	94,942	89.7	89.8	88.2	89.5
Food insecure	10,348	10,509	12,188	11,101	10.3	10.2	11.8	10.5
Without hunger.	6,402	6,820	8,353	7,786	6.4	6.6	8.1	7.3
With hunger.	3,946	3,689	3,835	3,315	3.9	3.6	3.7	3.1
With hunger among children [3] . .	(NA)	(NA)	331	255	(NA)	(NA)	0.9	0.7
Adult members	191,063	197,423	197,084	201,922	100.0	100.0	100.0	100.0
Food secure	172,862	178,631	174,964	181,586	90.5	90.5	88.8	89.9
Food insecure	18,200	18,792	22,120	20,336	9.5	9.5	11.2	10.1
Without hunger.	11,611	12,657	15,632	14,763	6.1	6.4	7.9	7.3
With hunger.	6,589	6,135	6,488	5,573	3.4	3.1	3.3	2.8
Child members	70,279	71,463	71,282	71,763	100.0	100.0	100.0	100.0
Food secure	58,048	59,090	57,255	58,868	82.6	82.7	80.3	82.0
Food insecure	12,231	12,373	14,027	12,895	17.4	17.3	19.7	18.0
Without hunger.	8,131	9,114	10,658	9,945	11.6	12.8	15.0	13.9
With hunger [4].	4,100	3,259	3,369	2,950	5.8	4.6	4.7	4.1
With hunger among children [3] . .	(NA)	(NA)	716	562	(NA)	(NA)	1.0	0.8

NA. Not available.

1. Adjusted data. These data are comparable to those of earlier years.

2. Data as collected. These data are comparable to those for 2000.

3. One or more children in these households was hungry because of the household's food insecurity. Percent distribution of households with hunger among children excludes households with no child from the denominator.

4. Most of these children did not, themselves, face hunger, but adults or older children in the household did.

Source: United States Census Bureau. (2002). *Statistical Abstract of the United States 2002*. Washington, D.C.: Government Printing Office. Retrieved from http://www.census.gov/prod/2003pubs/02statab/health.pdf.

Table 9.21
National School Lunch Program Participation and Federal
Costs: United States, Fiscal Years 1977 to 1999

(in Millions)

| | Participation 9 month average[1] | | | | Federal costs | |
Fiscal year	Free meals	Full- Reduced- meals[2]	price	Total[3]	Current dollars[4]	Constant 1999 dollars
1977	10.5	1.3	14.5	26.3	$2,111.1	$5,857.3
1978	10.3	1.5	14.9	26.7	2,293.6	5,945.0
1979	10.0	1.7	15.3	27.0	2,659.0	6,247.2
1980	10.0	1.9	14.7	26.6	3,044.9	6,298.5
1981	10.6	1.9	13.3	25.8	2,959.5	5,510.6
1982	9.8	1.6	11.5	22.9	2,611.5	4,528.5
1983	10.3	1.5	11.2	23.0	2,828.6	4,738.6
1984	10.3	1.5	11.5	23.3	2,948.2	4,744.1
1985	9.9	1.6	12.1	23.6	3,034.4	4,709.2
1986	10.0	1.6	12.2	23.8	3,160.2	4,786.9
1987	10.0	1.6	12.4	24.0	3,245.6	4,779.6
1988	9.8	1.6	12.8	24.2	3,383.7	4,785.7
1989	9.7	1.6	12.7	24.2	3,479.4	4,697.5
1990	9.9	1.6	12.8	24.1	3,676.4	4,727.6
1991	10.3	1.8	12.1	24.2	4,072.9	4,986.0
1992	11.1	1.7	11.7	24.5	4,474.5	5,317.4
1993	11.8	1.7	11.3	24.8	4,663.8	5,379.1
1994	12.2	1.8	11.3	25.3	4,994.5	5,613.2
1995	12.4	1.9	11.3	25.6	5,254.0	5,743.6
1996	12.6	2.0	11.3	25.9	5,441.0	5,786.3
1997	13.0	2.0	11.3	26.3	5,729.8	5,935.1
1998	13.0	2.2	11.3	26.5	5,872.1	5,984.8
1999	13.0	2.4	11.6	27.0	6,249.8	6,249.8

1. In order to reflect participation for the actual school year (September through May), these estimates are based on 9 month averages of October through May, plus September, rather than averages of the 12 months of the fiscal year (October through September).

2. The federal government provides a small subsidy for these meals.

3. Details may not sum to total because of rounding.

4. Includes cash payments and the value of "entitlement" commodities; does not include the value of "bonus" commodities. Overstates actual support for school lunches because a portion (less than $75 million a year) of commodity support included in the figures is used for other child nutrition programs.

Note: Constant dollars were calculated using the fiscal year CPI-U.

Source: United States House of Representatives, Committee on Ways and Means. (2000). *The 2000 Green Book: Background material and data on programs within the jurisdiction of the Committee on Ways and Means.* Retrieved from http://aspe.hhs.gov/2000gb/sec15.txt.

Table 9.22
School Breakfast Program Participation and Federal Costs: United States, Selected Fiscal Years 1977 to 1999

(in Millions)

Fiscal year	Participation 9 month average[1]				Federal costs	
	Free meals	Reduced-price meals	Full-price meals[2]	Total[3]	Current dollars[4]	Constant 1999 dollars
1977	2.0	0.1	0.4	2.5	$148.6	$412.3
1980	2.8	0.2	0.6	3.6	287.8	595.3
1981	3.0	0.2	0.5	3.8	331.7	617.6
1982	2.8	0.2	0.4	3.3	317.3	550.2
1983	2.9	0.1	0.3	3.4	343.8	576.0
1984	2.9	0.1	0.4	3.4	364.0	585.7
1985	2.9	0.2	0.4	3.4	379.3	588.7
1986	2.9	0.2	0.4	3.5	406.3	615.5
1987	3.0	0.2	0.4	3.7	446.8	658.0
1988	3.0	0.2	0.5	3.7	482.0	681.7
1989	3.1	0.2	0.5	3.8	507.0	684.5
1990	3.3	0.2	0.5	4.0	589.1	757.6
1991	3.6	0.2	0.6	4.4	677.2	829.0
1992	4.0	0.3	0.6	4.9	782.6	930.0
1993	4.4	0.3	0.7	5.4	868.4	1,001.6
1994	4.8	0.3	0.7	5.8	958.7	1,077.5
1995	5.1	0.4	0.8	6.3	1,181.8	1,291.9
1996	5.3	0.4	0.9	6.6	1,124.2	1,195.5
1997	5.5	0.9	6.9	6.6	1,212.7	1,256.2
1998	5.6	1.0	7.1	6.6	1,299.6	1,324.5
1999	5.7	1.1	7.4	6.6	1,354.8	1,354.8

1. In order to reflect participation for the actual school year (September through May), these estimates are based on 9 month averages of October through May, plus September, rather than averages of the 12 months of the fiscal year (October through September).

2. The Federal Government provides a small subsidy for these meals.

3. Details may not sum to totals due to rounding.

4. Does not include the value of any federally donated commodities. Fiscal year 1995 figure for Federal costs is not reduced for a "write-down" of approximately $50–$80 million for unclaimed obligations.

Note: Constant dollars were calculated using the fiscal year CPI-U.

Source: United States House of Representatives, Committee on Ways and Means. (2000). *The 2000 Green Book: Background material and data on programs within the jurisdiction of the Committee on Ways and Means.* Retrieved from http://aspe.hhs.gov/2000gb/sec15.txt.

Table 9.23
Special Supplemental Nutrition Program
for Women, Infants, and Children (WIC), Participation
and Federal Spending: United States, Selected Fiscal
Years 1977 to 1999

(Dollars in Millions)

Fiscal year	Participation (in thousands)				Federal spending	
	Women	Infants	Children	Total[1]	Current dollars[2]	Constant 1999 dollars
1977	165.0	213.0	471.0	848.0	$255.9	$710.0
1980	411.0	507.0	995.0	1,913.0	724.7	1,499.1
1981	446.0	585.0	1,088.0	2,119.0	874.4	1,628.1
1982	478.0	623.0	1,088.0	2,189.0	948.2	1,644.2
1983	542.0	730.0	1,265.0	2,537.0	1,123.1	1,881.5
1984	657.0	825.0	1,563.0	3,045.0	1,386.3	2,230.8
1985	665.0	874.0	1,600.0	3,138.0	1,488.9	2,310.7
1986	712.0	945.0	1,655.0	3,312.0	1,580.5	2,394.1
1987	751.0	1,019.0	1,660.0	3,429.0	1,663.6	2,449.9
1988	815.0	1,095.0	1,683.0	3,593.0	1,802.4	2,549.2
1989	951.8	1,259.6	1,907.0	4,118.4	1,929.4	2,604.9
1990	1,035.0	1,412.5	2,069.4	4,516.9	2,125.9	2,733.8
1991	1,120.1	1,558.8	2,213.8	4,892.6	2,301.1	2,817.0
1992	1,221.5	1,684.1	2,505.2	5,410.8	2,566.5	3,050.0
1993	1,364.9	1,741.9	2,813.4	5,920.3	2,819.5	3,252.0
1994	1,499.2	1,786.3	3,191.7	6,477.2	3,159.8	3,551.2
1995	1,576.8	1,817.3	3,500.1	6,894.2	3,451.0	3,772.6
1996	1,648.2	1,827.3	3,712.3	7,187.8	3,688.2	3,922.2
1997	1,710.5	1,863.0	3,835.4	7,408.9	3,845.7	3,983.5
1998	1,733.3	1,882.8	3,749.2	7,365.3	3,895.8	3,970.6
1999	1,742.5	1,897.6	3,671.4	7,311.5	3,955.6	3,955.6

1. Details may not sum to totals due to rounding.

2. Includes funding for studies, surveys, pilots, and farmers' market programs. Spending figures include adjustments for significant interyear carryovers and reflect spending by State WIC agencies derived both from current-year appropriations and prior-year amounts, adjusted for amounts carried forward into the next year.

Note: Constant dollars were calculated using the fiscal year CPI-U.

Source: United States House of Representatives, Committee on Ways and Means. (2000). *The 2000 Green Book: Background material and data on programs within the jurisdiction of the Committee on Ways and Means.* Retrieved from http://aspe.hhs.gov/2000gb/sec15.txt.

Figure 9.7
Comparison of Poverty Levels of WIC Participants Reporting
Income to Persons in the U.S. Population

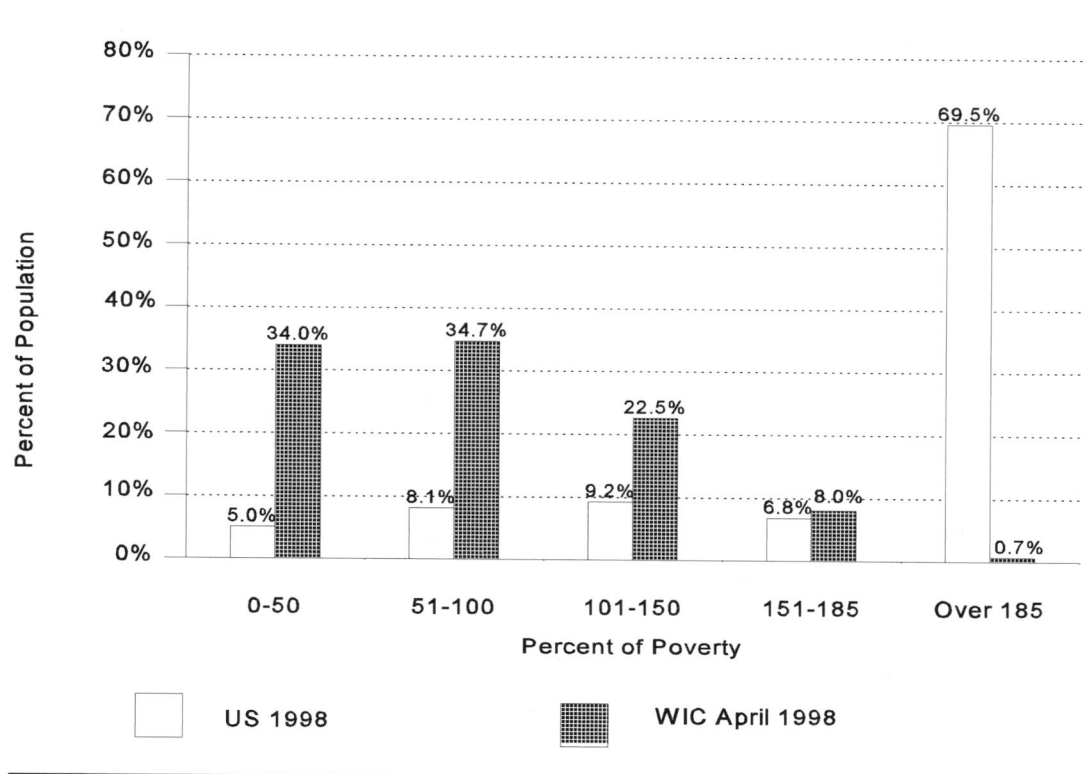

Source: Bartlett, S., Brown-Lyons, M., Moore, D., & Estacion, A. (1998). WIC participant and program characteristics 1998. Nutritional Assistance Program Report Series, Number WIC-00-PC. Washington, D.C.: U.S. Department of Agriculture, Food and Nutrition Service, Office of Analysis, Nutrition, and Evaluation. Retrieved from http://www.abtassoc.com/reports/ES-20006343640181.pdf.

Figure 9.8
Distribution of Individuals Enrolled in the WIC Program:
United States, April 1998

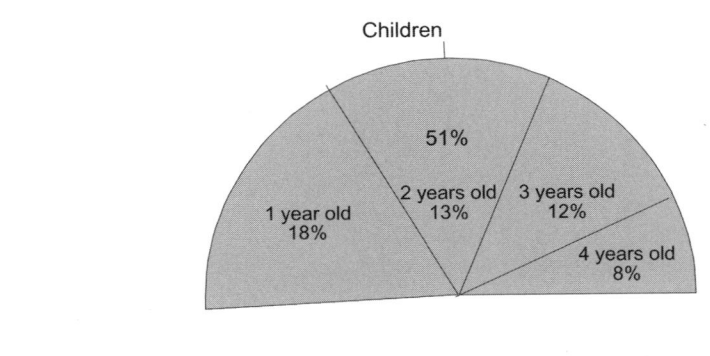
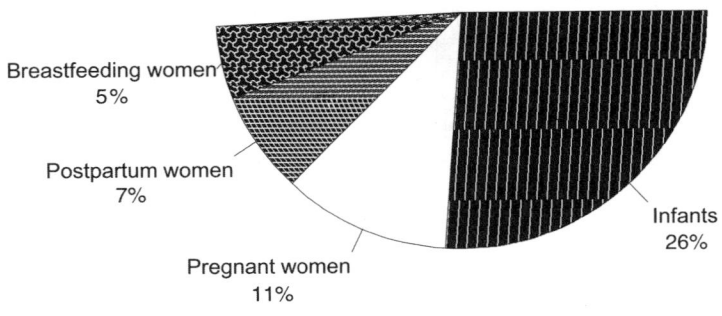

Source: Bartlett, S., Brown-Lyons, M., Moore, D., & Estacion, A. (1998). WIC participant and program characteristics 1998. Nutritional Assistance Program Report Series, Number WIC-00-PC. Washington, D.C.: U.S. Department of Agriculture, Food and Nutrition Service, Office of Analysis, Nutrition, and Evaluation. Retrieved from http://www.abtassoc.com/reports/ES-20006343640181.pdf.

10. Children and Youth Services

From the wild Irish slums of the 19th century Eastern seaboard to the riot-torn suburbs of Los Angeles, there is one unmistakable lesson in American history: A community that allows a large number of young men to grow up in broken families, dominated by women, never acquiring any stable relationship to male authority, never acquiring any rational expectations about the future—that community asks for and gets chaos. In such a society crime, violence, unrest, unrestrained lashing out at the whole social structure— these are not only to be expected, they are very nearly inevitable. (Daniel Patrick Monyhan, 1965, quoted in Ashcroft, 1995)

The safety and well-being of children is one of the paramount social concerns in the United States today, as it has been throughout most of its history. The threat to that well-being was a front-burner issue at the turn of the 20th century, and it had been for a couple of generations before that. All that has to be done to evidence this is to find and look at the many examples of protests made to stop what was considered the exploitation of children.

One high profile example occurred in 1887, when the then eleven-year-old child prodigy Josef Hofmann came to the United States to play piano recitals. Because of his age, the Society for the Prevention of Cruelty to Children protested to such an extent that the remainder of his U.S. tour had to be canceled. About this time, an anonymous donor (later found to be Alfred Cornig Clark of New York) provided the boy and his family with $50,000 with the stipulation that he could not return to the concert stage until he was at least 18.

Examples of the myriad lower profile cases of child exploitation from the turn of the twentieth century come from the coal mines in the United States and England. As the National Child Labor Committee reports to its readers in 1907:

> Child labor in the bituminous industry differs from that in the anthracite, as in the former there is no slate picking and the children employed are inside the mine. They work as runners,

drivers, door boys and couplers, while perhaps the larger percentage are employed with their fathers in loading coal.

> In one Pennsylvania mining borough where from 1,000 to 1,200 people are employed in the mines, it was estimated by several of the miners, two mine superintendents, the chief burgess and the superintendent of schools that between 175 and 200 boys under 16 were employed in the mines. . . . The general conditions of mining, so far as could be discovered by one who does not understand the technical problems of mining or of mining conditions, were about equal. One of these mines is operated by a large concern closely identified with a great railroad corporation, and there I discovered not less than ten per cent, and possibly fifteen per cent, of all the employees were boys under sixteen years of age. The other mine was an independent concern, and so far as we could find not a boy under sixteen years of age was employed. . . . This does not reflect upon the organization of the mine itself, for in other places we found the reverse true. The large corporations were freer from child employment than some of the independent concerns. This instance is given only to show that in the same locality the difference seemed entirely due to the attitude of the mining superintendents. . . .

> Here, as in the anthracite region, the cost in life and limb forms a large percentage of our national expenditure for the production of coal. In this industry as in others employing young children, the children bear more than their share of the risk, except that the miners and their laborers engage in the extra hazardous department of the industry. . . . The large percentage of accidents to mine workers under sixteen years of age and to non-English speaking workmen of all ages. (Lovejoy, 1907)

The passage of the Social Security Act in 1935 was an institutional watershed and a paradigm shift of tremendous proportions in social thinking; however, the beginning of the creation and expansion of a social safety net in this country was preceded by some attempts from a reluctant federal government to protect children. Because of the heretofore dislike of federalism, most of the laws and support systems in place were at the state levels. The child-welfare components of the Social Security Act layered federal funds over the existing state-level framework (Dobelstein, 1996).

Today, child welfare is still a major concern. The reason is somewhat different, but there is still the feeling of a higher than preferred acceptable level of life threatening events facing children. At the beginning of the twenty-first century, the issue is the creeping poverty that seems to be overtaking more and more children. The concern is that the deprivation that poverty engenders in children can lead to reduced health and quality-of-life issues.

"A main objective of public assistance is to make sure that children have a roof over their heads, heat in their homes, a minimally nutritious diet, and health care" (Schwartz and Volgy, 1992, 132). Current child welfare services in the United States "aim to improve the conditions of children and their families and to improve or provide substitutes for functions that parents have difficulty performing" (United States House of Representatives, Committee on Ways and Means, 2000, section 11, 1/93). This translates to approximately thirty federal programs for these types of services that are administered by four different cabinet-level agencies and five different committees within the House of Representatives. Significant components of these programs are run with and through state agencies and many non-profit, (per the IRS code 501(c)(3) designation) nongovernment agencies (NGOs).

Child welfare services provide a wide array of programs to help children cope with their surrounding environment and not get hurt or impaired as a result of potential or actual deprivation of care. Program activities range from the support and preservation of families and family development to the protection of abused or neglected children to adoption and foster care. Congress is concerned about recent trends affecting child welfare populations and programs, among them child abuse and neglect, substance abuse (especially children born of drug addicted parents with a chemical dependency), demographic shifts in which more children are living with relatives that are not their parents, and the potential that welfare reform may have on children. Most of the principal programs are authorized under programs that were initiated as part of the Social Security Act of 1935 or were added on as amendments over the years to meet the increasingly recognized importance of assisting children in poverty and attempting to reduce and eliminate the rising number of children that are in poverty. These programs reflect the reality that the primary reasons children receive social services are neglect and abuse, financial needs, emotional issues of the child or one or both parents, conflict between parent and child, abandonment, and the unwillingness of parents to care for the child (DiNitto and Dye, 1993). The number of children in poverty keeps increasing at alarming numbers, expanding what is already one of the largest, if not the largest single identified group in poverty. Social changes and current trends such as the rise of the single-parent (usually the mother) head of household family and "deadbeat" noncustodial parents influence how children enter into poverty. Uncollected child support is one of the key problems currently impacting children services, as reflected in a number of provisions stipulating collection as part of the revenue stream in the long-term of the programs in question.

The sobering reality is that children are two and-one-half times as likely to be poor if they live in single-parent, female-headed families; in 1996, about 24 percent of children lived in single-female head of household families, most of them with fathers that are living who by law are required to provide for them (Dobelstein, 1996).

Other than the programs provided under the Omnibus Reconciliation Act of 1990—the Child Care and Development Block Grant (CCDBG) and the At-Risk Child Care Program—that were discussed in chapter 9, the major federal programs in the social safety net that directly deal with children are the following:

Title IV-B of Social Security Act: Child Welfare Services Programs

Title IV-D of Social Security Act: Child Support Enforcement and Paternity Establishment Programs

Title IV-E of Social Security Act: Foster Care Program

Title IV-E of Social Security Act: Adoption Assistance Program

Title IV-E of Social Security Act: Adoption incentives programs

Title IV-E of Social Security Act: Foster Care Independence Program

Title XX of Social Security Act: Social Services Block Grants (SSBG)

These are the largest child welfare programs in the U.S. social safety net (United States House of Representatives, Committee on Ways and Means, 2000, section 11). As can be seen, most are authorized under titles IV-B and IV-E of the Social Security Act, containing the primary funding sources for welfare programs for states. Title IV-B funds may be used by the states to provide services to families and children without regard to family income, while Title IV-E funds are only provided to children who (a) still lived at home and (b) who would have been eligible for assistance under Aid to Families with Dependent Children (AFDC). Title IV-B funds also provide for the ability to conduct research activities and studies, demonstration activities, and training for child welfare staff training at private and public entities. Children who are recognized as having "special needs" under Title IV-E are eligible for the reimbursement of certain recurring adoption costs as part of the Adoption Assistance Program whereas only AFDC- or SSI-eligible "special needs" children qualify for matching federal adoption assistance payments. States may use funds from the Foster Care Independence Program for services facilitating the transition of children from foster care to independent living (regardless of AFDC foster care eligibility).

States are subject to penalties if their programs do not substantially address the elimination of identified barriers to adoption. States cannot discriminate based on age, color, or national origin. States also cannot delay the adoption or placement process because of agency jurisdictional issues. Overall, the federal government has identified the following outcomes for child welfare programs as a means of influencing state program development (United States House of Representatives, Committee on Ways and Means, 2000, section 11, 42/93):

- The reduction of the recurrence of child abuse and/or neglect:

  Recurrence in the past twelve months

- Reducing incidence of child abuse and/or neglect in foster care:

  Percent of substantiated or indicated maltreatment of a child by a foster parent or facilty staff member

- Increasing the permanency in foster care children:

  1. Percent who exited due to reunification
  2. Percent who exited due to adoption or legal guardianship
  3. Percent of special needs children who exited for each of the two previous reasons
  4. Percent of children age 12 or older who exited for each of the two previous reasons
  5. Percent breakdown of those who exited by race/ ethnic category based on the two reasons for exiting as defined above
  6. Age of entry into system for those emancipated (percent of those aged 12 or younger)

- Reduction in time in foster care to reunification without increasing re-entry:

  1. Percent reunified less than 12 months from latest removal
  2. Percent reunified 12–23 months from latest removal
  3. Percent reunified 24–35 months from latest removal
  4. Percent unified 36–47 months from latest removal
  5. Percent removed after 48 months from latest removal
  6. Percent of all entering foster care during reporting period reentered care within 12 months of prior foster care episode

- Reduction in time in foster care to adoption for all children:

  1. Percent reunified less than 12 months from latest removal
  2. Percent reunified 12–23 months from latest removal
  3. Percent reunified 24–35 months from latest removal
  4. Percent unified 36–47 months from latest removal
  5. Percent removed after 48 months from latest removal

  For children age 3 or older at time of entry into foster care:

  6. Percent reunified less than 12 months from latest removal
  7. Percent reunified 12–23 months from latest removal
  8. Percent reunified 24–35 months from latest removal
  9. Percent unified 36–47 months from latest removal
  10. Percent removed after 48 months from latest removal

- Increasing placement stability:

  1. Percent of no more than 2 placements less than 12 months from time of latest removal from home

2. Percent 12–23 months from time of latest removal from home
3. Percent 24–35 months from time of latest removal from home
4. Percent 36–47 months from time of latest removal from home
5. Percent 48 or more months from time of latest removal from home

- Reducing placement of young children in group homes or institutions:

  Percent children 12 or under placed in group home

TITLE IV-B: CHILD WELFARE SERVICES PROGRAMS

These programs provide funds for the care of children who do not or are not able to live with their parents. Protecting the children's mental and physical welfare is the main focus of the activities in these programs. Unlike so many other programs under the social safety net in the United States, there are no federal income eligibility requirements in order to receive child welfare services. Under subpart 1 of Title IV-B, 75 percent of federal matching grants go to states for services earmarked to protect children's welfare by:

- combating problems leading to neglect, abuse, exploitation, or crime by children
- preventing the unnecessary separation of children from their families and the restoration of children to their families when possible
- promoting the adoption of children when appropriate
- assuring adequate foster care when children cannot return home or be placed for adoption

Federal statutes do not impose a limit on the percentage of funds that have to be spent for each category of service. Instead, the litmus test for the amounts spent by the states is (a) that the states generate and submit a plan to the U.S. Department of Health and Human Services providing a detailed plan for how the funds are to be used, (b) there must be "significant portions" spent on each of the programs as proposed by the plan, and (c) each activity has to pass the evaluation by the Secretary of the U.S. Department of Health and Human Services as required under Title IV-B, subpart 2. The key programs supported under this matching grant include fall under the two headings of family preservation services and family support services.[1]

TITLE IV-D OF SOCIAL SECURITY ACT: CHILD SUPPORT ENFORCEMENT AND PATERNITY ESTABLISHMENT PROGRAMS

For the purpose of enforcing the support obligations owed by noncustodial parents to their children and the spouse (or former spouse) with whom such children are living, locating noncustodial parents, establishing paternity, obtaining child and spousal support, and assuring that assistance in obtaining support will be available under this part to all children (whether or not eligible for assistance under a State program funded under part A) for whom such assistance is requested, there is hereby authorized to be appropriated for each fiscal year a sum sufficient to carry out the purposes of this part. (42 U.S.C. 651, §451)[2]

The rationales for this program are rather straightforward. First of all, parents should pay for the well-being of their children. Parents have a responsibility to provide for the happiness and health of children, to the best of their ability. Second of all, children make up a significant portion of the poor in the United States, and they would be substantially helped materially (even, maybe, out of poverty itself) if the noncustodial parent were to provide the support that he or she morally should be contributing or legally is required to give as child support.[3]

Title IV-D, the Child Support Enforcement and Paternity Establishment Program (CSE), is the result of Congress coming to the conclusion that there had been a demographic shift: by 1975 the majority of children needed aid not because their parents were deceased but because a substantial number of parents who left the home and the rising number of noncustodial/nonresidential parents after divorce (mostly men for both categories) that were not contributing their fair share of the upbringing of these children. CSE provides federal matching funds to allow states to have programs that would (1) locate these missing parents, (2) determine paternity, (3) establish appropriate child support awards, and (4) collect child support payments. Although states administer the program, the federal government plays a significant role in the design, funding, monitoring, and the providing of technical assistance at the state level. The federal effort is headed by a separate organizational unit within the Department of Health and Human Services, the Federal Office of Child Support Enforcement (OCSE). It is this office that sets the standards that states have to follow when administering these four services. The assistant secretary in charge of this office is also responsible for the evaluation of the entire program; states have to annually review and report for compliance purposes.

Parents needing any, some, or all of these four services can apply for assistance for a nominal fee unless they are a Temporary Assistance for Needy Families (TANF), Title IV-E, or Medicaid recipient. CSE, in particular, plays a major role in the way TANF provides assistance to its eligible beneficiaries. TANF now requires states to increase the percentage of known deadbeat parents, become part of national communications network that includes the location and asset of parents, utilize more enforcement techniques,[4] and revise the rules specific to the distribution of past due child support payments to former recipients of public assistance (United States House of Representatives, Committee on Ways and Means, 2000, section 8, 2/81). Moreover, TANF requires applicants and recipients to assign their support rights to the state in order to receive benefits, along with their cooperation in establishing paternity of those children born outside of wedlock.

Many states have statutes that allow them to provide child benefits under TANF with the understanding that the benefit is a debit that will be due by the parent or parents on a one-to-one basis. Other states follow the common law practice based on the notion that a father is obligated to reimburse "any person who has provided his child with food, shelter, clothing, medical attention, or education" (United States House of Representatives, Committee on Ways and Means, 2000, section 8, 15/81). For example, if an individual who is receiving unemployment is found to be delinquent in child support, that individual is subject to having a portion of the benefit withheld. Working deadbeat parents, once located, may have their wages garnished. In other instances, liens are placed against real property. Filing for bankruptcy does not provide the noncustodial/nonresidential parent with relief of the debt or payment. The overall effect is that money collected under this program will go to reimburse the states for benefits given and, if there is something left over, then these funds will be provided to the household that is owed the child support. The reason for this overall effect is that the federal government provides incentives to the states to collect as many funds as possible, not only to remain in compliance, but as a means of generating some additional revenue.

How well have these efforts worked? To quote from the *Green Book Report 2000* (United States House of Representatives, Committee on Ways and Means, 2000, section 8, 53/81):

> In 1995, about 30 percent of the 13.7 million women and men rearing children alone had incomes below the poverty level. By comparison, only 22 percent of the custodial parents who received child support payments had incomes below the poverty level (U.S. Census Bureau, 1999, p. 5). Thus, child support appears to be associated with a modest reduction in poverty. If the child support program could collect support for a substantial fraction of the additional 9 million single parents who did not receive payments in 1995, the antipoverty impact of the program could be substantially improved.

TITLE IV-E OF SOCIAL SECURITY ACT: FOSTER CARE PROGRAM

The Foster Care Program under Title IV-E is a permanent entitlement providing states with open-ended matching funds for the costs of maintaining children who meet eligibility criteria in foster care. Part of the funds can be used for child placement, program administration, and training. Even though AFDC was replaced by TANF, states are still required to certify that they will continue to operate a Foster Care Program along with an Adoption Assistance Program (see next section). Eligible children under IV-E are also deemed to be eligible for Medicaid. The eligibility criteria for a child to be placed in foster care and for the state to receive reimbursement are:

1. the child must have been removed from a family that would have been eligible for AFDC as the program existed on July 16, 1996;

2. removal and foster care placement was based on a voluntary agreement signed by the child's parents (or guardians) or as a result of a judicial determination that remaining in the home was contrary to the child's welfare;

3. reasonable efforts were made to eliminate the need for removal; and

4. care and placement of the child become the state's responsibility.

Foster care placement can be done in private or public institutions as long as these are licensed and/or approved foster family homes or childcare institutions (that can accommodate a maximum of 25 children).

States must align the protection of foster care children to some portions of their prepared state plan under Title IV-B. Compliance is enforced by Title IV-E, requiring specific goals and procedures to meet those goals for children who meet eligibility criteria and are to remain in foster care more than twenty-four months. A critical consideration impacting program approval and federal reimbursement is the determination of how well reasonable efforts are identified and pursued in determining the appropriateness of the need for foster care and the level of support given.

Title IV-E reimbursement for foster care maintenance payments is a state's Medicaid matching rate, a rate that is inversely related to the state's per capita income, creating a matching-rate range from between 50 percent and 83 percent. States can opt to claim an open-ended matching rate of 50 percent (for child placement services and administrative costs), and a matching rate of 75 percent for personnel training for those employed at the agencies administering the program and new foster parents.

TITLE IV-E OF SOCIAL SECURITY ACT: ADOPTION ASSISTANCE PROGRAM

The Adoption Assistance Program is a permanently authorized, open-ended entitlement program that, as indicated in the previous section, is required of states that participate in TANF.[5] This program funds three types of activities: assistance payments for children who are adopted and qualify for the benefit, administrative costs, and training costs for professional staff and parents involved in adoptions (United States House of Representatives, Committee on Ways and Means, 2000, section 11).

A significant component of this program is the development of written adoption assistance agreements with parents that adopt children who are eligible for AFDC or SSI benefits and who have recognized special needs. Furthermore, matching federal funds are given to states that reimburse the nonrecurring adoption expenses of those adopting these children without regard to AFDC or SSI eligibility.[6] States also have the option of providing Medicaid coverage for those special needs children that do not qualify for AFDC or SSI and are adopted under a state-funded adoption program.[7] Some states provide adoption assistance subsidies, with the type of

payment different according to their preference. Not all children receiving these subsidies are eligible for Title IV-E federal funds.

The amount of assistance that may be given depends on the needs of the child and the economic abilities of the adoptive parents. No means-test can be used to determine parent eligibility, although their income level is taken into consideration; payments can change periodically as circumstances change. For those families who receive payments, "the payments may not exceed the amount the family would receive on behalf of the child under foster care" (United States House of Representatives, Committee on Ways and Means, 2000, 23/93).

TITLE IV-E OF SOCIAL SECURITY ACT: ADOPTION INCENTIVES PROGRAMS

Title IV-E encompasses incentive programs to states to enhance the opportunities for adopting foster children and foster children with special needs via incentive payments. Payments under these programs "equal $4,000 for each foster child whose adoption is finalized (over a certain baseline) and an additional $2,000 for each special-needs child whose adoption is finalized (over the baseline)" (United States House of Representatives, Committee on Ways and Means, 2000, section 11, 27/93).

TITLE IV-E OF SOCIAL SECURITY ACT: FOSTER CARE INDEPENDENCE PROGRAM

The Foster Care Independence Program is a capped entitlement program to help youth that eventually are to be emancipated from the foster care system when they attained adult status by turning age 18. This program is in response to data suggesting that many of the homeless youth found throughout the country seem to be the result of being let go of foster care. As Dobelstein (1996) found out, during the early 1990s, more than 75 percent of children in substitutive care had been there for two or more years, 60 percent had special needs, 39 percent were black, and 69 percent were more than 6 years old.

The program allows participating states to provide transitional independent living services to all youth in foster care who are between the ages of 16 and 18, and it applies to all foster care age youth regardless of whether or not they are Title IV-E eligible. It also provides follow-up services for up to 6 months after their emancipation from this form of care. States have the option of extending the independent living services and Medicaid coverage to former foster children up to age 21. To qualify, states have to submit a five-year plan which certifies that no more than 30 percent of program funds will be used for room and board for those in the 18- to 20-year-old bracket (United States House of Representatives, Committee on Ways and Means, 2000, section 11). The remainder of the funds is for juvenile delinquency programs, abstinence education, housing programs, programs for disabled youth, and school-to-work activities.

States have the flexibility to use these funds in meeting the generally stated purposes in the law. These overarching purposes include helping "eligible children make a transition to self-sufficiency through such services" as (United States House of Representatives, Committee on Ways and Means, 2000, section 11, 30/93):

- obtaining a high school diploma,
- career exploration,
- vocational training,
- job placement and retention,
- training in daily living skills,
- training in budgeting and financial management,
- substance abuse prevention, and
- preventive health services.

State success is measured by a series of outcome measures determined by the Secretary of Health and Human Services in the areas of educational attainment, the number of high school diplomas earned, employment, avoidance of dependency, homelessness rate for this age group, illegitimate births, incarceration, and high-risk behaviors.

TITLE XX OF SOCIAL SECURITY ACT: SOCIAL SERVICES BLOCK GRANTS (SSBG)

Title XX is a categorical aid-to-state programs by which the federal government provides incentives to states to enhance their social service systems to eligible individuals (see Chambers, 1986). This program is a capped entitlement program where the share each state receives is based on a formula that is statutorily defined. The formula represents a national funding ceiling which, in effect, caps how much money is available a priori for any given year. The funds are distributed in a block grant structure that allows states a wide discretion in terms of eligibility, disbursement amounts, programming, and administration, as long as these comply with the overall federal guideline requirements.

The purpose for the block grant is to allow each state to identify, pursue, and achieve a wide variety of social policies:

- Achieving or maintaining economic self-support to prevent, reduce, or eliminate dependency.

- Achieving or maintaining self-sufficiency, including the reduction or prevention of dependency.

- Preventing or remedying neglect, abuse, or exploitation of children and adults unable to protect their own interests, or preserving, rehabilitating or reuniting families.

- Preventing or reducing inappropriate institutional home care by providing for community-based care, home-based care, or other forms of less intensive care.

- Securing referral or admission for institutional care when other forms of care are not appropriate, or providing services to individuals in institutions (U.S. House of Representatives, Committee on Ways and Means 2000, section 10, 3/9).

Furthermore, the law creating Title XX allows the states authority to transfer up to 10 percent of the block grant annual allotment to one or up to all three of the three health care block grant programs[8] and the Low-Income Home Energy Assistance Program (please refer to chapter 8) (7/9). State participation is optional under Title XX because states are not required to provide any services; however, when they do, more than half of the states that provide services by using SSBG funds go directly or indirectly to children (Dobelstein, 1996).

Part of the welfare reform process undertaken by the passage the Personal Responsibility and Work Opportunity Reconciliation Act of 1996 (PRWORA) authorizes states to transfer a certain percentage of their state's TANF to Title XX or to the Child Care and Development Grant programs (please refer to chapter 8). Beginning in 2001, the entitlement is defined at $1.7 billion. From 2001 onwards, although states can transfer as much as 30 percent from TANF to Title XX, according to legislation passed in 1998,[9] the actual percent amount that can be transferred is 4.25 percent.

The best source of information for this data, interestingly enough is going to be the materials available at the state levels through the programs that work with TANF. For example, the state of Minnesota's experiment with the one-stop work center provide documentation of some of the "cutting edge efforts" in the area of childcare activities for parents receiving benefits under TANF and Title IV programs. The next best source of information is the *Green Book Report 2000* by the U.S. House of Representatives' Committee on Ways and Means. But for the most current information it is best to go to the TANF and Social Security Web sites, where some of the data is available with only a modicum of work on the researcher's part. A Web site that provides excellent links to many studies, statistics, and other publications is the U.S. Department of Health and Human Services Administration for Children and Families' National Child Care Information Network (http://nccic.org). Some significant works that are the basis for the analysis in this and the previous chapter are the U.S. Department of Health and Human Services, Office of the Assistant Secretary for Planning and Evaluation's report, *Trends in the Well-Being of America's Children and Youth 2000,* and the Center for Impact Research's study, *Knocking on the Door: Barriers to Welfare and Other Assistance for Teen Parents—A Three-City Research Study.*

All other chapters in this book provide a table describing what other countries provide in the social safety net for particular populations; please refer to these tables to make basic linkages to what is available in the area of child welfare. An excellent resource for information on government activities is the United Nations Development Programme series of *Human Development Reports*, with many of the key indicators already available in other chapters throughout this book. Another good source of information is the World Bank's *World Development Report 2000/2001.* Other good sources for international data can be found in the International Clearinghouse on International Developments in Child, Youth, and Family Policies at the Columbia University Web site, as well as the European Union Social Indicator Web pages (as indicated in earlier chapters).

NOTES

1. Please see the glossary for a description of these programs.

2. Retrieved from: http://www.ssa.gov/OP_Home/ssact/title04/0451.htm.

3. Data suggests that at least half of those children born in the late 1970s and early 1980s will live with a single parent prior to reaching adulthood, and for black children, the number is estimated to increase to about 80 percent. Poverty seems to be endemic among single-mothers who are heads of households: 38.7 percent of 8.9 million such households with children under 18 had incomes below the poverty threshold and around 16 percent of these families remained poor even with the mother working full-time (see United States House of Representatives, Committee on Ways and Means, 2000, section 8, 3/81).

4. Enforcement tools include, but may not be limited to the following (United States House of Representatives, Committee on Ways and Means, 2000, section 8, 8/81):

1. Imposing liens against real and personal property for amounts of overdue support;

2. Withholding State tax refunds payable to a parent who is delinquent in support payments;

3. Reporting the amount of overdue support to a consumer credit bureau upon request;

4. Requiring individuals who have demonstrated a pattern of delinquent payments to post a bond or give some other guarantee to secure payment of overdue support;

5. Establishing expedited processes within the State judicial system or under administrative processes for obtaining and enforcing child support orders and determining paternity. These expedited procedures include giving States authority to secure assets to satisfy payment of past-due support by seizing or attaching unemployment compensation, workers' compensation, judgments, settlements, lotteries, asset held in financial institutions, and public and private retirement funds;

6. Withholding, suspending, or restricting the use of driver's licenses, professional and occupational licenses, and recreational and sporting licenses of noncustodial parents who owe past-due support;

7. Denying passports to persons owing more than $5,000 in past-due support;

8. Requiring unemployed noncustodial parents who owe child support to a child receiving TANF benefits to participate in appropriate work activities;

9. Performing quarterly data matches with financial institutions; and

10. Voiding of fraudulent transfers of assets to avoid payment of child support.

11. Other tools can include the use of ITS tax refund to offset procedure for welfare and non-welfare families, and determine if any individuals receiving unemployment compensation owe child support.

5. For a more detailed discussion of TANF, please refer to chapter 7 in this book.

6. This may include a reimbursement of up to $2,000 per child from the federal government, with the state claiming up to 50 percent of these payments.

7. The Adoption and Safe Families Act requires states to provide health insurance coverage through Medicaid or other program with comparable benefits for when special needs children incur medical, mental health, or rehabilitative care costs.

8. The three health care block grants are the preventive Health and Health Services Block Grant; the Maternal and Child Health Services Block Grant; and the Alcohol, Drug Abuse, and Mental Health Services Block Grant.

9. In provisions included in the Transportation Equity Act of 1998.

PRINCIPAL SOURCES FOR ILLUSTRATIONS

Columbia University. (2003). *Poverty rates in nineteen rich countries, by age group.* The International Clearinghouse on International Developments in Child, Youth and Family Policies Web site. Retrieved from: http://www.childpolicyintl.org/contexttablespublicsector/table222.pdf.

Grogger, J, Karoly, L.A., and Klerman, J.A. (2002). *Consequences of welfare reform: A research synthesis.* (Report #: DRU-2676-DHHS). Washington, D.C.: Administration for Children and Families. Retrieved from: http://www.acf.dhhs.gov/programs/opre/welfare_reform/rand_report.pdf.

Shapiro, D.L., and Marcy, H.M. (April 2002). *Knocking on the door: Barriers to welfare and other assistance for teen parents—A three-city research study.* Chicago: Center for Impact Research. Retrieved from: http://www.impactresearch.org/documents/cirknockdoor.pdf

United States House of Representatives, Committee on Ways and Means. (2000). *The 2000 Green Book: Background material and data on programs within the jurisdiction of the Committee on Ways and Means.* Retrieved from: http://aspe.hhs.gov/2000gh.

World Bank (2001). *World development report 2000/2001: Attacking poverty.* Washington, D.C.: Author. Retrieved from: http://www.worldbank.org/poverty/wdrpoverty/report/index.htm

BIBLIOGRAPHY

Ashcroft, J. (1995). *Which will survive: The welfare state or the Republican revolution?* Heritage Foundation Lecture #539. Retrieved from: http://www.heritage.org/Research/Welfare/index.cfm.

Ashe, N. (2002). Adoption and special care glossary. *What you need to know about adoption web-site.* Retrieved from: http://adoption.about.com/library/glossary/bldef-specneeds.htm.

Chambers, D.E. (1986). *Social policy and social programs: A method for the practical public policy analyst.* New York: Macmillan Press.

DiNitto, D.M., and Dye, T.R. (1987). *Social welfare: Politics and public policy.* 2nd ed. Englewood Cliffs, NJ: Prentice Hall.

Dobelstein, A.W. (1996). *Social welfare: Policy and analysis.* Chicago: Nelson-Hall Publishers.

'Lectric Law Library. (2002). *'Lectric Law Lexicon Web site.* Retrieved from: http://www.lectlaw.com/def/g003.htm.

Lovejoy, O.R. (1907/2001). Child labor in the soft coal mines. *Child labor and the republic.* New York: National Child Labor

Committee. BoondocksNet Edition, 2001 retrieved August 1, 2003 from: http://www.boondocksnet.com/editions/clr/.

Oklahoma State Legislature. Definition of therapeutic foster care. *Revised statutes*. Retrieved from: http://www.policy.okdhs .org/ch75/Chapter_75-8/340-75-8/340_75-8-5._Definition_ of_therapeutic_foster_care.htm.

Schwartz, J.E., and Volgy, T.J. (1992). *The forgotten Americans*. New York: W.W. Norton and Company.

United States House of Representatives, Committee on Ways and Means. (2000). *The 2000 Green Book: Background material and data on programs within the jurisdiction of the Committee on Ways and Means*. Retrieved from: http://aspe.hhs .gov/2000gh.

United States Printing Office. (November 20, 2001). Section D: Administrative Wage Garnishment. *Federal Register*, vol. 66 (224), p. 58061.

Table 10.1
Impact of U.S. Welfare Reform as a Whole and Specific Reform Policies on Various Outcomes

Policy or Policy Bundle	Welfare Use (A)	Employment (B)	Earnings (C)	Food Stamps (D)	Medicaid (E)	Marriage (F)	Fertility (G)	Income (H)	Poverty (I)	Food Security (J)	Children's Health Coverage (K)	Savings (L)
(1) Financial Work Incentives	INCREASE	INCREASE	*	*	*	INCREASE		INCREASE	DECREASE	INCREASE	INCREASE	INCREASE
(2) Financial Work Incentives Tied to Hours Worked	INCREASE §	INCREASE	INCREASE	INCREASE		*		INCREASE	DECREASE	INCREASE		INCREASE
(3) Mandatory Work-related Activities	DECREASE	INCREASE	INCREASE	DECREASE	DECREASE	NO CHANGE	NO CHANGE	MIXED	DECREASE	DECREASE	DECREASE	
(4) Sanctions for non-compliance	DECREASE											
(5) Mandatory Work-Related Activities and Strong Financial Work Incentives	INCREASE	INCREASE	INCREASE	DECREASE	MIXED	*		INCREASE	DECREASE	*	INCREASE	*
(6) Mandatory Work-Related Activities and Weak Financial Work Incentives	DECREASE	INCREASE	INCREASE	DECREASE	DECREASE			INCREASE		*	DECREASE	
(7) Time Limits (Before Recipients Reach Limit)	DECREASE	INCREASE	*				*	*				
(8) Time Limits (After Recipients Reach Limit)	DECREASE	MIXED	*	*				*				*
(9) Family Cap	MIXED				*		MIXED					
(10) Parental Responsibility							*					
(11) Reform as a Bundle (Before Recipients Reach Time Limits)	DECREASE	INCREASE	INCREASE	DECREASE	MIXED	MIXED	MIXED	INCREASE	DECREASE	*	*	*

Policy or Policy Bundle	Child Abuse and Neglect (all ages) (M)	Preschool Age at Follow-Up			Grade School Age at Follow-Up			Adolescents at Follow-Up		
		Behavior Problems (N)	School Achievement Problems (O)	Health Problems (P)	Behavior Problems (Q)	School Achievement Problems (R)	Health Problems (S)	Behavior Problems (T)	School Achievement Problems (U)	Health Problems (V)
(1) Financial Work Incentives					DECREASE	MIXED	INCREASE	INCREASE	*	
(2) Financial Work Incentives Tied to Hours Worked		*	*	*	*	DECREASE	DECREASE	INCREASE	MIXED	*
(3) Mandatory Work-related Activities	*	MIXED	MIXED	MIXED	MIXED	MIXED	DECREASE	MIXED	INCREASE	MIXED
(4) Sanctions for non-compliance	*									
(5) Mandatory Work-Related Activities and Strong Financial Work Incentives					DECREASE	DECREASE	INCREASE	INCREASE	INCREASE	
(6) Mandatory Work-Related Activities and Weak Financial Work Incentives	*							*	*	
(7) Time Limits (Before Recipients Reach Limit)	*									
(8) Time Limits (After Recipients Reach Limit)										
(9) Family Cap	*									
(10) Parental Responsibility				*			DECREASE			
(11) Reform as a Bundle (Before Recipients Reach Time Limits)	*				MIXED	*	DECREASE	MIXED	INCREASE	*

LEGEND

DIRECTION	DIRECTION	DIRECTION	
Much evidence	Some evidence	Little evidence	No evidence

Knowledge base:

Notes: * Cell has up to three moderate or high-quality studies with no significant impacts or a single moderate-quality study with a significant impact.

§ These programs increase the sum of welfare payments and the earnings supplement provided outside the welfare system, although welfare payments per se may decrease.

Source: Grogger, J., Karoly, L.A., & Klerman, J.A. (2002). *Consequences of welfare reform: A research synthesis.* Report #: DRU-2676-DHHS. Washington, D.C.: Administration for Children and Families. Retrieved from http://www.acf.dhhs.gov/programs/opre/welfare_reform/rand_report.pdf.

Table 10.2

Federal Funding for Child Welfare, Foster Care, and Adoption Activities Under Titles IV-B and IV-E of the Social Security Act, Under Current Law: 1989 to 2005

(in Millions of Dollars)

Fiscal year	Title IV-B-1 Child Welfare Services Program	Title IV-B-2 Promoting Safe and Stable Families[1] Program	Total[2]	Title IV-E foster care State claims		Title IV-E Independent Living Program	Title IV-E adoption assistance State claims			Total
				Maintenance payments	Administration/ training[3]		Total[4]	Assistance payments	Administration/ training	
1989	$247	(5)	$1,153	$646	$507	$45	$111	$86	$24	$1,555
1990	253	(5)	1,473	835	638	50	136	105	31	1,912
1991	274	(5)	1,819	1,030	789	60	175	130	45	2,328
1992	274	(5)	2,233	1,204	1,029	70	220	161	58	2,796
1993	295	(5)	2,534	1,312	1,222	70	272	198	74	3,171
1994	295	60	2,750	1,371	1,375	70	347	249	98	3,522
1995	292	150	3,066	1,599	1,467	70	411	306	105	3,989
1996	277	225	3,098	1,503	1,595	70	483	361	122	4,153
1997	292	240	3,692	1,725	1,967	70	590	429	161	4,884
1998	292	255	3,714	1,932	1,782	70	697	512	185	5,027
1999 \6\	292	275	4,011	1,963	2,048	70	843	621	222	5,491
2000 (estimate)	292	295	4,398	2,120	2,278	105[7]	991	730	261	6,081
2001 (estimate)	292	305	5,013	2,384	2,629	140	1,161	856	305	6,911
2002 (estimate)	292	(8)	5,426	2,580	2,846	140	1,358	1,000	358	7,216
2003 (estimate)	292	(8)	5,759	2,781	2,978	140	1,575	1,160	415	7,766
2004 (estimate)	292	(8)	6,214	2,998	3,216	140	1,810	1,333	477	8,456
2005 (estimate)	292	(8)	6,702	3,231	3,471	140	2,079	1,531	548	9,213

1. In fiscal years 1998 and 1999, $16 and $18 million, respectively, lapsed.

2. Total includes administration, Statewide Automated Child Welfare Information System (SACWIS), and training expenditures, as well as maintenance payments.

3. Includes regular administration, SACWIS costs, child placement costs, and training.

4. Total includes administration and training expenditures and assistance payments. Differences in total due to rounding.

5. The IV-B-2 program did not begin operation until 1994.

6. Beginning in fiscal year 1999, title IV-E foster care and adoption assistance State claims data include Puerto Rico.

7. Does not include additional $35 million requested through a supplemental budget request.

8. Not authorised.

Note: Totals may differ from sum of amounts because of rounding.

Source: United States House of Representatives, Committee on Ways and Means. (2000). *The 2000 Green Book: Background material and data on programs within the jurisdiction of the Committee on Ways and Means.* Retrieved from http://aspe.hhs.gov/2000gb/sec11.txt.

Table 10.3
Participation in Child Welfare, Foster Care, and Adoption Activities Under Titles IV-B and IV-E of the Social Security Act, Under Current Law: 1988 to 2004

Fiscal year	Title IV-B-1 Child Welfare Services Program	Title IV-B-2 Promoting Safe and Stable Families Program	Title IV-E foster care assistance payments[1]	Title IV-E Independent Living Program[2]	Title IV-E adoption assistance payments[1]
1988..	NA	(3)	132,757	18,931	34,698
1989..	NA	(3)	156,871	44,191	40,666
1990..	NA	(3)	167,981	44,365	44,024
1991..	NA	(3)	202,687	45,284	54,818
1992..	NA	(3)	222,315	57,360	66,197
1993..	NA	(3)	231,100	57,918	78,000
1994..	NA	NA	245,000	71,081	91,200
1995..	NA	NA	260,800	73,137	106,200
1996..	NA	NA	273,600	85,261	124,700
1997..	NA	NA	289,400	84,309	146,900
1998..	NA	NA	306,500	87,446	168,400
1999[4]..	NA	NA	302,422	NA	195,243
2000 (estimated)............................	NA	NA	319,300	NA	223,900
2001 (estimated)............................	NA	NA	341,700	NA	256,400
2002 (estimated)............................	NA	(5)	357,100	NA	292,200
2003 (estimated)............................	NA	(5)	371,400	NA	330,200
2004 (estimated)............................	NA	(5)	386,300	NA	369,900

1. Average monthly number of recipients.
2. Estimated.
3. The IV-B-2 program did not begin operation until 1994.
4. Beginning in fiscal year 1999, data for average monthly number of recipients include Puerto Rico.
5. The IV-B-2 program is only authorised through 2001.
NA: Not available.

Source: United States House of Representatives, Committee on Ways and Means. (2000). *The 2000 Green Book: Background material and data on programs within the jurisdiction of the Committee on Ways and Means.* Retrieved from http://aspe.hhs.gov/2000gb/sec11.txt.

Table 10.4

Congressional Business Office (CBO) Baseline Projections for the Federal Foster Care and Adoption Assistance Programs: Fiscal Years 2000 to 2005

(in Millions of Dollars)

Program	2000	2001	2002	2003	2004	2005
Foster Care:						
Title IV-E caseload (in thousands)	314	325	334	342	349	356
Average monthly maintenance payments (Federal share)	$545	$564	$584	$605	$626	$648
Federal outlays (in millions of dollars):						
Maintenance payments	2,034	2,174	2,318	2,459	2,599	2,744
Administrative and child placement services	1,899	2,025	2,154	2,282	2,407	2,538
Training	206	218	230	241	253	264
Total outlays	4,139	4,417	4,702	4,983	5,259	5,546
Adoption Assistance:						
Title IV-E caseload (in thousands)	218	242	267	292	318	345
Average monthly payments (Federal share)	273	283	293	303	314	325
Federal outlays (in millions of dollars):						
Assistance payments	705	807	920	1,044	1,178	1,325
Administrative and child placement services	210	235	263	292	323	356
Training	39	44	49	55	62	69
Total outlays	953	1,086	1,232	1,391	1,564	1,750
Independent Living:						
Total outlays	70	123	140	140	140	140
Total outlays	5,171	5,625	6,074	6,514	6,962	7,436

Note: Numbers may not add to totals due to rounding.

Source: United States House of Representatives, Committee on Ways and Means. (2000). *The 2000 Green Book: Background material and data on programs within the jurisdiction of the Committee on Ways and Means.* Retrieved from http://aspe.hhs.gov/2000gb/sec11.txt.

Table 10.5
State-by-State Allocations for Title IV-B (Subpart 1) Child Welfare
Services: Selected Years 1989 to 2000

(in Thousands of Dollars)

State	1989 actual	1991 actual	1994 actual	1996 actual	1997 actual	1998 actual	1999 actual	2000 allotments
Alabama	$5,136	$5,634	$5,623	$5,106	$5,327	$5,244	$5,198	$5,250
Alaska	294	561	754	725	749	776	787	817
American Samoa	163	175	193	183	188	187	186	185
Arizona	3,797	4,307	5,034	5,015	5,466	5,291	5,752	5,764
Arkansas	3,095	3,369	3,424	3,178	3,359	3,349	3,213	3,301
California	23,100	26,521	31,732	31,049	32,760	33,893	34,075	34,160
Colorado	3,091	3,482	3,866	3,719	3,935	3,959	4,009	3,857
Connecticut	2,143	2,123	2,120	2,052	2,154	2,075	2,050	1,885
Delaware	654	716	726	713	756	688	689	701
District of Columbia	432	469	447	345	346	333	327	319
Florida	10,361	11,771	13,146	12,781	13,708	13,806	13,930	14,210
Georgia	7,301	8,002	8,426	8,032	8,502	8,479	8,584	8,679
Guam	342	375	351	329	340	338	336	335
Hawaii	1,119	1,247	1,204	1,117	1,179	1,207	1,189	1,196
Idaho	1,388	1,576	1,703	1,622	1,736	1,753	1,760	1,766
Illinois	10,773	11,488	11,773	11,067	11,684	11,633	11,663	11,556
Indiana	6,064	6,677	6,952	6,367	6,697	6,613	6,575	6,604
Iowa	3,074	3,223	3,475	3,223	3,358	3,310	3,318	3,290
Kansas	2,461	2,779	3,068	2,873	3,011	3,001	2,996	3,055
Kentucky	4,556	4,934	5,030	4,624	4,842	4,806	4,752	4,647
Louisiana	5,657	6,368	6,527	5,910	6,195	6,015	5,824	5,842
Maine	1,391	1,477	1,482	1,378	1,432	1,443	1,428	1, 406
Maryland	3,798	4,074	4,343	4,156	4,358	4,453	4,386	4,457
Massachusetts	4,418	4,498	4,708	4,579	4,792	4,624	4,681	4,627
Michigan	9,551	10,047	10,885	10,075	10,487	10,118	10,130	10,178
Minnesota	4,206	4,537	5,092	4,785	5,022	4,913	4,915	4,704
Mississippi	3,923	4,244	4,293	3,949	4,146	4,051	4,019	4,016
Missouri	5,235	5,654	6,146	5,727	5,998	6,055	6,078	6,066
Montana	1,049	1,125	1,207	1,158	1,203	1,201	1,183	1,176
Nebraska	1,744	2,087	2,071	1,879	1,968	1,991	1,995	2,002
Nevada	964	1,123	1,401	1,379	1,516	1,625	1,711	1,786
New Hampshire	1,024	498	1,087	1,096	1,152	1,137	1,135	1,134
New Jersey	5,465	5,412	5,224	5,368	5,669	5,679	5,542	5,718
New Mexico	2,072	2,282	2,510	2,418	2,541	2,530	2,511	2,535
New York	14,373	15,245	15,452	14,148	14,808	14,817	14,767	14,539
North Carolina	7,189	7,916	8,112	7,728	8,229	8,179	8,291	8,440
North Dakota	849	908	945	858	891	893	874	862
Northern Marianas	118	124	142	136	139	138	138	137
Ohio	10,429	12,195	12,878	11,853	12,386	11,996	11,901	11,397
Oklahoma	3,735	4,114	4,406	4,133	4,310	4,325	4,295	4,316
Oregon	2,850	3,162	3,556	3,321	3,531	3,582	3,580	3,594
Pennsylvania	11,236	12,011	12,148	11,076	11,583	11,515	11,350	11,347
Puerto Rico	3,674	7,100	8,105	7,480	7,787	7,722	7,662	7,631
Rhode Island	953	1,032	1,054	984	1,012	993	986	1,007
South Carolina	4,468	4,876	4,948	4,544	4,696	4,613	4,670	4,682
South Dakota	938	1,015	1,075	991	1,029	1,028	1,001	1,023
Tennessee	5,598	6,137	6,210	5,792	6,100	5,959	5,946	5,937
Texas	18,958	21,476	23,795	22,401	23,783	23,889	24,264	24,511
Utah	2,891	3,192	3,474	3,284	3,469	3,475	3,519	3,561
Vermont	583	717	715	674	703	710	701	685
Virginia	5,463	5,905	6,373	6,114	6,408	6,444	6,459	6,458
Virgin Islands	295	310	280	263	271	269	268	267
Washington	4,382	4,968	5,699	5,231	5,512	5,679	5,725	5,804
West Virginia	2,397	2,519	2,486	2,189	2,251	2,243	2,183	2,157
Wisconsin	5,077	5,442	6,022	5,574	5,854	5,742	5,729	5,748
Wyoming	382	689	724	638	661	671	662	659
Total	246,679	273,907	294,624	277,389	291,989	291,458	291,896	291,986

Note: Totals may differ from sum of state amounts due to rounding.

Source: United States House of Representatives, Committee on ways and Means. (2000). *The 2000 Green Book: Background material and data on programs within the jurisdiction of the Committee on Ways and Means.* Retrieved from http://aspe.hhs .gov/2000gb/sec11.txt.

Table 10.6
Title IV-B Promoting Safe and Stable Families[1]
Program: State-by-State Allocations

State	Fiscal year 1997 actual	Fiscal year 1998 actual	Fiscal year 1999 actual	2000 allotments
Alabama	$4,298,428	$4,587,680	$4,998,474	$5,467,218
Alaska	343,874	389,953	447,625	529,555
American Samoa	159,031	164,480	171,567	179,043
Arizona	4,126,491	4,495,927	4,774,662	5,070,424
Arkansas	2,106,230	2,202,087	2,412,199	2,716,339
California	29,852,578	33,398,317	37,749,671	40,544,805
Colorado	2,256,675	2,247,963	2,362,463	2,496,711
Connecticut	1,805,340	1,995,641	2,138,651	2,349,394
Delaware	451,335	481,706	522,229	586,057
District of Columbia	752,225	825,782	920,117	1,031,541
Florida	11,691,723	12,203,230	13,105,452	14,020,393
Georgia	6,297,197	6,766,829	7,559,881	8,335,896
Guam	274,029	286,517	302,757	319,890
Hawaii	773,717	894,598	1,019,589	1,222,967
Idaho	623,272	688,152	746,041	812,739
Illinois	8,682,824	9,404,745	10,046,684	11,393,553
Indiana	3,890,077	3,945,405	3,978,885	3,909,002
Iowa	1,504,450	1,536,873	1,641,290	1,760,182
Kansas	1,396,989	1,513,935	1,666,158	1,811,435
Kentucky	3,696,648	3,738,960	4,003,753	4,411,229
Louisiana	6,447,642	6,468,629	6,888,444	7,195,319
Maine	924,162	940,474	969,853	1,066,598
Maryland	3,030,392	3,303,130	3,680,469	4,079,010
Massachusetts	3,632,171	3,784,836	3,978,885	4,149,338
Michigan	7,995,076	8,349,578	8,952,491	9,485,814
Minnesota	2,600,549	2,752,608	2,934,428	2,998,745
Mississippi	4,019,030	4,197,728	4,327,037	4,532,892
Missouri	4,470,365	4,748,249	5,172,550	5,577,218
Montana	515,811	550,522	646,569	714,863
Nebraska	924,162	963,413	1,019,589	1,078,461
Nevada	752,225	848,721	920,117	1,049,293
New Hampshire	429,843	481,706	497,361	523,548
New Jersey	4,212,459	4,541,804	5,147,682	5,616,230
New Mexico	1,934,292	2,064,456	2,262,991	2,485,020
New York	15,237,926	(2)	(2)	(2)
North Carolina	4,814,239	5,069,387	5,520,703	6,068,954
North Dakota	343,874	344,076	348,152	379,765
Northern Marianas	121,935	125,114	129,247	133,608
Ohio	9,499,525	9,634,129	9,972,080	10,110,000
Oklahoma	2,750,994	3,004,931	3,232,844	3,490,646
Oregon	2,041,753	2,225,025	2,437,067	2,631,579
Pennsylvania	8,489,395	8,854,223	9,574,192	10,468,059
Puerto Rico	5,901,525	6,258,461	6,722,614	7,212,312
Rhode Island	752,225	825,782	895,249	989,602
South Carolina	3,116,360	3,349,007	3,556,128	3,927,057
South Dakota	429,843	458,768	472,493	533,640
Tennessee	5,287,066	5,551,093	5,669,911	5,999,983
Texas	21,169,757	22,892,526	24,793,426	26,985,190
Utah	1,096,099	1,123,982	1,143,929	1,225,329
Vermont	429,843	458,768	522,229	536,382
Virginia	3,933,061	4,404,173	4,874,134	5,300,937
Virgin Islands	222,094	231,404	243,510	256,282
Washington	3,481,726	3,830,713	4,351,905	4,833,043
West Virginia	2,493,088	2,523,224	2,287,859	2,486,708
Wisconsin	2,836,962	2,959,054	3,158,240	3,270,921
Wyoming	279,398	298,199	323,284	349,572
Subtotal	221,600,000	220,186,673	238,195,810	276,050,000
Set-asides:				
Indians (1 percent)	2,400,000	2,550,000	2,750,000	2,950,000
Research and evaluation	6,000,000	6,000,000	5,953,061	6,000,000
Courts	10,000,000	10,000,000	10,000,000	10,000,000
Subtotal	18,400,000	18,550,000	18,703,061	18,950,000
Lapsed funds	0	16,263,327	18,057,129	19,339,709
Total	240,000,000	255,000,000	274,956,000	295,000,000

1. The name of this program was changed from Family Preservation and Family Support in 1997 by Public Law 105–89.

2. New York did not apply for its allotment for these years; as a result, their funds lapsed.

Note: Totals may differ from sum of state amounts because of rounding.

Source: United States House of Representatives, Committee on Ways and Means. (2000). *The 2000 Green Book: Background material and data on programs within the jurisdiction of the Committee on Ways and Means.* Retrieved from http://aspe.hhs.gov/2000gb/sec11.txt.

Table 10.7
Foster Care Basic Monthly Maintenance Rates for Children Ages 2, 9, and 16:
Selected Years 1987 to 1998

	Age 2				Age 9				Age 16			
	1987	1991	1994	1998	1987	1991	1994	1998	1987	1991	1994	1998
Alabama	$168	$181	$205	$230rsc	$188	$202	$229	$254rsc	$198	$213	$241	$266rsc
Alaska[1]	428	561	588	652rsc	478	499	523	580rsc	565	592	621	689rsc
Arizona	223	247	297	403rs[2]	223	247	286	392rs[2]	282	305	365	471rs[2]
Arkansas	175	195	300	400rc	190	210	325	425rc	220	240	375	475rc
California	294	345	345	375rsc	340	400	400	436rsc	412	484	484	528rsc
Colorado	235	296	319	361rc[2]	266	296	319	361rc[2]	318	352	379	430rc[2]
Connecticut[1]	268	386	567	622rsc	302	424	586	642rsc	350	478	637	708rsc
Delaware[3]	264	301	342	410rsc	266	304	342	410rsc	342	1	440	511rsc
District of Columbia	304	304	431	445rsc	304	304	431	445rsc	317	317	519	536rsc
Florida	233	296	296	345rsc	233	296	296	355rsc	293	372	372	425rsc
Georgia[1]	300	300	300	338rsc	300	300	300	338rsc	300	300	300	338rsc
Hawaii	194	529	529	529rs[2]	233	529	529	529rs[2]	301	529	529	529rs[2]
Idaho	138	198	228	228rs	165	205	250	250rs	204	278	338	358rs
Illinois	233	268	322	343rsc	259	299	358	382rsc	282	325	390	415rsc
Indiana[4]	226	281	405	486rsc	245	330	462	536rsc	280	398	518	603rsc
Iowa	159	198	328	387rsc	201	243	342	409rsc	285	300	405	474rsc
Kansas	187	304	205	305rs[2]	245	304	277	305rs[2]	280	386	351	386rs[2]
Kentucky	248	265	263	375rsc	263	288	285	350rsc	300	333	330	398rsc
Louisiana	199	283	298	348rc[2]	232	316	331	331rc[2]	265	349	364	364rc[2]
Maine	244	296	296	325r[2]	250	304	304	334r[2]	291	353	353	389r[2]
Maryland	285	535	535	535rsc	285	535	535	535rsc	303	550	550	535rsc
Massachusetts	362	410	410	448rs	362	410	410	464rs	433	486	486	515rs
Michigan[5]	315	332	383	398rsc	315	332	383	398rsc	395	416	454	493rsc
Minnesota[1]	285	341	377	458rsc	285	341	377	458rsc	375	442	487	561rsc
Mississippi	130	145	175	225rc[2]	150	165	205	255rc[2]	160	175	250	300rc[2]
Missouri	174	209	212	316rs	212	255	259	364rs	232	281	286	392rs
Montana	283	307	330	345rs[2]	283	307	330	345rs[2]	354	384	416	435rs[2]
Nebraska	210	222	326	326rs[2]	210	291	394	393rs[2]	210	351	461	463rs[2]
Nevada	275	281	281	304rs[2]	275	281	281	304rs[2]	330	337	337	365rs[2]
New Hampshire	200	200	314	314rs[2]	251	251	342	342rs[2]	354	354	404	404rs[2]
New Jersey	203	244	272	294rs	215	259	288	312rs	253	305	340	368rs
New Mexico	236	258	308	308rs[2]	247	270	341	341rs[2]	259	281	367	367rs[2]
New York	312	353	367	367rs[2]	375	424	441	441rs[2]	434	490	510	510rs[2]
New York City	342	386	401	401rs[2]	403	455	473	473rs[2]	465	526	547	547rs[2]
North Carolina	215	265	315	315rs	215	265	365	365rs	215	265	415	415rs
North Dakota	240	260	265	317rsc	287	312	318	359rsc	345	416	424	469rsc
Ohio[6]	240	289	413	603rsc	270	328	413	603rsc	300	366	413	603rsc
Oklahoma	300	300	300	300rsc	360	360	360	360rsc	420	420	420	420rsc
Oregon	200	285	315	356rsc	234	295	327	370rsc	316	363	404	457rsc
Pennsylvania	558	303	315	312rc[2]	558	319	368	375rc[2]	558	377	473	482rc[2]
Rhode Island[7]	223	274	279	308rs	223	274	279	285rs	275	335	341	348rs
South Carolina	138	182	212	212rsc	158	209	239	239rsc	208	275	305	305rsc
South Dakota	188	237	259	353rsc	230	291	317	353rsc	276	349	382	424rsc
Tennessee	139	255	336	336rs	190	226	262	262rs	224	267	385	385rs
Texas	243	420	476	482rs[2]	243	420	476	482rs[2]	274	420	476	482rs[2]
Utah[1]	198	300	300	326rsc	198	300	300	326rsc	225	300	300	326rsc
Vermont	210	371	416	360rsc	249	371	416	360rsc	268	447	504	440rsc
Virginia	193	246	256	270rs	244	288	300	316rs	309	365	379	400rs
Washington	184	270	292	338rsc	227	332	359	410rsc	268	392	425	481rsc
West Virginia	161	161	161	400rsc	202	202	202	400rsc	242	242	242	400rsc

Table 10.7 (*continued*)

Wisconsin	163	231	276	289rsc	224	257	301	315rsc	284	324	361	374rsc
Wyoming	300	400	400	400rsc	300	400	400	400rsc	330	400	400	400rsc
Average monthly rates	239	294	329	NA	263	314	350	NA	307	365	407	NA

1. These States provided daily regular foster care maintenance rates which were converted to monthly rates using the formulas (daily rate) <greek-e> 365 <divide> 12. Alaska's base rate changes for regular family foster care became effective July 1, 1998.

2. 1998 data were not available. Data shown are for 1996, as reported to the American Public Human Services Association (formerly American Public Welfare Association).

3. The foster care maintenance rates provided in the table are midpoints. Delaware has a range of payments for each age. Delaware has a standard foster care payment and three levels of care with supplemental payments.

4. Basic monthly payment rates are State averages of rates set at the county level. They are estimated from daily maintenance payments of $16.20, $17.88, $20.10 and $27.35 respectively.

5. Michigan has two age ranges for payment rates in family foster care: 0–12 and 13–18.

6. Ohio's foster care rates range depending on the county: the rates provided in the table are the overall average for 88 counties, converted from Ohio's daily rate to a monthly rate. Rates are determined by the county agency, but must be within the approved uniform statewide standards for per diem foster care maintenance rates.

7. Regular family foster care basic monthly maintenance rates apply to age ranges. The amount presented for age 2 applies to ages 0–3; the amount for age 9 applies to ages 4–11; the amount for age 16 applies to ages 12 and older.

NA. Not available.

Note: States and/or counties supplement these basic rates with additional payments. For 1998, figures are coded for major items covered in the basic rate. Key: r = room and board; s = supervision; c = clothing.

Source: United States House of Representatives, Committee on Ways and Means. (2000). *The 2000 Green Book: Background material and data on programs within the jurisdiction of the Committee on Ways and Means.* Retrieved from http://aspe.hhs.gov/2000gb/sec11.txt.

Table 10.8

Federal Adoption Assistance Expenditures: Fiscal Years 1994 to 1999, and Average Number of Children Receiving Adoption Assistance, Fiscal Year 1999

(in Thousands of Dollars)

State	1994 claims	1995 claims	1996 claims	1997 claims	1998 claims	1999 claims	1999 average monthly number of children
Alabama	$1,830	$1,867	$1,786	$2,243	$2,492	$3,525	429
Alaska	1,070	1,286	1,562	1,914	2,232	2,840	731
Arizona	3,960	5,522	6,856	8,365	9,435	11,270	2,161
Arkansas	1,960	1,542	2,387	3,035	4,323	5,181	688
California	43,590	48,234	52,962	76,819	85,093	108,802	24,786
Colorado	3,230	3,316	4,361	5,420	7,888	10,358	2,992
Connecticut	6,310	7,122	6,040	4,507	12,369	10,341	1,748
Delaware	430	536	556	592	635	862	267
District of Columbia	1,970	1,847	1,987	2,676	3,273	4,434	485
Florida	.10,580	16,830	19,613	23,664	29,801	33,428	8,900
Georgia	3,320	4,364	4,864	6,913	11,156	15,193	3,570
Hawaii	480	610	980	1,183	2,026	2,802	675
Idaho	580	753	982	1,063	1,313	1,485	271
Illinois	13,060	16,801	19,362	27,246	35,494	55,526	16,242
Indiana	6,710	7,338	8,692	10,630	12,421	15,106	3,574
Iowa	3,870	4,976	6,591	11,347	12,238	15,792	2,670
Kansas	2,240	2,740	3,180	7,702	4,147	5,809	2,975
Kentucky	3,320	3,540	3,835	3,742	4,436	5,198	1,148
Louisiana	9,320	11,044	12,180	13,556	17,342	18,129	1,874
Maine	2,960	2,794	3,669	4,084	4,730	4,811	754
Maryland	2,880	3,633	4,491	5,447	6,271	8,197	2,179
Massachusetts[1]	8,380	9,603	11,147	12,585	12,648	17,699	4,552
Michigan	26,840	31,917	37,282	44,032	52,429	58,439	14,213
Minnesota	4,620	5,224	5,861	6,653	8,314	10,232	2,246
Mississippi	390	667	795	936	1,110	1,346	419
Missouri	5,190	6,743	6,270	7,432	8,775	10,998	3,341
Montana	760	905	1,330	1,258	2,866	2,339	501
Nebraska	1,560	1,771	2,062	2,332	2,881	3,287	877
Nevada	460	668	870	1,504	1,835	1,690	419
New Hampshire[2]	740	841	834	803	745	872	313
New Jersey	6,700	8,975	8,522	13,629	9,807	15,614	3,788
New Mexico	1,890	2,443	2,722	3,246	4,413	6,180	1,377
New York	72,590	89,816	100,466	114,405	123,605	134,508	32,759
North Carolina	2,550	4,229	5,258	6,783	8,962	11,035	3,506
North Dakota	500	460	544	635	827	1,139	202
Ohio	30,300	34,985	56,331	74,323	69,112	84,502	12,355
Oklahoma	.2,240	2,950	4,030	6,431	6,949	8,008	1,671
Oregon	3,300	4,020	4,936	6,178	8,668	10,776	4,081
Pennsylvania	4,263	5,440	6,820	8,090	10,273	12,385	2,760
Puerto Rico[3]	NA	NA	NA	NA	NA	54	92
Rhode Island	4,610	4,194	3,080	3,042	3,958	4,469	1,053
South Carolina	2,910	3,915	4,454	5,382	6,623	9,169	1,679
South Dakota	630	649	666	788	890	1,006	363
Tennessee	3,240	3,607	5,814	5,204	4,705	6,605	1,790
Texas	14,520	17,160	17,308	19,815	24,454	28,003	6,969
Utah	1,240	1,158	1,943	2,700	3,782	3,825	951
Vermont	1,860	1,947	2,080	2,664	3,325	3,970	667
Virginia	2,590	2,998	3,671	3,601	5,256	7,705	2,011
Washington	3,940	3,013	4,441	5,085	6,812	9,227	4,563
West Virginia	440	492	542	678	4,567	3,189	386
Wisconsin	7,730	9,056	10,339	13,122	14,503	17,382	3,211
Wyoming	60	24	51	105	123	172	68
Total	344,540	411,398	482,990	604,371	694,545	842,737	195,243

1. Fiscal year 1999 data include estimates for the third and fourth quarters.
2. Fiscal year 1999 data include estimates for the average monthly number of children.
3. Did not begin to participate until fiscal year 1999.
NA. Not applicable.
Note: Totals may differ from sum of State amounts because of rounding.

Source: United States House of Representatives, Committee on Ways and Means. (2000). *The 2000 Green Book: Background material and data on programs within the jurisdiction of the Committee on Ways and Means.* Retrieved from http://aspe.hhs.gov/2000gb/sec11.txt.

Table 10.9
Adoption Baselines, Number of Incentive-Qualifying Adoptions, and Incentive Payments, by State

State	1998 baseline (3-year average, 1995-97)	1998 incentive qualifying adoptions	Incentive payments for 1998 adoptions (in thousands)	1999 baseline (higher of 1997 or 1998)
Alabama	139	NA	0	136
Alaska	108	NA	0	109
Arizona	357	NA	0	474
Arkansas	138	251	$596	251
California	3,287	3,958	3,916	3,958
Colorado	417	560	892	560
Connecticut	207	229	88	278
Delaware	39	NA	0	33
District of Columbia	110	NA	0	132
Florida	987	1,549	2,744	1,549
Georgia	493	672	956	672
Hawaii	85	297	1,102	297
Idaho	44	NA	0	47
Illinois	2,200	4,656	14,606	4,656
Indiana	495	774	1,792	774
Iowa	350	517	790	517
Kansas	349	NA	0	421
Kentucky	211	NA	0	222
Louisiana	220	NA	0	284
Maine	108	112	24	112
Maryland	342	420	676	420
Massachusetts	1,116	1,137	84	1,161
Michigan	1,905	2,254	2,004	2,254
Minnesota	258	427	1,022	427
Mississippi	114	169	398	169
Missouri	557	616	236	616
Montana	115	144	116	144
Nebraska	185	NA	0	180
Nevada	149	NA	0	148
New Hampshire	45	50	20	50
New Jersey	621	755	870	755
New Mexico	147	197	200	197
New York	4,716	4,822	424	4,979
North Carolina	467	NA	0	694
North Dakota	47	83	144	83
Ohio	1,287	NA	0	1,400
Oklahoma	338	456	596	456
Oregon	445	665	1,248	665
Pennsylvania	1,224	1,494	1,260	1,526
Rhode Island	261	NA	0	226
South Carolina	256	465	1,064	465
South Dakota	56	58	8	58
Tennessee	328	NA	0	295
Texas	880	1,365	2,872	1,365
Utah	225	250	100	268
Vermont	75	116	214	116
Washington	607	759	620	759
West Virginia	182	211	128	220
Wisconsin	467	589	640	589
Wyoming	15	30	0	30

NA. Not available.

Source: United States House of Representatives, Committee on Ways and Means. (2000). *The 2000 Green Book: Background material and data on programs within the jurisdiction of the Committee on Ways and Means.* Retrieved from http://aspe.hhs.gov/2000gb/sec11.txt.

Table 10.10

Title IV-E Independent Living Awards Under Public Law 106-169, at Fiscal Year 2000 Appropriation Amount of $105 Million and Full Authorization Amount of $140 Million, by State

(in Thousands of Dollars)

State	Fiscal year 2000 appropriation amount of $105 million	Full authorization amount of $140 million	Funding under prior law
Alabama	$1,038	$1,269	$1,038
Alaska	500	500	13
Arizona	858	1,248	348
Arkansas	500	685	271
California	18,804	27,350	12,482
Colorado	1,419	2,064	826
Connecticut	1,134	1,650	755
Delaware	500	500	203
District of Columbia	1,092	1,092	1,092
Florida	4,163	6,055	987
Georgia	1,610	2,342	1,099
Hawaii	500	651	18
Idaho	500	500	107
Illinois	8,524	12,398	2,817
Indiana	1,405	2,044	1,020
Iowa	593	863	450
Kansas	717	1,030	717
Kentucky	984	1,432	792
Louisiana	1,358	1,535	1,358
Maine	566	713	566
Maryland	2,179	3,170	1,238
Massachusetts	2,353	3,422	636
Michigan	4,406	6,408	4,172
Minnesota	1,496	2,176	1,142
Mississippi	523	761	514
Missouri	2,112	3,072	1,295
Montana	500	500	244
Nebraska	765	1,113	436
Nevada	500	500	154
New Hampshire	500	500	320
New Jersey	2,298	2,298	2,298
New Mexico	500	500	207
New York	11,586	13,392	11,586
North Carolina	1,879	2,733	1,045
North Dakota	500	500	192
Ohio	2,861	3,072	2,861
Oklahoma	1,161	1,688	620
Oregon	1,197	1,741	931
Pennsylvania	4,638	5,578	4,638
Puerto Rico	1,126	1,637	NA
Rhode Island	500	500	315
South Carolina	810	1,178	580
South Dakota	500	500	193
Tennessee	1,622	2,359	778
Texas	2,900	4,218	1,842
Utah	500	500	202
Vermont	500	500	296
Virginia	1,362	1,393	1,362
Washington	1,664	2,421	825
West Virginia	521	714	521
Wisconsin	1,673	2,434	1,554
Wyoming	500	500	45
Total	102,900	137,900	70,000

NA. Not available.

Note: The allotments under the fiscal year 2000 appropriation amount of $105 million were provided by the U.S. Department of Health and Human Services. The allotments under the full authorization amount of $140 million are estimates based on the above data provided by the U.S. Department of Health and Human Services. Both allotment columns reflect the evaluation set-aside of 1.5 percent of $140 million ($2.1 million).

Source: United States House of Representatives, Committee on Ways and Means. (2000). *The 2000 Green Book: Background material and data on programs within the jurisdiction of the committee on Ways and Means.* Retrieved from http://aspe.hhs.gov/2000gb/sec11.txt.

Table 10.11
Title XX Social Services Block Grant
Funding Levels: 1982 to 2000

(in Millions of Dollars)

Fiscal year	Appropriation	Entitlement ceiling
1982	$2,400	$2,400
1983	2,675[1]	2,450
1984	2,700	2,700
1985	2,725[2]	2,700
1986	2,584[3]	2,700
1987	2,700	2,700
1988	2,700	2,750[4]
1989	2,700	2,700
1990	2,762[5]	2,800[6]
1991	2,800	2,800
1992	2,800	2,800
1993	2,800	2,800
1994	2,800[7]	2,800
1995	2,800	2,800
1996	2,381	2,381[8]
1997	2,500[9]	2,380[8]
1998	2,299[10]	2,380[8]
1999	1,909[11]	2,380[8]
2000	1,775[12]	2,380[8]

1. Amount includes an additional $225 million appropriated in the emergency jobs bill (public Law 98-8).

2. Amount includes $25 million earmarked for training of day care providers, licensing officials, and parents including training in the prevention of child abuse in child care settings (Public Law 98-473).

3. The entitlement ceiling for fiscal year 1986 was $2.7 billion. However, the Gramm-Rudman-Hollings legislation sequestration of funds for that period reduced the funding by $116 million to $2.584 billion.

4. The 1987 Budget Reconciliation Act (Public Law 100-203) included a $50 million increase in the Title XX entitlement ceiling for fiscal year 1988, however, these additional funds were not appropriated.

5. The fiscal year 1990 appropriation included a supplemental appropriation of $100 million (Public Law 101-198). The Gramm-Rudman-Hollings legislation sequestration of funds for fiscal year 1990 reduced the funding by $37.8 million to $2.762 billion.

6. OBRA 1989 (Public Law 101-239) included a permanent $100 million increase in the Title XX entitlement ceiling to $2.8 billion, beginning in fiscal year 1990.

7. The $2.8 billion appropriated amount shown does not include the $1 billion that OBRA 1991 made available on an entitlement basis under title XX for empowerment zones and enterprise communities.

8. At the time of the fiscal year 1996 appropriation, the entitlement ceiling for Title XX was still permanently set at $2.8 billion. However, the 1996 welfare reform law (Public Law 104-193) amended Title XX of the Social Security Act to set the entitlement ceiling at $2.381 billion for fiscal year 1996, and $2.380 billion for fiscal years 1997–2002. Under this legislation, the ceiling was scheduled to return to $2.8 billion for fiscal year 2003 and succeeding years.

9. Public Law 104-208 contained a $2.5 billion appropriation for Title XX, exceeding the ceiling established in the 1996 welfare reform law.

10. The fiscal year 1998 appropriations measure (Public Law 105-78) included $2.299 billion for Title XX despite the $2.38 billion ceiling established in the 1996 welfare reform law.

11. The Omnibus Consolidated Appropriations Act for fiscal year 1999 (Public Law 105-277) included an appropriation level of $1.909 billion for Title XX, once again, below the $2.38 billion ceiling established in Public Law 104-193.

12. The fiscal year 2000 Consolidated Appropriations Act (Public Law 106-113) set Title XX funding at $1.775 billion, of which $425 million may not be obligated to States until September 29, 2000.

13. Under the Transportation Equity Act (TEA, Public Law 105-178), the Title XX entitlement ceiling is scheduled to be permanently reduced to $1.7 billion beginning in fiscal year 2001.

NA. Not applicable.

Source: United States House of Representatives, Committee on Ways and Means. (2000). *The 2000 Green Book: Background material and data on programs within the jurisdiction of the Committee on Ways and Means.* Retrieved from http://aspe.hhs.gov/2000gb/sec10.txt.

Table 10.12

Title XX Social Services Block Grant Allocations by State and Territory: Selected Fiscal Years 1989 to 1998

(in Millions of Dollars)

State	1989	1993	1995	1996	1997	1998
Alabama	$45.1	$46.2	$45.1	$38.4	$40.3	$37.0
Alaska	5.9	6.2	6.4	5.5	5.8	5.3
American Samoa	0.2	0.1	0.1	0.1	0.1	0.1
Arizona	36.5	41.0	41.8	36.1	38.9	36.7
Arkansas	26.4	28.3	26.2	22.3	23.4	21.6
California	300.5	333.2	336.9	286.5	300.1	274.8
Colorado	36.4	38.9	37.9	32.7	34.9	32.6
Connecticut	35.5	38.8	35.8	30.1	31.3	28.5
Delaware	7.1	7.5	7.5	6.4	6.7	6.2
District of Columbia	7.0	6.8	6.4	5.3	5.4	4.8
Florida	130.0	144.8	147.2	125.6	133.2	123.3
Georgia	68.0	72.5	73.7	63.5	67.4	62.7
Guam	0.5	0.5	0.5	0.4	0.4	0.4
Hawaii	11.8	12.4	12.7	10.8	11.3	10.3
Idaho	11.2	11.3	11.6	10.1	10.8	10.1
Illinois	128.7	128.0	127.0	107.4	112.2	102.9
Indiana	61.3	62.1	61.8	52.4	54.9	50.5
Iowa	31.8	31.1	30.7	25.8	27.0	24.7
Kansas	27.4	27.7	27.5	23.2	24.4	22.3
Kentucky	41.5	41.3	41.0	34.8	36.5	33.6
Louisiana	50.1	47.2	46.8	39.4	41.2	37.8
Maine	13.1	13.7	13.5	11.4	11.8	10.8
Maryland	49.7	53.5	53.6	45.6	47.8	43.9
Massachusetts	65.0	67.4	65.5	55.2	57.7	52.8
Michigan	101.9	104.1	103.0	87.0	90.7	83.1
Minnesota	46.9	49.0	48.9	41.5	43.6	40.1
Mississippi	29.2	28.8	28.5	24.3	25.5	23.5
Missouri	56.4	57.3	56.7	48.0	50.4	46.3
Montana	9.1	8.9	9.0	7.7	8.2	7.6
Nebraska	17.8	17.7	17.5	14.8	15.5	14.2
Nevada	10.7	13.5	14.5	12.8	13.9	13.3
New Hampshire	11.4	12.4	12.1	10.3	10.9	10.0
New Jersey	84.9	86.5	85.0	72.3	75.5	69.1
New Mexico	16.5	17.0	17.3	14.8	15.8	14.7
New York	198.0	201.4	197.8	167.1	173.5	157.8
North Carolina	70.5	74.2	74.7	63.8	67.5	62.6
North Dakota	7.6	7.2	6.9	5.8	6.1	5.6
Northern Mariana Islands	0.1	0.1	0.1	0.1	0.1	0.1
Ohio	119.8	121.4	120.2	101.8	106.0	97.0
Oklahoma	36.8	35.2	35.1	29.7	31.1	28.5
Oregon	30.1	31.8	32.5	27.8	29.5	27.3
Pennsylvania	132.4	133.0	131.1	110.5	115.1	105.0
Puerto Rico	14.0	14.5	14.5	12.3	12.9	11.9
Rhode Island	10.9	11.2	11.0	9.2	9.5	8.6
South Carolina	37.6	39.0	39.3	33.4	35.0	32.0
South Dakota	7.9	7.8	7.8	6.6	6.9	6.3
Tennessee	53.5	54.6	54.8	46.8	49.4	45.7
Texas	185.8	190.2	192.7	165.5	175.5	162.9
Utah	18.5	19.3	19.8	17.1	18.2	17.0
Vermont	6.0	6.3	6.2	5.3	5.5	5.1
Virginia	64.5	69.3	69.6	59.6	62.6	57.6
Virgin Islands	0.5	0.5	0.5	0.4	0.4	0.4
Washington	49.7	54.5	56.1	48.2	51.0	47.3
West Virginia	21.4	20.1	19.8	16.7	17.4	15.9
Wisconsin	53.3	54.8	54.7	46.2	48.5	44.6
Wyoming	5.6	5.1	5.1	4.3	4.5	4.2
Total	2,700.0	2,800.0	2,800.0	2,381.0	2,500.0	2,299.0

Source: United States House of Representatives, Committee on Ways and Means. (2000). *The 2000 Green Book: Background material and data on programs within the jurisdiction of the Committee on Ways and Means.* Retrieved from http://aspe.hhs.gov/2000gb/sec10.txt.

Table 10.13
Use of Title XX Funds, by Expenditure
Category: Fiscal Years 1995 to 1998

Service	Percent of funds		
	1995	1996	1997
Adoption......................................	1.1	1.1	0.9
Case management......................	3.9	3.8	5.8
Congregate meals......................	0.0	0.0	0.1
Counseling..................................	1.3	1.4	1.7
Day care--adults.........................	0.8	1.5	0.9
Day care--children......................	14.7	14.8	12.9
Education/training.......................	0.9	0.5	0.7
Employment................................	1.1	1.2	1.2
Family planning..........................	1.1	1.3	1.2
Foster care--adults......................	0.7	0.3	0.4
Foster care--children...................	10.4	14.1	8.1
Health-related.............................	0.6	0.5	0.9
Home-based...............................	10.2	10.4	11.5
Home delivered meals................	0.5	0.6	0.8
Housing.......................................	0.2	0.2	0.2
Independent/transitional living.....	0.4	0.3	0.2
Information and referral...............	0.8	0.9	1.1
Legal..	0.4	0.4	0.4
Pregnancy and parenting...........	0.4	0.4	0.4
Prevention/intervention...............	6.8	5.2	5.4
Protective--adults........................	2.1	3.0	3.7
Protective--children.....................	11.0	6.7	7.0
Recreation..................................	0.1	0.1	0.1
Residential treatment..................	3.9	2.7	3.0
Special services--disabled..........	3.8	7.2	9.2
Special services--youth at risk.....	2.0	2.2	1.6
Substance abuse........................	0.3	0.3	0.3
Transportation.............................	0.6	0.6	0.5
Other..	5.6	4.8	6.0
Administrative costs....................	14.0	13.5	14.0
Total....................................	100.0	100.0	100.0

Source: United States House of Representatives, Committee on Ways and Means. (2000). *The 2000 Green Book: Background material and data on programs within the jurisdiction of the Committee on Ways and Means.* Retrieved from http://aspe.hhs.gov/2000gb/sec10.txt.

Table 10.14
Quality of Life Indicators

Economy	Growth of private consumption per capita Avg. annual growth rate (%), 1980–98	Distribution-corrected	Prevalence of child malnutrition % of children under age 5 1992–98[a]	Under-5 mortality rate Per 1,000 1980	1998	Life expectancy at birth Years 1998 Males	Females	Adult illiteracy rate % of people 15 and above 1998 Males	Females	Urban population % of total 1980	1999	Access to sanitation in urban areas % of urban pop. with access 1990–96[a]
Albania	..	..	8	57	31	69	75	9	24	34	41	97
Algeria	-2.3	-1.5	13	139	40	69	72	24	46	44	60	..
Angola	-9.5	..	..	261	204	45	48	..	..	21	34	34
Argentina	..	..	2	38	22	70	77	3	3	83	90	80
Armenia	..	..	3	..	18	71	78	1	3	66	70	..
Australia	1.7	1.1	0	13	6	76	82	..	..	86	85	..
Austria	2.0	1.5	..	17	6	75	81	..	..	65	65	100
Azerbaijan	..	..	10	..	21	68	75	..	..	53	57	67
Bangladesh	2.1	1.4	56	211	96	58	59	49	71	14	24	77
Belarus	-2.7	-2.1	..	..	14	63	74	0	1	57	71	..
Belgium	1.6	1.2	..	15	6	75	81	..	..	95	97	100
Benin	-0.4	..	29	214	140	52	55	46	77	27	42	54
Bolivia	0.1	0.1	8	170	78	60	64	9	22	46	62	77
Botswana	3.0	..	..	94	105	45	47	27	22	15	50	91
Brazil	0.7	0.3	6	80	40	63	71	16	16	66	81	74
Bulgaria	-0.8	-0.5	..	25	15	67	75	1	2	61	69	100
Burkina Faso	0.4	0.2	33	..	210	43	45	68	87	9	18	78
Burundi	-0.9	-0.6	..	193	196	41	44	45	63	4	9	60
Cambodia	..	..	..	330	143	52	55	43	80	12	16	..
Cameroon	-2.0	..	22	173	150	53	56	20	33	31	48	73
Canada	1.4	0.9	..	13	7	76	82	..	..	76	77	..
Central African Republic	-0.8	-0.3	23	..	162	43	46	43	68	35	41	..
Chad	..	..	39	235	172	47	50	51	69	19	23	74
Chile	4.0	1.7	1	35	12	72	78	4	5	81	85	82
China	7.2	4.3	16	65	36	68	72	9	25	20	32	58
Hong Kong, China	4.8	..	..	..	..	76	82	4	11	92	100	..
Colombia	1.2	0.5	8	58	28	67	73	9	9	64	73	76
Congo, Dem. Rep.	-4.5	..	34	210	141	49	52	29	53	29	30	23
Congo, Rep.	0.2	..	..	125	143	46	51	14	29	41	62	15
Costa Rica	0.8	0.4	5	29	15	74	79	5	5	43	48	100
Côte d'Ivoire	-2.2	-1.4	24	170	143	46	47	47	64	35	46	59
Croatia	..	..	1	23	10	69	77	1	3	50	57	71
Czech Republic	..	..	1	19	6	71	78	..	..	75	75	..
Denmark	1.8	1.4	..	10	..	73	78	..	..	84	85	100
Dominican Republic	0.0	0.0	6	92	47	69	73	17	17	51	64	76
Ecuador	-0.2	-0.1	..	101	37	68	73	8	11	47	64	87
Egypt, Arab Rep.	2.0	1.4	12	175	59	65	68	35	58	44	45	20
El Salvador	3.0	1.4	11	120	36	67	72	19	25	42	46	78
Eritrea	..	..	44	..	90	49	52	34	62	14	18	12
Estonia	-1.0	-0.7	..	25	12	64	75	..	..	70	69	..
Ethiopia	-0.4	-0.3	48	213	173	42	44	58	70	11	17	..
Finland	1.4	1.1	..	9	5	74	81	..	..	60	67	100
France	1.6	1.1	..	13	5	75	82	..	..	73	75	100
Georgia	..	..	..	..	20	69	77	..	..	52	60	..
Germany	..	..	..	16	6	74	80	..	..	83	87	..
Ghana	0.2	0.2	27	157	96	58	62	22	40	31	38	53
Greece	1.9	1.3	..	23	8	75	81	2	5	58	60	100
Guatemala	0.2	0.1	27	..	52	61	67	25	40	37	39	91
Guinea	1.0	0.6	..	299	184	46	47	..	..	19	32	..
Haiti	..	..	28	200	116	51	56	50	54	24	35	42
Honduras	-0.1	-0.1	25	103	46	67	72	27	27	35	52	81
Hungary	-0.1	-0.1	..	26	12	66	75	1	1	57	64	100
India	2.7	1.7	..	177	83	62	64	33	57	23	28	46
Indonesia	4.6	2.9	34	125	52	64	67	9	20	22	40	73
Iran, Islamic Rep.	0.5	..	16	126	33	70	72	18	33	50	61	89
Ireland	2.9	1.9	..	14	7	73	79	..	..	55	59	100
Israel	3.3	2.1	..	19	8	76	80	2	6	89	91	100
Italy	2.1	1.6	..	17	6	75	82	1	2	67	67	100
Jamaica	1.3	0.8	10	39	24	73	77	18	10	47	56	89
Japan	2.8	2.1	..	11	5	77	84	..	..	76	79	..
Jordan	-1.5	-1.0	5	..	31	69	73	6	17	60	74	..
Kazakhstan	..	..	8	..	29	59	70	..	..	54	56	..
Kenya	0.4	0.2	23	115	124	50	52	12	27	16	32	69
Korea, Rep.	6.5	4.4	..	27	11	69	76	1	4	57	81	100
Kuwait	..	..	2	35	13	74	80	17	22	90	97	100
Kyrgyz Republic	..	..	11	..	41	63	71	..	..	38	34	87
Lao PDR	..	..	40	200	..	52	55	38	70	13	23	70
Latvia	..	..	..	26	19	64	76	0	0	68	69	90
Lebanon	..	..	3	..	30	68	72	9	21	74	89	100
Lesotho	0.8	0.4	16	168	144	54	57	29	7	13	27	..
Lithuania	..	..	..	24	12	67	77	0	1	61	68	..
Macedonia, FYR	..	..	..	69	18	70	75	..	..	54	62	68
Madagascar	-2.2	-1.2	40	216	146	56	59	28	42	18	29	50
Malawi	0.8	..	30	265	229	42	42	27	56	9	24	70
Malaysia	2.9	1.5	20	42	12	70	75	9	18	42	57	100

Table 10.14 (*continued*)

Economy	Growth of private consumption per capita Avg. annual growth rate (%), 1980–98	Distribution-corrected	Prevalence of child malnutrition % of children under age 5 1992–98[a]	Under-5 mortality rate Per 1,000 1980	1998	Life expectancy at birth Years 1998 Males	Females	Adult illiteracy rate % of people 15 and above 1998 Males	Females	Urban population % of total 1980	1999	Access to sanitation in urban areas % of urban pop. with access 1990–96[a]
Mali	−1.0	−0.5	27	..	218	49	52	54	69	19	29	58
Mauritania	0.8	0.5	23	175	140	52	55	48	69	27	56	44
Mexico	0.2	0.1	..	74	35	69	75	7	11	66	74	81
Moldova	..	..	..	..	22	63	70	1	2	40	46	96
Mongolia	..	..	9	..	60	65	68	28	49	52	63	..
Morocco	1.9	1.2	10	152	61	65	69	40	66	41	55	69
Mozambique	−1.0	−0.6	26	..	213	44	47	42	73	13	39	53
Myanmar	..	..	43	134	118	58	62	11	21	24	27	42
Namibia	−1.4	..	26	114	112	54	55	18	20	23	30	77
Nepal	2.0	1.3	57	180	107	58	58	43	78	7	12	34
Netherlands	1.6	1.1	..	11	7	75	81	..	..	88	89	100
New Zealand	0.8	0.4	..	16	7	75	80	..	..	83	86	..
Nicaragua	−2.2	−1.1	12	143	42	66	71	34	31	50	56	34
Niger	−2.2	−1.1	50	317	250	44	48	78	93	13	20	71
Nigeria	−4.2	−2.1	39	196	119	52	55	30	48	27	43	61
Norway	1.6	1.2	..	11	6	76	81	..	..	71	75	100
Pakistan	2.0	1.4	38	161	120	61	63	42	71	28	36	53
Panama	2.4	1.2	6	36	25	72	76	8	9	50	56	99
Papua New Guinea	−0.6	−0.3	30	..	76	57	59	29	45	13	17	82
Paraguay	1.7	0.7	..	61	27	68	72	6	9	42	55	20
Peru	−0.4	−0.2	8	126	47	66	71	6	16	65	72	62
Philippines	0.8	0.4	30	81	40	67	71	5	5	38	58	88
Poland	..	..	..	..	11	69	77	0	0	58	65	100
Portugal	3.1	2.0	..	31	8	72	79	6	11	29	63	100
Romania	0.4	0.3	6	36	25	66	73	1	3	49	56	81
Russian Federation	..	..	3	..	20	61	73	0	1	70	77	..
Rwanda	−1.0	−0.7	29	..	205	40	42	29	43	5	6	..
Saudi Arabia	..	..	..	85	26	70	74	17	36	66	85	100
Senegal	−0.6	−0.4	22	..	121	51	54	55	74	36	47	83
Sierra Leone	−3.1	−1.2	..	336	283	36	39	..	..	24	36	17
Singapore	4.8	..	..	13	6	75	79	4	12	100	100	100
Slovak Republic	−2.1	−1.7	..	23	10	69	77	..	..	52	57	..
Slovenia	..	..	..	18	7	71	79	0	0	48	50	100
South Africa	−0.1	0.0	9	91	83	61	66	15	16	48	52	79
Spain	2.2	1.5	..	16	7	75	82	2	4	73	77	100
Sri Lanka	2.9	1.9	38	48	18	71	76	6	12	22	23	33
Sweden	0.7	0.5	..	9	5	77	82	..	..	83	83	100
Switzerland	0.5	0.3	..	11	5	76	82	..	..	57	68	100
Syrian Arab Republic	0.9	..	13	73	32	67	72	13	42	47	54	77
Tajikistan	..	..	..	..	33	66	71	1	1	34	28	83
Tanzania	0.0	0.0	31	176	136	46	48	17	36	15	32	97
Thailand	5.1	3.0	..	58	33	70	75	3	7	17	21	98
Togo	−0.1	..	25	188	144	47	50	28	62	23	33	57
Tunisia	1.1	0.7	9	100	32	70	74	21	42	52	65	100
Turkey	2.6	1.5	10	133	42	67	72	7	25	44	74	99
Turkmenistan	..	..	..	..	44	63	70	..	..	47	45	70
Uganda	1.9	1.2	26	180	170	42	41	24	46	9	14	75
Ukraine	..	..	..	..	17	62	73	0	1	62	68	70
United Kingdom	2.6	1.6	..	14	7	75	80	..	..	89	89	100
United States	1.9	1.1	1	15	..	74	80	..	..	74	77	..
Uruguay	2.6	1.5	4	42	19	70	78	3	2	85	91	56
Uzbekistan	5.5	3.7	19	..	29	66	73	7	17	41	37	46
Venezuela, RB	−0.8	−0.4	5	42	25	70	76	7	9	79	87	64
Vietnam	..	..	40	105	42	66	71	5	9	19	20	43
Yemen, Rep.	..	..	46	198	96	55	56	34	77	19	24	40
Zambia	−3.6	−1.8	24	149	192	43	43	16	31	40	40	40
Zimbabwe	0.4	0.2	16	108	125	50	52	8	17	22	35	99
World	**1.3 w**		**30 w**	**123 w**	**75 w**	**65 w**	**69 w**	**18 w**	**32 w**	**40 w**	**46 w**	**.. w**
Low income	1.4		..	177	107	59	61	30	49	24	31	56
Middle income	2.2		14	79	38	67	72	10	20	38	50	..
Lower middle income	3.6		15	83	39	67	72	10	23	31	43	59
Upper middle income	1.5		..	66	35	67	74	9	11	64	76	..
Low and middle income	1.9		..	135	79	63	67	18	33	32	41	..
East Asia & Pacific	5.6		22	82	43	67	71	9	22	22	34	61
Europe & Central Asia	..		8	..	26	65	74	2	5	59	67	..
Latin America & Caribbean	0.6		8	78	38	67	73	11	13	65	75	..
Middle East & North Africa	..		15	136	55	66	69	26	48	48	58	..
South Asia	2.6		51	180	89	62	63	35	59	22	28	46
Sub-Saharan Africa	−1.2		33	188	151	49	52	32	49	23	34	..
High income	2.2		..	15	6	75	81	..	..	75	77	..

Note: For data comparability and coverage, see the Technical Notes. Figures in italics are for years other than those specified.
a. Data are for most recent year available.

Source: The World Bank. (2001). *World Development Report 2000/2001: Attacking Poverty.* Washington, D.C.: Author. Retrieved from http://www.worldbank.org/poverty/wdrpoverty/report/tab2.pdf.

Table 10.15
Poverty Rates in Nineteen Rich Countries, by Age Group

	Year	Poverty rate[1] (% of population)			Rank of country		
		Overall	Children[2]	Aged[3]	Overall	Children2	Aged3
United States	1997	10.7	14.7	12.0	1	1	2
Italy	1995	8.9	14.1	4.7	2	2	5
Australia	1994	7.0	7.4	12.2	3	5	1
Japan[4]	1992	6.9	na	na	4	na	na
Canada	1994	6.6	8.5	1.2	5	3	14
United Kingdom	1995	5.7	8.3	4.0	6	4	7
Israel	1992	5.2	4.8	11.2	7	8	3
Spain	1990	5.1	7.0	3.9	8	6	9
Netherlands	1994	4.7	4.6	3.1	9	9	12
Sweden	1995	4.6	1.3	0.7	10	18	17
Germany[5]	1994	4.2	6.0	4.0	11	7	7
Switzerland	1992	4.0	4.4	3.1	12	10	12
Denmark	1992	3.6	2.1	3.7	13	15	10
France	1994	3.2	2.6	3.6	14	11	11
Norway	1995	3.0	2.2	0.7	15	13	17
Austria	1992	2.8	2.6	6.8	16	11	4
Finland	1995	2.1	1.5	0.9	17	17	15
Belgium	1992	1.9	1.6	4.2	18	16	6
Luxembourg	1994	1.3	2.2	0.9	19	13	15
Overall Average		4.8	5.3	4.5			

1. Poverty is measured at 40% median adjusted disposable personal income (ADPI) for individuals. Incomes are adjusted by E=0.5 where ADPI=adjusted DPI divided by household size (S) to the power E: ADPI=DPI/sE.
2. Children are under age 18.
3. Adults aged 65 and over.
4. Japanese data runs were made for LIS by Professor Tsuneo Ishikawa.
5. Includes all of Germany, including the eastern states of the former GDR.

Source: Columbia University. (2003). *Poverty rates in 19 rich countries, by age group*. The International Clearinghouse on International Developments in Child, Youth and Family Policies Web site. Retrieved from http://www.childpolicyintl.org/sipoverty/table323.pdf.

Table 10.16
Percentage of U.S. Teenage Parent Respondents to a Three-City Survey about Public Services They Receive

	CHICAGO		ATLANTA		BOSTON	
	Not Receiving TANF	Receiving TANF	Not Receiving TANF	Receiving TANF	Not Receiving TANF	Receiving TANF
FOOD STAMPS	*	96.1	44.4	78.1	23.4	36.2
WIC	*	86.3	64.6	71.2	83.7	86.7
MEDICAL CARD	*	99.7	80.0	94.6	93.6	99.6
CHILD CARE	*	44.9	25.3	45.1	11.2	66.3

* This question was not asked of Chicago respondents who were not receiving TANF benefits at the time of the survey.

Source: Shapiro, D.L., & Marcy, H.M. (April 2002). *Knocking on the door: barriers to welfare and other assistance for teen parents—A three-city research study.* Chicago: Center for Impact Research. Retrieved from http://www.impactre search.org/documents/cirknockdoor.pdf.

Figure 10.1
Response Received by U.S. Teen Parents When Soliciting Public Assistance in a Three-City Survey

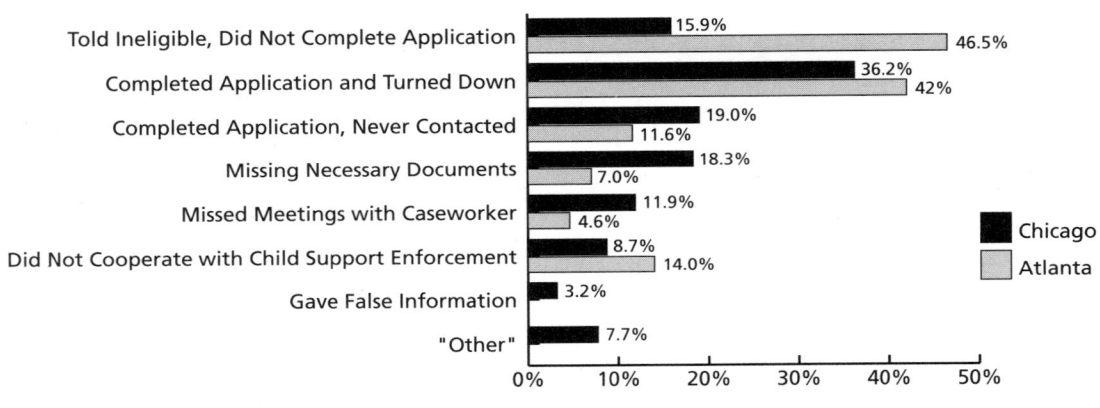

Note: Respondents could provide more than one response, thus the percentages add up to more than 100 percent. Reasons provided by less than 10 percent of respondents in Atlanta reflect the experiences of fewer than five respondents, and, therefore, percentages should be interpreted with caution.

Source: Shapiro, D.L., & Marcy, H.M. (April 2002). *Knocking on the door: barriers to welfare and other assistance for teen parents—A three-city research study.* Chicago: Center for Impact Research. Retrieved from http://www.impactresearch.org/documents/cirknockdoor.pdf.

Figure 10.2
Why U.S. Teens Receiving TANF Had Their
Benefits Reduced or Cut Off

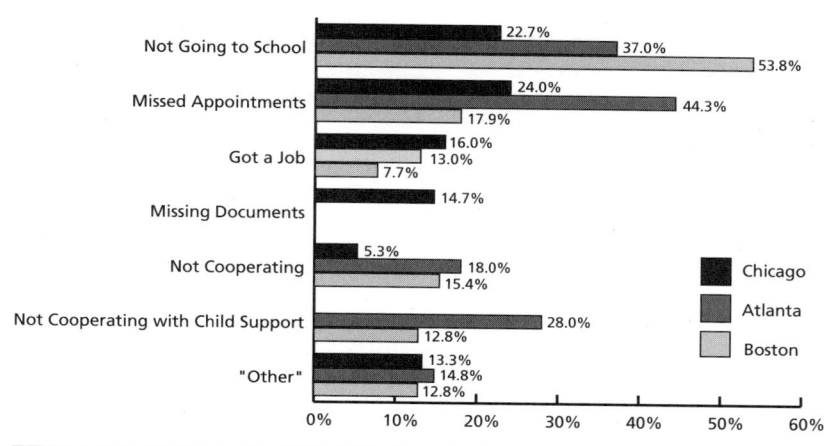

Note: Respondents could check more than one item, thus percentages add up to more than 100 percent.

Source: Shapiro, D.L., & Marcy, H.M. (April 2002). *Knocking on the door: Barriers to welfare and other assistance for teen parents—A three-city research study.* Chicago: Center for Impact Research. Retrieved from http://www.impactresearch.org/documents/cirknockdoor.pdf.

Glossary

Absolute poverty. That income below which a set of basic necessities cannot be afforded. The World Bank has defined relative poverty as the population earning less than one third of the national average income.

Absolute standard (threshold). A baseline measure used for comparative purposes. This measure defines threshold criteria that determine whether the item measured meets the criterion or criteria. These are developed by experts who take into consideration an individual's basic physiological needs like nutrition. Absolute standards differ from relative thresholds as commonly defined because the latter are developed by taking into account the actual expenditures generated by people. The United States prefers to use absolute standards while the European Union prefers to use relative thresholds in order to make cross-national comparisons simpler to analyze.

Active labor market policy (ALMP). Economic and labor policies enacted by national governments in which they interact with the labor markets with the aim to reduce the unemployment rate for individuals who want to work. These policies take the form of interventions centered on job placements, job training, and job creation (partial job churning).

Actuarial balance. The difference between the total summarized income rate (ratio of the present value of tax income to the present value of taxable payroll over a 75-year period) and the total summarized cost rate (ratio of the present value of expenditures to the present value of taxable payroll over a 75-year period).

Actuarial reduction. Reduction in the monthly benefit amount received when entitlement occurs prior to full retirement age if the beneficiary is a retired worker, spouse, or divorced spouse. Reduced monthly benefits are also given to surviving spouse or divorced spouse. Entitlement based on disability at ages 50–59 is payable if beneficiary is a surviving spouse or surviving divorced spouse.

Additional standard deduction for the elderly and the blind. Deductions in the IRS 1040 and equivalent forms that add deductions to reduce the adjusted gross income of the elderly and the blind. The standard deductions are additive, signifying that an individual who qualifies as elderly and blind is able to receive both deductions.

Adequate (standard of) living. Quality of life standard that presupposes the ability to comfortably meet one's needs, the ability to pursue areas and acquire items of interest, and have access to activities and services that the majority of the other individuals take for granted as part of their daily lives or routines.

Adjusted gross income (AGI). Income generated by an individual including wages, interest, capital gains, income from retirement accounts, and alimony that for tax and benefit purposes are adjusted downward as a result of specified deductions. For income tax purposes, deductions include contributions to retirement accounts and alimony paid by an individual. On a U.S. federal income tax form 1040, the adjusted gross income is the number you calculate and report at the bottom of page 1 and repeat at the top of page 2.

Adjustment. Changes made in the formula for the purpose of generating equivalencies between different measures or thresholds so that a scale can be generated.

Adoption. When an adult legally assumes the parental responsibilities of another (typically under age 18) via court action. An open adoption occurs when the court action allows the birth mother to retain some visitation privileges.

Adoption expenses tax credits. U.S. federal government legal provisions to reduce economic barriers to adoption. A tax credit of up to $5,000 ($6,000 when adopting a special-needs child from the United States) is provided to defray the one-time adoption expenses, with the credit phased out for those earning in excess of $75,000 and unavailable to families earning $115,000 or more. The tax credit is not available for foreign special-needs adoptions.

Age. According to the Social Security Administration, when looking at current-pay beneficiary data, classification is based on the age of the person at his or her last birthday.

For award purposes, age is determined to be either the age in a month of award or the age in year of award according to the tables used.

Aged beneficiary. A person who qualifies for benefits on basis of age rather than on child-care or disability.

Aged person. An individual who is 65 or older.

Aggregation. Combining of two or more kinds of economic categories into a single classification. Data used to develop the GDP and other measures as well as data on international trade, for example, aggregate goods and services into manageable groups.

Aid to Families with Dependent Children (AFDC). The original Title IV program under the Social Security Act of 1935. It was an income maintenance program shared by the federal and state governments that provided transitional financial assistance to needy families. Both levels of government shared in its cost. The federal government defined broad guidelines and program requirement while the states were responsible for program formulation, benefit determinations, and administration.

Allocation. The assignment of resources to a specified use, be these economic, social, individual, or temporal.

Allowance. Determination that a worker is entitled to cash disability benefit award or for a period of disability because of inability to work by reason of physical or mental impairment.

Annual earning test (AET). Determination of whether beneficiaries earning income in excess of maximum limits that require a reduction in benefits given to that individual.

Appropriated entitlement. Entitlements for which budgetary authority is given through annual appropriation acts.

Appropriation. Amount of funding generated by legislation for a program to spend in a fiscal year, at times also setting the terms under which funds may be spent.

Arbitrary (relative) standard. Measure or indicator based on judgments made by experts to determine the value or threshold that identifies (or describes) a condition.

Asset. Any item held by an individual or corporation that has an economic value attached to it. Cash, securities and other forms of investments, inventory, and property such as a car or a house, are considered types of assets.

At-Risk Child Care Program. Federal and program under the Aid to Families with Dependent Children (AFDC) providing child-care for children typically under age 13 from low-income working families not receiving assistance but need child-care services in order to accept or remain at work (or otherwise be at-risk of becoming eligible for assistance under AFDC guidelines).

Authorization. Legislation establishing or allowing a program or agency to continue by specifying general goals and administrative compliance requirements. These can set a ceiling on the amount of money that can be appropriated.

Average index monthly earnings (AIME). Resulting monthly earnings after indexing actual earnings to reflect the value of the individual's prior earnings relative to the national average earnings in the indexing year.

Balance of payments. The accounting of all of a country's domestic and international transactions for a given time period, usually for one year, based on payments received (receipts or credits) or payments meted out of the country (debits).

Baseline projections. Used to gauge the extent to which proposed legislation, if enacted, would alter current spending and revenue levels. These include the projection of receipts, outlays, and other budget amounts that would come to pass if there are no changes in existing policy.

Base year. Year used to compare the analysis of demographic and economic data. For example, in figuring out Social Security benefits, the years after 1950 leading upto the year a person becomes entitled to retirement or disability benefits. For survivor's benefits, the base years include the year of the worker's death.

Bend point. Dollar amount defining the AIME or PIA brackets that are part of the benefits formula.

Beneficiary. Person awarded benefits based on own earning record. Also, person designated and/or awarded benefits on basis of the earnings record of another.

Beveridge curve. A measure used by economists that traces the relationship between the unemployment rate, the job vacancy rate, and the non-accelerated inflation rate of unemployment (NAIRU, the rate of unemployment at which inflation is neither speeding up or slowing down). Movement along the curve (e.g., the rise and fall of unemployment and vacancy rates) reflects the state of the economic cycle.

Blindness-Visual Impairment. Typically defined as central visual acuity of 20/200 or less in the better eye with the use of a correcting lens, or a limitation in the fields of vision of less than 20 degrees (i.e., tunnel vision).

Block grants. In the United states, these are grants to states that can be used for a variety of purposes, funded by annual appropriations passed by Congress, and allocated to states by a determined formula. This type of grant to states typically provides states considerable flexibility in delivering outlined services to their beneficiaries.

Bounded rationality. Describes how policy makers look at decisions in terms of limited alternatives that are based on their assessment of the consequences created by the alternatives. Decisions are made by balancing the ability to achieve the most while minimizing unacceptable costs (economic and political).

Budget. The estimated government revenues and expenditures for a given year. The budget process consists of activities that encompass the development, implementation, and evaluation of a plan for the provision of services and capital assets, characterized by: (a) a long-term perspective, (b) linkages to broad goals, (c) results and outcomes, involvement and promotion of effective communication with stakeholders, and (d) incentives to government entities.

Capitation. Form of payment for services rendered by health-care providers by means of a prepaid, flat monthly fee for each covered plan member. Payment does not take into consideration the frequency or actual costs of providing services to that individual member.

Capped entitlement program. An entitlement program whose maximum funding is set by law. States can participate in these programs which are typically part of a matching grant structure. The amount of the funds they receive is based on a formula that determines how much of the total amount available nationwide goes to them.

Categorical grant. In the United States, an allocation of funds to a designated program for a specified purpose.

Child benefit. As defined by the Social Security Administration, monthly benefits to children of a retired, disabled, or deceased worker that was fully or currently insured. Benefits provided to unmarried children under 18 (19 if attending elementary or secondary school full time) and to disabled children 18 or older who become disabled before age 22. Under certain circumstances, benefits can be paid to stepchildren, grandchildren, or adopted children, and benefits for disabled children may continue if they marry certain other Social Security beneficiaries.

Child care. Time and activities devoted to the supervision and direct care of a child's needs, either at home or at a place designated and certified to provide such a service. Childcare is typically considered one of the responsibilities of parenthood; however, modern usage has expanded the concept of institutional care in lieu of the parent(s) ability to provide direct care and supervision.

Child Care and Development Block Grant (CCDBG). Federal program funded through a block grant to states and Native American tribes to assist low-income families with child care. States are given maximum flexibility in developing childcare policies and programs best suited to meet the needs of children and parents in the state as a means to encourage working parents to make their own decisions about childcare. The program also focuses on providing childcare to those individuals wanting independence from public assistance while providing states assistance in implementing health, safety, licensing, and registration standards established in state regulations.

Child Care and Development Fund (CCDF). A funding pattern description of federal funds provided through the annual appropriations process and entitlement funding for child care program support purposes through the states.

Child(ren). According to the U.S. Bureau of the Census, all unmarried, non-head of household individuals under age 18.

Child tax credit. A tax credit for each qualifying child in the household. A qualifying child is under the age of 17 who the taxpayer claims as a dependent exemption and is a son or daughter, descendant of the taxpayer, stepchild, or eligible foster child. Usually, the maximum amount for each child for each tax year cannot exceed the excess of the taxpayer's tax liability over the minimum tax liability. In the U.S., taxpayers with three or more children, the maximum credit amount cannot exceed the greater of (1) the general rule already described, or (2) an amount equal to the excess

of the sum of the taxpayer's regular income tax liability and the employee FICA share.

Chronic poverty. People in a situation in which the level of living of an individual, family, or group is below the standard of living of the community—either in terms of subsistence or normal standards of income required for at least modest participation in community life—for the majority, if not, the whole of their lives.

Claimant. Person on whose behalf the petition for benefits is filed.

Clinical Laboratory Improvement Amendments of 1988 (CLIA). All clinical laboratories must be properly certified to receive payments from Medicare or Medicaid payments for work done. Under this law, quality standards for all laboratory testing to ensure the accuracy, reliability, and timeliness of patient test results, regardless of where the test was performed, are established and monitored for compliance.

Competitive grants. Grants given in response to a request for proposal (RFP) from a sponsoring entity (government, NGO, or other private organization) that is open to applicants that are recognized as appropriate to perform the services asked for in the request for proposal. The review process is based on set guidelines that must be met in order to receive the award. Typically, these grants are awarded on the merit of the proposal in relation to proposal requirements, proposal evaluation criteria, and determination of applicant's ability to provide the asked for services.

Concurrent budget resolution. In the United States, it is the instrument passed by both houses of Congress but not signed by the president providing total budget authority, outlays, and deficit, and a subdivision of spending by functional category for the fiscal year.

Consolidated Omnibus Budget Reconciliation Act of 1986 (COBRA). Amends the Employee Retirement Income Security Act (ERISA), the Internal Revenue Code, and the Public Health Service Act to provide continuation of employer-sponsored group health coverage that otherwise might be terminated. The law generally covers group health plans maintained by employers with twenty or more employees. Key features are the provisions giving certain types of former employees, retirees, spouses, former spouses, and dependent children the right to temporary continuation of health coverage at group rates when coverage is lost due to certain specific events (reduction of hours, voluntary or involuntary termination of employment for reasons other than "gross misconduct").

Consumer price index (CPI). An indicator of consumer prices obtained by calculating the cost of a fixed "basket" of goods purchased on a monthly basis (including housing, electricity, food, and transportation). It is one of the most common indicators to determine inflation. Also called a cost-of-living index.

Consumer price index for urban wage earners and clerical workers (CPI-W). A relative measure of inflation prepared by the U.S. Department of Labor that is used to compute the annual COLA increases in benefits.

Consumption. Spending for purchasing done by individuals for the purpose of directly and indirectly acquiring and using goods and services (e.g., food, clothing, housing).

Continuing resolution. In the United States, legislation extending appropriations for specific ongoing programs when the regular appropriation has not been enacted by the beginning of the new fiscal year on October 1.

Contributions. Typically, taxes or other forms of payment similar to taxes to support a government program. Also, voluntary payments to a retirement plan, annuity, or other investment vehicle established by the individual. In the U.S., contributions include amounts paid by individuals and employers based on a percentage of an individual's earnings as required and determined by FICA, SECA, and state regulations for those state employees covered through voluntary agreements by states with social security.

Cost of living adjustment (COLA). Annual benefit increases to keep up with inflation rates.

Cost of living standard. How much it costs for individuals to meet the basic expectations of consumption requirements and expectations in a community. Also called "standard of living."

Counted income. Income and assets used to determine the income generation aspect of means-tests and other eligibility requirements for receiving benefits or aid.

Covered employee. Employees who qualify are eligible to receive benefits from a defined program by virtue of employment and/or contributions into the benefit scheme. For example, unemployment insurance schemes are based on worker and employer contributions into the system. Workers contributing into the scheme are considered "covered."

Creditable coverage. Prior health care coverage considered in determining allowable extent of pre-existing condition exclusion periods for individuals entering a group health plan or to determine if the individual is HIPAA eligible when seeking individual health coverage. Most health care falls under creditable coverage.

Currently insured status. A person who is covered under Social Security and is in process of meeting eligibility criteria, but who has not reached full retirement age. This means that the person is currently working and receiving credit for contributions during the years prior to retirement eligibility or determination of disability status.

Custodial parent. The parent who takes care and has direct oversight of the child(ren) most, if not all, of the time. The term also refers to that parent who the courts recognize as having custody, i.e., the legal responsibilities (food, clothing, shelter, education, economic and moral well-being) for the child(ren).

Deadbeat parent. A noncustodial parent that has a legal obligation to pay child support to the custodial parent, but who fails to meet the obligation and is in breach of divorce or legal decree and, typically, of laws concerning child protection and welfare.

Deceased worker. An individual who has died either after beginning to receive retirement benefits, or who has not reached retirement option age, and prior to placing any claims.

Deeming. The income and resources of certain persons who live with an SSI recipient when determining the amount of the payment: ineligible spouses of adult recipients, ineligible parents of child recipients under age 18, and the immigration sponsor for certain noncitizens.

Defined contribution plan. Required to satisfy specific funding stipulations in order to maintain participation and program solvency. An individual account for each participant, with benefits are largely based on the amount contributed; however, they tend to be affected by income, expenses, gains, and losses.

Dependent. Persons that are economically dependent on others for their economic well-being.

Dependent benefits. Monthly benefit paid to spouse or child of retired or disabled worker.

Dependent care tax credit. A non-refundable credit against income tax liability for up to 30 percent of a limited amount of employment-related dependent care expenses; limited to $2,400 for one qualifying dependent or $4,800 for two or more qualifying dependents (a dependent qualifies if under age 13 or a physically or mentally incapacitated dependent or spouse). Expenses that can be considered for this credit are those incurred directly in order to be able to be or remain gainfully employed. Expenses may not generally exceed an individual's earned income (if married, the earned income of the spouse making the lesser income). The credit rate is 30 percent, with it reduced to no less than 20 percent by one percentage point for each $2,000 of the adjusted gross income (AGI) above $10,000 (married couples are required to file a joint return for this credit, and their combined AGI is used for determination purposes).

Deprivation. The lack, loss, or inability to access of items that are at the least needed, or otherwise desired/wanted.

Direct assistance. Cash and/or services provided by a program directly to the beneficiary and not to the agency or organization providing the administration or services.

Disability insurance (DI). In the U.S., coverage that is part of Title II of the Social Security Act that allows for benefits for individuals who are determined to not be able to engage is substantial gainful activity for at least twelve months as a result of a medically verifiable condition beyond blindness.

Disability pension. Benefits paid to disabled employee and qualifying dependents.

Disabled child benefit. Monthly benefit to a disabled person who is 18 or older (son, daughter, or eligible grandchild) of retired, deceased, or disabled worker, whose disability began before age 22.

Disabled/disability. Inability to perform in a substantial gainful activity (SGA) due to medically determinable physical or mental impairment that may result in death or expected to continuously last longer than twelve months. Special rules typically apply to workers 55 or older whose disability is the result of blindness.

Discretionary programs. In the United States, programs funded by annual appropriations bills. At the federal level, "appropriated entitlements" such as veterans' compensation are exempt because expenditures are capped.

Discretionary spending cap. Limits placed on the total amount of budget authority and outlays for discretionary programs that legislatures may provide in a given fiscal year.

Diversification. A risk minimizing strategy based on having more than one type of asset, program, or strategy geared to ensure the well-being of an individual and/or his or her family or significant others.

Dividends. Income received from stock holdings and mutual funds accounts. Capital gains are not considered dividends.

Division of labor. The breakdown of tasks that are accomplished in a group or social setting, such as businesses and government agencies. Tasks are broken down into specified components, identified and then delegated to an individual or individuals whose duties and responsibilities center on the accomplishment of the identified task(s).

Drug addiction and alcoholism as Entitlement Disqualification. Legislation enacted in 1996 eliminated drug addiction and alcoholism (DA&A) as a basis for entitlement to Social Security and SSI disability benefits in the U.S. Individuals for whom drugs and/or alcohol is deemed a contributing factor material to the determination of disability will not be entitled to disability benefits. Those individuals already receiving disability benefits would cease receiving them, although they can request a new medical determination.

Earned income tax credit (EITC). A federal government tax-transfer program that provides tax reductions and wage supplements for low- and moderate-income working families through their income tax returns. Approximately seventeen states have a form of EITC based on the federal credit (all but one state). It has three phases, one where credits are earned as income increases, a second where the amount of credits flattens out and is maximized, and a third where a reduction or phase-out occurs as a result of the worker's income increasing.

Economy of scale. Increased operational efficiency in the use of resources. Costs or efforts are reduced because of increased activity or production. In terms of the latter, as production increases, it costs less to produce each unit.

Education IRAs. A trust or custodial account established expressly for the purpose of paying qualified higher education expenses of a named beneficiary. Contributions in the year 2000 were limited to $500 per year per beneficiary. Contributions are not deductible, and at present not included as part of income. As with other IRAs, there is a penalty for early withdrawal and use for purposes other than meeting the qualified higher education expenses.

EITC state nonrefundable credit. A state credit based on the percentage of the federal EITC credit that is credited to the taxpayer by reducing or eliminating the tax burden.

EITC state refundable credit. A state credit based on the percentage of the federal EITC credit that is paid to the taxpayer only if the credit is higher than the tax burden, i.e., the taxpayer gets a refund check.

Eligibility requirements. Defined criteria (usually by law or regulation) that determine whether or not a person, family, or other interested party is able to participate in and receive benefits from a program—the needed answers to the "who" and "what" questions. These provide the guidelines that provide the first step in the determination process, usually, the means-tests utilized by many programs to determine who can participate and qualify to receive benefits.

Eligible couple. Two persons, both qualifying for SSI, living together as married. Also, two persons living together meeting eligibility criteria.

Eligible worker. An individual that meets age and insured status requirements for retirement benefits whether or not he or she has filed for them.

Emergency advance payments. SSI payment that is available at the initial application for individuals who need immediate assistance prior to the commencement of regular payments. The advance is withheld from the first check.

Employee Retirement Income Security Act of 1974 (ERISA). U.S. federal law that provides detailed regulations for many aspects of defined contribution plans, providing detailed descriptions of the available benefits. It outlines which employees must receive a pension (if offered) and requires that employees become vested in their retirement programs after working for a given number of years and/or have reached a given age. The law makes provisions for survivors to receive benefits in case of an employee's death while still employed along with detailing the fiduciary and reporting responsibilities the retirement fund program must follow for compliance purposes. In addition, the law provides for grievance and appeals processes and gives participants the right to sue for benefits and breaches of fiduciary duty.

Employee. According to the Internal Revenue Service, an individual who performs services for a third party that pays that individual to perform those services, and who is subject to the employer's direction, rule, or control as to the method of performing or executing the services and the result to be effected or accomplished, with some stipulated legal limitations.

Employer. According to the Social Security Administration, (1) a corporation organized under the laws of the United States or any state, (2) a partnership if at least two-thirds of the partners are U.S. residents, (3) an individual who is a resident of the United States, or (4) a trust if all the trustees are U.S. residents.

Employer provided dependent care exclusion. The value of certain employer provided dependent care is excluded from an employee's gross income up to $5,000/year ($2,500 if married and filing separately). Programs meeting the requirements for this exclusion are that the program needs to be described in writing, satisfy certain non-discrimination rules, and provide notification of program to all employees. The type of care eligible is the same as that for the dependent care credit.

Engel's law. An observed phenomenon which states that the proportion a family spends on food decreases as that family's income increases.

Entitlement. A legal provision creating a binding obligation on the government to pay benefits to those individuals who meet statutory-defined eligibility criteria. In the area of social policy, these obligations take on the form of funds to provide assistance or services to those identified to have the obligation met. Those meeting eligibility criteria not receiving benefits have legal recourse in order to pursue the meeting of the obligation. Entitlements can be retroactive and precede the award date. There is also the term *technical entitlement* denoting an entitlement occurring when a beneficiary is entitled to benefits from more than one earning record, but who can only receive benefit from one of these earning records.

Entitlement program. A program mandating the payment of benefits to claimants meeting eligibility requirements that are established by statute, with amounts spent not controlled by annual appropriations. In certain programs, the existing appropriation line is permanent. In the United States, examples of entitlement programs include Social Security, Medicare and Medicaid.

Equality. The expectation that all people are to be treated alike by society and its organizations. The presumption is based on the view that no individual has a claim to preferential treatment without compelling reasons that are deemed legitimate to the claim.

Equity. A matter of fairness, centered on applying the rule to all. In early legal writing, it is referred to as "giving a person his or her due."

Extended benefits (EB) program. Federal-state program extending benefits to workers who had exhausted their benefits up to an additional thirteen weeks and, in some instances, second extension up to another eight weeks. The federal government and the states pay an equal share into this program; however, certain criteria must be in place for this program to become operable.

Extremely low income. Income below 30 percent of area median family income.

Factor. Often used as an input measure to production.

Fair Labor Standards Act of 1938. (FLSA) Federal law providing for minimum standards in wages and overtime entitlement. It also spells out administrative procedures by which covered work time must be compensated. The act also includes provisions related to child labor, equal pay, and portal-to-portal activities. In addition, the act exempts specified employees or groups of employees from the application of certain of its provisions. As of 1974, the act applies to government employees as well.

Fairness. Procedures and practices giving citizens a degree of sameness in decisions governing them. This is typically done by the establishment of obligations. Expectation and actions are based on the notion that institutions are fair and there is a voluntary exchange based on a perceived notion of benefit in the arrangement. It is these voluntary acts that lead to obligations that are normally owed to defined groups of individuals who recognize and follow through with the arrangements that make up the obligation and its end-result.

Family. According to the U.S. Bureau of the Census, a family is defined as a group of two or more persons related by birth, marriage, or adoption who live together.

Family average. The determination of what a typical family is within a society based on the number of adults and children, age, and/or wage earners on which formulae or decisions on benefit eligibility or monetary allocations are made.

Family budget. The spending levels of families based on their consumption patterns. It is a normative process in which consumption is based on meeting basic needs such as food, clothing, housing, transportation.

Family maximum benefit. The maximum monthly amount that may be paid on a worker's earnings record. Whenever the total of individual benefits exceeds this amount, each dependent or survivor benefits are proportionally reduced to bring the total within the allowable limit.

Family preservation services. A program under Title IV-B, subpart B that is a capped entitlement along with Family support services programs ($275 million in 1999, $295 million in 2000, $305 million in 2001), it is intended for children and families (including extended and adoptive families) that are at risk or in crisis. Services include helping children reunite with their biological families (if appropriate) or place them for adoption or other permanent placement, prevent children placement in foster care (including intense family preservation services), follow-up programs for families after a child has been returned from foster care, respite care to provide temporary relief for parents and other care givers (including foster parents), and parenting skills improvement training.

Family support services. A program under Title IV-B, subpart B that is a capped entitlement along with Family preservation services programs ($275 million in 1999, $295 million in 2000, $305 million in 2001), it is intended to reach families which are not yet in crisis, to prevent child abuse and neglect from occurring. These services are generally community-based activities designed to promote the well-being of children and the stability of families.

Family unit. A family or an individual. Size does not enter into the definition. A non–U.S. Bureau of the Census term, it has appeared in the poverty guidelines Federal Register notice since 1978 (Department of Health and Human Services, February 15, 2000).

Federal benefits rate. The benefit standards used to compute federal SSI payments. Benefit levels are reduced by one-third if an individual or couple is living in another person's household and receiving support and maintenance there.

Federal Insurance Contribution Act (FICA). Law setting rate for employee and employer contributions through a payroll tax that goes to fund the programs under Social Security. At present, the employee contribution rate is at 6.2 percent of gross earnings up to a maximum earning level in 2001 of $80,400. Employers match the contribution rate of 6.2 percent.

Federally administered payments. Federal SSI payments and those state supplements issues by the Social Security Administration on behalf of states.

Federal Unemployment Tax Act of 1939. Federal law authorizing the Internal Revenue Service to collect a federal employer tax used to fund state workforce agencies. Under the provisions of these laws, the costs of administering the UI and Job Service programs in all states are covered. It also requires the federal government to pay one-half of the cost of extended unemployment benefits (during periods of high unemployment) and provides for a fund from which states may borrow, if necessary, to pay benefits.

Fee-for-service plan. A health insurance plan where the insured person pays for services given by a healthcare provider. A participant submits a claim to the insurance company, and is reimbursed as long as the service is covered under the policy.

Financial adequacy. Having control of or access to sufficient financial resources to meet basic needs.

Fiscal year. A period of one year that defines reports and budget cycles. For many private firms, July 1 is a beginning date. For the U.S. federal government, October 1 begins the new funding year.

Food basket. The food items utilized in defining the food consumption nutritional requirements and acquisition costs for different size families. In the United States, the budget derived from these items reflects changes in the standard of living on a periodic basis (Citro and Michael, 1995).

Forecasting. The use of prior-released data to project revenues and expenditures. The resulting information is in the form of estimates because they are a "best guess" analysis of what is going to happen in a subsequent time period. Forecasting concurrent data means the use of prior-released data for comparing earlier data from the same time period as a means of adjusting data as it becomes definite to provide "accurate" trends to use in long-range forecasting activities that rely on historical data.

Formula-based grants. Grants from the U.S. federal government given to states based on the state's ability to prepare a plan that is approved by the federal government, whose funding is based on a specific formula.

Foster care. Typically, a program where the state places a child with adults other than parents or guardians on a 24-hour per day basis until the state determines otherwise. Foster parents are usually trained and certified by a state to assume care responsibility. However, there is a more intense form of foster care resulting from additional needs that the child may require. Therapeutic foster care (TFC) is specialized care for a child or youth with significant psychological, social, and emotional needs who will benefit from living in a family setting yet requires additional intensive or therapeutical services than traditional found in typical foster care.

Full benefits. Benefits provided to a person entitled to receive them that have not been reduced as a result of not meeting eligibility criteria or full retirement age.

Full employment. When all individuals wanting to work have a job that pays an adequate wage for the type of job performed.

Full-retirement age (FRA). The age at which an individual becomes entitled to unreduced benefits. The present age is 65; however, in the United States it is slowly increasing to age 67 by the year 2027.

Fully insured status. Worker meeting all age and eligibility criteria to qualify for retirement and/or disability benefits.

Gainful employment (activity)/substantial gainful employment. Compensated work that is of a sufficient amount to provide a significant amount of earnings to the individual. It is a formal determination for benefit levels based on the amount of money earned, and/or the number of hours worked, and the nature of the work itself.

Garnishment of wages. A court-ordered method or statutorily defined mechanism of collecting a debt in which a portion of a person's salary is paid to a creditor, often used to collect child support payments.

Gender neutral. Data, procedures, and language that do not have a specific reference to either gender.

Globalization. The increasing integration of the economies and societies of nations throughout the world resulting from the increasing flow of goods, services, capital, people, and information.

Government transfers. According to the U.S. Bureau of the Census, payments people receive from the following sources: unemployment compensation; state workers' compensation; Social Security (OASDI); Supplemental Security Income (SSI); public assistance (PA); veteran's benefits; government survivor benefits (OASI); government disability benefits (DI); government pensions; government educational assistance.

Gross (money) income. Moneys or benefits received before taxes are taken out by the various taxing authorities. Also known as gross earnings.

Gross domestic product (GDP). Measures the total output of goods and services for final uses within a country. It measures national performance and wealth through the consideration of the value of exports minus the value of imports.

Gross national income (GNI). Measures the total domestic and foreign income claimed by the residents of a nation. It comprises the GDP plus net factor income from abroad.

Gross national product (GNP). Measures in dollar value the overall performance of a nation's economy (goods and services). It looks at levels of consumption and investment along with government expenses.

Gross reference earnings. Earnings prior to taxes used as a threshold in determining eligibility under the U.S. unemployment insurance scheme.

Gross state product (GSP). In the United States, it is the rough equivalent of measuring production for each state. It is based on production activity and costs from all industries based in a state. A comparison between the GDP and the GSP will provide a statistical difference because the GSP does not take into account military expenditures along with different revision schedules.

Group insurance (group health plan). Health coverage sponsored by an employer or union for a group of employees, and typically for dependents. Retirees also may be able to participate in similar programs.

Group quarters. From 1983 onwards, non-institutional living arrangements for groups not living in conventional housing units or groups living in housing units containing ten or more unrelated people or nine or more people unrelated to the person in charge. Examples include a rooming house, staff quarters at a hospital, or a halfway house.

Head Start. A federal comprehensive child development program established in 1965 that serves eligible children from birth to age 5, pregnant women, and their families. The services provided are child-focused and have the overall goal of increasing the school readiness of young children in low-income families.

Health Insurance Portability and Accountability Act of 1996 (HIPAA). Protects the health insurance coverage for eligible workers and their families when they change or lose their jobs. The Act does this by ensuring that an individual receives credit for maintaining health coverage and limiting how a new employer may impose limits on healthcare coverage due to preexisting conditions.

Health Insurance Program (SCHIP). Program created in 1997 as part of the passed Balanced Budget Act that added Title XXI to the Social Security Act. Allows states to access funds to provide coverage to targeted low-income children through group health or other insurance plans. States are able to provide services through their Medicaid program while paying for the services through other funds, i.e., Title XXI funds.

Health maintenance organization (HMO). Under the Health Maintenance Organization Act of 1973, an HMO is a public or private entity which is organized under the laws of any state and which provides basic and supplemental health services to its members in the manner prescribed in the law. Members are required to pay a fixed fee on a period basis without regard to the frequency, extent, or kind of health service actually furnished (as defined by a community rating system of the costs associated with the basic health services offered under the program under U.S. Code 42, Chapter 6A, Subchapter XI). Examples of managed care organizations include the *group model HMO* (physician groups contracting with an agency that is fiscally responsible for covering enrollees, paying physicians on a per capita rate that is distributed among them),

staff model HMO (where physicians are employees of the HMO and paid a salary), *network model HMO* (HMO contracts two or more independent group practices to provide services and pay a fixed rate per enrollee to these groups), *independent practice associations* or IPA (HMO contracts with individual practice physicians or an association of them to provide services at a negotiated per capita rate), flat retainer or negotiated fee-for-service (FFS) to HMO members), *preferred provider organizations* or PPOs (combination of FFS indemnity plans and HMOs, typically run by organized insurers or providers, with contracts with network of service providers receiving payment based on a negotiated fee schedule and enrollees going to out-of-network providers pay additional out-of-pocket expenses), and *point of service* or POS (an open-ended HMO) based on a network of participating providers where employees select a primary care physician who determines referrals, with incentives to stay within the networks based on having additional out-of-pocket costs for going outside the system.

High deductible health plan. An employer-sponsored group health plan with annual deductible of no less than $1,500 and a maximum of $2,250 for individual and limits of $3,000 and $4,500 for family coverage.

Higher (tertiary) education. Education system (that includes public and private institutions) beyond that provided as part of basic instruction at the primary and secondary levels in order for children to learn those skills that prepare them for work opportunities and general citizenship obligations. Typically these systems include two- and four-year colleges and universities, with some of the universities providing postgraduate and professional training and/or technical training opportunities. These are distinct from some forms of postsecondary proprietary institutions that provide basic training skills for entry-level employment such as secretarial and paraprofessional skills.

High-risk pool. Coverage set up for individuals who are considered high risk as a result of preexisting, lifestyle conditions, combination of both, or other significant factor, and would otherwise not be able to get health insurance.

Hope Credit. In the U.S., a nonrefundable credit against federal income tax liability for qualified tuition and fees required for an eligible student attending an eligible educational institution. The credit is 100 percent of the first $1,000 of qualified tuition and fees per year, and 50 percent of the next $1,000. It is only available for the first two years of postsecondary education. A qualifying student is one that is enrolled in a degree, certificate, or other recognized academic program on at least a half-time basis. Eligibility is phased out for taxpayers with a modified adjusted gross income between $40,000 and $50,000 ($80,000 and $100,000 for joint returns).

Household. According to the U.S. Bureau of the Census, consists of all the persons who occupy a housing unit (house or apartment), whether or not they are related to each other. If there is a family living with another unrelated person, or if two unrelated persons lived in a house or apartment, both cases would be considered as two families and one household. The head of a family is referred to as a householder or head of household.

Household, own. Definition used to determine the federal benefit rate for adults who own their own living quarters, pay rent, pay a fair share of housing expenses, live in household composed of public assistance recipients only, are placed by agencies in private households, and children living with their parents.

Human capital. The ability and skills individuals have that they bring to a collective effort. It is seen as the sum of education, experience, and training. Ideally the combination of these factors provides a "value added" capability that leads to increased production.

Ideology. A way of thinking that characterizes and prescribes the way in which people who believe in this one manner value and judge cultural circumstances, events, people, products, and services based on this perspective.

Impairment-related expenses. Expenses an individual has in order to meet the costs associated with that person's disability. These expenses are identified and subtracted from the formula determining significant gainful activity for benefit determination purposes.

Income. Money accumulated by individuals as a result of exchanges made with the other elements of the community. There are two types, "earned" and "unearned." The former is the acquisition of money as a result of wages received in a labor exchange proposition (work), while the latter is the result of making money from asset accumulation, investments, gifts, and government transfers such as welfare. Also referred to as earnings.

Income determination. Identification of sources of moneys resulting from work or from receiving benefits (on a pretax or after-tax basis based on the reason for the determination) that is utilized to decide whether eligibility criteria are met.

Income maintenance. The ability to maintain a continuous stream of income that is, hopefully, sufficient to meet the minimum consumption needs of an individual or household. The concern is continuing a source of income during transition periods such as retirement, or in case of disability or other unforeseen events that have an adverse impact on the ability to earn income on a continuous basis as before.

Income, official definition of. Although shying away from a formal definition, the U.S. government asks questions about and considers the various forms of funds received from sources such as these: (1) Earnings; (2) Unemployment compensation; (3) Workers' compensation; (4) Social Security; (5) Supplemental security income; (6) Public assistance; (7) Veterans' payments; (8) Survivor benefits; (9) Disability benefits; (10) Pension or retirement income; (11) Interest; (12) Dividends; (13) Rents, royalties, and estates and trusts; (14) Educational assistance; (15) Alimony;

(16) Child support; (17) Financial assistance from outside of the household; (18) Other income.

Income, other. All other payments people receive regularly that cannot be otherwise included and accounted for as a form of revenue. Examples of this category include, but are not limited to, state programs such as foster child payments, military family allotments, and income received from foreign governments.

Income redistribution. Taxation policy held by government whose purpose it is to assist those in poverty to achieve more than a minimum standard of living. Taxes are levied in higher proportion to those earning higher incomes in order to redistribute these funds to those who are not capable of creating the same income opportunities.

Income replacement. Program that provides individuals with the means to replace their salaries or wages when they are not able to generate income from employment or private business.

Income-to-poverty ratios. According to the U.S. Bureau of the Census, it represents the ratio of family or unrelated individual income to their appropriate poverty threshold. Ratios less than 1.00 indicate that the income for the respective family or unrelated individual is below the official definition of poverty. A ratio of 1.00 or greater indicates income above the poverty level. For example, a ratio of 1.25 indicates that income was 125 percent above the appropriate poverty threshold (U.S. Census Bureau, 2002a).

Incrementalism. Political action strategy that focuses on making changes in "small measures" in order to create a series of changes that add to a major transformation of what is to be impacted.

Index. A statistical indicator that serves as a way to determine comparative standards when measuring an item or topic.

Individual health insurance. Insurance coverage that is sold by HMOs or other health insurance carriers to individuals who are not part of a group health plan. The insurance may be provided through a group or organization; however, it is not offered to individuals because they normally belong to a group such as employees.

Individual retirement account (IRA). A tax-deferred retirement account for individuals in the U.S. for up to $3,000 per year, with earnings tax-deferred until withdrawals begin at age $59\frac{1}{2}$ or later (or earlier, with a 10 percent penalty). Only those who do not participate in a pension plan at work or who do participate and meet certain income guidelines can make deductible contributions. Other individuals who want to establish an IRA can make contributions to it on a nondeductible basis.

Individual training account. As one of the requirements under the Workforce Investment Act of 1998, one-stop centers provide training assistance and other types of services based on an individual having the opportunity to choose training opportunities from eligible providers.

Inflation. A period of time when the price paid for purchased goods increases due to numerous factors such as higher production costs, transportation costs, supply and demand, and so forth.

In-kind. When money payments are substituted with services or other non-money forms of exchanges.

Institutionalization. Living arrangements for those living in public or private institutions, when more than 50 percent of care costs is met by Medicaid.

Insurance (insurance program or scheme). A plan or program whose purpose it is to protect against future losses by making current payments into the plan, spreading the risk among a pool of participants, and making it affordable to become part of the system. Some forms are required by law, others are optional. Typically, in many countries, social welfare programs are set up as an insurance program or scheme in which the person who is to receive the benefit prepays or participates in a contribution scheme in the form of payroll deduction and taxes. Often, a participant's employer is also required to contribute to the fund from which the benefits are eventually paid.

Insured (status). Having sufficient quarters of coverage to meet eligibility requirements for retired worker or disabled worker benefits, or to allow spouse, children, or survivors to be eligible to make benefit claims in case of the worker's retirement, disability, or death.

Interest income. Payments people receive (or have credited to accounts) from bonds, treasury notes, IRAs, certificates of deposit, interest bearing savings and checking accounts, and all other investments that pay interest.

Involuntary termination of employment. When a worker at a place of work looses the job as a result of condition outside his or her control. The employer makes the decision to terminate employment and acts on it. Examples of involuntary termination include, but are not limited to, downsizing, mergers, closing of firm or entire industry, lack of skills to keep other work at place of employment.

Job churning. Pattern of job availability based on the creation and elimination of jobs in various markets. This concept takes into account how jobs are developed by understanding that there will be jobs lost as a result of lack of demand as new technologies or supplanting markets are developed.

Job Training Partnership Act (JTPA). Legislation passed in 1982 that established programs to prepare youth and unskilled adults for entry into the labor force. It was also established to provide job training to those economically disadvantaged individuals facing serious barriers to employment that need such training to obtain productive employment.

Keynsian economics. An approach to economic political theory that espouses the notion that the role of government is to ensure full employment and maximize the flow of money throughout the economy to allow for profit making that, in turn, encourages production because of enhanced consumption. The emphasis is on government making decisions about the marketplace.

Lagging economic indicators. Economic variable, that fluctuates as the year goes by because of the ensuing events that impact and influence the economy. The term lagging is used because this information has to be revised; therefore, the information is already lagging current events. The GDP and unemployment rates are examples of lagging economic indicators.

Leading economic indicators. Economic indicators that are useful in forecasting events. These are also volatile in the sense that they change throughout the fiscal year's activities, but rather than being descriptive, these have the ability to provide insights to upcoming events.

Liberty. The freedom to act without constraints or interference from others because the action is protected by custom or law.

Lien. A legal claim on someone's property as security against a just debt. The type of (real) property to which a lien may be attached include land, vehicles, houses, antique furniture, and livestock.

Lifespan. Duration of a person's life, or how long a program or product lasts.

Lifetime learning credit. A nonrefundable credit against federal income tax liability for qualified tuition and fees required for an eligible student attending an eligible educational institution. The credit is 20 percent of up to $5,000 in qualified tuition and fees for a maximum credit of $1,000. As of December 31, 2002, the 20 percent credit was raised to $10,000 in qualified tuition for a maximum credit of $2,000. This credit is available for an unlimited number of years of education. It is also available with respect to any course of instruction at an eligible educational institution regardless of enrollment status. Eligibility is phased out for taxpayers with a modified adjusted gross income between $40,000 and $50,000 ($80,000 and $100,000 for joint returns).

Low (socio) economic status. Categorization identifying individuals as belonging to the lower tier of society based on their economic status as determined by income and consumption standards.

Low-income family. Families whose incomes do not exceed 80 percent of the median family income for the area.

Low-income housing credit. Tax credit that may be claimed by owners of residential property used for low-income rental housing for up to a period of 10 years. New construction and rehabilitation expenditures for low-income housing projects are for a maximum of 70 percent present value credit, claimed annually for 10 years. Acquisition costs of existing projects meeting the substantial rehabilitation requirements and costs of newly constructed projects receiving other federal subsidies are eligible for a 30 percent present value credit, also claimed annually for 10 years.

Macroeconomics. The study of aggregate performances in relationship of the GNP. It deals with the big picture—the analysis of income, employment, and price levels (Samuelson, 1976).

Maintenance of effort (MOE) requirement. State requirements under TANF that a state must spend at least a specified amount of state funds for benefits and ...vices for members of needy families each year. The stat... ust spend at least 80 percent (or 75 percent, if the stat... ...ets the TANF overall and two-parent participation rat... ...irements) of a historic state expenditure level for qu... ...tate expenditures—with the historical base being A... ...penditures in 1994.

Managed care plans. A... ...surance system character-...d providers providing health ized by a network of...this type of plan. Consequently, benefits to a de...ically managed through the net- HMOs are one-...ysicians acting as "gatekeepers." health care s... ...rticipation). Program required by work of p...ct payments. ...must join and pay contributions in the

Mandate...m state supplementation. Required by law, individuals converted to the Supplemental ...me (SSI) program from state assistance pro-... aged, blind, or disabled to insure that monthly ...not be less than the amount received under the ...ate programs.

...y spending. In the United States, spending that ...ccur in order to pay entitlement programs and the in-...t on government debt; this amounts to approximately ...-thirds of all spending at the federal-government level.

...rginalized. A social phenomenon linked to social status, typically at the lower end of a social structure. In the area of social policy, this concept refers to groups that are most often involuntarily placed outside the stream of social, economic, and political activities.

Means-test. Often referred to as an income test, it is when an agency utilizes the applicant's income (and at times other forms of assets) for eligibility determination purposes. Its purpose is to limit participation, benefits, and resources to those that meet the defined eligibility requirements, with income identifying the applicant's need.

Median income. The midpoint or half of a household's income as compared to the rest of the database (normally income figures from the Census or equivalent). This data is then utilized for income determination purposes for reports and eligibility requirements in certain public assistance programs.

Medicaid. Medicaid is a jointly-funded health insurance program by the federal and state governments for eligible low-income and needy people. According to the Centers for Medicare and Medicaid Services, it covers approximately 36 million individuals including children, the aged, blind, and/or disabled, and others who are eligible to receive federally assisted income maintenance benefits.

Medical savings account. A tax-sheltered savings account for paying medical bills. This account works in conjunction with a special low cost, "high deductible" health insurance policy, with the overall effect of providing comprehensive healthcare coverage that is affordable for those who qualify (currently, MSAs are limited to self-employed individuals and employees of small businesses with under fifty employees).

Medicare. Originally created as Title VIII of the Social Security Act in 1965, it is a health insurance program administered by the federal government for people who are 65 or older, qualifying disabled individuals under 65, and people with end-stage renal disease (permanent kidney failure treated through dialysis or transplantation). There are two components to it, Part A, for which recipients do not have to pay because they already contributed to the program through a payroll deduction plan (a tax), and Part B, for which most recipients have to pay because it is a voluntary program and payment is then taken from one's social security retirement (or railroad insurance, or civil service) monthly check. Part A provides hospital insurance while Part B principally covers non-hospital expenses and some other medical services not covered under Part A.

Minimum wage. The minimum remuneration amount set by law that a worker can receive for work performed.

Mitigation (mitigating circumstances). Action taken to reduce to a minimal or manageable level, or completely eliminate the negative impact of circumstances or events on individuals or households.

Multiple intelligences. A theory of cognitive learning that focuses on approaches to learning identified in individuals developed by Howard Gardner. These focus on a person's innate predilection for learning. There are eight types of intelligences identified in this theory: logical/mathematical, verbal/linguistic, visual/spatial, bodily/kinesthetic, musical/rhythmic, intrapersonal, interpersonal, and naturalist.

Multiplier. A number indicating the magnitude of a particula... policy or effect.

Needs. Items (such as food, clothing, shelter), services (such... medical care, utilities), or interactions (such as persona... teractions and relationships) considered essential to th... sic notions of an individual's existence.

Negative income tax. A taxation system in which s... are given to individuals, families, or households... below the poverty line. Those needing assistance... return and would receive benefits based on how... comes fell below identified levels.

Neoliberalism. Also known as "supply-side e... is an approach to economic political theory... reduce the amount of government interven... vate sector in order to allow the market t... essary corrections based on demand and... and services. The emphasis is on pers... and choice.

Noncustodial parent. The person who d... care, custody, or control of the child... of a court or regulatory decision... seen as having a formally recogni... the primary care of the child(ren)... sult of divorce proceedings or... noncustodial parents have a sp... to pay child support to assist... development of the child(ren...

Nontangible (intagible) asset. Non-physical or cash items that have an economic value attached to them (e.g., intellectual capital, human capital, earning power).

Normative. Typical of the group or class that helps define expectations and measures to determine whether those expectations are met.

Nutritious diet. The intake of food that meets the basic requirements defined to meet the needs of individuals in order to maintain their health and a lifestyle that is conducive to their overall well-being (physical and mental).

Obligation. Special social responsibilities social convention attaches to membership in formal or informal organized environments. It brings with it the expectations that for continued acceptance, certain behaviors and actions must occur in order to maintain a balance of legitimacy and fairness in the relationship.

Old-age pension (retired-worker benefit). Monthly benefit paid to a fully insured retired worker who is 62 or older, or to a person that is entitled under the transitionally insured status provision under the law.

Old-Age, Survivor, and Disability Insurance (OASDI). Program under social security systems paying monthly cash benefits to retired-worker beneficiaries, dependents, and the retired-worker's survivors on death and, in addition, to disabled-worker beneficiaries, their spouses and children, and for providing rehabilitation services to the disabled.

..., Survivor Insurance (OASI). Social Security providing monthly cash benefits to retired-worker beneficiaries and their spouses and children, and survivors of insured workers.

... Centers who purpose it is to provide assistance to individuals seeking work under the Workforce ... Act of 1998.

... Economic Co-operation and Development ... national organization made up of thirty ... share a commitment to democratic ... market economy. It has an active relationship with other nations, nongovernment ... Its purpose is to assist government ... responsiveness of key economic ... different geographical areas and ... policies by deciphering ... practices that work.

Owner-occupied housing (expense) tax deductions. Mortgage interest deductions on two classes of interest: interest on acquisition indebtedness ($1,000,000 total; $500,000 for married individuals filing a separate return) and interest on home equity indebtedness (lesser of $100,000–$50,000 for married person filing ... residence's fair market value, or the excess of the deductions are done as itemly, taxable income. Can also deduct loan period). These points (up front interest payments in computing house and paying real property taxes ... payments of ... chase of a

Pension plan. Program created for participants ... receive retirement income once they ... or pursue substantial gainful activity. Se... tions, government agencies, labor unions, are ... ization types, these can take on various forms ... options, profit sharing, defined plans, etc.

Pension. Compensation received by a retired person ... employer through a retirement plan and/or social se... benefits.

Per capita basis. Economic indicators broken down to a p... person average.

Police powers. The authority to establish and enforce legislation to regulate the actions of people to protect or promote the interests of public peace, safety, health and morals. (Refer to *Miller v. Board of Public Works*, 195 Cal. 477, 485, 234 Pac. 381 [1925])

Policy. A stated official standard that establishes the formally accepted goals that need to be accomplished to meet economic, political, or social aims.

Poor. A person who is unable to meet all of his or her basic needs to maintain life (for example, food, clothing, housing, and medical assistance).

Poverty. Lacking adequate resources to meet one's needs because of deprivation or inability to access these resources, which is why it is most typically defined in terms of income. The focus on resources means that there is a shortfall of consumption based on the lack of income necessary to reliably access those basic items and services as others in the community.

Poverty guidelines. In the United States, the official definition of poverty generated by the U.S. Department of Health and Human Services to use as the standards to determine eligibility requirements for many of the programs existing within the social safety net framework. The standard is generated as a result of tweaking and aligning the poverty thresholds provided by the Bureau of Statistics for different family categories.

Poverty line. The official or quasidefinition used by governments and other agencies to define who is poor and determine the level of individuals that fall within the definition. Typically, the line is defined either in terms of income or consumption patterns of individuals within a society. It is the absolute measure of the minimum standards of the community in respect to the amount of access to resources (typically income) necessary to partake in the consumption of goods or participation in acceptable, appropriate, and desirable social practices.

Poverty, official measure of. A set of money income thresholds that vary by family size and composition that a government agency uses to determine who is poor and who may be eligible for benefits and services, as a means to redistribute income to ensure these individuals have access to goods and services that other members of the community have.

Poverty thresholds. In the United States, it is the official definition of poverty for statistical and reporting purposes. The Bureau of Statistics generates the thresholds from data gathered and generated by the Census Bureau. The basic formula is based on determining food costs for different family (household) units times a multiplier (a factor of 3 for families of three or more) to account for the costs of other basic needs; the formula is updated annually to take into account a change in prices from one year to the next.

Pragmatic reasonableness. An action strategy that centers on increasing the credibility of individuals involved in a decision-making process by looking at the situation on a "real" basis, independent of their own personal preferences.

Prenatal care. Identified health needs for pregnant women and those services available to them as the fetus develops prior to birth.

Price index. Average price of a type of goods relative to a base year. A typical formula for quantities q and prices p^b, p^g in the base and given years is $I = 100\mathrm{S}p^g q/\mathrm{S}p^b q$.

Primary care physician. Physician who is the point of first contact with patients and takes on the continued responsibility for providing a person's medical care, usually a general practitioner.

Primary insurance amount (PIA). A formula-derived monthly amount payable to a retired worker beginning to receive benefits at the normal retirement age, or to a disabled-worker not already receiving a retirement benefit at a reduced level. Moreover, based on the worker's average monthly wage or indexed monthly earnings, it is the amount used as a base for computing all forms of benefits payable on the basis of an individual's earning record.

Procurement. For the federal government in the United States, the process of obtaining services, supplies, and equipment in conformance with applicable laws and regulations.

Producer price index (PPI). Measures the price of goods at the wholesale level in three category levels: crude goods, intermediate goods, and finished goods.

Profit sharing. An arrangement whereby an employer agrees to share a portion of its profits with employees in the form of cash, stocks or bonds redeemable immediately or deferred until retirement. The arrangement has a formula it uses to allocate the overall accumulation and distribution after retirement age is reached. Contributions are tax deductible only if plans are defined as an elective deferral plan.

Protestant ethic. Thesis developed by the German sociologist Max Weber (1864–1920) that stated that the religious zeal of Protestants gave a sense of calling and an ascetic ethic to laborers as well as to entrepreneurs and businessmen that led to higher productivity and creation of wealth. In other words, capitalism thrived because of personal drive and desire to earn and save as much as possible, and then give in the form of charity. Thus, personal industry is the measure by which individuals can take care of themselves.

Qualified state tuition programs. Two types of programs established and maintained by a state through which individuals can "buy" higher education for their children at a later date. The first type of program allows the purchase of tuition credits for a specified beneficiary that entitles that beneficiary to a waiver or payment of qualified higher education expenses. The second type of program allows individuals to make contributions of an account that is established for the purpose of meeting qualified higher education expenses.

Quality control/assurance. Quality control is a managerial process in an organization to provide stability. It is one of three basic processes through which quality can be managed, the other two being quality planning and quality improvement. Quality assurance's main purpose is to verify that quality control is maintained. Performance is evaluated after operations whereas quality control evaluates performance during operations.

Quality of life (QoL). An individual's perception of how he or she is satisfied with the choices and opportunities and resulting actions throughout life. Although this perception is individualized, it is also normalized because of the individual identifying himself or herself with the cultural mores of the community in which he or she lives, and the expectations these place on correctness and success vis-à-vis satisfaction. As a measure of how well an individual is doing, medical professionals, psychologists, economists, social workers, and policy professionals utilize the concept to define well-being.

Quarters of coverage (QCs). How credit is given for how long the individual has been covered under a program. A worker receives one quarter of credit, up to four per (the maximum allowed for any one year). No quarter credited from the quarter after death occurred, or quarter considered to be entirely covered under the of disability.

Real property. Assets owned by an individual that ble in nature: e.g., land, jewelry, vehicles, hous furniture, and livestock.

Reasonable effort. An element of the formula ing Title IV-E eligibility determination. Acc law and enacted legislation, reasonable ef lines provided to the state to follow in adr programs. In *Pennhurst State School an derman* (451 US 1, 101 S. Ct. 1531, [1981]) the U.S. Supreme Court state macy of Congress' power to legislate power thus rests on whether the knowingly accepts the terms of the 'contract.' There can, of course, be no knowing acceptance if a State is unaware of the conditions or is unable to ascertain what is expected of it. Accordingly, if Congress intends to impose a condition on the grant of federal moneys, it must do so unambiguously." In *Suter v. Artist M* (503 US 347, 112 S. Ct. *1360*, 118 L. Ed. 2d 1 [1992]) the Court made this determination as it applied to this area by indicating that "[the] term 'reasonable efforts' in this context is at least as plausibly read to impose only a rather generalized duty on the State, to be enforced not by private individuals, but by the Secretary [of Health and Human Services] in the manner previously discussed."

Reconciliation. In the United States, the process used by the federal government to amend tax and entitlement programs to meet the instructions in the budget resolution regarding outlay and revenue targets.

Redetermination. The periodic review for each SSI income recipient to ensure continued eligibility and appropriate level of payments.

Reduced (partial) benefits. Benefits given for those electing to retire before achieving fully retired status (ages 62–64) or who do not meet the other criteria for full-time benefits.

Regulatory compliance. Meeting the rules set forth by legislation or regulations that define the program in question.

Relative thresholds (standards). When standards and cutoffs of well-being in social settings are set by experts in a subjective (or arbitrary) manner. It is argued that in consequence, these standards do not provide a stable target to measure the effects of social programs because these change according to fluctuations in consumption levels rather than in fixed (quantified) real terms.

's, royalties, and estates and trusts. Net income derived the rental of a house, store, or other property. Also taken in from boarders or lodgers. Net royalty income periodic payments from estate or trust funds are red under these types of money revenues.

ion. The process of making decisions of or other needed assets and services are given program or recipients of actions am in question.

tual resources given to a program rated actions.

chological item that is considment to accomplish a task or

of the period in a person's er working, usually be- n age.

ed States, increasing desiring full retire- considered to be Inited States and by legislature. es and females

Retirement, early. Option to claim benefits prior to full retirement age. Benefits received under this option are actuarially reduced because person wanting benefits has not reached full retirement status. In the United States, the earliest age for a pension from Social Security is age 62.

Risk. The ability of an individual or family to face uncertainty in day-to-day life and to be able to cope with the unexpected consequences that uncertainty brings in the course of events. Typically seen in negative terms, it is considered as a planned or unplanned adverse event impacting one's life.

Risk management. The process of identifying and analyzing risk, the level of exposure to it, and determining a course of action to minimize its potential for an adverse effect.

Roth IRA. An individual retirement account (IRA) that has nondeductible contributions in order to generate tax-free growth.

Satisficing. Psychological perspective denoting the acceptance by a group or an individual of conditions, events, products, and services. The emphasis is on satisfactory rather than optimal outcomes from the point of view of that group or individual. In economics, this approach is in contrast with optimizing behavior that assumes that people attempt to optimize their opportunities.

School Lunch and Breakfast Program. A U.S. Federal government program providing federal cash along with federal food surpluses for the purpose of providing free or reduced cost breakfast and lunch for eligible children at schools and residential child care institutions that opt to be enrolled in this plan. This is an entitlement program for eligible low-income children that gives meals that meet the federal nutritional guidelines.

Self-employed. A person deriving income from operating a partnership or non-incorporated trade or business, i.e., a person who is working for himself or herself and whose activities in this area are the primary source of earned income.

Self-Employed Contribution Act (SECA). Federal law defining the amount of social security contributions that self-employed individuals must contribute. At present, the rate is set at 12.4 percent of earned net income in the United States. This distinction is typical in many countries, and participation is defined by legislation that normally makes participation either compulsory, voluntary, or both because of more than one available insurance-based pension scheme.

Shock (impact). Emotional or physical reaction to a sudden, typically unexpected event, often unpleasant that can result in an adverse effect or response leading to the creation of damage (emotional, physical, social, economic) of an individual.

Social benefit. Internal and external activities, decisions, events, and/or policies that are perceived to be in society's best interest rather than benefitting the private interest of a limited number of individuals.

Social Darwinism. A belief popular in the late nineteenth and into the twentieth century in England, parts of Europe, and the United States, applying Darwin's theory of evolution to social systems. The basic premise is that the strongest or fittest should survive and prosper while the weak and unfit should be allowed to die.

Social exclusion. A broad term utilized to refer to a situation whereby certain individuals and/or groups are deprived of the ability to identify with or participate in the activities of others. It is suggestive of a breakdown in the relationships that exists within a community between an identified class or group of individuals who share certain traits. Usually, the deprivation results in loss of social status, political clout, and/or economic loss.

Social safety net. For the purposes of this text, the social safety net is defined as having meeting the following criteria: (a) government or programs (at national, state or province, and/or local levels) that are designed to assist those needing assistance to maintain a basic standard of living as defined by the community; (b) defined by the powers that be as appropriate to provide available resources to those deemed eligible; (c) that may also be supported by private philanthropic or community-based nongovernment organizations (NGOs) whose purpose is to assist those in need of assistance in accordance to their own interests; and (d) whose performance can be measured in economic and social terms relating to the ability for the participants to at the least maintain if not enhance their quality of life.

Social security. Considered to be pensions and survivor benefits and permanent disability payments made by the Social Security Administration prior to deductions for medical insurance (U.S. Census Bureau, 2002).

Social Security Act. Public Law 74-271, enacted August 14, 1935. The Social Security Act consists of twenty titles, four have been repealed, and the remainder have been changed through subsequent amendments to the act.

Social Security Administration. An independent agency of the U.S. federal government, it is charged with the administration of the Title II OASDI programs and Title XVI Supplemental Security Income (SSI).

Social security trust fund. The four separate U.S. Treasury accounts in which the equivalent of taxes received under the Federal Insurance Contribution Act (FICA) are deposited to pay for the OASI, DI Benefit programs along with the HI and supplementary medical insurance (SMI) programs. Deposits also include contributions by state and local government employees, sums from the railroad retirement account, voluntary hospital and medical insurance premiums, and transfers of federal general revenues. Funds not distributed are invested in interest-bearing federal securities as required by law, with the interest earned also deposited into the trust fund.

Social welfare. A system that transfers resource allocations from one defined group to another defined group through a government agency or other accepted social organization that set the rules and roles of participants who administer the system and receive the benefits from the resource reallocation. For the purposes of this book, social welfare is part of the social safety net structure, with the social safety net structure encompassing other aspects of policy that impact other sectors such as financial and monetary, but whose impact on social issues is still critical.

Special interest(s) groups. Formal or informal groups that come together because of a similarity in points-of-view and/or goals, with the purpose of entering into a position of recognition and/responsibility who has access to the flow of information relevant to the group's interests and to make others aware of their opinions in order to influence or control the outcomes in these areas.

Spouse's benefit. Monthly benefit payable to spouse or divorced spouse of a retired-worker or disabled-worker under one of three conditions: (1) spouse is 62 or more and has an entitled child 16 or under of the worker under his or her care, or (2) divorced spouse was married to the worker for at least ten years prior to the divorce becoming final, or (3) a deemed spouse regardless of whether the legal spouse is entitled to benefits on the same earnings record.

Standard budget. A defined list of goods and services that families of particular size and make up require to consume over a year to live at a specified level of comfort.

State-administered supplementation. Payments to eligible persons based on state provisions, with payments varying in accordance to the recipient's living situation and geographical location within a state.

State supplementation, optional. Amount of benefits that may be paid to beneficiaries by some states to supplemental security income (SSI) recipients to approximate the total benefits paid with the state's cost of living standard.

Stock option(s). A program where a qualifying employee is capable of buying stock (usually common stock) in his or her company at a specified rate by a specifically defined time frame.

Student loan interest tax credits. A deduction of interest on qualified education loans, allowed only during the first sixty months in which interest payments are required.

Subsidy. Financial assistance or aid given by the government to individuals, organizations, and businesses as a result of program participation or as a form of temporary assistance to help through shortfall situations.

Substantial gainful activity. Work for which individual is compensated that is "substantial" in nature as determined from how much money was earned, and/or the number of hours worked, and the type of work involved.

Substitutive care. Term utilized for programs focused on providing services for children that are no longer part of their family. Foster care is a typical type of substitutive care.

Supplementary Security Income (SSI). Federally administered program for the needy aged, blind, and disabled that replaced the former federal-state programs of Old-Age Assistance, Aid to the Blind, and Aid to the Permanently and Totally Disabled.

Survivor benefits. Benefit payable to surviving members of the deceased family (based on definition and eligibility criteria for determining who qualifies as a surviving family member).

Survivor pension. Benefits allowed to a retired-worker's or disabled-worker's surviving member of the family based on the deceased's earnings record.

Survivor. A deceased worker's spouse, child(ren), and/or other qualifying dependents who are or may be entitled to benefits resulting from the worker's earnings record.

Tangible asset. Assets that are physical in nature such as cash, equipment, real estate, inventory, accounts receivable, etc.

Tax credits for the elderly and certain disabled individuals. Individuals that qualify are aged 65 or older and individuals, regardless of age, who are retired, on disability, and who were permanently and totally disabled at retirement. The maximum base for the credit for elderly or disabled individuals and married couples is $5,000 ($7,500 for a married couple filing jointly where only one of the two individuals qualifies or $3,750 for a married individual filing separately). For non-elderly disabled individuals, the base is the lesser amount of the applicable specified amount or the individual's annual disability income for the year. The maximum rate is reduced by the amount of certain nontaxable income such as untaxed social security benefits, railroad retirement, or veterans' non-service-related benefits.

Tax transfer system. Tax policy that has the effect of transferring income from one class of taxpayer to another, typically, from higher-income groups to lower-income groups. Tax transfers can also go to moderate-income earners dependent on legislative actions and social policy, although this class of individuals (or families, or households) typically receives a lower proportion of the transfer in relation to those identified as low-income.

Taxable Earnings. The U.S. Census Bureau recognizes three types of earnings: (1) *money wage or salary income*—the total income people receive for work performed as an employee during the income year; (2) *net income from non-farm self-employment*—net money income (gross receipts minus expenses) from one's own business, professional enterprise, or partnership where gross receipts include the value of all goods sold and services, and accepted expenses include costs of goods purchased, rent, heat, power, depreciation charges, wages and salaries paid, and business taxes (personal income taxes are not included); and (3) *net income from farm self-employment*—money income (gross receipts minus operating expenses) from the operation of a farm by a person on their own account (as an owner, renter, or sharecropper), with gross receipts including value of all products sold; payments from government farm programs; money received from the rental of farm equipment to others; rent received from farm property if payment is made based on a percent of crops produced; and incidental receipts from the sale of items such as wood, sand, and gravel. Operating expenses include terms such as cost of feed, fertilizer, seed, and other farming supplies; cash wages paid to farmhands; depreciation charges; cash rent; interest on farm mortgages; farm building repairs; and farm taxes (not state and federal personal income taxes) rendered.

Tax-exempt interest. Interest that is exempt from federal income tax, but may be subject to tax in certain state jurisdictions.

Temporary Assistance for Needy Families (TANF). Created by the Personal Responsibility and Work Opportunity Reconciliation Act (PRWORA) in 1997, it replaced the Aid to Families with Dependent Children and related welfare programs. This program centers on promoting work as the means of reducing the dependency of the poor on the benefits made available through the U.S. social safety net. The purposes behind TANF are to (1) assist needy families so children can be cared for in their own homes, (2) reduce the parents' dependency on welfare benefits by promoting job preparation, work, and marriage, (3) prevent out-of-wedlock pregnancies, and (4) encourage the formation and maintenance of two-parent families.

Terminated for cause. When an employee is permanently dismissed ("fired") from work as a result of not keeping with the duties and responsibilities of the job, and/or disruptive behavior, and/or the commission of illegal acts. Under these circumstances, the individual is deemed to have a responsibility in creating his or her unemployment status; therefore, jeopardizing the claim for unemployment benefits.

Termination of employment, voluntary. When an individual decides to leave the employer in order to pursue other opportunities or interests. The employee makes the decision and acts on it, not the employer.

Theoretical proposition. When conducting many forms of research, the model that is used as the basis for predicting what should happen based on the assumptions upon which the model rests.

Title II of the Social Security Act. Actual component of the Social Security Act that authorizes the creation of the social security trust funds and the OASI and DI programs along with the administrative regulations that make up its operational activities.

Trust fund. Assets held in a trust.

Uncertainty. Not having knowledge of what is going to happen next. Risk under these circumstances cannot be measured and the potential for an adverse effect is therefore increased.

Unearned income. Income that is not taxed as part of individual income such as interest, dividends, capital gains, or rents.

Unemployment. Used to refer collectively to people who are out of work. There are various types of unemployment situations ranging from those that are temporarily out of work to those who cannot work at all because of a lack of skills, a disability, a lack of desire to work, or a lack of need to work. It can be voluntary or involuntary depending on circumstances and personal preferences of economic or moral nature.

Unemployment compensation (UC). In the United States, payment of unemployment benefits through the unemployment insurance (UI) program.

Unemployment insurance (UI) program. A federal-state partnership that coordinates programs in each state that provides partial income replacement (as part of an income maintenance program) to regularly employed workers who become involuntarily unemployed.

Unemployment rate. Percentage of civilian population that is out of work.

Unreimbursed medical expense(s). Costs incurred by an individual that is not covered by that person's health plans. Some of these costs that may then be claimed as itemized deductions when filing income taxes include premiums paid for coverages for major medical, hospital, surgical, and physician's expenses, along with out-of-pocket amounts for treatment not covered by the health insurance plan.

Unrelated person. According to the U.S. Bureau of the Census, a person age 15 or older (other than an inmate of an institution) who is not living with any relatives. The person may live alone in a house or apartment or with other individuals who are not related to that person by birth, marriage, or adoption.

Utilization review. Process used by managed care plans to decide whether or not a patient receives the health care that the physician has recommended. The decision is based on the accepted standards of the profession, guidelines on what physicians normally would do under similar circumstances. The idea is to determine whether the care is medically necessary.

Vulnerability. Typically associated with the degree of openness to becoming hurt and succumbing to threats. It focuses on an individual's or household's degree of sensitivity to changing events and the ability to adapt to new and changing conditions, not to mention the level to which threats can be met, overcome, or overturned.

Wage. Renumeration given employees for work performed, based on hourly compensation, usually to lower-skilled workers.

Welfare economics. The branch of economics dealing with the impact of welfare on a nation's economy. Its focus is typically on competition, poverty, and allocations as these relate to an economy's efficiency and general equilibrium.

Welfare-to-Work (WtW). The Workforce Investment Act of 1997 (WIA) replaced in 2000 the Job Training Partnership Act of 1982 (JTPA) that provided for training assistance to disadvantaged youth and adults that met its eligibility requirement. WtW is part of the TANF system housed under the U.S. Department of Health and Human Services; however, it is administered through the U.S. Department of Labor. States and direct grant recipients administer the grants. The key administrative element is the Workforce Investment Boards that are the policy-making arm of the one-stop centers set up under the Workforce Investment Act programs.

Welfare-to-Work tax credit. An incentive for employers to hire TANF beneficiaries, it provides a tax credit on the first $20,000 of eligible wages paid to qualified long-term TANF recipients during the first two years of their employment. The credit works out to be: Year 1 = 35% of first $10,000 of eligible wages; Year 2 = 50% of first $10,000 of eligible wages; Maximum = $8,500 per qualified employee.

Windfall Elimination Provision (WEP). A modified benefit formula used by the Social Security Administration for determining the primary insurance amount estimating the windfall in benefits for individuals who have only minimal Social Security coverage and will receive a pension based on years of work in noncovered employment.

Women's, Infants, and Children's Nutrition Program (WIC). A federal assistance program administered by the states that provides an extra food allowance for children who are under five years of age, pregnant women, and postpartum women and their infants.

Worker. A person with earnings that can be credited for social security purposes on the basis of covered employment or self-employment during a given year.

Worker's compensation exclusion(s). When computing gross income, it does not include amounts received as worker's compensation for personal injuries or sickness. Worker's compensation benefits are not generally taxable. Payments made to coal miners (or survivors) for death or disability resulting from pneumoconiosis are excluded from gross income because payments are considered to be in the nature of worker's compensation.

Workforce Investment Act (WIA). Created by the Workforce Investment Act of 1997, its purpose is to coordinate the various training programs available to those who receive benefits in order to be able to go out and get work. The changes are seen as a response to the need for employers to have access to more and better-qualified workers and provide a means by which to streamline the transition process from welfare to work.

Workforce Investment Board. Local policy-making agencies that provide the guidance and the identification of the programs and activities of the localities one-stop centers that are part of the structure established by the Workforce Investment Act.

Working poor. In the United States, when a member or members of the family work, and still the family income falls twice below the federal poverty line. A working definition involves two statistical units, first, the *individual* to determine who is working and, second, the *household* to determine whether or not the person is poor.

Work opportunity tax credit. Available for employers hiring individuals from one or more of the eight targeted groups on an elective basis. The credit is typically equal to 40 percent of qualified wages (25 percent for employment of 400 or less hours). Normally, no more than $6,000 of wages during the first year of employment can be taken into account, meaning a maximum credit per individual of $2,400.

For summer youth program participants, the total credit amount is $1,200 (40 percent of up to $3,000 in first year wages). Targeted groups include: (1) TANF eligible families, (2) qualified ex-felons, (3) vocational rehabilitation referrals, (4) qualified summer youth employees, (5) qualified veterans, (6) youths who reside in an empowerment zone or enterprise community, (7) food stamp recipient families, and (8) certain SSI recipients.

Index

About the Author

FERNANDO F. PADRÓ is Assistant Professor and Coordinator of the Educational Counseling Program at Monmouth University.